CHARTERPARTIES AND BILLS OF LADING

AUSTRALIA
LBC Information Services
Sydney

CANADA and USA
Carswell
Toronto

NEW ZEALAND
Brooker's
Auckland

SINGAPORE and MALAYSIA
Thomson Information (S.E. Asia)
Singapore

The Bar Tournament.—Mr. Justice Scrutton (Vacation Judge) is interrupted by business when on the links.

SCRUTTON

ON

CHARTERPARTIES

and

Bills of Lading

Twenty-first Edition

BY

STEWART C. BOYD CBE Q.C.

Of Trinity College, Cambridge, Bencher of the Middle Temple;
One of her Majesty's Counsel

STEVEN BERRY

Of Exeter College, Oxford, and of Middle Temple
and Lincoln's Inn; One of Her Majesty's Counsel

ANDREW S. BURROWS Q.C. (Hon)

FBA, Of the Middle Temple; Norton Rose Professor of Commercial Law
in the University of Oxford and a Fellow of St Hugh's College

BERNARD EDER

Of Downing College, Cambridge; Bencher, Inner Temple; formerly
Visiting Professor, University College, London; One of
Her Majesty's Counsel

DAVID FOXTON

Of Magdalen College, Oxford, and of Gray's Inn;
One of Her Majesty's Counsel

AND

CHRISTOPHER F. SMITH

Of the Inner Temple

LONDON
SWEET & MAXWELL
2008

First Edition	(1886)	By T. E. Scrutton.
Second Edition	(1890)	By T. E. Scrutton.
Third Edition	(1893)	By T. E. Scrutton.
Fourth Edition	(1899)	By T. E. Scrutton.
Fifth Edition	(1904)	By T. E. Scrutton, K.C., and F. D. MacKinnon.
Sixth Edition	(1910)	By Sir T. E. Scrutton and F. D. MacKinnon.
Seventh Edition	(1914)	By Sir T. E. Scrutton and F. D. MacKinnon.
Eighth Edition	(1917)	By Sir T. E. Scrutton and F. D. MacKinnon, K.C.
Ninth Edition	(1919)	By Sir T. E. Scrutton and F. D. MacKinnon, K.C.
Tenth Edition	(1921)	By Sir T. E. Scrutton and F. D. MacKinnon, K.C.
Eleventh Edition	(1923)	By Sir T. E. Scrutton and F. D. MacKinnon, K.C.
Twelfth Edition	(1925)	By Sir S. L. Porter, K.C., and W. L. McNair.
Thirteenth Edition	(1931)	By Sir S. L. Porter, K.C., and W. L. McNair.
Fourteenth Edition	(1939)	By W. L. McNair and A. A. Mocatta.
Fifteenth Edition	(1948)	By Sir W. L. McNair, K.C., and A. A. Mocatta.
Sixteenth Edition	(1955)	By Sir W. L. McNair and A. A. Mocatta, Q.C.
Seventeenth Edition	(1964)	By Sir W. L. McNair, Sir A. A. Mocatta and M. J. Mustill.
		Second Impression (1971).
Eighteenth Edition	(1974)	By Sir A. A. Mocatta, M. J. Mustill, Q.C., and S.C. Boyd.
		Second Impression (1978).
		Third Impression (1980).
		Fourth Impression (1982).
Nineteenth Edition	(1984)	By Sir A. A. Mocatta, Sir M. J. Mustill, and S. C. Boyd, Q.C.
Twentieth Edition	(1996)	By Stewart C. Boyd, Andrew S. Burrows and David Foxton.
		Second impression (2001)
Twenty-first Edition	(2008)	By Stewart C. Boyd, Steven Berry, Andrew S. Burrows, Bernard Eder, David Foxton and Christopher Smith

Published by
Sweet & Maxwell Limited of
100 Avenue Road, London NW3
Computerset by Interactive Sciences Ltd, Gloucester
Printed in the UK by CPI William Clowes Beccles NR34 7TL

No natural forests were destroyed to make this product: only farmed timber was used and
replanted

A CIP catalogue record for this book is available from the British Library

ISBN 978 0 421 91510 7

PREFACE

The challenge when updating a long-established textbook is to ensure that the text remains relevant and accessible to the modern user, without compromising the strengths and characteristics which established the reputation of the text. T.E. Scrutton referred to this difficulty in the preface to the first edition published in 1886, noting of a number of competing texts that *"re-editing, to satisfactorily adapt such works to modern commerce, must also amount to re-writing"*.

The editors are conscious that, while editorial teams change, the book remains Scrutton's book, and readers have certain expectations both as to its style and content. We have taken the opportunity to restructure certain parts of the book, and to effect some editorial changes which will give the book a more modern feel. But we remain of the view that Scrutton's original approach—the identification of clear and succinct principles in the Articles, more extended discussion of the principles and the issues to which they give rise in notes, and examples illustrating the practical application of those principles in decided cases—remains of value to the modern reader.

When publishing the first edition in 1886, Scrutton noted in the Preface that *"the last twenty years have seen what almost amounts to a revolution in the shipping trade of Great Britain"*. In particular, he mentioned the supplanting of sailing ships by steamers and the invention of the electronic telegraph. The intervening 120 or so years have seen changes which are almost as revolutionary. Among these was the passage of the Carriage of Goods by Sea Act 1924 to give effect to the Hague Rules, and which for the first time regulated by statute the contract between ship and cargo. Since then, we have seen the passage of further COGSAs in 1971 and 1992, international conventions (such as the Hamburg Rules) intended to achieve greater uniformity and closer regulation of contracts of carriage, and other statutory reforms of the common law (for example the Contracts (Rights of Third Parties) Act 1999). All of these have been addressed in successive editions.

There have also been numerous other changes. The first edition of Scrutton did not include a chapter on time charters, whereas 20 pages are devoted to this topic in this edition, including references to important new decisions on the owner's obligation to obey orders (*The Hill Harmony* [2001]) and the recovery of damages for late re-delivery (*The Achilleas* [2007], although readers should note that, at the time of writing, we await the decision of the House of Lords on an appeal in this case). By contrast, there was extensive discussion of the law of blockade, stoppage in transit and of custom, the significance of which is much diminished in modern shipping, and this edition continues the process which began in earlier editions of condensing the discussion of topics which now have little practical importance.

In recent years there has been a discernable trend in the courts to address the particular issues which arise in shipping cases in the light of more general contractual principles. This has influenced decisions on the incorporation of terms (*The Spiros C* [2000], *The Hai Hing* [2000]), the determination of the contracting carrier (*The Starsin* [2003]), the date for the assessment of damages (*The Golden Victory* [2007]) and the duty to mitigate (*The Dynamic* [2003]). Although Scrutton addresses the specialist area of contracts of carriage, it is important that the book continues to reflect and be informed by developments in the law of contract (and tort) more generally.

There have been a number of significant developments in the law relating to charterparties and bills of lading since the 20th edition was published in 1996. Important areas include:

- developments in the general law of contract relating to mistake (*The Great Peace* [2002]) and third party rights (Contracts (Rights of Third Parties) Act 1999, considered in the charterparty context in *Nisshin v Cleaves* [2003] and *The Laemthong Glory* [2005]);
- determining the identity of the carrier under bills of lading (*The Starsin* [2003]);
- defining the circumstances in which a party in whom rights of suit are vested in COGSA 1992 will become subject to liabilities (*The Berge Sisar* [2001]);
- the owner's obligation to obey time charterer's orders (*The Hill Harmony* [2001]);
- guidance given by the House of Lords on the status of straight bills of lading in the *Rafaela S* [2005];
- liability for dangerous cargo under the Hague-Visby Rules (*The Giannis* NK [1998]);
- recovery of damages in time charterparty disputes (*The Golden Victory* [2007] and *The Achilleas* [2007], decision of the House of Lords pending);
- "clausing" bills of lading to reflect the condition of cargo on shipment (*The Arctic Star* [1996], *The Hawk* [1999], *The David Agmashenebeli* [2003] and *Sea Success v African Carriers* [2005]).

Responsibility for different parts of the book has been divided between the editors as follows:

Professor Andrew Burrows Q.C. (Hon): Chapters 1, 2, 3, 8 and 19.
Bernard Eder Q.C.: Chapters 15, 18, 20, and 21.
Steven Berry Q.C.: Chapters 9, 12, 13, and 14.
David Foxton Q.C.: Chapters 5, 6, 7 and 10.
Christopher Smith: Chapters 4, 11, 16 and 17, and the Appendices.
Responsibility for the book as a whole rests with the General Editor, Stewart Boyd Q.C.

                                                                    S.C.B.

CONTENTS

3. AGENCY

4. CHARTERPARTIES

5. THE BILL OF LADING AS A CONTRACT

6. BILLS OF LADING FOR GOODS ON A CHARTERED SHIP

10. THE BILL OF LADING AS A DOCUMENT OF TITLE

11. LIABILITY OF SHIPOWNER FOR LOSS OF, OR DAMAGE TO, GOODS CARRIED

12. PERFORMANCE OF THE CONTRACT—THE VOYAGE

APPENDICES

TABLE OF CASES

TABLE OF STATUTES

TABLE OF OVERSEAS ENACTMENTS

CHAPTER 1

NATURE, VALIDITY AND CONSTRUCTION OF THE CONTRACT

Article 1—Contracts of Affreightment

A1

WHEN a shipowner, or person having for the time being as against the shipowner the right to make such an agreement, agrees to carry goods by sea, or to furnish a ship for the purpose of so carrying goods, in return for a sum of money to be paid to him, such a contract is called a contract of affreightment (or a contract for the carriage of goods by sea) and the sum to be paid is usually called freight.

Depending on the manner in which the ship is employed, the contract of affreightment may be contained in a charterparty[1] or contained in, or evidenced by, a bill of lading.[2] But the classical division into charterparties and bills of lading is not exhaustive. Contracts of affreightment may be contained in or evidenced by documents which do not strictly fall into either category: e.g. freight contracts,[3] mate's receipts,[4] non-negotiable receipts,[5] sea waybills,[6] ship's delivery orders,[7] and through transportation documents.[8]

Article 2—Employment as a General Ship

A2

When the ship is put up for a particular voyage to carry the goods of any persons who may be willing to ship goods on her for that voyage, she is said to be "put on the berth" or employed as a general ship. After the goods are shipped, a document called a bill of lading[9] is issued, which serves as a receipt by the shipowner, acknowledging that the goods have been delivered to him for carriage.[10]

Besides acting as a receipt for the goods, the bill of lading serves also as:

(1) Evidence of the contract of affreightment between the shipper and the carrier[11] and, as between an indorsee of the bill of lading and the carrier, the bill of lading contains the contract of affreightment.[12]

---

[1] See Art.3, below.

[2] See Art.2, below.

[3] See, e.g. *Associated Portland Cement v Cory* (1915) 31 T.L.R. 442; *Bolckow, Vaughan v Cia Minera* (1917) 86 L.J.K.B. 439; *Pacific Phosphate Co v Empire Transport Co* (1920) 36 T.L.R. 750; *Cork Gas Consumers Co v Witherington R. Everett* (1920) 36 T.L.R. 599; *Larrinaga v Soc. Franco-Americaine* (1923) 29 Com.Cas. 1; *Cie Tunisienne de Navigation v Cie d'Armemente Maritime* [1971] A.C. 572.

[4] See Art.91.

[5] See p.414, below.

[6] See Arts 2 and 14.

[7] See Arts 2 and 14.

[8] See Arts 180–182.

[9] Also once called a *bill of loading*; the first use given in the N.E.D. is in 1599. A bill of lading, like a charterparty, used to be by "Indenture". See an example of 1538 ("This bylle indented and made, etc.") in Marsden, *Select Pleas of the Admiralty Court* (Selden Society, 1892), Vol. I, p.61.

[10] See Arts 57 to 65 as to the effect of representations in the bill of lading as to the number, condition, marks, etc. of the goods received.

[11] See Art.33 below.

[12] *Leduc v Ward* (1888) 20 Q.B.D. 473; see Art.14.

(2) A document of title, by the indorsement of which the property in the
goods for which it is a receipt may be transferred, or the goods pledged
or mortgaged as security for an advance.[13]

By the Carriage of Goods by Sea Act 1992, the lawful holder of the bill of
lading acquires all rights of suit and may become subject to all the liabilities
under the contract of carriage as if he had been a party to that contract.[14]

It has become increasingly common for liner companies and others to issue
documents called through bills of lading, which may evidence a contract for
carriage by land or air as well as by water. Such documents present special
problems, and it is doubtful to what extent they share the characteristics of the
conventional bill of lading.[15]

In some trades a sea waybill takes the place of the bill of lading. These are
used, generally for short journeys, where it is not contemplated that the goods
will be sold in transit. The sea waybill is non-negotiable and is not a document
of title. It is generally retained by the shipper and the carrier is entitled to deliver
the goods without it. The goods are claimed by the named consignee identifying
himself at the destination. Depending on the terms, the shipper may be permitted
to redirect the goods to another receiver.

Very similar to a sea waybill is a straight bill of lading which contrasts with the
usual "order" bill of lading because the words "to order" are deleted. A straight
bill of lading names a consignee and is non-negotiable and there is no power to
redirect the goods to another receiver. But it appears that, in contrast to the sea
waybill, the carrier must only deliver the goods against the surrender of the
document.[16]

A ship's delivery order may also replace the bill of lading. This is used where
goods covered by the bill of lading are sold to more than one person. In other
words, the ship's delivery order is used for splitting bulk cargoes. The bill of
lading holder obtains delivery orders for specified quantities of a bulk cargo
against surrender of the bill(s) of lading. The ship's delivery order contains an
undertaking by the carrier to deliver the specified quantity of goods to the order
of a named person.

The provisions of the Carriage of Goods by Sea Act 1992, which transfer to
third parties the rights (and sometimes liabilities) under the contract of carriage,

---

[13] See Chapter 10. This definition of a bill of lading was cited with approval in *Carrington Slipways Ltd v Patrick Operations Ltd* (1991) 24 N.S.W.L.R. 745.
[14] See Art.14.
[15] See Art.180. *Cf.* "the similar document of title" referred to in Art.I(*b*) of the Schedule to the Carriage of Goods by Sea Act 1971, below, p.382.
[16] See *MacWilliam Co Inc v Mediterranean Shipping Co (The Rafaela S)* [2005] UKHL 11; [2005] 2 W.L.R. 554. It was decided in that case that straight bills of lading are "bills of lading or similar documents of title" within Art.1(b) of the Hague-Visby Rules. See Treitel, "The Legal Status of Straight Bills of Lading" (2003) 119 L.Q.R. 608; Girvin, "Bills of Lading and Straight Bills of Lading: Principles and Practice" (2006) J.B.L. 86.

apply not only where the shipping documents are bills of lading but also where they are sea waybills and ship's delivery orders.[17]

Article 3—Employment as a Chartered Ship   A3

When the agreement is for the employment of the whole ship[18] on a given voyage or voyages or for a given period of time the contract of affreightment is almost always contained in a document called a charterparty,[19] the person entitled to the use of the ship is called the charterer, and the ship is said to be chartered or under charter.[20]

The charterer may intend to supply the cargo himself or to enter into sub-contracts of carriage with other shippers who provide all or part of the cargo, or to employ the vessel as a general ship. In each case a bill of lading will generally be issued when the goods are shipped. The bill of lading almost invariably contains words which purport to be provisions of the contract of affreightment and which often contradict the terms of the charter. This gives rise to a number of problems, which are discussed in Chapter 6.[21]

Article 4—Formation of the Contract   A4

A charterparty is usually signed before any steps are taken under the contract it contains, but its main provisions are almost always agreed in advance by correspondence, telex, or oral negotiation. Whether the parties are bound before the charter is signed will depend upon (i) whether they are *ad idem* and (ii) whether on the true construction of the language used in the negotiations, including the use of phrases such as "subject to contract" or "subject to signature of charterparty", it was the intention of the parties that they should be bound before signature of the formal document.[22] A fixture "subject to stem" does not

---

[17] See Art.14.

[18] Charters for part of a ship are relatively rare but occasionally used when bills of lading are inappropriate, e.g. between liner companies chartering space on one another's ships.

[19] *Charterparty*: in medieval Latin, *carta partita*, an instrument written in duplicate on a single sheet and then divided by indented edges so that each part fitted the other (whence the term "*indenture*"); only now used for this particular kind of shipping document. The first use given in the N.E.D. is in 1539. The phrase "*Chartre de freight ou endenture*" is used as early as 1375. (Black Book of the Admiralty, *Monumenta Juridica*, ed. Twiss, 1871, Vol. I. p.136). *Cf.* the absence of any definition of a "charter-party" in the Hamburg Rules notwithstanding Art.2.3, below, p.503.

[20] For a discussion of the various categories of charter and the more important characteristics of each as regards the relationships of the shipowner and charterer to one another and to third parties, see Chapter 4, below. Where the charterer himself charters the whole ship to a third party for the whole or part of the period or number of voyages covered by the original charter, the agreement is sometimes called a *sub-charter*.

[21] Below, p.66.

[22] *Soc. Portuguesa de Navios Tanquos v Polaris* [1952] 1 Lloyd's Rep. 71; affirmed CA, *ibid.* at p.407; *Zarati S.S. Co v Frames Tours* [1955] 2 Lloyd's Rep. 278; *Scancarriers A/S v Aotearoa International Ltd (The Barranduna)* [1985] 2 Lloyd's Rep. 419 (P.C.); *Hofflinghouse & Co Ltd v C-Trade S.A. (The Intra Transporter)* [1986] 2 Lloyd's Rep. 132; *Grace Shipping Inc v C.F. Sharp & Co (Malaya) Pte Ltd* [1987] 1 Lloyd's Rep. 207 (PC); *Star Steamship Soc. v Beogradska Plovidba (The Junior K)* [1988] 2 Lloyd's Rep. 583 ("subject to details"). The classic case on the objective approach to contract formation is *Smith v Hughes* (1871) L.R. 6 Q.B. 597, 607. See, generally, Howarth, "The Meaning of Objectivity in Contract" (1984) 100 L.Q.R. 265; De Moor, "Intention in the Law of Contract; Elusive or Illusory" (1990) 106 L.Q.R. 632.

result in a binding agreement unless the charterer obtains a berth and a cargo.[23]

Formerly a charterparty was made by deed,[24] but in modern times this is not usually so. Indeed it may be, and often is, made by word of mouth,[25] although almost invariably the intention of the parties is to reduce it to writing at a later stage. When the contract is reduced to writing, evidence of earlier or contemporaneous agreements is not admissible to contradict, vary, or add to the written terms. But there are a number of important exceptions to this rule,[26] and the rule does not in any case apply to a bill of lading, which as between the carrier and shipper does not contain the contract but is merely evidence of it.[27]

A5   **Article 5—Mistake in Entering into a Contract**

A contract of affreightment is governed by the normal contractual principles on mistake.[28] These will apply if the contract does not on its true construction provide for what should happen where the facts or law[29] are different from what either or both of the parties believed them to be. At common law it appears that a contract may be void if both parties entering into it made the same mistake (usually referred to as a common mistake) and the mistake was fundamental. What is "fundamentality" at common law is narrowly defined.[30] It most obviously includes the case where both parties believe that the subject matter of the contract is in existence, whereas in fact it has perished or been destroyed prior to the contract, or never existed.[31] At common law a contract may also be void if one party knew of the other's fundamental mistake (usually called a unilateral mistake). Again the types of unilateral mistake recognised to be fundamental at common law are narrow and principally include mistakes as to the identity of the other party.[32] It is also sometimes asserted that there is a third category of mistake (usually called mutual mistake) which may make the contract void in situations where each party is mistaken as to what the other is contracting for[33]: this is perhaps better viewed as a situation where, applying the normal objective

---

[23] *Kokusai Kisen Kabushiki Kaisha v Johnson* (1921) 8 Ll.L.R. 434. The charterer is under no legally enforceable obligation to obtain a berth and cargo, nor to take reasonable steps to do so.

[24] "A charterparty is usually under seal." (*Chitty on Pleading* 1816, Vol. III, p.93). Still earlier, "Charterparties . . . are made before Notaries or Scrivenors." Malynes, *Lex Mercatoria* (1686), p.99. As late as 1830 a report says that it was arranged "that the defendant's attorney should prepare a charterparty". (*Read v Rann* (1830) 10 B. & C. 438).

[25] It has been doubted whether a charter by demise can be constituted except by a document in writing: *Cory & Son v Dorman, Long & Co* (1936) 41 Com.Cas. 224. See, *contra*, as to a voyage charter, the dictum of Wigram V.-C. in *Lidgett v Williams* (1845) 14 L.J.Eq. 459, and contrast Lush J. in *Adamson v Newcastle S.S. Freight Association* (1879) 4 Q.B.D. 462 at pp.467, 468.

[26] See Arts 9 and 10, below. See also Chapter 8 below, as to the effect of representations.

[27] *The Ardennes* [1951] 1 K.B. 55, and see Art.32, below.

[28] See, generally, *Chitty on Contracts*, 29th edn (London: Sweet & Maxwell, 2004) ch.5.

[29] *Brennan v Bolt Burdon* [2004] EWCA Civ. 1017; [2005] Q.B. 303.

[30] *Bell v Lever Bros* [1932] A.C. 161; *Associated Japanese Bank v Credit du Nord* [1989] 1 W.L.R. 255. *The Great Peace Shipping Ltd v Tsavliris Salvage (International) Ltd (The Great Peace)* [2002] EWCA Civ. 1407; [2003] Q.B. 679.

[31] See, e.g. *Couturier v Hastie* (1856) 5 H.L.C. 673.

[32] See, e.g. *Cundy v Lindsay* (1878) 3 App. Cas. 459; *Lewis v Averay* [1972] 1 Q.B. 198.

[33] See, e.g. *Raffles v Wichelhaus* (1864) 2 H. & C. 906.

approach to the matter, there is no coincidence of offer and acceptance. In limited circumstances a signed contract may be held void under the doctrine of *non est factum*.[34]

A common mistake in the drawing up of a contract or, in some circumstances, a mistake of one party known to the other (i.e. a unilateral mistake) may provide grounds for equitable rectification.[35] This is so even though when rectified a necessary term has to be implied by the court.[36]

Previously there was an equitable doctrine of common mistake which rendered a contract voidable.[37] But in *The Great Peace*[38] this doctrine was excised, and *Solle v Butcher*[39] was overruled, on the basis that it was irreconcilable with the narrower common law doctrine of common mistake laid down in *Bell v Lever Bros*.[40]

Where a party is induced to enter into a contract by a misrepresentation the contract is voidable: and if the misrepresentation is made fraudulently or negligently the misrepresentee may claim damages in addition to, or as an alternative to, rescission.[41]

Article 6—Contracts entered into under Duress   A6

Traditionally the doctrine of duress was confined to threats to the person or to goods. Its recent expansion to encompass economic duress (which can include a threat to break a contract)[42] renders it worthy of mention in this work.[43] A contract of affreightment, as any other contract, may now be voidable for duress if the claimant entered into it because of an illegitimate threat.[44] It appears that a threat may be illegitimate even though what is threatened is not a crime or civil

---

[34] See *Saunders v Anglia Building Soc. (sub nom Gallie v Lee)* [1971] A.C. 1004.
[35] For common mistake, see *Vergottis v Ford* (1918) 34 T.L.R. 233; *Joint Danube and Black Sea Shipping Agencies v Iris* (1932) 43 Ll.L.R. 97; *Chandris v Dreyfus* (1934) 50 Ll.L.R. 141; *Federazione Italiana v Federal Co* (1949) 82 Ll.L.R. 717; *Rose v Pim* [1953] 2 Q.B. 450; *Joscelyne v Nissen* [1970] 2 Q.B. 86; *The Olympic Pride* [1980] 2 Lloyd's Rep. 67. For unilateral mistake, see *Roberts v Leicestershire CC* [1961] Ch. 555; *Riverlate Properties Ltd v Paul* [1975] Ch. 133; *Thomas Bates & Son Ltd v Wyndham's (Lingerie) Ltd* [1981] 1 W.L.R. 505; *The Olympic Pride* [1980] 2 Lloyd's Rep. 67, 72–73; *Commission for the New Towns v Cooper (G.B.) Ltd* [1995] Ch. 259.
[36] *Joint Danube and Black Sea Shipping Agencies v Iris, above.*
[37] See, e.g. *Solle v Butcher* [1950] 1 K.B. 671.
[38] *Great Peace Shipping Ltd v Tsavliris Salvage (International) Ltd (The Great Peace)* [2002] EWCA Civ. 1407; [2003] Q.B. 679.
[39] [1950] 1 K.B. 671.
[40] [1932] A.C. 161.
[41] See Art.55.
[42] For duress based on threatened breach of contract, see, e.g. *Occidental Worldwide Investment Corp v Skibs A/S Avanti (The Siboen and the Sibotre)* [1976] 1 Lloyd's Rep. 293; *North Ocean Shipping Co Ltd v Hyundai Construction Co Ltd (The Atlantic Baron)* [1976] 1 Lloyd's Rep. 293; *Vantage Navigation Corp v Suhail and Saud Bahwan Building Materials Inc (The Alev)* [1989] 1 Lloyd's Rep. 138; *Atlas Express Ltd v Kafco (Importers and Exporters) Ltd* [1989] Q.B. 833.
[43] See generally *Chitty on Contracts* (29th edn), ch.7. The language of economic duress now tends to be used for duress of goods; see, e.g. *Enimont Overseas A.G. v R. O. Jugotanker Zadar (The Olib)* [1991] 2 Lloyd's Rep. 108.
[44] The leading cases are *Universe Tankships Inc of Monrovia v International Transport Workers' Federation (The Universe Sentinel)* [1983] 1 A.C. 366; *Dimskal Shipping Co SA v International Transport Workers' Federation (The Evia Luck (No.2))* [1992] 2 A.C. 152.

wrong.[45] Conversely it may be that not every threatened breach of contract is illegitimate. In some circumstances it may be relevant to consider, in addition to the illegitimacy of the threat and its causal effect on the claimant, whether the claimant had a reasonable alternative to giving in to the pressure.[46]

A7   **Article 7—Effect of Illegality on a Contract of Affreightment**

A contract which is expressly or impliedly prohibited by statute is unenforceable, irrespective of the intention of the parties.[47] Similarly, where the contract cannot be performed without a violation of English law, as it stands at the date the contract is made, it is unenforceable whether the parties knew of the illegality or not when it was entered into.[48] If there is a subsequent change of the law, so that performance becomes illegal, the contract may be discharged under the doctrine of frustration.[49] If, however, prevention of performance by illegality is due to a party's own act (i.e. there is self-induced frustration) illegality will be no defence to the injured party's claim.[50]

Where a contract can be performed in two ways, one of which is legal and the other illegal, it will not be unenforceable[51] unless there is an intention to perform it in the way known to be illegal.[52] Where the intent is mutual the contract is unenforceable. If, however, the intent is unilateral, the contract is only unenforceable at the suit of the party who intended the illegality.[53]

Where some of the terms of a contract are unenforceable by reason of illegality and others are not, it may in certain circumstances be possible to "sever" the objectionable terms and to enforce the others.[54]

---

[45] See the *dictum* of Steyn L.J. in *CTN Cash and Carry Ltd v Gallaher Ltd* [1994] 4 All E.R. 714, 718; *R v Attorney General for England and Wales* [2003] UKPC 22 at [16]. This point is strengthened if one includes, as examples of duress, cases on actual undue influence involving threats: e.g. *Williams v Bayley* (1866) L.R. 1 H.L. 200.

[46] *Pao On v Lau Yiu Long* [1980] A.C. 614; *B & S Contracts and Design Ltd v Victor Green Publications Ltd* [1984] I.C.R. 419; *The Alev*, above; *Huyton SA v Peter Cramer* [1999] 1 Lloyd's Rep. 620; *DSND Subsea Ltd v Petroleum Geo-Services ASA* [2000] B.L.R. 530.

[47] *Mahmoud v Ispahani* [1921] 2 K.B. 716; *St. John Shipping Corpn v Joseph Rank* [1957] 1 Q.B. 267 at p.283; *Archbold's (Freightage) v Spanglett* [1961] 1 Q.B. 374; *Pheonix General Insurance Co of Greece SA v Halvanon Insurance Co Ltd* [1988] Q.B. 216. In *Tinsley v Milligan* [1994] 1 A.C. 340 the House of Lords rejected the "affront to public conscience" test for the enforceability of a contract affected by illegality. That discretionary test had been applied in, e.g. *Euro-Diam Ltd v Bathurst* [1990] 1 Q.B. 35; *Howard v Shirlstar Container Transport Ltd* [1990] 1 W.L.R. 1292.

[48] *Esposito v Bowden* (1857) 7 E. & B. 763; see also *Barker v Hodgson* (1814) 3 M. & S. 267 at p.270; *Atkinson v Ritchie* (1809) 10 East 530 at p.535.

[49] See Art.13 fn.182.

[50] *Monarch S.S. Co v Karlshamns* [1949] A.C 196 at pp.229–230, per Lord Wright; *Maritime National Fish v Ocean Trawlers* [1935] A.C. 524.

[51] *Waugh v Morris* (1873) L.R. 8 Q.B. 202; *The Teutonia* (1872) L.R. 4 P.C. 171 (but see *Reardon Smith Line v Ministry of Agriculture* [1962] 1 Q.B. 42); *Haines v Busk* (1814) 1 Marshall 191; *Hindley v General Fibre Co* [1940] 2 K.B. 517; *St. John Shipping Corp v Joseph Rank* [1957] 1 Q.B. 267 at p.286 (*Case 3*, below).

[52] *St. John Shipping Corp v Joseph Rank*, above, at p.286. See also *Cunard v Hyde* (1858) 27 L.J.Q.B. 408; and *Wilson v Rankin* (1865) L.R. 1 Q.B. 162, in which the claimant was held to have no illegal intention, and *Cunard v Hyde* (1859) 29 L.J.Q.B. 6, in which he was held guilty.

[53] *St. John Shipping Corp v Joseph Rank*, above, at p.283; *Archbold's (Freightage) v Spanglett*, above, at p.388.

[54] See *Chitty on Contracts*, 29th edn, Vol. I, §§ 16–188 to 16–197. Thus, in *Storer v Gordon* (1814) 3 M. & S. 308, where a ship was chartered to deliver an outward cargo on payment of freight, and carry home cargo, the seizure of the outward cargo by the Government before delivery was held to absolve the charterer from payment of freight, but not from the liability to load a return cargo.

An undertaking to indemnify a party against the consequences of making a false representation so as to deceive third parties is unenforceable.[55]

An English contract to perform an act in a foreign country is in general unenforceable (or, if the illegality is subsequent, discharged by frustration) if the performance is unlawful by the law of the country in question.[56]

Case 1. An Italian ship was chartered by an Englishman to carry wheat from Russia to England; before the ship arrived at the Russian port war was declared between England and Russia, and continued up to the day when the lay-days for loading would have expired. *Held,* that the declaration of war made commercial intercourse between England and Russia illegal, and that the contract was therefore discharged by English law.[57]

Case 2. C chartered in France A's ship to load pressed hay in France and proceed direct to London, "all cargo to be brought and taken from ship alongside". C's agent told the captain that the hay was to be landed at a particular wharf in London, and the captain assented. At the time of making the charter, the import of French hay into England was illegal by English law; though neither party knew of it. On arrival at London, when landing at the proposed wharf was found illegal, after eighteen days' delay beyond the lay-days, C unloaded the hay "alongside ship" for export in another vessel; this proceeding was not illegal. To an action by A for demurrage, C pleaded that the contract was void for illegality. *Held,* that the contract could be, and had been, performed legally, by taking the hay alongside for exportation, and, as there was no evidence of intention to perform it illegally with knowledge of its illegality, it was not void, and C was liable for demurrage.[58]

Case 3. In breach of ss.44 and 59 of the Merchant Shipping (Safety and Load Line Conventions) Act 1932, a ship arrived at a British port with her load line submerged. The holder of a bill of lading withheld part of the bill of lading freight on the ground that the contract of carriage had been performed in an illegal manner. *Held,* that the shipowners were entitled to recover the balance of freight, since: (i) contracts for the carriage of goods were not within the ambit of the Act; (ii) the fact that the contract was performed in an illegal manner did not render it unenforceable; and (iii) the shipowners could establish their right to freight without disclosing their illegal act.[59]

Note. Contracts with Enemies[60]

A. The test of enemy status, for the purpose of this matter, is not nationality but residence or commercial domicile. An enemy is one who resides or carries on business within enemy or enemy occupied[61] territory.[62]

---

[55] *Brown Jenkinson & Co v Percy Dalton* [1957] 2 Q.B. 621. See Art.61, below for the effect of this principle on the practice of issuing clean bills of lading for damaged goods against an indemnity from the shipper.

[56] *Reggazoni v Sethia* [1958] A.C. 301. See also *Foster v Driscoll* [1929] 1 K.B. 47; *Soc. Co-op Suisse v La Plata Cereal Co* (1947) 80 Ll.L.R. 530; *Royal Boskalis Westminster NV v Mountain* [1999] Q.B. 674. See also *Ralli v Compania Naviera* [1920] 2 K.B. 287 (charterers excused from paying full freight although it was neither contended nor held that the contract was frustrated). See generally, including a discussion of the impact on this principle of the Contracts (Applicable Law) Act 1990, *Dicey & Morris on The Conflict of Laws,* 14th edn (London: Sweet & Maxwell, 2006) paras 5–009, 32–230—32–243.

[57] *Esposito v Bowden* (1857) 7 E. & B. 763. See also *Avery v Bowden; Reid v Hoskins* (1856) 6 E. & B. 953.

[58] *Waugh v Morris* (1873) L.R. 8 Q.B. 202; see also *Cargo ex Argos* (1873) L.R. 5 P.C. 134, where illegality by French law, equivalent by English law to impossibility in fact, was met by the suggestion that the charterer might unload "alongside", and so act legally. (But see *Ralli v Compania Naviera Sota* [1920] 2 K.B. 287). Seizure by revenue officers will be prima facie proof of illegality of voyage, without proving actual condemnation: *Blanck v Solly* (1818) 1 Moore 531.

[59] *St. John Shipping Corp v Joseph Rank, Ltd* [1957] 1 Q.B. 267.

[60] On this subject and the legal effects of war generally, see Lord McNair, *Legal Effects of War,* 4th edn (New York: Cambridge University Press, 1967).

[61] *Sovfracht (V.O.) v Van Udens, etc.* [1943] A.C. 203.

[62] *Porter v Freudenberg* [1915] 1 K.B. 857. *Cf. Scotland v SA Territories Ltd* (1917) 33 T.L.R. 255. The distinction, however, is not always carefully preserved. In *Porter v Freudenberg,* in passages where an enemy's right to sue in our courts is discussed, "enemy" is used in the sense of nationality, not in that of domicile. It is laid down (and the rule is an old one) that an enemy may sue if he be within the realm by the licence of the Queen. If so, though he is "an enemy" by test of nationality, he may not, and in nearly all cases will not, be so by test of domicile. So in *Shaffenius v Goldberg* [1916] 1 K.B. 284, the plaintiff was not an "alien enemy" on the test of domicile but solely on that of nationality.

B. Any contract entered into after the outbreak of war between a British subject and an enemy is absolutely void for illegality unless made with the clear permission or licence of the Crown.[63]

C. As regards contracts entered into between a British subject and an enemy before the outbreak of war most of the questions that arise have now been settled. (i) A cause of action that before the war has accrued upon such a contract to the enemy is not destroyed by the outbreak of war, but the enemy's right to sue in British courts is suspended until after the end of the war.[64] In a case where the enemy was rather an artificial and not very hostile "enemy", the courts treated this rule as a matter of defence open to the British subject, which he could waive, and thereby remove the enemy's disability.[65] It can hardly be supposed that such complaisance by a British defendant in a suit by a resident in Germany would in either of the last two wars have had the same result. An exception to the rule arises in the case of an enemy within the realm by the licence of the Queen.[66] (ii) On a cause of action that on such a contract has accrued to a British subject he may sue the enemy during the war, provided that he can serve him with a writ under the rules of practice.[67] The enemy so sued may appear and defend, and may also appeal against any decision that is given against him.[68] (iii) The obligation of either party under such a contract to do anything during the war in performance of it ceases.[69] (iv) The chief difficulty, in regard to this topic, arises in regard to contracts, the terms of which, as to time of performance, would impose duties of performance after the war has ceased. All duty of performance during the war having disappeared under the last-mentioned rule, to what extent does the duty of performance survive, or revive, after the war is ended? The question is commonly put in the form—"Is the contract dissolved or only suspended?" In this question "suspended" means "temporarily cancelled", and not "postponed". And the question really means—"Is the contract dissolved or not?" For the alternative, "or suspended", only means that performance is for the time impossible though the contractual obligation is not dissolved.

The answer to the question depends on the particular circumstances of each case. The primary doctrine in issue is that of frustration (see Art.13, below) whereby the contract will be dissolved (i.e. discharged) if cessation of performance during the war will involve so radical an alteration in the whole substratum of the contract that to perform it when performance again becomes possible will be to carry out a new and different contract.[70] Alternatively it may be that the contract will be dissolved irrespective of frustration, because the continued existence of the contract will be contrary to the public policy of Great Britain as a belligerent.[71]

In fact the majority of contracts between a British subject and an alien who becomes an enemy in the technical sense discussed at the beginning of this Note will be dissolved by the outbreak of war. But this is not a necessary result in every case. If, for example, before

[63] *The Hoop* (1799) 1 C.Rob. 196; *Willison v Patteson* (1817) 7 Taunt. 439. Contrast *Shaffenius v Goldberg*, above.

[64] *Porter v Freudenberg*, above; *Sovfracht (V./O.) v Van Udens, etc.* [1943] A.C. 203.

[65] *Janson v Driefontein* [1902] A.C. 484.

[66] *Porter v Freudenberg*, above; *Shaffenius v Goldberg*, above. This may be a real exception in some cases (e.g. where a plaintiff is carrying on business in an enemy country but is resident in the realm by licence), but in most cases, as is pointed out in fn.62, above, is only an apparent exception: on the test of domicile such a plaintiff is not an "enemy".

[67] See fn.64, above.

[68] See fn.64, above.

[69] *Esposito v Bowden* (1857) 7 E. & B. 763.

[70] *Distington Co v Possehl* [1916] 1 K.B. 811; *Hirji Mulji v Cheong Yue S.S. Co* [1926] A.C. 497; *Fibrosa Spolka Ackcyjna v Fairbairn, Lawson, Combe Barbour Ltd* [1943] A.C. 32.

[71] *Zinc Corporation v Hirsch* [1916] 1 K.B. 541; *Clapham S.S. Co v Naamlooze, etc., Vulcaan* [1917] 2 K.B. 639; *Ertel, Bieber & Co v Rio Tinto Co* [1918] A.C. 260; *Naylor, Benzon & Co v Krainische Gesellschaft* [1918] 1 K.B. 331.

the outbreak of war, a British insurance company, in consideration of £10,000 paid down, agrees to pay an annuity to a person who subsequently becomes an enemy on the outbreak of war, the annuity could not be paid during the war (nor the amount of the annuity accruing during the period of the war be paid after the war ends)[72]; but the obligation to pay during the twenty years of the annuitant's life after the war will survive.

D. Cases may arise in the English courts where it is sought to recover damages for breach of a charter made between a neutral and an enemy: such an action might be brought either during or, more probably, after a war. It would seem that as a matter of public policy such an action would not be allowed to succeed here if it was part of the policy of England, at the time of the breach, to prevent performance of the contract.[73]

Article 8—Effects of Blockade   A8

A charter, the performance of which requires the running of a foreign blockade, is not illegal by the municipal law of England, though both parties knew of the blockade when the charter was entered into.[74] The only effect of such knowledge will be to prevent the delay caused by the blockade from putting an end to the charter.[75]

Running a blockade, by international law, involves the confiscation of the ship if captured on the voyage out or home, and of the cargo, if its owners knew or might have known of the blockade when they entered into the contract of carriage.[76]

Article 9—Construction of the Contract   A9

The rules of construction developed for contracts generally are equally applicable to charterparties and bills of lading.[77] The general approach is therefore an objective one by which the courts ascertain the intention of the parties by considering what meaning the document would convey to a reasonable person having all the background knowledge which would reasonably have been available to the parties in the situation in which they were at the time of the contract. In other words, one should construe a contract in its context.[78] The following more specific principles may be of assistance in construing charterparties and bills of lading:

---

[72] *Quaere*, see Lord McNair, *Legal Effects of War*, 4th edn, p.280.
[73] *O/Y Wasa S.S. Co v Newspaper Pulp & Wood Export* (1949) 82 Ll.L.R. 936 at p.960 (Dutch shipowners, Swiss charterers).
[74] *The Helen* (1865) L.R. 1 A. & E. 1; *Medeiros v Hill* (1832) 8 Bing. 231; *Moorsom v Greaves* (1811) 2 Camp. 626; *Naylor v Taylor* (1828) M. & M. 205.
[75] See Art.13, below; and see, as to contraband cargo, *Ex p. Chavasse* (1865) 11 Jur. (N.S.) 400. The effect of the Foreign Enlistment Act 1870 (33&34 Vict. c.90) must also be considered. As to this, see *United States v Pelly* (1899) 4 Com.Cas. 100.
[76] *The Mercurius* (1798) 1 Rob. 80; *The Alexander* (1801) 4 C.Rob. 93; *The Adonis* (1804) 5 C.Rob. 256 at p.259; *The Exchange* (1808) 1 Edw. 39 at p.42; *The James Cook* (1810) 1 Edw. 261; *Baltazzi v Ryder* (1858) 12 Moore P.C. 168. The headnote to the last case is not justified by the report, so far as it contradicts the text.
[77] For a detailed examination of the rules, see Lewison, *The Interpretation of Contracts* (4th edn, 2007).
[78] *Investors Compensation Scheme Ltd v West Bromwich Building Society* [1998] 1 W.L.R. 896. See also *Reardon-Smith Line Ltd v Hansen-Tangen* [1976] 1 W.L.R. 989, 996–997.

(i) Charters and bills of lading are to be construed in the light of the nature and details of the adventure contemplated by the parties to them.[79]

(ii) The construction to be given to charters and bills of lading is not an unnecessarily strict one, but such a one as with reference to the context and the object of the contract will best effectuate the obvious and expressed intent to the parties.[80]

(iii) Charters and bills of lading are to be construed according to their sense and meaning, as collected in the first place from the terms used understood in their plain, ordinary and popular sense,[81] unless they have generally in respect of the subject-matter, as by the known usage of trade or the like, acquired a peculiar sense, distinct from their popular sense; or unless the context evidently shows that they must in the particular instance, and in order to effectuate the immediate intention of the parties, be understood in some other special and peculiar sense.[82]

(iv) If the words are plain and unambiguous the fact that the parties have acted in a contrary sense in no way affects the true construction of the words.[83]

(v) If the words are fairly capable of two meanings, evidence of a course of conduct before or at the time of entering into the contract may determine the choice.[84]

(vi) Greater weight should attach to terms which the particular contracting parties have chosen to include in the contract than to pre-printed terms.[85]

(vii) In deciding who is the carrier, words on the face of a bill of lading should be given greater weight than those on the reverse side of the bill,

---

[79] *Mackill v Wright* (1888) 14 App.Cas. 106, per Lord Halsbury at p.114; Lord Watson at p.116; Lord Macnaghten at p.120; *Glynn v Margetson* [1893] A.C. 351; *Marifortuna Naviera SA v Govt. of Ceylon* [1970] 1 Lloyd's Rep. 247 at p.254. See also *Reardon Smith Line Ltd v Hausen-Tangen* [1976] 2 Lloyd's Rep. 621 per Lord Wilberforce at pp.624–626: "What the court must do is place itself in thought in the same factual matrix as that in which the parties were": and *L. Schuler v Wickman Machine Tool Sales Ltd* [1974] A.C. 235 per Lord Reid at p.251: "The fact that a particular construction leads to a very unreasonable result must be a relevant consideration. The more unreasonable the result the more unlikely it is that the parties can have intended it, and if they do intend it the more necessary it is that they shall make that intention abundantly clear".

[80] *Dimech v Corlett* (1858) 12 Moore P.C. 199 at p.224; so, per Brett M.R. in *Sailing Ship Garston v Hickie* (1885) 15 Q.B.D. 580. "The term 'port' is to be taken in its business, popular, or commercial sense, and not in its legal definition for revenue or pilotage purposes"; and see the same judge's remarks in *Stewart v Merchant's Marine Ins. Co* (1885) 16 Q.B.D. 619 at p.627. See also *Hall v Paul* (1914) 19 Com.Cas. 384.

[81] These words were cited with approval by the CA in *Royal Greek Government v Minister of Transport (Ilissos)* [1949] 1 K.B. 525 at p.528; and in *Mendl v Ropner* [1913] 1 K.B. 27 at pp.31, 32. See similarly *The Sea Queen* [1988] 1 Lloyd's Rep. 500, 502.

[82] Per Lord Ellenborough in *Robertson v French* (1803) 4 East 130 at p.135, cited by Bowen L.J. in *Hart v Standard Marine Ins. Co* (1889) 22 Q.B.D. 499 at p.501.

[83] *N.E. Ry v Hastings* [1900] A.C. 260 at p.263, per Lord Halsbury; *Wickman Tools v Schuler A.G.* [1974] A.C. 235 (HL).

[84] *Houlder Bros v Public Works Commissioner* [1908] A.C. 276 at p.285.

[85] See Art.11 below.

as that reflects the market practice of a reasonable reader of a bill of lading.[86]

(viii) Very obvious drafting mistakes can sometimes be "corrected" as a matter of construction rather than rectification.[87]

(ix) Evidence of a course of conduct after the contract has been entered into is not normally admissible to explain its terms.[88]

(x) Evidence of pre-contractual negotiations or of the parties' declarations of subjective intentions is normally not admissible.[89] But if the words are fairly capable of two meanings, evidence is admissible to show that the parties negotiated on an agreed basis that the words bore one of the two possible meanings.[90]

(xi) Charterparties often contain many redundant words and the presumption against surplusage is of little value in their construction.[91]

(xii) Exceptions or clauses introduced in favour of one party to the contract are to be construed most strictly against him.[92]

(xiii) Where different parts of the instrument are contradictory to each other, or of ambiguous agreement, the whole of the document must be considered to arrive at the general meaning.[93] The principle *noscitur a sociis* may determine the meaning of a clause or part of a clause.[94]

---

[86] *Homburg Houtimport BV v Agrosin Private Ltd, The Starsin* [2003] UKHL 12; [2003] 1 Lloyd's Rep. 571 at [15], [45–47], [82], [126], [183]. See Art.41 below.

[87] *ibid.* In this case a line in a Himalaya clause in a bill of lading specifying that the carrier had been acting for the benefit of his servants and agents was omitted by reason of "homoeoteleuton" (that is, a copy typist's error of reading from the same word in one line to the same word in another line missing out the passage in between). The House of Lords as a matter of construction read the line back into the bill of lading. For the relationship between construction and rectification, see A. Burrows, "Construction and Rectification" in A. Burrows and E. Peel (eds), *Contract Terms* (Oxford: Oxford University Press, 2007), p.77.

[88] *Houlder Bros v Public Works Commissioner*, above, at p.285; *Whitworth Street Estates v Miller* [1970] A.C. 583, per Lord Reid at p.603; Lord Hodson at p.606; Viscount Dilhorne at p.611; *Cie d'Armement Maritime v Cie Tunisienne de Navigation* [1971] A.C. 572, per Viscount Dilhorne at p.593; *Wickman Machine Tool Sales v Schuler* [1974] A.C. 235, distinguishing *Watcham v E. Africa Protectorate* [1919] A.C. 533 (ambiguous title to land); *The Tychy (No.2)* [2001] 2 Lloyd's Rep. 403.

[89] *Prenn v Simmonds* [1971] 1 W.L.R. 1381 (HL); *Investors Compensation Scheme Ltd v West Bromwich Building Society* [1998] 1 W.L.R. 896 at 913. For criticism, see G. McMeel, "Prior Negotiations and Subsequent Conduct—The Next Step Forward for Contractual Interpretation" (2003) 119 L.Q.R. 272; Lord Nicholls, "My Kingdom for a Horse: The Meaning of Words" (2005) 121 L.Q.R. 577.

[90] *Partenreederai M.S. Karen Oltmann v Scarsdale Shipping Co (The Karen Oltmann)* [1976] 2 Lloyd's Rep. 708. Cf. *Chartbrook Ltd v Persimmon Homes Ltd* [2007] EWHC 409 (Ch); [2007] 1 All E.R. (Comm) 1083.

[91] *Royal Greek Government v Minister of Transport (Ann Stathatos)* (1950) 83 Ll.L.R. 228 at p.235; *Grace v General S.N. Co* [1950] 2 K.B. 383 at p.392; *Chandris v Isbrandtsen-Moller* [1951] 1 K.B. 240 at p.245; *North River Freighters v President of India* [1955] 2 Lloyd's Rep. 73 at p.81; *Carga del Sur Compania Naviera v Ross T. Smyth* [1962] 2 Lloyd's Rep. 147 at p.154; *Soc. Carga Oceanica v Idolinoele Vertriebs GmbH* [1964] 2 Lloyd's Rep. 28 at p.33; *Inca Cia Naviera v Mofinol Inc* [1967] 2 Lloyd's Rep. 338 at p.350. Cf. per Somervell L.J. in *SA Maritime et Commerciale of Geneva v Anglo-Iranian Oil Co* [1954] 1 W.L.R. 492 at p.495.

[92] *Burton v English* (1883) 12 Q.B.D. 218 at p.220, per Brett M.R., and at p.222, per Bowen L.J.; *The Waikato* [1899] 1 Q.B. 56 (CA); *Christie & Vesey v Helvetia* [1960] 1 Lloyd's Rep. 540 at p.546. *Canada Steamships Ltd v R* [1952] A.C. 192. But cf. *Norman v Binnington* (1890) 25 Q.B.D. 475 at p.477; *Mendl v Ropner* [1913] 1 K.B. 27. See generally, E. Peel, "Whither *Contra Proferentem*?" in *Contract Terms* (eds A. Burrows and E. Peel, 2007) 53.

[93] Cf. *Elderslie v Borthwick* [1905] A.C. 93; *The Hibernian* [1907] p.277; *Nelson v Nelson* [1908] A.C. 16.

[94] *Compania Naviera Aeolus SA v Union of India* [1964] A.C. 868.

Difference in the size of type in which different parts are printed is not to be taken as a measure of the importance of the passages so printed.[95]

(xiv) When construing a clause in a standard form or charter, decisions on earlier and similar versions of the same clause are to be treated with reserve. The correct approach is to have regard only to the language of the actual clause in question.[96]

The construction of a charter or bill of lading is a question of law for the court, unless there is ambiguity,[97] or some peculiar meaning attached to the words of the document by reason of the custom of the trade or port to which the document relates. In these cases oral evidence will be admissible to assist in determining the special meaning of the words used.[98] Whether there is any ground for the admission of oral evidence on these points will be a question for the court.[99]

Case 1. A ship was chartered to proceed to X, a river port, and there load, "the master guaranteeing to carry 3,000 tons dead weight of cargo, upon a draught of twenty-six feet of water". The ship could carry such a cargo at such a draught in salt, but not in fresh, water. *Held*, that as the charter showed that both parties contemplated loading in a river, the guarantee must be applied to both fresh and salt water.[100]

Case 2. A ship was chartered to "proceed to loading-berth, North Dock, Swansea, and there load, always afloat, a full cargo . . . lighterage, if any, necessary to enable steamer to complete loading at North Dock, Swansea, to be at merchant's risk and expense". The vessel could have loaded "always afloat" in the North Dock, but could not at neap tides have got over the sill fully loaded. To avoid waiting till spring-tides, the shipowners moved the ship to another dock when partly loaded; the charterers claimed the cost of carrying cargo to the other dock. *Held*, that the clause as to lighterage was sufficiently ambiguous to admit extrinsic evidence in the shape of telegrams between the parties before signing the charter to explain it.[101]

A10   **Article 10—Evidence of Custom: when Admissible**

Evidence of custom may be admissible both for interpreting express terms and as the basis for implying terms into the contract.

So the customs of a trade[102] which regulate the performance of the contract, but do not change its intrinsic character, are tacitly incorporated in the contract, though not expressed in it,[103] on the ground that the parties to the contract must

---

[95] *Elderslie v Borthwick*, above.
[96] *Court Line v Finelvet (The Jevington Court)* [1966] 1 Lloyd's Rep. 683 at p.691.
[97] *The Curfew* [1891] p.131. Mere difficulty of construction is not ambiguity: a document is only ambiguous when, after full consideration, it is determined judicially that no interpretation can be given to it; *Higgins v Dawson* [1902] A.C. 1 at p.10 per Lord Davey, approving a dictum of Rigby L.J. in CA.
[98] See *Aktieselskab Helios v Ekman* [1872] 2 Q.B. 83 (CA), where oral evidence was admitted to explain what was meant by "alongside" and "delivery" at a particular port.
[99] *Bowes v Shand* (1877) 2 App.Cas. 455 at p.462; *Ashforth v Redford* (1873) L.R. 9 C.P. 20. As to evidence of usage, see Art.10.
[100] *The Norway* (1865) 3 Moore P.C. (N.S.) 245. *Cf. Hart v Standard Marine Co* (1889) 22 Q.B.D. 499; *Mackill v Wright* (1888) 14 App.Cas. 106.
[101] *The Curfew* [1891] p.131. See *The Nifa* [1892] p.411, when such evidence was rejected, there being no ambiguity.
[102] In this Article the expression "custom" is used in the sense of and includes "usage". In this sense it is to be distinguished from legal customs such as Borough English or gavelkind which are in effect local law.
[103] *Robinson v Mollett* (1875) L.R. HL 802 at pp.811, 819, 836. *Les Affreteurs Reunis v Walford* [1919] A.C. 801. *Palgrave, Brown v Turid* [1922] 1 A.C. 397.

be presumed to have contracted with reference to such customs.[104] Customs may be excluded by express words.[105]

Customs of trade may control the mode of performance of a contract, but cannot change its intrinsic character.[106] Thus if the express terms of the charter are inconsistent with the alleged custom, evidence of the custom will not be admissible.[107]

Evidence of custom is therefore admissible to explain ambiguous,[108] mercantile expressions in a charter or to add incidents, or to annex usual terms and conditions which are not inconsistent with the written contract between the parties, but not for any further purpose.[109]

In general, therefore, the term "loading" will be construed by the customs of the port of loading,[110] "discharge" by the customs of the port of discharge,[111] the method of payment of freight, in the absence of express provisions,[112] by the customs of the port where freight is payable[113]; for where the performance of a contract has reference to a particular trade the party contracting is necessarily obliged to make himself acquainted by due inquiry with the customs of that trade.[114]

Customs to be enforced by the courts must be—(1) reasonable[115]; (2) certain; (3) consistent with the contract[116]; (4) universally acquiesced in; (5) not contrary to law.[117]

---

[104] *Kirchner v Venus* (1859) 12 Moore P.C. 361 at p.399; *Novorossisk Shipping Co v Neopetro Co Ltd (The Ulyanovsk)* [1990] 1 Lloyd's Rep. 425, 431.

[105] *Brenda Co v Green* [1900] 1 Q.B. 518, "any custom of the port to the contrary notwithstanding". On the nature of a "custom of trade", see per Willes J. in *Meyer v Dresser* (1864) 16 C.B. (N.S.) 646 at p.662.

[106] *Mollett v Robinson* (1870) L.R. 5 C.P. 656, per Willes J.: see also L.R. 7 H.L. 802 at p.836; *The Nifa* [1892] p.411.

[107] See fn.103, above.

[108] e.g. "freight", which is a well-understood term in a contract, cannot be explained by custom: *Krall v Burnett* (1877) 25 W.R. 305; though its method of payment, which varies in each port, can: *Brown v Byrne* (1854) 3 E. & B. 703; *Falkner v Earle* (1863) 3 B. & S. 360; *The Norway* (1865) 3 Moore P.C. (N.S.) 245. Similarly evidence of custom cannot be given to explain the meaning of "alongside": but evidence of the *method* of delivering alongside can be given: see Art.83. Similarly evidence was admitted to explain the phrase "in regular turn"; *The Cordelia* [1909] p.27.

[109] *Robinson v Mollett* (1875) L.R. 7 H.L. 802 at p.815, per Mellor J.; *Produce Brokers Co v Olympia Oil Co* [1917] 1 K.B. 320.

[110] See Art.85.

[111] *Marzetti v Smith* (1883) 49 L.T. 580; *Petrocochino v Bott* (1874) L.R. 9 C.P. 355; *Aste v Stumore* (1884) C. & E. 319; *Marcelino Gonzalez v Nourse* [1936] 1 K.B. 565; *A/S Sameiling v Grain Importers (Eire) Ltd* [1952] 1 Lloyd's Rep. 313.

[112] *Gulf Line v Laycock* (1901) 7 Com.Cas. 1.

[113] See *Note*, at the end of this Article.

[114] per Willes J. in *Russian S.N. Co v De Silva* (1863) 13 C.B. (N.S.) 610 at p.617, and see cases and rules laid down in notes to *Wigglesworth v Dallison* (1779) 1 Smith L.C. 13th edn, p.597.

[115] *Hathesing v Laing* (1873) L.R. 17 Eq. 92 (Art.91 case 4).

[116] *Hudson v Clementson* (1856) 18 C.B. 213; *Hillstrom v Gibson* (1870) 8 Macpherson 463, where the words in the printed form of charter, "deliver according to the custom of the port", had been struck out of the charter; *The Alhambra* (1881) 6 P.D. 68 (CA); *Coverdale v Grant* (1884) 9 App. Cas. 470 at p.478; *Metcalfe v Thomson* (1902) 18 T.L.R. 706; *Kum v Wah Tat Bank Ltd* [1971] 1 Lloyd's Rep. 439 (PC). The custom must not only be consistent with the express words of the contract, but also its general tenor and any necessary implication from its express terms: *London Export Corporation v Jubilee Coffee Roasting Co* [1958] 1 W.L.R. 661.

[117] For discussion of these conditions, see *Ropner v Stoate Hosegood & Co* (1905) 10 Com.Cas. 73; *Sea S.S. Co v Price Walker & Co* (1903) 8 Com.Cas. 292, as to the growth and reasonableness of customs to discharge ships at a certain rate per day; *Walkers and Shaw, Re* [1904] 2 K.B. 152, where a custom was admitted; and *N.W. Rubber Co and Huttenbach, Re* [1908] 2 K.B. 907 at p.917. See also *Hogarth v Leith Seed Co*, 1909 S.C. 955; *Glasgow Navigation Co v Howard* (1910) 15 Com.Cas. 88; *Cunliffe-Owen v Teather & Greenwood* [1967] 1 W.L.R. 1421, 1438–9 (dealing with the usage of the Stock Exchange).

A custom is a reasonable and universal rule of action in a locality followed not because it is believed to be the general law of the land or because the parties following it have made particular agreements to observe it, but because it is in effect the common law within that place to which it extends, although contrary to the general law of the realm.[118]

Note. In a charter to discharge "according to the custom of the port", the jury were directed "that 'custom' in the charter did not mean custom in the sense in which the word is sometimes used by lawyers, but meant a settled and established practice of the port",[119] and the House of Lords approved this direction.[120] This seems to require a less rigorous standard of proof than in the case of a legal custom.[121] The nature of a binding custom has been thus illustrated: "In order that the shippers should be taken to have impliedly given leave to stow the goods on deck, the shipowners must prove a practice so general and universal in the trade, and in the particular port from which the goods were taken, that every one shipping goods there must be taken to know that other people's goods, if not his goods, might probably be stowed on deck."[122]

The practice of one or some merchants at a port will not make a custom,[123] though the practice of a particular line as to discharge may constitute a valid custom in dealings with that line.[124] A custom may be universal although only applicable to a particular form of charterparty.[125]

If a custom is once established, "contracting out" of it does not by itself destroy the custom. But if "contracting out" becomes so prevalent that the custom is only left operative in exceptional cases, then the custom itself must be held to have been abolished.[126] The practice of inserting express provisions in a particular class of contract to the same effect as the alleged custom is the strongest evidence that the custom does not exist.[127]

In practice it is difficult to establish a custom by affidavit evidence, or without evidence of instances of acceptance of the custom after an initial claim or dispute.[128]

(1) *Cases in which Evidence of Custom has been held Admissible*

Case 1. Charter between A and C, a foreigner, from Riga to Liverpool containing clauses: "the steamer to be discharged in ten working days. Discharging dock to be ordered on arrival at

---

[118] per Scrutton J., *Anglo-Hellenic Co v Dreyfus* (1913) 108 L.T. 36 at p.37, citing Tindal C.J. in *Lockwood v Wood* (1844) 6 Q.B. 50 at p.64. Therefore an attempt to prove a custom in a Russian port, supported only by evidence of the general law of Russia, which differed from English law, failed: *Angle-Hellenic Co v Dreyfus*, above.
[119] The practice must, however, amount to the acceptance of a binding obligation of a custom apart from a particular bargain; *Stathlorne S.S. Co v Baird*, 1916 S.C. (HL) 134.
[120] *Postlethwaite v Freeland* (1880) 5 App.Cas. 599 at p.616.
[121] See per Fletcher-Moulton L.J. in *North-West Rubber Co and Huttenbach, Re* [1908] 2 K.B. 907 at p.919, as to "the confusion between custom and what is customarily done". And see *Case 7*, below. As to the distinction between proof of custom and proof of a usual route, see *Reardon Smith Line v Black Sea and Baltic* [1939] A.C. 562.
[122] *Newall v Royal Exchange Shipping Co* (1885) 33 W.R. 342; reversed *ibid.* 868 at p.869; on the facts of which see *Royal Exchange Co v Dixon* (1886) 12 App.Cas. 11 at p.18. The practice of the only shipper at the port for thirty years has been held not to constitute a custom of the port: *Clacevich v Hutcheson* (1887) 15 Rettie 11. Otherwise at the port of Newlyn: *Temple v Runnalls* (1902) 18 T.L.R. 822. See also *Cazalet v Morris*, 1916 S.C. 952.
[123] *Lawson v Burness* (1862) 1 H. & C. 396.
[124] *Marcellino Gonzalez v Nourse* [1936] 1 K.B. 565.
[125] *Gripaios v Kahl Wallis & Co* (1928) 32 Ll.L.R. 328 (Centrocon).
[126] per Channell J., *Ropner v Stoate Hosegood* (1905) 10 Com.Cas. 73.
[127] See per Fletcher-Moulton L.J. in *North-West Rubber Co and Huttenbach, Re* [1908] 2 K.B. 907 at p.919; *Gulf Line v Laycock* (1901) 7 Com.Cas 1 at p.6; *Les Affreteurs Reunis v Walford* [1919] A.C. 801 at pp.807, 808.
[128] *Stag Line v Board of Trade* (1950) 83 Ll.L.R. 356 at pp.359, 360; *Bettany v Eastern Morning and Hull News Co* (1900) 16 T.L.R. 401.

Liverpool." Evidence was tendered of a custom of the port of Liverpool, that in the case of timber ships lay-days commenced on the mooring of the ship at the quay where she was to discharge. *Held* admissible, as explaining the meaning of "arrival at Liverpool"; inadmissible, if its effect was to vary or add to the terms of the charter, the evidence being admissible only upon the supposition that it was known to both parties.[129]

Case 2. A charter was made "on condition of the ship's taking a cargo of not less than 1,000 tons of weight and measurement". *Held*, that the proportions of weight and measurement tonnage were to be ascertained by oral evidence of the usage of the port of loading.[130]

Case 3. A bill of lading stating that goods shipped at X were deliverable at Z, "he or they paying freight for the said goods, five-eighths of a penny per pound—with 5 per cent primage and average accustomed". *Held*, that evidence of a custom of Z to deduct three months' discount on freight on goods from X was admissible.[131]

Case 4. A charter provided that a ship should deliver a cargo of timber "which should be taken from alongside at merchant's risk and expense". *Held*, that evidence of a custom that the ship should place the timber in barges alongside at its own expense was admissible as explaining "alongside" and "delivery".[132]

Case 5. A charter cargo was to be discharged at a certain rate per "working day". The charterer in answer to a claim for demurrage pleaded that by the custom of the port a "surf day" (i.e. a day when surf on the beach prevented lighters from discharging) was not a "working day". *Held*, that evidence of the custom was admissible to explain the meaning of "working day".[133]

(2) *Cases in which Evidence of Custom has been held Inadmissible*

Case 6. A bill of lading contained the clause "freight payable in London". Evidence was tendered that this meant by the custom of the steam shipping trade "freight payable in advance in London". *Held inadmissible*, the word "freight" being unambiguous, and there being nothing in the context to qualify it.[134]

Case 7. A charter to deliver "at Z, or so near thereto as the vessel could safely get." Evidence was tendered of a custom of the port of Z by which the consignee was only bound to take delivery at Z. *Held inadmissible*, as inconsistent with the charter.[135]

Case 8. A time charterparty contained a provision that a commission of 3 per cent on the estimated gross amount of hire was payable on signing the charter (ship lost or not lost) by the owners to certain brokers. Through the ship being requisitioned the charter was cancelled. To a claim by the charterers (as trustees for the brokers) for the commission, the owners pleaded that, by custom, commission was never payable to brokers except on hire earned and actually received. *Held*, that evidence of such custom was inadmissible as being inconsistent with the written contract.[136]

Case 9. A charter provided for a ship to carry timber to Yarmouth and to be discharged "always afloat . . . cargo to be taken from alongside at charterer's risk and expense". From lack of water the vessel could not "lie afloat" nearer than 13 feet from the quay. Evidence of a custom that the

---

[129] *S.S. Norden v Dempsey* (1876) 1 C.P.D. 654. As to the apparent conflict between this type of case and cases where customs of a port have been held to be binding on persons ignorant of them, see *Note* at the end of this Article.

[130] *Pust v Dowie* (1864) 5 B. & S. 20; see Art.47.

[131] *Brown v Byrne* (1854) 3 E. & B. 703. See also *Falkner v Earle* (1863) 3 B. & S. 360; and *The Norway* (1865) 3 Moore P.C. (N.S.) 245, and compare *Case 4*, below.

[132] *Aktieselskab Helios v Ekman* [1897] 2 Q.B. 83; *cf. Peterson v Freebody* [1895] 2 Q.B. 294, where no custom was alleged. See and contrast *Case 9* below. See as to a similar custom at Liverpool, *Cardiff S.S. Co v Jamieson* (1903) 19 T.L.R. 159; at London, *Glasgow Navigation Co v Howard* (1910) 26 T.L.R. 247; at Belfast, *Northmoor S.S. Co v Harland and Wolff* [1903] 2 I.R. 657.

[133] *British & Mexican Co v Lockett* [1911] 1 K.B. 264, *semble*, overruling *Bennetts v Brown* [1908] 1 K.B. 490.

[134] *Krall v Burnett* (1877) 25 W.R. 305. See also *Lewis v Marshall* (1844) 7 M. & G. 729, where evidence that "freight" included "passage money" was rejected. *Cockburn v Alexander* (1848) 6 C.B. 791.

[135] *Hayton v Irwin* (1879) 5 C.P.D. 130. *Cf. The Nifa* [1892] p.411. See also *Kearon v Radford* (1895) 11 T.L.R. 226, *Gulf Line v Laycock* (1901) 7 Com.Cas. 1, and *Hogarth v Leith Seed Co*, 1909 S.C. 955.

[136] *Les Affreteurs Reunis v Walford* [1919] A.C. 801.

shipowner must erect a staging across this gap, carry the timber across it, and dump it on the quay 10 feet from the edge was held inconsistent with the charterparty.[137]

Note. The line between admissibility and rejection of evidence of custom is very difficult to draw, and some of the cases, notably *Hutchinson v Tatham*,[138] are hard to reconcile with any clear principle. In one sense the contract must always be varied or added to by the admission of evidence of custom, inasmuch as the construction of the contract by the court would not be the same without the parol evidence, or else such evidence would be unnecessary. The best test whether a custom is, or is not, consistent with the contract is that of Lord Campbell C.J. "To fall within the exception of repugnancy the (custom) must be such as if expressed in the written contract would make it insensible or inconsistent."[139] The whole question was fully discussed in *Robinson v Mollet*.[140] Another difficulty arises from the apparent conflict between the dicta in *Kirchner v Venus*[141] and *S.S. Norden v Dempsey*,[142] to the effect that customs do not bind one ignorant of them, and such cases as *Robertson v Jackson*[143] and *Hudson v Ede*,[144] where customs of a port were held to bind persons ignorant of them. The explanation seems to be that, in the latter class of cases, custom is introduced to explain the meaning a word bears in the charter; e.g. the parties are presumed to have meant by "loading", "loading as carried out at the port of loading", but what this is can only be construed by the customs of the port of loading. The fact that a person who has contracted to "load" at a certain port is ignorant of how "loading" is conducted at that port cannot save him from being bound by the ordinary method of loading there. On the other hand, when, as in the former class of cases, something is sought to be added to the charter beyond the language the parties have used, or the essential character of the contract is sought to be varied, it may fairly be required that both parties be shown to have known of this addition, and therefore to have contracted without regard to it.

A11   **Article 11—Printed Forms of Contract**

Questions of construction frequently arise in the case of contracts of carriage effected by filling in printed forms, where parts of the printed form, left in by inadvertence, are in direct contradiction to clauses written, stamped on or typed in the form: in these cases the written, stamped on or typed clause should usually prevail, as clearly expressing the intention of the parties.[145] As Lord Bingham said in *The Starsin*, "[G]reater weight should attach to terms which the particular

---

[137] *Palgrave, Brown v Turid* [1922] 1 A.C. 397. *Cf. The Nifa* [1892] p.411.
[138] (1873) L.R. 8 C.P. 482.
[139] *Humfrey v Dale* (1857) 7 E. & B. 266 at p.275. "I accept and agree with this test," Lord Birkenhead L.C., *Palgrave, Brown v Turid* [1922] 1 A.C. 397 at p.406.
[140] (1875) L.R. 7 H.L. 802.
[141] (1859) 12 Moore P.C. 361 at p.399.
[142] (1876) 1 C.P.D. 654 at p.662. *Cf. Holman v Peruvian Nitrate Co* (1878) 5 Rettie 657 at p.663.
[143] (1845) 2 C.B. 412.
[144] (1868) L.R. 3 Q.B. 412; see also *Russian Steam Navigation Co v De Silva* (1863) 13 C.B. (N.S.) 610.
[145] See, as to words written in, or typed in, *Robertson v French* (1803) 4 East 130 at p.135; *Love v Rowtor Co* [1916] 2 A.C. 527; *Scrutton v Childs* (1877) 36 L.T. 212; *Glynn v Margetson* [1893] A.C. 351; *Hadjipateras v Weigall* (1918) 34 T.L.R. 360; *The Brabant* [1965] 2 Lloyd's Rep. 546; *Kum v Wah Tat Bank Ltd* [1971] 1 Lloyd's Rep. 439 at p.445 (P.C.); *Homburg Houtimport BV v Agrosin Private Ltd, The Starsin* [2003] UKHL 12; [2003] 1 Lloyd's Rep. 571 at [11], [45], [81], [183]. As to stamped clauses, see *Varnish v Kheti* (1949) 82 Ll.L.R. 525, and, as to typed clauses, *United British S.S. Co v Minister of Food* [1951] 1 Lloyd's Rep. 111 at p.114. Where in the margin of a bill of lading, which contained in print a long list of exceptions, including negligence, the words "At Merchant's Risk" were added in writing, it was held that the written words were only intended to sum up the effect of the printed matter, and did not supersede it as the effective agreement: *Briscoe v Powell* (1905) 22 T.L.R. 128.

contracting parties have chosen to include in the contract than to pre-printed terms probably devised to cover very many situations to which the particular contracting parties have never addressed their minds".[146] It is unnecessary to find a meaning in the particular contract for every word of a common printed form,[147] and it may be necessary, in order to give effect to the written words, actually to disregard printed words that are inconsistent.[148] It has been a matter of controversy whether the court may look at deletions from a printed form as showing the intention of the parties, but the weight of authority is now in favour of the view that the court may look at deletions.[149] On any view the court is not prevented from having regard to a clause which, although struck out, is referred to in words which are not struck out.[150]

Where both clauses are printed or both typewritten, a clause specifically designed to deal with a limited range of circumstances will, so far as concerns matters falling within that range, prevail over a clause of general application.[151]

Case 1. A charter contained a printed clause that cargo at Z "should be brought to and taken from alongside at risk and expense"; and a written clause: "cargo at Z as customary". The custom at Z is that the ship pays for the lighterage. *Held*, that of these contradictory clauses the written clause should prevail as being obviously intended by the parties.[152]

Case 2. A charter for outward voyage from X only, on a printed form, had a printed memorandum in the margin: "commission to be paid to C, to whom the vessel is to be addressed on her return to X". *Held*, that oral evidence was essential to show that the memorandum was part of the contract.[153]

Case 3. There was an inconsistency between the typed-in words on the face of the bill of lading "as agents for the carrier, Continental Pacific," and the standard terms (the "identity of carrier"

---

[146] *Homburg Houtimport BV v Agrosin Private Ltd, The Starsin* [2003] UKHL 12; [2003] 1 Lloyd's Rep. 571 at [11].

[147] per Brett J. and other judges in *Gray v Carr* (1871) L.R. 6 Q.B. 522 at pp.536, 550, 557; *Pearson v Göschen* (1864) 17 C.B. (N.S.) 353 at pp.373, 376; but see *McLean v Fleming* (1871) L.R. 2 Sc. & Div. 128.

[148] See *Love v Rowtor Co* [1916] 2 A.C. 527 at pp.535, 536. *Cf. Cunard Co v Marten* [1903] 2 K.B. 511. See also, the cases cited in Art.9, para. (viii).

[149] *Baumvoll v Gilchrest & Co* [1892] 1 Q.B. 253 at p.256; *cf.* per Lord Herschell [1893] A.C. 8 at p.15; *Gray v Carr* (1871) L.R. 6 Q.B. 522 at pp.524 (note) and 529; *Stanton v Richardson* (1874) L.R. 9 C.P. 390; *Glynn v Margetson* [1892] 1 Q.B. 337; [1893] A.C. 351 at p.357, per Lord Halsbury; *Caffin v Aldridge* [1895] 2 Q.B. 648; *Rowland S.S. Co v Wilson* (1897) 2 Com.Cas. 198; *Sanday v McEwan* (1922) 10 Ll.L.R. 359 at p.460; *Taylor v Lewis* (1927) 28 Ll.L.R. 329 at p.330; *Akties, Heimdal v Russian Wood Agency* (1933) 46 Ll.L.R. 1, per Scrutton L.J. at p.6; *Louis Dreyfus v Parnaso* [1959] 1 Q.B. 498 at p.515; *Thomasson v Peabody* [1959] 2 Lloyd's Rep. 296 at p.304; *Timber Shipping v. London and Overseas* [1972] A.C. 1 at pp.15–16, *Mottram Consultants Ltd v Bernard Sunley & Sons Ltd* [1975] 2 Lloyd's Rep. 197, 209 (HL); *Punjab National Bank v de Boinville* [1992] 3 All E.R. 104. The authorities in favour of the opposite restrictive view include *Sassoon v International Banking Corp* [1927] A.C. 711 at p.721; *Inglis v Buttery* (1878) 3 App.Cas. 552 at pp.569, 576; *S.S. Lyderhorn v Duncan* [1909] 2 K.B. 929 at p.941; *Manchester Canal Co v Horlock* [1914] 1 Ch. 453 at pp.463, 464; *Duncan and Pryce, Re* [1913] W.N. 117 (CA); *Cia Naviera Termar v Tradax Export SA* [1965] 1 Lloyd's Rep. 198 at p.204; *Tradax Export v Volkswagenwerk* [1969] 2 Q.B. 599 at p.607.

[150] *Reardon Smith Line v Central Softwood Buying Corporation* (1932) 42 Ll.L.R. 284 at p.291.

[151] *Mariofortuna Naviera SA v Govt. of Ceylon* [1970] 1 Lloyd's Rep. 247 at p.255; *Sabah Flour and Feedmills v Comfez Ltd* [1988] 2 Lloyd's Rep. 18.

[152] *Scrutton v Childs* (1877) 36 L.T. 212. See also *Alsager v St. Katharine's Docks* (1845) 14 M. & W. 794 at p.799; *Moore v Harris* (1876) 1 App.Cas. 318 at p.327, where the written clauses required the ship to deliver to a railway and forward to Toronto, and there was a printed clause, "goods to be taken from alongside by consignee immediately the vessel is ready to discharge, or otherwise they will be landed and stored at expense of consignee".

[153] *Hibbert v Owen* (1859) 2 F. & F. 502; see *Mackill v Wright* (1888) 14 App.Cas 106 at p.117.

clause and "demise" clause) on the reverse of the bill which said that the shipowner was the carrier. *Held*, that the typed-in words should prevail so that the charterer was the carrier.[154]

A12   **Article 12—Alterations in Contract**

A material alteration, addition, or erasure in a charter after signature, made and assented to by one party only, entitles the other party to avoid the charter.[155] A valid alteration may be effected by mutual consent.[156]

If, after the issue of a bill of lading the holder by forgery alters its terms, the question whether the bill of lading becomes a nullity or not depends upon whether the alteration goes to the essence of the contract evidenced by the bill of lading.[157]

A13   **Article 13—Frustration of Contract of Affreightment**

Under the doctrine of frustration, circumstances which delay the performance of a contract or render its performance impossible may discharge the parties.[158] This, in regard to charterparties, is commonly referred to under the phrase "frustration of the commercial purpose of the adventure".[159] Frustration occurs whenever the law recognises that supervening and unforeseen circumstances,[160] arising without default on the part of either party,[161] have rendered a contractual obligation incapable of being performed because in such circumstances performance would be a thing radically different from that which was undertaken by the

---

[154] *The Starsin* [2003] UKHL 12; [2003] 1 Lloyd's Rep. 571. See Art.41 below.
[155] *Croockewit v Fletcher* (1857) 1 H. & N. 893 at p.912; *Chitty on Contracts*, 29th edn (London: Sweet & Maxwell, 2004) Vol.I, §§ 25–020 to 25–027.
[156] *Hall v Brown* (1814) 2 Dow H.L. 367.
[157] *Kwei Tek Chao v British Traders and Shippers* [1954] 2 Q.B. 459 at p.476. Erasure of words indicating that the bill of lading was a "received for shipment" and not a "shipped" bill although material did not vitiate the contract of affreightment or prevent the bill of lading from being a document of title.
[158] The doctrine has in large measure been developed from the shipping cases dealing with delay. *Jackson v Union Marine Co* (1874) L.R. 10 C.P. 125 is the leading authority. *Hadley v Clarke* (1799) 8 T.R. 259, and *Touteng v Hubbard* (1802) 3 B. & p.291, referred to therein, must be treated as wrongly decided on the facts, if not on the law. Lord Finlay L.C. says so as to *Hadley v Clarke* in *Metropolitan Water Board v Dick, Kerr & Co* [1918] A.C. 119. For obvious reasons the question can rarely arise on a bill of lading. It would have arisen in *Embiricos v Reid* [1914] 3 K.B. 45, and the shipper must have succeeded if the shipowner had issued a bill of lading in respect of that portion of the cargo which had already been loaded and of which the shipper claimed redelivery. And see *Scottish Navigation Co v Souter* [1917] 1 K.B. 222, and *Baxter, Fell & Co v Galbraith & Grant* (1941) 70 Ll.L.R. 142.
[159] See *Note* at the end of this Article.
[160] In practice, frustration is rarely invoked in respect of contracts for the carriage of goods by sea because, as with many commercial contracts, the parties tend to include in their contracts "force majeure" clauses dealing with subsequent events. "Unforeseen circumstances" means circumstances for which the written contract makes no (*quaere*, full) provision: *Tatem v Gamboa* [1929] 1 K.B. 132 (Spanish civil war). See also *Bank Line v Capel* [1919] A.C. 435 (war-time requisition); *Anglo-Northern Co v Emlyn Jones* [1918] 1 K.B. 372 (outbreak of European war); *Blane Steamships v Minister of Transport* [1951] 2 K.B. 965 (constructive total loss); *Fibrosa v Fairbairn* [1943] A.C. 32, 40 (per Lord Simon); *Societe Franco Tunisienne v Sidermar* [1961] 2 Q.B. 278, 299–303; *The Eugenia* [1964] 2 Q.B. 226. *Cf. Banck v Bromley* (1919) 1 Ll.L.R. 494; subsequent proceedings (1920) 5 Ll.L.R. 124; *Monarch S.S. Co v Karlshamns* [1949] A.C. 196, 229. For a case in which provision in the charterparty precluded the operation of the doctrine when cargo carried under the charterparty was seized by an invading power see *Kuwait Supply Co v Oyster Management Inc (The Safeer)* [1994] 1 Lloyd's Rep. 637.
[161] "Reliance cannot be placed on self-induced frustration," per Lord Sumner in *Bank Line v Capel* [1919] A.C. 435 at p.452; *Maritime National Fish v Ocean Trawlers* [1935] A.C. 524; *Monarch S.S. Co v Karlshamns* [1949] A.C. 196 at p.229; *J. Lauritzen A.S. v Wijsmuller B.V. (The Super Servant Two)* [1990] 1 Lloyd's Rep. 1.

contract.[162] When the doctrine applies the contract ceases to bind either party.[163] If the frustrating event is proved, the onus of proving that it arose through the default of either party rests upon the party alleging such default.[164]

While in the ultimate analysis whether a contract was frustrated is a question of law, "that conclusion is almost completely determined by what is ascertained as the mercantile usage and the understanding of commercial men".[165] If events occur bringing about frustration, the contract is automatically terminated thereby and not by reason of the election of either party.[166]

The contract may be brought to an end in this way, whether it is still executory, or has been in part already performed,[167] and regardless of whether the parties have for a considerable time after the event not treated it as frustrated.[168]

If, judging reasonably[169] of probabilities[170] at the time he so claims, a party has rightly asserted the contract to be frustrated and at an end, he cannot afterwards be held liable on the ground that events have not turned out according to his expectations.[171]

---

[162] *Davis Contractors Ltd v Fareham U.D.C.* [1956] A.C. 14, per Lord Radcliffe at pp.728, 729; *National Carriers Ltd v Panalpina (Northern) Ltd* [1981] A.C. 675, at pp.688 and 717; *B.T.P. Tioxide Ltd v Pioneer Shipping Ltd and Armada Marine SA (The Nema)* [1982] A.C. 724, at 751, 752; *Edwinton Commercial Corp v Tsavliris Russ (Worldwide Salvage and Towage) Ltd, The Sea Angel* [2007] EWCA Civ 547; [2007] 2 All E.R. (Comm) 634.

[163] "The charterer is released from the charter. When I say *he* is, I think *both* are" (per Bramwell B., *Jackson v Union Marine Co* (1874) L.R. 10 C.P. 125 at p.144). "It would be monstrous to say that in such a case the parties must wait—for the obligation must be mutual—the shipper with cargo which might be perishable, or its market value destroyed, the shipowner with his ship lying idle, possibly rotting, the result of which might be to make the contract ruinous" (per Cockburn C.J., *Geipel v Smith* (1872) L.R. 7. Q.B. 404 at p.410).

[164] *Joseph Constantine v Imperial Smelting Corporation* [1942] A.C. 154.

[165] *The Nema, per* Lord Roskill at p.752, citing Lord Radcliffe in *Tsakiroglou v Noblee Thorl* [1962] A.C. 93 at p.124. An arbitrator's decision on frustration will not be interfered with by the courts if he has directed himself correctly on the law and has not reached a conclusion on the facts which no reasonable person could, on the facts found by him, have reached: Lord Roskill, above, at p.753 disapproving the holding of Kerr J. in *Trade and Transport Inc v Iino Katum Kaisha (The Angelia)* [1972] 2 Lloyd's Rep. 154. See also *International Sea Tankers Inc v Hemisphere Shipping Co Ltd (The Wenjiang)* [1982] 1 Lloyd's Rep. 128. For earlier cases on this aspect, see *Comptoir Commercial v Power* [1920] 1 K.B. 868; *British Movietonews v London and District Cinemas*, above, and *Davis Contractors v Fareham U.D.C.*, above.

[166] Bankes L.J., *Larrinaga v Société Franco-Americaine* (1922) 28 Com.Cas. 1 at p.2; Lord Sumner, *Bank Line v Capel* [1919] A.C. 435 at p.454; *Maritime National Fish v Ocean Trawlers* [1935] A.C. 524; *J. Lauritzen A.S. v Wijsmuller B.V. (The Super Servant Two)* [1990] 1 Lloyd's Rep. 1.

[167] *Embiricos v Reid* [1914] 3 K.B. 45; *Société Franco Tunisienne v Sidermar*, above, in which after a charter had been frustrated freight was recovered on a quantum meruit. The latter case was overruled on frustration in *The Eugenia*, above.

[168] *Kissavos Shipping Co v Empresa Cubana De Fletes (The Agathon)* [1982] 2 Lloyd's Rep. 211.

[169] The decision is objective, not subjective: per Bailhache J. in *Anglo-Northern Trading Co v Emlyn Jones* [1917] 2 K.B. 78 at p.85. A useful test is "would a reasonable man in the position of the party alleging frustration, after taking all reasonable steps to ascertain the facts then available, and without snapping at the opportunity of extricating himself from the contract, come to the conclusion that the interruption was of such a character and was likely to last so long that the subsequent performance or further performance of the contract would really amount to the performance of a new contract?" See Lord McNair's *Legal Effects of War*, 4th edn, pp.156 *et seq.* This was approved by Evershed M.R. in *Atlantic Maritime Co v Gibbon* [1954] 1 Q.B. 88 at p.113. The different views taken by each member of the CA on the facts demonstrate the difficulty of applying the principles of the doctrine.

[170] After-events ascertained at or before the trial of the issue may assist in determining what the probabilities were. See per Lord Sumner in *Bank Line v Capel* [1919] A.C. 435 at p.454, and per Lord Wright in *Denny Mott v Fraser* [1944] A.C. 265 at p.277. But see the not unreasonable criticism of this dictum per Sellers J. in *Atlantic Maritime Co v Gibbon* [1954] 1 Q.B. 88 at p.97 and the explanation by Devlin J. in *Universal Cargo Carriers v Citati* [1957] 2 Q.B. 401 at p.440.

[171] *The Savona* [1900] p.252; *Embiricos v Reid* [1914] 3 K.B. 45. *Query*, how far *Millar v Taylor* [1916] 1 K.B. 402, accords with this principle. It is probably best treated as a case of merely temporary suspension, but see *Atlantic Maritime Co v Gibbon* [1954] 1 Q.B. 88, where it was considered by the CA.

Where, under this principle, the obligations of the contract come to an end (or are discharged by impossibility of performance), the contract is not dissolved *ab initio*. It remains a good contract up to the moment of its dissolution and in respect of accrued obligations.[172] But money which has been paid under the contract for a consideration that has totally failed is recoverable by the payer, subject to the provisions of the Law Reform (Frustrated Contracts) Act 1943, where applicable.[173]

Note. Originally the rule of English law was that where a man has, so far as provided by the express terms of his contract, unconditionally contracted to do something, he is bound to do it or to pay damages, though supervening events may make performance by him impossible. In *Atkinson v Ritchie*[174] Lord Ellenborough said that the rights and duties of the parties to the contract "are conclusively fixed upon, and defined by, the terms of their own written contract. No exception (of a private nature at least) which is not contained in the contract itself, can be grafted upon it by implication, as an excuse for its non-performance. The rule laid down in the case of *Paradine v Jane*[175] has been often recognised in courts of law as a sound one, i.e. that "where the party by his own contract creates a duty or charge upon himself, he is bound to make it good if he may; notwithstanding any accident by inevitable necessity; because he might have provided against it by his contract". The rigour of this rule was maintained[176] until about the middle of the nineteenth century, when it was modified by the rule that a court may find that there was an implied term of the contract under which a contractor may be excused in the case of supervening impossibility. This was first clearly laid down in *Taylor v Caldwell*.[177] Earlier cases had in fact allowed this modification of the older rule, especially in cases as to personal services rendered impossible by death or illness,[178] but *Taylor v Caldwell* seems to be the first case which in terms lays down that there may be that implied term of which Lord Ellenborough had denied the possibility.

The theoretical basis for the doctrine has changed over the years. While for a long time

---

[172] Thus hire due but unpaid at the time of frustration is, apart from the effect of the Law Reform (Frustrated Contracts) Act 1943, recoverable; see below, Art.174. The same reasoning has been held to apply to the liability of a charterer, under the terms of a charter by demise, to indemnify the owner against liability for wreck removal, notwithstanding the frustration of the charter shortly after the ship had been on the rocks: *Blane Steamships v Minister of Transport* [1951] 2 K.B. 965 at pp.989, 1000. It may be doubted whether there was here any "accrued obligation". See, also, *Arab Bank v Barclays Bank* [1954] A.C. 495.

[173] *Fibrosa v Fairbairn* [1943] A.C. 32, overruling *Chandler v Webster* [1904] 1 K.B. 493. *Cf. Civil Service Society v General Steam Co* [1903] 2 K.B. 756; *Lloyd Royal Belge v Stathatos* (1917) 34 T.L.R. 70; *French Marine v Compagnie Napolitaine* [1921] 2 A.C. 494. The effect of the decision in the *Fibrosa* case was to bring the law of England into line with that of Scotland: see *Cantiere San Rocco v Clyde Shipbuilding Co* [1924] A.C. 226 (Sc.). See also, s.65 of the Indian Contract Act. In the case of contracts to which the Law Reform (Frustrated Contracts) Act 1943, applies a further adjustment of rights and liabilities falls to be made. The leading case applying the Act is *B.P. Exploration (Libya) Ltd v Hunt* [1979] 1 W.L.R. 783 (Robert Goff J.); [1983] 2 A.C. 352 (HL). See also *Gamerco SA v I.C.M./Fair Warning (Agency) Ltd* [1995] 1 W.L.R. 1226. The Act, however, does not apply "to any charterparty except a time charterparty or a charterparty by way of demise, or to any contract (other than a charterparty) for the carriage of goods by sea": see s.2(5)(*a*). The Act only applies to contracts governed by English law. For discussion on the Act, see an article by Lord McNair in 60 L.Q.R. 160. For the effect of frustration on an arbitration clause in a contract, see *Heyman v Darwins* [1942] A.C. 356; *Kruse v Questier* [1953] 1 Q.B. 669; *Fiona Trust & Holding Corp v Privalor* [2007] UKHL 40; [2007] 4 All E.R. 951.

[174] (1809) 10 East 530 at p.533.

[175] (1647) Aleyn 26.

[176] *Cf. Spence v Chodwick* (1847) 10 Q.B. 517, in which Pateson J., at p.528, and Wightman J., at p.530, both cite the passage from *Atkinson v Ritchie* quoted above.

[177] (1863) 3 B. & S. 826.

[178] *Cf.* e.g. *Hall v Wright* (1858) E.B. & E. 746.

the implied term approach of *Taylor v Caldwell* held sway,[179] recent cases of the highest authority favour Lord Radcliffe's statement,[180] cited in the Article above, sometimes called the "construction theory".[181]

Whatever the theoretical basis, it is clear that a contract may be frustrated in a variety of circumstances. The following may be taken as the most material:

(1) Where by a change in English law further performance of the contract becomes illegal[182] or where by a change in the law of a foreign country further performance becomes illegal in the agreed place of performance in that country.[183]

(2) Where in a contract for personal service the person engaged dies or becomes physically disabled.[184]

(3) Where the subject-matter of the contract or something essential for its performance is destroyed.[185]

(4) Where circumstances, of which the parties must have regarded the continued existence as essential to performance, cease to exist.[186]

(5) Where circumstances supervene which render performance of the contract in the time contemplated by both parties impossible.[187]

---

[179] *Taylor v Caldwell* (1863) 3 B. & S. 826; *Joseph Constantine v Imperial Smelting Corporation* [1942] A.C. 154; *British Movietonews v London and District Cinemas* [1952] A.C. 166. *Cf.* Lord Loreburn, *Tamplin v Anglo-Mexican Co* [1916] 2 A.C. 397 at p.404; "It is in my opinion the true principle for no court has an absolving power, but it can *infer* from the nature of the contract and the surrounding circumstances that a condition which is not expressed was a foundation upon which the parties contracted." But the implication must be necessary in order to effectuate the intention of the parties as revealed by the language they have used; see per Lord Atkinson in *Larrinaga v Société Franco-Americaine* (1923) 29 Com.Cas. 1 at p.11. In *Davis Contractors v Fareham U.D.C.* [1956] A.C. 696, Lords Reid and Somervell (at pp.721, 733) preferred the view that the doctrine of frustration depended not upon the operation of an implied term, but upon whether on its true construction, the contract was wide enough to apply to the new situation. *Cf.* Lord Radcliffe, at pp.728, 729. The implied term theory is "clearly still not incorrect": per Pearson J., in *Société Franco Tunisienne v Sidermar* [1961] 2 Q.B. 278 at p.294; see also per Diplock J. in *Port Line v Ben Line* [1958] 2 Q.B. 146 at p.162. See, however, the contrary view expressed by Lord Denning M.R. in *The Eugenia* [1964] 2 Q.B. 226 and the three cases in fn.162, above. Whatever the theoretical basis, the test applicable to the facts appears in most, if not all cases, to be the same: would performance in the new circumstances be fundamentally different or different in kind from that undertaken by the contract? For a critical analysis of the different theories on which the doctrine of frustration is based, see Lord McNair, *Legal Effects of War*, 4th edn, pp.166–177, and see per Lord Wright in *Denny Mott v Fraser* [1944] A.C. 265 at 274–276.

[180] See fn.162, above, and in particular per Lord Roskill in *The Nema*, above, at pp.751–752, where Lord Radcliffe's words are described as "the classic statement of the doctrine".

[181] per Lord Hailsham L.C. in *National Carriers Ltd v Panalpina (Northern) Ltd*, above, at p.688.

[182] *Baily v De Crespigny* (1869) L.R. 4 Q.B. 180 (convenant in a lease); *Duncan Fox v Schrempft and Bonke* [1915] 3 K.B. 355; *Arnhold Karberg v Blythe* [1916] 1 K.B. 495; *Metropolitan Water Board v Dick, Kerr & Co* [1918] A.C. 119; *Fibrosa Spolka Ackcynjna v Fairbairn, Lawson Combe Barbour Ltd* [1943] A.C. 32; *Denny Mott & Dickinson v James B. Fraser & Co Ltd* [1944] A.C. 265. *Cf. Walton Harvey Ltd v Walker and Homfrays Ltd* [1931] 1 Ch. 274.

[183] *Ralli v Compania Naviera* [1920] 2 K.B. 287. It should be noted, however, that it was neither contended nor held in that case that the contract was frustrated. The change in Spanish law merely made it illegal to pay the full charter freight; the sum permissible by Spanish law was recovered. See, also, *Soc. Co-op Suisse v La Plata Cereal Co* (1947) 80 Ll.L.R. 530 (prohibition of export of La Plata maize by Argentine law). *Cf. Kawasaki Steel Corp v Sardoil SpA (The Zuiho Maru)* [1977] 2 Lloyd's Rep. 552.

[184] *Robinson v Davison* (1871) L.R. 6 Ex. 269; *Poussard v Spiers* (1876) 1 Q.B.D. 410.

[185] *Taylor v Caldwell*, above; *Appleby v Myers* (1867) L.R. 2 C.P. 651; *Nickoll v Ashton* [1901] 2 K.B. 126; *Shipton Anderson v Harrison* [1915] 3 K.B. 676; *Gulnes v Imperial Chemical Industries* (1937) 43 Com.Cas. 96; *Tatem v Gamboa* [1939] 1 K.B. 132; *Blane S.S. Co v Minister of Transport* [1951] 2 K.B. 965 (constructive total loss of vessel under demise charter). *Cf. Aaby's Rederi v Lep Transport* (1948) 81 Ll.L.R. 465 (destruction by fire of majority of cargo charterer intended to load: no frustration of charter, which was not for a specific cargo).

[186] The Coronation cases; *Krell v Henry* [1903] 2 K.B. 740 (see Lord Wright's comments on this case in *Maritime National Fish v Ocean Trawlers* [1935] A.C. 524 at pp.528, 529); *Blakeley v Muller* [1903] 2 K.B. 760n.; *Chandler v Webster* [1904] 1 K.B. 493. The decision in *Herne Bay Co v Hutton* [1903] 2 K.B. 683, differs not as to the principle, but as to its application to the facts.

[187] *Jackson v Union Marine Co* (1874) L.R. 10 C.P. 125; *Horlock v Beal* [1916] 1 A.C. 486; *Scottish Navigation Co v Souter* [1917] 1 K.B. 222; *Hirji Mulji v Cheong Yue S.S. Co* [1926] A.C. 497; *The Penelope* [1928] p.180. See also *Court Line v Dant and Russell* (1939) 44 Com.Cas. 345 (ship under time charter caught in Yangtse above boom placed across the river by Chinese). "The commercial frustration of an adventure by delay

Whether the supervening obstacle involves such delay as to frustrate the commercial purpose of the adventure (or, in the wider phrase, creates impossibility of performance) depends on the facts in each case and must also be a question of probabilities. Some occurrences, e.g. a war or a blockade,[188] are of themselves so indefinite and serious in their likely duration that frustration may in most cases be assumed. Others, such as a strike,[189] will rarely warrant the assumption. In other cases, e.g. where a ship is damaged, the probabilities can be estimated by surveys or estimates as to the time[190] and the expense[191] that will be involved in repairing her.[192] Prolongation of a voyage by interruption of the contemplated route is capable in law of frustrating the contract of carriage, although a radical prolongation would be required to produce this result.[193]

"When this question arises in regard to commercial contracts . . . the principle is the same, and the language used as to 'frustration of the adventure' merely adapts it to the class of cases in hand".[194] The phrase, especially in its commoner and fuller form, "frustration of the commercial purpose of the adventure", is perhaps a little unfortunate. A slight variation in phrase or thought, makes it "the common purpose", and this suggests that the event, which has happened, or has failed to happen, must defeat both the respective objects for which the two parties made the contract, or must destroy the benefits which both respectively were to secure under it. But this can happen rarely, if ever: in most cases the object of one party—to receive payment for goods sold, or for services rendered, or the like—is fully capable of fulfilment.

During and immediately after the war of 1914–18 this doctrine was frequently in question in regard to the effect upon a charter of a requisition of the ship by the British Government.[195] In the first case in which that question came before the highest tribunal[196] there was a great conflict of judicial opinion. The case was decided in favour of the

---

means . . . the happening of some unforeseen delay without the fault of either party to a contract of such a character as that by it the fulfilment of the contract in the only way in which fulfilment is contemplated and practicable is so inordinately postponed that its fulfilment when the delay is over will not accomplish the only object or objects which the parties to the contract must have known that each of them had in view at the time they made the contract, and for the accomplishment of which object or objects the contract was made"; per Bailhache J. in *Admiral S.S. Co v Weidner* [1916] 1 K.B. 429 at pp.436, 437.

[188] "A state of war must be presumed to be likely to continue so long, and so to disturb the commerce of merchants, as to defeat and destroy the object of a commercial adventure like this": per Lush J., *Geipel v Smith* (1872) L.R. 7 Q.B. 404 at p.414; *Metropolitan Water Board v Dick, Kerr & Co* [1918] A.C. 119. But see Lord Sumner in *Akt. Nord-Osterso v Casper* (1923) 14 Ll.L.R. 203 at p.206 and *Vinava Shipping Co Ltd v Finelvet A.G. (The Chrysalis)* [1983] 1 Lloyd's Rep. 503.

[189] *Braemount S.S. Co v Andrew Weir* (1910) 15 Com.Cas. 101; *Ropner v Ronnebeck* (1914) 20 Com.Cas. 95; *Metropolitan Water Board v Dick, Kerr* [1917] 2 K.B. 1, per Scrutton L.J. at p.35. For a case where the charter was held to be frustrated after a strike, see *The Penelope* [1928] p.180. See, on this, *The Nema*, above [1982] A.C. at p.754. It is uncertain whether Merrivale P. regarded the coal strike or the embargo on the export of coal consequent upon it as the frustrating event.

[190] *Jackson v Union Marine* (1874) L.R. 10 C.P. 125.

[191] *Assicurazione v Bessie Morris* [1892] 2 Q.B. 652; *Carras v London and Scottish Assurance* [1936] 1 K.B. 291; *Kulukundis v Norwich Union* [1937] 1 K.B. 1.

[192] If the contract is really a speculative contract, the doctrine of frustration can rarely, if ever, apply: per Lord Sumner in *Larringaga v Société Franco-Americaine*, above.

[193] *The Eugenia* [1964] 2 Q.B. 226 at p.240; *The Captain George K* [1970] 2 Lloyd's Rep. 21 at p.31.

[194] per Lord Loreburn, *Tamplin v Anglo-Mexican Co* [1916] 2 A.C. 397 at p.404.

[195] It is often difficult to determine whether a ship has been requisitioned or whether a mere direction only has been given to her owner: see *Stella S.S. Co v Sutherland* (1920) 36 T.L.R. 724; *Bombay and Persia S.N. Co v Shipping Controller* (1921) 7 Ll.L.R. 226; *France Fenwick v R.* [1927] 1 K.B. 458. See also *China Mutual S.N. Co v Maclay* [1918] 1 K.B. 33. By s.17(1) of the Compensation (Defence) Act 1939, "requisition means, in relation to any property, take possession of the property or require the property to be placed at the disposal of the requisitioning authority". Difficulties still arise in applying this definition to the facts: see *Nicolaou v Minister of War Transport* (1944) 77 Ll.L.R. 495. The Crown's powers to retain possession of a ship under the prerogative power extend only for such period as possession is needed for the defence of the realm, and a requisition under the prerogative is, therefore, necessarily a temporary taking of possession: per Diplock J. in *Port Line v Ben Line Steamers* [1958] 2 Q.B. 146 at p.161. See also below, pp.34–40. For a clause in a time charter providing for cancellation if the vessel was "commandeered", see *Capel v Soulidi* [1916] 2 K.B. 365.

[196] *Tamplin v Anglo-Mexican Co* [1916] 2 A.C. 397.

charterer, who contended that the charter was still in force,[197] by three judges (Lord Buckmaster L.C., Lord Loreburn and Lord Parker) against two (Lord Haldane and Lord Atkinson). This division of opinion was chiefly in regard to the facts of the case, though there was some divergence as to the legal principle. And as regards the principle the division of opinion was rather between Lord Loreburn, Lord Haldane and Lord Atkinson on the one hand,[198] and Lord Buckmaster and Lord Parker on the other. This has produced the somewhat singular result that the principle deduced from that case, and subsequently applied by other courts in subsequent cases,[199] is really that laid down by Lord Loreburn alone, viz. that if the requisition was likely to outlast the whole remaining period of the charterparty the contract would be dissolved, but if the requisition was likely to last for a period substantially less than the remaining period of charter, it would not be dissolved. In the subsequent cases, in accordance with this, the evidence of shipbrokers was adduced and admitted to prove how long, from their experience, the parties as reasonable business men ought, at the date of the requisition, to have expected that it would last.

The view that the doctrine of frustration cannot apply to a time charterparty in its ordinary form was at one time entertained,[200] but this is erroneous.[201] Of course a time charterparty like any other contract is subject to the usual incidents of the law of contract; the suggestion was that the implication, under which it would be dissolved, was inconsistent with the express terms of the contract.

In relation to the requisitioning of ships during the war of 1914–18 another distinct question arose, viz. if the charter was not dissolved, was the charterer or the shipowner entitled to the hire paid by the Admiralty? Lord Parker alone in Tamplin's case[202] in an obiter dictum (since the point did not expressly arise, and was not argued[203]) suggested that the hire paid by the Admiralty would need to be apportioned between the two of them in accordance with the extent of their respective rights or interest in the ship's working during the period of the requisition. This principle was accepted and applied by courts of first instance in subsequent cases.[204] It is not easy to see why the charterer should have any interest in the hire paid by the Government, if it be remembered (i) that the charter is a contract by which the shipowner during a certain period agrees to do certain work for the

---

[197] In that case the Admiralty hire exceeded the chartered hire; hence it was the charterer who claimed that the charter remained effective. In later cases the relation of the two rates of hire, and in consequence the contentions of charterer and shipowner were usually reversed.

[198] "It will be found that the principles of law enunciated by Lord Loreburn and by the two leading dissentients are identical." Per Lord Finlay L.C., *Bank Line v Capel* [1919] A.C. 435 at pp.442, 443.

[199] e.g. *Countess of Warwick Co v Le Nickel Soc. Anon.* [1918] 1 K.B. 372; *Anglo-Northern Co v Emlyn Jones* [1918] 1 K.B. 372; *Heilgers v Cambrian Co* (1918) 34 T.L.R. 720. *Cf.* the numerous alternative tests discussed by Diplock J. in *Port Line v Ben Line Steamers* [1958] 2 Q.B. 146. Each yielded the same result, namely, that the charter was not frustrated.

[200] By Bailhache J. (fortified by the opinion of an anonymous arbitrator in an earlier case), in *Admiral Shipping Co v Weidner Hopkins* [1916] 1 K.B. 429. Lord Parker expressed a qualified approval of this view in *Tamplin v Anglo-Mexican Co*, above.

[201] *Scottish Navigation Co v Souter* [1917] 1 K.B. 222. See also the opinion of *Lord Sumner in Bank Line v Capel* [1919] A.C. 435; and *Edwinton Commercial Corp v Tsavliris Russ (Worldwide Salvage and Towage) Ltd, The Sea Angel* [2007] EWCA Civ 547; [2007] 2 All E.R. (Comm) 634 (no frustration of time charter *on the facts*). The doctrine was applied in unusual circumstances to a demise charter in *Blane S.S. Co v Minister of Transport* [1951] 2 K.B. 965.

[202] [1916] 2 A.C. 397 at p.428. Lord Parker's suggestion was based upon the terms of the Royal Proclamation under which ships were then requisitioned. It would seem that no question of apportionment could arise in connection with the requisitioning of ships by the Government during the war of 1939–45 in view of the definition of "owner" in the Compensation (Defence) Act 1939, though in certain circumstances the *whole* of the compensation due is held by the owner as trustee for the charterer: see s.4(3) of the Act, and *Port Line v Ben Line*, above, (p.39, below).

[203] It appeared to be assumed by the shipowner at all stages of that case that if the charter was not frustrated the charterer would receive all the Government hire, an assumption which the charterer was well content to accept.

[204] e.g. *Chinese Engineering Co v Sale* [1917] 2 K.B. 599; *London American Co v Rio de Janeiro, etc, Co* [1917] 2 K.B. 611; *Dominion Coal Co v Maskinonge Co* [1922] 2 K.B. 132 and *cf. Port Line v Ben Line*, above.

charterer, but is not a contract under which the charterer has any interest in the ship,[205] except that it is the vehicle with which the shipowner is to do the agreed work; (ii) that by the charter the charterer agrees to pay hire during the agreed period even if the shipowner by reason of restraint of princes is not doing his promised work; and (iii) that the "requisition" meant that the shipowner, under compulsion, agreed to do work for the Government instead of doing work for the charterer.

Case 1. A ship was chartered in November 1871 to proceed with all possible dispatch, dangers and accidents of navigation excepted, from Liverpool to Newport and there load iron for San Francisco. She sailed from L. to N. on January 2, 1872, but stranded on the way on January 3. The necessary repairs took till the end of August. On February 15 the charterers threw up the charter. The jury found that the time necessary for getting the ship off and repairing her was so long as to put an end, in a commercial sense, to the commercial speculation entered upon by the shipowner and charterer.[206] *Held*, that the charterer was justified in throwing up the charter.[207]

Case 2. C chartered a Greek ship to load a cargo of grain in the Sea of Azov and carry it to the United Kingdom. The ship arrived at the loading port on October 1, 1912, just before war broke out between Greece and Turkey. She commenced to load, but next day C stopped loading because the Turks were seizing and detaining Greek ships at the Dardanelles. War was declared on October 18. The lay-days expired on October 22. On October 21 C purported to cancel the charter. The ship was unable to leave the Black Sea until the war ended in September 1913. *Held*, that C was justified in treating the charter as at an end.[208]

Case 3. C chartered A's steamer on a time charter for sixty calendar months. The chartered period began on December 4, 1912, and would consequently end on December 4, 1917. In February 1915 the steamer was requisitioned by the British Government for war services. A claimed that the charterparty was determined or suspended[209] by this requisition. C claimed that it was not, being ready to continue to pay the monthly hire despite the requisition, and suggested that during the requisition he would receive the remuneration payable by the Government for use of the steamer. *Held*, that the requisition did not put an end to the charter.[210]

Case 4. A chartered his ship to C under a time charterparty form for "one Baltic round", freight being payable at so much per month until completion of such employment. The service began on July 4, 1914, and the vessel went to the Baltic to load under a sub-charter made by C with D. At the beginning of August 1914, when the war broke out, she was partly loaded, and some bills of lading had been issued by the captain to D. By reason of the war and orders of the Russian authorities the ship had to remain at her port of loading and was still there at the date of the action. On August 5,

---

[205] See Scrutton L.J. in *Elliott Tug Co v Shipping Controller* [1922] 1 K.B. 127; per Diplock J. in *Port Line v Ben Line Steamers* [1958] 2 Q.B. 146 and Bailhache J. in *Federated Coal Co v The King* (1922) 27 Com.Cas. 295: and in *Dominion Coal Co v Lord Curzon Co* (1922) 12 Ll.L.R. 490, especially the last.

[206] i.e. of both. Contrast the direction to the jury in *Case 1*, Art.52, below, where the delay was by breach of the shipowner's undertaking, and its limitation to the objects the *charterer* had in view.

[207] *Jackson v Union Marine* (1874) L.R. 10 C.P. 125. The question here was as to the time for repairs. In *Assicurazione v Bessie Morris* [1892] 2 Q.B. 652, on the shipowner's claim to put an end to the charter, the question was their expense. The decision that he must prove commercial impossibility to repair the ship for the voyage so far as regards the goods to be carried (i.e. commercially, destruction of the ship) illustrates the connection of these cases as to frustration with cases as to destruction of the subject-matter of a contract, like *Taylor v Caldwell* (1863) 3 B. & S. 826. See also *Carras v London and Scottish Assurance* [1936] 1 K.B. 291 and *Kulukundis v Norwich Union* [1937] 1 K.B. 1, and in particular the judgment of Scott L.J. in the latter case, at pp.41, 42.

[208] *Embiricos v Reid* [1914] 3 K.B. 45. *Cf. Geipel v Smith* (1872) L.R. 7 Q.B. 404.

[209] The claim that the charter was "suspended" was not seriously argued in the KBD, and not at all in the CA or HL. It is clearly not substainable. *Cf. Modern Co v Duneric S.S. Co* [1917] 1 K.B. 370.

[210] *Tamplin S.S. Co v Anglo-Mexican Co* [1916] 2 A.C. 397. So held by Lord Buckmaster L.C., Lord Loreburn and Lord Parker. The dissentient view of Lord Haldane and Lord Atkinson was really only on the question of fact whether the degree of interruption of performance of the contract amounted to its frustration. The question whether charterer or shipowner should receive the payments from the Government, or share them, was not raised or decided in the case, as Lord Parker points out at p.428.

C refused to pay further time hire. On November 6, A sued C for hire up to November 4. *Held*, that the charter was to be treated as frustrated and determined on and after the outbreak of war.[211]

Case 5. C chartered A's steamer for a voyage from X to Z and back at a monthly hire payable each month in advance. The first month's hire was paid and the ship placed at C's disposal. When she should have sailed from X on December 2, the authorities there refused to allow her to leave, and they did not release her until February 10 following. On December 12, C claimed that the charter was dissolved, and claimed repayment of the first month's hire. *Held*, (i) that the charter was dissolved on December 2, but (ii) that C could not recover back the first month's hire.[212]

Case 6. C chartered A's steamer by a charter dated February 16, 1915, for twelve months. The charter provided that the service should not begin before April 1, 1915, and if the steamer was not ready by April 30, 1915, C might cancel. She was not so ready, but C did not cancel. Just before her service was about to begin she was on May 11, 1915, requisitioned by the Government. On September 2, 1915, she was released. C then claimed that she must be placed at his disposal for twelve months. A claimed that the charter had been dissolved. *Held*, that the charter had been dissolved and that C's claim failed.[213]

Case 7. A ship was chartered on September 9, 1956, for a "trip out to India via Black Sea", hire being payable monthly. The war clause of the charter provided that "the vessel . . . nor to be ordered nor continued to any place or on any voyage . . . which will bring her within a zone which is dangerous . . . " The ship was delivered at Genoa on September 20, and after loading a cargo of metal goods, sailed from Odessa on October 25. On October 30 she arrived at Port Said, when the Canal Zone was "dangerous", and then entered the canal. On October 31 she was, trapped by the blocking of the canal. The southern end of the canal was not cleared until April 1957, but a passage north was cleared at the beginning of January and the ship reached Alexandria on January 12. However, on January 4 the charterers contended that the charter was frustrated and refused to continue the voyage via the Cape. *Held* (i) the charterers were in breach of the war clause; (ii) accordingly the charterers were not entitled to rely on the detention in the canal as a ground of frustration; (iii) the fact that the vessel would have had to proceed via the Cape did not frustrate the charter since the voyage round the Cape made no great difference except that it took a good deal longer and was more expensive than a voyage through the canal.[214]

---

[211] *Scottish Navigation Co v Souter; Admiral S.S. Co v Weidner* [1917] 1 K.B. 222. The facts in the second case were practically indistinguishable, except that the agreed employment of the ship was for "two Baltic rounds". It was agreed during the argument in the CA that a "Baltic round" ordinarily means a voyage from the United Kingdom to a Baltic port or ports, with leave to call at a port or ports substantially on the route thither, returning from the Baltic to a United Kingdom port with leave to call on the way back at a port or ports substantially on that route. For a very special case on the meaning of "one round voyage to the Kara Sea", see *Temple S.S. Co v Sovfracht* (1945) 79 Ll.L.R. 1 (HL).

[212] *Lloyd Royal Belge v Stathatos* (1918) 34 T.L.R. 70; *French Marine v Compagnie Napolitaine* [1921] 2 A.C. 494. But see now, the Law Reform (Frustrated Contracts) Act 1943.

[213] *Bank Line v Capel* [1919] A.C. 435; *cf. Maritime National Fish v Ocean Trawlers* [1935] A.C. 524.

[214] *The Eugenia* [1964] 2 Q.B. 226 (CA) overruling *Société Franco-Tunisienne v Sidermar* [1961] 2 Q.B. 278. This case was followed, *dubitante*, in *The Captain George K* [1970] 2 Lloyd's Rep. 21. See also *Tsakiroglou v Noblee* [1962] A.C. 93 (c.i.f. Hamburg from Port Sudan).

Chapter 2

PARTIES TO THE CONTRACT

The original parties to a contract of affreightment will normally be either the shipowner and charterer in a charterparty; or the shipper and carrier (who if the ship is a chartered ship may be the shipowner or the charterer)[1] in a bill of lading contract. But this chapter is concerned to examine when it is that other parties acquire (contractual) rights or liabilities under that contract.

A14   **Article 14—Persons acquiring rights and liabilities under the Carriage of Goods by Sea Act 1992[2]**

By s.2(1) of the Carriage of Goods by Sea Act 1992, "a person who becomes:

(a) the lawful holder of a bill of lading;

(b) the person who (without being an original party to the contract of carriage) is the person to whom delivery of goods to which a sea waybill relates is to be made by the carrier in accordance with that contract; or

(c) the person to whom delivery of the goods to which a ship's delivery order relates is to be made in accordance with the undertaking contained in the order,

shall (by virtue of becoming the holder of the bill or, as the case may be, the person to whom delivery is to be made) have transferred to and vested in him all rights of suit under the contract of carriage as if he had been a party to that contract."

Section 2(5) of the Act extinguishes certain rights of suit existing when the statutory transfer of rights of suit takes place. The effect of s.2(5) is as follows[3]:

---

[1] This is the "identity of carrier" issue: see Art.41 below.

[2] The Act is printed in full in Appendix 1, below. It was passed to give effect to the recommendations contained in the report of the Law Commission and the Scottish Law Commission on Rights of Suit in Respect of Carriage of Goods by Sea (Law Com. No. 196, Scot. Law Com. No. 130, H.C. 250), referred to hereafter as the "Report of the Law Commissions". The Act came into force on September 16, 1992, but nothing in the Act, including the repeal of the Bills of Lading Act 1855, has effect in relation to any document issued before that date: s.6(3). Similar legislation has been enacted in other jurisdictions e.g. Singapore (Bills of Lading Act, Cap 384, 1994 Ed) as to which see, for example, *The Shravan* [1999] 4 S.L.R. 197; *The Patraikos 2* [2002] 4 S.L.R. 232; *UCO Bank v Golden Shore Transportation Pte Ltd, The Asean Pioneer* [2005] SGCA 42.

[3] This summary is based on the Explanatory Note in the Report of the Law Commissions, p.51. For the policy considerations underlying the treatment of the rights of the shipper and intermediate holders, see the Report of the Law Commissions, paras 2.32 to 2.41.

   (i) The shipper under a bill of lading ceases to have contractual rights once someone else becomes the lawful holder of the bill of lading.[4]

   (ii) The intermediate holder of a bill of lading ceases to have contractual rights once someone else becomes the lawful holder of the bill of lading.[5]

   (iii) The transfer of rights under a sea waybill is without prejudice to the rights of an original party to the contract contained in or evidenced by the waybill.[6]

   (iv) Those intermediately entitled to delivery under the terms of a sea waybill cease to be entitled to rights of suit once someone else becomes entitled to delivery, e.g. where the consignee's name is changed before delivery.[7]

   (v) In the case of a ship's delivery order, the rights of the person entitled under the delivery order are in addition to any rights possessed by any person under the contract of carriage in relation to which the order is issued.[8] The shipowner can protect himself against the possibility of actions by both the bill of lading holder and holders of delivery orders by insisting on delivery up of the bill of lading in exchange for the delivery orders.

   (vi) Those intermediately entitled to delivery under a ship's delivery order cease to be entitled to rights of suit when someone else subsequently becomes entitled to delivery.[9]

Where loss or damage is sustained in consequence of a breach of the contract of carriage by a person other than the one to whom the rights of suit in respect of that breach are transferred by s.2(1), the person in whom the rights of suit are vested is entitled to exercise those rights for the benefit of the other person who has suffered the loss and damage to the same extent as they could have been exercised if they had been vested in that other person.[10] It is no answer to a claim brought by a person in whom rights of suit are vested under the Act that the loss and damage has been suffered by someone other than the claimant. The claimant

---

[4] s.2(5)(a). The rights which are extinguished in such a case are those under the contract contained in or evidenced by the bill of lading: s.5(1). Accordingly, if the shipper is a charterer, his rights of suit under the charter remain unaffected: see the Report of the Law Commissions, para.2.52.

[5] s.2(5)(b).

[6] s.2(5), tailpiece. Generally the shipper will be the only original party, unless he has contracted as agent for the consignee, and this is unlikely in a case where the shipper has reserved the right to alter the name of the consignee before delivery.

[7] s.2(5)(b). *Contra*, where the consignee was an original party to the contract: s.2(5), tailpiece.

[8] s.2(5), tailpiece.

[9] s.2(5)(b).

[10] s.2(4). See also Art.195.

will be liable to account for the proceeds of his claim to the person who has really suffered the loss and damage.[11]

Where a person in whom rights of suit are vested by virtue of s.2(1) of the Act:

(a) takes or demands delivery from the carrier of any of the goods to which the document relates;

(b) makes a claim under the contract of carriage against the carrier in respect of any of those goods; or

(c) is a person who, at a time before those rights were vested in him, took or demanded delivery from the carrier of any of those goods,

that person shall (by virtue of taking or demanding delivery or making the claim or, in a case falling within (c) above, of having the rights vested in him) become subject to the same liabilities[12] under that contract as if he had been a party to that contract.[13] The liabilities of original parties to the contract remain intact.[14]

Case. On arrival at the destination port, the buyers of a quantity of liquid propane took routine samples, before discharge, of the propane. On discovering from the samples that the propane was contaminated and not of the quality contracted for, the buyers rejected the cargo and sold the cargo on to sub-buyers to whom they subsequently indorsed the bill of lading. In a claim by the carriers against the buyers for breach of the obligation not to ship a dangerous cargo, the questions were whether the buyers had "demanded delivery" of the goods under s.3 and, if they had, did they remain subject to the liabilities under the contract of carriage, by reason of s.3, even after they had transferred their rights under that contract, by endorsement of the bill of lading, to the sub-buyers. *Held* that the buyers had not, by taking samples, demanded delivery; but, in any event, once the rights had been transferred by the buyer, by endorsement over to the sub-buyer of the bill of lading, the principle of mutuality between benefit and burden meant that they should not remain subject to the liabilities.[15]

It can be argued that ss 2 and 3 of the Act are to be given effect in any proceedings in the English Courts, regardless of the proper law governing the transfer of the bill of lading or other document.[16]

"Bill of lading." The expression "bill of lading" is not defined in the Act, but the Act does not apply to what is commonly called a "straight" bill,[17] i.e. one which is "incapable of transfer either by indorsement or, as a bearer bill, by delivery without indorsement",[18] such as a bill which is not made out "to order"

---

[11] See the Report of the Law Commissions, paras 2.24 to 2.29. The problems associated with causes of action for the benefit of others arise in a number of different fields, e.g. bailor and bailee, *cestui que* trust and trustee, principal and agent, etc., and it is there that one must turn for guidance on the solutions.

[12] For these words in the Bill of Lading Act 1855, s.1, see *Ministry of Food v Lamport & Holt Line* [1952] 1 Lloyd's Rep. 371 at p.382.

[13] s.3(1). See *Borealis AB v Stargas Ltd, The Berge Sisar* [2001] UKHL 17; [2002] 2 A.C. 205, *case* below.

[14] s.3(3).

[15] *Borealis AB v Stargas Ltd, The Berge Sisar* [2001] UKHL 17; [2002] 2 A.C. 205.

[16] The argument derives support from *Sewell v Burdick* (1884) 10 App. Cas. 74 at pp.85, 104. But *cf.* Contracts (Applicable Law) Act 1990, Sch.1, Arts 1.2(c) and 12. Toh [1994] L.M.C.L.Q. 280 rejects this argument in favour of a more modern choice of law approach.

[17] See Art.2 above.

[18] s.1(2)(a).

or "to assigns", or is marked "not negotiable".[19] Such a bill may nevertheless be a sea waybill within the meaning of the Act. A "received for shipment" bill which is not a straight bill is within the Act.[20]

"*Holder of a bill of lading*." References in the Act to the holder of a bill of lading are references to any of the following:

(a) a person with possession of the bill who, by virtue of being the person identified in the bill, is the consignee of the goods to which the bill relates;

(b) a person with possession of the bill as a result of the completion, by delivery of the bill, of any indorsement of the bill or, in the case of a bearer bill, of any other transfer of the bill;

(c) a person with possession of the bill as a result of any transaction by virtue of which he would have become a holder within paragraph (a) or (b) above had not the transaction been effected at a time when possession of the bill no longer gave a right (as against the carrier) to possession of the goods to which the bill relates.[21]

Paragraph (c) above refers to the case where the bill is transferred after the goods have been completely delivered to the person having a right under the bill of lading to claim them, so that the bill no longer operates as a document of title conferring constructive possession of the goods.[22] In such a case, however, the holder does not acquire rights of suit or become subject to liabilities under the Act unless he becomes the holder by virtue of a transaction effected pursuant to any contractual or other arrangements made before the time at which the right to possession of the goods ceased to attach to possession of the bill, or as a result of the rejection of goods or documents delivered to another person in pursuance of any such arrangements.[23]

"*Lawful holder*." A lawful holder is one who has become the holder of the bill in good faith.[24]

"*Sea waybill*." A sea waybill[25] is defined in the Act as "any document which is not a bill of lading but:

(a) is such a receipt for goods as contains or evidences a contract for the carriage of goods by sea; and

---

[19] The main consequence of this is that s.4 does not apply to such a document: see Art.59, below. For the underlying policy considerations, see the Report of the Law Commissions, para.2.50.

[20] s.1(2)(b). See the Report of the Law Commissions, para.2.48.

[21] s.5(2).

[22] See Art.95, below.

[23] s.2(2). The object of this provision is to prevent trafficking in bare causes of action: see the Report of the Law Commissions, para.2.43.

[24] s.5(2). See *UCO Bank v Golden Shore Transportation Pte Ltd* [2006] 1 S.L.R. 1 where the Singapore Court of Appeal considered a similar provision under its parallel Bills of Lading Act (Cap. 384, 1994 Rev Ed).

[25] See Art.2 above.

(b) identifies the person to whom delivery of the goods is to be made by the carrier in accordance with that contract".[26]

A sea waybill, like a bill of lading, is a document which contemplates that the goods to which it relates may become deliverable to a person other than the shipper. Unlike a bill of lading, however, it is not necessary for the document to leave the possession of the shipper before anyone else can take delivery under it. The consignee is named in the waybill or may be nominated by the shipper in accordance with its terms, and where the consignee is named, the waybill may make provision for his identity to be varied.[27] Delivery is made to the consignee without production of the waybill.

"*Ship's delivery order.*" A ship's delivery order[28] is defined in the Act as "any document which is neither a bill of lading nor a sea waybill but contains an undertaking which:

(a) is given under or for the purposes of a contract for the carriage of goods by sea of the goods to which the document relates, or of goods which include those goods; and

(b) is an undertaking by the carrier to a person identified in the document to deliver the goods to which the document relates to that person".[29]

The person entitled to delivery under a ship's delivery order does not become entitled to rights of suit or subject to liabilities otherwise than in respect of the goods to which the delivery order relates.[30]

The practice of issuing ship's delivery orders derives from the fact that a seller may wish to sell different parts of a bulk cargo shipped under a single bill of lading. It is undesirable for the shipowner to accept a surrender of the bill of lading and to issue a number of new ones[31]: the better and more usual practice is to issue a number of ship's delivery orders in exchange for the bill of lading.

"*Goods to which a document relates.*" The Act applies to goods to which a document relates even though the goods cease to exist after the issue of the document or cannot be identified (whether because they are mixed with other goods or for any other reason).[32]

"*All rights of suit*" includes the right to restrain by injunction threatened breaches of the contract of carriage by the shipowner.[33] The rights transferred

---

[26] s.1(3).
[27] This is recognised by s.5(3) of the Act.
[28] See Art.2 above.
[29] s.1(4).
[30] ss.2(3) and 3(2).
[31] *S.I.A.T. di del Ferro v Tradax* [1978] 2 Lloyd's Rep. 470 at p.493.
[32] s.5(4). For bills of lading for goods not shipped see Arts 59 to 62. For mixed goods, see Art.152.
[33] So held on the same words in the Bills of Lading Act 1855: *Wood v Atlantic Transport Co* (1900) 5 Com. Cas. 121.

include rights of suit in respect of breaches of the contract of carriage committed during the voyage but before the transfer takes place.[34]

"*The contract of carriage.*" In relation to a bill of lading or sea waybill this means the contract contained in or evidenced[35] by that bill or waybill.[36] In relation to a ship's delivery order it means the contract under or for the purposes of which the undertaking contained in the order is given.[37] The reference to the contract "evidenced by" the bill of lading or sea waybill must presumably be taken to exclude terms or incidents of the contract which are not evidenced by the document itself, and of which the transferee or consignee has no notice.[38] Thus, an indorsee or consignee will not be bound by acts of the shipper, which against the latter might amount to a waiver or give rise to an estoppel.[39]

Case. F, shippers of goods, indorsed to I a bill of lading stating that the goods were shipped at Fiume for Dunkirk. The ship deviated from the ordinary voyage between those ports and was lost on such deviation. I sued the shipowners, who pleaded that F knew of the intention to deviate before shipment. *Held,* that F's knowledge did not affect I.[40]

"*The same liabilities . . . as if he had been a party to that contract.*" Read in their widest sense these words would appear to impose a liability for matters arising at the port of shipment with which the transferee of obligations had nothing to do, such as the shipment of dangerous goods by the shipper in breach of warranty. It can be argued that this reading is incorrect.[41] However, the Law Commissions considered the matter, but decided not to distinguish between pre- and post-shipment liabilities, nor to make special provision exempting the consignee or indorsee from liability for the shipper's breach of warranty in respect of dangerous cargo.[42] It has been argued that the warranty that the cargo is not dangerous is a personal liability of the shipper not forming part of the contract of carriage.[43] Unless this is so, however, the transferee of rights of suit can only be sure of escaping such liability by abstaining from enforcing his rights under the Act.

Note. The Carriage of Goods by Sea Act 1992 was passed in order to remedy a number of flaws in the Bills of Lading Act 1855, which it repeals. The Report of the Law

---

[34] *Monarch S.S. Co v Karlshamns* [1949] A.C. 196 at p.218.
[35] See Art.33.
[36] s.5(1)(a).
[37] s.5(1)(b).
[38] *Rodger v Comptoir d'Escompte de Paris* (1869) L.R. 2 P.C. 393; *The Helene* (1865) B. & L. 415; at p.424; *The Emilien Marie* (1875) 44 L.J. Adm. 9; *Jenkyns v Usborne* (1844) 8 Scott N.R. 505; *Leduc v Ward* (1882) 20 Q.B.D. 475; *Hain v Tate & Lyle* (1936) 41 Com. Cas. 350; and the further cases cited at Art.90, fn.335, below. The case of defeat of stoppage *in transitu* by indorsement to a *bona fide* holder falls under this principle. It can be argued that all possible confusion would have been avoided if the 1992 Act had followed the Bills of Lading Act 1855 in referring only to the transfer of rights under the contract "contained in" the bill of lading.
[39] *Government of Swaziland Central Transport Administration v Leila Maritime Co Ltd (The Leila)* [1985] 2 Lloyd's Rep. 172.
[40] *Leduc v Ward*, above.
[41] 19th edn, p.28. The support for the view that the shipper remains liable for breach of his warranty that the goods are not dangerous is to be found in *Effort Shipping Co Ltd v Linden Management SA (The Giannis N.K.)* [1994] 2 Lloyd's Rep. 171; [1996] 1 Lloyd's Rep. 577; *The Athanasia Comninos and Georges Chr. Lemos* [1990] 1 Lloyd's Rep. 277.
[42] Report of the Law Commissions, paras 3.20 to 3.22.
[43] Carver, *Carriage by Sea*, (13th edn, 1984) p.68.

Commissions[44] contains a full discussion of the law as it stood before the Act and of the policy considerations underlying the reforms.

Before the passing of the Bills of Lading Act 1855 the indorsement of a bill of lading would not affect the contract contained in, or evidenced by, it and the indorsee could not sue or be sued on such contract, though he was the person really interested in the goods the subject of the contract.[45] The remedy adopted by s.1 of the Bills of Lading Act 1855 was to transfer rights of suit under the bill of lading contract to the consignee and to "every endorsee of a bill of lading to whom the property in the goods therein mentioned shall pass, upon or by reason of such consignment or endorsement". Unfortunately this proved ineffective in many cases where the property passed otherwise than upon or by reason of the consignment or endorsement of the bill of lading, either because it did not pass at all, although the buyer was on risk,[46] or because the indorsee did not obtain the full property in the goods,[47] or because the transfer of the bill of lading was in no way instrumental in passing the property.[48] The person really at interest could not sue in tort without assuming the burden of proving negligence and showing that he was the owner of or entitled to possession of the goods at the time of the negligence in question.[49] If the claim in tort got off the ground the shipowner could not avail himself of the protection of exceptions in the contract or under the Hague-Visby Rules. The buyer could ask his seller to assign the claim in contract, but could not compel him to do so.[50] Another expedient was for the receiver to rely on an implied contract on the terms of the bill of lading on the principle described in the next Article: but this depended on the facts of each case, which would not necessarily support the inference of contractual intention, particularly if the goods had been lost before arrival of the ship.[51]

Accordingly the Law Commissions recommended that the transfer of contractual rights should not be associated with the passing of property or risk, but should instead follow the transfer of possession of the bill of lading into the hands of a holder in good faith.[52] The Law Commissions recommended that the liabilities under the contract of carriage should be enforceable against the lawful holder if, but only if, he sought to enforce his rights under the contract,[53] and that the provisions regarding the transfer of rights and liabilities under the contract of carriage should be extended to sea waybills and ship's delivery orders, with power to the Secretary of State by subordinate legislation to extend the provisions to cases where a telecommunication system or other information technology is used for effecting transactions corresponding to those effected by bills of lading, sea waybills and ship's delivery orders.[54]

A15   **Article 15—Persons taking Delivery under the Bill of Lading or other Document**

Persons who are neither original parties to the contract of carriage nor within the provisions of the Carriage of Goods by Sea Act 1992[55] may nevertheless become

---

[44] For the full citation of this authority, see fn.2, above.
[45] *Thomson v Dominy* (1845) 14 M. & W. 403; *Howard v Shephard* (1850) 9 C.B. 297.
[46] e.g. *The Aliakmon* [1986] A.C. 785 (reservation of right of disposal).
[47] e.g. *Sewell v Burdick* (1884) 10 App. Cas. 74 (pledgee's limited special property).
[48] As in *The Delfini* [1990] 1 Lloyd's Rep. 252; or in the case of sales of undivided parts of bulk cargoes, where property did not pass until the goods were ascertained.
[49] See Art.120.
[50] *The Albazero* [1977] A.C. 774, per Lord Diplock at pp.845–846.
[51] See *The Aramis* [1989] 1 Lloyd's Rep. 213 at p.230.
[52] Report of the Law Commissions, paras 2.16 to 2.22.
[53] Report of the Law Commissions, paras 3.1 to 3.22.
[54] See ss.1(5), (6) and the definitions in s.5(1).
[55] See Art.14.

parties to a contract of affreightment with the shipowner if a new contract (commonly referred to as a *Brandt v Liverpool*[56] contract) can be found as a fact[57] in all the circumstances, e.g. from their having presented the bill of lading or other document[58] and taken delivery thereunder.[59] The test is objective and no contract will be inferred unless the conduct of the parties is consistent only with an intention to make such a contract.[60] A new contract may also be proved by evidence of previous dealings between the parties,[61] or of usage of trade.[62] The shipowner may be held liable under the new contract for failure to deliver the goods on the terms of the bill of lading.[63] He will not, however, have a claim under such a contract against the party presenting the bill of lading for breach of the shipper's warranty as to the fitness of the goods for carriage.[64]

Note. In the twenty or thirty years leading up to the passage of the Carriage of Goods by Sea Act 1992, the inadequacy of the Bills of Lading Act 1855, under modern conditions of business, to vest rights of suit in the person really at interest led to the principles summarised in this article being frequently invoked, if only to found an alternative cause of action in case a claim under the Act of 1855 should fail. Although the question whether a new contract was to be inferred is a question of fact, the courts were still faced with the issue whether the facts were capable in law of supporting the necessary implication. This in turn raised questions of offer and acceptance, consideration, and intention to contract.[65] The principles involved are not peculiar to the carriage of goods by sea, but are common to the formation of contracts of all kinds. The passage of the Carriage of Goods by Sea Act 1992 has reduced the practical importance of this line of authority, and it would seem that in all the leading reported cases in which a *Brandt v Liverpool* contract has been established the claimant would now have rights under the 1992 Act. Having said that, it would appear that *Brandt v Liverpool* contracts might still have a role to play in situations where the 1992 Act does not apply: for example, where the relevant

---

[56] See fn.63 below.
[57] It will not be inferred as a matter of law: see *Saunders v Vanzeller* (1843) 4 Q.B. 260; nor where the person presenting the bill at the same time repudiates liability under it: *S.S. County of Lancaster v Sharp* (1889) 24 Q.B.D. 158; nor where the bill clearly negatives such a contract: *Amos v Temperley* (1841) 8 M. & W. 798; *Howard v Tucker* (1831) 1 B. & Ad. 712; *Ward v Felton* (1801) 1 East 507; *Kennedy v Gouveia* (1823) 3 D. & R. 503.
[58] e.g. a ship's delivery order: *Peter Cremer Westfaelische GmbH v General Carriers SA* [1973] 2 Lloyd's Rep. 366.
[59] See as to demurrage, *Allen v Coltart* (1883) 11 Q.B.D. 782; *Palmer v Zarifi* (1877) 37 L.T. 790; *Dobbin v Thornton* (1806) 6 Esp. 16; *Jesson v Solly* (1811) 4 Taunt. 52; *Stindt v Roberts* (1848) 5 D. & L. 460; *Young v Moeller* (1855) 5 E. & B. 755; *Wegener v Smith* (1854) 15 C.B. 285; per Lord Selborne in *Sewell v Burdick* (1884) 10 App.Cas. 74 at p.89; *Scotson v Pegg* (1861) 6 H. & N. 295 (as explained by T.E.S.: see 19th ed. pp.29–30); *Benson v Hippius* (1828) 4 Bing. 455. See, as to freight, *Swan v Barber* (1879) 5 Ex.D. 130; *Sanders v Vanzeller* (1843) 4 Q.B. 260; *Cock v Taylor* (1811) 13 East 399; *Dougal v Kemble* (1826) 3 Bing. 383 at p.389; *Amos v Temperley* (1841) 8 M. & W. 798; *Kemp v Clark* (1848) 12 Q.B. 647; *White v Furness* [1895] A.C. 40, per Lord Herschell at pp.43, 44, *Lewis v M'Kee* (1868) L.R. 4 Ex. 58.
[60] *Ilyssia Cia. Naviera SA v Bamaodah (The Elli 2)* [1985] 1 Lloyd's Rep. 107; *The Aramis* [1989] 1 Lloyd's Rep. 213; *Cia Portorafti Commerciale SA v Ultramar Panama Inc (The Captain Gregos) (No. 2)* [1990] 2 Lloyd's Rep. 395; *Mitsui & Co Ltd v Novorossiysk Shipping Co (The Gudermes)* [1993] 1 Lloyd's Rep. 311. The reasoning in *The Aramis* is particularly important in holding that there was no *Brandt v Liverpool* contract made out.
[61] *Wilson v Kymer* (1813) 1 M. & S. 157; *cf. Taylor v Bell* [1968] 2 Lloyd's Rep. 63.
[62] *Dickenson v Lano* (1860) 2 F. & F. 188.
[63] *Brandt v Liverpool, etc. S.N. Co* [1924] 1 K.B. 575; *query*, whether there would have been any consideration for the implied contract if the bill of lading had been marked "freight prepaid" and no demurrage was due under it. See also *The St. Joseph* [1933] P. 119.
[64] *The Athanasia Comninos and Georges Chr. Lemos* [1990] 1 Lloyd's Rep. 277.
[65] See, e.g., the cases at fn.60, above. See also Treitel, "Bills of Lading and Implied Contracts" [1989] L.M.C.L.Q. 162.

shipping document presented does not fall within the Act or where the carrier delivers against an indemnity by the party taking delivery and there is no bill of lading or other relevant shipping document.

Case. Goods were shipped under a bill of lading to the order of F, who indorsed it to a banker, H, by way of pledge. H paid the freight, presented the bill of lading and took delivery of the goods. *Held*, though H could not sue under the Bills of Lading Act 1855, on the facts the shipowner was liable on an implied contract to deliver the goods on the terms of the bill of lading.[66]

A16A ## Article 16A—Persons acquiring rights under the Contracts (Rights of Third Parties) Act 1999[67]

The Contracts (Rights of Third Parties) Act 1999 has effected a wide-ranging reform of the privity of contract doctrine. What follows is an outline of the main provisions of the Act although, as we shall see, the effect of the Act on contracts for the carriage of goods by sea is limited by s.6(5)–(7).

The Act gives third parties the right to enforce a contract term where either the contract expressly confers that right on an expressly identified third party[68]; or the contract term purports to confer a benefit on an expressly identified third party unless, on a true construction of the contract, the parties did not intend the third party to have that right.[69] The third party may be expressly identified by name, class or description but need not be in existence when the contract is made.[70] It is made clear that, in addition to positive rights, the Act applies to the "enforceability" by third parties of negative rights (that is, exclusion and limitation clauses).[71]

If the third party has a right of enforceability, the default position is that the contracting parties cannot take away that right, without the third party's consent, by subsequently varying or rescinding the contract by agreement once a certain point has been reached. That point is either where the third party has communicated his assent to the term to the promisor[72]; or has relied on that term and the promisor knew of that reliance or ought reasonably to have foreseen it.[73] However, that is a default position only and the contracting parties can expressly agree in the contract that the third party's right is more or less secure than under that default position. The third party's right can be made less secure by expressly providing that the third party's consent is never needed prior to rescission or variation.[74] The third party's right can be made more secure by expressly providing that the third party's consent is always needed for rescission or

---

[66] See fn.63, above.
[67] See generally Treitel, "The Contracts (Rights of Third Parties) Act 1999 and the Law of Carriage of Goods by Sea" in Francis Rose (ed), *Lex Mercatoria: Essays in Honour of Francis Reynolds* (London: LLP, 2000) 345–379. The 1999 Act applies to contracts made on or after May 11, 2000: s.10(2).
[68] s.1(1)(a) and 1(3).
[69] s.1(1)(b), 1(2) and 1(3).
[70] s.1(3).
[71] s.1(6).
[72] s.2(1)(a).
[73] s.2(1)(b) and (c).
[74] s.2(3)(a).

variation irrespective of the third party's communication of assent or reliance.[75]

Defences that would have been available to the promisor had the promisee been suing are also available as defences to the third party's action (provided that the defence arises from or in connection with the contract and is relevant to the term the third party is seeking to enforce).[76] Again this is a default position only so that by an express term the contracting parties can expand the range of defences, so that a defence does not need to arise from or in connection with the contract[77]; or can narrow the range of defences.[78]

A promisee retains its rights to sue on the contract even though it is also enforceable by the third party.[79] The third party's right is therefore additional to, and does not replace, the promisee's rights: nor is there a statutory assignment of the promisee's rights to the third party. To avoid unacceptable double liability for the promisor, a court may reduce the third party's award to take account of a sum recovered (in relation to the same loss) by the promisee.[80]

There are specific sections dealing with the relationship between a third party's rights under the 1999 Act and the Unfair Contract Terms Act 1977[81] and the Arbitration Act 1996.[82] Existing statutory and common law exceptions to privity are not abolished[83]; and particularly importantly for this book, certain types of contract are excluded from the operation of the 1999 Act. By s.6(5)(a) contracts for the carriage of goods by sea, governed by the Carriage of Goods by Sea Act 1992, are excluded *except* for exclusion and limitation clauses in such contracts. This means that, with the exception of exemption clauses, contracts for the carriage of goods by sea contained in or evidenced by a bill of lading or sea waybill or for which there is an undertaking in a ship's delivery order are outside the 1999 Act.[84] The rationale for this is that third party rights in such contracts have been specifically dealt with in the regime enacted in the Carriage of Goods by Sea Act 1992 and the Legislature was anxious for that regime not to be undermined, or rendered less certain, by the general reform of privity enacted in the 1999 Act. But charterparties are within the scheme of the 1999 Act; as are exemption clauses even within bill of lading contracts and other contracts falling within the 1992 Act. The latter point means that a Himalaya clause in a bill of lading contract may be rendered straightforwardly enforceable by an expressly identified third party without the need to rely on the complex reasoning used at common law in, for example, *The Eurymedon*.[85]

---

[75] s.2(3)(b).
[76] s.3(2). See also, as regards exemption clauses, s.3(6).
[77] s.3(3).
[78] s.3(5).
[79] s.4.
[80] s.5.
[81] s.7(2).
[82] s.8. See *Nisshin Shipping Co Ltd v Cleaves & Co Ltd* [2003] EWHC 2602; [2004] 1 Lloyd's Rep. 38: *Case 1* below.
[83] s.7(1).
[84] s.6(6) and 6(7)(a).
[85] [1975] A.C. 154. See *Note* below.

Case 1. A chartering broker (Cleaves) had negotiated a number of charterparties on behalf of the shipowners (Nisshin). In each of the charterparties, Nisshin agreed with the charterers to pay Cleaves its commission. In each charterparty, there was also an arbitration clause by which the parties agreed to refer all disputes arising out of the contract to arbitration. *Held* that, applying s.1 of the 1999 Act, Cleaves had the right as a third party to enforce Nisshin's promise to pay it commission; and that, applying s.8 of the 1999 Act, it was entitled, and indeed bound (as a condition of enforcement), to enforce that right by arbitration.[86]

Case 2. By a contractual letter of indemnity given by the buyers of sugar to the charterers of the ship carrying the sugar, the receivers promised to indemnify the charterers against loss sustained by them. Under clause 1 of the letter of indemnity, the promise was to indemnify the charterers and their 'servants and agents' against loss caused by releasing the goods without the bill of lading. Under clause 3 the promise was to provide security for the ship's release and to indemnify the charterers against loss caused if the ship was arrested in connection with the delivery of the cargo. The question at issue was whether the third party shipowners could enforce clause 3 of the letter of indemnity given by the buyers to the charterers. *Held* that, applying s.1 of the 1999 Act, the shipowners as expressly identified third parties could enforce the clause in the letter of indemnity.[87]

Note. We have seen that the 1999 Act now affords a straightforward way by which third parties can be given the right to enforce exemption clauses. In contrast, the common law position on this question is complex. The starting point is that the doctrine of privity of contract means that exceptions in the contract of affreightment cannot generally be relied on by a person who is not a party to the contract, such as the master, a member of the crew, or an independent contractor (e.g. a stevedore or a sub-carrier under a through bill of lading).[88]

On the other hand it may be possible for a shipowner by a special clause (a so-called Himalaya clause)[89] in his form of bill of lading or in a charterparty to contract as agent on behalf of an independent contractor, such as a stevedore, and thereby secure for the latter the same protection against liability as that enjoyed by the shipowner.[90] It is not always easy, however, even by a special clause, to resolve all the difficulties in the way of extending the protection of exception clauses.[91] The courts will not allow a third party

---

[86] *Nisshin Shipping Co Ltd v Cleaves & Co Ltd* [2003] EWHC 2602; [2004] 1 Lloyd's Rep. 38.

[87] *Laemthong International Lines Co Ltd v Artis, The Laemthong Glory (No. 2)* [2005] EWCA Civ. 519; [2005] 1 Lloyd's Rep. 688.

[88] *Midland Silicones v Scruttons* [1962] A.C. 446; *Adler v Dickson* [1955] 1 Q.B. 158. It seems that no general principle is to be extracted from *Elder Dempster v Paterson Zochonis* [1924] A.C. 522, in which a shipowner sued in tort was held entitled to the protection of the exception clause in his time charterer's bill of lading signed by the master. In Singapore, the decision has been described as one of "doubtful authority": *The Golden Lore* [1980–1984] L.R.C. Comm. 133. But Lord Sumner's reliance on a notion of "bailment on terms" (which appears to mean that by entrusting the goods to the shipowners, the shipper may be taken to have impliedly agreed that the shipowner received the goods on the terms of the bill of lading which included the exemption from liability for bad storage has recently been given some support by Lord Goff in obiter dicta in *KH Enterprise (cargo owners) v Pioneer Container (owners)* [1994] 2 A.C. 324, 339–340 and in *The Mahkutai* [1996] A.C. 650. The failure of the claim in tort in *Pyrene v Scindia Navigation* [1954] 2 Q.B. 402, can be supported only on the implication of the facts there of a contract between the parties: see per Viscount Simonds in *Midland Silicones v Scruttons*, above, at p.471.

[89] See *Adler v Dickson*, above.

[90] *N.Z. Shipping v Satterthwaite Ltd, The Eurymedon* [1975] A.C. 154 (P.C.), in which it was held by a majority that the shipowner had authority to contract in the bill of lading on behalf of an independent contractor, a stevedoring company of which the shipowners were a subsidiary, and that by undertaking the discharge of cargo (which was damaged during discharge) the independent contractor provided consideration for the shipper's promise to extend the protection of the exceptions to the stevedore. This was followed unanimously in *Port Jackson Stevedoring Pty Ltd v Salmond (The New York Star)* [1981] 1 W.L.R. 138 (P.C.). For further support see *The Mahkutai* [1996] A.C. 650; and especially importantly, *Homburg Houtimport BV v Agrosin Private Ltd, The Starsin* [2003] UKHL 12; [2004] 1 A.C. 715 at [34], [93], [149–153] and [196–197]. See also *Godina v Patrick Operations Ltd* [1984] 1 Lloyd's Rep. 333 (N.S.W. Court of Appeal); *Hispanica de Petroleos SA v Vencedora Oceanica Navegacion SA (The Kapetan Markos N.L. (No. 2))* [1987] 2 Lloyd's Rep. 321; *Rockwell Graphic Systems Ltd v Fremantle Termonds Ltd* (1991) F.L.R. 294 (Aus.); *Carrington Slipways Pty Ltd v Patrick Operations Pty Ltd* [1991] 24 N.S.W.L.R. 745; *ITO International Terminal Operators Ltd v Miida Electronics Inc* [1986] 1 S.C.R. 752 (Can.).

[91] See the difficulties enumerated by Lord Reid in *Midland Silicones v Scruttons*, above, at p.474.

to take the benefit of an exemption clause where to do so would undermine the policy of the Hague-Visby rules under which the exemption clause is invalid.[92]

Alternatively, the shipowner may stipulate in the charterparty or bill of lading that the goods owner shall not sue the master, crew or sub-contractors for negligent carriage of the goods: the shipowner may be able to enforce such a stipulation by applying for proceedings against the master, crew or sub-contractor to be stayed under section 49 of the Supreme Court Act 1981.[93]

It is provided by Article IV bis, Rule 2 of the Carriage of Goods by Sea Act 1971, that a servant or agent of the carrier, not being an independent contractor, is entitled to avail himself of the defences the carrier is entitled to invoke under the rules, whether the action be founded in contract or tort.[94]

Case 1. The claimants were the owners (and consignees) of a drum of chemicals and they entered into a contract with the carriers for the carriage of the drum by sea to England from the United States. Under that contract, there was a term limiting the carriers' liability to $500 for loss of, or damage to, the goods. The carriers contracted with the defendant stevedores to unload the drum of chemicals in London. In doing so, the stevedores negligently damaged the drum. The claimants sued the stevedores in the tort of negligence for the damage to their drum. The stevedores argued that they were entitled to rely on the limitation clause in the contract between the claimants and the carriers so that their liability in tort was limited to $500. *Held* that, applying the privity of contract doctrine, the stevedores were not entitled to rely on the limitation clause in the contract to which they were not a party.[95]

Case 2. A contract for the carriage of goods by sea of a drilling machine was made between the claimant shipper and the carrier. The machine was damaged during unloading by the negligence of the defendant stevedores engaged by the carrier. A provision in the contract of carriage excluded the carrier from all liability unless an action was brought within one year after delivery of the goods. By a further term of the contract, the benefit of that limitation clause was said to protect not only the carrier but also every servant or agent or independent contractor of the carrier while acting in the course of its employment by the carrier. More than one year after the delivery of the goods, the claimant shipper brought an action in the tort of negligence against the defendant stevedores for damage to the machine. The stevedores argued that they were entitled to take the benefit of the one-year time limitation clause in the contract of carriage. *Held* that the stevedores were so entitled because the shipper made an offer of a unilateral contract to the stevedores, received by the carriers as agents for the stevedores, by which, in return for the stevedores unloading the goods, the shipper excluded the stevedores form liability after one year. The stevedores were therefore protected because they were parties to that unilateral contract (rather than being merely third parties to the contract of carriage).[96]

Case 3. The claimants were owners of a cargo of timber who had entered into a contract of carriage with the charterers of a ship. Under that contract, they excluded liability for negligent stowage. In their action in the tort of negligence against the shipowners, who were the actual performing carriers, one question was whether the shipowners could take the benefit of that exclusion. *Held* that they could not because to allow the actual carriers to take the benefit of that exclusion clause would undermine the Hague–Visby rules.[97]

---

[92] *Homburg Houtimport BV v Agrosin Private Ltd, The Starsin* [2003] UKHL 12; [2004] 1 A.C. 715 (where the third party was the actual performing carrier). The same policy objection would be given effect under the Contracts (Rights of Third Parties) Act 1999 by reason of s.3, especially s.3(6). *The Starsin* would therefore be decided in the same way under the 1999 Act.

[93] *Snelling v Snelling* [1973] 1 Q.B. 87; *Gore v Van der Lann* [1967] 2 Q.B. 31; *Nippon Yusen Kaisha v International Import and Export Co Ltd* [1978] 1 Lloyd's Rep. 206. Contrast *Neptune Orient Lines Ltd v J.V.C. (UK) Ltd* [1983] 2 Lloyd's Rep. 438.

[94] See the discussion on the rule, below, pp.409–411.

[95] *Midland Silicones Ltd v Scruttons Ltd* [1962] A.C. 446.

[96] *The Eurymedon* [1975] A.C. 154. For the further history of this case, see fn.90, above.

[97] *The Starsin* [2003] UKHL 12; [2004] 1 A.C. 715.

A16B   **Article 16B—Third Party Bound by the Terms of a Bailment or Sub-bailment**

The privity of contract doctrine dictates that normally a third party is not bound by a contract to which it is not a party. No reform of this "burden" side of privity has been made by the Contracts (Rights of Third Parties) Act 1999 which is purely concerned with extending benefits to third parties. Nevertheless it has been held at common law that when being sued in the tort of negligence for loss of goods (or, in so far as different, when being sued "in bailment"), a shipowner, who has no contractual relationship with the claimant owner of the goods, is entitled to rely on the terms of the sub-bailment under which it took possession of the goods.[98] This will be so where the sub-bailees knew that the property belonged to someone other than the bailees and where the owners had consented to the terms of the sub-bailment. As Lord Denning M.R. explained in *Morris v Martin & Son*[99] (a non-shipping case), "The owner is bound by the conditions if he has expressly or impliedly consented to the bailee making a sub-bailment containing those conditions, but not otherwise."

> *Case.* The claimants contracted with carriers for the carriage of their goods from Taiwan to Hong Kong. The carriers issued the claimants with bills of lading which provided that the carriers were entitled to sub-contract "on any terms" the carriage of the goods. The carriers sub-contracted the carriage to the defendant shipowners, who issued two feeder bills of lading acknowledging receipt of the claimants' goods for shipment. The feeder bills contained an exclusive jurisdiction clause providing that any claim or dispute arising under the bill of lading contract was to be determined in Taiwan unless the carrier otherwise agreed. The claimants' goods were lost when the defendants' ship sank following a collision. The claimants began an action in Hong Kong but a stay of the proceedings was granted by the Court of Appeal of Hong Kong and upheld by the Privy Council. It was *held* that, although there was no privity of contract between the claimants (the owners) and the defendants (the sub-bailees), the claimants were bound by the terms of the sub-bailment, including the exclusive jurisdiction clause, between the defendants and the carriers (the bailees).[100]

A17   **Article 17—Effect of a Charter on those with an Interest in the ship**

Apart from the shipowner and charterer, the following persons with an interest in the ship may be bound by, or otherwise affected by, a charterparty.[101]

(1) *Part-owner of Shares in Ship*

Any part-owner[102] of a ship may object to its employment in any particular way, though such employment is under a charter made by a managing owner

---

[98] *KH Enterprise v Pioneer Container, The Pioneer Container* [1994] 2 A.C. 324; *Case* below.

[99] [1966] 1 Q.B. 716, at p.729. This was also supported by *Gilchrist Watt & Sanderson Pty Ltd v York Products Pty Ltd* [1970] 1 W.L.R. 1262; and *Singer Co UK Ltd v Tees and Hartlepool Port Authority* [1988] 2 Lloyd's Rep. 164. But it was not followed by Donaldson J. in *Johnson Matthey & Co Ltd v Constantine Terminals Ltd* [1976] 2 Lloyd's Rep. 215. All those cases concerned clauses limiting or excluding the sub-bailees' liability to the owners of the goods.

[100] *The Pioneer Container* [1994] 2 A.C. 324. In *Sonicare v EAFT* [1997] 2 Lloyd's Rep. 48, Judge Hallgarten Q.C. applied *The Pioneer Container* in holding that terms limiting a warehouseman's liability applied because there had been an *implied* consent by a bailor to sub-bailment on those terms. See also *Sandeman Coprimar SA v Transitos y Transportes Integrales SL* [2003] EWCA Civ 113; [2003] Q.B. 1270 (bailor held to be bound by the CMR terms (i.e. the terms under the Convention on the Contract for the International Carriage of Goods by Road) of the sub-bailment which it had impliedly authorised).

[101] See Art.19, below, as to the circumstances in which an agent may be bound by a charterparty.

[102] The High Court in England is given Admiralty jurisdiction as to all questions between co-owners by the Supreme Court Act 1981, s.20(1).

appointed by himself. In such a case that part-owner will neither share the profits nor be liable for the losses of such voyage, but will be entitled, in an action of restraint, to a bond from his co-owners to secure the value of his share in the ship before she will be allowed to sail on the chartered adventure.[103] In such a case the co-owners who do not dissent divide the profits and losses in proportion to their shares.[104]

(2) *Purchaser*

The purchaser of the whole interest in a ship under charter is not by the purchase alone bound by (or entitled to the benefit of) the stipulations in the charter.[105]

The purchaser or assignee of a partial interest in a ship under charter is bound by the charter in existence, but is not liable for expenses or losses on charters which were completed before his purchase.[106]

Note. In *Lord Strathcona S.S. Co v Dominion Coal Co*[107] the Privy Council held that a purchaser of a ship who buys with knowledge of a charterer's rights may be restrained from dealing with the ship otherwise than in accordance with the charter. However, in *Port Line Ltd v Ben Line Steamers, Ltd*[108] Diplock J. held that the *Strathcona* case was wrongly decided, and refused to follow it. Diplock J. also held that even if the doctrine of the *Strathcona* case is good law, (i) it applies only where the purchaser has actual knowledge of the terms of the charter, and (ii) it gives the charterer no remedy against the purchaser except an injunction to restrain him from using the ship in a manner inconsistent with the charter. The charterer's claim for damages will be against the vendor only, who may then have a claim against the purchaser on his contract of sale.[109] But the *Strathcona* case was supported by Browne-Wilkinson J. in *Swiss Bank Corp v Lloyd's Bank Ltd*[110] on the ground that the purchaser commits the economic tort of knowing interference with another's contract.

Case. On November 5, 1954, C time-chartered a ship from A for a period of thirty months. On February 8, 1956, A (with the consent of C) sold the ship to Q, who was aware of the existence of the time charter, but did not know its terms. Q then demise-chartered the vessel back to A for the balance of the period of the time charter. On August 22, 1956, the ship was requisitioned, and the demise charter then terminated, by virtue of an express provision thereof. The requisition continued until November 26, 1956. Compensation was subsequently paid by the Crown to Q. *Held,* (i) The time charter between A and C was not frustrated by the requisition; (ii) a claim by C under the

---

[103] *The England* (1886) 12 P.D. 32; *The Talca* (1880) 5 P.D. 169. See also *Ouston v Hebden* (1745) 1 Wils. 101; *Haly v Goodson* (1816) 2 Mer. 77. As to the liabilities of sureties on such a bond, see *The Vivienne* (1887) 12 P.D. 185. As to the position of co-owners, *inter se*, see *Bennett v Maclellan* (1891) 18 Rettie 955. The majority of part-owners may not change the character of the ownership without the consent of the minority, as by turning their shares over to a limited company; *The Hereward* [1895] P. 284.

[104] *The Vindobala* (1887) 13 P.D. 42 at p.47, approving the dictum in *Abbot on Shipping*, 12th edn, p.66.

[105] *Port Line Ltd v Ben Line Steamers Ltd* [1958] 2 Q.B. 146.

[106] *The Vindobala*, above; *The Meredith* (1885) 10 P.D. 69; *Messageries Co v Baines* (1863) 7 L.T. (N.S.) 763. See *The Bonnie Kate* (1887) 57 L.T. 203, as to when part-ownership begins.

[107] [1926] A.C. 108.

[108] [1958] 2 Q.B. 146.

[109] See *Lorentzen v White Shipping Co* (1943) 74 Ll.L.R. 161. In that case the purchaser of a ship under charter had been obliged, in order to secure the release of the ship from arrest in U.S.A., to pay the time charterer a sum claimed by him as damages for breach of an initial warranty by the owner regarding the speed of the vessel. The purchaser was held entitled to recover the sum paid in discharge of the owner's liability to the time charterer.

[110] [1979] Ch. 548. The point did not arise on appeal: [1982] A.C. 584 (CA, HL). *Cf. Law Debenture Trust Corp Plc v Ural Caspian Oil Corp Ltd* [1993] 1 W.L.R. 138 (per Hoffmann J.); [1995] Ch. 152, C.A.

Strathcona doctrine[111] for the whole or part of the compensation moneys failed, because (a) the *Strathcona* case was wrongly decided, (b) even if it were not, the doctrine did not apply because Q had no actual knowledge of the terms of the time charter, and in any event the doctrine could give C no rights against Q except a right to restrain the use of the ship by Q in a manner inconsistent with the terms of the time charter; (iii) C was not "by virtue of a subsisting charter or contract of hiring the person who would be entitled to possession of or to use the vessel", and hence was not entitled to recover the compensation moneys from Q under s.4(3) of the Compensation (Defence) Act 1939.[112]

(3) *Mortgagor or Mortgagee*[113]

A mortgagor in possession has by statute[114] the powers of an ordinary owner, except that he must not materially impair the value of the mortgagee's security. The mortgagee out of possession is therefore bound by any charter which does not impair his security,[115] and the burden of proving that a charter is of such a nature is on him.[116]

He cannot object to a charter on the ground that its performance will involve the ship's leaving the jurisdiction, and so render the exercise of his rights more difficult; nor to an assignment of freight by the mortgagor as gross freight, the expenses of the voyage not being paid out of it[117]; nor to a charter making freight payable to a third party.[118]

But the mortgagee is not bound by a charter, entered into by the mortgagor after the mortgage, which does impair the mortgagee's security—e.g. a charter to carry contraband of war to a port of a belligerent power at a time when insurance against the risk of capture is impossible.[119] Similarly a mortgagee is entitled to interfere (by arresting the ship) with a bill of lading contract of carriage—even though this results in damage to the cargo—where allowing the ship to sail would have impaired the mortgagee's security because the ship was uninsured.[120]

---

[111] *Lord Strathcona S.S. Co v Dominion Coal Co* [1926] A.C. 108.

[112] *Port Line Ltd v Ben Line Steamers Ltd* [1958] 2 Q.B. 146.

[113] The rights of mortgagees to receive freight are discussed in Art.171.

[114] Merchant Shipping (Registration, Etc) Act 1995, Sch.1, para.10: "Except as far as may be necessary for making the ship or share available as a security for the mortgage debt, the mortgagee shall not by reason of the mortgage be deemed the owner of the ship or share and the mortgagor shall be treated as not having ceased to be the owner of the ship or share".

[115] *Keith v Burrows* (1877) 2 App.Cas. 636; *Collins v Lamport* (1864) 34 L.J. Ch. 196; *The Heather Bell* [1901] P. 272 (C.A.); *The Fanchon* (1880) 5 P.D. 173; *De Mattos v Gibson* (1858) 4 De G. & J. 276; *The Maxima* (1878) 39 L.T. 112; *Cory v Stewart* (1886) 2 T.L.R. 508; *The Keroula* (1886) 11 P.D. 92; *Laming v Seater* (1889) 16 Rettie 828; *The Myrto* [1977] 2 Lloyd's Rep. 243; *Anton Durbeck GmbH v Den Norske Bank ASA* [2005] EWHC 2497 (Comm); [2006] 1 Lloyd's Rep. 93. In *The Celtic King* [1894] P. 175, the mortgagee was *held* not bound without notice by a contract of employment for five years, which would impair his security by restricting his power of sale.

[116] *The Fanchon*, above. On the relations of mortgagees of shares and owners of other shares, see *The Orchis* (1890) 15 P.D. 38.

[117] *The Edmond* (1860) Lush. 57.

[118] *Cory v Stewart*, above. It is doubtful what dealings of the mortgagor will impair the mortgagee's security, i.e. a freight-earning ship. Lord Esher, in *Cory v Stewart*, above, goes so far as to suggest that, if the mortgagee considers the charter onerous, he should not enter into possession; but see *The Innisfallen* (1866) L.R. 1 A. & E. 72; *The Keroula* (1886) 11 P.D. 92. In *Laming v Seater* (1889) 16 Rettie 828, it was held that, when the mortgagor had contracted to insure the ship, the mortgagee was entitled to prevent her going to sea uninsured.

[119] *Law Guarantee Society v Russian Bank* [1905] 1 K.B. 815.

[120] *Anton Durbeck GmbH v Den Norske Bank ASA* [2005] EWHC 2497 (Comm); [2006] 1 Lloyd's Rep. 93.

A mortgagee of shares out of possession cannot maintain an action of restraint. (*Semble*, that he can, if in possession.[121]) A mortgagee out of possession cannot take possession if no sum is due to him under the mortgage and nothing is done by the mortgagor to impair the security, unless the collateral deed accompanying the mortgage contains special provisions for re-entry.[122] But if the mortgagor deals with the ship in a manner that impairs the security, the mortgagee may take possession without commencing any proceedings and even though there has been no actual default under the mortgage.[123]

(4) *Insurer*

An underwriter on a ship, by acceptance of notice of abandonment of a ship, becomes entitled to freight earned by her subsequently[124] but does not become entitled to the benefits or liable to the obligations of any pending contract of affreightment.[125]

---

[121] *The Innisfallen* (1866) L.R. 1 A. & E. 72; *The Keroula* (1886) 11 P.D. 92.
[122] *The Blanche* (1887) 58 L.T. 592; *The Cathcart* (1867) L.R. 1 A. & E. 314 at p.329; *The Heather Bell* [1901] P. 272 (CA).
[123] *The Manor* [1907] P. 339.
[124] *Stewart v Greenock Ins Co* (1848) 2 H.L.C. 159.
[125] *Hickie v Rodocanachi* (1859) 4 H. & N. 455.

CHAPTER 3

AGENCY

A18   **Article 18—When an Agent binds his Principal**[1]

A PERSON professing to act as agent will bind his alleged principal by a contract if that principal has:

(1) given him actual authority to make such a contract[2]; or

(2) represented that he has such authority and that representation has been relied on by the other party in entering into the contract[3];

(3) afterwards ratified the contract purporting to be made on his behalf.[4]

In an emergency, the authority of an agent to protect the interests of his principal may be enlarged (or a person not previously an agent may become one) by the necessity of the case and by the impossibility of communication with, or obtaining instructions from, his principal.[5]

Case. On a charter signed "C, *per proc.* of D" it was proved that D was allowed by C to act as his general agent. *Held*, that C was liable on the charter, though in making it D had exceeded C's special instructions.[6]

A19   **Article 19—When an Agent is Personally Liable**

A disclosed agent is normally neither entitled nor liable under the contract made on behalf of his principal i.e. the agent normally "drops out of the picture". But

---

[1] For a full discussion of this topic, see *Bowstead & Reynolds on Agency*, 18th edn (London: Sweet & Maxwell, 2006) Arts 1 to 32, 71 to 82. For the law on the relationship between agents and their principals (including the Commercial Agents (Council Directive) Regulations 1993, SI 1993/3053, which, as they deal with agents who buy or sell goods on behalf of others, are not directly relevant to this book) see *Bowstead & Reynolds on Agency*, 18th edn, Chs 6–7 and 11.

[2] Such authority may be given expressly, or implied from the circumstances of the case or by custom.

[3] The classic discussion of this notion of "apparent" or "ostensible" authority is Diplock L.J.'s in *Freeman and Lockyer v Buckhurst Park Properties Ltd* [1964] 2 Q.B. 480. See also *Baumvoll v Gilchrest & Co* [1892] 1 Q.B. 253, 263 (per Kay L.J.); *The Unique Mariner* [1978] 1 Lloyd's Rep. 438; *Egyptian International Foreign Trade Co v Soplex Wholesale Supplies Ltd (The Raffaella)* [1985] 2 Lloyd's Rep. 36; *Armagas Ltd v Mundogas SA (The Ocean Frost)* [1986] A.C. 717; *Polish Steamship Co v A. J. Williams Fuels (Overseas Sales) Ltd (The Suwalki)* [1989] 1 Lloyd's Rep. 511; *Ridgeway Maritime Inc v Beulah Wings Ltd (The Leon)* [1991] 2 Lloyd's Rep. 611; *First Energy (UK) Ltd v Hungarian International Bank* [1993] 2 Lloyd's Rep. 194; *Hirst v Etherington* [1999] Lloyd's Rep. P.N. 938.

[4] *Bolton Partners v Lambert* (1889) 41 Ch.D. 295; *Keighley Maxted & Co v Durant* [1901] A.C. 240; *The Borvigilant* [2002] 2 Lloyd's Rep. 630.

[5] This principle of "agency of necessity" is of particular importance in relation to the master's authority on the voyage to act in the interests of ship and cargo: see Arts.123 to 132, below. It was suggested by Lord Diplock in *China Pacific SA v Food Corp. of India (The Winson)* [1982] A.C. 939 that the phrase "agency of necessity" should be confined to the case where the question at issue is whether the agent has bound his principal to a contract with a third party and should not cover the case where the agent simply claims reimbursement from the principal (as was the issue in that case). See similarly *Bowstead & Reynolds on Agency*, 18th edn, Art.35. But the phrase has traditionally been used to include claims to reimbursement and the entitlement to dispose of the principal's property: see *Re F* [1990] 2 A.C. 1, 75; and Peel, *Treitel on The Law of Contract*, 12th edn (London, Sweet & Maxwell, 2007) para.16–041.

[6] *Smith v M'Guire* (1858) 3 H. & N. 554.

whether that is so depends, apart from custom or express agreement, on the intention of the parties, to be gathered in each case as a matter of construction from the terms of the contract as a whole.[7]

The description of the person in the body of the document and the form of his signature are the most material matters to be considered. The fact that the signature is qualified by the words "as agent" will generally be accepted as conclusive evidence that the signatory does not intend to contract personally. An agent wishing to protect himself from personal liability should, therefore, state in the body of the charter that it is made by him as agent for the charterer or shipowner, and sign it "D, as agent for the charterer" (or shipowner). In this case he cannot be sued on the charter, unless a custom exists which renders him personally liable.

In contrast, an undisclosed agent is normally both liable and entitled under the contract made on behalf of his principal (who will normally also be liable and entitled).[8]

Where an agent contracts for an unnamed principal, evidence of a custom that the agent is personally liable if he does not disclose his principal either at the time of the contract or within a reasonable time is admissible to render the agent liable, but not to exclude the principal's liability.[9]

It was at one time believed that, by trade custom, an English agent for a foreign principal was liable to the exclusion of the liability of the foreign principal. This custom no longer exists.[10] The fact that the principal carries on business abroad is, however, a relevant circumstance in determining whether the contract on its true construction admits the foreigner as a party, and whether the agent is personally liable.[10]

A person may by his conduct estop himself from denying that he is personally liable.[11]

---

[7] *Gadd v Houghton* (1876) 1 Ex.D. 357 (CA); *Hick v Tweedy* (1890) 63 L.T. 765; *Hough v Manzanos* (1879) 4 Ex.D. 104; *Brandt v Morris* [1917] 2 K.B. 784; *Universal Marine S.N. Co v McKelvie* [1923] A.C. 492; *Bridges & Salmon Ltd v The "Swan" (Owner)* [1968] 1 Lloyd's Rep. 5; *Tudor Marine v Tradax Export (The Virgo)* [1976] 2 Lloyd's Rep. 135 (CA); distinguished in *Jugoslavenska Linijska Plovidba v Holsman Trading A.S. Brusse & Sippellmport-Export (The Primorje)* [1980] 2 Lloyd's Rep. 74; and *Establissement Biretet Cie SA v Yukieru Kaiwan K.K. and Nissan Shipping Corp (The Sun Happiness)* [1984] 1 Lloyd's Rep. 381. The fact that the agent is personally liable does not mean that the principal cannot also be liable. See generally *Bowstead & Reynolds on Agency* 18th edn, Art.98. A person may be a party to a contract in two capacities, both as principal and agent; *The Sun Happiness* at p.384 per Lloyd J.
[8] *Humble v Hunter* (1842) 12 Q.B. 316; *Fred Drughorn Ltd v Rederiaktiebolaget Transatlantic* [1919] A.C. 203; *Said v Butt* [1920] 3 K.B. 497; *Dyster v Randall* [1926] 1 Ch. 932; *Siu Yiu Kwan v Eastern Insurance Co Ltd* [1994] 2 A.C. 199.
[9] per Bovill C.J. and Brett J., *Hutchinson v Tatham* (1873) L.R. 8 C.P. 482. See also brokers' cases; *Fairlie v Fenton* (1870) L.R. 5 Ex. 169; *Gadd v Houghton* (1876) 1 Ex.D. 357 (CA); *Southwell v Bowditch* (1876) 1 C.P.D. 100; reversed *ibid.* p.374 (CA); *Pike v Ongley* (1887) 18 Q.B.D. 708; see also *Dale v Humfrey* (1858) E.B. & E. 1004; *Fleet v Murton* (1871) L.R. 7 Q.B. 126; *Marikar v de Mel* [1946] A.C. 108.
[10] *Teheran-Europe v Belton (Tractors)* [1968] 2 Q.B. 545 (CA).
[11] *Herman v Royal Exchange Shipping Co* (1884) C. & E. 413.

(1) *Cases where an Agent has been held Personally Liable*[12]

Case 1. Charter between A and "D on behalf of C", afterwards referred to as "the parties": signed by A and D. *Held*, D was a party to the contract and could sue and be sued under it.[13]

Case 2. Charter between A and "D agent for C", signed "D". *Held*, D was personally liable.[14]

Case 3. Charter between A and "D, as agent for charterers . . . ship to load from agents of said freighters (= D) . . . captain to sign bills of lading at any freight required by charterers (= D) . . . This charter being entered into on behalf of others, it is agreed that all liability of charterers (= D) shall cease on completion of the loading", signed "D". *Held*, D was personally liable.[15]

(2) *Cases where Agent has been held* not *Personally Liable*

Case 4. B entered into a charter "between A and C", and signed it "B pro A". A had given B no authority to make this contract and did not adopt it. *Held*, that B, who had executed the charter in the name of another, and added his own name only as agent for that other, could not be treated as a party to the charter and sued upon it (*quaere*, unless it could be shown he was a real principal).[16]

Case 5. Charter between "B, acting for owners of the ship", and C: "B undertakes to pay demurrage on barges". *Held*, by Bramwell L.J., that B was not personally liable.[17]

Case 6. Charter between A and "D as agents for merchants". Signed "D, as agents for merchants". *Held*, that, apart from custom, D would not be personally liable.[18]

Case 7. Charter between "B agents for the owners" and "D charterers". The charter contained various stipulations as to "the charterers" and their obligations. The charter was signed "For and on behalf of D (as agents) J.A.M." *Held*, that D was not personally liable for demurrage.[19]

Case 8. Charter between "B, A's agent, and C, charterers", imposing sundry obligations on the charterers, without naming them, provided freight and demurrage to be paid in Glasgow by D. The charter was signed "For C, D". *Held*, D not liable personally for demurrage.[20]

A20   **Article 20—Who is the Principal?**

Although it appears from the words of the charter that a person contracts as a principal, or as an agent, it may be that other evidence indicates that that person is respectively an agent (for an undisclosed principal) or the true principal. To what extent is such evidence admissible?

---

[12] See also *Oglesby v Yglesias* (1858) E.B. & E. 930; *Schmaltz v Avery* (1851) 16 Q.B. 655; *Paice v Walker* (1870) L.R. 5 Ex. 173, which has been doubted by James L.J. in *Gadd v Houghton* (1876) 1 Ex.D. 357; *Weidner v Hoggett* (1876) 1 C.P.D. 533.

[13] *Cooke v Wilson* (1856) 1 C.B.(N.S.) 153.

[14] *Parker v Winlow* (1857) 7 E. & B. 942. *Cf. Hick v Tweedy* (1890) 63 L.T. 765.

[15] *Hough v Manzanos* (1879) 4 Ex.D. 104.

[16] *Jenkins v Hutchinson* (1849) 13 Q.B. 744. The proper remedy against B was on a breach of warranty; E. & B. 647. See Art.21.

[17] *Wagstaff v Anderson* (1880) 5 C.P.D. 171. Judgment proceeded partly on the ground that "shipbrokers do not usually act for themselves".

[18] *Hutchinson v Tatham* (1873) L.R. 8 C.P. 482; *Pike v Ongley* (1887) 18 Q.B.D. 708.

[19] *Universal Marine S.N. Co v McKelvie* [1923] A.C. 492, following *Gadd v Houghton* (1876) 1 Ex.D. 357, and overruling *Lennard v Robinson* (1855) 5 E. & B. 125.

[20] *Kimber Coal Co v Stone & Rolfe* [1926] A.C. 414.

The general rule appears still to be that evidence expressly to contradict a statement in the charter as to the parties to it will not be admitted,[21] in the absence of common mistake,[22] or parol agreement between the parties.[23]

There are, however, a number of important qualifications to the general rule.

(1) Where the charterparty contains a statement leaving it ambiguous whether a particular person was intended to be principal, evidence is admissible to show who is the true principal.[24] In particular, the description of a person in a charterparty as "charterer" or "disponent owner" is not inconsistent with his contracting as agent for another; and therefore the real undisclosed principal may prove the agency and sue in his own name.[24]

(2) Where a man purports to contract as agent for an unnamed principal, it is submitted that evidence is admissible to show that the agent himself is that unnamed principal, such a double character of the agent not being inconsistent with the terms of the charter[25]; or to prove a custom making the agent personally liable, so long as such custom does not exclude the liability of the unnamed principal.[26]

(3) Where a man purports to contract as agent for a named principal, it is submitted that evidence is admissible as in (2) to show that he is the true principal, so as to enable him to sue in his own name, provided the other party had notice of his position before action brought.[27]

Case 1. B signed a charter as "owner of the good ship *Anne*"; evidence was tendered to prove that he signed as agent for A, the real owner. *Held*, inadmissible to contradict the special description in the charterparty, or to allow A to sue.[28]

Case 2. In a printed charter between C and A, the name of K, who was not a party to the charter, was by mistake left as charterer. To the plea that A had not contracted with C, a reply that the

---

[21] *Humble v Hunter* (1848) 12 Q.B. 310; *Hill S.S. Co v Hugo Stinnes*, 1941 S.C. 324. The former case has been much discussed in the authorities, and was said by Scott L.J. in *Epps v Rothnie* [1945] K.B. 562, to be no longer good law. Many of the authorities are set out in the judgment of Morris J. in *O/Y Wasa S.S. Co v Newspaper Pulp and Wood Export* (1949) 82 Ll.L.R. 936, where at p.953 the learned judge said he would, if necessary, have been obliged to follow the view of Scott L.J. See also the cases discussed in the *Note* to this article, below.

[22] *Breslauer v Barwick* (1876) 36 L.T. 52.

[23] *Wake v Harrop* (1862) 1 H. & C. 202; *Cowie v Witt* (1874) 23 W.R. 76.

[24] *Drughorn v Rederiakt, Transatlantic* [1919] A.C. 203, in which *Humble v Hunter*, above, is distinguished; *O/Y Wasa S.S. Co v Newspaper Pulp and Wood Export*, above; *Siu Yin Kwan v Eastern Insurance Co Ltd* [1994] 2 A.C. 199 (P.C.); *cf. Asty Maritime Co Ltd v Rocco Giuseppe & Figli (The Astyanax)* [1985] 2 Lloyd's Rep. 109. *Quaere*, whether *Rederiakt, Argonaut v Hani* [1918] 2 K.B. 247, was rightly decided. Lord Shaw in *Drughorn's* case thought not. See generally, *Bowstead & Reynolds on Agency* (18th edn) Art.76; Peel, *Treitel on The Law of Contract* (12th edn) paras 16–056 to 16–057.

[25] *Schmaltz v Avery* (1851) 16 Q.B. 655; *cf. Cooke v Eshelby* (1887) 12 App.Cas. 271. *Schmaltz v Avery* was followed and applied in *Harper v Vigers* [1909] 2 K.B. 549, and *Sharman v Brandt* (1871) L.R. 6 Q.B. 720, was distinguished. In *Schmaltz v Avery*, above, at p.662, it is suggested that one who enters into a contract as agent cannot disclose himself as principal and recover if the other party relied on his character as agent and would not have contracted with him as principal. In *Harper v Vigers*, above, at p.563, Pickford J. found that the facts raised this position, but the point was not taken and the agent recovered. See also *Hill S.S. Co v Hugo Stinnes*, 1941 S.C. 324. See generally *Bowstead & Reynolds on Agency* (18th edn) Art.108.

[26] *Pike v Ongley* (1887) 18 Q.B.D. 708.

[27] *Jenkins v Hutchinson* (1849) 13 Q.B. 744; *Schmaltz v Avery*, above; *Gewa Chartering B.V. v Remco Shipping Lines Ltd (The Remco)* [1984] 2 Lloyd's Rep. 205.

[28] *Humble v Hunter* (1848) 12 Q.B. 310; see fn.21, above.

intention was to make a contract between A and C, but that K's name had been left in by mistake, was *held* good in law without rectifying the contract.[29]

Case 3. A charter with A, in the body of which D and Co. were expressed to be charterers, was signed by D, "For C and Co., D and Co., agents". In an action by A against D, D set up an express parol agreement between A and D that D's signature was only to be as agent, and was not to render him liable as principal. *Held*, a good defence.[30]

Note. It remains of interest to consider Scrutton's analysis (1st edn, pp.22–24) of four early cases that appeared to be inconsistent with the proposition that evidence will not be admitted expressly to contradict a statement in a charterparty as to the parties thereto:

"This proposition is apparently contradicted by the following four cases.[31] In *Schmaltz v. Avery*[32] D had entered into a charter between 'A and D, agents of the freighter', and containing the clause, 'this charter being concluded on behalf of another party, it is agreed that all responsibility on the part of D shall cease as soon as the cargo is shipped'. At the trial it was proved, no objection being taken to the evidence that D was the real freighter. The Court of Queen's Bench expressly noted that the evidence had not been objected to, and admitted that it, 'strictly speaking, contradicted the charter, yet,' they continued, 'the defendant does not appear to be prejudiced; for, as he was regardless who the real freighter was, it should seem that he trusted for his freight to the lien on the cargo' (and not to the person of any particular freighter). 'But there is no contradiction of the charter if the plaintiff can be considered as filling two characters, namely, those of agent and principal . . . he might contract as agent for the freighter, whoever that freighter might turn out to be, and might still adopt the character of freighter himself if he chose.'

In *Carr v. Jackson*,[33] where the charter was made between A and D, but contained the clause, 'this charter being concluded by D on behalf of another party resident abroad, D's liability is to cease on his shipping the cargo', Parke B. said: 'The defendant would have been responsible for the freight of the goods if it had been shown that he was the real principal in the matter, and the charter which professes to be entered into by him as agent would not preclude such evidence being given.'

In *Adams v. Hall*,[34] B entered into a charter as 'B for owners of ship S.' and signed it 'for owners, B'. In the court below three letters written by B were admitted without objection to prove that B was the owner of the S., and the Divisional Court, noting the absence of objection to the evidence, said that the signatures to the charter were consistent with B's ownership and that the letters did not contradict, but removed ambiguity in, the charter, and could therefore be used to explain the position of B.

In *Jenkins v. Hutchinson*,[35] B entered into a charter 'between A and C' and signed it 'B pro A'. A had given B no authority to make the charter, and did not adopt it. The court held that 'a party who executes an instrument in the name of another, whose name he puts to the instrument and adds his own name, as agent for that other, cannot be treated as a party to that instrument, and be sued upon it, *unless it be shown that he was the real principal*' (which seems to imply that evidence for such a purpose was admissible).

---

[29] *Breslauer v Barwick* (1876) 36 L.T. 52.
[30] *Wake v Harrop* (1862) 1 H. & C. 202.
[31] *Jenkins v Hutchinson* (1849) 13 Q.B. 744; *Schmaltz v Avery* (1851) 16 Q.B. 655; *Carr v Jackson* (1852) 7 Exch. 382; *Adams v Hall* (1877) 37 L.T. 70.
[32] (1851) 16 Q.B. 655 at pp.658, 663.
[33] (1852) 7 Exch. 382 at p.385.
[34] (1877) 37 L.T. 70.
[35] (1849) 13 Q.B. 744, 752; see Art.19, *Case 4*, above.

In one only of these four cases, *Carr v. Jackson*, did the question of the admissibility of the evidence directly arise, and even there, as the evidence tendered was itself held insufficient, its admissibility or inadmissibility was not vital. In two of them[36] such evidence was admitted without objection in the court below, and the higher court had to deal with it as already admitted; and in the fourth case[37] the court suggested that such evidence would have been admissible in a state of facts not before them. Moreover, in three out of the four cases[38] the evidence was admitted to prove that an agent professing to contract for an undisclosed principal was himself that principal, and in *Jenkins v. Hutchinson* the court suggested that such evidence might be admitted even where the principal was named; while in *Schmaltz v. Avery* the court held that such a change of front, the agent declaring himself as the principal, who was before undisclosed, was not inconsistent with the ordinary terms of such charterparties."

Article 21—Warranty of Authority   A21

Where a person effects a contract as agent, so describing himself as to escape personal liability on the contract, but has not in fact the authority he professes to have, so that his professed principal repudiates the contract, the alleged agent is liable for breach of an implied warranty that he has the authority that he professes to have.[39] The measure of damages for such a breach is what the claimant has in fact lost because he has not a binding contract with the alleged principal.[40]

A master or broker signing bills of lading for goods not on board will be liable for breach of warranty of authority to a consignee or indorsee who suffers damage by taking up and paying for the bills of lading in reliance on the statements which they contain.[41]

By telegraphic authority. In *Lilly v Smales*,[42] where an agent signing "by telegraphic authority of charterer, D, as agent", effected a charter which, through a mistake in transmission of the telegram instructing him, he had no authority to effect, Denman J. held that the warranty implied by such a signature was only that the agent had a telegram which, if correct, authorised such a charter as that which he signed.

Case. S, a sub-agent, effected a charter purporting to be made between A and "D agent for charterer C", on telegraphic instructions from D, an agent of C, the charterer, and signed "by telegraphic authority of D, S as agent". *Held*, that S warranted that he had authority from C, as well as from D, to sign the charter.[43]

---

[36] *Schmaltz v Avery; Adams v Hall*, above.
[37] *Jenkins v Hutchinson* (1849) 13 Q.B. 744.
[38] *Schmaltz v Avery; Carr v Jackson; Adams v Hall*, above.
[39] *Collen v Wright* (1857) 5 E. & B. 647; *Yonge v Toynbee* [1910] 1 K.B. 215; *V/O Rasnoimport v Guthrie* [1966] 1 Lloyd's Rep. 1; see *Salvensen v Rederi Nordstjernan* [1905] A.C. 302 as to misrepresentation by the principal's own agent. See generally *Bowstead & Reynolds on Agency* (16th edn) Arts 105–106.
[40] *Ex p. Panmure* (1883) 24 Ch.D. 367; *Firbank v Humphreys* (1886) 18 Q.B.D. 54; *V/O Rasnoimport v Guthrie*, above.
[41] *V/O Rasnoimport v Guthrie*, above; *Heskell v Continental Express* (1950) 83 Ll.L.R. 438. Reliance will usually be inferred from the fact of taking up and paying for the bills; *V/O Rasnoimport v Guthrie*, above, at pp.13–14: *cf. Silver v Ocean S.S. Co* [1930] 1 K.B. 416.
[42] [1892] 1 Q.B. 456.
[43] *Stuart v Haigh* (1893) 9 T.L.R. 488 (HL).

A22   **Article 22—Agents for the Crown**

Agents chartering on behalf of the Crown are not personally liable,[44] nor can they
be held liable for breach of warranty of authority.[45] It is doubtful whether the
Crown can be made liable as a principal under the doctrine of apparent
authority.[46]

A23   **Article 23—Classes of Agent—Master**

The ordinary authority of a master has lessened very much in modern times.[47]
Modern methods of communication have enabled the owner to perform much of
the master's work in foreign ports. The system of printed bills of lading and the
extensive development of regular lines of vessels, with their accompanying
agents[48] and branches abroad, have converted the master into little more than the
chief navigator of the ship. In the ports of loading and discharge he has
commonly very little to do, and, though on the voyage the necessity of the case
may (through the doctrine of agency of necessity) confer on him considerable
power,[49] increased facilities of communication have much diminished the cases
where, not being able to communicate with his owners, necessity arises. The
cases must therefore be read subject to the proviso that the position of the master
has materially altered; the master has been superseded partly by the owner and
partly by the broker and the broker's or master's authority is usually strictly
defined by the printed bill of lading.

 Thus, in the absence of express authority,[50] the master has no authority—

 (1) to charter the ship[51];

 (2) to vary the contract of affreightment[52];

---

[44] *Macbeath v Haldimand* (1786) 1 T.R. 172; *Unwin v Wolseley* (1787) 1 T.R. 674; *Gidley v Lord Palmerston*
(1822) 3 B. & B. 275. In exceptional cases the agent may by the form of the charter expressly make himself
liable, as in *Cunningham v Collier* (1785) 4 Douglas 233, where Lord Mansfield held such an agent liable.
[45] *Dunn v Macdonald* [1897] 1 Q.B. 555.
[46] *Att-Gen for Ceylon v Silva* [1953] A.C. 461. See *Bowstead & Reynolds on Agency* (18th edn) p.354 para.
8–044.
[47] For a statement of the "ordinary authority of a master" at that date, see *Grant v Norway* (1851) 10 C.B. 665 at
p.687.
[48] Voyage charters often provide that a vessel shall be addressed to an agent in a port of loading or discharge
nominated by the charterer. Such a nominee is agent for the ship and not the charterers: *Cosmar Cia Naviera v
Total Transport Corp (The Isabelle)* [1982] 2 Lloyd's Rep. 81, at p.86; affirmed CA [1984] 1 Lloyd's Rep.
366.
[49] See Arts 123–132, below.
[50] As in *Wiggins v Johnston* (1845) 14 M. & W. 609 (variation of charter); *Mercantile Exchange Bank v Gladstone*
(1868) L.R. 3 Ex. 233 at p.240 (agreement to carry goods freight free).
[51] Unless the master is in a foreign port and unable to communicate with the owners and the charter is a usual one
in its terms: *Walshe v Provan* (1853) 8 Ex. 843; *Thomas v Lewis* (1878) 4 Ex.D. 18; *The Fanny* (1883) 48 L.T.
771.
[52] *Grant v Norway* (1851) 10 C.B. 665 at p.687; *Sickens v Irving* (1859) 7 C.B.(N.S.) 165; *Burgon v Sharpe* (1810)
2 Camp. 529; *Margaronis v Peabody* [1964] 1 Lloyd's Rep. 173 at p.181; *President of India v Metcalfe Shipping
Co* [1970] 1 Q.B. 289 at p.305; *The Siam Venture and The Darfur* [1987] 1 Lloyd's Rep. 147. But *cf. Dillon v
Livingston* (1895) 11 T.L.R. 313; *Dawson Line v Akt. Adler* [1932] 1 K.B. 433 (agreement to accept freight on
bill of lading weight less two per cent in lieu of weighing); *Mitchell v Scaife* (1815) 4 Camp. 298 (rate of freight);
Holman v Peruvian Nitrate (1878) 5 Rettie 657 (demurrage).

(3) to issue bills of lading differing from the charter[53];

(4) to sign bills of lading for goods not shipped[54];

(5) to sign a second bill of lading for goods for which a bill has already been signed[55];

(6) to agree to carry goods freight free or to agree that freight shall be paid to a person other than the owners[56];

(7) to certify the quality, as distinct from the condition, of goods shipped[57];

(8) to settle claims for freight or demurrage.[58]

On most vessels sailing in a line the master has no authority to alter the printed bill of lading or to vary the rate of freight or to make engagements to carry goods.

The owner is bound by any term of a bill of lading within the apparent authority of the master, even if the master's authority has been expressly limited by the owner, unless the holder of the bill of lading knew that the master's authority was limited, in which case the owner is not bound beyond the master's express instructions.[59]

Case. Timber was shipped under a bill of lading signed by the master which stated it to be "shipped in good order and condition". It had, in fact, been damaged by oil before shipment, as the master knew, or could have known. *Held*, that it was within the authority of the captain to certify the *condition* of goods, and that the shipowners were as against an indorsee of the bill of lading bound by the admission.[60]

Article 24—Classes of Agent—Chartering Broker   A24

The authority of a chartering broker depends on his special instructions at the particular time, and, subject to any contrary agreement with his principal, may be withdrawn at any time. Thus, although he may have authority to effect a charter, he will not necessarily have authority to receive a revocation of an offer for a charter.[61]

---

[53] *Pickernell v Jauberry* (1862) 3 F. & F. 217; *Rodocanachi v Milburn* (1886) 18 Q.B.D. 67. However, most charters nowadays authorise the master to sign bills of lading "as presented": see Art.43.

[54] *Grant v Norway*, above. The decision on this point has been criticised, and in practice it has been rendered virtually obsolete by s.4 of the Carriage of Goods by Sea Act 1992 and Art.III, r.4 of the Hague-Visby Rules (see Arts 59–60, below).

[55] *Hubbersty v Ward* (1853) 8 Ex. 330. See also *The Atlas* [1996] 1 Lloyd's Rep 642, 649; *Daewoo Hong Kong Ltd v Mana Maritime Inc.* [1997] H.K.L.R.D. 1264 (Hong Kong).

[56] *Walshe v Provan* (1853) 8 Ex. 843 at p.850; *Reynolds v Jex* (1865) 7 B. & S. 86; *Arrospe v Barr* (1881) 8 Rettie 602; *The Canada* (1897) 13 T.L.R. 238. See also *Gibbs v Charleton* (1857) 26 L.J.Ex. 321.

[57] *Cox v Bruce* (1886) 18 Q.B.D. 147; and see Art.63.

[58] *Holman v Peruvian Nitrate* (1878) 5 Rettie 657: but *cf. Alexander v Dowie* (1857) 1 H. & N. 152.

[59] See *Grant v Norway* (1851) 10 C.B. 665; *Cox v Bruce* (1886) 18 Q.B.D. 147; *Reynolds v Jex* (1865) 7 B. & S. 86.

[60] *Compania, Vascongada v Churchill* [1906] 1 K.B. 237, followed in *Martineaus v Royal Mail Co* (1912) 17 Com.Cas. 176; *Silver v Ocean S.S. Co* [1930] 1 K.B. 416.

[61] *Raeburn v Burness* (1895) 1 Com.Cas. 22.

Broker's commission. In almost all charters a clause is inserted providing for the payment of a commission, usually a percentage upon the freight to be earned thereunder, to the broker[62] who has negotiated the contract. Such a clause does not make the broker a party to the charter,[63] but the charterer is entitled, and can be compelled by the broker, to sue, as trustee for the broker, upon the covenant by the shipowner in the charter to pay commission to the broker.[64] The broker may also now be able to enforce the promise of the payment of commission as a third party under the Contracts (Rights of Third Parties) Act 1999.[65]

A commission on "all hire earned" or "all hire paid and earned" does not entitle the broker to commission on hire which would have been earned but for the cancellation of the charter by the principals. Nor will the principals be guilty of a breach of contract if they cancel the charter, unless their object is merely to avoid paying commission.[66]

The commission is usually payable on freight as and when earned.[67] But it may be expressed to be payable on the signing of the charter upon the gross estimated freight, ship lost or not lost, or in like terms.[68] Under a clause by which commission was payable "on completion of loading, or should the vessel be lost", and the ship was lost on her way to the loading port, it was *held* that the broker could recover.[69]

The commission may be expressed to be payable on the freight, dead freight and demurrage, but, in the absence of such expression, "Commission at—per cent" will be payable on freight only.[70]

A25
Article 25—Classes of Agent—Loading Brokers

Loading brokers are agents appointed by owners of vessels trading as general ships in a regular line to procure cargoes for the vessels, and to receive payment of freight. They will advertise the dates of sailings in shipping papers and

---

[62] Some charters provide for the payment of commission to the charterers, in which case it seems to amount to a bonus or discount on the freight: *Westralian Farmers v King Line* (1932) 43 Ll.L.R. 378 at p.381.

[63] *White v Turnbull, Martin & Co* (1898) 3 Com.Cas. 183. The broker not being a party to the charter cannot sue the shipowner upon it as upon "any agreement relating to the carriage of goods in a ship or to the use or hire of a ship" under the Admiralty jurisdiction of the High Court and County Courts: Supreme Court Act 1981, s.20(2)(*h*); County Courts Act 1984, s.27: *The Nuova Raffaellina* (1871) L.R. 3 A. & E. 483.

[64] *Les Affreteurs Reunis v Walford* [1919] A.C. 801, approving and following *Robertson v Wait* (1853) 8 Exch. 299; *Re Western Counties* (1922) 10 Ll.L.R. 692; *Christie & Vesey v Helvetia* [1960] 1 Lloyd's Rep. 540.

[65] *Nisshin Shipping Co Ltd v Cleaves & Co Ltd* [2003] EWHC 2602; [2004] 1 Lloyd's Rep. 38. See above Art.16A.

[66] *White v Turnbull, Martin & Co* (1898) 3 Com.Cas. 183; approved in *French v Leeston Co* [1922] 1 A.C. 451; cf. *Broad v Thomas* (1830) 7 Bing. 99. Where brokers sued on a commission note providing for payment of commission on the exercise of an option of purchasing the vessel for £x. they were held not entitled to commission either on the terms of the note or on a *quantum meruit* when in fact the charterers purchased for £y: *Howard Houlder v Manx Isles* [1923] 1 K.B. 110; approved by Lord Wright in *Luxor v Cooper* [1941] A.C. 108 at p.145.

[67] A custom that commission is only payable on hire actually earned was held to have been proved in *Harley v Nagata* (1918) 23 Com.Cas. 121, but was held inconsistent with the charter in *Les Affreteurs Reunis v Walford* [1919] A.C. 801.

[68] *Les Affreteurs Reunis v Walford*, above.

[69] *Ward v Weir* (1899) 4 Com.Cas. 216. On a similar wording, but with the difference that the charter was a chartering "to arrive", the Scots courts came to a contrary conclusion: *Sibson v Barcraig Co* (1896) 24 Rettie 91.

[70] *Moor Line v Dreyfus* [1918] 1 K.B. 89.

elsewhere, and will sometimes supervise the stowage of the ship, though they do not normally accept responsibility to the shipowner for such stowage.[71] They are paid as a rule by a percentage commission on the freight engaged, and have a lien on the bill of lading, and so indirectly on the goods, for their charges.[72]

Loading brokers usually have authority to enter into contracts of affreightment on behalf of their principals and to sign and issue bills of lading, but in doing so their authority is limited to the same extent as that of the master signing and issuing bills of lading.[73]

Article 26—Classes of Agent—Managing Owners   A26

The managing owner is an agent appointed by the other owners to do what is necessary to enable the ship to prosecute her voyage and earn freight. Managing owners are rarely appointed nowadays to manage British ships, although they are sometimes appointed to manage foreign ships. The discussion of the authority of the managing owner of a British ship, which was included in earlier editions of this work,[74] has therefore been omitted.

Article 27—Classes of Agent—Forwarding Agents   A27

The term "forwarding agent" has several meanings. In the original sense, in which it is more or less synonymous with "shipping agent", it means a person employed by the shipper to enter into contracts of carriage with shipowners, but in the capacity of an agent only, and without personal liability as a carrier. The normal duties of a forwarding agent in this sense are: to ascertain the place and date of sailing, obtain a space allocation if required, prepare the bill of lading and send the draft to the loading brokers, arrange for the goods to be brought alongside, make the customs entry and pay any dues, and collect the signed bill of lading after shipment.[75]

Recently, however, the tendency has been for forwarding agents to undertake ancillary duties, such as packing, warehousing, cartage, lighterage, insurance, etc., and in some cases actually to undertake, as principal, the liability of a carrier for part for even the whole of the carriage of the goods to their destination.[76] They may also carry on a form of business known as "groupage" or "consolidation", in which parcels of cargo from different shippers are packed and

---

[71] See *Heskell v Continental Express* (1950) 83 Ll.L.R. 438 for an account of the duties of loading brokers.

[72] *Edwards v Southgate* (1862) 10 W.R. 528.

[73] See Art.23, above. See *United City Merchants v Royal Bank of Canada* [1983] 1 A.C. 168, in which a bill of lading was fraudulently dated by a loading broker showing goods as shipped on board before they had been, but the bill was held to be good tender under a banker's commercial credit, neither beneficiary nor banker knowing of the fraud.

[74] 17th edn, p.38.

[75] *Jones v European and General Express Co* (1920) 25 Com.Cas. 296; *Heskell v Continental Express* (1950) 83 Ll.L.R. 438; *Moto Vespa SA v Mat (Brittania Express) Ltd* [1979] 1 Lloyd's Rep. 175.

[76] In *Jones v European and General Express Co* (1920) 25 Com.Cas. 296, Rowlatt J. said that "a forwarding agent is not a carrier". This is no longer invariably true, and it may be doubted whether it is still exceptional for a forwarding agent to be a principal for sea-carriage, as was said in *Langley Beldon & Gaunt Ltd v Morley* [1965] 1 Lloyd's Rep. 297 at p.306.

despatched by them as a single consignment, often in a container provided by them.

It is often difficult to tell, in any given case, whether a person describing himself as a "forwarding agent" is in fact contracting as an agent or a principal. The fact that a person describes himself as a "forwarding agent" will not preclude him from being treated in law as a principal with the liability of a carrier, even if the carriage is not performed by him personally. Whether the forwarding agent has contracted as an agent or as a principal will turn on the construction of his contract with the shipper and the surrounding circumstances, particularly the relationship between the forwarding agent and the actual carrier. No single factor can be decisive, but the fact that the forwarding agent issues his own "house bill of lading",[77] that he is remunerated by taking his profit from a lump sum freight rather than on a commission basis,[78] that he has contracted for a lien in his own name,[79] that the carrying ship was owned by an associated company and managed by the forwarding agent,[78] that the forwarding agent agreed "to collect" rather than "to arrange for the collection of" goods from the shipper,[80] and that the forwarding agent held himself out as a "haulage, wharfage and lighterage contractor" although not owning any lighters,[81] have all been held to point towards the forwarding agent being a principal.[82]

The fact that the forwarding agent takes a bill of lading from the sea-carrier naming himself as shipper does not of itself make the forwarding agent liable as a carrier[83] although it may point to this result. But where, as is commonly the case where the forwarding agent is carrying on a groupage business, the forwarding agent books space at a concessionary rate of freight for the whole consignment in the hope of finding goods to fill it later, the inference is probably that the forwarding agent contracts as a principal. It is difficult to see how the shipper can be treated as a party, even by ratification, to a contract made before his existence is known, or, if the freight is not capable of being apportioned among the individual parcels in the consignment, how the shipper can be made liable to the actual carrier for the freight.

(1) *Forwarding agent as agent to arrange carriage*

The duties of a forwarding agent acting in the capacity of an agent only cannot be laid down in general terms, since they depend in each case on the terms of his

---

[77] *Troy v Eastern Co of Warehouses* (1921) 91 L.J.K.B. 632; *Landauer & Co v Smits & Co* (1921) 6 Ll.L.R. 577; but *cf. A. Gagniere & Co v Eastern Co of Warehouses* (1921) 7 Ll.L.R. 188 at p.189.

[78] *Lynch Bros Ltd v Edwards & Fase* (1921) 6 Ll.L.R. 371; *Troy v Eastern Co of Warehouses*, above; *Harris (Harella) Ltd v Continental Express Ltd* [1961] 1 Lloyd's Rep. 251, in which Paull J. doubted whether an "inclusive charge contract" could ever be a contract of agency only; *Harlow & Jones Ltd v P. J. Walker Shipping & Transport Ltd* [1986] 2 Lloyd's Rep. 141. Contrast *Marston Excelsior Ltd v Arbuckle, Smith & Co Ltd* [1971] 2 Lloyd's Rep. 306.

[79] *Laudauer v Smits & Co*, above. *Cf. Marston Excelsior Ltd v Arbuckle, Smith & Co Ltd* [1971] 2 Lloyd's Rep. 306.

[80] *Harris (Harella) Ltd v Continental Express Ltd*, above.

[81] *Elof Hansson Agency Ltd v Victoria Motor Haulage Co Ltd* (1938) 43 Com.Cas. 260.

[82] See also *Salsi v Jetspeed Air Services Ltd* [1977] 2 Lloyd's Rep. 57.

[83] *Platzhoff v Lebean* (1865) 4 F. & F. 545; *Langley, Beldon & Gaunt Ltd v Morley*, above.

contract with the shipper, which may be collected from the terms of booking notes, receipts, etc., or implied by custom or a course of dealing.

The forwarding agent has, however, been said to have a duty "to do all that he reasonably can to further the safe arrival of the goods to the consignee at destination",[84] and this may involve exercising reasonable care in employing the persons who are to perform the carriage.[85] He may be liable for delay due to his negligence,[86] or for failing to pass on instructions concerning the goods to the actual carrier.[87] While the goods are in his possession, he has the liability of a bailee.[88] It is submitted that he has a duty to examine the goods before shipment, and on delivery if he is responsible for receiving them at destination, to note their condition and any damage incurred and to give such notices as may be necessary to prevent claims from becoming time-barred.[89]

He has authority to incur reasonable charges for transport and storage if reasonably necessary, even if these were not originally contemplated, but where no fixed rate is quoted he must keep the charges as low as possible "consistently with the work being done with sufficient expedition" and may not make a secret profit on work performed by him personally,[90] although he is entitled to charge a fee for his services as an agent.[91]

Except where the goods are consigned under a transaction, such as a c.i.f. or f.o.b. sale, where it is usual for insurance to be effected by a third party,[92] he may be liable for failing to insure the goods, or at least for consigning the goods on "owner's risk" terms without first asking the shipper whether insurance is required: this seems to be the case whether or not the forwarding agent is aware that the goods may be specially valuable.[93] Where the forwarding agent is under a duty to insure the goods, he may do so by declaring the goods off an open cover, and he does not undertake that the insurers will be proper insurers, nor that they will pay claims without dispute.[94]

A forwarding agent employing another agent to perform his functions abroad may be vicariously liable for the negligence of that agent.[95]

A forwarding agent is by custom personally liable to the shipowner for freight and deadfreight for space booked by him, even if the shipowner knows that the

---

[84] *Langley, Beldon and Gaunt Ltd v Morley*, above.
[85] *C.A. Pisani & Co Ltd v Brown, Jenkinson & Co Ltd* (1939) 64 Ll.L.R. 340. See also *Marston Excelsior v Arbuckle, Smith & Co Ltd* [1971] 2 Lloyd's Rep. 306.
[86] *Jones v European & General Express Co*, above. *Cf. Marston Excelsior v Arbuckle, Smith & Co Ltd* [1971] 2 Lloyd's Rep. 306.
[87] See fn.84, above.
[88] *Armour & Co Ltd v Charles Tarbard Ltd* (1920) 37 T.L.R. 208; but *cf. Garside v Trent & Mersey* (1792) 4 T.R. 581, distinguished in *Hyde v Trent & Mersey* (1793) 5 T.R. 389.
[89] *Cf. Crawford and Law v Allan Line S.S. Co* [1912] A.C. 130, where there was an express undertaking to this effect. *Cf.* per Lord Atkinson at p.137.
[90] *Immediate Transportation Co Ltd v Speller, Willis & Co* (1922) 2 Ll.L.R. 645.
[91] *Marston Excelsior v Arbuckle, Smith & Co Ltd*, above, at p.310.
[92] *W.L.R. Traders (London) Ltd v British and Northern Shipping Agency Ltd* [1955] 1 Lloyd's Rep. 554.
[93] *Von Traubenberg v Davies, Turner & Co Ltd* [1951] 2 Lloyd's Rep. 462.
[94] *Jones v European and General Express Co* (1921) 90 L.J.K.B. 159.
[95] *Landauer & Co v Smits & Co* (1921) 6 Ll.L.R. 577.

space is booked by him only in his capacity as agent.[96] It seems that he is also liable as a principal to the shipowner for shipping dangerous cargo without giving notice to the shipowner of its dangerous character.[97]

A forwarding agent has a particular lien on the goods (and perhaps on the documents of title to the goods) while in his possession for his commission and any charges for work performed by him personally.[98] But it is doubtful whether, in the absence of agreement, his lien extends any further than this.[99] It certainly does not go so far as a general lien for all charges due to him by the shipper, and in any case it cannot be exercised while the goods are in the possession of the sea-carrier.[100]

The forwarding agent is entitled to recover from the shipper any increase in the freight which may properly be charged by the sea-carrier under the contract of affreightment, and which the forwarding agent has paid, e.g. where the forwarding agent has quoted rates based on the goods being of a certain weight or measurement, and they prove to be greater.[101]

Forwarding agents' "house bills of lading" are discussed below, in Article 180.

(2) *Forwarding agent as principal*

The position of a forwarding agent acting as a principal with the liability of a carrier is in many respects similar to that of a carrier issuing a through bill of lading.[102] The forwarding agent usually has the right to employ sub-contractors to perform all or part of the carriage; the right may be implied by custom,[103] or as a necessary implication in the case of a forwarding agent who does not operate his own ship or other facilities.

---

[96] *Anglo Overseas Transport Co Ltd v Titan Industrial Corporation (UK) Ltd* [1959] 2 Lloyd's Rep. 152; *Perishables Transport Co v N. Spyropoulos (London)* [1964] 2 Lloyd's Rep. 379; *Langley, Beldon & Gaunt Ltd v Morley* [1965] 1 Lloyd's Rep. 297.
[97] *Great Northern Ry. v L.E.P. Transport and Depository* [1922] 2 K.B. 743 (rail carriage).
[98] *Edwards v Southgate* (1862) 10 W.R. 528.
[99] But see per Devlin J. in *SA Angelo Castelletti v Transmarine Ltd* [1953] 2 Lloyd's Rep. 440 at p.449, as to the possibility of a lien for freight and charges paid by the forwarding agent.
[100] *Langley, Beldon and Gaunt Ltd v Morley* [1965] 1 Lloyd's Rep. 297.
[101] *Brushfield Sargent & Co v Holmwright Engineering Co* [1968] 1 Lloyd's Rep. 439.
[102] See Art.180.
[103] *Homecraft Weaver's Ltd v Ewer & Co Ltd* (1945) 78 Ll.L.R. 496; *cf. Garnham Harris and Elton Ltd v Ellis* [1967] 2 Lloyd's Rep. 22.

CHAPTER 4

CHARTERPARTIES

Article 28—Charterparties by Demise—Classification

CHARTERPARTIES may be categorised according to whether or not they amount to a demise or lease of the ship.[1]

A charter by demise operates as a lease of the ship itself, to which the services of the master and crew may or may not be superadded.[2] The charterer becomes for the time the owner of the vessel; the master and crew become to all intents his servants, and through them the possession of the ship is in him.[3] A charter by way of demise may be for time or for a particular voyage. In modern times, however, charters by way of demise are invariably expressed to be for a period of time.

Under a charter not by demise, on the other hand, the shipowner agrees with the charterer to render services by his master and crew to carry the goods which are put on board his ship by or on behalf of the charterer.[4] In this case, notwithstanding the temporary right of the charterer to have his goods loaded and conveyed in the vessel, the ownership and also the possession of the ship remain in the original owner through the master and crew, who continue to be his servants. Although the master, by agreement between the owner and charterer, may acquire authority to sign bills of lading on behalf of, and may be obliged to accept voyage instructions from, the latter, he nevertheless remains in all other respects the servant of the owner.[5]

Whether or not the charter amounts to a demise must turn on the particular terms of the charter. "The question depends, where other things are not in the way, upon this: whether the owner has by the charter, where there is a charter, parted with the whole possession and control of the ship, and to this extent, that he has given to the charterer a power and right independent of him, and without reference to him to do what he pleases with regard to the captain, the crew, and the management and employment of the ship. That has been called a letting or

---

[1] The main differences between charters by demise and charters not by demise are discussed in Art.29. The categories of charters not by demise are discussed in Art.30.

[2] A charter by demise of a ship without master or crew is sometimes called a "bareboat" or "net" charter. In contrast an ordinary time charter is sometimes called a "gross" charter; see, for an example of this usage, *Port Line v Ben Line Steamers* [1958] 2 Q.B. 146. This passage was cited with apparent approval in *The Rangiora* [2000] 1 Lloyd's Rep. 36.

[3] *Sandeman v Scurr* (1866) L.R. 2 Q.B. 86 at p.96. The language in the text is that of Cockburn C.J.

[4] *Sea and Land Securities v William Dickinson* [1942] 2 K.B. 65, per MacKinnon L.J. at p.69. See also Chapter 16, below.

[5] *Sandeman v Scurr* (1866) L.R. 2 Q.B. 86 at p.96; *Baumwoll v Furness* [1893] A.C. 8; *Manchester Trust v Furness, Withy & Co* [1895] 2 Q.B. 539 (CA); and see Art.43.

demise of the ship. The right expression is that it is a parting with the whole possession and control of the ship."[6]

Time charters almost always contain expressions such as "letting", "hiring", "hire", "delivery" and "redelivery", which are really apt only in charters by demise.[7] These expressions serve to distinguish such charters from voyage charters, but they do not in themselves characterise such charters as charters by demise. Indeed many time charters expressly provide that the charter should not be construed as a demise of the vessel.[8]

Note 1. At one time demise charters had largely fallen out of use,[9] but they are now more common. A time charter by demise may be used to finance the building or purchase of a vessel, the hire being fixed at a rate which reflects the capital cost of building or buying her, and the interest on the capital. The charterer by demise bears the commercial risk of operating the ship with a view to profit. The owner by demise bears the financial risk of building or buying the vessel for a fixed sum and letting her at a fixed rate of hire. His credit risk is secured by his ownership of the vessel, an agreed right to terminate the charter for failure to pay hire, and usually by guarantees and other securities such as assignments of freight, hire, and hull insurances.

Note 2. It has been held that "in ordinary commercial parlance the expression 'demise charterer' contemplates an agreement between owner and demise charterer" . But, even in the absence of a contract, where the person alleged to be the demise charterer has the rights and obligations equivalent to those of a demise charter ordinarily contained in a contract, that person will be treated as the demise charterer of the ship—at least for the purposes of establishing jurisdiction in rem over the ship.[10]

(1) *Charter* not *a Demise*

Case 1. A chartered a ship to C, to sail to X and load, from C's agent there, cargo to be stowed at merchant's risk and expense. The captain to sign bills of lading if required at any rate of freight without prejudice to the charter.

At X goods were shipped by shippers who knew nothing of the charter under a bill of lading signed by the master.

Held, that A had not parted with the possession of the ship; that the master was still A's servant, and that his signature to a bill of lading bound A. That the stowage of goods was by a stevedore appointed by the charterers, though ultimately paid by the owners, made no difference.[11]

---

[6] per Lord Esher in *Baumwoll v Gilchrest* [1892] 1 Q.B. 253 at p.259. *Cf.* per Lopes L.J. at p.261. Lord Esher's view was approved by the House of Lords: [1893] A.C. 8. See also *Wehner v Dene S.S. Co* [1905] 2 K.B. 92 and *The Guiseppe di Vittorio* [1998] 1 Lloyd's Rep. 136.

[7] *Italian State Railways v Mavrogordatos* [1919] 2 K.B. 305; *Sea and Land Securities v William Dickinson*, above; *A/S Tankexpress v Compagnie Financiere Belge des Petroles* [1949] A.C. 76 at p.90.

[8] See cl.27 of the New York Produce form.

[9] See *Herne Bay Co v Hutton* [1903] 2 K.B. 683 at p.689, per Vaughan Williams L.J.

[10] *The Guiseppe di Vittorio* [1998] 2 Lloyd's Rep. 136.

[11] *Sandeman v Scurr* (1866) L.R. 2 Q.B. 86. If A had parted with the possession and control of the ship, he would not have been bound by the acts of a master who was not his servant, even to shippers ignorant of the charter, *Baumwoll v Gilchrest & Co* [1892] 1 Q.B. 253; [1893] A.C. 8. *Steel v Lester*, below, is explained in that case by Lopes L.J. [1892] 1 Q.B. 253 at p.261, as turning on the owner's appointment of, and power of dismissing the captain. But a clause that the captain in signing bills of lading shall be the charterer's servant, will not free the owner from liability on such bills of lading to shippers ignorant of the clause: *Manchester Trust v Furness, Withy & Co* [1895] 2 Q.B. 539 (CA).

Case 2. A entered into a charter with C that his ship being staunch, "and so maintained by owners shall be placed under the direction of the charterer" for conveyance of goods within specified limits. "The steamer to be let for the sole use of charterers and for their benefit for six months . . . Charterers to have whole reach of hold and usual places of loading, room being reserved to owners for crew . . . Captain to use dispatch in prosecuting voyage, and crew to render customary assistance in loading; captain to sign bills of lading . . . and to follow the instructions of the charterers as regards loading . . . coals at cost of charterers, owners finding all ship's stores, and paying crew's wages . . . captain to furnish charterers with log and to use sails when possible to save coals . . . vessel to be returned at end of period by charterers."

As a fact, A paid the master and crew.

Held, that there was no demise; and that A was still responsible for acts of the master and crew, both to the public and to C.[12]

Case 3. A, registered as the "managing owner" of a ship under the Merchant Shipping Acts, made an agreement with E, the master, that E should take the ship wherever he chose, shipping whatever cargo he thought fit, engaging the crew, and paying A one-third of the net profits. A under this agreement had no control over the vessel. E made a charter, of which A knew nothing, with C, "between E, master for and on behalf of the owners". *Held,* that this agreement did not amount to a demise to E, but that A still remained liable to the public as "managing owner".[13]

(2) *Charter Amounting to a Demise*

Case 4. A by deed appointed E to command a ship on a certain voyage, paying a certain freight to A and retaining the surplus for himself; A had a super-cargo on board with power to supersede E if he misconducted himself. By another instrument E was to be paid wages by A. The deed or charter was made bona fide, and persons who shipped goods were aware of it. *Held* (by the House of Lords), that E was owner of the ship *pro tempore*, and was alone liable to shippers on the bill of lading.[14]

Case 5. A had purchased a ship for the purpose of selling it to C under an agreement which provided for payment of part of the purchase-money down, and part at the expiration of a charter of the same date. Under this charter A agreed to let and C to hire the steamer for four months, the charterer to provide and pay for provisions and wages of captain, officers, engineers and crew; owner to pay insurance and maintain steamer in an efficient condition during service; charterer to provide and pay for coal, port-charges, pilotage, etc. Payment for use and hire of vessel at rate of £750 per calendar month, hire to continue until delivery of ship to owners, unless lost. Owner had option of appointing chief engineer, to be paid by the charterer. Owner to have lien on cargoes for freights due under charter.

C appointed and paid captain, officers and crew; A appointed chief engineer. A was registered as owner and managing owner.

Held, that A had parted with the possession and control of the vessel, so that he was not liable to shippers ignorant of the charter on bills of lading signed by the master.[15]

Case 6 A ship which was legally and beneficially owned by the Republic of Ukraine was employed by B under an arrangement which permitted B to retain the right and power of ultimate decision over the use and exploitation of the ship. B enjoyed a wide degree of commercial discretion and was entitled to sell and mortgage the ship provided it obtained consent. *Held* B fell to be treated as a charterer by demise.[16]

---

[12] *Omoa Coal and Iron Company v Huntley* (1877) 2 C.P.D. 464.

[13] *Steel v Lester* (1877) 3 C.P.D. 121, explained by Lopes L.J. in *Baumwoll v Gilchrest & Co* [1892] 1 Q.B. 253 at p.261 as turning on the owner's power of appointing and dismissing the master; *cf. Associated Cement Co v Ashton* [1915] 2 K.B. 1; see also *Christie v Lewis* (1821) 2 B. & B. 410, and *Saville v Campion* (1819) 2 B. & Ald. 503; and compare with *Colvin v Newberry, Case* 4. See also *Dean v Hogg* (1834) 10 Bing. 345; *cf. Herne Bay Co v Hutton* [1903] 2 K.B. 683; and see *Lucas v Nockells* (1828) 4 Bing. 729.

[14] *Colvin v Newberry* (1832) 1 Cl. & F. 283.

[15] *Baumwoll v Furness* [1893] A.C. 8. See Art.41, below, and *Belcher v Capper* (1842) 4 M. & G. 502; *Meiklereid v West* (1876) 1 Q.B.D. 428.

[16] *The Guiseppe di Vittorio* [1998] 1 Lloyd's Rep. 136.

A29 **Article 29—Charterparties by Demise—Consequences of Classification**

Various consequences follow from a charter being construed as a demise[17]:—

(1) A charter by demise is a contract for the hire of a chattel, and is governed by the general law relating to contracts of hire. There will therefore be implied in a charter by demise the strict implied terms[18] as to, e.g. satisfactory quality and fitness for purpose laid down for contracts for the hire of goods by ss.6–10 of the Supply of Goods and Services Act 1982.[19] *Sed quaere* where the charter by demise is entered into to finance the purchase or building of the vessel.[20]

(2) The liability of a charterer under a charter by demise for damage to the ship will be subject to the ordinary common law exceptions.[21]

(3) The owner, not being in possession of the ship, has no lien at common law for freight due under the charter.

(4) The master of a demised ship is the servant of the charterer, not the owner.

(5) The owner is not liable to shippers, even if they did not know of the charter, or to the charterer, for acts of the master and crew.[22]

(6) Delivery to the master of goods bought by the charterer, unless the bill of lading is made deliverable to shipper or order, divests the unpaid vendor's rights of stoppage *in transitu*; under a charter not a demise, the master is a mere carrier, and not the charterer's agent, and the right of stoppage remains.[23]

(7) Bills of lading signed by the master bind the charterer but not the owner,[24] and a charterer by demise is therefore a "carrier" within the meaning of the Carriage of Goods by Sea Act 1971. (See Art.I(a) of Schedule to the Act in Chapter 20).

---

[17] This article as it appeared in the 20th Edn. Was referred to with apparent approval by Evans L.J. in *The Guiseppe di Vittorio* [1998] 1 Lloyd's Rep. 136 at p.160.

[18] Under the common law there was some doubt as to whether the implied term as to fitness for purpose was merely that the ship should on delivery be as fit for the purpose for which she was hired *as reasonable care and skill could make it*. See, e.g. *Reed v Dean* [1949] 1 K.B. 188; Goode, *Hire Purchase Law and Practice* 2nd edn (London: Butterworth, 1970) pp.231–235.

[19] As amended by the Sale and Supply of Goods Act 1994 and the Sale and Suply of Goods to Consumers Regulations 2002, SI 2002/3045. For the exclusion of such terms, see Supply of Goods and Services Act 1982, s.11. The main provisions of the Unfair Contract Terms Act 1977 are normally inapplicable to charterparties: see Sch.1, cl.2.

[20] By s.6(2)(a) of the Supply of Goods and Services Act 1982 a hire purchase agreement is not a contract for the hire of goods for the purposes of the Act. For the definition of hire purchase agreement see s.18(1) ibid and s.189(1) of the Consumer Credit Act 1974.

[21] e.g. Act of God: *Smith v Drummond* (1883) C. & E. 160.

[22] *Baumwoll v Furness* [1893] A.C. 8.

[23] *Berndtson v Strang* (1868) L.R. 3 Ch.App. 588; *ex p. Rosevear China Clay Co* (1879) 11 Ch.D. 560. See below Art.101.

[24] See Art.23.

(8) If a chartered ship earns salvage, the salvage reward goes to the charterer if the charter is a demise[25]; to the owner if the charter is not a demise.[26]

(9) Under a charter by way of demise wrongful acts of the master or crew can be barratry against the charterer, but not so under a charter not by way of demise.

(10) Where statutory duties are imposed on the "owner" of a ship, such as the payment of light dues, in the absence of express provisions in the charter, the charterer is liable if the charter is a demise, the owner if it is not.[27]

(11) A charterer not by demise cannot, since he is not in possession of the ship and so his claim is one for pure economic loss, recover as damages for negligence from a tortfeasor, who has damaged the ship, the loss of use of the ship during repairs for which time he may under the time charter remain liable to pay hire.[28]

(12) The Law Reform (Frustrated Contracts) Act 1943, applies to charters by demise (and time charters), but not to voyage charters.

(13) A charterer by demise is liable for collision caused by negligence of the demised ship.[29]

(14) A charterer by demise will be entitled to relief from forfeiture in appropriate circumstances if the owner seeks to withdraw the vessel.[30]

(15) A ship chartererd by demise to a person liable for maritime claims arising in connection with a different vessel may be arrested to secure the claims, whereas a ship which is time or voyage chartered to that person may not.[31]

Article 30—Charterparties not by Demise—Categories   A30

Charterparties not by way of demise fall into two main categories: (1) time charters and (2) voyage charters.

---

[25] See *Elliott Tug Co v Admiralty* [1921] 1 A.C. 137.
[26] See below, Art.147.
[27] *Cf. The Hopper No. 66* [1908] A.C. 126; *Trinity House v Clark* (1815) 4 M. & S. 288.
[28] *Chargeurs Réunis v English and American S.S. Co* (1921) 9 Ll.L.R. 464. *Elliott Steam Tug Co Ltd v The Shipping Controller* [1922] 1 K.B. 127, 139; *Candlewood Navigation Corp v Mitsui O.S.K. Lines Ltd* [1986] A.C. 1. *Cf. Morrison Steamship Co v Greystoke Castle (Cargo Owners)* [1947] A.C. 265 at pp.275, 279, 280, 296.
[29] *Fenton v Dublin S.S. Co* (1838) 8 A. & E. 835. On the liability of a ship *in rem* for a collision, when the charter amounts to a demise, see *The Tasmania* (1888) 13 P.D. 110; and Art.148. On the personal liability of the owner of a ship proceeded against *in rem*, see *The Dictator* [1892] P. 304.
[30] *More Og Romsdal Fylkesbatar A.S. v The Demise Charterers of the Ship "Jotunheim"* [2005] 1 Lloyd's Rep. 181; [2004] EWHC 671 (Comm). On the facts Cooke J. declined to grant relief. Contrast the position under a time charter discussed in Art.175 below.
[31] Supreme Court Act 1981 s.21(4). See *The Guiseppe di Vittorio* [1998] 1 Lloyd's Rep. 136.

Under the ordinary form of time charter, the shipowner agrees with the time charterer to render services for a named period[32] by his master and crew to carry goods put on board his ship by or on behalf of the time charterer.[33] The shipowner's remuneration is usually termed "hire"[34] and is generally calculated at a daily rate payable monthly, bi monthly or every two weeks.

A voyage charter differs from a time charter in many respects, but primarily in that it is a contract to carry specified goods on a defined voyage or voyages, the remuneration of the shipowner being a freight calculated according to the quantity of cargo loaded or carried, or sometimes a lump sum freight.[35]

In general, the principles set out in this work are common to all types of charter, with the exception of charters by demise, although some matters, such as demurrage, arise solely in relation to voyage charters or their hybrids. A number of matters peculiar to time charters require separate treatment, and are discussed in Arts 172A to 179.

Note Developments in chartering practice have, however, tended to obscure the distinction between time and voyage charters. For example, provision is sometimes made for a specific number of consecutive voyages or for as many voyages as the vessel can perform within a certain period. Such charters present their own problems,[36] although they constitute a sub-category of voyage charters by reason of the method by which the shipowner's remuneration is calculated. Other developments include the use of trip time charters where, although the charterparty relates to a specified trip (or voyage) the owner is paid hire (not freight) and the charterparty operates as a time charter for a period measured by the duration of the voyage.[37] A further development is the increasing use of 'slot charters' by which the charterer pays an agreed charge for use of a specified number of slots on a container vessel. Although such an arrangement only relates to part of the ship a slot charter (and, presumably, other charters that relate to part only of the relevant

---

[32] It is not uncommon for the period, instead of being defined in terms of time, to be defined as the time necessary to perform a defined voyage or "trip". A charter in this form is sometimes called a "time trip" charter: see, e.g. *Marbienes Compania Naviera SA v Ferrostaal A.G. (The Democritos)* [1975] 1 Lloyd's Rep. 386. In *Uni-Ocean Lines Pte. Ltd v C-Trade SA (The Lucille)* [1984] 1 Lloyd's Rep. 244 a charter in time charter form had no period of time and no clearly defined voyage or voyages to be performed, but merely provided for a range of places within which the ship might be traded.

[33] *Sea and Land Securities v William Dickinson* [1942] 2 K.B. 65, per MacKinnon L.J. at p.69.

[34] On the use of the term "hire", see p.56, above. An insurance on "freight" may include monthly hire under a time charter: *Inman v Bischoff* (1882) 7 A.C. 670 at p.678, per Lord Blackburn but in modern chartering usage "freight" does not include the remuneration paid under a time charter: *Care Shipping Corp v Itex Itagrani Export SA* [1993] 1 Q.B. 1. Cf. *Care Shipping Corp v Latin American Shipping Corp* [1983] Q.B. 1005.

[35] See *The Eugenia* [1964] 2 Q.B. 226 (CA).

[36] See, e.g. *Sterns v Salterns* (1922) 12 Ll.L.R. 385 (lump sum freight); *Ambatielos v Grace Brothers* (1922) 13 Ll.L.R. 227 (HL) (cancelling clause); *Corney v Barrelier* (1923) 16 Ll.L.R. 39 (frustration); *Dunford v Compania Maritime Union* (1911) 16 Com.Cas. 181 (delay); *Compagnie Primera, etc. v Compania Arrendataria* [1940] 1 K.B. 362 (deviation); *SA Maritime et Commerciale Geneva v Anglo-Iranian Oil Co* [1954] 1 W.L.R. 492 (substituted tonnage); *Hollis Bros v Bagley* [1958] 1 Lloyd's Rep. 484 (obligation to load by stated date); *Adamastos Shipping Co v Anglo-Saxon Petroleum* [1959] A.C. 133 (application of Hague Rules) and in CA [1957] 2 Q.B. 255 (seaworthiness, reasonable dispatch); *Suisse Atlantique v N.V. Rotterdamsche Kolen Centrale* [1967] 1 A.C. 361 (demurrage); *Agro Company of Canada Ltd v Richmond Shipping Ltd* [1973] 1 Lloyd's Rep. 392 (meaning of "final discharge" in Centrocon Arbitration Clause); *Skibsaktieselskapet Snefonn v Kawasaki Kisen Kaisha (The Berge Testa)* [1975] 1 Lloyd's Rep. 422 (completion date for last voyage read subject to tolerance of "about"); *Intermare Transport GmbH v Tradax Export SA (The Oakwood)* [1977] 1 Lloyd's Rep. 263 (last voyage).

[37] *Melvin International SA v Poseidon Schiffahrt GmbH (The Kalma)* [1999] 2 Lloyd's Rep. 374.

ship such as those common in the chemicals trade) is properly treated as a charter of the ship in question.[38]

Article 31—Chartered and Substituted Tonnage   A31

A contract may be of such a nature that one party may be entitled to perform his obligations under it vicariously,[39] or it may be of such a nature that he must perform them personally.[40] A charterparty, as regards the shipowner's obligations, is of the latter class.[41] It follows that if a man contracts as "owner" to provide a ship or ships under a charterparty he will, in the absence of anything in the charter to indicate the contrary, be bound, and entitled, to provide his own ship or ships, and cannot, and need not, provide a ship he has chartered.[42] A common alternative form is to contract as "Freight contractor", or "Chartered owner", or "Disponent", in which case chartered ships may or must be provided.[43]

Note: Provision is sometimes made in time or consecutive voyage charters for a change or changes in the ship performing the services thereunder. Thus, a provision giving the owner the right to substitute a similar vessel "at any time before or during the charter" on reasonable notice has been held to cover more than one substitution.[44] But an option to substitute does not in the absence of clear words survive the total loss of the chartered vessel, unless the option imposes an obligation on the owner to effect substitution.[45] Clear words are needed to convert a liberty to substitute into an obligation to substitute.[46]

---

[38] Certainly for the purposes of establishing Admiralty jurisdiction *in rem* under s.21 of the Supreme Court Act 1981—see *The Tychy* [1999] 2 Lloyd's Rep. 11.

[39] *British Wagon Co v Lea* (1880) 5 Q.B.D. 149. Such a contract is sometimes said to be "assignable", a word more accurately limited to the right to transfer the rights, not the obligations, of a contract.

[40] *Kemp v Baerselman* [1906] 2 K.B. 604.

[41] Lord Denman C.J. in *Humble v Hunter* (1848) 12 Q.B. 310 at p.317, *Fratelli Sorrentino v Buerger* [1915] 3 K.B. 367. In the last case the shipowner succeeded because upon the facts it was found that he was ready to perform personally and not vicariously; *cf. Omnium D'Enterprises v Sutherland* [1919] 1 K.B. 618. See also *Isaacs v McAllum* [1921] 3 K.B. 377. In *Dimech v Corlett* (1858) 12 Moo.P.C. 199 at p.223, the same view was taken of the charterer's obligations.

[42] *Cf. Alquife Mines v Miller*, Lloyd's List (1919) 1 Lloyd's Rep. 321 (HL).

[43] *Cf. Phosphate Co v Rankin* (1915) 21 Com.Cas. 248. So also if the contract is by "agents or owners" of ships to be named; *Cork Gas Co v Witherington* (1920) 36 T.L.R. 599.

[44] *SA Maritime et Commerciale of Geneva v Anglo-Iranian Oil Co* [1954] 1 W.L.R. 492.

[45] *Niarchos v Shell Tankers* [1961] 2 Lloyd's Rep. 496. The principle is so stated by McNair J. at p.506. But there seems no reason in principle why a clearly worded option should not survive the loss of the vessel even if it does not impose such an obligation: *Terkol Rederierne v Petroleo Brasiliero SA (The Badagry)* [1985] 1 Lloyd's Rep. 395.

[46] *Niarchos v Shell Tankers*, above, at p.506.

CHAPTER 5

THE BILL OF LADING AS A CONTRACT

A32   **Article 32—Issue of the Bill of Lading**

AFTER the shipment of goods under a contract of affreightment, the bill of lading is signed by the carrier or his agent[1] and delivered to the shipper, in exchange for the mate's receipt,[2] where one exists. The bill of lading should only be issued and dated when all of the cargo covered by the bill of lading has been loaded.[3]

Where the Carriage of Goods by Sea Act 1971 applies, the shipper may demand a bill of lading immediately the goods are received into the charge of the carrier.[4]

Where it is the shipper's duty to present bills of lading, he must do so within a reasonable time after the cargo is loaded, although the ship is lost before he presents them.[5] And when the cargo is loaded he must present the bill of lading in a reasonable time, even though the lay-days have not expired.[6] The master, in his turn, is bound to sign bills of lading in respect of each parcel shipped within a reasonable time of presentation and is not entitled to delay signing until all the cargo has been shipped.[7] When a bill of lading issued by the ship or on its behalf contains erroneous information, such as the date of shipment, the shipowner can correct the error provided the shipper retains the bills of lading.[8]

Note. The practice of issuing a "set"[9] of three original bills of lading is very ancient.[10] "Of the Bills of Lading there is commonly Three Bills of one tenor. One of them is enclosed in the letters written by the same Ship: another Bill is sent overland to the Factor or Party to whom the goods are consigned; the third remaineth with the Merchant, for his

---

[1] Usually the loading broker in the case of a ship in a regular line, otherwise the master or the ship's agents.
[2] See Art.91.
[3] *Mendala III Transport v Total Transport Corp (The Wilomi Tanana)* [1993] 2 Lloyd's Rep. 41. A charterer is entitled to present to the owner for signature a bill of lading for a parcel of cargo which has already been loaded, even though there remains cargo to be loaded at the port.
[4] See p.395, below.
[5] *Oriental S.S. Co v Tylor* [1893] 2 Q.B. 518 (CA). Where the charter provides that "the master is to sign bills of lading as presented", the owner's signature is not necessarily a sufficient compliance with the charter: *The Princess* (1894) 70 L.T. 388. A clause imposing a fixed sum for each day's failure to sign is a penalty, and will not be enforced, beyond the actual amount of damage proved: *Jones v Hough* (1879) 5 Ex.D. 115; *Rayner v Condor* [1895] 2 Q.B. 289; *The Princess*, above.
[6] *Nolisement v Bunge* [1917] 1 K.B. 160. The shipowner in respect of detention of his ship by delay in such presentation is entitled to recover damages for detention, and not merely to have relief from payment of dispatch money; *ibid.*
[7] *Halcyon S.S. Co v Continental Grain Co* [1943] K.B. 355. For a case where the shipowner, to enforce payment of freight owing on previous shipments, withheld the bill of lading though signed, see *Trucks and Spares v Maritime Agencies (Southampton)* [1951] 2 Lloyd's Rep. 345.
[8] *The Wilomi Tanana*, above.
[9] A letter of credit calling for a "full set of clean bills of lading" is not satisfied by tendering two bills of lading together with either an indemnity or an undertaking to produce the third bill: *Scott v Barclays Bank* [1923] 2 K.B. 1.
[10] *Cf.* the example, dated 1539, in Marsden, *Select Pleas in the Admiralty Court* (Selden Society, 1892), Vol.1, at p.89.

testimony against the Master, if there were any occasion of loose dealing."[11] *Barber v Meyerstein*[12] and *Glyn, Mills v E. & W. I. Docks*[13] are almost the only reported cases involving the kind of fraud that the existence of more than one bill of lading each of equal validity would seem to render so easy,[14] although frauds through the presentation of forged or falsely dated bills of lading have been the subject of numerous reported decisions.[15]

Article 33—Terms of the Bill of Lading   A33

The bill of lading is not the contract, for that has been made before the bill of lading was signed and delivered,[16] but it is excellent evidence of the terms of the contract,[17] and in the hands of an indorsee is the only evidence.[18] But it is open to the shipper to adduce oral evidence to show that the true terms of the contract are not those contained in the bill of lading, but are to be gathered from the mate's receipt,[19] shipping-cards,[20] placards, handbills[21] announcing the sailing of the ship, advice-notes, freight-notes,[22] undertakings or warranties by the broker, or other agent of the carrier.[23]

> *Case.* F. shipped a parcel of mandarins on A's ship in reliance upon an oral promise by the ship's agent that the ship would go direct to Z. The ship went first to Y to discharge other cargo and in consequence arrived late at Z, whereby F realised a lower market price for his mandarins and had to pay increased duty. The bill of lading issued to F contained a liberty clause that would have permitted the call at Y. *Held*, that evidence of the oral promise was admissible, the bill of lading not being itself the contract, and A was liable to F.[24]

Shippers cannot be required to accept bills of lading in accordance with the charter, if such charter involves unusual or onerous terms of which they were ignorant, and can demand their goods back, if shipped, at the ship's expense. The question would seem to be whether the shippers were, or should in reason have been, aware of the terms of the charter.[25]

---

[11] Malynes, *Lex Mercatoria* (1686), p.97.

[12] (1870) L.R. 4 H.L. 317.

[13] (1882) 7 App.Cas. 591.

[14] See also p.262 as to the master's duty to deliver to the holder of only one bill of a set.

[15] For example *Motis Exports Ltd v Dampskibsselskabet AF 1912 Aktieselskab and Aktieselskabet Dampskibsselskabet Svendborg* [1999] 1 Lloyd's Rep. 837; [2001] 1 Lloyd's Rep. 211; Paul Todd, "Delivery against forged bills of lading" [1999] L.M.C.L.Q. 449.

[16] In the hands of the charterer, it is usually no more than a receipt: see Art.35. This Article was cited with approval in *Cho Yang Shipping Co Ltd v Coral (UK) Ltd* [1997] 2 Lloyd's Rep. 641.

[17] per Lord Bramwell in *Sewell v Burdick* (1884) 10 App.Cas. 74 at p.105; *The Ardennes* [1951] 1 K.B. 55; *Heskell v Continental Express* (1950) 83 Ll.L.R. 438 at pp.449, 455; *Pyrene v Scindia Navigation* [1954] 2 Q.B. 402 at pp.419, 424.

[18] See Art.14.

[19] *De Clermont v General Steam Nav Co* (1891) 7 T.L.R. 187.

[20] *Peel v Price* (1815) 4 Camp. 243.

[21] *Phillips v Edwards* (1858) 3 H. & N. 813. *Cf. Anglo-Continental Holdiays v Typaldos Lines* [1967] 2 Lloyd's Rep. 61.

[22] See *Lipton v Jescott Steamers* (1895) 1 Com.Cas. 32, where the terms of a bill of lading were made part of the contract by references to it on advice-notes and freight-notes.

[23] *Runquist v Ditchell* (1800) 3 Esp. 64.

[24] *The Ardennes* [1951] 1 K.B. 55.

[25] *Peek v Larsen* (1871) L.R. 12 Eq. 378; *The Stornoway* (1882) 51 L.J.Adm. 27; *Watkins v Rymill* (1883) 10 Q.B.D. 178. So also where there are a charter and a sub-charter, and the shipper only knows of one, he will not be bound by the other: *Tharsis Sulphur Co v Culliford* (1873) 22 W.R. 46; *The Emilien Marie* (1875) 44 L.J.Adm. 9. So also where a mate's receipt not agreeing with the terms of the shipping note is tendered: *Armstrong v Allan* (1892) 8 T.L.R. 613. But contrast *Ralli v Paddington S.S. Co* (1900) 5 Com.Cas. 124, in which shippers, who knew of the existence of a charter, were *held* not entitled to demand their goods back from the

Note. Shippers are usually well aware of the terms on which goods are shipped in any regular line or trade, as the bills of lading are printed and sold by firms of stationers, the particulars of the goods being filled in by the shippers or their agents, who then leave them for signature at the office of the loading broker of the line.[26]

A shipper who has shipped under a particular form of bill of lading for some time without objection would accordingly be treated as bound by its terms,[27] although it would certainly be advisable for a shipowner to give him notice of any change in that form.[28] Clearly if the shipper or his agent himself fills up the bill of lading and tenders it to the master or ship's agent for signature, he will be bound by its printed conditions, whether or not he has read them or whether or not they are unusual.

However, the dictum of Mellish L.J. in *Parker v South Eastern Ry*[29] in its assumption that a person taking a bill of lading must necessarily be bound by all its terms, for he knows that the contract of carriage is contained in it, seems a little too sweeping in view of the actual course of business. Modern bills of lading contain a long list of excepted perils, exemptions from and qualifications of liability, printed in type so minute, though clear, as not only not to attract attention to any of the details, but to be only readable by persons of good eyesight.

A question may therefore arise whether the bill of lading really represents the terms of the contract to which the shipper agreed, as where it contains in small print very unusual clauses. Thus, in *Crooks v Allan*,[30] Lush J., in delivering judgment, said. "If a shipowner wishes to introduce into his bill of lading so novel a clause, as one exempting him from general average contribution . . . he ought not only to make it clear in words, but also to make it conspicuous by inserting it in such type and in such part of the document that a person of ordinary capacity and care could not fail to see it. A bill of lading is not the contract, but only evidence of the contract, and it does not follow that a person who accepts the bill of lading which the shipowner hands him, is necessarily and without regard to circumstances bound to abide by all its stipulations." So in *Lewis v M'Kee*[31] the captain was held not affected by a restrictive indorsement on a bill of lading, to which his attention was not called, and, *semble*, which he could not ordinarily and reasonably be expected to see. Two questions of fact arise: (1) Was the shipper actually aware of the particular clause? (2) If not, were reasonable means taken to inform him, and would a reasonable man have been aware of it?

The question is similar to that raised in cases where tickets (e.g. for a journey or for use of a cloakroom) contain exclusion clauses. In *Richardson v Rowntree*[32] the House of Lords approved questions left to a jury as follows: (1) Did the plaintiff know that there was writing or printing on the ticket? (2) Did she know that such writing or printing contained

---

master on his refusing to sign bills of lading except at the chartered rate of freight, which was higher than that contracted for by shippers with the charterers. See also *Peel v Price* (1815) 4 Camp. 243.

[26] See the account of the practice per Devlin J. in *Heskell v Continental Express* (1950) 83 Ll.L.R. 438 at p.449, and compare the remarks of Goddard L.C.J. in *The Ardennes* [1951] 1 K.B. 55 at p.60, cited with approval in *Ngo Chew Hong Edible Oil Pte. Ltd v Scindia Steam Navigation Ltd (The Jalamohan)* [1988] 1 Lloyd's Rep. 443.

[27] *Armour v Walford* [1921] 3 K.B. 473. But *cf. McCutcheon v MacBrayne* [1964] 1 W.L.R. 125 (HL).

[28] See *De Clermont v General Steam Navigation* (1891) 7 T.L.R. 187.

[29] (1877) 2 C.P.D. 416 at p.422.

[30] (1879) 5 Q.B.D. 38 at p.40; and see *Rodocanachi v Milburn* (1886) 18 Q.B.D. 67. See also the remarks of Hamilton J. In *Whinney v Moss S.S. Co* (1910) 15 Com.Cas. 114 at pp.122, 123.

[31] (1868) L.R. 4 Ex. 58.

[32] [1894] A.C. 217, approving *Parker v South Eastern Ry* (1877) 2 C.P.D. 416. See also (all being ticket cases) *Acton v Castle Mail Co* (1895) 1 Com.Cas. 135; *Marriott v Yeoward* [1909] 2 K.B. 987; *Cooke v Wilson* (1916) 85 L.J.K.B. 888; *Hood v Anchor Line* [1918] A.C. 837; *Thompson v London, Midland & Scottish Ry* [1930] 1 K.B. 41; *McCutcheon v MacBrayne* [1964] 1 W.L.R. 125; *Thornton v Shoe Lane Parking* [1971] 2 Q.B. 163; *Hollingworth v Southern Ferries Ltd (The Eagle)* [1977] 2 Lloyd's Rep. 70. See further *Watkins v Rymill* (1883) 10 Q.B.D. 178 (receipt for goods in repository). *Cf. Interfoto Picture Library Ltd v Stiletto Visual Programmes Ltd* [1989] Q.B. 433 (where the onerous clause was not an exclusion clause).

conditions relating to the terms of the contract of carriage? (3) Did the defendants do what was reasonably sufficient to give the plaintiff notice of the conditions?

A problem can occur with bills of lading generated by computer, that the face of the bill refers to terms and conditions printed overleaf but the reverse of the bill is blank. In these circumstances, the issue of whether the intended terms have been incorporated into the contract of carriage is likely to depend on any previous course of dealings between the parties, or the reasonable expectations in the particular trade as to the terms on which goods are usually carried.[33]

---

[33] For discussion of this issue see *Bua International Ltd v Hai Hing Shipping Co Ltd (The Hai Hing)* [2000] 1 Lloyd's Rep. 300 and see also *Stansted Shipping v Shenzen Nantian Oil Mills* [2000] All E.R. (D) 1175 upholding a finding of non-incorporation of the intended terms. For the suggestion that the bill could be rectified to incorporate the standard terms see Aikens, Lord and Bools, *Bills of lading* (2006) para.7.27.

CHAPTER 6

BILLS OF LADING FOR GOODS ON A CHARTERED SHIP

A34 **Article 34—General**

The issue of a bill of lading for goods on a chartered ship may create new obligations, but does not put an end to the obligations under the charterparty.[1] However, it gives rise to a number of special problems, which are discussed in the following Articles:

(1) Is such a bill of lading, in the hands of the charterer, evidence of a contract adding to or varying the terms of the contract contained in the charter, or is it merely a receipt for the goods?[2]

(2) If such a bill of lading, in the hands of the charterer, is merely a receipt for the goods, is it, in the hands of an indorsee from the charterer, a contract or evidence of a contract of affreightment?[3]

(3) To what extent is a holder of the bill of lading, other than the charterer, affected by the terms of the charter?[4]

(4) Is the contract of affreightment, if any, contained in the bill of lading, made with the shipowner or the charterer?[5]

(5) To what extent is a holder of the bill of lading, other than a charterer, bound by and entitled to rely on terms of the bill of lading differing from the charter?[6]

(6) If a bill of lading evidencing a contract of affreightment with the shipowner imposes more onerous terms on the shipowner than the charter, is the shipowner entitled to be indemnified by the charterer?[7]

A35 **Article 35—Bill of Lading in the Hands of Charterer**

Where the charterer is himself the shipper, and receives as such shipper a bill of lading in terms differing from the charter, the proper construction of the two documents taken together is that, prima facie and in the absence of any intention to the contrary, as between the shipowner and the charterer, the bill of lading,

---

[1] *Den of Airlie S.S. Co v Mitsui* (1912) 17 Com.Cas. 116; *Hogarth S.S. Co v Blyth* [1917] 2 K.B. 534 at p.550, per Scrutton L.J.; *Gardano and Giampieri v Greek Petroleum* [1961] 2 Lloyd's Rep. 259.
[2] See Art.35.
[3] See Art.36.
[4] See Arts 37, 38, 39, 40.
[5] See Art.41.
[6] See Art.42.
[7] See Art.43.

although inconsistent with certain parts of the charter, is to be taken only as an acknowledgment of the receipt of the goods.[8] Where the charterer becomes indorsee of a bill of lading, originally issued to a shipper other than the charterer, the bill of lading does not modify or vary the terms of the charterparty, at least where the charterparty provides that bills of lading are to be signed "without prejudice to this charterparty".[9]

If the holder of the bill of lading is merely an agent or factor of the charterer, he is in the same position as the charterer.[10] So also if the charterer takes a bill of lading in his own name, but as an agent for a third person, such third person is in the same position as the charterer.[11]

The bill of lading even though merely a receipt when issued may, when delivery of the goods is taken on presentation of the bill of lading, evidence a contract between the shipowner and the person taking delivery on the terms of the bill of lading.[12]

The fact that the bill of lading does not contain all the terms of the charter,[13] or that it contains terms not in the charter,[14] will not necessarily vary the contract between shipowner and charterer.[15]

But the parties to a charter may agree to vary it; and their agreement to vary may be expressed in the bill of lading given to the charterer.[16]

Case 1. C chartered A's ship, "master to sign bills of lading, at any rate of freight, and as customary at port of loading, without prejudice to the stipulations of the charter". C shipped goods under the charter, and the master signed a bill of lading, containing an exception of "negligence of the master and crew" which was not in the charter. The goods, whilst still owned by C, were lost through the master's negligence. *Held*, that the master had no authority to insert such a clause in the bill of lading, which could not prejudice the charter, but was a mere receipt for the goods shipped, and that the shipowners were therefore liable to C.[17]

Case 2. A ship was chartered, the charter containing a power to the master to sign bills of lading without prejudice to the charter and exceptions, inter alia, of "restraint of princes". A shipper, who was practically identified with the charterer, and fully aware of the charter, obtained a bill of lading containing only an exception of perils of the seas. The ship was delayed by restraint of princes. *Held*,

---

[8] *Rodocanachi v Milburn* (1886) 18 Q.B.D. 67, per Lord Esher at p.75; Lindley L.J. at p.78; *cf. Leduc v Ward* (1888) 20 Q.B.D. 475 at p.479; *Wagstaff v Anderson* (1880) 5 C.P.D. 171 at p.177, per Lord Bramwell: "To say that the bill of lading is a contract, superseding, adding to, or varying the former contract, is a proposition to which I can never consent": repeated less decidedly in *Sewell v Burdick* (1884) 10 App.Cas. 74 at p.105; *Temperley v Smyth* [1905] 2 K.B. 791 at p.802, per Collins M.R; *Krüger & Co v Moel Tryvan* [1907] A.C. 272 at p.278, per Lord Halsbury.

[9] *Love and Stewart v Rowtor* [1916] 2 A.C. 527; *President of India v Metcalfe Shipping Co* [1970] 1 Q.B. 289, explaining *Calcutta S.S. v Weir* [1910] 1 K.B. 759 and *Hogarth S.S. Co v Blyth* [1917] 2 K.B. 534 at p.551, per Scrutton L.J.; *Gardner Smith Pty. Ltd v The Ship Tomoe 8 (The Tomoe 8)* (1990) 19 N.S.W.L.R. 588. The law appears to be no different since the passing of the Carriage of Goods by Sea Act 1992: see the Report of the Law Commissions, para.2.53.

[10] *Kern v Deslandes* (1861) 10 C.B. (N.S.) 205; *Gledstanes v Allen* (1852) 12 C.B. 202; *Small v Moates* (1833) 9 Bing. 574; see also *President of India v Metcalfe Shipping Co*, above.

[11] *Delaurier v Wyllie* (1889) 17 Rettie 167.

[12] See Art.15.

[13] *The San Roman* (1872) L.R. 3 A. & E. 583 at p.592.

[14] *Rodocanachi v Milburn* (1886) 18 Q.B.D. 67; *Pickernell v Jauberry* (1862) 3 F. & F. 217; *Caughey v Gordon* (1878) 3 C.P.D. 419.

[15] See fn.8, above.

[16] For instances where such a variation has been effected, see *Gullischen v Stewart* (1884) 13 Q.B.D. 317; *Bryden v Niebuhr* (1884) C. & E. 241; *Davidson v Bisset* 1878 5 Rettie 709; and *Note*, below, p.68.

[17] *Rodocanachi v Milburn* (1868) 18 Q.B.D. 67.

that the contract of affreightment was to be found in the charter and bill of lading, and that the one exception in the bill of lading did not supersede the several exceptions in the charter.[18]

Case 3. D, as agent for C, negotiated a charter with A for a lump freight of £735, "the master to sign bills of lading at any rate of freight without prejudice to this charter". C shipped goods on his own account, and the master signed a bill of lading, making the goods "deliverable to C or assigns, paying freight as usual". C indorsed this bill to D, in part payment of advances on the cargo. *Held*, that D, both as agent for C and as having knowledge of the charter, was liable to A's lien for the whole freight due under the charter, and not merely for the freight in the bill of lading.[19]

Case 4. C agreed with A to ship oranges by A's ship at 4s. 6d. per box. E, A's master, then signed bills of lading for oranges shipped by C at 3s. 6d. per box. *Held*, that C was liable for freight at 4s. 6d. and was not relieved by the bill of lading.[20]

Case 5. Charterer (C) agreed to load a full cargo at a freight of "60s. per ton in full". The master was paid by the shipowner a fixed salary to include all charges and allowances. He signed a bill of lading making the goods "deliverable to order or assigns, he or they paying freight, etc., as per charter, with five per cent. primage for cash on delivery as customary". D, indorsees of the bill of lading as agents of C, received the cargo at the port of discharge. *Held*, that the master could not sue D for primage either for himself or for the owner.[21]

Case 6. A ship was chartered with the usual stipulations for freight and demurrage, and a cesser clause. The charterers shipped the cargo themselves, accepting the bills of lading, making the goods deliverable to themselves at the port of discharge, "they paying freight and all other conditions as per charter". In an action by shipowners against charterers as consignees under the bill of lading for demurrage at the port of discharge—*Held*, they were liable, for the bill of lading only incorporated those clauses of the charter which were consistent with its character as a bill of lading, and did not therefore incorporate the "cesser clause".[22]

Note. The cases of *Rodocanachi v Milburn*[23] and *Leduc v Ward*,[24] both in the Court of Appeal, brought into prominence the view that where a charter has been effected, and the charterer himself ships the cargo and takes a bill of lading for the shipment, such a bill of lading is only an acknowledgment of the receipt of the goods, unless there be an express provision in the documents (the charter and bill of lading) to the contrary. However in the cases of *Gullischen v Stewart*,[25] *Bryden v Niebuhr*,[25] and *Davidson v Bisset*,[26] the contract

---

[18] *The San Roman* (1872) L.R. 3 A. & E. 583 at p.592; an action *in rem* against the ship; though the charterer and shipper were nominally different firms, they were in fact almost identical, and the decision cannot, it is submitted, be supported, except on this ground. *Cf. The Patria* (1871) L.R. 3 A. & E. 436.

[19] *Kern v Deslandes* (1861) 10 C.B. (N.S.) 205, based, in *Fry v Mercantile Bank* (1866) L.R. 1 C.P. 689, on the position that D really represented C and sustainable on that ground; *sed quaere*, whether on the facts this was so. *Small v Moates* (1833) 9 Bing. 574, and *Gledstanes v Allen* (1852) 12 C.B. 202, are similar cases.

[20] *Pickernell v Jauberry* (1862) 3 F. & F. 217; *cf. Delaurier v Wyllie* (1889) 17 Rettie 167, where C was agent for the real shipper.

[21] *Caughey v Gordon* (1878) 3 C.P.D. 419. Here the master, without owner's authority, tried to introduce a new term into the contract, contrary to the charter, which could only be for owner's benefit. *Held*, he could not.

[22] *Gullischen v Stewart* (1884) 13 Q.B.D. 317. See also *Bryden v Niebuhr* (1884) C. & E. 241; *Davidson v Bisset* (1878) 5 Rettie 709; *Hill S.S. Co v Hugo Stinnes*, 1941 S.C. 324. If, instead of expressly incorporating some terms of the charter in the bill of lading, the owner had signed, and the charterers accepted, a bill of lading, binding themselves to pay demurrage and freight, without any reference to the charter, this case seems also to show that such a bill of lading would have overridden the cesser clause in the charter. Brett L.J., in giving judgment against the charterers, said: "Pushed to its legitimate conclusion, the argument for the charterers would free them from liability for freight." The argument was pushed so far, it is submitted, wrongly, by Denman J., in *Barwick v Burnyeat* (1877) 36 L.T. 250. In that case the charterers, who were also consignees, pleaded that the cesser clause, which exempted them by name after the ship's loading and payment of advance freight from subsequent liability, relieved them from any liability under a bill of lading accepted by them, making the goods deliverable "to order or assigns, he or they paying freight for the same, and other conditions as per charter": and they were *held* not liable for freight. This case was not cited in *Gullischen v Stewart* or *Bryden v Niebuhr*, but seems directly contrary to the principle of those decisions and must, it is submitted, be taken as overruled.

[23] (1886) 18 Q.B.D. 67.

[24] (1888) 20 Q.B.D. 475.

[25] See fn.22, above.

[26] 1878 5 Rettie 709. See also *Hill S.S. Co v Hugo Stinnes*, 1941 S.C. 324.

made between shipowner and charterer in the charter was in effect varied by the bill of lading and in *Gullischen v Stewart*,[27] Bowen L.J. speaks of the argument for the charterer as "rendering the bill of lading a nullity: it would be a useless form except as an acknowledgment that the goods had been put on board". It may be said that in *Gullischen v Stewart* and *Bryden v Niebuhr*,[27] the liability was not on the contract originally evidenced by the bill of lading, but on the contract implied from the charterer-consignee's taking the goods under the bill of lading by which he was consignee. But the Court of Appeal do not rest their judgment on this ground, for Brett M.R. says (at p.318): "The contract by a bill of lading is different from the contract by a charter, and the defendants are sued upon the contract contained in the bill of lading. It would be absurd to suppose that their liability upon the bill of lading would cease (under the cesser clause) upon the loading of the cargo." At any rate, in the Scots case of *Davidson v Bisset*,[28] no such question arose, and Lord Moncreiff there takes an intermediate view: "I should be disposed to say that in matters which relate to the details of the mode in which the contract of carriage is to be performed, the charter may be varied by the bill of lading, although the substance of the contract of affreightment is to be looked for in the charter." It is submitted that this limitation is unnecessary. If the parties to a charter wish to vary their contract, even in a substantial point, they can do so; and why not by a bill of lading?

Article 36—Bill of Lading in Hands of Indorsee from Charterer   A36

Although, as between shipowner and charterer, the bill of lading may be "merely in the nature of a receipt for the goods,[29] yet, where it is indorsed over, as between the shipowner and the indorsee, the bill of lading must be considered to contain the contract".[30]

Note. This view is so long established that it is scarcely open to question. It is, however, not easy to explain. The lawful holder has by statute[31] transferred to him all rights of suit under the contract of carriage, i.e. "the contract contained in or evidenced by" the bill of lading and may in certain circumstances become subject to liabilities under that contract. But in the case of the indorsement from the charterer-shipper of a bill of lading differing from the charter, there is, per Lord Esher in *Rodocanachi v Milburn*, no "contract contained in the bill of lading", but only a "mere receipt". How, then, can the indorsement pass what does not exist? Does a contract spring into existence on the transfer to the lawful holder, which had no existence before?[32] And, if so, what statutory authority is there for such a "creation", as opposed to the "transference" ordained by statute? It may be said, as in *Leduc v Ward*,[33] that between shipowner and indorsee the bill of lading must be considered to contain the contract, "because the shipowner has given it for the purpose of enabling the charterer to pass it on as the contract of carriage in respect of the goods". But this view, which appears to rest on some sort of estoppel against the shipowner, fails in the numerous cases where the variation from the charter is in favour of the shipowner and against the shipper and is also difficult to reconcile with the admitted

---

[27] See fn.22, above, at p.319.
[28] See fn.26, above.
[29] See Art.35, above.
[30] *Leduc v Ward* (1888) 20 Q.B.D. 475 at p.479, per Lord Esher.
[31] Carriage of Goods by Sea Act 1992, ss.2(1) and 5(1)(a). The former Bills of Lading Act 1855 contained similar wording.
[32] See per Lord Atkin in *Hain S.S. Co v Tate & Lyle* (1936) 41 Com.Cas. 350 at pp.356, 357.
[33] See fn.30, above.

law that a shipowner may repudiate against an indorsee for value a bill of lading, which his agent had no authority to give.[34]

Possibly the difficulty may be resolved by a consideration of the wording of the Carriage of Goods by Sea Act 1992 itself. Section 2(1) transfers to the lawful holder of the bill of lading all rights of suit "under the contract of carriage as if he had been a party to that contract". The definition of "contract of carriage" in s.5(1)(a) presupposes that the bill of lading does contain or evidence a contract: but if it is a mere receipt and the governing document is the charterparty it does not do so. As, however, the words of the statute must be given a sensible meaning, it is submitted that the true meaning is that the lawful holder has vested in him all rights of suit "as if there had been a contract in the terms contained in the bill of lading and he had been a party to that contract".

A37   **Article 37—Incorporation of Charter in Bill of Lading—General**

It is very common practice to include in bills of lading issued in respect of goods carried on a chartered ship, a provision purporting to incorporate into the bills some or all of the terms of the charterparty. There are numerous decisions on the effect of such provisions. It appears that in order to ascertain which, if any, terms of the charter are incorporated into the bills, an enquiry in three stages[35] must be carried out:

(1) The incorporating clause in the bill of lading must be construed in order to see whether it is wide enough to bring about a prima facie incorporation of the relevant term. General words of incorporation will be effective to incorporate only those terms of the charterparty which relate to the shipment, carriage or discharge of the cargo[36] or the payment of freight.[37] Which of those terms are incorporated into the bill depends on the width of the incorporating provision.[38] Where specific words of incorporation are used,[39] they are effective to bring about a prima facie incorporation even if the term in question does not relate to shipment, carriage or discharge,[40] and even if some degree of manipulation is required.[41] Where the intention is doubtful, the court will not hold that

---

[34] Art.23.
[35] It is possible that the first and second stages are alternative ways of describing the same process, but it is nevertheless convenient to keep them distinct.
[36] *The Annefield* [1971] P. 168 (CA), explaining and following *Thomas v Portsea* [1912] A.C. 1 (HL) and *The Merak* [1965] P. 223 (CA). For this reason, a clause in the charterparty concerning the approach voyage would not be incorporated: *Eridania SpA v Rudolf A. Oetker (The Fjord Wind)* [2000] 2 Lloyd's Rep. 191.
[37] per Lord Atkinson in *Thomas v Portsea*, above, at p.6, and Scarman J. in *The Merak*, above, at p.232.
[38] This aspect of the problem was not discussed in the more recent authorities, but there can be no doubt that the width of the incorporating clause is a very material consideration: see Art.39.
[39] *The Annefield*, above, per Lord Denning M.R. at p.184, and Cairns L.J. at p.186.
[40] *The Annefield*, above, per Lord Denning M.R. at p.184 and per Davis L.J. in *The Merak*, above, at p.254.
[41] *Siboti K/S v BP France S.A.* [2003] 2 Lloyd's Rep. 364; [2003] EWHC 1278 (Comm).

the term is incorporated.[42] If the incorporating clause in the bill of lading
is not wide enough of its own to bring about a prima facie incorporation
of the relevant term, then (*semble*) it will not be permissible to have
regard to the terms of the charterparty in order to effect an incorporation
which would otherwise fail.[43]

(2) If it is found that the incorporating clause is wide enough to effect a
prima facie incorporation, the term which is sought to be incorporated
must be examined to see whether it makes sense in the context of the bill
of lading[44]; if it does not, it must be rejected. This process should be
performed intelligently and not mechanically,[45] and must not be allowed
to produce a result which flouts common sense.[46] Where the term relates
to shipment, carriage or delivery, some degree of manipulation is
permissible to make its words fit the bill of lading,[47] but not where the
term relates to other matters.[48] Where the intention to incorporate a
specific clause is particularly clear, a greater degree of manipulation will
be permitted.[49]

(3) Where there is an incorporation which is prima facie effective, the term
in question must be examined to see whether it is consistent with the
express terms of the bill. If it is not, it will be rejected,[50] although terms
of the charterparty which are not incorporated for this reason may

---

[42] *The Annefield*, above, per Brandon J. at p.178, citing Lords Gorrell and Robson in *Thomas v Portsea*, above, at pp.9 and 11. These were cases on the incorporation of arbitration clauses, but it is submitted that the principle is of general application. This statement was cited with approval in *Ceval Alimentos v Agrimpex Trading (The Northern Progress) (No. 2)* [1996] 2 Lloyd's Rep. 319.

[43] *The Varenna* [1983] 2 Lloyd's Rep. 592 at pp.618 and 621-622 and *The Federal Bulker* [1989] 1 Lloyd's Rep. 103 at pp.108, 110 suggest that the enquiry ends with the bill of lading, although a different approach was adopted in *The Merak*, [1965] P. 223 and *The Annefield*, [1971] P. 168. In *Siboti K/S v BP France S.A.* [2003] 2 Lloyd's Rep. 364; [2003] EWHC 1278 (Comm), Gross J. indicated that if the issue had arisen, he would have followed the former, more recent, authorities. See further Art.40 below. If terms have successfully been incorporated, then in determining the meaning of the incorporated provision(s), it is legitimate to look at other, non-incorporated, terms: *Tradigrain SA v King Diamond Shipping SA (The Spiros C)* [2000] 2 Lloyd's Rep. 319 at paras 77-7.

[44] *Hamilton v Mackie* (1889) 5 T.L.R. 677, *Thomas v Portsea*, above, per Lords Gorrell and Robson at pp.10 and 11; *The Merak, supra, per* Sellers L.J. at p.250; *The Annefield*, above; *Porteus v Watney* (1878) 3 Q.B.D. 534 at p.542; *Gullischen v Stewart* (1884) 13 Q.B.D. 317; *Serraino v Campbell* [1891] 1 Q.B. 283 at p.289; *The Phonizen* [1966] 1 Lloyd's Rep. 150.

[45] *The Annefield*, above, per Cairns L.J. at p.186.

[46] *Miramar Maritime Corporation v Holborn Oil Trading Ltd* [1984] A.C. 676.

[47] *The Annefield*, above, per Lord Denning M.R. at p.184; *The Merak*, above, per Russell L.J. at p.260. *Cf. Miramar Maritime Corp v Holborn Oil Trading Ltd*, above ("charterer" not read as "receiver" so as to render receiver liable for demurrage). For "manipulation" so that incorporation of a charterparty clause for payment to a third party was construed, within the bill of lading, as providing for payment to the third party or such other person as the shipowner may direct see *Tradigrain SA v King Diamond Shipping SA (The Spiros C)* [2000] 2 Lloyd's Rep. 319.

[48] For this distinction, see *The Merak* [1965] P. 223, 260 (per Russell L.J.); *The Annefield* [1971] P. 168, 134 (per Lord Denning M.R.). *Contra* is *The Rena K* [1978] 1 Lloyd's Rep. 545, where Brandon J. was prepared to manipulate so as to give effect to the arbitration clause in a charterparty expressly mentioned by the incorporation clause in the bill of lading.

[49] *Siboti K/S v BP France S.A.* [2003] 2 Lloyd's Rep. 364; [2003] EWHC 1278 (Comm).

[50] *Gardner v Trechmann* (1884) 15 Q.B.D. 154, per Brett M.R. at p.157; *Akt. Ocean v Harding* [1928] 2 K.B. 371, per Scrutton L.J. at p.384; *Serraino v Campbell*, above, per Kay L.J. at p.301; *Vergottis v Robinson* (1928) 31 Ll.L.R. 23, per Roche J. at p.28; *Hogarth v Blyth* [1917] 2 K.B. 534 per Swinfen-Eady L.J. at p.549. See also *Red "R" S.S. Co v Allatini* (1909) 15 Com.Cas. 290 and *Agrosin Pte. Ltd v Highway Shipping Co Ltd (The Mata K)* [1998] 2 Lloyd's Rep. 614.

nevertheless negate the implication of terms which might otherwise be implied into the bill of lading.[51]

A38   **Article 38—Identification of the Charter**

Where the incorporating clause refers to, but does not identify, a charterparty, the court will assume that the reference is to any charter under which the goods are being carried.[52] Difficulties can arise where there are two charters, one between the shipowner and a charterer, and one between the charterer and a sub-charterer. It is submitted that a general reference will normally be construed as relating to the head charter, since this is the contract to which the shipowner, who issues the bill of lading, is a party. But this will not invariably be so, and the court may conclude, on examining the facts, that the intention was to incorporate the sub-charter[53]; or even, in extreme cases, that the bill of lading is so ambiguous as to be void.[54]

A reference to a void charterparty is valid to incorporate the terms of the document in which the purported charter is contained.[55]

Where the charterparty is not reduced to writing until after the bill of lading is issued, it will not be incorporated, although it suffices that the charterparty has been documented in such a way that its terms are readily ascertainable, even if no formal charterparty has been drawn up.[56] Where the charterparty is amended after signature, but before the issue of the bill of lading, the terms incorporated are those of the amended charter.[57] However, the terms of the bill of lading may, on their proper construction, permit the manner or mode of discharge of an incorporated obligation to be determined by the parties to the incorporated charterer, for example as to the bank account or person to whom freight should be paid or whether freight might be discharged by the direct payment of expenses on the shipowner's behalf.[58]

It not infrequently happens that where a printed form of bill provides for the incorporation of "the charterparty dated—", the parties omit to fill in the blank.

---

[51] *The Spiros C* [2000] 2 Lloyd's Rep. 319 (charterparty demurrage regime which put the responsibility of discharging upon receivers/charterers negatived implied term of bill of lading making shipper responsible for discharge, even though not incorporated).

[52] At any rate if it is a voyage charter: approved in *K/S A/S Seateam v Iraq National Oil Co (The Sevonia Team)* [1983] 2 Lloyd's Rep. 640 at p.644. The position is less clear where it is a time charter, the terms of which are in many respects inapposite to the carriage of goods on a voyage. The court might well hesitate to hold the consignee liable for, say, unpaid time charter hire: approved in *The Nanfri* [1978] 1 Lloyd's Rep. at p.591, per Kerr J.

[53] For example, where the charterer issues the bill. See *Lignell v Samuelson* (1921) 9 Lloyd's Rep. 361, where the charterer signed the bill on behalf of the master.

[54] *Smidt v Tiden* (1874) L.R. 9 Q.B. 446. We believe that the court would nowadays hesitate long before arriving at this conclusion.

[55] per Russell J. in *Akt. Ocean v Harding* [1928] 2 Q.B. 371 (CA).

[56] *Welex A.G. v Rosa Maritime Ltd (The Epsilon Rosa)* [2003] 2 Lloyd's Rep. 509; [2003] EWHC Civ 938 holding that on the facts of that case, a recap telex sufficiently reduced the terms of the incorporated charterparty into writing (c.f. *The Heidberg* [1994] 2 Lloyd's 287). See also *Tradigrain SA v King Diamond Shipping SA (The Spiros C)* [1999] 2 Lloyd's Rep. 91; [2000] 2 Lloyd's Rep. 319.

[57] *Fidelitas Shipping Co v Exportchleb* [1963] 2 Lloyd's Rep. 113 (CA). It remains unclear whether this would be the case where the amendment arises from informal exchanges rather than a formal addenda: *The Spiros C* [2000] 2 Lloyd's Rep. 319.

[58] *The Spiros C* [2000] 2 Lloyd's Rep. 319.

It is submitted that the effect is the same as if the reference were simply to "the charterparty", and that the omission does not demonstrate an intent to negative the incorporation.[59]

Article 39—Incorporating Provisions   A39

A wide variety of incorporating provisions is in common use. Several of these have been discussed by the courts. Some of the earlier decisions must be approached with caution, in the light of the more recent authorities.[60] The following is a summary of the decisions on various forms of clause.[61] In each instance, it must be recalled that even if the clause is wide enough to produce a prima facie incorporation, it will nevertheless be ineffective unless the incorporated term makes sense in the context of the bill of lading, and is consistent with its terms: see Article 37, above.

"Freight and all other conditions as per charter"

This is the narrowest form of incorporating clause in common use. The clause covers only such conditions of the charter as are to be performed by the consignee,[62] or are referable to the discharge and receipt of cargo.[63]

Thus the words do not incorporate charterparty exceptions clauses into the bill of lading.[64] Nor are they effective to incorporate a cesser clause,[65] nor a time charter indemnity and agency clause,[66] nor a clause in the charterparty that the bills of lading should be conclusive evidence of the arrival of cargo shipped.[67]

On the other hand, it has been held that the words are sufficient to incorporate provisions for demurrage at the discharging port,[68] for a lien in respect of loading

---

[59] Text approved by CA in *Pacific Molasses & United Molasses Trading Co v Entre Rios Compania Naviera (The San Nicholas)* [1976] 1 Lloyd's Rep. 8; see also *Bangladesh Chemical Industries v Tex-Dilan Shipping Co (The S.L.S. Everest)* [1981] 2 Lloyd's Rep. 389. *Cf. Finska Cellulosa v Westfield Paper Co* (1940) 46 Com.Cas. 87. We do not think that the decision in this case entails that the bill of lading incorporated a standard printed form of charter, if there was no binding charter at all.

[60] E.g. *Miramar Maritime Corporation v Holborn Oil Trading Ltd* [1984] A.C. 676, where the House of Lords doubted the correctness of earlier decisions, such as *Gray v Carr* (1871) L.R. 6 Q.B. 522 and *Porteus v Watney* (1878) 3 Q.B.D. 534.

[61] Whether arbitration clauses are incorporated is discussed separately in Art.40.

[62] *Serraino v Campbell* [1891] 1 Q.B. 283 (CA); *Russell v Niemann* (1864) 17 C.B. (N.S.) 163 at p.177; *Diederichsen v Farquharson* [1898] 1 Q.B. 150 (CA); *Manchester Trust v Furness Withy* [1895] 2 Q.B. 539 (CA); *Hogarth Shipping Co v Blyth* [1917] 2 K.B. 534. The statement of Lord Robson in *Thomas v Portsea* [1912] A.C. 1 at p.10, that the words incorporate only those terms which are *ejusdem generis* with the payment of freight seems unduly narrow.

[63] *Gullischen v Stewart* (1882) 11 Q.B.D. 186; 13 Q.B.D. 317.

[64] *Serraino v Campbell*, above; *Delaurier v Wyllie* (1889) 17 Rettie 167; *Diederichsen v Farquharson*, above; *Russell v Niemann*, above. See also *Moel Tryvan v Kruger* [1907] 1 K.B. 809; [1907] A.C. 272.

[65] *Gullischen v Stewart*, above. A cesser clause makes no sense in a bill of lading.

[66] *Manchester Trust v Furness Withy*, above.

[67] *Hogarth v Blyth*, above; but contrast *Fort Shipping Co v Pedersen* (1924) 19 Lloyd's Rep. 26 ("all conditions and exceptions"); *Oostzee Stoomvart v Bell* (1906) 11 Com.Cas. 214; *Evans v Webster* (1928) 34 Com.Cas. 173 ("all conditions terms and exceptions").

[68] *Gullischen v Stewart*, above; *Porteus v Watney*, above; see also *Van Liewen v Hollis* [1920] A.C. 239. Problems arise where there is more than one bill of lading. Both logic and the decided cases indicate that the consignee of each part cargo is liable for the whole of the demurrage due under the charter. This result is not commercially satisfactory. See the discussion at pp.287, 288.

port and discharging port demurrage,[69] and for a lien in respect of dead freight.[70] So also in the case of a clause providing that the vessel should discharge in a dock ordered by charterers.[71] The clause will also be sufficient to incorporate provisions in the charterparty identifying the person or account to whom the freight should be paid, as well as the rate of freight.[72]

Whether these words are sufficient to impose on the consignee a liability for loading port demurrage, as distinct from merely a lien, is less clear, but in principle it seems that they are not, since a provision relating to the rate at which cargo is to be loaded is not a condition to be performed by the consignee, nor is it relevant to the discharge and receipt of the cargo.[73]

"All conditions and exceptions"

An express reference to "exceptions" or to a "negligence clause" is sufficient to make the bill of lading subject to the excepted perils contained in the charterparty.[74]

"All the terms provisions and exceptions"

These are very wide words of incorporation, and are sufficient to bring into the bill of lading almost everything which is in the charterparty[75]—provided of course that the term makes sense in the context of the bill, and is not inconsistent with its express provisions.[76]

"All terms, conditions, clauses and exceptions"

This provision is perhaps the widest of those in common use. It has been held to be effective to incorporate into a bill of lading a clause which required "demurrage" to be paid if a discharging berth was not immediately available.[77]

---

[69] *Fedelitas Shipping Co v Exportchleb* [1963] 2 Lloyd's Rep. 113, per Pearson L.J. at p.125. See also *Gray v Carr* (1871) L.R. 6 Q.B. 522. The reason is that a lien for demurrage, even if incurred at the loading port, is material to the terms on which the consignee takes delivery of the cargo.

[70] *Kish v Taylor* [1912] A.C. 604 at p.614.

[71] *East Yorkshire S.S. Co v. Hancock* (1900) 5 Com.Cas. 266. The decision was on a wide form of incorporation, but the reasoning is equally applicable to the narrower forms.

[72] *India Steamship Co v Louis Dreyfus Sugar Ltd (The Indian Reliance)* [1997] 1 Lloyd's Rep. 52.

[73] See *Smith v Sieveking* (1855) 4 E. & B. 945; 5 E. & B. 589, approving *Wegener v Smith* (1854) 15 C.B. 285. The latter case indicates that receipt of the cargo by the consignee, under notice of a claim for demurrage, may be sufficient to justify the inference of an agreement to satisfy the claim. See Art.15.

[74] *The Northumbria* [1906] P.292; *Finska Cellulosa v Westfield Paper* (1940) 46 Com.Cas. 87; see also *Thomas v Portsea*, above, per Lord Gorrell at p.8. As to the incorporation of a conclusive evidence clause, see *Fort v Pedersen*, fn.67, above. In *The Modena* (1911) 16 Com.Cas. 292 it was held that these words did not incorporate the words "at charterer's risk", but this was a decision on special facts.

[75] *Vergottis v Robinson* (1928) 31 Ll.L.R. 23, per Roche J. at p.26.

[76] See Art.37, above. The decision in *Vergottis v Robinson* was to the effect that a clause requiring that charterers' agents should pay certain charges at the discharging port could not be read into the bill of lading. Possibly this would now be regarded as falling within the limits of permissible verbal manipulation: see p.71, above. In *Gorrisen v Challoner* (1925) 23 Ll.L.R. 61, it was held that a reference to "terms and conditions" incorporated a lien for dead freight and demurrage.

[77] *Roland-Linie Schiffahrt v Spillers (The Werrastein)* [1957] 1 Q.B. 109, "Demurrage" is a misnomer. For a discussion of this type of clause, see Art.80. For a decision on "all conditions terms and exceptions", see *Evans v Webster*, fn.67, above.

Similarly with a clause requiring the ship to discharge at a dock as ordered by the charterers.[78] "*All exceptions, limitations, provision, conditions and liberties herein benefiting the Carrier as if such provisions were expressly made for their benefit*". These words have been held, in the specific context of the "Himalaya" clause, not to extend to an exclusive jurisdiction clause in the charterparty, albeit it was recognised that the word "provision" had a wider import than "exclusions" and "limitations".[79]

Article 40—Incorporation of Arbitration and Jurisdiction Clauses[80]   A40

An arbitration or jurisdiction clause in a charterparty will be incorporated into a bill of lading if there are specific words of incorporation in the bill, even if some degree of verbal manipulation is called for,[81] and the clause does not conflict with the express terms of the bill. There are some authorities which suggest that an arbitration or jurisdiction clause will be incorporated by general words of incorporation in the bill, if the arbitration or jurisdiction clause or some other provision in the charter makes it clear that the clause is to govern disputes under the bill as well as under the charter.[82] However, more recent authorities have suggested that the wording of clauses in the charterparty cannot save an incorporation if the terms of the bill of lading are insufficiently wide to effect a prima facie incorporation.[83] This latter approach has the benefit that the transferee of a bill of lading will be able to ascertain from the terms of the bill itself whether the words of incorporation are sufficient to incorporate any arbitration or jurisdiction clause in the charterparty, and may be said to avoid the circularity inherent in the argument that the issue of whether or not a particular term of the charterparty has been made a term of the bill of lading turns on the language used in the charterparty. What is clear is that if there are no specific

---

[78] *East Yorkshire S.S. Co v Hancock*, above. The court did not have to decide whether "by charterers" meant "by consignees".

[79] *The Mahkutai* [1996] A.C. 650.

[80] The same approach is required for arbitration and jurisdiction clauses: *Siboti K/S v BP France S.A.* [2003] 2 Lloyd's Rep. 364; [2003] EWHC 1278 (Comm). Analogous issues may arise in determining the extent of provisions incorporated by a "Himalaya" clause: *The Mahkutai* [1996] 2 Lloyd's Rep. 1; [1996] A.C. 350 and *Air New Zealand Ltd v The Ship "Contship America"* [1992] 1 N.Z.L.R. 425 (shipowner unable to rely on arbitration clause in charter's bill of lading). For the position under the Hamburg Rules, see Article 22.2, below, p.510.

[81] For the general principle see Art.37, above. Where there is a specific incorporation it is now clear that some degree of verbal manipulation is permissible to make the clause fit the bill. If the clause referred to "disputes arising under this charterparty" it has been suggested that it is beyond the limits of manipulation: see per Cairns L.J. in *The Annefield* [1971] P. 168 at p.186 and *Navigazione Alta Italia SpA v Svenska Petroleum A.B., The Nai Matteini* [1988] 1 Lloyd's Rep. 452. But contrast on both these points, the decision of Brandon J. in *The Rena K* [1978] 1 Lloyd's Rep. 545 at p.551, of Webster J. in *The Oinoussin Pride* [1991] 1 Lloyd's Rep. 126, of the Court of Appeal in *Daval Aciers D'Usinor et de Sacilor v Armare S.R.L. (The Nerano)* [1996] 1 Lloyd's Rep. 1 and *The Delos* [2001] 1 Lloyd's Rep. 703. See also *Astro Valiente Compania Naviera v Government of Pakistan (The Emmanuel Colocotronis)* [1982] 1 Lloyd's Rep. 286. The decision of Staughton J. in the latter case was not followed by Hobhouse J. in *Skips A/S Nordheim v Syrian Petroleum Co Ltd (The Varenna)* [1983] 1 Lloyd's Rep. 416; upheld in the CA [1983] 2 Lloyd's Rep. 529.

[82] *The Merak*, [1965] P. 223 and *The Annefield*, [1971] P. 168, and see also Article 40 of the previous edition of this work.

[83] *The Varenna* [1983] 2 Lloyd's Rep. 592 at pp.618 and 621–622; *The Federal Bulker* [1989] 1 Lloyd's Rep. 103 at pp.108, 110 and *Siboti K/S v BP France SA* [2003] 2 Lloyd's Rep. 364; [2003] EWHC 1278 (Comm). The point was left open in *The Delos* [2001] 1 Lloyd's Rep. 703.

words of incorporation in the bill of lading, and no language in the charterparty to bolster an argument premised on general words of incorporation, the arbitration or jurisdiction clause is not incorporated into the bill.[84]

A41   **Article 41—Identity of Carrier**

When a bill of lading is issued for goods on a chartered ship, the question whether the bill of lading, in the hands of a shipper other than the charterer or of a bona fide holder for value is a contract with the shipowner or the charterer is one of some difficulty and it is difficult to lay down general rules.[85] In most cases, however, the position is as follows:

(i) If the charter is a demise,[86] so that the captain is the servant of the charterer and not of the owner, a bill of lading signed by the captain or by the charterer is a contract with the charterer, not the ship owner.[87]

(ii) If the charter is not a demise, a bill of lading signed by the master or by the charterer as authorised agent of the master[88] is usually a contract with the shipowner.[89] The contract may be with the owners even though the charter contains a clause that the captain shall sign bills of lading as agent for the charterers, if the holder of the bill of lading does not know of the clause.[90] If the bill of lading imposes terms on the shipowner which are more onerous than those under the charter, the shipowner may be able to look to the charterer for an indemnity.[91]

---

[84] It is submitted that this is the outcome of *The Annefield*, above; *The Merak*, above, *Thomas v Portsea* [1912] A.C. 1; *The Njegos* [1936] P. 90; *The Phonizen* [1966] 1 Lloyd's Rep. 150 and *The Federal Bulker* [1989] 1 Lloyd's Rep. 103. In *The Delos* above the incorporating words "*all the terms whatsoever*" were held to be insufficient to incorporate the arbitration clause. We do not think that the authority of the bill of lading cases is weakened by the previous decisions of the Court of Appeal on the incorporation of an arbitration clause in a colliery guarantee into a charterparty: *Weir v Pirie* (1898) 3 Com.Cas. 263 ("Subject in all respects to the colliery guarantee": *held* incorporated); *Clink v Hickie Bormann* (1898) 3 Com.Cas. 275 ("as per colliery guarantee form": *held* not incorporated). Very different considerations apply to incorporation into a charter from those which apply to a bill of lading.
[85] per Walton J. in *Samuel v West Hartlepool Co* (1906) 11 Com.Cas. 115 at p.125.
[86] For the meaning of this expression see Art.28, above.
[87] per Walton J., above, at p.125; *Baumwoll v Furness* [1893] A.C. 8; *Marquand v Banner* (1856) 6 E. & B. 232, as explained and criticised in *Gilkison v Middleton* (1857) 2 C.B. (N.S.) 1345 and *Wehner v Dene S.S. Co* [1905] 2 K.B. 92. See also *The Stolt Loyalty* [1993] 2 Lloyd's Rep. 281 at p.284.
[88] *Tillmanns v Knutsford* [1908] 1 K.B. 185.
[89] per Walton J., above, at p.126; per Channell J. in *Wehner v Dene S.S. Co* [1905] 2 K.B. 92 at p.98; *Baumwoll v Furness*, above; *Sandeman v Scurr* (1866) L.R. 2 Q.B. 86 (CA); *Limerick S.S. Co v Coker* (1916) 33 T.L.R. 103; *Turner v Haji Goolam* [1904] A.C. 826; *Molthes v Ellermans Wilson Line* [1927] 1 K.B. 710. See also *Michenson v Begbie* (1829) 6 Bing. 190; *Gilleison v Middleton* (1857) 2 C.B. (N.S.) 134; *Schuster v McKellar* (1857) 7 E. & B. 704; *Wastwater S.S. Co v Neale* (1902) 86 L.T. 266; *The Patria* (1871) L.R. 3 A. & E. 436; *Smidt v Tiden* (1874) L.R. 9 Q.B. 447; *Wagstaff v Andersen* (1880) 5 C.P.D. 171; *The Rewia* [1991] 2 Lloyd's Rep. 325; *MB Pyramid Sound N.V. v Briese—Schifforts GmbH & Co Kg* [1995] C.L.C. 886; *The Hector* [1998] 2 Lloyd's Rep. 287.
[90] *Manchester Trust v Furness, Withy & Co* [1895] 2 Q.B. 539. This is an application of the principle that secret limitations of a general authority do not affect a third party relying on the general authority.
[91] See Art.43, below.

(iii) Where the bill of lading is signed by the charterer in his own name, the contract is with the charterer and not the owner.[92] Where there is a plain identification of the charterer as the carrier on the front of the bill of lading by a term specifically included by the parties, the contract will be with the charterer, not the shipowner, even if the bill contains a printed demise clause or identity of carrier clause stating that the bill of lading contract is with the shipowner on the reverse.[93]

(iv) A bill may be a charterers' bill of lading even if the bill is signed by or on behalf of the master[94] although this will only be the case where the master (or the person signing on his behalf) has authority (actual or ostensible) to sign and does sign the bill of lading on behalf of the charterer and not the shipowner.[95]

If in form a bill of lading only constitutes a contract with the charterer, but in fact, as between charterer and shipowner, the charterer has authority to contract on behalf of the shipowner, it may be that the holder of the bill of lading can sue the shipowner upon it as an undisclosed principal.[96]

Case 1. A chartered a ship to C to sail to X, and load from C's agent there, cargo to be stowed at merchant's risk and expense: the captain to sign bills of lading, if required, at any rate of freight, without prejudice to the charter. At X goods were shipped by shippers, who knew nothing of the charter, under a bill of lading signed by the master. *Held*, that the shippers could sue A, the master having signed as his agent.[97]

Case 2. A chartered the *Ferndene* to C by a time charter, not a demise of the vessel, the captain to be under the orders of the charterers as to employment and the charterers agreeing to indemnify the owners from all consequences that might arise from the captain signing bills of lading. C sub-chartered the vessel to O, who contracted with F for the shipment of goods, for which the captain then signed bills of lading at the freight arranged between O and F. *Held*, the bills of lading constituted a contract between A and F.[98]

Case 3. A chartered the *Bombay* to C by a time charter not a demise; C sub-chartered to O, who knew of the charter. O shipped cargo under bills of lading signed by the master at the sub-charter freight, though the bill of lading contained no lien for that hire. A claimed a lien on the cargo for time

---

[92] *Samuel v West Hartlepool Co* (1906) 11 Com.Cas. 115; see also *The Roberta* (1937) 58 Ll.L.R. 15.9 at p.231, and (1938) 60 Ll.L.R. 84 (CA); *Walker v Dover Navigation Co* (1949) 83 Ll.L.R. 84 at p.90. This may well be so where the charterers are proprietors of a line of steamers; *cf. Herman v Royal Exchange Shipping Co* (1884) C. & E. 413; *The Okehampton* [1913] P. 173; and *Bathgate v Letricheux*, Lloyd's List, March 18, 1919.

[93] *Homburg Houtimport B.V. v Agrosin Private Ltd (The Starsin)* [2003] 1 Lloyd's Rep. 571; [2004] 1 A.C. 715; [2003] UKHL 12.

[94] *Harrison v Huddersfield* (1903) 19 T.L.R. 386.

[95] *The Rewia*, fn.88 above. For a case in which it was held that the bill of lading contract was not with the shipowner, notwithstanding the fact that the bill was signed by the master, see *Sunrise Maritime Inc v Uvisco Ltd (The Hector)* [1998] 2 Lloyd's Rep. 587 where a statement on the front of the bill of lading identified the charterer as the carrier. See also *The Venezuela* [1980] 1 Lloyd's Rep. 393.

[96] The possibility that both the charterer and the shipowner could be liable on the bill of lading contract on this basis was canvassed without decision by Rix LJ in *Homburg Houtimport BV v Agrosin Private Ltd (The Starsin)* [2001] 1 Lloyd's Rep. 437; [2001] EWCA Civ. 56. The argument that both the charterer and the shipowner were parties to the bills of lading under consideration was rejected in the House of Lords: [2003] 1 Lloyd's Rep. 571; [2004] 1 A.C. 715; [2003] UKHL 12.

[97] *Sanderman v Scurr* (1866) L.R. 2 Q.B. 86. See also *The Figlia Maggiore* (1868) L.R. 2 A. & E. 106.

[98] *Wehner v Dene S.S. Co* [1905] 2 K.B. 92; *cf. Wastwater S.S. Co v Neale* (1902) 86 L.T. 266; *Limerick S.S. Co v Coker* (1916) 33 T.L.R. 103; and *Molthes Rederi Aktieselskabet v Ellerman's Wilson Line* [1927] 1 K.B. 710.

charter hire. *Held*, that A was prevented by the issue of the bill of lading from claiming a lien for more than the sub-charter hire.[99]

Case 4. A chartered the *Lindenhall* to C; C made a freight contract with F for the carriage of oil at a named freight, C's form of bill of lading to be used. F shipped oil and received bills of lading signed by the captain on C's form at the contract rate of freight. *Held*, the contract in the bill of lading was between F and C, not A.[100]

Case 5. A ship was chartered with a clause, "In signing bills of lading it is expressly agreed that the captain shall only do so as the agent for the charterers; and the charterers hereby agree to indemnify the owners from all consequences and liabilities, if any, that may arise from the captain signing bills of lading or otherwise complying with the same." In other respects the master was the servant of the owners, in whom under the charter the possession and control of the ship remained. The master signed bills of lading containing the clause, "they paying freight and all other conditions as per charter". A claim was made by the shippers on the shipowners under the bill of lading. It was not proved that the shippers knew of the clause in the charter above quoted. *Held*, that the shippers were entitled to sue the shipowners and were not affected by constructive notice of the terms of the charter.[101]

Case 6. The face of the bill of lading contained a signature box with the words "as agent for C (The Carrier)". On the reverse of the bill was a prominent printed heading "Company's Standard Conditions", below which 35 conditions were set out, in two dense columns, in print which was very small but just legible by a painstaking and persistent reader. These terms defined the carrier as "the party on whose behalf this Bill of Lading has been signed", and included an "identity of carrier clause" providing that the contract was entered into with the owner of the vessel and a demise clause providing that the bill of lading would take effect as a contract of carriage with the shipowner or demise charterer and not the charterer. Held that the bill of lading was a contract between the shipper and the charterer. The language on the front of the bill of lading, which had been specifically inserted, plainly identified the charterer as the carrier, and took priority over the printed terms on the back of the bill of lading.[102]

Note. In an attempt to avoid the possibility that time charterers, other than by demise, might be held liable as parties to a bill of lading without being able, as owners of the ship, to claim the benefit of the shipowner's statutory right to limit his liability,[103] most modern bills of lading in use by liner companies have contained the following so-called "demise clause": "If the ship is not owned by or chartered by demise to the company or line by whom this bill of lading is issued (as may be the case notwithstanding anything that appears to the contrary) this bill of lading shall take effect only as a contract with the owner or demise charterer as the case may be as principal made through the agency of the said company or line who act as agents only and shall be under no personal liability whatsoever in respect thereof."[104]

---

[99] *Turner v Haji Goolam* [1904] A.C. 826. The judgments decide that the bills of lading were contracts between A and O; but the decision might also be supported on the ground that there was no contract between A and O giving a lien on his goods for time charter freight.

[100] *Samuel v West Hartlepool S. Nav Co* (1906) 11 Com.Cas. 115.

[101] *Manchester Trust v Furness, Withy & Co* [1895] 2 Q.B. 539 (CA).

[102] *Homburg Houtimport BV v Agrosin Private Ltd (The Starsin)* [2003] 1 Lloyd's Rep. 571; [2004] 1 A.C. 715; [2003] UKHL 12. For criticism of the decision see Aikens, Lord and Bools, *Bills of lading* (2006) para.7.69. See also *Ngo Chew Hong Edible Oil Pte. Ltd v Scindia Steam Navigation Ltd (The Jalamohan)* [1988] 1 Lloyd's Rep. 443 rejecting the suggestion that there was "anything anomalous" about the demise clause.

[103] For the origins of the clause see Lord Roskill (1990) 106 L.Q.R. pp.403–406. Article 1.2 of the Convention of Limitation of Liability for Maritime Claims 1976, which applies in the United Kingdom by virtue of s.186 of the Merchant Shipping Act 1995, extends to charterers and operators of ships the shipowner's right to limit. Nonetheless the clause is still in common use. See also Tetley (1999) 44 McGill L.J. 807–848, for a strong criticism of two Canadian decisions upholding the validity of the clause.

[104] *Quaere*, whether the clause would be sufficient to negative the personal liability of the time charterer in a case where the bill of lading holder has no notice that the ship is chartered or whether it would bind the shipowner who has not authorised the signature of the bill of lading on his behalf. Such authority is commonly included in time charters. Thus where the master is "to sign bills of lading as presented", the charterer or his delegate may sign on behalf of the master: see *The Berkshire* [1974] 1 Lloyd's Rep. 183 and *W. & R. Fletcher (New Zealand) Ltd v Sigurd Haavik A/S* [1980] 1 Lloyd's Rep. 560.

The decision in *The Starsin*, which gives greater weight to the terms of the front of the bill in determining the contractual carrier, may meet many of the criticisms which the identity of carrier clause has attracted.

Article 42—Bills of Lading Differing from Charter   A42

In the absence of any special provisions in the charter,[105] or express instructions, the master or broker has no actual authority by signing bills of lading differing from the charter to vary the contract the owner has already made.[106]

But, if without such authority he varies the contract on some point which would be within his authority as master if there were no charter, and the bill of lading is given to a shipper other than the charterer and ignorant of the terms of the charter, or, being given to the charterer, comes into the hands of a bona fide holder for value, the owner, if he recognises the master's contract of carriage, must also recognise all the terms of it.[107]

If, however, the variations are beyond the apparent authority of a master,[108] or if the holder of the bill of lading is aware of the limitation on the master's authority imposed by the terms of the charter or the difference in terms has been obtained by the fraud of a previous holder,[109] the owner will not be bound by the contract represented in the bill of lading to exist, even to a bona fide holder for value of such bills of lading.[110] Where the owner is relying on the bill of lading holder's knowledge of the terms of the charter, the onus is on the owner to prove such knowledge[111] and a clause in the bill of lading, "all conditions as per charter" will not give the holder constructive notice of such terms.[112]

Case 1. A ship was chartered with certain excepted perils, including "restraint of princes". F shipped goods in ignorance of the charter, and the master signed a bill of lading containing only an exception of "perils of the sea". In an action *in rem* by G the consignees, who also were ignorant of the charter, against ship, owner, and master, for failing to deliver through "restraint of princes", *held*, that the owner was liable and that the contract in the bill of lading was not affected by the contract in the charter of which F and G were ignorant.[113]

Case 2. A ship was chartered by C for a certain voyage, at a certain freight with a lien on the cargo for all freight, the master to sign bills of lading without prejudice to the charter. C shipped goods for which the master signed a bill of lading, making the goods deliverable to G, "paying freight as per margin, *i.e.* £196". C indorsed the bill for value to G. *Held*, that the owners, having by their master signed bills making the goods deliverable on payment of a certain freight, could, against consignees

---

[105] Such as "master to sign bills of lading as presented to him by charterers". See Art.43, below.
[106] See Art.23, above.
[107] *Mercantile Exchange Bank v Gladstone* (1868) L.R. 3 Ex. 233 at p.240; *The Patria* (1871) L.R. 3 A. & E. 436.
[108] See Art.23, above.
[109] *Mitchell v Scaife* (1815) 4 Camp. 298.
[110] *Grant v Norway* (1851) 10 C.B. 665; *Reynolds v Jex* (1865) 7 B. & S. 86; *Mercantile Exchange Bank v Gladstone*, above; *Gilkison v Middleton* (1857) 2 C.B. (N.S.) 134; *The Canada* (1897) 13 T.L.R. 238.
[111] *The Draupner* [1909] P. 219; [1910] A.C. 450; *The St. Cloud* (1863) 8 B. & L. 4.
[112] *Manchester Trust v Furness Withy* [1895] 2 Q.B. 539 at pp.545, 547, 549; see also *West Hartlepool Co v Tagart Beaton & Co* (1902) 18 T.L.R. 358 at p.360; 19 T.L.R. 251.
[113] *The Patria* (1871) L.R. 3 A. & E. 436. Otherwise if F had shipped through C, the charterer, as his agent: *Delaurier v Wyllie* (1889) 17 Rettie 167.

who had advanced money on faith of the statements in the bill of lading, only claim the bill of lading freight, and not the whole freight for which they had a lien under the charter.[114]

A43   **Article 43—"Master to Sign Bills of Lading as Presented"**

It is common to provide that "the master is to sign bills of lading [at any rate of freight] as presented by the charterer without prejudice to the charter" or other words authorising the charterer to prepare bills of lading and present them to the master or the ship's agents for signature.

Where bills are to be "without prejudice to the charter", this clause deprives the master of authority[115] to vary the contract between the shipowner and the charterer by issuing a bill of lading in terms different from the charter. This is so whether the charterer is himself the shipper,[116] or becomes the holder of the bill of lading by consignment or indorsement.[117]

What remains uncertain is the extent of the master's duty to issue or sign bills of lading in whatever terms the charterer chooses to present them. This will depend upon the terms of the charter and the nature of the variance between the terms of the bill of lading and the charter. On the proper construction of the charter, it may be the duty of the charterer only to present bills of lading which do not vary the provisions of the charter[118] with the result that if he does present bills which do vary them, the master may refuse to sign them, but that if he signs them, the charterer has broken his contract, and must make good to the shipowner any damages the latter sustains by reason of being liable on such bills to an extent greater than his liability under the charter.[119] The same facts may also give the shipowner a cause of action for an indemnity, in the alternative to his claim for damages.[120] However, the mere fact that the bills of lading do not contain a proper law or jurisdiction clause to ensure that the bill of lading terms are

---

[114] *Gilkison v Middleton* (1857) 2 C.B. (N.S.) 134. See also *Mitchell v Scaife* (1815) 4 Camp. 298. This case is distinguishable from cases like *Kern v Deslandes* (1861) 10 C.B. (N.S.) 205, by the fact that the holder was an indorsee for value, and not a mere agent or factor. Here, too, the owners seem to have authorised the signing of the bill of lading (see per Cockburn C.J.), and so varied their lien.

[115] If indeed he could have authority in the absence of such a clause: see Art.23.

[116] See Art.32.

[117] *President of India v Metcalfe Shipping Co* [1970] 1 Q.B. 289 (CA).

[118] As to the possibility, in the event of the charterer making out clean bills of lading as against mate's receipts not clean, of the shipowner obtaining indemnity from consequent claims by holders of the bills of lading, see *Leach v Royal Mail Co* (1910) 16 Com.Cas. 143. See also *Groves v Webb* (1916) 85 L.J.K.B. 1533, where wharfingers, who, at the request of the goods-owners, had issued clean warrants for goods subsequently found to be damaged, were held entitled to be indemnified by the goods-owner against claims by subsequent holders of the warrants. In view of the decision of the CA in *Brown Jenkinson & Co v Percy Dalton* [1957] 2 Q.B. 621, it may be doubted whether such an indemnity could now be obtained.

[119] This appears to be the view taken by the House of Lords in *Kruger v Moel Tryvan Ship Co* [1907] A.C. 272. In *Elder Dempster & Co v C.G. Dunn & Co* (1909) 15 Com.Cas. 49, both Lord Loreburn and Lord Gordell approved a cause of action based on a breach of warranty that bills of lading correctly stated marks; Lord Loreburn also approved a cause of action for an indemnity based on the request to sign the bills of lading. See also *Dawson Line v Akt. Adler* [1932] 1 K.B. 433. The authorities are reviewed by Mustill L.J. in *Naviera Mogor SA v Société Metallurgique de Normandie (The Nogar Marin)* [1988] 1 Lloyd's Rep. 413.

[120] *The Nogar Marin*, above; *Paros Shipping Corp v Nafta (G.B.) Ltd (The Paros)* [1987] 2 Lloyd's Rep. 269. In these circumstances, the act of presenting the bill to the master for signature will be a request to the shipowner to perform an act which he is not obliged to perform, and it is this request which can give rise to an obligation on the charterer's part to indemnify the shipowner as an alternative to the claim for damages: *Telfair Shipping Corp v Intersea Carriers SA (The Caroline P)* [1984] 2 Lloyd's Rep. 466. *Cf.: Gearbulk Pool Ltd v Seaboard Shipping Co* [2006] BCCA 552 (Can.) where the owner's claim for an indemnity was rejected on the facts.

interpreted in a manner consistent with the shipowner's obligations under the charter will not be a breach of contract.[121]

In other cases, however, the master may be bound within certain limits[122] to sign any bill of lading presented by the charterer. However, the terms of the contract in the charter will not be altered, and consequently, if the signing of the bill of lading exposes the shipowner to greater liability than under the charter, the charterer must indemnify him.[123]

In certain cases, the charter will make it clear that there is no breach of charter in presenting bills of lading for signature which expose the shipowner to greater liabilities than those he assumed under the charter. Thus where a clause contains the words "at any rate of freight", the master must sign a bill of lading which provides for a freight rate different from that payable under the charter. Indeed the charter may make it clear that the shipowner has taken the risk of owing wider obligations under the bill of lading than those assumed under the charter, in which case not only will there be no breach of charter in presenting such bills for signature but the shipowner will not be entitled to an indemnity in respect of any liability which may result.[124]

Where the charterer presents a bill of lading to the master for signature which contains factual inaccuracies—for instance as to the date of shipment, or the nature, quantity or condition of the cargo—the master will generally be under no duty to sign such a bill of lading.[125] Where he does so, and incurs a liability to the consignee as a result, the shipowner's right to an indemnity from the charterer will depend upon the nature of the inaccuracy and the master's knowledge of it. If the master knowingly signs a bill of lading which inaccurately records the date of shipment or the apparent order and condition of cargo, no right to an indemnity will be implied and any express indemnity will be unenforceable.[126] In any event, the master's conscious decision to sign the bill in these circumstances will break the causal link between the charterer's act in presenting the inaccurate bill and the liability.

Where the master is not aware of or reckless as to the inaccuracy of the bill, but would be aware of the true position had reasonable care been taken, then the

[121] *The Paros* above; *Orinoco Navigation Ltd v Ecotrade SA (The Ikariada)* [1999] 2 Lloyd's Rep. 365.

[122] The bill of lading must not contain extraordinary terms or terms which are manifestly inconsistent with the charter: *The Berkshire* [1974] 1 Lloyd's Rep. 185 at p.188; *W. & R. Fletcher (New Zealand) Ltd v Sigurd Haavik A/S* [1980] 1 Lloyd's Rep. 560; *Gulf Steel Co v Al Khalifa Shipping Co* [1980] 2 Lloyd's Rep. 261; *Garbis Maritime Corp v Philippine National Co (The Garbis)* [1982] 2 Lloyd's Rep. 283.

[123] The former part of this view appears to be that taken by the Privy Council in *Turner v Haji Goolam* [1904] A.C. 826, Case 3 in Art.41, and by Lord Esher in *Hansen v Harrold* [1894] 1 Q.B. 612.

[124] *Ben Shipping Co (Pte) Ltd v An Bord Bainne (The C Joyce)* [1986] 2 Lloyd's Rep. 285; *Boukadoura Maritime Corp v Soc. Anonyme Marocaine de l'Industrie et du Raffinage (The Boukadoura)* [1989] 1 Lloyd's Rep. 393; *Orinoco Navigation Ltd v Ecotrade SA (The Ikariada)* [1999] 2 Lloyd's Rep. 365.

[125] *The Nogar Marin*, above.

[126] *Brown Jenkinson & Co v Percy Dalton*, above and fn.117. The act of the master in these circumstances is said to be "manifestly unlawful in itself" as to which see *Rudolf A Oetker v I.F.A. Internationale Frachtagentur AG (The Almak)* [1985] 1 Lloyd's Rep. 557 at p.561; *The Nogar Marin*, above at p.417. By contrast a letter of indemnity was held to be enforceable when, at the charterer's request, the master removed the words "said to contain" from a bill of lading for 5,839 pieces of timber, it being expedient in order to avoid delay for the master to accept the charterer's description of the number of pieces rather than counting the number of pieces himself: *Malaysia Motors and General Underwriters (Pte.) Ltd v Abdul Karim* [1982] 1 M.L.J. 51 (Mal).

question of the shipowner's right to indemnify the charterer will depend upon the facts of the case. If the charterer's act in presenting the bill is properly to be characterised as a request to the master to sign the bill of lading with such qualifications as he thinks appropriate, rather than a request to sign the bill of lading in that form, no right of indemnity will be implied. The master should take reasonable steps to inspect the cargo before signing the bill of lading,[127] and there will not normally be any reason to imply an obligation to indemnify the shipowner against the consequences of the negligence of his own servant.[128]

Where however, the master is not negligent, and the correctness of the bill of lading details are within the knowledge of the charterer or the shipper, then the charterer will normally be obliged to indemnify the shipowner against any resultant liability.[129] This may be so even though it was within the master's power to check the details, if he acts reasonably in adopting them.[130]

Where the master inserts language into the bill of lading recording a view about the condition of the cargo which a reasonably observant master could not properly have held, this may have the result that the bill no longer records the apparent good order and condition of the cargo, placing the shipowner in breach of the bill of lading contract.[131]

Case 1. A chartered a ship to C under a charter containing a clause exempting A from liability for the negligence of A's master, E. C presented, and E signed, bills of lading, under the erroneous impression that they incorporated the negligence clause. In consequence, the cargo having been lost by the negligence of E, bona fide indorsees of the bills of lading recovered damages against A, which he, in turn, recovered against C, in the view of the House of Lords, as damages for breach of contract to present bills of lading in accordance with the charter.[132]

Case 2. A chartered a ship to C under a Gencon charterparty requiring the master, E, to sign bills of lading "without prejudice to the charter". Although damage to the cargo was apparent, C's agents, D, presented mate's receipts to E for signature which were clean. Negligently, E signed the receipts which were then presented to D's agents who prepared and issued clean bills of lading. A was held liable to the consignees of the cargo, G, and sued C for an indemnity. *Held*, that on the facts of this case, there was no need to imply an obligation on C's part either to present accurate mate's receipts for signature or to indemnify A against its liability as a result of clean bills being issued. The damage to the cargo was readily detectable by E and there was no reason to imply an obligation to protect A against the negligence of his own master.[133]

Case 3. A chartered a ship to C, "the master to sign bills of lading as presented without prejudice to the charter". C shipped goods, and presented bills in the ordinary form, which the master refused

---

[127] Although there is no implied term of the charterparty that the master will exercise reasonable care in signing mate's receipts or bills of lading: *The Almak*, above; *Trade Star Line Corp v Mitsui & Co Ltd (The Arctic Trader)* [1996] 2 Lloyd's Rep. 449 (which countenances the possibility of a narrower term that if requested to do so and if necessary to enable the charterers or their agents to issue bills of lading on behalf of the ship, the master or chief officer will sign mate's receipts which state the apparent order and condition of the goods received on board).

[128] *The Nogar Marin*, above, although *cf. The Almak*, above.

[129] *Elder Dempster & Co v Dunn* (1909) Com.Cas. 49; *The Nogar Marin*, above.

[130] *The Boukadoura*, above (quantity of liquid cargo loaded).

[131] *The David Agmashenebeli* [2003] 1 Lloyd's Rep. 92; [2002] EWHC 104 (Admlty); *Sea Success Maritime Inc v African Carriers* [2005] 2 Lloyd's Rep. 692 at p.699; [2005] EWHC 1542 (Comm); *Oceanfocus Shipping v Hyundai Merchant Marine (The Hawk)* [1999] 1 Lloyd's Rep. 176 at p.185. *Cf. The Arctic Trader* above suggesting that the master is under an absolute duty under Art.III r.3 of the Hague–Visby Rules accurately to record the apparent good order and condition of the cargo. See B. Parker, *Liability for incorrectly clausing bills of lading* [2003] L.M.C.L.Q. 201.

[132] *Krüger v Moel Tryvan* [1907] A.C. 272.

[133] *The Nogar Marin*, above.

to sign unless they contained the clause, "The vessel was not liable for duties on cargo, by non-arrival before July 1". *Held*, such refusal was a breach of the charter.[134]

Case 4. Under a voyage charter it was provided that the captain should sign bills of lading at the current or any rate of freight without prejudice to the charter. The captain signed bills making the freight payable in advance at a port of loading to the charterers, not the owners. *Held*, that such a term was beyond the authority conferred on him.[135]

Note. Charterparties now frequently contain a clause by which the charterer agrees to indemnify[136] the owner from any consequences that may arise from the captain following the charterer's instructions and signing bills of lading.

---

[134] *Jones v Hough* (1879) 5 Ex.D. 115.
[135] *The Canada* (1897) 13 T.L.R. 238. If the clause had been to sign bills of lading as presented, *submitted* he would have been bound to sign them though all freight was made payable in advance; *Janentzky v Langridge* (1895) 1 Com.Cas. 90, and *cf. The Shillito* (1897) 3 Com.Cas. 44. See also *West Hartlepool Co v Tagart, Beaton & Co* (1902) 19 T.L.R. 251; 8 Com.Cas. 133.
[136] See Art.179 for a discussion of indemnity clauses in time charters.

CHAPTER 7

TERMS OF THE CONTRACT

A44   **Article 44—Categorisation of Contractual Terms**

CONTRACTUAL terms fall into three categories[1]:

(1) "Conditions." If the promisor breaks a condition in any respect, however slight,[2] the other party can, if he wishes, by intimation to the party in breach, elect to be released from performance of his further obligation under the contract, claiming damages for any loss he has suffered; although he can, if he prefers, elect to maintain the contract in existence and content himself with proceeding for damages in respect of his loss.

(2) "Warranties." If the promisor breaks a warranty in any respect, however serious, the other party does not have a right to be released from his further obligations, but has only the right to recover damages.[3]

(3) "Innominate or intermediate terms", which are neither conditions nor warranties.[4] When an obligation of this type is broken, the right of the promisee to treat himself as discharged depends on whether the breach is sufficiently serious to go to the root of the contract.

Articles 45 to 53 contain a discussion of some of the terms which are commonly expressed or implied in charterparties and bills of lading.[5] Within the discussion it will be indicated whether the term is a condition, or a warranty, or is an innominate term.

---

[1] *Hongkong Fir Shipping Co v Kawasaki Kisen Kaisha* [1962] 2 Q.B. 26; *The Mihalis Angelos* [1971] 1 Q.B. 164; *Cehave NV v Bremer Handelgesellschaft mbH (The Hansa Nord)* [1976] Q.B. 44; *Bremer Handelsgesellschaft mbH v Vanden Arenne-Izegem PVBA* [1978] 2 Lloyd's Rep. 109, 113 (per Lord Wilberforce); *Federal Commerce & Navigation Co Ltd v Molena Alpha Inc (The Nanfri)* [1979] A.C. 757; *Bunge Corp v Tradax Export SA* [1981] 2 Lloyd's Rep. 1; *Compagnie General Maritime v Diakan Spirit SA (The Ymnos)* [1982] 2 Lloyd's Rep. 574; *Greenwich Marine Inc v Federal Commerce & Navigation Co Ltd (The Mavro Vetranic)* [1985] 1 Lloyd's Rep. 580; *Aktion Maritime Corp of Liberia v S. Kasmas & Brothers (The Aktion)* [1987] 1 Lloyd's Rep. 283. Previous cases in which the courts have categorised obligations as "conditions" are still good law, and it is plain from *The Mihalis Angelos* that, where appropriate, the court will not hesitate to add new instances to the category. The older cases in which it has been held that certain terms are *not* conditions should be approached with more caution, since until the recent attention which has been given to the third category, it may have been assumed that if a term was not a condition, it must be a warranty.

[2] Unless, no doubt, the breach is so slight as to be *de minimis*.

[3] In the older cases the word "warranty" is used with a variety of meanings. In the law of marine insurance it has an entirely different meaning from the one indicated in the text, for it is generally used to denote a fundamental term of the policy: Marine Insurance Act 1906, ss.33 *et seq.* No doubt there are several instances of terms in charterparties and bills of lading which are warranties in the present sense, but there are few reported cases where the courts have held that a breach, however serious, does not give the right to terminate the contract.

[4] There are several examples of this category of term in shipping law. Perhaps the most important is the undertaking of seaworthiness.

[5] Other terms are discussed at various stages of this book; see, e.g. below, Chapter 9, Arts 127, 149, 153.

Article 45—Undertakings implied in the Contract   A45

Apart from terms implied by statute or by custom, the court will imply into a contract all such terms as are *necessary* to give business efficacy to the contract as both parties must have intended. It is not sufficient to show that an implication would be *reasonable*, for it is not the function of the court to make a contract for the parties.[6]

In all contracts for the carriage of goods by sea,[7] there are implied in the absence of express stipulation to the contrary, the following undertakings[8] by the shipowner or carrier:

(1) That his ship is seaworthy.[9] In contracts to which the Carriage of Goods by Sea Act 1971 applies, this undertaking does not exist. It is replaced by an undertaking that the shipowner will before, and at the beginning of, the voyage exercise due diligence to make the ship seaworthy.[10]

(2) That his ship shall commence and carry out the voyage contracted for with reasonable dispatch.[11]

(3) That his ship shall carry out the voyage contracted for without unjustifiable deviation.[12] This is discussed in Articles 127 to 128.

The first two of these implied undertakings (but not the third) are innominate terms of the contract. Hence such breaches of these undertakings as defeat the commercial purpose of the voyage will justify the charterer of the ship or the owner of the goods carried in repudiating the contract to carry and claiming damages if he suffers any by reason thereof.[13] Such breaches as do not defeat the commercial purpose of the voyage will give rise only to an action for damages.[14]

---

[6] Generally as to implied terms, see *The Moorcock* (1884) 14 P.D. 64; *Hamlyn v Wood* [1891] 2 Q.B. 488; *Comptoir Commercial v Power* [1920] 1 K.B. 868, per Scrutton L.J. at p.899; *Shirlaw v Southern Foundries* [1939] 2 K.B. 206, per MacKinnon L.J. at p.227, "the officious bystander" test; *Compagnie Algerienne de Meunerie v Katana* [1960] 1 Lloyd's Rep. 132; *Liverpool C.C. v Irwin* [1977] A.C. 239 (HL); *Scally v Southern Health Board* [1992] 1 A.C. 294 (HL (N.I.)). In the last two cases the House of Lords implied a term in line with a wider notion of necessity than merely "business efficacy".

[7] Except time charters, to which the warranty of seaworthiness at the beginning of the voyage probably does not apply. See Art.177.

[8] These implied terms have stood for many years and it will rarely be necessary for any further implication to be made; per Hodson L.J. in *Compagnie Algerienne v Katana*, above.

[9] *Steel v State Line S.S. Co* (1877) 3 App.Cas. 72, and see Art.51.

[10] See s.3 of this Act and the Schedule thereto, Art.III, Rule 1, and notes in Chapter 20.

[11] *MacAndrew v Chapple* (1866) L.R. 1 C.P. 643, and see Art.52.

[12] *Scaramanga v Stamp* (1880) 5 C.P.D. 295. See also Rule 4 of Art.IV of the Schedule to the Carriage of Goods by Sea Act 1971 and the comment thereon in Chapter 20.

[13] *Freeman v Taylor* (1831) 8 Bing. 124; *Universal Cargo Carriers v Citati* [1957] 2 Q.B. 401 (*Case 3*, p.151, below); *Hongkong Fir Shipping Co v Kawasaki Kisen Kaisha* [1962] 2 Q.B. 26 (CA).

[14] *Clipsham v Vertue* (1843) 5 Q.B. 265; *Tarrabochia v Hickie* (1856) 1 H. & N. 183; *MacAndrew v Chapple* (1866) L.R. 1 C.P. 643; *The Hongkong Fir*, above, and Art.43.

A46   **Article 46—Ship's Class on the Register**

A statement in the charter of the ship's class on the register amounts only to a promise that the ship at the time of making the charter is actually so classed[15] and not that she is rightly so classed,[16] nor that she will continue to be so classed during the term of the charter, nor that the owners will omit no act necessary to retain her in that class.[17] The loss of class during the period of the charter may, however, have been caused by unseaworthiness, or some other breach of the shipowner's obligations, for which the charterer would have a remedy.

It is submitted that a statement of the ship's class is a condition of the contract, breach of which entitles the charterer to treat the contract as discharged.[18]

A47   **Article 47—Ship's Tonnage, or Dead Weight Capacity**

A statement of the ship's tonnage is an "innominate" term. A variation from the ship's tonnage as stated in the charter will not entitle the charterer to treat the charter as discharged unless the breach is so great as to go to the root of the contract.[19]   Where a charter contains a guarantee that a ship shall or can carry a certain number of tons dead weight, or is of a certain dead weight capacity, this, in the absence of indications to the contrary, is a guarantee of the abstract carrying capacity of the ship, without reference to any particular cargo proposed to be shipped.[20]

Where, however, the guarantee, on its proper construction, has reference to a cargo of a particular description proposed and made known to the owner for shipment on the contemplated voyage, the guarantee will relate to the capacity to carry that description of cargo.[21]

For a discussion of the relationship between a guaranteed capacity and an obligation to load a "full and complete cargo", see Art.86, below.

Case. A printed form of charter provided that the ship should carry a full and complete cargo of maize. There was also a clause, "The owners guarantee the ship's deadweight capacity to be 3,200 tons, and freight to be paid on this quantity." The ship could load a dead weight of 3,200 tons, e.g. with a cargo of coal, but she could not carry more than 3,081 tons of maize. *Held*, that there was no breach of the guarantee.[22]

---

[15] *Routh v Macmillan* (1863) 2 H. & C. 750.
[16] *French v Newgass* (1878) 3 C.P.D. 163.
[17] *Hurst v Usborne* (1856) 18 C.B. 144, approved in *French v Newgass*, above.
[18] See fn.15, above.
[19] See *Cargo Ships "El-yam" v "Invotra"* [1958] 1 Lloyd's Rep. 39 at p.52; so held in *Barker v Windle* (1856) 6 E. & B. 675, where the chartered tonnage was from 180 to 200 tons, the actual tonnage 258 tons; and *Gibbs v Grey* (1857) 2 H. & N. 22, where the difference was between 470 and 350 tons. See also *Harrison v Knowles* [1917] 2 K.B. 606, where it was held, on a contract for the sale of a ship, that the difference between 460 and 360 tons d.w.c. was a difference of degree and not of kind, and therefore did not constitute a breach of a condition. *Sed quaere*, and see *ibid.* [1918] 1 K.B. 608 (CA).
[20] *Millar v Freden* [1918] 1 K.B. 611; *Thomson v Brocklebank* [1918] 1 K.B. 655; *cf. Carnegie v Conner* (1889) 24 Q.B.D. 45, and *Societa Ungherese v Tyset Line* (1902) 8 Com.Cas. 25.
[21] *Mackill v Wright* (1888) 14 App.Cas. 106, per Lord Macnaghten at p.120, Lord Watson at pp.116, 117, Lord Halsbury at pp.114, 115. See also *Potter v New Zealand Shipping Co* (1895) 1 Com.Cas. 114. For a discussion of *Mackill v Wright* and the cases cited in fn.20 above, see 17th edn, p.77.
[22] *Millar v Freden* [1918] 1 K.B. 611 (CA). [*Sed quaere*, where the cargo is specified in the charter. T.E.S.]

Note. The term "tonnage" refers to register tons of 100 cubic feet, and has no reference to weight.

The term "tons" by itself would mean a weight of 20 cwt., but the full phrase "ton of 2240 lbs." is often used. So, too, nowadays is the phrase "x tons of 2000 kilograms", or "x metric tons". For payment of freight the ton is sometimes calculated at some specified number of cwt. less than twenty.

The term "tons weight or measurement" means that goods shipped are to be taken either by weight of 20 cwt., or by measurement of 40 cubic feet, a measure probably derived from the measure of 20 cwt. of salt water (= 35.7 cubic feet, the balance being the allowance for the hull carrying it). Whether goods are to be treated as weight or measurement goods for freight is at the option of the shipowner.[23]

The number of tons of 20 cwt. a vessel will lift is called her "dead weight capacity", for short, "dead weight", "d.w.", or "capacity".

Questions have arisen whether "dead weight capacity" is the vessel's lifting capacity for cargo only or whether in calculating that capacity the weight of bunkers, ship's stores and boiler feed water is to be included. It was held by a learned arbitrator in stating a special case, and not disputed when that case was argued before Lush J., that the weight of bunkers, ship's stores and boiler feed water was to be included, and at the same time it was held by Lush J. that water in the boilers was to be excluded as being part of the ship's equipment: *Soc. Minière du Tonkin v Sutherland & Co.*[24] "Capacity" is also applied to the "room" or number of cubic feet available for stowage in the holds of a ship, which may differ materially from the weight she can lift without putting her Plimsoll mark or load-line under water. Dry cargo ships nowadays are usually chartered either on dead weight, or bale capacity, or both.

Article 48—Ship's Name and National Character   A48

Substantial accuracy in the name of the vessel will be a condition of the contract.[25]

The national character of the vessel as stated in the charter may be a condition; e.g. in time of war, when neutrality is an important circumstance.[26] But a term as to national character cannot be inferred from the mere name of the ship.[27]

If a ship when chartered is in fact of a certain nationality it would be a breach of the charterparty by the owner if during its currency he changed her flag, e.g. by selling her to an owner of another nationality.[28] Damages for such breach may only be nominal, but in some circumstances may be substantial.[28]

---

[23] See *Pust v Dowie* (1864) 5 B. & S. 20.

[24] April 27, 1917, unreported. By the terms of the charter the ship was "guaranteed 4,700 tons deadweight all told".

[25] This statement by the author has appeared in all previous editions of this work. We know of no case supporting it, but substantial inaccuracy might seriously affect insurance of cargo.

[26] *Behn v Burness* (1863) 3 B. & S. 751 at p.757. During the Spanish-American War in 1898, lay arbitrators under a charter to nominate a first-class steamer held that a tender of a Spanish steamer was a bad tender, on the ground that, being liable to capture, she was not fit to carry the cargo. The CA declined to order a special case to be stated: *Hoyland v Ralli*, October 29, 1898.

[27] *Isaacs v McAllum* [1921] 3 K.B. at p.385.

[28] *Ibid.* See Art.17, as to the question whether the purchaser of a ship is bound by a charter affecting it. See also Art.31 as to provisions in charters allowing for a change in the ship performing the services thereunder.

A49   **Article 49—Speed of Ship**

A statement in a time charter of the ship's speed amounts to a promise, subject
to any protection afforded by an exception clause, that the ship at the time of her
delivery under the charter will be capable of the stated speed,[29] unless the
statement is qualified by words such as "without guarantee".[30] It is submitted
that an undertaking as to speed is not a condition, but is an "innominate" term
so that the charterer's right to treat the contract as discharged by a breach of the
undertaking will depend upon the gravity of the breach.

A50   **Article 50—Whereabouts of Ship and Time of Sailing**

Time clauses in mercantile contracts usually have the force of conditions.[31] Thus
a statement that the ship is in a certain position at the time of making the
charter,[32] or that she will be at a certain place by a certain day,[33] or that she will
be ready to receive cargo by a certain day,[34] or that she will sail on her voyage
by a certain day,[35] is usually a condition of the charter. The fact that failure to
comply with such a condition results from perils excepted in the charter will not
prevent its being a breach of such condition so as to entitle the charterers to
cancel, though the exception may protect the owner from a claim for damages.[36]

The words "expected ready to load" by a certain date mean that in view of the
facts known to the promisor when making his contract he honestly expects that
the vessel will be ready as stated and that his expectation is based on reasonable
grounds. This obligation is a condition, and any breach will entitle the charterer
to terminate.[37] The promise is broken if the promisor does not honestly expect,
or if he has no reasonable grounds for his expectation.[38] In considering the latter,

---

[29] *Cosmos Bulk Transport v China National Foreign Trade Transportation Corp (The Apollonius)* [1978] 1 Lloyd's
Rep. 53, differing from *Lorentzen v White Shipping Co* (1943) 74 Ll.L.R. 161, where it was held to apply only
at the time of making the charter. In the former case it was recognised that the warranty might have wider
application than that stated in the text. See further Art.177, below.
[30] *Losinjska Plovidba Brodarstovo DD v Valfracht Maritime Co Ltd* [2001] 2 Lloyd's Rep. 17.
[31] *Bunge Corp v Tradax* [1981] 2 Lloyd's Rep. 1 (HL). See also *Hyundai Merchant Marine Co Ltd v Karander
Maritime Inc (The Niizuru)* [1996] 2 Lloyd's Rep. 66..
[32] *Behn v Burness* (1863) 3 B. & S. 751; *Ollive v Booker* (1847) 1 Ex. 416; *Oppenheim v Fraser* (1876) 34 L.T.
524; *The Mihalis Angelos* [1971] 1 Q.B. 164.
[33] Submitted on the basis of *Corkling v Massey* (1873) L.R. 8 C.P. 395. See, however, *Associated Portland Cement
Manufacturers (1900) v Houlder* (1917) 22 Com.Cas. 279.
[34] *Oliver v Fielden* (1849) 4 Ex. 135; *Seeger v Duthie* (1860) 8 C.B. (N.S.) 45; *Shadforth v Higgin* (1813) 3 Camp.
385.
[35] *Glaholm v Hays* (1841) 2 M. & G. 257; *Van Baggen v Balnes* (1854) 9 Ex. 523; *Deffell v Brocklebank* (1817)
4 Price 36; *Bentsen v Taylor* [1893] 2 Q.B. 274.
[36] *Smith v Dart* (1884) 14 Q.B.D. 105; *Croockewit v Fletcher* (1857) 1 H. & N. 893. *Cf. Nickoll v Ashton Edridge*
[1901] 2 K.B. 126 (CA).
[37] *The Mihalis Angelos* [1971] 1 Q.B. 164; *Greenwich Marine Inc v Federal Commerce & Navigation Co Ltd (The
Mavro Vetranic)* [1985] 1 Lloyd's Rep. 581; *Geogas SA v Trammo Gas Ltd (The Baleares)* [1993] 1 Lloyd's Rep.
215 (CA). A statement as to the expected termination of the vessel's previous employment may likewise be a
term of the charter: *Goldberg v Bjornstad & Braekhus* (1921) 6 Ll.L.R. 73.
[38] *Sanday v Keighley, Maxted & Co* (1922) 27 Com.Cas. 296; *Finnish Government v Ford* (1921) 6 Ll.L.R. 188;
Monroe v Ryan [1935] 2 K.B. 28; *Cie Algerienne de la Meunerie v Katana* [1960] 1 Lloyd's Rep. 132; *The
Mihalis Angelos*, above. See also *Petroleum Export Corp v Kerr*, 32 F.2d 969 (1929). Contrast the position where
a time charterer gave an estimate of the length of a trip "without guarantee", where it sufficed that the estimate
was given in good faith, whether or not made on reasonable grounds: *Continental Pacific Shipping Ltd v
Deemand Shipping Co Ltd (The Lendoudis Evangelos II)* [1997] 1 Lloyd's Rep. 404.

regard will be had to such knowledge as the responsible officials of the shipowner have or ought to have, whether known to the shipowner or not.[39] The combination of the words "expected ready to load" and an express or implied undertaking that the vessel shall proceed to a port of loading with all reasonable despatch results in an obligation that wherever she may be she shall start at a time when, by so proceeding, she would normally arrive at the port of loading by the expected date.[40] An "estimated time of arrival" clause in a charterparty clause has the same effect.[41] This obligation is absolute and the exceptions in the charter will not excuse a failure to start in time unless the contract expressly so provides.[42] Nor is it necessary for the vessel to have completed its last fixture before the obligation of reasonable despatch arises, with the result that as soon as it becomes clear that the vessel will be unable to reach the loading port by the relevant date proceeding normally, the shipowner has committed an actual and not an anticipatory breach of contract.[43]

Case 1. A ship, on March 29, was described in the charter as "now sailed or about to sail". She did not in fact sail till April 23. *Held*, a breach of a condition.[44]

Case 2. A ship was chartered "now at sea, having sailed three weeks ago" to sail to X and there load a cargo. The ship had not in fact "sailed three weeks ago". *Held*, the statement was a condition and its breach entitled the charterer to throw up the charter.[45]

Case 3. Charter to proceed to X, "and on arrival there to load and to sail with June convoy, provided she arrived out and was ready to load sixty-five running days previous to the sailing of such convoy". The ship was not ready to load sixty-five days before the June convoy. *Held*, the breach only absolved her from sailing with the June convoy and did not free her altogether from her obligation to load and proceed.[46]

Case 4. A ship was chartered to proceed to X and there "load . . . the act of God and perils of the sea during the said voyage always excepted; should the steamer not be arrived at X free of pratique and ready to load on or before December 15, the charterers to have the option of cancelling or confirming the charter". Through dangers of the sea, the steamer, though at X, was not free of pratique by December 15, and the charterers cancelled. *Held*, that the clause as to excepted perils did not prevent them from so doing.[47]

Case 5. A ship was chartered "expected ready to load about July 1", with a cancelling date of July 20. At the date of the charter, the shipowner could not reasonably have estimated that the ship would arrive at the loading port "about July 1". On July 17, the charterers cancelled. *Held*, that they were

[39] *Efploia Shipping Co v Canadian Transport Co* [1958] 2 Lloyd's Rep. 449, in which the rule was applied to a statement in a time charter of the expected tonnage of bunkers on board on delivery.

[40] *Monroe v Ryan*, above; *Dreyfus v Lauro* (1938) 60 Ll.L.R. 94; *Evera SA Commercial v North Shipping Co* [1956] 2 Lloyd's Rep. 367. See the first two cases for a discussion as to the meaning of the word "about" when applied to an expected readiness date.

[41] *Mitsui O.S.K. Lines Ltd v Garnac Grain Co Inc (The Myrtos)* [1984] 2 Lloyd's Rep. 449.

[42] See the cases in fn.40, above and *Transworld Oil Ltd v North Bay Shipping Corp (The Rio Claro)* [1987] 2 Lloyd's Rep. 173. The exceptions do, however, apply after the vessel has started on the preliminary voyage: see below, p.117. See also *Geogas SA v Trammo Gas Ltd (The Baleares)* [1990] 2 Lloyd's Rep. 130 overruled on other grounds [1993] 1 Lloyd's Rep. 215 (CA).

[43] *Geogas SA v Trammo Gas Ltd (The Baleares)* [1993] 1 Lloyd's Rep. 215.

[44] *Bentsen v Taylor* [1893] 2 Q.B. 274 (CA). Cf. *Engman v Palgrave* (1898) 4 Com.Cas. 75, on words "now in Finland, bound to London".

[45] *Ollive v Booker* (1847) 1 Exch. 416.

[46] *Deffell v Brocklebank* (1817) 4 Price 36. See also *Davidson v Gwynne* (1810) 12 East 381; *Kidston v Monceau* (1902) 7 Com.Cas. 82.

[47] *Smith v Dart* (1884) 14 Q.B.D. 105. See also *Croockewit v Fletcher* (1857) 1 H. & N. 893. The excepted perils would protect the shipowner from an action by the charterer.

entitled to do so, on the ground of a breach of condition, although not under the cancelling clause.[48]

A51   **Article 51—Undertaking of Seaworthiness**

At common law a shipowner by contracting to carry goods on a voyage in a ship, in the absence of express stipulation,[49] impliedly[50] undertakes that his ship is seaworthy.[51] Where the Carriage of Goods by Sea Act 1971 applies, the common law absolute undertaking of seaworthiness is replaced by an undertaking that the shipowner will before and at the beginning of the voyage exercise due diligence to make the ship seaworthy.[52]

This implied undertaking arises not from the shipowner's position as a common carrier, but from his acting as a shipowner.[53] It does not apply to the approach voyage.[54]

The implied undertaking of seaworthiness is an innominate term. The right of the charterer to treat the contract as discharged in consequence of a breach of the undertaking depends on whether the breach goes to the root of the contract.[55]

Semble, if the initial unseaworthiness is sufficiently serious, the charterer may treat the contract as discharged even after the contract has been partially performed.[56]

In the case of a charter for consecutive voyages the shipowner is obliged to provide a seaworthy ship at the commencement of each voyage.[57] As to the undertaking of seaworthiness in a time charter, see pp.323–4, below.

The seaworthiness required is relative to the nature of the ship,[58] to the particular voyage contracted for,[59] and the particular stages of that voyage, being different for summer or for winter voyages, for river and lake, or for sea

---

[48] *The Mihalis Angelos* [1971] 1 Q.B. 164; *Greenwich Marine Inc v Federal Commerce & Navigation Co Ltd (The Mavro Vetranic)* [1985] 1 Lloyd's Rep. 581. See also *Corkling v Massey* (1873) L.R. 8 C.P. 395 and contrast *Associated Portland Cement Manufacturers v Houlder* (1917) 22 Com.Cas. 279.

[49] See Art.106, *Note 5*, below, as to the effect of exceptions on the implied undertakings in the contract of affreightment.

[50] As to express provisions to the effect that the ship shall be seaworthy, see p.95, below. As to unseaworthiness causing fire and its result upon the owner's statutory immunity under s.187 of the Merchant Shipping Act 1995, or upon an express exception of "fire", see Art.116.

[51] *Steel v State Line Steamship Co* (1877) 3 App.Cas. 72; *The Marathon* (1879) 40 L.T. 163; *Cohn v Davidson* (1877) 2 Q.B.D. 455; *Kopitoff v Wilson* (1876) 1 Q.B.D. 377; *Lyon v Mells* (1804) 5 East 428. As to the implied warranty for an unnamed tug that the tug is fit and efficient and properly supplied, see *The Undaunted* (1886) 11 P.D. 46; *The Marechal Suchet* [1911] P. 1; *The West Cock* [1911] P. 23; affirmed *ibid.* 208; *Fraser & White v Vernon* [1951] 2 Lloyd's Rep. 175. Contrast *Robertson v Amazon Tug Co* (1881) 7 Q.B.D. 598, a case where, however, the contract was neither one for towage services nor for hire; see the case distinguished in *Reed v Dean* [1949] 1 K.B. 188.

[52] See s.3 of the Act; below, p.379.

[53] *Kopitoff v Wilson* (1876) 1 Q.B.D. 377.

[54] *Compagnie Algerienne de Meunerie v Katana* [1960] 1 Lloyd's Rep. 132.

[55] *Hongkong Fir Shipping Co v Kawasaki Kisen Kaisha (The Hongkong Fir)* [1962] 2 Q.B. 26 (CA); *The Mihalis Angelos* [1971] 1 Q.B. 164 (CA); *Stanton v Richardson* (1874) L.R. 9 C.P. 390; affirmed 45 L.J.Q.B. 78 (HL); *Tully v Howling* (1877) 2 Q.B.D. 182; *Kish v Taylor* [1912] A.C. 604 at p.617; *The Europa* [1908] P. 84 at p.93; *New York and Cuba S.S. Co v Ericksen* (1922) 27 Com.Cas. 330; *Snia Societa v Suzuki* (1924) 29 Com.Cas. 284.

[56] *The Hongkong Fir*, above; *Snia Societa v Suzuki*, above.

[57] *Anglo Saxon Petroleum Co v Adamastos* [1957] 2 Q.B. 255 (reversed on another ground [1959] A.C. 133).

[58] *Burges v Wickham* (1863) 3 B. & S. 669.

[59] *Empresa Cubana Importada de Alimentos "Alimport" v Iasmos Shipping Co SA (The Good Friend)* [1984] 2 Lloyd's Rep. 586.

navigation,[60] whilst loading in harbour, and when sailing,[61] and varies with the particular cargo contracted to be carried.[62] At the commencement of loading the ship must be fit to receive her cargo and fit as a ship for the ordinary perils of lying afloat in harbour while receiving her cargo, but need not be fit for sailing.[63] On the completion of each stage she must have the degree of fitness which is required for the next stage.[64] The stages of a voyage for this purpose are usually marked by different physical conditions, e.g. river and sea.

As regards the supply of bunkers the obligation of seaworthiness has, at any rate in contracts of affreightment which permit calling at intermediate ports, been adjusted to meet commercial necessities by substituting (at the shipowner's option[65]) for the single obligation to make the vessel seaworthy once and for all at the commencement of the voyage a recurring obligation at the first port of each bunkering stage to supply the vessel with sufficient bunkers for that stage with a reasonable margin for contingencies, the owner having full discretion to fix, before the commencement of the voyage, the bunkering stages for the voyage, provided they are usual and reasonable. When once the stages have been fixed the presence of an intermediate bunkering port, at which it is possible but not intended that the vessel shall bunker, is irrelevant for the purpose of calculating the reasonable margin for contingencies.[66]

Whether or not initial unseaworthiness on leaving the first port of any predetermined bunkering stage can be cured on passage by bunkering at an intermediate bunkering port has not yet been decided.[67] The shipowner will be liable if, through the master's negligence, the ship sails with insufficient bunkers, even if the responsibility for supplying bunkers rests on the charterer.[68]

The undertaking of seaworthiness requires not merely that the shipowner will do and has done his best to make the ship fit, but that the ship really is fit in all respects to carry her cargo safely to its destination, having regard to the ordinary

---

[60] *Thin v Richards* [1892] 2 Q.B. 141; *Daniels v Harris* (1874) L.R. 10 C.P. 1; *Annen v Woodman* (1810) 3 Taunt. 299.

[61] *McFadden v Blue Star Line* [1905] 1 K.B. 697.

[62] *Stanton v Richardson* (1874) L.R. 9 C.P. 390; affirmed (1875) 45 L.J.Q.B. 78 (HL); *Tattersall v National Steamship Co* (1884) 12 Q.B.D. 297; *The Marathon* (1879) 40 L.T. 163; *Maori King v Hughes* [1895] 2 Q.B. 550 (CA) (refrigerating machinery); *Queensland Bank v P. & O. Co* [1898] 1 Q.B. 567 (CA) (bullion in a bullion room); *The Waikato* [1899] 1 Q.B. 56 (CA) (wool in an insulated hold). See also *Rathbone v McIver* [1902] 2 K.B. 378.

[63] *Reed v Page* [1927] 1 K.B. 743; *Svenssons v Cliffe S.S. Co* [1932] 1 K.B. 490, where the stage of loading was held not to be completed when the last sling of pit-props was on board, but not stowed. Although unseaworthy at the time of the accident there was no breach of warranty, the ship having been seaworthy at the commencement of the stage of loading. Cf. *The Stranna* [1938] P. 69 at pp.77, 84. See, also, as to when loading is completed. *Argonaut Navigation Co v Ministry of Food* [1949] 1 K.B. 572.

[64] *Reed v Page*, above. On the doctrine of stages in relation to a contract governed by the Hague-Visby Rules, see p.388.

[65] *Noemijulia S.S. Co v Minister of Food* [1951] 1 K.B. 223 at p.234.

[66] *The Vortigern* [1899] P. 140; *Thin v Richards* [1892] 2 Q.B. 141; *Northumbrian Shipping Co v Timm* [1939] A.C. 397. This extension of the doctrine of stages was first enunciated in *The Vortigern* and was applied to the warranty of seaworthiness under a voyage policy of insurance in *Greenock S.S. Co v Maritime Insurance Co* [1903] 2 K.B. 657.

[67] Gorrell Barnes J. in *The Vortigern*, suggested that it could. The point was left open in *Northumbrian Shipping v Timm*, above.

[68] *McIver v Tate* [1903] 1 K.B. 362, a time charter case.

perils to which such a cargo would be exposed on such a voyage.[69] The "ordinary perils" may include such treatment of the ship and cargo (e.g. fumigation) as by the local law of a port of call the cargo shipped must be exposed to.[70]

One test of seaworthiness is: Would a prudent owner have required that the defect should be made good before sending his ship to sea, had he known of it? If he would, the ship was not seaworthy.[71] The standard of seaworthiness may rise with improved knowledge of ship-building,[72] but the undertaking does not require absolute perfection, or an absolute guarantee of safe carriage. Thus, a ship may be seaworthy even though the shipowner knows that in the ordinary way cargoes of a particular kind carried in the vessel will inevitably suffer some minor damage.[73] In contrast, there will be an inevitable presumption of fact that a vessel is unseaworthy if there is some characteristic of it which prima facie endangers the safety of the vessel or its cargo or which renders it legally or practically impossible for the vessel to go to sea or to carry its cargo safely.[74] Seaworthiness need not be maintained at the cost of always introducing the latest or best appliances.[75] Nor does a defect that can be quickly remedied at sea make the ship unseaworthy,[76] unless the defect, although easily remediable, cannot be reached at sea to be remedied.[77] A temporary or minor impediment to discharge, such as a draft requiring lightening, will not render the ship unseaworthy, but a significant impediment to discharge, such as infestation of the ship and cargo, will do so.[78] A fitting which can with care be worked safely, may yet be so unusual and dangerous as to make the ship unseaworthy.[79] A ship may be unseaworthy even if the precise defect with the ship is not known.[80]

---

[69] *Hedley v Pinkney S.S. Co* [1894] A.C. 222 at p.227; *Maori King v Hughes* [1895] 2 Q.B. 550; *Steel v State Line Co* (1877) 3 App.Cas. 72 at p.86; *The Glenfruin* (1885) 10 P.D. 103; *The Good Friend*, above.

[70] *Ciampa v British India Co* [1915] 2 K.B. 774. Contrast *Compagnie Algerienne de Meunerie v Katana* [1960] 1 Lloyd's Rep. 132.

[71] *McFadden v Blue Star Line* [1905] 1 K.B. 697 at p.706. In *Kopitoff v Wilson* (1876) 1 Q.B.D. 377, where armour plates broke loose from their stowage and sank the ship, the question left to the jury was: "Was the ship at the time of sailing in a state, as regards the receiving and stowing of the plates, reasonably fit to encounter the ordinary perils that might be expected on a voyage at that season?" This test was applied in *Alfred C. Toepfer Schiffahrtsgesellschaft GmbH v Tossa Marine Co Ltd* [1985] 2 Lloyd's Rep. 325.

[72] See per Blackburn J. in *Burges v Wickham* (1863) 3 B. & S. 669 at p.693. Thus the HL in *The Mount Park S.S. Co v Grey, Shipping Gazette*, March 12, 1910, declined to interfere with the finding of a jury that a ship, seaworthy according to accepted standards of knowledge when she was built, was unseaworthy at the time in question owing to her owner's failure to incorporate a new device designed to avoid dangers inherent in the original specification: contrast *The Australia Star* (1940) 67 Ll.L.R. 110, a case of due diligence under the Carriage of Goods by Sea Act 1924, and see per Scrutton L.J. and Lord Sumner in *Bradley v Federal S.N. Co* (1926) 24 Ll.L.R. 446 at p.454, affirmed (1927) 27 Ll.L.R. 395 at p.396. See also *Western Canada S.S. Co v Canadian Commercial Corp* [1960] 2 Lloyd's Rep. 313 (Supreme Court of Canada).

[73] *M.D.C. v NV Zeevart Beurstraat* [1962] 1 Lloyd's Rep. 180 at p.186.

[74] *Athenian Tankers Management SA v Pyrena Shipping Inc (The Arianna)* [1987] 2 Lloyd's Rep. 376.

[75] *Virginia etc. Co v Norfolk etc. Co* (1912) 17 Com.Cas. 277.

[76] *Hedley v Pinkney* [1894] A.C. 222; *Leonard v Leyland* (1902) 18 T.L.R. 727; *The Diamond* [1906] P. 282; *Virginia etc. Co v Norfolk etc. Co* above; *The Pentland* (1897) 13 T.L.R. 430 (need for repair to one of two boilers preventing its use for a short time); *International Packers v Ocean S.S. Co* [1955] 2 Lloyd's Rep. 218 (locking bars which could be fitted at short notice during the voyage). The principle does not apply to such a thing as securing deck cargo by proper lashings: *Moore v Lunn* (1922) 38 T.L.R. 649.

[77] *Steel v State Line* (1877) 3 App.Cas. 72.

[78] *The Arianna*, above; *The Good Friend*, above.

[79] *The Schwann* [1909] A.C. 450.

[80] *Eridania SpA v Oetker (The Fjord Wind)* [2000] 2 Lloyd's Rep. 191 at p.199.

Unseaworthiness must relate to some attribute of the ship itself.[81] Bad stowage which endangers the safety of the ship may amount to unseaworthiness.[82] But bad stowage which affects nothing but the cargo damaged by it is bad stowage and nothing more, and still leaves the ship seaworthy for the adventure, even though the adventure is the carrying of the cargo.[83]

The undertaking of seaworthiness involves not only that the ship is herself fit to encounter the perils of the voyage, but also that she is fit to carry the cargo safely on that voyage.[84]

Inefficiency of the master or crew may constitute unseaworthiness,[85] and this inefficiency may consist of "disabling want of skill or disabling want of knowledge", e.g. as to the stability of the vessel[86] or her ballast and fuel system[87] or the operation of fire extinguishing systems,[88] or in mere shortage of numbers.[89] Furthermore, a disabling lack of will on the part of a member of the crew to use such skill and knowledge as he possesses may constitute incompetence and render the ship unseaworthy.[90] The master need not be in perfect health, provided that the owners adopt the ordinary standard of care in choosing a fit master.[91]

The shipowner must provide the ship with all necessary documents for the voyage,[92] namely those validly required by the law of the vessel's flag or by the laws, regulations or lawful administrative practices of governmental or local authorities at the vessel's ports of call, where known.[93]

---

[81] *A. Meredith Jones & Co Ltd v Vangemar Shipping Co Ltd (The Apostolis)* [1997] 2 Lloyd's Rep. 241 at p.257.

[82] *Northern Shipping Co v Deutsche Seereederei GmbH (The Kapitan Sakharov)* [2000] 2 Lloyd's Rep. 255 (stowage under deck of dangerous cargo which should have been stowed on deck); *Compania Sud America Vapores v M.S. E.R. Hamburg Schiffahrtsgesellschaft Mbh & Co KG* [2006] 2 Lloyd's Rep. 66; [2006] EWHC 483 (Comm) (as between shipowner and charterer, latter responsible under terms of time charter); *Transocean Liners Reederei GmbH v Euxine Shipping Co Ltd (The Imvros)* [1999] 1 Lloyd's Rep. 848 (same). See Baughen [2007] I.M.C.L.Q. 1.

[83] per Lord Sumner in *The Elder Dempster v Paterson Zochonis* [1924] A.C. 522; *The Thorsa* [1916] P. 257; *Wade v Cockerline* (1905) 10 Com.Cas. 115; *Bond v Federal SN Co* (1906) 22 T.L.R. 685; *Calcutta v Weir* (1910) 15 Com.Cas. 172; *Ingram v Services Maritime* [1913] 1 K.B. 538 at p.545.

[84] *Maori King v Hughes* [1895] 2 Q.B. 550 (CA) (defective refrigerating machinery); *The Waikato* [1899] 1 Q.B. 56 (CA) (implied undertaking that an insulated hold was fit to carry wool); *Queensland National Bank Ltd v Peninsular and Oriental Steam Navigation Co* [1898] 1 Q.B. 567 (CA) (carriage of specie; implied undertaking that bullion room was reasonably fit to resist thieves); *Tattersall v National S.S. Co* (1884) 12 Q.B.D. 297, see also the cases cited in fn.62, above. Contrast *The Thorsa*, above. If the ship is in fact fit to carry the cargo, the fact that there is a general belief that the presence on board of certain other goods makes it unfit does not justify the charterer in refusing to load: *Towse v Henderson* (1850) 4 Ex. 890. Text approved by Denning M.R. in *Actis Co v Sanko Steamship Co (The Aquacharm)* [1982] 1 Lloyd's Rep. 7 at p.9.

[85] *Hongkong Fir Shipping Co v Kawasaki Kisen Kaisha* [1962] 2 Q.B. 26; *The Makedonia* [1962] P. 190.

[86] *Standard Oil v Clan Line* [1924] A.C. 100 (failure to furnish the master with special information as to the type of the ship and her proper method of stowage, as supplied by the builders to the owner).

[87] *The Makedonia*, above.

[88] As in *Manifest Shipping & Co Ltd v Uni-Polaris Insurance Co Ltd and La Reunion Europeene (The Star Sea)* [1997] 1 Lloyd's Rep. 360; [2001] 1 Lloyd's Rep. 389.

[89] See *The Heinz Horn* [1970] 1 Lloyd's Rep. 191 (U.S. 5th Circuit CA).

[90] See fn.87, above.

[91] *Rio Tinto v Seed Shipping Co* (1926) 42 T.L.R. 381.

[92] *Levy v Costerton* (1816) 4 Camp. 389; *Dutton v Powles* (1862) 31 L.J.Q.B. 191; *Ciampa v Brit. India Co* [1915] 2 K.B. 774; *cf. Chellew v Appelquist* (1933) 38 Com.Cas. 218, and *The Makedonia*, above (plan of vessel's ballast and fuel system). But *cf. Wilson v Rankin* (1865) L.R. 1 Q.B. 162; *Alfred C. Toepfer Schiffahrtsgesellschaft GmbH v Tossa Marine Co Ltd* [1984] 1 Lloyd's Rep. 635 (vessel "fitted for the service" although lacking an I.T.F. certificate).

[93] *Alfred C. Toepfer Schiffahrtsgesellschaft GmbH v Tossa Marine Co Ltd* [1985] 2 Lloyd's Rep. 239 (vessel "fitted for service" although lacking I.T.F. certificate).

The undertaking of seaworthiness also comprises a duty to have on board suitable loading and discharging tackle for the ordinary purposes of loading and discharging.[94] This duty will be implied even where the charter provides that the cargo is to be loaded and discharged free of expense to the vessel.[94]

The undertaking, express or implied, that a ship is fit for a particular cargo is not excluded by a provision that the ship is to be fitted or cleaned before loading to the satisfaction of the charterer's inspector.[95]

If unseaworthiness arises in the course of the voyage, and the shipowner has an opportunity to remedy it, he is bound to do so before proceeding on the voyage, but cannot require the charterer to wait if the delay will be such as to go to the root of the contract.[96]

The burden of proving unseaworthiness rests upon the party who asserts it and the party intending to rely upon unseaworthiness must plead it with sufficient particularity. But where a ship, shortly after leaving port and without any apparent reason sinks or leaks, the mere facts afford prima facie evidence of unseaworthiness, which must be rebutted.[97]

Irrespective of whether the charterer can treat the contract as discharged for breach of the implied undertaking of seaworthiness, the shipowner will be liable in damages[98] for loss *caused* by[99] breach of that undertaking unless he is expressly protected from such liability by exceptions in the charter or bill of lading.[100] Liability may arise if unseaworthiness is *a* cause of the loss, though other causes, for which the shipowner may be covered by express exceptions, may contribute.[101]

---

[94] *Hang Fung Shipping Co v Mullion* [1966] 1 Lloyd's Rep. 511; *Madras v P. & O.* (1923) 16 Ll.L.R. 240.

[95] *Petrofina SA v Cia Italiana Transporto* (1937) 42 Com.Cas. 286, applying *Sleigh v Tyser* [1900] 2 Q.B. 335 although the fact of such approval may be relevant in considering whether due diligence has been exercised: *The Good Friend*, above.

[96] This obligation arises, not from the undertaking of unseaworthiness, unless the doctrine of stages applies, but from the duty to take care: *Worms v Storey* (1855) 11 Ex. 427; *The Rona* (1884) 51 L.T. 28; *Thin v Richards* [1892] 2 Q.B. 141; *Assicurazione v Bessie Morris S.S. Co* [1892] 2 Q.B. 652 (CA). See also *The Vortigern* [1899] P. 140.

[97] *Madras v P. & O.* (1924) 18 Ll.L.R. 93 at p.96; *Anderson v Morice* (1875) L.R. 10 C.P. 609, affirmed (1876) 1 App.Cas. 713; *Pickup v Thames and Mersey* (1878) 3 Q.B.D. 594; *Ajum Goolam v Union Marine* [1901] A.C. 362; *Lindsay v Klein* [1911] A.C. 194; *Waddle v Wallsend* [1952] 2 Lloyd's Rep. 105 at p.139.

[98] These may include damages and costs the charterer has to pay to other persons by reason of the unseaworthiness: *Scott v Foley, Aikman & Co* (1899) 5 Com.Cas. 53.

[99] The shipowner will not be liable on the ground of unseaworthiness if the latter does not cause the loss: *The Europa* [1908] P. 84; approved in *Kish v Taylor* [1912] A.C. 604. Contrast the cases of deviation in which on one view of the law the deviation need not cause the loss: *Thorley v Orchis S.S. Co* [1907] 1 K.B. 660, below, p.234. Contrast also the effect of unseaworthiness in a voyage policy of marine insurance: Marine Insurance Act 1906, s.39.

[100] As in *The Laertes* (1887) 12 P.D. 187. For cases where exceptions did not protect him, see *The Glenfruin* (1885) 10 P.D. 103; *The Undaunted* (1886) 11 P.D. 46; *Seville v Colvils & Co* (1888) 15 Rettie 616; *Gilroy v Price* [1893] A.C. 56; *Maori King v Hughes* [1895] 2 Q.B. 550; *Queensland Bank v P. & O. Co* [1898] 1 Q.B. 567; *The Waikato* [1899] 1 Q.B. 56 (CA); *Thompson and Norris Manufacturing Co v Ardley* (1929) 35 Ll.L.R. 248 (old London Lighterage Clause). See the general discussion of the relation of other terms in the contract to express or implied terms as to seaworthiness in *Bank of Australasia v Clan Line* [1916] 1 K.B. 39. See generally below, Art.106 *Note 5*. Even if an exception applies to unseaworthiness on the voyage, the shipowner is liable if having an opportunity to repair the ship he by negligence (not covered by exceptions) proceeds without repairing it: see above, fn.96 and *Hellenic Steel Co v Svolamar Shipping Co Ltd (The Komninos S)* [1990] 1 Lloyd's Rep. 541.

[101] See per Lord Wright in *Smith, Hogg v Black Sea and Baltic Insurance* [1940] A.C. 997 and again, in *Monarch S.S. Co v Karlshamns* [1949] A.C. 196 at p.226, and the comment on *Case 9*, below.

Note. Charters frequently contain *express* provisions regarding seaworthiness, such as that the ship is "tight, staunch and strong and in every way fitted for the voyage" at the date of the charter or shall be so when proceeding to her loading port or berth. This express provision is not dissimilar to the implied undertaking of seaworthiness, though the terms in which it is framed may enlarge the common law obligation by applying at an earlier time than the commencement of loading or sailing.[102] There may, however, be differences between an obligation of seaworthiness, and one that the vessel be "in every way fitted for service and carriage".[103] Where a charterparty contains such a term, and is also subject to the Hague or Hague-Visby Rules so far as the carrying voyage is concerned, it will be a matter of construction whether the obligation of seaworthiness is an absolute one for the period up to the carrying voyage, and an obligation of due diligence during that voyage, or an obligation of due diligence throughout, although the latter is the more obvious construction.[104]

The inclusion of an express provision as to seaworthiness may also have somewhat unexpected consequences upon the application of exception clauses to cases of damage caused by unseaworthiness. If there is an implied obligation as to seaworthiness, exception clauses will, unless their wording is quite clear, be read as not applying to breaches of the implied obligation.[105] If, however, there is an express undertaking of seaworthiness, exceptions will be read as applying to the consequences of a breach of it.[106]

Case 1. F shipped goods under a bill of lading, which excepted "perils whether or not arising from negligence of A's servants, risk of craft or hull, or any damage thereto, etc". Sea water entered through the negligence of some of the crew in leaving a lower port insufficiently fastened. *Held*, that if this were so at the beginning of the voyage the ship was then unseaworthy and the exceptions of the bill of lading did not protect the shipowner, as they do not apply till the voyage has begun.[107] That such a bill of lading contained an implied undertaking that the ship was, at the time of its departure, reasonably fit for accomplishing the services which the shipowner engaged to perform.[108]

Case 2. A ship was chartered to proceed to the East Indies and take on board a cargo of, *inter alia*, wet sugar. The ship was seaworthy for any cargo except wet sugar, for which she had not pumps of sufficient capacity. *Held*, that the charter implied an undertaking that the ship was fit to carry wet sugar, and that, as the ship could not be made fit without a delay unreasonable under the circumstances of the contract, the charterer was justified in throwing up the charter.[109]

Case 3. A ship was chartered on March 4, "for twelve months, for as many consecutive voyages as the said ship can enter upon after completion of the present voyage" from X to Z. When the ship

---

[102] *Stanton v Richardson* (1874) L.R. 9 C.P. 390; affirmed (1875) 45 L.J.Q.B. 78 (HL); *Scott v Foley, Aikman & Co* (1899) 5 Com.Cas. 53; *New York and Cuba Mail S.S. Co v Eriksen* (1922) 27 Com.Cas. 330. It is submitted that "tight, staunch and strong" apply to a ship's machinery as well as to her hull. See also *The Asia Star* [2007] 3 SLR 1 (Sing.) as to the effect of an express warranty that the vessel's tanks be "epoxy coated".

[103] *Athenian Tanker Management SA v Pyrena Shipping Inc* [1987] 2 Lloyd's Rep. 376.

[104] The latter conclusion was reached in *Eridania SpA v Rudolf A. Oetker (The Fjord Wind)* [2000] 2 Lloyd's Rep. 191 (reversing a decision that the nature of the seaworthiness obligation varied at [1999] 1 Lloyd's Rep. 307).

[105] See p.199, below and *Hellenic Steel Co v Svolamar Shipping Co Ltd (The Komninos S)* [1990] 1 Lloyd's Rep. 541.

[106] *Tattersall v National S.S. Co* (1884) 12 Q.B.D. 297; *Morris v Oceanic S.S. Co* (1900) 16 T.L.R. 533, as explained in *Bank of Australasia v Clan Line* [1916] 1 K.B. 39; *Elder Dempster v Paterson Zochonis* [1923] 1 K.B. 420, per Bankes L.J. at p.436; *Atlantic Shipping Co v Dreyfus* [1922] 2 A.C. 250; *Cosmopolitan Shipping Co v Hatton* (1929) 35 Com.Cas. 113, per Scrutton L.J. at p.121. *Cf. Minister of Materials v Wold S.S. Co* [1952] 1 Lloyd's Rep. 485 at p.498.

[107] In charters, both the carrying voyage and the chartered voyage, which need not coincide with the carrying voyage; in bills of lading, the carrying voyage: *Hudson v Hill* (1874) 43 L.J.C.P. 273; *Barker v M'Andrew* (1865) 18 C.B. (N.S.) 759; *Christie & Vesey v Helvetia* [1960] 1 Lloyd's Rep. 540; *Transworld Oil Ltd v North Bay Shipping Corp (The Rio Claro)* [1987] 2 Lloyd's Rep. 173.

[108] *Steel v State Line Steamship Co* (1877) 3 App.Cas. 72; *Gilroy v Price* [1893] A.C. 56.

[109] *Stanton v Richardson* (1875) L.R. 9 C.P. 390; affirmed (1875) 45 L.J.Q.B. 78 (HL). "Seaworthiness" has a wide meaning, "reasonably fit to carry the cargo contracted for". *Cf.* the judgments in *Steel v State Line*, above, and *Case 4*, below.

had completed that voyage, she was found to be unseaworthy and the necessary repairs delayed her for two months. The charterer threw up the charter. *Held*, by the whole court that he was justified: by Brett J., on the ground that the ship was not reasonably fit for the purpose for which she was chartered and could not be made fit within any time which would not have frustrated the object of the adventure[110]: by Kelly C.B., Mellish L.J. and Amphlett J.A., on the ground that, the charter being for a specified time, the charterer was not bound to accept the ship for a time shorter than or substantially different from such specified time.

Case 4. F shipped cattle under a bill of lading agreeing that the shipowner was not liable for accidents, disease or mortality, and under no circumstances for more than £5 per animal. The ship, after carrying a cargo of cattle on a previous voyage, was improperly cleaned, and F's cattle took foot-and-mouth disease. *Held*, there was a duty on the shipowner to have the ship reasonably fit for the carriage of the goods he had contracted for, and that, such duty being neglected, the limitations of liability did not apply.[111]

Case 5. A steamer sailed from the Philippines for Liverpool, under a contract giving liberty to call at coaling-ports and excepting the negligence of master and engineer. At Colombo she coaled with the intention of bunkering next at Suez, though in fact she had on completion of coaling insufficient coal to reach that port. Off Perim, a coaling station, the engineer negligently informed the master that there was sufficient coal to reach Suez and the master in consequence did not put into Perim to coal. Coal ran short before she reached Suez. *Held*, that there was a breach of the warranty of seaworthiness in that when Suez was fixed as the next bunkering port the next stage of the voyage became Colombo/Suez and she had insufficient coal for that stage. As she did not in fact bunker at Perim it was not necessary to decide whether her initial unseaworthiness on leaving Colombo could have been cured by bunkering at Perim.[112]

Case 6. A ship sailed from an Eastern port with a foul bill of health. At Naples lemons were shipped under a bill of lading for London. Marseilles was the next port of call and under French law the ship, coming from an Eastern port without a clean bill of health, had to be fumigated. The lemons were damaged by the fumigation. *Held*, that the ship was not seaworthy at Naples for the carriage of the lemons.[113]

Case 7. C, by a charter incorporating the Harter Act, chartered a turret ship from A. She was structurally seaworthy when she left port with C's cargo on board. Her master, a competent seaman but without special knowledge of the effects of her peculiar design on her stability, ordered two water-ballast tanks to be emptied whilst on passage and the ship capsized and the goods were lost. *Held*, that the lack of special knowledge constituted unseaworthiness. *Held*, further, that as A had not passed on to the master special instructions as to stability received from her builders he had not exercised due diligence to make her seaworthy.[114]

Case 8. F shipped palm oil in butts on board A's ship, chartered to C, under bills of lading issued by C. The bills of lading contained an exception of bad stowage but not of unseaworthiness. Palm-kernels of other shippers were stowed immediately on top of the palm oil and crushed the butts with loss of oil, there being no permanent or temporary 'tween-decks to carry the weight of the palm kernels. *Held*, bad stowage and not unseaworthiness and neither A nor C was liable.[115]

Case 9. Timber was shipped at Soroka for Garston under a charter providing that the shipowner should not be liable for loss resulting (i) from unseaworthiness unless caused by want of due diligence on the part of the shipowner to make his ship seaworthy, and (ii) act, neglect or default of the master in the navigation or management of the ship. When the ship sailed she was inherently unstable by

---

[110] *Tully v Howling* (1877) 2 Q.B.D. 182.
[111] *Tattersall v National S.S. Co* (1884) 12 Q.B.D. 297. Contrast *The Thorsa* [1916] P. 257; and see the discussion of the relation of bad stowage to unseaworthiness in *Elder Dempster & Co v Paterson Zochonis* [1924] A.C. 522 and fn.83, above.
[112] *The Vortigern* [1899] P. 140. The latter point was also left open in *Northumbrian Shipping Co v Timm* [1939] A.C. 397. *Cf. Thin v Richards* [1892] 2 Q.B. 141; *Biccard v Shepherd* (1861) 14 Moore P.C. 471; *Dixon v Sadler* (1839) 5 M. & W. 405; *McIver v Tate Steamers* [1903] 1 K.B. 362.
[113] *Ciampa v British India Co* [1915] 2 K.B. 774. Contrast *Compagnie Algerienne de Meunerie v Katana* [1960] 1 Lloyd's Rep. 132.
[114] *Standard Oil Co v Clan Line* [1924] A.C. 100.
[115] *Elder Dempster & Co v Paterson Zochonis* [1924] A.C. 552. As to A's protection, see Chapter 2.

loading an excessive deck cargo. On passage she put into Stornoway to take on extra bunkers and in the course of bunkering she fell on her beam ends. There was no finding that the act of taking on extra bunkers was negligent. *Held*, that the shipowners had failed to exercise due diligence to make the ship seaworthy and were liable for the consequential loss.[116]

Case 10. In May 1939, C shipped a cargo of soya beans on A's British ship for carriage from the Far East to one or two out of a number of Continental ports at C's option. The ship should have completed the voyage by July, but owing to unseaworthiness and consequential repairs *en route* was not ready to leave Port Said till September 24. War had broken out between Great Britain and Germany on September 3 and the Admiralty in consequence ordered the ship to discharge at Glasgow. Shortly after arrival at Glasgow, H, to whom C had sold the cargo, took up and paid for the bill of lading. H required the goods in his factory in Sweden, where he could get no replacement, and having transhipped the cargo from Glasgow sued A for the cost of transhipment, as damages suffered by unseaworthiness. *Held*, that the likelihood of war and a consequential diversion of the ship, if delayed, were reasonably foreseeable at the date of the bill of lading and that the damage suffered was in the legal sense caused by unseaworthiness.[117]

## Article 52—Undertaking of Reasonable Dispatch				A52

The shipowner impliedly undertakes[118] that his vessel shall be ready to commence the voyage agreed on and to load the cargo to be carried, and shall proceed upon and complete the voyage agreed upon, with all reasonable dispatch.[119]

This implied undertaking is an innominate term of the contract. Hence if by a breach of this undertaking there is such delay as "goes to the root of the whole matter, deprives the charterer of the whole benefit of the contract, or entirely frustrates the object of the charterer in chartering the ship,"[120] the charterer may refuse to perform his part of the contract altogether.[121]

---

[116] *Smith, Hogg v Black Sea and Baltic Insurance* [1940] A.C. 997. It is difficult to extract the *ratio decidendi* of this case. Lord Wright (with whom Lord Atkin agreed) held that the unseaworthiness being a cause of the disaster "or, if it be preferred, a real or effective or actual cause", though in his opinion the epithets "add nothing", it was immaterial that there may have been other co-operating causes covered by exceptions. Lord Porter (with whom Lord Romer agreed) decided against the shipowner on the ground that the unseaworthiness was the cause of the loss since the master's act in taking on extra bunkers would have been safe if the ship had not been unstable. He preferred not "to decide what would be the result if the loss were attributable partly to the coaling and partly to the unseaworthiness, or to determine whether the fact that the unseaworthiness was a substantial cause, even though some other matters relied upon were a substantial cause also, would be enough to make the owner liable". Lord Maugham expressed no preference for either view. In *Monarch S.S. Co v Karlshamns* [1949] A.C. 196 at pp.225 *et seq*. Lord Wright further elaborated his view, pointing out that to cause damage unseaworthiness must nearly always operate by means of and along with the specific and immediate peril. See, also, per Devlin J. in *Heskell v Continental Express* (1950) 83 Ll.L.R. 438 at p.458. *Cf. Wayne Tank Co v Employers Liability Ltd* [1974] Q.B. 57, per Roskill L.J. at p.73.

[117] *Monarch S.S. Co v Karlshamns* [1949] A.C. 196.

[118] *Louis Dreyfus & Co v Lauro* (1938) 60 Ll.L.Rep. 94; *Fyffes Group Ltd and Caribbean Gold Ltd v Reefer Express Lines Pty Ltd and Reefkrit Shipping Inc (The Kriti Rex)* [1996] 2 Lloyd's Rep.171 at p.191.

[119] In the case of a charter for consecutive voyages, the obligation to proceed with reasonable dispatch entails that the ship shall complete as many voyages as possible within the period of the charter. *Anglo-Saxon Petroleum Co v Adamastos Shipping Co* [1957] 2 Q.B. 255 (reversed on other grounds [1959] A.C. 133). See also s.14, Supply of Goods and Services Act 1982. Sometimes there may be an express obligation providing for utmost dispatch as in *Tidebrook v Vitol (The Front Commander)* [2006] 2 Lloyd's Rep. 251.

[120] per Willes J., *MacAndrew v Chapple* (1866) L.R. 1 C.P. 643 at p.648.

[121] *Freeman v Taylor* (1831) 8 Bing. 124; *Tully v Howling* (1877) 2 Q.B.D. 182; *Universal Cargo Carriers v Citati* [1957] 2 Q.B. 401. This is an application of the general principle that default in performance by one party may be of such a nature as to entitle the other to regard it as a repudiation of the whole contract; *Hurst v Usborne* (1856) 18 C.B. 144 was wrongly decided (see per Bramwell B., *Jackson v Union Marine* (1874) L.R. 10 C.P. 125 at p.147), and *Hudson v Hill* (1874) 43 L.J.C.P. 273 cannot be regarded as satisfactory.

In contrast, if the delay is not so serious as to have this result, the charterer cannot refuse to load,[122] but the shipowner will be liable for damages,[123] unless the delay was caused by an excepted peril.[124]

Time charters commonly contain an express obligation that the master shall prosecute all voyages with the utmost dispatch, but the exception clause may be sufficiently widely drawn to protect the shipowner from the consequences of a breach of this obligation.[125]

Delay during the course of the voyage may constitute a deviation, as to which see Art.127, below.

When the Hamburg Rules apply, the implied obligation of reasonable despatch is replaced by an express liability for delay unless the carrier can prove that he, his servants or agents took all measures that could reasonably be required to avoid the delay. Delay occurs when the goods have not been delivered at the port of discharge within the time expressly provided for, or, in the absence of such agreement, within the time which it would be reasonable to require of a diligent carrier having regard to the "circumstances of the case".[126] A person entitled to make a claim for delay can elect to treat the goods as lost if they remained undelivered more than 60 days after the time for delivery.[127]

Case 1. A's ship was chartered to C to proceed to the Cape, there deliver cargo, and thence to proceed with all convenient speed to Bombay, where C was to load cotton. The ship stayed eight days longer at the Cape than was necessary, and then loaded cattle for Mauritius. Proceeding to Bombay *via* Mauritius, she arrived six weeks later than she would have done by proceeding direct. C refused to load. It was left to the jury to say whether the delay was such as to put an end to the ordinary objects C might have had in view when he made the contract. The jury found a verdict for C. *Held*, a proper direction and a new trial refused.[128]

Case 2. A ship which was in London was chartered as "bound to Nantes" to load there and proceed to Z. Before proceeding to Nantes the ship went to Newcastle. The charterer alleged unreasonable delay and refused to load. *Held*, that such an allegation was only a ground for an action for damages, and would not support a repudiation of the charter unless it was also alleged that the delay frustrated the object of the voyage.[129]

Case 3. A ship was chartered "with all convenient speed, having liberty to take an outward cargo for owner's benefit, direct on the way, to proceed to X and there load a full cargo". The ship deviated to Y, which was not "direct on the way" to X, and arrived at X a few days late. The charterer refused

---

[122] *Clipsham v Vertue* (1843) 5 Q.B. 265; *Tarrabochia v Hickie* (1856) 1 H. & N. 183. *Cf. Bornmann v Tooke* (1808) 1 Camp. 377; *Collard v Carswell* (1892) 19 Rettie 987; *Kidston v Monceau* (1902) 7 Com.Cas. 82 and *Hongkong Fir Shipping Co v Kawasaki Kisen Kaisha* [1962] 2 Q.B. 26 (CA).

[123] *Medeiros v Hill* (1832) 8 Bing. 231; *M'Andrew v Adams* (1834) 1 Bing.N.C. 29; *MacAndrew v Chapple* (1866) L.R. 1 C.P. 643; *The Wilhelm* (1866) 14 L.T. 636. *Cf. Engman v Palgrave* (1898) 4 Com.Cas. 75; and *Associated Portland Cement Co v Houlder* (1917) 22 Com.Cas. 279. Whether damage caused by delay is too remote or not will depend on whether the loss incurred could be reasonably anticipated as the result of delay; *Monarch S.S. Co v Karlshamns* [1949] A.C. 196 at p.215, per Lord Porter, thus reconciling the last cited case and *The Wilhelm*, above.

[124] *Barker v M'Andrew* (1865) 18 C.B. (N.S.) 759; *Donaldson v Little* (1882) 10 Rettie 413. See also Art.103; Art.106, *Note 5*.

[125] *Istros v Dahlstroem* [1931] 1 K.B. 247 (Baltime form of charter). *Tor Line v Alltrains Group of Canada (The T.F.L. Prosperity)* [1984] 1 Lloyd's Rep. 123 (HL). *Cf. Suzuki v Beynon* (1926) 42 T.L.R. 269 and *Marifortuna Naviera SA v Government of Ceylon* [1970] 1 Lloyd's Rep. 247.

[126] See Art.5.2 below.

[127] See Art.5.3 below.

[128] *Freeman v Taylor* (1831) 8 Bing. 124. *Cf. Tully v Howling* (1877) 2 Q.B.D. 182.

[129] *Clipsham v Vertue* (1843) 5 Q.B. 265. *Cf. Tarrabochia v Hickie* (1856) 1 H. & N. 183.

to load. It was admitted that the object of the voyage was not frustrated, and the whole court *held* that the charterer was not entitled to repudiate the charter, but had his remedy in damages.[130]

Case 4. A ship, then at X, was chartered to "proceed to the usual loading place there, guaranteed for cargo in all October, and there load and proceed to Z", with an exception of certain perils "during the voyage". The vessel started for the usual loading place, but was prevented by excepted perils from arriving there until after considerable delay. The charterer loaded cargo, but sued the shipowners for damages. *Held*, that passage to the place of loading was part of the voyage, and the shipowner was protected by the exceptions from the claim.[131]

Article 53—Dangerous Goods   A53

By the common law[132] there is an implied (probably innominate) term in a contract of affreightment that the shipper of goods will not ship goods of such a dangerous character or so dangerously packed that the shipowner or his agent could not by reasonable knowledge and diligence be aware of their dangerous character, unless notice be given to the shipowner or his agent of such dangerous character; and the shipper is therefore strictly liable for damage resulting from the shipment of such dangerous goods.[133] Put another way, unless the shipowner knows or ought to know the dangerous character of the goods, there will be an implied warranty by the shipper that the goods are fit for carriage in the ordinary way and are not dangerous.[134]

But when the shipowner or his agent has full opportunities of observing the dangerous character of such goods, he is treated as having such notice and the shipper therefore is not liable.[135] On the same principle, where both parties agree that a specific cargo shall be shipped, the nature of which is known to both of them, and when the particular difficulty which may arise is also known to both

---

[130] *MacAndrew v Chapple* (1866) L.R. 1 C.P. 643. *Cf. Medeiros v Hill* (1832) 8 Bing. 231; and *M'Andrew v Adams* (1834) 1 Bing. N.C. 29. The last is a good example of the double undertaking (a) expressly to arrive by a certain date, under penalty of a cancelling clause, (b) impliedly to use reasonable dispatch. Arrival within the time specified under (a) did not relieve the shipowner from damages for breach of (b).

[131] *Barker v M'Andrew* (1865) 18 C.B.(N.S.) 759; *Minister of Materials v Wold S.S. Co* [1952] 1 Lloyd's Rep. 485 at p.499. *Cf. Monroe Bros v Ryan* [1935] 2 K.B. 28.

[132] Certain special goods are also dealt with by statutory penalties: see Merchant Shipping Act 1894, s.449 (as amended by Merchant Shipping (Registration, Etc) Act 1993, Sch.4, para.11) and Merchant Shipping Act 1979, s.21. The Nuclear Installations Act 1965 imposes strict liabilities in relation to accidents occurring during the carriage of nuclear or radioactive matter in certain specified circumstances. Rule 6 of Art.IV in the Schedule to the Carriage of Goods by Sea Act 1971 also deals with dangerous goods. (See Section XX, below.) Many bills of lading contain special provisions as to risky or hazardous goods, e.g. glass, specie, etc., or provide for the shipment of "lawful merchandise" only; see below, p.155.

[133] *Brass v Maitland* (1856) 6 E. & B. 470; *Hutchinson v Guion* (1858) 5 C.B. (N.S.) 149; *Williams v East India Company* (1802) 3 East 192 at pp.200, 201; *Farrant v Barnes* (1862) 11 C.B. (N.S.) 553, in which see dictum per Willes J. at p.563; *Bamfield v Goole, etc., Transport Co* [1910] 2 K.B. 94; *Ministry of Food v Lamport & Holt* [1952] 2 Lloyd's Rep. 371 at p.382; *Micada Cia Naviera v Texim* [1968] 2 Lloyd's Rep. 59 (goods unsafe without shifting boards); *Effort Shipping Co Ltd v Linden Management SA (The Giannis N.K.)* [1993] 2 Lloyd's Rep. 171; [1996] 1 Lloyd's Rep. 577; [1998] 1 Lloyd's Rep. 337; [1998] A.C. 605.

[134] *Bamfield v Goole, Transport Co* [1910] 2 K.B. 94; *Brass v Maitland*, above. In the dissentient judgment of Crompton J. in *Brass v Maitland* and in *Acatos v Burns* (1878) 3 Ex.D. 282, there are various dicta to the effect that the warranty of the shipper is less extensive and is limited by the actual or imputed knowledge of the shipper as to the danger. But this limitation was not accepted by the CA. in *Bamfield v Goole, Transport Co*. See also *G.N. Ry v L.E.P. Co* [1922] 2 K.B. 742, *Burley v Mayor, of Stepney* (1947) 80 Ll.L.R. 289 and *The Athanasia Comninos and Georges Chr. Lemos* [1990] 1 Lloyd's Rep. 277 and *Effort Shipping Co Ltd v Linden Management SA (The Giannis N.K.)* [1996] 1 Lloyd's Rep. 577; [1998] 1 Lloyd's Rep. 337; [1998] A.C. 605.

[135] *Acatos v Burns* (1878) 3 Ex.D. 282, which seems thus reconcilable with *Brass v Maitland* and other cases, though some of its dicta are more sweeping. See *Bamfield v Goole, Transport Co*, above; *Greenshields v Stephens* [1908] A.C. 431; and *Transoceanica v Shipton* [1923] 1 K.B. 31, where the principle of *Acatos v Burns* was applied.

parties at the time the shipment is contracted for, the charterer is not liable for any damage or delay caused by the shipment of that cargo,[136] unless the cargo possesses some special and not obvious characteristic which creates a danger outside the range of the dangers which a carrier of that type of cargo should foresee and guard against[137] or, where the risks are of the same kind as the carrier should foresee, they are of a difference of degree which approximates to a difference in kind.[138]

Goods may be dangerous within this principle if owing to legal obstacles as to their carriage or discharge they may involve detention of the ship.[139] In certain circumstances goods may be dangerous because of their propensity to contaminate the vessel's holds and thereby damage future cargos.[140]

The charterer will be liable for the cost of discharging and reloading the cargo if properly and reasonably incurred (*semble*, even if the shipowner is under no legal obligation to reload).[141]

Note. It does not appear to have been considered whether if the shipowner contracts to ship specified goods, not ordinarily matter of commercial knowledge, without knowing, as the fact is, that they are dangerous to the ship, or to other goods, or likely to infect the ship, he can refuse to take them on learning their character. It would seem that if the danger can be avoided by expense and care on his part, he must take them, but if it cannot be so avoided, he is not bound to carry them.

Case 1. F shipped on board A's ship sixty casks described as "bleaching powder", apparently sufficiently packed; in fact the powder contained chloride of lime, which corroded the casks and damaged the rest of the cargo. *Held*, that in the absence of notice to A of the dangerous character of the goods, F was liable for the resultant damage, unless the powder was so well known an article that masters of ships ought to know of its dangerous character. F pleaded that he shipped the goods, packed as he received them from third persons, without negligence. *Held*, by Lord Campbell and Wightman J., no defence; by Crompton J., a good defence.[142]

Case 2. A, shipowners, received for shipment from F a quantity of salt cake with permission to stow it in bulk. In ignorance of its nature they stowed it next to casks, which corroded, letting out the brine they contained, which damaged the salt cake. F sued A for the negligent stowage. *Held*, proof that F concealed the dangerous nature of salt cake from A, and that it would not be known to masters in the ordinary course of business, was a good defence. *Held*, also, the mere fact that F authorised stowage in bulk was no defence, as he did not authorise negligent stowage in bulk.[143]

Case 3. F shipped maize in A's ship, apparently in good order and condition; on the voyage it sprouted and was evidently in bad condition and dangerous. The jury found that it was dangerous when shipped, that its state could not have been ascertained by the use of reasonable means and that

---

[136] *Owners of S.S. Sebastian v de Vizcaya* [1920] 1 K.B. 332; *The Domald* [1920] P. 56; *General Feeds Inc v Burnham Shipping Corp (The Amphion)* [1991] 2 Lloyd's Rep. 101.
[137] *Atlantic Oil Carriers v British Petroleum Co* [1957] 2 Lloyd's Rep. 55 at p.95.
[138] *The Athanasia Comninos*, above; *The Amphion*, above. See also *Elders Grain Co Ltd v The "Ralph Misener"* [2005] FCA 139 (Can.), a case decided under Art.IV r.6 of the Hague Rules concerning the spontaneous combustion of a cargo of alfalfa pellets.
[139] *Mitchell v Steel* [1916] 2 K.B. 610; *Effort Shipping Co Ltd v Linden Management SA (The Giannis N.K.)* [1993] 2 Lloyd's Rep. 171; [1996] 1 Lloyd's Rep. 577; [1998] 1 Lloyd's Rep. 337; [1998] A.C. 650.
[140] *Sig. Bergessen D.Y. & Co v Mobil Shipping & Transportation Co (The Berge Sund)* [1993] 2 Lloyd's Rep. 453 at p.463; *The Giannis N.K.*, above (other cargos on same voyage).
[141] *Micada Cia Naviera v Texim*, above.
[142] *Brass v Maitland* (1856) 6 E. & B. 470.
[143] *Hutchinson v Guion* (1858) 5 C.B. (N.S.) 149.

the shipowner had full opportunities of examining it. *Held*, that F was not liable for any damage or delay occasioned by such shipment.[144]

Case 4. F shipped rice on A's ship which he had chartered for a voyage to the Piraeus. The discharge of rice there could only take place with the permission of the British Government. F knew this; A did not and could not reasonably have known it. The ship was delayed in consequence. *Held*, that F was liable to A for damages for the delay.[145]

Case 5. F loaded a cargo of ground-nut extraction meal pellets on A's ship. The pellets were infested with insects. As a result, the ship was refused entry to a number of countries and was ordered to dump its cargo of wheat at sea. *Held* the pellets were a dangerous cargo. The pellets posed a danger to other cargo because the shipment and voyage were to countries where the imposition of a quarantine and an order for dumping of the entire cargo was to be expected.[146]

---

[144] *Acatos v Burns* (1878) 3 Ex.D. 282. Both shipper and shipowner knew that the cargo was maize and that in certain circumstances maize was liable to sprout. There was "the clearest notice to the carrier of the nature of the goods he was requested to carry" (per Fletcher Moulton L.J., *Bamfield v Goole, Co* [1910] 2 K.B. 94 at p.111). *Cf. Greenshields v Stephens* [1908] A.C. 431 and *Atlantic Oil Carriers v British Petroleum* [1957] 2 Lloyd's Rep. 55 at p.95.

[145] *Mitchell v Steel* [1916] 2 K.B. 610. Where a cargo of barley was mixed with foreign substances, whereby the action of the grain elevator was impaired and the discharge delayed, an attempt by the shipowner to extend the doctrine of this case and claim damages for the delay was unsuccessful; *Transoceanica v Shipton* [1923] 1 K.B. 31. *Semble*, on the grounds that the shipowner had full opportunity of knowing the nature of the cargo. See also remarks of Roche J. (obiter) in *Rederiaktiebolaget Transatlantic v Board of Trade* (1924) 30 Com.Cas. 117.

[146] *Effort Shipping Co Ltd v Linden Management SA (The Giannis N.K.)* [1993] 2 Lloyd's Rep. 171; [1996] 1 Lloyd's Rep. 577; [1998] 1 Lloyd's Rep. 337, [1998] A.C. 605, a decision on Art.IV r.6 of the Hague-Visby Rules.

CHAPTER 8

REPRESENTATIONS

A54   **Article 54—Representations: General**

So far as concerns the law of charterparties and bills of lading, representations may be arranged in the following categories:

(1) Representations which induce the party to whom the representation is made to enter into the contract, but which do not become terms of the contract.[1]

(2) Representations which become contractual terms either by virtue of incorporation into the contract or by constituting a contract collateral to the main contract.[2]

(3) Representations which, although not forming part of the contract, are contained in the document which constitutes, or is evidence of, the contract.[3]

A55   **Article 55—Representations Inducing Contracts**

The effect of a representation which induces a person to enter into a contract, but which does not become a term of the contract, depends on whether the representation was made fraudulently, negligently, or innocently.

If the representation was fraudulent, the party relying on it may rescind the contract (subject to the bars of affirmation, delay, counter-restitution being impossible, and third party rights) and may also recover damages for the tort of deceit.[4]

Where the representation was not fraudulent, but was made without due care, the party acting on the representation may have one or both of two remedies. First, if he has suffered loss as a result of entering into a contract with the misrepresentor, he may recover damages under s.2(1) of the Misrepresentation Act 1967.[5]

---

[1] See Art.55, below.

[2] See Art.56, below.

[3] See Art.57, below.

[4] For an authoritative definition of "fraud", see *Derry v Peek* (1889) 14 App.Cas. 337, per Lord Herschell at p.374. "Fraud is proved when it is shown that a false representation has been made (1) knowingly, or (2) without belief in its truth, or (3) recklessly, careless whether it is true or false."

[5] It is possible that the claimant may also have a cause of action in tort, under the doctrine of *Hedley Byrne v Heller* [1964] A.C. 465, see Art.61, below. See also *Oleificio Zucchi v Northern Sales* [1965] 2 Lloyd's Rep. 496, at p.519. As regards a contract entered into with the misrepresentor, the point is academic, since the claimant obtains the same rights, with a more favourable burden of proof, under the Misrepresentation Act. Furthermore, it has been held that the wider remoteness test for deceit may apply to a claim under s.2(1): *Royscot Trust Ltd v Rogerson* [1991] 2 Q.B. 297.

Once the claimant has proved that he entered into the contract after[6] the representation was made and as a result thereof[7] has suffered loss, the burden is on the
defendant to relieve himself from liability by proving that he had reasonable
ground to believe and did believe up to the time the contract was made that the
facts represented were true.[8] The injured party may also rescind the contract (subject to the four bars listed above). But a court or arbitrator seised of the dispute has
a discretion under s.2(2) of the Misrepresentation Act to declare the contract subsisting and award damages in lieu of rescission, if of opinion that it would be equitable to do so, having regard to the nature of the misrepresentation and the loss that
would be caused by it if the contract were upheld, as well as to the loss that rescission would cause to the party making the representation.

Finally, there is the case where the representation is neither fraudulent nor negligent. Here, the innocent party may rescind the contract (subject to the four bars)
but has no right to damages. The arbitrator or court, has, however, the same discretion as in the case of negligent misrepresentation to award damages in place
of rescission.[9]

Most of the reported shipping cases on misrepresentation are concerned with
representations by the shipowner. But there is no reason why representations by
the shipper or charterer should not also found a claim.[10]

Article 56—Representations Forming Terms of a Contract   A56

A representation made before the contract is concluded may become a term of the
contract by being expressly reproduced in the contractual document. This was at
onc time the only way in which it could obtain contractual force, since the general rule was that oral evidence could not be admitted to vary the terms of the
charter. It has, however, now become common for the courts to give effect to
written or oral representations not embodied in the contract, by treating them as
collateral promises, the consideration being the act of entering into the main contract.[11] Thus, damages have been recovered for breach of oral warranties as to the
vessel's cargo capacity,[12] draught[13] and intended route.[14]

When the representation has become a term of the contract, or of a collateral
contract the representee can either bring a claim based on the misrepresentation
or can enforce the representation as a term of the contract. In the latter case, the
claim is governed by the same rules as apply to other contractual terms. These
rules are summarised in Art.44, above. The main practical consequences of

---

[6] And, presumably, "in consequence of. . . . " The same point arises on s.2(2).
[7] "Thereof" presumably refers to the act of entering into the contract.
[8] s.2(1) Misrepresentation Act 1967.
[9] s.2(2) of the Misrepresentation Act, which unlike s.2(1), applies to innocent as well as negligent misstatements.
   If the situation is not one in which rescission would have been available there is no discretion to award damages:
   Government of Zanzibar v British Aerospace (Lancaster House) Ltd [2000] 1 W.L.R. 2333.
[10] See Art.65.
[11] See *De Lassalle v Guildford* [1901] 2 K.B. 215; *Heilbut v Buckleton* [1913] A.C. 30; *Chitty on Contracts*, 29th
   edn, Vol.I, §§12–003 to 12–007.
[12] *Hassan v Runciman* (1904) 10 Com.Cas. 19.
[13] The unreported case, cited 17th edn, p.71.
[14] *The Ardennes* [1951] 1 K.B. 55.

enforcing a term as part of the contract, as distinct from as a misrepresentation inducing the contract are as follows[15]:

(1) The right of the injured party to treat the contract as terminated[16] depends upon the nature of the term and the magnitude of the breach, and not (as in the case of misrepresentation) on the discretion of the court or arbitrator,[17] or the existence or non-existence of the various circumstances which bar the right to rescind.[18]

(2) The injured party is always entitled to recover damages for the loss resulting from breach of the term; his right does not, as in the case of a misrepresentation, depend on whether the breach is fraudulent, negligent or innocent.[19]

(3) The aim of damages for a breach of contract is to protect the claimant's expectation interest by putting the claimant into as good a position as if the contract had been performed.[20] In contrast the aim of damages for a fraudulent or negligent misrepresentation is to protect the claimant's reliance interest by putting the claimant into as good a position as if no representation had been made.[21]

(4) The test of remoteness of damage for breach of contract[22] appears to be more restrictive than for tortious misrepresentation (whether sued for at common law or under s.2(1) of the 1967 Act).[23]

(5) The cause of action triggering the usual limitation period of six years accrues at the date of the breach for breach of contract but at the date of the loss for tortious misrepresentation.[24]

---

[15] Tortious misrepresentations also avoid certain statutory limitations of liability: see p.110, below.

[16] The right to treat the contract as terminated for a breach of condition or serious breach differs from the right to rescind for misrepresentation. The former operates prospectively, whereas rescission involves avoidance of the contract *ab initio*.

[17] Under s.2(2) of the Misrepresentation Act: see Art.54.

[18] In *Pennsylvania Shipping Co v Cie National* (1936) 42 Com.Cas. 45 at p.49. Bransom J. held that the charterer could throw up the charter on the ground that the representation had become embodied in the contract as a condition. This view seems preferable to that of Roche J. in *Compagnie Paris Orleans v Leeston* (1919) 1 Ll.L.R. 235.

[19] Unless, of course, the term is one which involves no more than that the party honestly or reasonably believes it to be true—as in the case of the statement that a ship is "expected ready to load" see Art.50, above.

[20] The classic authority is *Robinson v Harman* (1848) 1 Exch. 850, 855. See Article 192, below.

[21] *Doyle v Olby (Ironmongers) Ltd* [1969] 2 Q.B. 158; *Smith New Court Ltd v Scrimgeour Vickers (Asset Management) Ltd* [1997] A.C. 254. See further, contrasting estoppel and tortious misrepresentation, p.110, below. The measure of damages awarded at the court's discretion in lieu of rescission under s.2(2) of the 1967 Act is not yet settled: see *William Sindall Plc v Cambridgeshire CC* [1994] 1 W.L.R. 1016.

[22] *Hadley v Baxendale* (1854) 9 Exch. 341; *Koufos v Czarnikow Ltd, The Heron II* [1969] 1 A.C. 350. See Article 192, below.

[23] For fraudulent misrepresentation at common law and for liability under s.2(1), all direct loss is recoverable: *Doyle v Olby (Ironmongers) Ltd* [1969] 2 Q.B. 158; *Smith New Court Ltd v Scrimgeour Vickers (Asset Management) Ltd* [1997] A.C. 254; *Royscot Trust Ltd v Rogerson* [1991] 2 Q.B. 297. For negligent misrepresentation at common law the normal tort test, as laid down in *Overseas Tankship (UK) Ltd v Morts Dock & Engineering Co Ltd, The Wagon Mound* [1961] A.C. 388, applies. See Article 192, below.

[24] See, e.g. *Forster v Outred & Co* [1982] 1 W.L.R. 86. Moreover the Latent Damage Act 1986 does not apply to a claim for breach of contract: *Iron Trade Mutual Insurance Co Ltd v J. K. Buckenham Ltd* [1990] 1 All E.R. 808; *Société Commerciale de Reassurance v E.R.A.S. (International) Ltd* [1992] 2 All E.R. 82n. On the inapplicability of the Hague-Visby Rules time-limit to tortious misrepresentation, see p.110, below.

Article 57—Representations in Bills of Lading   A57

Bills of lading usually contain statements as to the description, quantity, nature, marks and packing of the goods, and similar matters. These statements are not representations inducing the contract, nor are they terms of the contract in the sense discussed above.[25] Nevertheless, they may confer important rights on third parties who, in reliance on the statements, take up and pay for the bills of lading under contracts of purchase or pledge. The representation may operate in three ways:

(1) By estoppel. If the requirements of an estoppel are satisfied, the shipowner is precluded from denying the accuracy of the statement, and this may enable the third party to make good a claim in contract for loss or damage in transit.[26] There is also a statutory estoppel in certain cases.[27]

(2) As prima facie evidence of the facts represented.[28]

(3) As the foundation of a direct action in tort, if the statement is fraudulent or negligent.[29]

The choice between employing the misrepresentation as the foundation of a direct action in tort, or as evidence or an estoppel is of practical importance, since it may affect the measure of damage, and the application of the Hague-Visby Rules and statutes limiting liability.[30] Articles 58–61 look at each of those three legal methods in turn. Articles 62–64 then focus on particular representations in bills of lading.

Article 58—Estoppel at Common Law   A58

In order to establish an estoppel, it must be shown that[31]:

(1) The statement embodied a representation of fact;

(2) The maker intended that the representation should be relied upon; and

---

[25] *Cf. V/O Rasnoimport v Guthrie* [1966] 1 Lloyd's Rep. 1, 14
[26] See Art.58, below.
[27] See Art.59, below.
[28] See Art.60, below.
[29] See Art.61, below.
[30] See p.110, below.
[31] *Silver v Ocean Steamship Co* [1930] 1 K.B. 416 at p.133. Estoppel has developed in a variety of ways. The kind of estoppel dealt with in this Article is known as "estoppel in pais", as distinct from, e.g. "promissory estoppel", or "estoppel by convention". See generally on the different types of estoppel, *Amalgamated Investment & Property Co Ltd v Texas Commerce International Bank Ltd* [1982] Q.B. 84; *Lokumal & Sons v Lotte Shipping Co Pte. Ltd (The August Leonhardt)* [1985] 2 Lloyd's Rep. 28; *Baird Textiles Holdings Ltd v Marks & Spencer Plc* [2001] EWCA Civ 274; [2002] 1 All E.R. (Comm) 737. As in the second case, estoppel has often been relevant, outside the context of this Article, in relation to whether a time bar under the Hague-Visby Rules or elsewhere in a charterparty has been extended: see also, e.g. *The Stolt Loyalty* [1993] 2 Lloyd's Rep. 281.

(3) The party asserting the estoppel in fact relied upon the representation to his detriment.[32]

As to requirement (1), it is plain that there can be no estoppel without a representation. It is possible, by the use of phrases such as "quantity unknown"[33] or "believed to be",[34] to negative an estoppel which would otherwise have arisen.

As to requirement (2), the shipowner will in most, although not necessarily all, cases be taken to know and intend that the representation will be relied upon.[35] In particular, he can envisage the likelihood that in reliance on the representation of "good order and condition", a purchaser will take up and pay for the bill of lading, or a banker will advance money upon the security of it.[36]

Finally, as to requirement (3), there must be reliance on the representation by the party asserting the estoppel.[37] In the absence of contrary evidence, the fact that a holder of a bill of lading containing a representation of a type which is commonly relied upon—such as a statement of the condition of the goods on shipment—has taken up and paid for the bill of lading is sufficient to show that he relied upon it.[38] This presumption may, however, be rebutted by proof that it was clearly known to the person taking up the bill of lading that the representation was untrue,[39] but it is not enough to establish that his purchase contract required him to take the goods subject to an allowance if he would nevertheless have rejected the goods.[40]

A59   **Article 59—Estoppel by Statute**

By s.4 of the Carriage of Goods by Sea Act 1992,[41] a bill of lading which (a) represents goods to have been shipped on board a vessel or to have been received for shipment on board a vessel, and (b) has been signed by the master of the vessel or by a person who has the express, implied or apparent authority of the carrier to sign bills of lading, is, in favour of a person who has become the lawful

---

[32] It may be that in some cases the party raising the estoppel can succeed without proof of reliance, on the basis of the doctrine propounded by Winn L.J. in *Panchaud Frères v Ets General Grain* [1969] 2 Lloyd's Rep. 109. The boundaries of this doctrine have not yet been defined.

[33] See p.112, below. Sometimes the disclaimer takes an extreme form, such as "weight, quantity, number, contents, condition and quality unknown". Although this type of claim reduces the commercial value of the document, it is not objectionable in theory, nor does it offend the Hague-Visby Rules, unless the shipper has made a demand for a bill of lading in compliance with Art.III, r.3; *Noble Resources Ltd v Cavalier Shipping Corp (The Atlas)* [1996] 1 Lloyd's Rep. 642.

[34] Such a phrase is commonly used where goods are shipped in a closed package, and where the shipowner does not wish to commit himself by any representation as to the nature, quantity or condition of the goods.

[35] If the shipowner is assured by the shipper that the bill of lading will not be negotiated, it may be that the element of intention is absent.

[36] See *Brown Jenkinson v Percy Dalton* [1957] 2 Q.B. 621.

[37] It appears that provided the reliance is not *de minimis*, it need not be commensurate with the damages which the plaintiff is entitled to recover by establishing the estoppel.

[38] *Silver v Ocean S.S. Co* [1930] 1 K.B. 416; *cf. V/O Rasnoimport v Guthrie* [1966] 1 Lloyd's Rep. 1, 14.

[39] *Evans v Webster* (1928) 34 Com.Cas. 172.

[40] *Peter Cremer Westfaelische GmbH v General Carriers SA* [1973] 2 Lloyd's Rep. 366, explaining *The Skarp* [1935] P. 134; and *Dent v Glen Line* (1940) 45 Com.Cas. 244 at pp.257–259.

[41] See Appendix 1.4, below.

holder of the bill, conclusive evidence as against the carrier of the shipment of
the goods or, as the case may be, of their receipt for shipment.

Note. Section 4 of the Carriage of Goods by Sea Act 1992 abolishes, as against a person who has become the lawful holder of a bill of lading, the decision in *Grant v Norway*[42]
that the master cannot bind the carrier by his signature of a bill of lading for goods not
shipped. The section embodies the recommendations in Ch.4 of the Report of the Law
Commission and the Scottish Law Commission on Rights of Suit in Respect of Carriage
of Goods by Sea,[43] which endorsed criticisms of the decision in earlier editions of this
work[44] and by other authors.[45]

Section 3 of the Bills of Lading Act 1855 is repealed.[46] This had been intended to overcome the decision in *Grant v Norway*: but since it provided for the bill of lading to be conclusive evidence only against "the master or other person signing the same" it was of little
practical value.

The statutory estoppel does not apply to documents other than bills of lading,[47] such as
sea waybills and ship's delivery orders. In this respect, the Law Commissions were not
prepared to recommend extending the statutory protection beyond that afforded by Art.III,
r.4 of the Hague-Visby Rules,[48] which do not apply to non-negotiable documents.[49] Nor
does the estoppel apply in favour of any person other than one who has become the lawful
holder of the bill of lading.[50] In particular this does not include the original shipper of the
goods.[51]

The section does not confer a cause of action for the non-delivery of goods
represented to have been shipped, but merely raises an estoppel against the person signing the bill.[52] But where there is no underlying contract,[53] and hence no
other possible cause of action, it may be that, in order to give effect to the intention underlying the section, one should regard s.4 "as a statutory exception to the
general rule that estoppel does not give rise to a cause of action".[54]

Where the contract of carriage is governed by the Hague-Visby Rules, a bill of
lading which shows the leading marks,[55] the number, quantity, or weight of the
goods, and their apparent order and condition is, by virtue of Art.III, r.4, conclusive evidence of such receipt when the bill of lading has been transferred to a
third party acting in good faith.

The bill of lading may, by contract, be made conclusive evidence of the quantity shipped.[56]

---

[42] (1851) 10 C.B. 665.
[43] Law Com. No. 196: Scot Law Com. No. 130: HC 250.
[44] See 19th edn, p.115.
[45] Reynolds, "Warranty of Authority" (1967) 88 L.Q.R. 189, 193; *Bowstead & Reynolds on Agency* (16th edn,
1996) p.370.
[46] Carriage of Goods by Sea Act 1992, s.6(2).
[47] For the meaning of "bill of lading" in the 1992 Act, see Art.14, above.
[48] See s.1(6)(b) of the Carriage of Goods by Sea Act 1971, below, p.377.
[49] Paras 4.8 to 4.12 of the Report.
[50] For the meaning of "holder" and "lawful holder" in the 1992 Act, see Article 14, above.
[51] *Agrosin Pte Ltd v Highway Shipping Co Ltd, The Mata K* [1998] 2 Lloyd's Rep. 614, 616.
[52] See, with regard to s.3 of the 1855 Act, *V/O Rasnoimport v Guthrie* [1966] 1 Lloyd's Rep. 1.
[53] As in a case like *Heskell v Continental Express Ltd* [1950] 1 All E.R. 1033.
[54] *Carver on Bills of Lading*, (2nd edn, 2005) para.2.020.
[55] For a discussion of marks, see Art.64, below.
[56] See pp.111–112, below.

A60 ### Article 60—The Bill of Lading as Prima Facie Evidence

Where the contract of carriage is governed by the Hague-Visby Rules, a bill of lading which shows the leading marks, the number, quantity, or weight of the goods, and their apparent order and condition is, by virtue of Art.III, r.4, prima facie evidence (in favour of the original shipper) of the receipt by the carrier of the goods as therein described.[57] Apart from the Hague-Visby Rules, the bill of lading is prima facie evidence of certain matters.[58]

A61 ### Article 61—Tortious Misrepresentation

In addition to founding an estoppel, a representation in a bill of lading may give rise to an action in tort at the suit of a person who relies upon the representation, and thereby suffers loss.

Thus, if a bill of lading contains a statement as to the apparent condition of the goods, or the date of shipment, or a similar matter, and the master or ship's agent signs the bill knowing the statement to be untrue, the person so signing is liable in fraud to anyone who suffers loss by relying on the representation, e.g. by taking up and paying for a "clean" bill of lading, which he would have rejected if the true condition of the goods had been stated.[59] So also if he acts recklessly, not caring whether the statement is true or false.[60] Furthermore, the shipowner should also be held liable, at least where the statement is of a type which is commonly included in a bill of lading, such as the date of shipment,[61] for it is in the course of the master or agent's employment to issue bills of lading containing such statements. Vicarious liability of this type will not necessarily extend to everything which is included in a bill of lading, and in particular it appears on the authorities as they stand at present that the shipowner will not be liable in tort if the bill of lading represents that goods are on board when in fact they are not.[62]

If the master or agent issues bills of lading containing representations which he knows to be false, in return for an agreement by the person tendering the bill for signature to indemnify him against any liability which may ensue, the indemnity

---

[57] For the text of Art.III, r.4, see p.391 below.

[58] e.g. shipment of the goods (see Art.62, below).

[59] *The Saudi Crown* [1986] 1 Lloyd's Rep. 261; *Hunter Grain Pty Ltd v Hyundai Merchant Marine Co Ltd* 117 A.L.R. 507. As to reliance in the case of estoppel, see Art.58, above. The rule that in certain cases reliance is to be presumed is perhaps no more than a rule of evidence, and the court may well require strict proof of reliance in a case of fraud.

[60] See the definition of fraud, cited at Art.55, fn.4, above.

[61] *The Saudi Crown* [1986] 1 Lloyd's Rep. 261; *Blue Nile Co Ltd v Emery Customs Brokers (S) Pte Ltd* [1992] 1 S.L.R. 296 [Sing.].

[62] According to *Grant v Norway* (1851) 10 C.B. 665 the master has no authority to bind the shipowner to an estoppel in such a case, and although ostensible authority and course of employment are not the same thing, it would be curious if the master's acts could bind the owner in tort but not in contract. Indeed it was assumed in the reasoning in *The Saudi Crown* [1986] 1 Lloyd's Rep. 261, albeit that that was distinguishable as concerning a representation as to the date of the bill of lading, that *Grant v Norway* did apply to a claim in tort for misrepresentation. The decision in this case was criticised in earlier editions: see 19th edn, Art.60. Its importance has been much diminished although it has not formally been overruled by s.4 of the Carriage of Goods by Sea Act 1992 (see Art.59, above) and Art.III, r.4 of the Hague-Visby Rules (see p.390 below).

is unenforceable, for the issuing of the bill in such circumstances is fraudulent.[63] Such an indemnity may, however, be valid if there is a genuine doubt about the condition of the goods.[64]

It is submitted that the person signing the bill of lading, and also the ship-owner, may be liable, even in the absence of deliberate fraud or recklessness, if incorrect statements are made in the bill through want of due care to ensure that they are correct.[65] Such a liability would arise:

(1) If the act of issuing the bill was performed without due care—e.g. if insufficient steps were taken to check that the bill conformed with the mate's receipt.

(2) If the information on which the statement on the bill was based was not collected or checked with due care—e.g. if the ship's officer did not take the requisite steps to ascertain the apparent condition of the goods, or the marks on the goods. The court may well proceed with caution when faced with allegations that there has been negligence of this type. In each case, the question is whether the master or agent has proceeded with lack of *reasonable* care, and this must be decided with reference to the nature of the cargo, the circumstances of the loading, and the exigencies of the trade. The court is likely to be slow in implying any duty of care which might unduly increase the burdens on the ship's officers, or delay the proper conduct of loading.

It is unlikely that, in addition to the right of action at common law discussed above, a person who takes up and pays for a bill of lading[66] containing an inaccurate representation may have a remedy for negligent misstatement under the Misrepresentation Act 1967 because that only applies as regards misrepresentations made by one contracting party to the other. By virtue of s.2(1) of the Carriage of Goods by Sea Act 1992[67] the lawful holder of a bill of lading has transferred to him all rights of suit under the contract of carriage as if he had been a party to that contract. The argument would be that such a lawful holder has entered into a contract after a misrepresentation has been made to him by the

---

[63] *Brown Jenkinson v Percy Dalton*, above. So far as *Leach v Royal Mail Co* (1910) 16 Com.Cas. 143 and *Groves v Webb* (1916) 85 L.J.K.B. 1533 decide the contrary, they must be regarded as overruled. The practice of issuing such indemnities is nevertheless widespread, and the indemnity is almost invariably honoured.

[64] *Ibid.* per Morris L.J. There will, it is submitted, be few cases where a master who entertains doubts about the condition of the goods could issue a clean bill of lading without his conduct being described as reckless. The practice, however usual, of employing an indemnity as a means of settling an argument between the shipper and the master is not, it is thought, one which the court would encourage.

[65] No such claim has so far been brought to judgment in England, but it is submitted that the relationship between the shipowner and a person who becomes holder of the bill is one which satisfied the tests laid down in *Hedley Byrne v Heller* [1964] A.C. 465. On this point see *Rudolf A. Oetker v I.F.A. Internationale Frachtagentur AG (The Almak)* [1985] 1 Lloyd's Rep. 557 at p.560 drawing attention to the possible effect of the decision in *Grant v Norway* on such a claim.

[66] Similar arguments would apply in the case of persons deriving rights of suit under the Carriage of Goods by Sea Act 1992 in respect of sea waybills or ship's delivery orders.

[67] See Art.14.

shipowner, and that he can accordingly rely upon s.2(1) of the Misrepresentation Act. We submit that this argument is unsound. The Carriage of Goods by Sea Act does not create a new contract between the shipowner and the holder, but rather brings about a species of statutory assignment of the original agreement between the shipper and shipowner. This is not the kind of transaction to which the Misrepresentation Act is directed.

In many respects the tortious remedies indicated above will be no more than alternatives to the more usual contractual remedies which the bill of lading holder pursues through the medium of the estoppel. There are, however, certain respects in which the different causes of action may produce different practical results.

First, the measure of damage will not necessarily be the same. When the holder brings a successful claim for cargo damage, using the representation as proof that the goods began the voyage in good condition, he recovers the difference between the sound arrived value of the goods, and their actual arrived value. Where he sues in tort on the ground that he was induced to take up the bill of lading and pay the price of the goods by a wrongful representation in the bill, his measure of damage will be the loss resulting from his so doing: which will normally be the difference between the price and the actual arrived value.[68] If the market has changed during the voyage, the two measures of damage will be different.

Secondly, it is submitted that neither the Hague-Visby Rules time-limit under Art.III, r.6,[69] nor the limit of liability under Art.IV, r.5,[70] applies to tortious claims of the type discussed above. Whilst neither rule is limited in its application to claims for loss or damage to cargo, the rules are concerned only with claims "in connection with" the goods,[71] and which are also in some way related to the carriage of the goods.[72] A cause of action based directly on a wrongful statement in a shipping document, not founded on any allegation of fault in the carriage itself, is not the type of claim with which the rules were intended to deal.[73]

A62   **Article 62—Representations as to Quantity**

At common law, a master cannot bind the carrier by his signature of a bill of lading for a quantity of goods not shipped.[74] But, as we have seen, the effect of this has been reversed by statute so that the bill of lading is conclusive evidence of the quantity of goods shipped in favour of a person who has become the lawful holder of the bill.[75] The bill of lading is prima facie evidence (in favour of the

---

[68] Art.56, above.
[69] p.392, below.
[70] pp.406–407, below.
[71] See Art.III, r.8, below, p.396.
[72] See also Art.IV bis, r.1, below, p.410.
[73] So held by Roskill J. in chambers.
[74] *Grant v Norway* (1851) 10 C.B. 665; *Rasnoimport v Guthrie* [1966] 1 Lloyd's Rep. 1.
[75] Carriage of Goods by Sea Act 1992, s.4. See to similar effect, the Hague-Visby Rules Art.III, r.4. See Art.59 above.

original shipper) both under the Hague-Visby Rules (if they apply)[76] and at common law,[77] that the goods were shipped, and the burden of disproving it lies on the shipowner. The evidence to displace the bill of lading must show not merely that the goods may not have been shipped but that they were not[78]; the statement in the bill of lading is not to be displaced merely by a consideration of the balance of probabilities.[79] The evidence may, for example, be rebutted by conclusive evidence that after receipt by the shipowner none of the goods were lost or stolen, and that he has delivered all that he received[80]; or by evidence of disputed tallies, of the mate's receipts and of the ship's draught.[81]

The master or agent cannot bind the owner by signing a second bill of lading for goods for which he has already signed a bill.[82] Such a bill has no binding effect, even in the hands of a bona fide holder for value. A clause, known as "the conclusive evidence clause" is sometimes inserted in bills of lading.[83] This clause reads: "The bill of lading shall be conclusive evidence against the owner of the quantity of cargo received", or is in similar terms. With such a clause[84] the shipowner will be liable for short delivery though it is otherwise clear that the timber was not "received" or "taken on board".[85] To free himself, the shipowner must prove loss by excepted perils after "taking on board"; loss by excepted perils alongside the ship will not do.[86] The conclusive evidence clause may be employed in bills of lading to which the Hague-Visby Rules apply, since it increases and does not purport to decrease, the liability of the shipowner. Unless the shipowner disclaims recourse to Art.III, r.5, he will be entitled to an indemnity from the shipper in respect of the quantity stated in writing by the shipper to have been shipped in excess of that in fact shipped.

Sometimes the clause provides that the bill of lading shall be conclusive "unless error be proved". In this case, the bill of lading is no more than prima

---

[76] Art.III, r.4.
[77] *Smith v Bedouin* [1896] A.C. 70; *Harrowing v Katz* (1894) 10 T.L.R. 400; [1896] A.C. 73 (HL); *Bennett and Young v Bacon* (1897) 2 Com.Cas. 102; *Att-Gen of Ceylon v Scindia* [1962] A.C. 60 (PC), in all of which the evidence was not displaced. For the evidential position with regard to liquid cargos see *Amoco Oil Co v Parpada Shipping Co Ltd (The George S)* [1989] 1 Lloyd's Rep. 369 (*sed quaere*); *Anonima Petroli Italiana SpA v Marlucidez Armadora SA (The Filiatra Legacy)* [1990] 1 Lloyd's Rep. 354; [1991] 2 Lloyd's Rep. 337.
[78] *Smith v Bedouin*, above, at p.79.
[79] *Hain v Herdman and MacDougal* (1922) 11 Ll.L.R. 58 (HL).
[80] As in *Sunday v Strath S.S. Co* (1920) 26 Com.Cas. 277.
[81] As in *Hine v Free, Rodwell & Co* (1897) 2 Com.Cas. 149.
[82] *Hubbersty v Ward* (1853) 8 Ex. 330.
[83] *Semble*, that a master signing bills of lading for charterers has no authority to bind his owners by a bill of lading containing this clause: *Thin v Liverpool Brazil Co* (1901) 18 T.L.R. 226.
[84] The variation of "delivered to the ship" instead of "received" makes no difference: *Crossfield v Kyle S.S. Co* [1916] 2 K.B. 885.
[85] See *Lishman v Christie* (1887) 19 Q.B.D. 333; *Evans v Webster* (1928) 34 Com.Cas. 172; *Crossfield v Kyle* [1916] 2 K.B. 885. Where with such a clause the bill of lading specifies quantities of different sorts of goods (e.g. deals and boards), the shipowner is equally bound as to both, so that if there is a short delivery of deals and an over-delivery of boards, he cannot take the two together as representing the total quantity of both: *Mediterranean Co v Mackay* [1903] 1 K.B. 297; discussed in *Lauro v Dreyfus* (1937) 59 Ll.L.R. 110 at p.116; *Nordborg (Owners) v Sherwood* [1939] P. 121.
[86] *Fisher v Calder* (1896) 1 Com.Cas. 456. Shipowners have sometimes met the difficulty by adding to the statement of cargo shipped in the bill of lading a marginal note: "so many timbers of above lost alongside", or similar words. This seems to make the bill of lading contain no conclusive statement of quantity shipped: *Lohden v Calder* (1898) 14 T.L.R. 311. See also *Oostzee Stoomvart v Bell* (1906) 11 Com.Cas. 214.

facie evidence. But the actual source of the error must be proved; mere inference as to the existence of an error will not suffice.[87]

Where the statement of the amount or quantity of the goods in the bill of lading is qualified by such words as "weight or quantity unknown" or "said to contain —packed by shippers" there is no representation as to quantity being made so that there is no statutory estoppel under either s.4 of the Carriage of Goods by Sea Act 1992 or the Hague-Visby Rules[88]; and the bill of lading is not even prima facie evidence against the shipowner of the amount or quantity shipped save that such amount or quantity is not drastically at odds with the quantity actually loaded[89] and the onus is on the cargo-owner of proving what in fact was shipped.[90] Where the carriage is governed by the Hague-Visby Rules, Art 3, r.3 lays down that, if the shipper so demands, the carrier is bound to issue a bill of lading showing the number of packages or pieces, or the quantity, or weight, as the case may be, as furnished in writing by the shipper. A bill of lading stating, for example, "weight or quantity or number unknown" would not comply with this requirement although there is an exemption from the requirement where the carrier has "no reasonable means of checking" which would be the case with containerised goods.

A63   **Article 63—Representations as to Condition on Shipment**

Where the bill of lading states, as it almost invariably does, that the cargo was "shipped in good order and condition" or "shipped in apparent good order and condition", the shipowner is estopped[91] as against an indorsee for value of the bill[92] and against a person rightfully presenting the bill of lading and taking delivery thereunder[93] from proving that they were not in apparent good order and condition, unless it was clearly known to the indorsee or person presenting the bill that the statement was untrue or is proved that he did not act upon the faith of the statement. In the absence of contrary evidence the fact that the holder of a bill of lading containing such a statement has taken it without objection is suffi-cient to show that he relied upon it.[94]

---

[87] *Royal Commission on Sugar Supply v Hartlepools Seatonia S.S. Co* [1927] 2 K.B. 419; but *cf. Lauro v Drefus* (1937) 59 Ll.L.R. 110 at p.117.

[88] *Noble Resources Ltd v Cavalier Shipping Corp, The Atlas* [1996] 1 Lloyd's Rep. 642; *Agrosin Pte Ltd v Highway Shipping Co Ltd, The Mata K* [1998] 2 Lloyd's Rep. 614; *Ace Imports Pty Ltd v Companhia de Navegacio Lloyd Brasilero, The Esmeralda I* (1987) 10 N.S.W.L.R. 32; [1988] 1 Lloyd's Rep. 206.

[89] *Conoco (UK) Ltd v Limai Maritime Co Ltd (The Sirina)* [1988] 2 Lloyd's Rep. 613.

[90] *New Chinese Co v Ocean S.S. Co* [1917] 2 K.B. 664; *Att-Gen of Ceylon v Scindia* [1962] A.C. 60 (PC). See *Craig Line v North British Co,* 1921 S.C. 114; *Jessel v Bath* (1867) L.R. 2 Ex 267; *Lebeau v General Steam Navigation* (1872) L.R. 8 C.P. 88; *Ace Imports Pty Ltd v Companhia de Navegacao Lloyd Brasileiro, The Esmeralda I* (1987) 10 N.S.W.L.R. 32 [1988] 1 Lloyd's Rep. 206; *Rederiaktiebolaget Gustav Erikson v Dr Fawzi Ahmed Aboli Ismail* [1986] 2 Lloyd's Rep. 281. Where the master subsequently stamps a bill recording the quantities, then notwithstanding a statement that "weight or quantity unknown", he may be held as a matter of objective construction to have adopted the figures: *ibid.*

[91] The words are not words of contract: *Compania Vasconzada v Churchill* [1906] 1 K.B. 237; *The Skarp* [1935] P. 134.

[92] *Compania Vasconzada v Churchill,* above; *The Tromp* [1912] P. 337.

[93] *Brandt v Liverpool* [1924] 1 K.B. 575.

[94] See Art.58, above.

In the case of perishable goods, apparent good order and condition includes apparent ability to withstand ordinary methods of transport.[95]

These clauses only admit as against the shipowner that a package was shipped externally to all appearances in good condition. They constitute no admission as to the internal condition of the goods,[96] or as to their quality.[97]

Sometimes the words "shipped in good order or condition" are omitted. It is submitted that in such a case the bill is not even prima facie evidence of the condition of the goods on shipment.[98]

Bills of lading not infrequently include the words "contents unknown" or "quality unknown". These do not alter the effect of the bill, since in any event the words "in apparent good order and condition" do not involve any representation as to quality, or as to the nature of the contents.[99] Furthermore, the effect of the words "in apparent good order and condition" is not nullified by the addition of "condition unknown".[100]

The practice is now developing of including in the bill of lading a definition of "good order and condition" which makes it clear that the representation does not imply that the cargo is free from the type of defect which commonly affects the cargo in question, e.g. rust (metal goods) or moisture (timber). There appears to be no reason why these clauses should not be valid: and they do not appear to offend the Hague-Visby Rules.[101]

Where the Hague-Visby Rules apply, the carrier is bound on demand of the shipper to issue a bill of lading showing the apparent order and condition of the goods.[102] By virtue of the rules, and quite apart from common law, such a bill of lading is prima facie evidence of the receipt of the goods by the carrier in the order and condition stated and conclusive evidence of such receipt when the bill of lading has been transferred to a party acting in good faith.[103]

A container packed by the shipper is usually acknowledged as "one container in apparent good order and condition said to contain [the contents] as declared by the shipper". An acknowledgement in this form does not bind the carrier to any representation as to the condition or description of the contents.[104] Moreover, the requirement under the Hague-Visby rules to issue, on demand of the shipper, a

---

[95] *Dent v Glen Line* (1940) 45 Com.Cas. 244.
[96] *The Peter der Grosse* (1875) 1 P.D. 414, affirmed (1876) 34 L.T. 749 (CA); but see *Craig v Delargy*, 1879 6 Rettie 1269; *Witzler v Collins* (1879) 35 Am.Rep. 327.
[97] *Cf. Cox v Bruce* (1886) 18 Q.B.D. 147.
[98] It might be argued that if the bill does not state that the goods were in bad condition on shipment this carries an inference that they were in good condition, but this is not considered to be correct: see *The Isle de Panay* (1925) 267 U.S. 260 and *Tokio Marine & Fire Insurance Co v Retla S.S. Co* [1970] 2 Lloyd's Rep. 91 (US 9th Circuit CA).
[99] *Martineaus v Royal Mail Co* (1912) 17 Com.Cas. 176; *National Petroleum Co v "Athelviscount"* (1934) 48 Ll.L.R. 164; *cf. The Ida* (1875) 32 L.T. 541.
[100] *The Skarp* [1935] P. 134.
[101] See *Tokio Marine & Fire Insurance Co v Retla S.S. Co*, above.
[102] Art.III, r.3.
[103] Art.III, r.4. This evidence is, on the wording of the rules, available even to a claimant who has not given value or who cannot prove reliance on the representation.
[104] See Art.62 above.

bill of lading showing the apparent order and condition of the goods does not apply where the carrier "has no reasonable means of checking" which would be the case with containerised goods.

A64   **Article 64—Representations as to Marks**

The shipowner is estopped from showing that goods shipped were marked otherwise than as stated in the bill of lading if the marks denote the commercial character or description of the goods but not if they are merely inserted for ease of identification.[105] However, where the contract of carriage is governed by the Hague-Visby Rules, a bill of lading which shows the leading marks necessary for identification of the goods is, by virtue of Art.III, r.4, prima facie evidence of the receipt by the carrier of the goods as therein described and conclusive evidence of such receipt when the bill of lading has been transferred to a third party acting in good faith.[106]

The master has no authority to bind the shipowner by representations in the bill of lading as to the quality of the goods shipped, and therefore a statement by the master in the bill of lading as to marks denoting the quality of the goods does not estop the shipowner from showing that the goods shipped were of a different quality.[107]

The shipowner usually requires as a condition of assuming liability for the goods that they shall be correctly marked or marked in a particular way.[108]

Such a provision will generally only excuse the shipowner from delivering the actual goods shipped if the goods have become mixed and unidentifiable.[109] The words "correctly marked" in such a provision apparently mean "marked in accordance with the marks on the bills of lading".[110]

Where the Hague-Visby rules apply, the carrier, on demand of the shipper, is bound to issue a bill of lading showing the leading marks necessary for identification provided such marks are clearly shown on the goods or their cases or coverings in such a manner as should remain legible until the end of the voyage.[111] But there is an exemption from this requirement where the carrier has "no reasonable means of checking" which will be the case with containerised goods.

---

[105] *Parsons v New Zealand Shipping Co* [1900] 1 Q.B. 714; [1901] 1 K.B. 548 (CA), the difference of opinion in the Court of Appeal turned on the question of fact whether the marks did or did not denote the commercial character or description of the goods. See also *Compania Importadora v P. & O.* (1927) 28 Ll.L.R. 63.
[106] See p.391, below, for the full text of the rule.
[107] *Cox v Bruce* (1886) 18 Q.B.D. 147.
[108] *Cox v Bruce*, above; *Parsons v New Zealand Shipping Co*, above: *Compania Importadora v P. & O.*, above; see also Art.IV, r.2(*o*) of the Hague-Visby Rules, below, p.399. Such a clause will be invalidated by Art.III, r.8 of the Hague-Visby Rules if it purports to extend the exception in Art.IV, r.2(*o*): *British Imex v Midland Bank* [1958] 1 Q.B. 542.
[109] *Sandeman v Tyzack* [1913] A.C. 680; and see Art.152, below, for the general principles applicable to mixed and unidentifiable goods.
[110] *Parsons v New Zealand Co*, above, per A. L. Smith, M.R., and Collins L.J. (Romer L.J. doubting).
[111] Art.3 r.3.

Article 65—Representations by the Shipper   A65

Most of the authorities on misrepresentations deal with misrepresentations by the carrier. However, Art.IV, r.5(*h*) of the Hague-Visby Rules[112] contains an important statutory provision dealing with misrepresentations by the shipper. The rule provides that the carrier shall not be responsible for loss or damage to or in connection with goods[113] if the nature or value thereof has been knowingly misstated by the shipper in the bill of lading. The provision appears to presuppose that the bill of lading has been drawn up by the shipper, and its application to the not uncommon case where the bill of lading is drawn up by the carrier from information supplied by the shipper is uncertain. It is submitted that the carrier ought in such circumstances to be treated as the agent of the shipper to draw up the bill of lading unless he has reasonable grounds for suspecting that the information furnished to him by the shipper is incorrect.[114]

The rule does not apply unless the misstatement is contained in the bill of lading; but it is submitted that if the misstatement, although not contained in the bill of lading, is contained in a document forming part of the contract evidenced by the bill of lading (such as the booking form submitted by the shipper) the rule would be satisfied by an application to rectify the bill of lading so as to incorporate the misstatement into it.[115]

Apart from the Hague-Visby Rules, a misstatement by the shipper as to the nature or value of the goods will entitle the carrier to invoke the remedies discussed in Art.55 above.[116]

Article III, r.5 of the Hague-Visby Rules provides that the shipper shall indemnify the carrier against loss, damage and expenses arising or resulting from inaccuracies in the marks, number, quantity and weight of the goods as furnished by the shipper.[117] There may also be a similar right to an indemnity at common law where the shipowner has no reason to doubt the accuracy of the particulars inserted in the bill of lading by the shipper.[118]

---

[112] See below, p.407.
[113] See below, p.398, for a discussion of the meaning of these words.
[114] Compare the provisions of Art.III, rr.3 and 5.
[115] See *Pendle & Rivett v Ellerman Lines* (1928) 33 Com.Cas. 70.
[116] See e.g. *Lebeau v General Steam Navigation* (1872) L.R. 8 C.P. 88.
[117] See p.391, below.
[118] *Elder Dempster v Dunn* (1909) 15 Com.Cas. 49. See also Art.43, above.

CHAPTER 9

PERFORMANCE OF CONTRACT: LOADING

A66   **Article 66—Performance of Contract before Loading**

UNDER a contract of affreightment whereby some goods but not a complete cargo are to be carried, e.g. under a contract evidenced in a bill of lading, the bill of lading is not signed till the goods are shipped and therefore as a rule does not provide for anything previous to shipment. The contract is, however, generally made before shipment and may in principle provide for matters occurring before shipment.

If a binding contract has been made by way, for example, of a booking note,[1] but the goods are afterwards "shut out" for want of room, the contract of affreightment is prima facie broken and an action will lie against the shipowner. Such actions, which clearly lie at law, are in practice almost unknown. Extra freight paid for the goods shut out could probably be recovered,[2] as would storage charges, and demurrage for railway trucks in which goods shut out were stored has been recovered in the port of London under special circumstances. Whether or not loss of profits on goods shut out can be recovered will depend upon whether this type of loss is too remote on normal principles.[3]

A67   **Article 67—Shipowner's Duty under a Charter before Loading: "To proceed to a Port and there Load"**

Where the vessel is not at the loading port at the date of the charter, the chartered voyage is not be the same as the carrying voyage, but may include a preliminary approach voyage, as in a charter "to proceed to a port and there load".[4] Terms in the charter as to the position of the vessel, the time of sailing, "estimated time of arrival", and "expected ready to load", may identify when the preliminary voyage must start.[5] Subject to such terms, the shipowner's first duty is to proceed to his port of loading with reasonable speed.[6] If the charter is for a definite voyage or adventure there may also be an obligation, which may be a condition,

---

[1] Some engagements of cargo space are, however, not binding contracts, being either too informal, or containing qualifications negating contractual intent, or both: e.g. *Heskell v Continental Express* (1950) 83 Ll.L.Rep. 438, 449, 452–453.

[2] See *Featherston v Wilkinson* (1873) L.R. 8 Ex. 122.

[3] Bigham J. in the unreported case of *Hecker v Cunard S.S. Co* in July 1898 held that such losses could not usually be recovered, but this may not lay down any general principle applicable in modern circumstances.

[4] See Brett L.J. in *Nelson v Dahl* (1879) 12 Ch.D. 568 at pp.581–584.

[5] As to which, see Art.50 above.

[6] This is often an express term and, if not, will be implied: *Fyffes Group v Reefer Express, the "Kriti Rex"* [1996] 2 Lloyd's Rep. 171 at 190–191. In the case of a charter for consecutive voyages the obligation to proceed to the first port of loading with reasonable dispatch applies to each of the voyages: *Anglo-Saxon Petroleum v Adamastos Shipping Co* [1957] 2 Q.B. 255 (reversed on other grounds [1959] A.C. 133).

to arrive in reasonable time,[7] and by a fixed day, if such be named in the charter.

The excepted perils in the charter apply to events during this preliminary voyage.[8] They do not ordinarily apply to earlier events.[9]

If it be unnecessary for the ship to proceed immediately to her loading port in order to get there by the date agreed, or the "expected ready" date, the owner commits no breach of contract by entering into an intermediate charter; but he runs the risk that perils of the seas encountered on the intermediate charter voyage will prevent him fulfilling his obligations under the original charter, and the exception clause in the latter will not ordinarily protect him, being inapplicable before the commencement of the preliminary voyage.

The port to which the ship is to proceed may be named in the charter, in which case the ship is bound to go there, the shipowner being usually protected by the clause "or as near as she can safely get"; or it may be left to the charterer to name, being "a port as ordered", or "to be nominated", the shipowner being sometimes protected by its description as a "safe port".[10] Where the charter provides that a ship is to load or discharge at a port "to be nominated", once the port has been effectively nominated, its status will be as if it had been written into the charter from the outset.[11] Frequently, charters contain an express provision entitling the charterer to revoke and replace a nomination.[12] Such a clause will be interpreted in the context of the charter, such that if the charter allows the charterer to send the vessel to three discharge ports, the clause will not enable the charterer to send the vessel to more than three effective discharge ports.[15]

Case 1. A ship was chartered on December 28, when lying at U, to proceed forthwith to X and there load, perils excepted "which may prevent the loading or delivery of the cargoes during the said voyage". Owing to delays caused by excepted perils, the ship did not reach X till July 28 and the charterers refused to load. The jury found that the delay did not defeat the commercial object of the adventure. *Held*, that "forthwith" meant without unreasonable delay[13]; that the exceptions in the charter applied to the preliminary voyage to the port of loading, and that the charterers were not justified in throwing up the charter.[14]

---

[7] *Jackson v Union Marine Insurance Co* (1874) L.R. 10 C.P. 125.

[8] *Barker v M'Andrew* (1865) 18 C.B.(N.S.) 759; *Hudson v Hill* (1874) 43 L.J.C.P. 273; *Minister of Materials v Wold S.S. Co* [1952] 1 Lloyd's Rep. 485 at pp.498–499. On the relation of excepted perils to implied undertakings, see Art.106, *Note* 5.

[9] Because they do not apply to events occurring before the ship begins the chartered service: see *Monroe Bros v Ryan* [1935] 2 K.B. 28: *Case 2*, below. See also *Dreyfus v Lauro* (1938) 60 Ll.L.R. 94; *Christie & Vesey v Helvetia* [1960] 1 Lloyd's Rep. 540 at p.547, per Pearson J.; *Transworld Oil Ltd v North Bay Shipping Corp (The Rio Claro)* [1987] 2 Lloyd's Rep. 137. In *Evera SA Commercial v North Shipping Co* [1956] 2 Lloyd's Rep. 367 reference to the intermediate charter voyage was made in the charter, but not sufficiently clearly to make the beginning of the chartered voyage contingent upon the conclusion of the previous one.

[10] See Art.69.

[11] *Reardon Smith Line v Ministry of Agriculture, Fisheries and Food* [1963] A.C. 691.

[12] *Bulk Shipping AG v I.P.C.O. Trading SA (The Jasmine B)* [1992] 2 Lloyd's Rep. 39.

[13] On the meaning of "forthwith", see also *Roberts v Brett* (1865) 11 H.L.C. 337. Cf. *Forest Oak S.S. Co v Richard* (1899) 5 Com.Cas. 100, where the words "to proceed immediately" were held to allow the ship to go to a coaling-port first.

[14] *Hudson v Hill*, above. The ship made her outward voyage by Rio, which ordinarily would be a breach entitling the charterer to throw up the charter (*M'Andrew v Adams* (1834) 1 Bing.N.C. 29) but was allowed by a special clause in the charter. The findings of the jury were contradictory and unsatisfactory, and, if the sugar season was over, it is difficult to reconcile some remarks of Brett J. with the present law. If the jury had found commercial frustration, the charterers could have thrown up the charter, but the shipowner would have been protected from an action by the exceptions.

Case 2. On August 2, A chartered the *R.* to C "expected ready to load about September 11" to proceed with all convenient speed to X and there load a cargo; there was an exception clause exempting A from liability for unavoidable accident or hindrances beyond A's control. On August 31, A chartered the *R.* to carry stone from P to F "expected ready to load P on or about September 6/7". Owing to prolonged gales the *R.* was unable to load at P until September 11 and in consequence could not commence loading at X before September 18. *Held*, A committed no breach of his charter with C by entering into the charter of August 31, but that the *R.* had not proceeded with all convenient speed to X, that the exception clause did not apply until the *R.* had begun her voyage to X, and that A was liable for extra expenses incurred by C owing to the delay.[15]

A68   **Article 68—Cancelling Clause**

A cancelling clause is a contractual right in the charter to cancel, irrespective whether the owner is in breach, if the vessel does not arrive ready to load by the cancelling date. The excepted perils do not apply to the cancelling clause.[16]

Where there is a cancelling clause and the ship cannot get to the port of loading by her cancelling date, she is yet bound to proceed, unless the delay by excepted perils is such as to put an end to the charter.[17] The shipowner cannot, when the cancelling date is past, call upon the charterer to declare whether he will load the vessel or not.[18] Where the charterer, having refused to declare what he would do, and the shipowner having refused to proceed, the charterer applied to the court for an injunction to restrain the shipowner from using the ship for any purposes other than those of the charter (i.e. in practice though not in form to compel the shipowner to proceed), the court refused his application, leaving him to his remedy in damages, if any.[19]

A charterer is not entitled to cancel (*semble* under the clause as distinct from any right he may have to rescind at common law) before the cancelling date even though it is clear that the owner will be unable to tender the ship in time.[20] But if the charterer gives notice of cancellation in such circumstances, and the owner accepts it without demur, this will amount to a cancellation by agreement.[20] In deciding whether the charterer is entitled to cancel under a cancelling clause, it is for the charterer to establish the right he claims.[21] He cannot cancel if in breach of contract he has nominated a port which the ship cannot reach by her cancelling date.[22]

---

[15] *Monroe v Ryan* [1935] 2 K.B. 28, distinguished in *Pinch & Simpson v Harrison Whitfield & Co* (1948) 81 Ll.L.R. 268, where Denning J. held that the charterers were entitled to rely upon an exception of frosts although these had set in before the charter voyage started. See also *Dreyfus v Lauro* (1938) 60 Ll.L.R. 94; *Evera SA Commercial v North Shipping Co* [1956] 2 Lloyd's Rep. 367.

[16] *Smith v Dart* (1884) 14 Q.B.D. 105.

[17] *Shubrick v Salmond* (1765) 3 Burrows 1637.

[18] So held in America in *The Progreso* (1872) 50 Fed. Rep. 835; and then in England in *Moel Tryvan (Owners) v Weir* [1910] 2 K.B. 844. See also *Thode v Gimeno* [1961] 2 Lloyd's Rep. 138. An express clause is sometimes inserted in a charter whereby the shipowner on arrival of the cancelling date can call upon the charterer to elect whether he will cancel or not: see *Bank Line v Capel* [1919] A.C. 435 and *Christie & Vesey v Helvetia* [1960] 1 Lloyd's Rep. 540.

[19] *Buckley v Tatem* (1900) 83 L.T. 121. The position may now be different if the ship is unique, or otherwise irreplaceable, such that damages will not be an adequate remedy: see *Lauritzencool v Lady Navigation* [2005] EWHC 2607 (Comm); [2005] 1 Lloyd's Rep. 260, approved at [2005] EWCA Civ 579; [2005] 2 Lloyd's Rep. 63, a time charter case.

[20] *Christie & Vesey v Helvetia* [1960] 1 Lloyd's Rep. 540; *The Madeleine* [1967] 2 Lloyd's Rep. 224; *The Mihalis Angelos* [1971] 1 Q.B. 164 (CA). The owner's damages claim will, however, be affected, and may be rendered nominal, by the fact that the right to cancel would have accrued and been exercised.

[21] *Noemijulia S.S. Co v Minister of Food* [1951] 1 K.B. 223 at p.228; *The Madeleine* [1967] 2 Lloyd's Rep. 224 at p.237.

[22] *Shipping Corp of India v Naviera Letasa SA* [1976] 1 Lloyd's Rep. 132.

A cancelling clause in a consecutive voyage charter may, according to the words used, have the effect (if the option given be exercised) of cancelling the whole charter and not merely one of the voyages under it.[23]

The exercise by the charterer of his right to cancel does not necessarily debar him from asserting a claim for damages against the shipowner for failure to send the ship to load.[24]

The charterer may lose his right to cancel if not exercised in time. If the time for cancelling is not specified, it will probably be a reasonable time.[25]

Article 69—"To proceed to a safe Port"   A69

Where a charter, whether for voyage or time, expressly provides that a ship shall go to a safe port or berth to be nominated or ordered by the charterer, the charterer is obliged so to nominate or order, and in so doing, warrants that the port or berth is safe.[26]

Where the charter names the port or berth, and also uses the word "safe" to describe the port or berth, it will generally be interpreted as a warranty by the charterer that the named port or berth is safe.[27]

If the charter provides for the nomination of a port or berth, but is silent as to its safety, a warranty that the port or berth is safe will probably be implied, but this is not invariable and may depend on the specific terms of the charter.[28]

If the charter provides for the ship to go to a named port or berth, or to one or more as ordered out of a number of named ports or berths, but contains no provision as to safety, the charterer will probably not be under any obligation as to the safety thereof.[29] It is frequently said that the charterer will nevertheless be

---

[23] *Ambatielos v Grace Brothers* (1922) 12 Ll.L.R. 227 (HL).

[24] *Nelson v Dundee East Coast S.S. Co*, 1907 S.C. 927; *Marbienes Comp. Naviera v Ferrostaal (The Democritos)* [1976] 2 Lloyd's Rep. 149.

[25] See e.g. *Moel Tryvan v Weir* [1910] 2 K.B. 844.

[26] *Kodros Shipping Corp of Monrovia v Empreso Cubana De Fletes (The Evia)* [1983] 1 A.C. 736 (HL): [1982] 2 Lloyd's Rep. 307. *Compania Naviera Maropan v Bowaters* [1955] 2 Q.B. 68 (CA); *Reardon Smith Line v Australian Wheat Board* [1956] A.C. 266 (PC); *Leeds Shipping Co v Société Française Bunge* [1958] 2 Lloyd's Rep. 127 (CA) (voyage charters) and *Grace v General S.N. Co* [1950] 2 K.B. 383 (time charter), following *Limerick v Stott* [1921] 1 K.B. 568 and Greer L.J. in *Lensen S.S. Co v Anglo-Soviet* (1935) 40 Com.Cas. 320 at p 329.

[27] *AIC Ltd v Marine Pilot (The Archimidis)* [2008] EWCA Civ 175; *Ullises Shipping v Fal Shipping (the Greek Fighter)* [2006] EWHC 1729 (Comm) paras 312–313; *STX Pan Ocean v Ugland (The Livanita)* [2007] EWHC 1317 (Comm) paras 17–22. In the *Livanita* the Judge declined to answer the related questions whether an owner could rely on a safe port warranty if the port was named and he knew, at the date of the charterparty, that the port was unsafe, or if the unsafety was reasonably predictable and expected.

[28] *Aegean Sea v Repsol, the "Aegean Sea"* [1998] 2 Lloyd's Rep. 39 at 67–68, commenting obiter on inter alia Art.69 of the 20th edn of this work. The point has not been decided but the balance of opinion in the cases supports the implication: see *Reardon Smith Line v Ministry of Agriculture* [1960] 1 Q.B. 439 at p.488, per Wightman J. in *Ogden v Graham* (1861) 1 B. & S. 773 at p.779, and per Roche J. in *Brostrom v Dreyfus* (1932) 38 Com.Cas. 79 at p.85, cited with apparent approval by Morris L.J. in *Compania Naviera Maropan v Bowaters* [1955] 2 Q.B. 68 at p.105; Cooke *et al*, *Voyage Charters*, 3rd edn (2007), paras 5.37–5.38. The alternative view is that the only limitation in such circumstances on the charterer's freedom of choice is not to nominate an "impossible" port: see per Willmer L.J. in *Reardon Smith Line v Ministry of Agriculture* [1962] 1 Q.B. 42 at pp.109, 110; *the "Aegean Sea"* [1998] 2 Lloyd's Rep. 39 at 67.

[29] See per Dixon C.J. obiter in the High Court of Australia in *Reardon Smith Line v Australian Wheat Board (the "Houston City")* [1954] 2 Lloyd's Rep. 148 at p.153, a dissenting judgment generally approved by the PC *ibid*. In *The A.P.J. Priti* [1987] 2 Lloyd's Rep. 37 no such warranty was implied, although there were other indications in the charter that the shipowner had taken the risk of proceeding to the port in question.

under an implied obligation not to nominate an impossible port.[30] However, this will depend both on the terms of the charter and the nature of the impossibility. Where the nature of the impossibility results from the inherent inability of the ship safely to enter one of the ports, then in the absence of the word "safe", the shipowner may be held to have taken upon himself the task of ascertaining that his ship is capable of entering all the alternative ports.[31] Further, whilst the charterer may be under an obligation not to nominate a port which has become impossible after the contract was concluded, this restriction on the charterer's right of selection is less likely to be implied when the impossibility existed at the date of the contract.

Where the safety of the berth is warranted, but not the safety of the port, then the charterer's obligation is to nominate a berth which can be approached safely from within the port and which was itself safe, save insofar as affected by hazards or risks which affect the port as a whole or all of the berths within it.[32]

The charterer's obligations regarding the safety of the port are related primarily to the moment when the order is given.[33] Presumably, where there is a warranty, and the port is named in the charter, the obligations relate to the date of the charter. At that moment the port must be prospectively safe, i.e. its characteristics, both permanent[34] and temporary, must be such that in the absence of some unexpected[35] and[36] abnormal event[37] it will be safe for the ship at the time when she actually arrives there.[38]

If the charterer complies with this primary obligation by nominating a safe port, he may (at least under a period time charter) have the right, and come under

---

[30] See per Dixon C.J. obiter, *Reardon Smith Line v Australian Wheat Board* [1954] 2 Lloyd's Rep. 148 at p.153; the CA in *Compania Naviera Maropan v Bowaters* [1955] 2 Q.B. 68 and in *Stag Line v Ellerman and Papayanni* (1949) 82 Ll.L.R. 826 at p.831. See also *Eurico SpA v Philipp Bros (The Epaphus)* [1986] 2 Lloyd's Rep. 387 at p.391; [1987] 2 Lloyd's Rep. 215. See also above, fn.28

[31] *The Epaphus* [1986] 2 Lloyd's Rep. 387 at p.392; [1987] 2 Lloyd's Rep. 215. It is submitted that whilst this will be the position where the charter identifies the alternative ports or makes it clear that the vessel must be able to enter every port in the range, this will not necessarily be the position where the charter merely specifies a loading or discharge range from which one port is to be chosen.

[32] *Atkins International H.A. v Islamic Republic of Iran Shipping Lines (The A.P.J. Priti)* [1987] 2 Lloyd's Rep. 37; *Ullises Shipping v Fal Shipping (The Greek Fighter)* [2006] EWHC 1729 (Comm) paras 320–323.

[33] The propositions in the following three paragraphs of the text are based on the leading speech of Lord Roskill in *The Evia*, above, with which all the other members of the House agreed.

[34] The expression "inherently" safe and unsafe is used more than once in *The Evia*. It is believed that this word is not an essential part of the doctrine there laid down, but merely describes a port which by its geographical or other features always tends to expose a vessel to risk (although it may be noted that in *Reardon Smith Line v Australian Wheat Board*, above, which is cited as an illustration of an inherently unsafe port, the defect in the mooring facilities was only temporary). Quite plainly, on the cases, a port may be unsafe by reason of matters which do not amount to a permanent attribute of the port.

[35] The word "unexpected" cannot, we suggest, be understood as directing attention solely to the question whether the charterer actually expected the event to occur which made the port unsafe. If he did expect it, then he was in breach of duty. But even if he did not, he ought to be held liable if a reasonable person in his position would have expected the occurrence.

[36] The requirements that the event shall be unexpected and abnormal are cumulative. An event may be highly abnormal, and yet, if in the special circumstances it is to be expected, the charterer will be in breach if he does not give a fresh order; see, e.g. *Uni-Ocean Lines v C-Trade (The Lucille)* [1983] 1 Lloyd's Rep. 387, affirmed [1984] 1 Lloyd's Rep. 244.

[37] Until the decision in *The Evia*, above, the reference to an abnormal occurrence in the passage from the judgment of Sellers L.J. in *Leeds Shipping Co v Société Française Bunge*, above, p.131 had been widely understood as conveying that the normality or otherwise of the event was an essential element in deciding whether the port is unsafe. In the light of the statement of the law by the House of Lords, the importance of this factor is much reduced, if not entirely eliminated, for reasons given in *The Lucille*, above, at p.394.

[38] *The Evia*, above, at p.757.

a further obligation, to nominate another port, if the port first nominated thereafter becomes unsafe as the result of a supervening event. In such a case, the charterer must withdraw the original nomination, and substitute an order to a safe port. This secondary obligation subsists throughout the voyage to the port, and whilst the ship is at the port, whether loading or discharging has been completed or not: always provided, however, that it is still possible for the ship to avoid the new danger by leaving the port. If the new danger cannot be avoided, so that another port cannot effectively be nominated, the charterer will not be liable if the danger causes the ship to suffer damage whilst in the port.

It has not yet been decided whether the charterer's secondary right and obligation to nominate a fresh port if the original choice becomes unsafe applies where the contract in question is a voyage charter or a time charter for a defined trip. The better view is not.[39]

The requirement that the port shall be prospectively safe when the order is given does not entail that the port must be safe at that particular moment, merely that it will be safe on arrival, subject to unexpected or abnormal occurrences. Thus, if the port is unsafe when the order is given, but in all human probability[40] the obstacle will be removed before the ship arrives, the charterer is not placed in breach of duty if an unexpected event prevents the port from being made safe, although he may then be under the secondary obligation to make a fresh nomination.

Whether a port is a "safe port" is in each case a question of fact and degree[41] and must be determined with reference to the particular ship concerned,[42] assuming that she is properly manned and equipped and navigated and handled without negligence and in accordance with good seamanship.[43]

---

[39] The point was expressly left open in *The Evia, ibid.* p.765. A general right or obligation to change the port is difficult to fit into a charter for a defined voyage or trip from and to a particular named port or ports and difficult to reconcile with the rule that where a port is nominated it is treated as if written into the charter, particularly in those cases where there is no express liberty to change ports (such as a clause qualifying the port by "or so near thereto as she may safely get"). The rule in the *Evia* can be justified in the case of a period time charter because the charterer's employment of the ship is not defined in relation to any particular voyage(s) or trip(s). There is another and different problem, namely the effect on third parties when the charterer performs his secondary obligation to name an alternative safe port. For example, the shipowner may have issued bills of lading for carriage to the nominated port. The charterer may have sub-chartered for a voyage to that port. The House of Lords envisaged that this could be dealt with by the use of suitable words in the contract with the third party (*ibid.* p.766). No doubt this solution is practicable as regards the charterer's contracts (although no form of sub-charter or bill of lading in common use contains such a provision), but it is not so easy to see what words could be devised to protect the shipowner when the right and duty to renominate is not in his hands. Perhaps the answer is that compliance with a proper renomination would be a reasonable deviation under the bills of lading.

[40] This is the test prescribed by *The Evia: ibid.* p.757. It requires a high degree of probability that the risk will in due course be eliminated, before the nomination can be regarded as valid.

[41] *Palace Co v Gans Line* [1916] 1 K.B. 138; *Bornholm (Owners) v. Exporthleb* (1937) 58 Ll.L.R. 59. If the vessel has to dismantle her masts in order to reach the port (*Goodbody and Balfour, Re* (1899) 5 Com.Cas. 59), or to cut her mast to get out when light (*Limerick S.S. Co v Stott* [1921] 1 K.B. 568 at p.575), it is not "safe".

[42] e.g. absence of tugs necessary to enable a vessel of a particular length to enter a port may make the port unsafe: *Brostrom v Dreyfus* (1932) 38 Com.Cas. 79. See also *Palm Shipping Inc v Vitol SA (The Universal Monarch)* [1988] 2 Lloyd's Rep. 483.

[43] *Leeds Shipping Co v Société Française Bunge* [1958] 2 Lloyd's Rep. 127 (CA); *The Dagmar* [1968] 2 Lloyd's Rep. 566; *G.W. Grace v General Steam Navigation Co* [1950] 2 K.B. 383; *Kristiansands Tankrederei v Standard Tankers (Bahamas) (The Polyglory)* [1977] 2 Lloyd's Rep. 353. If the port cannot safely be negotiated without the exercise of more than ordinary prudence and skill, it is not safe: *The Polyglory*, above.

As a broad statement of the law a port will not be safe unless in the relevant period of time, the particular ship can reach it, use it[44] and return from it without, in the absence of some abnormal occurrence, being exposed to danger which cannot be avoided by good navigation and seamanship.[45] A port which would otherwise be unsafe may become a safe port if the charterer gives the owner sufficient warning of the dangers of the port to enable the vessel to avoid them.[46] The absence of a proper system of weather forecasts, navigational aids, and so forth, which if present would enable a ship to use the port without danger, may render the port unsafe.[47]

A port will be unsafe if, apart from natural and physical causes, there is danger to ship and cargo in proceeding to and entering and using the port from political causes.[48] However a political risk will normally only be sufficient to render a port prospectively unsafe if the risk is such that a reasonable master or shipowner would decline to send his vessel there.[49]

The shipowner may be entitled to recover for breach of the charterer's undertaking to nominate a safe port even if the ship suffers no physical damage: for example if it suffers delay through some obstacle to safe entry or departure.[50]

However, a temporary danger or obstacle, such as neap tides,[51] will not render a port unsafe; to do so the danger or obstacle must be operative for a period which, having regard to the nature of the adventure and of the contract, would be sufficient to frustrate the commercial object of the adventure.[52] Even a delay of sufficient length will not in itself be a breach, but will merely evidence a breach of the charterer's promise at the time of nomination.[53]

---

[44] A port will not necessarily be unsafe if a ship has to leave it in certain states of the weather (see *Leeds Shipping Co v Société Française Bunge*, above, at p.131, commenting on the statement of Morris L.J. in *Compania Naviera Maropan v Bowaters* [1955] 1 Q.B. 68 at p.105; *The Dagmar*, above; *Islander Shipping Enterprises SA v Empresa Maritima del Estado SA (The Khian Sea)* [1979] 1 Lloyd's Rep. 545); or, *semble*, tides: see *Carlton S.S. Co v Castle Mail Co* [1898] A.C. 486. See also Art.72, below.

[45] *Leeds Shipping Co v Société Française Bunge*, above, at p.131, approved in *The Evia*, above, at p.760.

[46] *The Dagmar*, above, (weather forecasts).

[47] *The Dagmar*, above; *Islander Shipping Enterprises v Empresa Maritima Delesiato (The Khian Sea)* [1979] 1 Lloyd's Rep. 545. These cases were explained in *The Evia*, above, at p.763, as being concerned with ports where there was no proper system. It is not clear what the position would be if the charterer nominated a port where the system was proper but where it broke down through isolated human error. Consistently with the reasoning in *The Evia*, it would seem that the charterer is not liable in such a case.

[48] *The Teutonia* (1872) L.R. 4 P.C. 171 at pp.181, 182: *Ogden v Graham* (1861) 1 B. & S. 773; *Palace Co v Gans Line* [1916] 1 K.B. 138. This was assumed to be the law in *Vardinoyannis v The Egyptian General Petroleum Corp (The Evaggelos Th)* [1971] 2 Lloyd's Rep. 200, and *The Lucille*, above.

[49] *K/S Penta Shipping A/S v Ethiopian Shipping Lines Corp (The Saga Cob)* [1992] 2 Lloyd's Rep. 545, CA. See also *Pearl Carriers Inc v Japan Lines Ltd (The Chemical Venture)* [1993] 1 Lloyd's Rep. 508.

[50] This was assumed in *Unitramp v Garnac Grain Co (The Hermine)* [1979] 1 Lloyd's Rep. 212, and *The Lucille*, above.

[51] *Aktieselskabet Eriksen v Foy, Morgan & Co* (1926) 25 Ll.L.R. 442. See also *Carlton S.S. Co v Castle Mail Co* [1898] A.C. 486, and Art.70, below.

[52] *The Hermine*, above, as explained in *The Evia*, above, at p.762; *Independent Petroleum v Seacarriers (The Count)* [2006] EWHC 3222 (Comm); [2007] Lloyd's Law Reports Plus 60.

[53] *The Hermine*, above, and *The Evia*, above. This doctrine gives rise to problems. We believe the correct understanding to be that in this, as in other situations, the parties must ask themselves at the time of the order, whether the port is prospectively safe, i.e. whether it is likely (if "likely" is the right standard) that the ship will be able to use the port without a delay sufficient to frustrate the adventure. If a reasonable person would answer in the affirmative, the fact that the delay unexpectedly proves to be prolonged, does not render the charterer liable. Nevertheless, the delay actually experienced is one of the items of evidence, in the light of which, with hindsight, the court will decide whether the port was prospectively safe.

Dangers likely to be incurred on the voyage to the port, or in the course of leaving it, may affect its safety[54] and a port is not necessarily safe because at the moment when the vessel gets to it, and in the weather then prevailing, she can get into it with safety.[55]

The dangers which render a port unsafe need not necessarily be in close proximity to the working area of the port. If the only means by which the vessel can reach or leave the port are subject to hazards, the port will be unsafe even if the hazards are a considerable distance away.[56]

If an unsafe berth or port is nominated, the ship can refuse to obey the order.[57] If the ship complies with the order, the shipowner will, in the absence of a waiver or estoppel, be entitled to recover in respect of damage suffered by the ship through the reasonable compliance of the master with the order, but the ordinary rules as to remoteness, causation and mitigation apply to the damages recoverable.[58]

Where a ship is ordered to an unsafe port and the master acts negligently in entering or remaining in the port, the charterer will be free from liability if, but only if, the negligence is sufficiently serious to sever the causal connection between the order and the damage to the vessel.[59]

Case 1. A German vessel was chartered to proceed to Y, "where she shall receive orders from charterer's agent within three days of arrival to proceed to any one safe port in Great Britain or on the Continent between Havre and Hamburg"; at Y the ship was ordered to Dunkirk, then a safe port; before reaching Dunkirk war broke out between France and Germany, rendering it unsafe for the ship to enter Dunkirk; she therefore proceeded to Dover. *Held* (i) there was no breach in ordering the ship to Dunkirk, (ii) the shipowners were entitled at Dover to exercise their lien for freight.[60]

Case 2. A ship under time charter providing that she was to be employed only between good and safe ports was ordered to Hamburg. At the time of the order and during the voyage to and from Hamburg the weather was exceptionally cold and a great deal of ice formed in the Elbe. The ship was damaged by ice-blocks on the way to and from Hamburg. The master acted reasonably and as an intelligent observer would have expected. *Held* (1) Hamburg was not a safe port since an ordinarily prudent and careful master could not reach it and leave it in safety; (2) the charterers were in breach of the time charter in ordering the ship to Hamburg; (3) the act of the master in proceeding to and

---

[54] *Palace Co v Gans Line* [1916] 1 K.B. 138 (risk of torpedo); *Grace v General Steam Navigation Co* [1950] 2 K.B. 383 (ice in the Elbe on way to Hamburg).

[55] *Johnston v Saxon Queen Co* (1913) 108 L.T. 564; *The Polyglory*, above.

[56] See the cases cited in *Transoceanic Carriers v Cook Industries (The Mary Lou)* [1981] 2 Lloyd's Rep. 272, at pp.280–281 (the point did not arise in *The Evia*, which overruled *The Mary Lou* on other grounds). On the other hand the undertaking of safety does not entail that every spot in the port must be safe: see *Mediolanum Shipping Co v Japan Lines* [1984] 1 Lloyd's Rep. 136.

[57] See the cases cited in fn.26, above, and *Ogden v Graham* (1861) 1 B. & S. 773 (politically unsafe); *The Alhambra* (1881) 6 P.D. 68 (insufficient water); *West v Wrights (Colchester)*; (1935) 40 Com.Cas. 186 (unsafe berth).

[58] See fn.26, above. See also *Motor Oil Hellas (Corinth) Refineries SA v Shipping Corp of India (The Kanchenjunga)* [1987] 2 Lloyd's Rep. 509; [1989] 1 Lloyd's Rep. 354; [1990] 1 Lloyd's Rep. 391.

[59] This is the position established by the cases cited, above, including in particular *Leeds Shipping Co v Société Française Bunge*, above, and *Cia Naviera Maropan v Bowaters* [1955] 2 Q.B. 68. In the United States the more equitable rule prevails that liability can be divided between the parties according to the degree of fault (see *Ore Carriers of Liberia v Navigem Company* [1971] A.M.C. 513), but this result does not appear to be open in England on the cases as they stand at present.

[60] *The Teutonia* (1872) L.R. 4 P.C. 171. See the discussion of the *ratio decidendi* of this difficult case in *Reardon Smith Line v Ministry of Agriculture* [1962] 1 Q.B. 42 (CA) and the *Note* following Art.66 in the 18th edn.

from Hamburg was no *novus actus interveniens*; (4) the charterers were liable for the damage to the ship.[61]

Case 3. Ship time chartered. Clause 2 provided that she was to be employed between good and safe ports. She was ordered in March 1980 to load a cargo of cement in Cuba for carriage to Basrah on the west bank of the Shatt-al-Arab waterway. She berthed on August 20, and completed discharge on September 22. As a result of war between Iran and Iraq breaking out after August 20, the port became unsafe during discharge in that no ship was able from sometime before September 22, onwards to escape. *Held*, by the House of Lords, that as Basrah was at the time of the order prospectively safe for the ship to go there, discharge and leave the port, and that her departure was prevented by unexpected and abnormal events that had suddenly occurred after the arrival, there had been no breach by the charterers of clause 2.[62]

A70   Article 70—"To proceed to a Port as ordered"

If a charterparty provides for a ship to proceed to a port as ordered, it is the obligation of the charterer to furnish the requisite orders within whatever time may be specified, or if no time be specified, within a reasonable time. If the charterer fails to give orders within the appropriate time, the ship must await those orders until the delay becomes such as to frustrate the voyage. Unless and until frustration occurs the master is not entitled to proceed to some port of his own choice.[63]

If the ship is to proceed to a port of call for orders as to a port of discharge and if at the port of call the charterer will only name a port which is impossible of access, he commits a breach of contract, and the shipowner, on discharging the goods at the port of call, if that is a reasonable place for such discharge, can claim freight under a *quantum meruit*,[64] and also damages for any detention of the ship at the port of call due to the charterer's refusal to nominate a proper port.[64] But this principle will apply only if the port is impossible or at least subject to such delay as will frustrate the commercial object of the adventure. The charterer is not obliged to consider the owner's convenience when selecting the port.[65]

If the charterer orders the vessel to a port falling outside the charterparty range, such an order has been said itself to be a breach of contract. If the shipowner complies with the order in circumstances in which there is no waiver of his right to damages, he can recover damages for this breach of contract. Alternatively, the shipowner may claim a *quantum meruit* for the extra-contractual service he has provided.[66]

---

[61] *Grace v General S.N. Co* [1950] 2 K.B. 383. See also *Compania Naviera Maropan v Bowaters* [1955] 2 Q.B. 68; *Reardon Smith Line v Australian Wheat Board* [1956] A.C. 266 (PC); *Leeds Shipping Co v Société Française Bunge* [1958] 2 Lloyd's Rep. 127 (CA).

[62] *The Evia*, above.

[63] *The Timna* [1970] 2 Lloyd's Rep. 409, explaining *Sieveking v Maas* (1856) 6 E. & B. 670 and *Proctor, Garratt, Marston v Oakwin S.S. Co* [1926] 1 K.B. 244. The point was not discussed on appeal [1971] 2 Lloyd's Rep. 91.

[64] *Aktieselskabet Olivebank v Dansk Fabrik* [1919] 2 K.B. 162. In the above case the shipowner was apparently held entitled to recover the whole charterparty freight upon his quantum meruit.

[65] *Dobell v Green* [1900] 1 Q.B. 526; *Bulman v Fenwick* [1894] 1 Q.B. 179; *Reardon Smith Line v Minister of Agriculture* [1962] 1 Q.B. 42.

[66] *Batis Maritime Corp v Petroleos del Mediterraneo SA (The Batis)* [1990] 1 Lloyd's Rep. 345. There are dicta of Lord Mustill in *Torvald Klaveness v Arni (The Gregos)* [1995] 1 Lloyd's Rep. 1 at 9 which make it unclear whether the giving of an invalid order will itself always be a breach of contract.

The charterer may be entitled to order, and the owner obliged to obey an order, that the vessel should not proceed to berth, even if that would put the charterer in breach of his other obligations under the charterparty, such as to load the cargo within the laytime.[67]

Note. The question of giving notice to charterers and waiting at a port of call for orders is, in practice, generally regulated by special stipulations in the charterparty. For instance: "Orders as to port of discharge are to be given to the Master within twenty-four hours after receipt by consignees of Master's telegraphic report to consignees . . . of his arrival at the port of call and for any detention waiting for orders after the aforesaid twenty-four hours, the Charterers or their agents shall pay the steamer thirty shillings sterling per hour."[68] For an alternative form of clause, see *Case 2*, below.

Case 1. A ship was chartered to proceed to X, and there load timber "to a coal port or a good and safe port on the Firth of Forth, or to London, or to a good and safe port on the East Coast of Great Britain as ordered at Y". She loaded at X and proceeded to Y for orders; she received no orders there, so, after waiting a reasonable time, proceeded to Leith, "a good and safe port on the Firth of Forth", and there discharged. *Held*, that in the absence of orders the master was justified in proceeding after a reasonable time, and was not bound to communicate with the charterer; that in such a case he should [might?] go to the place to which he thought it would be most to the advantage of the charterer to go.[69]

Case 2. A clause provided that the master was to telegraph for orders as to the loading port on arrival at the port of outward discharge and that if orders were not received before the completion of discharge the vessel should proceed to X for orders. *Held*, that an application for orders by the master was a condition precedent to the charterers' obligation to wait until the vessel arrived at X before nominating the loading port, and that in the absence of any such application the charterers were entitled to exercise their common law right to give orders within a reasonable time.[70]

Article 71—"So near thereto as she can safely get"   A71

A ship chartered to load or unload a named port or dock or berth, "or so near as she can safely get", if prevented on her arrival from reaching the place of loading or unloading, is bound to wait a reasonable time before adopting the alternative place of loading or discharge, if by so waiting she can get to the port or dock or berth named for loading or unloading.[71]

This reasonable time will be fixed by commercial considerations, and by the nature of the voyage in which the ship is engaged.[72] The interests of both parties have to be considered in determining what, from a commercial point of view,

---

[67] *Novorossisk Shipping v Neopetro (The Ulyanovsk)* [1990] 1 Lloyd's Rep. 425, doubted in part in *Total v Arcadia (The Eurus)* [1998] 1 Lloyd's Rep. 351, 355.

[68] As to the effect of this clause, see *Proctor, Garratt, Marston v Oakwin S.S. Co* [1926] 1 K.B. 244, and *Ethel Radcliffe S.S. Co v Barnett* (1926) 31 Com.Cas. 222.

[69] *Sieveking v Maas*, above. Lord Campbell's remarks in this case seem inconsistent with *Rae v Hackett*, above, where charterer's failure to name a port was held to justify the shipowners in proceeding; but there the port to be named was the port of loading—in this case the port of discharging, and all it was necessary to decide was that the shipowner was not liable to an action for proceeding without orders. We have, however, altered Lord Campbell's "should" to "might" to cover the two cases.

[70] *Thode v Gimeno* [1961] 2 Lloyd's Rep. 138 (CA).

[71] *Dahl v Nelson* (1881) 6 App.Cas. 38, and *The Varing* [1931] P. 79.

[72] per Lord Blackburn (1881) 6 App.Cas. 38 at p.54: "What would be the effect on the object of the contract, and the damage to each party caused by the delay?" Per Brett L.J. (1879) 12 Ch.D. 568 at p.593: "Notice must be taken of what the particular adventure in each case is." See also *Reardon Smith Line v Ministry of Agriculture* [1962] 1 Q.B. 42 at pp.87, 113. The time will certainly be unreasonable if the delay is such as to frustrate the adventure.

would be reasonable.[73] Thus in tidal rivers or harbours she is usually bound to wait till ordinary spring tides[74]; in icebound rivers or seas till the ice melts[75]; in case of delay by congestion in docks, a time reasonable from a commercial point of view. The obstacle preventing her from reaching the named port, dock or berth need not be physical.[76]

If a blockade intervenes, *semble* the shipowner will not be entitled to deliver at another port, even if this is a reasonable course to take, and so become entitled to freight, at any rate in the absence of proof that such port is as near to the named port as the ship can safely get.[77]

If the clause applies it gives liberty to go to another sufficiently near place, which may include a different port. The test whether the ship has reached a place sufficiently near to come within the protection of the phrase is whether she is within an area or zone or within a range of proximity not beyond the reasonable contemplation of the parties as fair and reasonable men.[78]

Case 1. A ship was chartered to proceed "to the Z Docks, or so near thereto as she can safely get". She reached the dock gates on August 4; but the docks were quite full, though application had been made on the ship's behalf on July 16, and at least five weeks would elapse before the ship could be discharged. *Held*, that the shipowner was bound to wait a reasonable time to go into the docks, but that if he could only go in by waiting an unreasonable time, he was entitled to call upon the charterer to take delivery outside the dock gates at charterer's expense. *Held*, also, that the delay required to enter the docks in this case was unreasonable.[79]

Case 2. A ship was chartered to proceed to a berth within certain limits in the port of Plymouth, or "as near as she could safely get". She could not at neap tides get to the berth named, but could at spring tides. She arrived at neap tides. *Held*, that she must wait till spring tides; the delay by tides in a tidal harbour being in the ordinary and regular course of navigation.[80]

---

[73] *Athamas (Owners) v. Dig Vijay Cement Co* [1962] 2 Lloyd's Rep. 120.

[74] *Parker v Winlow* (1857) 7 E. & B. 942; *Bastifell v Lloyd* (1862) 1 H. & C. 388; *Schilizzi v Derry* (1855) 4 E. & B. 873. *Cf. The Curfew* [1891] P. 131. It apparently will not alter the case if the low tides occur in the middle of the ship's loading time, so that she has to go away and return to complete her loading: *Carlton S.S. Co v Castle Mail Co* [1898] A.C. 486.

[75] *Schilizzi v Derry* (1855) 4 E. & B. 873 at p.886; *Metcalfe v Britannia Iron Works* (1877) 2 Q.B.D. 423; and see *Nelson v Dahl* (1879) 12 Ch.D. 568, per Brett L.J. at p.593. *Sed quaere*; see fn.8, below and *Grace v General S.N. Co* [1950] 2 K.B. 383.

[76] *Dahl v Nelson* (1881) 6 App.Cas. 38. See *Reardon Smith Line v Ministry of Agriculture* [1962] 1 Q.B. 42 at pp.87, 113.

[77] *Castel & Latta v Trechman* (1884) C. & E. 276; the report is unsatisfactory; it does not show whether Constantinople was the nearest safe port. The decision may be doubted. *Cf. St. Enoch Co v Phosphate Co* [1916] 2 K.B. 624. But this is now frequently provided for by express clauses. See *Nobel's Explosives v Jenkins* [1896] 2 Q.B. 326, and Art.68, above. But if there is no prospect of the removal of the obstacle within a reasonable time, the master or shipowner may throw up the contract: *Geipel v Smith* (1872) L.R. 7 Q.B. 404. In that case he will still have the duty of providing for the cargo in the way most beneficial to its owner (see Arts 123, 129), and he will be entitled to recover any expenses incurred in so doing: *Cargo ex Argos* (1873) L.R. 5 P.C. 134, and Arts 129, 163, below. As to the possibility of a claim by the shipowner against the charterer rather than the cargo owner see *Adelfamar SA v Silos E. Mangimi Martini SpA (The Adelfa)* [1988] 2 Lloyd's Rep. 466.

[78] *Athamas (Owners) v. Dig Vijay Cement Co* [1963] 1 Lloyd's Rep. 287 (CA), *Case 5*, below. Mere mileage is not the test (*ibid.*). What is the nearest safe port must be a question of fact in each case: *East Asiatic Co v Tronto Co* (1915) 31 T.L.R. 543. It does not, of course, follow that the nearest safe port, though possibly the most convenient to the shipowner, is the port most beneficial to the cargo-owner. The master must act reasonably in his selection, having regard to the consignees' convenience as well as the ship's: *Renton v Palmyra* [1957] A.C. 149 at pp.173–174.

[79] *Dahl v Nelson* (1881) 6 App.Cas. 38; *The Varing* [1931] P. 79.

[80] *Parker v Winlow* (1857) 7 E. & B. 942: *Aktieselskabet Eriksen v Foy, Morgan & Co* (1926) 25 Ll.L.R. 442. See also *Bastifell v Lloyd* (1862) 1 H. & C. 388. Per Bramwell B. at p.395, "it would be different if there were only one or two tides in the year".

Case 3. Ship chartered, "to Galatz, or so near thereto as she should safely get". She reached the mouth of the Danube, ninety-five mile from G., on November 5, but there was not then enough water to enable her to cross the bar; she remained there till December 11, when the anchorage was no longer safe, and she accordingly proceeded to Odessa, the nearest safe port. There was water enough on the bar on January 7. *Held*, there had been no performance of the charter; the rising of the Danube at the beginning of the year being a well-known incident in Danube navigation, the master was bound to wait.[81]

Case 4. Charter "to Taganrog, or so near as she could safely get and deliver the cargo afloat". On arriving at Kertch, three hundred miles by sea, seven hundred by land, from T., the ship was prevented by ice from entering the Sea of Azof. She claimed under the clause to deliver at Kertch. *Held*, this was not a delivery under the charter, the obstruction being only temporary, and such as must be incident in every voyage to a frozen sea.[82]

Case 5. Charter to "Saigon, always afloat, where the vessel is to discharge part cargo such quantity to be . . . sufficient to enable the vessel thereafter to proceed safely to and to enter and discharge the balance of the cargo at one safe place, always afloat, Pnom-Penh, or so near thereto as she may safely get". The ship discharged a part cargo at Saigon, but the Pilotage Authority refused to take her to Pnom-Penh, on the ground that the depth of water was insufficient to enable the lightly laden ship to navigate the river in safety. The ship accordingly discharged the balance of her cargo at Saigon. The distance between Saigon and Pnom-Penh by water is 250 miles. The ship would have had to wait five months before the depth of water was sufficient to allow her to proceed to Pnom-Penh. *Held*, the shipowners were entitled to discharge the whole of the cargo at Saigon and to recover the full freight for two-port discharge.[83]

Note 1. The question of the disposition of the cargo on bills of lading or charters where the vessel is prevented from reaching her port of destination, is often dealt with by clauses of this kind: "In case of the blockade[84] or interdict of the port of destination, or if without such blockade or interdict the entering of the port of discharge should be considered unsafe by reason of war, infectious disorder, quarantine disturbances, ice, or from any other cause,[85] the master to have the option of landing the goods at any other port[86] he may consider safe, at shipper's risk and expense, when the ship's responsibility shall cease"; or: "when the navigation of the continental ports is obstructed by ice,[87] the goods to be landed at the nearest available port at the risk and expense of the consignor, such delivery being considered final"; or: "should hostilities render it unsafe for the steamer or her cargo to proceed to the port of destination, she has liberty to discharge her cargo at any near available port, and there end her voyage, giving shippers due notice of such fact".

---

[81] *Schilizzi v Derry* (1855) 4 E. & B. 873. Lord Campbell, p.886, compared detention by insufficient water to detention by ice. But his statement that the vessel was bound to get within the ambit of the port before discharging at a substituted place was queried by Lord Blackburn in *Dahl v Nelson* (1881) 6 A.C. 38 at p.51. On the latter case see *Athamas (Owners) v. Dig Vijay Cement Co* [1963] 1 Lloyd's Rep. 287.

[82] *Metcalfe v Britannia Iron Works* (1877) 2 Q.B.D. 423 (CA). It is doubtful whether the conclusion of fact here would now be arrived at. See also *Grace v General S.N. Co* [1950] 2 K.B. 383.

[83] *Athamas (Owners) v. Dig Vijay Cement Co* [1963] 1 Lloyd's Rep. 287 (CA).

[84] See the meaning of the word discussed in *Government of Republic of Spain v North of England S.S. Co* (1938) 61 Ll.L.R. 44 at p.57.

[85] To which phrase the doctrine of *ejusdem generis* must be applied.

[86] For the meaning of "neighbouring safe and convenient port" in such a clause see *Associated Lead Manufacturers v Ellerman & Bucknall* [1956] 2 Lloyd's Rep. 167, and see *Renton v Palmyra* [1957] A.C. 149 at pp.173, 174.

[87] "Obstruction" or "inaccessibility" in such a clause must arise from obstacles that prevent the port being reached except after inordinate delay. And the "opinion of the master" must be exercised fairly as between both parties: *Tillmanns v Knutsford* [1908] 2 K.B. 385 at p.406, per Farwell L.J.; *Government of Republic of Spain v North of England S.S. Co* (1938) 61 Ll.L.R. 44 at p.57 (discretion of the master). Where on a voyage from England to Vladivostock the ship was delayed for three days by ice, upon which the master went to Nagasaki, but just after he turned back the ice cleared away so that ships could get into Vladivostock, it was held that the shipowners were not protected under the clause "Should a port be inaccessible on account of ice . . . or should entry at port be deemed by the master unsafe in consequence of war, disturbance, or any other cause, it shall be competent for the master to discharge at some other safe port": *Knutsford v Tillmanns* [1908] A.C. 406.

The Chamber of Shipping has from time to time approved various War Risks Clauses giving the shipowners wide liberties.[88]

This power is sometimes given the master "in case of apprehension of such prevention, or in case of war or hostilities rendering the further prosecution of the voyage in the opinion of the master[89] or owners unsafe". Without such clauses as these, though the master might delay or deviate to avoid danger, he could not land the goods or give up the intention of proceeding to the original port of destination, at any rate till such delay had ensued as to defeat the commercial purpose of the adventure; *semble*, even then he would not be entitled to freight; though he might be entitled to the expenses of delivery. (See Arts. 163, 168.)

Note 2. In the years shortly before 1939 charters to load at Russian ports during periods of the year when these are usually icebound frequently contained special clauses relating to the provision of icebreaker assistance to enable ships to enter and leave the loading ports free of expense to owners. The decision in each turned on the special words used and the particular facts proved.[90] Once a breach of the obligation to provide such assistance is established the charterers will be liable for damage caused to ships by the ice, unless they can prove that the same damage would have been suffered if there had been no breach.[91]

A72   **Article 72—"Safely"**

"Safely" means "safely, as a laden ship".[92] In the absence of a specific clause, such as a lightening or ship to ship transfer clause, the ship therefore is not bound to load part of her cargo in the port and then take on board outside the port the part of the cargo she could not safely load in port.[93] Neither is she bound to unload before reaching the port, to enable herself to proceed to a port she could not reach in safety at her laden draught of water.[94]

If the ship is to load in a tidal harbour or a river with a bar and her loading is being completed at neap tides, the captain is not entitled to sail with less than a full cargo, though that is all with which at the then state of the tides he can get out: he must complete his cargo and wait for the spring tide that will enable him to leave.[95]

Case 1. A ship was chartered "to a safe port as ordered, or as near thereto as she can safely get, and always lie and discharge afloat". The ship was ordered to Lowestoft, where the vessel could not

---

[88] See, e.g. *Luigi Monta v Cechofracht* [1956] 2 Q.B. 552, where the words "compliance with orders given by the Government of the Nation under whose flag the vessels sails . . . or by any other Government" had to be construed in relation to the Chinese Nationalist Government in Formosa.

[89] See fn.83, above.

[90] *Anastassia v Ugleexport Charkow; Russian Wood Agency v Dampskibsselskabet Heimdal* (1934) 39 Com.Cas. 238; *Danneberg v White Sea Timber Trust* (1935) 41 Com.Cas. 60.

[91] *Akties. Steam v Acros; Akties. Bruusgaard v Arcos* (1933) 39 Com.Cas. 158; *Danneberg v White Sea Timber Trust* (1935) 41 Com.Cas. 60; *Rendal v Arcos* (1937) 43 Com.Cas. 1 at pp.14, 15.

[92] *Shield v Wilkins* (1850) 5 Ex. 304; *AIC v Marine Pilot (The Archimidis)* [2007] EWHC 1182 (Comm) para.40, approving this passage from the 20th edn of this work.

[93] *The Alhambra* (1881) 6 P.D. 68 (CA); *Shield v Wilkins* (1850) 5 Ex. 304. See also *Hayton v Irwin* (1879) 5 C.P.D. 130 (CA). She may in a tidal harbour be bound, after commencing loading to one spring tide, to wait until the next spring tide to complete it; *Carlton S.S. Co v Castle Mail Co* [1898] A.C. 486.

[94] *Shield v Wilkins*, above; *Erasmo Tregalia v Smith's Timber Co* (1896) 1 Com.Cas. 360, a charter to discharge at Sutton Bridge; *Reynolds v Tomlinson* [1896] 1 Q.B. 586 (Gloucester and Sharpness); *Hall v Paul* (1914) 19 Com.Cas. 384 (King's Lynn).

[95] *Gifford v Dishington* (1871) 9 Macpherson 1045; *Cf. The Curfew* [1891] P. 131.

"lie always afloat", without previously discharging some of her cargo outside the port. *Held*, that the shipowner was not bound to go to such a port, but only to one where the vessel on her laden draught of water could always lie afloat safely.[96]

Case 2. A ship was chartered to X, "or so near thereto as she can safely get". X is a bar-harbour; the ship was loaded inside the bar as deep as the water on the bar would allow. *Held*, that the charterer was not entitled to require the ship to complete loading at her own expense outside the bar, for she could not be said to "safely get" to a place from which she could not safely get away with a full cargo, and her going inside the bar was therefore only for the charterer's accommodation. According to the terms of the charter, she need not have crossed the bar at all.[97]

Case 3. A vessel was chartered to proceed "to a safe port, or as near thereto as she can safely get, and deliver same . . . to discharge as customary with all possible dispatch, cargo to be taken from alongside ship at merchant's risk and expense". She was ordered to Z, but could get no nearer than Y. The shipowner claimed to deliver enough at Y to lighten his vessel, at charterer's expense; the charterer set up a custom at the port of Z that the ship must get to Z at her own expense. *Held*, that the custom was inconsistent with the contract, and the charterer must pay the expense of lightening.[98]

Note 1. At all times of the tide and always afloat. This clause will relieve the ship of the duty of waiting in a tidal river or harbour till the tide serve her to proceed to the dock or wharf where she is to discharge: under it the charterer will be required to name a loading or discharging berth, where she can lie "always afloat at all times of the tide". The clause "always afloat" alone will not justify a vessel in declining to go to a berth where she cannot lie continuously always afloat, if she can do so partly before and partly after neap tides.[99] So where the ship is chartered "to load as customary always afloat at such wharf or anchorage as the charterers may direct", and the charterers direct her to a wharf where she can load part of her cargo afloat, but will afterwards require to load the rest of her cargo from lighters at an anchorage (that being a customary method of loading in the port), the charterers commit no breach of the charter.[100]

Case. A ship was chartered to Z, "or as near thereto as she may safely get, at all times of tide and always afloat". She arrived at Y on September 5, but the tides would not allow her to proceed to Z, "always afloat", till September 9. *Held*, that the vessel had "arrived at Z", for purposes of demurrage, on September 5.[101] If chartered "to load *always* afloat", and she is ordered to a berth where she can always lie afloat, but which she can only get to and from at certain times of tides, she is bound to wait for suitable tides.[102]

Note 2. A dock as ordered on arriving, if sufficient water.

---

[96] *The Alhambra*, above.
[97] *Shield v Wilkins*, above. If she had not crossed the bar the charterer must have borne the expense of loading outside by lighters: *Trindade v Levy* (1860) 2 F. & F. 441; but if, having gone inside, she had loaded a full cargo, and been obliged to unload to get out, she must have paid the expense of loading outside, and must carry the full cargo to earn her freight: *General Steam Navigation Co v Slipper* (1862) 11 C.B. (N.S.) 493. Where a vessel chartered to load always afloat in a dock could do so, but could not leave the dock except at spring tides: *Held*, that she was bound to load in the dock and wait for spring tides, and was not entitled to go to another dock when partly loaded and require the charterers to lighter her cargo to her: *The Curfew* [1891] p.131.
[98] *Hayton v Irwin* (1879) 5 C.P.D. 130. There was no express decision that the ship was bound to proceed to Z after lightening. It is submitted that she was not, if Y was outside the port of Z (*The Alhambra* (1881) 6 P.D. 68), and if Y was in the port of Z the lay-days would begin to count from her readiness to unload at Y, in the absence of any custom of the port; *Nielson v Wait* (1885) 16 Q.B.D. 67.
[99] *Carlton S.S. Co v Castle Co* [1898] A.C. 486. In that case, however, the ship was chartered to load in Senhouse Dock. The Superior Courts did not say what was to happen to her during the time when she would have taken the ground if she stayed in the dock; and it is doubtful whether the decision would apply to a case where "a safe berth" was to be named. Perhaps the ship must wait outside till after the first neap tides.
[100] *Aktieselskabet Inglewood v Miller* (1903) 8 Com.Cas. 196.
[101] *Horsley v Price* (1882) 11 Q.B.D. 244. Without the clause "at all times of the tide", the ship must have waited at her own expense until the 9th: *Parker v Winlow* (1857) 7 E. & B. 942.
[102] *The Curfew* [1891] p.131.

Case. A ship was chartered to proceed to Z to discharge in "a dock as ordered on arriving, if sufficient water, or as near thereto as she may safely get, always afloat". On arriving at Z she was ordered to the C dock, but there was not for four weeks sufficient water in the C dock. *Held*, that there must be "sufficient water" in the dock when the order is given, and that, if there is not, the ship is not bound to discharge in the dock named.[103]

Note 3. The Scots cases *Hillstrom v Gibson*[104] and *Dickinson v Martini*,[105] which follow *Hillstrom v Gibson* and certain dicta in the English cases of *Capper v Wallace*[106] and *Nielsen v Wait*,[107] cannot be accepted as sound. They are inconsistent with the decision in *The Alhambra*[108] and subsequent cases in which *The Alhambra* has been followed.

The Alhambra in effect decides that where the ship is to go to "a safe port", it must be a port to which she can go as a loaded ship, and the master is not bound to discharge part of his cargo short of the destination, in order, with a lighter craft, to get to that destination and discharge the remainder. *Hillstrom v Gibson* and *Dickinson v Martini* are inconsistent with this. In *Capper v Wallace*[109] (decided the year before *The Alhambra*) the court, on the authority of *Hillstrom v Gibson*, said that it is the duty of the master so to lighten his ship. In *Nielsen v Wait*[110] (in which *The Alhambra* was not cited) there is a dictum of Pollock B. based upon *Hillstrom v Gibson*, to the same effect.

The Alhambra has since been followed and approved in several English cases, viz.: *Reynolds v Tomlinson*,[111] *Erasmo Treglia v Smith's Timber Co*,[112] and in *Hall Brothers v Paul*,[113] and the principle it lays down may now be considered as firmly established.[114]

A73   **Article 73—Loading under a Charter—Duty of Shipowner**

At the port of loading the rights of the shipowner and the obligations of the charterer as regards loading the cargo, apart from the special provisions[115] altering the general principle, depend on the following facts:

(1) The ship must be at the place where she is bound to be ready for cargo (Art.74), or, if there is the provision in the charter and the circumstances justify its application, "so near thereto as she can safely get". (Arts 71, 72, 74.)

(2) The ship must be, so far as she is concerned, ready to load. (Art.75.)

(3) The charterer must have notice of the above facts. (Art.76.)

---

[103] *Allen v Coltart* (1883) 11 Q.B.D. 782.
[104] 1870 8 Macpherson 463.
[105] 1874 1 Rettie 1185.
[106] (1880) 5 Q.B.D. 163.
[107] (1885) 14 Q.B.D. 516.
[108] (1881) 6 P.D. 68.
[109] (1880) 5 Q.B.D. 163 at p.166.
[110] (1885) 14 Q.B.D. 516 at pp.522, 523.
[111] [1896] 1 Q.B. 586.
[112] [1896] 1 Com.Cas. 360.
[113] (1914) 19 Com.Cas. 384. Sankey J. there expressly disapproved of *Hillstrom v Gibson* and the dicta in *Capper v Wallace* and *Nielson v Wait*.
[114] In the first seven editions of this work the conflict of these cases was discussed in much greater detail in the equivalent of this *Note*. In view of the repeated affirmation of the principle of *The Alhambra*, the elaboration of the point seems no longer necessary.
[115] As to which, see below, Arts 77 to 81.

When these conditions are fulfilled the vessel is "an arrived ship", and the lay-days, or days allowed for loading the ship, begin, unless there are special provisions regulating when time begins.[116]

In some cases upon the happening of the above three events the charterer will also be bound to load the cargo.

In other cases the charterer will be bound to load the cargo only when:

    (4) The ship is at the place at which the charterer is bound to load the cargo. (Art.74.)

In other words, of the above events (1) may coincide with (4) or may precede it.

The above principles as to the rights and obligations as to loading at the port of loading also apply to discharging at the port or place of discharge *except* that (3) "Notice of readiness" is not always necessary at the port of discharge. (See Art.150.)

Article 74—Where the Ship must be ready to Load[117]—Where the   A74 Charterer is bound to Load

As mentioned in Art.73, one must distinguish (1) the place at which the ship reaches the contractual destination and becomes an "arrived ship" under the charter, so that (subject to special provisions) her lay-days begin, from (2) the place at which the charterer is bound to put the cargo on board the ship.

These two points depend in every case upon the terms of the charter. They may coincide, or the first may precede the second, as appears below.[118]

A. If the charter is to proceed to a specified and actual "loading spot",[119] i.e. a named wharf, or a specific berth at a quay, or within a dock,[120] then (1) the ship will only be an "arrived ship" when she gets to the named "spot", and (2) the charterer will only be bound to load the ship when she gets to the named spot (i.e. the two points coincide).[121] Mere arrival in fact at the berth is not enough: the ship must be there by permission of the authorities, if any, and of right.[122]

---

[116] As to which, see below, Arts 77 to 81.
[117] Similar principles apply to discharging and accordingly the cases cited in this Article relate both to ports of loading and ports of discharge.
[118] The leading cases on this topic are *Nelson v Dahl* (1879) 12 Ch.D. 568, *Leonis Co v Rank* [1908] 1 K.B. 499 and, in particular, *Oldendorff v Tradax Export* [1974] A.C. 479 (HL).
[119] *Cf.* Kennedy L.J. as to this phrase, *Leonis Co v Rank*, above, at p.521.
[120] This kind of charter is often called a "berth" charter to distinguish it from a "port" charter, as to which see C. below. It is sometimes difficult to apply this dichotomy to the words used: e.g. *North River Freighter v President of India* [1956] 1 Q.B. 333.
[121] Brett L.J., *Nelson v Dahl*, above, at pp.581, 584; *Strahan v Gabriel* (unreported, cited (1879) 12 Ch.D. 568 at p.590); *Watson v Borner* (1900) 5 Com.Cas. 377.
[122] *Good v Isaacs* [1892] 2 Q.B. 555.

The position is the same if the charter is to proceed to a wharf or quay or berth, "to be named by the charterer", the effect of this provision being as if the berth "named" was actually specified in the charter.[123]

B. If the charter is to proceed to a named dock (i.e. an area containing several possible "loading spots"), or to a dock "as ordered" or "to be named",[124] then (1) the ship will, in the absence of any custom of the port regulating the matter, be an "arrived" ship when she gets inside the specified dock and is, so far as she is concerned, ready to load,[125] but (2) the charterer will be entitled to select the actual berth at which he will load the ship and he is not bound to load her till she gets there.[126]

In this case the two points do not coincide.[127] But in such a case by the custom of the port the ship may not be an "arrived" ship until she has got, not merely into the area of the named dock, but also into a berth where loading can take place within that dock.[128]

C. The same rule applies, *mutatis mutandis*, where the charter is to proceed to a "port", or to "a port as ordered",[129] or other area larger than the "dock" dealt with in B. In the same way (1) the ship is, subject to the effect of custom, an arrived ship when she comes to rest within the named port[130] or area and is at the immediate and effective disposition of the charterer,[131] but (2) the charterer can

---

[123] *Tharsis Sulphur Co v Morel* [1891] 2 Q.B. 647; *Murphy v Coffin* (1883) 12 Q.B.D. 87; *Good v Isaacs* [1892] 2 Q.B. 555; *Bulman v Fenwick* [1894] 1 Q.B. 179; *Modesto v Duprè* (1902) 7 Com.Cas. 105; *Aktieselskabet Inglewood v Millar* (1903) 8 Com.Cas. 196; *Stag Line v Board of Trade* [1950] 2 K.B. 194; *Graigwen (Owners) v. Anglo-Canadian Shipping Co* [1955] 2 Lloyd's Rep. 260. *Cf. Hull S.S. Co v Lamport* (1907) 23 T.L.R. 445, where the berth "to be named" under the charter was named in the bill of lading but the vessel could not discharge there. *Parker v Winlow* (1857) 7 E. & B. 942, if rightly decided, must have fallen within this principle. See *Leonis Co v Rank* [1908] 1 K.B. 499 at p.514. For the position where the charter is to proceed to a ready quay berth "as ordered" see Art.81, below. As to damages for not loading "in regular turn", see Art.193, *Note*, below.

[124] *Tapscott v Balfour* (1872) L.R. 8 C.P. 46. It is "precisely as if that dock had been expressly named in the charter originally", *ibid.* p.52. *Cf. Norden S.S. Co v Dempsey* (1876) 1 C.P.D. 654 at p.655.

[125] *Tapscott v Balfour*, above; *Randall v Lynch* (1810) 2 Camp. 352; Brett L.J., *Nelson v Dahl* (1879) 12 Ch.D. 568 at pp.581, 582, 584, *Davies v McVeagh* (1879) 4 Ex.D. 265, if rightly decided, must be under this principle; see Brett L.J. (1879) 12 Ch.D. 568 at p.590. In *Monsen v Macfarlane* [1895] 2 Q.B. 562, the charter was "to proceed to a customary loading place in the—Dock as required by the charterers". If this had stood alone the case would have fallen under A. above and been governed by *Tharsis Sulphur Co v Morel*, above. But the charter went on "to be loaded as per colliery guarantee". By the colliery guarantee the undertaking was "to load in fifteen days after the ship is ready in Dock at G." It was held that the guarantee was incorporated that the ship was therefore to be "ready in dock", and the case was governed by the principle of *Tapscott v Balfour*, above. See also *Thorman v Dowgat S.S. Co* [1910] 1 K.B. 410, in which *Monsen v Macfarlane* was followed and *Shamrock S.S. Co v Storey* (1898) 5 Com.Cas. 21 distinguished.

[126] *The Felix* (1868) L.R. 2 A. & E. 273. That the charterer has this right to select the actual loading berth does not have the same result so far as the starting of lay-time is concerned as if the charter was expressly "to proceed to a berth as selected by the charterer" (see above under A.); see *Leonis Co v Rank* [1908] 1 K.B. 499 at pp.515, 516. *Sanders v Jenkins* [1897] 1 Q.B. 93, seems to have been wrongly decided upon an assumption to the contrary of this. But once the charterer has made his selection in the exercise of his implied right to so do, he cannot change the berth so selected without the agreement of the shipowner: *Anglo-Danubian Transport Co v Ministry of Food* (1949) 83 Ll.L.R. 137; approved, *Reardon Smith Line v Ministry of Agriculture* [1962] 1 Q.B. 42 at pp.90, 113.

[127] They might, if the dock were so small a basin that to be inside it would be to be alongside the only berth within it.

[128] *Norden S.S. Co v Dempsey* (1876) 1 C.P.D. 654.

[129] *Brown v Johnson* (1842) 10 M. & W. 331; *Thiis v Byers* (1876) 1 Q.B.D. 244.

[130] In applying this rule "port" must be given its commercial and not its geographical or legal meaning: see below, text to fn.134.

[131] *Oldendorff v Tradax Export* [1974] A.C. 479; *Federal Commerce and Navigation Co v Tradax Export SA (The Maratha Envoy)* [1977] 2 Lloyd's Rep. 301 (i); *Leonis Co v Rank* [1908] 1 K.B. 499. See also *Brown v Johnson* (1842) Car. & M. 440; *Pyman v Dreyfus* (1889) 24 Q.B.D. 152; *Jaques v Wilson* (1890) 7 T.L.R. 119; *Van Nievelt v Forslind* (1925) 30 Com.Cas. 263. The rule is not affected by the words "whether in berth or not".

select the actual berth or "loading spot" at which he is to do the loading.[132] "Port" in this context includes not merely "that part of the port where a ship can be loaded when a berth is available",[133] but the whole area of the port "in its commercial sense", i.e. the port as understood by shippers, charterers and shipowners.[134] This may or may not coincide with the legal area of the port: the area within which the port authority exercises powers regulating the movements and conduct of ships may be some indication, although powers over matters such as pilotage are sometimes exercised far beyond the limits of the port in its commercial sense.[135]

Where the ship proceeds at once to the berth selected by the charterer, she becomes an arrived ship when she gets there, but not before.[136] If she has to wait for the berth to become vacant she may become an arrived ship before reaching the berth if, but only if, she has come to rest within the port[137]; and is at the immediate and effective disposition of the charterer.[138] This will be presumed if she is at a place where waiting ships usually lie, unless in some extra-ordinary circumstances, proof of which would lie on the charterer.[139] If she is at some other place, then it is for the owner to prove that she is at the immediate and effective disposition of the charterer[140]: she must normally be at a place where she counts for turn and where orders to proceed can be communicated to her in time for her to reach the berth as it becomes vacant.[141]

But, even if she is within the port in its business sense, the custom of the port may prevent her from being an "arrived" ship.[142] It may by custom be necessary for her to have arrived in some particular part,[143] or in a dock,[144] or in some particular dock,[145] within that port.

---

[132] *The Felix* (1868) L.R. 2 A. & E. 273; *Pyman v Dreyfus* above; *The Mary Thomas* (1896) 12 T.L.R. 511. Once the charterer has selected the berth he has no right to change it without the consent of the shipowner: *Anglo-Danubian Transport Co v Ministry of Food* (1950) 83 Ll.L.R. 137; approved *Reardon Smith Line v Ministry of Agriculture* [1962] 1 Q.B. 42 at pp.90, 113. See also *Venizelos A.N.E. of Athens v Soc. Commerciale de Cereales et Financière SA* [1974] 1 Lloyd's Rep. 350.

[133] This was the test approved in *The Aello*, [1961] A.C. 135, now overruled.

[134] *Oldendorff v Tradax Export* [1974] A.C. 479 at pp.535, 552–553, 559, 561; *The Maratha Envoy* (above). See also *S.S. Garston v Hickie, Borman & Co* (1885) 15 Q.B.D. 580. See also *President of India v Olympia Sauna Shipping Co SA (The Ypatia Halcoussi)* [1984] 2 Lloyd's Rep. 455.

[135] *Oldendorff v Tradax Export*, above, pp.535, 553, 561. The usual waiting anchorage may be outside the port in its commercial sense, e.g. Glasgow (Tail-of-Bank) and Hull (Spurn Head): *ibid*. pp.535, 559.

[136] *Oldendorff v Tradax Export* [1974] A.C. 479, at pp.535, 553.

[137] *ibid*. pp.535, 552, 561.

[138] *ibid*. pp.390–391, 397, 407, 414–415.

[139] *ibid*. pp.535, 553, 561.

[140] *ibid*. pp.391, 407, 414, 415.

[141] *ibid*. pp.560, 561. *Semble*, if for some reason due to the conditions of the port and not of the ship, the port authority order her to some place other than the usual waiting place, she is there an arrived ship: *ibid*. p.407.

[142] per Kennedy L.J., *Leonis Co v Rank* [1908] 1 K.B. 499 at p.520. Proof as regards a foreign port of the rules of the law of the country as a whole, differing from the English law as to an arrived ship, will not suffice to support an allegation of such a custom: *Anglo-Hellenic Co v Dreyfus* (1913) 108 L.T. 36.

[143] *Brereton v Chapman* (1831) 7 Bing. 559; *Kell v Anderson* (1842) 10 M. & W. 498; *Thiis v Byers* (1876) 1 Q.B.D. 244.

[144] *Brown v Johnson* (1842) 10 M. & W. 331. In that case "it must have been assumed or proved that the usual place of unloading ships in the port of Hull was in a dock"; Brett L.J., *Nelson v Dahl* (1879) 12 Ch.D. 568 at p.586.

[145] *Nielsen v Wait* (1885) 16 Q.B.D. 67. But evidence of such a custom may be inadmissible as being inconsistent with the terms of the charter, *Reynolds v Tomlinson* [1896] 1 Q.B.D. 586. In the latter case *Nielsen v Wait* was distinguished, but it is difficult to reconcile it with *The Alhambra* (1881) 6 P.D. 68.

D. Where the charter provides that the ship shall proceed to a berth, or dock, or port, "or so near thereto as she can safely get", the point where the ship becomes "an arrived ship" in each of the foregoing three cases may not be the actual named point but the substituted point "near thereto" under the provision.[146] The circumstances in which the shipowner is entitled to go to such substituted point have been discussed in Arts 71 and 72, below.

E. Where the charterer has the right to select, under the foregoing rules, the place to which the ship must proceed in order that she may be an "arrived" ship, he must exercise his right of selection reasonably. He need not select, in the interests of the shipowner, a place that is then free and accessible,[147] so long as he selects one that is likely to be free in a reasonable time.[148] In determining what is a reasonable selection of a place of loading by the charterer it is material to consider how far access to it is prevented or delayed "by obstacles caused by the charterer or in consequence of the engagements of the charterer". For if the ship is prevented by such causes "the lay-days commence to count as soon as the ship is ready to load, and would, but for such obstacles or engagements, begin to load at that place."[149]

If co-operation by the charterers over documentary requirements is necessary for the ship to become an "arrived" ship, it is likely to be implied that the charterers are bound to act with reasonable despatch and in accordance with the practice of the port to enable the ship to become an arrived ship.[150]

If the charterer under a "berth" charter will not name any berth he will be liable for any damages occasioned by his refusal or delay.[151]

When the ship has become an "arrived" ship, but the charterer has still the right to select the berth at which he will load her, it does not much matter how

---

[146] Whether the ship has become "an arrived ship" by reaching such a substituted point may involve a doubtful and difficult question of fact: *The Fox* (1914) 83 L.J.P. 89.

[147] *Murphy v Coffin* (1883) 12 Q.B.D. 87; *Tharsis Co v Morel* [1891] 2 Q.B. 647; *Reardon Smith Line v Ministry of Agriculture* [1962] 1 Q.B. 42 (CA) (affirmed in part [1963] A.C. 691 (HL)). See as to colliery guarantees *Dobell v Green* [1900] 1 Q.B. 526 (CA).

[148] per Bowen L.J., *Tharsis Co v Morel*, above, at p.652; *Akt. Olivebank v Dansk Fabrik* [1919] 2 K.B. 162. In *Bulman v Fenwick* [1894] 1 Q.B. 179, the CA appears to have held that the only limitation to the charterer's power to select a berth is that he must not choose one that is so blocked that the obstacle cannot be removed in a time consistent with the commercial adventure; see also *Reardon Smith Line v Ministry of Agriculture*, above. The nomination must not be of an "impossible" place, e.g. one at which delay would frustrate the commercial object of the adventure: per Willmer L.J. [1962] 1 Q.B. 42 at p.113; or at which cargo cannot be discharged: *Hull SS v Lamport* (1907) 23 T.L.R. 445. If the cause of delay is one which the parties must have contemplated, as neap tides, they must wait till the tides are suitable: *Carlton S.S. Co v Castle Mail Co* [1898] A.C. 486. If the owner, without waiting for the charterer to select a berth, proceeds to one of his own choice he must bear the expense of proceeding to the one selected, if selected reasonably, by the charterer: *The Felix* (1868) L.R. 2 A. & E. 273.

[149] per Kennedy J., *Aktieselskabet Inglewood v Millar* (1903) 8 Com.Cas. 196 at p.201. See also *Watson v Borner* (1900) 5 Com.Cas. 377; *The Deerhound* (1901) 6 Com.Cas. 104. But see also and contrast *Harrowing v Dupré* (1902) 7 Com.Cas. 157; *Quilpue v Brown* [1904] 2 K.B. 264 (CA). The unsatisfactory cases, *Ashcroft v Crow Orchard Co* (1874) L.R. 9 Q.B. 540, and *Wright v New Zealand Co* (1879) 4 Ex.D. 165, might conceivably be explained upon this principle, but probably they should be considered to have been wrongly decided. See 19th edn, *Note* to Art.157.

[150] *Sunbeam Shipping v President of India (The Atlantic Sunbeam)* [1973] 1 Lloyd's Rep. 482.

[151] *Stewart v Rogerson* (1871) L.R. 6 C.P. 424. Presumably the breach is of an "innominate obligation" (see Art.44) and not of a condition, as in the case of a port charter, with similar consequences: see fn.152, below. This is sometimes expressly catered for (as in the Gencon charter), e.g. "time lost in waiting for berth to count as loading time": see Art.79.

or when he exercises his selection of the berth for loading: any delay will be at his risk of paying demurrage or damages for detention. The charterer will be in breach if the berth is not nominated in sufficient time to enable the ship to be loaded within the lay-days.[152] In the absence of express provision or custom the shipowner is not bound to shift from the selected berth to another at his own expense to suit the convenience of the charterer.[153]

Case 1. A ship was chartered to take coals to London, the vessel to be delivered in five working days: she entered the port of L at Gravesend on March 9, but was not allowed to proceed to the Pool, the usual place for the discharge of colliers, till March 20. *Held*, that the lay-days were to be reckoned from the time of the ship's arrival at the ordinary place of discharge, according to the usage of the port of L for such vessels.[154]

Case 2. A ship was chartered "to proceed to a port in the Bristol Channel, or so near thereto as she may safely get at all times of the tide and always afloat, eight running days, Sundays excepted, to be allowed the merchants for loading and discharging the cargo". The steamer was ordered to Gloucester and arrived at Sharpness, within the port of Gloucester, but seventeen miles from the usual basin for discharging grain cargoes; at S she unloaded sufficient grain to enable her to proceed to the basin. The shipowner claimed to date his "running days" from commencing to discharge at S. A custom of the port of Gloucester was proved that vessels too heavily laden to proceed beyond S were lightened at S, and that the time of unloading at S and G counted in the lay-days, but not the time of proceeding from S to G. *Held*, a reasonable custom, and not inconsistent with the charter, though in its absence the lay-days would have run consecutively, Sundays excepted, from commencing to discharge at S.[155]

Case 3. A ship was chartered to proceed to any dock at Z, as ordered by charterers, and there load coal in the usual and customary manner. She was ordered to the W docks. Coal is usually loaded in the W docks from tips, sometimes from lighters. By the dock regulations of Z no coal agent is allowed to have more than three vessels in the dock at the same time. The vessel was ready to go into the dock on July 3, but the charterer's agent having already three vessels in the dock she was not admitted till July 11, and could not get under the tips till July 22. *Held*, that the lay-days commenced on July 11, and that the words "load in the usual and customary manner" referred to the manner and not the place of loading.[156]

Case 4. A ship was chartered to "proceed to the Mersey, and deliver her cargo at any safe berth as ordered on arrival in the dock at Garston . . . , to be discharged when berthed with all dispatch as customary". On arrival at the dock a berth was ordered by the harbourmaster, as customary, but

---

[152] *Universal Cargo Carriers v Citati* [1957] 2 Q.B. 401 at p.429. The breach is of an "innominate obligation" and not of a condition, so that if the delay is so long as to frustrate the commercial object of the charter, the shipowner may treat the contract as repudiated, but not otherwise: *ibid.*, and see Art.44.

[153] *King Line v Moxey, Savon & Co* (1939) 62 Ll.L.R. 252. *Cf. Radcliffe S.S. Co v Exporthleb* (1939) 64 Ll.L.R. 250.

[154] *Kell v Anderson* (1842) 10 M. & W. 498, explained in *Oldendorff v Tradax Export*, above, at p.559 by Lord Diplock. The case of *Ford v Cotesworth* (1870) L.R. 5 Q.B. 544, is not inconsistent with this. There the charter was to proceed to Lima and deliver in the usual and customary manner. The ship proceeded to Callao, the usual port of discharge for L., but was prevented from discharging for seven days by acts of the Government; and it was held that if there had been a time fixed for the discharge it would have begun on arrival at the usual place of discharge, but that, as there was no fixed time, reasonable diligence only was required, and the delay from the time of arrival was not unreasonable under the circumstances. In *Thiis v Byers* (1876) 1 Q.B.D. 244, where there was a fixed time named, the lay-days counted from the arrival at the usual place of discharge. See also *Brereton v Chapman* (1831) 7 Bing. 559.

[155] *Nielsen v Wait* (1885) 16 Q.B.D. 67 (CA), where the decision proceeded on different grounds from that of Pollock B. in the court below (1885) 14 Q.B.D. 516. But see *Reynolds v Tomlinson* [1896] 1 Q.B.D. 586, where a vessel chartered to a safe port and ordered to Gloucester, where she could not get without being lightened, refused to proceed beyond Sharpness, and the Divisional Court rejected evidence of the above custom, as contradicting the provision to proceed to a safe port. See also *M'Intosh v Sinclair* (1877) I.R. 11 C.L. 460; *Caffarini v Walker* (1876) I.R. 10 C.L. 250.

[156] *Tapscott v Balfour* (1872) L.R. 8 C.P. 46. See also *Shadforth v Cory* (1863) 32 L.J.Q.B. 379. In *Norden S.S. v Dempsey* (1876) 1 C.P.D. 654, a custom for timber ships at Liverpool that the lay-days should begin on reaching a particular place in the dock, was proved and held binding.

owing to the crowded state of the dock the vessel did not reach it for some time. *Held*, that the obligation of the charterers did not commence till the vessel was in berth.[157]

Case 5. A vessel was chartered to proceed to H, cargo to be discharged at usual fruit berth, as fast as steamer could deliver as customary and where ordered by charterers. On arrival the ship was ordered to a usual fruit berth, and moored there, but without permission of the officials controlling the quay, and was ordered away the next morning. *Held*, that the obligations of the charterers to unload did not commence till the ship was in a usual fruit berth as ordered by charterers with the assent of the harbour authorities.[158]

Case 6. A ship was chartered to discharge cargo at a (named) quay at Z. The ship arrived and found the only quay berth occupied by another ship. The shipowner offered to discharge across the other ship, if the charterer would pay the additional expense. The charterer refused. *Held*, that the lay-days did not begin till the ship was alongside the quay, the place named where the voyage was to end.[159]

Case 7. A ship was chartered to proceed to a customary loading place in the R dock, Grimsby, and here receive a cargo of coal, "to be loaded as customary at Grimsby as per colliery guarantee". The guarantee provided that the ship could be loaded in fifteen colliery working days after she was "ready in Dock at Grimsby". The ship was ready in dock on September 3, but did not get under the spout at a customary loading place till October 10. *Held*, that the lay-days began on September 3. *Semble*, that but for the colliery guarantee they would have begun when the ship could first get into a customary loading berth selected by charterers.[160]

Case 8. Charter to proceed to a safe port as ordered, and there load. Ship ordered to Bahia Blanca. She arrived at B.B., anchored off the pier and gave notice of readiness. Charterers desired her to load alongside the pier, to which, after considerable delay, she proceeded. *Held*, that lay-days began when the ship was ready off the pier, and not merely when she got alongside.[161]

Case 9. A ship was chartered to carry grain to one of six ports at the charterers' option. The charterers ordered her to discharge at Liverpool/Birkenhead. On January 3 she anchored at Mersey Bar anchorage on the instructions of the port authority and waited for a berth to become available. She did not berth until January 21. Mersey Bar anchorage is within the legal, administrative and fiscal area of the port of Liverpool/Birkenhead, and is the usual waiting place for grain ships discharging at the port, but it is some 17 miles from the nearest grain discharging berth. *Held*, she was an "arrived" ship at Mersey Bar Anchorage.[162]

A75   **Article 75—Readiness to Load**

A ship to be ready to load[163] must be completely ready in all her holds so as to afford the charterer complete control of every portion of the ship available for cargo.[164] A charter for the "full reach and burden" of the ship refers only to her

---

[157] *Tharsis Co v Morel* [1891] 2 Q.B. 647; *Modesto v Dupré* (1902) 7 Com.Cas. 105.
[158] *Good v Isaacs* [1892] 2 Q.B. 555.
[159] *Strahan v Gabriel* (1879) 12 Ch.D. 590, *cit.* per Brett L.J.
[160] *Monsen v Macfarlane* [1895] 2 Q.B. 562; *Thorman v Dowgate S.S. Co* [1910] 1 K.B. 410.
[161] *Leonis Co v Rank* [1908] 1 K.B. 499, explained in *Oldendorff v Tradax Export*, case 9 below.
[162] *Oldendorff v Tradax Export* [1974] A.C. 479 (HL), overruling *The Aello* [1961] A.C. 135, explaining and applying *Leoni Co v Rank* [1908] 1 K.B. 499, and discussing *Shipping Developments Corp v Sojuzneftexport (The Delian Spirit)* [1972] Q.B. 103 (CA) *Cf. The Maratha Envoy*, above, where the usual waiting place was not within the port.
[163] The same principles apply, *mutatis mutandis*, to readiness to discharge: *Government of Ceylon v Société Franco Tunisienne* [1960] 2 Lloyd's Rep. 352 at p.357. A ship may be ready to discharge even if the owner is unwilling, by reason of exercising a lien, to discharge: *Rashtriya Chemicals v Huddart Parker (The Boral Gas)* [1988] 1 Lloyd's Rep. 342.
[164] *Groves, Maclean & Co v Volkart* (1884) C. & E. 309; *Oliver v Fielden* (1849) 4 Ex. 135; *Balley v De Arroyave* (1838) 7 A & E. 919; *Noemijulia S.S. Co v Minister of Food* [1951] 1 K.B. 223 at pp.236, 239. A ship is not ready to discharge the charterparty cargo if some of it is overstowed by other cargo: *Government of Ceylon v Société Franco-Tunisienne* [1960] 2 Lloyd's Rep. 352. Nor is she ready to load if her holds are infested: *Compania de Naviera Nedelka v Tradex Internacional SA (The Tres Flores)* [1974] Q.B. 264 (CA). However, where a ship is herself ready to discharge the cargo but the infested state of the cargo precludes discharge of the cargo, this does not affect the readiness of the ship: *Eurico SpA v Philipp Brothers (The Epaphus)* [1987] 2 Lloyd's Rep. 215. In practice the ship is considered "ready to load" though stiffening ballast, or cargo used for

structural capacity at the date of charter,[165] and means all the space of the vessel proper to be filled with cargo.[166]

A ship may be ready to load so as to prevent the cancelling clause from operating although she may not have complied with some requirement necessary before lay-time starts.[167]

The degree of necessary readiness of the ship for her part is relative to that of the charterer or the consignees for theirs. Therefore the ship need not be absolutely ready (e.g. by having all her gear fixed up for the work) at a time when the charterer or consignees are not in a position to do any of their part of the work, so long as the ship can be absolutely ready at the earliest time the charterers or consignees can be ready to perform their part in loading or discharging.[168] Nor apparently need the ship have obtained free pratique provided that the practice in the port and the actual medical condition of the crew are such that pratique can subsequently be obtained without delaying the loading or discharge.[169] Similarly, the ship can be ready to load, for the purpose of starting lay-time, even if she has not yet complied with all the local routine formalities.[170] It is sufficient that the ship is ready in a businesslike and mercantile sense.[171] However, where a ship needs to take on board water for her boilers on arrival, which would have the effect of making the ship stop work, she was not ready to load.[171]

Where there is more than one port of loading with optional cargoes and the charterer seeks to cancel on the ground of the insufficiency of the loading gear, he must prove that at the cancelling date the ship was in such a condition that the shipowner would necessarily be unable to load some cargo which the charterer was entitled to call upon him to take on board at the first or some subsequent port.[172]

---

stiffening the ship, has yet to be put on board her. But to be "ready for stiffening" is not to be "ready to load"; *Sailing Ship Lyderhorn v Duncan* [1909] 2 K.B. 929.

[165] *Japy Freres v Sutherland* (1921) 26 Com.Cas. 227.

[166] *Weir v Union S.S. Co* [1900] A.C. 525 at p.532. The clause does not in the absence of custom give the charterers any right, or deprive the owners of their right, to carry passengers: *Shaw Savill v Aitken* (1883) C. & E. 195; *Soc. Anon. Commercial v National SS Co* [1935] 2 KB 313. It does not give the charterers the right to carry cargo in cabins: *Mitcheson v Nicoll* (1852) 7 Ex. 929

[167] Thus it has been sufficient to prevent the cancelling clause from operating that the ship was herself ready to receive cargo though not in berth (*Hick v Tweedy* (1890) 63 L.T. 765) and although notice of readiness has not been given: *Aktiebolaget Nordiska Lloyd v Brownlie & Co* (1925) 30 Com.Cas. 307. See also *Aktieselskabet Inglewood v Millar's Karri* (1903) 8 Com.Cas. 196 at p.200; *Noemijulia S.S. Co v Minister of Food* [1951] 1 K.B. 223 at pp.236, 239.

[168] *Antclizo Shipping Corp v Food Corp of India (The Antclizo No.2)* [1992] 1 Lloyd's Rep. 558 at p.564; *Unifert International S.A.R.L. v Panous Shipping Co Inc (The Virginia M)* [1989] 1 Lloyd's Rep. 603. See also *Armement Deppe v Robinson* [1917] 2 K.B. 204; *The Tres Flores*, above; *Gerani Compania Naviera v General Organisation for Supply Goods (The Demosthenes)* [1982] 1 Lloyd's Rep. 275; *The Aello* [1961] A.C. 135. *Quaere* whether the doctrine of *Budgett v Binnington* [1891] 1 Q.B. 35, applies before the ship is ready: *ibid.*

[169] *Shipping Development Corp v V/O Sojuzneftexport (The Delian Spirit)* [1972] 1 Q.B. 103 at p.124, distinguishing *The Austin Friars* (1894) 10 T.L.R. 633 and applying *Armement Deppe v Robinson*, above. See also *The Tres Flores*, above, and *Sidermar v Apollo Corp (The Apollo)* [1978] 1 Lloyd's Rep. 200 at 205.

[170] *The Aello*, above (police and berthing permits).

[171] *The Virginia M*, above.

[172] *Noemijulia S.S. Co v Minister of Food* [1951] 1 K.B. 223 (CA). *Cf. New York & Cuba S.S. Co v Eriksen* (1922) 27 Com.Cas. 330, per Greer J. at p.335, an authority not cited to the CA *Sun S.S. Co v Watson & Youell Shipping Agency* (1926) 42 T.L.R. 240, in which it was decided that all shifting boards had to be in position before the

In addition to the requirements set out above, a charter may stipulate further requirements before the ship is ready to load.[173]

Case 1. A ship was chartered with a power to the charterers to cancel the charter if the ship were not ready to load on or before May 31. On that day she had only discharged two of her holds, and was not completely discharged till the middle of the next day. *Held*, the charterers were entitled to cancel.[174]

Case 2. A ship was under charter to load nitrate after discharging an outward cargo of coal. She was to have stiffening supplied by charterers on receipt of forty-eight hours' notice of readiness to receive it. Charterers to have the right to cancel if ship not ready to load cargo on or before noon of January 31. On January 27 the ship had discharged enough coal to need stiffening, and the captain gave notice to the charterers, requiring 700 tons of stiffening. The balance of the coal cargo could not have been discharged by noon of January 31. *Held*, that the charterers were entitled to cancel.[175]

Case 3. A charter provided that the charterer was to have the full reach and burden of the ship "including tween and shelter decks, bridges, poop, etc. (provided same are not occupied by bunker coals and/or stores)": There were optional cargoes, optional ports of loading and a cancelling date for the first port. *Held*, (i) No. 3 lower hold, which was designed as a reserve bunker space, was within the proviso; (ii) the burden was upon the charterer to show that this hold, which contained some coal at the cancelling date, was not reasonably required for the purpose of the ship having enough bunkers for the whole voyage; (iii) the absence of mainmast and after derricks was immaterial so far as the right to cancel was concerned unless the charterer proved the ship would necessarily be unable to load at the first or some subsequent port cargo which the charterer was entitled to ship.[176]

Case 4. A charter to load grain provided for notice of readiness at the roads. Notice was given. The vessel was at the roads for some 8 days. Subsequently it was discovered that the holds were infested and fumigation was required, which took some 4 hours. *Held* the vessel was not ready before fumigation and the notice was invalid.[177]

A76   **Article 76—Notice to Charterer of Readiness to Load**

The shipowner must give notice to the charterer of the ship's readiness to load her cargo at the place agreed on in the charter.[178] Unless otherwise provided the notice may be oral.[179]

If notice of a specified number of hours is provided for, this may, in the absence of express provision to the contrary, run during Sundays and holidays and other time when lay-time does not run under the charter.[180]

When there is a stipulation for written notice to be given and for lay-time to begin a specified time thereafter, no agreement that lay-time shall start sooner nor

---

ship could be said to be ready to load, was distinguished by the CA on the ground that the only cargo concerned there was grain in bulk and that the question at issue was the starting of lay-time and not the right to cancel.
[173] For example in charters to India, it is sometimes provided that the ship must be entered at the Customs House, as to which see *The Antclizo No. 2*, above.
[174] *Groves, Maclean & Co v Volkart* (1884) C. & E. 309.
[175] *Sailing Ship Lyderhorn v Duncan* [1909] 2 K.B. 929.
[176] *Noemijulia S.S. Co v Minister of Food* [1951] 1 K.B. 233 (CA).
[177] *Compania de Naviera Nedelka v Tradax (The Tres Flores)* [1973] 2 Lloyd's Rep. 247.
[178] *Stanton v Austin* (1872) L.R. 7 C.P. 651; *Fairbridge v Pace* (1844) 1 C. & K. 317. In *Gordon v Powis* (1892) 8 T.L.R. 397, under the clause, "Captains or owners to telegraph advising probable arrival, and at least eight clear days' notice shall be given previous to requiring cargo", it was held that a telegram advising ship's departure from the last port did not satisfy notice of readiness for cargo required. In *Burnett S.S. Co v Olivier & Co* (1934) 48 Ll.L.R. 238, where there was an express clause providing that notice of readiness should be given, it was held that this applied to the first only of three ports of loading.
[179] *Franco-British S.S. Co v Watson & Youell* (1921) 9 Ll.L.R. 282 at p.284.
[180] *Borg (Owners) v. Darwen Paper Co* (1921) 8 Ll.L.R. 49.

a waiver of the stipulation as to notice will be inferred from the mere loading or discharge of the ship before notice is given.[181]

Unless the charter provides to the contrary, facts entitling notice to be given, such as arrival and readiness, must exist at the time notice is given, and not only at its expiry, for the notice to be valid. If a notice is invalid for this reason it will not become valid when the facts change so as to justify a notice being given.[182]

Where an invalid notice of readiness is given lay-time may not begin even when the ship commences loading or unloading. It will only do so where there is waiver by the charterers of the invalidity by accepting the notice with knowledge of the invalidity, or by loading or discharging with knowledge of the invalidity and without reservation; or if there is otherwise a contractual variation or estoppel.[183] By contrast to the normal position, a charter may indicate that laytime is to run after the service of a notice, even if the ship was not in fact ready, provided that the notice was served in good faith.[184]

If the charterers accept the notice so as to give rise to waiver or estoppel, it has been said that acceptance cannot be withdrawn unless induced by fraud.[185]

If an owner gives notice of readiness which is premature because it is before the first permissible layday then, by contrast with a notice which is invalid due to the ship being unready, or not being an arrived ship, it takes effect at the earliest layday.[186] Similarly if a charter restricts the times of day at which a notice may be given, such as "within office hours" , a notice given out of hours which is received by the charterers will take effect from the next time at which it could validly have been given.[187]

Case 1. A ship was chartered to proceed direct to S dock, and there load in the usual and customary manner. In an action by shipowner against charterers for not loading, the latter pleaded that by reason of want of notice of the ship's arrival at the S dock and her readiness to load, the charterers were unable to load her. *Held*, a good defence, if proved.[188]

---

[181] *Pteroti v National Coal Board* [1958] 1 Q.B. 469; see *Nelson v Nelson* [1908] A.C. 108. *Cf. Franco-British S.S. Co v Watson & Youell* (1921) 9 Ll.L.R. 282 at p.284, where written notice was not required, and *Kawasaki Kisen v Bantham S.S. Co* [1938] 1 K.B. 805 at p.813 (notice of delivery under time charter).

[182] *Transgrain Shipping BV v Global Transporte Oceanico SA (The Mexico I)* [1988] 2 Lloyd's Rep. 149; [1990] 1 Lloyd's Rep. 507 (CA), where the ship was unready, disapproving *Government of Ceylon v Société Franco-Tunisienne* [1960] 2 Lloyd's Rep. 352 at p.358; *Glencore v Navios (The Mass Glory)* [2002] EWHC 27 (Comm); [2002] 2 Lloyd's Rep. 244 and *Glencore v Flacker Shipping (The Happy Day)* [2002] EWCA Civ 1068; [2002] 2 Lloyd's Rep. 487, where the ship had not arrived. Masters have been advised, in case of doubt, to give and go on giving notices: *Zim v Tradax (The Timna)* [1970] 2 Lloyd's Rep. 409, 411.

[183] *Glencore v Flacker Shipping (The Happy Day)* [2002] EWCA Civ 1068; [2002] 2 Lloyd's Rep. 487, 510–511 para.85, following a review of older authorities. Older examples of waiver or estoppels include *Surrey Shipping v Compagnie Continental (The Shackleford)* [1978] 2 Lloyd's Rep. 154 and *Sofial v Ove Skou (The Helle Skou)* [1976] 2 Lloyd's Rep. 205.

[184] *United Nations Food and Agriculture Organisation—World Food Programme v Caspian Navigation Inc (The Jay Ganesh)* [1994] 2 Lloyd's Rep. 358. See also *Cobelfret N.V. v Cyclades Shipping Co Ltd (The Linardos)* [1994] 1 Lloyd's Rep. 28.

[185] *Sofial SA v Ove Skou Rederi (The Helle Skou)* [1976] 2 Lloyd's Rep. 205, explained as a case of waiver in *Glencore v Flacker Shipping (The Happy Day)* [2002] EWCA Civ 1068; [2002] 2 Lloyd's Rep. 487.

[186] *Tidebrook v Vitol SA (The Front Commander)* [2006] 2 Lloyd's Rep. 251. If the charterer accepts the premature notice, there may be waiver so as to give effect to the notice before the first permissible layday.

[187] *Galaxy v Novorossisk (The Petr Schmidt)* [1998] 2 Lloyd's Rep. 1.

[188] *Stanton v Austin*, above.

Case 2. A ship was chartered to proceed to A and there load; she arrived at A with a cargo on owner's account. Her arrival was entered at the Custom House, but no notice was given to the charterer of her readiness to load homeward cargo. *Held*, the charterer was not liable for failing to provide a cargo.[189]

Case 3. A ship gave notice of readiness to discharge when not ready. She became ready to charterers' knowledge. After further delay she commenced discharge. *Held* laytime did not commence before discharge (the charterers having conceded that laytime did commence on discharge).[190]

Case 4. The ship gave notice of readiness under a berth charter before arrival at the berth. The charterers knew this and commenced discharge without any reservation of rights. *Held* that by commencing discharge with knowledge of the invalidity of the notice and without any reservation or rights the charterers had waived the invalidity of the notice.[191]

Note. As to notice of readiness to discharge, see Art.150.

A77   **Article 77—Special Demurrage Clauses**[192]

Articles 73 to 76 set out the requirements which must, in the absence of special provision, be fulfilled before the ship is arrived, and lay-time begins to run against the charterer. However, express provisions are commonly inserted in charterparties which either dispense with the fulfilment of one or more of these requirements, or stipulate that although lay-time proper does not begin until the requirements are fulfilled, nevertheless some other form of time shall start to count upon the happening of a specified event. These provisions may for convenience be grouped under the following headings:

(1) Clauses which dispense with one or more of the pre-conditions to "arrival".[193]

(2) Clauses which provide that certain types of waiting time are to "count as" loading or discharging time. Provisions of this type require the "special" time to be brought into the calculation of lay-time and demurrage.

(3) Clauses which provide that certain types of waiting time are to be paid for at a stipulated rate. Under provisions of this type, waiting time does not enter into the calculation of lay-time or demurrage.

---

[189] *Fairbridge v Pace*, above. What amount of notice will suffice is doubtful. If the charterers are proved to be otherwise aware of the readiness to load, *quaere* whether express notice would be required when there is no stipulation for written notice: see *Franco-British S.S. Co v Watson & Youell*, above, at p.284.

[190] *Transgrain Shipping BV v Global Transporte Oceanico SA (The Mexico I)* [1988] 2 Lloyd's Rep. 149; [1990] 1 Lloyd's Rep. 507 (CA).

[191] *Glencore v Flacker Shipping (The Happy Day)* [2002] 2 Lloyd's Rep. 487.

[192] This expression was suggested in H. Tiberg. *The Law of Demurrage* (4th edn, 1995) pp.259 *et seq.*

[193] In *R. Pagnan & Fratelli v Finagrain Compagnie Commerciale et Financiere SA (The Adolf Leonhardt)* [1986] 2 Lloyd's Rep. 395 at p.397, Staughton J. observed that such clauses are used where the parties do not like the legal test of when a ship has reached its destination.

(4) Clauses which place upon the charterer an obligation to give the ship immediate access to a berth.

These various provisions differ both as to their nature and their effects. The following Articles discuss, in relation to each type of clause, whether time can begin notwithstanding that the prerequisites of arrival are not fulfilled; how the running of time is calculated; whether the running of time is interrupted or postponed by the operation of excepted perils; and how, if at all, the running of this "special" time is affected, if lay-time in the strict sense is also running.

Article 78—Clauses which dispense with the prerequisite of "arrival"   A78

It is possible by express provision to provide that lay-time shall begin to run notwithstanding that one or more of the prerequisites of "arrival" have not been fulfilled. In practice, by far the most common type of clause is one which ensures that time begins to run when the ship has reached a particular point, even though she has not yet attained the location at which she can become arrived.[194] Amongst these clauses are the following:

(i) "Time to discharge to begin when the vessel is reported at the Custom House". Clauses in this and similar forms are effective to start the lay-time running even though the vessel has not become an arrived ship.[195]

(ii) "In the event of the vessel . . . being unable to berth immediately upon arrival . . . time to count from next working period after vessel's arrival at . . . anchorage."[196]

(iii) "Whether in berth or not."[197]

(iv) "Berth or no berth."[198]

---

[194] It is known, but less common, to have clauses which can operate to *postpone* the running of lay-time until a point after arrival. Examples are clauses which fix the lay-time by reference to a "colliery guarantee" or a "regular turn", see *Monsen v Macfarlane* [1895] 2 Q.B. 562 (colliery guarantee); *US Shipping Board v Strick* [1926] A.C. 545; *Moor Line v Manganexport* (1936) 55 Ll.L.R. 114; *The Themistocles* (1949) 82 Ll.L.R. 232 (regular turn); and the Indian cases in which the vessel must have been entered at Customs House, see *Antclizo Shipping v Food Corp of India (The Antclizo No.2)* [1992] 1 Lloyd's Rep. 558.

[195] *Horsley Line v Roechling*, 1908 S.C. 866; *The Graigwen* [1955] 2 Lloyd's Rep. 260; *Compania Argentina de Navegacion de Ultrauar v Tradax Export (The Puerto Rocco)* [1978] 1 Lloyd's Rep. 252.

[196] *Cia Nav. Termar v Tradax* [1966] 1 Lloyd's Rep. 566 (HL). An exclusion of "time used in shifting" in a clause of this type does not exclude time spent in waiting at anchorage for sufficient depth of water to proceed.

[197] *Northfield S.S. Co v Compagnie L'Union des Gaz* [1912] 1 K.B. 434; *Bulk Transport Group Shipping Co Ltd v Seacrystal Shipping Ltd (The Kyzikos)* [1989] 1 Lloyd's Rep. 1; [1989] A.C. 1264. This clause is effective to advance the running of lay-time where no berth is available but not where a berth is available but cannot be reached due to fog: *ibid. Aliter* where the charter is in a "port" form where it is inappropriate and indeed surplusage: *Carga del Sur Na SA v Ross T. Smythe & Co Ltd* [1962] 2 Lloyd's Rep. 147; *The Johanna Oldendorff* [1974] A.C. 479 at p.553; *The Martha Envoy* [1978] A.C. 1.

[198] *Société Anonyme Marocaine de l'Industrie du Raffinage v Notos Maritime Corp (The Notos)* [1987] 1 Lloyd's Rep. 503 in which it was held that the shipowner could give a valid Notice of Arrival when she reached the customary anchorage whether or not a berth was available.

(v) "Whether in port or not."[199]

Clauses of this type, which provide that lay-time is to begin at an arbitrary point, are to be distinguished from those which add a further prerequisite to the commencement of lay-time, leaving unaffected the requirement that the ship shall be "arrived". In each case, the particular words of the charter must be construed.[200]

The computation of time under clauses of this type does not normally raise any special problem. Since the time simply forms part of the ordinary lay-time, it is calculated in the same manner as lay-time,[201] and is interrupted or postponed by the operation of the perils comprised in the lay-time exception clauses.[202]

A79   **Article 79—Clauses which Provide that Waiting Time is to Count as Loading or Discharging Time**

The "Gencon" form of charter provides: "Time lost in waiting for berth to count as loading time." A similar clause relates to time spent in waiting at the discharging port.[203] It is not uncommon for this formula to be inserted into other forms of charter, and other clauses to a similar effect are also in use. Such clauses may advance the commencement of laytime in berth charters,[204] and in port charters where the usual waiting place is outside the limits of the port.[205]

When the clause applies it does not have the effect of enabling the shipowner to count as laytime periods when excepted causes, such as holidays, bad weather and strikes, would have prevented laytime from running had the vessel been in berth,[206] or, in the case of a port charter, had she been an arrived ship.[207] It is irrelevant that notice of readiness has not been given, because it cannot be owing to no berth being available.[208]

---

[199] *R. Pagnan & Fratelli v Finagrain Compagnie Commerciale Agricole et Financiere SA (The Adolf Leonhardt)* [1986] 2 Lloyd's Rep. 397. To take advantage of such a clause, the ship must be within a usual waiting area for ships seeking to enter the port.

[200] Contrast *The Graigwen*, above, with *Akt. Inglewood v Millar's Karri Forests* (1903) 8 Com.Cas. 196 and *Sanders v Jenkins* [1897] 1 Q.B. 93, which have similar clauses. See also per Kennedy J. in *Modesto v Dupre* (1902) 7 Com.Cas. 105 at pp.110–111.

[201] e.g. by reference to weather working days (if the lay-time is so expressed) and not chronological days. So also with Sundays, holidays, etc.

[202] See *Reardon Smith v East Asiatic* (1938) 44 Com.Cas. 10 and *The Amstelmolen* [1961] 2 Lloyd's Rep. 1 on the effect of the "Centrocon" strike clause on the running of time under a clause employing the words "whether in berth or not".

[203] Sometimes "as lay-time" is substituted for "loading" or "discharging" time: *Aldebaran Compania Maritima SA v Aussenhandel AG (The Darrah)* [1977] A.C. 157; the change does not affect the construction.

[204] The clause was originally intended to be used in "berth" charters. Many of the problems to which it has given rise stem from its use in "port" charters. Sometimes the effect of the clause is negated by another clause in the charterparty relieving the charterer from liability for events or hindrances outside his control: *Navrom v Callitsis Ship Management SA (The Radauti)* [1987] 2 Lloyd's Rep. 276; [1988] 2 Lloyd's Rep. 416.

[205] *The Maratha Envoy* [1978] A.C. 1 at p.10 and *The Werrastein* [1957] 1 Q.B. 109, though again *The Darrah*, above, shows that the occurrence of causes, excepting the running of lay-time, would affect the calculation of the relevant time lost.

[206] *The Darrah*, above, reversing *The Loucas N* [1971] 1 Lloyd's Rep. 215.

[207] *The Darrah*, above, per Lord Diplock, [1977] A.C. at p.168.

[208] *The Werrastein*, above.

It is submitted that the time spent in waiting should be added into the lay-time calculation from moment to moment as it is lost and should not be added in at the end.[209] Time can be lost although the ship is not ready to load or discharge, provided that her unreadiness does not cause delay.[210]

Article 80—Clauses which Require Waiting Time to be Paid for   A80

Charterparties sometimes provide that once a particular point has been reached, all time waiting thereafter will be "paid" for. Thus, in the "Austral" form the discharging clause stipulates that "if such discharging place is not immediately available, demurrage in respect of all time waiting thereafter shall be paid" at the demurrage rate.[211]

Clauses of this type are different from those discussed in the preceding Articles, since the waiting time neither ranks as lay-time nor is brought into the lay-time calculation.[212] It follows that waiting time can run against the shipowner notwithstanding that the ship is not within the geographical limits of the port[213] and no notice has been given.[214] Similarly, waiting time can start even though the vessel is not, at the moment when she begins to wait, physically ready to load.[214] Since the clause does not purport to make the waiting time a part of lay-time, it should logically continue to run even on days—e.g. Sundays and holidays —when the running of lay-time is suspended. Whether the running of waiting time is prevented or interrupted by excepted perils depends on the wording of the exception.

Article 81—Clauses requiring the immediate availability of a berth   A81

Some forms of clause require the charterer to nominate a "ready quay berth"[215] or a berth which is "reachable upon arrival" or "always accessible".[216] The word "arrival" does not require the vessel to have satisfied the requirements of an arrived ship. The word means arrival at the point, whether within or outside the

---

[209] Adopting the view of Donaldson J. for the reasons given by him in *The Loucas N.* [1970] 2 Lloyd's Rep. 482 at p.486, differing from the decision on this point, given without reasons, by Diplock J. in *Government of Ceylon v Soc. Franco-Tunisienne (The Massalia)* [1960] 2 Lloyd's Rep. 352.

[210] This appears to be the combined result of *The Massalia*, above, where time was "lost" notwithstanding that the charterers' cargo was over-stowed with other cargo, and the dicta of Donaldson J. in *The Loucas N*, above, at p.485, which envisaged that there would be a deduction if the ship required time to uncover hatches or rig cargo gear. For another case of a part cargo overstowed above the cargo carried under the charter, where it was held there was no time lost until after the overstowed cargo had been discharged; see *Agios Stylianos Compania Naviera v Maritima Associates International (The Agios Stylianos)* [1975] 1 Lloyd's Rep. 426.

[211] *Roland-Linie Schiffahrt v Spillers* [1957] 1 Q.B. 109.

[212] The word "demurrage" in the "Austral" clause is clearly not used in its technical sense.

[213] In *Roland-Linie v Spillers*, above, time began to run notwithstanding that the ship, for reasons of draught and lack of space, had to wait some 22 miles away from the discharging place and outside the legal, geographical and fiscal limits of the port.

[214] This is so as regards "time lost waiting for berth" and must be so, *a fortiori*, in relation to the "Austral" clause.

[215] i.e. a berth which is ready for loading upon a ship's arrival: *Harris v Jacobs* (1885) 15 Q.B.D. 247.

[216] See e.g. *Seacrystal Shipping v Bulk Transport (The Kyzikos)* [1989] 1 Lloyd's Rep. 1.

fiscal or commercial limits of the port, where the indication or nomination of a particular loading place would become relevant if the vessel were to be able to proceed without being held up.[217]

A berth is not "reachable" if it is occupied by another vessel.[218] Nor is the berth reachable on arrival if there is insufficient depth of water in the berth or in the port[219] or if the berth cannot be reached due to a ban on night navigation at the port, bad weather or the absence of tugs.[220] The charterer must nominate a berth which the vessel can reach on arrival proceeding normally,[221] that is to say without waiting in the port in the ordinary way.[222]

Time lost by the ship as a result of the berth not being "ready" or "available" or "accessible" does not count towards the lay-time. If the ship is not an "arrived" ship, breach by the charterer of these clauses does not entitle or require the owner to give notice of readiness.[223] The owner's remedy is to recover damages for the delay. It is submitted that the computation of damages should take into account delays which would have occurred in any event if the ship had berthed at once.[224]

Since the clause is not concerned with lay-time, it is submitted that the time which is excluded from lay-time (e.g. time on Sundays and holidays) is not excluded from the computation of the damages. Similarly it is submitted that exceptions clauses which are concerned exclusively with lay-time do not exempt the charterer from liability for failure to nominate a ready or reachable berth.

Notwithstanding that the charterers may be in breach of their obligation to nominate a berth "reachable upon arrival", nevertheless from the time the vessel is an arrived ship the charterers are entitled to the full use of the permitted lay-time and the owners cannot recover damages at large for the breach during the running of such time, and cannot recover both demurrage and damages for the same delay.[225]

Note. The clause applied notwithstanding words excusing the charterers from liability for delay in getting into berth due to "any reason over which Charterer has no control", because the exclusion did not apply to the obligation to designate and procure the berth,

---

[217] *The Angelos Lusis*, [1964] 2 Lloyd's Rep. 28 *per* Megaw J. at pp.33–34, followed in *The President Brand* [1967] 2 Lloyd's Rep. 38, and *The Delian Spirit* [1971] 1 QB 103.
[218] *Soc. Cargo Oceanica v Idolineole (The Angelos Lusis)* [1964] 2 Lloyd's Rep. 28. See also *The Delian Spirit* [1971] 1 Q.B. 103; *Nereide SpA Navigazione v Bulk Oil International (The Laura Prima)* [1982] 1 Lloyd's Rep. 1.
[219] *The President Brand* [1967] 2 Lloyd's Rep. 338.
[220] *K/S Arnt J. Moerland v Kuwait Petroleum Corp (The Fjordaas)* [1988] 1 Lloyd's Rep. 336; *Palm Shipping Inc v Kuwait Petroleum (The Sea Queen)* [1988] 1 Lloyd's Rep. 500; *Sale v Turkish Cargo Lines (The Amiral Fahri Engin)* [1993] 1 Lloyd's Rep. 75.
[221] *Soc. Cargo Oceanica v Idolineole (The Angelos Lusis)*, above.
[222] *Palm Shipping Inc v Kuwait Petroleum*, above.
[223] *The Mass Glory* [2002] 2 Lloyd's Rep. 244 at 249–250.
[224] Because a computation of damages involves a comparison of the shipowner's actual financial position with his position as it would have been had there been no breach.
[225] *Shipping Developments Corp v V/O Sojuzneftexport (The Delian Spirit)* [1972] 1 Q.B. 103 (CA), approving *The President Brand* [1967] 2 Lloyd's Rep. 338; *The Mass Glory* [2002] EWHC (Comm) 27; [2002] 1 Lloyd's Rep. 244.

and only applied when the delays occurred by a cause occurring after the berth had been designated and procured by the charterer.[226]

Article 82—Duty of Charterer to Furnish Cargo   A82

In the absence of express stipulations it is the absolute non-delegable duty of the charterer,[227] if he can legally do so, to furnish a cargo according to the charter. This duty may be resolved into three parts:

A. The cargo must reasonably comply with the terms of the charter.

B. The charterer must bring the cargo to the loading place, if it is not already there.

C. The charterer must perform his part of the operation of putting the cargo on board the vessel.

A. *The cargo* must be one reasonably complying with the terms of the charter.[228] If the charter is for a specified description of cargo and the charterer ships goods of a different description, the shipowner can claim the market rate of freight for that other cargo if in excess of the chartered freight.[229]

Where the charterer is under the obligation to load a cargo that may be constituted in various ways, e.g. a full and complete cargo of "wheat and/or maize and/or rye", the fact that he has made all arrangements for shipping one kind, e.g. wheat, will not relieve the charterer from his obligation to load an alternative cargo, e.g. maize or rye, if by an excepted peril during the process of loading he is prevented from loading the wheat.[230] But in such a case it seems that he is allowed a reasonable time for making his alternative arrangements.[231]

B. Whether a charter is in the berth or port category,[232] if the ship cannot arrive so as to enable lay-time to commence unless cargo is available for her (owing, for

---

[226] *Nereide v Bulk Oil (The Laura Prima)* [1982] 1 Lloyd's Rep. 1; *Sametiet M/T Johs Stove v Istanbul Petro Rafinerisi A/S (The Johs Stove)* [1984] 1 Lloyd's Rep. 38. See also *Palm Shipping Inc v Kuwait Petroleum (The Sea Queen)*, above.

[227] *Triton v Vitol (The Nikmary)* [2003] EWCA Civ 1715; [2004] 1 Lloyd's Rep. 55 at 60, para.11.

[228] *Holman v Dasnieres* (1886) 2 T.L.R. 480; affirmed *ibid*. p.607. See also *Stanton v Richardson* (1872) L.R. 7 C.P. 421. Thus a charter to load a cargo of pitch in bulk will, *semble*, not be satisfied by a cargo which has melted and has to be dug out of the trucks; a "cargo of machinery" without any particular description of it, by a single piece of machinery to ship which the master must cut open his decks. *Cf. Isis Co v Bahr & Co* [1900] A.C. 340.

[229] *Steven v Bromley* [1919] 2 K.B. 722. *Cf. Chandris v Isbrandtsen-Moller* [1951] 1 K.B. 240.

[230] *Brightman v Bunge y Born* [1924] 2 K.B. 619, affirmed on other grounds [1925] A.C. 799; *South African Dispatch Line v Owners of S.S. "Niki"* [1960] 1 Q.B. 518 (CA). In the latter case the use of the phrase "the cargo intended for shipment . . . cannot be provided" in the exceptions clause did not take the case out of the principle. Contrast *Reardon Smith Line v Ministry of Agriculture* [1963] A.C. 691 (HL), where the words of the charter were held to confer a true option as to alternative cargoes, which the charterer was free to exercise or not as he thought fit.

[231] See the cases in fn.230, above. The allowance of a reasonable time has not yet been the subject of decision in the HL, though it was approved by Lord Atkinson in *Brightman v Bunge y Born* [1925] A.C. 799 at p.814, and discussed in *Reardon Smith Line v Ministry of Agriculture* [1963] A.C. 691 at p.717, per Lord Radcliffe and at p.732, per Lord Devlin. See also *Venizel A.N.E. v Soc. Commerciale de Cereales et Financiére SA* [1974] 1 Lloyd's Rep. 350.

[232] See, above, Art.74.

example, to regulations of the harbour-master) the charterer, in the absence of any relevant exception, is under an absolute obligation to provide the cargo or such part of it as may be necessary in time to enable the ship to become arrived and, in default of this obligation, will be liable in damages to the shipowner for delay caused by the non- availability of such cargo.[233] When the arrival of the ship is not affected by the non-availability of cargo, the charterer must[234] make and carry out arrangements for delivery of the cargo at the ship's side at the place of loading in time to load her within the agreed time after her arrival[235] and in ordinary circumstances nothing which prevents him from doing so will relieve him from his express or implied obligation to load in a fixed or reasonable time, as the case may be.[236] But where there are several loading places in the port and the charterer has supplied a cargo at one of them and is prevented from loading by the operation of an excepted peril he is excused from loading at any of the other loading places so long as the prevention is only temporary and the delay does not exceed a reasonable time.[237]

Stipulations and exceptions in a charter as to the obligation to load usually apply to C. only, i.e. the operation of putting the cargo on board and not to B., i.e. the bringing of the cargo to the port of loading.[238] They may, however, sometimes apply to B.[239]

---

[233] *The Aello* [1961] A.C. 135 applying *Ardan S.S. Co v Weir* [1905] A.C. 501, and distinguishing *Little v Stevenson* [1896] A.C. 108. The latter must now be taken to have been decided on its special facts and *Jones v Green* [1904] 2 K.B. 275 to have been overruled, unless supportable on the state of knowledge of the parties: see *The Aello* [1961] A.C. at pp.176, 185, 221, which is not overruled on this point by *Oldendorff v Tradax Export* [1974] A.C. 479. See also *Triton v Vitol (The Nikmary)* [2003] EWCA Civ 1715; [2004] 1 Lloyd's Rep. 55 at pp.61–62, para.15. It is not sufficient for the charterer to do all that is reasonable as Greer J. thought was his obligation: *Vergottis v Cory* [1926] 2 K.B. 344, followed in *Hogarth v Cory* (1926) 32 Com.Cas. 174 (PC). The Shipowner's remedy is by way of damages; he cannot claim that his ship must be deemed to have arrived so as to enable lay-days to commence: *The Aello*, above; *The Maratha Envoy* [1978] A.C. 1 (HL).

[234] This obligation is not a condition: *Chandris v Isbrandtsen-Moller* [1951] 1 K.B. 240; *Universal Cargo Carriers v Citati* [1957] 2 Q.B. 401 at pp.429, 430. Although, therefore, failure to make the cargo available at the appropriate time will entitle the shipowner to damages, he will not be entitled to treat the charter as repudiated unless the delay, actual or probable, is such as would frustrate the commercial object of the charter; *Universal Cargo Carriers v Citati*, above, at pp.430–435. See, also, *Hongkong Fir Shipping Co v Kawasaki Kisen Kaisha* [1962] 2 Q.B. 26.

[235] *Vergottis v Cory* [1926] 2 K.B. 344 at p.356; *Universal Cargo Carriers Corp v Citati* [1957] 2 Q.B. 401 at p.429; *Triton v Vitol (The Nikmary)* [2003] EWCA Civ 1715; [2004] 1 Lloyd's Rep. 55 at pp.61 paras 13–14.

[236] See Lord Selborne in *Grant v Coverdale* (1884) 9 App.Cas. 470 at pp.475, 476; and Lord Blackburn in *Postlethwaite v Freeland* (1880) 5 App.Cas. 599 at p.619; *Ardan S.S. Co v Weir* [1905] A.C. 501. As the duty to provide cargo devolves on the charterer alone, he does not come within the principle of *Ford v Cotesworth* (1868) L.R. 4 Q.B. 127 at pp.133, 134; affirmed (1870) 5 Q.B. 544. But *quaere* whether since *Ralli v Compania Naviera* [1920] 2 K.B. 287, foreign law preventing the charterer alone procuring a cargo would not be a good defence. In *Kirk v Gibbs* (1857) 1 H. & N. 810, where a charterer had contracted to load a full cargo and to procure the necessary Peruvian Government pass for loading, it was held no defence that that Government would only grant a pass for less than full cargo. So, if the duty to load is on the shipowner alone, as in *Hills v Sughrue* (1846) 15 M. & W. 253. As to discharging, see *Kruuse v Drynan* (1891) 18 Rettie 1110; *Granite S.S. Co v Ireland* (1891) 19 Rettie 124.

[237] *Lewis v Dreyfus* (1926) 31 Com.Cas. 239. Cf. *Seabridge Shipping v Antco Shipping Co* [1977] 2 Lloyd's Rep. 367.

[238] *Grant v Coverdale* (1884) 9 App.Cas. 470; *Kay v Field* (1883) 10 Q.B.D. 241; *Ardan S.S. Co v Weir* [1905] A.C. 501. Thus "loaded *with usual despatch*" does not relate to the facilities which the charterers may have in their trade for getting the cargo alongside the vessel, but to putting it on board: *Kearon v Pearson* (1861) 7 H. & N. 386. Cf. *The Sheila* [1909] p.31, note ("customary turn by the G. W. Ry.").

[239] But to do so they must be clearly worded: *Triton v Vitol (The Nikmary)* [2003] EWCA Civ 1715; [2004] 1 Lloyd's Rep. 55 at 60, para.11; *Arden S.S. Co v Mathwin*, 1912 S.C. 211; *Pinch & Simpson v Harrison, Whitfield & Co* (1948) 81 Ll.L.R. 268 ("provision of cargo").

Thus, in the absence of express provisions covering the case the charterer will not be relieved from such obligations by:

(i) Causes preventing a cargo from being obtained, such as strikes,[240] bankruptcy of merchants supplying the cargo,[38] or non-existence of such cargo[241]; or

(ii) Causes preventing a cargo when obtained from being transmitted to the port of loading, such as ice,[242] bad weather,[243] railway delays[244] or Government orders.[245]

The charterer may, however, be relieved from such obligations:

(i) If any exception in the charter *expressly* applies to the act of bringing the cargo to the place of loading.

(ii) If any exception in the charter *by implication*[246] applies to the act of bringing the cargo to the place of loading. The implication will arise, for instance, if the circumstances of business in relation to the contractual cargo are such that the charterer cannot have the goods ready at that loading place but must necessarily convey them from a particular place in a particular manner. If such transit is prevented by a cause falling within the exceptions the charterer will be excused. He must show, however, that no other method of bringing the cargo to the loading place was available.[247]

(iii) If the parties contracted in reference to a cargo from a particular source and were aware of the existence of a state of things which might delay

---

[240] per Lord Selborne, *Grant v Coverdale* (1884) 9 App.Cas. 470 at p.476; *Stephens v Harris* (1887) 57 L.J.Q.B. 203. Even with the exception of "strikes" and a strike causing delay, the charterer is not absolved if he has not made a proper contract for purchase of the cargo, under which contract delay might have been avoided: *Dampsk. Danmark v Poulsen*, 1913 S.C. 1043.

[241] *Hills v Sughrue* (1846) 15 M. & W. 253. *Cf. Ashmore v Cox* [1899] 1 Q.B. 436.

[242] *Grant v Coverdale*, above; *Kay v Field*, above; *Kearon v Pearson*, above.

[243] *Fenwick v Schmalz* (1868) L.R. 3 C.P. 313.

[244] *Adams v Royal Mail Steam Co* (1858) 5 C.B. (N.S.) 492; *Elliott v Lord* (1883) 52 L.J.P.C. 23.

[245] *Semble*, from *Ford v Cotesworth* (1868) L.R. 4 Q.B. 127; and see *Case* 4 below. *Quaere*, whether since *Ralli v Compania Naviera* [1920] 2 K.B. 287 this requires modification.

[246] *Furness v Forwood* (1897) 2 Com.Cas. 223 ("stoppage of trains and miners"); *Petersen v Dunn* (1895) 1 Com.Cas. 8 ("strikes, lock-outs of pitmen and others"). *Cf. Fenwick v Schmalz* (1868) L.R. 3 C.P. 313.

[247] *Hudson v Ede* (1868) L.R. 3 Q.B. 412, as explained by Lord Selborne in *Grant v Coverdale* (1884) 9 App.Cas. 470 at p.477, and by the Court of Appeal in *Stephens v Harris* (1887) 57 L.J.Q.B. 203, and *Brightman v Bunge y Born* [1925] A.C. 799. Contrast *Matheos v Dreyfus* [1925] A.C. 654 at pp.662, 666 and *Lewis v Dreyfus* (1926) 31 Com.Cas. 239, as to the burden of proving an alternative practicable mode or place of loading. *Hudson v Ede* was followed by Charles J. in *Allerton S.S. Co v Falk* (1888) 6 Asp.M.C. 287, on facts applicable to the salt trade in the Mersey. In *The Alne Holme* [1893] P. 173 and *Hain S.S. Co v Canadian Transport Co* (1942) 73 Ll.L.R. 80 (lighterage from Taku Bar to Tientsin), the same principle was applied to the port of discharge. See also *Furness v Forwood Bros* (1897) 2 Com.Cas. 223 (ore coming by rail to Poti); *Richardsons & Samuel, Re* [1898] 1 Q.B. 261 (oil coming by rail to Batoum); *Smith v Rosario Nitrate Co* [1894] 1 Q.B. 174 (CA) (nitrate coming down to Iquique).

the provision of a cargo from such source and such delay in fact occurs, provided that the delay is not unreasonable.[248]

C. The charterer must perform his part of the operation of putting the cargo on board, unless excused by express exceptions, the causes excepted being proved not merely to exist but also directly to prevent the loading of the ship.[249] If the charterer proves that the usual and proper method of loading was prevented by an excepted peril, the onus shifts to the shipowner to prove the existence of an alternative practicable method.[250] If this be shown, the charterer cannot escape liability unless he proves that no time would have been saved by adopting the alternative method.[251]

Voyage charters generally include laytime provisions stipulating the time within which the charterer must load (and discharge) and demurrage provisions providing for liquidated damages for breach. See Art.157, *Charterer's undertaking to load in a Fixed Time*; and Art.158, *Charterer's undertaking to load in a Reasonable Time* and Chapter 14 generally.

When once the loading is completed the charterer's obligation is fulfilled,[252] and subsequent delays,[253] such as by ice,[254] or failure to procure clearance,[255] must fall on the shipowner, unless caused by the charterer, e.g. by his not presenting bills of lading for signature[256] or by failing to co-operate in obtaining the necessary clearance for the vessel from the port of loading.[257]

Case 1. A ship was chartered to "proceed to Cardiff East Bute Dock and there load iron in the customary manner . . . cargo to be supplied as fast as steamer can receive . . . time to commence from the vessel's being ready to load, excepting in case of hands striking work, or frost, or floods, or any other unavoidable accidents preventing the loading".

The charterer's agent had his own iron at a wharf in a canal outside the dock, but there were other agents with wharves in the dock, and it was possible, though expensive, to bring the iron from the wharf to the dock by land. Frost stopped the transit of the iron by the canal, though it would not have stopped the loading if the cargo had been in the dock. *Held*, that the charterers were liable for the

---

[248] *Harris v Dreesman* (1854) 23 L.J.Ex. 210 (*Case 5*, below). *Jones v Green* [1904] 2 K.B. 275, if not overruled by *Ardan S.S. Co v Weir* [1905] A.C. 501 and *The Aello* [1961] A.C. 135, appears to fall under this principle.

[249] per Lord Blackburn, *Postlethwaite v Freeland* (1880) 5 App.Cas. 599 at p.619; *The Village Belle* (1874) 30 L.T. 232. Thus the perils must prevent the loading of cargo by any ship; e.g. the order of an invading army that *no* grain shall be exported: *Bruce v Nicolopulo* (1855) 11 Ex. 129. Generally a cause which prevents or delays the provision of a cargo is not a cause "preventing or delaying loading". Cf. *Arden S.S. Co v Mathwin*, 1912 S.C. 211; *Pinch & Simpson v Harrison, Whitfield & Co* (1948) 81 Ll.L.R. 268.

[250] *Matheos v Dreyfus* [1925] A.C. 654 at pp.662, 666.

[251] *Reardon Smith Line v Ministry of Agriculture* [1962] 1 Q.B. 42 at pp.94, 122 (CA) (this point did not arise in the HL).

[252] *Smith v Wilson* (1817) 6 M. & S. 78.

[253] *Nolisement v Bunge* [1917] 1 K.B. 160.

[254] *Pringle v Mollett* (1840) 6 M. & W. 80. For special clauses imposing an obligation on charterers to provide icebreaker assistance to enable a ship to enter or leave a port of loading, Art.71 *Note 2*, above.

[255] *Barret v Dutton* (1815) 4 Camp. 333. Otherwise if the charterer fails to provide necessary documents or information.

[256] *Nolisement v Bunge* [1917] 1 K.B. 160.

[257] *Margaronis Navigation Agency v Peabody & Co* [1964] 1 Lloyd's Rep. 173. There is probably an equivalent duty on the part of the shipowner to co-operate with the charterer to enable the ship to complete and be released from the loading operation: *Total Transport Corp v Amoco Transport Co (The Altus)* [1985] 1 Lloyd's Rep. 423 at p.430.

delay, as the frost did not prevent the loading, but only the transit of the cargo to the place of loading by one of the ways usual at the Port.[258]

Case 2. A shipowner agreed to send his ship to X and there find and take on board a full cargo of guano. There was no guano at X within a reasonable time of the ship's arriving. *Held*, the shipowner was absolutely bound to find and load a full cargo.[259]

Case 3. A ship was chartered to proceed to X and there load coals in customary manner. The loading was delayed by a dispute between the railway and the colliers as to rates of carriage and by a strike of colliers. *Held*, that the charterers were liable for the delay.[260]

Case 4. A ship is chartered to load cattle at an English port; though the loading of cattle already at that port would not be prohibited, their transfer to that port is forbidden by Order in Council. *Submitted*, the charterer would be liable for delay arising from such Order.[261]

Case 5. A ship was chartered to load at S colliery. Before signing the charter both parties knew that the colliery engine had broken down and was being repaired. *Held*, that if the engine was repaired and the ship loaded in a reasonable time, the charterer was not liable, as the owners signed the charter knowing of the breakdown of the engine.[262]

Case 6. A ship was chartered to proceed to X "and there load grain; the cargo to be brought to and taken from alongside the ship at the ports of loading and discharge at the charterer's expense and risk . . . thirty running days for loading . . . detention by ice not to be reckoned as lay-days". All grain loaded at X was brought by river from U, ninety miles off. Owing to ice between U and X the cargo was detained in transit to X. *Held*, that the conveyance from U by water, being the only method used, must be considered as part of the act of loading, and that the exception as to ice relieved the charterer from liability.[263]

Case 7. A ship chartered with thirty running days for loading finished her loading on February 25, but owing to a fire at the custom-house her clearances could not be obtained till March 9, when she sailed. *Held*, that, as it was the duty of the owner to obtain clearances, the charterer was not liable for the delay.[264]

Case 8. A ship was chartered to discharge in forty-eight hours, except in case of "strike . . . detention by railway or cranes . . . or any other cause beyond the control of the charterers which might impede the ordinary loading and discharging of the vessel"; owing to a railway strike, railway wagons to receive coal were not forthcoming; the cargo could have been discharged on the quay. *Held*, that the charterers were not protected by the exceptions.[265]

Case 9. A ship was chartered to load at New York a cargo of steel billets at 23s. a ton. The charterer shipped 1,208 tons of steel billets and 987 tons of general merchandise. At the time of

---

[258] *Grant v Coverdale* (1884) 9 App.Cas. 470. See also *Kay v Field* (1883) 10 Q.B.D. 241, and *The Rookwood* (1894) 10 T.L.R. 314 (CA). In *Kearon v Pearson* (1861) 7 H. & N. 386, it was said "that time for loading has no reference to the place whence the cargo is to come", i.e. "usual dispatch" could not be construed "usual dispatch of cargo coming from a particular colliery", but "usual dispatch of persons having a cargo ready for loading". Cf. *The Sheila* [1909] P. 31, note.

[259] *Hills v Sughrue* (1846) 15 M. & W. 252; but see the observations on this case in *Clifford v Watts* (1879) L.R. 5 C.P. 577, where Brett and Willes JJ. treat it as a contract by the charterer to find a full cargo, which it certainly was not.

[260] *Adams v Royal Mail Steam Co* (1858) 5 C.B. (N.S.) 492.

[261] On authority of *Ford v Cotesworth* (1870) L.R. 5 Q.B. 544; if export from the English or foreign port were actually forbidden, the charterer would be excused. See *Ralli v Compania Naviera* [1920] 2 K.B. 287.

[262] *Harris v Dreesman* (1854) 23 L.J.Ex. 210.

[263] *Hudson v Ede* (1868) L.R. 3 Q.B. 412, as explained by Lord Selborne in *Grant v Coverdale* (1884) 9 App.Cas. 470. The dictum of Willes J. approved by the court in *Hudson v Ede*, that "whenever there was no access to the ship by reason of excepted perils from any one of the storing places from which goods were conveyed direct to the ship, the exception in the charter would apply", must be taken as overruled by *Coverdale v Grant*, unless "any one" means "all". See also *Stephens v Harris* (1887) 57 L.J.Q.B. 203; and *"Matheos" (Owners) v. Dreyfus* [1925] A.C. 654. Cf. *Allerton S.S. Co v Falk* (1888) 6 Asp.M.C. 287 and the cases cited in fn.247, above.

[264] *Barret v Dutton* (1816) 4 Camp. 333.

[265] *Granite S.S. Co v Ireland* (1891) 19 Rettie 124. Cf. *Kruuse v Drynan* (1891) 18 Rettie 1110.

shipment that market rate for general goods was higher than 23s. a ton. *Held*, that the shipowner could claim the higher market rate of freight on the 987 tons.[266]

Case 10. A ship was ordered to Buenos Aires to load maize. Owing to a system of traffic control operated by the port authorities, she could not get into the commercial area so as to become an arrived ship, although there were empty berths there, until the charterers had maize available for her to load, and she was forced to wait in the outer anchorage. There was nothing the charterer could have done to make the cargo available earlier. *Held*, she could not be deemed to be an arrived ship, so as to enable time to commence whilst at the anchorage but the charterers were liable in damages for the time lost waiting until, on cargo becoming available, she was permitted to berth.[267]

A83   Article 83—"Alongside"

In ordinary circumstances goods to be brought to or taken from "alongside" must be delivered immediately alongside, i.e. to or from the ship's tackle in such a position that the consignee can begin to act upon them.[268] The word "alongside" is not ambiguous: the shipowner must deliver alongside. No evidence of a custom increasing his obligation can be given.[269] But so long as the cargo is delivered alongside, the mutual obligations of shipowner and receiver may be ascertained by evidence of the customary method of discharge; e.g. the shipowner may be obliged by custom to stack the cargo on shore or stow it in barges, but he cannot be required in dealing with it to place it in a position which is not alongside the ship.[270] The incidence of this customary method may, however, be excluded by apt words, e.g. "any custom of the port to the contrary notwithstanding".[271]

The shipowner's duty does not begin till the goods are under his charge.[272]

If the shipowner takes the goods for loading before they have been brought to the place to which it is the duty of the charterer under the charter to bring them, he cannot, without express agreement to that effect, claim from the charterer any extra expense incurred in so doing.[273]

A84   Article 84—Charterer's Refusal or Inability to Load

If the charterer expressly or by conduct refuses to load the vessel, the shipowner need not wait till the end of the days allowed for loading before he can sue for

---

[266] *Steven v Bromley* [1919] 2 K.B. 722.
[267] *The Aello* [1961] A.C. 135, overruled on other points by *Oldendorff v Tradax Export* [1974 A.C. 479.
[268] *Petersen v Freebody* [1895] 2 Q.B. 294, where no custom was alleged. See *Avon S.S. Co v Leask* (1890) 18 Rettie 280, where "delivery alongside" is contrasted with "delivery at ship's rail"; on the words "ex car from alongside", see *Isis S.S. Co v Barh & Co* (1898) 3 Com.Cas. 325. As to the words "discharge onto wagons . . . within reach of shore crane tackle", see *Dampskip Selskab Svendborg v L.M. & S. Ry.* [1930] 1 K.B. 83. The words "to be delivered from the ship's tackle" are not inconsistent with a practice so to discharge into lighters and then onto the quay: *Marcelino Gonzalez v Nourse* [1936] 1 K.B. 565.
[269] *Palgrave, Brown v Turid* [1922] 1 A.C. 397, overruling *Stephens v Wintringham* (1898) 3 Com.Cas. 169. See also *Hillas & Co v Rederi Aktiebolaget Aeolus* (1926) 32 Com.Cas. 69 (Hull); *Northmoor S.S. Co v Harland & Wolff* [1903] 2 I.R. 657 (Belfast); *The Rensfjell* (1924) 40 T.L.R. 458 (West Hartlepool and Sunderland); *Anglo-Oriental Navigation Co v Brocklebank* (1927) 27 Ll.L.R. 359 (jute at Dundee); *Dalgleish S.S. Co v Williamson* (1935) 40 Com.Cas. 312 (cork at Heysham).
[270] *Smith, Hogg & Co v Bamberger* [1929] 1 K.B. 150; *Aktieselskab Helios v Ekman* [1897] 2 Q.B. 83 (CA) (London); *Glasgow Navigation Co v Howard* (1910) 15 Com.Cas. 88 (London).
[271] *Brenda S.S. Co v Green* [1900] 1 Q.B. 518.
[272] per Lord Selborne in *Coverdale v Grant* (1884) 9 App.Cas. 470 at p.475. See also *British Columbia Co v Nettleship* (1868) L.R. 3 C.P. 499.
[273] *Holman v Dasnieres* (1886) 2 T.L.R. 480; affirmed *ibid.* p.607. In *Fletcher v Gillespie* (1826) 3 Bing. 635, there was such an express agreement.

a breach of the contract to load, but may accept such anticipatory breach and treat it as final.[274] If the shipowner does not accept the refusal as final, the charterer may retract it and may begin to load at any time before the lay-days have expired.[275]

Again, where the charterer refuses to load and the shipowner does not accept such refusal as final, if the contract becomes illegal before the lay-days have expired,[276] the doctrine of frustration will operate in the normal way so that the charterer will be absolved from the performance of his contract.

If the charterer is wholly and finally disabled from finding and loading a cargo before the expiry of a time sufficient to frustrate the adventure, the shipowner will be entitled to treat the charter as at an end even though the charterer has never refused to load and has insisted that he is ready, able and willing to do so.[277] If, however, by words or conduct the charterer professes inability to perform the charter, that is sufficient to constitute an anticipatory breach which the shipowner may accept and, in such circumstances, it will be irrelevant whether or not the charterer was able to perform.[278]

Case 1. A by his agent agreed to carry C's goods in his ship, the shipment to commence on August 1. On July 21, A wrote to C saying that his agent had no authority to make the contract; on July 23, A still repudiated it, but offered a substituted contract. C gave A notice that he would hold A bound by the original contract, but that, if A failed to perform it, C would make other arrangements. On August 1, A wrote that he was prepared to ship the goods, making no reference to the original contract. C declined, having made other arrangements. *Held,* that C had a right to treat A's repudiation as a final breach.[279]

Case 2. An English ship was chartered to proceed to X and there load a cargo in forty-five running days. The vessel was ready to load on March 9; between March 1 and April 1 the charterer repeatedly refused to load, but the captain stayed on at X ready to load. On April 1, and before the expiration of the running days, war broke out between England and Russia; the captain finally sailed on April 22. *Held,* that as the captain had never accepted the refusal to load as final, the charterer had the whole of the running days to perform his contract in, and, as before then the performance became illegal, he was discharged.[280]

Case 3. A ship chartered to load at X arrived there on July 12. The charterer had failed to nominate a shipper prepared to accept notice of readiness or a loading berth, or to provide a cargo by July 18. The shipowners thereupon cancelled the charter and ordered the ship away from X three days before the lay-days were due to expire. An arbitrator found that the shipowner should on July 18 have inferred from the charterer's conduct (i) he was willing to perform if he could; (ii) he could not have

---

[274] *Danube & Black Sea Ry. v Xenos* (1863) 13 C.B. (N.S.) 825; *Universal Cargo Carriers v Citati* [1957] 2 Q.B. 401 at pp.436, 437 and *Evera SA Commercial v North Shipping Co* [1956] 2 Lloyd's Rep. 367 at p.377. As regards his duty, in that case, to mitigate the damages, see *Note 4* to Art.192, below.
[275] *Reid v Hoskins* (1856) 6 E. & B. 953.
[276] As in *Esposito v Bowden* (1857) 7 E. & B. 763; *Avery v Bowden* (1856) 6 E. & B. 953 at p.962.
[277] *Universal Cargo Carriers v Citati* [1957] 2 Q.B. 401. Whether the charterer was unable to perform is to be determined in the light of all the evidence at the trial, whether relating to events which occurred before or after the critical date and whether or not known to the shipowner at the time: *ibid*, p.450. Whether the shipowner will, apart from sailing away, be able to recover damages will depend, inter alia, upon whether the charterer is protected by exceptions or can rely upon illegality by the local law.
[278] *ibid*, p.437. See, also, *Evera SA Commercial v North Shipping Co* [1956] 2 Lloyd's Rep. 367 at p.377.
[279] *Danube Co v Xenos*, above. This case follows the principle of *Hochster v De la Tour* (1853) 2 E. & B. 678; *Frost v Knight* (1872) L.R. 7 Ex. 111; discussed in *Johnstone v Milling* (1886) 16 Q.B.D. 460 (CA).
[280] *Reid v Hoskins* (1856) 6 E. & B. 953.

performed by the end of the lay-days or within a reasonable time thereafter; but (iii) he could have performed before the delay became so long as to frustrate. *Held*, (1) the obligations to nominate a berth and to provide a cargo were warranties, breaches of which would not entitle the shipowners to cancel unless they persisted or would persist for sufficiently long to frustrate the commercial object of the venture; (2) the arbitrator's second finding did not amount to a finding that the charterer had renounced the contract, since the relevant period was not a reasonable time but a time sufficient to frustrate the venture; but (3) the case should be remitted to the arbitrator to decide whether the charterer was in fact, on July 18, willing and able to perform the charterparty within such time as would not have frustrated the commercial object of the venture.[281]

As to the charterer's obligations to load within the lay time, and demurrage, see:

Demurrage: see Chapter 14, Arts 154–160, below.

Loading in fixed time: see Art.157, below.

Loading in reasonable time: see Art.158, below.

Loading with customary dispatch: see Art.158, below.

A85   **Article 85—Loading**

Stipulations as to loading or unloading in a charter or bill of lading are to be construed with reference to the customs of the port of loading or discharge,[282] unless such customs contradict or vary express stipulations in the charter or bill of lading.[283] At common law loading is a joint operation between shipper or charterer and the shipowner, responsibility for which is considered further in Article 90.

Note. The admissibility of evidence of custom or usage is more fully discussed in Art.11.

Case 1. A ship was chartered to load at X "a full and complete cargo of sugar, molasses, and/or other lawful produce". Evidence was tendered of a custom at X that a full cargo of sugar and molasses meant a cargo composed of particular kinds of package, i.e. hogsheads of sugar and puncheons of molasses. *Held*, admissible.[284]

Case 2. A ship was chartered to proceed to X and there load in the customary manner a full and complete cargo of M coke, "to be loaded in regular turn". The vessels for M coke were loaded by

---

[281] *Universal Cargo Carriers v Citati* [1957] 2 Q.B. 401. The arbitrator found the charterer willing but unable [1957] 2 Lloyd's Rep. 311.

[282] *Carali v Xenos* (1862) 2 F. & F. 740 seems to show that it may not be sufficient to follow the usual custom of the docks, if unusual damage can be prevented from occurring by special exertion.

[283] per Lord Blackburn in *Postlethwaite v Freeland* (1880) 5 App.Cas. 599 at p.613, who curiously enough omits the qualification that the custom must not contradict the writing: *Aktieselskab Helios v Ekman* [1897] 2 Q.B. 83 (CA); *Cuthbert v Cumming* (1856) 11 Ex. 405; *Leidemann v Schultz* (1853) 14 C.B. 38; *Pust v Dowie* (1864) 5 B. & S. 20; *The Skandinav* (1881) 51 L.J.Ad. 93; *Brenda S.S. Co v Green* [1900] 1 Q.B. 518. See also *Benson v Schneider* (1817) 7 Taunt. 272; *Nielsen v Neame* (1884) 1 C.& E. 288; *Fullagsen v Walford* (1883) C. & E. 198.

[284] *Cuthbert v Cumming* (1856) 11 Ex. 405. *Cf. Mikkelsen v Arcos* (1925) 42 T.L.R. 3; *Angfartygs A/B Halfdan v Price and Pierce* (1939) 45 Com.Cas. 23.

the M colliery in the order of their entry in a book, and not of their readiness to load and this ship was so loaded. The jury found that the ship was loaded according to the practice of the M Colliery, but that it was not an established or known custom, and that "regular turn" meant "order of readiness", not "order of entry in the book". *Held*, that the charterer was liable for demurrage.[285]

Case 3. A sailing vessel was chartered to proceed to X for coals and load "in regular turn"; there is only one colliery at X, and the practice of that colliery is to supply steamers in their order of readiness, and sailing vessels in their order, but to postpone sailing vessels to steamers; and this applies to all coal vessels at X. The owner was ignorant of this usage. *Held*, that this usage was the custom of the port and that "regular turn" was to be construed according to it, the owner's ignorance being immaterial.[286]

Article 86—To Load a Full and Complete Cargo[287]   A86

"Full and complete cargo" means a full and complete cargo according to the custom of the port of loading.[288]

Where the charter provides that a ship is "to load a full and complete cargo", there is a mutual obligation on the charterer to tender and load and the owner to load a full and complete cargo.[289]

Where a vessel is chartered as of a certain capacity, and the charterer undertakes to load a "full and complete cargo", he cannot limit his obligation to the capacity named in the charter, but must load as much cargo[290] as the ship will carry with safety.[291]

But where a certain number of tons is stipulated for in the clause as to "cargo", that number and not the actual capacity of the vessel will constitute the approximate measure of the charterer's obligation.[292]

---

[285] *Lawson v Burness* (1862) 1 H. & C. 396; see also *Leidemann v Schultz* (1853) 14 C.B. 38 and *Robertson v Jackson* (1845) 2 C.B. 412.

[286] *King v Hinde* (1883) 12 Ir.L.R.C.L. 113. The Scottish case of *Stephens v Macleod* (1891) 19 Rettie 38 appears to contradict this, and is, it is submitted, erroneous.

[287] For undertakings by the shipowner as to the ship's tonnage or dead weight capacity, and Art.75, above, as to the meaning of the expression "full reach and burthen".

[288] *Cuthbert v Cumming* (1856) 11 Ex. 405 at p.409; and see Art.85. See also *Colonial Ins. Co v Adelaide Ins. Co* (1886) 12 App.Cas. 128 at p.134.

[289] *China Offshore v Giant Shipping (The Posidon)* [2001] 1 Lloyd's Rep. 697, 701–702; *Margaronis Navigation Agency v Peabody & Co* [1965] 1 Q.B. 300. Where there is more than one usual method of loading, the charterer may fulfil his obligation of loading a full and complete cargo by adopting one of those methods notwithstanding that by the adoption of another of those methods more goods could have been shipped; *Angfartygs A/B Halfdan v Price and Pierce* (1939) 45 Com.Cas. 23.

[290] "Cargo" usually means an entire shipload: *Kreuger v Blanck* (1870) L.R. 5 Ex 179; *Borrowman v Drayton* (1876) 2 Ex.D. 15 (but not necessarily a "full and complete cargo"); *Miller v Borner* [1900] 1 Q.B. 691. See also *Harrison and Micks, Lambert & Co, Re* [1917] 1 K.B. 755 and *Paul v Pim, Jun.* [1922] 2 K.B. 360. But a contract to load a "cargo" stated to be less than the capacity of the vessel leaves the shipowner at liberty to load other cargo: *Caffin v Aldridge* [1895] 2 Q.B. 648 (CA). As to "dead weight capacity", see Art.47.

[291] *Furness Withy v Black Sea (The Roman Karmen)* [1994] 1 Lloyd's Rep. 644, *Heathfield v Rodenacher* (1896) 2 Com.Cas. 55 (CA); *Thomas v Clarke* (1818) 2 Stark. 450; *Hunter v Fry* (1819) 2 B. & Ald. 421. *Cf. Red. Urania v Zachariades* (1931) 41 Ll.L.R. 145. Where the cargo contracted for varies in size or weight or condition according to the time of year, the charterer will fulfil his obligation by supplying a full and complete cargo of the goods in their normal condition at the time of shipment: *Isis Co v Bahr & Co* [1900] A.C. 340. But where charterers, having contracted to load a full and complete cargo, fail to load the ship within the lay-days with the result that she can only carry a winter instead of a summer cargo, they are guilty of a breach of contract for which the damages are the difference between the freight earned by a summer and that earned by a winter cargo: *Aktieselskabet Reidar v Arcos* [1927] 1 K.B. 352.

[292] *Morris v Levison* (1876) 1 C.P.D. 155; *Alcock v Leeuw* (1884) C. & E. 98; *Miller v Borner* [1900] 1 Q.B. 691.

On the other hand a charter for a full and complete cargo, subject to stipulated maximum and minimum quantities, obliges the charterer to load either a full and complete cargo or the stated maximum, whichever is the less, the owners giving a warranty that the ship can carry the minimum.[293] If a charter in this form also provides that the quantity is to be in owner's option to be declared by the master on commencement of loading, the amount declared establishes the quantity to be loaded.[294] But where the master makes a declaration not provided for by the charter, the declaration does not convert the obligation to load "a full and complete cargo" into an obligation to load the quantity declared.[295]

The charterer is bound to put on board goods equivalent to the cargo stipulated for or to a full and complete cargo, though, owing to their destruction before the ship sails, they may not all be carried in the ship.[296] But when the charterer has loaded goods which have been destroyed by an excepted peril, he is not bound, nor is he entitled, to load other goods in the same space, and the shipowner has the right to fill that space with goods and take the freight thereon.[297]

Where the charterer fails to load a full and complete cargo, the shipowners may, if such course is reasonable, fill up with other cargo in order to minimise the damages and may delay for a reasonable time in so doing.[298]

Where the charter calls for a "full and complete cargo", the charterer is entitled to keep the ship in port during the lay-days for as long as a full and complete cargo is not loaded, even if cargo is deliberately withheld by the charterer.[299]

Where the ship is stowed in a manner that does not make full use of her hold, but the charterer or his agents saw the stowage and made no objection, the shipowner will not be liable for not loading a full and complete cargo.[300] The charterer may however not be liable.[301]

---

[293] *Carlton S.S. Co v Castle Mail Packets* (1897) 2 Com.Cas. 173 at p.177; *Jardine, Matheson & Co v Clyde S.S. Co* [1910] 1 K.B. 627; *Louis Dreyfus v Parnaso* [1960] 2 Q.B. 49. In *Jardine, Matheson & Co v Clyde S.S. Co* it was also decided that where the charterer is given the use of the ship, except the bunkers, he is not required to load cargo in the cross-bunker forward of the engine-room, which could, with coal burning ships, usually be used either for cargo or for fuel: see *ibid.* 15 Com.Cas. 193. See also *Noemijulia S.S. Co v Minister of Food* [1951] 1 K.B. 223.

[294] *Louis Dreyfus v Parnaso* [1960] 2 Q.B. 49. Harman L.J., at p.59, said that the option need not be exercised and that no declaration need be made; *sed quaere.* Apparently the declaration by the master may be qualified, as by the word "about": *ibid.* As to the latitude given by this word, see, *Case 1,* below, and the cases there footnoted.

[295] *Margaronis Navigation Agency v Peabody & Co* [1965] 1 Q.B. 300 at p.316; but *cf.* per Pearson L.J. at [1965] 2 Q.B. 430 at p.446.

[296] Thus in *Jones v Holm* (1867) L.R. 2 Ex. 335, where, when a ship had loaded part of her cargo she caught fire, and the cargo on board being damaged had to be sold: *Held,* that the charterer was not bound to replace the damaged cargo, but was bound to supply so much as would with the undamaged cargo make a "full and complete cargo". But see *Strugnell v Friedrichsen* (1862) 12 C.B. (N.S.) 452, where the discharge of three-quarters of the cargo under similar circumstances at the master's request, and at the charterer's expense, was held to free the charterer from any further liability apparently on the ground that the contract had been discharged by mutual consent.

[297] *Aitken v Ernsthausen* [1894] 1 Q.B. 773. This seems to be so whether the rate of freight is a rate per ton or a lump sum: *cf. Weir v Girvin & Co* [1900] 1 Q.B. 45.

[298] *Wallems Rederi A/S v Muller & Co* [1927] 2 K.B. 99.

[299] See Art.157.

[300] *Hovill v Stephenson* (1830) 4 C.P. 469.

[301] *Furness v Tennant* (1892) 8 T.L.R. 336.

The charterer is entitled to the full benefit of the use of the ship, and the shipowner is not entitled to impair that full benefit by loading more bunker coals than are reasonably necessary for the chartered voyage.[302]

To be "lawful merchandise" within the common provision limiting the use of a ship to the carriage of such cargo, the goods must be of a type which it is lawful to load at the port of loading and to carry to and discharge at the port ordered by the charterers for discharge.[303]

Case 1. A vessel was chartered "to load a full and complete cargo of iron, say about 1,100 tons". The deadweight capacity of the ship was 1,210 tons. The charterer furnished 1,080 tons. *Held*, that the charterer was only bound to "load about 1,100 tons"; that 3 per cent was a fair margin; hence that he should have loaded 1,133 tons.[304]

Case 2. A ship was guaranteed to carry 2,600 tons deadweight, and charterers undertook to load a full and complete cargo at a named freight "all per ton deadweight capacity as above". A full and complete cargo would be 2,950 tons. *Held*, (1) charterers should load 2,950 tons; (2) freight was payable on that quantity at the named rate.[305]

Article 87—Broken Stowage   A87

Where there is a charter "to load a full and complete cargo", if the cargo loaded leaves room that may be filled with "broken stowage", such broken stowage must be provided unless the custom of the port of loading does not require it.[306]

Case. A ship was chartered "to load at X a full and complete cargo of sugar, molasses, and/or other produce". The charterer filled the ship with sugar, in hogsheads and molasses in puncheons, but did not fill up with broken stowage. Evidence of a custom at X that "full and complete cargo of sugar and molasses" meant cargo so stowed without broken stowage, held admissible, and the custom reasonable. *Held*, therefore, that the charterer had fulfilled his obligation.[307]

---

[302] *Darling v Raeburn* [1907] 1 K.B. 846. In *Carlton S.S. Co v Castle Mail Co* (1897) 2 Com.Cas. 173 (not reversed on this point on appeal), the shipowner was held entitled to ship more bunkers than were necessary for the chartered voyage, but this was on proof that such a course was customary. As to considerations which may limit the amount which the owners can reasonably be required to load see *Furness Withy (Australia) Pty v Black Sea Shipping Co* [1994] C.L.C. 180.

[303] *Leolga v John Glynn* [1953] 2 Q.B. 374. In *Vanderspar v Duncan* (1891) 8 T.L.R. 30, government guns and ammunition were held on proof of usage not to be "lawful merchandise". See also *Potter v New Zealand S. Co* (1895) 1 Com.Cas. 114.

[304] *Morris v Levison* (1876) 1 C.P.D. 155. But see *Miller v Borner* [1900] 1 Q.B. 691, on the words "a cargo of about 2,800 tons", and *Jardine, Matheson & Co v Clyde S.S. Co* [1910] 1 K.B. 627 (cited in n.95, p.161), on the words "a cargo of beans not less than 6,500 but not exceeding 7,000 tons". A cargo of so many tons, "or thereabouts", is frequently taken to allow a margin of five per cent either way. This sort of usage is old: "If the ship be fraighted for 200 Tuns or thereabouts, this addition (*or thereabouts*) is within five Tuns commonly taken and understood" (Malynes, *Lex Mercatoria*, 1686, p.100). In *Alcock v Leeuw* (1884) C. & E. 98, a charter to ship "empty petroleum barrels as required by the master, say about 5,000", was held to allow the master 10 per cent margin on either side of 5,000. In *SA L'Industrielle Russo-Belge v Scholefield* (1902) 7 Com.Cas. 114, a custom of the Newcastle coal trade that the word "*about*" gave the vendor an option of five per cent either way was proved and upheld by the CA. A shortfall of 331 tons on 10,400 (or 3.18 per cent) is within the margin permitted by the word "about": *Louis Dreyfus v Parnaso* [1960] 2 Q.B. 49 (CA). In *Efploia v Canadian Transport* [1958] 2 Lloyd's Rep. 449 at p.458, "about 600/700 tons" was assumed to give a range of 575/725 tons. Where the word "*about*" is not used, see *Harland v Burstall* (1901) 6 Com.Cas. 113. See also *Thornett and Yuills, Re* [1921] 1 K.B. 219 and *Red. Urania v Zachariades* (1931) 41 Ll.L.R. 145. The margin expressly permitted by "about" will still be subject to the rule "*De minimis non curat lex*": *Shipton v Weil* (1912) 17 Com.Cas. 153.

[305] *Heathfield S.S. Co v Rodenacher* (1896) 2 Com.Cas. 55 (CA).

[306] *Cole v Meek* (1864) 15 C.B. (N.S.) 795; see also *Duckett v Satterfield* (1868) L.R. 3 C.P. 227.

[307] *Cuthbert v Cumming* (1856) 11 Ex. 405. *Cf. Mikkelsen v Arcos* (1925) 42 T.L.R. 3; *Angfartygs A/B Halfdan v Price and Pierce* (1939) 45 Com.Cas. 23.

A88   **Article 88—Deck Cargo**

Goods are to be loaded in the usual carrying places.[308]

The shipowner or master will only be authorised to stow goods on deck: (1) by a custom binding in the trade, or port of loading, to stow on deck goods of that class on such a voyage,[309] or (2) by express agreement with the shipper of the particular goods so to stow them.[310]

Deck stowage not so authorised is a breach of contract by the shipowner who will in principle be liable under his contract of carriage for damage happening to such goods caused by such stowage.[311]

Whether exceptions of the charter or bill of lading apply to protect the shipowner is a matter of construction. There is no rule of law that, because unauthorised loading of deck cargo is a fundamental breach, such exceptions are inapplicable.[312] Even if there are any special principles of construction relating to the application of exceptions to deviation, they do not apply to deck cargo.[313] Normal principles of construction of exemption clauses apply, not always with consistent results.[314]

If by his bill of lading the shipowner is authorised to carry either under deck or on deck, he is not bound to inform the shipper that he is going to carry on deck, so as to enable the latter to insure his goods as deck cargo.[315]

---

[308] *Mitcheson v Nicoll* (1852) 7 Ex. 929; *Royal Exchange Co v Dixon* (1886) 12 App.Cas. 11 at p.16. See below, Arts 119, 133. Where by the charter charterers were to have "the full reach of the vessel's hold from bulkhead to bulkhead, including the half-deck", *held*, that the freight for goods stowed on deck was due to the shipowners: *Neill v Ridley* (1854) 9 Ex. 677. As to cross-bunkers, see *Jardine Matheson & Co v Clyde S.S. Co* (1910) 15 Com.Cas. 193.

[309] Such as existed in *Gould v Oliver* (1837) 4 Bing.N.C. 134, and was attempted to be proved in *Newall v Royal Exchange Co* (1885) 33 W.R. 432; reversed *ibid*, p.868, and *Royal Exchange Co v Dixon* (1886) 12 App.Cas. 11.

[310] As in *Burton v English* (1883) 12 Q.B.D. 218; *Wright v Marwood* (1881) 7 Q.B.D. 62; *Johnson v Chapman* (1865) 19 C.B. (N.S.) 563.

[311] *Newall v Royal Exchange Co*, below. This case is also reported in (1885) 1 T.L.R. 178, 490, but in neither report are the grounds of the judgment very clear. Before Cave J., at the trial, it was assumed that there was a binding custom to load on deck at the shipowner's risk: Cave J. held that this custom excluded the terms of the bill of lading; that therefore the shipowner was liable as a common carrier, but that as the goods, owing to the custom, were properly stowed on deck, the master was the agent of the shipper in making a jettison and the shipper's only right was to a general average contribution. In the Court of Appeal it was held that there was no such binding custom, that therefore the goods were improperly stowed on deck and the master had not the authority of the shipper to jettison them; that consequently the remedy of the shipper was not for a general average contribution; and that the shipowner could not protect himself by the exceptions in the bill of lading, because those exceptions only applied to goods properly stowed. The House of Lords, *sub nom. Royal Exchange Co v Dixon* (1886) 12 App.Cas. 11, upheld the view of the Court of Appeal.

[312] *Kenya Railways v Antares Co Pte Ltd (The Antares)* [1987] 1 Lloyd's Rep. 424, CA, disapproving a passage to the contrary in the 19th edn of this work at p.167. For deviation cases, see below, Art.127.

[313] *Daewoo v Klipriver (The Kaptian Petko Voivoda)* [2003] EWCA Civ 451; [2003] 2 Lloyd's Rep. 1, 12–15, paras 13–23, commenting on the passage in the 20th edn of this work at p.168, and overruling *Wibau Maschinenfabric Hartman SA v Mackinnon Mackenzie & Co (The Chanda)* [1989] 2 Lloyd's Rep. 494 in which Hirst J. held that as a matter of construction, the exceptions and limitations contained in the bill of lading did not apply to unauthorised deck carriage. *Nelson Pine Industries Ltd v Seatrans New Zealand Ltd (The Pembroke)* [1995] 2 Lloyd's Rep. 290 (N.Z.) in which the package limitation clauses in the Hague/Hague-Visby Rules were held as a matter of construction not to apply to cargo carried on deck in breach of contract and *JJ Case (Australia) Pty. Ltd v Tasman Express Line Ltd (The Canterbury Express)* (1990) 102 F.L.R. 59 (Aus), might not now be decided the same way.

[314] See e.g. *The Fantasy* [1991] 2 Lloyd's Rep. 391, *The Danah* [1993] 1 Lloyd's Rep. 351, *LD Seals v Mitsui (The Darya Tara)* [1997] 1 Lloyd's Rep. 42, *The Visurgis* [1999] 1 Lloyd's Rep. 218, *Transocean v Euxine (The Imvros)* [1999] 1 Lloyd's Rep. 848 and *Sunlight v Ever Lucky* [2004] 2 Lloyd's Rep. 174.

[315] *Armour v Walford* [1921] 3 K.B. 473.

The peculiar position of goods stowed on deck puts them in a special relation to claims for general average.[316]

Goods carried on deck and stated to be so carried in the bill of lading are not "goods" within the meaning of the Carriage of Goods by Sea Act 1971. A mere liberty to carry on deck without the statement in the bill of lading does not exclude the application of the Act.[317] If the bill of lading provides for carriage on deck, but they are carried under deck, the Act apparently applies to them. *Quaere* as to the result if they start the voyage on deck and in the course of it are restowed under deck. See Article I(c) and notes thereto in Chapter 20.[318]

Article 89—Ballast and Dunnage   A89

The shipowner having to furnish a seaworthy ship is bound to provide sufficient ballast and dunnage to make the ship seaworthy and the ship is not ready to load until she is so provided.[319] The shipowner cannot require the charterer to provide such a cargo as will render it unnecessary for the shipowner to load ballast.[320]

The shipowner under a voyage charter may carry freight-paying merchandise as ballast, if it takes no more room than ballast would have done and does not interfere with the cargo shipped by the charterer.[321]

Note. Dunnage is the name given to the provision made in stowage to protect goods, by the use of various articles, from damage by contact with the bottom or sides of the vessel or with other goods. Shifting boards are to be treated as part of the ship's proper equipment rather than as dunnage,[322] and in the absence of express provision in the charter the owners will be liable for the cost of fitting them.[323]

Case 1. A ship was chartered "to load a full and complete cargo of copper, tallow, hides, or other goods".[324] The charterer provided tallow and hides, but no copper. In consequence, the ship had to

---

[316] See below, Arts 119, 136.

[317] *Svenska Traktor Akt. v Maritime Agencies (Southampton)* [1953] 2 Q.B. 295.

[318] For the position under the Hamburg Rules see Art.9.1 below.

[319] *Sailing Ship Lyderhorn v Duncan* [1909] 2 K.B. 929; *Harlow & Jones Ltd v P.J. Walker Shipping and Transport Ltd* [1986] 2 Lloyd's Rep. 141. The charterer sometimes contracts to ship ballast at ship's expense: and, if so, may, in the absence of express stipulation be liable for delay in such shipment: see for such stipulation *Sanguinetti v Pacific Steam Navigation Co* (1877) 2 Q.B.D. 238. For special clause as to dunnage, see *The Cressington* [1891] p.152, where it was held that the certificate of a surveyor on the point before sailing is not conclusive against the charterer even when the charter requires such a certificate to be furnished. *Cf. Sleigh v Tyser* [1900] 2 Q.B. 333; *Petrofina, SA v Cia. Italiano Trasporto Olii Minerali* (1937) 42 Com.Cas. 286.

[320] *Moorsom v Page* (1814) 4 Camp. 103; *Irving v Clegg* (1834) 1 Bing.N.C. 53; *Southampton S. Colliery Co v Clarke* (1870) L.R. 6 Ex. 53; *Weir v Union S.S. Co* [1900] A.C. 525.

[321] *Towse v Henderson* (1850) 4 Ex. 890. *Semble*, the shipowner may use cargo as ballast or dunnage, provided it can be so stowed as to take no harm, though this will rarely happen; hence, dictum of Sir R. Phillimore in *The Marathon* (1879) 40 L.T. 163 at p.166.

[322] *Wye Co v Compagnie P.O.* (1922) 10 Ll.L.R. 85, in which charterers agree to provide "all dunnage required".

[323] *Rederi A/B Unda v Burdon & Co* (1937) 42 Com.Cas. 239. *Cf. Aktieselskapet Skagerack v Saremine* (1939) 64 Ll.L.R. 153, where charterers were held liable for the cost of shifting boards; *sed quaere*.

[324] For other cases on special charters as to proportion of goods to be shipped, see *Cockburn v Alexander* (1848) 6 C.B. 791; *Warren v Peabody* (1849) 8 C.B. 800; *Capper v Forster* (1837) 3 Bing.N.C. 938; *Southampton S. Colliery Co v Clarke* (1870) L.R. 6 Ex. 53.

keep in her ballast and so lost freight. *Held*, that the charterer was justified in shipping such a cargo.[325]

Case 2. A ship was chartered "to carry a full and complete cargo of merchandise, 100 tons of rice or sugar to be shipped previous to any other cargo as ballast". The charterer completed the loading with such light goods that more than 100 tons of ballast was required. *Held*, that the shipowner must supply it.[326]

A90   **Article 90—Loading, Stowage and Stevedores**

At common law loading is a joint operation of the shipper or charterer and of the shipowner. In the absence of custom or express agreement[327] it is the duty of the former at his risk and expense to bring the cargo alongside and lift it to the ship's rail[328]; it is then the duty of the owner by his master to receive load and stow the cargo properly.[329] Stowing and lashing the cargo are part of the operation of loading.[330] If the master or shipowner himself directs the stowage, he is bound to exercise the same skill as a properly qualified stevedore.[331] If he fails to do so, the shipper has an action against the owner or master.[332]

As between shipper and shipowner the employment of a stevedore by the shipowner does not relieve him from liability under his contract to carry as contained in the bill of lading, and, unless protected by express agreement, he will therefore be contractually liable for damage done in or by negligent stowage,[333] though he will have his remedy against the stevedore.

A shipper who takes an active interest in the stowage cannot afterwards be heard to complain of patent defects in the stowage of which he made no complaint at the time.[334] The knowledge and consent of the shipper would

---

[325] *Moorsom v Page* (1814) 4 Camp. 103.

[326] *Irving v Clegg* (1834) 1 Bing.N.C. 53.

[327] A contract of carriage subject to the Carriage of Goods by Sea Act 1971 may place the responsibility for loading and discharging on the shipper or receiver, notwithstanding Arts I and III, r. 2 of the Rules (see below), and may do so by in corporation of a charterparty; see *Jindal Steel v Islamic Shipping (The Jordan II)* [2004] UKHL 49; [2005] 1 Lloyd's Rep. 57 (HL), approving the summary in the 20th edn of this work at pp.430–431. It remains unclear whether the incorporation into the bill of lading of a charterparty under which stowage is the responsibility of "the charterer" is sufficient to transfer responsibility to the shipper or receiver: *Balli Trading Ltd v Afalona Shipping Co Ltd (The Coral)* [1993] 1 Lloyd's Rep. 1 (CA).

[328] *Harris v Best* (1892) 68 L.T. 76; *Argonaut Navigation Co v Ministry of Food* [1949] 1 K.B. 572 (CA); *Pyrene Co v Scindia Navigation Co* [1954] 2 Q.B. 402 at pp.414, 416. The division of duties at the ship's rail instead of alongside is somewhat out of keeping with modern methods and apparently does not apply in Scotland: *ibid.* and *Glengarnock Iron and Steel Co v Cooper* (1895) 22 R. 672.

[329] *Jindal Steel v Islamic Shipping (The Jordan II)* [2004] UKHL 49; [2005] 1 Lloyd's Rep. 57 at p.61, para. 11 per Lord Steyn; *Blaikie v Stembridge* (1860) 6 C.B. (N.S.) 894; *Sandeman v Scurr* (1866) L.R. 2 Q.B. 86. *Cf. Ballantyne v Paton*, 1912 S.C. 246. The ship must have suitable tackle available for the ordinary purposes of loading and discharging, even if the goods are to be "loaded free of expense to the vessel": *Hang Fung Shipping Co v Mullion* [1966] 1 Lloyd's Rep. 511; *cf. Madras v P. & O.* (1923) 16 Ll.L.R. 240 at p.243. For the obligations of shipowner and charterer as to the opening and closing of hatches, see *S.G. Embiricos v Tradax* [1967] 1 Lloyd's Rep. 464.

[330] See the cases in fn.328, above, and *Svenssons v Cliffe S.S. Co* [1932] 1 K.B. 490.

[331] *Anglo-African Co v Lamzed* (1866) L.R. 1 C.P. 226; *Swainston v Garrick* (1833) 2 L.J.Ex. 255, and see *Note 1*, below.

[332] See fn.329, above.

[333] *Sandeman v Scurr* (1866) L.R. 2 Q.B. 86; *The Figlia Maggiore* (1868) L.R. 2 A. & E. 106; *The St. Cloud* (1863) B. & L. 4; *Hayn v Culliford* (1878) 4 C.P.D. 182.

[334] *Hutchinson v Guion* (1858) 5 C.B. (N.S.) 149 at p.162; *Hovill v Stephenson* (1830) 4 C. & P. 469; *Major v White* (1835) 7 C. & p.41; *Ohrloff v Briscall* (1866) L.R. I P.C. 231; *The Santamana* (1923) 14 Ll.L.R. 159; *Ismail v Polish Ocean Lines* [1976] 1 Lloyd's Rep. 489. The statement in the text was approved by the Supreme court of Canada in *Mannix v Paterson* [1966] 1 Lloyd's Rep. 139. See also *M.S.C. Mediterranean Shipping Co SA v Alianca Bay Shipping Co Ltd* [1985] 2 Lloyd's Rep. 217.

probably not be a good defence against a person claiming under the Carriage of Goods by Sea Act 1992.[335]

Whether the charterer or owner is ultimately liable for bad stowage will depend on the terms of the charter as to stowage.[336] Voyage and time charters frequently contain express provisions dealing with the cost, or responsibility, or both, for loading, stowage and stevedores. The NYPE form of time charter provides "charterers are to load, stow and trim the cargo at their expense under the supervision of the captain", which transfers responsibility to the charterers.[337] Adding the words " . . . and responsibility" after the word "supervision" transfers responsibility back to the shipowner.[338] A clause in a booking note that "the Merchant shall tender and load . . . the cost of loading, stowing and discharging the goods shall be borne by the merchant" transferred responsibility to the shipper.[339]

A clause requiring the charterer to pay for loading, stowage (and discharge), or that the owners will be free of expense for these matters, will not necessarily transfer responsibility.[340] Clauses dealing with responsibility for loading and stowage are likely to be interpreted widely to include all cargo operations, e.g. planning, lashing, trimming, and perhaps even hatch handling.[341] If responsibility for stowage is transferred to the charterer the master has the right to intervene on grounds of seaworthiness, but does not owe the charterer the duty to do so, and the owner will only be liable to the charterer for bad stowage if the master actually intervenes causatively.[342]

In case of bad stowage either the charterer or owner will have his remedy against the stevedore, unless the damage results from defects in gear supplied by the ship.[343]

Where the charter requires the owner to employ a stevedore nominated by the charterer, the latter is under an implied duty to nominate a stevedore who is

---

[335] As to the position under the Bills of Lading Act 1855 see *Ohrloff v Briscall*, above; *The Helene* (1865) B. & L. 415, 429; *Government of Swaziland Central Transport Administration v Leila Maritime Co Ltd (The Leila)* [1985] 2 Lloyd's Rep. 172. *Cf. Leduc v Ward* (1888) 20 Q.B.D. 475; *Hain S.S. Co v Tate & Lyle* (1936) 41 Com.Cas. 350. The position may differ where the Hague or Hague-Visby Rules apply, when a defence under Article IV, r.2(i) may be available: *Ismail v Polish Ocean Lines*, above.

[336] *Union Castle Co v Borderdale Co* [1919] 1 K.B. 612.

[337] *Canadian Transport v Court Line* [1940] A.C. 934. The right to supervise does not give rise to a duty to the charterer to intervene: *Transocean v Euxine (The Imvros)* [1999] 1 Lloyd's Rep. 848; *Compania Sud American v MS ER Hamburg* [2006] EWHC 483 (Comm); [2006] 2 Lloyd's Rep. 66.

[338] *M.S.C. Mediterranean Shipping v Alianca (The Argonaut)* [1985] 2 Lloyd's Rep. 217; *AB Marintrans v Comet Shipping (The Shinjitsu Maru No.5)* [1985] 1 Lloyd's Rep. 568; *Alexandros Shipping v MSC Mediterranean (The Alexandros P)* [1986] 1 Lloyd's Rep. 421

[339] *A.Meredith Jones v Vangemar (The Apostolis No.2)* [2000] 2 Lloyd's Rep. 337 at pp.346–347.

[340] *Jindal v Islamic Solidarity (The Jordan II)* [2003] EWCA Civ 144; [2003] 2 Lloyd's Rep. 87 (CA The point did not arise in the HL); *Govt of Ceylon v Chandris* [1965] 2 Lloyd's Rep. 204.

[341] *Alexandros Shipping v MSC Mediterranean (The Alexandros P)* [1986] 1 Lloyd's Rep. 421; *The Visurgis* [1999] 1 Lloyd's Rep. 218; *Jindal v Islamic Solidarity (The Jordan II)* above; *C.V.S. Flintermar v Sea Malta (The Flintermar)* [2005] EWCA Civ 17; [2005] 1 Lloyd's Rep. 409. *Compania Sud American v MS ER Hamburg* [2003] EWCA 483 (Comm); [2006] 2 Lloyd's Rep. 66.

[342] *Transocean v Euxine (The Imvros)* [1999] 1 Lloyd's Rep. 848; *Compania Sud American v MS ER Hamburg* [2006] EWHC 483 (Comm); [2006] 2 Lloyd's Rep. 66.

[343] See *Cases* below. The owner is primarily liable to pay the stevedore. See *Eastman v Harry* (1876) 33 L.T. 800 and *Brittania S.S. Co v Bunge* (1929) 35 Com.Cas. 163. As to the liability to pay for winchmen, where stevedores provided by the charterers and paid by the ship would not use winches worked by the crew, see *Sociedad Anonima Commercial, etc. v National S.S. Co* (1932) 38 Com.Cas. 88.

competent but there is no implied term that the stevedores nominated will exercise reasonable care.[344]

It is very usual to find a provision in charterparties whereby the charterer secures the right to appoint a stevedore, and under such a clause a question often arises whether a stevedore so appointed is, as between the owners and the charterers,[345] the servant of the owners or the charterers. No general rule can be derived from the cases.[346] Where, however, the responsibility for stowage is not transferred from the owner to the charterer, and remains with the owner, it seems probable that in most cases the stevedore, though appointed or nominated by the charterer, is the servant of the shipowner.

In an attempt to resolve some of the difficulties of identifying responsibility for stowage and acts of stevedores various clauses and agreements have been devised which attempt to apportion the responsibility between owners and charterers. The most usual are the Berth Standard of Average Clause (commonly attached to the Baltime Charter) and the Inter-Club New York Produce Exchange Agreement (which is sometimes expressly incorporated into the New York Produce Exchange form of time charter). These clauses and agreements have given rise to their own difficulties.[347]

With a general ship loading cargo at more than one port, the shipowner at a later port may shift, and even temporarily put ashore, cargo loaded at an earlier port, if that is necessary for the proper stowage of the vessel on the voyage and the exceptions of the bill of lading protect him as to damage sustained by such cargo while so removed.[348] A common clause provides that, if the vessel is destined for two ports of discharge, the master shall be informed at the time of loading so as to arrange the stowage, or the vessel shall be left in "seaworthy trim" to proceed between the ports of discharge.[349] A provision in such a clause that "any expense" incurred by the shipowners in shifting cargo shall be paid by the charterers entitles the shipowner to recover additional disbursements made as a result of the necessity to shift the cargo, but does not render the charterer liable for delay.[350] "Seaworthy trim" involves not only leaving the vessel on an even

---

[344] *Overseas Transportation Co v Mineralimportexport* [1971] 1 Lloyd's Rep. 514; on appeal [1972] 1 Lloyd's Rep. 201; *Maceio v Clipper Shipping (The Clipper Sao Luis)* [2000] 1 Lloyd's Rep. 645.

[345] As between the owners and consignees or indorsees, if the latter are ignorant of the provisions of the charter and if under the charter the owners retain possession and control of the ship, an appointment of a stevedore by the charterers will not absolve the owners from responsibility for bad stowage: *Swainston v Garrick* (1833) 2 L.J.Ex. 255; *Sandeman v Scurr* (1866) L.R. 2 Q.B. 86.

[346] Article 90 *Note 2* at pp.173–175 of the 20th edn of this work contained an analysis of the cases, many of some antiquity. In bad stowage cases the more usual issue is which party is responsible for stowage, rather than whose servant is the stevedore, though terms as to the appointment of the stevedore may be relevant to responsibility for stowage.

[347] See *Clan Line Steamers Ltd v Ove Skou Rederi A/S* [1969] 2 Lloyd's Rep. 155 and *Filkos Shipping Corp v Shipmair B.V.* [1983] 1 Lloyd's Rep. 9 (Berth Standard of Average Clause); *D/S A/S Idaho v Peninsular and Oriental S.N. Co (The Stathnewton)* [1983] 1 Lloyd's Rep. 219, *The Holstencruiser* [1992] 2 Lloyd's Rep. 378, *Ocean Focus v Hyundai (The Hawk)* [1999] 1 Lloyd's Rep. 176, *The Elpa* [2001] 2 Lloyd's Rep. 596, *Kamilla v AC Oersleff's (The Kamilla)* [2006] EWHC 509 (Comm); [2006] 2 Lloyd's Rep. 238 (Inter-Club N.Y.P.E. Agreement).

[348] *Bruce, Marriott & Co v Houlder* [1917] 1 K.B. 72.

[349] See *Britain S.S. Co v Dreyfus* (1935) 51 Ll.L.R. 196.

[350] *Chandris v Government of India* [1956] 1 Lloyd's Rep. 11; *The Argobeam* [1970] 1 Lloyd's Rep. 282.

keel, but also with such steps having been taken (by way of bagging the part cargo) as may be necessary to enable the ship to meet the perils of the sea on the passage to the next port.[351] Lay-time does not run during the time taken to put the vessel into seaworthy trim.[352]

The owner who has employed an independent contractor as stevedore is not vicariously liable in tort to persons damaged in the course of the stevedore's work, unless the damage results from defects in gear supplied by the ship. In any other case, their remedy, if any, is against the stevedore.[353] But the general tort principle that the employer of an independent contractor incurs no liability for the acts of his contractor and his servant is subject to exceptions, as when the act is unlawful or in its nature dangerous, or is controlled or interfered with and directed by the employer. Generally, therefore, persons suffering damage by reason of the contractor's negligence in the operation of loading, apart from the contract of carriage, can only sue the contractor, and this is the explanation of *Murray v Currie*[354]; as the work was not so dangerous, per se, as to bring it within the exception, nor did the employer control the contractor's work.

In contrast, the dictum of Willes J. in *Murray v Currie* that, "The shipowner would not have been liable to the charterer (shipper), if the wrongful act of the stevedore had caused damage to any part of the cargo",[355] is, it is submitted, unsound. In the absence of express agreement to the contrary the operation of loading is one which the carrier is legally bound to perform under his contract of carriage and he cannot get rid of his liability by employing an independent contractor, though he may have a remedy over against the contractor.

Case 1. A ship was chartered by C to load a cargo not exceeding what the ship could reasonably carry. "C's stevedore to be employed by the ship, and the cargo . . . to be brought alongside at C's risk and expense." C did not appoint a stevedore and the owners did not load a full cargo. *Held*, that the condition that C should appoint a stevedore was not a condition precedent; that, even if he did not, the owners and their master were bound to take on board as much cargo as the ship could reasonably carry and that the master was bound to use the same skill as a qualified stevedore in stowing it.[356]

Case 2. C chartered a ship from A, with a clause, "stevedore of outward cargo to be appointed by charterer, but to be paid by and act under captain's orders". Other shippers, knowing of the charter, shipped goods which were stowed by the stevedore appointed by the charterer; the captain did not interfere with their stowage. *Held*, that the shippers could not sue the master for bad stowage.[357]

Case 3. A chartered a ship to C, to sail to X, and load from C's agents there "cargo to be brought to and taken from alongside at merchant's risk and expense". Goods were shipped by F, ignorant of the charter. The stevedore was appointed by the charterers, though ultimately paid by owners. *Held*, that F could sue A on bills of lading signed by the master.[358]

---

[351] *Britain S.S. Co v Dreyfus*, above, and *The Argobeam*, above, at p.291.
[352] *The Argobeam*, above.
[353] *Murray v Currie* (1870) L.R. 6 C.P. 24: *Cameron v Nystrom* [1893] A.C. 308.
[354] (1870) L.R. 6 C.P. 24.
[355] *Ibid*, at p.27.
[356] *Anglo-African Co v Lamzed* (1866) L.R. 1 C.P. 226.
[357] *Blaikie v Stembridge* (1860) 6 C.B. (N.S.) 894.
[358] *Sandeman v Scurr* (1866) L.R. 2 Q.B. 86. *Semble*, that A could sue C for the damages F recovered from him. But *cf. Baumvoll v Gilchrest & Co* [1892] 1 Q.B. 253, where the ship was out of its owner's possession and control and the owner was held not liable on bills of lading signed by the master.

Case 4. K, a stevedore, in unloading A's ship, employed L, a member of A's crew, assigned to him by A, but under the orders of and paid by K. Through L's negligence M, a fellow-workman, was injured. *Held*, that K, and not A, was liable.[359]

Case 5. C sued A and E, his captain, for negligent stowage of A's ship chartered by C, whereby damage was done to the cargo. A proved that C and his broker were on board from time to time during the loading, saw what was being done, and made no objection to it. *Held*, a good defence.[360]

A91   Article 91—Mate's Receipt

On delivery of goods by a shipper to the shipowner or his agent the shipper will, unless there is a custom of the port to the contrary, obtain a document known as a "mate's receipt". Apart from special contract[361] the goods are then in the shipowner's possession and at his risk.[362] The shipowner will hold them on the terms of his usual bill of lading, even before its signature; but this is frequently expressly provided for in the mate's receipt.[363]

As a general rule the person in possession of the mate's receipt, where one exists, is the person entitled to bills of lading, which should be given in exchange for that receipt, and he can sue for wrongful dealing with the goods. The shipowner will be justified in delivering bills of lading to him if he has received no notice of and does not know of other claims.[364]

But the mate's receipt is also a recognition of property in any person named therein as owner, an acknowledgment that the shipper holds the goods on his account.[365] The master will therefore be justified in delivering bills of lading to such a person; or to a person proved to be the owner of the goods,[366] even though the mate's receipt is not produced, if he has received no notice of other claims and is satisfied the goods are on board.[367]

The mate's receipt is not a document of title to the goods shipped and mere indorsement or transfer of it without notice to the shipowner or his agent does not pass the property in the goods. But there is no reason in principle why a mate's receipt should not become a document of title by custom,[368] and, whether or not

---

[359] *Murray v Currie* (1870) L.R. 6 C.P. 24.
[360] *Ohrloff v Briscall* (1866) L.R. 1 P.C. 231. But the knowledge of the lighterman who brought the goods to the ship will not be sufficient to affect the shipper: *Figlia Maggiore* (1868) L.R. 2 A. & E. 106.
[361] See Art.106, *Note 3*. Such special contract may also be contained in the shipping note tendered by the shipper and signed by or for the shipowner. Thus in *Armstrong v Allan* (1892) 8 T.L.R. 613, the shipping note contained the clause "no goods to be received on board unless a clean receipt can be given". The captain received the goods, but would not give "a clean receipt"; and the shipper was held entitled to demand his goods back.
[362] *British Columbia Co v Nettleship* (1868) L.R. 3 C.P. 499; *Cobban v Downe* (1803) 5 Esp. 41.
[363] Cf. *De Clermont v General Steam Navigation Co* (1891) 7 T.L.R. 187. *Semble*, that the *risk* is only that of an ordinary bailee until shipment: *Nottebohn v Richter* (1886) 18 Q.B.D. 63.
[364] *Craven v Ryder* (1816) 6 Taunt. 433; *Thompson v Trail* (1826) 6 B. & C. 36; *Falke v Fletcher* (1865) 18 C.B. (N.S.) 403.
[365] *Evans v Nichol* (1841) 4 Scott's N.R. 43; *Craven v Ryder* (1816) 6 Taunt. 433. The majority of receipts do not contain an owner's name.
[366] *Cowasjee v Thompson* (1845) 5 Moo.P.C. 165.
[367] *Hathesing v Laing* (1873) L.R. 17 Eq. 92; *Nippon Yusen Kaisha v Ramjiban Serowgee* [1938] A.C. 429; *Kum v Wah Tat Bank* [1971] 1 Lloyd's Rep. 439 (PC). In practice lightermen and agents frequently detain the mate's receipt as security for disputed accounts; but shipowners in these cases often disregard the mate's receipt and deliver bills of lading to the shipper.
[368] *Kum v Wah Tat Bank* [1971] 1 Lloyd's Rep. 439 (PC), where however a custom to this effect was rejected as being inconsistent with the words "non-negotiable" contained in the receipt itself. See Art.11, above, as to the admissibility of evidence of customs generally.

it is a document of title, a valid pledge of the goods may be effected by delivery of the goods to the ship coupled with delivery of the mate's receipt to the pledgee, if that is the intention of the parties.[369]

Statements in the mate's receipt are not conclusive against the shipowner, but throw on him the burden of disproving them.[370]

Quaere, whether a mate's receipt is a "document of title" within the meaning of r.7 of Art.III in the Schedule to the Carriage of Goods by Sea Act 1971, so that on having the name of the carrying ship "noted" upon it, it is to be "deemed to constitute a shipped bill of lading". (See notes to Art.I(b) and Art.III, r.7, in Chapter 20, below.)

Note. A *clean receipt* is one in which the acknowledgment of the receipt of the goods is not qualified by any reservation as to their quality or quantity.[371] So also *a clean bill of lading* is one in which there is nothing to qualify the admission that so many packages are shipped in good order and condition.[372] *Claused* when applied to a mate's receipt or bill has no settled meaning, but generally refers to a notation qualifying other statements as to the description or apparent condition of the goods.[373]

Case 1. F, shippers, delivered to A's servants on the quay goods for shipment by A's vessel alongside, and received a mate's receipt; one of the cases was left behind. *Held*, that A was liable for its loss.[374]

Case 2. F sold sugar f.o.b. to H: F shipped the sugar on A's ship receiving a "mate's receipt"—"Received on board the *X*, for and on account of F." H resold to K; K obtained bills of lading from A's captain. Before the ship sailed H failed. F claimed to stop *in transitu*. The jury found that by shipping under the mate's receipt F did not intend to divest his lien. *Held*, that F was entitled to the bills of lading, and not K, the property being still in F.[375]

Case 3. F sold goods to H f.o.b., took a bill from H in payment and shipped them on A's ship, getting mate's receipt. H failed, while the bill was running. F claimed to stop *in transitu*. A's captain had made out the bills of lading in H's name, without production of mate's receipts. *Held*, that, F being absolutely paid by bill,[376] the right to stop *in transitu* was gone; that the property was therefore in H and that the possession by F of the mate's receipts was immaterial.[377]

Case 4. H, acting as agent for C F, bought goods and shipped them in A's vessel, chartered to C F, obtaining a mate's receipt for them. C F indorsed the receipts to H, who kept them as security for his payment by C F, but gave no notice to A's captain. C F obtained bills of lading from the captain and indorsed them to a bank. The bank and H both claimed the goods. H set up a custom of Bombay that mate's receipts were negotiable instruments, indorsement of which passed the property, and that captains were bound not to give bills of lading except on the production of the mate's receipt. *Held*, that such a custom was bad; that A's captain, knowing C F to be the owners of the goods and having

---

[369] *ibid.* See also *Evans v Nichol*, above; *Bryans v Nix* (1839) 4 M. & W. 775.
[370] *Biddulph v Bingham* (1874) 30 L.T. 30; *Nippon Yusen Kaisha v Ramjiban Serowgee*, above. Contrast the effect of a statement in a bill of lading by the master within his authority. See Arts 25 and 62.
[371] *Armstrong v Allan* (1892) 8 T.L.R. 613.
[372] *Restitution S.S. Co v Pirie* (1889) 61 L.T. 330 at p.333. See also *Canada and Dominion Sugar Co v Canadian (W.I.) Steamships* [1947] A.C. 46.
[373] *Sea Success v African Maritime (The Sea Success)* [2005] EWHC 1542 (Comm); [2005] 2 Lloyd's Rep. 692.
[374] *British Columbia Co v Nettleship* (1868) L.R. 3 C.P. 499. The delivery must be to a recognised agent of the shipowner, as master, mate or dock company, not merely on board the ship, or to the crew: *Cobban v Downe* (1803) 5 Esp. 41; *Mackenzie v Rowe* (1810) 2 Camp. 482.
[375] *Craven v Ryder* (1816) 6 Taunt. 433.
[376] See Art.101.
[377] *Cowasjee v Thompson* (1845) 5 Moo.P.C. 165.

no notice of any other claim, was justified in giving bills of lading to C F, and that the holders of the bills of lading had precedence over the holder of the mate's receipts.[378]

Case 5. F shipped goods in A's ship, and received a mate's receipt: "Received on board the *A* from F, to be delivered to G." F had arranged with G that these goods should be consigned to him as security for advances, and forwarded the receipt to G. F failed, and A claimed a lien on the goods for other debts due from F to A. *Held,* that G, as holder of the mate's receipt, acknowledging that the goods were held to be delivered to him, was entitled to sue A for the goods.[379]

Case 6. C orally chartered a ship from A and loaded in it iron supplied by H. A's mate gave a receipt for 330 tons; there was no bill of lading. On arrival there were only $326\frac{1}{2}12$ tons of iron. C had paid H for 330 tons on the mate's receipt. C sued A for the price of $3\frac{1}{2}12$ tons short. A's mate proved that he had delivered all that he had received. *Held,* that A was not liable, the mate's receipt being only prima facie evidence, which A could contradict.[380]

A92   **Article 92—Cesser Clause**

Charters frequently contain a clause to the effect that the charterer's liability shall cease on shipment of the cargo.[381] This clause, known as the "lien and exemption clause", or "cesser clause",[382] is usually inserted in consideration of the granting to the shipowner of a lien, which he would not otherwise possess, on the cargo for demurrage and dead freight.[383]

The tendency of the courts is to hold that the exemption granted to the charterer is co-extensive with the lien conferred on the shipowner by the bill of lading. This conclusion has been reached by two different routes. First, by holding that the creation of an effective lien is a condition precedent to the cesser of the charterer's liability.[384] Secondly, by holding that if, through the fault of the charterers, the bill of lading does not confer a lien, the owners have an independent cause of action against them for failing to include an appropriate provision in the bill of lading.[385]

---

[378] *Hathesing v Laing* (1873) L.R. 17 Eq. 92; *Nippon Yusen Kaisha v Ramjiban Serowgee* [1938] A.C. 429 (gunny trade at Calcutta).

[379] *Evans v Nichol* (1841) 4 Scott's N.R. 43; *Kum v Wah Tat Bank* [1971] 1 Lloyd's Rep. 439 (PC).

[380] *Biddulph v Bingham* (1874) 30 L.T. 30.

[381] In the Approved Baltimore Berth Grain Charterparty a strange clause, somewhat analogous to a cesser clause, appears as follows: "This contract shall be completed and superseded by the signing of Bills of Lading on the same form as in use by regular line steamers from loading port to port of destination, or if port of destination be one to which there is no regular line of steamers from loading port, this contract shall be superseded by the signing of Bills of Lading in the form customary for such voyages for grain cargoes, which Bills of Lading shall, however, contain the following clauses . . . " For some of the difficulties ensuing as between charterer and shipowner, see *N.V. Reederji Amsterdam v President of India* [1960] 2 Lloyd's Rep. 82; *Tradax v Volkswagenwerk* [1969] 1 Lloyd's Rep. 494. The clause does not take effect unless Bills of Lading are signed which satisfy the requirement of the clause both as regards form and content: *Moscow V/O Export Khleb v Helmville Ltd (The Jocelyne)* [1977] 2 Lloyd's Rep. 121; see also *Oriental Maritime v Ministry of Food (The Silva Plana)* [1989] 2 Lloyd's Rep. 371.

[382] e.g. "The Owners or Master shall have an absolute lien on the cargo for the recovery of all Bill of Lading freight, dead-freight and demurrage, but the Charterers' liability shall cease upon the shipment of the cargo, and payment of dead-freight, difference in freight and demurrage provided such cargo be worth the Bill of Lading freight at the port of shipment" (Centrocon Charter).

[383] See Art.196.

[384] *Clink v Radford* [1891] 1 Q.B. 625 (CA); *Hansen v Harold* [1894] 1 Q.B. 612 (CA); *Dunlop v Balfour* [1892] 1 Q.B. 507 (see especially the judgment of Wright J.); and the judgment of Harman L.J. in *Fidelitas Shipping Co v Exportchleb* [1963] 2 Lloyd's Rep. 113 and *Action SA v Britannic Shipping Corp Ltd (The Aegis Britannic)* [1987] 1 Lloyd's Rep. 119. See also *Gray v Carr* (1871) L.R. 6 Q.B. 522 at p.544 and *French v Gerber* (1877) 2 C.P.D. 247 at p.250.

[385] *Fidelitas Shipping v Exportchleb*, above, per Pearson L.J., as explained in *Overseas Transportation Co v Mineralimportexport* [1971] 1 Lloyd's Rep. 514 at pp.518–519; [1972] 1 Lloyd's Rep. 201 (CA).

Where, therefore, no lien at all has been granted to the shipowner, the courts have been slow to relieve the charterer from liabilities arising either before or after the shipment of the cargo[386]; but, where the words make it clear that such was the intention of the parties, they have held the charterer relieved,[387] even though the effect of such a decision was to leave the shipowner without remedy.[388]

Similarly, where a lien has been granted to the shipowner the courts have held the charterer excused from claims for which the shipowner has a lien[389] or some other security on the cargo,[390] but have treated him as liable for claims for which the shipowner has no such lien,[391] or which the express words of the clause show that he was intended to be liable for.[392]

It is not, however, enough to include in the bill of lading a clause purporting to create a lien. The charterer's liability will not cease unless the lien is in fact effective. Thus, if the local law or practice at the port of discharge is such that no lien can be exercised by the owner, then the cesser clause does not protect the charterer from liability.[393]

The rule that the cesser clause does not protect the charterer against claims for which no lien is given by the bill of lading applies even when the form of bill of lading to be signed is specified in the charterparty and one is signed in that specified form.[394]

The fact that the charterer is also the consignee of the cargo will not destroy his exemption under such a clause,[395] unless he is consignee under a bill of lading incorporating and so reviving the liabilities of the charter, in which case the cesser clause will be held inapplicable to the new contract as regards liabilities accruing after the shipment of the cargo.[396]

---

[386] *Christoffersen v Hansen* (1872) L.R. 7 Q.B. 509.

[387] *Oglesby v Yglesias* (1858) E.B. & E. 930; *Milvain v Perez* (1861) 3 E. & E. 495.

[388] The charterer is generally but not always relieved (see *Jennesen v Secretary of State for India* [1916] 2 K.B. 702) by the cesser clause from liabilities accruing after the shipment of the cargo; there has been a conflict of opinion whether he is in addition relieved from liabilities accruing before such shipment; and, though the authorities now establish that he is (for example see *Fidelitas Shipping Co v Exportchleb*, above), if a corresponding lien is given to the shipowner, yet several judges, and notably Lord Esher, while recognising that the authorities decide this, have thought that on principle the decisions should have been the other way. See per Brett J. in *Gray v Carr* (1871) L.R. 6 Q.B. 522 at p.537 and in *Kish v Cory* (1875) L.R. 10 Q.B. 553 at p.559; also per Coleridge L.C.J. in the latter case at p.557, and per Grove J. at p.562; but, as the latter learned judge says "The authorities, however, are too strong to be overruled even by a court of error."

[389] *Francesco v Massey* (1873) L.R. 8 Ex. 101; *Kish v Cory* (1875) L.R. 10 Q.B. 553; *Bannister v Breslauer* (1867) L.R. 2 C.P. 497; *Sanguinetti v Pacific Steam Navigation Co* (1877) 2 Q.B.D. 238.

[390] *French v Gerber* (1877) 2 C.P.D. 247 at p.250.

[391] *Clink v Radford* [1891] 1 Q.B. 625; *Hansen v Harrold* [1894] 1 Q.B. 612; *Dunlop v Balfour* [1892] 1 Q.B. 507; *Lockhart v Falk* (1875) L.R. 10 Ex. 132; *Francesco v Massey*, above. Contrast, however, the judgment of Pearson L.J. in *Fidelitas Shipping Co v Exportchleb*, above.

[392] *Lister v Van Haansbergen* (1876) 1 Q.B.D. 269; *Pederson v Lotinga* (1857) 28 L.T. (O.S.) 267.

[393] *Overseas Transportation Co v Mineralimportexport* [1972] 1 Lloyd's Rep. 201 (CA); *Maritime Transport Operator v Louis Dreyfus (The Tropwave)* [1981] 2 Lloyd's Rep. 159. This result is sometimes achieved by express provision in the charterparty: see, for example, the "Gencon" form, discussed in *"Z" Steamship Co v Amtorg* (1938) 61 Ll.L.R. 97, where the owners' claim failed because they did not attempt to exercise their lien. See also *The Aegis Britannic*, above.

[394] *Jennesen v Secretary of State for India* [1916] 2 K.B. 702.

[395] *Sanguinetti v Pacific Steam Navigation Co* (1877) 2 Q.B.D. 238.

[396] *Gullischen v Stewart* (1884) 13 Q.B.D. 317 (demurrage at port of discharge) and *Bryden v Niebuhr* (1884) C & E. 241 (demurrage at port of call), which, it is submitted, overrule *Barwick v Burnyeat* (1877) 36 L.T. 250.

Case 1. A ship was chartered with no provision as to rate of loading or demurrage at port of loading, but with such provisions relating to the port of discharge, and also a clause: "The charterers' liability under this charter to cease on the cargo being loaded, the owners having a lien on the cargo for the freight and demurrage." On a claim by the shipowners for damages for detention at the port of loading, *held*, that as no lien was given for such damages under the name "demurrage", the cesser clause did not free the charterers.[397]

Case 2. A ship was chartered at a lump freight, the liability of the charterers to cease on the vessel being loaded, the master and owners having a lien[398] on the cargo for all freight and demurrage under the charter. The charterers had under the charter the privilege of rechartering the vessel at any rate of freight without prejudice to the charter, the captain to sign bills of lading ... at the current or any rate of freight without prejudice to the charter.

The charterers rechartered and presented bills of lading showing freight payable by weight delivered in London for a sum sufficient to satisfy the balance of freight due under the charter, but without any provision for lien. The captain signed them. On the voyage the cargo diminished in weight so that the bill of lading freight (payable on weight delivered in London) was insufficient to cover the freight due under the charter, leaving a balance still unpaid. The shipowners sued the charterers for this balance. The charterers pleaded the cesser clause. *Held*, no defence, as the cesser clause only relieved the charterers to the extent to which an effective lien was given to the shipowners.[399]

Note 1. The importance of the decision in *Hansen v Harrold*[14] is in the frequent cases where, there being a cesser clause in the charter with a lien for demurrage, demurrage is alleged to have been incurred at the port of loading, but is disputed. The captain is asked under the terms of the charter to sign bills of lading as presented, which give no lien for demurrage. He fears that if he does so, the cesser clause will prevent his owners from recovering demurrage at all. It appears to follow from *Hansen v Harrold*[400] that if, owing to the terms of the bill of lading, the shipowner has no effective lien for demurrage, the charterer will not be relieved by the cesser clause from a claim for demurrage. See, for a dispute of this kind settled by agreement, *Anderson v English & American Co*[401]; other similar cases have arisen in arbitrations. The decision in *Janentsky v Langridge*[402] does not conflict with this, for if the cesser clause did not operate because there was no lien for the freight unpaid, yet the charterers were only liable on right delivery of the cargo and this had not taken place.

Note 2. Even in the case of charters containing a cesser clause such as "this charter being entered into on behalf of others, it is agreed that all liability of agents shall cease on shipping of the cargo", or similar words, the agent has sometimes been held liable. Thus in *Schmaltz v Avery*,[403] Patteson J., delivering the judgment of the court, said: "There is nothing in the argument that the plaintiff's responsibility is expressly made to cease 'as soon as the cargo is shipped', for that limitation plainly applies only to his character as agent, and, being real principal, his responsibility would unquestionably continue after the cargo was shipped." On the other hand, in *Oglesby v Yglesias*[404] it was held by Erle and Crompton JJ. that the agent, though personally liable on the charter, was freed by such a clause from all liability after shipping of cargo.

---

[397] *Clink v Radford* [1891] 1 Q.B. 625 (CA).
[398] For the effect of the particular form of these words, see *Fidelitas Shipping Co v Exportchleb* [1963] 2 Lloyd's Rep. 113, particularly per Pearson L.J. at pp.122, 124.
[399] *Hansen v Harrold* [1894] 1 Q.B. 612 (CA); see *Williams v Canton Co* [1901] A.C. 462.
[400] [1894] 1 Q.B. 612. See, however, per Pearson L.J. in *Fidelitas Shipping Co v Exportchleb* [1963] 2 Lloyd's Rep. 113.
[401] (1895) 1 Com.Cas. 85.
[402] (1895) 1 Com.Cas. 90.
[403] (1851) 16 Q.B. 655 at p.663.
[404] (1858) E.B. & E. 930.

Of these contradictory decisions, that in *Oglesby v Yglesias*[404] seems the more consistent with principle. If the plaintiffs relied on the defendant's charterer as principal, then with their eyes open they have agreed to the insertion of a clause directly limiting his liabilities, and the erroneous recital that he acts for another will not affect the question. And this is not inconsistent with the case of *Gullisch*en v Stewart[405]; for there, though persons exempted from liability after loading by a cesser clause were yet held liable for freight, it was on the subsequent contract in the bill of lading; on the charter alone they would, it is submitted, have been exempt. *Barwick v Burnyeat*[406] even exempts them on charter and bill of lading together but is, it is submitted, wrong.

Article 93—Demurrage and Cesser Clause   A93

Where no demurrage in the strict sense of the term[407] is stipulated for in the provisions as to lay-days, but a lien for demurrage is given by the cesser clause to the shipowner, such a lien will include damages for detention at the port of loading and the charterer will therefore not be liable for such damages.[408]

Where demurrage in the strict sense of the term is stipulated for in the charter, after provisions as to both loading and discharging, it applies to both: if then a lien for demurrage is given together with a cesser clause, such a lien applies only to demurrage in the strict sense[409] [and not to damages for detention beyond the agreed days on demurrage].[410] The charterer will therefore be freed from liability for demurrage at the port of loading[411] [but not for damages for detention at the port of loading[412]].[413]

Where there is a stipulation for demurrage at the port of discharge, but none at the port of loading, the term "demurrage" can only be taken to apply to the port of discharge; and the shipowner will therefore have no lien for damages for detention at the port of loading, while the charterer will be liable for such damages.[414]

Case 1. A ship was chartered to load in regular turn in the customary manner... "this charter being concluded by C on behalf of another party resident abroad, it is agreed that all liability of C in every respect and as to all matters and things *as well before* as during and after the shipping of the cargo shall cease as soon as he has shipped the cargo". *Held*, that by this clause the charterers, on shipment of the cargo, were protected from liability for delay in loading.[415]

Case 2. A ship was chartered by C "to load in fifteen working days, the vessel to be discharged at the rate of thirty-five tons per working day, and ten days on demurrage over and above her said lay-days, C's liability to cease when ship is loaded, the captain having a lien upon the cargo for freight

---

[405] (1884) 13 Q.B.D. 317.
[406] (1877) 36 L.T. 250. See fn.22, Art.35, above.
[407] Agreed damages to be paid for the delay of the ship in loading and unloading beyond an agreed period, such delay not being caused by default of the shipowner: see Art.154.
[408] *Bannister v Breslauer* (1867) L.R. 2 C.P. 497; only to be supported on this ground; *cf. Clink v Radford* [1891] 1 Q.B. 625, per Bowen L.J. at p.631.
[409] *Kish v Cory* (1875) L.R. 10 Q.B. 553.
[410] *Gray v Carr* (1871) L.R. 6 Q.B. 522.
[411] *Francesco v Massey* (1873) L.R. 88 Ex. 101; *Kish v Cory*, above.
[412] *Gray v Carr; Francesco v Massey*, above.
[413] The parts in brackets are not yet clear law. The whole subject of demurrage and the cesser clause was discussed at length in earlier editions: see 17th edn, pp.161–167.
[414] *Clink v Radford* [1891] 1 Q.B. 625; *Dunlop v Balfour* [1892] 1 Q.B. 507; *Lockhart v Falk* (1875) L.R. 10 Ex. 132; *Gardiner v Macfarlane*, (1889) 16 Rettie. 658.
[415] *Milvain v Perez* (1861) 3 E. & E. 495. See also *Oglesby v Yglesias* (1858) E.B. & E. 930.

and demurrage". A claim was made against C for five days' demurrage and fourteen days' detention beyond the days on demurrage. On the trial C was held liable both for demurrage and for damages for detention. He appealed as to demurrage, admitting he was liable for damages for detention. *Held*, that as the owner had a lien for demurrage, C was not liable for it.[416]

Case 3. A ship was chartered by C to carry rice, calling at a port for orders "to be forwarded within forty-eight hours after her notice of her arrival had been given to and received by charterer's agents in London, or lay-days to count . . . Liability of C to cease as soon as cargo is on board, provided the same is worth the freight at port of discharge, but the owners of the ship to have an absolute lien on the cargo for all demurrage." C delayed orders at the port of call and ordered the ship to a port which was not good and safe. *Held*, that C was exonerated by the cesser clause, the term "lay-days to count" giving the owner some protection by his lien on the cargo.[417]

Case 4. A ship was chartered to load in the customary manner, proceed to Z, and then deliver, "the cargo to be discharged in ten working days. Demurrage at £2 per 100 tons register *per diem*. The ship to have an absolute lien on cargo for freight and demurrage, the charterer's liability to any clauses in this charter ceasing when he has delivered the cargo alongside ship." The ship was delayed in loading. *Held*, that demurrage in the clause giving the lien only applied to demurrage at the port of discharge and that the charterer was therefore liable for damages for detention at the port of loading.[418]

Case 5. A ship was chartered to load a full and complete cargo . . . "this charter being concluded by C for and on account of another party, it is agreed that all liability of C shall cease as soon as the cargo is shipped, loading excepted, the owner agreeing to rest solely on his lien on the cargo for freight, demurrage, and all other claims". *Held*, that the charterers were liable for delay in loading.[419]

Case 6. A ship was chartered by C "to load and unload with all dispatch . . . C's liability to cease when the cargo is shipped, provided the same is worth the freight on arrival at the port of discharge, the captain having an absolute lien on it for freight and demurrage". *Held*, that demurrage applied to delay at the port of loading, that the owner had therefore a lien for it, and that the charterer was not liable.[420]

---

[416] *Francesco v Massey* (1873) L.R. 8 Ex. 101. See also *Kish v Cory* (1875) L.R. 10 Q.B. 553 (CA).

[417] *French v Gerber* (1877) 2 C.P.D. 247 (CA).

[418] *Lockhart v Falk* (1875) L.R. 10 Ex. 132; *Gardiner v Macfarlane*, (1889) 16 Rettie 658; see *Clink v Radford* [1891] 1 Q.B. 625; *Dunlop v Balfour* [1892] 1 Q.B. 507.

[419] *Lister v Van Haansbergen* (1876) 1 Q.B.D. 269. This case turns on express evidence of intention in the words "loading excepted". So also *Pederson v Lotinga* (1857) 28 L.T. 267 may be supported as turning on a clause to pay demurrage at the port of loading, day by day, and is so construed by Blackburn J. in *Christoffersen v Hansen* (1872) L.R. 7 Q.B. 509 at p.514. In *Rederiaktieselskabet Superior v Dewar* [1909] 2 K.B. 998, demurrage was "to be paid day by day as falling due", but there was no cesser clause, and *Pederson v Lotinga* was held to be inapplicable.

[420] *Bannister v Breslauer* (1867) L.R. 2 C.P. 497. This case has been much doubted, but never formally overruled.

CHAPTER 10

THE BILL OF LADING AS A DOCUMENT OF TITLE

Article 94—Indorsement of the Bill of Lading

A94

GOODS shipped under a bill of lading may be made deliverable to a named person, or to a name left blank, or "to bearer", and in the first two cases may or may not be made deliverable to "order or assigns".

Bills of lading making goods deliverable "to order" or "to order or assigns" are by mercantile custom negotiable[1] instruments, the indorsement and delivery of which may affect the property in the goods shipped.[2] Bills of lading which are not negotiable instruments are sometimes known as "straight bills".[3] Although not negotiable, a "straight" bill of lading is a "bill of lading or other similar document of title" within s.1(4) of the Carriage of Goods by Sea Act 1971,[4] but not a bill of lading for the purposes of the Carriage of Goods by Sea Act 1992 by virtue of s.1(2)(a) of that Act and (semble) not a document of title at common law, save in the limited sense that production is required to entitle the holder to delivery.[5]

Indorsement is effected either by the shipper or consignee writing his name on the back of the bill of lading, which is called an "indorsement in blank", or by his writing "Deliver to I [or order], F", which is called an "indorsement in full".[6]

The shipper may, if he has retained the right of disposal of the goods, delete the name of the consignee and either leave the bill deliverable to a name left blank or insert the name of another consignee.[7]

---

[1] See *Note* 1, below.

[2] Custom of merchants, as found in the special verdict in *Lickbarrow v Mason* (1794) 5 T.R. 683; discussed by Lords Selborne and Blackburn in *Sewell v Burdick* (1884) 10 App.Cas. 74; and in *Blackburn on Sale*, 3rd edn, pp.343–347. As to whether through bills of lading, combined transport bills of lading or "received for shipment" bills of lading are negotiable instruments, see Art.182, below.

[3] The issue of whether a bill of lading is a "straight" or "order" bill of lading can involve fine issues of construction, particularly where (as is often the case) the standard terms on the reverse of the bill of lading have been prepared to allow for the fact that the bill may take either form. For cases on this issue see *International Air and Sea Cargo GmbH v Chitral (Owners) (The Chitral)* [2000] 1 Lloyd's Rep. 529 (held to be a "straight" bill) and *Parsons Corp v C.V. Scheepvaartonderneming (The Happy Ranger)* [2002] 2 Lloyd's Rep. 357; [2002] EWCA Civ 694 (held to be an "order" bill). On the characteristics of "straight" bills of lading see further *Voss v Apl Co Pte Ltd* [2002] 2 Lloyd's Rep. 707 (Sing.). For the origin of the description "straight" bill see Treitel (2003) 119 L.Q.R. 608.

[4] *J.I. Macwilliam Co Inc v Mediterranean Shipping Co SA (The Rafaela S)* [2005] 1 Lloyd's Rep. 347; [2005] UKHL 11. See generally Professor Sir Guenter Treitel, Q.C., F.B.A "The Legal Status of Straight Bills of Lading" (2003) 119 L.Q.R. 608.

[5] A straight bill is not capable of transferring symbolic possession of goods, and does not therefore meet this characteristic of documents of title at common law.

[6] This passage was cited with approval in *Keppel Tatlee Bank Ltd v Bandung Shipping Pte. Ltd* [2003] 1 Lloyd's Rep. 619 (Sing.).

[7] *Ishag v Allied Bank International* [1981] 1 Lloyd's Rep. 92, 98–99; *Elder Dempster Lines v Ishag* [1983] 2 Lloyd's Rep. 548.

So long as the goods are deliverable to a name left blank, or to bearer, or the indorsement is in blank, the bill of lading may pass from hand to hand by mere delivery, or may be redelivered without any indorsement to the original holder, so as to affect the property in the goods.[8]

But the holder of the bill may at any time fill in the blank either in the bill or indorsement, or restrict by indorsement the delivery to bearer, such power being given to him by the delivery to him of such a bill of lading.[9] Thereafter, transfer of the bill will require special indorsement, unless the bill is subsequently indorsed in blank by a lawful holder.[10]

Semble. A bill of lading which does not contain some such words as "to order", or "to order or assigns", or which is indorsed in full but without such words,[11] is not a negotiable instrument.[12]

Note 1. "Negotiable" as a term of art describes an instrument which can give to a transferee a better title than that possessed by the transferor. A bill of lading is not "negotiable" in this sense: the indorsee does not get a better title than his assignor.[13] Indeed a bill of lading is "negotiable" only in a popular, and not in a technical, sense.[14] For it is "negotiable" to the same extent as a cheque marked "not negotiable", i.e. it is "transferable".[15] The special verdict in *Lickbarrow v Mason*[16] uses the words "negotiable and transferable".[17]

Note 2. As the Schedule to the Carriage of Goods by Sea Act 1971 is couched in popular language, Art.VI therein makes provision for a "non-negotiable document", which is not to be a bill of lading. "Non-negotiable" here probably means not transferable. See notes to Art.VI in Chapter 20, below.

---

[8] per Lord Selbourne in *Sewell v Burdick* (1884) 10 App.Cas. 74 at p.83. The inference that an assignment of property is contemplated will be weaker from an indorsement in blank than from one in full.

[9] See fn.2, above.

[10] *Keppel Tatlee Bank Ltd v Bandung Shipping Pte. Ltd* [2003] 1 Lloyd's Rep. 619 (Sing.): a case in which bills indorsed in blank were transferred to K, who specially indorsed them in favour of S. S returned the bills to K, but without any special or blank indorsement. It was held that K did not become the lawful holder of the bills: the effect of K's prior special indorsement was that the bills ceased to be bearer bills, and there had been no subsequent special or blank indorsement which made K once more the lawful holder by virtue of the subsequent transfer from S. See also *East West Corp v DKBS 1912* [2003] 1 Lloyd's Rep. 239, [2003] Q.B. 1509; [2003] EWCA Civ 174.

[11] i.e. "deliver to A".

[12] *Henderson v Comptoir d'Escompte de Paris* (1873) L.R. 5 P.C. 253 at p.260; see also *Soproma v Marine & Animal By-Products Corp* [1966] 1 Lloyd's Rep. 367 at pp.373, 390; *International Air and Sea Cargo GmbH v Chitral (owners) (The Chitral)* [2000] 1 Lloyd's Rep. 529; *Melissa (HK) Ltd v P&O Nedlloyd (HK) Ltd* [1999] 3 H.K.L.R.D. 674 (Hong Kong); *The Brij* [2001] 1 Lloyd's Rep. 431; *Carewins Development (China) Ltd v Bright Fortune Shipping Ltd* [2006] 4 H.K.L.R.D. 131 (Hong Kong).

[13] *cf.* Lord Campbell, *Gurney v Behrend* (1854) 3 E. & B. 622 at pp.633, 634. One case in which the indorsee gets more than the indorser has (whether it can be called "a better title" is a nice question) is in the case where a previous vendor's right of stoppage *in transitu*, valid against the indorser, is not available against the indorsee. Hence the phrase of that most learned judge, Sir James Shaw Willes, that negotiable instruments "includes bills of lading as against stoppage in *transitu* only" (*Fuentes v Montis* (1868) L.R. 3 C.P. 268 at p.276). Secondly, the indorsee of the bill of lading may get more favourable contractual rights than were possessed by the indorser, as in *Leduc v Ward* (1888) 20 Q.B.D. 475; *Hain S.S. Co v Tate & Lyle* (1936) 41 Com.Cas. 350; see also Art.14, above. And thirdly, the assignor who has a defeasible title (e.g. one liable to be put aside on the ground of his fraud) may validly pass the property to an assignee, as in *Pease v Gloahec* (1866) L.R. 1 P.C. 219. See also an article by R. E. Negus in 37 L.Q.R. 442.

[14] *Kum v Wah Tat Bank* [1971] 1 Lloyd's Rep. 439 at p.446, per Lord Devlin (PC).

[15] But see *Hibernian Bank v Gysin and Hanson* [1939] 1 K.B. 483.

[16] See fn.2, above.

[17] This note was cited with approval in *J.I. Macwilliam Co Inc v Mediterranean Shipping Co SA (The Rafaela S)* [2003] 2 Lloyd's Rep. 113; [2002] EWCA Civ 556.

Article 95—Effects of Indorsement   A95

The indorsement and delivery of a bill of lading by the person entitled to hold it have effects depending partly on custom and partly on statute.

A. *By mercantile custom*[18] such an indorsement and delivery of a bill of lading, made after shipment of the goods and before complete delivery[19] of their possession has been made to the person having a right under the bill of lading to claim them (exhaustion),[20] transfers such property[21] as it was the intention of the parties to the indorsement to transfer.[22]

B. *By the Carriage of Goods by Sea Act* 1992,[23] the lawful holder of a bill of lading has transferred to him all the rights and may become subject to liabilities under the contract evidenced in the bill of lading.[24]

C. *By the Carriage of Goods by Sea Act* 1971, the indorsement to a third party of a bill of lading issued to a charterer may create a contract in different terms from the charterparty, even though the bill of lading expressly incorporates the charterparty.[25]

Article 96—Effects on Property of Indorsement by Mercantile Custom   A96

The presumed intention of the parties in indorsing a bill of lading may vary widely according to the circumstances.

It may be an intention:

(1) To transfer absolutely the property in the goods,[26] subject only, if the price be unpaid, to the right of the unpaid vendor[27] to stop the goods in their transit to the vendee as a means of reasserting his lien on the goods for the price unpaid, known as the right of stoppage *in transitu*.[28]

(2) To pass the property on certain conditions, as on the acceptance of bills of exchange for the price.[29]

---

[18] As stated in the special verdict in *Lickbarrow v Mason* (1794) 5 T.R. 683. See fn.2, above.
[19] i.e. complete physical surrender of the goods: *Barclays Bank v Customs & Excise Commissioners* [1963] 1 Lloyd's Rep. 81.
[20] *Barber v Meyerstein* (1870) L.R. 4 H.L. 317; *Barclays Bank v Customs & Excise Commissioners*, above (pledges of the bills of lading before delivery of the goods), *The Delfini* [1988] 2 Lloyd's Rep. 599, 609 on appeal, [1990] 1 Lloyd's Rep. 252. *Cf. The Future Express* [1992] 2 Lloyd's Rep. 79; [1993] 2 Lloyd's Rep. 542. For a review of the authorities concerning the "exhaustion" of a bill of lading as a document of title, see, in particular, the judgment of Judge Diamond Q.C. at [1992] 2 Lloyd's Rep. 79, 96–100 doubting that a bill can become exhausted other than by delivery against one of the original bills. Wrongful delivery of the goods, apart from the bill of lading, does not render the bill ineffective as a symbol of property; and its indorsement, even after such wrongful delivery, may still pass the property: *Short v Simpson* (1866) L.R. 1 C.P. 248.
[21] Strictly speaking, the property is transferred, not by the indorsement, but by the contract under which the indorsement is made: see per Lord Bramwell (1884) 10 App.Cas. 74 at p.105.
[22] *Sewell v Burdick* (1884) 10 App.Cas. 74. The bill does not amount to an attornment by the shipowner, in advance, to any consignee or indorsee, regardless of whether the parties intended the property to pass: *The Future Express*, above.
[23] Below, Appendix I.
[24] Art.14.
[25] See *Note* to Art.I(*b*) and Art.III, r.3(4) in Chapter 20, below.
[26] See Art.97.
[27] See Art.98.
[28] See Art.101.
[29] See Arts 99, 102.

(3) To effect a mortgage of the goods as security for an advance.[30]

(4) To effect a pledge of the goods for the same purpose.[31]

(5) To pass no property at all in the goods.[32]

Note. The decision in *Sewell v Burdick*[33] made it clear that the effect of the indorsement of a bill of lading depends entirely on the particular circumstances of each indorsement and that there is no general rule that indorsement passes the whole legal property in the goods, as had been strongly contended by Brett M.R. in the court below,[34] and in *Glyn, Mills & Co v East and West India Docks*.[35] In the light of this decision, the special verdict in *Lickbarrow v Mason*[36] which recites that "the property is transferred by indorsement", must be read "the property which it was the intention to transfer is transferred"[37]; and many *obiter dicta* on the subject, such as the statement of Lord Hatherley in *Barber v Meyerstein*,[38] that, when goods are at sea, assigning the bill of lading is parting with the "whole and complete ownership of the goods", and of Lord Westbury in the same case, that the transfer of the bill of lading for value "passes the absolute property in the goods", must be taken as overruled, or strictly limited to the circumstances of the particular case.[39]

A97   **Article 97—Intention to transfer the whole Property by Indorsement of the Bill of Lading**

Property in goods at sea may be completely passed by indorsement and delivery of the bill of lading under which the goods are shipped in exchange for payment of the price.

Note 1. The question of the passing of property in goods shipped is not of great importance to the shipowner, as he is safe in delivering to the holder of the first bill of lading duly presented, if he has no notice or knowledge of other claims,[40] while if he has such knowledge, though probably in strict law he must either deliver at his peril to the rightful claimant or interplead,[41] yet in practice he can almost always obtain in exchange for delivery of the goods an indemnity against legal proceedings, which will render him virtually safe.[42]

Note 2. The property in goods shipped under a bill of lading may be passed without indorsement of such bill,[43] and it would seem that subsequent indorsement of the bill of lading to a different person will have no effect in passing the property, unless the circumstances of the case warrant the application of the Factors Act. The ordinary operation of the law as to the sale of goods which transfers the property in them is not

---

[30] See Art.102.
[31] See Art.103.
[32] See Art.104.
[33] (1884) 10 App.Cas. 74.
[34] (1884) 13 Q.B.D. 159 at p.167.
[35] (1882) 6 Q.B.D. 475 at p.480.
[36] (1794) 5 T.R. 683.
[37] As suggested by Lord Selborne (1884) 10 App.Cas. 74 at p.80.
[38] (1870) L.R. 4 H.L. 325 at p.335.
[39] See (1884) 10 App.Cas. 74 at pp.81, 104.
[40] *Glyn, Mills v East & West India Dock Co* (1882) 7 App.Cas. 591; see Art.151.
[41] per Lord Blackburn (1882) 7 App.Cas. 591 at p.611.
[42] Unless the decision in *Brown Jenkinson & Co Ltd v Percy Dalton (London) Ltd* [1957] 2 Q.B. 621 applies to such an indemnity.
[43] *Meyer v Sharpe* (1813) 5 Taunt. 74; *Nathan v Giles* (1814) 5 Taunt. 558.

affected by the existence of a bill of lading relating to those goods, by the indorsement of which, as *one* of the methods recognised by that law, the property may be passed.[44] And, in truth, "property does not pass by indorsement of the bill of lading, but by the contract in pursuance of which the indorsement is made".[45]

Note 3.[46] In a contract for the sale of goods upon "c.i.f." terms,[47] the contract, unless otherwise expressed, is for the sale of goods to be carried by sea,[48] and the seller performs his part by shipping goods of the contractual description[49] on board a ship bound to the contractual destination,[50] or purchasing afloat goods so shipped,[51] and tendering, within a reasonable time after shipment,[52] the shipping documents, to the purchaser, the goods during the voyage being at the risk of the purchaser.[53] In such a contract of sale of "unascertained goods"[54] the property probably passes to the purchaser only when the bill of lading is indorsed to and accepted by him.[55] The sending of a notice of appropriation, although it will make the goods the subject-matter of the contract ascertained, is not an "unconditional appropriation" so as to pass the property to the buyer if the seller retains the bills of lading against payment of the price and thus reserves the *jus disponendi.*[56]

The term "shipping documents" in such a contract of sale ordinarily means (1) a bill of lading; (2) a policy of insurance; (3) an invoice.[57] They may be tendered even though

---

[44] *cf.* per Parke B., *Bryans v Nix* (1839) 4 M. & W. 775 at pp.790, 791.

[45] per Lord Bramwell, *Sewell v Burdick* (1884) 10 App.Cas. 74 at p.105.

[46] McCardie J. referred to this Note with approval in *Manbre Saccharine Co v Corn Products Co* [1919] 1 K.B. 198 at p.202.

[47] "Not every contract which is expressed to be a c.i.f. contract is such": per Lord Porter in *Comptoir d'Achat v Luis de Ridder* [1949] A.C. 293 at p.309; see, also, below, p.175, fn.76.

[48] *L. Sutro & Co and Heilbut Symons & Co, Re* [1917] 2 K.B. 348.

[49] *Harland & Wolff v Burstall* (1901) 6 Com.Cas. 113. They must be of a fitness and quality to withstand the effects of normal transit to the port of destination: per Diplock J. in *Mash & Murrell v Emanuel* [1961] 1 Lloyd's Rep. 46; reversed [1961] 2 Lloyd's Rep. 326 (CA), without consideration of this point. Compare an article on "Deterioration of Goods in Transit" [1962] J.B.L. 351.

[50] *Lecky v Ogilvy* (1897) 3 Com.Cas. 29 (the two Tripolis). See also *Ceval Alimentos SA v Agrimpex Trading Co Ltd (The Northern Progress) (No. 2)* [1996] 2 Lloyd's Rep. 319 (tender bad when bill of lading incorporated charterparty term requiring sellers to divert the carrying ship to a different destination in defined circumstances) and *Soules CAF v PT Transap of Indonesia* [1999] 1 Lloyd's Rep. 917 (tender bad when bill of lading provided for delivery at range of ports wider than range in sale contract). The seller must pay any expenses necessary to secure delivery at the contractual destination, e.g. lighterage to a wharf at the point of discharge in addition to the ocean freight when that wharf is the destination named in the c.i.f. contract: *Acme Wood Co v Sutherland* (1904) 9 Com.Cas. 170. But of course the buyer, as indorsee of the bill of lading, must pay any demurrage at the port of discharge which the shipowner can claim under it and cannot seek to recover this back from the seller.

[51] The decision on service out of the jurisdiction of the House of Lords in *Johnson v Taylor* [1920] A.C. 144, rendered obsolete, see now C.P.R. 6.20(6), seems to overlook this possibility. A seller who has not shipped goods may yet perform his c.i.f. contract of sale: see also, *Vantol v Fairclough, Dodd & Jones* [1955] 1 Lloyd's Rep. 546 at p.552. The point was mentioned, but not dealt with in the HL: [1956] 2 Lloyd's Rep. 437 at p.447.

[52] *Groom v Barber* [1915] 1 K.B. 316. If the first tender is bad the seller can make a second tender which may be good, if he can do so within the time required by the contract for performance: *Borrowman v Free* (1878) 4 Q.B.D. 500; *Hyundai Merchant Marine Co Ltd v Karander Maritime Co Ltd (The Niizuru)* [1996] 2 Lloyd's Rep. 66.

[53] *Tregelles v Sewell* (1862) 7 H. & N. 574; *Groom v Barber,* above.

[54] Sale of Goods Act 1979, ss.16–18 which in the case of unascertained goods forming part of an identified bulk must now be read subject to the Sale of Goods (Amendment) Act 1995 on which see *Benjamin's Sale of Goods* 7th (2006) paras 18–285 to 18–307.

[55] *Wait v Baker* (1848) 2 Exch. 1; *The Miramichi* [1915] P. 71 at p.78. *Cf.* Kennedy J., *Ryan v Ridley* (1902) 8 Com.Cas. 105 at p.107. If the bill of lading is indorsed to the buyer and posted to him, probably the property would pass on its being put into the post. *Cf. Badische Anilin v Basle Co* [1898] A.C. 200 at pp.203, 204. There are however, dicta to the effect that the property may pass upon shipment of the goods. See *Ireland v Livingston* (1872) L.R. 5 H.L. 395 at p.409; *Biddell v E. Clemens Horst & Co* [1911] 1 K.B. 934 at p.956; *Comptoir D'Achat v Luis de Ridder* [1949] A.C. 293 at p.309. *Cf. Groom v Barber* [1915] 1 K.B. 316 at p.324. Though the property passes, payment may by the terms of the contract be postponed: *Dupont v British S. Afr. Co* (1901) 18 T.L.R. 24. See generally *Benjamin's Sale of Goods* 7th (2006) paras 19–098 to 19–109.

[56] *Bailey v Ross T. Smyth* (1940) 45 Com.Cas. 292 (HL), where the question of passing of property under a c.i.f. contract is elaborately discussed.

[57] per Blackburn J. in *Ireland v Livingston* (1872) L.R. 5 H.L. 395 at p.406; *Bailey v Ross T. Smyth,* above.

at the date of tender the seller knows that the goods have been lost and can never arrive.[58]

(1) *The bill or bills of lading*[59] must be in a form[60] usual in the trade,[61] and must cover the whole transit of the goods from the port of shipment to the port of arrival,[62] so that the buyer in possession of the bill of lading may not only be able to get delivery of the goods if they arrive, but also will be able to sue the carrier for loss or damage occurring at any stage of the transit. It must be for the contractual quantity and not for a larger quantity[63] and must be signed within a reasonable time after shipment.[64] A delivery order or a ship's release will not suffice unless, as is common, the contract expressly so provides.[65] The bill of lading must be effective at the time of tender, e.g. must not have been avoided or frustrated by war at that time though valid when issued.[66] Where the sale contract requires the bill of lading to be on liner terms, there will be a right of rejection of documents if the bill does not so provide.[67]

(2) Ordinarily an actual *policy*[68] must be tendered,[69] and an insurance broker's cover note or certificate that an insurance has been effected will not suffice.[70] It must be tendered

---

Blackburn J., *loc. cit.*, also mentioned the charterparty as one of the necessary documents. But neither in *Biddell v E. Clemens Horst & Co*, above, nor in *Johnson v Taylor* [1920] A.C. 144, is the charterparty mentioned; and in *Finska Cellulosa v Westfield Paper Co* (1941) 46 Com.Cas. 87 at p.91, Caldecote L.C.J., doubted whether the charterparty need be tendered. It is probably not required, even if some of the terms have been incorporated into the bill, unless necessary to determine whether or not the tendered documents comply with the terms of the contract of sale (as in *SIAT di dal Ferro v Tradax Overseas SA* [1990] 1 Lloyd's Rep. 53). Additional documents and details are frequently required by the contract: the provision of these will usually be obligatory, but the contract may on its true construction be directory only as to some of the additional requirements: *John Martin v Taylor* [1953] 2 Lloyd's Rep. 591.

[58] *Manbré Saccharine Co v Corn Products Co* [1919] 1 K.B. 198.

[59] For a detailed discussion see *Benjamin's Sale of Goods* 7th edn (2006) paras 19–025 to 19–041.

[60] As to whether a through bill of lading, combined transport bill of lading or "received for shipment" bill of lading may be tendered, see Art.182.

[61] e.g. whether the vessel must be a steamer or may be a sailing vessel: *Ranson v Manufacture d'Engrais* (1922) 13 Ll.L.R. 205; or as to route: *Shipton v Weston* (1922) 10 Ll.L.R. 762; but see *Tsakiroglou v Noblee* [1962] A.C. 93; the route must be a reasonable one at the time of shipment; or as to the inclusion of a special war risks clause: *Finska Cellulosa v Westfield Paper Co* (1941) 46 Com.Cas. 87. See *Burstall v Grimsdale* (1906) 11 Com.Cas. 280.

[62] See fn.60, above.

[63] *Keighley Maxted Bryan & Co, Re (No. 2)* (1894) 70 L.T. 155.

[64] *Foreman & Ellams v Blackburn* [1928] 2 K.B. 60.

[65] *Heilbut Symons v Harvey* (1922) 12 Ll.L.R. 455.

[66] *Karberg v Blythe* [1916] 1 K.B. 495; *Baxter, Fell & Co v Galbraith & Grant* (1941) 70 Ll.L.R. 142.

[67] *Soon Hua Seng Co Ltd v Glencore Grain Ltd* [1996] 1 Lloyd's Rep. 398.

[68] For a detailed discussion see *Benjamin's Sale of Goods* 7th (2006) paras 19–042 to 19–052.

[69] per Blackburn J. in *Ireland v Livingston* (1872) L.R. 5 H.L. 395 at p.406. In *Wilson, Holgate & Co v Belgian Grain Co* [1920] 2 K.B. 1, Bailhache J. was unable to find that since the decision in *Ireland v Livingston*, above, any custom had arisen obviating the necessity for a tender by the seller of an actual policy if the buyer required it, and decided that a broker's cover note or certificate of insurance would not suffice. He considered, however, that American certificates of insurance stood on a different footing and were equivalent to policies, "being accepted in this country as policies". But McCardie J. in *Diamond Alkali Export Corp v Bourgeois* [1921] 3 K.B. 443, held that an American certificate which did not purport to be a policy and did not contain all the terms of the insurance was a bad tender. And in *Scott v Barclays Bank* [1923] 2 K.B. 1, the CA, reversing Sankey J. (1922) 12 Ll.L.R. 502, held that an American certificate in similar terms was not an "approved policy" and could be refused. In practice, certificates of insurance are constantly accepted and some forms of c.i.f. contracts expressly provide that they shall suffice; see *Burstall v Grimsdale* (1906) 11 Com.Cas. 280; *John Martin v Taylor* [1953] 2 Lloyd's Rep. 591. We suggest that where the contract is silent as to the form of insurance document and in the absence of evidence as to custom or course of dealing, the insurance document, in order to constitute a good tender, (1) must profess to be a policy, (2) must be capable of being sued upon, and (3) must incorporate all the terms of the insurance either in the document itself or by reference to some well-known or readily accessible document. See *Malmberg v Evans* (1924) 30 Com.Cas. 107. It may be possible to prove either by custom or by the course of dealing between the parties that a document not conforming with these tests must be accepted. This, however, is doubtful; see per Atkin L.J. in *Malmberg v Evans* (1924) 30 Com.Cas. 107, and per McCardie J. in *Diamond Alkali Corp v Bourgeois* [1921] 3 K.B. 443 at p.458. *Quaere*, whether an English c.i.f. buyer can complain if the policy tendered is in the currency of the country from which the goods are exported and not in sterling. See *Malmberg v Evans*, above, at p.116.

[70] If the contract requires an "approved policy" this imports an objective standard and requires a policy to which no "reasonable commercial objection can be taken", and which therefore ought to be approved: *Scott v Barclays*

even if the goods have arrived in safety,[71] and may be tendered even though the seller knows that before the tender the goods have been lost.[72] It must cover only the goods mentioned in the bill of lading and invoice, and cover them for an amount at least reasonably equivalent to the value of the goods at the port of shipment, though not necessarily their whole value at their destination.[73] It must be made "upon the terms current in the trade"[74] as regards such points as the perils insured against (e.g. as to the f. c. & s. clause) and the quantum of the risk (e.g. as to the f.p.a. franchise) covered.

The best way of approaching the consideration of all questions on c.i.f. sales is to realise that this form of the sale of goods is one to be performed by the delivery of documents representing the goods,[75] i.e. of documents giving the right to have the goods delivered or the possible right, if they are lost or damaged, of recovering their value from the shipowner or from underwriters.[76] The seller performs his contract by tendering the documents and breaks it by failing to tender them. In order to be in a position to perform by so tendering it may be necessary for him to ship the goods, though not invariably, since he may buy documents for goods already afloat.[77] In holding that the seller breaks his contract by failing to ship the goods[78] did the House of Lords in *Johnson v Taylor* sufficiently distinguish between performance of the contract and the doing of something which is, or may be, a necessary step towards ability to perform the contract?

From the fact that the contract is performed by the delivery of documents it results that various rules in the Sale of Goods Act 1979, which is primarily drafted in relation to the sale and delivery of goods on land, can only be applied to c.i.f. sales *mutatis mutandis*.[79]

Bank [1923] 2 K.B. 1 at pp.14, 17. *Cf. Hodgson v Davies* (1810) 2 Camp. 530 at p.532, and *Smith v Mercer* (1867) L.R. 3 Ex. 51 at p.54, as to "approved bill".

[71] *Orient Co v Brekke* [1913] 1 K.B. 531.

[72] *Manbré Saccharine Co v Corn Products Co* [1919] 1 K.B. 198 at p.205. *Cf. Hickox v Adams* (1876) 34 L.T. 404.

[73] *Tamvaco v Lucas* (1861) 1 B. & S. 185. *Contrast Loders v Bank of New Zealand* (1929) 33 Ll.L.R. 70. See also *Strass v Spillers* [1911] 2 K.B. 759 (honour policies). As to the liability of the vendor, if policies turn out to be invalid or worthless, see *Cantiere Meccanico v Constant* (1912) 17 Com.Cas. 182 at pp.183, 188, 192, *Semble*, the seller would be similarly liable if the bill of lading tendered was a forgery: with which position contrast that in *Leather v Simpson* (1871) L.R. 11 Eq. 398, and *Guaranty Trust v Hannay* [1918] 2 K.B. 623. As to insurance against all risks, see *Yuill v Scott-Robson* [1908] 1 K.B. 270, and *Vincentelli v Rowlett* (1911) 16 Com.Cas. 310.

[74] per Hamilton J., *Biddell v E. Clemens Horst Co* [1911] 1 K.B. 214 at p.220. If the seller has to pay advance freight on shipment, he may presumably insure the advance freight by a separate policy which he keeps himself, and intimate to the buyer that on the arrival of the ship the amount of the advance freight should be paid to the seller in place of payment of freight to the shipowners. Or he may insure the goods for their full arrived value (thereby treating the advance freight as representing the enhanced value of the goods at destination), and invoice the buyer for the full c.i.f. price.

[75] The difference between Scrutton J. in *Karberg v Blythe* [1915] 2 K.B. 379 at p.388, and Bankes L.J. and Warrington L.J., *ibid.* [1916] 1 K.B. 495, is one of language rather than of substance. *Cf. Manbré Saccharine Co v Corn Products Co* [1919] 1 K.B. 198 at p.203. See also *Soules CAF v PT Transap of Indonesia* [1999] 1 Lloyd's Rep. 917 at p.918 (*"essentially a documentary transaction"*); *Trasimex Holdings SA v Addax BV* [1999] 1 Lloyd's Rep. 28 at p.32; *Cargill International SA v Bangladesh Sugar & Food Industries Corp* [1996] 2 Lloyd's Rep. 524 affirmed [1998] 1 W.L.R. 461.

[76] In some trades there is in use a form which is in terms expressed to be a c.i.f. contract, but also provides (i) for payment on landed weights; (ii) for payment as to any goods arriving damaged with an allowance; and (iii) for the contract to be void as to any portion shipped but not arriving. Except in name this is not a c.i.f. contract. The buyer will, however, be able to sue on the bill of lading in cases of damage, holding any sum recovered as trustee for the seller: *Paul v National S.S. Co* (1937) 43 Com.Cas. 68; *Obestain Inc v National Mineral Development Corp Ltd (The Sanix Ace)* [1987] 1 Lloyd's Rep. 465; *The Aramis* [1987] 2 Lloyd's Rep. 58; and probably also in cases of shortage: see *The Arpad* (1933) 46 Ll.L.R. 182 and 51 Ll.L.R. 115 at pp.117, 118; *Ministry of Food v Australian Wheat Board* [1952] 1 Lloyd's Rep. 297 at p.311, and *cf. Den of Airlie v Mitsui* (1912) 17 Com.Cas. 117.

[77] See, above, p.173, fn.51.

[78] *Johnson v Taylor* [1920] A.C. 144. See now C.P.R. 6.20(6).

[79] *cf. E. Clemens Horst Co v Biddell* [1912] A.C. 18. So in s.51 of the Act "the time when the goods ought to have been delivered" means, in regard to failure to deliver under a c.i.f. contract, the time when in the normal course the shipping documents ought to have been tendered, not the time when the goods would themselves have arrived: *Sharpe v Nosawa* [1917] 2 K.B. 814. *Cf. Produce Brokers Co v Weis & Co* (1918) 87 L.J.K.B. 472. In *Kwei Tek Chao v British Traders and Shippers* [1954] 2 Q.B. 459 at p.486, Devlin J. expressed the view that

And there may be cases in which the buyer must pay the full price for delivery of the documents, though he can get nothing out of them, and though in any intelligible sense no property in the goods can ever pass to him, i.e. if the goods have been lost by a peril excepted by the bill of lading, and by a peril not insured by the policy, the bill of lading and the policy yet being in the proper commercial form called for by the contract.[80]

Under a c.i.f. contract, "payment against shipping documents", the price is due upon, or within a reasonable time after, tender of the documents,[81] irrespective of the arrival of the ship,[82] and notwithstanding that the buyer has had no opportunity of inspecting the goods to ascertain whether they are in accordance with the contract.[83] By paying against documents the buyer does not, however, lose his right of rejection on the grounds, e.g. of the goods being not of the contractual description. In such cases the buyer can, after inspecting the goods and rejecting them, recover the price previously paid against documents.[84] In other words the buyer has two possible grounds of rejection, one in respect of the documents and the other in respect of the goods.[85] If, however, the ground for rejecting the goods is one which is evident from the shipping documents themselves, the buyer may in appropriate circumstances lose the right of rejection if he takes up the documents without objection.[86]

A98   **Article 98—Unpaid Vendor's Securities**

Where goods are shipped by a vendor in pursuance of his buyer's order for delivery to the buyer, such shipment prima facie passes the property to the buyer, delivery to the ship being equivalent to delivery to him.[87]

But under these circumstances the unpaid vendor has the right to stop the goods *in transitu*,[88] though they are made by the bill of lading deliverable to the vendee.[89]

An unpaid vendor frequently insists on more than this security for the price and deals with the bill of lading so as to prevent the property in the goods from passing to the vendee on their shipment, either by:

---

delivery of the goods under s.35 of the Act meant in the case of a c.i.f. contract transfer of possession by delivery of the documents of title.

[80] *Groom v Barber* [1915] 1 K.B. 316; *Weis v Credit Co* [1916] 1 K.B. 346; see also *Law v Brit. Am. Tobacco Co* [1916] 2 K.B. 605; and *Clark v Cox, McEuen & Co* (1920) 25 Com.Cas. 94.

[81] If the buyer refuses to accept the documents, the seller's claim against him is for damages for breach of contract, not for the price: *Stein v County Co* (1916) 115 L.T. 215.

[82] *Ryan v Ridley* (1902) 8 Com.Cas. 105. See also *Polenghi v Dried Milk Co* (1904) 10 Com.Cas. 42. Where, as is common, the contract provides for payment "on arrival of the vessel", and the vessel is lost and so never arrives, payment, in the absence of anything to indicate the contrary, must be made at the time when she ought to have arrived. In short, "on arrival of the vessel" specifies the time when, and not a condition upon which, payment is to be made. *Cf. Fragano v Long* (1825) 4 B. & C. 219. Contrast the case of goods sold "to arrive". See *Benjamin's Sale of Goods* 7th edn (2006), paras 21–022 to 21–024.

[83] *E. Clemens Horst v Biddell* [1912] A.C. 18.

[84] *Polenghi v Dried Milk Co* (1904) 10 Com.Cas. 42.

[85] *Kwei Tek Chao v British Traders and Shippers* [1954] 2 Q.B. 459; *Berger & Co v Gill & Duffus SA* [1984] 1 Lloyd's Rep. 227 (HL).

[86] *Panchaud Frères SA v Establissements General Grain* [1970] 1 Lloyd's Rep. 53 (CA). Goods shipped out of time; date of shipment appeared in shipping documents: by taking up documents without objection, the buyer lost the right to rely upon the late shipment as a ground for rejecting the goods.

[87] *Shepherd v Harrison* (1871) L.R. 5 H.L. 116 at p.127.

[88] See below, Art.101.

[89] *Ex p. Banner* (1876) 2 Ch.D. 278 at p.288.

A. Reserving to himself the *jus disponendi*.[90]

B. Conditional indorsement of the bill of lading.[91]

Article 99—Reservation of Jus Disponendi by Unpaid Vendor   A99

The unpaid vendor may take from the master a bill of lading making the goods deliverable to his order or to his agent, and may forward this bill to his agent, with instructions not to indorse it to the vendee except on payment for the goods.

If he takes the bill in this form on his own behalf, and not as agent for, or on behalf of, the purchaser, he prima facie thereby reserves to himself the power of absolutely disposing of the goods, known as the *jus disponendi*, and no property will pass to the purchaser by the shipment.[92] Payment or tender of the price will pass the property to the purchaser,[93] unless the *jus disponendi* has been reserved by the vendor for some other purpose than that of securing the contract price.[94]

Article I of the Schedule to the Carriage of Goods by Sea Act 1971, speaks of "the moment at which a bill of lading regulates the relations between a carrier and a holder". The meaning of "regulates the relations" is obscure. Presumably when a charterer, as unpaid vendor, has sent forward a bill of lading, reserving the *jus disponendi*, the bill of lading "regulates the relations" between the shipowner and the purchaser when the bill of lading is indorsed to the purchaser with the intention of passing the property, i.e. generally on the payment of the purchase price (see Chapter 20 below).

Note. It has been discussed whether the *jus disponendi* is merely a vendor's lien, or is some right in the vendor concomitant with property in the vendee, or operates as an act of the vendor which prevents the property from passing to the vendee on shipment of the goods and postpones the vesting of the property till certain conditions are satisfied. *Ogg v Shuter*[95] shows that it is more than a vendor's lien. The judgment in *Mirabita v Ottoman Bank*[96] declines to decide between the last two alternatives, but the language of Cotton L.J. in the same case appears to show that to speak of the vendor's *jus disponendi* is another way of saying that the property has not passed to the vendee, whatever may be his rights

---

[90] See Art.99.

[91] See Art.100; and also Sale of Goods Act 1979, s.19.

[92] *Shepherd v Harrison* (1871) L.R. 5 H.L. 116; *Mirabita v Ottoman Bank* (1878) 3 Ex.D. 164 at p.172; *Ogg v Shuter* (1875) 1 C.P.D. 47; *Gabarron v Kreeft* (1875) L.R. 10 Ex. 274; *Bailey v Ross T. Smyth* (1940) 45 Com.Cas. 292 (HL); *Transpacific Eternity SA v Kanematsu Corp (The Antares III)* [2002] 1 Lloyd's Rep. 233 at p.236: see Sale of Goods Act 1979, s.19(1)(2) and see further *Eridania SpA v Rudolf A. Oetker (The Fjord Wind)* [1999] 1 Lloyd's Rep. 307 at p.355; *Center Optical (Hong Kong) Ltd v Jardine Transport Services (Hong Kong) Ltd* [2001] 2 Lloyd's Rep. 678 at p.783 and *Evergreen Marine Corp v Aldgate Warehouse (Wholesale) Ltd* [2003] 2 Lloyd's Rep. 597 at [30]–[33]; [2003] EWHC 667 (Comm). *Cf: Tang He, Re* [2001] 1 H.K.L.R.D. 451 (Hong Kong).

[93] *Mirabita v Ottoman Bank*, above.

[94] *Wait v Baker* (1848) 2 Ex. 1.

[95] (1875) 1 C.P.D. 47.

[96] (1878) 3 Ex.D. 164.

under the contract of sale. In the Prize Court, where in many cases it has been necessary to decide precisely when the property in goods sold has passed, it has been held that the reservation of the *jus disponendi* by the seller does prevent the property passing to the buyer.[97]

A100   **Article 100—Conditional Indorsement by Unpaid Vendor**

The unpaid vendor may draw a bill of exchange on the vendee for the price, and either:

A. Forward it for acceptance, together with a copy of the bill of lading,[98] sending also an indorsed bill of lading to his agent[99]; or

B. Discount it at a bank, depositing an indorsed bill of lading as security for the advance and leaving the bank to present the bill of exchange for acceptance or payment together with the bill of lading.[100]

In case A, the vendee cannot retain the bill of lading, or obtain the indorsed bill of lading unless he accepts the bill of exchange.[101] But if being in possession of the indorsed bill of lading he transfers it by indorsement to an innocent holder for value, that holder obtains under the Factors Act 1889, a good title to the goods, though the vendee has not accepted the bill of exchange.[102]

In case B, the vendee cannot obtain the bill of lading from the bank unless he accepts the bill or pays the amount due; but if, before the bank realises the goods to satisfy its claim, the vendee tenders the amount claimed, the property in the goods will at once pass to him,[103] and he will be entitled to the bill of lading, unless the *jus disponendi* has been reserved by the vendor with some other intention than that of securing the contract price.[104]

The vendee is not entitled to require delivery of all copies of the bill of lading before accepting bills of exchange, if the copy tendered is in fact effectual to pass the property; nor, *semble*, can he claim that they should be delivered at such a time that they can be forwarded to arrive at the port of destination before the ship, but only that the shipper shall forward them with all reasonable dispatch.[105]

---

[97] *cf.*, e.g. *The Miramichi* [1915] P. 71 at p.78.

[98] In *Coventry v Gladstone* (1867) L.R. 4 Eq. 493, an attempt failed to set up a custom to deliver bills of lading, not when bills of exchange were accepted, but when they were paid.

[99] *Shepherd v Harrison* (1871) L.R. 5 H.L. 116.

[100] *Turner v Trustees of Liverpool Docks* (1851) 6 Ex. 543. Where a bank presents a bill of exchange with bills of lading annexed, it is not taken to guarantee that the latter are genuine: *Leather v Simpson* (1871) L.R. 11 Eq. 398; *Baxter's Leather Co v Chapman* (1874) 29 L.T. 642; *Guaranty Co v Hannay* [1918] 2 K.B. 623 (CA).

[101] *Shepherd v Harrison* (1871) L.R. 5 H.L. 116. See also Sale of Goods Act 1979, s.19(3), and *Cahn v Pockett's S.S. Co* [1899] 1 Q.B. 643. For special facts under which the consignee who had received bills of lading was held not bound to accept bills of exchange drawn against him, see *Depperman v Hubbersty* (1852) 17 Q.B. 766; for special facts in which the consignee was held to be bound, see *Imperial Ottoman Bank v Cowan* (1874) 31 L.T. 336; *Hoare v Dresser* (1859) 7 H.L.C. 290.

[102] *Cahn v Pockett's S.S. Co* [1899] 1 Q.B. 643.

[103] *Mirabita v Ottoman Bank* (1878) 3 Ex.D. 164.

[104] *Wait v Baker* (1848) 2 Ex. 1. See also *Barber v Taylor* (1839) 5 M. & W. 527; *Gilbert v Guignon* (1872) L.R. 8 Ch. 16.

[105] *Sanders v Maclean* (1883) 11 Q.B.D. 327.

In all these cases the vendor, by reserving the *jus disponendi*, is prima facie presumed to intend to retain the property in the goods,[106] and the burden of disproving this intention lies on those who dispute it.[107]

Case 1. P requested V in Brazil to purchase cotton for him. V did so and forwarded it to England, taking a bill of lading deliverable to V's order and describing the cotton in the invoice as "shipped on account and at the risk of P". V forwarded to his agent W the invoice and two bills of lading; W sent on to P the invoice and one bill of lading, indorsed, and a bill of exchange for the price of the cotton. P refused to accept the bill of exchange, but kept the bill of lading, which he handed to his brokers, who paid the freight on the cotton and got a delivery order from the shipowners. Meanwhile, W obtained delivery of the cotton under the second bill of lading. *Held*, that W's action reserved to him the *jus disponendi* and the property in the cotton: that P could not keep the bill of lading without accepting the bill of exchange, and that W was justified in taking possession of the cotton.[108]

Case 2. V purchased goods in X, as agents for P in England, with the proceeds of bills drawn by V on P and discounted in X. On shipping, V took bills of lading making the goods deliverable to P and forwarded them to P by post, with notice of the bills of exchange drawn. While the goods were *in transitu* P became bankrupt, having accepted some of the bills, but having paid none. *Held*, that the property had passed absolutely to P, subject only to V's right to stop *in transitu*.[109]

Case 3. V shipped guano to P, as the result of a correspondence, which objected to the proposed price, but asked the captain to bring some other goods as well. P insured the cargo. V took a bill of lading, making the goods deliverable to V or order, but before it was indorsed to P the ship was wrecked. The jury found that V had intended the shipment to pass the property to P and had not intended to keep the guano in his own hands; and this verdict was sustained by the court who *held* that the property was in P from the time of shipment.[110]

Case 4. V sold potatoes to P, payment to be by cash against bill of lading, and took a bill of lading deliverable to V or order. The ship arrived on January 26. W, the agent of V, presented on January 27 the bill of lading to P, who refused to pay the draft for the price annexed, on the plea of short shipment. There was in fact no short shipment; and on February 2, W sold the potatoes, P on the same day giving notice that he claimed them, but not tendering the price. *Held*, that until P paid or tendered cash against the bill of lading, the possession (*quaere* property) was in W, with a power to sell the goods.[111]

Case 5. V purchased cotton by P's orders and shipped it on P's ship, V taking a bill of lading making the cotton deliverable at Z, "to order or assigns, paying for freight for the cotton nothing, being owner's property". V indorsed the bill in full: "Deliver to the bank of Z, or order"; drew bills of exchange on P and discounted them at another bank on the security of an indorsed bill of lading. V also forwarded to P an invoice stating that the goods were shipped "by order and for account of P and to him consigned". P became bankrupt before the goods arrived; V paid the bills of exchange and claimed to stop the goods *in transitu*; the representatives of P claimed the goods on arrival. *Held*, that by the terms of the bill of lading, V reserved to himself the *jus disponendi* in the goods and did

---

[106] The property and right of possession to goods shipped have been held to be transferred to the vendee on the facts of the following cases: *Walley v Montgomery* (1803) 3 East 585; *Coxe v Harden* (1803) 4 East 211; *Ogle v Atkinson* (1814) 5 Taunt. 759; *Wilmshurst v Bowker* (1844) 7 M. & G. 882; *Key v Cotesworth* (1852) 7 Ex. 595; *Joyce v Swann* (1864) 17 C.B. (N.S.) 84; *Castle v Playford* (1872) L.R. 7 Ex. 98; *Ex p. Banner* (1876) 2 Ch.D. 278; *Mirabita v Ottoman Bank* (1878) 3 Ex.D. 164; *Colonial Ins Co v Adelaide Ins Co* (1886) 12 App.Cas. 128. The property and right of possession were held to have been reserved by the vendor and shipper in the following cases: *Craven v Ryder* (1816) 6 Taunt. 433; *Ruck v Hatfield* (1822) 5 B. & Ald. 632; *Brandt v Bowlby* (1831) 2 B. & Ad. 932; *Ellershaw v Magniac* (1843) 6 Ex. 570; *Wait v Baker* (1848) 2 Ex. 1; *Van Casteel v Booker* (1848) 2 Ex. 691; *Jenkyns v Brown* (1849) 14 Q.B. 496; *Turner v Trustees of Liverpool Docks* (1851) 6 Ex. 543; *Moakes v Nicolson* (1865) 19 C.B. (N.S.) 290; *Falke v Fletcher* (1865) 18 C.B. (N.S.) 403; *Shepherd v Harrison* (1871) L.R. 5 H.L. 116; *Ogg v Shuter* (1875) 1 C.P.D. 47; *Gabarron v Kreeft* (1875) L.R. 10. Ex. 274; *Bailey v Ross T. Smyth* (1940) 45 Com.Cas. 292 (HL). As to the general presumption arising from the seller taking the bill of lading in his name see Art.99 above.
[107] *Joyce v Swann* (1864) 17 C.B. (N.S.) 84.
[108] *Shepherd v Harrison* (1871) L.R. 5 H.L. 116. See also *Barrow v Coles* (1811) 3 Camp. 92 and *Cahn v Pockett's S.S. Co* [1899] 1 Q.B. 643.
[109] *Ex p. Banner* (1876) 2 Ch.D. 278.
[110] *Joyce v Swann* (1864) 17 C.B. (N.S.) 84.
[111] *Ogg v Shuter* (1875) 1 C.P.D. 47.

not lose it by indorsing the bill to the bank, and that he consequently was entitled to the goods as against P's representatives.[112]

Case 6. V shipped 600 tons umber upon a ship chartered for P, under a bill of lading deliverable to V or assigns. P insured the umber. V drew a bill of exchange for the price and forwarded it for discount to the Z bank with the bill of lading. P declined to pay the bill, but afterwards, and before the bank dealt with the cargo, tendered the amount of the bill of exchange and demanded the bill of lading. The bank refused and sold the umber. *Held*, that the refusal and sale were wrongful and that the property passed to P on his tender made before the bank had realised.[113]

Case 7. V agreed to sell to P corn for cash or acceptance on handing over a bill of lading. V sent P the charter of the ship made in V's name, in which the corn was loaded, and took a bill of lading deliverable to G or assigns. When the cargo reached its destination, V left the invoice and an unindorsed bill of lading with P, who raised disputes as to the quality of the cargo, but afterwards tendered the price. V refused to accept it. *Held*, that no property in the corn passed to P, either at shipment, or by tender of the price.[114]

Case 8. V agreed to sell to P iron, payment in cash at L, in exchange for bills of lading. V took a set of three bills of lading, forwarded two duly indorsed to his agents in L, and retained the third himself. On August 3, V's agents tendered the two bills to P, who refused to pay cash unless all three were tendered. V's agents accordingly procured the third, and tendered the three to P on August 9. P refused to pay cash on the ground that the tender was so late that he could not forward them so as to reach the port of destination before the ship. *Held*, (1) that the tender of what was in fact a bill effectual to pass the property was good, though the purchaser, in the absence of the other bills of the set, did not know it was effectual.[115] (2) *Semble*,[116] that so long as V used reasonable diligence in tendering the bill of lading to P, it was not necessary that he should tender it in time for it to reach the port of destination before the carrying ship.[117]

A101   Article 101—Stoppage in transitu

Under certain conditions a vendor, who has forwarded goods in such a manner that the property, though not the actual possession, has passed to the purchaser,[118] has the right of resuming possession of the goods during their transit to the purchaser.[119]

This resumption of possession by the vendor does not amount to termination of the contract,[120] but is the exercise by an unpaid vendor[121] of his right to insist on his lien for the price.[122]

---

[112] *Turner v Trustees of Liverpool Docks* (1851) 6 Ex. 543.

[113] *Mirabita v Imperial Ottoman Bank* (1878) 3 Ed.D. 164.

[114] *Wait v Baker* (1848) 2 Ex. 1, distinguished in *Mirabita v Imperial Ottoman Bank*, above, as a case where there was no appropriation of the goods and no passing of the property until the bill of lading, which the vendor had taken to his own order, had been handed over unconditionally to the purchaser. See also *Ellershaw v Magniac* (1843) 6 Ex. 570; *Gabarron v Kreeft* (1875) L.R. 10 Ex. 274.

[115] Thus if the third bill had been indorsed to I, before the tender of the other two to P, the tender would not be effective, but P was not entitled to require proof of the effectiveness of the tender, a state of things productive of some hardship.

[116] per Brett M.R. at pp.336, 338. Cotton L.J. at p.340, and Bowen L.J. at p.344, express themselves not unfavourably to this view, but decline finally to decide it.

[117] *Sanders v Maclean* (1883) 11 Q.B.D. 327 (CA).

[118] It is beyond the scope of this work to discuss exhaustively the cases when property passes on shipment; the method of reserving property in the vendor by taking bills of lading which make the goods deliverable to his order has been dealt with above: Art.99. On the question of appropriation of goods not specific, the reader is referred to *Benjamin's Sale of Goods* 7th edn (2006) paras 5–059 to 5–130.

[119] On the right of stoppage in transitu see *Benjamin's Sale of Goods* 7th edn (2006) paras 15–061 to 15–091.

[120] *Kemp v Falk* (1882) 7 App.Cas. 573 at p.581; *Humberson, Re* (1846) De Gex 262; *Wentworth v Outhwaite* (1842) 10 M. & W. 436.

[121] It depends on the character of unpaid vendor and not on the nature of a lien; for other persons who are entitled to liens have yet no right to stop *in transitu* after they have lost possession: *Kinloch v Craig* (1790) 3 T.R. 783.

[122] Statement of law by Cotton L.J. in *Phelps v Comber* (1885) 29 Ch.D. 813 at p.821. The right is not affected by the Bills of Sale Acts: *Ex p. Watson* (1877) 5 Ch.D. 35 at p.44.

This right, known as the right of stoppage *in transitu*, may be exercised:

   (i) by an unpaid vendor of goods and others in an analogous position;

   (ii) on the insolvency of the vendee;

   (iii) as against such vendee, and all persons claiming under him;

   (iv) except as against an indorsee or transferee of the bill of lading or other document of title for such goods, who has given valuable consideration for such indorsement or transfer, in ignorance of any circumstances which would prevent such indorsement or transfer from acting as a valid transfer of a property or interest in the goods;

   (v) at any time before the vendee has acquired possession of the goods by himself or his agent and so terminated the transit.

Note. This Article contains only the general principles of the doctrine of stoppage *in transitu*, a subject of considerable technicality. Earlier editions of this work contained a valuable discussion of the whole topic under the headings (i) to (v) set out in this Article.

Article 102—Indorsement of Bill of Lading as a Mortgage   A102

The effect of indorsement of a bill of lading may be to show an intention to pass, and therefore to pass, the legal estate in the goods to the indorsee as security by way of mortgage for an advance, leaving the indorser an equitable right to redeem them.[123]

Article 103—Indorsement of Bill of Lading as a Pledge   A103

The indorsement may have the effect of giving the indorsee an equitable interest as security by way of pledge for an advance, accompanied by a power to obtain delivery of the goods when they arrive, and if necessary to realise them for the purpose of the security.[124] If such goods are not delivered to the pledgee of the bill of lading, he can bring an action for wrongful interference with them, unless the defendant's parting with the goods was before the plaintiff acquired his title.[125]

---

[123] *Sewell v Burdick* (1884) 10 App.Cas. 74. As to the difference, in general, between a mortgage and a pledge, see *Morritt, Re* (1886) 18 Q.B.D. 222 at pp.232, 235.

[124] *Sewell v Burdick*, above. The person indorsing the bill of lading as security for advances still retains sufficient interest in the goods to enable him to bring an action for damage to them: *The Glamorganshire* (1888) 13 App.Cas. 454.

[125] *Bristol, etc. Bank v Midland Ry* [1891] 2 Q.B. 653; as explained in *Margarine Union v Cambay Prince S.S. Co* [1969] 1 Q.B. 219; *Hannam v Arp* (1928) 30 Ll.L.R. 306 at p.309 (CA); *The Future Express* [1992] 2 Lloyd's Rep. 79; [1993] 2 Lloyd's Rep. 542; *Cf. London Joint Stock Bank v British Amsterdam Co* (1910) 16 Com.Cas. 102.

An indorsement of bills of lading in blank and their deposit so indorsed by way of security for money advanced,[126] without more, will be held to be a pledge.[127]

Note. It is impossible to state with any confidence what dealings with a bill of lading will amount to a mortgage as distinguished from a pledge. Probably none of the ordinary commercial dealings with bills of lading amounts to mortgages and the difference between mortgages and pledges is immaterial from a commercial point of view, as it lies chiefly in the exact legal remedies for enforcing the security.

Case 1. F shipped goods to Z on A's ship taking a bill of lading making the goods deliverable to F or assigns. F indorsed the bill in blank, and deposited it with I as security for an advance. I never claimed the goods under the bill of lading. *Held*, that the transaction amounted to a pledge of the goods represented by the bill of lading.

Case 2. F sold cheese to G and shipped it on board A's ship taking bills of lading to order of F or assigns. F drew bills of exchange on G for the price, which he sold to the T Bank, with bills of lading attached indorsed in blank. The T Bank forwarded the bills to their agents in London with a hypothecation note of the goods attached. On arrival of A's ship, A deposited the goods with X, instructing them to hold the goods to his order. G induced X to deliver the goods to him without any order from A, and then by fraud G induced the Z bank to take up the bills of exchange, receiving with them the bills of lading. Z got delivery orders from A and presented them to X. When it was found that G had procured X to deliver to him the goods without any order from A, Z sued X for conversion. *Held*, that Z were pledgees of the goods and could sue for conversion.[128]

A104   **Article 104—Ineffectual Indorsements**[129]

An indorsement of the bill of lading may pass no property or title to the indorsee, as:

(1) Where the indorser has no property to pass[130]; having, e.g. already indorsed one bill of lading of a set so as to pass the property[131]; or

(2) Where there is no consideration for the indorsement[132]; or

(3) Where the circumstances show that no property was intended to pass, as in the case of an indorsement to an agent to enable him to sell, or to stop *in transitu*[133]; or

(4) Where the indorsee knows of facts which prevent the indorsement from being effective,[134] as the open insolvency of a consignee who has not paid the price of the goods[135]; or

---

[126] It will require the stamp suitable for a pledge and not for a mortgage: *Harris v Birch* (1842) 9 M. & W. 591.

[127] *Sewell v Burdick*, above.

[128] *Bristol, etc. Bank v Midland Ry* [1891] 2 Q.B. 653.

[129] This article must be read subject to the provisions of the Factors Acts, with which it is beyond the province of this work to deal.

[130] *Finlay v Liverpool S.S. Co* (1870) 23 L.T. 251 at p.255; *Gurney v Behrend* (1854) 3 E. & B. 622 at p.634; *The Future Express* [1992] 2 Lloyd's Rep. 79; [1993] 2 Lloyd's Rep. 542. *Cf. Delaurier v Wyllie* (1889) 17 Rettie 167 (as to the iron).

[131] *Barber v Meyerstein* (1870) L.R. 4 H.L. 317.

[132] *Sewell v Burdick* (1884) 10 App.Cas. 74 at p.80, per Lord Selborne; *Waring v Cox* (1808) 1 Camp. 369.

[133] *Waring v Cox*, above; *Patten v Thompson* (1816) 5 M. & S. 350; *Tucker v Humphrey* (1828) 4 Bing. 516.

[134] *Dick v Lumsden* (1793) 1 Peake 189; *Cuming v Brown* (1807) 1 Camp. 104; *Gilbert v Guignon* (1872) L.R. 8 Ch. 16.

[135] See 17th edn, Art.66.

(5) Where at the time of the indorsement the shipowner has already delivered the goods to a person entitled to have them delivered to him[136]; or

(6) where, although the bill of lading has been indorsed in favour of another person, that person has not obtained possession of the bill as a result of the completion of the indorsement by delivery.[137]

But where the indorser has the property, even though such property has been obtained by fraud, an indorsement for valuable consideration to a bona fide indorsee, before the original owner or indorser has obtained a legal rescission of the transfer, will pass the property.[138]

Case 1. Goods consigned to P were in course of transit landed at a sufferance wharf on the Thames, subject to a stop for freight by A and to a stop for advances by I, a mortgage on security of a set of three bills of lading. P obtained from K a loan, with which he redeemed the bill from I and indorsed two to K as security for his advance. P obtained another advance from M, to whom he indorsed the third bill. With this advance the stop for freight was removed and M obtained the goods from the sufferance wharf on production of his indorsed bill. *Held,* that the property in the goods having passed to K by the first indorsement, the second conferred no property on M, and K could recover from him the goods or their value.[139]

Case 2. V shipped to P oilcake, sending the bill of lading to V's agent, W, with instructions not to part with it "without first receiving payment". P gave W a bill of exchange accepted by K, and promised immediate payment in cash, on which W delivered to P the indorsed bill of lading. P indorsed the bill of lading to I, who took it bona fide and for value. P and K then became bankrupt, without paying W. *Held,* that though P had obtained the bill of lading by fraud, he could transfer the property in the goods by its indorsement to I, a bona fide holder for value.[140]

---

[136] As to whether a bill will be exhausted by delivery to a person entitled to the goods where delivery has not been made against the surrender of the bill see *The Future Express* [1992] 2 Lloyd's Rep. 279 (holding no); *Motis Exports v Dampskibs AF 1912 Akt* [2000] 1 Lloyd's Rep. 211 (dicta to the same effect) but *cf.* Channell J., *London Joint Stock Bank v British Amsterdam* (1910) 16 Com.Cas. 102 at p.105; *Enichem Anic SpA v Ampelos Shipping Co Ltd (The Delfini)* [1990] 1 Lloyd's Rep. 252 at p.269. For discussion of the decision in *The Future Express* see Aikens, Lord and Bools, *Bills of lading* (2006) paras 2.97–2.98 suggesting (it is submitted, correctly) that delivery to the person entitled to the goods will exhaust the bill even if delivery is not made against presentation of the bill.
[137] *Aegean Sea Traders Corp v Repsol Petroleo SA (The Aegean Sea)* [1998] 2 Lloyd's Rep. 39 (bill of lading indorsed in favour of R and posted to R not effective where R did not receive the bill into his possession and accept delivery of it).
[138] *Pease v Gloahec* (1866) L.R. 1 P.C. 219; *The Argentina* (1867) L.R. 1 A. & B. 370; *Nippon Yusen Kaisha v Ramjiban Serowgee* [1938] A.C. 429. This is an application of the normal principle that the power to rescind a transaction is defeated by the claim of a bona fide purchaser for value without notice.
[139] *Barber v Meyerstein* (1870) L.R. 4 H.L. 317.
[140] *The Argentina* (1867) L.R. 1 A. & F. 370.

CHAPTER 11

LIABILITY OF SHIPOWNER FOR LOSS OF, OR DAMAGE TO, GOODS
CARRIED

A105   **Article 105—Liability of Shipowner in Absence of Express Stipulations**

IN the absence of express stipulations in the contract of affreightment,[1] and
subject to certain statutory exemptions from, and limitations of, liability,[2] all
shipowners who are common carriers for reward[3] (i.e. who offer their ships as
general ships for the transit of the goods of any shipper) are liable[4] for any loss
of or damage to such goods in transit, unless caused by the act of God, or the
Queen's enemies, or by the inherent nature[5] of the goods themselves, or by their
having been properly made the subject of a general average sacrifice.[6]

Quaere, whether a shipowner who is not a common carrier has the same
liability as a common carrier,[7] or is only liable as a bailee for the exercise of due
care and diligence.[8] If he has the liability of a common carrier he will be liable
for damage to the goods carried resulting from causes other than the act of God
or the Queen's enemies, or the vice of the goods themselves, though such damage
could not be prevented by reasonable care and diligence on his part and that of
his servants. If he has only the liability of a bailee he will be free where he can
prove that he and his servants have exercised reasonable care and diligence.

At common law all shipowners who contract to carry goods undertake
absolutely, in the absence of express provisions negativing such undertaking, that
their ship is seaworthy at the beginning of the voyage,[9] and that they will proceed
on the voyage with reasonable dispatch[10] and without unnecessary deviation.[11]

---

[1] See *Lipton v Jescott Steamers* (1895) 1 Com.Cas. 32.
[2] Of the statutes applicable the Carriage of Goods by Sea Act 1971 (see Chapter 20), is the most important. See
also Merchant Shipping Act 1995, s.185 (limitation of amount of damages); s.186 (exclusion of liability for fire,
valuables), below, Appendix I. For the position under the Hamburg Rules See Art.4.1, Appendix VI, below.
[3] If a carrier is to have no reward he comes within Lord Holt's sixth category of bailments (*Coggs v Bernard*
(1703) 2 Ld.Ray. 909 at p.918) and is only liable for loss due to negligence.
[4] *Nugent v Smith* (1876) 1 C.P.D. 19, 422; *Liver Alkali Co v Johnson* (1874) L.R. 9 Ex. 338. Per Brown L.J. in
Pandorf v Hamilton (1886) 17 Q.B.D. 670 at p.683. See Arts 107, 108. This liability is not removed by a practice
of the shipowner to insure at the cost of the goods owner and by his direction: *Hill v Scott* [1895] 2 Q.B. 371.
The liability is not assumed by a warehouseman who undertakes to have goods brought by barge from the ship
to his warehouse and carries out that arrangement by sub-contract with a lighterman: *Consolidated Tea Co v
Oliver's Wharf* [1910] 2 K.B. 395.
[5] The phrase "inherent vice" is commonly used of this ground of exemption. See Art.111, below.
[6] See Arts 133–138, below.
[7] per Brett J. in *Nugent v Smith* (1876) 1 C.P.D. 19 at p.33, and *Liver Alkali Co v Johnson* (1874) L.R. 9 Ex. 338
at p.344.
[8] per Cockburn C.J. in *Nugent v Smith*, above, at pp.434, 438; compare Lord Herschell at p.510 and Lord
Macnaghten at p.515 of *The Xantho* (1887) 12 App.Cas. 503; Lord Watson at p.526 of *Hamilton v Pandorf*
(1887) 12 App.Cas. 518; and Note, below. See also per Willes J. in *Notara v Henderson* (1872) L.R. 7 Q.B. 225
at p.236; *Grill v General Iron Colliery Co* (1886) L.R. 1 C.P. 600 at p.612.
[9] *Steel v State Line* (1878) 3 App.Cas. 72, and Art.45.
[10] See Art.52.
[11] See Arts 127, 128.

Note: In the law, as thus stated, there are two disputed points:

(1) Whether the owner of a ship or lighter hired to carry a specific cargo on a particular voyage, as distinguished from a general ship plying habitually between particular ports and carrying the goods of all comers, is in the absence of express agreement a common carrier and therefore liable, in the absence of express stipulations, for all damage resulting in transit, unless from the act of God or the Queen's enemies or vice in the goods themselves.

(2) Whether, apart from the liabilities of a common carrier, every shipowner or master who carries goods on board his vessel for hire is, in the absence of express stipulations, subject to the liability of an insurer, except as against the act of God or the Queen's enemies or inherent vice in the goods, or whether he is only liable for loss shown to have arisen from negligence on his part or that of his servants.

The practical importance in the case of ships is not very great, as the difference in the law would chiefly affect ships chartered to one shipper without any express stipulations in the charter, an unusual case; but it is important in the case of lighters, which are frequently let out for hire in that way.

A. The first question was discussed in *Liver Alkali Co v Johnson*.[12] There, A was a lighterman and let out his flats to any customer who applied for them; his flats did not ply between any fixed points, but each voyage was fixed by the particular customer; a special bargain was made with each customer, though not for the use of a particular flat; but no flat was carrying goods for more than one person on the same voyage. A let a flat on these terms to C to carry salt from L to W; on the voyage, without A's negligence, the flat was wrecked. C sued A for the damage to the salt. The court, consisting of Kelly C.B., Martin, Bramwell and Cleasby BB. held A a common carrier, and therefore liable. Kelly C.B. laid stress on the fact that no particular vessel was hired, saying: "No doubt, if each particular voyage had been made under a special contract containing stipulations applicable to that voyage only, the case would have been different," which seems to distinguish the case of a ship specifically chartered to a particular shipper.

In the Exchequer Chamber the majority of the court (Blackburn, Mellor, Archibald and Grove JJ.) affirmed this judgment[13] on the ground that a lighterman, carrying on business as described, "does, in the absence of something to limit his liability, *incur the liability of a common carrier* in respect of the goods he carries". Brett J., while agreeing that A was liable, put his liability on the ground that[14] "by a recognised custom of England, every shipowner who carries goods for hire in his ship, whether by inland navigation, or coastways, or abroad, undertakes to carry them at his own absolute risk, the act of God or the Queen's enemies excepted", unless he limits this liability by express agreement. He emphatically held that A was not a common carrier, on the ground that he did not undertake to carry goods for, or charter his flat to, the first comer (and therefore was not liable to an action for refusing to do so, the essential characteristic of a common carrier). The rest of the court had expressly abstained[15] from examining whether A was a carrier so as to be liable to such an action, and had confined themselves to deciding that he "had the liability of" (*quaere*, the same liability as) "a common carrier". In *Nugent v Smith*,[16] Cockburn C.J. repeated Brett J.'s objection: "I cannot help seeing the difficulty that stands in the way of *Liver Alkali Co v Johnson*; namely, that it is essential to the character of a common carrier that he is bound to carry the goods of all persons applying to him, while

---

[12] (1872) L.R. 7 Ex. 267. *Cf. Hill v Scott* [1895] 2 Q.B. 371. See also *Consolidated Tea Co v Oliver's Wharf* [1910] 2 K.B. 395, as to a wharfinger who incidentally undertakes lighterage.
[13] (1874) L.R. 9 Ex. 338 at p.341.
[14] *ibid.* p.344.
[15] *ibid.* p.340.
[16] (1876) 1 C.P.D. 423 at p.433.

it has never been held, and, as it seems to me, never would be held, that a person who lets out vessels to individual customers on their application was liable to an action for refusing the use of such vessel if required to furnish it."[17]

The judgment, however, may be supported on narrow grounds: (1) It only applies, according to the judgment of the court below, to cases where no specific vessel is chartered or hired, but there is a contract to carry so much cargo; the case of a specific charter is expressly excluded. (2) The court above did not decide that A was a common carrier, but only that a lighterman contracting to carry goods in some vessel or other, has the same liability as a common carrier. The case therefore may be confined to the calling of lighterman; and whether a lighterman has the liabilities of a common carrier is a question of fact in each particular case.[18] Traditionally the leading lightermen on the Thames have expressly declined to take the liability of common carriers and carry on the terms of various clauses, which are not so clearly expressed as might be desired.[19]

B. The liability of an insurer, said to be undertaken, in the absence of express agreement, by all shipowners lending their vessels for hire, rests on the authority of Brett J. (later Lord Esher), who expressed that opinion in 1874, in the *Liver Alkali* case, and repeated it in 1875, in *Nugent v Smith*,[20] where he said, Denman J. concurring, "The true rule is that every shipowner or master who carries goods on board his ship for hire is, in the absence of express stipulation to the contrary, subject by implication . . . by reason of his acceptance of the goods to be carried, to the liability of an insurer, except as against the act of God or the Queen's enemies . . . not because he is a common carrier, but because he carries goods in his ship for hire." As the ship there was a general ship, this was *obiter dictum*, but in the Court of Appeal, Cockburn C.J., admitting that the point was not involved in the case, took occasion to dissent entirely from the view of Brett J. in a very elaborate judgment, in which he held that no such liability existed, but that shipowners, other than of general ships, were only bailees, and bound to use ordinary care and diligence.

On this two questions arise: (1) as to the history of the rule; (2) as to its present position.

(1) As to its history, the view of Brett J. was[21] that the common law of England as to bailments is founded on the Roman law, that therefore bailees are liable only for ordinary care unless they fall within certain classes, who are absolute insurers, the historical origin of these classes being found in the Praetor's Edict.[22] This historical view was persuasively attacked by Oliver Wendell Holmes in his work on the Common Law.[23]

---

[17] See the case also discussed in *Watkins v Cottel* [1916] 1 K.B. 10. And see *Belfast Ropework Co v Bushell* [1918] 1 K.B. 210.

[18] *Tamvaco v Timothy* (1882) 1 C. & E. 1.

[19] See *Tate v Hyslop* (1885) 15 Q.B.D. 368 at p.370; *Thomas v Brown* (1899) 4 Com.Cas. 186 at p.189; *Price v Union Lighterage Co* [1904] 1 K.B. 412; *Rosin, etc., Co v Jacobs* (1909) 14 Com.Cas. 78, 247; affirmed 15 Com.Cas. 111; *Travers v Cooper* [1915] 1 K.B. 73; *Brewster v Beckett* (1929) 34 Ll.L.R. 337; *Kilroy Thompson v Perkins and Homer* [1956] 2 Lloyd's Rep. 49 (meaning of "in transit"); *Shawinigan v Vokins* [1961] 2 Lloyd's Rep. 153 (meaning of "reckless"). The London Lighterage Clause was formerly of such universal application on the Thames that its terms were sometimes implied without express mention: see *Lawrence v Produce Brokers* (1920) 4 Ll.L.R. 231; *Lynch v Edwards* (1921) 6 Ll.L.R. 371: *Armour v Tarbard* (1921) 37 T.L.R. 208; but this did not apply to amendments (due to *Thompson & Norris Manufacturing Co v Ardley* (1929) 35 Ll.L.R. 248) of the clause not brought to the notice of the goods owner: *Elof Hansson Agency v Victorian Motor Haulage* (1938) 43 Com.Cas. 260.

[20] (1875) 1 C.P.D. 19 at p.33. See also *Paterson Steamships v Canadian Co-operative Wheat Producers* [1934] A.C. 538 at p.544.

[21] (1875) 1 C.P.D. 19 at p.29.

[22] Dig. IV, 9.

[23] (1882) London, pp.175–205.

Cockburn C.J. took the view[24] that the strict liability of carriers was introduced by custom in the reigns of Elizabeth I and James I as an exception to the ordinary rule that bailees were bound to use ordinary care.[25]

Holmes maintained that the stricter liability is the older of the two and that the present liability of carriers is therefore a survival of the old rules.[26]

(2) As to the rule of law prevailing, cases in the House of Lords,[27] supported as they are by several dicta of Willes J., e.g. "the shipowner's exemption is from liability for loss which could not have been avoided by reasonable care, skill, and diligence"[28]; . . . "The contract in a bill of lading is to carry with reasonable care unless prevented by the excepted perils"[29]; and also by the judgments in *Laurie v Douglas*,[30] where a direction to the jury that "a shipowner was only bound to take the same care of goods as a person would of his own goods, i.e. an ordinary and reasonable care", was held a proper direction, and in *The Duero*,[31] cast doubt on the view advocated by Lord Esher. The question so far as it is of practical importance is fully discussed below.[32]

Article 106—The Effect of Excepted Perils in the Contract of Affreightment

A106

Charterparties contain an undertaking by the shipowner and charterer to perform their respective parts of the contract, unless prevented[33] by certain perils excepted in the contract, provided that such perils could not have been avoided by reasonable care and diligence on the part of the person prevented by them from performing the contract and of his servants. Bills of lading contain an undertaking by the shipowner or carrier to deliver safely the goods set forth in them, unless prevented by certain perils known as "excepted perils" or exceptions, provided that such perils and their consequences could not have been avoided by reasonable care and diligence on the part of the shipowner or carrier

---

[24] (1876) 1 C.P.D. 423 at p.430.

[25] Liability of innkeepers, *Calye's Case* (1584) 8 Co. 32. Of common carriers by land, *Woodliffs Case* (1596) Moore 462; Owen 57. Of common carriers by water, *Rich v Kneeland* (1613) Hob. 17: Cro.Jac. 330. The first case cited for the general liability of shipowners is *Morse v Slue* (1671) 2 Keb. 866; 3 Keb. 72 at pp.112, 135; 2 Lev. 69; 1 Vent. 190, 238; 1 Mod. 85; Sir T. Raym. 220. The reason for the liability of a common carrier is stated by Lord Holt (*Coggs v Bernard* (1703) 2 Ld.Raym. 909 at p.918), and by Lord Mansfield (*Forward v Pittard* (1785) 1 T.R. 27 at p.34) to be the avoidance of collusion whereby the carrier "may contrive to be robbed on purpose and share the spoil".

[26] The fuller discussion of the historical question is beyond the scope of this work. The reader may refer to Holmes C.J., c. 5, Bailments, and to the following cases: *Southcote v Bennett* (1601) 4 Rep. 83b; Cro.Eliz. 815 (adversely discussed by Lord Holt in *Coggs v Bernard* (1703) 2 Ld. Raym. 909, and *Sir W. Jones on Bailments*, 3rd edn, pp.41–45); *Rich v Kneeland*, above: *Symons v Darknoll* (1628) Palmer 523; *Nicholls v Moore* (1661) 1 Sid. 36; *Mathews v Hopkins* (1667) 1 Sid. 244; *Morse v Slue*, above; *Goff v Clinkard* (1750) 1 Wils. 282n.; *Dale v Hall* (1750) 1 Wils. 281; *Barclay v Cuculla* (1784) 3 Dougl. 389; *Trent, etc., Navigation v Ward* (1785) 3 Esp. 127; *Forward v Pittard* (1785) 1 T.R. 27; *Lyon v Mells* (1804) 5 East 428.

The two English exceptions to the carrier's liability, which are different from the Roman ones, have each a purely English history. The exception, "the act of God", results from the discharge of contractors from performance rendered impossible by the act of God (Holmes, 202); that of "the King's enemies", from the result of the rule that the bailee had no action against them, they not being amenable to civil process; and that therefore it was not fair that the bailor should sue him (Holmes, 177, 201; *Marshal of Marshalsea's Case*, Y.B. 33 Hen. 6. f. 1 pl. 3).

[27] *The Xantho* (1887) 12 App.Cas. 503; *Hamilton v Pandorf* (1887) 12 App.Cas. 518.

[28] *Notara v Henderson* (1872) L.R. 7 Q.B. 225 at p.236.

[29] *Grill v General Iron Screw Collier Co* (1866) L.R. 1 C.P. 600 at p.612.

[30] (1846) 15 M. & W. 746; doubted on other grounds in *The Accomac* (1890) 15 P.D. 208.

[31] (1869) L.R. 2 A. & E. 393.

[32] Below, *Note* 1.

[33] *Meling v Minos Shipping Co* [1972] 1 Lloyd's Rep. 458, applying *Polemis and Furness Withy, Re* [1921] 3 K.B. 560. On the question how far the exceptions protect the charterer, as well as the shipowner, see *Note* 2.

and his servants.[34] For the consequences resulting solely from the occurrence of these perils, the shipowner or charterer under a charterparty,[35] the shipowner or carrier under a bill of lading, are not liable. In considering whether the breach complained of is *caused* by an excepted peril, the immediate, the direct,[36] or dominant[37] cause, and not the remote cause, is looked to.[38]

The court will place a narrow construction on an exceptions clause or liberty to the extent necessary to avoid inconsistency with the main purpose of the contract.[39] However, there is now no rule of law which disentitles a party who has committed a "fundamental breach" of contract from relying on a provision of the contract which excludes or limits his liability. The question whether, and to what extent, such a provision is to be applied to a serious breach of contract is a matter of construction of the contract itself.[40] But it remains an open question whether the long-established rule that an unjustified deviation is always treated as a breach to which such a provision does not apply, unless the charterer or goods-owner affirms the contract of carriage is still good law.[41]

Where the Carriage of Goods by Sea Act 1971 applies it is necessary to consider whether any particular exception in the bill of lading is permitted, and whether any additional exception is imported by that Act.[42] Under the Hamburg Rules, the traditional categories of exceptions (most of which, with the exception of errors in the navigation and management of the vessel, are merely examples of causes of loss where the shipowner is not at fault) are eschewed. Instead the carrier will generally be liable for loss, damage or delay occurring when the goods are in his charge, unless he establishes that all measures that could

---

[34] The authorities for this statement are discussed in *Note* 1 below. See also per Lord Esher in *Bulman v Fenwick* [1894] 1 Q.B. 179, as to strikes; *The Glendarroch* [1894] P. 226 (CA); per Collins M.R. in *Dunn v Currie* [1902] 2 K.B. 614 at p.621; *Searle v Lund* (1903) 20 T.L.R. 390; *Dampskibsselskabet Danmark v Poulsen*, 1913 S.C. 1043.

[35] On the relation between exceptions in the charter and bill of lading where the charterer is also the shipper, see Chapter 6.

[36] per Lord Sumner in *Becker Gray v London Assurance Corp* [1918] A.C. 101 at p.114.

[37] per Lord Dunedin in *Leyland S.S. Co v Norwich Union* [1918] A.C. 350 at p.363.

[38] *Causa proxima, non remota, spectatur.* See, for illustrations of this rule, *Leyland S.S. Co v Norwich Union* [1918] A.C. 350; *The Xantho* (1887) 12 App.Cas. 503; *Hamilton v Pandorf* (1887) 12 App.Cas. 518; *Letricheux v Dunlop* (1891) 19 R. 209; *The Christel Vinnen* [1924] P. 208 (CA); and individual exceptions, below. In *Smith & Service v Rosario Nitrate Co* [1893] 2 Q.B. 323 at p.328, delay on the voyage by barnacles, which had accumulated while the ship was detained in port by restraints of princes, was *held* covered by the exception. As to the position where loss is due to the concurrence of unseaworthiness (not excepted) and of an excepted peril, see *Smith Hogg v Black Sea and Baltic* [1940] A.C. 997 (*Case* 9, Art.51, above), and comment thereon in fn.116.

[39] *Glynn v Margetson* [1893] A.C. 351 (wide liberty to deviate would be inconsistent with contractual voyage); *Sze Hai Tong v Rambler Cycle Co* [1959] A.C. 576 (PC) (clause exempting shipowner from liability for events occurring after discharge did not permit him deliberately to deliver goods without production of bills of lading); *Motis Exports v Dampskibsselskabet AF 1912* [1999] 1 Lloyd's Rep. 837; *Mitsubishi Corp v Eastwind Transport Ltd (The Irbenskiy Proliv)* [2005] 1 Lloyd's Rep. 383; [2004] EWHC 2924 (Comm). Contrast *Renton v Palmyra* [1957] A.C. 149 (clause in a bill of lading permitting the shipowner in certain events beyond his control to deliver the goods short of their destination was not inconsistent with the main purpose of the contract). See also: *Trafigura Beheer BV v China Navigation Co Ltd* [2001] 1 H.K.L.R.D. 17 (Hong Kong); *Carewins Development (China) Ltd v Bright Fortune Shipping Ltd* [2006] 4 H.K.L.R.D. 131 (Hong Kong).

[40] *Photo Production Ltd v Securicor Transport Ltd* [1980] A.C. 827; *Suisse Atlantique v NV Rotterdomsche Kolen Centrale* [1967] 1 A.C. 361; *George Mitchell (Chesterhall) Ltd v Finney Lock Seeds Ltd* [1983] 2 A.C. 803.

[41] See below, Art.127.

[42] See Art.III, r.8, and Art.IV, rr.1 and 2, in Chapter 20, below.

reasonably be required to avoid the occurrence causing the loss, damage or delay were taken.[43]

Note 1. It is submitted that the statement in the first paragraph of the text is the true result of the cases in the House of Lords,[44] though language is there used apparently capable of another construction. Thus, Lord Herschell in *The Xantho*, at p.510, said: "The true view" (of the difference between a policy of marine insurance and a contract of affreightment) "appears to me to be presented by Willes J.[45] when he said: 'A policy of insurance is an absolute contract to indemnify for loss by perils of the sea, and it is only necessary to see whether the loss comes within the terms of the contract and is caused by perils of the sea, the fact that the loss is partly caused by things not distinctly perils of the sea, does not prevent it coming within the contract. In the case of a bill of lading it is different, because there the contract is to carry with reasonable care unless prevented by the excepted perils. If the goods are not carried with reasonable care, and are consequently lost by perils of the sea, it becomes necessary to reconcile the two parts of the instrument, and this is done by holding that if the loss through perils of the seas is caused by previous default of the shipowner, he is liable for his breach of his contract.' "

This view finds some support in cases of the early nineteenth century, e.g. in the decision of the Court of Exchequer in *Laurie v Douglas*,[46] where a direction to the jury that a shipowner was only bound "to take the same care of goods as a person would of his own goods, i.e. an ordinary and reasonable care", was held a proper direction. But if the contract is as stated by Willes J., and approved by Lord Herschell, "to carry with reasonable care, unless prevented by the excepted perils", the exceptions become meaningless; there is need for any excepted perils. For no loss is caused by an excepted peril, which the shipowner could have prevented by reasonable care. No peril is an "act of God", if it could have been prevented by reasonable foresight and care.[47] No peril is a "peril of the sea", "which could be foreseen as one of the necessary incidents of the adventure".[48] It would be sufficient that the contract should read, "to carry with reasonable care". If the shipowner did so, he would not be liable for damage which could not be prevented by reasonable care, without the addition of any list of excepted perils. If he did not do so, he would be liable for his omission whatever perils were excepted.

Some light is perhaps thrown on the meaning of the House of Lords by another dictum of Willes J.[49]: "The exception in the bill of lading only exempts the shipowner from the absolute liability of a common carrier, and not from the consequences of the want of reasonable skill, diligence, and care." This appears to represent the contract as stated above, and as one: (1) to carry absolutely at shipowner's risk; (2) unless the damage is caused by excepted perils; (3) provided the shipowner and his agents have used reasonable care to prevent such damage.[50] The view is supported by the language of Lord Macnaghten in *The Xantho*, at p.515, where he classes the implied engagement of reasonable care with the implied warranty of seaworthiness, and also, more recently by

---

[43] See Art.5.1, below.
[44] *The Xantho* (1887) 12 App.Cas. 503; *Hamilton v Pandorf* (1887) 12 App.Cas. 518.
[45] *Grill v General Iron Screw Collier Co* (1866) L.R. 1 C.P. 600 at p.612. See Lord Sumner's view in *Becker Gray v London Assurance Corp* [1918] A.C. 101 at p.113.
[46] (1846) 15 M. & W. 746; see on this case *The Accomac* (1890) 15 P.D. 208.
[47] *Nugent v Smith* (1876) 1 C.P.D. 423; *Nichols v Marsland* (1876) 2 Ex.D. 1.
[48] *The Xantho* (1887) 12 App.Cas. 503, per Lord Herschell at p.509.
[49] *Notara v Henderson* (1872) L.R. 7 Q.B. 225 at pp.235, 236.
[50] This proviso may itself be excluded by the exception known as the "negligence clause"; *cf.* Art.118.

Lord Wright.[51] In this second view, if damage be caused by a peril not excepted, the shipowner is not protected, though he has used due diligence.

The various principles of construction applied to contracts of affreightment and policies of marine insurance lead to different legal results from similar facts. Thus in a bill of lading whose only exception is "perils of the seas", where damage results from a storm, the shipowner will still be liable, if it is proved that the stowage was negligent, and that such negligence co-operated with the storm to damage the goods.[52] In a policy of insurance the underwriter would be liable for damage from a storm as a peril of the sea, though it was proved that the ship became unseaworthy on the voyage through negligence of the owner's servants.[53]

Before 1887[54] there was some authority for saying that this difference in construction arose either from the different meaning of such terms as "perils of the sea" in the two documents, or from the application of the maxim, "*Causa proxima, non remota, spectatur*", to policies and not to bills of lading. But the House of Lords[54] in 1887 decided that each of these views was erroneous; and that the explanation of the different results already pointed out is to be found in the undertaking of the shipowner in the contract of affreightment, that he and his servants or agents shall be not negligent, which is confined in the policy to an undertaking by the assured that he himself will not contribute to the loss by his own wilful misconduct, without reference to the acts of his servants or agents.

Note 2. Mutuality of exceptions. It is obvious that exceptions, of which the most typical is "perils of the seas", were originally inserted in charterparties for the protection of the shipowner. How far they can also be relied upon by the charterer, as limiting his obligations, is purely a question of the construction of the particular charterparty. In many modern charters the various perils are expressed to be "always *mutually* excepted": in which case beyond question the charterer can claim their benefit, though many of them rarely have any bearing upon his obligations to load, or discharge, cargo, and to pay freight, etc. As to charterparties in which it is not made clear that the exceptions are to be "mutual", there is some conflict of authority. The point seems to be first directly discussed by Lord Alvanley in *Touteng v Hubbard*,[55] when he says, "I will first consider for what purpose and for whose benefit the words 'restraints of princes during the said voyage always excepted' were introduced. It appears to me that they were introduced for the benefit of the master, not of the merchant." The first occasion on which any judge suggested that an exception in the charter might avail the charterer seems to be in a dictum of Martin B. in 1870.[56]

The question has subsequently been often raised. In *Barrie v Peruvian Corp*[57] the charterer was prevented from loading by a storm which destroyed the loading pier: he was

---

[51] In *Paterson Steamships v Canadian Co-operative Wheat Producers* [1934] A.C. 538 at p.545, and *Smith Hogg v Black Sea and Baltic* [1940] A.C. 997 at p.1004.

[52] *The Oquendo* (1877) 38 L.T. 151; *The Catherine Chalmers* (1875) 32 L.T. 847.

[53] *Walker v Maitland* (1821) 5 B. & Ald. 171; *Davidson v Burnard* (1868) L.R. 4 C.P. 117; *Redman v Wilson* (1845) 14 M. & W. 476. For further illustration of the difference in principle, consider *Cory v Burr* (1883) 8 App.Cas. 393; *West India Telegraph Co v Home etc., Insurance Co* (1880) 6 Q.B.D. 51; *Taylor v Dunbar* (1869) L.R. 4 C.P. 206; *Pink v Fleming* (1890) 25 Q.B.D. 396; *Reischer v Borwick* [1894] 2 Q.B. 548; *Leyland S.S. Co v Norwich Union Insurance Co* [1917] 1 K.B. 873.

[54] *Thames and Mersey Insurance Co v Hamilton* (1887) 12 App.Cas. 484; *The Xantho, ibid.* p.503; *Hamilton v Pandorf, ibid,* p.518.

[55] (1802) 3 P. & B. 291 at p.298. He relies on the decision of Lord Kenyon in *Blight v Page* (1801) 3 P. & B. 295n. Other early cases to the same effect are *Sjoerds v Luscombe* (1812) 16 East 201; and *Storer v Gordon* (1814) 3 M. & S. 308.

[56] *Ford v Cotesworth* (1870) L.R. 5 Q.B. 544 at p.548.

[57] (1896) 2 Com.Cas. 50.

held entitled to rely on the exception of "perils of the seas". This was followed as an authority, but its correctness doubted, by Bigham J. in *Newman and Dale, Re*.[58] It was not followed in *Braemount S.S. Co v Weir*,[59] which concerned a time charterparty. In *Cazalet v Morris*[60] and in *Aktieselskabet Frank v Namaqua Co*,[61] the ordinary exceptions clause was held not to apply for the benefit of the charterer, but in both these cases the question of construction was influenced by the fact that the charters also contained special clauses expressly limiting the obligations of the charterer.[62]

No general rule can be laid down, the matter being one of construction in each case, though it appears that prima facie and certainly in their historical origins, exceptions in a charterparty were and still are intended for the protection of the shipowner.[63]

Note 3. List of exceptions. The early bills of lading and charterparties do not contain any exceptions at all.[64] The first provision of this kind was "the danger of the sea only excepted".[65] As the result of a case tried in 1795,[66] the exceptions were enlarged to read "the act of God, the King's enemies, fire, and all and every other dangers and accidents of the seas, rivers, and navigation of whatever nature and kind soever excepted". This clause has been still further extended, until, as has been said, "there seems to be no other obligation on the shipowner than to receive the freight".

Exceptions are so numerous that an exhaustive enumeration is impossible; but the following is believed to be a tolerably comprehensive list of exceptions which have come before the courts for judicial interpretation[67]:

The act of God.[68]

The King's enemies.[69]

Pirates,[70] robbers, thieves, whether on board or not, pilferage.[70]

---

[58] [1903] 1 K.B. 262.

[59] (1910) 15 Com.Cas. 101. In fact even if it had been held that "strikes" was an exception in favour of the charterer, he must have failed in the case on the principle of *Brown v Turner Brightman* [1912] A.C. 12.

[60] 1916 S.C. 952.

[61] (1920) 25 Com.Cas. 212 at pp.217, 218.

[62] See also *Akt. General Gordon v The Cape Copper Company Ltd* (1921) 26 Com.Cas. 289 (CA) and *Cantiere Navale Triestina v Russian Soviet Export Agency* [1925] 2 K.B. 172 (CA).

[63] See, in particular the judgment of Scrutton L.J. in *Akt. General Gordon v The Cape Copper Co Ltd*, above, the approval therein by Bankes L.J. of the judgment of Bailhache J. in *Ralli Brothers v Compania Naviera Sota y Aznar* [1920] 1 K.B. 614, at pp.635–7 (point not dealt with in the CA) and per Atkin L.J. in *Cantiere Navale Triestina v Russian Export Agency*, above, at p.212.

[64] See charterparties and bills of lading between 1531 and 1541 printed in Marsden, *Select Pleas in the Admiralty Court* (Selden Society (1892), Vol. I, at pp.35, 61, 89, 95, 112); West's *Symboleography*: editions 1632 and 1647, printing (s.656) a charterparty dated 1582, and (s.659) a bill of lading dated 1598; Malynes, *Lex Mercatoria* (1686), p.99, setting out the terms of a charterparty from London "to the town of Saint Lucar de Barameda in Spain" and back again. The early charterparty, like the early marine insurance policy, began with the words, "In the name of God, Amen." (West's *Symboleography*, ss.655, 656.) A bill of lading as late as 1766 would begin, "Shipped by the Grace of God", and would end, "And so God send the good ship to her desired port in safety, Amen." (*Wright v Campbell* (1767) 4 Burr. 2046 at p.2047.) A charterparty in French, made at Constantinople between Greeks, and dated June 12, 1920, was headed, "Au nom de Dieu."

[65] *Cf. Wright v Campbell*, above.

[66] *Smith v Shepherd*, McLachlan, 6th edn, p.433; Abbot, 14th edn, pp.473, 578. There were in that case no exceptions at all, but the decision alarmed shipowners as to their liability. They tried, according to Lord Tenterden, to get a bill passed limiting their common law liability. It passed the Commons but was thrown out by the Lords. Whereupon they generally amended their bills of lading.

[67] The application of exceptions in particular cases may be affected by the considerations set forth in *Note 5* at the end of this Article.

[68] See Art.108.

[69] See Art.109.

[70] See Art.114.

Barratry of master and mariners.[71]

Arrest and restraints of princes, rulers, and peoples.[72]

Strikes,[73] lock-outs, or stoppage of labour from whatever cause.[73]

In case of strikes, etc., time not to count.[74]

In case of delay by reason of strikes no claim for damages to be made by owners of ship.[75]

Leakage,[76] ullage,[77] spiles,[78] jettison.[79]

Injurious effects of other goods.[80]

Not liable for loss of goods under any circumstances whatsoever.[81]

Owners are responsible for no loss or damage or delay arising from any other cause whatsoever.[82]

The owners not to be responsible in any other case nor for damage or delay whatsoever and howsoever caused.[83]

Fire.[84]

Perils of boilers, steam, or steam machinery,[85] and consequence of defects therein or damages thereto, escape of steam, explosion.

Risks of steam navigation.[86]

Perils of navigation.[87]

Detention by ice.[88]

Breakdown of steamer.[89]

---

[71] See Art.117.

[72] See Art.110.

[73] See Art.113.

[74] *Held*, to relieve charterers from liability for demurrage only to the extent that time in discharging was in fact lost owing to strikes, etc.: *London and Northern Co v Central Argentine Ry* (1913) 108 L.T. 528; *Central Argentine Ry v Marwood* [1915] A.C. 981. But see, as to the latter, *Reardon Smith Line v Ministry of Agriculture* [1962] 1 Q.B. 42 at pp.77, 106, 127 (CA). (This point did not arise in the HL).

[75] *Held*, when inserted in a charter providing for discharge in a fixed time, with a fixed rate of demurrage, to excuse the charterer from liability for demurrage when incurred by reason of a strike: *Moor Line v Distillers Co*, 1912 S.C. 514. But see also *Westoll v Lindsay*, 1916 S.C. 782.

[76] See Art.115.

[77] = leakage.

[78] = the leakage resulting from holes stopped by a peg called a "spile" bored in a cask for the purpose of getting at its contents, which are sometimes replaced by water. The effect of the exception will be to free shipowner from liability for leakage and watering, unless the shipper proves negligence.

[79] See Art.119.

[80] See Arts 53, 115.

[81] *Held* to cover wilful default and misfeasance by shipowner's servants: *Taubman v Pacific S.S. Co* (1872) 26 L.T. 704.

[82] *Held*, in the context of the remainder of the Gencon exceptions clause, to be limited to loss, damage or delay of or to goods: *Louis Dreyfus v Parnaso* [1959] 1 Q.B. 498, reversed on other grounds [1960] 2 Q.B. 49.

[83] *Held*, in the context of the remainder of the Baltime exceptions clause, *not* to extend to financial loss, such as the loss suffered by the charterers from the master's refusal to enter a port nominated by them: *Tor Line v Alltrans Group of Canada (The T.F.L. Prosperity)* [1984] 1 Lloyd's Rep. 123 (HL), disapproving *Nippon Yusen Kaisha v Acme Shipping Corp* [1972] 1 Lloyd's Rep. 1. See also *Sunlight Mercantile Pte v Ever Lucky Shipping Co Ltd* [2004] 1 S.L.R. 171; [2004] 2 Lloyd's Rep. 174 where the Singapore Court of Appeal declined to follow *The Imvros* [1999] 1 Lloyd's Rep. 848.

[84] See s.186 of the Merchant Shipping Act 1995, discussed in Art.116.

[85] Does not apply if the defect was due to negligence (*Siordet v Hall* (1828) 4 Bing, 607); or if the machinery was unseaworthy at starting, though the defect was latent: *The Glenfruin* (1885) 10 P.D. 103; *The Maori King v Hughes* [1895] 2 Q.B. 550.

[86] = physical risks, incidental to ships propelled by steam machinery, such as breakdown of engine, disabling of screw, etc.: *Mercantile S.S. Co v Tyser* (1881) 7 Q.B.D. 73.

[87] Includes collision by the negligence of another ship: *Garston S.S. Co v Hickie, Borman* (1886) 18 Q.B.D. 17.

[88] *Hudson v Ede* (1868) L.R. 3 Q.B. 412; *Kay v Field* (1883) 10 Q.B.D. 241; *Matheos (Owners) v Dreyfus* [1925] A.C. 654. For special clauses dealing with ice-breaker assistance, see above, Art.71, *Note* 2.

[89] *Traae and Lennard, Re* [1904] 2 K.B. 377.

Latent defect.[90]

Risk of craft,[91] risk of storage afloat or on shore, save risk of boats so far as ships are liable.[92]

At ship's risk.[93]

At ship's risk (when signed for alongside) *but in all other respects* the act of God, etc., excepted.[94]

Goods to be forwarded at ship's expense, but owner's risk.[95]

At shipper's risk, at charterer's risk.[95]

Collision.[96]

Detention by railways.[97]

Perils of land transit.[98]

Force majeure.[99]

Accidents.[100]

Accidents to hull.[101]

---

[90] "Latent defect" means a defect which could not be discovered on such an examination as a reasonably careful skilled man would make: *Dimitrios N. Rallias* (1922) 13 Ll.L.R. 363; *Brown v Nitrate Producers S.S. Co* (1937) 58 Ll.L.R. 188. The exception of "latent defect" by itself does not qualify an express or the implied warranty of seaworthiness: *The Christel Vinnen* [1924] P. 208; *Minister of Materials v Wold S.S. Co* [1952] 1 Lloyd's Rep. 485 at p.497. But the addition of such words as "even existing at the time of shipment" will do so: *Cargo ex Laertes* (1887) 12 P.D. 187. "Latent defect in the machinery" in a marine policy does not cover a weakness of design: *Jackson v Mumford* (1902) 8 Com.Cas. 61 at p.68, per Kennedy J.; contrast *Western Canada S.S. Co v Canadian Commercial Corp* [1960] 2 Lloyd's Rep. 313 (Supreme Court of Canada), a Hague Rules case. "Latent defects in hull machinery and appurtenances" does not cover bunker coal liable to spontaneous combustion: *Tempus Shipping Co v Dreyfus* [1930] 1 K.B. 699 at p.705.

[91] = without risk or liability to the owner of the craft in respect of the carriage of the goods: *Webster v Bond* (1884) C. & E. 338; but *held* not to protect shipowner from loss by negligence or unseaworthiness: *The Galileo* [1915] A.C. 199.

[92] *Held* to protect from liability for any loss occurring to goods in boats, which shipowners would not be liable for had it occurred in ships: *Johnston v Benson* (1819) 4 Moore C.P. 90.

[93] In reference to goods alongside, *held* by the CA in *Nottebohn v Richter* (1886) 18 Q.B.D. 63, to mean "at the same risk as if they were on board the ship under the charter" (i.e. subject to the excepted perils), and it was suggested that without such a clause the shipowner's liability would only be for reasonable care till the goods reached the ship; see also *The Brabant* [1956] 2 Lloyd's Rep. 546.

[94] *Held*, distinguishing *Nottebohn v Richter*, above, to put the risk of goods while alongside absolutely on the shipowner: *Dampskibsselskabet S. v Calder* (1911) 17 Com.Cas. 97.

[95] See *Note* 3 to Art.118.

[96] See Art.112.

[97] *Letricheux v Dunlop*, 1891 19 Rettie 209. *Cf. Mein v Ottmann* (1904) 6 Fraser 276; *Turnbull v Cruikshank* (1905) 7 Fraser 265; *Glasgow Navigation Co v Iron Ore Co*, 1909 S.C. 1414. This exception usually covers matters preventing a cargo being brought by rail to the port of shipment; *Furness v Forwood* (1897) 2 Com.Cas. 223; *Richardsons & Samuel, Re* [1898] 1 Q.B. 261 (CA) otherwise if, though a cargo is stopped on the railway, other cargo can be obtained at a commercial though higher price at the port of shipment. But see *Bunge y Born v Brightman & Co* [1925] A.C. 799.

[98] Perils of the roads—*held* to mean "perils peculiar to roads"; whether marine roads, or anchorages, or land roads, was not decided: *De Rothschild v Royal Mail Co* (1852) 7 Ex. 734 at p.743. Compare Lord Herschell on "perils of the sea", *The Xantho* (1887) 12 App.Cas. 503 at p.509.

[99] *Yrazu v Astral Co* (1904) 9 Com.Cas. 100. *Cf. Matzoukis v Priestman* [1915] 1 K.B. 681; *The Concadoro* [1916] 2 A.C. 199; *Zinc Corporation v Hirsch* [1916] 1 K.B. 541; *Lebeaupin v Crispin* [1920] 2 K.B. 714; *Marifortuna Naviera SA v Govt. of Ceylon* [1970] 1 Lloyd's Rep. 247; *Mamidoil-Jetoil Greek Petroleum Company SA v Okta Crude Oil Refinery AD* [2003] 1 Lloyd's Rep. 1.

[100] *The Torbryan* [1903] P. 194; *Fenwick v Schmalz* (1868) L.R. 3 C.P. 313; *Wade v Cockerline* (1904) 10 Com.Cas. 47; affirmed *ibid.* 115. Shortage of labour occasioned by the prevalence of plague is not an "accident preventing or delaying the discharge"; *Mudie v Strick* (1909) 14 Com.Cas. 135. The wilful refusal of the officers and crew to sail except in convey is not an "accident": *Royal Greek Government v Minister of Transport (The Illissos)* [1949] 1 K.B. 7 at p.13; affirmed *ibid.* 525 (CA). See also the term "accident" discussed in *Denholm v Shipping Controller* (1920) 4 Ll.L.R. 426, reversed upon another point (1921) 7 Ll.L.R. 66; *Akt. Frank v Namaqua Copper* (1920) 25 Com.Cas. 212; *The Apollonius* [1978] 1 Lloyd's Rep. 53 at p.66 and fn.36, p.214.

[101] *Wade v Cockerline* (1904) 10 Com.Cas. 47; affirmed *ibid.* p.115; *Svenssons v Cliffe S.S. Co* [1932] 1 K.B. 490 at p.500, *held*, to cover breaking away of bulwarks when deck cargo shot overboard.

Accidents to cargo.[102]

Improper opening of valves.[103]

Not liable for negligence of shipowner's servants.[104]

Error in judgment by master.[105]

Exceptions of all liability, or limited liability, in respect to particular goods,[106] such as glass, specie, precious stones, cattle, etc.

Exceptions as to the amount of liability for goods.[107]

£x on any one cargo.[108]

Not accountable beyond net invoice price of goods.[109]

Not liable for any claim[110] notice[111] of which is not given within certain time.[112]

Any claim must be made in writing and claimant's arbitrator appointed within three months of final discharge, and, where this provision is not complied with, the claim shall be deemed to be waived and absolutely barred.[113]

---

[102] *Burrell v Green* [1914] 1 K.B. 293; *Tynedale S.S. Co v Anglo-Soviet Shipping Co* (1935) 52 Ll.L.R. 282 at p.285; *Royal Greek Government v Ministry of Transport (The Ann Stathatos)* (1950) 83 Ll.L.R. 228.

[103] *Held* to include improperly leaving valves open: *Mendl v Ropner* [1913] 1 K.B. 27.

[104] See Art.118.

[105] Does not cover mistake as to the obligations of the charterparty: *Knutsford Co v Tillmanns* [1908] A.C. 406. See also *Lord S.S. (Owners) v Newsum* [1920] 1 K.B. 846; *Glafki Shipping Co SA v Pinios Shipping Co No. 1* [1947] 1 Lloyd's Rep. 660; *Whistler International Ltd v Kawasaki Kisen Kaisha Ltd (The Hill Harmony)* [2001] 1 Lloyd's Rep. 147.

[106] *Semble*, that these do not apply, unless the ship is seaworthy at starting: *The Glenfruin* (1885) 10 P.D. 103; *Leuw v Dudgeon* (1867) L.R. 3 C.P. 17 (note); *Tattersall v National S.S. Co* (1884) 12 Q.B.D. 297.

[107] *Baxter's Leather Co v Royal Mail Co* [1908] 1 K.B. 796; affirmed [1908] 2 K.B. 626 (CA). See *Mantoura v David* (1926) 32 Com.Cas. 1. If there are no invoices, the exception does not apply: *Cosmopolitan Shipping Co v Hatton* (1929) 35 Com.Cas. 113. If the damage is by unseaworthiness and there is no special provision in the bill of lading as to liability for unseaworthiness, these clauses do not protect the shipowner. If, however, there is a special provision as to liability for unseaworthiness, these clauses do avail to protect him: *Bank of Australasia v Clan Line* [1916] 1 K.B. 39, which thus reconciles the apparently divergent cases *Tattersal v National Co* (1884) 12 Q.B.D. 297, and *Morris v Oceanic* (1900) 16 T.L.R. 533; *Elder Dempster v Paterson Zochonis* [1923] 1 K.B. 420 at p.436. This very difficult, if not heroic, feat of reconciliation was previously attempted on other grounds in *Wiener v Wilsons* (1910) 15 Com.Cas. 294 at p.303. See also *Atlantic Co v Dreyfus* [1922] 2 A.C. 250 and *Cosmopolitan Shipping Co v Hatton*, above, per Scrutton L.J. at pp.116–121. The incorporation of the Carriage of Goods by Sea Act 1971, and the similar American and Dominion statutes nullifies such a limitation of liability: see *Hordern v Commonwealth Line* [1917] 2 K.B. 420; and below, Chapter 20, Art.III.

[108] *Clan Line v Ove Skou Rederi A/S* [1969] 2 Lloyd's Rep. 155 (a decision on an indemnity clause in a time charter).

[109] *Nelson v Nelson* [1906] 2 K.B. 804. See also fn.110, below.

[110] Refers to claims for damage, whether apparent or latent: *Moore v Harris* (1876) 1 App.Cas. 318. As to indorsement of claim on bill of lading, see *Mikkelsen v Arcos, Ltd* (1925) 42 T.L.R. 3. For a case where a similar clause was held inapplicable to the loss of a ship and cargo, see *Cosmopolitan Shipping Co v Hatton* (1929) 35 Com.Cas. 113.

[111] This need not be precisely formulated but will suffice if it indicates a head of damage arising from breach of a clause in the charter or bill of lading. There is a presumption of fact, rebuttable by evidence, that an agent acting for his principal in a transaction, but not authorised to accept notice, will have acted in the usual way by passing on a notice given to him; *Rendal v Arcos* (1937) 43 Com.Cas. 1 (HL).

[112] See fn.110, above and *Evergos Naftiki Eteria v Cargill Plc (The Voltaz)* [1997] 1 Lloyd's Rep. 35. Voyage charters frequently provide that demurrage claims are barred unless the claim, supported by relevant documents, is made within a certain period—as to which see *Mabanaft International Ltd v Erg Petroli SpA (The Yellow Star)* [2000] 2 Lloyd's Rep. 637.

[113] *Held* not void as ousting the jurisdiction of the court, but in a claim for loss by unseaworthiness to be subject to the principle of *Bank of Australasia v Clan Line*, above; *Atlantic Co v Dreyfus* [1922] 2 A.C. 250. See also *Ford v Compagnie Furness* [1922] 2 K.B. 797 and *Bede S.S. Co v Bunge y Born* (1927) 43 T.L.R. 374. If the cargo could never be discharged because it had been lost the clause does not apply: *Denny, Mott v Lynn Shipping Co* [1963] 1 Lloyd's Rep. 339. The clause is inconsistent with the 12-month time limit under the Hague Rules and so avoided by Art.III, r.8 of the Rules where they apply: *The Ion* [1971] 1 Lloyd's Rep. 541; and see Chapter 20, Art.III, below. The clause bars a claim even though the cause of action giving rise to the claim has not arisen or come to the knowledge of the claimant until too late to enable him to comply with the clause: *The Himmerland* [1965] 2 Lloyd's Rep. 353. Where the clause is incorporated in a consecutive voyage charter, the expression "final discharge" refers to discharge of cargo on the voyage out of which the claim arises: *Agro Company of Canada Ltd v Richmond Shipping Ltd* [1973] 1 Lloyd's Rep. 392.

Not liable for damage, unless goods are marked in a particular way.[114]

Ship's liability to cease when goods are free of the ship's tackle.[115]

Not liable for any damage capable of being covered by insurance.[116]

Not responsible for any damage to goods however caused which can be covered by insurance.[117]

Not liable for loss or damage even if such loss or damage result from a cause for which, but for this special agreement to the contrary, the steamer would have been liable.[118]

Owners to give time-charterers the benefit of their protection and indemnity club insurances so far as club rules allow.[119]

Not liable for failure to notify consignee.[120]

Exceptions expressly negativing the shipowner's warranty of seaworthiness.[121]

Certificate of surveyor to be accepted as proof of seaworthiness,[122] or of due diligence to make seaworthy.[123]

The maintenance by the owners of the vessel's class shall be considered a fulfilment of every duty, warranty, or obligation, whether before or after the commencement of the voyage.[124]

Liberty to call at intermediate ports for any purpose, to touch and stay at other ports either in or out of the way, to tow and assist vessels in all situations,[125] and perform salvage services to vessels and cargo, without being deemed a deviation.[126]

Owners only liable for ship damage, etc.[127]

---

[114] See Art.64.

[115] A clause in this form was held sufficient to protect the shipowner where a servant of the landing agents fraudulently misappropriated the goods in collusion with the consignees; *Chartered Bank v British India S.N. Co* [1909] A.C. 369. Where, however, the ship's agent deliberately, but without fraud, delivered the goods without production of the bills of lading, it was held that a very similar clause did not apply; *Sze Hai Tong v Rambler Cycle Co* [1959] A.C. 576 (P.C.); see also *Comp. Importadora de Arroces v P. & O.* (1927) 28 Ll.L.R. 63.

[116] The question is whether an underwriter in the ordinary way of business would insure against the particular peril. This exception does not relieve the shipowner from liability to general average: *Crooks v Allan* (1879) 5 Q.B.D. 38; or from damage caused by the negligence of himself or his servants: *Price v Union Lighterage Co* [1904] 1 K.B. 412; *Mersey Shipping and Transport Co v Rea* (1925) 21 Ll.L.R. 375 (but see and contrast the clause next quoted in the text above); or from damage caused by unseaworthiness: *Nelson v Nelson* [1908] A.C. 16; "damage" covers total or partial destruction, but not abstraction of goods: *Taylor v Liverpool S.S. Co* (1874) L.R. 9 Q.B. 546; *Aira Force S.S. Co v Christie* (1892) 9 T.L.R. 104 (CA) (owner under time charter to pay for insurance). See also *The Rossetti* [1972] 2 Lloyd's Rep. 116.

[117] This, despite the very slight difference from the last-quoted clause, *does* protect the shipowner from liability for negligence of his servants because it contains words referring to causation: *Travers v Cooper* [1915] 1 K.B. 73. See Art.118, Note 1. See also *Kuwait Maritime Transport Corp v Rickmers Linie KG (The Danah)* [1993] 1 Lloyd's Rep. 351.

[118] *Varnish v The Kheti* (1949) 82 Ll.L.R. 525.

[119] *Canadian Transport Co v Court Line* [1940] A.C. 934. *Cf. The Auditor* (1924) 18 Ll.L.R. 464 (benefit of insurance on the goods).

[120] *E. Clemens Horst Co v Norfolk, etc., Co* (1906) 11 Com.Cas. 141.

[121] See Art.51; and *Cargo ex Laertes* (1887) 12 P.D. 187; *Rathbone v McIver* [1903] 2 K.B. 378; *Upperton v Union Castle Co* (1903) 9 Com.Cas. 50; *Nelson v Nelson* [1908] A.C. 16; *South American Syndicate v Federal Co* (1909) 14 Com.Cas. 228.

[122] *South American Syndicate v Federal Steam Co* (1909) 14 Com.Cas. 228. *Cf. Walters v Joseph Rank* (1923) 39 T.L.R. 255; *Studebaker Distributors v Charlton S.S. Co* [1938] 1 K.B. 459.

[123] *The Australia Star* (1940) 67 Ll.L.R. 110.

[124] *Held*, following *Nelson v Nelson* [1908] A.C. 16, too vague to protect the shipowner from the consequences of unseaworthiness due to bad stowage: *Ingram v Services Maritimes* [1913] 1 K.B. 538.

[125] See below, Art.128; and *Leduc v Ward* (1888) 20 Q.B.D. 475. For United Kingdom towage conditions and cases thereon, see *The Uranienborg* [1936] P. 21; *G.W. Ry v Royal Norwegian Government* (1945) 78 Ll.L.R. 152; *Guy v Glen Line* [1948] P. 159.

[126] *Potter v Burrell* [1897] 1 Q.B. 97.

[127] Ship damage—such damage as happens by the insufficiency of the ship, or the negligence of those in charge of her: *East India Co v Tod* (1788) 1 Bro.P.C. 405.

The owners only to be responsible for delay in delivery of the vessel or for delay during the currency of the charter and for loss or damage to goods on board if caused by want of due diligence on the part of the owners or their managers.[128]

The owners not to be responsible for damage or delay whatsoever and howsoever caused.[129]

Inability of ship to execute or proceed on the voyage.[130]

Or otherwise.[131]

Such as.[132]

Viz. et. cetera.[133]

Interventions of sanitary, customs, or other constituted authorities which may hinder the loading.[134]

Unavoidable accidents and hindrances.[135]

Obstructions beyond charterer's control.[136]

Other causes beyond charterer's control.[137]

---

[128] *Held*, not to excuse postponement of delivery under the charter caused by delays in the course of construction: *Christie & Vesey v Helvetia* [1960] 1 Lloyd's Rep. 540 (Baltime exceptions clause). See also on this clause *The T.F.L. Prosperity* [1984] 1 Lloyd's Rep. 123, in which the HL disapproved *Westfal-Larsen v Colonial Sugar* [1960] 2 Lloyd's Rep. 206 (Austr.); and *The Brabant* [1965] 2 Lloyd's Rep. 546.

[129] *Held* in the context of clause 13 of the Baltime charter not to include financial loss: *The T.F.L. Prosperity*, above, in which the HL disapproved. *Nippon Yusen Kaisha v Acme Shipping Corp* [1972] 1 Lloyd's Rep. 1 (CA). See, also the similar words of the "Gencon" exceptions clause, *held* in *Dreyfus v Parnaso* [1959] 1 Q.B. 498 to cover only loss or damage to the goods.

[130] Inability to proceed from lack of men through smallpox is within the exception *Beatson v Schank* (1803) 3 East 233.

[131] See *Norman v Binnington* (1890) 25 Q.B.D. 475; *Baerselmann v Bailey* [1895] 2 Q.B. 301; *The Waikato* [1899] 1 Q.B. 56; *The Torbryan* [1903] P. 194; *Packwood v Union Castle Co* (1903) 20 T.L.R. 59; *Smackman v General Steam Co* (1908) 13 Com.Cas. 196.

[132] *Held*, to limit a general exception to the class or classes of matters specifically enumerated: *Diana Maritime Corp v Southerns* [1967] 1 Lloyd's Rep. 114 at p.123. Where, however, the words appeared in brackets, the matters specifically enumerated were held to be intended as examples and not to limit the general words which proceeded them: *Micada Cia Naviera v Texim* [1968] 2 Lloyd's Rep. 57.

[133] *Ambatielos v Jurgens* [1923] A.C. 175.

[134] *Watson Brothers v Mysore Manganese Co* (1910) 15 Com.Cas. 159; *Hogarth v Cory* (1926) 32 Com.Cas. 174 ("Government regulations and restrictions . . . affecting the normal shipment of the cargo").

[135] *Crawford & Rowatt v Wilson* (1896) 1 Com.Cas. 277, *held*, to cover a rebellion during which discharging could only proceed as ordered by a naval officer. See also *Aktieselskabet Argentina v Von Laer* (1903) 19 T.L.R. 151, and *Phosphate Co v Rankin* (1915) 21 Com.Cas. 248. "Unavoidable" means unavoidable by ordinary diligence: *Granger v Dent* (1829) M. & M. 475. *Cf. Dampskibsselskabet Danmark v Poulsen*, 1913 S.C. 1043, fn.147, p.282.

[136] Includes the obstruction due to a glut of ships preventing access to berths: *Larsen v Sylvester* [1908] A.C. 295; *Leonis Co v Rank* (1908) 13 Com.Cas. 161, 295; *Reardon Smith Line v East Asiatic Co* (1938) 44 Com.Cas. 10; *The Amstelmolen* [1961] 2 Lloyd's Rep. 1 (the exception in the last two cases was held to be operative notwithstanding that the laytime clause contained the words "whether in berth or not"). In *The Loucas N.* [1971] 1 Lloyd's Rep. 215, Lord Denning M.R. described the decision in *The Amstelmolen* as unsatisfactory. In *S.S. Milverton Co v Cape Town Gas Co* (1897) 2 Com.Cas. 281, held to cover refusal of authorities to let a ship enter dock though *semble* this was unnecessary as the ship had never reached her destination. See also *Ambatielos v Jurgens* [1923] A.C. 175. *Quaere* whether "obstructions on railways" would cover a "ca'canny" movement: *Brightman v Bunge y Born* [1924] 2 K.B. 619.

[137] As to the effect on these wide words of the doctrine of *ejusdem generis*, see Note 4, below. In *France, Fenwick v Spackman* (1912) 18 Com.Cas 52 at p.57, Bailhache J., obiter, expressed the view that the cause to excuse must be abnormal and, if it "always would" prevent performance, the clause would not protect. Similarly in *Ciampa v British India S.N. Co* [1915] 2 K.B. 774, in which that case was cited, Rowlatt J. held that the words "restraints of princes . . . or any circumstances beyond the shipowner's control" did not cover the fumigation of the ship at a port of call under the local law to which the ship was inevitably "doomed" before the commencement of the voyage. It appears that the necessity for fumigation was known to the shipowner but not to the shipper before sailing, but the existence of knowledge does not appear to have formed any part of the judgment. In *Induna S.S. Co v British Phosphate Commissioners* [1949] 2 K.B. 431, Sellers J. doubted whether either of the above judgments was intended to lay down any general principle and these doubts appear to have been shared by the CA in *Reardon Smith v Ministry of Agriculture* [1962] 1 Q.B. 42 at pp.83, 107, 128. (The point did not arise in the HL) The cases are all collected in the judgment in the Q.B.D., *ibid.* [1960] 1 Q.B. 439 at pp.493–495. See also *Compagnie Algerienne de Meunerie v Katana* [1960] 1 Lloyd's Rep. 132.

Any circumstances beyond the shipowner's control.[138]

Any other hindrance of whatsoever nature beyond the charterers' control.[138]

Causes that "prevent" or "hinder" performance.[139]

If the ship is prevented from entering the port or is likely to be delayed thereat for an unreasonable time.[140]

Note 4. Ejusdem generis. The general rule of construction that where specific words are followed and amplified by the addition of general words, the latter are to be confined in their application to things of the same kind as the preceding specific words, has often to be taken into consideration upon the interpretation of charterparties and bills of lading.[141] Thus the words "or other causes beyond charterer's control" (following the words "strikes, lockouts, accidents to railways, factories or machinery") were, in *Richardsons & Samuel, Re*,[142] restricted to matters *ejusdem generis*, and held not to cover (1) an arrangement in the port that vessels should load in turn of their arrival; (2) a dismissal of hands preparing cargo for shipment because there was no work for them to do and consequent delay when the cargo came forward. On the other hand, in *Lockie v Craggs*,[143] upon a shipbuilding contract, similar words were applied to include delays affecting a previous vessel, whose presence was contemplated by the parties to the contract. In *Allison and Richards, Re*[144] the words were "riots, strikes, lock-outs, or any cause beyond charterer's control", and it was held that delay through colliers taking an unauthorised holiday was due to a cause within the general words as being *ejusdem generis* with the special words. In *Tillmanns v Knutsford*,[145] upon the words "should entry at a port be deemed by the master unsafe in consequence of war, disturbance, or any other cause", it was held that ice was not within the general words, not being *ejusdem generis* with the preceding special words. In *Mudie v Strick*,[146] on the words "strikes, lock-outs, civil commotions, or any other causes or accidents beyond the control of the consignees", it was held that shortage of labour occasioned by plague was not within the general words of the exception. In *Thorman v Dowgate S.S. Co*[147] it was held that delay by reason of the number of ships waiting in the dock to come to the loading tips was not within the exception of "strikes of pitmen or workmen, frosts or storms, delays at spouts caused by stormy weather, and any accidents stopping the working, leading [*sic*], or shipping of the cargo, also suspensions of labour, lock-outs, delay on the part of the railway company, or

---

[138] *Held*, in *Reardon Smith Line v Ministry of Agriculture* [1962] 1 Q.B. 42 at pp.75, 102, 127, to cover restrictions on loading bulk wheat imposed by the executive authority in the port consequent upon a strike. (The point did not arise in the HL.) See also the cases cited in the next note and *Crawford & Rowat v Wilson* (1895) 1 Com.Cas. 154.

[139] See *Wilson v Tennants* [1917] 1 K.B. 208; [1917] A.C. 495, and the cases therein discussed. Increased cost of performance (unless so great as to amount to commercial impossibility) is not covered: *ibid*. See also *Phosphate Co v Rankin* (1915) 21 Com.Cas. 248. The words "affecting" or "interfering with" may have a wider meaning.

[140] *Diana Maritime Corp v Southerns* [1967] 1 Lloyd's Rep. 114. The shipowner must take into account the interest of both parties to the contract before invoking a clause in this form giving him liberty to discharge the goods at an alternative place of delivery. He must take into account all matters which he knows or as a reasonably sensible shipowner ought to know as affecting a particular consignee.

[141] The text of the contract and the surrounding circumstances may, however, indicate that no limitation on the prima facie meaning of the general words is intended: see fn.153 below.

[142] [1898] 1 Q.B. 261. *Cf. Northfield Co v Compagnie des Gaz* [1912] 1 K.B. 434.

[143] (1901) 7 Com.Cas. 7.

[144] (1904) 20 T.L.R. 29, 584.

[145] [1908] 1 K.B. 185; affirmed [1908] 2 K.B. 385; affirmed [1908] A.C. 406.

[146] (1909) 14 Com.Cas. 135. Upon the facts a new trial was ordered by the CA (*ibid*. p.227), but the judgment of Pickford J. remains unaffected as to the principle.

[147] [1910] 1 K.B. 410. *Cf. Hain S.S. Co v Canadian Transport Co* (1942) 73 Ll.L.R. 80.

any other cause beyond the charterer's control."[148] In *Jenkins v Watford*[149] a shortage of labour was held not to be within the ambit of the clause, "insurrections, riots, fire, frost, floods, strikes, lock-outs, accidents to mills or machinery or other unavoidable hindrances beyond charterer's control".

It must be remembered that the question is whether a particular thing is within the genus that comprises the specified things. It is not a question (though the point is often so put in argument), whether the particular thing is like one or other of the specified things. The more divers the specified things the wider must be the genus that is to include them: and by reason of the diversity of the genus that includes them may include something that is not like any one of the specified things.[150]

Another aspect of this is "the rule that, if the particular words exhaust a whole genus, the general words must refer to some larger genus".[151]

General words may be subject to some limitation even though only one specific word be used: e.g. "with liberty to call at any ports in order for bunkering or other purposes".[152]

And, in regard to this rule of construction it must also be remembered that "prima facie general words are to be taken in their larger sense, unless you can find that in the particular case the true construction of the instrument requires you to conclude that they are intended to be used in a sense limited to things *ejusdem generis* with those which have been specifically mentioned before".[153] And the words of the document may themselves make the application of the rule of *ejusdem generis* impossible. Thus, in *Larsen v Sylvester*,[154] the general words were "any other unavoidable accidents or hindrances of what kind soever", and it was held that the words "of what kind soever" made it impossible to limit the generality of the words to one kind, i.e. the genus of the preceding specified causes.

Where general words were followed by specific words with "etc." at the end of them, it was held that the doctrine of *ejusdem generis* did not apply to limit the full meaning of the general words.[155]

---

[148] See also *Abchurch S.S. Co v Stinnes*, 1911 S.C. 1010. And see *Arden S.S. Co v Mathwin*, 1912 S.C. 211, in which the fact that a colliery had restricted its output was held not to be within an exception of "stoppage at collieries".

[149] (1918) 87 L.J.K.B. 136; *cf. Hadjipateras v Weigall* (1918) 34 T.L.R. 360.

[150] This paragraph was quoted with approval and the whole doctrine of *ejusdem generis* discussed by McCardie J. in *Owners of S.S. Magnhild v McIntyre* (1920) 25 Com.Cas. 347. (His judgment was reversed on other grounds, 26 Com.Cas. 185.) Greer J., however, in *Aktieselskabet Frank v Namaqua Co* (1920) 25 Com.Cas. 212, preferring to follow *Cullen v Butler* (1816) 5 M. & S. 461, and *Thames and Mersey Insurance Co v Hamilton* (1887) 12 App.Cas. 484, rather than *Knutsford v Tillmanns* [1908] A.C. 406, said that the right test to apply was to ask whether the alleged exception was like any of those specially enumerated. He repeated this view in *Adelaide S.S. Co v R.* (1923) 29 Com.Cas. 165 at p.170. An intermediate view, but rather closer to that of Greer J. than to that stated in the text, was expressed by Devlin J. in *Chandris v Isbrandtsen-Moller* [1951] 1 K.B. 240. See, also, *Coates v Diment* [1951] 1 All E.R. 890 at p.898.

[151] per Willes J., *Fenwick v Schmalz* (1868) L.R. 3 C.P. 313 at p.315.

[152] *Stag Line v Foscolo, Mango & Co* [1932] A.C. 328.

[153] per Lord Esher M.R., *Anderson v Anderson* [1895] 1 Q.B. 749 at p.753. This principle was applied in *Chandris v Isbrandtsen-Moller*, above, to a clause "excluding acids, explosives, arms, ammunition or other dangerous cargo". There was nothing in the text of the charter or the circumstances in which it was made to suggest that the parties intended "other dangerous cargo" to have some limited meaning.

[154] [1908] A.C. 295. In *France Fenwick v Spackman* (1912) 18 Com.Cas. 52, this case was followed in construing the words "or any cause whatsoever". See also *Reardon Smith v Ministry of Agriculture* [1962] 1 Q.B. 42 (CA) on "any other hindrance of whatsoever nature", and *Siderman v Apollo Corp (The Apollo)* [1978] 1 Lloyd's Rep. 200 at p.205. Contrast *Thorman v Dowgate Co* [1910] 1 K.B. 410, on the words "or any other cause".

[155] "Causes over which the charterers have no control—viz., quarantine, ice, hurricanes, blockades, clearing of the steamer after last cargo is taken on board, etc." *Held*, to include a strike: *Ambatielos v Jurgens* [1923] A.C. 175. And see p.196, fn.132, above, for the effect of the words "such as".

Note 5. Implied undertakings and exceptions. The implied undertakings in a contract of affreightment,[156] e.g. to provide a seaworthy ship, to proceed without unreasonable delay, and without unjustifiable deviation, are not affected by exceptions in the bill of lading, unless these latter clearly negative them[157]; thus the breakdown of a crankshaft, unseaworthy at starting, does not come within the exception "breakdown of machinery"; in other words, exceptions are to be construed "as exceptions to the liability of a carrier, not as exceptions to the liability of a warrantor".[158] However, if clear words are used, it is unnecessary for the exception to make express reference to unseaworthiness.[158] Furthermore, exceptions do not interfere with the operation of express conditions such as a "cancelling clause".[159] Where goods are stowed improperly on deck the question of whether exceptions will apply depends on the proper construction of the contract in question.[160]

As regards the effect of deviation upon exceptions, see Art.127, below.[161]

As regards the effect of unseaworthiness causing fire upon the shipowner's statutory immunity under s.186 of the Merchant Shipping Act 1995, see Art.116, below.

As regards the time during which the exceptions apply and their relation to the burden of proof, see Art.107.

Article 107—Operation of Exceptions   A107

Exceptions in the contract of affreightment, unless otherwise clearly worded, limit the shipowner's liability during the whole time he is in possession of the goods as carrier and therefore apply during the loading and discharging of the goods.[162] So far as the charterer is concerned they are co-extensive with the charterer's obligations.[163]

Exceptions can be successfully relied upon even though the event preventing performance is operating at the date of the contract.[164]

The arrival of the ship,[165] coupled with failure to deliver the goods, is prima

---

[156] See Arts 51, 52, 127.
[157] *The Glenfruin* (1885) 10 P.D. 103; *The Christel Vinnen* [1924] P. 208; *Rathbone v McIver* [1903] 2 K.B. 378; *Elderslie v Borthwick* [1905] A.C. 93; *Nelson v Nelson* [1908] A.C. 16 as explained by Lord Macnaghten in *Chartered Bank v British Indian S.N. Co* [1909] A.C. 369 at p.375; *Thompson & Norris Manufacturing Co v Ardlay* (1929) 34 Ll.L.R. 248; *The Rossetti* [1972] 2 Lloyd's Rep. 116; *Sunlight Mercantile Pte. Ltd v Ever Lucky Shipping Company Ltd* [2004] 2 Lloyd's Rep. 174; [2004] 1 S.L.R. 171. Contrast *The Cargo ex Laertes* (1887) 12 P.D. 187; *Bond v Federal S.N.* (1905) 21 T.L.R. 438, per Channell J. at p.440, where the exceptions in terms qualified these obligations and *Transocean Liners Reederei GmbH v Euxine Shipping Co Ltd (The Imvros)* [1999] 1 Lloyd's Rep. 848. See also *Houston v Sansinena* (1893) 68 L.T. 567 (HL); *Searle v Lund* (1903) 19 T.L.R. 509.
[138] *Varnish v Kheti* (1949) 82 Ll.L.R. 525 at p.529.
[159] *Smith v Dart* (1884) 14 Q.B.D. 105; but see *Donaldson v Little* (1882) 10 Rettie 413.
[160] *Daewoo Heavy Industries Ltd v Klipriver Shipping Ltd* [2003] EWCA Civ 451. in which the carrier was held entitled to rely on Art.IV r.5 of the Hague Rules even though the cargo in question was wrongfully carried on deck.
[161] As to the effect of deviation in cases to which the Carriage of Goods by Sea Act 1971, applies, see *Notes* to Art.IV, r.4, in Chapter 20, below.
[162] *Norman v Binnington* (1890) 25 Q.B.D. 475; *The Carron Park* (1890) 15 P.D. 203; per Wright J. in *De Clermont v General Steam Navigation Co* (1891) 7 T.L.R. 187; and see *Note* 2 to Art.118. For the position under the Carriage of Goods by Sea Act, see Chapter 20, below.
[163] *Pinch & Simpson v Harrison, Whitfield & Co* (1948) 81 Ll.L.R. 268.
[164] *Induna S.S. Co v British Phosphate Commissioners* [1949] 2 K.B. 430 at p.437; *Reardon Smith Line v Ministry of Agriculture* [1962] 1 Q.B. 42 at pp.83, 107, 128 (CA). (The point did not arise in the HL.) The question is one of construction in each case. The relevance of the parties' knowledge (at the date of the contract) of the actual or probable operation of the event is discussed in the two cases cited (in the latter in the Q.B.D. at [1960] 1 Q.B. 439 at pp.493–495). See the contrary view based on the particular facts, taken, obiter, by Kerr J. in *Trade and Transport Inc v Tino Kaiun Kaisha (The Angelia)* [1972] 2 Lloyd's Rep. 154.
[165] The non-arrival of the ship is not evidence of negligence at all: *Boyson v Wilson* (1816) 1 Stark. 236.

facie evidence of breach of contract,[166] and probably of negligence,[167] by the shipowner. The shipowner must show that the cause of the loss was one of the excepted perils in the bill of lading, or that the goods were not shipped,[168] in order to free himself.[169] Thus, when there are concurrent causes of damage, partly excepted and partly not excepted, the shipowner must prove *how much* damage was due to the excepted causes.[170] Where however the breach of contract by the shipper or charterer is a concurrent cause of loss, it is for the shipper or charterer to prove how much damage was due to the shipowner's breach.[171]

If the shipowner makes a prima facie case to this effect, the shipper must then disprove it[172] by showing that the real cause of the loss was something not covered by the exceptions, as, for instance, the negligence of the shipowner or his servants, where negligence is not one of the excepted perils,[173] or unseaworthiness,[174] where unseaworthiness is not excepted, or, perhaps, that there has been a deviation[175]; and unless he can prove one of these, the shipowner will be protected.[176]

If when loss or damage has occurred the goods owner proves facts as to the cause of the loss which are consistent with negligence on the part of the shipowner or his servants, but such evidence leaves it in doubt whether the actual cause of the loss or damage was such negligence, the onus is upon the shipowner to prove that the loss was not due to negligence,[177] or to show a way in which the loss might have occurred without his negligence, in which case the onus still remains on the goods owner.[178]

Exceptions in the bill of lading will not relieve either the shipowner or shipper from their obligations to contribute in general average,[179] unless they are clearly intended to give such relief.[180]

---

[166] *The Xantho* (1886) 2 T.L.R. 704. Lord Herschell's remarks in (1887) 12 App.Cas. 503 at p.512 were not approved by the CA in *The Glendarroch* [1894] P. 226. As to the burden of proof under a time charter, see *The Roberta* (1938) 60 Ll.L.R. 84.

[167] See *Baxter's Leather Co v Royal Mail Co* [1908] 1 K.B. 796; affirmed [1908] 2 K.B. 626. Proof of failure to deliver and nothing more does not establish "wilful misconduct" against the carrier: *Smith v G.W. Ry* [1922] A.C. 178.

[168] See Art.62, as to the effect on the burden of proof of representations in the bill of lading of the quantity of goods shipped.

[169] See fn.167, above.

[170] *Gosse Millerd v Canadian Government Merchant Marine* [1929] A.C. 223, per Lord Sumner, at p.241; *The Mekhanik Evgrafov and The Ivan Derbenev* [1987] 2 Lloyd's Rep. 634; see also below Chapter 20, Art.III.

[171] *C.H.Z. "Rolimpex" v Efavrysses Compania Naviera SA (The Panaghia Tinnou)* [1986] 2 Lloyd's Rep. 580.

[172] As to the onus of proof, see *The Northumbria* [1906] P. 292; *London & N.W. Ry v Ashton* [1920] A.C. 84.

[173] *The Glendarroch* [1894] P. 226, and see also, below, Chapter 20, Art.III.

[174] See Arts 51 and 106.

[175] See Art.127, below; *Hunt & Winterbotham v B.R.S.* [1962] 1 Q.B. 617, where however it was said that the shipper might by his pleading put the carrier to strict proof that there had been no deviation such as to deprive the carrier of the benefit of exceptions.

[176] *The Norway* (1865) 3 Moore P.C.(N.S.) 245; *Muddle v Stride* (1840) 9 C. & P. 380; *Czech v General Steam Co* (1867) L.R. 3 C.P. 14. See also *Williams v Dobie* (1884) 11 Rettie 982; *Cunningham v Colvils* (1888) 16 Rettie 295; *Minister of Food v Reardon Smith Line* [1951] 2 Lloyd's Rep. 265. This paragraph was cited with approval by Simon L.C. in *Joseph Constantine v Imperial Smelting Corporation* [1942] A.C. 154.

[177] *Travers v Cooper* [1915] 1 K.B. 73; *cf. L.N.W. Ry v Ashton* [1920] A.C. 84. Contrast *Smith v G.W. Ry* (1922) 27 Com.Cas. 247.

[178] *The Kite* [1933] P. 154, following Lord Dunedin's dissenting opinion in *Ballard v North British Ry*, 1923 S.C. 43 at p.54 (HL).

[179] *Schmidt v Mail S.S. Co* (1876) 45 L.J.Q.B. 646; *Crooks v Allan* (1879) 5 Q.B.D. 38.

[180] See *Walford v Galindez* (1897) 2 Com.Cas. 137.

Exceptions in the charterparty will, in the absence of clear words, operate only so as to excuse what would otherwise be a breach. They will not operate so as to extend time for performance (such as the laytime provided for loading and discharge).[181]

Case. Goods shipped under a bill of lading, excepting "perils of the sea", were delivered damaged. The shippers sued and the shipowners proved damage by sea water through stranding. *Held*, that unless the shipper proved negligent navigation as causing the stranding, the shipowner succeeded.[182]

Article 108—Act of God   A108

The exception "act of God" includes any accident as to which the shipowner can show that it is due to natural causes, directly and exclusively, without human intervention, and that it could not have been prevented by any amount of foresight, pains and care, reasonably to be expected from him.[183]

Note. A stricter view than this was taken by Brett and Denman JJ. in the court below,[184] but was negatived by the Court of Appeal, Mellish L.J. saying: "I think that in order to prove the cause of the loss was irresistible, it is not necessary to prove that it was absolutely impossible for the carrier to prevent it, but that it is sufficient to prove that by no reasonable precaution under the circumstances could it have been prevented." This view is supported by *Nichols v Marsland*,[185] in which the jury found that a flood was "so great that it could not reasonably have been anticipated, though if it had been anticipated the effect might have been prevented", and the Court of Appeal held that such a flood was an "act of God".

Collision by negligence of another ship, and "pirates", appear to be "perils of the sea", but not "acts of God". On the other hand, the exception "act of God" appears to cover such causes of loss as frost, lightning, etc., which are not perils peculiar to the sea.[186]

Case 1. A, a common carrier between L and A, took on board a mare of F's. No bill of lading was signed. Partly by more than ordinarily bad weather, partly by the conduct of the mare, without any negligence by A's servants, the mare was seriously injured. *Held*, that A was not liable for injuries resulting from these concurrent causes, which he could not by reasonable care and foresight have prevented, and was accordingly protected by the common law exception to a common carrier's liability of act of God or inherent nature of the goods themselves.[187]

Case 2. Goods were shipped under a bill of lading excepting the "act of God". The vessel having to start the next morning, the captain filled his boiler overnight, and, frost coming on, the tubes burst,

---

[181] *Cero Navigation Corp v Jean Lion & Cie (The Solon)* [2000] 1 Lloyd's Rep. 292 in which Thomas J stated that it was established law that once a vessel was on demurrage no exceptions would operate to prevent demurrage continuing to be payable unless clearly worded so as to have that effect. See also Arts 157, 158, below.
[182] *The Glendarroch* [1894] P. 226.
[183] per James L.J. in *Nugent v Smith* (1876) 1 C.P.D. 423 at p.444; see Cockburn C.J. at pp.437, 438; Mellish L.J. at p.441. *Cf. The Marpesia* (1892) L.R. 4 P.C. 212; and for discussions of "inevitable accident", *The Merchant Prince* [1892] P. 179; *The Albano* (1892) 8 T.L.R. 425. See fnn 100 and 135 above. In this case it appears that the principle of *The Glendarroch* [1894] P. 226, that the shipowner need not negative negligence, but the goods owner must affirmatively prove it, does not apply.
[184] (1875) 1 C.P.D. at p.34.
[185] (1876) 2 Ex.D. 1. See, however, the discussion of *Nichols v Marsland* in *Greenock Corp v Caledonian Ry* [1917] A.C. 556.
[186] See Art.112, below. As to the history of the phrase "act of God", see O. W. Holmes, *Common Law*, p.202, and fn.183, above.
[187] *Nugent v Smith* (1876) 1 C.P.D. 19; reversed *ibid.* 423.

damaging the goods. *Held*, that the negligence of the captain excluded the exception though frost was an "act of God".[188]

A109   **Article 109—The Queen's Enemies**

This exception refers to the enemies of the sovereign of the shipowner.[189] It probably only refers to states recognised as at war with the sovereign and not to piratical or traitorous subjects,[190] or to states at peace with the sovereign.[191]

The word "war" in a provision in a charterparty is not to be construed in accordance with the tests of international law, but is to receive the business or commercial meaning in which it would be understood in its context.[192]

The Carriage of Goods by Sea Act 1971, in Rule 2 of Article IV of the Schedules, includes "Act of War" and "Act of Public Enemies" in the list of statutory exceptions. The meaning of the latter phrase is not clear, but presumably the two phrases together cover the action of any belligerent, and (*quaere*) of pirates also.[193]

Case 1. F, merchants in Russia, shipped wheat on a ship belonging to A, a subject of the Duke of Mecklenburg, to be carried to England under a bill of lading containing an exception "the King's enemies". The Duke was at war with Denmark and the ship was captured by the Danes. *Held*, that the exception certainly included enemies of the shipowner's sovereign, and the shipowner was therefore freed.[194]

Case 2. F shipped goods under a bill of lading excepting "the Queen's enemies". Ship and goods were confiscated by the Spanish courts for violations of the revenue laws, Spain being at peace with England. *Held*, that such confiscation did not come within the exception.[195]

A110   **Article 110—Arrests or Restraints of Princes, Rulers and Peoples**[196]

This exception applies to forcible interferences by a state or the government of a country taking possession of the goods by a strong hand, such as arrest, embargoes[197] or blockades[198]; to the operation of the common law as to trading with the enemy upon the outbreak of war[199]; to government action for other purposes, indirectly resulting in the detention of the goods[200]; to state prohibition

---

[188] *Siordet v Hall* (1828) 4 Bing. 607. Rats causing a leak are not an "act of God"; *Dale v Hall* (1750) 1 Wils. 281. *Sed quaere*, whether on principle if the shipowner could show that no care or diligence reasonably to be expected to him could prevent there being some rats on a ship, he would not bring himself within the exception.
[189] *Russell v Niemann* (1864) 17 C.B. (N.S.) 163.
[190] See the *Marshal of Marshalsea's Case*, and comments thereon, Holmes' *Common Law*, pp.177, 201: *Forward v Pittard* (1785) 1 T.R. 27, per Lord Mansfield at p.34.
[191] *Spence v Chodwick* (1847) 10 Q.B. 517.
[192] *Kawasaki Kisen, etc. v Bantham S.S. Co (No. 2)* [1939] 2 K.B. 544. In relation to attacks carried out by terrorists see the decision of the Court of Appeal in *IF P&C Insurance Ltd (Publ) v Silversea Cruises Ltd* [2004] 1 Lloyd's Rep. IR 696; [2004] EWCA Civ 769.
[193] See below, p.401.
[194] *Russell v Niemann* (1864) 17 C.B.(N.S.) 163.
[195] *Spence v Chodwick*, above. It would be a "seizure" under an insurance policy: *Cory v Burr* (1883) 8 App.Cas. 393 at p.405.
[196] "Revolutions, riots, or émeutes" are occasionally added.
[197] *Rotch v Edie* (1795) 6 T.R. 413. *Seabridge Shipping v Antco Shipping* [1977] 2 Lloyd's Rep. 367.
[198] *Geipel v Smith* (1872) L.R. 7 Q.B. 404.
[199] *British and Foreign Co v Sanday* [1916] 1 A.C. 650.
[200] *Rodocanachi v Elliott* (1874) L.R. 9 C.P. 518. It may protect the shipowner from the consequences of detention, e.g. when the detention of the ship caused a growth of barnacles: *Smith & Service v Rosario Nitrate Co* [1893] 2 Q.B. 323 at p.328.

of discharge, either temporarily, as in quarantine, or permanently, as where a cargo becomes tainted and so within a prohibition against import[201]; to the decrees of a Prize Court after capture[202]; or to embargoes imposed by the government of the shipowner[203]; or to the risk of such proceedings.[204] A shipowner can rely on "restraint of princes" when the power of restraint operates only against his person and though his ship is beyond the region where the restraining power can deal with her.[205]

It does not apply to ordinary legal proceedings in the courts of a state or their result,[206] to the application of the local law at a port of call to facts existing before the commencement of the voyage, such law being then known to the party claiming protection,[207] nor to the proceedings of a number of people not professing to act legally or by government authority.[208] It does not apply to restrictions on navigation as to sea routes imposed by a belligerent for the safety of shipping, to action taken to avoid the risk of loss by restraint of princes,[209] nor to the threats of an arbitrary belligerent which suggest danger to neutral ships.[210] Nor does it apply where the seizure of the ship results from the negligence of the shipowner or his agents in taking on board cargo of such a description as occasions the seizure.[211] The exception may apply to matters preventing the cargo from arriving at the port of loading.[212]

In r.2 of Art.IV of the Schedule to the Carriage of Goods by Sea Act 1971, this exception is enlarged by adding the words "or seizure under legal process".[213]

Case 1. Goods were insured[214] from Japan to London via Marseilles and/or Southampton, by a line of steamers whose practice was to send goods by land from Marseilles to Boulogne via Paris. One of the risks insured against was "arrests, restraints, and detainments of all kings, princes, and peoples". On arriving at Paris the goods were detained by the siege of Paris by the Germans, though not by any express order dealing with the goods. *Held*, a peril insured against.[215]

Case 2. A ship chartered to load nitrate at Iquique, with an exception of "restraints of princes and rules, political disturbances or impediments, during the said voyage always mutually excepted", was detained: (1) by civil war at the port of loading preventing loading; (2) by civil war preventing cargo

---

[201] *Miller v Law Accident Ins Co* [1903] 1 K.B. 712 (CA). *Cf. British and Foreign Co v Sanday*, above.
[202] *Stringer v English and Scottish Marine Ins Co* (1870) L.R. 5 Q.B. 599; and see *Panamanian Oriental S.S. Co v Wright* [1971] 1 Lloyd's Rep. 487.
[203] *Aubert v Gray* (1861) 3 B. & S. 163.
[204] *Nobel's Explosives v Jenkins* [1896] 2 Q.B. 326; *Phosphate Co v Rankin* (1915) 21 Com.Cas. 248. As to the amount of risk necessary, compare *Miller v Law Accident Ins Co*, above, with *Brunner v Webster* (1900) 5 Com.Cas. 167.
[205] *Furness, Withy & Co v Rederiaktiebolaget Banco* [1917] 2 K.B. 873.
[206] *Finlay v Liverpool & G.W. Co* (1870) 23 L.T. 251; *Crew, Widgery & Co v G.W. Steamship Co* [1887] W.N. 161; contrast *Panamanian Oriental S.S. Co v Wright* [1971] 1 Lloyd's Rep. 487.
[207] *Ciampa v British India Co* [1915] 2 K.B. 774; *Induna S.S. Co v British Phosphate Commissioners* [1949] 2 K.B. 430. But see these cases discussed in *Reardon Smith v Ministry of Agriculture* [1960] 1 Q.B. 439 at pp.493–495; *affirmed* [1962] 1 Q.B. 42 at pp.83, 107, 128 (CA). (The point did not arise in the HL) See also, fn.164, above.
[208] *Nesbitt v Lushington* (1792) 4 T.R. 783.
[209] *Becker Gray v London Assurance Co* [1918] A.C. 101.
[210] *Bolckow, Vaughan & Co v Compania Minera, etc.* (1916) 32 T.L.R. 404.
[211] *Dunn v Currie* [1902] 2 K.B. 614.
[212] *Smith v Rosario Nitrate Co* [1894] 1 Q.B. 174; Art.82.
[213] See p.339, below.
[214] We have used insurance cases, as illustrations, when the different principles of construction do not affect the case. See definition in Rule 10 of the First Schedule to the Marine Insurance Act 1906.
[215] *Rodocanachi v Elliott* (1874) L.R. 9 C.P. 518.

coming down to such port; (3) by seizure by one faction to compel payment of export dues already paid to the other faction. *Held*, that all three causes were within the exception.[216]

Case 3. F shipped goods under bill of lading excepting "acts or restraints of princes or rulers". The goods were detained by an order of the State of New York in a civil action. *Held*, not to come within the exception.[217]

Case 4. Goods were insured against "arrests, restraints, and detainment of all kings, princes and peoples". The vessel was seized by a tumultuous mob, and the goods taken out of her. *Held*, not within the perils insured against, as "peoples" means "the governing power of the country".[218]

Case 5. Goods were shipped from London to Japan on a bill of lading excepting "restraint of princes". They were contraband of war. On arrival at Hong Kong war broke out between China and Japan and there was well-founded fear of capture if the ship proceeded. *Held*, that delivery in Japan was prevented by a restraint of princes within the exception.[219]

Case 6. A cargo of cattle on a voyage from London to Buenos Aires became infected with disease during the voyage and their landing was therefore prohibited by an administrative order issued under the ordinary law of the Argentine Republic. *Held*, to be a restraint of princes.[220]

Case 7. A cargo of rice was shipped from Rangoon to Galatz. While on the voyage an official of the Romanian Government informed the agents of the ship that the law of Romania prohibited the landing of rice from Rangoon. Thereupon the ship did not proceed to Galatz. In fact there was no such prohibition in the law of Romania. *Held*, the shipowners were not protected by the exception "restraint of princes".[221]

Case 8. Cargo was insured by British assured on a British steamer to Hamburg. The insured perils included restraints of princes. War with Germany broke out during the voyage. The ship put into a British port and discharged the cargo. The assured gave notice of abandonment to the cargo underwriters. *Held*, that there was a constructive total loss by restraint of princes.[222]

Case 9. A Swedish ship was chartered to British charterers for six months to perform voyages within certain limits. The charter contained an exception of "restraint of princes". During the period the ship was at Cardiff and was ordered by the charterers to load for Genoa, which was within the said limits. The shipowners refused to go on the ground that a new Swedish law had forbidden Swedish ships to carry goods for freight except to or from Swedish ports, and relied on the exception. Under the law the owner and master were liable to penalties for its breach. *Held*, that, though the Swedish Government were not in a position to interfere with the ship, the shipowner was entitled to rely on the exception.[223]

Case 10. A German ship, insured against restraint of princes, and bound from Calcutta to Hamburg, was at sea when on August 4, 1914, war broke out between England and Germany. The master, to avoid risk of capture, put into a neutral port, where the voyage was abandoned. If the ship had proceeded she would probably have been captured. *Held*, the loss of voyage was not caused by restraint of princes, but by the voluntary act of the captain.[224]

---

[216] See fn.212, above.
[217] *Finlay v Liverpool and G.W. Co* (1870) 23 L.T. 251; *Crew, Widgery & Co v G.W. Steamship Co* [1887] W.N. 161.
[218] *Nesbitt v Lushington* (1792) 4 T.R. 783. This would be a "seizure". See *Note*, below.
[219] *Nobel's Explosives Co v Jenkins* [1896] 2 Q.B. 326. See, however, *Watts, Watts & Co v Mitsui* [1916] 2 K.B. 826; varied [1917] A.C. 227, on anticipation that a peril will operate, as distinguished from anticipation as to the duration of a peril in operation. And see *Case 10*, below.
[220] *Miller v Law Accident Insurance Co* [1903] 1 K.B. 712.
[221] *Brunner v Webster* (1900) 5 Com.Cas. 167.
[222] *British and Foreign Co v Sanday* [1916] 1 A.C. 650.
[223] *Furness, Withy & Co v Rederiaktiebolaget Banco* [1917] 2 K.B. 873.
[224] *Becker, Gray & Co v London Assurance* [1918] A.C. 101.

Note The phrase, "capture and seizure", common in insurance policies, rarely, if ever, occurs in bills of lading. The two words have been defined in *Cory v Burr*[225] thus: "Capture" includes every act of seizing or taking by an enemy or belligerent.[226]

"Seizure" includes every act of taking forcible possession, either by lawful authority or by overpowering force, whether such seizure be justified by law or not, or whether it be belligerent or not: thus a seizure of a ship by coolie passengers was held a "seizure".[227]

The difference, therefore, between the three exceptions is this:

"The King's Enemies" covers belligerent acts of states, other than that of the owner of the vessel.

"Restraint of princes or rulers" includes this and also covers restraints of the sovereign power in peace, whether of the carrier's country or not, other than the ordinary consequences of legal proceedings.[228]

"Capture and seizure" includes all captures or seizures resulting from the above sources and also seizures resulting from ordinary legal proceedings or from private overwhelming force.

Article 111—Inherent Vice, Insufficiency of Packing   A111

The shipowner is not liable for loss of or damage to the goods caused by their "inherent vice".[229] By "inherent vice" is meant the unfitness of the goods to withstand the ordinary incidents of the voyage,[230] given the degree of care which the shipowner is required by the contract to exercise in relation to the goods.[231] Thus a tendency of the goods to heat, discolour, rot, or evaporate, or to destroy their packing, or the inherent restiveness or phrensy of an animal, or defective packing, may all constitute inherent vice.

It may be that the exception does not apply to the extent that the damage has been aggravated by the shipowners' unjustifiable deviation.[232] Where the

---

[225] (1883) 8 App.Cas. 393 at p.405.

[226] *Semble*, whether lawful or unlawful: *Powell v Hyde* (1855) 5 E. & B. 607 (seizure by Russia before outbreak of Crimean War). "Risk of seizure or capture" includes risk of sinking by submarine: *Tonnevold v Finn Friis* [1916] 2 K.B. 551.

[227] *Kleinwort v Shephard* (1859) 1 E. & E. 447. See also *Johnston v Hogg* (1883) 10 Q.B.D. 432; *Ionides v Universal Marine Ins Co* (1863) 14 C.B.(N.S.) 259; *Kuwait Airways Inc v Kuwait Insurance Co* [1999] 1 Lloyd's Rep. 803; *Bayview Motors Ltd v Mitsui Marine and Fire Insurance Co Ltd* [2002] 1 Lloyd's Rep. 652; [2002] EWHC 21 (Comm).

[228] The "restraint of princes" in *Miller v Law Accident Insurance Co*, above, was held by the CA also to be a "detention", within the words "capture, seizure, and *detention*".

[229] *Story on Bailments*, § 492a; *Kendall v London & S.W. Ry* (1872) L.R. 7 Ex. 373; *Blower v G.W.R.* (1872) L.R. 7 C.P. 655; *Nugent v Smith* (1876) 1 C.P.D. 423; *The Barcore* [1896] P. 294; *Lister v Lancashire and Yorks Ry* [1903] K.B. 878; *Internationale Guano v MacAndrew* [1909] 2 K.B. 360; *Gould v S.E. and Chatham Ry* [1920] 2 K.B. 186; *L.N.W.R. v Hudson* [1920] A.C. 324; *Bradley v Federal Steam Navigation* (1927) 27 Ll.L.R. 395; *White v "Hobsons Bay"* (1933) 47 Ll.L.R. 207; *Potts v Union S.S. Co* [1946] N.Z.L.R. 276; *Albacora S.R.L. v Westcott & Laurance Line* [1966] 2 Lloyd's Rep. 53; *The Flowergate* [1967] 1 Lloyd's Rep. 1; *Chris Foodstuffs v Nigerian National Shipping Line* [1967] 1 Lloyd's Rep. 293; *Westcoast Food Brokers Ltd v The Ship "Hoyanger" and Westfal-Larsen & Co A/S (The Hoyanger)* [1979] 2 Lloyd's Rep. 79. *Cf.* s.55(2)(c) of Marine Insurance Act 1906, and s.33 of the Sale of Goods Act 1979.

[230] *Cf.* the formulation of Gorrel Barnes J. in *The Barcore*, above, at p.297: " . . . its own want of power to bear the ordinary transit in a ship."

[231] *Gatoil International Inc v Tradax Petroleum Ltd (The Rio Sun)* [1985] 1 Lloyd's Rep. 350. For the degree of care required of a common carrier, see above, pp.201–204, and the cases in fn.229, above, decided before the Carriage of Goods by Sea Act 1924. For the degree of care required under that Act and that of 1971 see the later cases and Art.III, rr.1 and 2, of the Hague–Visby Rules, below.

[232] *Internationale Guano v MacAndrew* [1909] 2 K.B. 360. But this may now be a matter of construction: see below, Art.127.

inherent vice has rendered the ship unseaworthy, the court will consider whether the loss was caused by the state of the ship or the state of the cargo.[233]

The shipowner may rely on the exception even if he knew of the inherent vice[234] although his knowledge may affect the degree of care required of him.[235]

The shipowner may be estopped from relying on the exception by a statement in the bill of lading to the effect that the goods were "shipped in apparent good order and condition".[236]

Case. A cargo of wet salted fish turned out damaged by bacteria present in the fish on shipment. The damage could have been prevented by refrigeration, but the shipowner could not reasonably have known that; the ship had no refrigerated hold. In an action on bills of lading incorporating the Hague Rules, *held*, that the shipowner was protected by the exception of inherent vice; his obligation under the Hague Rules was merely to carry the fish according to a system which was sound in the light of all the knowledge which he had or ought to have had about the nature of the fish. The fish were therefore unfit to stand the treatment which the contract required of the shipowner.[237]

A112   **Article 112—Perils of the Sea**

The term "Perils of the Sea",[238] whether in policies of insurance, charterparties, or bills of lading, has the same meaning,[239] and includes any damage to the goods carried caused by sea-water, storms, collision, stranding, or other perils peculiar to the sea or to a ship at sea, which could not be foreseen and guarded against by the shipowner or his servants as necessary or probable incidents of the adventure.

Where there is an accidental incursion of sea-water into a vessel at a part of the vessel, and in a manner, where sea-water is not expected to enter in the ordinary course of things, and there is consequent damage, there is prima facie a loss by

---

[233] *Empresa Cubana Importada de Alimentos "Alimport" v Iasmos Shipping Co SA (The Good Friend)* [1984] 2 Lloyd's Rep. 586.

[234] *Gould v S.E. and Chatham Ry Co* [1920] 2 K.B. 186; *Barbour v S.E. Ry*, 34 L.T. 67.

[235] *Internationale Guano v MacAndrew* [1909] 2 K.B. 360; *Albacora S.R.L. v Westcott & Laurance Line* [1966] 2 Lloyd's Rep. 53; *The Rio Sun*, above.

[236] *Silver v Ocean S.S. Co* [1930] 1 K.B. 416; *Potts v Union S.S. Co* [1946] N.Z.L.R. 276; Art.63, above.

[237] *Albacora v Westcott & Laurance Line* [1966] 2 Lloyd's Rep. 53 (HL). The shipowner's obligation to make the ship seaworthy, under Art.III, r.1, was not discussed, but presumably the same principle applies. See, however, *The Erik Boye* (1929) 34 Ll.L.R. 442.

[238] This exception is often expanded into "all and every other dangers and accidents of the seas, rivers, and [steam] navigation of whatsoever nature and kind excepted".

[239] Collected from the judgments in *Thames and Mersey Insurance Co v Hamilton* (1887) 12 App.Cas. 484; *The Xantho, ibid.* 503; *Hamilton v Pandorf, ibid.* 518. See *Goodfellow Lumber Sales v Verreault* [1971] 1 Lloyd's Rep. 185, where the Supreme Court of Canada arrived at a very similar view of the law. See also *The Sabine Howaldt* [1971] 2 Lloyd's Rep. 78 (US Circuit CA). But though the phrase "perils of the sea" has the same meaning in policies of insurance and in contracts of affreightment, it does not follow that in all cases where the goods owner can succeed against the cargo underwriters for a loss by perils of the sea the shipowner would be able to sustain a defence of "perils of the sea", since the shipowner may be precluded from relying upon the defence on proof that the perils of the sea were brought into operation by negligence (*The Glendarroch* [1894] P. 226) or (possibly) that unseaworthiness was a contributory cause: *Smith, Hogg v Black Sea & Baltic* [1940] A.C. 997 and fn.116, Art.51, above. Rule 7 in Sch.I to the Marine Insurance Act 1906, provides as follows: "The term 'perils of the seas' refers only to fortuitous accidents or casualties of the seas. It does not include the ordinary action of the winds and waves." As to the need for an antecedent fortuity see *566935 BC Ltd v Allianz Insurance Co of Canada* [2007] Lloyd's Rep. IR 503; [2006] B.C.J. 2754. But *cf: General China Metals Industries Co Ltd v Malaysian International Shipping Corp, Berhad* (1999) 196 C.L.R. 161 (Aust.) where it was held that sea and weather conditions whichh may reasonably be foreseen and guarded against may nevertheless constitute a "peril of the sea".

perils by the sea.[240] Damage incurred not by an incursion, may also be a loss by perils of the sea.[241] If a prima facie case of loss by perils of the sea is made out, it is for the goods owner to establish such negligence as would disentitle the shipowner to rely upon the defence of perils of the sea.[242]

Such damage will include all natural and necessary consequences of perils of the sea,[243] but no consequences which do not necessarily and immediately follow from the occurrence of such perils, such as deterioration of goods by reason of delay caused by sea perils.[244]

The shipowner will be liable for incidents that must occur on the voyage, such as taking the ground in the ordinary course of navigation,[245] and for perils which, though occurring on the sea, are not peculiar to the sea, or to a ship on the sea, such as rats eating the cargo,[246] and damage done by explosion of boilers, or bursting of steam valves,[247] or damage to the ship by cargo being dropped upon it in loading.[248]

The equivalent statutory exception contained in Art.IV, r.2, of the Rules scheduled to the Carriage of Goods by Sea Act 1971, is "Perils, dangers and accidents of the sea or other navigable waters".

Note. As so defined, "perils *of* the sea", which are not the same as perils *on* the sea,[249] will include those "acts of God" where the effective cause is one peculiar to the sea. Thus frost or lightning,[250] as effective causes of loss, will be acts of God, but not perils of the sea; damage by swordfish or icebergs would be a peril of the sea, if the shipowner could not have prevented it by reasonable care. There are dicta in the judgments of the House of Lords which suggest that the limitation in the definition, "peculiar to the sea", is too narrow; e.g. per Lord Halsbury[251]: "Some effect must be given to the words, 'perils *of the sea*'; the sea, or *the vessel being on the sea*, has nothing to do with" (a rat's eating cargo in the hold of a ship); and again, per Lord Bramwell[252]: "The damage to the donkey-engine was not through it being in a ship or at sea"—"all perils, losses, and misfortunes of a marine character, or of a character incident to a ship as such", a wider phrase which Lord Herschell also uses[253]: "damage of a character to which a marine adventure is

---

[240] *Canada Rice Mills v Union Marine* [1941] A.C. 55 at p.68.

[241] *Canada Rice Mills v Union Marine*, above: closing of ventilators in heavy weather resulting in the cargo heating.

[242] *The Glendarroch* [1894] P. 226: and see fn.239, p.403, below.

[243] *Cf. Montoya v London Assurance Co* (1851) 6 Ex. 451 at p.458; *Jackson v Union Marine Ins Co* (1874) L.R. 10 C.P. 125.

[244] *Taylor v Dunbar* (1869) L.R. 4 C.P. 206; *Pink v Fleming* (1890) 25 Q.B.D. 396. *Cf. Field S.S. Co v Burr* [1899] 1 Q.B. 579 (CA).

[245] See below.

[246] *Laveroni v Drury* (1852) 8 Ex. 166; *Kay v Wheeler* (1867) L.R. 2 C.P. 302, *Hamilton v Pandorf* (1887) 12 App.Cas. 518.

[247] *Thames and Mersey Ins Co v Hamilton* (1887) 12 App.Cas. 484; overruling *West India Co v Home and Colonial Ins Co* (1881) 6 Q.B.D. 51.

[248] *Stott v Marten* [1916] 1 A.C. 304.

[249] per Lord Herschell in *The Xantho* (1887) 12 App.Cas. 503 at p.509. See the similar remark as to "perils of the roads", by Parke B. in *De Rothschild v R. M. Steam Packet Co* (1852) 7 Ex. 734 at p.743. "Rain is not a peril of the sea, but at most a peril on the sea": see per Lord Wright in *Canada Rice Mills v Union Marine* [1941] A.C. 55 at p.64.

[250] The suggestion, *arguendo*, by Pollock C.B. in *Lloyd v General Coll. Co* (1864) 3 H. & C. 284 at p.290, that lightning is a peril of the sea, is, it is submitted, erroneous.

[251] *Hamilton v Pandorf* (1887) 12 App.Cas. 518 at p.523.

[252] *Thames and Mersey Ins Co v Hamilton* (1887) 12 App.Cas. 484 at p.492.

[253] *ibid.* p.498.

subject". But these dicta again must be limited by the result of the decisions, as when Lord Halsbury says,[254] that "sea perils cannot be enlarged into perils whose only connection with the sea is that they arise from machinery which gives motive power to ships". Perhaps the phrase "peculiar to the sea, or to a ship at sea", is most consistent with the authorities, and we have therefore adopted it.

Some previous definitions must clearly be revised. That by Lush J.: "Casualties arising from the violent action of the elements as distinguished from their silent natural gradual action"[255] must be altered by substituting for "violent" "unexpected", or "out of the ordinary course of the adventure". For a ship running on a sunken rock in calm weather does not suffer from the violent action of the elements, but does incur a loss by perils of the sea. Again, the definition by Lopes L.J. in *Pandorf v Hamilton*[256]: "Sea-damage occurring at sea and nobody's fault", is clearly not exhaustive. Sea-damage, through the fault of somebody (e.g. another ship), will be a peril of the sea both under a policy of insurance and a contract of affreightment, though by reason of implied undertakings the shipowner, in the case of negligence of the crew, may not be protected under a charter. And it is not clear what sea-damage it is which does not occur at sea.

The exception includes:

(1) Damage by sea-water, whether it enters the ship through negligence of another ship in collision,[257] or through holes made by rats,[258] or worms,[259] or swordfish, or icebergs, or cannon shot,[260] or through some obstruction getting into a seacock so as to prevent its being closed.[261]

(2) Damage to the goods by rough weather beyond the ordinary wear and tear of the voyage, the stowage not being negligent.[262]

(3) Captures by pirates[263] or wreckers.[264]

(4) Damage received while in dock without negligence, if the docking is in the course of the voyage[265]; but not if the docking is not in pursuance of a voyage: as where the ship was blown over in a graving dock by a squall.[266]

(5) Stranding not incurred as part of the navigation, unless the shipper proves negligence.[267] Thus damage through taking the ground in the ordinary course of

---

[254] *ibid.* p.491.

[255] *Merchant Trading Co v Universal Marine Co* (1874) L.R. 9 Q.B. 596, *cit. Cf. Sassoon v Western Assurance Co* [1912] A.C. 561.

[256] (1885) 16 Q.B.D. 629 at p.633; approved by Lord Bramwell in *Thames and Mersey Ins Co v Hamilton* (1887) 12 App.Cas. 484 at p.492, and *Hamilton v Pandorf, ibid.* at p.526; and Lord Macnaghten in *Hamilton v Pandorf, ibid.* at p.531.

[257] *The Xantho* (1887) 12 App.Cas. 503. *Cf. Buller v Fisher* (1799) 2 Peake 183.

[258] *Hamilton v Pandorf* (1887) 12 App.Cas. 518.

[259] *Cf. Rohl v Parr* (1796) 1 Esp. 445.

[260] *Cullen v Butler* (1816) 5 M. & S. 461, as corrected by Lord Herschell, 12 App.Cas. 509. But this would be a war risk rather than a marine risk: *Leyland v Norwich Union* [1918] A.C. 350. *Cf. Davidson v Burnand* (1868) L.R. 4 C.P. 117; *The Cressington* [1891] P. 152; *Blackburn v Liverpool Co* [1902] 1 K.B. 290, where there was a negligence clause and the engineer negligently let water into the wrong tank.

[261] *McFadden v Blue Star Line* [1905] 1 K.B. 697.

[262] *Lawrence v Aberdein* (1821) 5 B. & A. 107; *Gabay v Lloyd* (1825) 3 B. & C. 793; *The Catherine Chalmers* (1875) 32 L.T. 847. This covers damage through exceptionally rough weather preventing the ventilators being used for an unusual time, whereby the heat from the boilers, damaged the cargo; *The Thrunscoe* [1897] P. 301. See, also, *Canada Rice Mills v Union Marine* [1941] A.C. 55 at p.70, where it is stated that the exceptional nature of the weather is immaterial; *Neter v Licences and General Insurance* (1944) 77 Ll.L.R. 202. See also *Great China Metal Industries Co Ltd v Malaysian International Shipping Corp Berhad (The Bunge Seroja)* [1999] 1 Lloyd's Rep. 512.

[263] *Pickering v Barkley* (1648) Styles 132. See Art.114, below.

[264] *Bondrett v Hentigg* (1816) Holt N.P. 149. *Quaere*, if this accords with the principle of later decisions?

[265] *Laurie v Douglas* (1846) 15 M. & W. 746; *Devaux v J'Anson* (1839) 5 Bing.N.C. 519, as criticised by Lord Herschell in *Thames and Mersey Ins Co v Hamilton* (1887) 12 App.Cas. 484 at p.497.

[266] *Phillips v Barber* (1821) 5 B. & Ald. 161.

[267] *The Norway* (1865) B. & L. 404.

navigation in a tidal harbour, or hauling up on the beach to repair, will not be a peril of the sea.[268] But it will be a peril of the sea, if owing to stress of weather something different from the ordinary course of navigation occurs without negligence: as where a heavy swell bumps the ship on a hard bottom,[269] or where damage is caused in the ordinary course of navigation by an unseen peril, which could not have been detected by reasonable care, as where a ship takes the ground over an unknown hole and strains herself,[270] or where a vessel is driven by stress of weather into a tidal harbour where she takes the ground.[271]

(6) Loss of deck cargo whilst loading in calm weather due to the vessel for no discoverable reason suddenly heeling over.[272]

The exception will *not* include:

(1) Damage by sea-water entering the vessel solely through the operation of natural causes, as by the ordinary decay or wear and tear of the vessel.[273]

(2) Damage resulting from the ordinary wear and tear of the voyage which must be provided against by proper packing by the shipper, proper stowage by the ship-owner.

(3) Damage arising from inherent inability of the cargo to stand the effect of the voyage.[274]

(4) Any cases where the damage can be proved by the goods owner to result from negligence on the part of the shipowner or his servants in the stowage or management of the vessel.[275]

(5) Damage resulting from initial unseaworthiness of the vessel.[276]

(6) Damage from war.[277]

(7) Damage from confiscation by foreign courts, or the consequences of actions at law.[278]

(8) Barratrous acts of the crew,[279] or intentional scuttling.[280]

(9) Damage done directly by rats, or vermin, to the cargo.[281]

---

[268] *Magnus v Buttemer* (1852) 11 C.B. 876; *Thompson v Whitmore* (1810) 3 Taunt. 227.

[269] *Fletcher v Inglis* (1819) 2 B. & Ad. 315. *Cf. Bishop v Pentland* (1827) 7 B.C. 219, where a rope broke and the ship fell on her side.

[270] *Letchford v Oldham* (1880) 5 Q.B.D. 538. See also *Rayner v Godmond* (1821) 5 B. & A. 225.

[271] *Corcoran v Gurney* (1853) 1 E. & B. 456. *Cf. Barrow v Bell* (1825) 4 B. & C. 736.

[272] *The Stranna* [1937] P. 130; affirmed [1938] P. 69 where the clause included "perils of the sea even when occasioned by negligence".

[273] *Sassoon v Western Assurance Co* [1912] A.C. 561; *Sinda Timber Enterprises (Pte) Ltd v Owners of the Benoi VI* [1987] 2 M.L.J. 123 (Sing.); *566935 BC Ltd v Allianz Insurance Co of Canada* [2007] Lloyd's Rep. IR 503.

[274] *The Barcore* [1896] P. 294 (deals changing colour after shipment in the wet).

[275] *The Glendarroch* [1894] P. 226. Per Lord Herschell, *The Xantho* (1887) 12 App.Cas. 503 at p.510; *The Oquendo* (1877) 38 L.T. 151; *The Freedom* (1871) L.R. 3 P.C. 594; *The Figlia Maggiore* (1868) L.R. 2 A. & E. 106; *Leesh River Tea Co v British India Steam Navigation Co* [1966] 1 Lloyd's Rep. 450, affirmed on this point at [1966] 2 Lloyd's Rep. 193.

[276] *The Glenfruin* (1885) 10 P.D. 103, and see Art.51; *The Christel Vinnen* [1924] P. 208 (CA).

[277] *The Patria* (1871) L.R. 3 A. & E. 436.

[278] *Spence v Chodwick* (1847) 10 Q.B. 517; *Benson v Duncan* (1849) 3 Ex. 644.

[279] *The Chasca* (1875) L.R. 4 A. & E. 446.

[280] *Samuel v Dumas* [1924] A.C. 431; see also *The Christel Vinnen* [1924] P. 208 (CA).

[281] *Kay v Wheeler* (1867) L.R. 2 C.P. 302; *Laveroni v Drury* (1852) 8 Ex. 166. *Cf. Hamilton v Pandorf* (1887) 12 App.Cas. 518; *Dale v Hall* (1750) 1 Wils. 281 has decided that "rats" are not the "act of God", on which see fn.188, above.

Case 1. Goods were lost through a collision with another ship, neither vessel being to blame. *Held*, that such a collision was a peril of the sea.[282]

Case 2. Goods were damaged through a collision caused by the negligence of the carrying ship. *Held*, not protected by the exception of perils of the seas.[283]

Case 3. Goods were damaged by a collision caused by the negligence of the other ship, wind and waves not contributing. *Held*, a peril of the sea.[284]

Case 4. Cattle were insured against the perils of the sea; they were properly stowed, but the violence of the weather killed some and bruised others. *Held*, damage by perils of the seas.[285]

Case 5. Goods were damaged when the vessel encountered very heavy weather . Although the conditions encountered had been forecast the trial judge found that the vessel was seaworthy and that the owners had complied with their duties properly and carefully to load, handle, stow and carry the cargo. *Held*, damage by perils of the sea—knowledge of the weather likely to be encountered was critical to the assessment of whether the owner had complied with his duties but provided he had done so the defence succeeded.[286]

Case 6. Goods shipped were stowed in a place especially exposed to the waves and in rough weather were damaged by salt water. *Held*, that the improper stowage took the damage out of the protection of the exception.[287]

Case 7. Owing to bad weather a ship's hatches were kept closed and the cargo putrefied. *Held*, that improper stowage and lack of ventilation took the case out of the exception "perils of the seas".[288]

Case 8. Rice was damaged by heating due to the closing of ventilators to prevent the incursion of sea water in rough weather. *Held*, damage to the rice by such an incursion through the ventilators would have been a loss by perils of the sea and that the damage by heating caused by action to prevent such incursion was also damage by perils of the sea.[289]

Case 9. Goods were shipped with an exception "all and every the dangers and accidents of the seas and navigation". While the ship was discharging her cargo in dock, moored to a barge and a lighter, she capsized, owing to ropes breaking, and the goods were damaged. *Held*, a "danger of navigation" within the exception.[290]

Case 10. Goods were damaged by sea water let into the hold by the barratrous act of the crew in boring holes in the ship. *Held*, not protected by the exception of perils of the sea.[291]

---

[282] *Buller v Fisher* (1799) 2 Peake 183.

[283] *Lloyd v General Colliery Co* (1864) 3 H. & C. 284.

[284] *The Xantho* (1887) 12 App.Cas. 503.

[285] *Lawrence v Aberdein* (1821) 5 B. & A. 107; see also *Tatham v Hodgson* (1796) 6 T.R. 656.

[286] *Great China Metal Industries Co Ltd v Malaysian International Shipping Corp Berhad (The Bunga Seroja)* [1999] 1 Lloyd's Rep. 512.

[287] *The Oquendo* (1877) 38 L.T. 151; see also *The Catherine Chalmers* (1875) 38 L.T. 847.

[288] *The Freedom* (1871) L.R. 3 P.C. 594 at p.603; see also *The Figlia Maggiore* (1868) L.R. 2 A. & E. 106; *The Thrunscoe* [1897] P. 301; *cf. Canada Rice Mills v Union Marine* [1941] A.C. 55. But where the putrefaction is caused by extraordinary delay owing to bad weather, *semble*, that the shipowner will not be excused by the exception "perils of the sea"; though he may be by the plea of inherent vice in the goods themselves: *The Barcore* [1896] P. 294. Such damage would not be a peril of the sea, for which underwriters would be liable: see *Taylor v Dunbar* (1869) L.R. 4 C.P. 206; *Tatham v Hodgson*, above; *Pink v Fleming* (1890) 25 Q.B.D. 396.

[289] *Canada Rice Mills v Union Marine* [1941] A.C. 55; *Neter v Licences and General Insurance* (1944) 77 Ll.L.R. 202.

[290] *Laurie v Douglas* (1846) 15 M. & W. 746; see *The Accomac* (1890) 15 P.D. 208; *cf. Devaux v J'Anson* (1839) 5 Bing.N.C. 519, as criticised by Lord Herschell in *Thames and Mersey Ins Co v Hamilton* (1887) 12 App.Cas. 484 at p.497.

[291] *The Chasca* (1875) L.R. 4 A. & E. 446.

Case 11. Goods were damaged on the voyage by rats. The ship-owner, who had two cats and a mongoose on board, and had employed a professional rat-catcher, was found to have taken every precaution. *Held*, that such damage by rats was not a peril of the sea or of navigation.[292]

Case 12. On a voyage rats ate a hole in a leaden pipe, and so let sea water into the ship, damaging her cargo. *Held*, a peril of the sea.[293]

Case 13. A ship was fired into in mistake for an enemy and sea water entered through the shot-holes. Damage done by sea water is a peril of the sea.[294]

Case 14. A donkey-engine accidentally exploded: *Submitted*, that if the explosion damaged goods directly, such damage would not be a peril of the sea; but that if it admitted sea water to the goods, the damage in that case would be a peril of the sea.[295]

Case 15. A ship was scuttled by some of her crew on the owner's instructions. *Held*, not a peril of the sea.[296]

Article 113—Strikes   A113

A "strike" is "a general concerted refusal by workmen to work in consequence of an alleged grievance".[297] The exception "strikes or lock-outs" covers refusals of men or masters to carry on work or business by reason of and incidental to labour disputes.[298] It does not cover dismissals of men to save expense[299] or (*semble*) men leaving work for fear of disease.[300]

---

[292] *Kay v Wheeler* (1867) L.R. 2 C.P. 302. *Cf.* Godolphin, "A view of the Admiral Jurisdiction", 1685: "The master . . . may not sail without one cat or more in his vessel." So Malynes, *Lex Mercatoria* (1686), p.102: The master "must answer for any harm which Rats do in a Ship to any Merchandise for want of a Cat". So earlier in a charterparty of "the *Anne* of Hull" of June 10, 1532, it is provided that the shipowner shall supply "a doge [sic] and a cat with all other necessaries". Marsen, *Select Pleas of the Admiralty Court* (Selden Society, 1892), Vol. I, p.37.

[293] *Hamilton v Pandorf* (1887) 12 App.Cas. 518.

[294] *Cullen v Butler* (1816) 5 M. & S. 461, as corrected by Lord Herschell in *The Xantho* (1887) 12 App.Cas. 503 at p.509. See *Leyland v Norwich Union* [1918] A.C. 350, as to war risk.

[295] *Thames & Mersey Ins Co v Hamilton* (*The Inchmaree*) (1887) 12 App.Cas. 484; *Hamilton v Pandorf*, above.

[296] *Samuel v Dumas* [1924] A.C. 431.

[297] per Sankey J., *Williams v Naamlooze, etc.* (1915) 21 Com.Cas. 253 at p.257; the definition did not claim to be exhaustive. The "grievance" in that case was the crew's objection to face the dangers of German mines and submarines. The suggestion in *Stephens v Harris* (1887) 57 L.T. 618, that the grievance must be as to the rate of wages, is too narrow; *ibid*. "Strikes" includes sympathetic strikes even though the men on strike may themselves have no grievance and even though the strike is directed only at a particular class of ships or cargo: *Seeberg v Russian Wood Agency* (1934) 50 Ll.L.R. 146; *J. Vermaas Scheepvaartbedrif NV v Association Technique de l'Importation Charbonniére* [1966] 1 Lloyd's Rep. 582. A strike may be discontinuous, e.g. a refusal to work night, but not day, shifts: *Tramp Shipping Co v Greenwich Marine Inc* (*The New Horizon*) [1975] 2 Lloyd's Rep. 314.

[298] *Richardsons & Samuel, Re* [1898] 1 Q.B. 261 at pp.267, 268. As to the phrase "general strike", see *Aktieselskabet Shakespeare v Ekman* (1902) 18 T.L.R. 605. In *Allison and Richards, Re* (1904) 20 T.L.R. 584, it was held that delay through colliers taking an unauthorised holiday was within the exception, "time lost through strikes, lockouts, or any other cause beyond the charterers' control". In *Gordon Co v Moxey Savon & Co* (1913) 18 Com.Cas. 10, it was held that "stoppage" of work by a strike may extend beyond the actual ending of the strike, e.g. where colliers cannot in fact resume the getting of coal for some days after they are willing to resume work. But "stoppage" in such a clause means an entire absence of output, and not merely a deficiency, however, great: *Aktieselskabet Adalands v Whitaker* (1913) 18 Com.Cas. 229. See also *Arden S.S. Co v Mathwin*, 1912 S.C. 211; *Miguel de Larrinaga S.S. Co v Flack* (1925) 21 Ll.L.R. 284. As to whether a "ca'canny" movement is an obstruction on railways, see *Brightman v Bunge y Born* [1924] 2 K.B. 619. Where a ship moored end on to a quay was not discharged owing to a declaration of the presidents of two co-operative societies of labour (published some months before and since acted on) that vessels were not to be discharged while so moored, the delay was held not to be within an exception of "hands striking work": *Horsley Line v Roechling*, 1908 S.C. 866. As to an exception of "strike of any class of workmen essential to the discharge", see *Langham S.S. Co v Gallagher* [1911] 2 I.R. 348; and *Dampskibsselskabet Svendborg v Love*, 1915 S.C. 543.

[299] *Richardsons & Samuel, Re*, above.

[300] *Stephens v Harris* (1887) 57 L.T. 618; the point was left open on appeal; *Mudie v Strick* (1909) 14 Com.Cas. 135.

The employer must use reasonable exertions to carry on his business and obtain men.[301] Strikes preventing cargo from coming to the port of loading may be within the exemption.[302]

A strike may prevent cargo being loaded within the lay-days notwithstanding that the strike has been settled before the ship's arrival.[303] "The consequences of any strike" will include congestion in a port due to a strike, but continuing after the strike has ended.[304]

An exception of "strike preventing loading" will not entitle the charterer to decline to load by reason of a strike of the crew which may delay the ship's sailing.[305]

An exception of "strikes", expressed to be mutually operative, will not absolve the charterer from paying hire for time during which he has been prevented by a strike from employing the ship.[306]

As to the effect of strikes on demurrage, see Arts 157, 158.

Case. Several tramp ships were severally chartered to proceed to one of a number of named places as ordered by the charterers to load full and complete cargoes of wheat in bulk. The charters contained an exception providing "lay or working days shall not count at ports of loading during any time when the loading of cargo is delayed by strikes or any other hindrance of whatsoever nature beyond the charterers' control". The charterers ordered the ships to Vancouver where, between February 17 and May 7, 1953, a strike of elevator men at five out of the seven elevators available to load wheat in bulk was in operation. Some of the orders were given before the strike started and some during its operation. The charterers had made reasonable and proper arrangements with the Canadian Wheat Board, a statutory authority with a monopoly over the export of Canadian grown wheat, for securing delivery of wheat to the ships in time. As a result of the strike the local manager of the Board, acting reasonably in the circumstances, limited the wheat available from the two working elevators to liners, thus excluding the chartered ships, which were delayed for substantial periods after arrival at Vancouver, in some cases after the strike had ended. In actions against the charterers for demurrage, *held* by McNair J. and Sellers and Willmer L.JJ. that loading was delayed by "strikes" or alternatively by a "hindrance" within the exception (by Donovan L.J. on the latter ground only) and

---

[301] *Bulman v Fenwick* [1894] 1 Q.B. 179 at p.185. A charterer cannot rely on delay from a strike, if by having made a proper contract with the suppliers of the cargo the delay could have been avoided: *Dampskibsselskabet Danmark v Poulsen*, 1913 S.C. 1043.

[302] *The Alne Holme* [1893] P. 173. See also *Leonis v Rank (No. 2)* (1908) 13 Com.Cas. 161; affirmed *ibid.* at p.295; *Reardon Smith Line v Ministry of Agriculture* [1962] 1 Q.B. 42 (CA) (the point did not arise in the HL) and contrast *Sametiet M/T Johs Stove v Istanbul Petrol Rafinerisi A/S (The Johs Stove)* [1984] 1 Lloyd's Rep. 38, where an arbitrator's finding of fact that although there was congestion and a strike the effective cause of the vessel being unable to get into the nominated berth was not the strike but congestion, which was not included in the exceptions in the demurrage clause.

[303] *Leonis v Rank (No. 2)* (1908) 13 Com.Cas. 161, affirmed *ibid.* at p.295 (CA) ("strike of railway employees or other labour connected with the working, loading or delivery of the cargo proved to be intended for the steamer"). *Reardon Smith Line v Ministry of Agriculture* [1962] 1 Q.B. 42 (CA). A different result was reached in *Westoll v Lindsay*, 1916 S.C. 782 ("if cargo cannot be loaded by reason of strike . . . the days shall not count during the continuance of such strike"). Contrast *Central Argentine Ry v Marwood* [1915] A.C. 981, in which *Leonis v Rank (No. 2)* apparently was not cited. In *Westoll's* case Lord Johnston at p.780 expressed the view that the decision in *Central Argentine Ry v Marwood* was in conflict with and so overruled *Leonis v Rank (No. 2)*. *Sed quaere.* The two cases can probably be reconciled on their particular facts and the difference in the language of the clause; see the explanations of *Central Argentine Ry v Marwood* in *Reardon Smith Line v Ministry of Agriculture* above, at pp.77, 106, 127. In *J. Vermaas Scheepvaartbedrif NV v Association Technique de l'Importation Charbonniére* [1966] 1 Lloyd's Rep. 583, "time lost through existing strikes preventing or delaying the discharging" was held to apply only to strikes existing at the time when the vessel was available and ready to discharge.

[304] *Salamis Shipping (Panama) SA v Meerbeech & Co* [1971] 2 Q.B. 550 (CA). The case also deals with problems arising under the "Gencon" charter general strike clause and the option there given to receivers of keeping a vessel waiting until a strike is at an end "paying half demurrage after expiration of the time provided for discharging".

[305] *Ropner v Ronnebeck* (1914) 20 Com.Cas. 95.

[306] *Brown v Turner Brightman* [1912] A.C. 12; *cf. Aktieselskabet Lina v Turnbull*, 1907 S.C. 507.

that the charterers were accordingly protected as regards delays both during the currency of the strike and during the period after it had ended when congestion due to the strike still prevailed.[307]

Article 114—Pirates, Robbers by Land or Sea, Thieves   A114

Piracy is "robbery and depredation on the sea or navigable rivers, etc., or by descent from the sea upon the coast, by persons not holding a commission from an established civilised state".[308]

The exception "robbers" refers to robbers by violence external to the ship,[309] and does not include secret theft.[310]

The exception "thieves" refers to thieves external to the ship,[311] and does not apply to thefts committed by men in the service of the ship, such as stevedores.[311]

Thefts or mutinous seizure by the crew, if reasonable precautions have been taken to prevent them, are probably barratry.

It seems doubtful how far "pirates, robbers, and thieves" or "pilferage" are permissible exceptions under the Carriage of Goods by Sea Act 1971. "Piracy" is probably within the words "Act of public enemies" in r.2 of Art.IV of the Schedule; and for loss by robbery, theft or pilferage as well as loss by piracy the shipowner (if the theft, etc., could not have been prevented by reasonable skill and care) may be exempt as being loss "by a cause arising without the actual fault or privity of the shipowner or without the fault or neglect of his agents or servants".[312]

Case 1. A box of diamonds was shipped with the exceptions, "pirates, robbers, thieves, barratry of master and mariners". The box was stolen before delivery; there was no evidence to show by whom. *Held*, that thieves meant "thieves external to the ship", that even if theft by the crew was barratry, still as the ship owners must prove the loss to fall within one of the exceptions[313] (and it might have been the act of a passenger, who was certainly not within the exceptions), the shipowner was liable.[314]

Case 2. Goods were shipped from P to London, under exceptions, "robbers, the dangers of the seas, roads, and rivers". The goods were stolen in transit by rail from Southampton to London. *Held*, that the loss was not by "dangers of the roads" and that "robbers" meant robbers by violence and the shipowner was liable.[315]

---

[307] *Reardon Smith Line v Ministry of Agriculture* [1960] 1 Q.B. 439; affirmed [1962] 1 Q.B. 42 (CA). (The point did not arise in the HL [1963] A.C. 691.)

[308] The definition of the *New English Dictionary*. See *Republic of Bolivia v Indemnity* [1909] 1 K.B. 785; *Piracy Jure Gentium, Re* [1934] A.C. 586 (P.C.); and *Athens Maritime Enterprises Corp v Hellenic Mutual War Risks Association (Bermuda) Ltd* [1982] 2 Lloyd's Rep. 483.

[309] *De Rothschild v Royal Mail Co* (1852) 7 Ex. 734. The phrase "assailing thieves" is sometimes used.

[310] *Taylor v Liverpool S.S. Co* (1874) L.R. 9 Q.B. 546. Cf. *The Prinz Heinrich* (1897) 14 T.L.R. 48. Rule 9 of Sch.I of the Marine Insurance Act 1906, reads: "The term 'thieves' does not cover clandestine theft or a theft committed by any one of the ship's company, whether crew or passengers."

[311] *Steinman v Angier Line* [1891] 1 Q.B. 619.

[312] *City of Baroda (Owners) v Hall Line* (1926) 42 T.L.R. 717; *Hourani v Harrison* (1927) 32 Com.Cas. 305; *Potts v Union S.S. Co of New Zealand* [1946] N.Z.L.R. 276; *Leesh River Tea v British India Steam Navigation Co* [1966] 2 Lloyd's Rep. 193. And see Chapter 20, below.

[313] *Semble*, that if the shipowner had proved theft by the crew, i.e. prima facie barratry, the onus of proving negligence of the owner or master would then be on the shipper.

[314] *Taylor v Liverpool S.S. Co* (1874) L.R. 9 Q.B. 546.

[315] *De Rothschild v Royal Mail Co* (1852) 7 Ex. 724.

Note. Loss by pirates relieves the shipowner of the burden of proving that the loss was not caused by his negligence.[316] But in so far as it is still good law that pirates are a peril of the sea,[317] the advantage of the additional exception is not very great. Mutinous seizure by the passengers has been held "piracy" under an insurance policy.[318]

In ships which usually carry bullion in a bullion room, there is an implied warranty that the bullion room is reasonably fit to resist thieves: unless this is complied with, the ship is unseaworthy.[319]

A115   **Article 115—Loss or Damage from Leakage,[320] Breakage, Heat, Sweat, Rust, etc.**

If reasonable care is used in the stowage of goods, this exception protects the shipowner from liability for any damage or loss to the goods which leak, break, heat, sweat, rust, etc.

It does not by itself protect him from liability for damage resulting from negligent stowage[321] (though it throws the burden of proving such negligence on the shipper),[322] nor the liability for damage to goods from the leakage, etc., of other goods.[323]

Case 1. Goods were shipped, "to be free of breakage, leakage, or damage". On discharge the goods were found damaged by oil. There was no oil in the cargo, but oil was used in the donkey-engine in an adjacent part of the ship. *Held*, that the exception did not relieve the owner from liability for the negligence of his servants, but threw the burden of proving such negligence on the shipper.[324]

Case 2. Sugar was shipped "not liable for leakage". It was damaged by leakage from other sugar which accumulated owing to insufficient means of drainage. *Held*, that the accumulation of leakage was the cause of the damage and that the exception did not cover this.[325]

Case 3. Palm-baskets and barrels of oil were shipped "not accountable for rust, leakage or breakage". The oil leaked and damaged the palm-baskets. *Held*, the exception only covered the leakage of the oil and not the damage to the baskets by such leakage.[326]

---

[316] *Czech v General Steam Co* (1867) L.R. 3 C.P. 14.
[317] So decided as long ago as 1648 in *Pickering v Barkley* (1648) Styles 132, and in other old cases. *Quaere* if the decision is consistent with modern definitions of perils of the sea (see Art.112, above).
[318] *Palmer v Naylor* (1854) 10 Exch. 382.
[319] *Queensland Bank v P. & O. Co* [1898] 1 Q.B. 567. See fn.84, Art.51, above.
[320] An attempt to limit "leakage" to "ordinary leakage", said by the custom of trade to be one per cent, failed in *Ohrloff v Briscall* (1866) 4 Moore P.C.(N.S.) 70 at p.77.
[321] *Phillips v Clark* (1857) 2 C.B.(N.S.) 156, see per Willes J. See also *The Pearlmoor* [1904] P. 286 and *Hellenic Steel Co v Svolomar Shipping Co Ltd (The Komninos S)* [1990] 1 Lloyd's Rep. 541.
[322] *Czech v General Steam Co* (1867) L.R. 3 C.P. 14; *Craig v Delargy* (1879) 6 Rettie 1269; *The Glendarroch* [1894] P. 226.
[323] *The Nepoter* (1869) L.R. 2 A. & E. 375; *Thrift v Youle* (1877) 2 C.P.D. 432; *Ministry of Food v Lamport & Holt* [1952] 2 Lloyd's Rep. 371. This source of liability is often met by an exception of "contact with or smell or evaporation or taint from other goods": or "injurious effects from other goods".
[324] See fn.322, above.
[325] *The Nepoter* (1869) L.R. 2 A. & E. 375. *Case 3* shows that the exception did not cover the damage by leakage, even without accumulation.
[326] *Thrift v Youle* (1877) 2 C.P.D. 432. So "rust" only covers rust of the goods themselves, not damage done by contact with other rusty goods: *Barrow v Williams* (1890) 7 T.L.R. 37. The words "the vessel is not to be accountable for leakage" in the charter of a tanker were held not to apply to leakage from one tanker to another: *Steaua Romana, etc. v A/S Oljefart II* (1934) 50 Ll.L.R. 21 at p.23.

Case 4. Maize was shipped under a bill of lading containing inter alia exceptions of "loss or damage . . . arising from sweating . . . decay . . . heat". The maize was damaged by becoming heated on the voyage, which was due to improper stowage. *Held*, that the shipowners were liable.[327]

Article 116—Fire   A116

By s.186 of the Merchant Shipping Act 1995,[328] the owner or part owner, and any charterer, manager, or operator of a United Kingdom ship[329] is not liable for any loss of or damage to goods by reason of fire[330] on board.[331] A person may lose his exemption under this section if it is proved that the loss resulted from his personal act or omission, committed with the intent to cause such loss or damage or recklessly and with knowledge that such loss or damage would probably result.[332]

The exemption under this section is not conditional upon the fulfilment of the implied warranty of seaworthiness.[333] Therefore proof that the fire was caused by unseaworthiness will not destroy the statutory protection, as it would deprive a shipowner of the benefit of an exception of "fire" in his bill of lading. Nor will such proof deprive him of his right to contribution in general average.[334]

It is possible to contract out of the benefit of this section.[335] Where, therefore, goods are shipped under a bill of lading which contains an exception of "fire", and which also contains an express or implied promise to be liable for loss due to unseaworthiness, the shipowner has been held to have agreed to be liable for loss or damage from fire caused by unseaworthiness, and thereby to have waived the benefit of the section.[336] But such an agreement will only be inferred from some special undertaking in the bill of lading to be liable for fire caused by unseaworthiness: it will not be inferred merely from (a) the insertion of "fire" as an excepted peril, and (b) the existence of the implied warranty of seaworthiness in the bill of lading.[337]

---

[327] *The Pearlmoor* [1904] P. 286. See also, on "sweat damage", *Bowring v Amsterdam London Insurance Co* (1930) 36 Ll.L.R. 309 at pp.326, 327.

[328] See Appendix I.

[329] I.e. a ship registered in the United Kingdom: Merchant Shipping Act 1995, s.1(3).

[330] "Damage by reason of fire" includes damage by smoke and by water used to put out fire: *The Diamond* [1906] P. 282. But mere heating which has not arrived at the stage of incandescence or ignition is not "fire": *Tempus Shipping Co v Louis Dreyfus* [1930] 1 K.B. 699.

[331] The statute only deals "with fire on board". Thus, a fire on board a public lighter bringing goods to the ship is not within the section: *Morewood v Pollok* (1853) 1 E. & B. 743. But the damage need not have been consummated on board. Thus, where maize heated by fire in the bunker coal on board the ship was discharged into lighters and there caught fire as a consequence of being heated by the fire on board, the shipowner was held protected: *Tempus Shipping Co v Louis Dreyfus*, above. Where a bill of lading covers goods elsewhere than on board (e.g. in craft or on quay during transhipment) an exception of "fire whether on board, in craft or on quays or wharves" may be desirable to supplement the protection of the statute. The danger to the shipowner of including an exception of "fire" (as shown by the *Virginia Carolina* case, below) may be avoided by adding a clause "nothing in this bill of lading shall be deemed in any way to limit or affect the operation of section 186 of the Merchant Shipping Act 1995". The exception of "fire unless caused by the actual fault or privity of the carrier" occurs in Art.IV, r.2, of the Schedule to the Carriage of Goods by Sea Act 1971, but the operation of s.186 of the Merchant Shipping Act 1995 is expressly saved by the Carriage of Goods by Sea Act 1995, s. 6(4), and Art.VIII of the Rules.

[332] Merchant Shipping Act 1995, s.186 and Sch.7, Part I, Art.4. See Art.198, below.

[333] *Virginia Carolina Co v Norfolk, etc., Co* [1912] 1 K.B. 229; *Dreyfus v Tempus Shipping Co* [1931] A.C. 726.

[334] *Dreyfus v Tempus Shipping Co*, above.

[335] *Cf. The Satanita* [1897] A.C. 59.

[336] *Virginia, etc., Co v Norfolk, etc., Co*, above.

[337] *Ingram v Services Maritimes* [1914] 1 K.B. 541; *Dreyfus v Tempus Shipping Co*, above.

An exception of "fire" is very commonly inserted in bills of lading. In view of the provisions of the statute this will not generally be necessary for the protection of the owner, the charterer, the manager or the operator of a United Kingdom ship, but may be necessary in the case of fire not on board.[338] In some cases its insertion will actually increase the liabilities of the shipowner.[339]

An exception of fire in a charterparty will not protect charterers against liability for loss by fire caused by the negligence of their servants.[340]

If a fire results from spontaneous combustion, due to the dangerous condition of the goods, of which the shipowner could not reasonably know, the statute or the exception "fire" will protect him, but shippers of other goods damaged will have their remedy against the shippers of the dangerous goods.[341]

Neither the exception "fire on board", nor the provision of s.186 of the Merchant Shipping Act 1995, relieves the shipowner from the liability for general average contribution to the owner of goods damaged by water used in extinguishing a fire on board.[342]

Fire caused by lightning will be an "act of God".

In the Hamburg Rules, the burden of proving that fire resulted from the fault or neglect of the carrier, his servants or agents, rests upon the claimant.[343] This is the only instance under the Rules where the claimant bears the burden of proving fault, rather than the carrier the absence of fault.

A117   **Article 117—Barratry of Master or Mariners**

This exception covers any wilful act of wrongdoing by the master or mariners against the ship and goods without the privity of the shipowner, even though with the intention of benefiting him. Barratry of the mariners includes any crime or fraud causing loss of or damage to the goods,[344] committed by them under such circumstances that they could not reasonably have been prevented by the owner or the master.

Acts to the best of a man's judgment, though erroneous, or through honest incompetence, or illegal acts done by the owner's instructions, or acts whose commission has only been rendered possible by the owner's negligence in

---

[338] See fn.331, above.

[339] *Virginia, etc, Co v Norfolk & Co*, above.

[340] *Polemis v Furness, Withy* [1921] 3 K.B. 560. *Semble*, on the ground that, since shipowners would not be protected by the exception in the case of a fire caused by negligence, the exception being "mutual", must be given the same effect in the case of charterers, even though the primary obligation which the exception qualifies is different in the two cases: see per Horridge J. in *Fagan v Green* [1926] 1 K.B. 102 at p.108. See also *Hollier v Rambler Motors Ltd* [1972] 2 Q.B. 71 (CA).

[341] See above, Art.53.

[342] *Schmidt v Royal Mail Co* (1876) 45 L.J.Q.B. 646; *Greenshields v Stephens* [1908] A.C. 431.

[343] Art.5.4(a), below.

[344] An exception of "loss or damage by barratry" applies not only to physical damage to cargo, but to extra expense incurred by the receivers in discharging the cargo in consequence of the barratrous acts of the crew: *Compania Naviera Bachi v Hosegood* (1938) 60 Ll.L.R. 236.

appointing a drunken or incapable captain,[345] will not come under the exception "barratry".[346]

Negligence, even amounting to reckless carelessness, will not constitute barratry; there must be an intention to injure the ship or goods.[347]

The following acts are barratrous:

Boring holes in a ship to scuttle it[348]; illegal trading with the enemy, or smuggling[349]; intentional breach of port rules so that the ship is forfeited or detained[350]; intentional breach of blockade without owner's authority[351]; fraudulent deviation from course[352]; preventing discharge in order to obtain extra wages.[353]

The following acts are not barratrous:

Deviation, unless accompanied by fraud or crime[354]; failure to observe rules of navigation, without fraud, though such failure is by statute to be taken as wilful default[355]; stowing goods on deck, in spite of shipper's remonstrance.[356]

"Barratry" appears to be an exception that is null and void under the Carriage of Goods by Sea Act 1971.[357]

## Article 118—Negligence of the Master, Mariners and other Servants of the Shipowner	A118

The tendency of the courts is to construe this and similar exceptions strongly against the shipowner[358]; they will not protect him from the consequences of his

---

[345] See per Brett L.J. in *Chartered Mercantile Bank of India v Netherlands India S.N. Co* (1883) 10 Q.B.D. 521 at p.532.

[346] *Arnould on Marine Insurance* (16th edn), §§ 809 *et seq.*, Lord Hardwicke, in *Lewen v Swasso* there cited; Lord Ellenborough in *Earle v Rowcroft* (1806) 8 East 126 at p.139; *Atkinson v G.W. Insurance Co* (1872) 27 L.T. 103 (Am.). See definition in r.11 of Sch.1 to the Marine Insurance Act 1906; and as to the application of this definition to charterparties and bills of lading, see *Compania Naviera Bachi v Hosegood* (1938) 60 Ll.L.R. 236 at p.242.

[347] Channell J. *Briscoe v Powell* (1905) 22 T.L.R. 128 at p.130. The recklessness presumably may be so great as to be in itself evidence of intention. See the discussion of "wilful misconduct" in *Forder v G.W. Ry* [1905] 2 K.B. 532, and in *Smith v G.W. Ry* [1922] 1 A.C. 178.

[348] *The Casca* (1875) L.R. 4 A. & E. 446; *Ionides v Pender* (1873) 27 L.T. 244.

[349] *Earle v Rowcroft* (1806) 8 East 126; *Havelock v Hancill* (1789) 3 T.R. 277; *Pipon v Cope* (1808) 1 Camp. 434.

[350] *Knight v Cambridge* (1724) 1 Str. 581, cited in *Earle v Rowcroft*, above, at p.135; *Robertson v Ewer* (1786) 1 T.R. 127.

[351] *Goldschmidt v Whitmore* (1811) 3 Taunt. 508.

[352] *Ross v Hunter* (1790) 4 T.R. 33; *Mentz Decker & Co v Maritime Co* (1909) 15 Com.Cas. 17.

[353] *Compania Naviera Bachi v Hosegood* (1938) 60 Ll.L.R. 236.

[354] *Earle v Rowcroft*, above; *Phyn v Royal Exchange Co* (1798) 7 T.R. 505.

[355] *Grill v General Colliery Co* (1866) L.R. 1 C.P. 600 at p.610.

[356] *Atkinson v G.W. Insurance Co* (1872) 27 L.T. 103 (Am.).

[357] This observation was approved, obiter, in *Leesh River Tea Co v British India Steam Navigation* [1966] 1 Lloyd's Rep. 450 at p.458 (reversed on other grounds at [1966] 2 Lloyd's Rep. 193). See Art.III, r.8, and Art.IV, r.2, below, in which no changes were made from the similar rules in the 1924 Act.

[358] *Price v Union Lighterage Co* [1904] 1 K.B. 412; *The Pearlmoor* [1904] P. 286. *Cf.* fn.257, above, and cases there cited. See also *Note* 1 at the end of this Article. *Cf.* also *Rosin, etc. Co v Jacobs* (1909) 14 Com.Cas. 78; reversed *ibid.* 247 (CA); affirmed (1910) 15 Com.Cas. 111 (HL); where the words were held to be unambiguous. So where a charter for livestock excepted negligence and unseaworthiness in a general exceptions clause and in another part provided that the ship should provide water for the cattle, it was held by Mathew J. that the exceptions did not operate to excuse a failure to fulfil the positive agreement to provide water: *Vallée v Bucknall* (1900) 16 T.L.R.362. But an exception limiting liability beyond a certain amount may apply, although the loss is caused by negligence: *Baxter's Co v Royal Mail Co* [1908] 2 K.B. 626.

own personal negligence,[359] as in negligently appointing a drunken or incompetent captain, or in negligently giving orders that no pilot should be employed.[360]

But where the master is himself owner or part owner and is sued as such, the exception "negligence of the master" will protect him as to his negligence as master, though not as to his negligence as owner.[361]

This exception will not apply, unless clearly worded to that effect, to relieve the shipowner from the consequences of a breach of his implied undertaking[362] that the ship should be seaworthy at starting.[363]

Where an exception of negligence of the shipowner's servants is clearly expressed, full effect will be given to it, so that even the most culpable recklessness on their part will not render him liable.[364]

The Carriage of Goods by Sea Act 1971, like its predecessor of 1924 imitating the American Harter Act 1893, draws an implied distinction between negligence in the navigation or in the management of the ship and negligence otherwise than in such navigation or management. From consequences of the former it allows the shipowner to be relieved, from those of the latter it does not. Neither Act attempts the task of defining the meaning or effect of the words "navigation or management" of the ship, but their meaning has been the subject of considerable discussion in the cases which are referred to in the notes to this Article.

Case 1. Cargo was shipped under an exception, "negligence or default of master or mariners or others performing their duties". Through careless stowage by master and crew the cargo was damaged. *Held*, the exception freed the shipowner from liability.[365] *Secus*, if the stowage had made the ship unseaworthy at starting.[366]

Case 2. Sugar was shipped under an exception of "loss from any act, neglect, or default of the pilot, master, or mariners in navigating the ship . . . the captain, officers and crew of the vessel in the transmission of the goods, as between the shipper and the ship, shall be considered the agents of the shipper". The sugar was negligently stowed. *Held*, by Denman J., that the damage did not occur "in

---

[359] For a case where personal negligence of the shipowner was proved, see *City of Lincoln v Smith* [1904] A.C. 250, and contrast *Anglo-Argentine Co v Westoll*, discussed *ibid.* p.255. (Reported also, *The Times*, May 15, 1900).

[360] per Brett L.J. in *Chartered Mercantile Bank of India v Netherlands India S.N. Co* (1883) 10 Q.B.D. 521 at p.532; *Norman v Binnington* (1890) 25 Q.B.D. 475 at p.477. See also *Worms v Storey* (1855) 11 Ex. 427 at p.430 (repairs); *Grill v General Colliery Co* (1868) L.R. 1 C.P. 600; 3 C.P. 476 at p.481 (navigation); *Laurie v Douglas* (1846) 15 M. & W. 746 (management of cargo), discussed in *Notara v Henderson* (1872) L.R. 7 Q.B. 225 at p.236; and *The Accomac* (1890) 15 P.D. 208 at 211.

[361] *Westport Coal Co v McPhail* [1898] 2 Q.B. 130.

[362] *Steel v State Line Co* (1878) 3 App.Cas. 72; and Art.47.

[363] See Art.51, above. See also *The Glenfruin* (1885) 10 P.D. 103, where though "accidents to machinery" were excepted in the bill of lading, loss caused by the breaking of a crankshaft through a latent flaw, not discoverable by diligence on the part of the shipowner, was held not within the exception: *Tattersall v National Steam Ship Co* (1884) 12 Q.B.D. 297. So an exception of "Neglect . . . of stevedores or servants . . . in loading, stowing or otherwise" was held not to protect the shipowner where bad stowage constituted unseaworthiness: *Ingram v Services Maritimes* [1913] 1 K.B. 538. See also *Elder Dempster v Paterson Zochonis* [1924] A.C. 522 and compare *The Thorsa* [1916] P. 257.

[364] *Briscoe v Powell* (1905) 22 T.L.R. 128. *Cf. The Torbryan* [1903] P. 35; affirmed *ibid.* p.194. So in *Marriott v Yeoward* [1909] 2 K.B. 987 it was held that even felonious acts by a servant of the shipowner were covered by "any act, neglect, or default, whatsoever" of servants, etc.

[365] *The Duero* (1869) L.R. 2 A. & E. 393.

[366] *Elder Dempster v Paterson Zochonis* [1924] A.C. 522.

navigating the ship"; by Court of Appeal that the damage, resulting from the act of the stevedore, was not within the exception.[367]

Case 3. A ship was chartered to proceed to X and there load sugar, the shipowners not to be responsible "for any act, neglect, or default, whatsoever of their servants during the said voyage". During the loading one of the engineers negligently left open a valve, whereby water entered and damaged the cargo. *Held,* that "voyage" included the whole time during which the vessel was performing the contract contained in the charter and that the exceptions exempted the shipowner from liability.[368]

Case 4. Cargo was carried under an exception of "any act, negligence, or default of master or crew in the navigation of the ship in the ordinary course of the voyage". In discharging cargo in dock, through the removal of a bilge-pump, water entered the hold and damaged the cargo. *Held,* by Butt J., that the damage was caused by joint negligence of an engineer and shore workmen and was not within the exception. *Held,* by the CA, that, assuming there was negligence of the crew, it was not in navigating the ship, or in the ordinary course of the voyage, and the exceptions did not apply.[369]

Case 5. Cargo was carried under an exception of "negligence or default of pilot, master, mariners, engineers, or other persons in the service of the ship, whether in navigating the ship or otherwise". Whilst the ship was being loaded, the goods were damaged by the negligence of the shipowner's men. *Held,* that the exception protected the shipowner from liability.[370]

Case 6. A cargo was shipped under the exceptions "perils of the sea . . . and other accidents of navigation even when occasioned by the negligence of the master". On the voyage perils of the sea caused a leak through which water entered; the master negligently omitted to stop the leak, whereby water continued to enter. *Held,* the exceptions freed the shipowner from liability.[371]

Case 7. A cargo of tin plates was shipped under a bill of lading to which the Carriage of Goods by Sea Act 1924 applied. After the cargo was shipped it became necessary to leave the hatches open so that workmen might go in and out of the hold in order to remove the tail shaft liner. By the negligence of the shipowner's servants the open hatches were not properly protected from rain and the cargo suffered damage. *Held,* that this negligence was not negligence in the management or navigation of the ship.[372]

Case 8. The Charterers of a vessel under a time charter which incorporated Art.IV r.2(a) of the Hague–Visby Rules ordered the vessel to proceed by one of two available routes. The master declined to do so. *Held,* the order was one as to the employment of the vessel and the master's decision was, therefore, not one made "in the navigation" of the ship and the exception did not apply.[373]

Note 1. The general principles of construction relating to whether an exception clause excludes liability for negligence are perhaps most authoritatively set out in *Canada*

---

[367] *Hayn v Culliford* (1878) 3 C.P.D. 410; affirmed (1879) 4 C.P.D. 182. *Cf. The Ferro* [1893] P. 38, where the words were "navigation or management," and the stevedore's negligence stowage was held not to come within them on both of the grounds taken in *Hayn v Culliford*. The expression "loss by negligence of servants" has been held to protect the shipowner from a claim by the cargo-owner, where the goods were by the negligence of his servants delivered to the wrong consignee: *Smackman v General Steam Co* (1908) 13 Com.Cas. 196.

[368] *The Carron Park* (1890) 15 P.D. 203.

[369] *The Accomac* (1890) 15 P.D. 208; doubting *Laurie v Douglas* (1846) 15 M. & W. 746. For a Scottish decision on similar words, see *Gilroy v Price*, 1891, 18 Rettie 569; reversed on another ground in [1893] A.C. 56.

[370] *Norman v Binnington* (1890) 25 Q.B.D. 475; see *Baerselman v Bailey* [1895] 2 Q.B. 301, where one passage at the end of the judgment in *Norman v Binnington* is disapproved: see also *De Clermont v General Steam Navigation Co* (1891) 7 T.L.R. 187 and *Packwood v Union Castle Co* (1903) 20 T.L.R. 59.

[371] *The Cressington* [1891] P. 152; so if the sea-water was negligently admitted to the wrong tank by the engineer: *Blackburn v Liverpool Co* [1902] 1 K.B. 290. Contrast *The Christel Vinnen* [1924] P. 208 (CA), where the shipowner was held liable for damage caused by unseaworthiness, though that damage could have been minimised if the master had not been negligent.

[372] *Gosse Millerd v Canadian Govt. Merchant Marine* [1929] A.C. 223.

[373] *Whistler International v Kawasak iKisen Kaisha Ltd (The Hill Harmony)* [2001]1 Lloyd's Rep. 147.

Steamship Lines v The King.[374] Negligence is most obviously excluded where the exception clause uses the word "negligence" or a synonym for it. But general words such as "not responsible for damage, however caused" will normally be construed as excluding liability for negligence where the defendant could realistically only have been liable for negligence; but will normally not be construed as excluding liability for negligence, as opposed to strict liability, where the defendant's liability can be strict.

It has been held that "error of navigation" does not protect against the negligence of the owners and their servants because, even if it were the law that a carrier's liability encompasses negligence only, the legal position is unclear[375] and therefore protection against the possibility of strict liability could reasonably have been sought.[376]

Note 2. The form of the exception in cases to which the Carriage of Goods by Sea Act 1971 applies has now been stereotyped by Art.IV, r.(2)(a) of the Schedule to that Act in the words "Act, neglect, or default of the master, mariner, pilot, or the servants of the carrier in the navigation or in the management of the ship."[377]

Both this wording and that used in the earlier contractual exceptions, in the Harter Act, and in other Acts which copied the wording of the Harter Act, have given rise to considerable discussion. Two main questions appear to arise: (1) Over what period of time or place does the exception extend? (2) What is comprehended in the words "navigation or management of the ship"?[378] The authorities are not in a very satisfactory condition, but in view of the vagueness of the words to be construed this is hardly surprising.

(1) It seems that the exceptions in the contract of affreightment, unless otherwise worded, limit the shipowner's liability during the whole time in which he is in possession of the goods as carrier.[379] Accordingly an exception of negligence "during the voyage" was held by Sir J. Hannen to cover negligence during loading and to apply to the whole time during which the vessel was engaged in performing the contract contained in the charter,[380] and an exception of "damage in navigating the ship, or otherwise" was held to cover damage done during loading.[381] So also in club policies of insurance. In *Good v London Mutual Association*,[382] a sea-cock and bilge-cock were left open whilst the ship was moored alongside the quay at a coaling port, with the result that water entered the

---

[374] [1952] A.C. 192 (P.C.). See also *Travers v Cooper* [1915] 1 K.B. 73; *Pyman v Hull and Barnsley Co* [1915] 2 K.B. 729; *Rutter v Palmer* [1922] 2 K.B. 87; *Calico Printers' Association v Barclays Bank* (1931) 36 Com.Cas. 197; *Alderslade v Hendon Laundry* [1945] K.B. 189; *Varnish v The Kheti* (1949) 82 Ll.L.R. 525; *Hollier v Rambler Motors Ltd* [1972] 2 Q.B. 71; *Gillespie Bros v Bowles Transport* [1973] 1 Q.B. 400; *Smith v South Wales Switchgear Ltd* [1978] 1 W.L.R. 165; *Lamport & Holt Lines v Coubro & Scrutton (The Raphael)* [1982] 2 Lloyd's Rep. 42; *Industrie Chimiche Italia Centrale v Nea Ninemia Shipping Co (The Emmanuel C)* [1983] 1 Lloyd's Rep. 310; *E.E. Caledonia Ltd v Orbit Valve Co Europe* [1993] 2 Lloyd's Rep. 418 (indemnity clause).

[375] Arts 105–106, above.

[376] *Industrie Chimiche Italia Centrale v Nea Ninemia Shipping Co (The Emmanuel C)* [1983] 1 Lloyd's Rep. 310. The same conclusion was reached in *Seven Seas Transportation Ltd v Pacifico Guior Marine Corp* [1984] 1 Lloyd's Rep. 588.

[377] See Chapter 20, below.

[378] *Semble*, the owner would be covered if his crew improperly abandoned his ship: *Bulgaris v Bunge & Co* (1933) 38 Com.Cas. 103 at p.114.

[379] *Norman v Binnington* (1890) 25 Q.B.D. 475 at p.478; *The Carron Park* (1890) 15 P.D. 203, per Wright J. in *De Clermont v General Steam Navigation Co* (1891) 7 T.L.R. 187 at p.188.

[380] *The Carron Park*, above.

[381] *Norman v Binnington*, above. *Cf. The Glenochil* [1896] P. 10, in which an exception "faults in management" was held to cover putting water into the ballast tanks while the cargo was being discharged, without ascertaining that the pipes were in order. See also *Blackburn v Liverpool Co* [1902] 1 K.B. 290; and *The Rodney* [1900] P. 112.

[382] (1871) L.R. 6 C.P. 563. In *The Warkworth* (1884) 9 P.D. 20; affirmed *ibid.* p.145, negligent inspection of the steam steering gear by an overlooker on shore, whereby the ship steered badly and did damage, was held "improper navigation", within s.54 of the Merchant Shipping Act 1862 which limited the owner's liability, and Bowen L.J. defined it as "improper navigation by the owner of the ship or his agents, including using a ship which is not in a condition to be so employed".

hold and damaged the cargo. This was held "improper navigation" within the policy; Willes J. defining the phrase as "something improperly done with the ship or part of the ship in the course of the voyage". Being asked *arguendo* whether bad stowage would be improper navigation, Willes J. said: "Certainly, unless in a port where stevedores are employed," the qualification being the point taken by the Court of Appeal in *Hayn v Culliford*.[383] Smith J. qualified this as "bad stowage which affects the safe sailing of the ship". In *Carmichael's* case,[384] a cargo of wheat was damaged through improper caulking of a cargo-port by the shipowner's servants before the voyage commenced: and it was held by the Court of Appeal that this was "improper navigation" within the policy, because it affected the safe sailing of the ship with regard to the safety of the goods on board during the voyage. On the other hand, in *Canada Shipping Co v British Shipowner's Association*[385] a cargo of wheat was damaged by being stowed in a dirty hold, and this was held by the Court of Appeal not to be improper navigation. The distinction between these two cases appears to depend not upon the time when the negligence first took place, which in both cases was before the ship sailed on her voyage, but upon the fact that in the former case the safe sailing of the ship was affected whereas in the latter the safe sailing of the ship was not, but the proper and careful carriage of the cargo alone was interfered with. In *The Accomac*,[386] where a pipe was left open through the joint negligence of the ship's engineer and shore workmen repairing the ship, whereby water entered and damaged the cargo in the course of its discharge, the CA held that this negligence was neither in navigation nor in the ordinary course of the voyage, and they doubted the decision in *Laurie v Douglas*,[387] where the capsizing of a ship while moored in dock was held a danger of navigation. In *The Glenochil*[388] the pumping of water into the ballast tank to secure stability was held to be management of the ship, notwithstanding that she was moored alongside the quay and in process of being discharged. In *The Southgate*,[389] where water entered through a valve improperly left open while the vessel was moored with cargo in her before starting, Barnes J. seems to have thought that the accident was one of "navigation", while he decided that it was clearly an "accident of the sea and other waters". It would seem that "navigation in the course of the voyage" cannot be extended to beyond the actual sailing of the ship (though it is submitted on the whole course of the authorities that the better view would have been to consider the words as applicable to the whole adventure the shipowner undertakes, i.e. the management and conduct of his ship as a cargo-carrying vessel); but that "management", and, perhaps, "navigation" by itself, will extend to the whole of such adventure.

(2) The words "management and navigation" appear to have been construed for the first time by an English court in *The Ferro*,[390] where Sir F. Jeune and Barnes J. held under a bill of lading excepting "damage from any act, neglect, or default of the pilot, master, or mariners in the navigation or management of the vessel": (i) that the stevedore's negligence was not covered; (ii) that, if it was, improper stowage was not "navigation or management of the vessel". The meaning of these words was further considered in a number of cases determined before the passing of the Carriage of Goods by Sea Act 1924. In *The Glenochil*,[391] where the engineer pumped water into the ballast tank to secure

---

[383] *Hayn v Culliford* (1878) 3 C.P.D. 410; affirmed (1879) 4 C.P.D. 182.
[384] *Carmichael v Liverpool S.S. Association* (1887) 19 Q.B.D. 242.
[385] (1889) 23 Q.B.D. 342.
[386] (1890) 15 P.D. 208. See, also, on joint negligence of the crew and a third party, *Minister of Food v Reardon Smith Line* [1951] 2 Lloyd's Rep. 265.
[387] (1846) 15 M. & W. 746.
[388] [1896] P. 10.
[389] [1893] P. 329.
[390] [1893] P. 38.
[391] [1896] P. 10.

stability,[391] without inspecting the pipes, and the water through a broken pipe damaged the cargo, the Divisional Court held that this was in the "management", even if it was not in the "navigation" of the vessel. Both in *The Rodney*,[392] where the boatswain in trying to get water out of the forecastle by freeing a pipe with a rod broke the pipe so that water got to the cargo; and in *Rowson v Atlantic Transport Co*,[393] where butter was damaged by the negligent working of refrigerating machinery, the casualty was held to be a "fault in management". In *The Renée Hyaffil*[394] the master stayed in a port of call from his fear of German submarines or mines, and the cargo was damaged by the delay; it is not surprising that the court held that this was not "a fault or error in navigation or management". In *Owners of S.S. Lord v Newsum*,[395] an error of the master in choosing the route he should pursue was held not to be "negligence, default, or error in judgment in the management or navigation of the ship". In *Toyosaki v Société les Affreteurs*[396] it was held that neglect by the master to give orders to keep steam up in port was not "negligence, default, or error in judgment of the master in the management of the steamer".

Since the passing of the Act of 1924 the meaning of the words has been considered more particularly in *Hourani v Harrison*,[397] *Gosse Millerd v Canadian Govt. Merchant Marine*,[398] *Foreman & Ellams v Federal S.N. Co*,[399] *Leesh River Tea Co v British India Steam Navigation Co*[400] and *International Packers v Ocean S.S. Co*.[401] In the first the loss was occasioned by the theft of the servants of the stevedore who was employed in discharging the ship at her destination; in the second a cargo of tin plates was damaged by rain-water making its way through improperly covered hatches, which were left open to enable workmen to enter and leave the hold in order to execute repairs to the ship; in the third a cargo of meat was damaged by the mismanagement of the refrigerating machinery used for cooling the cargo; and in the fourth the cover of a storm valve on a sanitary pipe was stolen by a stevedore. In each of these cases it was held that the injury did not occur in the management or navigation of the ship. In the fifth case[2] the application of these principles excused from liability. There locking bars had been provided for securing the hatchway covers after the tarpaulin had been battened down, pursuant to Lloyd's Register Rules and the Load Line (Amendment) Rules 1946. They had not, however, been used and in consequence heavy seas stripped these tarpaulins from the hatch covers of a hold in the well deck and water entered the hold and damaged the cargo, though its amount was insufficient to endanger the ship. It was *held* that there had been a failure of the ship's main defences against seaworthiness constituting "neglect to take reasonable care of the ship or some part of its as distinct from the cargo". The principles[402]

---

[392] [1900] P. 112.
[393] [1903] 2 K.B. 666. Some of the judges in treating it as a fault in management of the ship relied on the fact that the refrigerating machinery was used to cool the ship's provisions as well as the cargo. If it had cooled only the cargo the decision would apparently have been otherwise.
[394] (1916) 32 T.L.R. 660.
[395] [1920] 1 K.B. 846.
[396] (1922) 27 Com.Cas. 157; and see *Suzuki v Beynon* (1926) 42 T.L.R. 269.
[397] (1927) 32 Com.Cas. 305 (CA).
[398] [1929] A.C. 223 (HL).
[399] [1928] 2 K.B. 424.
[400] [1966] 1 Lloyd's Rep. 450; [1966] 2 Lloyd's Rep. 193 (CA).
[401] [1955] 2 Lloyd's Rep. 218 at pp.230, 234.
[402] Different considerations applied in construing the words "improper management of the ship" in s.1 of the Merchant Shipping Act 1900, which were to be construed more widely: *The Athelvictor* [1946] P. 42. In that case the negligence of the crew in leaving open certain sea valves, whereby petrol escaped and subsequently ignited, was held to come within the statute and thus entitle the shipowners to limit their liability. Pilcher J., however, expressed the view that had the matter arisen on a claim by cargo-owners for loss of the petrol made on a bill of lading, incorporating the Harter Act or Carriage of Goods by Sea Act, the facts of the case would not have been covered by an exception of negligence in the management of the ship. In *The Teal* (1949) 82 Ll.L.R. 414, the same judge applied the words to improper stowage of dangerous cargo which endangered the safety of the ship.

upon which the decisions depended were summarised as follows in the dissenting judgment of Greer L.J.,[403] which was approved in the House of Lords in *Gosse Millerd v Canadian Govt. Merchant Marine*.[404] If the cause of the damage is solely or even primarily a neglect to take reasonable care of the cargo, the ship is liable. But if the cause of the damage is a neglect to take reasonable care of the ship or some part of the ship, as distinct from the cargo, the ship is released from liability. If, however, the negligence is not negligence towards the ship but only a negligent failure to use the apparatus of the ship for the protection of the cargo the ship is not so relieved.[405] Presumably *The Touraine*[406] (where Hill J. held (following *The Rodney*) that the fracture of a water pipe leading from the seamen's wash-house, by the negligent use of an iron rod, after the commencement of the voyage, in order to clear the pipe of an obstruction and put the wash-house floor in proper order, was negligence in the management of the ship) was so decided because the clearing of the pipe was management of the ship in a matter affecting the ship as a ship and not primarily affecting either the cargo or the apparatus of the ship for the protection of the cargo. In *Caltex Refining Co Pty Ltd v BHP Transport Ltd (The Iron Gippsland)*[407] the negligence consisted in a failure properly to operate the inert gas system. Even though it was accepted that the system existed fundamentally for the protection of the vessel, it was held that this was achieved through the management of cargo and accordingly this was not an act in the management of the vessel. In *Whistler International v KawasakiKisen Kaisha Ltd (The Hill Harmony)*[408] it was held that, in circumstances where the master had no rational justification for preferring one route to another, a decision taken as to the route to be sailed was an act which related to the employment of the vessel and not to navigation. In *CSAV v MS ER Hamburg Schiffahrtsgesellschaft mbH & Co KG*[409] it was assumed for the purpose of deciding various preliminary issues that the explosion on board (which damaged both the ship and cargo) was caused by the fact that bunkers were heated to a temperature above that required to keep the fuel oil reasonably thin for pumping. Morison J. held that, although the heating of the bunkers indirectly adversely affected the cargo, it was properly categorised as an act neglect or default in the management of the ship.

The question whether a particular person is a "servant" of the carrier within the meaning of the exceptions would seem to depend upon the capacity in which that person was acting at the time when the negligence occurred, e.g. a stevedore would not be included under the words "pilot, master or mariners" (*The Ferro*[410]), but might be included if employed direct by the steamer: *Hourani v Harrison*,[411] and *Machu v L. & S. W. Ry.*[412]

Note 3. "*At owner's risk*", "*at shipper's risk*", "*at merchant's risk*". It is now clear that these expressions will not exempt the charterer or owner from his own negligence.[413] In

---

[403] [1928] 1 K.B. 717 at p.749.
[404] See fn.398, above. See also *Rey Banano del Pacifico C.A. v TransportesNavierosEcuatorianos (The Isla Fernandina)* [2000] 2 Lloyd's Rep. 15 in which this page of the 20th edn was referred to with apparent approval by Langley J. at p.35.
[405] See *The Farrandoc* [1967] 2 Lloyd's Rep. 276.
[406] [1928] P. 58.
[407] (1994) 34 N.S.W.L.R. 29. *Sed quaere.*
[408] [2001]1 Lloyd's Rep. 147.
[409] [2006] EWHC 483 (Comm).
[410] [1893] P. 38.
[411] (1927) 32 Com.Cas. 305.
[412] (1848) 2 Ex. 415.
[413] *Svenssons v Cliffe S.S. Co* [1932] 1 K.B. 490 at pp.496–499; *Exercise Shipping Co Ltd v Boy Maritime Lines Ltd (The Fantasy)* [1991] 2 Lloyd's Rep. 391; [1992] 1 Lloyd's Rep. 235; *The Visurgis* [1999] 1 Lloyd's Rep. 218. Suggestions to the contrary in *Wade v Cockerline* (1905) 10 Com.Cas. 47 and *Burton v English* (1883) 12 Q.B.D. 218 cannot stand in the light of subsequent authority.

The Galileo,[414] a bill of lading provided for transhipment "at shipper's risk" and with "liberty to the ship to convey goods in lighters to and from steamers at risk of the owners of the goods". The shipowner was held liable for loss of goods at the port of transhipment, caused by the unseaworthiness of a lighter used to store the goods pending shipment. In *The Forfarshire*,[415] "all transporting at owner's risk" appeared in a towage contract by which repairers agreed to provide all means of transportation. The clause was held not to cover loss due to the deficiency of the tackle provided. In *Whitworth v Pacific S.N. Co*,[416] the words "lighterage at owner's risk" did not excuse the shipowner from liability for negligent stowage in a lighter at the port of discharge. In *The Fantasy*, a provision that cargo could be shipped on deck "at charterer's risk" was held not to exempt the shipowner from the negligent performance by the master of the shipowner's express contractual obligation to tighten and check the lashing, but would have exempted the shipowner from liability for any negligence of third parties to whom he had delegated the performance of his contractual duties.[417] In *Sunlight Mercantile Pte Ltd v Ever Lucky Shipping Co Ltd*[418] the bills of lading provided that the cargo was shipped on deck "at shipper's risk" and this wording was held not to protect the ship owner from liability for unseaworthiness.[419]

A119   **Article 119—Exception of Jettison**

This exception will cover all claims made under the bill of lading and arising from the jettison of goods properly stowed; but will not in the absence of clear words cover claims arising out of the jettison of goods improperly stowed on deck.[420]

It is submitted that it will not protect the shipowner against claims for general average contribution arising from proper jettison of goods.[421] Apart from an express exception of jettison, the shipowner will be protected in the case of jettison properly made for the common safety.[422]

A120   **Article 120—Who can sue for Failure to carry Goods safely**

A. *In tort*, there can sue:

The legal owner or person with possessory title[423] to the goods at the time of

---

[414] [1915] A.C. 1991.

[415] [1908] P. 339.

[416] (1926) 25 Ll.L.R. 573. See also *Mitchell v London & York Ry* (1875) L.R. 10 Q.B. 256, and *Mersey Shipping and Transport Co v Rea* (1925) 21 Ll.L.R. 375.

[417] [1991] 2 Lloyd's Rep. 391; [1992] 1 Lloyd's Rep. 235. See also *JJ Case (Australia) Pty Ltd v Tasman Express Line Ltd (The Canterbury Express)* (1990) 102 F.L.R. 59 (Aus); *Sunlight Mercantile Pte Ltd v Ever Lucky Shipping Co Ltd* [2004] 1 S.L.R. 171 (Sing.); [2004] 2 Lloyd's Rep. 174; *PT Soonlee Metalindo v Synergy Shipping Pte Ltd* [2007] 4 S.L.R. 51 (Sing.).

[418] [2004] 2 Lloyd's Rep. 174.

[419] But see the decision of Langley J. in *Transocean Liners Reederei GmbH v Euxine Shipping Co Ltd (The Imvros)* [1999] 1 Lloyd's Rep. 848 in which the owners were held to be under no responsibility for loss of or damage to cargo carried on deck even though the ship was unseaworthy. Although this conclusion was doubted in *Sunlight Mercantile* it can be justified on the basis that the ship was unseaworthy only because of a breach by Charterers of their obligations in relation to lashing. Langley J. held that the owners had complied with their obligations in relation to seaworthiness.

[420] *Royal Exchange S. Co v Dixon* (1886) 12 App.Cas. 11 and *Newall v Royal Exchange Co* (1885) 1 T.L.R. 490 read in the light of *Kenya Railways v Antares Co Pte Ltd (The Antares No. 2)* [1987] 1 Lloyd's Rep. 424 at p.429 (CA) and *Daeoww Heavy Industries Ltd v Klipriver Shipping Ltd* [2003] EWCA Civ. 451.

[421] On authority of *Schmidt v Royal Mail Co* (1876) 45 L.J.Q.B. 646; *Crooks v Allan* (1879) 5 Q.B.D. 38.

[422] See Art.133.

[423] *Semble*, this includes the immediate right to possession of, e.g. a bailee: *Transcontinental Express Ltd v Custodian Security Ltd* [1988] 1 Lloyd's Rep. 128; *The Hamburg Star* [1994] 1 Lloyd's Rep. 399.

the tort complained of[424] whether or not such person is a party to the bill of lading.[425]

The consignee of goods will be deemed to have an interest in the goods unless the contrary appear.[426]

The nominal shipper cannot sue in tort if he ships merely as agent for the real owner.[427]

B. *In contract*, there can sue:

(1) The shipper,[428] unless he acted merely as agent for another, in which case the principal can sue[429] and the agent cannot.[430]

(2) The charterer, who may recover substantial damages if he is the owner or entitled to possession of the goods even if they are not at his risk.[431] If he himself had no interest in the goods, he may recover substantial damages for the benefit of the person who does have such an interest if, but only if, the charterparty does not contemplate that the carrier will enter into separate contracts of carriage with whomsoever may become the owner of the goods.[432]

---

[424] *Margarine Union v Cambay Prince S.S. Co* [1969] 1 Q.B.D. 219 (negligence); *Leigh and Sillivan Ltd v Aliakmon Ltd* [1986] A.C. 785 (negligence). See also *Mitsui & Co Ltd v Flota Mercante Grancolombiana SA* [1988] 2 Lloyd's Rep. 208; *Nippon Yusen Kaisha v Ramjiban Serourgee* [1938] A.C. 429 (conversion). In *Obestain Inc v National Mineral Development Corporation Ltd (The Sanix Ace)* [1987] 1 Lloyd's Rep. 465, 468, Hobhouse J. said that a legal owner's claim might be defeated if he has a bare proprietary title without any right to possession of the goods. But it should be noted that the refusal to allow those without a proprietary interest in the goods to sue in the tort of negligence flows simply from the classification of the loss as purely economic. Nor can a time charterer, not in possession of a ship or goods, recover in negligence from a tortfeasor, who has damaged the ship or caused the loss of the goods, damages for the loss of the use of the ship under the time charter or the loss of freight in respect of the carriage of the goods: *Remorquage a Hélice v Bennetts* [1911] 1 K.B. 243; *The Okehampton* [1913] P. 173; *Chargeurs Réunis v English and American S.S. Co* (1921) 9 Ll.L.R. 464; *Elliott Steam Tug Co Ltd v The Shipping Controller* [1922] 1 K.B. 127, 139; *Candlewood Navigation Corp v Mitsui O.S.K. Lines Ltd* [1986] A.C. 1; *cf. Morrison Steamship Co v Greystoke Castle (Cargo Owners)* [1947] A.C. 265 at pp.275, 279, 280, 296. Art.29, above. As regards the position of an equitable owner of goods, the House of Lords in *Leigh & Sillavan Ltd v Aliakmon Ltd* [1986] A.C. 785, 812, held that, unless the equitable ownership conferred a possessory title (as in *Healey v Healey* [1915] 1 K.B. 938) the equitable owner could not sue in the tort of negligence for damage to the goods unless he joined the legal owner as a party to the action. For a consideration of the position in circumstances where the damage is progressive see *Homburg Houtimport BV v Agrosin Private Ltd (The Starsin)* [2003] 1 Lloyd's Rep. 571; [2003] UKHL 12.
[425] But see the doubt of Maugham L.J. in *The Arpad* [1934] P. 189 at p.231, as to whether there is a right of action in tort in a case based simply on non-delivery.
[426] *Coleman v Lambert* (1839) 5 M. & W. 502 at p.505; *Tronson v Dent* (1853) 8 Moore P.C. 419 at p.458. As to bailees, not liable over to their bailor, see *The Winkfield* [1902] P. 42, in which case it is very doubtful whether the alleged bailee has possession at all.
[427] *Moores v Hopper* (1807) 2 B. & P.N.R. 411; but *cf. The Winkfield*, above.
[428] The shipper under a bill of lading within the Carriage of Goods by Sea Act 1992 loses his right to sue once another person becomes the lawful holder of the bill: see Art.16.
[429] *Anderson v Clark* (1824) 2 Bing. 20; *Fragano v Long* (1825) 4 B. & C. 219.
[430] See fn.428, above.
[431] *The Sanix Ace*, above.
[432] *The Albazero* [1977] A.C. 774 explaining *Joseph v Knox* (1813) 3 Camp. 320; *Dunlop v Lambert* (1839) 6 Cl. & Fin. 600 at p.626. In the shipping context it is difficult to conceive of any circumstances in which the principle in *Dunlop v Lambert* could now be invoked, except perhaps in the case of a charterparty which expressly provided that bills of lading should not be issued. But in the realm of defective buildings the principle of *Dunlop v Lambert* was invoked by the House of Lords in *Linden Gardens Trust Ltd v Lenesta Sludge Disposals Ltd* [1994] 1 A.C. 85 (and see also *Darlington B.C. v Wiltshier Northern Ltd* [1995] 1 W.L.R. 68) so as to enable the owner of a building to recover substantial contractual damages based on the loss of a subsequent owner to whom assignment was prohibited. For a dubious application of the principle in Singapore see *The Neptune Agate* [1994] 3 S.L.R. 786.

(3) Any person in whom rights of suit are rested under the Carriage of Goods by Sea Act 1992.[433]

(4) Any person who, by presenting the bill of lading and taking delivery of the goods thereunder, or otherwise, has made a new implied contract of carriage with the shipowner.[434]

A121   **Article 121—Who can be sued for Negligent Carriage of the Goods**

A. *The shipowner.* (1) *In tort*[435] if he is or was in possession of the goods by his agents, there being no charter amounting to a demise[436]; (2) *in contract*, by any person with whom he has contracted, or by the assignees of such person.

B. *The charterer.* (1) *In tort*, if he is or was in possession of the goods, his charter amounting to a demise; (2) *in contract*, by any person with whom he has contracted, or the assignees of such person.

C. *The master.* (1) *In tort*, if he is or was in possession of the goods or the goods were lost or damaged by his negligence[437]; (2) *in contract*, by any person to whom he has made himself personally liable on a contract.[438]

D. *Members of the crew*, if they have negligently handled or cared for the goods and thus caused loss or damage.[439]

E. *An independent contractor*,[440] employed by someone in contractual relationship with the goods owner.[441]

Note. The question of the extent (if any) to which third parties can rely on (or are bound by) the terms and conditions of (and in particular any exemption clauses contained in) the contract of carriage is dealt with in Chapter 2.

---

[433] Art.14. For the measure of damages see Art.195, below.

[434] See Art.15.

[435] *The Termagant* (1914) 19 Com.Cas. 239; *Lee Cooper v Jeakins* [1967] 2 Q.B. 1; *cf. Margarine Union v Cambay Prince S.S. Co* [1967] 2 Lloyd's Rep. 315.

[436] See Art.28; and *cf. Baumwoll v Furness* [1893] A.C. 8.

[437] See the decision of the CA in *Adler v Dickson* [1955] 1 Q.B. 158, and particularly the judgment of Jenkins L.J. at p.713, and also *Midland Silicones v Scruttons* [1962] A.C. 446.

[438] But apparently the master, if sued on a bill of lading signed by himself merely as agent for the charterers, cannot be sued in contract: see per Bingham J. in *Repetto v Millar's Karri and Jarrah Forests* (1901) 6 Com.Cas. 129 at p.135. "The master therefore could not sue, and it follows as a consequence that he cannot sue."

[439] See fn.437, above, and *Lee Cooper v Jeakins* [1967] 2 Q.B. 1.

[440] *Lee Cooper v Jeakins*, above, in which the principle of *Donoghue v Stevenson* [1932] A.C. 562 was applied to render liable in tort to the goods owner a carrier by land employed by a forwarding agent for negligence of the carrier's driver in failing to protect the goods against theft. On the question whether an independent contractor is entitled to the benefit of exceptions in the contract of carriage, see the *Note* at the end of this Article.

[441] A sub-contractor employed under a contract which is within the apparent authority of his immediate employer cannot be held liable in tort to the goods-owner, if he obeys his immediate employer's instructions under the contract and commits no breach of its terms: *Mayfair Photographic v Baxter Hoare* [1972] 1 Lloyd's Rep. 410.

CHAPTER 12

PERFORMANCE OF THE CONTRACT—THE VOYAGE

Article 122—"Final Sailing"[1]

A VESSEL has finally sailed from her port of loading when she has passed the limits of the port,[2] ready for her voyage with the purpose of proceeding on her voyage and without any intention of coming back.[3]

The fact that she is towed and has no sail set, or that she is driven back into port by a storm, will not prevent her having "finally sailed".[3] But if her clearances are not on board, or she is not ready for sea, the fact that she has left the port will not constitute final sailing.[4]

The term "port" is to be taken in its business, popular, and commercial sense,[5] and not in its legal definition for revenue or pilotage purposes.[6]

"*Port Charges*" include all charges a vessel has to pay before she leaves a port and therefore includes light dues, where such are claimable,[7] but the term does not include pilotage dues.[8]

Case 1. A ship was chartered, the owners to receive one-third of the freight within eight days "from final sailing from her last port in the United Kingdom". She was loaded at Penarth, and towed out eight miles, bringing her three miles into the Bristol Channel, outside the commercial, but inside the fiscal port of Cardiff. She then cast anchor, owing to threatening weather. A storm arose, which drove her ashore within the commercial port of Cardiff. *Held*, that she had finally sailed from her last port, so as to entitle her owners to an advance of one-third of the freight.[9]

---

[1] Whether a vessel has "finally sailed" is chiefly of importance in determining whether "advance freight" is payable. See *Case 1*, below.
[2] "Sailing" in insurance cases, where there is a warranty to sail before a particular day, has been held to be "breaking ground", i.e. leaving her moorings ready for sea, though not leaving port; see Parke B. in *Roelandts v Harrison* (1854) 9 Ex. 444 at p.456. See also *Mersey Mutual v Poland* (1910) 15 Com.Cas. 205.
[3] *Price v Livingstone* (1882) 9 Q.B.D. 679; *Roelandts v Harrison* (1854) 9 Ex. 444; *S.S. Garston v Hickie, Borman & Co* (1885) 15 Q.B.D. 580; approved by Lord Watson in *Hunter v Northern Ins Co* (1888) 13 App.Cas. 717 at p.733; *Leonis Co v Rank* [1908] 1 K.B. 499 at pp.519 *et seq.*; *Hall Bros v Paul* (1914) 19 Com.Cas. 384; *Goodbody and Balfour, Re* (1899) 5 Com.Cas. 59 (port of Manchester). "Port" may mean a usual place of loading within a legal port. *The Mary Thomas* (1896) 12 T.L.R. 511.
[4] *Thompson v Gillespy* (1855) 5 E. & B. 209; *Hudson v Bilton* (1856) 6 E. & B. 565.
[5] See fn.3, above. See also *President of India v Olympia Sauna Shipping Co SA (The Ypatia Halcoussi)* [1984] 2 Lloyd's Rep. 455.
[6] On the other hand, in *Caffarini v Walker* (1876) I.R. 10 C.L. 250, and *M'Intosh v Sinclair* (1877) I.R. 11 C.L. 456, the "port of Newry" was taken in its legal and fiscal sense and not as a geographical expression. On the distinction, see also, *Nicholson v Williams* (1871) L.R. 6 Q.B. 632. In *Nielsen v Wait* (1885) 14 Q.B.D. 516, the "port of Gloucester" seems to be taken as the legal or fiscal port. In *S.S. Garston v Hickie, Borman & Co*, above, Brett M.R. said, "the port may extend beyond the place of loading and unloading; if the port authorities are exercising authority over ships within a certain space of water, and shipowners are submitted to that jurisdiction, that is the strongest evidence that that space of water is accepted as the commercial port".
[7] *Newman v Lamport* [1896] 1 Q.B. 20. *Cf. Scales v Temperley S.S. Co* (1925) 23 Ll.L.R. 312.
[8] *Whittal v Rahtkens* (1907) 12 Com.Cas. 226. *Cf. Societa Ungherese v Hamburg SA Ges.* (1912) 17 Com.Cas. 216. As to "dock dues" see *The Katherine* (1913) 30 T.L.R. 52, and *The Hamlet* [1924] P. 224, where it was held that "dock dues" meant dock dues computed on the correct basis. As to "dues on cargo", see *London Transport Co v Bessler* (1908) 24 T.L.R. 531.
[9] *Price v Livingstone* (1882) 9 Q.B.D. 679. In *Roelandts v Harrison*, and S.S. *Garston v Hickie, Borman & Co*, above, fn.3 the port was also the port of Cardiff, the ship in each case was ready to sail, and on her way to sea, but had not got inside the commercial port.

Case 2. A ship being loaded and cleared, came into the roads and cast anchor three miles from X harbour, not intending to return. The shrouds and cables were not ready for sailing, bills of lading were not signed, and the mate was not on board. She was lost the same day, before the deficiencies were supplied. *Held*, she had not finally sailed.[10]

A123   **Article 123—Master's Authority on the Voyage**[11]

The master on a voyage occupies a double position. First as agent of the shipowner he has the duty of doing what is necessary to carry out the contract[12] and of taking reasonable care of the goods entrusted to him.[13] If extraordinary steps are necessary,[14] such as sale,[15] borrowing money on bottomry,[16] salvage agreements,[17] transhipment,[18] jettison,[19] deviation or delay,[20] he has power to bind his owner by his action, provided that there is no possibility of communicating with him.[21] However, except where circumstances render him an agent of necessity, he has no implied authority to enter into salvage agreements on behalf of cargo owners, however reasonable the terms may be.[22]

He can also bind the charterer by his actions in doing what is necessary on the charterer's part to carry out the contract, but not beyond, except by express instructions.[23]

Note. Thus the captain is the agent of the owners in providing those necessaries for the voyage which by the terms of the charter are to be paid for by the owners, or necessaries for the ship's sailing where it is in the interest of the owners that the ship should sail[24]; he is the agent of the charterers for providing those necessaries for the voyage which are by the charter to be paid for by the charterers, e.g. bunkers[25]; but in the latter case he is agent of the shipowners to see that the vessel starts with a sufficient supply of bunkers and is thus seaworthy.[26]

---

[10] *Thompson v Gillespy* (1855) 5 E. & B. 209; see also *Hudson v Bilton* (1856) 6 E. & B. 565.

[11] The master's authority with regard to contracts for the employment of the vessel, signing bills of lading, etc., rests on different principles from those discussed in this and the following articles, and is discussed in Art.23.

[12] *The Turgot* (1886) 11 P.D. 21; *The Beeswing* (1885) 53 L.T. 554.

[13] *The Hamburg* (1864) B. & L. 253 at p.272; *The Gratitudine* (1801) 3 C.Rob. 240; *Notara v Henderson* (1872) L.R. 7 Q.B. 225; *Assicurazione v Bessie Morris S.S. Co* [1892] 2 Q.B. 652 at p.659 (CA) and Art.129, below.

[14] See Art.125.

[15] See *Australasian S.N. Co v Morse* (1872) L.R. 4 P.C. 222; and Arts 130, 132.

[16] See *The Karnak* (1869) L.R. 2 P.C. 505, and Art.132, below.

[17] *The Renpor* (1883) 8 P.D. 115, and Art.147.

[18] *The Soblomsten* (1866) L.R. 1 A. & E. 293, and Art.131. If on its true construction, any contractual liberty to tranship does not apply after the abandonment of the voyage, and there are no circumstances of necessity, the master has no power to tranship the cargo to its destination: *The Kota Sejarah* [1991] 1 M.L.J. 136.

[19] *Burton v English* (1883) 12 Q.B.D. 218, and Art.133.

[20] See Arts 127, 128.

[21] As to the lessened authority of the master in modern times owing to the increased facility of communications, see Art.23. And see Art.126, below.

[22] *Industrie Chimiche Italia Centrale v Alexander G. Tsavliris & Sons Maritime Co (The Choko Star)* [1990] 1 Lloyd's Rep. 516; *The Pa Mar* [1999] 1 Lloyd's Rep. 338 at 341–342.

[23] *The Turgot* (1886) 11 P.D. 21; *The Beeswing* (1885) 53 L.T. 554. See also *Petrinovic v Mission Francaise* (1942) 71 Ll.L.R. 208.

[24] Thus where the owners were to receive time hire, and the ship was detained through failure of the charterers to supply coal as per charter, it was held that the master had no authority to bind the owners for his orders for coal, as the owners gained nothing by expediting the sailing of the ship: *The Turgot* (1866) 11 P.D. 21. See also *Citizens Bank v Wendelin* (1886) 2 T.L.R. 240.

[25] *The Beeswing* (1885) 53 L.T. 554; *Morgan v Castlegate S.S. Co* [1893] A.C. 38.

[26] *McIver v Tate Steamers* [1903] 1 K.B. 362; *The Vortigern* [1899] P. 140.

Secondly the duty of acting as agent of the cargo-owner for the protection of his interests may devolve upon the master from its possession of the goods[27]; his primary duty is to carry on the cargo safely in the same bottom, yet in exceptional circumstances it may be both his right and his duty to deal with the cargo in some other way. Thus, if his action is necessary[28] and it is impossible to communicate with, or obtain instructions from, the cargo-owner,[29] the action of the master will bind the cargo-owner,[30] as in salvage agreements,[31] sale,[32] borrowing money on *respondentia*,[33] transhipment,[34] and drying or conditioning goods,[35] jettison,[36] delay or deviation.[37] The master is aways the appointed agent for the ship: he is in special cases of necessity the involuntary agent for the cargo-owner; but the foundation of his authority is the prospect[37] of benefit, direct or indirect, to the cargo-owner. Thus he may sell part of the cargo to carry on the rest, but may not sell the whole cargo unless it cannot profitably be carried further. He may not repair the ship at the sole expense of the cargo without reasonable prospect of benefit to such cargo, and such a prospect would not exist in the case of goods not injured by delay.[38]

Article 124—Master's Authority, whence derived   A124

Under the doctrine of "agency of necessity", the authority of the master, in the absence of express instructions, to deal with the ship and goods in a manner not consistent with the ordinary carrying out of the contract, as by selling the goods, thowing them overboard, or pledging them for advances of money depends on two circumstances:

(1) The necessity for the action (Art.125).

(2) The impossibility of communicating with, or obtaining instructions from, his principals, whether shipowners or cargo-owners (Art.126).

The significance of establishing an agency of necessity can vary.[39] It may mean that the principal is bound to a contract with a third party. It may entitle the agent to reimbursement from the principal of the necessary expenses incurred.[40] Or it may afford the agent a defence to an action in tort (*e.g.* for conversion).

---

[27] *cf. Hansen v Dunn* (1906) 11 Com.Cas. 100.
[28] See Art.125.
[29] See Arts 23 and 24.
[30] *The Gratitudine* (1801) 3 C.Rob. 240; and see Arts 120–126.
[31] *The Renpor* (1883) 8 P.D. 115; *Industrie Chimiche Italia Centrale v Alexander G. Tsavliris & Sons Maritime Co (The Choko Star)* [1990] 1 Lloyd's Rep. 516. See also Art.134.
[32] See *Australasian S.N. Co v Morse* (1872) L.R. 4 P.C. 222; and Arts 126, 132. See also *Sims v M.R. Co* [1913] 1 K.B. 103.
[33] *The Onward* (1873) L.R. 4 A. & E. 38; *Kleinwort v Cassa Marittima* (1877) 2 App.Cas. 156, and Arts 132, 134.
[34] *The Soblomsten* (1866) L.R. 1 A. & E. 293, and Art.131.
[35] Art.129.
[36] *Burton v English* (1883) 12 Q.B.D. 218, and Art.134.
[37] The fact that the cargo ultimately derives no benefit is immaterial, if there was a reasonable prospect of it: *Benson v Chapman* (1849) 2 H.L.C. 696 at p.720.
[38] *The Onward*, above, at pp.57, 58; see also per Brett M.R. and Bowen L.J. in *The Pontida* (1884) 9 P.D. 177 at p.180; *The Gratitudine* (1801) 3 C.Rob. 240 at pp.257, 261.
[39] See Art.18, above.
[40] This has alternatively been justified as a right correlative to the duty on the "agent" as a bailee of the property to preserve it: see *China Pacific SA v Food Corp of India (The Winson)* [1982] A.C. 939: *Enimont Overseas AG v Rojugotanker Zadar (The Olib)* [1991] 2 Lloyd's Rep. 108, 116.

A125   **Article 125—Necessity**

Action will be *necessary* if, some action being called for, the action taken is such as a prudent man with full knowledge of the facts would approve as being likely to prove beneficial in the interests of the adventure.[41] The mere fact that the master acts in good faith is not sufficient.[42] Nor will it be sufficient, although his acts ultimately benefit the cargo-owner, if he acts under the orders of a competent authority or by virtue of his obligations to his employers in regard to the safety of his ship.[43]

Note. Thus, if money can be obtained from the shipowner's or cargo-owner's agent in the port, or raised on personal credit, the master will not be justified in binding the ship or cargo by a bottomry bond; but if the carriage of the cargo cannot be completed with profit to the cargo-owner without raising money on security of the cargo such a course will be justified.[44]

So, also, if damaged wool can either be sold as it is, or can be dried, repacked, and sent on, but at a cost to the owner clearly exceeding any possible value of it when so treated, the commercial necessity for the sale will arise; but if the goods can be carried on and delivered in a merchantable state, though damaged, the master will not be justified in selling.[45]

Where such a necessity of dealing with the cargo arises, the captain in dealing with the cargo acts as the agent of the cargo-owner[46]; if no such necessity exists,[47] or if the necessity arises from wrongful acts or omissions on the part of the shipowner or his servants,[48] or if the captain professes to act for the shipowner,[49] he will be treated as the agent of the shipowner.[50]

A126   **Article 126—Communication with Cargo-owners**

The master, before dealing with the cargo in a manner not contemplated in the contract must, if possible,[51] communicate with the owners of the cargo as to what should be done. For the master's authority to bind the cargo-owners rests upon the fact that the circumstances require immediate action in the interests of the cargo, and that nobody but the master can decide what shall be done in time to take such immediate action. If the cargo-owners can be communicated with and

---

[41] *The Onward* L.R. 4 A. & E. 38 at p.58; *Australasian S.N. Co v Morse* (1872) L.R. 4 P.C. 222 at p.230; *Atlantic Insurance Co v Huth* (1880) L.R. 16 Ch. 474 at p.481. *Cf. Phelps, James & Co v Hill* [1891] 1 Q.B. 605.

[42] *Tronson v Dent* (1853) 8 Moore P.C. 419 at pp.448 *et seq*; the owner may be liable for an erroneous, though bona fide, use of the master's discretion; *Ewbank v Nutting* (1849) 7 C.B. 797.

[43] *Gillespie Bros v Burns, Philip* (1946) 79 Ll.L.R. 393 (N.S.W.). See also *Ningxia Yinchuan v AJ Brendon Shipping* [1998] 3 S.L.R. 154 (Sing.)

[44] *The Onward*, above.

[45] Arts 130–132.

[46] *Burton v English* (1883) 12 Q.B.D. 218.

[47] As in the case of improper jettison or sale.

[48] As in the case of jettison resulting from improper stowage on deck: *Newall v Royal Exchange S. Co* (1885) 1 T.L.R. 178; reversed *ibid.* p.490.

[49] As in cases of transhipment, in which the captain does not abandon the shipowner's voyage and forward the goods in the interests of the cargo-owner, but continues the voyage in another ship in the interests of the shipowner in order to earn freight for him. *Cf. Hansen v Dunn* (1906) 11 Com.Cas. 100.

[50] *Newall v Royal Exchange S. Co*, above.

[51] Given modern means of communication, it will be rare for communication to be practically impossible: see *F, Re* [1990] 2 A.C. 1, 75. As to the lessened authority of the master in modern times due to the increased facility of communications, see Art.23.

they give directions in time, the necessity for the master's action does not arise.[52] But the necessity remains, and the master may again take such action as appears necessary, if it proves impossible to obtain instructions because, although the cargo-owners have been communicated with, they have failed to give instructions.[53]

The possibility of communication must be estimated by consideration of the facts rendering immediate action necessary, the distance of the master from the cargo-owners, and his means of communicating with them, the cost and risk incidental to the delay resulting from the attempt to make such communication, and the probability of failure after every exertion has been made.[54]

The necessity for communication with cargo-owners will be much lessened in cases where the action of the master primarily affects the ship, as in repairs of the ship, or deviations by necessity, causing delay, or where, the ship being a general one, there are many owners of cargo.[55]

Such communication need only be made where an answer can be obtained from the cargo-owners, or there is reasonable expectation that it can be obtained, before it becomes necessary to take action. If there are reasonable grounds for such an expectation, the master should use every means in his power to obtain such an answer.[56]

The information furnished must be full, and must include a statement of any measure, such as sale, raising money on bottomry, etc., which the master proposes to take.[57]

If the master communicates and receives instructions, he is bound to follow them, if consistent with his duty to the shipowner; if he can communicate and does not do so, he cannot justifiably take any action on behalf of the cargo-owners.[58]

Article 127—Shipowner's Duty to Proceed without Deviation and with reasonable despatch   A127

In the absence of express stipulations to the contrary, the owner of a vessel, whether a liner or general ship or a ship chartered for a particular voyage or under

---

[52] *The Hamburg* (1863) 2 Moore P.C.(N.S.) 289 at p.323, explaining *The Bonaparte* (1853) 8 Moore P.C. 459. See also *International Packers v Ocean S.S. Co* [1955] 2 Lloyd's Rep. 218 at p.238. The above passage deals with the question of action to be taken by the captain in the interests of the cargo and as agent for the cargo-owners. But where the captain is dealing with the cargo in the interests of the shipowner (e.g. where the ship has been damaged and it is a question whether to repair her and complete the voyage), the absence of instructions from the cargo-owners will not absolve the shipowner from liability for neglect causing damage to the cargo while his own course of action is being considered. See *Hansen v Dunn* (1906) 11 Com.Cas. 100.

[53] *The Karnak* (1869) L.R. 2 P.C. 505; *China Pacific SA v Food Corp of India (The Winson)* [1982] A.C. 939.

[54] *The Karnak* (1869) L.R. 2 P.C. 505 at p.513; *The Onward* (1873) L.R. 4 A. & E. 38.

[55] *Phelps, James & Co v Hill* [1891] 1 Q.B. 605. If this case lays down that it is never necessary to communicate with cargo-owners where steps are to be taken, affecting their cargo, and inconsistent with the contract, it is submitted it goes too far. The authorities in this article do not seem to have been cited to the court.

[56] *Australasian S.N. Co v Morse* (1872) L.R. 4 P.C. 222.

[57] *The Onward* (1873) L.R. 4 A. & E. 38; *Kleinwort v Cassa Marittima* (1877) 2 App.Cas. 156.

[58] *The Hamburg* (1863) 2 Moore P.C.(N.S.) 289. See also *Springer v G.W. Ry* [1921] 1 K.B. 257; and *Sims v M.R. Co* [1913] 1 K.B. 103.

a time charter,[59] impliedly undertakes to proceed in that ship[60] by a usual and reasonable route without unjustifiable departure from that route and with reasonable despatch.[61] Prima facie the route is the direct geographical route[62]; but evidence is admissible to prove what route is a usual and reasonable route for the particular ship at the material time, provided that it does not involve any inconsistency with the express words of the contract.[63] A route may be a usual and reasonable route though followed only by ships of a particular line and though recently adopted.[64] Where the route which is usual and reasonable at the time that the contract is entered into subsequently becomes obstructed, the owner may, unless the contract is thereby frustrated, be obliged to proceed by the route which is usual and reasonable at the time of the voyage.[65]

Departure from the route so ascertained is *justifiable* if necessary to save life or to communicate with a ship in distress as the distress may involve danger to life,[66] or if it is involuntary, e.g. as the result of necessity[67]; but in the absence of express stipulations to the contrary it is *not justifiable*, except in cases to which the Carriage of Goods by Sea Act 1971, applies,[68] if only necessary to save property of others.[69]

Departure from the route so ascertained may also be justified by express stipulations (e.g. "liberty" or "deviation" clauses) in the contract; but any such stipulation, however widely phrased, must be construed with reference to the contract route ascertained in accordance with the foregoing principles.[70] In considering the construction of such clauses a distinction will be drawn between deviation clauses which, if construed literally, would in effect enable the shipowner to nullify the contract at will, and clauses stating what the rights and

---

[59] *Whistler v Kawasaki (The Hill Harmony)* [2001] 1 Lloyd's Rep. 147 (HL), a time charter case. The master is obliged to follow the time charterer's instructions as to route, being instructions as to "employment", except where the instructions expose the ship to risks to her safety beyond the normal ones which the shipowner agreed to bear: see [2001] 1 Lloyd's Rep. At pp.152–153, 160.

[60] *Balian v Joly Victoria* (1890) 6 T.L.R. 345 (CA).

[61] *Davis v Garrett* (1830) 6 Bing. 716: *Scaramanga v Stamp* (1880) 5 C.P.D. 295 (CA); *Louis Dreyfus v Lauro* (1938) 60 Ll.L.Rep. 94, *Fyffes v Reefer Express (The Kriti Rex)* [1996] 2 Lloyd's Rep. 171 at 191. The obligation is subject to a *de minimis* limitation: *Lyric Shipping Inc v Intermetals Ltd (The Al Taha)* [1990] 2 Lloyd's Rep. 117. See also Art.45, above.

[62] *Achille Lauro v Total* [1968] 2 Lloyd's Rep. 247.

[63] An obligation to proceed with "utmost despatch" may require the shortest and quickest route, even if there is evidence of a different usual route: *Whistler v Kawasaki (The Hill Harmony)* [2001] 1 Lloyd's Rep. 147, 149 per Lord Bingham. It will require the vessel to proceed at maximum speed consistent with normal navigation: *Ease Faith v Leonis* [2006] EWHC 232 (Comm); [2006] 1 Lloyd's Rep. 673 at 693–694, paras 129–133.

[64] This statement of the general principle is based on Lord Porter's speech in *Reardon Smith Line v Black Sea and Baltic General Insurance* [1939] A.C. 562 at p.584. The earlier cases on the route to be followed, which are not easy to reconcile, were *Davis v Garrett* (1830) 6 Bing. 716; *Leduc v Ward* (1888) 20 Q.B.D. 475; *Glynn v Margetson* [1893] A.C. 351; *White v Granada* (1896) 13 T.L.R. 1; *Evans v Cunard* (1902) 18 T.L.R. 374; *Morrison v Shaw, Savill* [1916] 2 K.B. 783; *Frenkel v MacAndrews* [1929] A.C. 545.

[65] *The Eugenia* [1964] 2 Q.B. 226; *The Captain George K* [1970] 2 Lloyd's Rep. 21; and see Art.14.

[66] *Scaramanga v Stamp*, above.

[67] *Lavabre v Wilson* (1779) 1 Dougl. 284; even though the necessity arises from original unseaworthiness; *Kish v Taylor* [1912] A.C. 604. See also Art.128, below.

[68] See Art.IV, r.4 of the Schedule to the Act and comment thereon, below.

[69] *Scaramanga v Stamp*, above.

[70] *Leduc v Ward* (1888) 20 Q.B.D. 475; *Glynn v Margetson* [1893] A.C. 351; *Hadji Ali Akbar v Anglo-Arabian* (1906) 11 Com.Cas. 219; *Morrison v Shaw, Savill* [1916] 2 K.B. 783; *Connolly, Shaw Ltd v A/S Det Nordenfjeldske D/S* (1934) 49 Ll.L.R. 183; *Islamic Investment v Transocean (The Nour)* [1999] 1 Lloyd's Rep. 1 at 8–9, and *Note* at the end of this Article.

obligations of the parties are to be in the event of obstacles beyond their control arising to prevent or impede performance according to the primary terms of the contract.[71]

Unjustifiable departure from the contract route unless involuntary (e.g. resulting from error of judgment as to route) constitutes a deviation.[72]

Delay in performing the contract voyage may also constitute a deviation,[73] just as delay in carrying out the insured voyage may constitute a deviation under an insurance policy.[74]

An owner whose ship without justification deviates thereby commits a fundamental breach of his contract of carriage. However, it is now unclear whether classification of the breach as fundamental adds anything to saying that there has been a breach of condition. What is uncontroversial is that the other party to such contract, on becoming aware of the deviation, can *either* treat the breach as a repudiation bringing the contract to an end and claim damages *or* elect to waive the deviation as a final repudiation and treat the contract as still subsisting, reserving his right to damages.[75] In the latter case all the terms of the contract will remain in force and the shipowner will be able both to enforce any rights arising out of the contract and to rely on any exception clause which may be applicable to a casualty occurring before or after the deviation, and will be liable only for damages resulting from the deviation itself.[76] But what if the charterer or goods-owner chooses the former option? In the past the significance of classifying the breach as fundamental was that, if the innocent party chose to

---

[71] *Renton v Palmyra* [1957] A.C. 149 at pp.164, 172, 174.

[72] *Rio Tinto Co v Seed Shipping Co* (1926) 24 Ll.L.R. 316.

[73] Taking a ship in tow "has been held to be equivalent to a deviation, and rightly so, seeing that the effect . . . is necessarily to retard the progress of the towing vessel, and thereby to prolong the risk of the voyage": per Cockburn C.J. in *Scaramanga v Stamp* (1880) 5 C.P.D. 295 at p.299. See also *The Renée Hyaffil* (1916) 32 T.L.R. 83, 660; *Att-Gen v Smith* (1918) 34 T.L.R. 566; *Brandt v Liverpool S.N. Co* [1924] 1 K.B. 575 at pp.597, 601, and Art.128. Delay consequent upon the master taking in other cargo in mitigation of the shipowner's claim for dead freight under a charter will not, if his action was reasonable, constitute a deviation: *Wallems Rederi A/S v Muller & Co* [1927] 2 K.B. 99.

[74] Marine Insurance Act 1906, ss.48, 49. The effect of a deviation may not be the same on a policy as on a contract of affreightment; see *Internationale Guano v MacAndrew* [1909] 2 K.B. 360 at p.365.

[75] Statement in the text approved by MacKinnon L.J. in *Compagnie Primera, etc. v Compania Arrendataria, etc.* [1940] 1 K.B. 362 at p.375. In that case deviations on the first of two voyages under a consecutive voyage charterparty, which was not severable, were held to relieve the charterer from his obligations as regards the second voyage.

[76] *Hain S.S. Co v Tate & Lyle* (1936) 41 Com.Cas. 350 at pp.354, 355, 363, 371: *cf. Paterson Steamships v Robin Hood Mills* (1937) 58 Ll.L.R. 33 at p.39. For cases prior to this authoritative statement in the House of Lords, see *Balian v Joly, Victoria* (1890) 6 T.L.R. 345; *The Dunbeth* [1897] P. 133; *Joseph Thorley v Orchis* [1907] 1 K.B. 660; *Internationale Guano v MacAndrew* [1909] 2 K.B. 360; *Morrison v Shaw, Savill* [1916] 2 K.B. 783; and contrast *The Europa* [1908] P. 84 (effect of breach of warranty of seaworthiness). Where the contract of carriage is still largely unperformed when knowledge of the deviation comes to the charterer as in *Hain S.S. Co v Tate & Lyle*, it is clear that the latter must unambiguously accept the owner's conduct as a repudiation if he wishes to bring the contract to an end. It frequently happens, however, that the voyage has been performed and bills of lading presented before the fact of deviation is discovered, as was the case with the bill of lading holders in *Hain S.S. v Tate & Lyle*. In these circumstances it will rarely, if ever, be in the bill of lading holder's interest to waive his rights to treat the contract of carriage as at an end, and it is submitted that in the absence of clear conduct by him amounting to waiver, he will be able to rely on the deviation: see *Hain S.S. Co v Tate & Lyle* (1936) 41 Com.Cas. 350 at pp.356, 361, 364. It has been suggested that a claim to refer a dispute as to a deviation to arbitration under the provisions of a clause in a charter might amount to a waiver of the deviation as amounting to repudiation: see *US Shipping Board v Bunge y Born* (1924) 41 T.L.R. 73 (CA). *Sed quaere*, the point was not discussed in the HL ((1925) 42 T.L.R. 174), and see *Heyman v Darwins* [1942] A.C. 356, and *Woolf v Collis Removal Service* [1948] 1 K.B. 11 (CA). On waiver of deviation, see also *Temple S.S. Co v Sovfracht* (1945) 79 Ll.L.R. 1 at p.11 (HL); *US Shipping Board v Masters* (1923) 14 Ll.L.R. 208.

terminate the contract, he was able to avoid any clauses excluding or limiting liability. The controversial question is whether that fundamental breach doctrine still applies to deviation cases even though its use as a rule of law has otherwise been abolished by the House of Lords in the *Suisse Atlantique* case[77] and *Photo Production Ltd v Securicor Ltd*.[78] Any breach, however serious, can now generally be excluded by an appropriately worded exclusion clause: whether it does so or not is a question of construction.

On one view, the fundamental breach doctrine lives on in respect of deviation. This derives some support from *dicta* of Lord Wilberforce in the *Photo Production* case: "It may be preferable that [the deviation cases] should be considered as a body of authority *sui generis* with special rules derived from historical and commercial reasons."[79] If this view prevails then where the charterer or goods-owner elects to terminate the contract for deviation, he can claim the delivery of his goods, and since the exceptions contained in the contract are inapplicable, the shipowner will be liable for any loss or damage which the goods may have sustained, unless he can show (1) that the loss or damage was occasioned either by the act of God, or by the King's enemies, or by inherent vice of the goods, *and* (2) that the said loss or damage must equally have occurred even if there had been no deviation.[80] And it is probably immaterial whether the loss or damage arises before, or during, the deviation, or after it has ceased.[81]

The alternative view is that the fundamental breach doctrine has been abolished even for deviation so that, where the charterer or goods-owner elects to terminate, the applicability of contractual exceptions clauses is a matter of construction. This view has been favoured by Lloyd and Longmore L.JJ. "the

---

[77] [1967] 1 A.C. 361.

[78] [1980] A.C. 827. See also *George Mitchell (Chesterhall) Ltd v Finney Lock Seeds Ltd* [1983] 2 A.C. 803. See generally M. Dockray, [2000] LMCLQ 76.

[79] [1980] A.C. 827, 845.

[80] i.e. the shipowner will have the benefit of the common law exceptions of a common carrier if he can show that loss by one of those excepted causes was not, and could not have been, occasioned by the deviation: *Morrison v Shaw, Savill* [1916] 2 K.B. 783; *Lilley v Doubleday* (1881) 7 Q.B.D. 510; *Haine S.S. Co v Tate & Lyle* (1936) 41 Com.Cas. 350; *Rendal v Arcos* (1937) 43 Com.Cas. 1 at p.14; *Temple S.S. Co v Sovfracht*, above. In *Hain's* case. Lord Wright, at pp.361, 369, uses language which raises a doubt whether the shipowner will even have the benefit of the common law exceptions of a common carrier. In *Morrison v Shaw, Savill* only the second of the propositions in the text above is insisted on as necessary; but the cause of loss in question was admittedly the King's enemies. Theoretically, it is submitted, the shipowner must also prove the first proposition. Practically, proof of the second proposition is hardly possible as regards any cause of loss except inherent vice of the goods. Contrast the decision of the PC in *Paterson Steamships v Robin Hood Mills* (1937) 58 Ll.L.R. 34, where it was held that a deviation, after which the ship resumed her contractual course, and ran on the rocks, through negligent navigation, had nothing to do with the loss, and that, accordingly, even assuming the owners to have been privy to the deviation, the loss occurred without the actual fault or privity of the owners within s.503 of the Merchant Shipping Act 1894.

[81] Pickford J. in *Internationale Guano v Macandrew* [1909] 2 K.B. 360, commenting on *Joseph Thorley v Orchis Co* [1907] 1 K.B. 660, suggests that this is not correct as regards loss or damage occurring on the voyage *before* the deviation takes place. But in that case Pickford J. was dealing with damage arising from inherent vice of the goods. And his decision was based on the grounds that the shipowner proved (1) loss by inherent vice, and (2) that this loss must have occurred even if there had been no deviation. In the case of loss covered by an exception in the bill of lading (e.g. sea-perils) occurring before the deviation, the shipowner, it is submitted, would not be entitled to rely on the exception. The deviation has displaced and destroyed his special contract. *Cf. per* Lord Maugham in *Hain S.S. Co v Tate & Lyle* (1936) 41 Com.Cas. 350 at p.371: "the charterers become entitled to treat the contract as at an end as *from the date of the repudiation*". *Cf.* also *Thiess Bros v Australian Steamships* [1955] 1 Lloyd's Rep. 459 (N.S.W.) where freight payable on shipment, and to be considered earned lost or not lost, was held recoverable after an unjustifiable deviation leading to a heavy loss of cargo.

deviation cases should now be assimilated to the ordinary law of contract".[82] It is likely to prevail.

The effect of deviation upon the shipowner's right to freight has not been finally determined. In the event of a deviation not treated as a repudiation of the contract of carriage it is clear that the contractual right to freight remains unimpaired. In the case of a deviation accepted as a repudiation of the contract of carriage, the shipowner may lose his contractual right to freight but it is probable that if the goods are nevertheless carried to their destination the shipowner will be entitled subject to clear contractual terms to the contrary, to recover a reasonable sum as freight on a restitutionary *quantum meruit* basis.[83]

Similarly, in the case of a deviation accepted as a repudiation, provisions as to discharging in a fixed time will no longer bind the charterer, though he will probably still be bound to discharge in a reasonable time.[84]

Deviation rendered necessary by a breach of the warranty of seaworthiness[85] may be a permissible deviation, in the sense that it will not enable the contract of carriage to be discharged so as to deprive the shipowner of the benefit of its terms,[86] the necessity for the deviation being judged by the *existence* of the peril not by the *cause* of the peril; but, *semble*, the shipowner would under such circumstances be deprived, on the ground of breach of warranty of seaworthiness, of any right to claim contribution in general average in respect of the expenses at the port of refuge to which he deviates.[87] Unless waived by the cargo-owner a deviation will prevent a shipowner from recovering general average contribution in respect of expenses incurred as the result of a casualty occurring after the deviation.[88]

Rule 4 of Art.IV of the Schedule to the Carriage of Goods by Sea Act 1971, deals with deviation in terms that are capable of various interpretations. If a shipowner deviates from the voyage agreed by his bill of lading and cannot bring

---

[82] *Kenya Railways v Antares Co Pte. Ltd (The Antares)* [1987] 1 Lloyd's Rep. 424, 430; *State Trading Corp of India Ltd v M. Golodetz Ltd* [1989] 2 Lloyd's Rep. 277, 289; *Daewoo v Klipriver (The Kapitan Petko Voivoda)* [2003] EWCA Civ 451; [2003] 2 Lloyd's Rep. 1 at 13 para.14, in which the other members of the CA agreed generally with Longmore LJ.

[83] *Hain S.S. Co v Tate & Lyle* (1936) 41 Com.Cas. 350, in particular, per Lord Wright, at pp.368, 369; *Balian v Joly, Victoria* (1899) 6 T.L.R. 345; *Joseph Thorley v Orchis* [1907] 1 K.B. 660 at pp.667, 669. For an award of a reasonable freight on a *quantum meruit* in the case of frustration see *Société Franco Tunisienne v Sidermar* [1961] 2 Q.B. 278, subsequently overruled by the CA on another point in *The Eugenia* [1964] 2 Q.B. 226.

[84] *US Shipping Board v Bunge y Born* (1924) 40 T.L.R. 541; affirmed (1924) 41 T.L.R. 73; affirmed (1925) 42 T.L.R. 174. *Quaere*, as to effect of deviation on right to demurrage already accrued at port of loading. Probably it would be unaffected.

[85] In *Monarch S.S. Co v Karlshamns* [1949] A.C. 196 at p.202, the qualification "unless the vessel's condition was known to the owners before sailing" was introduced by Lord Porter with whom Lords Uthwatt, du Parcq and Morton agreed. There is no reference to this qualification in the speeches in *Kish v Taylor* [1912] A.C. 604, nor do the facts of that case as stated indicate whether or not there was such knowledge. Probably Lord Porter's qualification is intended to deal with the situation where the owners knew that the condition of the vessel on sailing was such as inevitably to necessitate deviation so that the deviation when it occurred was voluntary, and to draw the distinction between such American cases as *The Willdomino* (1927) 272 U.S. 718, on the one hand and *The Malcolm Baxter* (1928) 31 Ll.L.R. 200 on the other; in the latter case (as in *Monarch S.S. Co v Karlshamns*, above) such knowledge was negatived.

[86] *Kish v Taylor* [1912] A.C. 604.

[87] *Strang v Scott* (1889) 14 App.Cas. 601; see *Kish v Taylor*, above, at pp.619, 620.

[88] *Hain S.S. Co v Tate & Lyle* (1936) 41 Com.Cas. 350 at p.361. The shipowner will be unable to prove that the casualty must have occurred had he not been in fault by deviating.

himself within r.4 of Art.IV of the Schedule, the traditional view was that he will not be able to rely on the exceptions in r.2 of Art.IV, or *semble* the other statutory exceptions.[89] If, however, as seems likely, deviation cases have been assimilated to the ordinary law of contract, the question would need to be revisited as a straightforward issue of construing the Hague–Visby Rules.[90]

Note. Express[91] stipulations limiting this implied undertaking are usually introduced into charters and bills of lading, e.g.:

"With liberty to call at any ports in any order, to sail without pilots, and to tow and assist vessels in distress, and to deviate for the purpose of saving life or property."

Such a clause allows the shipowner to take on board cargo at the port of call, unless he has already contracted for the whole reach of the ship,[92] but not to go out of the course of the original voyage to discharge such cargo.[93]

The clause "liberty to tow and assist vessels in all situations" will protect a ship in towing off a stranded vessel, though no life is in danger and though the vessel towing is wrecked and her cargo lost,[94] and though the towage delays the chartered adventure, if it does not frustrate its commercial object.[95]

All these clauses must be construed in the light of the commercial adventure undertaken by the shipowner.[96] Thus a clause giving leave "to call at any ports" will only allow the shipowner to call at ports which will be passed in the ordinary course of the named voyage in their geographical order[97]: the addition of the words "in any order" will allow the shipowner to depart from the geographical order[98]; but even when there are general words which, literally construed, would give liberty to call at ports outside the geographical voyage, these will be cut down, by the special description of the voyage undertaken, to ports on the course of that voyage. What, however, is the voyage must be determined in the light of commercial practice as well as by consideration of geography,[99] and, until the voyage has been so determined, no question of deviation can arise.[100]

---

[89] *Stag Line v Foscolo, Mango* [1932] A.C. 328.

[90] The words *"in any event"* in Art.III r.6 and Art.IV r.5(a) probably mean that those rules, at least, apply in cases of deviation: see the discussion in *Daewoo v Klipriver (The Kapitan Petko Voivoda)* [2003] EWCA Civ 451; [2003] 2 Lloyd's Rep. 1 at 12–15 paras 10–22.

[91] If an *express* liberty to deviate is granted, no implied liberty inconsistent therewith can be presumed: *United States Shipping Board v Bunge y Born* (1925) 31 Com.Cas. 118.

[92] *Caffin v Aldridge* [1895] 2 Q.B. 648 (CA).

[93] *The Dunbeth* [1897] P. 133.

[94] *Stuart v British and African Navigation Co* (1875) 32 L.T. 257.

[95] *Potter v Burrell* [1897] 1 Q.B. 97.

[96] Approved per McCardie J. in *Armour v Walford* [1921] 3 K.B. 473 at p.478. See *Renton v Palmyra* [1957] A.C. 149 as to the distinction between clauses purporting to give the shipowner liberty, in effect, to nullify the contract and those designed to deal with the occurrence of emergencies beyond the control of the parties.

[97] *Leduc v Ward* (1888) 20 Q.B.D. 475: *Glynn v Margetson* [1893] A.C. 351; *White v Granada S.S. Co* (1896) 13 T.L.R. 1; *Islamic Investment v Transocean (The Nour)* [1999] 1 Lloyd's Rep. 1.

[98] *Glynn v Margetson* [1893] A.C. 351: see also *Evans v Cunard Co* (1902) 18 T.L.R. 374. The words of such a clause may, however, be wide, enough to entitle the shipowner even to alter the named destination of the ship, and (by virtue of a clause giving liberty to tranship) to forward the goods by another ship from the new destination; *Hadji Ali Akbar v Anglo-Arabian, etc., Co* (1906) 11 Com.Cas. 219. Addition of the words "although in a contrary direction to or out of or beyond the route of the said port of delivery" will protect the shipowner unless the use of the liberty is such as to frustrate the contract: *Connolly, Shaw, Ltd v A/S Det Nordentjeldske D/S* (1934) 49 Ll.L.R. 183. In *Thiess v Australian Steamships* [1955] 1 Lloyd's Rep. 459 (N.S.W.) a widely drafted modern deviation clause was *held* inapplicable since the deviation was in no way connected with the contract voyage.

[99] *Evans v Cunard Co* (1902) 18 T.L.R. 374, where the bill of lading described the goods as shipped from Bari in Italy on a vessel bound for Liverpool, and on proof that vessels of this line invariably proceeded via the Adriatic and thence by Levantine or Black Sea ports before proceeding to Liverpool, it was held that calling at Constantinople was covered in the liberty "to stay at any ports . . . whether in or out of the customary route".

[100] *Frenkel v MacAndrews* [1929] A.C. 545, where a bill of lading issued at Malaga merely stated that the goods

Whether any particular port is an "intermediate port", within the meaning of a general liberty to call at intermediate ports, is a question of fact in each case, to be decided upon consideration of all the circumstances—e.g. the class and size of the ship, the nature of the voyage, the usual and customary course, the usual and customary ports of call, and the nature and position of the port in question.[101]

A clause in bills of lading is not uncommon to this effect: "With liberty to carry the goods or any part of them beyond their port of destination, and to tranship, land, and store them either on shore or afloat, and reship and forward them at the shipowner's expense but at merchant's risk."[102]

For other liberty clauses, dealing inter alia, with events such as war, blockade, hostilities, ice, etc., which may entitle the ship to go to other than the named port of destination, see Art.71, *Note* 1.

Case 1. A ship was chartered to proceed from X to Z; on her voyage she went to the assistance of a vessel in distress and agreed to tow her to Y (out of her course); while thus towing she was wrecked. The jury found the deviation not reasonably necessary to save life, but reasonably necessary to save property. *Held*, that such a deviation was unjustifiable, and that the cargo-owners could recover against the shipowner.[103]

Case 2. Oranges were shipped at Malaga, under a bill of lading, stating shipment on board a steamer, "now lying in the port of M, bound for Liverpool with liberty to proceed to and stay at any port or ports in any rotation in the Mediterranean, Levant, Black Sea or Adriatic, or on the coasts of . . . Spain . . . for the purpose of delivering coals, cargo, or passengers or any other purpose whatever". The steamer, on leaving Malaga, proceeded to B, a port two days off in the opposite direction to L, where she loaded cargo and then returned and proceeded to L. By reason of this delay the oranges were rotten on arrival at L. *Held*, that the general words must be limited by the specified voyage, and only allowed the ship to call at ports fairly and substantially in the ordinary course of the voyage, and that they did not justify the actual deviation.[104]

Case 3. Cargo of H was shipped in New Zealand on a liner for carriage to London. The bill of lading contained a general liberty to call at intermediate ports. The ship left the usual track to London in order to land other cargo at Havre. When approaching Havre the vessel was torpedoed by a German submarine and H's cargo was lost. *Held*, (i) that there was a deviation, Havre not being an intermediate port within the liberty, and (ii) that, as the shipowner could not prove that the cargo must have been lost by King's enemies if there had been no deviation, he was liable to pay damages for the loss.[105]

---

had been shipped "with destination to Liverpool", evidence was admitted to prove one of the customary routes was via ports east of Malaga (via Levant) and not direct (*directo*); compare *Reardon Smith Line v Black Sea and Baltic General Insurance* [1939] A.C. 562. These two decisions of the HL turned on the determination of the contractual route and not on the interpretation of "liberty" or "deviation" clauses. The cases on the latter point were, however, elaborately discussed.

[101] *Morrison v Shaw, Savill* [1916] 2 K.B. 783. See especially Swinfen-Eady L.J., *ibid.* p.795.
[102] The conditions of such a clause must be strictly complied with in order that the shipowner may enjoy the protection given: *Cunard S.S. Co v Buerger* [1927] A.C. 1. The liability of the shipowner may depend not only upon the exact language used but also upon the surrounding circumstances with reference to which it was used. Contrast *Sargant v East Asiatic Co* (1915) 21 Com.Cas. 344 with *Broken Hill Co v P. & O.* [1917] 1 K.B. 688. In the former case, on the terms of the clause as set out in the text, the shipowner was held not entitled, after the goods had arrived at their port of destination, to carry them on to another port and thence to ship them back. In the latter case, though the terms of the clause were indistinguishable, he was held to be so entitled on the ground that both parties must have had in mind as part of the surrounding circumstances the fact that the carrying vessel was a mail steamer.
[103] *Scaramanga v Stamp* (1880) 5 C.P.D. 295.
[104] *Glynn v Margetson* [1893] A.C. 351. This was the case of a tramp steamer, and a printed form of bill of lading, giving extensive liberties to deviate had been used with the words "now lying at Malaga and bound for Liverpool" inserted in writing. *Cf.* Bray J. in *Sutro & Co and Heilbut, Symons & Co, Re* [1917] 2 K.B. 348 at p.367. In the case of a regular liner, with the whole bill of lading in print, other considerations might arise. See *Frenkel v MacAndrews* [1929] A.C. 545, and the explanation of the ratio decidendi of that case in *Reardon Smith Line v Black Sea and Baltic* [1939] A.C. 562. *Cf. Hadji Ali Akbar v Anglo-Arabian Co* (1906) 11 Com.Cas. 219; *Connolly, Shaw Ltd v A/S Det Nordenfjeldske D/S* (1934) 49 Ll.L.R. 183.
[105] *Morrison v Shaw, Savill* [1916] 2 K.B. 783.

Case 4. C chartered A's ship to carry a cargo of sugar from three ports in the West Indies to the UK. After loading at the first two ports the ship deviated on her way to the third port X, but with knowledge of the deviation C loaded her on her arrival at X. On leaving X she stranded, heavy general average expenditure was incurred for the salvage of the cargo, part of which was subsequently transhipped and carried to the UK. H presented the bills of lading in ignorance of the deviation, and in order to obtain the goods from A, who was claiming a lien for general average contribution, entered into a Lloyd's average bond. *Held*, (1) that C had waived the deviation by loading at X; (2) that A had a lien on the goods for general average contribution; (3) that H was not affected by C's waiver and (4) was not liable to pay the contractual freight on the goods shipped at the first two ports, nor in the circumstances on a quantum meruit, but (5) was liable for general average contribution on the terms of the bond.[106]

Case 5. Timber was shipped at Canadian ports to London under bills of lading providing that, should it appear that strikes would prevent the vessel from entering the port of discharge or their discharging in the usual manner and leaving again safely and without delay, the master might discharge at any safe and convenient port and that such discharge should be deemed due fulfilment of the contract. Whilst the ship was on passage a strike broke out in London, followed by a strike at Hull, and the shipowners caused her to proceed to Hamburg and discharge the timber, which was there made available to bill of lading holders on payment of full freight. In an action against shipowners to recover as damages the expenses of storage at Hamburg and of forwarding the timber from Hamburg, *held*, that the shipowners were protected by the bill of lading provisions which dealt with the rights and obligations of the parties in the event of obstacles beyond their control preventing or impeding performance of the contract in accordance with its primary terms.[107]

A128   **Article 128—Master's Authority to delay and deviate in Cases of Necessity**

A master, if his ship has been so damaged as to necessitate repairs[108] or if he received credible information that by proceeding on the direct course of the voyage his ship or his cargo will be exposed to some imminent peril, as by hostile capture, pirates, icebergs, or other dangers of navigation, will be both entitled[109] and bound[110] to make a reasonable deviation, or to incur a reasonable delay, in order to ascertain the nature of, or to avoid, the danger, or to repair the damage.[111] It is not necessary that the danger should be common to ship and cargo: it will be sufficient if it affects either of them.[112] And the deviation will be justified even though the necessity for it arises from unseaworthiness.[113]

---

[106] *Hain S.S. Co v Tate & Lyle* (1936) 41 Com.Cas. 350 (HL).

[107] *Renton v Palmyra* [1957] A.C. 149. It was decided that the provision relied upon was not avoided by the Canadian Water Carriage of Goods Act 1936.

[108] cf. *Phelps, James & Co v Hill* [1891] 1 Q.B. 605. It would seem from this case that where the ship is a general ship, and therefore there are many owners of cargo, it will rarely, if ever, be necessary to communicate with them for authority to delay, or deviate, even if one of the objects of such action is reconditioning of cargo: *sed quaere*; and see fn.55 to Art.126.

[109] *The Teutonia* (1872) L.R. 4 P.C. 171 at p.179; *Nobel v Jenkins* [1896] 2 Q.B. 326; *The San Roman* (1872) L.R. 5 P.C. 301; *The Wilhelm Schmidt* (1871) 25 L.T. 34; *The Express* (1872) L.R. 3 A. & E. 597; *The Heinrich* (1871) L.R. 3 A. & E. 424; *Pole v Cetcovitch* (1860) 9 C.B.(N.S.) 430. Where the danger was foreseen by the shipowner, who after consideration gave his master orders to pursue a certain course, the master had no power to deviate from that course in consequence of that danger: *The Roebuck* (1874) 31 L.T. 274.

[110] He need not put into port or delay in port merely for the purpose of reconditioning cargo; but being in port he may not carry on damaged cargo with the certainty that it will perish or greatly deteriorate on the voyage: *Notara v Henderson* (1870) L.R. 5 Q.B. 346; *The Gratitudine* (1801) 3 C.Rob. 240 at p.259; *Vlierboom v Chapman* (1844) 13 M. & W. 230.

[111] See fn.108, above.

[112] *The Teutonia*, above.

[113] *Kish v Taylor* [1912] A.C. 604.

If the master delays or deviates unreasonably, or to a greater extent than a prudent man under the circumstances would adopt, the cargo-owner has the option previously discussed[114] whether to treat the master's conduct as a repudiation bringing the contract to an end or to treat the contract as still subsisting, reserving his right to damages.

If the delay or deviation is reasonable, the charterers cannot obtain the goods short of the port of destination, without payment of full freight.[115]

Case 1. A Prussian ship with a contraband cargo was chartered from X to an English port for orders; thence to any safe port in England or the Continent between Havre and Hamburg; she received orders to proceed to Dunkirk, and had arrived off that port on June 16, when she informed that war had broken out between France and Prussia. The captain sailed to the Downs to inquire, and anchored there on June 17 (Sunday); on the 18th, the shipowner ordered him not to go into Dunkirk; on the 19th he put into Dover; and there was informed that war between France and Prussia, imminent from June 10, had been declared on the 19th. *Held*, that putting back to the Downs to obtain information and the delay on the 19th were justifiable, and that the goods-owners could not obtain their goods at Dover without payment of full freight.[116]

Case 2. Coffee was shipped on a German ship, under a bill of lading containing only an exception of perils of the seas, from America to Hamburg. Near Falmouth the master was informed that war had broken out between France and Germany, and he accordingly put into F on August 23. Hamburg was then blockaded by the French Fleet, and remained blockaded till September 18. During all that time and until November 7, the English Channel and North Sea were rendered unsafe by French cruisers. On September 18, when the blockade was raised, the goods-owners offered full freight for the goods delivered either at F or at Hamburg. The master refused to proceed to Hamburg on the ground of the danger of capture, and refused to deliver the cargo. *Held*, that the master's delay (of fifty days, September 18 to November 7) was unreasonable, and his refusal to proceed to H a breach of the contract[117]; and that the goods-owners were therefore entitled to the cargo at F.

Case 3. Goods were shipped at Swansea on a general ship starting from Bristol, and calling at S to New York. The ship put into Queenstown with damage to ship and cargo through bad weather. The captain communicated with the shipowners at Bristol, who ordered him to return there. He did not communicate with the cargo-owners. When in the Avon the ship and cargo were lost by an excepted peril. Cargo-owners sued the shipowners for loss on a deviation. It was proved that the ship, but not the cargo, could be repaired at Queenstown; that ship and cargo could be repaired and cargo sold at Swansea, sixty miles short of Bristol; that ship could be advantageously repaired and cargo sold at Bristol, though there was no evidence as to whether the cargo could be reconditioned there. The jury found the master had acted reasonably and the deviation was justified. The Court of Appeal refused to disturb their verdict, and *held*, that under the circumstances there was no necessity to communicate with the cargo-owners and obtain their sanction.[118]

---

[114] See Art.127, above.

[115] *The Teutonia*, below.

[116] *The Teutonia* (1872) L.R. 4 P.C. 171. *The San Roman, The Heinrich, The Express, and The Wilhelm Schmidt*, all arose out of similar circumstances, and in effect decided that reasonable apprehension of capture justifies delay or deviation. The latter part of the decison in *The Teutonia* is best explained as a decision on equitable principles on the unusual facts of the case: *Reardon Smith Line v Ministry of Agriculture* [1962] 1 Q.B. 42 at pp.90, 117, 129. See also *Aktieselskabet Olivebank v Dansk Fabrik* [1919] 2 K.B. 162 and compare *St. Enoch Co v Phosphate Co* [1916] 2 K.B. 624.

[117] *The Patria* (1871) L.R. 3 A. & E. 436. It is difficult to understand this case, as the same judge had held a longer delay from similar causes reasonable in other cases (e.g. *The San Roman* 53 days; *The Express*, 170 days). The absence of the exception "restraint of princes" in the bill of lading may make the difference (see Art.110). The decision was that the master's refusal to proceed to Hamburg amounted to a repudiation of the charter which the goods-owners accepted by instituting proceedings. Sir R. Phillimore suggested that on the refusal of the master to proceed to H the goods-owners were entitled to their goods on payment of a pro rata freight, but it seems clear that such a refusal if wrongful would entitle them to their goods without payment of any freight at all. *Medeiros v Hill* (1832) 8 Bing. 231, shows that, if the parties knew of the blockade when the charter was entered into, the existence of the blockade would be no defence to an action for not proceeding towards the blockaded ports.

[118] *Phelps, James & Co v Hill* [1891] 1 Q.B. 605. See fn.55 to Art.126.

A129   **Article 129—Master's Duty to take care of Goods**[119]

The master, as representing the shipowner, has the duty of taking reasonable care of the goods entrusted to him, by doing what is necessary to preserve them on board the ship during the ordinary incidents of the voyage, e.g. by ventilation, pumping or other proper means.[120]

He has also the duty of taking reasonable measures though necessitating expense to prevent or check the loss or deterioration of the goods even by reason of accidents for the necessary consequences of which the shipowner is by reason of the bill of lading under no original liability, and the shipowner will be liable[121] for any neglect of such duty by the master.

The master is entitled to estimate the extent of delay to the adventure by the probabilities of the case and, if he is justified by them in not incurring the delay, he will not afterwards be held liable because his expectations are falsified by events.[122] The place, the season, the extent of the deterioration, the opportunities at hand, the interests of other persons in the adventure whom it might be unfair to delay for the sake of the part of the cargo in peril, all the circumstances affecting risk, trouble, delay, and inconvenience, must be taken into account. The performance of the duty cannot be insisted on if it involves deviation, but reasonable delays in a port of call for purposes connected with the voyage, though not necessary to its completion, will not amount to deviation.[123]

As the master has to exercise a discretionary power, his owner will not be liable unless it is affirmatively proved that the master has been guilty of a breach of duty.

Semble, the master will have a lien on the goods for any expenses incurred in the performance of such duty.[124]

Case 1. F shipped beans on the S, on a voyage to Z, the bill of lading giving leave to call at ports on the voyage. The vessel called at Y, and on her way out came into collision, whereby the beans were damaged by salt water; she put back to Y. The wet beans might have been warehoused and dried at Y, with material benefit to them, and without reasonable delay to the adventure. The ship proceeded to L without drying them. *Held*, that the shipowners were liable to F for the master's failure to dry the beans, though protected by the bill of lading from liability for the damage immediately caused by the collision.[125]

---

[119] Rule 2 of Art.III of the Schedule to the Carriage of Goods by Sea Act 1971, provides that: "Subject to the provisions of Article IV the carrier shall properly and carefully . . . handle . . . carry keep care for . . . the goods carried", and the principles to be applied in determining whether there has been a breach of the duty imposed by this rule are the same as the common law principles summarised in the present Article: *International Packers v Ocean S.S. Co* [1955] 2 Lloyd's Rep. 218.

[120] *Notara v Henderson* (1870) L.R. 5 Q.B. 346; affirmed (1872) L.R. 7 Q.B. 225, per Willes J. at p.235; *Tronson v Dent* (1853) 8 Moore P.C. 419; *Australasian S.N. Co v Morse* (1872) L.R. 4 P.C. 222; *International Packers v Ocean S.S. Co*, above. *Cf. Garriock v Walker* (1873) 1 Rettie 100; *Adam v Morris* (1890) 18 Rettie 153; *Phelps, James & Co v Hill* [1891] 1 Q.B. 605; *Hansen v Dunn* (1906) 11 Com.Cas. 100; *Gatoil International Inc v Tradax Petroleum Ltd (The Rio Sun)* [1985] 1 Lloyd's Rep. 350. See also s.13 of the Supply of Goods and Services Act 1982. For a discussion whether, in case of wreck of the ship, the shipowners may charge for the services of agents in saving, conditioning, and forwarding the goods, see *Rose v Bank of Australasia* [1894] A.C. 687.

[121] This is not, like the authority to tranship, a power for the benefit of the shipowner only to secure his freight: *De Cuadra v Swann* (1864) 16 C.B.(N.S.) 772.

[122] *The Savona* [1900] P.252.

[123] See fn.120, above.

[124] *Hingston v Wendt* (1876) 1 Q.B.D. 367. See per Blackburn J. at p.373.

[125] *Notara v Henderson* (1872) L.R. 7 Q.B. 225. See also *The Rio Sun*, above.

Case 2. A ship carrying a cargo of maize from the Plate to Port Elizabeth put into Cape Town in a damaged condition. The captain communicated with his owners, with underwriters on ship, freight and cargo, and with owners of cargo. Unreasonable delay ensued while it was being considered whether the ship should be repaired to continue the voyage, be towed with the cargo, or the cargo transhipped to earn freight, and owing to the conflict of interests in these various courses the cargo was damaged by being kept on board during this delay. *Held*, that the shipowner was liable to the cargo-owners for the damage.[126]

Article 130—Master's Power to sell damaged or perishable Goods   A130

The condition of the goods may be such that immediate sale is the wisest course in the interests of the cargo-owner; in such a case the master, if he cannot communicate with the cargo-owner or obtain his instructions, will be entitled and bound to sell them.[127] Such a condition will arise if the master cannot convey the goods or cause them to be conveyed to their destination as merchantable articles, either at all or without expenditure clearly exceeding their value after their arrival at their destination.[128] If, however, the master can, but does not, communicate with the cargo-owner before selling the goods, the cargo-owner will be entitled to recover[129] damages for conversion,[130] even though the sale is reasonable.[131]

Case 1. Maize was shipped on a voyage from X to Z; at Y, an intermediate port, it was found heated and sprouting; the master transhipped it into lighters, and informed the shipper's agent by telegraph on March 10 and 13 of its condition, suggesting that it could not be carried on. He received two telegrams in reply that the shipper wished the grain to be forwarded. On March 27 the captain telegraphed again: "Have held survey which reports grain unfit for shipment; will be sold tomorrow by public auction"; and it was sold on the 28th. The sale was a prudent measure, but not one of such urgent necessity as to give no time or opportunity for communicating with the owner. *Held*, that no case was made out entitling the master to sell, as he was bound to have awaited the result of his communication of the proposed sale to the owner.[132]

Case 2. The ship R., with a mixed cargo of metal and perishable articles, was wrecked, on April 19, in Algoa bay fifty miles from Port Elizabeth. The consul there, on April 22, advised the captain to sell the ship and cargo, which he did on April 30. The captain did not go to P. E., or make any attempt to raise money for salvage, or to induce others to attempt the salvage. He had no funds in his hands. There was conflicting evidence as to whether such attempts, if made, would have been successful, but much evidence that the course adopted was the most prudent. *Held*, that no necessity for the sale existed, such as would make the master the agent of the cargo-owner to effect a sale, and that the sale was therefore void.[133]

---

[126] *Hansen v Dunn* (1906) 11 Com.Cas. 100.

[127] *Australasian S.N. Co v Morse* (1872) L.R. 4 P.C. 222; *Acatos v Burns* (1878) 3 Ex.D. 282; *Tronson v Dent* (1853) 8 Moore P.C. 419; *Atlantic Insurance Co v Huth* (1880) 16 Ch.D. 474; *Vllerboom v Chapman* (1844) 13 M. & W. 230, and see Arts 125, 126. As to German law, see *The August* [1891] P. 328; *The Industrie* [1894] P. 58.

[128] *Atlantic Insurance Co v Huth*, below, at p.481.

[129] As to the person liable for unjustifiable sale by master, see *Wagstaff v Anderson* (1880) 4 C.P.D. 283, and Art.119.

[130] *Springer v G.W. Ry.* [1921] 1 K.B. 257; *cf. Sims v Midland Ry Co [1913] 1 K.B. 103.* See also *Prager v Blatspiel* [1924] 1 K.B. 566 (no necessity for the sale of furs).

[131] *Acatos v Burns* above.

[132] *Acatos v Burns* (1878) 3 Ex.D. 282. See also *Australasian S.N. Co v Morse* (1872) L.R. 4 P.C. 222.

[133] *Atlantic Insurance Co v Huth* (1880) 16 Ch.D. 474. The sale was held to be void by English law which was assumed to be the law applicable to the transaction. Proof that the sale was valid by the law of the place where it was made, even though void by English law, would have been a defence to the purchasers: *Cammell v Sewell* (1860) 5 H. & N. 728. But the carrier would still be responsible to the owners of the cargo for any sale not justified by the law of the flag or by the terms of the contract of carriage.

A131　　　　　　**Article 131—Master's Power of Transhipment**

Where a vessel in which goods are shipped is hindered by an excepted peril from completing the contract voyage, the shipowner must, if the obstacle can be overcome by reasonable expenditure or delay, do his best to overcome it.[134] It is only where an excepted peril renders the completion of the voyage physically impossible, or so clearly unreasonable as to be impossible from the business point of view, that the shipowner is justified in throwing up the voyage without the consent of the charterer or shipper.[135] The test of whether completion of the voyage is impossible from a business point of view may depend on the possibility of effecting repairs or the cost of repairs. In either case the question to be considered is the repair necessary to enable the ship to complete the voyage with the particular cargo carried.[136]

Where the shipowner is prevented from completing the contract voyage by a peril which cannot be overcome in a reasonable time, or by damage which cannot be repaired at a reasonable expense, he is not *bound* either to repair or tranship[137]; though, if he elects to do neither, he must hand over his cargo to the cargo-owner[138] freight free, or, if the cargo-owner is not present to receive it, and cannot be communicated with, the master must act for the best as the cargo-owner's agent.[139] He has, however, the *right* to earn his freight either by repairing his own ship and proceeding to the port of destination, or by transhipping the goods into another vessel to be forwarded thither,[140] and he may delay the transit a reasonable time for either of these purposes.[141] If he spends an unreasonable time in making up his mind which course to adopt, and the cargo is damaged during the delay, the shipowner will be liable to the cargo-owner for the damage.[142]

In case of justifiable transhipment by the master as agent for the shipowner, the cargo-owner will be bound to pay the full freight originally contracted for, though the transhipment was effected by the shipowner at a smaller freight.[143]

---

[134] *Ferruzzi France SA & Ferruzzi SpA v Ocean Maritime Inc (The Palmea)* [1988] 2 Lloyd's Rep. 261.

[135] *Assicurazione v Bessie Morris S.S. Co* [1892] 1 Q.B. 571 at p.581; affirmed [1892] 2 Q.B. 652 (CA); *Carras v London and Scottish Assurance* [1936] 1 K.B. 291; *Kulukundis v Norwich Union* [1937] 1 K.B. 1. See also *The Savona* [1900] P. 252.

[136] *Kulukundis v Norwich Union* [1937] 1 K.B. 1, in particular the judgment of Greene L.J. *Cf.* the judgment of Scott L.J. In exceptional circumstances the shipowner may not be excused although repair of his ship is physically or commercially impossible, if it is possible to get the goods to their destination by reasonable means, such as lighters: *ibid.* pp.18, 19, *Cf.* per Goff J. in *Western Sealanes Corp v Unimarine (The Pythia)* [1982] 2 Lloyd's Rep. 160 at p.166.

[137] There is no *duty* to tranship: *Kulukundis v Norwich Union* [1937] 1 K.B. 1 at pp.17, 18, 37, 38. For earlier discussions of the point, see *Shipton v Thornton* (1838) 9 A. & E. 314, and *Hansen v Dunn* (1906) 11 Com.Cas. 100. In *Terkol Rederierne v Petroleo Brasiliero SA (The Badagry)* [1985] 1 Lloyd's Rep. 395 at p.398, this statement was approved by Sir John Donaldson M.R., who described the principle as anomalous.

[138] See per Bowen L.J. *Svendsen v Wallace* (1884) 13 Q.B.D. 69 at p.88.

[139] The extent of the shipowner's duty to care for and discharge the cargo after the frustration of the voyage is discussed by Roskill J. in *The Medina Princess* [1965] 1 Lloyd's Rep. 361 at p.522 and in *Adelfamar SA v Silos E. Morgimi Mortini SpA (The Adelfa)* [1988] 2 Lloyd's Rep. 466.

[140] See per Lawrence J. in *Cook v Jennings* (1797) 7 T.R. 381 at p.385; and per Lindley J. in *Hill v Wilson* (1879) 4 C.P.D. 329 at p.333; *De Cuadra v Swann* (1864) 16 C.B. (N.S.) 772.

[141] *The Bahia* (1864) B. & L. 292; *The Soblomsten* (1866) L.R. 1 A. & E. 293; *Cargo ex Galam* (1863) B. & L. 167; *The Gratitudine* (1801) 3 C.Rob. 240; *Shipton v Thornton* (1838) 9 A. & E. 314 at pp.332 *et seq.*

[142] *Hansen v Dunn* (1906) 11 Com.Cas. 100.

[143] *Shipton v Thornton*, above; *The Bernina* (1886) 12 P.D. 36.

Semble, the master cannot, without express authority, bind the cargo-owner to more unfavourable terms in the contract of transhipment, as by wider exceptions,[144] or to pay a larger freight than that originally contracted for, unless communication with the cargo-owner is impossible, and forwarding the cargo on such terms as would appear to a reasonable man to be the most beneficial course of the interests of the cargo.[145]

If the hindrance of the ship's voyage is not caused by an excepted peril, the shipowner is not entitled as of right to tranship on his own account on terms more onerous to the shipper than the original contract (though he may be bound to do so on account of the cargo-owner); but he is liable for delay or failure to deliver.[146]

Note. In many bills of lading (especially through bills of lading and bills issued by regular steamship lines) there is an express provision that the shipowner shall have liberty to tranship[147] and forward the goods "by any other line",[148] or "by any other steamer or steamers". The terms of such clauses vary considerably, but there is not usually much doubt as to their meaning.

Where in such a clause there was liberty to tranship and forward "at ship's expense but at shipper's risk", it was *held* that the phrase "at shipper's risk" applied only to the process of transhipment, and did not supersede the general provisions of the bill of lading as to the transit after transhipment to the destination.[149]

Case 1. F shipped goods on board the S, at a named freight for a voyage from X to Z; on the voyage at Y the necessity for transhipment arose, and the master made a contract for the forwarding of the goods to Z at a freight which, together with pro rata freight from X to Y, was less than the original freight agreed upon. On arrival at Z, F refused to pay more than such pro rata and forwarding freight. *Held*, that he was bound to pay the freight originally agreed upon.[150]

Case 2. A shipowner carried goods under a contract of affreightment which did not except negligence of the master and crew. The ship was so injured by the negligence of her master as to be unable to complete the voyage; and the master thereupon transhipped the cargo into another vessel under a contract containing an exception of negligence of the master and crew. Such vessel was lost by negligence of the master and crew. *Held*, that the transhipment being for the benefit of the shipowner he could not bind the cargo-owner by more onerous exceptions and was therefore liable for the loss.[151]

Case 3. A ship chartered (with perils of the sea excepted) by C to proceed to London ran ashore near Gibraltar. Ship and cargo were damaged; the ship was repaired in six weeks at a cost of £750, and proceeded to the United Kingdom with another cargo. Some of the original cargo was sold, some with the consent of its owners was transhipped; the latter cargo could have been carried to London in the repaired ship without unreasonable delay, and C never consented to the original voyage being abandoned. *Held*, that the shipowner, as he could repair within a reasonable time, and at a cost less

---

[144] *The Bernina*, above.
[145] *Gibbs v Grey* (1857) 2 H. & N. 22, where it was held that the master had no power to bind the consignee to ship a full cargo, or, *semble*, to pay a higher freight than the current at the time; and see *Cargo ex Argos* (1873) L.R. 5 P.C. 134 at p.165; *Shipton v Thornton* (1838) 9 A. & E. 314 at p.336.
[146] *Shipton v Thornton* above; *The Bernina*, above.
[147] "Liberty to tranship" is sufficiently wide to cover putting goods into lighters in order to complete the voyage: *Marcelino Gonzalez v Nourse* [1936] 1 K.B. 565. But presumably only if this is a reasonable course.
[148] Which phrase does not mean that the substituted ship must be a "liner": *Hadji Ali Akbar v Anglo-Arabian Co* (1906) 11 Com.Cas. 219.
[149] *Stuart v British and African Co* (1875) 32 L.T. 257; *Whitworth v Pacific S.N. Co* (1926) 25 Ll.L.R. 573; and see *Notes* at end of Art.118.
[150] *Shipton v Thornton* (1838) 9 A. & E. 314. See *Matthews v Gibbs* (1860) 30 L.J.Q.B. 55.
[151] *The Bernina* (1886) 12 P.D. 36.

than the value of the ship when repaired, was bound to remedy the effect of the excepted perils and carry on the cargo in the same ship.[152]

Case 4. A ship was chartered with the usual exception of perils of the seas to proceed to Valparaiso to load a cargo. Whilst so proceeding she stranded in the Straits of Magellan and was subsequently abandoned by her owner to the salvors, the cost of repairs exceeding the ship's repaired value. *Held*, the shipowner was discharged from further performance of the charter, since it was impossible in a commercial sense to repair the ship.[153]

A132   **Article 132—Master's Power of raising Money on Cargo**

The master will be entitled to raise money on the cargo to enable him to complete the contract voyage when the master cannot obtain money in any other way, if such course is the most beneficial for the cargo-owner, and if the cargo-owner cannot be communicated with, or, being communicated with, omits to give any instructions whatever.

Money may be so raised by one of two methods: (1) By a sale of part of the cargo[154]; in which case the goods-owner may either treat the proceeds of the sale as a loan to the shipowner whether the vessel reaches her destination or not, no freight being payable on the goods sold; or, if the vessel reaches her destination, he may pay the freight which would have been earned if the goods sold had been carried to their destination and claim an indemnity against any loss occasioned to him by the sale.[155] (2) By loan on the security of the cargo.[156]

A133   **Article 133—Jettison**[157]

The captain's authority to jettison goods properly stowed arises in the case of necessity,[158] i.e. where a prudent man in the interest of the adventure would take such a course.[159]

Where such necessity arises the captain in making the jettison acts as agent of the cargo-owner; if no such necessity exists, or if the goods jettisoned were improperly stowed, e.g. on deck, and the jettison is therefore unjustified the captain acts only as the agent of the shipowner, who is liable for his acts[160] unless protected by exceptions.[161]

---

[152] *Assicurazione v Bessie Morris S.S. Co* [1892] 2 Q.B. 652.
[153] *Carras v London and Scottish Assurance* [1936] 1 K.B. 291; *Kulukundis v Norwich Union* [1937] 1 K.B. 1. It was decided in the latter case that the relevant repairs were those necessary to enable the vessel to carry her cargo to its destination. Whether these be permanent or temporary will depend on what the necessities of each case demand.
[154] See Arts 125, 126.
[155] See *Hopper v Burness* (1876) 1 C.P.D. 137, and Art.168 on freight.
[156] Where ship, cargo and freight together are hypothecated, the transaction is known as *bottomry*; where cargo alone is hypothecated it is generally known as *respondentia*. See *Busk v Fearon* (1803) 4 East 319; *Glover v Black* (1763) 3 Burr. 1394; *Cargo ex The Sultan* (1859) Swabey 504. *Bottomry* and *respondentia* bonds are now little used, and the discussion of them appeared in earlier editions of this work has therefore been omitted: see 17th edn, Arts 107–108.
[157] As to the exception of "jettison", see Art.119.
[158] It is almost impossible that the question of communicating with the cargo-owner should arise, except perhaps in a case of stranding.
[159] *Burton v English* (1883) 12 Q.B.D. 218 at pp.220, 223; *Morrison Steamship Co v Greystoke Castle (Cargo Owners)* [1947] A.C. 265; and see Art.125.
[160] *Royal Exchange Shipping Co v Dixon* (1886) 12 App.Cas. 11; *Dixon v Royal Exchange Shipping Co* (1884) 1 T.L.R. 178; reversed *ibid.* p.490.
[161] It is doubtful whether the phrase "at merchant's risk" would protect him, though there are dicta to the contrary in *Burton v English*, above. See Arts 119, 136.

Note. Jettison made in a time of common peril seems first mentioned in a reported case in 1609,[162] but rather as affording a defence to the person making the jettison on a claim for trespass to the goods, than as raising any question of general average. But there is record of what was apparently a claim for general average arising from jettison of a ship's boat and oars and of cargo in 1540.[163]

<h2 style="text-align:center">Article 134—General Average[164]					A134</h2>

All loss which arises in consequence of extraordinary[165] sacrifices made or expenses incurred for the preservation of the ship and cargo comes within the general average, and must be borne proportionately by all who are interested.[166]

To give rise to a claim for general average contribution[167]:

(1) There must be a common danger,[168] during a common maritime adventure,[169] which must be real, and not merely apprehended by the master, however reasonably.[170]

(2) There must be a necessity for a sacrifice.[171]

---

[162] *Mouse's Case* (1609) 12 Co Rep. 63.

[163] The *Trinity James* or *The Chance*, Marsden, *Select Pleas of the Admiralty Court* (Selden Society, 1892), Vol. 1, p.95.

[164] Arts 134–146 state the common law on this subject. This is substantially affected by the York-Antwerp Rules 1994 (as to which see Appendix II), which are almost invariably made applicable by express terms in charters and bills of lading. The subject of general average is so entirely in the hands of average adjusters, and so ably dealt with in the work of Lowndes and Rudolf, *The Law of General Average and the York-Antwerp Rules*, 12th edn (London: Sweet & Maxwell, 1997) (the 13th edn is imminent) that we have not thought it necessary to treat it in any length or detail. We do not know when "average adjusters" first practised as a special profession. In *Crofts v Marshall* (1836) 7 C. & P. 597 at p.606, on December 19, 1836, "Mr. Richards (a Settlor of Averages at Lloyd's) was then called"; and in *Pirie v Steele* (1837) 8 C. & P. 200 at p.203, in 1837, Mr Richards being called, said "I am a taker of averages."

[165] Not expenses incurred to avert an ordinary peril on that voyage at that time: *SA Nouvelle v Spillers* [1917] 1 K.B. 865.

[166] per Lawrence J. in *Birkley v Presgrave* (1801) 1 East 220 at p.228; see also per Brett M.R. in *Svendsen v Wallace* (1884) 13 Q.B.D. 69 at p.73. *Cf.* the statutory definition in the Marine Insurance Act 1906, s.66(2), and the less stringent test laid down by Rule A of the York-Antwerp Rules 1924, discussed in *The Seapool* [1934] P. 53. See also the elaborate opinions of the majority of the Lords in *Morrison Steamship Co v Greystoke Castle (Cargo Owners)* [1947] A.C. 265. It would seem to follow from these that if the shipowner or master properly incurs a general average expenditure or sacrifice he is acting not only on behalf of the other interests, but *as their agent*. In consequence, as was decided in that case, those interests have a right to sue a third party (such as a colliding ship) whose negligence has caused the danger giving rise to the expenditure or sacrifice and are not limited to rights of subrogation exercised through and in the name of the carrying ship. Other and more startling results may follow, as was pointed out in the dissenting opinion of Lord Simonds. Thus could cargo-owners be sued as principals in respect of contracts made in a port of refuge by the master, and if so, for what proportion of such contractual liability?

[167] *Pirie v Middle Dock Co* (1881) 44 L.T. 426.

[168] See *Walthew v Mavrojani* (1870) L.R. 5 Ex. 116; *Royal Mail Co v Bank of Rio* (1887) 19 Q.B.D. 362; *Hamel v P. & O. Co* [1908] 2 K.B. 298. It is not, however, necessary that there should be a contribution legally recoverable to make the act giving rise to the contribution a general average act. Where ship, cargo and freight belong to the same owner, so that no legal claim for contribution arises, a voluntary sacrifice to save them may yet be a general average act, giving rise to a claim on underwriters for a general average loss: *Montogmery v Indemnity Ins Co* [1902] 1 K.B. 734 (CA).

[169] The common maritime adventure may continue after the end of the voyage while there is cargo on board: see *Whitecross Wire v Savill* (1882) 8 Q.B.D. 653; *Trade Green v Securitas Bremer (The Trade Green)* [2000] 2 Lloyd's Rep. 451 at 454–455.

[170] *Watson v Firemen's Fund Co* [1922] 2 K.B. 355. "Mere bona fides on the part of the captain is not sufficient: it must be shown that those circumstances did in fact exist which give rise to the right of contribution"; Brett L.J., *Whitecross Wire Co v Savill* (1882) 8 Q.B.D. 653 at p.662.

[171] *Pirie v Middle Dock*, above.

(3) The sacrifice must be voluntary.[172]

(4) It must be a real sacrifice, and not a mere destruction and casting off of that which had become already lost and consequently of no value.

(5) There must be a saving of the imperilled property through the sacrifice.[173]

(6) The common danger must not arise through any default for which the interest claiming a general average contribution is liable in law,[174] even if the liability cannot be enforced owing to lapse of time. Therefore the fact that the common danger arises from the nature of the cargo (e.g. from spontaneous combustion of coal) does not prevent the cargo-owner from claiming contribution for sacrifice of the cargo, unless he was guilty of some breach of contract or of duty in shipping it.[175]

In the case of deviation made necessary by a breach of the warranty of seaworthiness, although the contract of carriage is not thereby repudiated or displaced,[176] yet the shipowner, by reason of the breach of warranty (unless exempted by exceptions from liability therefor) would be debarred from claiming contribution in general average towards, e.g. the expenses at the port of refuge to which he deviates.[177] Similarly, a deviation to which no exception clause applies will, unless waived by the cargo-owner, prevent the shipowner recovering general average contribution in respect of expenses incurred as a result of a casualty occurring after the deviation.[178]

For the position obtaining when Rule D of the York-Antwerp Rules 1994, applies and there has been fault by the party claiming contribution, see the discussion in Appendix II.[179]

Note. The office of the bill of lading is to provide for the rights and liabilities of the parties in reference to the contract to carry, and it is not concerned with liabilities to contribution in general average where a loss has been occasioned by a sacrifice properly made for the general benefit.[180] But express clauses, such as "General average payable

---

[172] *Shepherd v Kottgen* (1877) 2 C.P.D. 585. The sacrifice is voluntary even when it is made by order of the port authorities. The master assenting if it was made for the benefit of ship and cargo: *Papayanni v Grampian S.S. Co* (1896) 1 Com.Cas. 448; probably not if for the benefit of other ships. *Cf. Athel Line v Liverpool and London War Risks Association* [1944] K.B. 87 (obedience of master in convoy to naval orders without any knowledge of risks on which they were based).

[173] *Pirie v Middle Dock Co*, above. See also *Chellew v Royal Commission* [1922] 1 K.B. 12.

[174] *Strang v Scott* (1889) 14 App.Cas. 601 at p.608: *Schloss v Heriot* (1863) 14 C.B.(N.S.) 59; *Goulandris Bros v Goldman* [1958] 1 Q.B. 74; *State Trading Co of India v Doyle Carrier Inc* [1991] 2 Lloyd's Rep. 55; *Guinomar v Samsung (The Kamsar Voyager)* [2002] 2 Lloyd's Rep. 57 at 65–66. Thus in *The Carron Park* (1890) 15 P.D. 203, the shipowner succeeded in recovering a general average contribution for expenditure occasioned by the negligence of his servants, from liability for which he was protected by an exception in the bill of lading: approved in *Milburn v Jamaica Fruit Co* [1900] 2 Q.B. 540 (CA), and in *Dreyfus v Tempus Shipping Corp.* [1931] A.C. 726. Even if the exceptions clause only protects against physical loss of or damage to the goods themselves, the shipowner is entitled to recover contribution from cargo in respect of expenditures incurred to preserve it from such loss or damage not withstanding that the peril was brought about by his own breach of contract: *The Makedonia* [1962] 1 Lloyd's Rep. 316 at p.341.

[175] *Greenshields v Stephens* [1908] A.C. 431.

[176] *Kish v Taylor* [1912] A.C. 604.

[177] *Strang v Scott* (1889) 14 App.Cas. 601; *Kish v Taylor*, above.

[178] *Hainn S.S. Co v Tate & Lyle* (1936) 41 Com.Cas. 350 at p.361 (HL).

[179] Below.

[180] per Lush J. in *Schmidt v Royal Mail S.S. Co* (1876) 45 L.J.Q.B. 646; and *Burton v English* (1883) 12 Q.B.D. 218.

according to York-Antwerp Rules 1994", almost invariably affect the common law as to liability for general average; again the presence of the negligence clause in the bill of lading may enable the shipowner to recover general average contribution for sacrifices rendered necessary by the negligence of his master, though without such a clause he could not.[181]

The clause "not to be liable for any damage capable of being covered by insurance" does not free the shipowner from liability to general average contributions.[182]

Article 135—Classes of General Average Loss   A135

The following sacrifices or expenses may give rise to a claim for a general average contribution:

A. Sacrifices—

  (1) of cargo:

    (i) by jettison (Art.136);
    (ii) by fire, directly or indirectly (Art.137);
    (iii) by sale, or other sacrifices of value[183] (Art.138);

  (2) of ship or tackle (Art.139);

  (3) of freight (Art.140).

B. Expenditure at sea in replacing a general average loss, or in a port of refuge (Arts 141, 142).

Article 136—General Average Loss—Jettison of Cargo   A136

Where cargo stowed in a proper part of the ship is properly jettisoned for the common good, its owner is entitled to a general average contribution from the other interests in the adventure: i.e. the ship, the freight, and the rest of the cargo.[184] He can enforce this claim either by a direct action against each of the owners of the ship or cargo,[185] or by claiming through the master, who is his agent for that purpose, a lien on each parcel of goods saved to satisfy it proportionate liability.[186] An interest whose fault has led to the jettison is not entitled to a general average contribution in respect thereof,[187] but innocent

---

[181] See fn.174, above.
[182] See fn.180, above.
[183] As in *Anglo-Argentine Co v Temperley* [1899] 2 Q.B. 403, where cattle were diminished in value by the shipowner's putting into an infected port to repair sea damage. Damage to cargo caused by discharging it in order to repair damage to the ship sustained by the perils of navigation, the cargo being in no danger, does not give rise to a claim for general average contribution: *Hamel v P. & O. Co* [1908] 2 K.B. 298.
[184] *Strang v Scott* (1889) 14 App.Cas. 601 at p.606. But see fn.174, above. See Arts 119, 134, above; as to the amount of contributions, see *Fletcher v Alexander* (1868) L.R. 3 C.P. 375. It has been held in America that the lien will also attach to damages recovered from a wrong-doing ship: *Armour v Green Star S.S. Co Ltd* (1931) Ll.L.R. 199; and *cf. The Empusa* (1879) 5 P.D. 6.
[185] *Dobson v Wilson* (1813) 3 Camp. 480.
[186] See fn.184, above.
[187] But see York-Antwerp Rules 1994, Rule D, printed in Appendix II, and fn.174, above.

owners of cargo jettisoned in consequence of the fault of another interest are not thereby deprived of their remedy.[188]

Cargo stowed on deck (which is not a usual or proper place of stowage), if jettisoned, does not give rise to a general average contribution from the other interests in the adventure, unless it is so stowed in pursuance of a recognised custom of the trade or port, or by consent of all the other interests in the adventure.[189]

If the cargo is shipped on deck by agreement between its owner and the shipowner, there being no custom so to load, the owner of such cargo, if jettisoned, has no right to a general average contribution either against other cargo-owners, or, if there are other cargo-owners, against the shipowner or the person entitled to the freight[190]; but, if there is no other cargo-owner, such a jettison may give rise to such a contribution from the ship and freight,[191] even though such cargo according to the charter is to be carried "at merchant's risk".[192]

The clause "at merchant's risk" protects the shipowner from liability for improper jettison, resulting from acts of the crew done as the servants of the shipowner, but not from liability for general average contribution in respect of a proper jettison which is made by the captain as agent of the cargo-owner. If the goods are stowed on deck without the merchant's consent or a binding custom so to stow, and are then jettisoned, the shipowner will be liable for such a jettison as a breach of his contract to carry safely in the absence of an effective exception.[193]

Case 1. F shipped in A's ship twenty-six pieces of timber. There was a custom in the timber trade to carry lumber on deck. F's goods were placed on deck, and were properly jettisoned. *Held*, that F was entitled to a general average contribution from ship to freight: *semble*, also from cargo.[194]

Case 2. C F shipped in A's ship a full cargo of timber, under a charter whereby C F's timber on deck was properly jettisoned. *Held*, C F was entitled to recover a contribution to his loss from A.[195]

Case 3. F shipped cattle on A's ship, agreeing they should be carried on deck: there were other owners of cargo. On the voyage the cattle were properly jettisoned. *Held*, that F was not entitled to a general average contribution either against A or against the other cargo-owners.[196]

---

[188] See fn.184, above.

[189] *Strang v Scott* (1889) 14 App.Cas. 601 at p.608; *Wright v Marwood* (1881) 7 Q.B.D. 62 at p.67. See *Burton v English* (1883) 12 Q.B.D. 218 (CA) for such an agreement, and *Gould v Oliver* (1837) 4 Bing.N.C. 134, for such a custom; the custom also exists in the coasting trade; it was not proved in *Dixon v Royal Exchange Shipping Co* (1884) 1 T.L.R. 178; reversed *ibid.* p.490. As to deck stowage on inland waters, see *Apollinaris Co v Nord Deutsche Co* [1904] 1 K.B. 252. See also r.1 of the York-Antwerp Rules, Appendix II.

[190] *Wright v Marwood*, above; not so, if there is a custom so to load; *Gould v Oliver* above.

[191] *Johnson v Chapman* (1865) 19 C.B.(N.S.) 563; discussed in *Wright v Marwood* (1881) 7 Q.B.D. 62 at p.69.

[192] The statement in the text is based on dicta in *Burton v English* (1883) 12 Q.B.D. 218 at p.220, the authority of which is now doubtful. See *Svenssons v Cliffe S.S. Co* [1932] 1 K.B. 490 at pp.496–499. See Art.118.

[193] *Royal Exchange S.S. Co v Dixon* (1886) 12 App.Cas. 11; *Newall v Royal Exchange Steamship Co* (1885) 1 T.L.R. 490; see also per Lush L.J. in *Schmidt v Royal Mail Co* (1876) 45 L.J.Q.B. 646 at p.648.

[194] *Gould v Oliver* (1837) 4 Bing.N.C. 134.

[195] *Johnson v Chapman* (1865) 19 C.B.(N.S.) 563.

[196] *Wright v Marwood* (1881) 7 Q.B.D. 62.

Case 4. F shipped timber on A's ship, which was not a general ship, under a charter, "the steamer shall be provided with a deck-load if required at full freight, but a merchant's risk". There was a custom to carry such timber on deck: on the voyage the deck timber was properly jettisoned. *Held*, that F was entitled to a general average contribution from A.[197]

Case 5. Cotton was shipped by F under bills of lading excepting "jettison" and "stranding". Some of the cotton was stowed on deck without F's consent; the ship stranded, and the deck cotton was properly jettisoned. An attempt to prove a custom to stow on deck failed. *Held*, that the cargo-owner was entitled to recover the full value of the cotton from the shipowner.[198]

Article 137—General Average Loss—Cargo damaged by Fire,[199] directly   A137
or indirectly

Damage to the cargo by pouring water on it,[200] or by scuttling the ship to extinguish fire, or by burning it as fuel for the engines to avert the loss of ship and cargo,[201] gives rise to a claim for general average contribution by the owner of the cargo destroyed or damaged.[202] There must be a real fire: damaged done by pouring in water when the captain thinks there is fire, when in fact there is none, however, reasonable, his belief, is not the subject of contribution.[203]

Case. F had shipped wire on board the *S.* to be carried to Z. The *S.* arrived and proceeded to discharge her cargo; about 100 tons remained on board, including the plaintiff's wire, when fire broke out, which was extinguished by pouring water into the hold, whereby the wire was damaged. *Held*, that F was entitled to a general average contribution from the owner of the *S.*[204]

Article 138—General Average Loss—Sale of Cargo, or other Sacrifice of   A138
its Value

Sale of part of the cargo to furnish money for repairs to enable the ship to prosecute the voyage[205] or to release the master from arrest that he may prosecute the voyage[206] will only give rise to a claim for general average against the rest of the cargo, if the rest of the cargo can be carried on in no other way, and it is more beneficial to the cargo to be carried on than to stay where it is[207]: any other kind of sale will only give rise to personal claim against the shipowner.[208]

---

[197] *Burton v English* (1883) 12 Q.B.D. 218. The authority of the case on this point is not affected by the doubts expressed in fn.192, above.

[198] *Royal Exchange Steamship Co v Dixon* (1886) 12 App.Cas. 11.

[199] As to the exception of "fire" and the statutory protection given by s.186 of the Merchant Shipping Act 1995, see Art.116 and fn.342, Art.116, above.

[200] *Papayanni v Grampian S.S. Co* (1896) 1 Com.Cas. 448.

[201] *Walford v Galindez* (1897) 2 Com.Cas. 137. If the ship was insufficiently supplied with fuel at starting, the owner of the cargo burnt will be entitled, in the absence of appropriate exceptions in the contract of affreightment, to recover its full value from the shipowner, while in consequence other owners of cargo will not be liable to contribute to general average: *Robinson v Price* (1876) 2 Q.B.D. 91; affirmed *ibid.* p.295; *The Vortigern* [1899] P. 140.

[202] *Whitecross Wire Co v Savill* (1882) 8 Q.B.D. 653; in which the Court of Appeal for the first time decided this question, which they had left undecided in *Stewart v West India S.S. Co (1873) L.R. 8 Q.B. 362. See also Achard v Ring* (1874) 31 L.T. 647. an exception "fire on board" in the bill of lading will not relieve the owner from liability for general average contribution to the owner of goods damaged by water used in extinguishing such fire: *Schmidt v Royal Mail S.S. Co* (1876) 45 L.J.Q.B. 646; *Greenshields v Stephens* [1908] A.C. 431.

[203] *Watson v Firemen's Fund Co* [1922] 2 K.B. 355.

[204] See fn.202, above.

[205] *Hallett v Wigram* (1850) 9 C.B. 580.

[206] *Dobson v Wilson* (1813) 3 Camp. 480.

[207] *Hallett v Wigram* above.

[208] *Hopper v Burness* (1876) 1 C.P.D. 137; in which the payment of freight on cargo thus sold is discussed; and see Art.132, on master's power of raising money on cargo.

The value of a cargo may be sacrificed in whole or part in other ways, e.g. where putting into a port of refuge renders it illegal to land the cargo at its port of destination, as in the case of cattle touching at an infected port. The loss of value due to such a sacrifice is made good in general average.[209]

A139

Article 139—General Average Loss—Sacrifice of Ship, Machinery or Tackle

Sacrifice of ship, machinery, or tackle, necessary for the safety of the whole adventure, and not incurred in carrying out the shipowner's original contract, will give rise to a general average contribution,[210] unless:

(1) The thing sacrificed was at the time in such a condition that it would have been certainly lost, even if the rest of the adventure was saved, as when a mast is cut away, which is either certain to go overboard, or has already gone overboard and is hanging as a wreck, or[211]:

(2) The sacrifice was rendered necessary by the actionable default of the shipowner, as in providing a ship insufficiently equipped,[212] in which case he must bear all the loss.

Damage done to the ship by a voluntary and intentional stranding,[213] or by knowingly causing her to come into collision, in avoiding a common peril, may be a general average sacrifice of the ship.[214]

Case 1. A ship sailed well equipped, having a donkey-engine and a sufficient supply of coal for all purposes other than pumping purposes; she met with heavy weather and leaked considerably, the donkey-engine was used to pump, and it was only by this steam pumping that the leak was kept under; the coal ran short, and some of the spare spars and cargo were used for fuel. *Held*, that the sacrifice of the spars and cargo was a general average loss.[215]

Case 2. A ship ran aground and was in danger. The engines were intentionally worked to get her off, at the risk of straining them, and they were strained. *Held*, that the damage to the engines and the coal consumed were subjects of general average contribution.[216]

Case 3. A sailing ship, with auxiliary screw, was damaged by perils of the sea, so that practically she had lost all her power of sailing; instead of repairing her sailing gear, she proceeded with her voyage under steam alone, at a very heavy expenditure in coals. *Held*, that such expenditure did not

---

[209] *Anglo-Argentine Co v Temperley* [1899] 2 Q.B. 403.
[210] *Birkley v Presgrave* (1801) 1 East 220; *Price v Noble* (1811) 4 Taunt. 123; *Wilson v Bank of Victoria* (1867) L.R. 2 Q.B. 203. Tipping the ship by the head, in order to repair the propeller, whereby water damaged the cargo, has been held a general average sacrifice; *M'Call v Houlder* (1897) 2 Com.Cas. 129. So, also, damaging the engines by working on them with knowledge of the risk to get a ship off is a general average sacrifice: *The Bona* [1895] P. 125 (CA). As to calculation of the amount of general average sacrifice where it follows previous damage, and the ship becomes a constructive total loss, see *Henderson v Shankland* [1896] 1 Q.B. 525 (CA).
[211] *Shepherd v Kottgen* (1877) 2 C.P.D. 585. See *Corrie v Coulthard* (1877) 3 Asp.M.L.C. 546n.
[212] See *Robinson v Price* (1877) 2 Q.B.D. 91 at p.95; *Wilson v Bank of Victoria* (1867) L.R. 2 Q.B. 203; *The Vortigern* [1899] P. 140.
[213] The decision to breach must be reasonable: *Anglo-Grecian Steam Trading Co v T. Beynon & Co* (1926) 24 Ll.L.R. 122.
[214] *Austin Friars Co v Spillers & Bakers* [1915] 3 K.B. 586. See also *The Seapool* [1934] P. 53.
[215] *Robinson v Price* (1877) 2 Q.B.D. 91; affirmed *ibid.* 295.
[216] *The Bona* [1895] P. 125.

give rise to a general average contribution because it was incurred in carrying out the shipowner's original contract.[217]

Case 4. A ship met with a storm which caused part of the rigging to give way; the mainmast in consequence began to lurch, and was cut away by the captain's orders; if it had not been cut away it would have gone overboard very shortly, at great risk to the ship. *Held,* that the cutting away of the mast, then practically worthless, did not give rise to a claim for general average contribution.[218]

Article 140—General Average Loss—Sacrifice of Freight   A140

Sacrifice of freight by the shipowner, by an act whereby the cargo is preserved, gives rise to a general average contribution against the cargo.[219]

The freight to be considered is the bill of lading, not the chartered freight.[220]

Case 1. F shipped coal on A's ship to be carried to Z; on the voyage the coal took fire by spontaneous combustion; the ship and cargo were in immediate danger of total destruction by fire, but, by jettison of cargo, and pouring water on it, and discharging it at Y, the ship and a large portion of the cargo were saved from destruction. It was found impossible to carry the cargo to its destination, and it was accordingly sold at Y. By reason of such measures, the ship was prevented from earning her freight by delivering at Z. *Held,* that the shipowner was entitled to a general average contribution from the cargo on account of the freight thus lost.[221]

Case 2. A cargo of coals became so heated that it was impossible to carry it with safety to its destination. The master accordingly put into a port of refuge and discharged the coal, which was sold. The sale involved a loss of freight, but was effected at a time when both ship and cargo were in safety. *Held,* the sale did not amount to a general average act and the loss of freight was not a general average sacrifice.[222]

Article 141—General Average Loss—Extraordinary Expenditure by   A141
Shipowner

Extraordinary expenditure voluntarily[223] incurred, or extraordinary loss of time and labour voluntarily accepted, may also give rise to a general average contribution, provided that in each case the sacrifice is made for the common safety in a time of danger.[224] But the expense must be both extraordinary and incurred to avoid a common peril.[225]

Such general average contribution must cover not only the voluntary sacrifice, but also expenses directly caused by, or in consequence of, the voluntary sacrifice.[226]

Thus when the cargo has been placed in safety, it will not be liable to

---

[217] *Wilson v Bank of Victoria,* above.
[218] *Shepherd v Kottgen* (1877) 2 C.P.D. 585.
[219] *Pirie v Middle Dock Co* (1881) 44 L.T. 426. It was also suggested that the cargo was not entitled to general average contribution from the ship: (1) because the loss arose from vice in the cargo (as to which see *Greenshields v Stephens* [1908] A.C. 431); (2) because there was really no loss, the cargo selling for more at Y than it would have realised after paying freight at Z. The case is discussed by Bingham J. in *Iredale v China Traders Ins Co* [1899] 2 Q.B. 356.
[220] *cf. The Leitrim* [1902] P. 256. Loss of time is not made good as demurrage on ship, loss of interest on cargo, or loss of time hire by charterer: *Wetherall v London Ass. Co* [1931] 2 K.B. 448.
[221] *Pirie v Middle Dock Co,* above.
[222] *Iredale v China Traders Ins Co* [1900] 2 Q.B. 515.
[223] See fn.172, above.
[224] per Bowen L.J., *Svendsen v Wallace* (1884) 13 Q.B.D. 69 at pp.84, 85. See also per Lawrence J. in *Birkley v Presgrave* (1801) 1 East 220. The sentence in the text is in the words of Bowen L.J. It is not quite clear what he meant by "extraordinary loss of time", as to which see fn.220, above.
[225] *cf. SA Nouvelle v Spillers* [1917] 1 K.B. 865.
[226] See fn.224, above.

contribute to expense afterwards incurred by the shipowner for the purposes of earning his freight, as in getting off a stranded vessel,[227] or making arrangements for the further carrying of the cargo in his own vessel, under circumstances when the cargo might have stayed where it was, or have been carried on by other vessels, with equal advantage.[228] But expenses incurred by the shipowner, or his agents, as agents of the cargo-owner or in the sole interests of the cargo, in preserving the cargo, must be borne by the cargo.[229]

A142   **Article 142—Expenses in Port of Refuge**

Where a ship on her voyage runs into a port of refuge to repair a general average sacrifice, such as cutting away a mast, the expenses of repairing the sacrifice, of warehousing and reloading goods necessarily unloaded for the purpose of repairing the injury, and expenses incurred for pilotage with other charges on the vessel on leaving port, are also the subject of general average.[230]

The amount of liability to a third party, incurred as the natural consequence of a general average act, is to be treated as general average expenditure. Thus if, in time of common peril, the ship is run into a dock to preserve her from sinking, and in doing so the risk of injuring the dock wall is intentionally and knowingly incurred, the liability of the shipowner to the dock-owner for the injury done is a subject of general average contribution.[231]

Where a ship on her voyage, in consequence of damage not the subject of a general average contribution, such as springing a leak, puts into a port of refuge, and, in order to repair the ship, the cargo is necessarily landed, the expenses of reloading the cargo to enable the ship to prosecute her voyage are not the subject of a general average contribution from the cargo,[232] nor is damage to the cargo sustained in discharging it, in order to repair the ship, the cargo being in no danger.[233]

Semble, that in principle the expenses of unloading the cargo will or will not be the subject of general average, according as the cargo is not or is safe in the ship without removal.[234]

---

[227] *Walthew v Mavrojani* (1870) L.R. 5 Ex. 116; *Job v Langton* (1856) 6 E. & B. 779; *Royal Mail Co v Bank of Rio* (1887) 19 Q.B.D. 362.

[228] *Schuster v Fletcher* (1878) 3 Q.B.D. 418. For circumstances in which the shipowner may make such charges, see *Rose v Bank of Australasia* [1894] A.C. 687, in which *Schuster v Fletcher*, above, was disapproved.

[229] See per Montague Smith J. and Hannen J. in *Walthew v Mavrojani*, above, at pp.125, 126. Montague Smith J. suggests the case of "perishable goods landed on a desert island in a distant and unfrequented part of the world". *Semble*, that this is not general average, but that, the original venture being at an end, the cargo-owner must bear the whole expense: see *Cargo ex Argos* (1872) L.R. 5 P.C. 134. As to the possibility of a claim by the shipowner against the charterer rather than the goods-owner see *Adelfamar SA v Sibs E. Mangimi Martini SpA (The Adelfa)* [1988] 2 Lloyd's Rep. 466.

[230] *Atwood v Sellar* (1880) 5 Q.B.D. 286. See also *Plummer v Wildman* (1815) 3 M. & S. 482, as explained in *Svendsen v Wallace* (1884) 13 Q.B.D. 69 at p.90; *Hallett v Wigram* (1850) 9 C.B. 580.

[231] *Austin Friars Co v Spillers & Bakers* [1915] 3 K.B. 586.

[232] *Svendsen v Wallace* (1884) 13 Q.B.D. 69; affirmed (1885) 10 App.Cas. 404. See also *Power v Whitmore* (1815) 4 M. & S. 141; *Hallett v Wigram*, above; *Walthew v Mavrojani* (1870) L.R. 5 Ex. 116.

[233] *Hamel v P. & O. Co* [1908] 2 K.B. 298.

[234] In practice they are charged as general average; but see per Brett M.R. (1884) 13 Q.B.D. 69 at p.76; per Bowen L.J. *ibid.* at p.88, and per Lord Blackburn (1885) 10 App.Cas. 404 at p.414. These expenses are expressly chargeable under Rule X(a) of the York-Antwerp Rules 1994, printed in Appendix II.

Semble, that the expenses of warehousing the cargo are to be borne by the cargo.[235]

Semble, that pilotage expenses and port dues out are not the subject of general average.[236]

Note. The distinction in fact between *Atwood v Sellar*,[237] and *Svendsen v Wallace*,[238] is that in the first case the ship put into port to repair a general average sacrifice; in the second to repair a particular average loss, or one liable to be borne by the ship alone[239]; though such putting into port is probably a general average sacrifice in itself. The difference in principle is not clear, and seems to be rather a question of the continuity of the transaction, unloading the cargo not being a necessary consequence of putting into port, which was the general average sacrifice in *Svendsen v Wallace*; though it is of the voluntary sacrifice of the ship, which was the general average act in *Atwood v Sellar*. But it is impossible to feel that *Atwood v Sellar* is satisfactory as an authority. *Da Costa v Newnham*[240] must be taken as overruled: and *Morgan v Jones*[241] as either overruled or limited to its own very special facts.[242]

Article 143—Master's Duty to collect General Average Contribution   A143

Where a general average loss has occurred on a voyage, the shipowner or master has a right to retain cargo until he is paid or tendered the amount due on it for general average[243]; he is under a duty to persons entitled to a general average contribution from the cargo to take all reasonable precautions to protect their interests either by obtaining deposits in cash or suitable bonds and guarantees, and is liable to an action if he omits to do so.[244] But *semble*, he need not institute legal proceedings to enforce such bonds or guarantees unless indemnified by the parties interested.

It is also the duty of the master to furnish to all cargo-owners all the accounts and particulars necessary for adjusting general average.[245] If he omits to do so,

---

[235] See fn.232, above.
[236] So per majority of CA in *Svendsen v Wallace*, above. But see Rule X(a) of the York-Antwerp Rules 1994, printed in Appendix II.
[237] (1880) 5 Q.B.D. 286.
[238] (1885) 10 App.Cas. 404.
[239] *Jackson v Charnock* (1880) 8 T.R. 509; *Hallett v Wigram* (1850) 9 C.B. 580.
[240] (1788) 2 T.R. 407. See per Brett M.R. in *Svendsen v Wallace* (1884) 13 Q.B.D. 69 at p.80 and per Bowen L.J., *ibid.* at p.90.
[241] (1857) 7 E. & B. 523. See per Brett M.R. in *Svendsen v Wallace*, above, at p.80 and per Bowen L.J., *ibid.* at p.93; *Royal Mail Co v Bank of Rio* (1887) 19 Q.B.D. 362 at pp.371, 377.
[242] The practice of English adjusters will be found in the Rules of Practice of the Association of Average Adjusters printed in the Annual Reports of the Association. See also the York-Antwerp Rules, 1994, Appendix II.
[243] See per Lord Esher and Lindley L.J. in *Huth v Lamport* (1886) 16 Q.B.D. 735; *Simonds v White* (1824) 2 B. & C. 805 at p.811. For a clause exempting the goods from lien, but making the shippers liable, see *Walford v Galindez* (1897) 2 Com.Cas. 137.
[244] *Strang v Scott* (1889) 14 App.Cas. 601, at p.606; *Crooks v Allan* (1979) 5 Q.B.D. 38; *Nobel's Explosives v Rea* (1897) 2 Com.Cas. 293. *Hallett v Bousfield* (1811) 18 Ves. 187, is a doubtful authority; see *Strang v Scott*, above at p.606. Some bills of lading exempt the master from this duty, e.g. "shipowner not to be bound to exercise his lien for general average contribution". The master is under no duty to persons entitled to salvage from the cargo to detain it until he obtains a bond from the cargo-owners to pay such salvage: *The Raisby* (1885) 10 P.D. 114, and Art.147.
[245] *Huth v Lamport*, above, and see *The Norway* (1864) B. & L. 377 at p.397.

the cargo-owner who fails to tender a sufficient sum in consequences of such omission, is not liable for such failure.[246]

If he does furnish such particulars, the cargo-owner must either pay the sum demanded, or tender the right sum, at his peril.

If, as in practice, the master demands a particular security[247] for the payment by the cargo-owner of the amount found on adjustment to be due, such security must be a reasonable one.[248]

Case. A, shipowners, had a lien on cargo in their ship, for general average. They required the cargo-owner to make a deposit of 10 per cent on the value of the goods in the name of A, or B, his average adjuster or A and B; and to execute a bond, the "Liverpool Bond", providing that such deposit should be security for general average and that the persons in whose name it stood might pay out from time to time such sums as they thought right to A or his master on account of their disbursements. All questions of general average to be adjusted by B, with appeal to arbitrators whose decision should be final. *Held*, that such a requirement was unreasonable, and its continued demand released the cargo-owner from the necessity of tendering.[249]

A144   Article 144—Who can sue for General Average Contribution

(1) The shipowner, or, if the charter amounts to a demise, the charterer: they have also a possessory lien on the cargo for the general average contribution due from it.[250]

(2) The cargo-owner, who can sue another cargo-owner,[251] the shipowner, or the person entitled to the freight, for general average contribution due from them. He has not after adjustment a maritime lien on the ship for the contribution due from it, nor will such a personal debt support a bottomry bond on the ship given in a subsequent voyage.[252]

(3) The person entitled to the freight for contributions due from the other interests in the adventure.[253]

A145   Article 145—Who can be sued for General Average Contribution

There are liable for general average contribution:

(1) The shipowner, for that due from the ship (unless she is under a charter amounting to a demise, in which case the charterer is liable), and from the chartered freight.[254]

---

[246] See per Lord Esher and Lindley L.J. in *Huth v Lamport* (1886) 16 Q.B.D. 735; *Simonds v White* (1824) 2 B. & C. 805.

[247] *Semble*, that if the master obtains from the cargo-owners the form of security usual at the port of discharge he will be protected: *Simonds v White*, above; *The Raisby* (1885) 10 P.D. 114.

[248] *Huth v Lamport*, above. The clause in some bills of lading, "In case of average, a deposit sufficient to cover the estimated contribution to be paid at port of discharge if so required by the master" seems both unnecessary and unworkable. The master has his lien without it, and the method of "estimating", which is the difficulty, is not provided for.

[249] *Huth v Lamport* (1886) 16 Q.B.D. 735.

[250] See Arts 143, 184.

[251] *Strang v Scott* (1889) 14 App.Cas. 601; *Dobson v Wilson* (1813) 3 Camp. 480.

[252] *The North Star* (1860) Lush. 45; *quaere*, whether a lien for general average by foreign law will support a bond.

[253] *Pirie v Middle Dock Co* (1881) 44 L.T. 426.

[254] As to the liability of chartered freight on a round voyage, see *Williams v London Assurance Co* (1813) 1 M. & S. 318; *Carisbrook Co v London and Provincial Co* [1902] 2 K.B. 681.

(2) The charterer[255] for that due from the ship, if the charter amounts to a demise[256] in respect of his interest in bill of lading freight,[257] and[258] in respect of his interest in advance freight.[259]

(3) The cargo-owner.

(4) The consignee of cargo who has taken delivery of the goods under a bill of lading is not liable for general average, unless:

(a) He is the owner of the goods; or

(b) The bill of lading under which he takes the goods stipulates that he shall pay average; or

(c) He has notice from the master or his lien for average, and after that takes the goods.[260]

(5) The shipper, though the property in the goods has passed from him may be liable under special clauses in the bill of lading.[261]

Article 146—General Average Contribution, how adjusted   A146

In the absence of special agreement,[262] the amount to be contributed in general average is adjusted when the voyage is terminated by the delivery of the goods or otherwise and according to the law of the place of delivery.[263] The fact that the voyage has been temporarily suspended while the ship is repaired at a port of refuge, does not justify an average adjustment at such port.[264]

If after the shipowner has incurred general average expenditure at a port of refuge both ship and cargo are lost while completing the voyage, the shipowner cannot claim contribution from the owners of cargo.[265]

---

[255] See fn.251, above.

[256] See fn.252, above.

[257] See *The Leitrim* [1902] P. 256.

[258] *Pirie v Middle Dock Co*, above.

[259] *Frayes v Worms* (1865) 19 C.B.(N.S.) 159.

[260] *Scaife v Tobin* (1832) 3 B. & A. 523. He would not be liable if he merely had notice that the goods were liable for general average, but not that the master claimed a lien (*ibid.*). He may also be liable under the terms of a Lloyd's average bond for the proportion of general average to which the shippers or owners may be liable to contribute, if the bond is entered into in consideration of the shipowner giving up his lien: *Hain SS Co v Tate & Lyle* (1936) 41 Com.Cas. 350.

[261] *Walford v Gallndez* (1897) 2 Com.Cas. 137.

[262] e.g. "Average, if any, to be adjusted according to British custom" which makes the custom of English average adjusters, though contrary to the law, part of the contract, *Stewart v West India Co* (1873) L.R. 8 Q.B. 362, See also *Goulandris Bros v Goldman* [1958] 1 Q.B. 74, at pp.90, 91, per Pearson J. Today the usual clause is "General average to be adjusted according to York-Antwerp Rules 1994." These rules are printed in Appendix II. The usual clause does not have the effect of delaying the running of time under the Limitation Act 1980, until after an adjustment has been prepared: *Chandris v Argo Insurance* [1963] 2 Lloyd's Rep. 65.

[263] *Simonds v White* (1824) 2 B. & C. 805; *Dalglish v Davidson* (1824) 5 D. & R. 6. The shipowner is under no obligation to employ an average stater at any particular place, or at all. He may make his own statement: *Wavertree S.S. Co v Love* [1897] A.C. 373; *Chandris v Argo Insurance*, above.

[264] *Hill v Wilson* (1879) 4 C.P.D. 329; see also *Fletcher v Alexander* (1868) L.R. 3 C.P. 375; *Mavro v Ocean Insurance Co* (1875) L.R. 10 C.P. 414.

[265] So held by Sankey J. as matter of the common law: *Chellew v Royal Commission* [1921] 2 K.B. 627. In the CA the decision was affirmed only on the effect of the York-Antwerp Rules: [1922] 1 K.B. 12.

A147 **Article 147—Salvage**[266]

If cargo is saved from loss or damage on a voyage by persons other than those who have undertaken to carry it, the salvors are entitled to remuneration and reward for their services, known as *salvage*.[267] Salvage by professional salvors is usually governed by the terms of agreements on the Lloyd's Open Form and such agreements may bind cargo owners if made by the master managers or owners on their behalf as agents of necessity.[268] The fact that the owners of the salvage vessel are also owners of the vessel responsible in whole or in part for the collision necessitating the salvage does not debar their claim to salvage remuneration: probably, too, the owners of a salving vessel which is herself in part responsible for the collision, are entitled to salvage.[269]

No salvage is payable by cargo owners unless some cargo is saved, and it is payable proportionately to the cargo saved.[270] Ship and cargo must each pay its own share of salvage; neither can be made liable for salvage due from the other without an express agreement to pay it,[271] or unless the shipowner is liable to indemnify the cargo-owners for such payment, on the ground that the necessity for the salvage was caused by his breach of contract[272]; but either or both, if saved, may be liable to pay salvage for life saved, though, if life is saved, but not cargo or ship, the cargo-owner or shipowner will not be liable to pay life salvage.[273]

The authority of the master to bind the cargo to pay salvage is derived from necessity and benefit to the cargo.[274] It is no part of the duty of the master of the salved ship to protect the salvors by obtaining a bond from the cargo-owners for their proportion of any salvage that may be due before allowing the cargo-owners to take away their goods.[275]

---

[266] See generally on salvage, *Kennedy's Law of Salvage* 6th edn (London: Sweet & Maxwell, 2001).

[267] The Crown is now in the same position as regards the law relating to civil salvage as a private person, both as regards salvage claims against and by the Crown, subject to s.29 of the Crown Proceedings Act (1947) (exclusion of proceedings *in rem* against the Crown) (so far as consistent with the Salvage Convention) and except for ss.225–227 of the Merchant Shipping Act 1995: see MSA 1995, s.230(1), (2). Crown Proceedings Act 1947, s.8. Different Government Departments may, however, for procedural purposes not be treated as identical parties: see *The Susan v Luckenbach* [1951] P. 197 at p.203.

[268] *The Choko Star* [1990] 1 Lloyd's Rep. 516; *The Pa Mar* [1999] 1 Lloyd's Rep. 338 at 342—343.

[269] The *Beaverford v The Kafiristan* [1938] A.C. 136; *The Susan V Luckenbach* [1951] P. 197. These cases also suggest that a claim for salvage may be defeated by the defence of circuity of action if the claimant is owner of the ship solely responsible for the collision necessitating the salvage and no question of limitation of liability arises.

[270] *The Longford* (1881) 6 P.D. 60; see also *Semco v Lancer (The Nagasaki Spirit)* [1997] 1 Lloyd's Rep. 323, 326–327. The general rule that no salvage is payable if no property is saved has been altered in cases where salvage services have prevented or minimised damage to the environment see Art.14 of the Salvage Convention of 1989, incorporated into English law in 1994.

[271] *The Pyrennee* (1863) B. & L. 189; *The Raisby* (1885) 10 P.D. 114; a case of an agreement to salve, and not an agreement to pay a particular sum for salvage. For instances of such express agreement, see *The Prinz Heinrich* (1888) 13 P.D. 31; *The Cambrian* (1887) 57 L.T. 205.

[272] *Scaramanga v Marquand* (1886) 53 L.T. 810; *Duncan v Dundee Shipping Co* (1878) 5 Rettie 742.

[273] See the Merchant Shipping Act 1894, s.544, and *The Renpor* (1883) 8 P.D. 115; *The Mariposa* [1896] P. 273; *Cargo ex Sarpedon* (1877) 3 P.D. 28; *The Fusilier* (1865) 3 Moore P.C.(N.S.) 51. In *The Annie* (1886) 12 P.D. 50, the ship was raised, but sold for less than the cost of raising her, and it was *held* that there was nothing to which a claim for life salvage could attach.

[274] *The Renpor* (1883) 8 P.D. 115 at p.118.

[275] *The Raisby* (1885) 10 P.D. 114.

Where, however, the shipowners have paid, or made themselves personally liable to pay, a sum of money for the preservation of the ship and cargo, they will, if such payment is justifiable and did not result from the fault of the shipowners,[276] have a lien on the cargo for the sum that they have paid[277]; though the fact that they have bona fide and reasonably paid a certain sum is not conclusive that that sum is the basis on which the liability of the cargo-owners is to be reckoned.[278]

The charterer of a vessel which renders salvage services is not entitled, in the absence of special clauses,[279] to salvage for those services[280] unless the charter amounts to a demise, so that at the time of the salvage he is in possession of the vessel.[281]

Case. The *R.*, owned by A, rendered salvage services to the *S.*, owned by K, and chartered to A, the charter not amounting to a demise. *Held*, that A was entitled to salvage from the *S*.[282]

Article 148—Collision   A148

The cargo laden on board a vessel at the time of collision cannot be sued in the Admiralty Court for the damage[283] even though it belongs to the owner of the ship, or to the charterer under a charter amounting to a demise.[284]

The owner of cargo on board a ship sued for collision can only be compelled to pay into court the amount of freight due from him to the shipowner, less the costs of payment in.[285]

The owner of a cargo lost by a collision in which both ships are in fault may of course recover his whole loss against the owner of the ship that is carrying his cargo, unless prevented by exceptions in the bill of lading. But he may make an alternative claim against the stranger ship,[286] in which case he can recover his loss against the two ships in the proportions in which they have been found to be in fault.[287] If the stranger ship is alone in fault, he may either recover the whole loss against her, or he may recover it from the carrying ship, unless prevented by

---

[276] *The Ettrik* (1881) 6 P.D. 127. See also *The Makedonia* [1962] 1 Lloyd's Rep. 316 at p.341.

[277] *Briggs v Merchant Traders' Co* (1849) 13 Q.B. 167, *Cox v May* (1815) 4 M. & S. 152.

[278] *Anderson, Tritton & Co v Ocean S.S. Co* (1884) 10 App.Cas. 107. For the conditions rendering a salvage agreement void, see *The Rialto* [1891] P. 175; *The Mark Lane* (1890) 15 P.D. 135.

[279] For such a special clause, held to divide equally the net profit on the salvage operations, see *Brooker v Pocklington* [1899] 2 Q.B. 690.

[280] *The Collier* (1866) L.R. 1 A. & E. 83; *The Waterloo* (1820) 2 Dods. 433; *The Alfen* (1857) Swabey 189. The charterer may have a claim against the owner for delay or deviation in rendering the salvage: *The Alfen*, above.

[281] *The Maria Jane* (1850) 14 Jur. 857; *The Scout* (1872) L.R. 3 A. & E. 512; *Elliott Tug Co v Admiralty* [1921] 1 A.C. 137, and Art.28.

[282] See fn.169, above.

[283] *The Victor* (1860) Lush. 72; *The Leo* (1862) Lush. 444.

[284] If it were a demise, the charterer would be liable for collision caused by negligence of the chartered ship: *Fenton v Dublin S.S. Co* (1838) 8 A. & E. 835.

[285] *The Leo*, above; *The Flora* (1866) L.R. 1 A. & E. 45.

[286] *Thorogood v Bryan* (1849) 8 C.B. 115, to the contrary, is now overruled by *The Bernina* (1887) 13 App.Cas. 1. The fact that the owner of the stranger ship is also the owner of the carrying ship, and protected by exceptions in the bill of lading, will not help him: *Chartered Merc. Bank v Netherlands Co* (1883) 10 Q.B.D. 521.

[287] Under the Merchant Shipping Act 1995, s.187.

exceptions in the contract of affreightment[288]; if the carrying ship alone is at fault, he may recover the whole loss from her unless prevented by exceptions in the contract of affreightment.[289] As distinct from loss suffered by the cargo-owner through physical damage to his cargo caused by a collision, he may recover from the stranger wrongdoing ship the contribution he has had to make to the carrying ship in respect of a general average sacrifice or expenditure properly incurred by that ship, although liability to contribute may only arise by virtue of the special terms of the contract of affreightment, namely, clauses excepting the carrying ship from liability in negligence and incorporating the provisions of the York-Antwerp Rules 1994, including Rule D.[290]

---

[288] As he almost certainly would be under the exception of perils of the seas: *the Xantho* (1887) 12 App.Cas. 503.

[289] See *The Xantho*, above, and Art.112, above. On the liability of a ship *in rem* for a collision, where the charter amounts to a demise, see *The Tasmania* (1888) 13 P.D. 110 and Art.28.

[290] *Morrison Steamship Co v Greystoke Castle (Cargo Owners)* [1947] A.C. 265.

CHAPTER 13

PERFORMANCE OF THE CONTRACT—UNLOADING

Article 149—Unloading   A149

AT the port of discharge it is the duty of the master to proceed to the place of discharge provided by the contract[1] and the shipowner may be restrained by injunction from discharging cargo in a place not so agreed.[2] Difficult questions may arise as to who has the right of naming the discharging berth where the cargo is deliverable to several consignees or indorsees of bills of lading. In the case of a general ship this right is vested in the master, subject to any controlling custom of the port. In the case of a ship under a charter this right belongs:

(1) if the charterers hold the bills of lading, to the charterers;

(2) if the bills of lading are not held by the charterers, to the bills of lading holders, if all agree on the place of discharge, or to the majority of the bills of lading holders so long at any rate as the minority do not dissent;

(3) if there is no agreement, to the charterers or possibly to the bill of lading holders with the preponderating interest.[3]

Apart from special provisions, it is the duty of the shipowner at common law to get the goods out of the ship's hold, to put them on the ship's deck or alongside[4] and to have suitable tackle available for the ordinary purposes of discharging[5]: but the duty of providing, and making proper use of, sufficient means for the discharge of the cargo, when it has been got up out of the hold, lies in general upon the charterer.[6] In the absence of any limitations by the terms of the charter or bill of lading, the charterers or consignees must take delivery at the time and under the conditions stated in the following Articles, and must take delivery continuously in ordinary working hours from that time.[7]

This duty must be fulfilled when:

---

[1] See Art.73.

[2] *Wood v Atlantic Transport Co* (1900) 5 Com.Cas. 121.

[3] *The Felix* (1868) L.R. 2 A. & E. 273; *Ireland v Southdown S.S. Co* (1926) 32 Com.Cas. 73; *Co-op Wholesale Society v Embiricos* (1928) 30 Ll.L.R. 315; *Malozzi v Carapelli SpA* [1975] 1 Lloyd's Rep. 229.

[4] *Ballantyne v Paton*, 1912 S.C. 246. The shipowner is not in the absence of a custom of the port bound to separate cargoes which have been loaded in bulk, e.g. bones, hornes, piths and hoofs mixed; *Clacevich v Hutcheson* (1887) 15 Rettie 11; nor to bag bulk cargo; *British Oil and Cake Mills v Moor Line* (1935) 41 Com.Cas. 53; *Akt. Sameiling v Grain Importers (Eire)* [1952] 1 Lloyd's Rep. 313; nor to bulk bagged cargo; *Atlantic Shipping Co v Bunge y Born* (1931) 39 Ll.L.R. 292. See also fn.24, below. For the meaning of "bulk cargo", see *Hird v Rea* (1939) 63 Ll.L.R. 261. For the meaning of "homogeneous" cargo, see *Chandris v Union of India* [1956] 1 Lloyd's Rep. 11. For the custom of London as to timber, see *Akt. Helios v Ekman* [1897] 2 Q.B. 83 (CA), and Art.83, and see, as to Liverpool, *Cardiff S.S. Co v Jamieson* (1903) 19 T.L.R. 159.

[5] The obligation to provide suitable tackle arises even though the cargo is to be "discharged free of expense to the vessel": *Hang Fung Shipping Co v Mullion* [1966] 1 Lloyd's Rep. 511; see also *Madras v P. & O.* (1923) 16 Ll.L.R. 240 at p.243. For the respective obligations of shipowner and charterer as to the opening and closing of hatches, see *S. G. Embiricos v Tradax* [1967] 1 Lloyd's Rep. 464.

[6] per Lord Selborne in *Poslethwaite v Freeland* (1880) 5 App.Cas. 599 at p.608.

[7] *Zillah v Midland Ry* (1903) 19 T.L.R. 63.

(1) The ship is at the place where the carrying voyage is to end. (Arts 69–74.)

Where the charter provides that the vessel is to unload at a port or place to be nominated, the same principles apply to the nomination of the port of discharge as to the nomination of the port of loading.[8] The charter may provide that the nomination of the discharge port must take place by a certain time.[9] The act of nomination of the discharge port or place may take the form of issuing or causing to be issued bills of lading referring to that port or place.[10] There will be no such nomination where bills of lading have been issued which themselves provide for a port or place to be nominated.[11]

Neither the master nor any agent of the shipowner is entitled to demand of the consignee before the ship's arrival whether he will receive the goods consigned to him. A refusal to perform the contract made before the ship's arrival is not a final breach of the contract, unless it is accepted as such by the shipowner, or is still unretracted at the time of the ship's arrival, in which case it becomes an actual as distinct from an anticipatory breach of the contract.[12]

(2) She is ready to discharge.[13]

In the absence of an express provision, notice to the charterer of the above facts is not necessary, but when they are fulfilled the lay-days allowed for discharging begin (Art.150).[14]

As in the case of loading,[15] so in the case of discharging it appears that where the contract of carriage is subject to the Carriage of Goods by Sea Act 1971, the parties may validly agree, notwithstanding Art.III, rr.2 and 8, of the Schedule to the Act, that the charterer or consignee is responsible for discharge.[16]

---

[8] See Articles 69–74, above.

[9] For instance the Gencon charter which provides that the nomination must be made "on signing bills of lading".

[10] *Heinrich Hanno & Co v Fairlight Shipping Co (The Kostas K)* [1985] 1 Lloyd's Rep. 231. This will be the case where the bills are issued to a third party. *Quaere* where the bills remain in the hands of the charterer. Cf. *A/S Tank v Agence Maritime L. Strauss* (1939) 65 Ll.L.Rep. 87.

[11] As to the duties of the bills of lading holder to nominate in this situation see *Gatoil International Inc v Tradax Petroleum Ltd (The Rio Sun)* [1985] 1 Lloyd's Rep. 350 at p.359.

[12] *Ripley v M'Clure* (1849) 4 Ex. 345, as modified and explained by *Hochster v De la Tour* (1853) 2 E. & B. 678; *Frost v Knight* (1870) L.R. 5 Ex. 322; which cases are discussed in *Johnstone v Milling* (1886) 16 Q.B.D. 460; *Mersey Steel Co v Naylor Benzon* (1884) 9 App.Cas. 434 at pp.438, 439; a repudiation which is not "accepted" as such by the innocent party is a "thing writ in water", see per Asquith L.J. in *Howard v Pickford Tool Co* [1951] 1 K.B. 417 at p.421.

[13] The same principles apply *mutatis mutandis* as to readiness for loading: See Art.75, above.

[14] As to the time when the ship's responsibility ends, see *British Shipowners' Co v Grimond* (1876) 3 Rettie 968; *Knight S.S. Co v Fleming*, 1898 25 Rettie 1070; *The Jaederen* [1892] P. 351, per Barnes J. at p.358, and Art.153, Note 3, below.

[15] See above, Art.90.

[16] *Jindal Steel v Islamic Shipping (The Jordan II)* [2004] UKHL 49; [2005] 1 Lloyd's Rep. 57 (HL), approving the summary in the 20th edn of this work at pp.430–431. It remains unclear whether the incorporation into the bill of lading of a charterparty under which stowage is the responsibility of "the charterer" is sufficient to transfer responsibility to the shipper or receiver: *Balli Trading Ltd v Afalona Shipping Co Ltd (The Coral)* [1993] 1 Lloyd's Rep. 1 (CA).

Article 150—Notice of Readiness to discharge not required   A150

In the absence of special contract[17] or custom, the shipowner is not bound to give notice of his readiness to unload either to the charterers or to shippers or consignees under bills of lading.[18]

If, however, the charterers or consignees have been prevented by the shipowners' wrongful act or omission from learning by reasonable diligence of the ship's readiness to unload, they will to that extent be discharged.[19]

Where the ship arrives already on demurrage, days on demurrage begin to count on arrival, even if notice of readiness would have been required under the charterparty for the commencement of the laydays.[20]

Case 1. A ship carried goods under a bill of lading, "to be taken out in fourteen days after arrival, or to pay 10s. a day demurrage". The ship was ready to deliver on October 3, but the goods were not landed till October 29. The consignees pleaded: (1) no notice of arrival: *Held*, unnecessary[21]; (2) that the ship was wrongly entered in the custom-house as *Die Treue* instead of *The Treue*: *Held*, that an entry by the shipowner so inaccurate as to mislead a person using reasonable diligence would have relieved the consignee from liability demurrage; but that it was not proved here that reasonable diligence had been used, and that therefore the consignees were liable.[22]

Case 2. Under a charter: "the ship to be addressed to charterers' agents free of commission", the ship, in breach of the charter, was addressed by the shipowners to other agents, who gave no notice to consignees, whereby delay occurred and the latter were sued for demurrage. It being proved that the charterers' agent would have given such notice: *Held*, that the shipowner could not claim demurrage, the liability for which arose from his own breach of contract.[23]

Unloading accordance to custom of port of discharge, see Arts 85 and 158.
Demurrage in unloading, see Chapter 14.

Article 151—Duty of Master as to Delivery at Port of Discharge   A151

In the absence of statutory provisions, customs of the port of discharge[24] or express stipulations in the charter or bill of lading, the master on the arrival of the

---

[17] See the cases on notice of readiness to load in Art.76, below. In bills of lading there commonly appears, "Party to be notified—". Where the name of the consignee is inserted in this space there is an obligation upon the shipowner to give notice to him of the arrival of the goods: *E. Clemens Horst Co v Norfolk, etc., Co* (1906) 11 Com.Cas. 141. A common clause provides that time for discharging is to commence twenty-four hours after arrival at or off the port the port of discharge. In the absence of qualification this means twenty-four hours by the clock: if the twenty-four hours expire during a period excepted as laytime such as a holiday, time for discharge will commence when the first working period thereafter is reached: *Borg (Owners) v Darwen Paper Co* (1921) 8 Ll.L.R. 49.
[18] *Harman v Mant* (1815) 4 Camp. 161; *Harman v Clarke* (1815) 4 Camp. 159; *Nelson v Dahl* (1879) 12 Ch.D. 568, per Brett L.J. at p.583; and *cf. Major v Grant* (1902) 7 Com.Cas. 231.
[19] *Houlder v General Steam Navigation Co* (1862) 3 F. & F. 170; *Bradley v Goddard* (1863) 3 F. & F. 638, *Harman v Clarke*, above.
[20] *Pagnan v Tradax* [1969] 2 Lloyd's Rep. 150. It is thought that a clearly worded clause could postpone commencement of days on demurrage until the expiry of notice of readiness notwithstanding the rule "once on demurrage, always on demurrage". *Cf.* Art.155 below.
[21] In *Houlder v General Steam Navigation Co*, above, an attempt to prove a custom to give notice to consignees failed.
[22] *Harman v Clarke*, above.
[23] *Bradley v Goddard* (1863) 3 F. & F. 638.
[24] In London, for example, delivery to the dock authority is, as regards the ship's liablity, equivalent to delivery to the consignee: *Petrocochino v Bott* (1874) L.R. 9 C.P. 355. *Cf. Grange v Taylor* (1904) 9 Com.Cas. 223, where the bills of lading were for undivided portions of a bulk cargo, the whole of which was delivered to the Dock Company, and the shipowner was held under no obligation to divide up the portions correctly. *Cf. P. & O. Co v Leetham* (1915) 32 T.L.R. 153 as to a custom of Hull.

ship at its destination must allow the consignee a reasonable time to receive the goods, and cannot discharge his liability by landing them immediately on the ship's arrival.[25]

The shipowner is both bound and entitled to deliver the goods against production of an original bill of lading provided he has no notice of any other claim or better title.[26] The holder of the bill of lading, who presents it at a reasonable time, is entitled, in the absence of custom to the contrary, to have the goods delivered to him direct from the ship, existing liens being satisfied.[27]

If a person claims the goods as entitled to them, but is unable to produce the bill of lading, the captain can, of course, deliver them to him on his giving security, or an indemnity, against possible adverse claims by others. Under a bill of lading contract, he is under no obligation to do so,[28] nor, save in exceptional circumstances, can he be ordered to effect such delivery under a time or voyage charter.[29]

The shipowner or master is justified in delivering the goods to the first person who presents to him a bill of lading, making the goods deliverable to him, though that bill of lading is only one of a set, provided that he has no notice of any other claims to the goods, or knowledge of any other circumstances raising a reasonable suspicion that the claimant is not entitled to the goods.[30] If he has any such notice or knowledge, he must deliver at his peril to the rightful owner,[31] or must interplead.[32] He is not entitled to deliver to the consignee named in the bill of lading, without the production of the bill of lading, and does so at his risk if the consignee is not in fact entitled to the goods.[33]

---

[25] *Bourne v Gatliff* (1844) 11 Cl. & Fin. 45 at p.70. See also *Proctor, Garratt, Marston v Oakwin S.S. Co* [1926] 1 K.B. 244; *Turner, Nott & Co v Lord Mayor, etc., of Bristol* (1928) 31 Ll.L.R. 359. For an English port without customs, see *Fowler v Knoop* (1878) 4 Q.B.D. 299.

[26] *Motis Exports v Dampskibsselskabet AF 1912* [2000] 1 Lloyd's Rep. 211, 216 para.19.

[27] *Erichsen v Barkworth* (1858) 3 H. & N. 601 at p.616; reversed on another point (1858) 3 H. & N. 894. In the absence of express stipulation or custom the shipowner cannot discharge the cargo on to the quay and there sort it. He must, if required, deliver to each consignee separately: *The Varing* [1931] P. 79, per Scrutton L.J. at pp.84, 89.

[28] *Gatoil International Inc v Tradax Petroleum Ltd (The Rio Sun)* [1985] 1 Lloyd's Rep. 350 at p.361; see also *Motis Exports v Dampskibsselskabet AF 1912* [2000] 1 Lloyd's Rep. 211, 216 para.19; *Carewins Development (China) Ltd v Bright Fortune Shipping Ltd* [2006] 4 H.K.L.R.D. 131 (Hong Kong); *Voos Peer v APL Co Pte Ltd* [2002] 4 S.L.R. 481 (Sing.)

[29] *Kuwait Petroleum Corp v I & D Oil Carriers Ltd (The Houda)* [1994] 2 Lloyd's Rep. 541. It would appear that the Court does have the jurisdiction to order the discharge of a cargo without production of bills of lading on production of a suitable letter of indemnity where the bills have been lost.

[30] *Glyn, Mills & Co v East and West India Dock Co* (1882) 7 App.Cas. 591; *The Tigress* (1863) 1 B. & L. 38. See also *Caldwell v Ball* (1786) 1 T.R. 205.

[31] In answer to a claim by the indorsee of a bill of lading the shipowner is entitled to plead that the shipper of the goods had no property in them and that therefore no property has passed to the indorsee: *Finlay v Liverpool and G.W. S.S. Co* (1870) 23 L.T. 251.

[32] per Lord Blackburn in *Glyn, Mills & Co v East and West India Dock Co*, above, at pp.611, 614. The opinion in *Fearon v Bowers* (1753) 1 H.Bl. 364n, and any dicta approving it in *The Tigress*, above, to the effect that the captain is not concerned to examine who had the better right on different bills of lading, are overruled by the principal case. The shipowner is not entitled to interplead if he has issued bills of lading to more than one person for the same goods: *Elder Dempster Lines v Zaki Ishag* [1923] 2 Lloyd's Rep. 548.

[33] *The Stettin* (1889) 14 P.D. 142; *London Joint Stock Bank v Amsterdam Co* (1910) 16 Com.Cas. 102; *Sze Hai Tong Bank v Rambler Cycle Co* [1959] A.C. 576 at p.586 (P.C.) *MB Pyramid Sound NV v Briese-Shiffarts GmbH & Co KG (The Ines)* [1995] 2 Lloyd's Rep. 144; *The Tareechai Marine* [1995] 1 M.L.J. 413 (Mal.). Cf. *The Cherry* [2003] 1 S.L.R. 471 (Sing.).

The shipowner is liable if he delivers to someone who is not in fact the holder of the bill of lading even if he does so without negligence.[34] Clauses exempting the shipowner from loss or damage "after discharge" do not apply to "misdelivery" (in the sense of delivery to a party who is not the holder of the original bill of lading).[35] In principle, however, very clear words might protect the shipowner against such misdelivery.[36]

Misdelivery by the master will not affect the property in the goods, so as to confer any better right on the claimant than he originally had, as against persons claiming on another bill of lading of the set.[37]

In some cases—for instance when the cargo can be discharged and held under lien ashore—it may be so unreasonable for the shipowner to refuse to discharge the cargo that he cannot claim demurrage from delay resulting from his refusal to do it.[38]

Semble, that a warehouseman, with whom the goods have been warehoused under statutory powers, is in the same position as the shipowner as to the delivery of the goods.[39]

Case. Goods were shipped and consigned to G to be delivered in Z under three bills of lading marked First, Second, Third, respectively. G indorsed the bill of lading marked "First" to a bank as security for a loan. On the arrival of the goods at Z they were landed into warehouses by the master under a stop for freight due on them. G produced to the warehouseman the bill marked "Second", unindorsed, and was entered in their books as the owner. G then paid the freight, and gave a delivery order to P, to whom the warehouseman delivered bona fide and without knowledge of the bank's claim. *Held*, that the warehouseman was not liable to the bank for wrongful delivery of the goods.[40]

Article 152—Goods of Different Owners Mixed and Unidentifiable—Delivery   A152

Where goods of one description, shipped under different bills of lading, have become mixed and unidentifiable in the course of the voyage the owners of the

---

[34] *Motis Exports v Dampskibsselskabet AF 1912* [2000] 1 Lloyd's Rep. 211, where on the assumed facts the shipowner delivered against production of a forged bill.
[35] *SA Sucre Export v Northern River (The Sormovskiy 3068)* [1994] 2 Lloyd's Rep. 266, *MB Pyramid Sound v Breese (The Ines)* [1995] 2 Lloyd's Rep. 144; *Motis Exports v Dampskibsselskabet AF 1912* [2000] 1 Lloyd's Rep. 211; *East West v DKBS 1912* [2003] EWCA Civ 83; [2003] 1 Lloyd's Rep. 239; *Trafigura Beheer v Mediterranean Shipping (The MSC Amsterdam)* [2007] EWCA Civ 794; [2007] 2 Lloyd's Rep. 622, paras 28–32.
[36] See e.g. *Chartered Bank of India v British India* [1909] AC 369, *Trafigura Beheer v Mediterranean Shipping (The MSC Amsterdam)* [2007] EWCA Civ 794; [2007] 2 Lloyd's Rep. 622, para.29. Some of the language of Lord Denning in *Sze Hai Tong v Rambler* [1959] A.C. 576 might suggest that it is not possible to exclude liability for misdelivery because it would be against the *"main object and intent of the contract"*; but the case is properly treated as a matter of construction of the exemption clause: see *East West v DKBS 1912* [2003] 1 Lloyd's Rep. 239 at 258–259 para.65.
[37] *Barber v Meyerstein* (1870) L.R. 4 H.L. 317.
[38] *Carlberg v Wemyss Co* 1915 S.C. 616; *The Siam Venture and Darfur* [1987] 1 Lloyd's Rep. 147. Where the shipowner does not have the option of delivering the cargo ashore but retaining control of it pending the production of bills of lading, it will generally not be unreasonable to refuse to discharge the cargo. If the master of a time-chartered vessel at the request of the time-charterers delivers his cargo without production of the bills of lading, the owner will be entitled to be indemnified by the time-charterers against subsequent liability to the holders of the bills of lading: *Strathlorne S.S. Co v Andrew Weir & Co* (1934) 40 Com.Cas. 168; *A/S Hansen-Tengens Rederi III v Total Transport Corp (The Sagona)* [1984] 1 Lloyd's Rep. 194. Cf. *ED & F Man Ship Ltd v Heng Hong (The MV Aksu)* [1999] 1 S.L.R. 200. But see *Brown Jenkinson & Co v Percy Dalton* [1957] 2 Q.B. 621.
[39] See *Glyn, Mills & Co v East and West India Dock Co* (1882) 7 App.Cas. 591, per Lords Selborne and Cairns at p.597; Lord O'Hagan at p.601; Lord Blackburn at pp.609, 614; Lord Watson at p.614; *contra*, per Lord FitzGerald at p.617; and per Brett L.J. (1882) 6 Q.B.D. 475 at p.486.
[40] *Glyn, Mills & Co v East and West India Dock Co*, above.

goods so mixed become tenants in common of the whole of the mixed goods in the proportions in which they have severally contributed to that whole.[41] It will therefore be the duty of the shipowner to deliver the indistinguishable goods, or their proceeds, to the various holders in proportion to the extent to which full delivery on each bill of lading remains unsatisfied by the delivery under it of its proper identifiable goods. Similarly, in so far as the shipowner can prove that the co-ownership of the goods is of pecuniary value to the bill of lading holder, the damages recoverable (subject to an exceptions clause) from the shipowner for failure to deliver will be reduced.[42]

The shipowner may be relieved of his duty of apportioning the goods among the bill of lading holders by the provisions of the various bills of lading, or by the custom of the port as to discharge.[43]

In some cases a penal rule has been applied that where the goods of A have been wrongfully mixed by B with the goods of B, so that the goods of A are unidentifiable, A is sole owner of the mixture.[44] This is not the general rule, which is that where B wrongfully mixes the goods of A with goods of his own (*semble* with goods of C), which are substantially of the same quality and nature, and they cannot in practice be separated, the mixture is owned in common in the proportion to the quantities contributed to the mixture. A is entitled to receive a quantity equal to that of his goods which went into the mixture and to sue for damages caused by reason of the admixture.[45]

Note. The statement in the text as to the principle of apportionment where the doctrine of *commixtio* applies is correct, and is of simple application, when the parcels of cargo shipped have all arrived at their destination. But where the position is complicated by a part of the whole cargo having been lost at sea, as well as by part arriving unidentifiable, difficult problems may arise. The difficulty is to determine in what proportions the various bill of lading holders have contributed to the bulk of unidentifiable goods. This would necessitate also the ascertainment of the proportions in which the various holders contributed to the amount of goods lost at sea.

Obviously the problem can be solved only by making assumptions.[46] One possible method would be to assume that the goods lost at sea were contributed by the various consignments in proportion to their original amounts when shipped. Another method would be to assume that the unmarked and unidentifiable bulk has been contributed by the various consignments in proportion to their original amounts when shipped. In *Spence v*

---

[41] *Spence v Union Marine Co* (1868) L.R. 3 C.P. 427, following *Buckley v Gross* (1863) 3 B. & S. 566, and *Jones v Moore* (1841) 4 Y. & C. 351; *Sandeman v Tyzack & Branfoot Co* [1913] A.C. 680; *Gill & Duffus (Liverpool) Ltd v Scruttons* [1953] 2 Lloyd's Rep. 545; *Smurthwaite v Hannay* [1894] A.C. 494 at p.505 (per Lord Russell of Killowen C.J.); *Indian Oil Corp Ltd v Greenstone Shipping SA (The Ypatianna)* [1987] 2 Lloyd's Rep. 280; Birks, "Mixing and Tracing" (1992) 45(2) C.L.P. 69.

[42] *Sandeman v Tyzack & Brandfoot Co* [1913] A.C. 680, 697 (per Lord Moulton).

[43] *Grange v Taylor* (1904) 9 Com.Cas. 223; *Petrocochino v Bott* (1874) L.R. 9 C.P. 355 (both as to London); *P. & O. Co v Leetham* (1915) 32 T.L.R. 153 (as to Hull): *Gill & Duffus (Liverpool), Ltd v Scruttons* [1953] 2 Lloyd's Rep. 545 (master porter's duties at Liverpool).

[44] *Lupton v White* (1608) 15 Ves. 342; *Sandeman v Tyzack* [1913] A.C. 680, 695 (per Lord Moulton).

[45] *India Oil v Greenstone Shipping (The Ypatianna)* [1987] 2 Lloyd's Rep. 286, 298; *Glencore v MTI* [2001] 1 Lloyd's Rep. 284, 329–330 esp. at para.185.

[46] In *Sandeman v Tyzack* [1913] A.C. 680 the House of Lords (Scotland) refused to make such an assumption *against* the alleged co-owner: i.e. the *commixtio* principle was held not to apply because it could not be proved that any of the defenders' original bales were among the remaining unidentified bales.

Union Marine Co, above, there was a loss of part of the whole shipment at sea, and also an arrival of unmarked and unidentifiable bales. The court seems to have *held* that the amount paid in by the defendants was, in any case, enough without going into the nice questions involved in ascertaining how much the plaintiffs had in fact lost. The headnote in the *Law Reports* (not apparently justified by the judgment) says: "All the owners became tenants in common of the cotton which arrived at Liverpool and could not be identified . . . the share of each owner's loss in the cotton totally lost . . . *and his share in the remainder which arrived at Liverpool* being in the proportion that the quantity shipped by him bore to the whole quantity shipped." This is to apply the two methods suggested above both at once, but this is impossible in almost every case. There is no necessary connection at all between the proportion of goods lost (assuming them to have been lost in the proportions of the original shipments) and the resulting proportion of unidentifiable goods.

There is, however, a principle upon which the same percentage can be applied both to the bales lost at sea and to the unidentifiable arrived bales, and can be applied in every case, viz. the share of each consignee's loss in the bales lost at sea, and equally his share in the unmarked arrived bales is in the proportion which the difference between the number of marked bales delivered to each consignee and the number of marked bales shipped to each consignee bears to the total of such differences for all the consignments.[47] And this, it is submitted, should be the rule applied in such cases.[48]

Article 153—The Master's Power to land or carry on the Goods at   A153 Common Law

While the master is not, as a general rule, bound to unload except on production of the bill of lading, he is not bound to keep goods on board his ship if no bill of lading is produced.

If the consignee or holder of the bill of lading does not claim delivery within a reasonable time, the master may land and warehouse the cargo in a statutable[49] warehouse at the expense of its owners, still preserving his lien on it, and it is his duty to act reasonably[50] in doing so rather than render the charterers, if they are not the defaulting consignees, liable for demurrage.[51]

In such a case the warehouseman holds the goods as the common agent of the shipowner and of the consignee or indorsee of the bill of lading; agent of the shipowner to retain the goods and his lien for freight; agent of the consignee or

---

[47] Thus, suppose A ships 500 bales marked RS, and B ships 100 bales marked MN. A's consignee has delivered to him 450 marked RS. B's consignee has delivered 10 marked MN. There have been lost at sea 100 bales (marks unknown), and there arrive 40 without marks and unidentifiable.

 A shipped 500 and has had delivered 450, i.e. 50 were in the 100 lost at sea, or are partly in the 40 unmarked. B shipped 100 and has had delivered 10, i.e. 90 were in the lost 100 at sea, or are partly among the 40 unmarked. A is short 50 and B is short 90, i.e. 140 altogether. If 5/14ths of the 100 lost at sea were A's and 9/14ths were B's, then A lost 35 5/7ths and B lost 64 2/7ths. There remain unaccounted for 14 2/7ths of A's, i.e. 5/14ths of the 40 unmarked, and 25 5/7ths of B's, i.e. 9/14ths of the 40 unmarked. If the headnote to *Spence v Union Marine Co* were applied to this case it would mean that 5/6ths of the 100 lost at sea came out of A's consignment, and 5/6ths of the 40 unmarked belong to A. But A has only lost 50 altogether, either by loss at sea or by loss of marks!

[48] See, for an adaptation of this, *Gill & Duffus (Liverpool), Ltd v Scruttons* [1953] 2 Lloyd's Rep. 545.

[49] i.e. a warehouse, on the goods in which the lien of the shipowner is preserved by some statute.

[50] See *Smailes v Hans Dessen* (1906) 12 Com.Cas. 117.

[51] *Howard v Shepherd* (1850) 9 C.B. 297 at p.321; *Erichsen v Barkworth* (1858) 3 H. & N. 601, reversed, however, on appeal: (1858) 3 H. & N. 894. This power is also given by express provision in most bills of lading. See *Note* 1.

indorsee to hold or deliver the goods for him on his producing the bill of lading and paying the freight.[52]

Semble, that if there are no statutable warehouses, delivery into which preserves his lien, he can still retain it by hiring a warehouse for the purpose.[53]

If, in unloading by the master owing to the delay or absence of the consignee, difficulties arise from the inaccurate description of goods in the bill of lading, the consignee must bear the resulting loss.[54]

If the master is forbidden to land the goods by the port authorities, or cannot obtain warehouse accommodation, he may, and must, at their owner's expense,[55] deal with them in the manner both most reasonable to preserve his lien and most convenient in his judgment for their owner.

Note 1. Many bills of lading have some such clause as the following:
"The shipowner shall be entitled to land these goods on the quays of the dock where the steamer discharges immediately on her arrival, and upon the goods being so landed the shipowner's responsibility shall cease. This clause is to form part of this bill of lading, and any words at variance with it are hereby cancelled" (known as the *London Clause*).[56]

Note 2. Where by the terms of his contract the shipowner has to deliver the cargo, he must pay any expenses necessarily involved in the process of delivering, e.g. the expenses of providing bags in which coffee beans escaping from bags broken on board the ship must be replaced in order to effect their discharge.[57]

Note 3. When the ship's liability is to cease is usually expressly provided in the bill of lading, e.g.: "Ship's responsibility ceases immediately the goods are discharged from the ship's deck"; or "the goods, etc. . . . as soon as they are discharged over the ship's side shall be at risk of the shipper or consignee"; or "goods at risk of consignee from ship's tackles"; or as in the *London Clause* as above; or "The ship's responsibility ceasing when delivering into lighter when the goods are over the ship's side level with the rail." Clauses of this nature are not likely to apply where the goods are misdelivered to a party who is not the holder of the original bill of lading: see Art.151 above. In the absence of any such express provision, the question must be decided by the custom of the port of discharge; and, if no such custom can be proved, the general rule appears to be "that goods are delivered when they are so completely in the custody of the consignee that he may do as

---

[52] See Willes J., *Meyerstein v Barber* (1866) L.R. 2 C.P. 38 at p.50.
[53] *Mors le Blanch v Wilson* (1873) L.R. 8 C.P. 227; *Kokusar Kisen Kabushiki Kaisha v Cook* (1922) 12 Ll.L.R. 343 at p.345.
[54] *Shirwell v Shaplock* (1815) 2 Chit. 397.
[55] *Cargo ex Argos* (1872) L.R. 5 P.C. 134; *Mors le Blanch v Wilson* (1873) L.R. 8 C.P. 227; *Edwards v Southgate* (1862) 10 W.R. 528. See Art.163. As to the possibility of claiming against the charterer see *Adelfamar SA v Sibs E Mangimi Martini SpA (The Adelfa)* [1988] 2 Lloyd's Rep. 466.
[56] See, for instances of the operation of such a clause, *Alexiadi v Robinson* (1861) 2 F. & F. 679; *Wilson v London, etc., Steam Co* (1865) L.R. 1 C.P. 61; *Oliver v Colven* (1879) 27 W.R. 822; *Major v Grant* (1902) 7 Com.Cas. 231. The clause does not apply in the case of goods landed not in the docks but at a wharf: *Produce Brokers' Co v Furness Withy* (1912) 17 Com.Cas. 165. It sometimes contains an option to discharge into craft hired by the shipowner. "Craft" may cover sailing barges if dumb barges are exhausted: *United States Shipping Board v Vigers* (1924) 41 T.L.R. 26.
[57] *Leach v Royal Mail Co* (1910) 16 Com.Cas. 143. As to the liability for discharging expenses under the "Centrocon" charter in the case of the shipment of optional cargoes, see *Lykiardopulo v Bunge y Born* [1934] 1 K.B. 680, the cases there cited: *Woodfield S.S. Co v Bunge y Born* (1933) 45 Ll.L.R. 14; and *Hain S.S. Co v Minister of Food* [1949] 1 K.B. 492 (CA).

he pleases with them", in other words, when they pass from agents of the shipowner to agents of the consignee.[58]

Note 4. There is often a clause in bills of lading requiring claims for damaged[59] goods to be made within a certain time, as before removal, or within seven days after the goods are landed, or within one month of steamer's arrival.

See also r.6 in Art.III of the Schedule to the Carriage of Goods by Sea Act 1971.[60] By r.8 of Art.III such clauses are invalidated in cases to which the Act applies.[61]

---

[58] See *British Shipowners Co v Grimond* (1876) 3 Rettie 968 at p.972, and *Knight S.S. Co v Fleming* (1898) 25 Rettie 1070. *Cf. The Jaederen* [1892] P. 351, per Barnes J. at p.358, as to cases where the whole discharge is done by a dock company as agents for shipowner and charterer.

[59] This includes both apparent and latent damage: *Moore v Harris* (1876) 1 App.Cas. 318. See also Art.106, *Note 3,* above.

[60] Below, Chapter 20.

[61] *Australasian United Co v Hunt* [1921] 2 A.C. 351, and *Coventry Sheppard v Larrinaga S.S. Co* (1942) 73 Ll.L.R. 256.

CHAPTER 14

DEMURRAGE

A154   **Article 154—Nature of Demurrage**

DEMURRAGE,[1] in its strict meaning, is a sum agreed by the charterer to be paid as liquidated damages[2] for delay[3] beyond a stipulated or reasonable time for loading or unloading, generally referred to as the lay-days or lay-time. Where the sum is only to be paid for a fixed number of days, and a further delay takes place, the shipowner's remedy is to recover unliquidated "damages for detention" for the period of the delay. The phrase "demurrage" is sometimes loosely used to cover both these meanings.[4]

"Dispatch money", "dispatch rebate" or sometimes simply "dispatch" is a rebate of freight allowed to the charterer at a daily rate for loading or discharging in less than a stipulated or reasonable time.[5]

A stipulation as to demurrage is one for the benefit of the charterer as well as of the shipowner, i.e. a charterer, at the price of paying the agreed demurrage, is entitled to keep the ship for the agreed time, or, if not agreed, such a time as will not frustrate the commercial object of the adventure,[6] beyond the lay-days; the shipowner is not entitled to sail away directly the lay-days have expired, treating the provision for demurrage as merely for his protection if he allows the ship to remain beyond the lay-days,[7] even though the charterer is in breach of contract, unless, at the time the ship sails, the charterer is wholly and finally disabled from loading (or discharging) before the expiry of a time that will frustrate the commercial object of the adventure. Equally, an order given by the charterer to the shipowner which will necessarily involve lay-time being exceeded is not a

---

[1] "Demurrage" is an elastic term and there is a tendency to extend its meaning, e.g. so as to cover delay caused by failure to nominate a loading port, see *Trading Soc. Kwik-Hoo-Tong v Royal Commission on Sugar Supply* (1924) 19 Ll.L.R. 90; *cf. The Varing* [1931] P. 79 at pp.89, 93. See Arts 77 to 82 for so-called "special demurrage" clauses.

[2] See *Note* 1, below.

[3] See *Note* 2, below. See *Navico AG v Vrontados Naftiki Etairia P.E.* [1968] 1 Lloyd's Rep. 379 for a discussion of the commercial basis of demurrage. A clause providing for an agreed sum by way of demurrage is not an exceptions clause: *Suisse Atlantique v N.V. Rotterdamsche Kolen Centrale* [1967] A.C. 361. *Cf. Interfoto Picture Library Ltd v Stiletto Visual Programmes Ltd* [1988] Q.B. 433.

[4] For a discussion of the resulting difficulties, see Art.93. An exception relieving a charterer from liability for "damages for delay" in a charterparty, which also provides for "demurrage" in the strict sense, may relieve him not only from liability for damages for detention but also for demurrage. See *Moor Line v Distillers Co*, 1912 S.C. 514; and *Westoll v Lindsay*, 1916 S.C. 782.

[5] *Navico AG v Vrontados Naftiki Etairia P.E.*, above.

[6] *Universal Cargo Carriers Corp v Citati* [1957] 2 Q.B. 401. See also per Scrutton L.J. in *Inverkip S.S. Co v Bunge* [1917] 2 K.B. 193 at p.201.

[7] *Wilson & Coventry v Thoresen* [1910] 2 K.B. 405; *Aktieselskabet Reidar v Arcos* [1927] 1 K.B. 352 at p.361; *Proctor, Garratt, Marston v Oakwin S.S. Co* [1926] 1 K.B. 244; *Ethel Radcliffe S.S. Co v Barnett* (1926) 31 Com.Cas. 222; *Novorossisk Shipping Co Ltd v Neopetro Co Ltd* [1990] 1 Lloyd's Rep. 425 at p.430. But *quaere* whether, there being no provision for demurrage, the charterer can insist on the ship remaining for a reasonable time after expiration of the lay-days on paying damages for detention: *Wilson & Coventry v Thoresen*, above.

non-contractual order and the shipowner will be obliged to obey such an order unless it will entail frustrating delay.[8]

Stipulations for demurrage may be:

(1) *Exhaustive:* as "ten days for loading and demurrage at £20 per diem afterwards", which covers all delay. On such a provision the shipowner cannot say that the provision for £20 a day demurrage only applies to a reasonable time, and that thereafter he can claim damages for detention. If the contract is not repudiated or frustrated, he can only claim the agreed rate of demurrage,[9] even though the delay by the charterer may be wilful so as, for example, to limit the number of voyages that can be performed and thus the freight payable under a charter for consecutive voyages to be performed within a stated period.[10]

(2) *Partial:* as "ten days to load, ten days on demurrage at £20 per diem", when all delay after twenty days will give rise to damages for detention: or "demurrage at £20 per diem",[11] when demurrage will begin at a time ascertained, except that it must be when a reasonable time for loading has elapsed.

(3) *Absent:* as "ten days to load", or "load according to the custom of the port", or simply "load", where all unexcused delay will give rise to "damages for detention".

Note 1. It has long been established that Lord Trayner's statement in *Lilly v Stevenson*[12] that "days stipulated by the merchant on demurrage are just lay-days but lay-days that have to be paid for" is not correct, and that demurrage is liquidated damages for breach of contract: *Aktieselskabet Reidar v Arcos*,[13] *Superfos Chartering A/S v N.B.R. (London) Ltd (The Saturnia).*[14] It is for this reason that clauses which purport to exclude or reduce liability to pay demurrage are in the nature of exceptions clauses and fall to be construed accordingly.[15]

---

[8] See fn.6, above; *Novorossisk Shipping Co Ltd v Neopetro Co Ltd*, above; doubted obiter in *Total v Arcadia (The Eurus)* [1998] 1 Lloyd's Rep. 351 at 355 per Staughton L.J.

[9] *Western S.S. Co v Amaral Sutherland* [1913] 3 K.B. 366; *Inverkip S.S. Co v Bunge* [1917] 2 K.B. 193; see also *Britain S.S. Co v Donugol* (1932) 44 L.L.L.R. 123 (detention due to breach of obligation to provide icebreaker covered by demurrage clause). See *Universal Cargo Carriers Corp v Citati* [1957] 2 Q.B. 401 on this generally and as to what may constitute a repudiation. It has not been decided whether damages for detention can be recovered at large if the shipowner allows his ship to stay on after a frustrating delay.

[10] *Suisse Atlantique v NV Rotterdamsche Kolen Centrale* [1967] A.C. 361.

[11] *Cf. Harris v Jacobs* (1885) 15 Q.B.D. 247, in which Brett L.J. laid down that "such a payment was in the nature of demurrage; the clause as to demurrage in a charter being elastic enough in the ordinary construction of a charter to comprise such a damage as this", and cited as authority his own judgment in *Sanguinetti v Pacific Co* (1877) 2 Q.B.D. 238 at p.252, for criticisms on which see *Note* to Art.55 in the 17th edn. See also Art.93, above. The Scottish courts take a stricter view of "demurrage": cf. *Gardiner v Macfarlane* (1889) 16 Rettie 658; and cf. the English courts in *Clink v Radford* [1891] 1 Q.B. 625, and *Dunlop v Balfour* [1892] 1 Q.B. 507. For the effect of a stipulation to load "on conditions of *colliery guarantee*", see *Restitution Steamship Co v Pirie* (1889) 61 L.T. (N.S.) 330; affirmed (1889) 6 T.L.R. 50 (CA); *Monsen v Macfarlane* [1895] 2 Q.B. 562 (CA); *Saxon S.S. Co v Union S.S. Co* (1900) 5 Com.Cas. 381; *Shamrock S.S. Co v Storey* (1899) 5 Com.Cas. 21; *Thorman v Dowgate SS. Co* [1910] 1 K.B. 410.

[12] 1895 22 Rettie 278.

[13] [1927] 1 K.B. 352 at 361.

[14] [1987] 2 Lloyd's Rep. 43 at 45.

[15] *The Saturnia*, above and Art.155, below.

Note 2. The charterer or consignee cannot, in answer to a claim for demurrage, plead that the shipowner could have, and ought to have, lessened the amount of the delay by landing the goods, and so mitigated the claim for demurrage. In *The Arne*,[16] where there was a clause in the bill of lading providing that if the consignee did not take delivery immediately after arrival the goods might be landed by the ship at the expense and risk of the goods owner, it was held that this was an option given to the shipowner for his protection, and that the consignee could not rely on it as an answer to a claim for demurrage. The same principle was laid down by Lindley L.J. in *Hick v Rodocanachi*.[17] On the other hand, the shipowner cannot claim demurrage for delay caused only by his own unreasonable conduct[18]: in certain circumstances, therefore, he might be unable to claim demurrage caused by his own exercise of a lien for freight on the cargo, when he might have landed the cargo, subject to his lien. This principle is recognised in *Lyle Co v Cardiff*,[19] and in *Smailes v Hans Dessen*,[20] though in both cases it was held that the exercise of the lien was reasonable,[20] and the shipowner was therefore not debarred from his claim for demurrage. For this reason also, demurrage was not interrupted when the shipowner exercised a contractual lien over cargo and the shipowner could not have discharged the cargo ashore and yet preserved the lien: *Rashtriya Chemicals & Fertilizers Ltd v Huddardt Parker Industries Ltd (The Boral Gas).*[21]

Note 3. The provisions as to demurrage quantify the whole of the damages for delay arising from the charterer's breach of contract in delaying the ship beyond the agreed time and the charterer's liability for such damages is limited to the amount of demurrage. Thus in *Suisse Atlantique v NV Rotterdamsche*,[22] where the charterer under a consecutive voyage charter deliberately delayed the ship beyond the agreed lay-days on a number of the voyages, thereby reducing the number of voyages which could be performed under the charter, the shipowner's claim for lost freight was limited to the amount of demurrage.

Where the charterer is in breach of a separate obligation under the charter beyond the obligations to load or discharge cargo within the lay-days, and as a consequence there is delay to the ship at the loading or discharging port, the charterer's liability for such delay is likewise limited to the amount of demurrage: *Inverkip Steamship Co v Bunge & Co.*[23] However, where there is a further breach of charter and this causes loss in addition to delay, damages will be recoverable. In *Chandris v Isbrandtsen-Moller*[24] dangerous cargo was shipped in breach of contract which caused delay in discharge, but no damage to the ship. As the shipowner had not treated the charterer's conduct as a repudiation, he was limited as regards delay in discharge to the demurrage figure. However he recovered the cost of surveying the cargo as damages, as this was a different head of loss to that resulting from the detention of the vessel.

Delay in loading or discharging may itself place the charterer in breach of a further obligation under the charter, e.g. to load a full and complete cargo, which causes a further head of loss beyond the detention of the vessel. In these circumstances, damages are

---

[16] [1904] P. 154.

[17] [1891] 2 Q.B. 626 at p.632.

[18] In *Robinson v British Aluminium Co* (November 1915), unreported, it was held by Bailhache J., under this principle, that it was unreasonable for the shipowner to exercise a lien for a claim for demurrage when the consignees offered to deposit the amount claimed in joint names in a bank. *Cf.* also *Alexiadi v Robinson* (1861) 2 F. & F. 679; *Möller v Jecks* (1865) 19 C.B. (N.S.) 332, and *Carlberg v Wemyss Co*, 1915 S.C. 616. This is an instance of the general principle that a shipowner cannot claim for demurrage caused by his own fault: see *Note* to Art.155, below.

[19] (1899) 5 Com.Cas. 87.

[20] (1906) 12 Com.Cas. 117.

[21] [1988] 1 Lloyd's Rep. 342. See also *Gill Duffus SAS v Rionda Futures Ltd* [1994] 2 Lloyd's Rep. 67 at 76.

[22] [1965] 1 Lloyd's Rep. 166; *ibid.* p.533 (CA); [1967] 1 A.C. 361 (HL).

[23] [1917] 2 K.B. 193.

[24] [1951] 1 K.B. 240.

recoverable in addition to demurrage for delay. This is one interpretation of the decision in *Aktieselskabet Reidar v Arcos*,[25] the facts of which are given below.

Where there is no further breach of charter beyond the failure to load or discharge within the lay-days, but the charterer's breach causes the shipowner damage in addition to the detention of the ship, the position is not clear but it is submitted that the better interpretation of *Aktieselskabet Raidar v Arcos* is that these losses can be recovered in addition to demurrage.[26]

Case. A chartered his ship to B to load a full and complete cargo of timber for the United Kingdom. The charter provided for loading in a fixed time and for demurrage at a fixed rate per day thereafter. By default[27] of B the fixed time for loading was exceeded and demurrage became payable. If the ship had been loaded within the fixed time, the ship would have loaded and earned freight on a summer deck load. In fact, owing to the delay, she sailed with a winter deck load only. *Held*, (1) that on the expiration of the fixed lay-days B was in breach; (2) that A, in addition to demurrage at the fixed rate, was entitled to recover the difference in freight between a summer and a winter deck load as damages.[28]

Article 155—Demurrage, when payable—Damages for Detention   A155

Demurrage becomes payable when the lay-days allowed for loading or unloading have expired. Such lay-days begin when the ship arrives at the place agreed upon in the charter for the commencement of lay-days,[29] and is there ready to proceed to her loading or discharging berth and prepared to load or discharge when she gets there.[29] They run continuously[30] in the absence of express agreement[31] or custom of the port[32] to the contrary or unless covered by an express exception.[33]

When the lay-days have expired, demurrage in the absence of express agreement[34] runs continuously from the end of the lay-days until the loading or discharging is completed. Nor is the charterer or bill of lading holder excused by the absence of the ship from the port of loading[35] or by the inability of the ship to load or discharge, e.g. if she is damaged by collision or by any other cause, unless due to the default of the shipowner[36] or covered by an express exception[37];

---

[25] [1927] 1 K.B. 352 as explained in *Suisse Atlantique v NV Rotterdamsche*, above.
[26] *Aktieselskabet Reidar v Arcos*, above, at pp.358, 362 per Bankes L.J.; p.363 per Atkin L.J.; *Total Transport Corp v Amoco Transport (The Altus)* [1985] 1 Lloyd's Rep. 423; *Adelfamar SA v Silos E. Mangimi Martini SpA (The Adelfa)* [1988] 2 Lloyd's Rep. 466 at 472. Cf. *Suisse Atlantique v NV Rotterdamsche Kolen Centrale*, above at pp.389–90; pp.407–8; p.418; *Richco International Ltd v Alfred C. Toepfer International GmbH* [1991] 1 Lloyd's Rep. 136; *Pentonville v Transfield (The Johnny K)* [2006] 1 Lloyd's Rep 666 at 670 para.33.
[27] Where a clause provided that demurrage would be paid provided the detention occurred "by default of the charterers or their agents", Pearson J. held that detention beyond the lay-days itself constitutes a "default" unless the detention was caused by an excepted peril: *NV Reederij Amsterdam v President of India* [1960] 2 Lloyd's Rep. 82: this point was not dealt with on appeal; [1961] 2 Lloyd's Rep. 1.
[28] *Aktieselskabet Reidar v Arcos* [1927] 1 K.B. 352: see *Note* 3, above.
[29] See Arts 71 and 74, above.
[30] *M'Intosh v Sinclair* (1877) 11 I.R.C.L. 456; *Nielsen v Wait* (1885) 16 Q.B.D. 67.
[31] e.g. "Sundays and holidays excepted."
[32] *Nielson v Wait*, above, where a custom of the port of Gloucester not to reckon in the lay-days the time occupied in moving the ship from one place of discharge to another was held good. In *Dickinson v Martini* (1874) 1 Rettie 1185, time spent in lightening outside the port, in order to proceed to a port of discharge, was included in the lay-days. See Art.71, above.
[33] See *Note*, below.
[34] e.g. if lay-days except "Sundays and holidays" and demurrage is "per like day" or "per like hour": *Rayner v Condor* (1895) 1 Com.Cas. 80; and contrast *Aktieselskabet Gimle v Garland*, 1917, 2. S.L.T. 254.
[35] *Tyne and Blyth Co v Leech* [1900] 2 Q.B. 12.
[36] *Cantiere Navale Triestina v Russian Soviet Naphtha Export Agency* [1925] 2 K.B. 172. See also fn.120, below.
[37] See *Note*, below.

for the charterer is, on the expiration of the lay-days, in breach of his obligations as to loading or discharging.[38] However, in order to be entitled to claim demurrage, the shipowner is under an obligation to have the vessel ready and available to load or discharge and demurrage does not run if the ship is employed for the owner's own purposes.[39] Thus, if the shipowner removes the vessel from the charterer's disposition, e.g. for bunkering,[40] or to discharge other cargo carried under concurrent charters,[41] or if when on demurrage at the first port of loading she is moved to a second loading port named in the charter,[42] no demurrage is payable for the period when the vessel is so removed from the charterer's disposition or is on passage.[43]

It is a general principle that, where there is a stipulation for work to be done in a limited time, and the other party by his conduct renders it impossible or impracticable for the other party to do his work within the stipulated time, then the one whose conduct caused the trouble can no longer claim liquidated damages.[44] The principle would appear to apply to demurrage clauses because they are liquidated damages clauses. If so applied then, where the shipowner causes delay which prevents the charterer from loading or discharging within the lay-time, he would be disentitled from claiming demurrage at all, not merely for the period of the delay caused by him. This drastic solution does not, however, appear to have been applied in a demurrage case, and is not consistent with those cases in which the consequence of the shipowner's removal of the ship has been that he is disentitled to demurrage for the period of removal.[45]

When once a vessel is on demurrage no exceptions will operate to prevent demurrage continuing to be payable unless the exceptions clause is clearly worded so as to have that effect.[46]

---

[38] *Aktieselskabet Reidar v Arcos* [1927] 1 K.B. 352, per Atkin L.J. at p.363.

[39] *Ellis Shipping Corporation v Voest Alpine Intertrading (The Lefthero)* [1991] 2 Lloyd's Rep. 599 at p. 608; *Stolt v Landmark* [2002] 1 Lloyd's Rep. 786.

[40] *Ropner Shipping Co & Cleeves Valleys Collieries, Re* [1927] 1 K.B. 879. See also *Petrinovic v Mission Française* (1942) 71 Ll.L.R. 208 (final removal for safety of ship and cargo).

[41] *Stolt v Landmark* [2002] 1 Lloyd's Rep. 786.

[42] *Breynton v Theodoridi* (1924) 19 Ll.L.R. 409, in which the meaning of "lighterage for owner's account" was also discussed. When the ship has become an arrived ship and then proceeds to an additional port not named in the charter at the charterer's request, demurrage will continue: *Ricargo Trading SA v Spliethoff's Berrachting-skantor BV (The Tassos IV)* [1983] 1 Lloyd's Rep. 648.

[43] Statement in text approved by CA: *Surrey Shipping Co v Compagnie Continentale (The Shackleford)* [1978] 2 Lloyd's Rep. 155 at p.161. See, also, the admirable summary of the common law position per Sir John Donaldson M.R. in *Mosvolds Rederi A/S v Food Corp of India (The King Theras)* [1984] 1 Lloyd's Rep. 1 (CA). A premature acceptance of notice of readiness may cause time to count before the ship is in berth: *ibid.* See also, *Ricargo Trading v Spliethoff's Bevrachtingskantor (The Tassos IV)* [1983] 1 Lloyd's Rep. 648.

[44] *Dodd v Churton* [1897] 1 Q.B. 562; *Trollope & Colls v North West Met. Hospital Board* [1973] 1 W.L.R. 601, 607–608. The principle, though stated in construction cases, has been said to apply to "*all contracts*": see Chitty L.J. in *Dodd v Churton* [1897] 1 Q.B. 562 at 568.

[45] See fn.43 above; in none of which, however, was the *Dodd v Churton* point taken.

[46] *Lilly v Stevenson* 1895 22 Rettie 278; *Rederi Transatlantic v Compagnie Française des Phosphates* (1926) 32 Com.Cas. 126 ("and demurrage not to accrue"); *Compagnie Naviera Aeolus v Union of India* [1964] A.C. 868 (Centrocon Strike Clause) where the text was approved by Lord Reid at p.879 and *Marc Rich & Co Ltd v Tourloti Compania Naviera SA (The Kalliopi A)* [1988] 2 Lloyd's Rep. 101 where Staughton L.J., in approving the text, described the principle as a "rule of construction imposed on the parties by law"; *Ellis Shipping v Voest Alpine (The Lefthero)* [1992] 2 Lloyd's Rep. 109; *Cero v Jean Lion (The Solon)* [2000] 1 Lloyd's Rep. 292; *Frontier v Swissmarine (The Cape Equinox)* [2005] 1 Lloyd's Rep. 390 at 392 para.10 ("*an ambiguous clause cannot give the charterers any protection*"). See further *Note*, below.

Damages for detention (where demurrage is not provided for) become payable either:

(1) On the expiration of the specified lay-days, if any, as above; or

(2) On the expiration of a reasonable time for loading or unloading when no lay-days are specified; or

(3) On the expiration of the fixed number of days for which demurrage has been stipulated.

A charterer may also be liable for damages for detention of the ship during the voyage caused by his shipping cargo that involves such detention.[47]

He may also be liable for damages for detention of the ship if by his breach of contract he delays her in the course of the voyage, e.g. by failure, at a port of call for orders, to give orders in due time,[48] or by his delay in presenting bills of lading for signature,[49] or by his wrongful insistence on a particular method of discharge resulting in delay to the ship in reaching her discharging place.[50]

Where damages for detention are claimed rather than demurrage, for instance because the demurrage rate was only specified to apply for a set period of time which has been exceeded or because the ship has been detained prior to becoming an arrived ship, the demurrage rate may be used as evidence of the market value of the vessel during the period of detention.[51] However, this will not be done when there is alternative evidence of the earning capacity of the ship.[52]

Note. Exceptions must usually be explicit if they are to apply to lay-time and demurrage.[53] A general exceptions clause will not normally be read as applying to provisions for lay-time and demurrage such as "berth reachable on arrival": *Sametiet M/T Johs Stove v Istanbul Petrol Rafinerisi (The Johs Stove)*.[54] Where the charter relieves the charterer from "liability" for certain events, this will not prevent the running of lay-time because there is no contractual obligation to discharge on these days.[55] Even if such a clause is capable of applying to the obligations concerning the time for loading and discharging cargo, it will not normally be held to apply once the vessel is on demurrage. The general principle of construction is sometimes referred to as "once on demurrage always on demurrage".[56] Thus in *Dias Compania Naviera v Louis Dreyfus Corporation*

---

[47] See Art.53.
[48] *Aktieselskabet Olivebank v Dansk Fabrik* [1919] 2 K.B. 162, and see Art.70.
[49] See Art.197.
[50] *The Varing* [1931] P. 79 (CA).
[51] *Rashtriya Chemicals & Fertilizers Ltd v Huddardt Parker Industries Ltd* [1988] 1 Lloyd's Rep. 342 at 345.
[52] *SIB International S.R.L. v Metallgesellschaft Corp (The Noel Bay)* [1989] 1 Lloyd's Rep. 361 at p.366 (CA).
[53] *The Solon* [2000] 1 Lloyd's Rep 292. Examples of explicit words are in cll.6 & 7 of the Asbatankvoy form, stating that delays from particular causes "*shall not count as used laytime or demurrage*": see *Triton v Vitol (The Nikmary)* [2004] EWCA Civ 1715; [2004] 1 Lloyd's Rep. 55.
[54] [1984] 1 Lloyd's Rep. 38.
[55] *Freedom Maritime Corp v International Bulk Carriers SA (The Khian Captain)* [1985] 2 Lloyd's Rep. 212.
[56] e.g. *Superfos Chartering A/S v N.B.R. (London) Ltd (The Saturnia)* [1987] 2 Lloyd's Rep. 43 (CA) although this usage of the maxim has been criticised: *Ellis Shipping Corp v Voest Alpine Intertrading (The Lefthero)* [1992] 2 Lloyd's Rep. 109 (CA).

(The Dias)[57] a term to the effect that time used in fumigating a ship's hold was "to not count" was held to apply to lay-time and did not prevent demurrage from continuing to accrue. Nor do the provisions of Part I of the Gencon charter strikes clause: *Superfos Chartering A/S v N.B.R. (London) Ltd (The Saturnia)*.[58] The rule of construction applies even if the excepting event had begun to operate before the vessel went on demurrage: *The Lefthero*. Even if the clause makes it clear that it is intended to except the charterer from liability, this is not sufficient to exclude liability for demurrage if the words can sensibly be construed to apply to other obligations or liabilities.[59] However certain general exceptions clauses do, on their proper construction, apply when the ship is on demurrage.[60]

Article 156—Demurrage and Dispatch Money, how calculated

Stipulations as to demurrage and lay-days must be strictly limited to those ports to which they are applied in the charter; a reasonable time for loading and unloading will be allowed at other ports on the voyage, to which such stipulations are not applied.[61] Where there is a stipulation as to lay-time, the charterer will bear the burden of showing that one of the exceptions to the running of lay-time—such as weather preventing working of the vessel—has occurred.[62]

A stipulation as to cancelling the charter will not, unless it clearly so provides, apply after the vessel is on demurrage.[63]

When the stipulations in a charter as to loading and unloading differ materially, it will not be allowable in the absence of express provision to lump together the days for loading and discharging, an intention to separate them being inferred.[64]

Provision is not infrequently made to the effect that the charterer shall have the right "to average" the days for loading and discharging in order to avoid demurrage.[65] When the charterer exercises this option[66] the correct method of giving effect to the clause is to work out the position separately for the two operations of loading and discharging and then, for the purpose of calculating the demurrage to be paid or dispatch money earned, to set off the time saved in one

---

[57] [1978] 1 Lloyd's Rep. 325 (HL).
[58] [1987] 2 Lloyd's Rep. 43 (CA).
[59] *Islamic Republic of Iran Shipping Lines v Ierax Shipping Co of Panama (The Forum Craftsman)* [1991] 1 Lloyd's Rep. 81; *Marc Rich & Co Ltd v Tourloti Compania Naviera SA (The Kalliopi A)* [1988] 2 Lloyd's Rep. 101 although *cf. President of India v N.G. Livanos Maritime Co (The John Michalos)* [1987] 2 Lloyd's Rep. 188.
[60] e.g. the Centrocon strikes clause: *Mosvolds Rederi A/S v Food Corp of India* [1986] 2 Lloyd's Rep. 68.
[61] See *Marshall v Bolckow, Vaughan & Co* (1881) 6 Q.B.D. 231; *Niemann v Moss* (1860) 29 L.J.Q.B. 206; *Avon S.S. Co v Leask* (1890) 18 Rettie 280. For other cases where special stipulations as to demurrage were construed, see *Marshall v De la Torre* (1795) 1 Esp. 367; *Stevenson v York* (1790) 2 Chit. 570; *Sweeting v Darthez* (1854) 14 C.B. 538.
[62] *Freedom Maritime Corp v International Bulk Carrier SA (The Khian Captain)* [1985] 2 Lloyd's Rep. 212.
[63] See *Steel Young v Grand Canary* (1904) 9 Com.Cas. 275.
[64] See fn.59, above.
[65] Mention of avoiding demurrage is sometimes omitted: see fn.66, below, and *Alma S.S. Co v Salgaoncar* [1954] 2 Q.B. 94.
[66] The charterer electing to take dispatch money at port of loading will be debarred from averaging the days to save demurrage at port of discharge: *Oakville Co v Holmes* (1899) 5 Com.Cas. 48. Not so, however, if the charterer's agent agrees at port of loading, without authority to do so, to take dispatch money: *Love v Rowtor* [1916] 2 A.C. 527.

operation against the excess time used in the other.[67] An alternative provision, also quite frequently used,[68] is that time for loading and discharging shall be "reversible". This gives the charterer the option to add together the days allowed for both operations and, when the option is exercised, has the same effect as a provision for a specified time for both loading and discharging.[69]

Note. There are few branches of the law which raise nicer points than those arising out of clauses defining lay-time for loading and discharging, and providing for the calculation of demurrage and dispatch money. Any statement of principles is difficult, however, because of the variety of language used in the clauses. The authorities are grouped below by reference to the more important phrases used and are considered apart from the effect of any custom of the port.[70]

Days mean consecutive calendar days of twenty-four hours commencing at midnight, and include Sundays and holidays.[71] If the ship is not ready to load till part of the day has expired, the charterer is not bound to commence loading her until the commencement of the next calendar day; but if he does any work on the partial day it may be evidence of an agreement to treat it as a whole day.[72] In the absence of express stipulation part of a calendar day used in loading or discharging counts as a whole day.[73] *Secus*, where the lay-

---

[67] The statement in the text is based upon the decision of Devlin J. in *Alma S.S. Co v Salgaoncar* [1954] 2 Q.B. 94, following Hamilton J. in *Watson Brothers v Mysore Manganese Co* (1910) 15 Com.Cas. 159, and distinguishing *Moliere S.S. Co v Naylor, Benzon & Co* (1897) 2 Com.Cas. 92, where Kennedy J. decided otherwise on the strength of evidence as to practice. The effect of adopting this method is that the time saved, which may be set off, may include not only lay-days, but also Sundays and holidays. This seems questionable in principle, since what are to be "averaged" are lay or working days, not lay-days plus Sundays and holidays.

[68] There are others, e.g. "any hours saved in loading to be added to the hours allowed for discharging": *Rowland S.S. Co v Wilson* (1897) 2 Com.Cas. 198, where it was held that this provision applied only to avoid demurrage, although this was not expressed, and not also to increase dispatch money. See also *Rederi Transatlantic v Compagnia Française des Phosphates* (1926) 32 Com.Cas. 126 ("days not consumed in loading may be added to time for discharging and any extra time consumed in loading may be deducted from time for discharging").

[69] *Fury Shipping Co v State Trading Co of India (The Atlantic Sun)* [1972] 1 Lloyd's Rep. 509, in which it suited the charterer not to exercise the option and thus save more dispatch money. For earlier cases, see *Love v Rowtor* [1916] 2 A.C. 527; *Verren v Anglo-Dutch Brick Co.* (1929) 34 Ll.L.R. 56; affirmed *ibid.* 210; and *Alma S.S. Co v Salgaoncar* [1954] 2 Q.B. 94 at p.104. In *"Z" Steamship Co v Amtorg* (1938) 61 Ll.L.R. 97, Goddard J. held, obiter, under the special clauses there, that dispatch money could be earned on time saved in loading and the same time could be used under the reversible provisions to avoid demurrage on discharge: *sed quaere*. It is submitted that if the charterer requires payment of dispatch money on loading, he can no longer avail himself of the reversible provisions. The latter were not, however, expressed to be at the charterer's option. See also *Chadwick Weir v Dreyfus* (1923) 14 Ll.L.R. 108 (dispatch paid on loading not forfeited by delay in discharge).

[70] As in *Cochran v Retberg* (1800) 3 Esp. 121, where the then custom of the port of London was proved to consider days as working days only, excluding Sundays and holidays; and *Nielsen v Wait* (1885) 16 Q.B.D. 67.

[71] *Nielsen v Wait*, above. The running day, or day of twenty-four hours, during which the ship is running, is opposed to the working day; for which see p.276 below. But under the clause "to be loaded at the rate of 200 tons per running day . . . time to count twelve hours after written notice of readiness is given", the "running day" was held to mean periods of twenty-four hours beginning twelve hours after the receipt of the notice: *Leonis S.S. Co v Rank* (1907) 13 Com.Cas. 161; *Hain S.S. Co v S.A. Comercial de Exportacion y Importacion (The Trevarrack)* (1934) 49 Ll.L.R. 86. See also *Verren v Anglo-Dutch Brick Co* (1929) 34 Ll.L.R. 56; affirmed *ibid.* (CA). The decision of Roche J., doubted by Scrutton L.J. on appeal, suggests that provisions in a charter as to when time is to start may cause a departure from the calendar day other than in the case of "running" days, e.g. "working" days and (*quaere*) "weather working" days. On the latter see also *Horsley Line v Roechling*, 1908 S.C. 866; *"Z" Steamship Co v Amtorg* (1938) 61 Ll.L.R. 97 at p.101, and below.

[72] *The Katy* [1895] P. 56; *Brown v Johnson* (1842) 10 M. & W. 331; *Niemann v Moss* (1860) 29 L.J.Q.B. 206. This passage was applied in *Thomasson Shipping Co v Peabody* [1959] 2 Lloyd's Rep. 296 at p.304.

[73] *Commercial S.S. Co v Boulton* (1875) L.R. 10 Q.B. 346 (ship on demurrage used part of a calendar day: there was no provision for demurrage being payable pro rata for part of a day); see also the report of the same case as to the ship *Boston* in (1875) 3 Asp. Mar. Law Cas. (N.S.) 111. *Cf. Horsley Line v Roechling*, 1908 S.C. 866.

days are artificial periods of twenty-four hours.[74] The provision of so many days or working days[75] for loading or discharging does not by itself mean that the ship can be compelled to work twenty-four hours a day.[76]

Sundays and holidays excepted. This provision excepts Sundays and holidays from the lay-days, even though work is done upon them, unless some actual agreement to count them as lay-days is proved. This agreement will not be inferred from the fact that work is done.[77] A "non-working holiday" is a public holiday on which work is not ordinarily done without substantial extra payment.[78] A day may be a holiday according to local law although it is also a working day.[79] Neither a wet day, nor the usual half-holiday on Saturday is included in the phrase "general or local holidays".[80] A day on which as the result of a statutory forty-hour week men engaged in a particular trade do not work except at higher wages is not an "official or local holiday".[81] Whether a day is a holiday or not is a question of fact depending on the law, practice or custom applicable in the port.[82]

Working days means all days on which work is ordinarily done at the port, excluding Sundays and holidays.[83] It is a day of work as distinguished from a day of play or rest.[84] It is immaterial that on a working day the charterer is prevented from loading, unless the cause of delay is covered by an exception.[85] Evidence of custom is admissible to explain the meaning of "working day".[86] The number of hours in a working day on which a ship must load must be settled by the custom of the port, or express or implied agreement.[87]

Cargo to be discharged at the average rate of not less than—tons per day. Such a clause, where the tonnage of the cargo, divided by the average rate of discharge, gives a fraction over a day, does not allow the charterer the whole of the last day. It is doubtful how the fraction is to be computed; probably by the proportion of hours used to the hours in the working day; but it is arguable that the charterer is only entitled to the number of days, and cannot claim the fraction over.[88]

---

[74] *Verren v Anglo-Dutch Brick Co* (1929) 34 Ll.L.R. 56; *Reardon Smith Line v Ministry of Agriculture* [1963] A.C. 691, per Lord Devlin at p.739.

[75] As to which see below.

[76] *Reardon Smith Line v Ministry of Agriculture*, above, per Lord Devlin at p.738.

[77] *Nelson v Nelson* [1908] A.C. 108, overruling *Houlder v Weir* [1905] 2 K.B. 267; *Whittal v Rahtkens* [1907] 1 K.B. 783, and *Blanckelow v Lamport* [1907] 1 K.B. 787n.

[78] *Panagos Lyras v Joint Danube and Black Sea, etc.* (1931) 47 T.L.R. 403.

[79] *Chief Controller of Chartering of the Govt. of India v Central Gulf S.S. Corp* [1968] 2 Lloyd's Rep. 173.

[80] *Love v Rowtor Co* [1916] 2 A.C. 527 at p.536; *Hain S.S. Co v SA Comercial de Exportacion y Importacion (The Trevarrack)* (1934) 49 Ll.L.R. 86.

[81] *"Z" Steamship Co v Amtorg* (1938) 61 Ll.L.R. 97.

[82] *Akt. Westfall-Larsen v Russo-Norwegian Transport* (1931) 40 Ll.L.R. 259; *Hain Steamship Co v SA Comercial de Exportacion y Importacion (The Tregantle)* (1932) 48 T.L.R. 363; *Chief Controller of Chartering of the Govt. of India v Central Gulf S.S. Corp*, above.

[83] *Nielsen v Wait* (1885) 16 Q.B.D., 67 at p.71. A Saturday, though a half-holiday, must be treated as a working day: *Robert Dollar Co v Blood Holman & Co* (1920) 4 Ll.L.R. 343; *Reardon Smith Line v Ministry of Agriculture* [1963] 1 Lloyd's Rep. 12 at p. 42 (HL).

[84] *Reardon Smith Line v Ministry of Agriculture* [1963] 1 Lloyd's Rep. 12 at pp.31, 39.

[85] *Holman v Peruvian Nitrate Co* (1878) 5 Rettie 657, where a "surf day" was held a working day. But contrast *British and Mexican Co v Lockett* [1911] 1 K.B. 264.

[86] e.g. in some ports a day observed as the Mohammedan Friday is not a working day; *Reardon Smith Line v Ministry of Agriculture*, above, at p.39, per Lord Devlin. See also *British and Mexican Co v Lockett*, above, overruling *Bennetts v Brown* [1908] 1 K.B. 490.

[87] *Reardon Smith Line v Ministry of Agriculture*, above, per Lord Devlin at p.40; *Nielsen v Wait*, above.

[88] *Yeoman v R.* [1904] 2 K.B. 429. Cargo 2,364 tons; rate 210 tons a day = 11 days 54/210ths. The charterer was held not entitled to claim 12 days. *Cf. Horsley Line v Roechling*, 1908 S.C. 866. In *Houlder v Weir* [1905] 2 K.B. 267, upon a similar clause, Channell J. held that it related primarily to the number of days, not hours, and if the calculation gave a fraction of a day at the end the charterer was entitled to a whole day. He distinguished *Yeoman v R.* on the ground that there was in that case a provision for payment of demurrage per day "and pro rata", which made the case an exception to the rule. But (1) if the rate is 100 tons a day and the cargo is 950 tons, and if he has ten days to discharge, surely the charterer discharges at the average rate of 95 tons a day, not 100 as agreed, and (2) the Court of Appeal in deciding *Yeoman v R.* do not appear to have rested their decision merely on the provision as to payment "pro rata".

When there are two or more ports of discharge the time taken at all must be aggregated before demurrage or dispatch can be calculated.[89]

The weight of cargo actually loaded or discharged and not the nominal cargo on which freight may be payable must be used for the calculation.[90]

"*Cargo to be loaded at the average rate of—tons per hatch per weather working day.*" This provision requires the stipulated rate to be multiplied by the number of hatches which the vessel possesses, the product being divided into the tonnage of cargo carried.[91]

Cargo to be loaded at an average rate of not less than 150 metric tons per available workable hatch per day. A "working hatch" is a hatch into which there is still cargo to be loaded or from which there is still cargo to be discharged. In practice this means that the permitted lay time is ascertained by dividing by 150 the greatest weight of cargo loaded into any one hold and then making any necessary adjustments if loading into any hatch was prevented by non-availability.[92]

"*Cargo to be discharged at the average daily rate of 1000 mt basis 5 or more available working hatches pro rata if less number of hatches per weather working day.*" In contrast with the previous wording, this wording provides an overall rate for the ship rather than a rate per hatch. In consequence, provided there are five hatches available when the ship commences discharging, the daily rate will apply. If a hatch becomes temporarily unavailable during loading or discharging, the relevant period will not count as lay-time, but the lay-time available will not increase simply because loading or discharge of a particular hold is complete.[93]

"*One running day for every 400 tons up to 2,800 tons, and for all quantities in excess 500 tons per day.*" With a cargo of 3,800 tons this means the 400 tons rate for the first 2,800 tons, and the 500 tons rate for the balance. It does not provide two separate rates for the whole contents of vessels under and over 2,800 tons respectively.[94]

"*To count as lay-time.*" A provision that a certain period of time, e.g. overtime, is "to count" as lay-time will normally be construed as if it were intended for the benefit of the shipowner. Conversely, a provision that time is "not to count" as lay-time will normally be construed as if it were intended for the benefit of the charterer.[95] It will not, however, avoid the running of demurrage since in default of the clearest words "time", which is or is not to count, is lay-time and not time on demurrage.[96] Sometimes a clause provides that in certain circumstances time is to count as *used lay-time*. Here, if the lay-time clause provides that certain days—such as Saturdays, Sundays and holidays—are to count as lay-time if used, these days will be treated as lay-time for the purposes of such a clause.[97]

---

[89] *United British S.S. Co v Minister of Food* [1951] 1 Lloyd's Rep. 111, not following *The Themistocles* (1949) 82 Ll.L.R. 232, which on this point was, it is submitted, incorrectly decided, certain days being counted twice over for the purpose of dispatch money as the result of treating separately the time taken in loading at each of two ports; *Cia Naviera Azuero SA v British Oil & Cake Mills* [1957] 2 Q.B. 293. See also *Salgoancar v Goulandris Bros.* [1954] 1 Lloyd's Rep. 56 (different rates for loading in berth and in stream).

[90] *Hain S.S. Co v Minister of Food* [1949] 1 K.B. 492 (CA) (optional cargo shipped under Centrocon charter): for the method of calculation when a cargo less than the agreed weight is shipped see *Bedford Steamship Co Ltd v Navico AG (The Ionian Skipper)* [1972] 2 Lloyd's Rep. 273.

[91] *The Theraios* [1971] 1 Lloyd's Rep. 209 (CA). Thus, a rate of 120 tons per hatch per day is, for a five hatch ship, equivalent to a rate of 600 tons per day.

[92] *Compania de Navegacion Zita v Louis Dreyfus* [1953] 2 Lloyd's Rep. 472, applying *The Sandgate* [1930] P. 30. See also, *Cargill Inc v Rionda de Pass Ltd (The Giannis Xilas)* [1982] 2 Lloyd's Rep. 511; *Cargill v Marpro Ltd (The Aegis Progress)* [1983] 2 Lloyd's Rep. 570.

[93] *President of India v Jebsens (UK) Ltd* [1991] 1 Lloyd's Rep. 1.

[94] *Turner v Bannatyne* (1903) 9 Com.Cas. 83; affirmed *ibid.* p.306. See also fn.74, above.

[95] *The Stamatios Embiricos* [1971] 1 Lloyd's Rep. 574; and *cf.* the cases on "time lost in waiting for berth to count as loading time," cited in Art.79.

[96] *The Dias* [1978] 1 Lloyd's Rep. 325 (HL); *Food Corp of India v Carras (The Delian Leto)* [1983] 2 Lloyd's Rep. 496.

[97] *Huyton SA v Inter Operators SA (The Stainless Emperor)* [1994] 1 Lloyd's Rep. 298.

Per working day of twenty-four hours: This means that each twenty-four hours on which work was done is to count as a conventional day, though the hours might be on several days.[98]

Colliery working days means all days on which the colliery works in normal times and under normal circumstances, excluding Sundays and holidays, which are not port holidays. It includes days on which the colliery would work ordinarily, but does not work owing to a strike.[99]

Weather working day means a working day[100] that is not unavailable to work because of weather; in other words a fine working day.[101] A fine Saturday, though a half holiday, would, therefore, in the absence of any express provision, count as a whole weather working day.[102] When bad weather[103] occurs for part of a weather working day a reasonable apportionment should be made of the day according to the incidence of the weather upon the length of the day that the parties either were working or might be expected to have been working at the time; the apportionment is a question of fact for the judge or arbitrator.[104] It is immaterial that even if the weather had been fine, no attempt would have been made to work.[105]

---

[98] *Forest S.S. Co v Iberian Ore Co* (1899) 5 Com.Cas. 83; *Watson Bros v Mysore Managanese Co* (1910) 15 Com.Cas. 159. *Cf. Orpheus v Bovill* (1916) 114 L.T. 750; and see the comment thereon in *Alvion S.S. Co v Galban Lobo* [1955] 1 Q.B. 430 (CA). But "per working day of twenty-four consecutive hours" was held to mean twenty-four actually consecutive hours, whether by day or night: *Turnbull v Cruikshank* (1905) 7 Fraser 265.

[99] *Saxon Ship Co v Union S.S. Co* (1900) 5 Com.Cas. 381. The length of the working day or holiday is usually defined by the colliery guarantee. But under such a document the artificial extension of non-working days was held only to apply to lay-days, and not to demurrage days: *Saxon v Union S.S. Co*, above, overruling *Clink v Hickie Borman (No. 2)* (1899) 4 Com.Cas. 292.

[100] As to which, see above.

[101] *Reardon Smith Line v Ministry of Agriculture* [1963] A.C. 691 per Lord Radcliffe at p.722. The HL reviewed all the earlier authorities and disapproved the decision of the CA in *Alvion S.S. Co v Galban Lobo* [1955] 1 Q.B. 430, in so far as it decided that a weather working day was a day during the ordinary working hours of which (i.e. hours during which work is done at standard rates) weather allows the relevant work to be done. "Weather permitting working day" means the same as "working day weather permitting": *Magnolia Shipping Co of Limassol v Joint Venture, etc. of Brussels (The Camelia)* [1978] 2 Lloyd's Rep. 182. The provision of so many "running hours weather permitting" means that number of hours during which the weather permitted loading; in a port charter the words are applicable whether the ship is in berth or waiting for a berth: *Dow Chemical (Nederland) v. B.P. Tanker Co Ltd (The Vorros)* [1983] 1 Lloyd's Rep. 579 (CA). See also, *Gebr. Broer B.V. v Saras Chinica* [1982] 2 Lloyd's Rep. 436.

[102] *Reardon Smith Line v Ministry of Agriculture*, above.

[103] If weather renders the berth unsafe but does not interfere with the actual operation of loading, lay-time continues to run: *Compania Crystal v Herman & Mohatta* [1958] 1 Lloyd's Rep. 616. *Quaere* whether a mere threat of bad weather can render a day "non-weather working". See also *Bennetts v Brown* [1908] 1 K.B. 490 (days on which surf prevented lighters discharging ashore *held* "weather working days") and *Damps. Botnia v Bell* [1932] 2 K.B. 569 (days on which ice prevented loading of timber floated alongside *held* not "weather working days").

[104] *Reardon Smith Line v Ministry of Agriculture* [1963] A.C. 691 (HL); approving at p.740 the decision of Pearson J. in *The Azliero* [1957] 2 Q.B. 293. See, also, the reference to an unreported decision in the HL cited at some length in *A/S Uglands Rederi v The President of India (The Danita)* [1976] 2 Lloyd's Rep. 377, at p.380. This case, like *The King Theras* [1984] 1 Lloyd's Rep. 1 (CA), dealt with difficulties that seem not infrequently to arise in calculating lay time and demurrage under charters providing for the ocean-going vessel to discharge into lightening vessels many miles out at sea from the discharging ports of Madras and Calcutta. The form of charter used was the Baltimore Berth Grain charter with special adaptations by the Indian Supply Commission.

The principle of apportionment by reference to the fraction of the working day during which, but for weather, work might have been expected to have been carried out, is a refinement on the rough rule first applied in *Branckelow S.S. Co v Lamport & Holt* [1897] 1 Q.B. 570. The reference in a charter to a 24-hour basis for the calculation of weather working days will presumably alter the principle of apportionment set out above: see *Compania Naviera Azuero v British Oil and Cake Mills* [1957] 1 Lloyd's Rep. 312 at p.325 and *Reardon Smith Line v Ministry of Agriculture* [1960] 1 Q.B. 439 at pp.515–517. When, as is usually the case in modern charters, the weather working day does not run from midnight to midnight and Saturdays intervene, the incidence of bad weather may raise nice mathematical problems in applying the principle of apportionment.

[105] *Reardon Smith Line v Ministry of Agriculture* [1963] A.C. 691, per Lord Devlin at p.740 and *A/S Uglands Rederi v President of India (The Danita)* [1976] 2 Lloyd's Rep. 377. "Weather permitting working day" means a working day on which work would have been done but for weather preventing it: *The Camelia* [1978] 2 Lloyd's Rep. 182.

Dispatch Money. Where "dispatch money" was to be paid at 10s. per hour on any time saved in loading or discharging, and four days were saved, it was held that they were to be taken as of twenty-four, and not of twelve, hours each, the "dispatch money" being payable on the time saved, or running hours, and not on the working hours.[106] The clause "Sundays and fete days excepted" has been held to apply both to dispatch money and lay-days,[107] and therefore where the charterer, by speed in loading, dispatched the ship four days earlier than he was bound to do by the charter, but of the four days two were "Sundays or holidays," which were excepted from the lay-days, he was only allowed dispatch money on two days. He could not save days to which he was not entitled as lay-days by the charter.

Each case turns on the construction of the particular words used, but the phrase "all time saved" in loading and discharging will probably suffice to enable dispatch money to be calculable on Sundays and holidays saved as well as on lay-days saved.[108] On the other hand, if the words are "all working time saved" Sundays and holidays are excluded from the days saved.[109]

Case 1. A ship chartered "to load and discharge as fast as the ship can work, but a minimum of seven days to be allowed merchants, and ten days on demurrage over and above the said laying days". *Held*, that from the context "days" meant "working", not "running" days.

The ship came into dock on Tuesday evening at 5 p.m., reached her berth on Wednesday, at 8 a.m., and continued unloading till 8 p.m. She began again at 4 a.m., on Thursday, and finished at 8 a.m. *Held*, she was liable for two days' demurrage (the lay-days having been exhausted at the port of loading).[110]

Case 2. By charter seven running days were allowed for discharging; the vessel arrived on Saturday and was cleared by 10 a.m., when she gave notice of readiness to discharge. The charterers at first declined to receive cargo, but afterwards received it from 1 p.m. to 4 p.m., when work stopped. *Held*, that charterers' conduct amounted to an agreement that Saturday should be counted as a lay-day, though they were not otherwise bound to take discharge on that day at all.[111]

Case 3. A ship was chartered "to be loaded in X in fourteen days, and to be discharged, weather permitting, at not less than twenty-five tons per working day, holidays excepted". *Held*, that the days for loading must be taken as "running days", the days for unloading as working days.[112]

Case 4. A charter provided: "Cargo to be loaded and discharged as fast as steamer can receive and deliver during working hours. If longer detained £12 per diem demurrage." *Held*, that saving of time at the port of discharge could not be set off against delay at port of loading.[113]

---

[106] *Laing v Holloway* (1878) 3 Q.B.D. 437.
[107] *The Glendevon* [1893] P. 269; approved, *dissentiente* Fletcher Moulton L.J., by the Court of Appeal in *Nelson v Nelson* [1907] 2 K.B. 705. The House of Lords did not discuss this point, and the headnote in [1908] A.C. 108 is inaccurate. In *Royal Mail Co and River Plate Co, Re* [1910] 1 K.B. 600, where by the charter dispatch money was to be paid for "each running day saved", Bray J. distinguished *The Glendevon* and followed *Laing v Holloway*, above. Bray J. also expressed his agreement with the dissentient judgment of Fletcher Moulton L.J. in *Nelson v Nelson*, holding that *The Glendevon* was wrongly decided. See also *Mawson v Beyer* [1914] 1 K.B. 304, in which the foregoing cases are discussed and the principles to be deduced therefrom collated; *The Themistocles* (1949) 82 Ll.L.R. 232; and *Bulk Transport Corp v Sissy Steamship Co Ltd (The Archipelagos)* [1979] 2 Lloyd's Rep. 289.
[108] Based upon *The Themistocles*, above, and *Mawson v Beyer*, above.
[109] *Thomasson v Peabody* [1959] 2 Lloyd's Rep. 296. When dispatch money is payable on all working time saved and the lay-days are defined as weather working days, the calculation of dispatch money must be made to the number of working (*semble* weather working) days saved and not by reference to calendar days: *ibid.*
[110] *Commercial S.S. Co v Boulton* (1875) L.R. 10 Q.B. 346; *Hough v Athya*, 1879 6 Rettie 961.
[111] *The Katy* [1895] P. 56.
[112] *Niemann v Moss* (1860) 29 L.J.Q.B. 206.
[113] *Avon S.S. Co v Leask* (1890) 18 Rettie 280; following *Marshall v Bolckow Vaughan* (1881) 6 Q.B.D. 231.

Article 157—Charterer's Undertaking: to Load or Unload in a Fixed Time

Charterparties, in regard to the time for loading or discharge, fall into two classes,[114] (1) for discharge in a fixed time, (2) for discharge in a time not definitely fixed.[115] If a charterparty is to fall within the first class the provision for a fixed time must be in plain and unambiguous terms.[116]

If by the terms of the charter the charterer has agreed to load or unload within a fixed period of time,[117] that is an absolute and unconditional engagement, for the non-performance of which he is answerable, whatever be the nature of the impediments which prevent him from performing it,[118] unless such impediments are covered by exceptions in the charter,[119] or arise from the loading or unloading being illegal by the law of the place where they have to be performed[120] or arise

---

[114] *Hulthen v Stewart* [1903] A.C. 389; *Van Liewen v Hollis* [1920] A.C. 239.

[115] As to (2) see Art.158.

[116] Lord Macnaghten in *Hulthen v Stewart*, above at p.394; *Van Liewen v Hollis*, above.

[117] The effect is the same, if the days can be calculated, as where the rate of loading or discharge per day is fixed; cf. *Alexander v Aktieselskabet Hansa* [1920] A.C. 88; *Aktieselskabet Gimle v Garland*, 1917, 2 S.L.T. 254; or "per weather working day"; *Van Nievelt v Forslind* (1925) 30 Com.Cas. 263. But in *Dobell v Watts* (1891) 7 T.L.R. 622, a clause. "Cargo to be loaded as fast as vessel can receive in ordinary working hours, and to be received as customary as fast as steamer can deliver in ordinary working hours—not less than one hundred standards a day loading or discharging", was held by the CA not a clause obliging the charterer to receive one hundred standards a day, and so fixing the number of lay-days, but a clause for the benefit of charterers only. See also *Love v Rowtor Co* [1916] 2 A.C. 527, where a printed form of charterparty for discharge in a reasonable time was by written words turned into one for a fixed time. In consequence a reference in the print to "customary discharge" was neglected as insensible and inapplicable. Cf. *Baird v Price Walker* (1916) 115 L.T. 227, and *N.V. Reederij Amsterdam v President of India* [1960] 2 Lloyd's Rep. 82. The point was not raised on appeal.

[118] per Lord Selborne in *Postlethwaite v Freeland* (1880) 5 App.Cas. 599 at p.608. For a striking example of the absolute nature of the obligation, see *Porteus v Watney* (1878) 3 Q.B.D. 223; affirmed *ibid.* p.534. In *Potter v Burrell* [1897] 1 Q.B. 97, under a charter for a series of ships "as nearly as possible a steamer a month" to be loaded in a fixed time; owing to excepted perils, two steamers arrived at the same time and could not with the resources of the port be loaded in the fixed time. *Held*, by the CA, that as the shipowner was not liable for the delay, the charterer was not excused by it. See, however, *Nelson v Nelson* [1908] A.C. 108, where a similar question was differently decided. The headnote of the report is inadequate and inaccurate. *Potter v Burrell* does not appear to have been cited. For the provision "two voyages per month, fortnightly", see *The Melrose Abbey* (1898) 14 T.L.R. 202.

[119] See *Note* 1 at end of this Article. For an illustration of this, see *Granite S.S. Co v Ireland* (1891) 19 Rettie 124, where the excepted peril occurred, but did not prevent the discharge of the ship, only the removal of its cargo from the quay when discharged. See also *Aktieselskabet Argentina v Von Laer* (1903) 19 T.L.R. 151. The addition of the words "provided the steamer can deliver at this rate" will not relieve the charterer in a case where the steamer is in fact prevented by existing circumstances, but in normal circumstances is of a capacity so to deliver: *Northfield S.S. Co v Compagnie de Gaz* [1912] 1 K.B. 434; *Alexander v Aktieselskabet Hansa* [1920] A.C. 88. In some charters these words have been altered to "provided the steamer with the men and appliances actually employed by her can deliver at this rate". This seems to achieve the results unsuccessfully contended for by charterers in the above two cases.

[120] See *Ralli v Compania Naviera* [1920] 2 K.B. 287, which overrules *Blight v Page* (1801) 3 B. & P. 295n., and *Barker v Hodgson* (1814) 3 M. & S. 267. See Art.7, above. Illegality to excuse the charterer must actually prevent loading and not merely shorten the time available for it: *Compania Crystal de Vapores v Herman & Mohatta (India), Ltd* [1958] 1 Lloyd's Rep. 616, at p.624. Illegal orders of the authorities will not protect the charterer, who has his remedy against them: *Bessey v Evans* (1815) 4 Camp. 131; *Gosling v Higgins* (1808) 1 Camp. 451; *The Newport* (1858) Swabey 335. Compare the principle involved in *Evans v Bullock* (1877) 38 L.T. 34; *Ronneberg v Falkland Islands Co* (1864) 17 C.B.(N.S.) 1; *Sully v Duranty* (1864) 3 H. & C. 270. See also, as to prevention by executive acts of authorities not acting under the ordinary law, *Cantiere Navale Triestina v Russian Soviet Naphtha Export* [1925] 2 K.B. 172. Where a ship otherwise ready to load is prevented from loading by quarantine, the lay-days stipulated in the charter will not begin to run till the quarantine has expired: *White v Winchester* (1886) 13 Rettie 524; *The Austin Friars* (1894) 10 T.L.R. 633.

from the fault of the shipowner or those for whom he is responsible[121] or from a frustrating event.[122]

Thus after the ship is ready to load or unload at the agreed place,[123] the charterer will not, in the absence of express exceptions,[124] be released from his contract by delay resulting from the crowded state of the docks,[125] bad weather,[126] or ice preventing loading,[127] insufficient supply of cargo,[128] or strikes of persons for whom the shipowner is not responsible, even though the shipowner is prevented by the same cause from performing his share of the work[129]; and when there is a provision for demurrage, the charterer (at the price of paying the demurrage) can insist on the ship remaining for a reasonable time for complete loading.[130] On the other hand, the charterer is entitled to keep the

---

[121] *Alexander v Aktieselskabet Hansa* [1920] A.C. 88, in which Lord Finlay, at p.94, quotes the text above with approval; *Overseas Transportation Co v Mineralimportexport* [1971] 1 Lloyd's Rep. 514 at p.519; *Budgett v Binnington* [1891] 1 Q.B. 35; *Benson v Blunt* (1841) 1 Q.B. 870; *The Anna* (1901) 18 T.L.R. 25; *Hansen v Donaldson* (1874) 1 Rettie 1066, where discharge was impeded by the insufficiency of the shipowner's crew; as to this case see also *Alexander v Aktieselskabet Hansa*, above; *Petrinovic v Mission Française* (1942) 71 Ll.L.R. 208 (final removal of ship for safety of ship and cargo). Where loading or discharge is a joint operation, it follows from *Budgett v Binnington* that the inability of the shipowner to do his part will only excuse the charterer when it is that alone which prevents the charterer from doing his share of the work: *Leeds S.S. Co v Duncan Fox* (1932) 42 Ll.L.R. 123. In *Harris v Best* (1892) 68 L.T. 76, delay was caused by restowing some cargo that had shifted, and restowing other cargo to enable fresh cargo to be properly stowed. The stevedore was employed and paid by the owners. *Held*, the charterers were not liable for demurrage for this delay, the stevedore being the owner's servant; see also *Overseas Transportation Co v Mineralimportexport*, above, where the charter did not clearly state whose servants the stevedores were to be. There must, however, be a "fault" on the part of the shipowner, and the fact that the delay is due to the voluntary act of the owner will not of itself suspend the running of lay-time. Thus, in *Houlder v Weir* [1905] 2 K.B. 267, it was held that where the charterer was delayed towards the end of discharge by reason of the shipowner's necessary operation of taking in ballast to stiffen the ship, the charterer was responsible for demurrage during that delay. Similarly, in *Compania Crystal de Vapores v Herman & Mohatta (India) Ltd* [1958] 1 Lloyd's Rep. 616, Devlin J. held that lay-time continued to run during a period when the ship was ordered away from her berth by the harbourmaster, to avoid possible damage from bore tides. Contrast *Gem Shipping Co v Babanaft (Lebanon) S.A.R.L. (The Fontevivo)* [1975] 1 Lloyd's Rep. 339: lay-time stopped when ship left Lattakia owing to crew being afraid of air raids. See also *President of India v Moor Line* [1958] 2 Lloyd's Rep. 205 (High Court of Australia) (no breach by shipowner in failing to receive cargo "continuously" owing to inability to obtain stevedores to work overtime) and compare *Ropner Shipping Co and Cleeves Western Valleys Anthracite Collieries, Re* [1927] 1 K.B. 879, applied in *Blue Anchor Line v Toepfer (The Union Amsterdam)* [1982] 2 Lloyd's Rep. 432. See also *Total Transport Corp v Amoco Transport Co (The Altus)* [1985] 1 Lloyd's Rep. 423 in which Webster J. stated that lay-time can be "suspended or interrupted by an act of a shipowner which has the effect of preventing the completion of loading or the commencement of the voyage even without a breach of contract on his part, if that act constitutes a fault falling short of a breach of contract or if it lacks lawful excuse".

[122] *Adelfamar SA v Silos E. Mangimi Martini SpA (The Adelfa)* [1988] 2 Lloyd's Rep. 466.

[123] See Arts 71, 74, above, and *Tharsis Co v Morel* [1891] 2 Q.B. 647.

[124] As regards the application of exceptions to events delaying or hindering the charterer after discharge from the ship, see Art.82, above.

[125] *Randall v Lynch* (1810) 2 Camp. 352; *Brown v Johnson* (1843) 10 M. & W. 331; *Tapscott v Balfour* (1872) L.R. 8 C.P. 46. Where, however, the charter provided for discharge, "in regular turn with other vessels at the average rate of 30 tons a day", and the commencement of the discharge was delayed by the vessel having to wait her turn according to the custom of the port, the charterer was held not liable for the delay: *The Cordelia* [1909] P. 27. Nor was he held liable even with the addition of the words "commencing when written notice is given of steamer being ready to load": *United States Shipping Board v Strick* [1926] A.C. 545. *Cf. Moor Line v Manganexport* (1936) 55 Ll.L.R. 114.

[126] *Thiis v Byers* (1876) 1 Q.B.D. 244. See also *Cia. Crystal de Vapores v Herman & Mohatta (India) Ltd*, above.

[127] *Barret v Dutton* (1815) 4 Camp. 333. A provision that loading shall take place at a certain rate per weather working day may suffice, if ice prevents loading: *Damps. Botnia v Bell* [1932] 2 K.B. 569.

[128] See Art.82.

[129] See fn.119, above and fn.142, below.

[130] *Wilson and Coventry v Thoresen* [1910] 2 K.B. 405. *Quaere* whether, in the absence of any provision for demurrage, he can similarly insist at the price of paying damages for detention: *ibid.*

ship the whole of the lay-days though he could have loaded her in less time.[131]

The provisions of the charter as to fixed days must be limited to the ports to which they expressly refer,[132] and a reasonable time will be allowed for loading or unloading at ports not expressly provided for.[133]

Note 1. The occurrence of an obstacle preventing loading or unloading, which is within an exception, does not excuse the charterer absolutely, but only in so far as it in fact prevents him from fulfilling his contract. Thus, in *Elswick S.S. Co v Montaldi*,[134] where the charterer, who had to discharge at an average rate of 500 tons a day, was behind his time, and then a strike occurred, delaying, but not preventing, the discharge, Bigham J. held the charterer excused only to the extent to which the strike delayed the discharge of that cargo which, had the charterer used due diligence before, would have remained on board at the time when the strike occurred.[135]

Note 2. Onus of proof. The charterer in order to gain the protection of an exception must prove not only the existence of the excepted cause, but also that he could not by reasonable exertion or precaution have prevented the operation of the cause. He is not entitled to fold his arms and do nothing.[136]

Note 3. Where an obstacle, which is within an exception, prevents loading or discharging in the method adopted by the charterer, but does not affect other available methods, the charterer is allowed a reasonable time to make up his mind whether the obstacle will continue, and to make arrangements for using the other methods available if it continues.[137]

Note 4. Charterparties often provide for loading at an average rate of so many tons per day. In such a case the charterer is under no obligation to load any cargo on any particular day and is not in breach until such time as it is clear that he cannot in any event maintain the stipulated average.[138]

Note 5. Extensions of loading time on account of bad weather take two forms. In some charterparties the rate of loading is calculated "per weather working day".[139] In such a case it is immaterial that the charterer did not attempt to load on a particular day if on that day bad weather would have prevented loading.[140] Other charterparties provide that any time lost through work being impossible owing to bad weather is to be added to the lay-

---

[131] *Petersen v Dunn* (1895) 1 Com.Cas. 8; *Margaronis Navigation Agency v Peabody* [1964] 1 Lloyd's Rep. 173. If, however, the charterer does complete the loading before the lay-days expire he cannot keep the ship in port by delay in presenting the bill of lading: *Nolisement v Bunge* [1917] 1 K.B. 160; or by failing to co-operate in obtaining necessary clearance from the port of loading: *Margaronis Navigation Agency v Peabody*, above.

[132] *Marshall v De la Torre* (1795) 1 Esp. 367; *Stevenson v York* (1790) 2 Chit. 570.

[133] *Sweeting v Darthez* (1854) 14 C.B. 538. See also *Fowler v Knoop* (1878) 4 Q.B.D. 299.

[134] [1907] 1 K.B. 626.

[135] *Cf. London and Northern Co v Central Argentine Ry* (1913) 108 L.T. 527; *Central Argentine Ry v Marwood* [1915] A.C. 981.

[136] *Dampskibsselskabet Svendborg v Love*, 1915 S.C. 543, per Lord Dunedin; *Bulman v Fenwick* [1894] 1 Q.B. 179; *Burnett S.S. Co v Danube and Black Sea, etc.* [1933] 2 K.B. 438.

[137] *Lewis v Dreyfus & Co* (1926) 31 Com.Cas. 239; *Brightman v Bunge y Born* [1924] 2 K.B. 619; *South African Dispatch Line v S.S. Niki (Owners)* [1960] 1 Q.B. 518. See also *Reardon Smith Line v Ministry of Agriculture* [1963] A.C. 691 (HL).

[138] See per Scrutton L.J. in *Burnett S.S. Co v Danube and Black Sea, etc.* [1933] 2 K.B. 438 at p.447.

[139] See also, above, Art.156, *Note*.

[140] *Cia Naviera Azuero SA v British Oil & Cake Mills* [1957] 1 Lloyd's Rep. 312; *Reardon Smith Line v Ministry of Agriculture* [1963] A.C. 691 at p.740 (HL).

days or is not to count. In this case the charterer must prove not only that bad weather occurred, but also that it did in fact prevent him from loading.[141]

Case 1. A ship was chartered to unload in the London Docks, forty days being allowed as lay-days; owing to the crowded state of the docks the vessel was detained forty-one days over the lay-days. *Held*, that the charterer was liable for delay.[142]

Case 2. A ship was chartered to load at London, with thirty running days; owing to frost the loading of the ship was prevented. *Held*, the charterer was liable for the delay.[143]

Case 3. A charter to discharge at Bristol allowed a fixed number of days for discharging. The custom at Bristol was that discharge was the joint act of the charterer and shipowner. Discharge was prevented by a strike of labourers, which prevented both shipowner and charterer from performing their part of the discharge. *Held*, that as the charterer was not prevented from discharging by the fault of the shipowner or persons for whom the shipowner was responsible, he was not excused for delay beyond the fixed lay-days.[144]

Article 158—To Load or Unload—In Reasonable Time—According to the Custom of the Port—As Customary—With Customary Dispatch

If no fixed time for loading (or unloading) is stipulated in the charter, the law implies an agreement on the part of the charterer to load or discharge the cargo within a reasonable time,[145] and, so far as there is a joint duty in loading or unloading, that the merchant and shipowner shall each use reasonable diligence in performing his part.[146]

In the absence of express provisions, there is an absolute undertaking on the part of the charterer to have cargo ready to load,[147] and a reasonable time for loading then begins.[148] On a like principle, at the other end of the voyage, what

---

[141] *Burnett S.S. Co v Danube and Black Sea, etc.*, above. Under a charter providing for loading and discharge in four days "with the usual exceptions of . . . frosts", it was *held* that the charterer did not escape liability for demurrage when frosts did not prevent the operation of discharge, but would have damaged the cargo had discharge taken place: *Henry & MacGregor v Galbraith & Roy* (1940) 66 Ll.L.R. 71.

[142] *Randall v Lynch* (1810) 2 Camp. 352.

[143] *Barret v Dutton* (1815) 4 Camp. 333.

[144] *Budgett v Binnington* [1891] 1 Q.B. 35; *Leeds S.S. Co v Duncan Fox* (1932) 42 Ll.L.R. 123; 37 Com.Cas. 213; *semble* that where the shipowner saves a claim for demurrage by paying the labourers extra wages he can recover that sum from the charterers: *ibid.*

[145] *Hick v Raymond* [1893] A.C. 22. Per Lord Selborne in *Postlethwaite v Freeland* (1880) 5 App.Cas. 599 at p.608; *Van Liewen v Hollis* [1920] A.C. 239. The time is unfixed whenever there is not a definite time expressed or implied (as in Art.157). The obligation is the same whether the charter is altogether silent as to the time, as in *Hick v Raymond*, above; or stipulates for "customary dispatch", as in *Postlethwaite v Freeland*, above; or, "as fast as steamer can deliver" (*Good v Isaacs* [1892] 2 Q.B. 555); or both the last phrases (*Hulthen v Stewart* [1903] A.C. 389); or, "as fast as master shall require" (*Sea S.S. Co v Price Walker* (1903) 8 Com.Cas. 292 at p.296). Nor is the obligation altered by a provision that time is to count on arrival of the steamer: *Bargate Co v Penlee Co* (1921) 26 Com.Cas. 168; nor by a provision that a ready berth is to be given: *Glen Line v Royal Commission* (1922) 10 Ll.L.R. 510. Discharge with more than customary dispatch can be secured by such words as "to be discharged continuously, any custom of the port to the contrary notwithstanding"; *Maclay v Spillers* (1901) 6 Com.Cas. 217. *Cf. Crown S.S. Co v Leitch*, 1908 S.C. 506. "Forthwith" = without unreasonable delay: *Hudson v Hill* (1874) 43 L.J.C.P. 273; *Forest Oak Co v Richard* (1899) 5 Com.Cas. 100; *Total Transport Corp. v Amoco Transport Co (The Altus)* [1985] 1 Lloyd's Rep. 423.

[146] *Ford v Cotesworth* (1868) L.R. 4 Q.B. 127 at p.137; affirmed (1870) L.R. 5 Q.B. 544; *Cunningham v Dunn* (1878) 3 C.P.D. 443 (CA). Illegality by foreign law may either be taken into account in estimating reasonable time, as in the above cases, or treated as an absolute defence; *Ralli v Compania Naviera* [1920] 2 K.B. 287.

[147] And exceptions, unless clearly expressed otherwise, apply only to actual loading, not to procuring of cargo to be loaded. See Art.82; and *cf. Dampskibsselskabet Danmark v Poulsen*, 1913 S.C. 1043.

[148] *Ardan S.S. Co v Weir* [1905] A.C. 501, which apparently overrules *Jones v Green* [1904] 2 K.B. 275, unless distinguishable as suggested in Art.82, fn.233, above. The analogous case of *Barque Quilpué v Brown* [1904] 2 K.B. 264 turns on knowledge by the shipowner of the method of loading. See also Art.82, above; *The Aello* [1961] A.C. 135 and *Wilson v Thoresen* [1910] 2 K.B. 405.

is in question is the reasonable time for *discharge*. Therefore difficulties in getting the cargo away to an ulterior destination after the actual discharge are not to be taken into account.[149]

"A reasonable time" means reasonable under the circumstances then existing, other than self-imposed inabilities of either shipowner or charterer,[150] and should be estimated with reference to the means and facilities then available at the port, the course of business at the port,[151] the customary methods employed at the port, and the character of the port with regard to tides and otherwise.[152] Thus, where a strike at the port of loading or discharge prevents a diligent consignee from doing his part of the work in spite of reasonable exertions on his part, he will not be liable for the consequent delay.[153] But where a strike prevents a method of discharge selected by a consignee from being available he must within a reasonable time arrange for another method, if one is available.[154]

This obligation to load or unload in a reasonable time imports without express reference a stipulation that the work shall be done in the manner customary in the port.[155] But an express provision, "according to the custom of the port", or "with customary dispatch" or "as customary", though usually unnecessary,[156] is very commonly inserted.[157] In consequence, every impediment arising out of that custom or practice which the charterer or shipowner could not have overcome by the use of any reasonable diligence[158] ought to be taken into consideration.

---

[149] *Langham S.S. Co v Gallagher* [1911] 2 Ir.R. 348; *Dampskibsselskabet Svendborg v Love*, 1915 S.C. 543.

[150] But this limitation does not make the charterers liable for delay arising from the previous engagements, not of the charterers or their agents, but of the consignees to whom the charterers have sold the cargo: *Watson v Borner* (1900) 5 Com.Cas. 377; *The Deerhound* (1901) 6 Com.Cas. 104. Nor does it extend to a case in which delay is due to the engagements of the charterers or shipowners themselves, when those engagements are reasonably made in the normal carrying on of their business, and do not create such an exceptional state of circumstances as the parties to the charter on signing it cannot be taken to have contemplated: *Harrowing v Dupré* (1902) 7 Com.Cas. 157; *Quilpué v Brown* [1904] 2 K.B. 264. Contrast *Aktieselskabet Inglewood v Millar's Karri* (1903) 8 Com.Cas. 196.

[151] *Hick v Raymond* [1893] A.C. 22; *Postlethwaite v Freeland* (1880) App.Cas. 599, per Lord Selborne at p.609; *Hulthen v Stewart* [1903] A.C. 389; *The Arne* [1904] P. 154.

[152] *Carlton S.S. Co v Castle Mail Co* [1898] A.C. 486.

[153] See fn.149, above.

[154] *Fitzgerald v Lona* (1932) 44 Ll.L.R. 212; *Rederiaktiebolaget Macedonia v Slaughter* (1935) 40 Com.Cas. 227 (London lightermen strike). *Cf. Brightman v Bunge y Born* [1924] 2 K.B. 619; affirmed [1925] A.C. 799; *South African Dispatch Line v S.S. Niki (Owners)* [1960] 1 Q.B. 518 (CA) and *Reardon Smith Line v Ministry of Agriculture* [1963] A.C. 691 (HL).

[155] See per Lord Blackburn, *Postlethwaite v Freeland* (1880) 5 App.Cas. 599 at p.613; A. L. Smith L.J., *Lyle v Cardiff Corp* [1900] 2 Q.B. 638 at p.643; Collins M.R., *Temple v Runnalls* (1902) 18 T.L.R. 822 at p.823; Lord Herschell thought otherwise: *Hick v Raymond* [1893] A.C. 22 at p.30. But, if the charterer has not got cargo ready to load, he cannot under a charter to load in the "usual and customary manner" escape liability for ensuing delay by an allegation that he has done his best to load: *Ardan S.S. Co v Weir* [1905] A.C. 501.

[156] Theoretically an express reference to "the custom of the port" might impose on the charterer a greater obligation than would rest upon him if there were no such words—e.g. if by the custom of the port he is bound to do something which in the existing conditions of the port he cannot in fact do even with the exercise of reasonable diligence. This principle was applied, and such a custom found, in *Aktieselskabet Hekla v Bryson* (1908) 14 Com.Cas. 1. But that decision has been overruled by the HL in *Van Liewen v Hollis* [1920] A.C. 239, and it may be doubted if any such custom can in fact exist.

[157] On the other hand, if the charter is expressly one for discharge in a fixed time a reference in its printed form to "customary dispatch" is insensible and inapplicable: *Love v Rowtor Co* [1916] 2 A.C. 527.

[158] *Carali v Xenos* (1862) 2 F. & F. 740: the shipowner had contracted to forward goods by foreign steamer, but missed the last steamer of the season; he had discharged according to the custom of the port, but could by diligence have expedited the discharge of these goods so as to catch the steamer. *Held*, that he was liable for the delay, apparently on the ground that he had not used what was due diligence under the circumstances.

The express stipulations and the implied obligation as to customary dispatch refer to the customary manner of discharge, and only indirectly to the time usually occupied in discharging in such customary manner.[159]

"Custom", or "customary" does not mean "custom" in the strict legal sense, but a settled and established practice of the port.[160]

Article 159—Who are liable for Demurrage provided for in a Charter

Where there is a charter containing express stipulations as to demurrage, there will be liable on it, for demurrage:

(1) The charterer,[161] unless (A) there is a cesser clause in the charter[162]; and (B) he has been freed by a new contract on the bill of lading.[163]

(2) The parties to the bill of lading, if the charterparty stipulations as to demurrage are expressly incorporated in the bill of lading[164]; or persons taking goods without protest under such bill of lading[165] provided that the charterparty stipulations can sensibly be read as imposing liability on the bill of lading holder[166]. The bill of lading may incorporate the charterparty in terms which make it clear that the receivers are to have no liability for demurrage.[167]

Case 1. A ship was chartered with the usual stipulations for freight, demurrage and a cesser clause. The charterers shipped the cargo themselves and accepted a bill of lading, making the goods deliverable to themselves, at port of discharge, "they paying freight and all other conditions as per charter". In an action by shipowners against charterers as consignees under the bill of lading for demurrage at the port of discharge, *Held*, that they were liable, as the bill of lading only incorporated those clauses of the charter which were consistent with its character as a bill of lading, and, therefore, though it incorporated the provisions as to demurrage, did not incorporate the cesser clause.[168]

Case 2. C chartered a ship from A, to pay a named freight, sixteen lay-days and demurrage at £2 per day. C shipped a cargo consigned to G in London, under a bill of lading, "paying freight as per charter", with a memorandum in the margin, "there are eight working days for unloading in London". G was sued by A for demurrage. *Held*, that as the bill of lading did not clearly show that

---

[159] *Dunlop v Balfour* [1892] 1 Q.B. 507 at p.520; *Castlegate S.S. Co v Dempsey* [1892] 1 Q.B. 854 at pp.861, 862; *Metcalfe v Thompson* (1902) 18 T.L.R. 706. *Cf. Sea S.S. Co v Price Walker* (1903) 8 Com.Cas. 292; *Ropner v Stoate Hosegood & Co* (1905) 10 Com.Cas. 73; and *Akties. Glittre v Gabriel, Wade & English* (1926) 24 Ll.L.R. 372.

[160] See Art.11, above. For further discussion of the nature of the charterer's obligation to load or unload in a reasonable time see the 19th edition at pp.323–327. It is now rare for charters not to make specific provision as to the time for loading or unloading.

[161] See the cases on charterparty freight, Art.169.

[162] See Art.92; *cf. Hick v Rodocanachi* [1891] 2 Q.B. 626.

[163] *Gullischen v Stewart* (1884) 13 Q.B.D. 317.

[164] They were held to be incorporated in *Porteus v Watney* (1878) 3 Q.B.D. 534; *Wegener v Smith* (1854) 15 C.B. 285; *Gray v Carr* (1871) L.R. 6 Q.B. 522; not to be incorporated in *Chappel v Comfort* (1861) 10 C.B.(N.S.) 802; *Smith v Sieveking* (1855) 4 E. & B. 945. See as to words incorporating the charter, *Serraino v Campbell* (1890) 25 Q.B.D. 501 and as to incorporation generally, see Art.37, above.

[165] *S.S. County of Lancaster v Sharp* (1889) 24 Q.B.D. 158; and see Art.17, and fn.170, below.

[166] *Miramar Maritime Corp v Holborn Oil (The Miramar)* [1984] 1 A.C. 676, in which it was held that the shippers under the bill of lading were not liable for discharge port demurrage, where the bill of lading incorporated the charterparty and the charterparty made "charterers" liable for demurrage; see also *Tradigrain v King Diamond (The Spiros C)* [2000] 2 Lloyd's Rep. 319.

[167] *SA Sucre Export v Northern River Shipping Ltd (The Sormovsky 3068)* [1994] 2 Lloyd's Rep. 266 at p.286.

[168] *Gullischen v Stewart*, above.

the conditions as to demurrage in the charter were incorporated in the bill of lading, G was not liable.[169]

Case 3. Under a bill of lading of goods deliverable to G, "he paying for said goods as per charter, with primage and average accustomed", G was held not liable for demurrage at the port of loading due under the charter.[170]

Case 4. C chartered a ship from A, "fifty running days to be allowed for loading, and ten days on demurrage over and above the said laying days at £8 per day", the owner to have a lien for demurrage; there was a cesser clause. C shipped goods under a bill of lading "to be delivered as per charter to G, he paying freight and all other conditions or demurrage as per charter". The ship was detained at her port of loading ten days on demurrage and eighteen days besides. A claimed a lien against G for demurrage and damages for detention. *Held*, that G was liable for the demurrage, but not for the damages for detention, which were not clearly included in the bill of lading.[171]

Article 160—Who are liable for Demurrage provided for in Bill of Lading

Where there is an express stipulation as to demurrage contained in a bill of lading,[172] demurrage due under it will be payable:

(1) By the shipper or consignor[173];

(2) By every person presenting such bill of lading and demanding delivery under it, if there can be inferred from such demand an agreement in fact to pay it[174];

(3) Under a bill of lading within the Carriage of Goods by Sea Act 1992,[175] by any person to whom rights of suit have been transferred under the Act and who takes or demands delivery of the goods or makes a claim under the contract of carriage against the carrier.[176]

Where there is an obligation to discharge, there is an obligation to discharge in a reasonable time. It is doubtful whether there is an implied contract by the consignor to unload the goods (and therefore to do so in a reasonable time). In any event there is no such implication into a bill of lading which seeks to incorporate, albeit ineffectively, a regime which would excuse a shipper from liability for discharge and place it solely on the receiver or

---

[169] *Chappel v Comfort*, above.
[170] *Smith v Sieveking* (1855) 4 E. & B. 945.
[171] *Gray v Carr* (1871) L.R. 6 Q.B. 522.
[172] There is no liability to pay demurrage on a holder of a delivery order addressed by the shipper to the shipper's agent at the port of discharge, since this creates no contract between the holder and the shipowner: *Tradax Internacional v R. Pagnan & Fratelli* [1968] 1 Lloyd's Rep. 244. *Quaere*, whether a person taking delivery of goods under a ship's delivery order might not be liable for demurrage if the demurrage provisions of the bill of lading were incorporated in the delivery order.
[173] *Cawthorn v Trickett* (1864) 15 C.B.(N.S.) 754.
[174] See Art.17.
[175] Appendix I; see also Art.16.
[176] See Art.16.

charterer.[177] If there is an implied contract, the shipowner and not the master is entitled to sue.[178]

Note. If there are a number of bills of lading, each stipulating for a fixed number of lay-days, and a fixed sum for demurrage, or each incorporating such stipulations from a charterparty, can the shipowner proceed against each of the indorsees or consignees and recover the whole amount from each? The cases of *Leer v Yates,*[179] *Straker v Kidd,*[180] and *Porteous v Watney*[181] appear to show that he can. This result, at first sight,[182] seems so outrageous that much doubt upon the point has naturally been expressed. In the case of a demurrage clause incorporated from a charterparty there would seem to be a way out of the difficulty by holding that each holder of the bill of lading has undertaken that the stipulation of the charterparty shall be fulfilled, i.e. that the shipowner shall receive the sum (e.g. £10 a day) named therein, and if the shipowner has received this from one consignee, another can contend that the obligation of the charterparty has been fulfilled so as to absolve him. This was a suggestion of Thesiger L.J.,[183] though it was not supported by the other members of the Court of Appeal. But if there is a separate contract expressed in each bill of lading—so many lay-days for discharge, and so much per day for demurrage—it is very difficult to see any escape from the liability of each and every holder or consignee for the whole amount. The conscience of the shipowner may be made easier if he sues all the consignees for the charterparty demurrage without claiming the whole amount from each of them.[184] The defendants are not likely to raise the defence, which strictly is available to them, that their liability is several, not joint.[185] Where the shipowner recovers demurrage under the bill of lading at a rate which exceeds that to which he is entitled under the governing charter, he is entitled to recover the larger amount but will hold any excess on trust for the charterer.[186]

---

[177] *Tradigrain v King Diamond (The Spiros C)* [2000] 2 Lloyd's Rep. 319. The proposition that " There is contained in every bill of lading an implied contract by the consignor to unload the goods in a reasonable time", in the 20th edn of this work, and dating back to the editorship of Lord Justice Scrutton, based inter alia on *Fowler v Knoop* (1878) 4 Q.B.D. 299, is difficult to reconcile with *The Miramar,* was doubted in *Tradigrain v King Diamond* [2000] 2 Lloyd's Rep. 319 at pp.332–336 paras 59-81 (Rix L.J.), and is probably incorrect.

[178] *Brounker v Scott* (1811) 4 Taunt. 1; *Evans v Forster* (1830) 1 B. & Ad. 118. In *Cawthorn v Trickett* (1864) 15 C.B.(N.S.) 754, the master who was a part owner and managing owner, was held entitled to sue the consignor on an express contract that the ship should be unloaded in regular turn. Where an express contract is made with him in the bill of lading, the master can sue for demurrage, as he can for freight: *Jesson v Solly* (1811) 4 Taunt. 52; and see Art.171.

[179] (1811) 3 Taunt. 387.

[180] (1878) 3 Q.B.D. 223.

[181] *ibid.* p.227; affirmed *ibid.* p.534. The correctness of the decision was doubted in *Miramar Maritime Corp v Holborn Oil Trading Ltd* [1984] A.C. 76.

[182] There are considerations, however, which are pertinent on the side of the shipowner. If a charterer ships a cargo with an obligation in the charterparty as to its discharge in a certain time and then, for the convenience of the charterer, many bills of lading for small parcels are issued, the shipowner (especially if there is the usual cesser clause) may have no practical means of enforcing his right to have the steamer discharged in proper time, if he is limited, as against each holder of a bill of lading, to his default in taking delivery of his own parcel.

[183] (1878) 3 Q.B.D. 534 at p.540. *Quaere* whether the bill of lading holder who pays can recover a contribution from other bills of lading holders under the Civil Liability (Contribution) Act 1978 or in restitution.

[184] As was apparently done in *The Lizzie* (1918) 23 Com.Cas. 332; reversed *sub nom. Van Liewen v Hollis* [1920] A.C. 239 (HL). In *Roland-Linie Schiffahrt v Spillers* [1951] 1 Q.B. 109, bill of lading holders were held liable under a clause providing that if a discharging place should not be immediately available, demurrage should be paid for all time waiting thereafter: the amount due was recovered rateably from the various defendants: *ibid.* p.123.

[185] The US Shipping Board has used a provision in bills of lading to this effect: "Cargo to be discharged at the rate of —— tons per day, with demurrage £ —— per day payable *pro rata* freights", i.e. the whole demurrage is to be apportioned among the holders of the bills of lading in proportion to the freight they severally have to pay. *Cf. US Shipping Board v Durrell* [1923] 2 K.B. 739, where the CA held that there was no implied condition that all the bills of lading should be in the same terms, and no prevention in law arose from the fact that some consignees were under less onerous obligations as to discharge and demurrage than others: see (1924) 29 Com.Cas. 157.

[186] *The Sormovsky 3068,* above.

Difficulties have arisen in cases of two charters of the same ship on the same voyage whether the shipowner can recover demurrage at a cumulative rate for part of the time used in discharging. The answer may depend on whether the two charters can be read together as one,[187] or not, as when the charterers are different.[188]

---

[187] As in *Sarma Navigation v Sidermar (The Sea Pioneer)* [1982] 1 Lloyd's Rep. 13.
[188] *Agios Stylianos Comp. Nav. v Maritime Associates International Ltd of Lagos* [1975] 1 Lloyd's Rep. 426. See also, *Transamerican S.S. Corp v Tradax Export (The Oriental Envoy)* [1982] 2 Lloyd's Rep. 266.

CHAPTER 15

FREIGHT

Article 161—Freight: What it is

"FREIGHT", in the ordinary mercantile sense, is the reward payable to the carrier for the carriage and arrival of the goods in a merchantable condition,[1] ready to be delivered to the merchant.[2] The true test of the right to freight is the question whether the service in respect of which the freight was contracted to be paid has been substantially performed,[3] or, if not, whether its performance has been prevented by the act of the cargo-owner.[4]

Under the simple contract to pay freight[5] no freight is payable if the goods are lost[6] on the voyage,[7] or for any other reason, except the fault of the merchant alone,[8] are not delivered at the port of destination.

From the signing and delivery of bills of lading[9] while the goods are in course of carriage without unreasonable delay, and until they are delivered to the merchant, the master of the ship has a lien on them for the freight due for such carriage, and cannot be compelled to part with them till such freight is paid and the bills of lading delivered up.[10]

These incidents of freight exist by rule of law, and do not need a bill of lading or other written contract between the parties to support them, though they may be excluded by such a written contract.[10]

---

[1] *Asfar v Blundell* [1896] 1 Q.B. 123.

[2] The definition of the Judicial Committee in *Kirchner v Venus* (1859) 12 Moore P.C. 361 at p.390, is, "Freight is the reward payable to the carrier for the safe carriage and delivery of goods." But *Dakin v Oxley* (1864) 15 C.B.(N.S.) 646 at p.665, shows that *safe* carriage in the sense of delivery of goods in good condition is not necessary, and cases like *Cargo ex Argos* (1873) L.R. 5 P.C. 134, and *Cargo ex Galam* (1863) B. & L. 167, show that actual delivery of goods is not essential, readiness to deliver sufficing. "Freight as used in the policy of insurance, imports the benefit derived from the employment of the ship": per Lord Tenterden in *Flint v Flemyng* (1830) 1 B. & Ad. 45 at p.48, approved by Lord Blackburn in *Inmann S.S. Co v Bischoff* (1882) 7 App. Cas. 670 at p.678. Lord Blackburn added that the word included the monthly hire of the ship for time, but this usage is nowadays confined to marine insurance: *Care Shipping Corp v Itex Itagrani Export SA* [1993] Q.B. 1. The clause dealing with freight on optional cargo in the Centrocon charter refers to the gross, not net, freight: *Hain S.S. Co v Minister of Food* [1949] 1 K.B. 492.

[3] per Willes J., *Dakin v Oxley* (1864) 15 C.B.(N.S.) 646 at p.664; *Kirchner v Venus* (1859) 12 Moore P.C. 361 at p.398, and Chapter 18, on Lien, below. Cf. *The Industrie* [1894] P. 58.

[4] *Cargo ex Argos*, above; *Cargo ex Galam*, above; and Art.163.

[5] See fn.2, above.

[6] A guarantee of a gross freight of £900 will be payable if the freight is less than £900, though the vessel is lost on the voyage, as the breach occurs at the port of loading: *Carr v Wallachian Co.* (1867) L.R. 2 C.P. 468.

[7] As to whether a charter includes one voyage or two, so that freight is payable for a part of the chartered services, though the ship is lost in performing the other part, see *Mackrell v Simond* (1776) 2 Chit. 666. The clause "ship lost or not lost" is now very usual. This clause does not bar a claim for loss of freight where the ship is lost otherwise than by an excepted peril: *Great Indian Ry v Turnbull* (1885) 53 L.T. 325.

[8] See Art.164.

[9] *Tindall v Taylor* (1854) 4 E. & B. 219 at p.27; *Thompson v Trail* (1826) 2 Car. & p.334. And see Art.185 on Liens, below.

[10] *Dakin v Oxley* (1864) 15 C.B.(N.S.) 646 at p.664; *Kirchner v Venus* (1859) 12 Moore P.C. 361 at p.390. It would perhaps be more accurate to say that during the voyage the master is entitled to keep the goods because by his contract he is entitled to carry them and earn freight, and that when he has performed the voyage and earned the freight he is entitled to hold them under the lien that then arises to enforce payment of the freight.

The term "freight" will be presumed to have its ordinary mercantile meaning,[11] unless evidence is found in the charter or bill of lading which negatives this. But where the contract sued upon is an oral contract, evidence may be given that the parties by using the term "freight" intended advance freight.[12]

Case: Goods were shipped under a bill of lading with the words "Freight payable in London." Evidence was tendered that by the custom of the steam shipping trade this meant "freight payable in advance in London". *Held*, inadmissible, the word "freight" being well understood, and there being no words here to qualify it.[13]

Note 1. Freight is usually payable, under a voyage charter, in accordance with the express provisions of the charter, thus: a certain proportion of the freight, or a certain lump sum on sailing; remainder on delivery, either by cash or by specified bills. If the charter is a round charter, or there are loading and discharging expenses in the course of the voyage, the charter may require such disbursements to be advanced against the freight by the charterers or their agents.

Where the charterers propose to put the ship up as a general ship, and the captain may sign bills of lading at a lower rate of freight than the charter, the shipowners may protect themselves thus: "Any difference between charter and bill of lading freight to be settled at port of loading before sailing; if in vessel's favour to be paid in cash, at current rate of exchange less insurance; if in charterer's favour, by captain's draft, payable three days after ship's arrival at port of discharge."[14]

Note 2. Stipulations as to the payment of freight in the bill of lading vary very much. It is very common to find the freight made due and payable "on shipment of the goods" or "in exchange for bills of lading" or "on or before the departure of the vessel". A usual clause is "The freight shall be deemed earned as the cargo is loaded on board and shall be discountless and non-returnable, vessel and/or cargo lost or not lost." Sometimes this clause is coupled with a further clause making all or part of the freight payable within a certain number of days after signing and releasing the bills or completion of discharge. Under this clause, an indefeasible right to the payment of freight accrues on loading, and the shipowner will not lose the right to payment of full freight merely because the vessel is lost[15] or the shipowner commits a repudiatory breach of contract which is accepted as

---

[11] *Krall v Burnett* (1877) 25 W.R. 305; *Lewis v Marshall* (1844) 7 M. & G. 729; *Blakey v Dixon* (1800) 2 B. & P. 321. This will allow the introduction of usages of the particular trade or practices of merchants creating rights between the parties to a contract in respect of some matter which is not in terms provided for by the contract; see per Willes J. in *Meyer v Dresser* (1864) 16 C.B.(N.S.) at p.662, and Art.11, above. So *Brown v Byrne* (1854) 3 E. & B. 703, where a custom at Liverpool as to discount from freight was held binding. See also *Russian Steam Navigation Co v De Silva* (1863) 13 C.B.(N.S.) 610; *The Norway* (1865) 3 Moore P.C.(N.S.) 245. In *Meyer v Dresser*, above, evidence of a particular method of payment of freight, tendered as a "general custom of merchants", was rejected as a mere mode of carrying on business; and in *Kirchner v Venus*, above, evidence of custom as to freight was held inadmissible on the ground that one of the parties, being ignorant of it, could not have intended, or be presumed to have intended to be bound by it: *sed quaere*; and see *Note* following Art.11. In *Stuart v Bigland* (January 24, 1886), unreported (CA) "to pay out of freight collected" was held to mean out of gross, not net, freight.
[12] *Lidgett v Perrin* (1861) 11 C.B.(N.S.) 362; *Andrew v Moorehouse* (1814) 5 Taunt. 435; and see Art.10.
[13] *Krall v Burnett*, above. See also *Mashiter v Buller* (1807) 1 Camp. 84, criticised by Brett J. in *Allison v Bristol Marine Ins Co.* (1876) 1 App.Cas. 209 at p.218.
[14] See *Ralli v Paddington S.S. Co* (1900) 5 Com.Cas. 124.
[15] *Karin Vatis Vagres Compania Maritima SA v Nissho-Iwai America Corp (The Karin Vatis)* [1988] 2 Lloyd's Rep. 330.

bringing the contract to an end[16] before the events which are to trigger the payment of freight take place. Where the bill of lading provides that freight is payable as per a charterparty, the whole manner or mode of collection of the freight is delegated to the charterer at any rate until the shipowner steps in to claim his freight upon the failure of the time charterer.[17] Where the freight is to be paid on delivery it is sometimes secured thus: "Freight and primage for the said goods to be paid at destination, but if the consignee for any reason, perils of the sea excepted, refuses to pay the same, shippers hereby undertake to pay amount here on demand", or "to be delivered after safe arrival at Z to G, freight for the said goods as per margin being paid first in London". The clause "ship lost or not lost", almost always appears. A provision is sometimes inserted for the payment of double freights on goods incorrectly described.

Article 162—Advance Freight   A162

Where money is to be paid by the shipper to the shipowner before the delivery of the goods for ship's disbursements[18] or otherwise, such payment will be treated as an advance of freight or as a loan according to the intention of the parties as expressed in the documents.[19] A stipulation that it shall be paid "subject to the insurance", or "less insurance", will indicate that the payment is an advance of freight.[20]

If it is an advance of freight,[21] it must be paid, though the goods are (after the due date of payment,[22] but before payment) lost by excepted perils, and it will not be recoverable from the shipowner if the goods are after payment so lost.[23] Where the vessel is lost and the charter thus frustrated, or the charter is otherwise determined before the expiry of the number of days permitted for payment after signing bills of lading, the question of whether or not the freight is payable will

---

[16] *Colonial Bank v European Grain & Shipping Ltd (The Dominique)* [1989] 1 Lloyd's Rep. 431.

[17] *Tradigrain SA v King Diamond Shipping SA (The Spiros C)* [2000] 2 Lloyd's Rep. 319; *India S.S. v Louis Dreyfus Sugar Ltd (The Indian Reliance)* [1997] 1 Lloyd's Rep. 52.

[18] Under a clause "Cash for disbursements to be advanced at port of loading on account of freight not exceeding £150 in all", the charterer is not entitled to advance the maximum sum named if the shipowner prefers to find the cash himself: *The Primula* [1894] P. 128; see also *The Red Sea* [1896] P. 20. As to a "vessel's ordinary disbursements", see *Dene S.S. Co v Mann, George* (1949) 82 Ll.L.R. 846.

[19] *Allison v Bristol Marine Insurance Co* (1876) 1 App.Cas. 209 at pp.217, 233, in which all the cases are discussed by Brett J., and *Kirchner v Venus* (1859) 12 Moore P.C. 361, is explained. See also *Coker v Limerick S.S Co Ltd* (1918) L.J.K.B. 767.

[20] *Allison v Bristol Marine Ins Co* (1876) 1 App.Cas. 209 at p.229; *Hicks v Shield* (1857) 7 E. & B. 633; *Jackson v Isaacs* (1858) 3 H. & N. 405, in which the charterer was to deduct cost of insurance from advance freight. See also *Frayes v Worms* (1865) 19 C.B.(N.S.) 159.

[21] A similar liability for freight, though not payable in advance or upon shipment, is often imposed by a clause in the bill of lading to this effect: "Freight to be considered earned, and must be paid, ship and/or cargo lost or not lost." *Cf.: Great Indian Peninsular Ry v Turnbull* (1885) 53 L.T. 325; *Mansfield v Maitland* (1821) 4 B & Ald 582.

[22] *Cf. Oriental S.S. Co v Tylor* [1893] 2 Q.B. 518, where, the freight being due on signing bill of lading, it was held payable where the ship was lost before signing bill of lading, but after it should have been presented, and signed; otherwise if the loss is before the due date of payment. Thus in *Smith v Pyman* [1891] 1 Q.B. 742, where the freight was payable in advance "if required" and the ship was lost before request, it was held the freight was not payable; and in *Weir v Girvin & Co* [1900] 1 Q.B. 45, where the freight was payable three days after sailing and part of the cargo was burnt before sailing, it was held that freight was not payable on the cargo burnt.

[23] *Anon.* (1684) 2 Shower 283; *De Silvale v Kendall* (1815) 4 M. & S. 37; *Byrne v Schiller* (1871) L.R. 6 Ex. 20; affirmed *ibid.* p.319; *Saunders v Drew* (1832) 3 B. & Ad. 445. For the explanation of this rule, which is peculiar to English law, and probably arose from the long voyages of the East India trade, see Brett J. in *Allison v Bristol Marine Insurance Co* (1876) 1 App.Cas. 209 at p.223. As to Scots Law, see *Note*, below.

depend upon whether the charter intended to give the shipowner an indefeasible right to freight, with the provisions as to payment merely being a mechanism to determine the time of payment, or whether these are intended to be conditions precedent to the right to freight.[24] A provision that freight is "deemed earned" will normally render advance freight irrecoverable and enable a shipowner to recover any balance of freight to be payable on the completion of the voyage, even when the voyage is not completed.[25] In the absence of a clause securing the shipowner's right to freight, advance freight will be recoverable if the shipowner has not fulfilled the condition precedent of starting the carriage of the goods on the agreed voyage in a seaworthy ship within a reasonable time.[26]

It will also be recoverable as part of the damages for non-delivery of the goods if they are lost by a peril not excepted.[27]

If advance freight is not paid at the time specified, there will not be a lien for it on the goods carried, without express stipulation[28] nor in any event if the voyage is abandoned before the voyage is begun.[29] Where the advance freight is payable "if required", the shipowner cannot require its payment after the shipper has ceased to be able to insure his risk.[29]

Any payments for ship's use by the person liable to pay freight made before such freight is due and without authority from the contract of affreightment, will be treated as loans rather than as prepayment of freight.[30]

If the payment in advance is regarded as a loan by the shipper to the shipowner, whether on security of the freight or not,[31] it is repayable, if freight to that amount is not due from the shipper, whether the ship is lost or not, and it cannot be insured by either party.[32]

In the absence of anything in the contract to indicate a contrary result, a payment of advance freight is a payment on account of the whole sum which would otherwise be payable on the cargo delivered at destination: it is not to be treated as the total of proportionate advances of the agreed freight upon each ton of goods shipped.[33]

---

[24] *Karin Vatis Vagres Compania Maritime SA v Nissho-Iwai America Corp (The Karin Vatis)* [1988] 2 Lloyd's Rep. 330; *Colonial Bank v European Grain & Shipping Ltd (The Dominique)* [1989] 1 Lloyd's Rep. 431 (HL). Compare *Compania Naviera General v Kerametal Ltd (The Lorna 1)* [1983] 1 Lloyd's Rep. 373 which Mustill L.J. suggested was consistent with *The Dominique*: [1988] 1 Lloyd's Rep. 215 (CA).

[25] *The Karin Vatis*, above; *The Dominique*, above; *Ellis Shipping Corp v Voest Alpine Intertrading (The Lefthero)* [1991] 2 Lloyd's Rep. 599.

[26] *Ex p. Nyholm, re Child* (1873) 29 L.T. 634.

[27] *G. Indian Peninsula Ry v Turnbull* (1885) 53 L.T. 325; *Rodocanachi v Milburn* (1886) 18 Q.B.D. 67; *Dufourcet v Bishop* (1886) Q.B.D. 373.

[28] *How v Kirchner* (1857) 11 Moore P.C. 21; *Kirchner v Venus* (1859) 12 Moore P.C. 361; *Tamvaco v Simpson* (1886) L.R. 1 C.P. 363, see the judgment of Willes J.; *Ex p. Nyholm, re Child* (1873) 29 L.T. 634; and see Arts 185, 190, 191, below.

[29] *Smith v Pyman* [1891] 1 Q.B. 742.

[30] *Tanner v Philips* (1972) 42 L.J.Ch. 125; *The Salacia* (1862) 32 L.J.Adm. 43; and see Art.171.

[31] It may not involve a set-off against the freight.

[32] *Watson v Shankland* (1873) L.R. 2 H.L. (Sc.) 304; *Manfield v Maitland* (1821) 4 B. & Ald. 582; *Allison v Bristol Marine Insurance Co* (1976) 1 App.Cas. 209 at pp.229, 253.

[33] *Allison v Bristol Marine Ins Co* (1876) 1 App.Cas. 209.

Note 1. The decision in *Allison v Bristol Marine Insurance Co*[34] was that the advance freight was not to be regarded distributively as a payment of so much per ton, leaving a balance per ton of the cargo delivered to be paid on delivery, but the advance was to be treated as a payment in advance of the whole amount payable on delivery. Thus if 500 tons are shipped at a freight of £2 a ton, and if £500 is paid as advance freight, and if on the voyage 250 tons are lost by an excepted peril, the shipowner must deliver the remaining 250 tons without receiving any payment for freight. He cannot say that the £500 was an advance of £1 upon each ton shipped, and therefore claim £250 as the balance of £1 per ton upon the 250 tons delivered: on the other hand: if 400 tons are lost on the voyage, the charterer cannot claim repayment of £300 of the advance of £500.

In *Allison's* case the courts apparently were only concerned with rights under the charterparty as between shipowner and charterer, or if there was a bill of lading in the hands of an indorsee from the charterer, it was only one bill for the whole cargo. The judges did not need to consider what would be the position if there were separate bills of lading for parts of the cargo, with the usual clause as to "freight payable as per charterparty", in the hands of different consignees. Thus, suppose in the case put above two bills of lading were issued for the 500 tons shipped, the first 300 tons in Hold No. 1 stating that £300 has been paid as advance freight, and that balance of freight is payable on delivery as per charterparty; and the second for 200 tons in Hold No. 2 stating that £200 has been paid as advance freight, and with the same clause. On the voyage 250 tons out of Hold No. 1 are lost. Presumably the shipowner, on delivering 50 tons to the holder of the first bill of lading, can recover no further freight from him: for more than £2 a ton on 50 tons has been paid in advance. But from the holder of the second bill of lading, to whom he delivers his full 200 tons the shipowner can surely claim £200, since that is £2 a ton on the 200 tons delivered less £200 paid in advance. In the result the shipowner on the whole voyage would get £700, i.e. £500 as advance freight, and £200 from the second consignee at the port of delivery. But on the charterparty alone and from the charterer, if he had not indorsed any bills of lading, he would only have got £500 altogether, as is stated above. It is difficult to see how, when bills of lading are issued for parts of the cargo, the advance freight can fail to become distributive at least in regard to the quantities under each bill of lading. For there seems no ground on which the holder of the second bill of lading could assert that he need pay no freight on delivery. His contract in the bill of lading is surely to pay £2 a ton on the 200 tons delivered to him less that part of the £500 paid in advance, which must be treated as advance freight on his goods.[34]

Note 2. There is a divergence between the English and Scots law as to the recoverability of payments on account of freight. The English law is as stated above in the text. By Scots law, however, an advance of freight by charterers to owners may, unless the parties contract expressly or by clear implication that it shall not be recoverable, be recovered by the charterers in the event of the total loss of the ship even by excepted perils upon the ordinary legal principle of failure of the consideration for the payment, i.e. the contract work of carrying and right delivery of the cargo.[35]

Case 1. Goods were shipped under a charter "to be delivered on being paid freight £5 per ton delivered. . . . Cash for ship's disbursements to be advanced to the extent of £300, free of interest, but subject to insurance. . . . The freight to be paid on unloading and right delivery of cargo as follows,

---

[34] The example is T.E.S.'s own.
[35] *Watson & Co v Shankland* (1871) 10 M. 142, affirmed on another point in (1873) L.R. 2 H.L.(Sc.) 304. See *Cantiare San Rocco v Clyde Co* [1924] A.C. 226.

in cash, less two months' interest at 5 per cent and if required £300 to be paid in cash on arrival at port of loading, less two months' interest." D, agent for the charterer, C, advanced £300; the ship was lost on the voyage, and C claimed £300 from A, the shipowner, as a loan. *Held*, that the charter, and the provision for insurance, showed conclusively that the advance was for freight, and not as a loan, and therefore could not be recovered, though the ship was lost.[36]

Case 2. Goods were shipped under a charter, "Sufficient cash for ship's disbursements to be advanced, if required, to the captain by charterers (C) on account of freight at current rate of exchange subject to insurance only." The whole freight was £735. C advanced at X £160, being allowed £5 for insurance. C did not insure the £160. The ship was lost by perils not excepted, and C claimed to recover £8,400, the price for which the goods were sold "to arrive", less £575 balance of freight. The shipowners claimed to deduct £735—the whole freight. *Held*, they were not entitled to do so, as C's damage was the amount he would have to receive less the amount he would have to pay on arrival of the goods.[37]

Case 3. Under a charter, with a clause, "One-third freight, if required to be advanced, less 3 per cent for interest and insurance", the ship sailed and was wrecked on her voyage. After the wreck, the shipowner "required" payment for the first time of one-third freight. *Held*, that the charterer was under no liability to pay advance freight till required by the shipowner, and that this requirement could not be made when the voyage could not be performed.[38]

A163   **Article 163—Back Freight**

When the ship is either ready to deliver cargo at the port of destination, or is prevented by excepted perils from reaching that port,[39] but the merchant does not take delivery or forward instructions within a reasonable time, the master, if he does not tranship in the interests of the shipowner,[40] has the power and duty to deal with the cargo in the owner's interest at the owner's expense. He may land and warehouse it, or, if this is impracticable, may carry it in his ship, or forward it in another ship to such place as may be most convenient for its owner, and can charge the owner with remuneration for and expenses of such carriage under the name of *"back freight"*.[41]

Case. Oil was shipped from X to Havre, under a bill of lading. "Goods to be taken out within twenty-four hours after arrival." On reaching Havre the landing of oil was forbidden; attempts to land it at other ports near failed. The ship returned to Havre, transhipped the oil into lighters in the harbour, unloaded the rest of the cargo, reshipped the oil and brought it back to X. The shipper made no

---

[36] *Hicks v Shield* (1857) 7 E. & B. 633. See also *Allison v Bristol Insurance Co*, above; and for a curious case of advance freight, see *The Thyatira* (1883) 8 P.D. 155.

[37] *Rodocanachi v Milburn* (1886) 18 Q.B.D. 67. See *Dufourcet v Bishop* (1886) 18 Q.B.D. 373.

[38] *Smith v Pyman* [1891] 1 Q.B. 742; but see *Oriental S.S. Co v Tylor* [1893] 2 Q.B. 518, where under the clause of "one-third of the freight to be paid on signing a bill of lading", freight was held recoverable, as damages for not presenting bills of lading, where shippers had delayed presenting bill of lading till after ship had sunk and then refused to present it or pay advance freight.

[39] *Semble*, that, in case the ship is prevented by excepted perils from reaching her port of destination, the shipowner can recover expenses and back freight incurred in the interests of the cargo-owner; *vide Notara v Henderson* (1879) L.R. 5 Q.B. 346, and Arts 127, 129. Where the voyage is prevented by its illegality, back freight may be recoverable where such illegality was not known to the shipowner, but not where it was: *Heslop v Jones* (1787) 2 Chit. 550.

[40] Art.131.

[41] *Cargo ex Argos* (1873) L.R. 5 P.C. 134, settling the doubt of Mansfield C.J. in *Christy v Row* (1808) 1 Taunt. 300 at p.316. See Art.153. See also *Chan Sew Nang v Sindo Pasir Pte Ltd* (1980) 1 M.L.J. 462 (Sing). As to the possibility of making such a claim against the charterer, see *Adelfamar SA v Silos E. Mangimi Martini SpA (The Adelfa)* [1988] 2 Lloyd's Rep. 466.

request for the delivery of the goods at Havre. *Held*, that the shipowner was entitled to the freight and expenses of the return journey to X as well as the original freight from X to Havre.[41]

Article 164—Shipowner's Right to Full Freight   A164

The shipowner is entitled to the full freight stipulated in the charter or bill of lading:

(1) When he delivers the goods in a merchantable condition,[42] at the port of destination[43] or is ready to deliver them, but the consignee does not take delivery within a reasonable time.[44]

(2) Where a lump sum as freight has been stipulated for and he has delivered, or is ready to deliver, some part of the goods.[45]

(3) Where, the necessity of transhipment having arisen, he has transhipped, and so caused the goods to be delivered, even though at a less freight than that originally contracted for.[46]

(4) Where he has been prevented from delivering the goods solely by the default of the freighter, as, e.g. if the freighter refuses to accept delivery at the port of destination,[47] or requires delivery of the goods at an intermediate port,[48] refuses to name a safe port to which the ship can proceed and enter.[49]

Case 1. F shipped cement under a bill of lading: "Freight to be paid within three days after the arrival of ship before the delivery of any portion of the goods specified in this bill of lading." The vessel arrived, but on the day of arrival a fire accidentally broke out which necessitated the scuttling of the ship, and the cement was so acted upon by water as to cease to exist as cement. *Held*, that the master must be ready to deliver before freight was payable, and therefore no freight was due.[50]

Case 2. F shipped petroleum on A's ship to be delivered at Havre, to be taken by F within twenty-four hours of ship's arrival at Havre. At Havre the port authorities refused to allow the petroleum to be landed or the ship to come to the ordinary place of discharge in the port. The ship was allowed to anchor in the outer port, and F could have taken delivery of the petroleum there into lighters. F made no application to the ship for the goods. *Held*, that A had done all that was required on his part, and was entitled to full freight.[51]

Article 165—Lump Freight   A165

Lump freight is a gross sum stipulated to be paid for the use of the entire ship or a portion thereof; it will therefore be payable if the shipowner is ready to perform

---

[42] *Asfar v Blundell* [1896] 1 Q.B. 123.
[43] Delivery need not be to the consignee, if it is in a manner approved by him: see *Fenwick v Boyd* (1846) 15 M. & W. 632.
[44] *Duthie v Hilton* (1868) L.R. 4 C.P. 138 at p.143; *Cargo ex Argos* (1873) L.R. 5 P.C. 134; and per Lord Mansfield in *Luke v Lyde* (1759) 2 Burr. 883.
[45] See Art.165.
[46] *Shipton v Thornton* (1838) 9 A. & E. 314; *Matthews v Gibbs* (1860) 30 L.J.Q.B. 55, is not inconsistent with this, but turns on special facts; and see Art.131.
[47] *Cargo ex Argos* (1873) L.R. 5 P.C. 134.
[48] *The Bahia* (1864) B. & L. 292; *Cargo ex Galam* (1863) 2 Moo.P.C.(N.S.) 216; *The Soblomsten* (1886) L.R. 1 A. & E. 293; *Luke v Lyde* (1759) 2 Burr. 882 at p.888.
[49] *The Teutonia* (1872) L.R. 4 P.C. 171 cannot now be explained on this ground: see *Note* to Art.66 in the 18th edition; *Aktieselskabet Olivebank v Dansk Fabrik* [1919] 2 K.B. 162.
[50] *Duthie v Hilton* (1868) L.R. 4 C.P. 138; *Asfar v Blundell* [1896] 1 Q.B. 123 (dates).
[51] *Cargo ex Argos*, above.

his contract, though no goods are shipped, or though part of the goods shipped is not delivered. If any goods are shipped, some must be delivered to entitle the shipowner to lump freight.[52] Provision that freight shall be computed on intake quantity may have similar effect to one for a lump freight.[53]

If there is a charterparty for a cargo at a lump freight, and bills of lading for separate parcels provide that freight shall be payable as per charterparty, each holder of a bill of lading will be liable for such proportion of the lump freight as his parcel bears to the whole cargo shipped.[54]

Note 1. The delivery of some of the goods which entitles the shipowner to the whole lump freight may be delivery (1) in the chartered ship, or (2) (if the use of such substituted method is permissible in the circumstances and under the charterparty) in a substituted ship,[55] (3) by other means, e.g. by delivering them to the port of destination from the wreck of the chartered ship.[56]

Note 2. Lump sum freights and guarantees of capacity, etc.—In *S.S. Heathfield v Rodenacher*[57] a ship was guaranteed by owners to carry 2,600 tons dead weight; and the charterer contracted to load a full and complete cargo at a named rate "all per ton dead weight capacity as above". The ship could carry 2,950 tons, and the Court of Appeal held that freight was payable at the named rate on 2,950 tons: *sed quaere.* In *S.S. Rotherfield v Tweedie*,[58] the charterers, in a Danube berthnote, agreed to load a full cargo of wheat at a named rate per ton on the guaranteed dead weight capacity of 4,250 tons. "Owners guarantee steamer can carry 4,250 tons dead weight." The ship carried a full cargo of 3,950 tons, which with bunkers made up the 4,250 tons guaranteed. *Held*, freight was only payable on 3,950 tons. Both these decisions seem to strike out of the charters part of their provisions.

Case 1. A ship was chartered to load a full cargo, proceed to Z, and there deliver the same on being paid " a lump freight of £315". On the voyage, part of the cargo, properly loaded, was lost through perils of the sea. *Held*, that on delivery of the remainder the full freight of £315 was payable.[59]

---

[52] *The Norway* (1865) 3 Moore P.C.(N.S.) 245; *Robinson v Knights* (1873) L.R. 8 C.P. 465; *Merchant Shipping Co v Armitage* (1873) L.R. 8 C.P. 469; varied (1873) L.R. 9 Q.B. 99. *Cf. London Transport v Trechman* [1904] 1 K.B. 635. Dr. Lushington in *The Norway* (1865) 12 L.T. 57 had expressed the opinion that where short delivery of goods was not due to excepted perils, the freighter might deduct pro rata freight for the goods not delivered, though he could not deduct their value, nor could he deduct the freight if the short delivery were due to exceptional perils. The Judicial Committee, reversing him on the question of fact, held that the short delivery was due to excepted perils, but also said: "We do not mean to express an opinion that even if the jettison and sale had been attributable to the negligence of the master there ought to be a deduction. Perhaps, in this case, the proper remedy of the shipper would have been by a cross-action." Coleridge C.J. expresses a doubt whether this is correct in *Merchant Shipping Co v Armitage* (1873) L.R. 9 Q.B. 99 at p.107. Most of the cases as to lump sum freight are considered in *Thomas v Harrowing S.S. Co* [1915] A.C. 58.
[53] *Shell International Petroleum v Seabridge Shipping (The Metula)* [1978] 2 Lloyd's Rep. 5: Exxonvoy charter.
[54] *Brightman v Miller, Shipping Gazette,* June 9, 1908; *cf.* and contrast *Red "R" S.S. Co v Allantini* (1909) 14 Com.Cas. 303; affirmed (1910) 15 Com.Cas. 290; *Mazarakis v Bunge y Born* (1926) 25 Ll.L.R. 169; *Hain S.S. Co v Minister of Food* [1949] 1 K.B. 492.
[55] As in *Rederiaktiebolaget Transatlantic v Board of Trade* (1924) 30 Com.Cas. 117.
[56] *Thomas v Harrowing S.S. Co* [1915] A.C. 58. The judgments in this case indicate that under certain forms of lump sum charters the arrival of the chartered ship itself is a condition precedent to the right to freight.
[57] (1896) 2 Com.Cas. 55.
[58] (1897) 2 Com.Cas. 84.
[59] *Robinson v Knights* (1873) L.R. 8 C.P. 465.

Article 166—Full Freight for Delivery of Damaged Goods, or for Short   **A166**
Delivery

The shipowner will be entitled to full freight:

(1) If he is ready to deliver in substance at the port of destination the goods loaded even though they are in a damaged condition. The freighter will not be entitled to make a deduction from the freight for the damage, but will have a separate cause of action or counterclaim for the damage, unless caused solely by excepted perils or by the vice of the goods themselves. The question is whether the substance delivered is identical commercially with the substance loaded, though it may have deteriorated in quality.[60]

Case 1. Coal shipped under a charter had by the negligence of the master so deteriorated in quality as not to be worth its freight. The charterer therefore abandoned it to the shipowner and claimed to be discharged from freight. *Held,* he was not entitled to abandon, and was liable for the whole freight, his remedy being by cross-action.[61]

Case 2. Dates shipped under a lump-sum charter were under water for two days in the Thames. They were condemned by the Sanitary Authority as unfit for human food, and were unmerchantable as dates. They, however, looked like dates, and were of considerable value for distillation into spirit. *Held,* by the Court of Appeal, that, as the thing delivered was not in a business sense the thing shipped no freight was payable.[62]

Case 3. A assigned all earnings of the vessel to a Bank. A then chartered the vessel to C for a single voyage under a Gencon charter. The cargo was shipped on board, bills of lading were issued and the vessel proceeded on the voyage. The Bank gave notice of the assignment to C. Whilst taking on bunkers at Colombo, the vessel was arrested by a third party creditor. Whilst still under arrest and after considerable delay, C transhipped (at considerable expense) the cargo onto another vessel. Held: (i) that the freight had accrued due; (ii) that C was liable to pay the outstanding freight in full to the Bank as assignee; (iii) that, although A had wrongfully repudiated the charter, C was not entitled to set-off C's loss (including the cost of transhipment).[63]

---

[60] *Dakin v Oxley* (1864) 15 C.B.(N.S.) 646, per Willes J. at pp.664 *et seq.*; *Melhuish v Garrett* (1858) 4 Jur.(N.S.) 943; *Shields v Davis* (1815) 6 Taunt. 65; *Asfar v Blundell* [1896] 1 Q.B. 123; *St. John Shipping Co v Rank* [1957] 1 Q.B. 267 at p.291; *The Brede* [1974] Q.B. 233; *Aries Tanker Corp v Total Transport (The Aries)* [1977] 1 Lloyd's Rep. 334 (HL); *Elena Shipping Ltd v Aidenfield Ltd (The Elena)* [1986] 1 Lloyd's Rep. 425 in which the no set-off rule was applied to a breach occurring before the loading voyage was performed; *Colonial Bank v European Grain & Shipping Ltd (The Dominique)* [1989] 1 Lloyd's Rep. 431 in which the no set-off rule was applied to advance freight notwithstanding a repudiatory breach of charter. The rule established in *The Aries* may be avoided by a special clause allowing e.g. a deduction from freight of the c.i.f. value of cargo short delivered: *Lakeport Navigation Company Panama v Anonima Petroli Italiana (The Olympic Brilliance)* [1982] 2 Lloyd's Rep. 205; *Protank Shipping v Total Transport Corp* [1997] 2 Lloyd's Rep. 42 and also where the claim to be set-off is itself a liquidated sum: *Colonial Bank v European Grain & Shipping Ltd (The Dominique)* [1987] 1 Lloyd's Rep. 239 although per *contra Freedom Maritime Corp v International Bulk Carriers SA (The Khian Captain No. 2)* [1986] 1 Lloyd's Rep. 429. The necessity of relying upon a set-off or counterclaim, as distinct from a defence, becomes material in the case of the freighter's claim being time-barred, as by the Centrocon Arbitration Clause or the Hague–Visby Rules. The CA held in *Federal Commerce and Navigation v Molena Alpha (The Nanfri)* [1978] 2 Lloyd's Rep. 132, that the principle established as regards freight, does not apply to hire, but the HL did not deal with the point: [1979] 1 Lloyd's Rep. 201. See also Art.174.

[61] *Dakin v Oxley* and *The Aries*, above.

[62] *Asfar v Blundell* [1896] 1 Q.B. 123. *Quaere* whether this decision was right; the consignees took the cargo and sold it for £2,400. Perhaps they could not have been compelled to take delivery, but, if they did, it is submitted they ought to pay freight. The distinction between *Melhuish v Garrett*, above, and *Duthie v Hilton* (1868) L.R. 4 C.P. 138, where cement was affected by water, so as to become a solid mass, and it was held that no freight was due, is presumably that the substance there was something different from the substance loaded, though the brick-dust and the solid cement would seem equally useless to the shipper. Willes J., in *Dakin v Oxley*, above, at p.667, puts the question thus: "What was the thing for the carriage of which freight was to be paid, and whether that thing, or any and how much of it, has substantially arrived." See also, *Montedison v Icroma (The Caspian Sea)* [1980] 1 Lloyd's Rep. 91.

[63] *Colonial Bank v European Grain & Shipping Ltd (The Dominique)* [1987] 1 Lloyd's Rep. 239.

(2) On a contract for a lump sum as freight, the shipowner is entitled to full freight even though he delivers less goods than the quantity named in the bill of lading, if he delivers all that were loaded.[64] Statements of contents or weight contained in the bill of lading are binding against the shipper or consignee for the purposes of freight, if the goods are delivered as received.[65]

A167   **Article 167—Freight pro rata for Short Delivery**

If the shipowner, contracting to load a full cargo, only loads and carries part of it,[66] or if, having loaded a full cargo, he only delivers part of it, he will, in the absence of a stipulation for lump freight,[67] only be entitled to freight pro rata on the quantity delivered; and the freighter can counterclaim for short delivery[68] not solely caused by excepted perils, or by the vice of the goods themselves.[69]

Note. Where, after shipment, part of a cargo is burnt, there being an exception of fire, the shipper is relieved from replacing it, or from paying freight on it; the shipowner is not entitled to demand freight on it, or fresh cargo in its place, but may himself furnish fresh cargo in its place, on which he will be entitled to freight. His right to ship fresh cargo appears to arise whether the freight is a lump freight or per ton.[70]

A168   **Article 168—Freight pro rata for Delivery short of Place of Destination**

A contract to carry goods for freight payable at the agreed destination is a contract "to do an entire work for a specific sum".[71] Accordingly, the shipowner "can recover nothing unless the work is done, or unless it can be shown that it was the defendant's fault that the work was incomplete, or that there is something to justify the conclusion that the parties have entered into a fresh contract".[71]

It follows that if the contract is governed by English law,[72] where the shipowner delivers the goods to the merchant short of the port of destination, he

---

[64] *Davidson v Gwynne* (1810) 12 East 381; *Blanchet v Powell* (1874) L.R. 9 Ex. 74; *Meyer v Dresser* (1864) 16 C.B.(N.S.) 646; *The Norway* (1865) 3 Moore P.C.(N.S.) 245; *Jessel v Bath* (1867) L.R. 2 Ex. 267. By express agreement the cargo-owner may have a right to deduct the cost of cargo short delivered from the freight, as in *S.S. Garston v Hickie, Borman (No. 2)* (1886) 18 Q.B.D. 17, where the clause was: "less cost of cargo delivered short of bill of lading quantity"; *The Olympic Brilliance*, above.

[65] *Tully v Terry* (1873) L.R. 8 C.P. 679. See also *Cavas v Bingham* (1853) 2 E. & B. 836 and *Jessel v Bath* (1867) L.R. 2 Ex. 267. They may by agreement be made binding as against the shipowner: *Lishman v Christie* (1887) 19 Q.B.D. 333, where the clause was: "the bill of lading to be conclusive evidence of the quantity received, as stated therein". Cf. *Mediterranean Co v Mackay* [1903] 1 K.B. 297; and *Crossfield v Kyle S.S. Co* [1916] 2 K.B. 885.

[66] *Ritchie v Atkinson* (1808) 10 East 295.

[67] Willes J. suggests in *Dakin v Oxley*, below, an exception if the delivery of the whole cargo is made a condition precedent to the payment of any freight; but such a case is rare.

[68] Over-delivery under one bill of lading will not in itself be any defence to a shipowner against a consignee's claim for short delivery under another bill of lading: *Nordborg (Owners) v Sherwood* [1939] P. 121.

[69] *Dakin v Oxley* (1864) 15 C.B.(N.S.) 646 at p.665; *The Norway* (1865) 3 Moore P.C.(N.S.) 245; *Spaight v Farnworth* (1880) 5 Q.B.D. 115; *Mediterranean Co v Mackay* [1903] 1 K.B. 297.

[70] *Aitken Liburn v Ernsthausen* [1894] 1 Q.B. 773 (CA); *Weir v Girvin & Co* [1900] 1 Q.B. 45 (CA).

[71] Blackburn J., *Appleby v Myers* (1867) L.R. 2 C.P. 651 at p.661.

[72] For a foreign ship under English charter, see *The Industrie* [1894] P. 58; *The Patria* (1871) L.R. 3 A. & E. 436. See also *The Adriatic* [1931] p.241.

can only claim freight proportional to the amount of voyage completed, known as freight pro rata *itineris peracti*, or freight pro rata, if an express or implied agreement to that effect exists with the merchant[73]; or, secondly, on a claim for damages, if he has by the act of the cargo-owner been prevented from completing the carriage to the agreed destination, provided that freight pro rata *itineris peracti* is the true measure of damages.[74]

An agreement to pay pro rata freight will not be implied from the mere fact that the merchant receives his goods at the request of the shipowner at an intermediate port.[75]

To justify a claim for pro rata freight there must be such a voluntary acceptance of the goods by their owner, at a port short of their final destination, or such a dealing, or neglect to deal with them there, as to raise a fair inference that the further carrying of the goods (the shipowner having a right to carry them further) was intentionally dispensed with by the goods-owner.[76]

Thus where the goods are arrested, and the goods-owner, knowing of their arrest, takes no step to release them, and allows them to be sold, a claim for pro rata freight arises.[77] But, where the shipowner has no longer a right to carry on, as where he abandons the ship and cargo, or where he delays repairs or transhipment beyond a reasonable time, and the goods-owner elects to treat the charter as at an end,[78] the goods-owner, who receives his goods, will not thereby give the shipowner any claim for freight pro rata.[79]

A sale by the master, though justifiable in the interests of the cargo, gives him no claim for pro rata freight, if the goods-owner has not been consulted, whether

[73] *Osgood v Groning* (1810) 2 Camp. 466; *The Newport* (1858) Swabey 335; *Luke v Lyde* (1759) 2 Burr. 882; *Dakin v Oxley* (1864) 15 C.B.(N.S.) 646 at p.665. It is possible that the shipowner can recover to the extent that the merchant has been incontrovertibly benefited by the carriage of goods: *Proctor & Gamble Philippine Manufacturing Corp v Peter Cremer GmbH & Co (The Manila (No. 2))* [1988] 3 All E.R. 843. See generally Goff and Jones: *The Law of Restitution* 7th edn (London: Sweet & Maxwell, 2007) paras 1–023 to 1–026, 20–006, 20–053 to 20–054.
[74] See Art.164. *Aktieselskabet Olivebank v Dansk Fabrik* [1919] 2 K.B. 162 is a good example of such a claim.
[75] *The Soblomsten* (1866) L.R. 1 A. & E. 293; *Cook v Jennings* (1797) 7 T.R. 381; *Metcalfe v Britannia Iron Works* (1877) 2 Q.B.D. 423; *Thornton v Fairlie* (1818) 8 Taunt 354.
[76] *Osgood v Groning*, above; *The Newport*, above; *Christy v Row* (1808) 1 Taunt 300; *Liddard v Lopes* (1809) 10 East 526; *Mitchell v Darthez* (1836) 2 Bin.N.C. 555. *Cf.: Petrinovic v Mission Française* (1942) 71 Ll. L.R. 208.
[77] *The Soblomsten* (1866) L.R. 1 A. & E. 293; Lord Mansfield's remark in *Luke v Lyde* (1759) 2 Burr. 882 at p.888 that "If the merchant abandons all, he is excused freight, and he may abandon all though they are not all lost" must be read with the comments of Willes J. in *Dakin v Oxley* (1864) 15 C.B.(N.S.) 646 at p.665, who substitutes "decline to accept" for "abandon"; in which case the goods-owner, by declining to accept his goods short of the place of destination at pro rata freight, will compel the master either to carry or send them on at the full freight (see Arts 131, 163, 164), or to give them up to their owner there, without requiring any freight.
[78] *The Cito* (1881) 7 P.D. 5. If the shipowner, having abandoned ship and cargo so as to put an end to the contract of affreightment, afterwards regains possession from salvors, he will not thereby revive the contract or regain any right to freight: *The Arno* (1895) 8 Asp.M.C. 5. On this see *Bradley v Newsom* [1919] A.C. 16. To constitute abandonment there must be neither intention to return nor hope of recovery. The decision of the majority of the House of Lords that the facts in that case were not abandonment, and that full freight was still payable when the abandoned ship was brought in, will startle at any rate some commercial lawyers, who will prefer the dissentient judgment of Lord Summer.—(T. E. S.) See also *Court Line v R.* (1945) Ll.L.R. 390 (time-charter hire to end on vessel becoming constructive total loss: alleged abandonment).
[79] *The Kathleen* (1874) L.R. 4 A. & E. 269; *The Cito* (1881) 7 P. & D. 5 (CA); *The Leptir* (1885) 52 L.T. 768; *The Arno*, above.

such consultation was possible or not,[80] or, having been consulted, has not acquiesced.[81]

Case 1. A chartered vessel on the voyage became disabled, and was on October 2 towed into an English port, where she and the cargo were arrested in a salvage suit on October 7. The master took the necessary steps to defend the suit, but on October 24 abandoned the vessel; the owners of the cargo had been informed of the suit and of the probable sale of the cargo, but gave no instructions. The cargo was sold by the order of the court. *Held*, that the owners of the cargo by their inaction had waived their right to have the voyage completed at a time when the master had not lost his right to tranship, and that the cargo-owners were therefore liable to pay pro rata freight.[82]

Case 2. A ship was chartered to proceed to Taganrog and deliver cargo. Owing to ice in the Sea of Azof she could get no further than Kertch, 300 miles by sea from T., and would have had to wait till the spring to complete her voyage. The captain proposed to discharge the cargo; the consignees objected. The captain delivered the cargo to the custom-house at Kertch, claiming a lien on it for freight; the custom-house gave it up to the consignees, who gave the captain a receipt for it, but declined to pay freight. *Held*, that the shipowner was not entitled to full freight, for he had not completed the voyage, nor to pro rata freight, for there was no express or implied contract to pay it.[83]

Case 3. A ship on a voyage to Z was, owing to perils of the sea, abandoned by her crew. She was found derelict by another ship, which brought her into an English port. *Held*, that upon satisfying the cargo's liability to the salvors the cargo-owners were entitled to their goods without payment of any freight, the contract of affreightment being at an end by justifiable abandonment of the ship, and the shipowner having therefore no right to carry on by transhipment.[84]

Case 4. A ship, *S.*, on a chartered voyage met with storms, and signals of distress were made to the ship *R*. The *S.*'s master and crew went on board the *R.*, but without taking clothes or baggage; on seeking to return to the *S.* they were not allowed; the master of the *R.* sent some of his own crew on board the *S.*, and the *S.*'s crew helped to navigate the *R. Held*, that there was no such abandonment as to put an end to the contract of carriage (as there was either no abandonment or an unjustifiable one); that the shipowners were therefore entitled at least to pro rata freight, if the consignees required delivery of the cargo.[85]

Case 5. Goods were shipped in July 1914 at an American port on the British steamer *St. H.* under a bill of lading for delivery at Hamburg. During the voyage the war with Germany began on August 4. The consignees, owners of the goods and British subjects, on the ship being diverted to Manchester, took delivery of the goods there. *Held*, that the shipowners had no claim against them for any freight.[86]

---

[80] *Vlierboom v Chapman* (1844) 13 M. & W. 230; *Hopper v Burness* (1876) 1 C.P.D. 137; *Acatos v Burns* (1878) 3 Ex.D. 282 (CA).

[81] *Hill v Wilson* (1879) 4 C.P.D. 329. To render himself liable to pro rata freight, the goods-owner, having had an option of having the goods sent on to their destination, or of accepting them at the intermediate port, must accept the goods at the intermediate port: *Hill v Wilson*, above, at p.335. See also *Blasco v Fletcher* (1863) 14 C.B.(N.S.) 147. *Semble*, however, that while the captain must protect the interests of the goods, he should also protect the interests of the ship, and should not let the goods go without the payment of pro rata freight.

[82] *The Soblomsten* (1866) L.R. 1 A. & E. 293. *Semble*, the shipowner was entitled to full freight, as the master, being entitled to tranship, was prevented by the default of the cargo-owners: see *The Bahia* (1864) B. & L. 292. The case cited is distinguishable from such cases as *Hopper v Burness* (1876) 1 C.P.D. 137, as there the sale was by the master; here the master was in no way responsible for it.

[83] *Metcalfe v Britannia Iron Works Co* (1877) 2 Q.B.D. 423. See also *Castel v Trechman* (1884) C. & E. 276.

[84] *The Cito* (1881) 7 P.D. 5, but see and contrast *Case 6*, below; see also *The Kathleen* (1874) L.R. 4 A. & E. 269; *Curling v Long* (1797) 1 B. & p.634; *The Arno* (1895) 8 Asp.M.C. 5. On the rights of underwriters to freight, see *Hickie v Rodocanachi* (1859) 4 H. & N. 455; *Miller v Woodfall* (1857) 8 E. & B. 493; *Guthrie v North China Ins Co* (1902) 7 Com.Cas. 130.

[85] *The Leptir* (1885) 52 L.T. 768. *Semble*, that if the owners were willing to tranship and carry on, the consignees were not entitled to their goods without full freight being paid. In this case the suit was by salvors; the shipowners put in no appearance, and would seem to have abandoned all intention of carrying on, in which case they would have no right to any freight.

[86] *St. Enoch Co v Phosphate Co* [1916] 2 K.B. 624. *Cf. East Asiatic Co v Tronto S.S. Co* (1915) 31 T.L.R. 543; *Petrinovic v Mission Française* (1942) 71 Ll.L.R. 208. In the Prize Court a different principle applies; *cf. The Juno* [1916] P. 169. The plaintiffs in *Case 5*, above, attempted in the Prize Court to secure a practical reversal of the judgment in the K.B.D. but failed in the P.C. See *The St. Helena* [1916] 2 A.C. 625.

Case 6. A timber-cargo was shipped at Archangel on the *Jupiter* in July 1916, under a charterparty for carriage to Hull, with an exception of King's enemies, and freight to be paid on delivery. Off the coast of Scotland a German submarine stopped the ship, drove her crew into boats, and exploded bombs to sink her. The Germans then towed the crew, who thought their vessel was sunk, five miles away, and left them. A few days later the vessel and the cargo, not having been sunk in fact, were brought by salvors into Leith. The charterers at once telegraphed to the owner claiming to have the cargo delivered freight free at Leith, but the owner at once replied repudiating this claim, and claiming to be entitled to complete the voyage. *Held,* that in these circumstances the owner was entitled to complete the voyage, and the contract was not determined by any "abandonment" of the vessel or voyage.[87]

Note. Hopper v Burness[88] reconciles the case of *Baillie v Moudignliani*[89] and *Hunter v Prinsep,*[90] showing that mere receipt of the produce of the sale of goods at an intermediate port by their owner cannot be treated as the receipt of the goods themselves, so as to give rise to a claim for freight pro rata. Brett J. puts the cargo-owner's position thus:

(1) If the goods are sold for a higher price at the intermediate port than they would fetch at the port of destination, he can treat the proceeds as a forced loan, and claim them at once without paying pro rata freight.

(2) If they are sold for a smaller price, he can similarly treat the actual proceeds as a forced loan,[91] but he can also claim an indemnity for the difference of the price if, but not unless, the ship arrives at the port of destination,[92] and he must then deduct the freight that would have been due on the delivery of the goods there if carried.

Article 169—Amount of Freight   A169

Freight is payable according to the express stipulations of the charter or bill of lading,[93] or, failing them, according to the custom of the trade or port.[94] In the case of tankers, freight is now commonly fixed by reference to published scales of standard rates.[95] If no rate of freight is expressly agreed, the shipowner will be entitled to a reasonable sum.[96]

Similarly, if a charter is for the carriage of specified goods[97] at a named freight, but the charterer ships goods of a different description, the shipowner can claim

---

[87] *Bradley v Newsom* [1919] A.C. 16. Some people would have thought this voyage abandoned, as did Lord Sumner, but wrongly according to the majority in the House of Lords—(T. E. S.). For a reference to *Ex p. Cheeseman* (1763) 2 Eden 181, as a case which curiously anticipates this one, we are indebted to the learning and courtesy of Mr. Gerald Fitzgibbon, K.C., of Dublin. See also *Court Line v R.* (1945) 78 Ll.L.R. 390, where *Bradley v Newsom* was followed in the case of a claim for time-charter hire.

[88] *Hopper v Burness*, above.

[89] *Park on Insurance* (1775), P. 90.

[90] *Hunter v Prinsep* (1808) 10 East 378.

[91] This has been doubted by Pollock C.B. in *Atkinson v Stephens* (1852) 7 Ex. 567.

[92] *Atkinson v Stephens*, above.

[93] There may be an express agreement for the payment of freight outside that in the bill of lading: *Hedley v Lapage* (1816) Holt 392.

[94] See Art.10; and *cf. Young v Jarrah Co* (1899) 4 Com.Cas. 96. As to the rate of exchange where the freight is payable in a foreign currency see fn.95, below, and Art.192, fn.30.

[95] For cases arising out of the use of such scales, see *Achille Lauro v Total* [1969] 2 Lloyd's Rep. 65 (Suez Canal clause); *Agenor Shipping Co v Société des Petroles Miroline* [1968] 2 Lloyd's Rep. 359 (devaluation); *Sanko S.S. Co Ltd v Propet Co Ltd* [1970] 2 Lloyd's Rep. 235; *Total v Liberian Transocean* [1972] 1 Lloyd's Rep. 399 (devaluation); *The Yoho Maru* [1973] 1 Lloyd's Rep. 409 (effect of amendments to scale); *The Mersin* [1973] 1 Lloyd's Rep. 532 (effect of amendment); *Mitsui O.S.K. Lines v Agip SpA* [1978] 1 Lloyd's Rep. 263 (amendment); *Pole Star Compania Naviera SA v Koch Marine SA* [1979] 1 Lloyd's Rep. 581.

[96] *Cf. Ursula Bright Co v Ripley* [1903] 8 Com.Cas. 171; and see Supply of Goods and Services Act 1982, s.15.

[97] When the shipowner delivers a quantity of goods in excess of that specified in a bill of lading a contract to pay freight on the surplus may be found as a fact, but does not arise by implication of law: *Nordborg (Owners) v Sherwood* [1939] P. 121.

that as to the latter there is no agreed rate of freight, and the charterer must pay the market rate as a reasonable remuneration for services rendered outside the contract.[98]

Thus if the goods shipped belong to the shipowner, and therefore no freight is due from him for their carriage, but a freight, whether substantial[99] or nominal,[100] is inserted in the bill of lading as payable, that freight will be payable by assignees of the bill of lading or person taking delivery under it, other than the owner or his agents.

Case 1. E, master of a ship owned by A, carried a cargo of wheat "on owner's account", purchased on the credit of R, to whom E gave bills of lading for "wheat shipped on owner's account, deliverable to P's order at freight of 1s. per ton", and bills of exchange for the price, which A accepted. A had mortgaged his ship to M. A sold the cargo *in transitu* to K, the sale note running "as cargo is coming on ship's account, freight to be computed at £2 15s. per ton". A indorsed the bill of lading, which he had received from P on his acceptance of the bills of exchange, to K, with a note: "The freight assigned is at the rate of £2 15s. per ton, and not the nominal amount of 1s. per ton." On ship's arrival, M, as mortgagee, took possession, and claimed freight at £2 15s. from K, who refused to pay more than 1s. *Held*, that M was only entitled to the freight named in the bill of lading, the larger sum being in reality part of the purchase-money, and no claim of *quantum meruit* being possible in face of the express contract.[101]

Case 2. D, as agent for C, purchased and paid for rice to be carried to Z in C's ship. The rice was then shipped under the bills of lading, "to be delivered to D or assigns, freight for the said goods at £4 5s. per ton". C assigned the freight to M during the voyage. *Held*, that on arrival D was bound to pay M the freight in the bill of lading, and was not entitled to set off the price of the rice due from C to himself.[102]

Where freight is payable on goods according to their weight or measurement, and owing to swelling,[103] expansion after hydraulic pressure[104] or shrinkage, the same goods are larger or smaller at the port of destination than when loaded, freight will be payable in the absence of express stipulation or usage on the amount shipped and not on the amount delivered.[105]

Case 1. A ship was chartered to load a full and complete cargo and deliver on being paid freight at £2 7s. 6d. per ton. The bill of lading showed 2,644 quarters shipped; owing to heat the corn

---

[98] *Steven v Bromley* [1919] 2 K.B. 722; and see pp.156, 161. The principle is that where A having contracted with B does work outside that which he has undertaken, and B accepts the benefit of that, an agreement by B to pay reasonably for the work may be implied: see *Rederi Sverre v Phs. Van Ommeren* (1921) 6 Ll.L.R. 193. See also *Greenmast Shipping Co SA v Jean Lion et Cie. SA (The Saronikos)* [1986] 2 Lloyd's Rep. 277; *Batis Maritime Corp v Petroleos del Mediterroneo SA (The Batis)* [1990] 1 Lloyd's Rep. 345.
[99] *Weguelin v Cellier* (1873) L.R. 6 H.L. 286.
[100] *Keith v Burrows* (1877) 2 App.Cas. 636; *Brown v North* (1852) 8 Ex. 1; *Turner v Trustees of Liverpool Docks* (1851) 6 Ex. 543. The shipowner may, however, have a lien as unpaid vendor for the balance of the price, representing what would be freight if the shipowner and original goods-owner were different: *Swan v Barber* (1879) 5 Ex.D. 130.
[101] *Keith v Burrows* (1877) 2 App.Cas. 636.
[102] *Weguelin v Cellier* (1873) L.R. 6 H.L. 286.
[103] *Gibson v Sturge* (1855) 10 Ex. 622; *Spaight v Farnworth* (1880) 5 Q.B.D. 115, per Bowen L.J. at p.118. Malynes, *Lex Mercatoria* (1686), p.100, may be taken to indicate the same principle: "If a woman be carried over and be delivered of a child on the voyage, yet there is nothing to be paid for the passage of the child."
[104] *Buckle v Knoop* (1867) L.R. 2 Ex. 333.
[105] *Dakin v Oxley* (1864) 15 C.B.(N.S.) 646, per Willes J. at pp.665, 666. On the terms "gross invoice weight, gross landing weight", see *Leech v Glynn* (1890) 6 T.L.R. 306.

swelled, and 2,785 quarters were delivered. *Held*, that freight was payable on the quantity shipped, and not on its measurement at the port of discharge.[106]

Case 2. Clause in a bill of lading, "Freight . . . to be paid . . . on the gross weight at the port of discharge . . . it being expressly agreed that freight is to be considered as earned and must be paid ship and/or cargo lost or not lost." Part of the goods (nitrate) was dissolved by sea water on the voyage. But for this the cargo on delivery would have weighed 93 tons more than the cargo actually delivered did weigh. *Held*, that freight was payable on this 93 tons.[107]

So, where the freight is payable according to quantity or measurement, the method of weighing or measuring, in the absence of express indication or custom to the contrary,[108] must be determined by the custom of the port of loading.[109]

Where freight is payable on a basis of measurement at the port of loading, it is the charterer's duty to have it so measured, and if that be neglected the shipowner can recover as damages the cost of so measuring it at the port of discharge.[110]

Case. A ship was chartered, "freight at the rate of 35s. per 180 English cubic feet taken on board, as per Gothenburg custom". The cargo was not measured at the Baltic port of shipment; but, on arrival at Hull, was there measured for the payment of freight. *Held*, that it should be measured according to the G. custom, and not the custom of the port of discharge.[111]

---

[106] *Gibson v Sturge*, above. To meet this, the clause "freight payable according to net weight delivered" was sometimes introduced into shipping documents; and in *Coulthurst v Sweet* (1866) L.R. 1 C.P. 649, under a bill of lading with that clause, the shipowner was held not entitled to demand freight on the weight named in the bill of lading, or to require the consignee to pay the expense of weighing. Willes J. said: "In the absence of any custom to govern the matter, the person who wants to ascertain the quantity must incur the trouble and expense of weighing." In this dictum of Willes J. the word "wants" apparently means "desires in order to be in a position to present an enforceable demand for freight". But even when freight is payable as to part "on final out-turn being ascertained", actual measurement at the port of discharge may not be a condition precedent to a right to freight. The master may establish his claim by production of the bill of lading figure coupled with proof that no cargo has been lost on passage: *Petersen v Ronassen & Son* (1926) 31 Com.Cas. 347. See also *Marwood v Taylor* (1901) 6 Com.Cas. 178.

In *Spaight v Farnworth*, above, the words were "freight payable on timber on intake measure of quantity delivered". This was held to mean on the quantity delivered taken at the actual measures of the port of shipment. In *London Transport Co v Trechman* [1904] 1 K.B. 635, under the words "deliver the cargo . . . on being paid freight at the rate of 10s. 6d. per ton gross weight shipped payable on right and true delivery of the cargo", it was held that freight was only payable on the cargo delivered, not on the amount of cargo shipped, but upon the shipping weight of the cargo so delivered. A more complicated clause is found in *Tully v Terry* (1873) L.R. 8 C.P. 679. In *Christie v Davis Coal Co* (1899) 95 Fed. 837; (1901) 110 Fed. 1006, a charterparty providing for a full cargo of coal deliverable on being paid freight at and after the rate of $165 per ton on the quantity intaken was held to be a lump sum contract. See also *Oostzee Stoomvart Maats v Bell* (1906) 11 Com.Cas. 214; and *New Line Ltd v Bryson* 1910 S.C. 409 (freight "per intaken Gothenburg standard", and cargo in fact never measured on shipment).

[107] *Pacific Steam Co v Thomson*, 1920 S.C. (HL) 159.

[108] *Nielsen v Neame* (1884) C. & E. 288, where freight was to be paid "45s. per St. Petersburg standard hundred", and the method of calculating St. P. standard hundreds used at the port of discharge was taken, on evidence of a custom to that effect. See also *Bottomley v Forbes* (1838) 5 Bing.N.C. 121.

[109] *Pust v Dowie* (1865) 34 L.J.Q.B. 127; *The Skandinav* (1881) 51 L.J.Adm. 93 (CA); and see Art.86, n.90, above.

[110] *Merryweather v Pearson* [1914] 3 K.B. 587. See also *Petersen v Ronaasen & Son* (1926) 31 Com.Cas. 347.

[111] *The Skandinav*, above. The two cases of *Moller v Living* (1811) 4 Taunt. 102 and *Geraldes v Donison* (1816) Holt N.P. 346 are not inconsistent with this. In *Moller v Living* there was a contract to pay freight at £14 per last on a quantity stated in the bill of lading as "100 lasts in 2,092 bags". The voyage was from D to L. There were 2,092 bags on board, and they contained 100 lasts by L measure but not by D measure: *held*, that the specific description in the bill of lading negatived any question of different measures, and freight was payable on the 100 lasts. If the description had been simply "100 lasts", the question would arise, and it did in *Geraldes v Donison*, above, where following a usage of merchants, it was held that the bill of lading weight was subject to check by weighing at the port of delivery, the court there suggesting that the clause "weights unknown" in the bill of lading introduced the custom. But in *Tully v Terry* (1873) L.R. 8 C.P. 679 that clause was held not to interfere with the captain's right under the charter to be paid freight on the invoice quantity in the bill of lading; the object of the clause being explained to be "to protect the captain against any mistake that might occur in the invoice quantity in the bill of lading, in case of alleged short delivery or deterioration, not caused by his default". See above, Art.62.

A170   **Article 170—Freight: When Payable**

When freight is payable on delivery of the cargo, payment and delivery are concurrent acts.[112] The merchant is not entitled to have the goods unless he is ready to pay the freight. The shipowner is not entitled to the freight unless he is ready to deliver the cargo.[113] The master is entitled to refuse to discharge the cargo unless freight is paid for each portion as delivered[114]; *semble*, also, that the merchant need only pay freight *pari passu* with delivery.

Note 1. Stipulations as to the time of payment of freight vary considerably in practice, but in very many cases freight is payable at the port of loading, sometimes on delivery of bills of lading, sometimes with fourteen days' credit. In the former case, where the bill of lading contains a clause "freight paid in London", the delivery of the bill of lading acts as a receipt for freight.

Note 2. Charterparties frequently provide that some part of the freight should be payable in advance—for instance upon signing and issuing bills of lading—and the balance thereafter. In *Minerals and Metals Trading Corp of India Ltd v Encounter Bay Shipping Co Ltd (The Samos Glory)*[115] the balance of freight was payable "after completion of discharge and settlement of demurrage", and it was held that the obligation to pay the balance of freight only accrued when the demurrage liability had been determined by agreement or award.

For freight on fodder, under a special cattle contract, see *Holland v Pritchard* (1896) 12 T.L.R. 480; and *British & South American Co v Anglo-Argentine Co* (1902) 18 T.L.R. 382, in which case a charter for carriage of freight free of fodder "necessary for the voyage" was held to mean "necessary *in fact* as found at the port of discharge", not necessary according to the estimate formed on shipment.

Under some charters, freight may be paid at receiver's option on quantity delivered or on bill of lading quantity, less two per cent. Such an option need not be exercised by the consignee till the time for payment arrives: *The Dowlais* (1902) 18 T.L.R. 683; but may be exercised by the receiver when he is required to pay advance freight: *English Coaling Co v Tatem* (1919) 63 S.J. 336. An attempt to prove a customary right to such an option, without express provision in the bill of lading failed in *Gulf Line v Laycock* (1901) 7 Com.Cas. 1. In such a case, the charge for stevedoring will be on the quantity on which freight is payable: *The Hollinside* [1898] P. 131. If the charterer presents a bill of lading for signature which understates the weight, and the receivers exercise their option under the clause to pay freight on bills of lading quantity less two per cent, the charterer will be liable to indemnify the shipowner for the loss of freight incurred: *Dawson Line v Adler* [1932] 1 K.B. 433.

For special clauses as to freight, where the cargo is to consist of several articles at various rates, see *Capper v Forster* (1837) 3 Bing.N.C. 938; *Cockburn v Alexander* (1848) 6 C.B. 791; *Warren v Peabody* (1849) 8 C.B. 800; *Southampton Co v Clarke* (1870) L.R. 6 Ex. 53.

For special phrases, e.g. *Freight in full for the voyage: Sweeting v Darthez* (1854) 14 C.B. 538; *Highest freight paid on same voyage: Gether v Capper* (1856) 18 C.B. 866; *Alternative freights: Gibbens v Buisson* (1834) 1 Bing.N.C. 283 and *Fenwick v Boyd* (1846) 15 M. & W. 632.

[112] *Vogemann v Bisley* (1897) 2 Com.Cas. 81. It may be that the consignee is entitled to ascertain what goods are on board before payment.

[113] *Paynter v James* (1867) L.R. 2 C.P. 348; *Yates v Ralston* (1818) 2 Moore C.P. 294; *Tate v Meek* (1818) 2 Moore C.P. 278; *Yates v Meynell* (1818) 2 Moore C.P. 297; *Duthie v Hilton* (1868) L.R. 4 C.P. 138.

[114] *Black v Rose* (1864) 2 Moore P.C.(N.S.) 277; *Brown v Tanner* (1868) L.R. 3 Ch. 597, which decides that the freight under a charter is not due under the contract till all the cargo is delivered, and which turns partly on the special words "freight to be collected by the charterers", would not prevent the master from claiming his lien on each part of the cargo. In *Suart v Bigland* (January 24, 1886), unreported (CA), a clause "to pay out of freight collected" was held to mean "out of gross freight collected", and not to justify postponement of payment till all freight was collected.

[115] [1986] 2 Lloyd's Rep. 603. See also *Food Corp of India v Achilles Halcoussis (The Petros Hadjikyriakos)* [1988] 2 Lloyd's Rep. 56; *Antclizo Shipping Corp v Food Corp of India (The Antclizo No. 2)* [1991] 2 Lloyd's Rep. 485. *Cf. President of India v La Pintada* [1983] 1 Lloyd's Rep. 37.

Article 171—Freight: To Whom Payable   **A171**

To whom freight is payable depends on the terms of the contract of affreightment, or, if no person is named therein, on the person with whom the contract was made, to whom or to his agent freight is payable, subject to any subsequent dealing, such as assignment of the freight or mortgage of the ship. It may be payable to:

(1) The shipowner.

(2) The master.

(3) The broker.

(4) A third person.

(5) The charterer.

(6) An assignee of the freight.

(7) A mortgagee of the ship.

(1) *The Shipowner*

Where freight is due from the charterer under a charter, or from the shipper under a bill of lading where there is no charter, the shipowner, in the absence of express stipulation, is prima facie entitled to receive the freight.[116] He may give authority to collect such freight to any person he pleases.[117]

The loading broker (where freight is payable at the port of loading) and the master, when freight is payable on delivery, have ordinarily authority from the shipowner to collect freight,[117] and payment to either of them will be good payment, discharging the shipper or consignee, unless the owner has given the shipper or consignee notice not to pay either of them,[118] or unless there is any custom of the trade or port to the contrary or unless the contract otherwise provides. Payment to the master before freight is due will be treated as an advance to the master rather than as payment of freight.[119]

A charter incorporating a lien on sub-freights will give the shipowner a right (where e.g. his time-charterer has defaulted) to step in and claim payment of sub-freights to himself provided that they have not already been paid.[120]

---

[116] *Smith v Plummer* (1818) 1 B. & A. 575 at p.581; *Atkinson v Cotesworth* (1825) 3 B. & C. 647 at p.649.
[117] *The Edmond* (1860) Lush 57. For a curious case where the shipper was held to have made a new contract with the shipowner to the exclusion of the charterer, see *Hoyland v Graham* (1896) 1 Com.Cas. 274.
[118] *Atkinson v Cotesworth*, above.
[119] *Smith v Plummer*, above.
[120] See Art.174. *Cf. Trading SA v King Diamond Shipping SA (The Spiros C)* [2000] 2 Lloyd's Rep. 319

(2) *The Master*

The master may be entitled to sue in person for freight:

(i) where the express contract was made with him[121];

(ii) where a contract to pay freight to him is inferred as a fact from the consignee or some other person taking delivery of the goods.[122]

The master, however, cannot sue for freight where he has signed the bill of lading only as agent for the shipowner.[123]

The master who receives freight from consignees has usually no right to retain it against his owner for in the absence of express agreement or statutory procedure,[124] the master has no lien for wages, or advances made abroad on ship's account, on either ship or freight.[125]

(3) *The Broker*

The broker who has acted as loading broker to the ship,[126] sometimes collects the freight he has engaged. Payment to him in the absence of any express notice not to do so will usually discharge the person paying.

(4) *A Third Person*

(i) Where freight is made payable by the charter or bill of lading to a third person, that person can only sue in the name of the shipowner, but payment to the shipowner, apart from such a suit, will not discharge the person paying, unless the third person was only to receive payment as agent for the shipowner.[127]

(ii) Payment to a person entitled to receive the beneficial produce of a contract to pay freight will absolve the payer[128]: thus payment of freight to the obligee under a bottomry bond binding ship and freight,[129] or payment in to the Court of Admiralty, by the monition of the court, in a suit *in rem* against ship and freight

---

[121] As in *Seeger v Duthie* (1860) 8 C.B.(N.S.) 45 at p.56; *Shields v Davis* (1815) 6 Taunt 65.

[122] *Brouncker v Scott* (1811) 4 Taunt 1. A contract with the master personally would rarely, if ever, be inferred nowadays.

[123] *Repetto v Millar's Co* (1901) 6 Com.Cas. 129, where the bill of lading incorporated the charter, and the charter required the master to sign bills of lading as presented at any rate of freight without prejudice to the charter.

[124] As to masters of British ships, see Merchant Shipping Act 1995, s.41. As to the seamen's lien for wages on freight due under a charter and sub-charter, see *The Andalina* (1886) 12 P.D. 1.

[125] *Smith v Plummer* (1818) 1 B. & A. 575. See also, if freight is made payable to agent of ship's husband, he cannot retain it as against owners in satisfaction of a debt due to him by ship's husband: *Walshe v Provan* (1853) 8 Ex. 843.

[126] See Art.41. In *Dunlop v Murietta* (1886) 3 T.L.R. 166 (CA), A in Glasgow instructed B in Liverpool to make a charter; B did so with C, through D in London. A ratified the charter signed by D; A instructed B to get the advance freight sent "either directly or through you". B passed on this letter to D. D showed the letter to C and obtained the freight, and absconded. *Held*, that C had not paid A.

[127] *Kirchner v Venus* (1859) 12 Moore P.C. 361 at p.398.

[128] *Morrison v Parsons* (1810) 2 Taunt. 407 at p.415.

[129] *Benson v Chapman* (1849) 2 H.L.C. 696.

by an obligee of a bottomry bond,[130] is a bar to an action for freight by the shipowner.

(5) *The Charterer*

The circumstances in which bill of lading freight is payable to the charterer are discussed in Art.41.

(6) *Assignee of Ship or Freight*[131]

The assignee of a ship or of its freight[132] is entitled to all freight due after the assignment, which the assignor had at the time of assignment the right to transfer,[133] from the moment at which he has gone through the forms necessary to complete his title.[134]

The assignee of a share in the ship is entitled to his share in the freight under similar circumstances.[135]

Case. A, in June 1854, sold by bills of sale 24/64ths of his ship to B, 40/64ths to Q. B. registered his bill of sale in November. In December, A assigned the freight to be earned on a voyage then in progress to E, and E gave notice thereof to C, the charterer. In January 1855, Q registered his bill of sale. *Held,* B was entitled to 24/64ths: E to 40/64ths of the freight.

Note. If the assignment is in writing and absolute, and not by way of charge,[136] the assignee, after giving to the person liable to pay freight notice of the assignment, can sue in his own name.[137] Where these conditions are not complied with the assignee should normally join the assignor as a party to the proceedings.[138] An assignment, absolute in form, may be looked into to see whether it is in substance by way of charge.[139] Notice of the assignment of freight to the person liable to pay it takes it out of the order and disposition of the assignor.[140]

(7) *Mortgagee of Ship and Freight*

A mortgagee who has not entered into possession of the mortgaged ship has no absolute right to the freight the ship may be earning, and cannot compel its payment to himself by simply giving notice to the person liable to pay it.[141]

---

[130] *Place v Potts* (1855) 5 H.L.C. 383.

[131] See Art.17(4) as to the position of underwriters on ship who have accepted abandonment.

[132] An assignment of freight to be earned is good: *Leslie v Guthrie* (1835) 1 Bing.N.C. 697; *Lindsay v Gibbs* (1856) 22 Beav. 522, overruling *Robinson v Macdonnell* (1816) 5 M. & s.228.

[133] But if the shipowner subsequently mortgages the ship to a mortgagee who has no notice of the previous assignment, the right of the mortgagee to the freight will prevail over that of the assignee: *Wilson v Wilson* (1872) L.R. 14 Eq. 32.

[134] See *Lindsay v Gibbs*, above; *Morrison v Parsons* (1810) 2 Taunt. 407; *Gardner v Cazenove* (1856) 1 H. & N. 423; *Boyd v Mangles* (1849) 3 Ex. 387.

[135] *Lindsay v Gibbs*, above.

[136] See *Burlinson v Hall* (1884) 12 Q.B.D. 347; *Tancred v Delagoa Bay Co* (1889) 23 Q.B.D. 239.

[137] Law of Property Act 1925, s.136. See *Smith v S.S. Zigurds* [1934] A.C. 209 for form of notice.

[138] See *De Pothonier v De Mattos* (1858) E.B. & E. 461; *Wilson v Gabriel* (1863) 4 B. & s.243; *Weguelin v Cellier* (1873) L.R. 6 H.L. 286 as to set-off. See generally *Chitty on Contracts* (29th edn, 1994) para.19–022.

[139] *Gardner v Cazenove* (1856) 1 H. & N. 423.

[140] *Douglas v Russell* (1831) 4 Sim. 524.

[141] *Keith v Burrows* (1877) 2 App.Cas. 636; *Liverpool Marine Co v Wilson* (1872) L.R. 7 Ch. 507 at p.511; *Gardner v Cazenove* (1856) 1 H. & N. 423; *Dean v M'Ghie* (1826) 4 Bing. 45; *Kerswill v Bishop* (1832) 2 C. & J. 529; *Willis v Palmer* (1859) 7 C.B.(N.S.) 340.

On taking actual or constructive possession[142] he then becomes entitled to all the freight that the ship is in course of earning, whether under an express contract,[143] or, if none exists, under a *quantum meruit.*[144] He is not entitled to freight which has become due previously to his taking possession, but is still unpaid at that time.[145]

The mortgagee of the ship, when entitled to freight, is not liable to have that right defeated by an assignee of the freight under an assignment previous to the mortgage, provided that the mortgagee took his security without notice of the assignment.[146]

Case 1. A mortgaged his ship, charters and freight to M, and subsequently chartered her, and mortgaged the freight to N, "the freight to be paid on unloading and right delivery of the cargo". The ship arrived in port, and most of the cargo had been delivered to the consignees, when M took possession. *Held*, that as no freight was payable under the charter till the whole cargo was delivered, M was entitled by taking possession to the whole freight under the charter.[147]

Case 2. A mortgaged his ship to M, and afterwards chartered her to C, the charter providing that C should make advances not exceeding £150 on account of freight, the balance £450, to be paid on delivery of the cargo. C advanced abroad £300. On the ship's arrival, M took possession, and claimed £450 balance of freight from C. C claimed to deduct £150 for advances. *Held*, that the advance of £150 beyond the £150 warranted by the charter was simply a loan, and not a prepayment of freight, and that therefore C was not entitled to deduct it from the freight due.[148]

A172   **Article 172—Freight: By Whom Payable**

Freight is prima facie payable according to the terms of the contract of affreightment, and by the person with whom such contract is made.[149] The shipper may have contracted as agent for the consignee, so as to make the consignee liable for the freight.[150] If the consignee is the owner of the goods, he is also prima facie liable to pay freight for them, as being the person with whom the contract of carriage is presumed to be made.[151]

Entry of the goods at the custom house is prima facie evidence that the person in whose name they are entered is their owner and liable to pay freight for them, but he can rebut this presumption by showing that his entry was made merely as agent.[152]

---

[142] As by giving notice to the mortgagee and charterer, the ship being at sea, and actual possession impossible; *Rusden v Pope* (1868) L.R. 3 Ex. 269; or, where the mortgagor is ship's husband by his removal by the other part owners and the mortgagee: *Beynon v Godden* (1878) 3 Ex.D. 263.

[143] But no more, even though the freight in the contract is nominal: *Keith v Burrows*, above.

[144] *Gumm v Tyrie* (1864) 4 B. & s.680; affirmed (1865) 6 B. & S. 298.

[145] *Shillito v Biggart* [1903] 1 K.B. 683. See also *Cato v Irving* (1842) 5 De G. & M. 210 at p.224 and *Keith v Burrows* (1877) 2 App.Cas. 636. If, however, on his taking possession there is cargo on board subject to a lien for freight which has accrued, "the mortgagee succeeds to the lien and can enforce it": Mellish L.J., *Keith v Burrows* (1877) 2 C.P.D. 163 at p.165. As to priority of mortgagees, see *Liverpool Co v Wilson* (1872) L.R. 7 Ch. 507 at p.511; *Brown v Tanner* (1868) L.R. 3 Ch. 597.

[146] *Wilson v Wilson* (1872) L.R. 14 Eq. 32.

[147] *Brown v Tanner* (1868) L.R. 3 Ch. 597.

[148] *Tanner v Phillips* (1872) 41 L.J.Ch. 125. In *The Salacia* (1862) 32 L.J.Adm. 43, the charter authorised "necessary, ordinary expenses"; see Art.162.

[149] *Cho Yang Shipping v Coral (UK) Ltd* [1997] 2 Lloyd's Rep. 641; *cf.: Evergreen Marine Corp v Aldgate Warehouse Ltd* [2003] EWHC 667 (Comm); [2003] 2 Lloyd's Rep. 597.

[150] *Dickenson v Lano* (1860) 2 F. & F. 188; *Taylor v Bell* [1968] 2 Lloyd's Rep. 63 at p.70.

[151] *Coleman v Lambert* (1839) 5 M. & W. 502; *Dickenson v Lano* (1860) 2 F. & F. 188.

[152] *Ward v Felton* (1801) 1 East 507; *Wilson v Kymer* (1813) 1 M. & S. 157; *Artaza v Smallpiece* (1793) 1 Esp. 23.

A new contract to pay freight may be inferred as a fact from demand of the goods, and their delivery by the master without insisting on his lien.[153] Freight may be payable by:

(1) The shipper.

(2) Any person in whom rights of suit against the carrier are vested under s.2(1) of the Carriage of Goods by Sea Act 1992, and who takes or demands delivery from the carrier of those goods or who makes a claim under the contract of carriage against the carrier.

(1) *The Shipper*

From shipment of goods upon a vessel for a certain voyage a contract by the shipper to pay freight for such goods is implied.[154]

From this implied contract the shipper may be freed, either by express contract in the bill of lading, or by delivery by the master of a bill of lading with an indorsement freeing the shipper, whose terms are known to the master when he delivers the goods.[155] The shipper does not free himself from such liability by indorsing the bill of lading,[156] even to the shipowner.[157] Nor will the presence of the clause in the bill of lading, "to be delivered to consignee of assigns, he or they paying freight for the same", free the shipper, if the master deliver under such a bill to the consignee without insisting on his lien for freight,[158] unless the master was offered cash by the consignees, and for his own convenience took a bill of exchange, which was afterwards dishonoured, in which case the shipper will be freed.[159]

Case. A chartered ship to D to carry iron at 7s. 3d. per ton; the next day, D, professing to act as A's broker, chartered it to C to carry iron at 8s. per ton; each charter contained clauses making freight payable on signing bill of lading, and giving the owner an absolute lien for freight. Neither A nor C knew of the other charter, and D had no authority to make it as broker for A. C shipped his iron under bills of lading signed by the master making the goods deliverable to "consignees, he or they paying freight as per charter". The master did not demand freight on signing bills of lading, and he delivered to the consignees without insisting on his lien. C paid 8s. per ton to D, who became bankrupt. A sued C for the freight at 7s. 3d. *Held*, there was neither an express nor an implied contract on which A could sue C, the parties never having been *ad idem*.[160]

---

[153] See Art.15.
[154] *Domett v Beckford* (1833) 5 B. & Ad. 521; *G.W. Ry v Bagge* (1885) 15 Q.B.D. 625; *Shephard v De Bernales* (1811) 13 East 565; *Christy v Row* (1808) 1 Taunt. 300; *Cho Yang Shipping v Coral (UK) Ltd* [1997] 2 Lloyd's Rep. 641.
[155] *Lewis v M'Kee* (1868) L.R. 4 Ex. 58, a case of consignee; see for the general principles, *Watkins v Rymill* (1883) 10 Q.B.D. 178.
[156] Carriage of Goods by Sea Act 1992, s.3(3).
[157] *Fox v Nott* (1861) 6 H. & N. 630.
[158] *Shephard v De Bernales* (1811) 13 East 565. Such clauses are inserted for the benefit of the master, confirming his lien, and not of the shipper.
[159] *Marsh v Pedder* (1815) 4 Camp. 257; *Tapley v Martens* (1800) 8 T.R. 451; *Strong v Hart* (1827) 6 B. & C. 160.
[160] *Smidt v Tiden* (1874) L.R. 9 Q.B. 446.

The words "freight prepaid" in the bill of lading do not of themselves mean that the shipper is not liable for the freight if it has not in fact been paid.[161]

(2) *Persons subject to liabilities under the Carriage of Goods by Sea Act 1992*

The position of persons taking or demanding delivery of the goods or making a claim against the carrier under the contract of carriage under bills of lading, sea waybills and delivery orders, is discussed in Art.16, above.

---

[161] *Cho Yang Shipping v Coral (UK)* [1997] 2 Lloyd's Rep. 641 *cf: India S.S. v Louis Dreyfus Sugar Ltd (The Indian Reliance)* [1997] 1 Lloyd's Rep. 52

CHAPTER 16

TIME CHARTERS

Article 172A—Time Charters: Characteristics   A172A

As set out in Art.30, above, charterparties not by way of demise fall into two main categories: time charters and voyage charters. A time charter is strictly speaking not a contract of carriage but a contract of hire and services. The owner under a time charter undertakes (for the period of the charter) various obligations. These generally include the obligation to make the vessel available to the charterer and the obligation to keep the hull, machinery and equipment in a thoroughly efficient state. The charterer undertakes to pay hire at the agreed rate and has the right to exploit the earning capacity of the vessel. Although ownership and possession of the vessel remain with the owner (who bears the expense of maintaining the vessel and the crew), the right to make use of the vessel is granted to the charterer.[1]

The terms of the charterparty will need to make provision for a large number of matters including its duration, the hire payable, the rights and obligations of the parties as to payment of hire and when (if at all) the obligation to pay hire is to be suspended, the day to day obligations of the parties in relation to the exploitation of the vessel and redelivery of the vessel at the end of the period. Most, if not all, disputes in relation to time charterparties depend upon the particular wording agreed between the parties and the proper construction of the charterparty in question. But some matters of general principle can be derived from the reported decisions and these are discussed below.

Article 173—Time Charters: Duration   A173

Disputes as to the duration of a time charter usually concern its termination and not its beginning. However, special provision may be made for time to count, or for the charterer to be in breach, if no berth is available for the vessel when she arrives at the port where her service is to start.[2]

Where a time charter is for a stated period, the date for redelivery should be regarded as an approximate date only,[3] unless there is a clear agreement to the

---

[1] See the speeches of Lord Bingham of Cornhill and Lord Hobhouse in *Whistler International v Kawasaki Kisen Kaisha Ltd (The Hill Harmony)* [2001] 1 Lloyd's Rep. 147. See also the analysis of the off hire clause in *Hyundai Merchant Marine Co Ltd v Furnace Withy (Australia) Pty (The Doric Pride)* [2006] 2 Lloyd's Rep. 175; [2006] EWCA 599.

[2] *Anders Utkilens Rederi A/S v Compagnie Tunisienne de Navigation (The Golfstraum)* [1976] 2 Lloyd's Rep. 97: charterer held to be in breach because of the absence of "such available berth where she can safely lie always afloat". The New York Produce Exchange form makes special provision for hire to accrue during the period of non-availability of a berth for delivery.

[3] *Hyundai Merchant Marine Co Ltd v Gesuri Chartering Co Ltd (The Peonia)* [1991] 1 Lloyd's Rep. 100; *Chiswell Shipping v National Iranian Tanker Co (The World Symphony and World Renown)* [1992] 2 Lloyd's Rep. 115.

contrary.[4] In the absence of such an agreement, the charterer commits no breach of contract if he sends the ship on her last voyage with reasonable grounds for expecting that she will be redelivered within a reasonable time of the stipulated date.[5] The margin or tolerance otherwise allowed at common law is often expressly provided for by phrases defining the period of the charter, such as "12 months, 15 days more or less", etc.[6] If this is done, no further tolerance will be implied.[7] The last voyage will be a legitimate one if reasonably calculated to end within the implied or agreed tolerance. If, through no fault of either side, the voyage does not finish within the tolerance, hire continues payable at the charter rate until the end of the period of express or implied tolerance, and, in the absence of an exonerating clause, the owner may recover damages for the period thereafter.[8] In general such damages will be assessed by reference to the market rate for the period of the over-run, but there is no rule limiting the damages to this amount and in appropriate circumstances the owner will be able to recover other reasonably foreseeable losses.[9] In the event that delay beyond the period of express or implied tolerance becomes frustrating in nature, the shipowner can bring the charter to an end.[10]

If the charterer orders the vessel on a last voyage which is not calculated to end within the implied or agreed tolerance, he will be in breach.[11] The legitimacy of

---

[4] As there was held to be in *Watson v Merryweather* (1913) 18 Com.Cas. 294.

[5] *Gray v Christie* (1889) 5 T.L.R. 577, approved and applied in *London and Overseas Freighters v Timber Shipping Co (The London Explorer)* [1972] A.C. 1 (HL).

[6] As in *The London Explorer*, above, as interpreted by the CA in *The Alma Shipping Corp of Monrovia v Mantovani (The Dione)* [1975] 1 Lloyd's Rep. 115. In his speech in *The London Explorer*, which differed in its reasoning from that of Lord Morris, Lord Reid used the word "legitimate" to describe a final voyage ordered by time charterers, which was calculated to comply with the implied or express tolerance. This was taken up and developed by Lord Denning in *The Dione*, above, and has been extensively used in later cases: *Marbiennes Comp. Nav. v Ferrostaal (The Democritos)* [1975] 2 Lloyd's Rep. 149; *Gulf Shipping Lines v Comp. Nav. Alanje (The Aspa Maria)* [1976] 2 Lloyd's Rep. 643; *Mareva Navigation v Canaria Armadora (The Mareva A.S.)* [1977] 1 Lloyd's Rep. 368 and *Jadranska Slobodna Plovidba v Gulf Shipping Line (The Matija Gubec)* [1983] 1 Lloyd's Rep. 24. See further fn.7

[7] *The Peonia*, above; *The World Symphony and World Renown*, above. See also *Bocimar NV v Farenco Navigation Company Ltd* [2002] EWHC 1617 (QB) in which the Charterers sought permission to appeal against a decision by arbitrators that no margin should be implied where the charterparty was for a period of 11 to 14 months. Aikens J. dismissed the application, commenting that the decision of the arbitrators was "probably, if not almost certainly" correct. It is, however, quite possible for the parties to agree that the Charterers should be able to give orders for a further voyage even if it will end after the expressly agreed tolerance—see *Petroleo Brasiliero SA v Kriti Akti Shipping Co SA (The Kriti Akti)* [2004] 1 Lloyd's Rep. 712; [2004] EWCA Civ 116.

[8] *The Peonia* above; *The World Symphony and World Renown*, above. Conflicting views on this point are expressed in *The London Explorer*, above, and *The Dione*, above, both of which cases were reviewed by the Court of Appeal in *The Peonia*. Where the charterparty rate exceeds the market rate, the terms of the charter may provide that the charterparty rate is to be paid until the actual, rather than contractual, redelivery (as in *The Peonia*).

[9] *Transfield Shipping Inc v Mercator Shipping Inc.* [2007] EWCA Civ. 901, a decision which is said to have created a fair degree of uncertainty in the market—see Weale at [2008] L.M.C.L.Q. 6.

[10] *The Peonia*, above per Saville J. See also *Torvald Klaveness A/S v Arni Maritime Corp (The Gregos)* [1995] 1 Lloyd's Rep. 1 at p.9. In *Edwinton Commercial Corp & Anor v Tsavliris Russ (Worldwide Salvage & Towge) Ltd (The Sea Angel)* [2007] 1 C.L.C. 876; [2007] EWCA Civ 547 the Court of Appeal rejected the argument advanced by the charterers of the vessel, who asserted that because they were prevented by the unreasonable actions of port authority from redelivering the vessel for a period of 3 months at the end of a charter for 20 days the contract was frustrated.

[11] In *Torvald Klaveness A/S v Arni Maritime Corp (The Gregos)* [1993] 2 Lloyd's Rep. 335, certain doubts were expressed as to whether the mere giving of a non-contractual order could constitute a breach of contract. These doubts were echoed by Lord Mustill in the House of Lords, [1995] 1 Lloyd's Rep. 1 at p.9 where, however, the proposition was assumed to be correct. It is submitted that, as the authorities cited by Lord Mustill show, this principle is now too well-established by authority to be departed from and is, in any event, correct.

the charterer's order will be provisionally assessed at the time when it is given, but such an order cannot be insisted upon if circumstances have rendered it illegitimate when the time for performance arrives.[12] If the owner proceeds on the illegitimate voyage, hire will be payable at the charter rate up to the end of the tolerance period, and at the current market rate for the excess period thereafter.[13]

The charterer will not be in repudiatory breach of contract simply by reason of having given an illegitimate voyage order.[14] If, however, the owner refuses to proceed on the illegitimate voyage, and the charterer refuses to order the vessel on a legitimate voyage in circumstances in which he is contractually obliged to give an order, the owner may accept the charterer's conduct as a repudiation and sue for damages.[15]

The charterparty may provide that the owner has a further option to complete her last voyage. In the absence of clear words to the contrary,[16] such a clause will only apply to voyages which it was reasonably believed would be completed within the charter period and any express or implied tolerance, and does not render legitimate what would otherwise be an illegitimate voyage order.[17]

Under a time charter for six or seven (in charterer's option) consecutive voyages during 1910, under which the sixth voyage was not completed until January 6, 1911, it was held that the charterer could not exercise his option to send the vessel on a seventh voyage in 1911.[18]

Under a time charter "for the term of six calendar months", hire to continue until redelivery with a provision for payment "half-monthly in advance in London except for the last half-month, which time to be estimated and paid in advance up to such time as steamer is expected to be redelivered", it was held

---

[12] *The Gregos*, above.

[13] *The Dione*, above; *Shipping Corp of India Ltd v NSB Niederelbe Schiffahrtsgesellshaft mbh (The Black Falcon)* [1991] 1 Lloyd's Rep. 77. In *Hector v Sovfracht* [1945] K.B. 243 there was a special clause in the charter to this effect. On current market rate see *Arta Shipping Co v Thai Europe Tapioca Service (The Johnny)* [1977] 2 Lloyd's Rep. 1. Where these are not too remote, further damages (such as the loss of a subsequent fixture) can be claimed: *The Gregos* [1993] 2 Lloyd's Rep. 335 (although the question of remoteness must be tested when the contract is concluded and not, as suggested in that case, at the time of the last voyage order). In *Transfield Shipping Inc. of Panama v Mercator Shipping Inc. of Monrovia* [2006] 7 EWCA Civ 901 (in which this footnote was referred to in the judgment at first instance and on appeal) the vessel was redelivered late and the claimants (owners) were obliged to agree to a reduction in the hire payable on her next fixture in order to obtain an extension of the cancelling date. It was held that they were entitled to recover the resulting loss from the charterers. The shipowner could, as a matter of common law, seek an indemnity against any loss suffered in compliance with such an order: *The Gregos* [1995] 1 Lloyd's Rep. 1 at p.9 [1994] C.L.C. 1,188. It is submitted that the shipowner could, in the alternative, claim a quantum meruit for the provision of an extra-contractual service: *The Batis* [1990] 1 Lloyd's Rep. 345. Where the charter rate exceeds the market rate, the terms of the charter may enable the shipowner to claim that higher rate (as in *The Peonia*). Even if this is not so, such a rate should, in principle, be recoverable: *Torvald Klaveness A/S v Arni Maritime Corp (The Gregos)* [1992] 2 Lloyd's Rep. 40 at p.42. This approach may be justified by treating the illegitimate order as an offer to complete the non-contractual voyage at the charterparty rate.

[14] *The Gregos* [1995] 1 Lloyd's Rep. 1, in which it was held that such a breach was a breach of an innominate term. The point had been left open in *The Peonia*, above.

[15] *The Dione*, above, at p.118 per Lord Denning; *The Gregos*, above.

[16] For a case in which a clause was held to have had this effect see *The World Symphony and World Renown*, above. *Sed quaere*.

[17] *The Peonia*, above; *The World Symphony and World Renown*, above.

[18] *Dunford & Co v Compania Anonima Maritima Union* (1911) 16 Com.Cas. 181.

that the engagement was for six months certain. The charterer could not therefore redeliver the steamer in the last half-month and avoid payment of hire for the period between redelivery and the expiration of six months.[19]

A clause is not uncommon to the effect that in the event of, e.g. war, charterers are to have the option of cancelling or suspending the charter. It is doubtful whether "suspending" means merely cutting the period during which the cause operates out of the agreed period of hire, or further postponing the agreed termination of the hiring by the addition of the suspended period: the former view seems preferable. The option must be exercised within a reasonable time after the occurrence of the event.[20]

Time charters sometimes contain a clause giving the charterer the option of extending the period of the charter: the exercise of such an option is irrevocable, as is a notice that the charterer does not intend to exercise the option.[21]

Time charters generally require the charterer to give notice of pending redelivery (often a certain number of days' approximate notice followed by a specified number of days definitive notice). Where the charterer fails to do so the owner will be entitled to recover damages in respect of his resulting loss.[22]

In a trip time charterparty it is common for the charterer to give an estimate of the expected duration of the trip—usually "without guarantee". In such cases the charterer's obligation is to give an estimate that he genuinely believes to be correct and the charterer will not, in the absence of bad faith, be liable for damages if the expected duration is exceeded.[23]

A174   Article 174—Time Charters: Payment of Hire

Under a time charter the charterer remains liable to pay hire throughout the contractual period, unless (1) his liability is suspended by an express provision in the charter,[24] or (2) the owner, in breach of his contractual duties, fails to

---

[19] *Reindeer S.S. Co v Forslind* (1908) 13 Com.Cas. 214.

[20] *Kawasaki Kisen Kabushiki, Kaisha v Belships* (1939) 63 Ll.L.R. 175. Another clause provides that in case of war "steamer not to be sent on any voyage before owners have been able to cover her full value against war risk". If when war breaks out the ship has started on her voyage but puts into a port for bunkers, the clause does not apply to the passage from that port to her final destination: *Westralian Farmers v Dampskibsselskab Orient* (1939) 65 Ll.L.R. 105. Where the charterparty contains a clause permitting cancellation in the event of war the Court will take this into account in assessing damage for repudiation of the charterparty. In *Golden Strait Corp v Nioopon Yusen Kubishika Kaisha (The Golden Victory)* [2007] UKHL 12 the Charterers repudiated the charterparty when it had nearly four years left to run. Fifteen months later the Second Gulf War broke out and the House of Lords concluded that it was appropriate to take this fact, and the probability that if it had not already been repudiated the charterparty would have been cancelled, into account in assessing damages.

[21] *Marseille Fret SA v D. Oltmann Schiffahrts GmbH & Cook G. (The Trado)* [1982] 1 Lloyd's Rep. 157. See also *Atlantic Lines & Navigation Co Inc. v Didymi Corp* [1984] 1 Lloyd's Rep. 583 ("narrowing" the agreed tolerance).

[22] In *UBC Chartering Ltd v Shipping Co Ltd (The Liepaya)* [1999] 1 Lloyd's Rep. 649 the charterer was obliged to give 15 days' notice of expected redelivery but in fact gave one day's notice. The owner recovered hire at the charterparty rate for 14 days.

[23] *Continental Pacific Shipping Ltd v Deemand Shipping Co Ltd (The Lendoudis Evangelos II)* [1997] 1 Lloyd's Rep. 404.

[24] Such as the off-hire clause: see Art.176.

render the services promised under the charter,[25] or (3) the charter is frustrated.[26]

Thus in the absence of express agreement hire is payable[27] during detention for breach of blockade,[28] by embargo,[24] bad weather[29] or repairs,[30] unless the delay involved is so great as to frustrate the contract.[31]

The charterer cannot rely on an excepted peril such as strikes or restraint of princes, even when expressed to be mutual, as excusing him from paying hire during time in which by such excepted peril he is unable to use the ship.[32]

The right of the charterer in paying hire, which is almost invariably made payable in advance, to make deductions, for example, in respect of breach of contract by the shipowner or disbursements made to or on behalf of the master, is recognised in certain circumstances. Some deductions, such as master's disbursements, may be expressly permitted by the time charter, usually subject to the vouching of payments. Such express provisions will not, however, deny the charterer's right to equitable set-off in other circumstances.[33]

This right, not applicable to a claim for freight under a voyage charter,[34] does not arise in every case where there are cross-claims, nor every case where there are cross-claims arising out of the same contract. The charterer will only have a right of deduction where the breach of the shipowner has deprived or prejudiced him in his use of the ship,[35] and then only such hire as was due in respect of the period in which the charterer has been deprived of or prejudiced in the use of the ship.[36] Thus the right does not apply to cross-claims based upon conversion of

---

[25] *Sea and Land Securities v William Dickinson* [1942] 2 K.B. 65 (CA); *Akt. Tankexpress v Compagnie Financiere Belge des Petroles* (1947) 80 Ll.L.R. 365 (CA); affirmed [1949] A.C. 76 (HL). The decision of the CA in the former case left open the question whether strictly the charterer's obligation to pay hire is suspended or whether his right is to claim damages the measure of which would be at any rate the amount of hire for the period of refusal of the charter services. But in the latter case, Atkinson J. held (1946) 79 Ll.L.R. 45 that the charterer's obligation to pay hire was suspended and, as the CA was equally divided on the point, his judgment stood on appeal. The HL decided this case on another point, but the remarks of Lords Porter [1949] A.C. 76 at p.91 and du Parcq at p.106 suggest, contrary to the view of Atkinson J. and Bucknill L.J. and in accord with that of Tucker L.J., that there is no half-way house between acceptance of the repudiation and continuance of the charter with the consequent obligation to continue to pay hire. See, also, per Bailhache J. in *Admiral S.S. Co v Weidner* [1916] 1 K.B. 429 at p.436.
[26] See Art.14 and Law Reform (Frustrated Contracts) Act 1943.
[27] Where hire is earned at the end of each period specified it may, unless a contrary intention appears (as in *Gibbon v Mendez* (1812) 2 B. & Ald. 17), be recovered by the shipowner although only payable under a charter at longer intervals during one of which the ship may be lost: *Havelock v Geddes* (1809) 10 East 555.
[28] *Moorsom v Greaves* (1811) 2 Camp. 626. *Cf. Radcliffe v Compagnie Generale* (1918) 24 Com.Cas. 40 (detention due to fitting armament and waiting for gun crew).
[29] See fn.21, above.
[30] *Havelock v Geddes* (1809) 10 East 555; *Ripley v Scaife* (1826) 5 B. & C. 167.
[31] See Art.14.
[32] *Brown v Turner Brightman* [1912] A.C. 12; *Aktieselskabet Lina v Turnbull*, 1907 S.C. 507.
[33] *Federal Commerce and Navigation v Molena Alpha Inc. (The Nanfri)* [1978] Q.B. 927 (CA) per Lord Denning M.R. and particularly by Goff L.J. at p.988; see, also, *Santiren Shipping Ltd v Unimarine (The Chrysovalandou Dyo)* [1981] 1 Lloyd's Rep. 159. The point was deliberately not dealt with in the HL [1979] A.C. 757.
[34] *Aries Tanker Corp v Total Transport (The Aries)* [1971] 1 Lloyd's Rep. 334 (HL), upholding *Henriksens Rederi A/S v Rolimpex (The Brede)* [1974] 1 Q.B. 233, distinguished in the case of time charter hire in *The Nanfri*, above, by Denning M.R. and Goff L.J., approving *Compania Sud Americana de Vapores v Shipmair B.V. (The Teno)* [1977] 2 Lloyd's Rep. 289, where the earlier cases are fully discussed.
[35] *Leon Corp v Atlantic Lines & Navigation Co Inc. (The Leon)* [1985] 2 Lloyd's Rep. 470.
[36] *Century Textiles & Industry Ltd v Tomoe Shipping Co (Singapore) Pte Ltd (The Aditya Vaibhav)* [1991] 1 Lloyd's Rep. 573.

bunkers[37] or damage to cargo.[38] Making deductions from hire, unless fully justified both as to the right to deduct or set-off and as to quantum, may be fraught with danger that the owner may be entitled to withdraw his ship.[39]

It appears to be generally accepted that (a) a charterer is not entitled to deduct from a monthly instalment due in advance a sum in respect of a known future off-hire period, which will begin during that month; (b) such a deduction is however permissible from the next monthly hire payment, if the vessel is then back on hire.[40] If a vessel is off-hire at the due date for a monthly instalment in advance, the charterer has the option of not paying until just before the vessel returns on hire, or paying on the due date subject to a deduction in respect of a period off-hire during the previous month.[41] If on the due date for payment a sum of hire is due, payment by the charterer of a smaller sum, bona fide but incorrectly believing that sum is all that is due after taking credit for earlier payments made covering a period during part of which the vessel went off-hire, will not avail him. Bona fides is no protection nor is part payment of a smaller sum than that due owing to a miscalculation of the justifiable deduction.[42] However, special facts showing that the owner knew that the charterer had made a miscalculation in paying a smaller sum than that due and had thwarted the charterer in his endeavour to find out whether the owner accepted the charterer's calculation may give rise to an equitable estoppel against the owner.[43]

Provision is usually made in time charters for hire at a certain rate per calendar month or per day and at the same rate for any part of a month to continue until redelivery, with payments to be made in cash monthly (or every 14 days or semi-monthly) in advance. The charterer in such a case is liable to pay a month's hire in advance, though the vessel will probably be redelivered before the end of the relevant period. However, the shipowner is under an implied obligation to re-pay any unearned hire.[44] But if during the relevant period the charter is frustrated,[45] payment of hire due but not paid before the date of frustration and the adjustment

---

[37] *The Leon*, above although the status of overriding fraud was left open at p.476.

[38] *The Teno*, above, per Parker J. at p.297 and *The Nanfri*, above, per Denning M.R. at p.976 and Goff L.J. at p.981. Lord Salmon in *The Mihalios Xilas* [1979] 2 Lloyd's Rep. 303 (HL) at p.313 said, obiter, that the only exception to the obligation on the charterer to pay full hire on or before when due was where the parties by their course of conduct had agreed that the owner's liabilities might be deducted from hire, if discharge of them by the charterer could be vouched.

[39] per Goff L.J. in *The Nanfri*, above, at pp.981–982. As to the right of withdrawal see Art.175, below.

[40] *Tradax Export v Dorada Compania Naviera (The Lutetian)* [1982] 2 Lloyd's Rep. 140 at p.149. For cases on off-hire clauses, see Art.176, below.

[41] *The Lutetian*, above.

[42] *The Lutetian*, above, at p.154. See also *Western Bulk Carriers K/S v Li Hai Maritime Inc (The Li Hai)* [2005] EWHC 735 (Comm) in which the amount underpaid was only some US$500. In that case owners would have been entitled to withdraw but for the fact that they failed to serve a notice complying with the requirements of the charterparty.

[43] *The Lutetian*, above, at p.158.

[44] *Pan Ocean Shipping Co Ltd v Credit Corp Ltd (The Trident Beauty)* [1994] 1 Lloyd's Rep. 365; *Tonnelier v Smith* (1897) 2 Com.Cas. 258 (CA); *Stewart v Van Ommeren* [1918] 2 K.B. 560; *French Marine v Compagnie Napolitaine* [1921] 2 A.C. 494. The same principle applies in relation to the return of hire paid in advance when the owner justifiably withdraws the ship: *The Mihalios Xilas* [1979] 2 Lloyd's Rep. 303 (HL). Hire paid in advance can be assigned unconditionally and the right of the assignee to receive it will not be defeated by any subsequent failure of the ship owner to earn the hire.

[45] As to which see *Edwinton Commercial Corp v Tsavliris Russ (Worldwide Salvage and Towage) Ltd (The Sea Angel)* [2007] 1 C.L.C. 876; [2007] EWCA Civ 547.

of overpaid hire will be governed by the Law Reform (Frustrated Contracts) Act 1943. In most cases the result will probably be that hire will only be payable up to the date of frustration. Prima facie the charterer would be entitled to recover hire paid in respect of the period after that date. However s.1(3) of the Act entitles a party who has conferred a benefit upon the other pursuant to the contract prior to the date of the frustrating event to recover a sum from the other in an amount which the Court considers just having regard to the value of the benefit. In assessing what sum should be awarded, the Court will consider the amount of any expenses incurred before the time of discharge by the benefited party, including any sums paid or payable by him to the other party, and the effect in relation to the benefit of the circumstances giving rise to the frustration of the contract.[46] If during the period in respect of which hire has been paid in advance the ship comes off hire, the charterer can recover the overpaid hire on the ground of failure of consideration.[47]

Time charters usually provide that owners shall have a lien upon all cargoes[48] and all sub-freights for any amounts due under the charter.[49] So far as concerns sub-freights, this operates as an equitable assignment by way of security.[50]

The lien does not come into operation until payment of hire is due.[51] The phrase "sub-freights" does not apply to hire payable under a time-charter but only to freight payable under a bill of lading or a voyage charter.[52] The lien must be exercised against the consignee liable to pay the sub-freight, and money paid by him to the charterer's agent cannot be followed into the hands of such agent unless the freight has been received by him after notice from the shipowner that

---

[46] For an example of the operation of the Act under a time charter see *Ocean Tramp Tankers Corp v Sovfracht (The Eugenia)* [1963] 2 Lloyd's Rep. 155 overruled on the question of frustration, *ibid* 381.

[47] *Stewart v Van Ommeren*, above; *The Mihalios Xilas*, above. *Cf. The Eugenia* [1963] 2 Lloyd's Rep. 155 (QBD), reversed on the issue of frustration [1964] 2 Q.B. 226 (CA). This appears to be a restitutionary remedy, albeit that contrary to the traditional rule, the failure of consideration may be partial and not total. Commonly there will be an express contractual right to repayment: See *The Trident Beauty*, above.

[40] There is no implied obligation on the shipowner's part to exercise any lien over cargo at the charterer's request: *Cosemar SA v Marimarna Shipping Co Ltd (The Mathew)* [1990] 1 Lloyd's Rep. 323.

[49] These are the words of Clause 18 of the New York Produce Exchange form; the Baltime clause includes the words "belonging to the time-charterers": see *Care Shipping Corp v Latin American Shipping Corp (The Cebu)* [1983] 1 Lloyd's Rep. 302 and *Itex Itagrani Export SA v Care Shipping Corp (The Cebu No. 2)* [1990] 2 Lloyd's Rep. 316.

[50] *The Cebu*, above; *The Cebu (No. 2)*, above. See also *The Nanfri* [1979] A.C. 757; *G. & N. Angelakis Shipping Co SA v Compagnie National Algerienne de Navigation (The Attika Hope)* [1988] 1 Lloyd's Rep. 439 (in which it was held that the priority of successive assignments followed the rule in *Dearle v Hall*); In *Welsh Irish Ferries Ltd, (in receivership and liquidation) (The Ugland Trader), Re* [1985] 2 Lloyd's Rep. 372 and *Anangel Glory Compania Naviera SA v M. Golodetz Ltd (The Anangel Glory)* [1988] 1 Lloyd's Rep. 45. In these last two cases, it was held that as the lien on sub-freights operated as an equitable assignment by way of charge, it was void as against the liquidator or administrator of a corporate charterer unless registered as a charge on book debts under s.95 of the Companies Act 1948, now ss.395 *et seq* of the Companies Act 1985. The position was reversed by s.396(2)(g) Companies Act 1985 as inserted by s.93 Companies Act 1989. This footnote was referred to with apparent approval by Rix LJ in *Tradigrain SA v King Diamond Shipping SA (The Spiros C)* [2000] 2 Lloyd's Rep. 319 at p.323.

[51] *Wehner v Dene S.S. Co* [1905] 2 K.B. 92; *Mutual Export Corp v Asia Australia Express Ltd (The Lakatoi Express)* (1990) 19 N.S.W.L.R. 285 (Aus.).

[52] This seems to be the better view: See *Itex Itagrani Export SA v Care Shipping Corp (The Cebu No. 2)* [1990] 2 Lloyd's Rep. 316 not following *Care Shipping Corp v Latin American Shipping Corp (The Cebu)* [1983] 1 Lloyd's Rep. 302. See also *Mutual Export Corp v Asia Australia Express Ltd (The Lakatoi Express)* (1990) 19 N.S.W.L.R. 285 (Aus.), in which it was held that no lien could be exercised in respect of any quantum meruit claim by the head owners. *Quaere* whether the lien applies to sub-sub voyage charter freight, and whether this will depend on whether the intervening charters are voyage or time charters.

he claims a lien on it.[53] Until the lien is exercised, the charterer is free to deal with the sub-freights as his own.[54] A clause giving the charterer a lien on the ship for money paid in advance and not earned probably confers no real lien, since the ship is not in the charterer's possession.[55]

When the time charter requires hire to be paid "in cash", payment may be made by any commercially recognised method of transferring funds, the result of which is to give the transferee the unconditional right to the immediate use of the funds,[56] i.e. the equivalent of cash or as good as cash.[57]

Time charters often contain a clause providing for the hire to be adjusted if the vessel's speed or consumption varies from the figures agreed in the charter.[58]

Note. In all contracts (which includes charters) "month" means calendar month[59] unless the context otherwise requires: Law of Property Act 1925, s.61. So far as concerns charterparties this was so decided in *Jolly v Young*[60] in 1794. It is not uncommon in charterparties to stipulate that a month shall mean thirty days. Another usual clause is that "a day's hire shall be calculated on the basis of 1/30th of a month's hire of the ship". In the absence of such a clause a day's hire must be calculated by reference to the number of days in the calendar month in which the broken period occurs. Under a clause to pay freight per month and at the same rate for any part of a month it has been held that a part of a day must be reckoned as a whole day.[61]

A175   **Article 175—Time Charters: Right of Withdrawal of Ship**

A usual clause in time charters provides that in default of punctual and regular payment of hire or on any breach of this charterparty, the shipowner shall have the right to withdraw the vessel from the service of the charterers.[62] Under this clause a withdrawal cannot be temporary or suspensory; a valid withdrawal cancels the charter.[63]

---

[53] *Tagart Beaton v Fisher* [1903] 1 K.B. 391; *Molthes Rederei A/S v Ellerman's Wilson Line* [1927] 1 K.B. 710; *Cascade Shipping Inc. v Eka Jaya Agencies (S) Pte Ltd* [1992] 1 S.L.R. 197, [1993] 1 S.L.R. 980 (Sing.) in both of which the apparent conflict between *Tagart Beaton v Fisher* and *Wehner v Dene S.S. Co* [1905] 2 K.B. 92 is discussed.

[54] *The Annangel Glory*, above; *Tradigrain SA v King Diamond Shipping SA (The Spiros C).* [2000] 2 Lloyd's Rep. 319.

[55] See per Lord Sumner in *French Marine v Compagnie Napolitaine* [1921] 2 A.C. 494 at p.516 and *Ellerman Lines v Lancaster Maritime Co (The Lancaster)* [1980] 2 Lloyd's Rep. 497. Such a "lien" gives the charterer no right to trace the proceeds of an insurance policy on the ship: *ibid.*

[56] *The Brimnes* [1972] 2 Lloyd's Rep. 465, approved CA [1975] Q.B. 929: see also *The Effy* [1972] 1 Lloyd's Rep. 18.

[57] *A/S Awilco v Fulvia SpA Di Navigazione (The Chikuma)* [1981] 1 Lloyd's Rep. 371 (HL).

[58] e.g. *Showa Oil Tanker Co Ltd v Maravan SA (The Lorissa)* [1983] 2 Lloyd's Rep. 325.

[59] A calendar month is computed by proceeding from the given day in one month to the day with the corresponding number in the next month: *Freeman v Reed* (1863) 4 B. & S. 174.

[60] (1794) 1 Esp. 187; see also *Turner v Barlow* (1863) 3 F. & F. 946; *Bruner v Moore* [1904] 1 Ch. 305.

[61] *Angier v Stewart* (1884) C. & E. 357, following *Commercial S.S. Co v Boulton* (1875) L.R. 10 Q.B. 346.

[62] In the absence of an express right of withdrawal, the shipowner cannot withdraw the vessel for late payment of hire unless the late payment amounts to a repudiation of the charter: see fn.85 below. For the text of this clause in the New York Produce Exchange form of time charter, see *Mardorf Peach v Attica Sea Carriers Corp of Liberia (The Laconia)* [1977] A.C. 850 at p.867, and for the version in the Baltime form see, e.g. *Kawasaki Kisen Kaisha v Bantham S.S. Co.* [1938] 2 K.B. 790 at p.791. See also Clause 11a. N.Y.P.E '93 form.

[63] *Steelwood Carriers of Monrovia v Evimeria Compania Naviera of Panama (The Agios Giorgis)* [1976] 2 Lloyd's Rep. 192; *Aegnoussiotis Corp of Monrovia v A/S Kristian Jebsen Rederie of Bergen (The Aegnoussiotis)* [1977] 1 Lloyd's Rep. 268; *International Bulk Carriers v Evlogia Shipping Co (The Mihalios Xilas)* [1978] 2 Lloyd's Rep. 186, per Donaldson J. at p.191.

"Punctual and regular" payment means payment on the day it is due.[64] In the absence of the words "punctual and regular", hire must still, unless there are special circumstances which excuse it, be paid on the due date.[65] Unless there is special provision to the contrary, the charterer will have up to midnight on the due date by which to pay.[66]

"Default" means a failure without excuse to pay hire on the due date: neither deliberate non-performance nor negligence is required.[67] It would seem that the charterer will be in default and that the ship may be withdrawn if there has only been part payment by the due date.[68] Payment or tender after the due date will not of itself deprive the shipowner of the right of withdrawal.[69]

"Any breach of this charterparty" means any repudiatory breach, and accordingly does not give a right to withdraw the ship for non-repudiatory breaches.[70]

The shipowner need not make a demand for payment before exercising his right of withdrawal[71] but, save in very exceptional circumstances,[72] withdrawal involves notice to the charterer to be given within a reasonable time after the default.[73] The right of withdrawal probably applies to the first as well as to the subsequent payments.[74]

---

[64] *Italian State Rys v Bitzas* (1917) 79 Ll.L.R. 463n.; *Akt. Tankexpress v Compagnie Financière Belge des Petroles (The Petrofina)* [1949] A.C. 76, overruling the decision in *Nova Scotia Co v Sutherland* (1899) 5 Com.Cas. 106, that payment a day or two late may constitute "punctual payment"; *Mardorf Peach v Attica Sea Carriers Corp of Liberia (The Laconia)* [1977] A.C. 850; [1977] 2 Lloyd's List Rep. 315. See also, *Budd v Johsnon Englehart* (1920) 1 Ll.L.R. 27 (hire reaching shipowner the day after due date held to have been paid promptly within the meaning of any reasonable interpretation of the charter); *quaere* whether the decision would now be followed. See also, *Maclaine v Gatty* [1921] 1 A.C. 376; *Kawasaki Kisen Kabushiki Kaisha v Bantham S.S. Co* [1938] 1 K.B. 805.

[65] *Akt. Tankexpress v Compagnie Financière Belge des Petroles*, above; *The Laconia*, above. The special circumstances in the former case were that hire was despatched by cheque in the way payment had always previously been made and accepted, but the letter was held up in the post owing to the outbreak of war.

[66] *The Afovos* [1983] 1 Lloyd's Rep. 335 (HL).

[67] *Akt. Tankexpress v Compagnie Financière Belge des Petroles*, above.

[68] *Tradax Export SA v Dorada Compania Naviera (The Lutetian)* [1982] 2 Lloyd's Rep. 140 at p.154. See *China National Foreign Trade Transportation Corp v Evlogia Shipping Co (The Mihalios Xilas)* [1979] 2 Lloyd's Rep. 303 (HL). The point was left undecided in *The Laconia*, above, per Lord Wilberforce at p.872. However the HL overruled the decision of the CA in *Empresa Cubana de Fletes v Lagonosi Shipping Co (The Georgis C)* [1971] 1 Q.B. 488 that "default of payment" meant "default of payment and for so long as default continues".

[69] *The Laconia*, above, in particular per Lords Wilberforce at p.19 and Salmon at pp.323–324. Where the charter provides for payment to a named bank for account of the owners, payment is sometimes made through an intermediary bank by a series of book entries: in the ordinary way this does not amount to payment or tender unless and until the owners can ascertain whether it has been made and, *semble*, it is available for the owners to draw upon: *Zim Israel Navigation v Effy Shipping Corp* [1972] 1 Lloyd's Rep. 18; see also *The Brimnes* [1972] 2 Lloyd's Rep. 465 at p.480; [1975] Q.B. 929 (CA) and above, fn.56. The onus of proving late payment rests upon the owners: *Tropwood AG v Jade Enterprises (The Tropwind)* [1977] 1 Lloyd's Rep. 397, per Kerr J.

[70] *Antaios Compania Naviera SA v Salen Rederierna A.B. (The Antaios No. 2)* [1984] 2 Lloyd's Rep. 235.

[71] *Tyrer and Hessler, Re* (1902) 7 Com.Cas. 166.

[72] *The Georgis C.*, above, at pp.504, 506, 507.

[73] *The Laconia*, above: discussed and applied in *Gatoil Anstaft v Omenniol (The Balder London)* [1980] 2 Lloyd's Rep. 489 *The Antaios No. 2*, above. Notice given by telex during business hours is treated as having been received when it was sent: *The Brimnes*, above, at p.480. Where notice is sent outside of office hours this presumption does not apply. *Schelde Delta Shipping B.V. v Astarte Shipping Ltd (The Pamela)* [1995] 2 Lloyd's Rep. 249. See discussion on the sufficiency of notice without actual withdrawal: *Tropwood A.G. v Jade Enterprises (The Tropwind)* [1982] 1 Lloyd's Rep. 232 (CA).

[74] *Kawasaki Kisen Kaisha v Bantham S.S. Co* [1938] 1 K.B. 805 (point not discussed on appeal [1938] 2 K.B. 790); but contrast the view of Roche J. in *Budd v Johnson Englehart* (1920) 2 Ll.L.R. 27. In the former case the shipowner failed solely because he had not given notice of the deadweight capacity of his vessel, which was straight from the builder's yard, and the first instalment of hire could not therefore be properly calculated.

Many time charterers include what have been called "anti-technicality" clauses in order to prevent, on rising rates of hire, what may be regarded as unmeritorious withdrawals of vessels. These have often taken the form of requiring shipowners to give charterers a prescribed period of notice within which to pay before the vessel may be withdrawn.[75] Notice under such a clause cannot be conditional and cannot be given until after there has been a breach of the obligation to pay hire.[76] However, it is the time when the notice is received by the charterer which matters, not when it was sent by the owner.[77] In considering whether the owner has given adequate notice the starting point is to consider the wording of the anti technicality clause and determine what it requires—but in general terms the notice (as well as being unconditional) must be unambiguous.[78]

The court has no jurisdiction to apply the equitable doctrine of relief against forfeiture to the exercise by an owner of his express right of withdrawal of his ship in default of payment of hire when due.[79]

The shipowner may by agreement or conduct waive the right to withdraw, but mere forbearance to exercise the right of withdrawal for a limited time will not operate as a waiver.[80] He may also lose the right if at the due date for payment of hire he is unjustifiably withholding the services of the vessel.[81]

If the shipowner withdraws the ship he cannot recover any hire for the period after withdrawal even though withdrawal takes place in the middle of a period for which hire is payable in advance,[82] nor is the position different if "redelivery" does not take place immediately upon notification of withdrawal.[83] But he can

---

[75] *Antaios Compania Naviera v Salen Rederierna (The Antaios)*, above, *Oceanic Freighters Corp v M.V. Libyaville Redeerei und Schiffahrts GmbH (The Libyaville)* [1975] 1 Lloyd's Rep. 537 at pp.554–555; *Afovos Shipping Co v R. Pagnan and F.Lli (The Afovos)* [1980] 2 Lloyd's Rep. 469 at p.480; *Italmare Shipping Co v Ocean Tanker (The Rio Sun)* [1981] 2 Lloyd's Rep. 489 (CA) at p.496, and per Parker J. [1982] 1 Lloyd's Rep. 404. See, also, the references by Lord Wilberforce in *The Laconia*, above, at p.869, to three "lenient" forms of withdrawal clauses.

[76] *The Afovos*, above, [1983] 1 Lloyd's Rep. 335 (HL) and *The Lutetian*, above, [1982] 2 Lloyd's Rep. 140 at p.155.

[77] *Schelde Delta Shipping B.V. v Astarte Shipping Ltd (The Pamela)* [1995] 2 Lloyd's Rep. 249.

[78] *Western Bulk Carriers K/S v Li Hai Maritime Inc. (The Li Hai)* [2005] EWHC 735 (Comm.).

[79] *Scandinavian Trading Tanker v Flota Petrolena Ecuatoriana (The Scaptrade)* [1983] 2 Lloyd's Rep. 253 (HL). This had been earlier discussed by Lloyd J. in *The Afovos* [1980] 2 Lloyd's Rep. 469, who was inclined to favour relief, as also had been Lord Simon of Glaisdale in *The Laconia*, above, at p.874. Contrast the position of a charterer by demise as to which in *More Og Romsdal Fylkesbatar A.S. v The Demise Charterers of the Ship "Jotunheim"* [2005] 1 Lloyd's Rep. 181; [2004] EWHC 671 (Comm) Cooke J. concluded that the Court would have jurisdiction to grant relief from forfeiture in appropriate cases.

[80] *The Mihalios Xilas* [1979] 2 Lloyd's Rep. 303 (HL); *Nova Scotia Co v Sutherland* (1899) 5 Com.Cas. 106; *Tyrer and Hessler, Re* (1902) 7 Com.Cas. 166; *Langfond S.S. Co v Canadian Forwarding Co* (1907) 96 L.T. 559; *Modern Co v Duneric S.S. Co* [1917] 1 K.B. 370; *Wulfsberg v Weardale Co* (1916) 85 L.J.K.B. 1717 (issue of writ claiming hire on same day as notice of withdrawal); *Temple S.S. Co v Sovfracht* (1945) 79 Ll.L.R. 1 at p.11 (HL); *Bird v Hildage* [1948] 1 K.B. 91. If, however, a method of payment has been accepted in the past, an owner cannot insist upon a more correct fulfilment of the charter without giving reasonable notice of his intention; *Akt. Tankexpress v Compagnie Financière Belge des Petroles* [1949] A.C. 76 at pp.93, 98 and 104, applying *Panoutsos v Raymond Hadley* [1917] 2 K.B. 473; *Zim Israel Navigation v Effy Shipping Corp* [1972] 1 Lloyd's Rep. 18. See also *The Brimnes*, above, at pp.483–487.

[81] *Akt. Tankexpress v Compagnie Financière Belge des Petroles* (1946) 79 Ll.L.R. 451; affirmed (1947) 80 Ll.L.R. 365 (CA). But the better view probably is that hire will still be due unless the charterer accepts the owner's conduct as a repudiation and brings the charter to an end: see [1949] A.C. 76 and see Art.174, fn.25 above.

[82] *Wehner v Dene S.S. Co* [1905] 2 K.B. 92. Hire paid in advance will be returnable if the withdrawal is justified: *ibid.* and *The Mihalios Xilas*, above. cited with approval in *Petroleum Shipping Ltd v Vatis (The Riza)* [1997] 2 Lloyd's Rep. 314 at p.321.

[83] *Italian State Railways v Mavrogordatos* [1919] 2 K.B. 305.

claim damages for the remainder of the agreed period of hire based upon the charterer's repudiation of the charter if the charterer's conduct is such as to amount to a repudiation.[84] Payment a few days late, as the result of an oversight, will not normally be a repudiation.[85] If there is cargo on board at the time of withdrawal and the shipowner carries it to its destination, no doubt he is entitled to remuneration for that service, but the exact nature of this right has not been judicially determined.[86] Where the cargo is carried under bills of lading issued by the owner, he will be obliged to complete the voyage[87] but will be able to recover freight from the shipper unless the bills are marked freight pre-paid or freight has already been paid to the charterer or his agent.[88] Where cargo has been carried under a charterer's bill of lading, the shipowner's duty as bailee is to take reasonable care of the cargo and to deliver it at the destination in the bill of lading: if the freight has not been prepaid, the shipowner may have a claim for a quantum meruit.[89]

Case. Ship under time charter at a fixed rate of hire per month payment to be made in cash, monthly, in advance, in London. In default of such payment the owners were to have the faculty of withdrawing the vessel from the service of the charterers. There was the usual off-hire clause specifying a number of events on the occurrence of which hire should cease, none of which was applicable to the facts. Hire normally became due on the 27th of each month. On the outbreak of war in September 1939, during the currency of the charter, a dispute arose as to a voyage the charterers intended the vessel to make and pending its settlement the owners refused to place the ship at the charterers' disposal for loading. The dispute was settled on September 25, on which day the owners cabled the master to load, but the cable did not reach him and he accordingly did not place his ship at the charterers' disposal for loading. On the same day the charterers sent from Brussels a letter to Hambros Bank, London, enclosing a cheque for a month's hire from September 27: this was in accordance with previous practice in remitting hire. Hambros Bank did not receive the cheque until October 3. On September 30 owners gave the charterers notice they cancelled the charter for non-payment of hire. Neither party knew by October 3 when hire was tendered that the master was still refusing to load. *Held*, by Atkinson J. and Bucknill L.J., that the owners were not entitled to cancel since on September 27, they had withdrawn the ship from the service of the charterers, who were therefore not in breach for non-payment of hire. Tucker L.J. considered that although the owners were in breach of contract entitling the charterers to damages, the charterers were not thereby relived of the obligation to pay hire and were therefore in default, thus entitling the owners to withdraw the ship. As the CA was equally divided, the decision of Atkinson J. stood on appeal. In the HL the charterers succeeded on the ground that payment had been made in the previously accepted way.[90]

---

[84] *Leslie Shipping Co v Welstead* [1921] 3 K.B. 420. Contrast *Rutherford Sender & Co v Goldthorpe* [1922] 1 K.B. 508.

[85] See *Empresa Cubana de Fletes v Lagonisi Shipping Co* [1971] 1 Lloyd's Rep. 7 at p.14; *The Brimnes* [1972] 2 Lloyd's Rep. 465 at p.482.

[86] The law is so stated in the 11th edition of this work at p.397, the last edition for which Scrutton and MacKinnon L.JJ. were responsible. See also *Wulfsberg v Weardale Co*, above, and the discussion of the right to recover freight after deviation, Art.127, above. A similar question arises in relation to cargo left on board after frustration: *cf. Soc. Franco-Tunisienne, etc. v Sidermar* [1961] 2 Q.B. 278 (overruled on the issue of frustration by *The Eugenia* [1964] 2 Q.B. 226). In our view the right is best viewed as restitutionary: see Burrows', *Law of Restitution* (1993) pp.279–280 and 282.

[87] *Tropwood A.G. v Jade Enterprises (The Tropwind)* [1982] 1 Lloyd's Rep. 232 (CA) per Lord Denning M.R.

[88] *Ngo Chew Hong Edible Oils Pte Ltd v Scandia Steam Navigation Co Ltd (The Jalamohan)* [1988] 1 Lloyd's Rep. 443.

[89] *J. Gasden Pty Ltd v Strider 1 Ltd (The AES Express)* (1990) 20 N.S.W.L.R. 57 (Aus.) (in which it was held that no quantum meruit was payable where the cargo was being carried under charterer's freight pre-paid bills, it being a "necessary incident" of the withdrawal that the shipowner assumed the charterer's obligations under the bills).

[90] *Akt. Tankexpress v Compagnie Financière Belge des Petroles* (1947) 80 Ll.L.R. 365 (CA); affirmed [1949] A.C. 76. See fn.81, above.

A176   **Article 176—Time Charters: Off-hire Clause**

Provision is usually made in time charters for hire to cease[91] in certain specified events.[92] If hire is withheld under such a provision it is for the time charterer to establish facts bringing him within the language of the clause.[93]

The wording of the off-hire clause varies,[94] but it frequently takes the form that in the event of loss of time from deficiency of men[95] or stores, breakdown of machinery, damage,[96] and other specified events preventing the (full) working of the vessel[97] for more than twenty-four working hours, the payment of the hire shall cease until she be again in an efficient state to resume her service.[98] The

---

[91] Charters sometimes provide the time shall not cease completely, but shall be reduced *pro rata* to the degree of inefficiency of the ship. See *The H. R. MacMillan* [1974] 1 Lloyd's Rep. 311 (CA): vessel with three cranes, hire to be reduced *pro rata* in the event of a breakdown of a crane or cranes.

[92] A clause providing that should the vessel become a constructive total loss the hire should cease as from the day of the casualty resulting in such loss operates if the events are such as would substantiate such a claim if made under any normal policy of marine insurance, even though the owner had not insured and was carrying the risk himself: *Court Line v R.* (1945) 78 Ll.L.R. 390 (CA).

[93] *Sea and Land Securities v Dickinson* [1942] 2 K.B. 65; *Leolga v John Glynn* [1953] 2 Q.B. 374 at p.383.

[94] For special variants, see *Magnhild v McIntyre* [1921] 2 K.B. 97, where time lost through grounding when "trading to shallow harbours, rivers, or ports where there are bars" was for the charterers' account: see also *Court Line v Finelvet (The Jevington Court)* [1966] 1 Lloyd's Rep. 683; *Traae and Lennard, Re* [1904] 2 K.B. 377; *Burrell & Sons v Green* [1914] 1 K.B. 293; reversed *sub nom. Burrell & Sons v Hind, Rolph & Co* [1915] 1 K.B. 391 and *Royal Greek Government v Minister of Transport (Ann Stathatos)* (1950) 83 Ll.L.R. 228 (accident to cargo). For the joint effect of the off-hire clause and a special clause providing that all derelicts and salvage shall be for owners' and charterers' equal benefit, see *Booker v Pocklington S.S. Co* [1899] 2 Q.B. 690. For the meaning of "fault" in an off-hire clause see *Sig. Bergessen D.Y. A/S v Mobil Shipping and Transportation Co (The Berge Sund)* [1992] 2 Lloyd's Rep. 460; [1993] 2 Lloyd's Rep. 453 (CA).

[95] This means normal crew, not gun crews; *Radcliffe v Compagnie Generale* (1918) 24 Com.Cas. 40. It deals with numerical insufficiency and does not therefore apply to a complete crew who are on strike: *Royal Greek Government v Minister of Transport (Ilissos)* [1949] 1 K.B. 525 (CA). *Quaere* whether inability of the crew to work owing to sickness would be within the words of the clause: *ibid.* at p.529. Want of a crew owing to smallpox was held in an old case to come within the words "ship's inability to proceed": *Beatson v Schank* (1803) 3 East 233.

[96] Under the words "deficiency of men or stores, breakdown of machinery, or any other cause", it has been held that the chartered ship was off hire while collision damage was being repaired even though the Crown was liable for the cost of repairs: *Adelaide S.S. Co v R. (No. 2)* [1926] A.C. 172. See also *The Essex Envoy* (1929) 33 Com.Cas. 61 (ship *held* off hire during repair of collision damage incurred before date of charter and even though ship would have been otherwise idle). (The decision on the latter point seems doubtful.) In the case of damage to a ship due to the negligence of the pilot, charterers were held entitled to put the ship off hire during the time taken for repairs although they were, under the charter, to provide and pay for "pilotage", such a provision not making the pilot the charterers' servant: *Fraser v Bee* (1900) 17 T.L.R. 101. Contrast *Brys & Gylsen v J. & J. Drysdale & Co* (1920) 4 Ll.L.R. 24 on the effect of the words "provide and pay". As to liability under a towage contract for a ship under time charter, see *The Basis* (1950) 84 Ll.L.R. 306. The word "*whatsoever*" is often added after the words "*any other cause*", but where it is not these words are to be construed *ejusdem generis* the preceding list—see *Andre & Cie SA v Orient Shipping (Rotterdam) BV (The Laconian Confidence)* [1997] 1 Lloyd's Rep. 139.

[97] In *Court Line v Dant & Russell* (1939) 44 Com.Cas. 345 at p.352, Branson J. held that these words were not apt to cover a case where a ship was in every way sound and well found, but was prevented from trading as desired by the charterers, e.g. by being confined to the upper reaches of the Yangtse River through a boom placed across it. Again in *Actis Co Ltd v Sanko S.S. Co (The Aquacharm)* [1982] 1 Lloyd's Rep. 7, where the ship had to be lightened to pass through the Panama Canal, she was held to be not off-hire. The fact that a ship was boycotted by shore labour because she did not have an I.T.F. Blue Card did not constitute a cause affecting the "efficient working of the vessel": *Sanko S.S. Co Ltd v Fearnley and Eger A/S (The Manhattan Prince)* [1985] 1 Lloyd's Rep. 140. But a lengthy testing and disinfection of the ship's holds before free pratique would be granted did put the ship off-hire during time so lost: *The Apollo* [1978] 1 Lloyd's Rep. 200 at p.206. Where additional cleaning was necessary for reasons unconnected with any fault or breach of contract by the shipowner, the vessel will not be off-hire because cleaning is the very service required by the charterer: *The Berge Sund*, above. See also *Belcore Maritime Corp v F.Lli. Moretti Cereal SpA (The Mastro Georgis)* [1983] 2 Lloyd's Rep. 66 and compare with *C.A. Venezolana de Navegacion v Bank Line Ltd (The Roachbank)* [1987] 2 Lloyd's Rep. 498 at 500; [1988] 2 Lloyd's Rep. 337 (CA). (vessel not off-hire which had picked up refugees and was refused permission to enter port).

[98] *Eastern Mediterranean Maritime (Liechtenstein) v Unimarine (The Marika)* [1981] 2 Lloyd's Rep. 622: hire resumed when ship refloated after grounding. Not all off-hire clauses take this form: see text to fn.109, below.

clause often ends, after the words "the payment of hire shall cease", with "for the time lost thereby".[99] Prevention under such a clause includes partial interference,[100] but a ship may be in an efficient state to discharge her cargo and her owners be thus entitled to hire, although she is not in an efficient state to put to sea.[101] The charterer, however, will probably not be entitled to put the ship off hire where the event giving rise to the loss of time was due to his breach of contract.[102]

Under the above clause, if damage prevents the working of the vessel for more than twenty-four hours, hire ceases from the beginning of the period, and not from the end of the twenty-four hours.[103] In the case of defects in machinery, which may be slow in becoming apparent, a "breakdown in machinery" under the clause occurs and hire ceases from the point of time at which the defects became so serious as to make it reasonably necessary to put into a port for repairs.[104] The off-hire clause does not usually qualify other express obligations of the charterer, such as to pay for all bunkers; the charterer may therefore have to pay for bunkers consumed during an off-hire period,[105] unless, of course, the event which put the vessel off hire was itself caused by the shipowner's breach of contract.

Hire begins again, not when the ship is in the same position as when she broke down,[106] but when she has been repaired and is again efficient to resume her service. It may thus be payable for the time in which, having been repaired, she is proceeding to another port in order to reload cargo discharged there to enable her to repair,[107] or proceeding to the position from which she turned back for

---

[99] Where a ship was refloated after grounding hire was held to restart at once, notwithstanding shipping movements that might have taken place during her grounding preventing her going straight into berth: *Eastern Mediterranean (Liechtenstein) v Unimarine (The Marika)* [1981] 2 Lloyd's Rep. 622. The vessel will only go off-hire for the time that the full working of the vessel immediately required is prevented by one of the listed events; *The Pythia* [1982] 2 Lloyd's Rep. 160 at pp.168–169. Another ending is "from the hour when detention or inefficiency begins until she be again in an efficient state to resume her service, at the place where the accident occurred and any fuels consumed shall be made good by owners to charterers": *The Teno* [1977] 2 Lloyd's Rep. 289 (Baltime Form).

[100] *Hogarth v Miller* [1891] A.C. 48 (ship had to be towed owing to breakdown of her high pressure engine, although she assisted the tug with her low pressure engine); *Tynedale S.S. Co v Anglo Soviet Shipping Co* (1936) 41 Com.Cas. 206 (loss of mast preventing use of forward winches during discharge).

[101] *Hogarth v Miller*, above. In *The H. R. MacMillan*, above, where the words "the period of such inefficiency" appeared in a special form of off-hire clause, it was held that the question was whether the vessel was efficient for the work in hand.

[102] *Nourse v Elder Dempster* (1922) 13 Ll.L.R. 197 (loss of time and expenses due to faulty bunkers the provision of which was the charterers' responsibility under the charter); or the shipowner may recover as damages the amount of hire lost under the off-hire clause: *Leolga v John Glynn* [1953] 2 Q.B. 374. The statement in the text is suggested by remarks of Greer J. in the former case. These were, however, obiter as the facts did not come within the language of the off-hire clause. In the case of a charter with the Crown difficult questions arise in the application of this principle where the act giving rise to the delay has been due to the acts of the Crown otherwise than as charterers: *Board of Trade v Temperley S.S. Co* (1927) 27 Ll.L.R. 230. See also *Larrinaga S.S. Co v R.* [1945] A.C. 246 at p.262 (naval orders to a ship under charter to the Crown are not "charterers' orders").

[103] *Meade King v Jacobs* [1915] 2 K.B. 640. This may be avoided by express provision: see clause 14 of the charter in *Vogemann v Zanzibar Co* (1902) 7 Com.Cas. 254.

[104] *Giertsen v Turnbull*, 1908 S.C. 1101. Marine growth due to a ship being kept inactive in a tropical port for three months is not a "defect in the hull": *Santa Martha Baay Sheepvaart, etc. v Scanbulk A/S (The Rijn)* [1981] 2 Lloyd's Rep. 267, at p.272.

[105] *Vogemann v Zanzibar Co* [1923] 2 K.B. 141. This result is often avoided by qualifying the charterers' obligation to pay for bunkers by the words "while the ship is on hire".

[106] Though a special clause sometimes provides for this: *The Pythia* [1982] 2 Lloyd's Rep. 160 at p.168.

[107] *Smailes v Evans* [1917] 2 K.B. 54.

repairs. The charterer may therefore have to pay twice for part of the voyage.[108]

The form of off-hire clause discussed above causes hire to cease from the occurrence of the stipulated event, and the off-hire period thus started continues until it ends on the occurrence of another event. There are, however, other forms of clause, which require the period of off-hire to be calculated in terms of the net time lost to the charterer.[109]

The off-hire clause does not necessarily exhaust the charterer's remedies in respect of the events which bring the clause into operation. If the occurrence of the event constitutes a breach of contract by the owner, the charterer may (depending on the construction of the clause) also be entitled to recover damages.[110]

Prepaid hire can be recovered in respect of that portion of time already paid for during which the ship is inefficient, as money paid for a consideration which has failed or as a matter of contractual obligation.[111] The charterer may not, however, make a deduction from hire in respect of an expected, future, off hire event, however certain it appears to be that the vessel will be off hire.[112]

Case. A vessel broke down in her high-pressure engine on a voyage from the West Coast of Africa to the Elbe, and put into the Canary Islands, where she was pronounced unfit to proceed. A tug was engaged as a general average expenditure, and brought her home with the use of her low-pressure engine. *Held*, that under the off-hire clause, no freight was payable from the Canary Islands to the Elbe, as the ship was not in an efficient state for proceeding at sea; but that hire was due for the time during which she was discharging cargo on the Elbe, as she was efficient for that purpose, though not for proceeding to sea as a steamer.[113]

A177   **Article 177—Time Charters: Owner's and Charterer's Obligations**

A time charter not by way of demise includes an undertaking of seaworthiness at the beginning of the time[114] but there is by Scots law no such warranty at the

---

[108] *Vogemann v Zanzibar Co*, above. In *Traae and Lennard, Re* [1904] 2 K.B. 377, where the clause was "detention by ice to be for the account of the charterers, unless caused by breakdown of steamer", the steamer was damaged by stranding in the course of her voyage at St. Petersburg, and her repairs detained her so long that she could not get to St. Petersburg before the winter ice set in and waited at Reval. The court upheld the award giving her hire from her port of repair to Reval, but refusing it while waiting at Reval till St. Petersburg opened in the spring.

[109] For an example of such clauses, see *The H. R. MacMillan* [1974] 1 Lloyd's Rep. 311 (New York Produce Exchange Form) and *The Teno*, above, and text to fn.99, above. It has been said that the court leans to construe clauses as "period" clauses rather "time lost" clauses: *Navigas International Ltd v Trans-Offshore Inc. (The Bridgestone Maru No. 3)* [1985] 2 Lloyd's Rep. 62.

[110] See *The H. R. MacMillan*, above.

[111] *Stewart v Van Ommeren* [1918] 2 K.B. 560. But see Lord Roche in *Tynedale S.S. Co v Anglo-Soviet Shipping Co* (1936) 41 Com.Cas. 206 at p.219. Charters commonly provide for an express right of repayment. For example: "Any hire paid in advance to be adjusted accordingly." A list of perils said to be "always mutually excepted" will not prevent the charterer recovering hire paid in advance if the ship is lost by one of the perils: *Meling v Minos Shipping Co* [1972] 1 Lloyd's Rep. 458. See also *The Trident Beauty*, above and Art.174, fn.47, above.

[112] *Western Bulk Carriers K/S v Li Hai Maritime Inc (The Li Hai)* [2005] EWHC 735 (Comm).

[113] *Hogarth v Miller* [1891] A.C. 48. The suggestion made by Lord Watson and Lord Herschell in *Hogarth v Miller*, at pp.60 and 64, that if the shipowner had engaged a tug at his own cost he might have recovered something on the basis of a quantum meruit for the time occupied in the towage does not appear to have been acted upon in subsequent cases and it may be doubted whether it is in accordance with principle. For discussion of the validity of a claim for a quantum meruit by owners against time charterers, see *The Pythia* [1982] 2 Lloyd's Rep. 160 at p.167.

[114] *Giertsen v Turnbull*, 1908 S.C. 1101.

beginning of each voyage under the charter.[115] Probably the same is true in English law.[116] If the master proceeds on such a voyage without using an opportunity to remedy the unseaworthy condition of his ship the owner will be liable for his negligence unless protected by exceptions.[117] A charter for consecutive voyages or for a "round trip" does not rank as a time charter for the purposes of this rule, and therefore the shipowner under such a charter is obliged to provide a seaworthy ship at the commencement of each voyage or at the commencement of each stage of the trip.[118]

A clause in common use in time charters provides that the owners will maintain the vessel in a thoroughly efficient state in hull and machinery during the service. Whether a clause of this nature creates an absolute obligation (subject to excepted perils) to maintain the ship in a seaworthy condition throughout the voyage, or whether it merely places the obligation on the owners of bearing the expenses of maintenance and of taking all reasonable and proper steps for restoring the vessel's efficiency after accidents, will depend on the precise words used, and, in particular, on the wording and effect of the exceptions clauses.[119] It may also depend upon whether the defect in question was present on delivery of the vessel into service or only arose thereafter.[120]

Time charters sometimes contain clauses purporting to incorporate the provisions of the Hague–Visby Rules, and since the Rules apply only to voyages and to bills of lading, this often gives rise to difficulty[121] particularly in relation to the obligation to exercise due diligence to make the ship seaworthy "before and at the beginning of the voyage". The effect of this is no doubt to cut down the absolute undertaking of seaworthiness to an obligation to exercise due diligence, but it is uncertain whether the obligation attaches at the beginning of the charter or at the beginning of each voyage under the charter. The latter position seems more satisfactory where the charter requires the master to sign bills of lading for each voyage which themselves incorporate the Hague-Visby Rules, but the question must always turn on the construction of the charter as a whole.[122] The incorporation of the Hague or Hague–Visby Rules into time

---

[115] *Giertsen v Turnbull*, above. Contrast *Park v Duncan*, 1898 25 Rettie 528, where sending the ship to sea on a subsequent voyage with insufficient coals was held a breach of the express provisions of the charter.

[116] In time policies of insurance there is no implied warranty of initial seaworthiness owing to the hardship of requiring the shipowner to undertake that his vessel is seaworthy at a time when she is at sea beyond his control, a time at which such policies frequently begin to run: *Gibson v Small* (1853) 4 H.L.C. 353; Marine Insurance Act 1906, s.39. There is also the difficulty of deciding what constitutes seaworthiness for a definite time, but for unknown voyages. These considerations do not apply so strongly to time charters other than by demise, which usually, though not always, commence with the vessel's starting from port for a known voyage.

[117] *Worms v Storey* (1855) 11 Ex. 427; *The Rona* (1884) 51 L.T. 28.

[118] *Anglo-Saxon Petroleum Co v Adamastos Shipping Co* [1957] 2 Q.B. 255 (CA) (reversed on another ground [1959] A.C. 133); *McIver v Tate* [1903] 1 K.B. 362 ("round trip").

[119] Contrast *Anglo-Saxon Petroleum Co v Adamastos*, above, and *Minister of Materials v Wold S.S. Co* [1952] 1 Lloyd's Rep. 485 at p.499 with *Giertsen v Turnbull*, 1908 S.C. 1101, *Snia Societa v Suzuki* (1924) 29 Com.Cas. 284 at p.290, and *Tynedale S.S. Co v Anglo-Soviet Shipping Co* (1936) 41 Com.Cas. 206. See also Art.178 on the effect of such a clause when coupled with an obligation on the part of the charterer to "redeliver in the same good order and condition".

[120] *Poseidon Schiffahrt GmbH v Nomadic Navigation Co Ltd (The Trade Nomad)* [1999] 1 Lloyd's Rep. 723.

[121] See Chapter 20, below.

[122] See, e.g. *Adamastos v Anglo-Saxon Petroleum Co* [1959] A.C. 133 (consecutive voyage charter).

charters may also give rise to difficulties when property belonging to the chatrerer is lost or damaged but when the relevant property is on board fortuitously (such as lashing or loading equipment) and is not being carried under any contract of carriage[123] or when claims are made for breach of the charterparty which are not in respect of a particular cargo.[124]

Time Charterers generally provide that, whilst owners are to remain responsible for the navigation of the vessel, the master is to be under the orders of the Charterers as regards employment and is to prosecute his voyages with the utmost despatch. A decision as to which of two possible routes to sail on a particular voyage is, certainly in the absence of a rational (presumably navigational) reason for preferring one route, a matter of employment rather than navigation. Thus a decision to proceed by the longer route will be a breach of the obligation of utmost despatch and an order to sail the shorter route will be an order in relation to the employment rather than navigation of the vessel.[125]
Clause 8 of the New York Produce form of time charter provides that time charterers are to load, stow, trim and discharge the cargo at their expense under the supervision of the master. This does not mean that whenever discharging is necessary the charterers must pay for it. In general, the obligations of time charterers as to discharging will only apply to the designated discharging place, unless they have ordered the discharge or it has been agreed as a variation that the cargo shall be discharged at an alternative place. Time charterers are generally under no obligation to order discharge at a different discharging place from that designated, though they have the right to do so.[126] It is not uncommon for the words "and responsibility" to be added after the word "supervision", in which case the owners will remain liable for the consequences of negligent stowage and no term will be implied to the effect that the stevedores appointed by the Charterers would take reasonable care.[127] But where the words "and responsibility" are not added it appears that the Charterers will remain responsible for the consequences of poor stowage even where they render the ship unseaworthy[128] but not, in the absence of other expressly agreed terms, where cargo is stowed on deck.[129] Where the charterer is obliged, by clause 8, to discharge the cargo this refers to the physical acts involved in the unloading of the cargo and will not, without more, impose a wider obligation to, for example, provide security where the port authority declines to permit discharge to take place until security has been provided.[130] Charterers' obligations as to discharge are often performed by receivers acting on their behalf, but if receivers acting at

---

[123] As to which see *Grimaldi Compagnia di Navagazione SpA v Sekihyo Lines Ltd (The Seki Rolette)* [1998] 2 Lloyd's Rep. 638. It appears that the Hague/Hague Visby limitation period of one year will apply to claims for loss of or damage to such equipment even though they are not carried under a contract of carriage.
[124] *The Marinor* [1996] 1 Lloyd's Rep. 301
[125] *Whistler International Ltd v Kawasaki Kisen Kaisha Ltd* [2001] 1 Lloyd's Rep. 147.
[126] *Western Sealanes Corp v Unimarine (The Pythia)* [1982] 2 Lloyd's Rep. 160 at pp.164–165, per Goff J.
[127] *Macieo Shipping Ltd v Clipper Shipping Lines Ltd (The Clipper Sao Luis)* [2000] 1 Lloyd's Rep. 645.
[128] See *CSAV v MS ER Hamburg Schiffahrtsgesellschaft mbH &Co. KG* [2006] EWHC 484 (Comm).
[129] *L.D. Seals N.V. v Mitsui OSK Lines Ltd (The Darya Tara)* [1997] 1 Lloyd's Rep. 42.
[130] *Nippon Yusen Kaisha Ltd v Scindia Steam Navigation Co Ltd (The Jalagouri)* [2000] 1 Lloyd's Rep. 515.

one discharge port give orders to the vessel to discharge more than she has been ordered by Charterers to discharge, Charterers will not be responsible for the unauthorised order.[131]

Time charters generally include express terms obliging the charterer to employ the ship only between safe ports and places.[132] Even where there is no express term a warranty of safety will generally be implied[133] although some forms of time charter specifically provide that the charterer is only obliged to use due diligence to ensure that the vessel is employed between safe ports and will only be liable for loss and damage caused by a failure to exercise due diligence.[134]

Time charters commonly include clauses dealing with the responsibility for the payment of war-risk premiums.[135]

Time charters usually provide that the charterer shall provide and pay for all bunker fuel, which is, so far as unconsumed, to be taken over by the owners on redelivery at an agreed price. It is a question of construction whether such bunkers remain the property of the charterer until consumed, and whether any remaining unconsumed bunkers vest in the owner on the termination of the charter by redelivery, cancellation, frustration, breach or otherwise. During the currency of the charter the owner is the bailee of any bunkers that are the property of the charterer and has a duty to see that they are used to carry out the charterer's orders.[136] *Semble*, the owner is not obliged to keep his own bunkers separate from those of the charterer. *Quaere*, whether the charterer is entitled during or after the currency of the charter to remove bunkers that are his property.

Time charters frequently contain a warranty by the shipowner as to the speed and bunker consumption of the chartered ship. It is as a matter of construction whether such a warranty applies to the vessel at the date of delivery, or throughout the charter period. In the absence of a contrary term, the warranty will apply on the date of delivery, although the shipowner will be obliged to maintain the vessel thereafter.[137] Where information about the vessel's speed and consumption is contained within a typed description clause claused "all details 'about'—all details given in good faith but without guarantee" then there is no

---

[131] *Merit Shipping Co Inc v T.K. Boesen A/S (The Goodpal)* [2000] 1 Lloyd's Rep. 638.

[132] As in *Maintop Shipping Co Ltd v Bulkindo Lines Pte Ltd (The Marinicki)* [2003] 2 Lloyd's Rep. 655; [2003] EWHC 1894 (Admlty.)

[133] *The Evaggelos TH* [1971] 2 Lloyd's Rep. 200.

[134] See, for example, *Dow Europe SA v Navoklav Inc* [1998] 1 Lloyd's Rep. 306.

[135] For the problems to which such clauses give rise see *World Magnate Shipping Ltd v Rederi A/B Soya* [1975] 2 Lloyd's Rep. 498; *Schiffahrtsagentur Hamburg Middle East Line GmbH v Virtue Shipping Corp (No. 2)* [1981] 2 Lloyd's Rep. 300, and cases there cited; *International Sea Tankers Inc v Hemisphere Shipping Co Ltd (The Wenjiang)* [1982] 1 Lloyd's Rep. 128; *Ocean Star Tankers SA v Total Transport Corp (The Taygetos)* [1982] 2 Lloyd's Rep. 272; *Phoenix Shipping Co v Apex Shipping Corp (The Apex)* [1982] 2 Lloyd's Rep. 407; *Telfair Shipping Corp v Athos Shipping Co SA (The Athos)* [1981] 2 Lloyd's Rep. 74, on appeal [1983] 1 Lloyd's Rep. 127; *Islamic Republic of Iran Shipping Lines v P. & O. Bulk Shipping Ltd (The Discaria)* [1985] 2 Lloyd's Rep. 489.

[136] *The Span Terza* [1984] 1 Lloyd's Rep. 119 (HL) Under the usual form of charter the property in the bunkers remains vested in the charterer until redelivery. See also *Forsythe International (UK) Ltd v Silver Shipping Co Ltd (The Saetta)* [1993] 2 Lloyd's Rep. 268.

[137] *Arab Maritime Petroleum Transport Co v Luxor Trading Panama (The Al Bida)* [1986] 1 Lloyd's Rep. 142; [1987] 1 Lloyd's Rep. 124 (CA).

warranty.[138] Where a breach of the speed warranty results in an under-consumption of fuel, the shipowner may be able to set off the value of this under-consumption in assessing damages.[139] A speed and consumption warranty will normally be given for defined conditions of "good weather". Any shortfall in performance in those conditions will apply, with appropriate adjustments, in conditions falling outside the defined "good weather" conditions.[140]

Note: Although a large number of time charters are on the New York Produce Exchange form, a number of P&I Clubs which were members of the International Group (and insured both owners and charterers in respect of their potential liabilities to cargo owners) considered that it failed to provide sufficient clarity as to the respective liability of owners and charterers for cargo claims. It had proved a "fertile ground for legal disputes"[141] and this led to the signature of the Inter-Club New York Produce Exchange Agreement 1984 which has since been replaced by an Agreement of 1996.[142] In cases to which it applies[143] the Inter-Club Agreement "cuts right across any allocation of functions and responsibilities based on the Hague Rules" and "provides a more or less mechanical apportionment of financial liability".[144]

A178   **Article 178—Time Charters: Condition on Redelivery**

Time charters usually provide that the charterer shall redeliver the vessel in the same good order and condition (fair wear and tear excepted) as when delivered to him. If on redelivery the vessel has by the charterer's breach of contract been damaged, his liability is for damages (i.e. cost of repair and loss of profit during repair), but he is not liable for hire during the period occupied by the repairs.[145]

The phrase "redeliver in the same good order and condition" must be read in the light of the charterparty as a whole. For instance, if, as is usual, the charter imposes on the shipowner responsibility for maintaining the ship and for insurance,[146] the charterer is clearly not liable under this clause for defects in maintenance existing at the time of redelivery and probably not for insurable damage, though if such damage results from the charterer's breach of contract under other clauses of the charter, e.g. sending the ship to an unsafe berth, the charterer would be liable under that other clause. Indeed, there is some ground

---

[138] *Japy Freres v Sutherland* (1921) 26 Com. Cas. 227; *Continental Pacific Shipping Ltd v Demand Shipping Co Ltd* [1997] 1 Lloyd's Rep. 404; *Losinjska Plovidba Brodarstovo DD v Valfracht Maritime Co Ltd* [2001] 2 Lloyd's Rep. 17.

[139] *Ocean Glory Compania Naviera SA v A/S P.V. Christensen (The Ioanna)* [1985] 2 Lloyd's Rep. 165.

[140] *Exmar N.V. v B.P. Shipping Ltd (The Gas Enterprise)* [1993] 2 Lloyd's Rep. 352.

[141] Per Morison J. in *Transpacific Discovery SA v Cargill International SA (The Elpa)* [2001] 2 Lloyd's Rep. 596.

[142] The 1996 Inter-Club New York Produce Exchange Agreement is printed in Appendix IV, below.

[143] As to which see *The Holstencruiser* [1992] 2 Lloyd's Rep. 378; *The Hawk* [1999] 1 Lloyd's Rep. 176; *Transpacific Discovery SA v Cargill International SA (The Elpa)* [2001] 2 Lloyd's Rep. 596.

[144] *D/S A/S Idaho v The Peninsular and Oriental Steam Navigation Co (The Strathnewton)* [1983] 1 Lloyd's Rep. 219.

[145] *Wye S.S. Co v Compagnie P. O.* [1922] 1 K.B. 617; *Black Sea & Danube Shipping Co v Goeland Transport & Trading Co* (1942) 74 Ll.L.R. 192 at p.195.

[146] For a case on the meaning in a time charter of "war risk, if any required, for charterers' account", see *Holland v Watson, Munro* (1915) 32 T.L.R. 169.

for concluding that under the clause the charterer incurs no liability as regards defects in the condition of the ship on redelivery unless those defects have arisen from his contractual default.[147] It has, however, been held that the words "fair wear and tear excluded" will not necessarily protect the charterer even when the damage to the ship has been caused without negligence.[148] But this is doubtful.

Note: In *Bulfracht (Cyprus) Ltd. v Boneset Shipping Co. Ltd. (The Pamphilos)*[149] the vessel underperformed during service as a result of her hull becoming encrusted with marine growth. The arbitrators concluded that owners were entitled to recover hire deducted in respect of the time thereby lost because the underperformance was caused by owner's compliance with charterer's order. They also concluded that Charterers were not, however, in breach of their redelivery obligations by redelivering the vessel with her hull in the same state. *Held*, by Colman J., that there was nothing inconsistent in the two findings and the marine growth could properly be treated as fair wear and tear.

Article 179—Time Charters: Indemnity of Shipowner   A179

The shipowner may be entitled, either by implication of law or by express agreement, to be indemnified by the time-charterer against loss falling upon him in consequence of the latter's acts or of complying with the latter's requests or orders.[150] Thus, such a right of indemnity may (subject to the express terms of the charter) be implied by law[151] if the master of a time-chartered vessel at the request of the time-charterers delivers the cargo without production of bills of lading; the shipowner is then entitled to be indemnified against subsequent liability to the holders of the bills of lading.[152]

Time charters usually contain an express indemnity clause.[153] Such clauses vary in detail but a common form is as follows: "the captain (although appointed

---

[147] See per Scrutton L.J. in *Limerick v Stott* [1921] 2 K.B. 613 at p.621 and per McCardie J. in *Wye S.S. Co v Compagnie P. O.*, above, at p.621. See the former case also for a discussion of the phrase "ice-bound port".

[148] *Chellew Navigation Co v Appelquist* (1933) 38 Com.Cas. 218. The actual decision turned on a finding by the umpire that the damage was not "fair wear and tear". See also *C.P.R. v Board of Trade* (1925) 22 Ll.L.R. 1 (HL), a case of a liner hired as a troopship.

[149] [2002] 2 Lloyd's Rep. 681; [2002] EWHC 2292 (Comm).

[150] The question of when a cause of action accrues against such an indemnity is a matter of construction: *Telfair Shipping Corp v Intersea Carriers SA (The Caroline P)* [1984] 2 Lloyd's Rep. 466.

[151] In *Triad Shipping Co v Stellar Chartering and Brokerage Inc (The Island Archon)* [1994] 2 Lloyd's Rep. 227 Evans L.J. held that the right to an indemnity would be implied both as a matter of law and to give the charterparty business efficacy—see also *Action Navigation Inc v Bottigliere di Navigaziione SpA (The Kitsa)* [2005] 1 Lloyd's Rep. 432; [2005] EWHC 177 (Comm).

[152] *Strathlorne S.S. Co v Andrew Weir* (1934) 40 Com.Cas. 168 (CA). There was also an indemnity clause in the time charter but the courts did not base their decisions on this. See also *Kruger & Co Ltd v Moel Tryvan Ship Co Ltd* [1907] A.C. 272, and *Elder Dempster v Dunn* (1909) 15 Com.Cas. 49 for voyage charter cases where the shipowners were held entitled to be indemnified by the charterers against liability to bill of lading holders: in the former case because of the absence of an exception of negligence in the bill of lading although there was such an exception in the charter; in the latter case because bills of lading were presented and signed for goods, some of which were unmarked. Contrast *Brown Jenkinson & Co v Percy Dalton (London)* [1957] 2 Q.B. 621. See also Art.43.

[153] It is common for time charters in the N.Y.P.E. form to incorporate the Inter-Club Agreement, which provides when and in what circumstances the shipowner and charterer can seek a complete or partial indemnity from the other in respect of cargo claims. As to the operation of the Inter-Club Agreement see *Ben Line Steamers Inc v Pacific Steam Navigation Inc (The Benlawers)* [1989] 2 Lloyd's Rep. 51; *A/S Iverans Rederei v K.G. M.S. Holstencruiser Seeschiffahrtsgesellschaft mbH & Co (The Holstencruiser)* [1992] 2 Lloyd's Rep. 378. The Shelltime 4 form of time charterparty includes an express indemnity at clause 13.

by the owners) shall be under the orders[154] and direction of the charterer as regards employment, agency, or other arrangements, and the charterer hereby agrees to indemnify the owners for all consequences or liabilities that may arise from the captain signing bills of lading[155] by the orders of the charterer or their agents or otherwise complying with such orders or direction". The range of the protection thus afforded to the shipowner will in all cases depend upon the exact language used.

Although this important clause must, like any other clause in a charter, be construed in relation to the scheme of the charter as a whole, it has been held not to be limited in its application to matters outside the scope of other clauses in the charter, though the result be considerable overlapping between the general terms of the indemnity clause and the special provisions of other clauses.[156] However, other provisions of the charterparty may preclude the implication of an indemnity in respect of matters expressly provided for.[157]

Although the exact scope of the clause is not settled[158] the following would seem to have been established by the limited number of authorities upon the clause:

(1) it does not extend to navigation or incidents of navigation, which remain the responsibility of the shipowner[159];

(2) "employment" means employment of the ship and not employment of persons[160];

(3) "such orders" are not limited to the signing of bills of lading or other documents[161];

---

[154] *Grace v General S.N. Co* [1950] 2 K.B. 383, at p.396: but the shipowners remain liable for his acts, unless protected by exceptions: *Baynes v Ballantyne* (1898) 14 T.L.R. 399 (HL). The master's duty is to act reasonably on receipt of orders. Some orders are of their nature such that they would, if the master were to act reasonably, require immediate compliance. Others would require a great deal of thought and consideration before a reasonable master would comply with them: *Midwest Shipping Co v Henry* [1971] 1 Lloyd's Rep. 375. See, also, *The Teutonia* [1872] L.R. 4 P.C. 171, 179. However, there is no finite list of situations in which a master may reasonably delay before acting on an order: the duty of the master on receiving an order is to act in a reasonable and prudent manner, and in time of war this may involve delay in acting on an order until the authority of the party giving the order is established: *Kuwait Petroleum Corp v I & D Oil Carriers Ltd (The Houda)* [1994] 2 Lloyd's Rep. 541.

[155] See *Milburn v Jamaica Co* [1900] 2 Q.B. 540; and Art.40.

[156] So held by Devlin J. in *Royal Greek Government v Minister of Transport (Ann Stathatos)* (1950) 83 Ll.L.R. 228 at pp.234, 235. The alternative view, which until the point is decided in a higher court must still be arguable, is that the clause should be regarded as a residuary one and deals only with matters not specifically covered elsewhere in the charter. An example would be loss or damage due to deviation or change of voyage on the instructions of the charterers after bills of lading have been signed: see the argument of the Attorney-General in *Larrinaga S.S. Co v R.* [1945] A.C. 246 at p.251. (Quaere whether the master would be obliged to obey such instructions if they involved a breach of his bill of lading contract).

[157] *The Berge Sund*, above.

[158] Per Thomas J. in *Aegean Sea Traders Corp v Repsol Petroleo SA (The Aegean Sea)* [1998] 2 Lloyd's Rep. 39 at p.69.

[159] *Weir v Union S.S. Co* [1900] A.C. 525, per Lord Davey at p. 533; *Larrinaga S.S. Co v R.* [1945] A.C. 246, per Lord Wright at p.256. See also *Park v Duncan* (1898) 25 Rettie 528 (bunkers). The charterer has no right to require the shipowner to take on board more bunkers than are needed for the purposes of the charter: *Mammoth Bulk Carriers Ltd v Holland Bulk Transport B.V.* [1978] 1 Lloyd's Rep. 346. In *Newa Line v Erechthion Shipping Co SA (The Erechthion)* [1987] 2 Lloyd's Rep. 180 Staughton J. characterised an order to proceed to such berth as the Harbour Authority should nominate so as to lighten there as an order as to employment, whereas an instruction from the pilot as to where or how the ship should anchor was a matter of navigation.

[160] *Larrinaga S.S. Co v R.*, above; see in particular Lord Wright at p.256, and Lord Porter at p.261.

[161] *Royal Greek Government v Minister of Transport (Ann Stathatos)* (1950) 83 Ll.L.R. 228 at p.233. See also Art.43.

(4) an order to load a particular cargo is an order as to employment and the consequences of complying with such an order are within the scope of the indemnity[162];

(5) the ordinary expenses of trading under the charterparty and, in particular, of trading to a warm water port which the Charterers were entitled to nominate, are not within the scope of the indemnity. [163]

(6) (*semble*) the consequences of complying with an order to go to an unsafe port or berth are within the scope of the indemnity.[164]

Notwithstanding the apparently wide ambit of the clause, its protection may on the facts be difficult to secure owing to the intervention of some fresh act or event breaking the chain of causation between the order and the damage.[165]

---

[162] *Portsmouth S.S. Co v Liverpool and Glasgow Salvage Association* (1929) 34 Ll.L.R. 459; *Royal Greek Government v Minister of Transport (Ann Stathatos)*, above; *Deutsche Ost-Afrika-Linie GmbH v Legent Maritime Co Ltd* [1998] 2 Lloyd's Rep. 71. This so even if the cargo is not dangerous or unusual: *The Athanasia Comninos and Georges Chr. Lemos* (1979) [1990] 1 Lloyd's Rep. 277. There will be no indemnity however where the charterer has no choice in the cargo and the shipowner has contracted to carry the specific cargo in question: *The George Chr. Lemos* [1991] 2 Lloyd's Rep. 107n.

[163] *Action Navigation Inc v Bottigliere di Navigazione SpA (The Kitsa)* [2005] 1 Lloyd's Rep. 432; [2005] EWHC 177 (Comm).

[164] So held by Greer L.J. in *Lensen S.S. Co v Anglo-Soviet S.S. Co* (1935) 40 Com.Cas. 320 at p.329. This was, however, only one of the grounds of his decision, since he also agreed with Slesser L.J. that the charter was subject to an implied term that the berth should be safe. This view of Greer L.J. was treated as a guiding authority by Devlin J. in *Royal Greek Government v Minister of Transport (Ann Stathatos)*, above, at p.234. *Cf.* the view of Morris J. in *Stag Line v Ellerman & Papayanni Lines* (1949) 82 Ll.L.R. 826 at p.836.

[165] As in *Royal Greek Government v Minister of Transport (Ann Stathatos)*, above, and *A/B Helsingfors S.S. Co v Rederi A/B Rex* [1969] 2 Lloyd's Rep. 52. See also *Vardinoyannis v Egyptian General Petroleum Corp* [1971] 2 Lloyd's Rep. 200 and *Newa Line v Erechthion Shipping Co SA*, above, in which it is suggested that the negligence of the master will not always break the chain of causation. The authorities stressing the requirement for the loss to be a direct consequence of the order may have to be reconsidered in the light of more recent authorities on causation: *The Berge Sund*, above at p. 462. See also *Action Navigation Inc v Bolligliere di Navigazione SpA (The Kitsa)* [2005] 1 Lloyd's Rep. 432; [2005] EWHC 177 (Comm) as to the need for there to be a direct causal link between the order given and the loss or expense suffered and *Ullises Shipping Corp v FAL Shipping Co Ltd (The Greek Fighter)* [2006] EWHC 1729 (Comm) in which Colman J. held that charterers' orders to load a particular cargo were not (on the hypotheses in question) a sufficiently predominant cause of the subsequent loss to trigger either the express indemnity contained in the Shelltime 4 form of charterparty or any right to an implied indemnity.

CHAPTER 17

THROUGH BILLS OF LADING, COMBINED TRANSPORTATION,
CONTAINERS

A180   **Article 180—Through bills of lading**

"THROUGH bill of lading" is an expression loosely used to mean a document containing a contract for the carriage of goods from one place to another in separate stages, of which at least one stage is a conventional sea transit[1]. The sea transit may itself be divided into separate stages to be performed by different shipowners by a process of transhipment. The sea transit is often coupled with a stage of transit by some other means, e.g. by road, rail or air, in which case the through bill of lading is sometimes called a "combined transport bill of lading".

The multiplicity of different types of through bills of lading makes it difficult to lay down hard and fast principles governing the liabilities and relationships of the various parties involved. Most of the relevant authorities turn on the construction of particular clauses in through bills of lading and are not of general application; and although there is a considerable amount of nineteenth century authority on the liabilities of successive rail-carriers, the decisions are not always directly applicable to the different problems raised by sea-carriage. An attempt has been made in this Article, however, to set out such general principles as can be extracted from the authorities.

In the case of rail carriage by successive railway companies, the rule was that the company receiving the goods from the shipper, issuing the through ticket and receiving the through freight, was prima facie liable as a carrier for the whole distance.[2] But the railways cases probably depend in part on the fact that the same rolling stock, and often the same driver and guard, were commonly used for the entire journey. With the possible exception of "roll-on, roll-off" carriage, where the carrying vehicle is carried by sea together with the goods, there is no analogous situation under a through bill of lading. The rule must therefore be applied with caution to the different circumstances of a through transit involving sea-carriage.[3] The presumption, if it exists at all in relation to sea-carriage, can

---

[1] In *J. I. Macwilliam Co Inc v Mediterranean Shipping Co SA (The Rafaela S)* [2003] 2 Lloyd's Rep. 113; [2002] EWCA Civ 556 Rix L.J. (referring to this article in the 20th edn) described the expression "Through Bill of Lading" as being "loose and ambiguous".

[2] *Bristol & Exeter Ry v Collin* (1859) 7 H.L.C. 194. See also *Thomas v Rhymney Ry Co* (1871) L.R. 6 Q.B. 266 and the cases there cited. The dissenting judgment of Lord Denning in *Midland Silicones v Scruttons* [1962] A.C. 446, contains a valuable analysis of the railway cases. The liabilities of successive air carriers are governed by the Carriage by Air Act 1961. The liabilities of successive road crriers are governed by the Carriage of Goods by Road Act 1965.

[3] *Cf.* however, *Greeves v West India & Pacific S.S. Co Ltd* (1870) 22 L.T. 615; *Logan & Co v Highland Ry Co* (1899) 2 Sess.Cas. (5th Series) 292; *Aberdeen Grit Co v Ellerman's Wilson Line*, 1933 S.C. 9, in which the company issuing the through bill of lading was held responsible for the whole journey.

in any case be excluded by the terms of the through bill of lading,[4] or by the surrounding circumstances, so as to show that the issuing company is not responsible for those parts of the carriage which it does not perform personally. Thus, the through bill of lading may provide for "transhipment at shipper's risk"[5] or limit the issuing company's liability to that of a forwarding agent for land carriage beyond the port of discharge.[6]

Where the company issuing the through bill of lading is responsible for the whole transit, the other companies concerned are usually to be treated as sub-contractors to that company, and not as parties to the through bill of lading.[7] But where all the companies involved have an arrangement by which they co-operate in providing through carriage, even if they are not technically a partnership, the company issuing the through bill of lading may be held to do so as agent for the other companies concerned, and clauses in the bill of lading for the benefit of the carrier will, so far as their wording allows, be construed as being for their benefit.[8] In exceptional circumstances the companies concerned may be jointly liable for the whole transit[9]; but it is not uncommon for the companies concerned to issue the through bill of lading "severally and not jointly".[10]

The fact that the company issuing the through bill of lading is not responsible for part of the transit will not prevent the company from recovering the full freight for each stage of the transit if the through bill of lading so provides.[11] Freight, if payable in advance, is usually payable for the whole journey, and should the goods be lost on one of the stages, the shipper is not entitled to a pro rata return of the freight for other stages as if the consideration had failed,[12] even if calculated separately for each stage and even if the issuing company has not paid over any part of the freight relating to stages of the journey to be performed by other companies.[13]

Through bills of lading commonly contain provisions incorporating "all conditions expressed in the regular forms of bills of lading in use by the

---

[4] *Moore v Harris* (1876) 1 App.Cas. 318; *Kitts v Atlantic Transport Co Ltd* (1902) 7 Com.Cas. 227; *E. Clemens Horst Co v Norfolk and North American S.S. Co* (1906) 11 Com.Cas. 141; *Crawford & Law v Allan Line S.S. Co* [1912] A.C. 130; see also, as to rail carriage, *Fowles v G.W.R.* (1852) 7 Ex. 698 (contrast *Bristol & Exeter Ry v Collins*, above); and, as to canal traffic, *Hyde v Trent & Mersey* (1793) 5 Term Rep. 389.

[5] See *Note 3* to Art.118.

[6] *Cliffe v Hull & Netherlands S.S. Co* (1921) 6 Ll.L.R. 136.

[7] *Bristol & Exeter Ry v Collins* (1859) 7 H.L.C. 194. The sub-contractors may be liable in tort for loss or damage to the goods. See Art.121. However the sub-contractors may be able to rely upon the terms of their own bill of lading against the goods owner: *The Pioneer Container* [1994] 1 Lloyd's Rep. 593 (P.C.).

[8] *Gill v Manchester Ry Co* (1873) L.R. 8 Q.B. 186; *Hall v North Eastern Ry Co* (1875) L.R. 10 Q.B. 437; *Barrat v Great Northern Ry Co* (1904) 20 T.L.R. 175; see also *Reader v South-Eastern & Chatham Ry Co* (1921) 38 T.L.R. 14 and *Wilson v Darling Island Stevedoring Co* [1956] 1 Lloyd's Rep. 346 at p.357, per Fullagar J. (High Ct. of Australia).

[9] *Hayes v S. Wales Ry Co* (1859) 9 Ir.C.L.R. 474.

[10] e.g. *The Hibernian* [1907] P. 277; *Crawford & Law v Allan Line S.S. Co* [1912] A.C. 130; *Walker v Dover Navigation Co Ltd* (1950) 83 Ll.L.R. 84.

[11] *The Hibernian* [1907] P. 277; *Kitts v Atlantic Transport Co Ltd* (1902) 7 Com.Cas. 227; *cf. Leech v Glynn & Son* (1890) 6 T.L.R. 306. In *Britannia v Factor Pace* [1998] 2 Lloyd's Rep. 420 the Claimant was a freight forwarder and had paid the freight due for the whole of the through carriage (by a number of different means of transport) of the Defendant's goods from the United Kingdom to Russia. *Held* the Claimant was entitled to recover the sums due as freight—that is to say without regard to any alleged counterclaims or set offs.

[12] *Greeves v West India Co* (1870) 22 L.T. 615.

[13] *Troy v Eastern Co of Warehouses* (1921) 26 Com.Cas. 340.

company" or to the effect that "all goods are carried subject to the conditions of persons by whom the goods may be conveyed". The effect of such provisions is to incorporate the conditions referred to into the through bill of lading, even if they are unknown to the shipper, but not to relieve the company issuing the through bill of lading from its responsibility as a carrier (subject to those conditions) while the goods are out of its possession.[14] If the terms of the through bill of lading and the ocean bill of lading are at variance, they will be construed, so far as possible, so as to give effect to both sets of conditions consistently.[15] Where the two sets of conditions cannot be construed consistently, it is submitted that the terms of the through bill of lading should prevail.

Terms which would be implied if the shipper made a direct contract with the company carrying as a sub-contractor may be implied in the through bill of lading so as to apply to the company issuing the through bill of lading.[16]

It is not always easy to tell whether provisions in the through bill of lading are to be construed as applying only to the company issuing the through bill of lading and to the stage of transit performed by that company, or whether they are to be construed as applying, *mutatis mutandis*, to the other companies and to the stages performed by them. Each case must, it is submitted, turn on its own facts.[17]

A company accepting goods in apparent good order and condition under a through bill of lading cannot rely on a clause limiting its responsibility to the stage of the transit which it performs in person, unless it proves that the loss or damage complained of took place during a stage of the transit for which it was not responsible.[18] Where, as often happens, particularly in the case of goods carried in containers, it is impossible to discover when the damage took place, the carrier may have great difficulty in discharging the burden of proof.

Each successive carrier may be estopped by statements in the through bill of lading, or in the ocean bills of lading incorporated in the bill of lading, or by receipts issued by it to the previous carrier, or by failure to notify damage or shortages to the previous carrier, from denying that he received the goods from the previous carrier in apparent good order and condition.[18]

A carrier under a through bill of lading is not as a rule the agent of the shipper to assent to bad stowage by a successive carrier to whom he has delivered the goods, so as to prevent the shipper from complaining of the bad stowage.[18]

---

[14] *E. Clemens Horst Co v Norfolk & North American S.S. Co* (1906) 11 Com.Cas. 141; *The Hibernian* [1907] P. 277; *Aberdeen Grit Co v Ellerman's Wilson Line*, 1933 S.C. 9; *cf. Crawford & Law v Allan Line S.S. Co* [1912] A.C. 130.

[15] e.g. *E. Clemens Horst Co v Norfolk & North American S.S. Co* (1906) 11 Com.Cas. 141 (notification); *The Hibernian* [1907] P. 277 (lien for inland freight exercisable by sea-carrier).

[16] *Armour & Co Ltd v Charles Tarbard Ltd* (1920) 37 T.L.R. 208; *Lynch Bros v Edwards & Fase* (1921) 6 Ll.L.R. 371; *Elof Hansson Agency Ltd v Victoria Motor Haulage Co Ltd* (1938) 43 Com.Cas. 260 (London Lighterage Clause); *cf.* also *The Galileo* [1915] A.C. 199.

[17] *Cf. Moore v Harris* (1876) 1 App.Cas. 318; *Leech v Glynn & Son* (1890) 6 T.L.R. 306; *Wiener v Wilsons & Furness* (1910) 15 Com. Cas. 294; *Crawford & Law v Allan Line S.S. Co* [1912] A.C. 130; and seen fn.7, above.

[18] *Crawford & Law v Allan Line S.S. Co*, above.

Note 1: In cases where transhipment takes place it will not always be clear whether the parties have entered into a single contract for through transportation from a place or port of loading to a final destination, or whether there are, in fact, two contracts for separate stages of the overall transportation. In *J.I. Macwilliam Co Inc v Mediterranean Shipping Co SA*[19] the cargo was carried from Durban to Felixstowe and then transhipped for carriage to Boston. A single (straight) bill of lading was issued for the voyage to Felixstowe. *Held,* on the facts, that there were 2 separate contracts of carriage. The significance of the distinction was that the cargo was alleged to have been damaged during the voyage from Felixstowe to Boston meaning that (if there were 2 voyages) the port of shipment was Felixstowe and the more generous package limitation of the Hague–Visby Rules applied.[20]

Note 2: Combined transport may arise (and the bill of lading fall to be treated as a combined transport bill) even where there is no or no significant inland transport prior to loading or subsequent to discharge of the cargo. Thus in *East West Corp v DKBS 1912 and AKTS Svendborg*[21] the Court of Appeal held that certain of the relevant bills were, on a proper construction of the boxes completed on the front of the bills, combined transport bills. The significance of this was that the carrier remained liable throughout the period when the goods were under its aegis rather than for the more limited period (subsequent to loading but prior to discharge) which would otherwise have been the case.

Article 181—Application of International Conventions to Combined   A181
Transportation

The application to through bills of lading of the various international conventions governing carriage by sea, road, and air is a matter of some complexity.

The application of the "Hague-Visby Rules" scheduled to the Carriage of Goods by Sea Act 1971 to through bills of lading is discussed in Chapter 20.[22]

The Convention on the Contract for the International Carriage of Goods by Road (the "CMR Convention"), scheduled to the Carriage of Goods by Road Act 1965, applies "to every contract for the carriage of goods by road in vehicles for reward, when the place of taking over of the goods and the place designated for delivery, as specified in the contract, are situated in two different countries, of which at least one" is a party to the Convention.[23]

It is not clear to what extent the CMR Convention applies to the carriage of goods partly by road and partly by sea. Article 2, para.1, makes the following provisions for "roll-on, roll-off" traffic:

---

[19] [2003] 2 Lloyd's Rep. 113; [2002] EWCA Civ 550.
[20] As to which see Chapter 20, below.
[21] [2003] 1 Lloyd's Rep. 239; [2003] EWCA Civ 83.
[22] Below, Chapter 20, p.369 (application to goods after transhipment); pp.381, 390, 395 (application to "received for shipment" bills of lading and combined transport bills of lading); p.384 (application to goods transhipped into lighters); p.392 (time for notice of loss or damage); p.396 (whether a transhipment clause is permitted by the Rules).
[23] Carriage of Goods by Road Act 1965, Sch, Art.1, para.1. The parties to the Convention are set out in the Carriage of Goods by Road (Parties to Convention) Order 1967 SI 1967/1683 as amended by SI 1980 No. 697. The Convention does not apply to traffic between the United Kingdom of Great Britain and Northern Ireland and the Republic of Ireland (Protocol of Signature).

"Where the vehicle containing the goods is carried over part of the journey by sea, rail, inland waterways or air, and . . . the goods are not unloaded from the vehicle, this Convention shall nevertheless apply to the whole of the carriage. Provided that to the extent that it is proved that any loss, damage or delay in delivery of the goods which occurs during carriage by other means of transport was not caused by an act or omission of the carrier by road, but by some event which could only have occurred in the course of and by reason of the carriage by that other means of transport, the liability of the carrier by road shall be determined not by this Convention but in the manner in which the liability of the carrier by the other means of transport would have been determined if a contract for the carriage of goods alone had been made by the sender with the carrier by the other means of transport in accordance with the conditions prescribed by law for the carriage of goods by that means of transport. If, however, there are no such prescribed conditions, the liability of the carrier by road shall be determined by this Convention."

Arguably the CMR Convention is only intended to apply to combined road and sea carriage in the circumstances set out in Art.2, since otherwise it would be in conflict with the Carriage of Goods by Sea Act 1971; but this is by no means clear from the wording and in respect of multi-modal carriage performed partly by air and partly by road it appears that the CMR will in fact apply to the whole carriage regardless of whether the non-road leg was conducted by roll-on roll-off transport.[24] Even when Art.2, para.1 applies, it is doubtful how far the court will go in applying "the Conditions prescribed by law for the carriage of goods by that means of transport". Presumably the United Kingdom Carriage of Goods by Sea Act 1971, will be applied to goods shipped at ports in the United Kingdom; but it is by no means clear to what extent an English court ought to apply the conditions prescribed by any foreign law for such carriage.

Detailed discussion of the provisions of the CMR Convention in so far as they may apply to carriage by sea is outside the scope of this work, but it should be noted that many of the common law rules governing sea-carriage are substantially modified by the CMR Convention, e.g. stoppage in transit (Art.12), lien (Art.13) frustration, abandonment of the voyage, and alternative delivery (Arts 14 to 16), dangerous goods (Art.22), privity of contract and vicarious immunity of servants and sub-contractors (Art.28). The CMR Convention imposes compulsory levels of liability on the carrier (Arts 17 to 29 and Art.41), including a one-year period of limitation (Art.32) and a monetary limit of liability of 25 gold francs per kilogram (Art.23), but these and other limitations of the carrier's liability cannot be relied on if the damage was caused by his wilful misconduct or default (Arts 29 to 32). The Convention provides a code of jurisdiction and procedure for claims (Arts 30 to 33), and provisions for claims against and between successive carriers (Arts 34 to 40).

---

[24] *Quantum Corporation Inc v Plane Trucking Ltd* [2002] 2 Lloyd's Rep. 25; [2002] EWCA Civ 350.

In the case of carriage partly by air and partly by sea, the provisions of the Warsaw Convention as amended at the Hague 1955, scheduled to the Carriage by Air Act 1961, may be applicable to the air carriage. But the provisions of the Warsaw Convention do not in any event apply to the sea carriage,[25] and they are therefore not discussed in this work.[26]

Article 182—Through bills of lading as commercial documents   A182

The increasing use of through bills of lading and similar documents in commerce has given rise to some uncertainty as to how far they possess the same legal characteristics as a conventional bill of lading. For instance, bankers advancing money under documentary credits will wish to know whether a through bill of lading is a transferable document of title capable of being the subject of an effective pledge.[27] The question whether it is a "bill of lading" for the purposes of the Carriage of Goods by Sea Act 1971 is also of importance, for if it is not within the Act, the contract of carriage contained in it is not binding as between the shipowner and the transferee of the through bill of lading[28]; the shipowner may thus find that he is unable to recover freight and demurrage from the transferee, and yet may be exposed to an action in tort[29] for loss of or damage to the goods, in which he will be unable to rely on exceptions in the through bill of lading.[30] Another problem is whether a through bill of lading can validly be tendered under a c.i.f. or f.o.b. contract of sale.

The difficulties spring largely from the fact that neither a through bill of lading nor a combined transport bill of lading nor a bill of lading in the form "received for shipment" is within the custom as found in 1794 in *Lickbarrow v Mason*,[31] by which bills of lading first became judicially recognised as transferable documents of title. But it is submitted that there would now be little difficulty in establishing that all three types of document are by custom treated as transferable documents of title.[32] A "received for shipment" bill of lading is undoubtedly within the Carriage of Goods by Sea Act,[33] and there seems no reason to doubt that the other forms of bill of lading are also within the Act.[34]

---

[25] Carriage by Air Act 1961, Sch, Art.31(1).

[26] The reader is referred to the standard works on the law of carriage by air, e.g. *Shawcross & Beaumont on Air Law*.

[27] The related questions of whether a through bill of lading or similar document is a "document of title" for the purposes of the Factors Acts and the Sale of Goods Act 1979, are outside the scope of this work. But see the *Note* following Art.68 in the 17th edn of this work.

[28] A new contract on the terms of the bill of lading may, however, be inferred where the transferee presents it and demands delivery of the goods under it: see Art.17.

[29] See Art.121.

[30] He may be able to rely on the doctrine of bailment on terms: *K.H. Enterprise (Cargo Owners) v Pioneer Container (Owners)* [1994] 1 Lloyd's Rep. 593 (PC).

[31] (1794) 5 T.R. 683.

[32] So held in relation to "received for shipment" bills of lading in *The Malborough Hill* [1921] 1 A.C. 444 (Privy Council): doubted in *Diamond Alkali v Bourgeois* [1921] 3 K.B. 443 (obiter) by McCardie J. The Privy Council was apparently prepared to take judicial notice of the custom, whereas McCardie J. was not. See also *Kum v Wah Tat Bank Ltd* [1971] 1 Lloyd's Rep. 439 (Privy Council) in which a custom rendering a mate's receipt a negotiable document of title was held inconsistent with the express terms of the receipt.

[33] s.1(2)(b).

[34] See the Report of the Law Commissions, para.2.49.

The inclusion of a clause giving the shipowner liberty to tranship the goods or to carry them in a substitute ship would not, it seems, prevent the document being a document of title and a "bill of lading" within the Act, at least where the shipowner remains responsible for the carriage of the goods even in the event of transhipment or substitution.[35] But it is less certain that a bill of lading providing that in the event of transhipment the shipowner accepts no responsibility beyond that of a forwarding agent would be a document of title or within the Act. Such a document would not be a good tender under a c.i.f. contract[36] unless it was the usual or only available form in the trade.[37]

Unless a bill of lading in the form "received for shipment" is the usual form in the trade, it is not, in the absence of agreement, a good tender under a c.i.f. or f.o.b. contract.[38] The defect is commonly remedied by stamping on the bill of lading the words "shipped on board" together with the date, the name of the vessel and the port of loading.[39] Even where a "received for shipment" bill of lading is a good tender the goods must in fact have been shipped within the contract period.[40]

A through bill of lading may by agreement or usage be considered a good tender under a c.i.f. contract; but a c.i.f. contract providing for tender of a through bill of lading is not satisfied by the tender of an "ocean bill of lading" issued by a carrier to whom the goods have been transhipped at an intermediate port[41] unless there is a further agreement or usage permitting such tender.[42]

A "house bill of lading" issued by a forwarding agent acting solely in the capacity of an agent to arrange carriage is not a bill of lading at all,[43] but at most a receipt for the goods coupled with an authority to enter into a contract of carriage on behalf of the shipper. It is not a document of title, nor within the Carriage of Goods by Sea Act 1992,[44] and it is unlikely that it would ever be regarded as a good tender under a c.i.f. contract.

A combined transport bill of lading providing for carriage partly by sea and partly by some other means of transport is not a valid tender under a c.i.f. contract, in the absence of agreement or usage to that effect; if the express terms

---

[35] *The Marlborough Hill*, above.
[36] *Holland Colombo Trading Society Ltd v Segu Mohamed Khaja Alawdeen* (1954) 2 Lloyd's Rep. 45 (Privy Council); *cf.* also *Fischel & Co v Spencer* (1922) 12 Ll.L.R. 36 which, however, turned on the particular finding of fact by the arbitrators.
[37] *Plaimar Ltd v Waters Trading Co Ltd* (1945) 72 C.L.R. 304 (High Court of Australia).
[38] *Diamond Alkali v Bourgeois* [1921] 3 K.B. 443; *Yelo v S.M. Machado & Co Ltd* [1952] 1 Lloyd's Rep. 183; but *cf. The Marlborough Hill*, above. In *Weis v Produce Brokers Co* (1921) 7 Ll.L.R. 211 the arbitrators found as a fact that the bill of lading was the usual form for the named vessel: *cf.* also *United Baltic Corp v Burgett & Newsam* (1921) 8 Ll.L.R. 190: *Suzuki & Co v Burgette and Newsam* (1922) 10 Ll.L.R. 223; *Kwei Tek Chao v British Traders and Shippers* [1954] 1 Lloyd's Rep. 16 at p.24.
[39] *Cf.* Art.III, r.7 of the Hague–Visby Rules, below, Chapter 20.
[40] *Suzuki & Co v Burgett & Newsam* (1922) 10 Ll.L.R. 223.
[41] *Hansson v Hamel & Horley Ltd.* [1922] 2 A.C. 36; *Landauer & Co v Craven Speeding Bros* [1912] 2 K.B. 94, explaining *Cox, McEuen & Co v Malcolm & Co* [1912] 2 K.B. 107.
[42] *N.V. Arnold Otto Meyer v Aune* [1939] 3 All E.R. 168.
[43] *A. Gagniere & Co v Eastern Co of Warehouses* (1921) 7 Ll.L.R. 188, affirmed (CA) (1921) 8 Ll.L.R. 365; see also *Emilio Clot v Compagnie Commerciale du Nord* (1921) 8 Ll.L.R. 380. *Carrington Slipways Pty Ltd v Patrick Operations Pty Ltd* (1991) 24 N.S.W.L.R. 745.
[44] It is not, it is submitted, a sea waybill within the Act because the receipt is not given by or on behalf of the person with whom the contract of carriage is made.

of the contract provide for carriage by sea, evidence of such a usage will not be admitted.[45] If there is no agreed or customary or usual route at the time of shipment, that route must be chosen which is reasonable.[46]

Article 183—Containers[47]   A183

The use of containers as a method of carrying goods is common, particularly in the field of combined transportation.[48] The container is essentially no more than a sophisticated form of package, and it is thought that where the goods have been stowed in the container by the shipper, the carrier would be entitled to rely on a defence of "inherent vice" or "insufficiency of packing" if the goods were damaged because of some defect in the container or in the manner of stowage.[49] Where, however, the carrier has supplied the container to the shipper, the carrier has the liability of a hirer (subject to appropriate exceptions in the contract of carriage), and warrants that the container is as fit for the purpose for which it is hired as reasonable care and skill can make it.[50] The warranty is not excluded by the fact that the shipper has been given an opportunity to examine the container.[51] A container packed by the shipper is usually acknowledged as "one container in apparent good order and condition said to contain [the contents] as declared by the shipper". An acknowledgement in this form does not, it is thought, bind the carrier to any representation as to the condition or description of the contents so as to constitute an estoppel in favour of an indorsee of the bill of lading.[52] It may, however, amount to a sufficient enumeration of packages or units within the container to mean that the amount of the carrier's package limitation is fixed by reference to the number of packages or units so stated.[53]

---

[45] *L Sutro & Co and Heilbut, Symons & Co* [1917] 2 K.B. 348 as explained in *Tsakiroglou & Co Ltd v Noblee Thorl GmbH* [1962] A.C. 93.

[46] *Tsakiroglou & Co Ltd v. Noblee Thorl GmbH,* above.

[47] The general principles set out in this Article will apply equally to pallets, flats, transportable tanks, etc. See para.B.12, below, for a discussion of limitation of liability under Art.IV, r.5 of the Hague–Visby Rules as it applies to containers.

[48] See Art.27 (forwarding agents) for a discussion of "groupage" or "consolidation" business.

[49] See Art.112 above, and Art.IV, rule 2 of the Hague–Visby Rules, below; and *cf.* Art.53 as to the position if the defect in the container renders the goods dangerous.

[50] *Cf. Hyman v Nye* (1881) 6 Q.B.D. 685. See also ss.6–10 of the Supply of Goods and Services Act 1982.

[51] *Cf. Jones v Page* (1867) 15 L.T. 619.

[52] See Art.57 for a discussion of estoppels based on representations in bills of lading.

[53] This would appear to be the position under the Hague–Visby Rules: *El Greco (Australia) Pty Ltd v Mediterranean Shipping Co SA* [2004] 2 Lloyd's Rep. 537; [2004] FCAFC 202; *sed quaere* under the Hague Rules: *The River Gurara* [1998] 1 Lloyd's Rep. 225.

CHAPTER 18

LIEN

A184   **Article 184—Kinds of Lien**

A SHIPOWNER may have a lien on goods carried for charges incurred in carrying them:

(1) at common law; or

(2) by express agreement.[1]

By common law he has a lien for:

(i) freight[2];

(ii) general average contributions[3];

(iii) expenses incurred by the shipowner or master in protecting and preserving the goods.[4]

There are possessory liens depending on the possession of the goods.

A possessory lien does not arise whether at common law or, it is submitted, by express agreement if possession of the goods was unlawful at the time at which the lien is said to have attached.[5] If, therefore, a charterer or shipper without express, implied or ostensible authority of the owner, wishes to ship goods under charter or bill of lading, it would seem that the shipowner would not be able to set up his common law lien for freight, on a lien expressly given him by charter or bill of lading, against a claim in detinue by the owner of the goods.[6] *Quaere*, whether this principle would apply in the case of the exercise by a shipowner of a lien for general average contribution, the goods having, *ex hypothesi*, benefited by the general average act.

---

[1] See Art.191. As to other types of lien including maritime liens generally see: Jones, *A Treatise on the Law of Liens, Common Law, Statutory and Maritime*, 2nd edn (2005 reprint); Thomas, *Maritime Liens;* Jackson, *Enforcement of Maritime Claims,* 4th edn (London: Informa, 2005), pp. 459–604.

[2] See Arts 185–189. On a through bill of lading, where part only of the goods are delivered, the lien on the goods delivered for freight may by the terms of the document include freight for carriage on the first stage of the goods lost on the second stage: *The Hibernian* [1907] P. 277 (CA); and see Art.180.

[3] See Arts 143–146.

[4] See Arts 129, 147 and *Hingston v Wendt* (1876) 1 Q.B.D. 367 at pp.372, 373. In that case the plaintiff had given up possession of the goods and so lost his lien, but he recovered on a contract made by the defendant's agent to pay the charges in consideration of the goods being released: *ibid.* p.371.

[5] *Tappenden v Artus* [1964] 2 Q.B. 185.

[6] We know of no case where the principle has been applied to the case of carriage by sea. It may have arisen on the unusual facts of *Finlay v Liverpool and G.W. S.S. Co* (1870) 23 L.T. 161 at p.251. For an excellent discussion of the principles, see *Waugh v Denham* (1865) 16 Ir.C.L.R. 405. See, also, *Story on Bailment*, s.588, and *Parsons on Shipping*, Vol. I, p.180. A common carrier, obliged by law to carry the goods, can maintain his lien for freight against the owner, provided that, when he received the goods for carriage, he did not know that possession of them was unlawful as against the true owner; *Waugh v Denham, above*, and the cases there cited.

Article 185—Common Law Lien for Freight   A185

The common law lien for freight, which is a possessory lien, only exists where the agreed time for payment of freight is contemporaneous with the time of delivery of the goods.[7]

In the absence of express agreement[8] there is, therefore, no lien for:

(1) Advance freight, or freight payable before the delivery of the goods.[9]

(2) Freight agreed to be paid after the delivery of the goods, or not due when the goods are claimed.[10]

Case. C chartered a ship from A, to proceed to L. at 77s. 6d. per ton freight and hire, £250 to be advanced in cash on signing bills of lading and clearing at the custom house, and remainder on delivery at L. Ship to have an absolute lien for freight, dead freight, and demurrage. After the ship was loaded, and before she sailed, C failed, and his trustee disclaimed the charter. A claimed a lien on the cargo for at least the £250. *Held*, that, being advance freight, there was no lien for it by common law or custom, and that the clause in the charter was not enough to give a lien for it as it was not "freight".[11]

Article 186—On what Goods   A186

The common law lien for freight applies to all goods coming to the same consignee on the same voyage for the freight due on all or any part of them,[12] but not to goods on different voyages under different contracts.[13]

Article 187—For what Amount[14]   A187

When, the ship being chartered, the consignee is the charterer or his agent, he will be bound by the lien for freight due under the charter,[15] unless a new contract exonerating him has been made in the bill of lading.[16]

---

[7] See per Brett J. in *Allison v Bristol Marine Insurance Co* (1876) 1 App.Cas. 209 at p.225, explaining *Kirchner v Venus* (1859) 12 Moore P.C. 361 at p.390.

[8] See Art.191

[9] *How v Kirchner* (1857) 11 Moore P.C. 21; *Kirchner v Venus* (1859) 12 Moore P.C. 361; Ex p. *Nyholm, re Child* (1873) 29 L.T. 634; *Nelson v Association for Protection of Wrecked Property* (1874) 43 L.J.C.P. 218; *Tamvaco v Simpson* (1866) L.R. 1 C.P. 363; *Gardner v Trechmann* (1884) 15 Q.B.D. 154. The case of *Gilkison v Middleton* (1857) 2 C.B.(N.S.) 134, adversely criticised in *Kirchner v Venus*, is distinguishable on the ground that a lien for all freight due under the charter was expressly given by the charter; though, as this was not incorporated in the bill of lading, to make consignees for value liable for it seems contrary to such cases as *Fry v Mercantile Bank* (1866) L.R. 1 C.P. 689. In *Neish v Graham* (1857) 8 E. & B. 505, there was no such express lien, and it must be taken as overruled.

[10] *Foster v Colby* (1858) 3 H. & N. 705; *Thompson v Small* (1845) 1 C.B. 328; *Alsager v St Katherine's Docks* (1845) 14 M. & W. 794; *Lucas v Nockells* (1828) 4 Bing. 729; the agreement to receive payment subsequently is treated as a waiver of the lien. See also *Canadian Pacific (Bermuda) Ltd v Lagon Maritime Overseas (The Fort Kipp)* [1985] 2 Lloyd's Rep. 168 in which a stipulation that freight was payable after the completion of discharge precluded the exercise of a contractual lien for freight.

[11] *Ex p. Nyholm, re Child* (1873) 29 L.T. 634.

[12] *Sodergren v Flight* (1796), unreported, cited 6 East 622; *Perez v Alsop* (1862) 3 F. & F. 188.

[13] *Bernal v Pim* (1835) 1 Gale 17.

[14] See Art.169, Amount of Freight.

[15] *McLean v Fleming* (1871) L.R. 2 Sc. & Div. 128 at pp.133, 134; *Kern v Deslandes* (1861) 10 C.B. (N.S.) 205; *Campion v Colvin* (1836) 3 Bing (N.S.) 17; *Small v Moates* (1833) 9 Bing. 574; *Gledstanes v Allen* (1852) 12 C.B. 202. These cases, in view of later law, e.g. *Fry v Mercantile Bank* (1866) L.R. 1 C.P. 689, must be limited strictly to the charterer and persons identical with him in interest, and many dicta in them are now no longer law.

[16] As in *Gullischen v Stewart* (1884) 13 Q.B.D. 317; and suggested by Willes J. in *Pearson v Göschen* (1864) 17 C.B.(N.S.) 353 at p.374. As to new contracts in the bill of lading, see Arts 36, 42; and *Rodocanachi v Milburn* (1886) 18 Q.B.D. 67.

Where the consignee is an indorsee for value of the bill of lading from the charterer, or represents a shipper other than the charterer, whether aware of the charter or not, he will only be bound by the lien for freight contained in the charter, as distinguished from the freight specified in the bill of lading if a clear intention to that effect is shown in the bill of lading.[17] If a shipper ships goods in ignorance of the charter, he can decline to accept bills of lading for them in accordance with the charter but in an unusual form, and can demand his goods back free of expense, the liens in the charter or otherwise not attaching to them.[18]

Case. C chartered a ship from A: "The ship to have a lien on cargo for freight, 70s. per ton . . . to be paid on unloading of the cargo." C shipped goods under a bill of lading: "Freight for the goods payable in L. as per charter", and indorsed the bill of F for value. *Held*, that against F the shipowners had a lien only for the freight due for the goods included in the bill of lading, and not a lien for the whole chartered freight.[19]

A188
Article 188—Lien: how waived

The shipowner's lien for freight may be waived: as by acceptance of a bill for the freight[20]; by making the freight payable after the deliver of the goods[21]; or by delivery without requiring payment, unless such delivery was induced by fraud.[22]

A189
Article 189—Lien: how maintained

The shipowner may do what is reasonable to maintain his lien, e.g. he may bring the goods back from their destination, if the lien is not discharged there.[23] He will not lose his lien by consenting to hold as agent for the consignee,[24] nor by warehousing the goods ashore, in his own, a statutable, or (semble) a hired warehouse.[25] If the discharge of the cargo is delayed by the proper exercise of his lien by the shipowner, he will be entitled to recover demurrage for the delay.[26] A

---

[17] *Pearson v Göschen* (1864) 17 C.B.(N.S.) C.B.(N.S.) 352; *Foster v Colby* (1858) 3 H. & N. 705; *Fry v Mercantile Bank* (1866) L.R. 1 C.P. 689; *Gardner v Trechmann* (1884) 15 Q.B.D. 154; *The Norway* (1864) B. & L. 226; *Red "R." S.S. Co v Allatini* (1909) 14 Com.Cas. 303; affirmed (1910) 15 Com.Cas. 290. See also above, Arts 36, 37. So far as *Gilkison v Middleton* (1857) 2 C.B.(N.S.) 134 is contrary to this, it must be taken as overruled. See Art.185, fn.9.
[18] *Peek v Larsen* (1871) L.R. 12 Eq. 378; *The Stornoway* (1882) 51 L.J. Adm. 27; and Art.33 above. Contrast *Ralli v Paddington* (1900) 5 Com.Cas. 124.
[19] *Fry v Mercantile Bank*, above; *cf. Red "R." S.S. Co v Allatini*, above.
[20] *Tamvaco v Simpson* (1866) L.R. 1 C.P. 363; *Horncastle v Farran* (1820) 3 B. & A. 497.
[21] *Foster v Colby* (1858) 3 H. & N. 705; *The Fort Kipp*, above.
[22] *Semble*, that, as such a delivery would not prevent stoppage *in transitu*, neither would it waive the lien: See 17th edn, Art.71.
[23] *Edwards v Southgate* (1862) 10 W.R. 528; *Cargo ex Argos* (1873) L.R. 5 P.C. 134.
[24] *Allan v Gripper* (1832) 2 C. & J. 218; *Kemp v Falk* (1882) 7 App.Cas. 573 at p.584.
[25] *The Energie* (1875) L.R. 6 P.C. 306; *Mors Le Blanch v. Wilson* (1873) L.R. 8 C.P. 227. See also per Willes J., *Meyerstein v Barber* (1866) L.R. 2 C.P. 38 at p.54. In the latter case he will be able to recover warehouse charges as well as the principal sum in dispute: *Anglo-Polish S.S. Line v Vickers* (1924) 19 Ll.L.R. 121 at p.125. Similarly, the shipowner does not lose his lien by depositing goods in a warehouse, if he is compelled by law to do so; *Wilson v Kymer* (1813) 1 M. & S. 157, at p.160.
[26] *Lyle v Cardiff Corp* (1899) 5 Com.Cas. 87 at p.94. Not so, however, if the exercise of the lien is unreasonable. See *Note 1* to Art.153. *Cf.: Rashtriya Chemicals and Fertilisers Ltd v Huddart Parker Industries Ltd (The Boral Gas)* [1988] 1 Lloyd's Rep. 342. If the lien is not properly exercised (eg because the owner insists on payment of an exhorbitant sum) the owner will be liable in damages: *Gericke Pte Ltd v Nortrans Shipping Pool Pte Ltd (The Hamlet Arabia)* [1998] 1 S.L.R. 489 (Sing.).

lien for hire under a time charter may be validly exercised by remaining off the port of discharge until arrears of hire have been paid.[27]

It is submitted that in the absence of express agreement or statutory powers,[28] the owner or captain has no power to sell goods on which he has a lien to realise the freight due to them, unless the goods, having been abandoned by all persons entitled to them, have become his property.[29]

Lien for General Average: see Art.143.
Lien for Expenditure on Cargo: See Art.129.

Article 190—Liens not supported by Common Law[30]

A190

There is no lien at common law[31]:

(1) for dead freight[32];

(2) to the holders of a bill of exchange drawn against a particular cargo, on such cargo, in the absence of express intention to give such a lien[33];

(3) to the shipowner, for wharfage dues on overside goods[34];

(4) for port charges, though the charterer has agreed to pay them[35];

(5) for demurrage, or damages for detention[36];

(6) on goods shipped on ship's account.[37]

Article 191—Lien by Express Agreement

A191

Where a lien for certain charges is expressly stipulated for, the fact that such lien is inconvenient, or that the lienee is under no contractual obligation to pay the chargee,[38] will be no answer to the express terms of the agreement.[39] But the

---

[27] *Santiren Shipping Ltd v Unimarine (The Chrysovalandou-Dyo)* [1981] 1 Lloyd's Rep. 159.
[28] See, for example, the power of the Court to order a sale of property which is of a perishable nature or which for any other good reason it is desirable to sell quickly under CPR Part 25.1(1)(c)(v); and also the power of the Court to order a sale under s.44 of the Arbitration Act 1996, as to which see, e.g. *Stelios Maritime Ltd v Ibeto Cement Co (The Stelios B)* (2007) 711 L.M.L.N. 2
[29] *Enimont Overseas A.G. v Ro Jugstanrev Zadar (The Olib)* [1991] 2 Lloyd's Rep. 108.
[30] See also Art.185.
[31] As to lien by agreement for some of these things, see Art.191.
[32] *Phillips v Rodie* (1812) 15 East 547. See Art.194.
[33] *Robey v Ollier* (1872) L.R. 7 Ch. 695; *Phelps v Comber* (1885) 29 Ch.D. 813; *Ex p. Dever, re Suse* (1884) 13 Q.B.D. 766; *Frith v Forbes* (1862) 4 De G.F. & J. 409, the one case in which an express intention to give such a lien has been found, has been so doubted, see especially *Phelps v Comber*, above, as to be a very unsafe authority to follow; see *Brown v Kough* (1885) 29 Ch.D. 848.
[34] See Art.152 and *Notes* in the 19th edn; *Bishop v Ware* (1813) 3 Camp. 360. If, however, the goods have been justifiably landed under Art.152, the wharf-owner will have a lien for such wharfage dues.
[35] *Faith v East India Co* (1821) 4 B. & Ald. 630.
[36] *Birley v Gladstone* (1814) 3 M. & S. 205, and see Art.94.
[37] *Swan v Barber* (1879) 5 Ex.D. 130.
[38] *Miramar Maritime Corp v Holborn Oil Trading Co Ltd* [1983] 2 Lloyd's Rep. 319; [1984] A.C. 676 (HL).
[39] *McLean v Fleming* (1871) L.R. 2 Sc. & Div. 128 at p.135. The fact that a clause giving the lien is in the bill of lading is not conclusive that it is part of the contract between the parties: see *Crooks v Allan* (1879) 5 Q.B.D. 38, and Art.33.

agreement for a lien will be limited that for which it is expressly given[40] and must be read subject to the express terms of the charter.[41]

Thus there may be liens by express agreement for:

(1) dead freight[42];

(2) demurrage or damages for detention[43];

(3) advance freight[44];

(4) charterparty freight, as against the holder of the bill of lading[45];

(5) "all charges whatsoever"[46];

(6) "all moneys becoming in any way due to the shipowners under the provisions of the bill of lading";

(7) "all fines, and expenses, or losses by detention of or damage to vessel or cargo, caused by incorrect description of goods, or shipment of dangerous goods without notice";

(8) "all previously unsatisfied freight and charges on other goods due in respect of any shipment by any steamer or steamers of this line from either shipper or consignee, such lien to be made available at shipowner's option by sale otherwise"[47];

(9) "when the goods are carried at a through rate of freight, the inland proportion thereof, together with the other charges of every kind (if any), are due on delivery of the goods to the ocean steamship, and the

---

[40] Thus a lien for "all freights, primages and charges" will not include a lien for interest on freight, even though the bill of lading stipulates for interest on freight: *E. Clemens Horst Co v Norfolk, etc. Co* (1906) 11 Com.Cas. 141. Nor does a lien for "all charges whatsoever" cover a lien for dead freight: *Red. "Superior" v. Dewar & Webb* [1909] 1 K.B. 948; affirmed [1909] 2 K.B. 998 (CA).

[41] *Canadian Pacific (Bermuda) Ltd v Logan Maritime Overseas (The Fort Kipp)* [1985] 2 Lloyd's Rep. 168. See also *Jarl Trä AB v Convoys Ltd* [2003] EWHC 1488 (Comm); [2003] 2 Lloyd's Rep. 459 with regard to the circumstances in which a sub-bailee is entitled to exercise a lien against the cargo-owner.

[42] See Art.196, see also *Red. "Superior" v Dewar & Webb*, above. As to how far there can be a lien for unliquidated damages under the head of dead freight, see *Note* to Art.196.

[43] See Art.93. As to a lien at the port of discharge for demurrage accrued at the port of loading, see *Red. "Superior" v Dewar & Webb* [1909] 2 K.B. 998, distinguishing *Pederson v Lotinga* (1857) 28 L.T.(O.S.) 267, and *Gardner v Trechmann* (1884) 15 Q.B.D. 154. As to how far there can be a lien for unliquidated damages for detention, see Art. 93. See also *Faith Maritime Co Ltd v Feoso (Singapore) Pte Ltd* [2003] 3 S.L.R. 556 (Sing.).

[44] See Art.162. Where a lien is given for advance freight under a time charterparty, under which hire is payable in advance fortnightly, the lien for each instalment cannot be exercised until it falls due: *Wehner v Dene S.S. Co* [1905] 2 K.B. 92.

[45] See Arts 37–39, 169, 187.

[46] *Semble*, is confined to charges specifically mentioned in the charterparty: *Red. "Superior" v Dewar & Webb* [1909] 2 K.B. 998 (CA), reversing on this point Bray J. in the court below. But see *Fidelitas Shipping Co v Exportchleb* [1963] 2 Lloyd's Rep. 113, where Harman L.J. at p.121, thought demurrage was covered by the word "expenses" and Pearson L.J. at p.126, thought it was covered by the word "charges". The clause gave the shipowners a lien for "freight and all other charges and expenses due under the contract of carriage".

[47] See *Whinney v Moss S.S. Co Ltd* (1910) 15 Com.Cas. 114, for a clause even more sweeping than the above. Such a clause does not give a right of lien superior to the right of an unpaid vendor who stops *in transitu: United States Co v G. W. Ry* [1916] 1 A.C. 189.

shipowner or his agent shall have a first lien on the goods in whole or part until payment thereof."[48]

(10) "all sub-freights for any amounts due under this charter".[49]

(11) "lien on the ship for all monies paid in advance and not earned".[50]

Where the charter is for a number of voyages, the question of whether a lien can be exercised on one voyage for sums due in respect of another is a matter of construction.[51]

---

[48] On this clause, in a through bill of lading, see *The Hibernian* [1907] P. 277, and Art.180.
[49] See Art.174; *The Juridical Nature of a Lien on Sub-Freights* [1989] L.M.C.L.Q. 191; *Lien on Sub-Freights* [2002] L.M.C.L.Q. 289.
[50] As to the effect of such a provision, see *Ellerman Lines Ltd v Lancaster Maritime Ltd (The Lancaster)* [1980] 2 Lloyd's Rep. 497.
[51] *Rashtriya Chemicals & Fertilisers Ltd v Huddart Parker Industries Ltd (The Boral Gas)* [1988] 1 Lloyd's Rep. 342.

CHAPTER 19

DAMAGES[1]

A192   **Article 192—Rules of Damages**

Contract. The usual aim of damages for breach of contract is to put the claimant into as good a position as it would have been in if the contract had been performed.[2] This is commonly referred to by academic commentators as the protection of the claimant's expectation interest[3] or performance interest.[4] While damages can be alternatively claimed on the basis of being put into as good a position as if no contract had been made the courts will not thereby knowingly allow a claimant to escape from a bad bargain.[5]

Note. Although the alternative basis is often regarded as the protection of the claimant's reliance interest, the rule against escape from a bad bargain suggests that it may be better viewed as merely an alternative way of protecting the expectation interest under which the claimant has the benefit of a presumption, rebuttable by the defendant, that it would at least have recouped its reliance expenses had the contract been performed.[6]

These aims are subject to certain restrictions, the most important of which is that damages cannot be recovered for loss that is too remote.[7] The test for remoteness in contract is that the loss should be such as may fairly and reasonably be considered either arising naturally, i.e. according to the usual course of things, from such breach of contract itself, or such as may reasonably be supposed to have been in the contemplation of both parties, at the time they made the contract, as the probable result of the breach of it.[8]

---

[1] As to damages for detention of the ship, see Chapter 14, Demurrage.

[2] See, e.g., *Robinson v Harman* (1848) 1 Exch 850, 855; *Monarch S.S. Co v Karlshamns* [1949] A.C. 196, 220 (*Case* 10, Art.51, above); *Czarnikow v Koufos* [1969] 1 A.C. 350, 414; *Ruxley Electronics & Construction Ltd v Forsyth* [1995] 3 W.L.R. 118, 122, 131–132.

[3] This was the terminology first coined by Fuller and Perdue in their seminal article "The Reliance Interest in Contract Damages" (1936–1937) 46 Yale L.J. 52 and 373.

[4] Friedmann, "The Performance Interest in Contract Damages" (1995) 111 L.Q.R. 628.

[5] *C & P Haulage v Middleton* [1983] 3 All E.R. 94; *C.C.C. Films (London) v Impact Quadrant Films Ltd* [1994] 3 All E.R. 298.

[6] *Commonwealth of Australia v Amann Aviation Pty Ltd* (1991) 66 A.J.L.R. 123; Andrew Burrows, *Remedies for Torts and Breach of Contract*, 3rd edn (Oxford: Oxford University Press, 2004) 70–72.

[7] The duty to mitigate and contributory negligence are dealt with in the notes below. Other restrictions on contractual damages include causation (see, e.g. *Monarch Steamship Co Ltd v Karlshamns Oljefabriker (A.B.)* [1949] A.C. 196; *Galoo Ltd v Bright Grahame Murray* [1994] 1 W.L.R. 1360; and that damages for mental distress are recoverable only where an important object of the contract was to obtain mental satisfaction or where the mental distress is directly consequent on physical inconvenience (see, e.g. *Jarvis v Swans Tours Ltd* [1973] Q.B. 233; *Watts v Morrow* [1991] 1 W.L.R. 1421); *Farley v Skinner* [2001] UKHL 49; [2002] 2 A.C. 732.

[8] *Hadley v Baxendale* (1854) 9 Ex. 341 at p.354, per Alderson B.

This classic statement of the law on remoteness in contract, approved and applied in a multitude of cases,[9] has often been treated as laying down two rules, the second beginning with the word "or". The better view, however, is that there is but one rule with two branches, the second dealing with special circumstances, known to both parties at the time of making the contract, without which knowledge the damage caused could not reasonably be considered as having been fairly and reasonably within the contemplation of the parties at that time.[10] It is quite unnecessary, when special circumstances exist to the knowledge of both parties, that the contract should make provision, in the event of a breach, for liability in damages due to such circumstances.[11]

In contrasting the remoteness tests in contract and tort, it has been stressed that the true test in contract is not whether the damage caused was reasonably foreseeable at the date of the breach as the consequence of the breach, but whether the party in breach should reasonably have contemplated that, at the time the contract was made, the damage (or type of damage) suffered[12] was liable to be the result of the breach, or was a serious possibility or a real danger.[13]

An account of profits[14] or restitutionary damages,[15] aimed at a disgorgement of gains made by the breach of contract, may exceptionally be awarded where normal compensatory damages are inadequate. But an account of profits has been

---

[9] See in particular, *Hall v Pim (Junior)* (HL) (1927) 33 Com.Cas. 324; *Banco de Portugal v Waterlow* [1932] A.C. 452; *Monarch S.S. Co v Karlshamns* [1949] A.C. 196 (Case 10, Art.51, above); *Czarnikow v Koufos* [1969] 1 A.C. 350; *Jackson v Royal Bank of Scotland Plc* [2005] UKHL 3; [2005] 1 W.L.R. 377; *Hammond v Bussey* (1887) 20 Q.B.D. 79 was one of the earliest of a long line of cases applying the principle to costs incurred in reasonably defending an action by a third party.

[10] *Czarnikow v Koufos*, above, per Lord Reid at p.385; per Lord Upjohn at pp. 421–422. "These two things, 'arising naturally from' or 'the probable result of' the breach, need not be antithetically treated; they may run into each other and, indeed, be one"; per Lord Shaw in *Hall v Pim (Junior)* above at p.334. See also *Victoria Laundry v Newman Industries* [1949] 2 K.B. 528; *Satef-Huttenes Albertus SpA v Paloma Tercera Shipping Co SA (The Pegase)* [1981] 1 Lloyd's Rep. 175, at p.182; *Kpohraror v Woolwich Building Society* [1996] 4 All E.R. 119; *Transfield Shipping Inc v Mercator Shipping Inc, The Achilleas* [2007] EWCA Civ 901; [2007] 2 Lloyd's Rep. 555.

[11] *Czarnikow v Koufos*, above per Lord Upjohn at p.422, and per Diplock L.J. in the CA [1966] 2 Q.B. 695 at p.728.

[12] For the emphasis on the "type" of damage, see *H. Parsons (Livestock) Ltd v Uttley Ingham & Co Ltd* [1978] Q.B. 791; *Transworld Oil Ltd v North Bay Shipping Corp (The Rio Claro)* [1987] 2 Lloyd's Rep. 173. *Brown v K.M.R. Services Ltd* [1995] 4 All E.R. 598.

[13] [1969] 1 A.C. 350 per Lord Reid at p. 388; Lord Morris at p.406; Lord Hodson at p.410 and Lords Pearce and Upjohn at pp.414 and 425. The phrase "on the cards" favoured by Asquith L.J. in delivering the judgment of the CA in *Victoria Laundry v Newman Industries* [1949] 2 K.B. 528 was disapproved by all five Law Lords in *Czarnikow v Koufos*, above. The former case, however, contains "a most valuable analysis of the rule": per Lord Morris [1969] 1 A.C. 350 at p.399; See, also, *Aruna Mills v Gobindram* [1968] 1 Q.B. 655 at p.668; *Allan Peters v Brocks Alarm* [1968] 1 Lloyd's Rep. 387 at p.392; *Parsons (Livestock) Ltd v Uttley Ingham and Co Ltd* [1978] Q.B. 791; *Satef-Huttenes Albertus SpA v Paloma Tercera Shipping Co SA (The Pegase)* [1981] 1 Lloyd's Rep. 175; *Islamic Republic of Iran Shipping Lines v Ierax Shipping Co of Panama (The Forum Craftsman)* [1991] 1 Lloyd's Rep. 81.

[14] *Attorney General v Blake* [2001] 1 A.C. 268; *Esso Petroleum Co Ltd v Niad* [2001] All E.R. (D) 324.

[15] *Wrotham Park Estate Co Ltd v Parkside Homes Ltd* [1974] 1 W.L.R. 798; *Experience Hendrix LLC v PPX Enterprises Inc* [2003] EWCA Civ 323; [2003] 1 All E.R. (Comm) 830. There is on-going controversy as to whether these damages are better viewed as compensatory (compensating for "loss of an opportunity to bargain") rather than restitutionary. Controversially, Chadwick L.J. in *WWF-World Wide Fund for Nature v World Wrestling Federation Enterntainment Inc* [2007] EWCA Civ 286; [2008] 1 W.L.R. 445, at [59] described both "damages on the *Wrotham Park* basis" and an account of profits as compensatory.

refused by arbitrators for the withdrawal, and profitable use, of a ship in breach of a charterparty.[16]

Exemplary damages cannot be awarded for breach of contract.[17]

Tort. The usual aim of damages in tort is to put the claimant into as good a position as it would have been in if the tort had not been committed.[18] And, although the result will often be the same, the general rule of remoteness in tort is different from that in contract and imposes a wider liability. The defendant will be liable for any type of damage which is reasonably foreseeable as liable to happen even in the most unusual case, unless the risk is so small that a reasonable man would in the whole circumstances feel justified in neglecting it.[19] Other differences between the rules on damages in tort and contract include that, in contrast to contract, exemplary damages[20] can sometimes be awarded for a tort. As with breach of contract, an account of profits and restitutionary damages can sometimes be awarded for a tort.[21]

Note 1. Penalty provisions. In many charters there appears a clause in some such terms as "Penalty for non-performance of this agreement estimated amount of freight." Such a clause is inoperative, and is neglected by the court.[22] It is also well-established, although on general principles[23] less obvious, that it is equally a penalty clause and inoperative (rather than being a valid limitation clause) if in the form, "Penalty for non-performance of this agreement proved damages not exceeding the estimated amount of freight."[24] In past editions of this work, it has been said to be "a mystery why the clause survives, except upon the supposition that chartering brokers regard it as a piece of sacred ritual".[25]

---

[16] *AB Corp v CD Company, The Sine Nomine* [2002] 1 Lloyd's Rep. 805 noted by Beatson, "Courts, Arbitrators and Restitutionary Liability for Breach of Contract" (2002) 118 L.Q.R. 377.

[17] *Addis v Gramophone Co Ltd* [1909] A.C. 488; *Perera v Vandiyar* [1953] 1 W.L.R. 672. For criticism see Cunnington, "Should Punitive Damages be Part of the Judicial Arsenal in Contract Cases?" (2006) 26 Legal Studies 369.

[18] *Livingstone v Rawyards Coal Co* (1880) 5 App. Cas. 25 at p.39; *Shearman v Folland* [1950] 2 K.B. 43 at p.49; *British Transport Commission v Gourley* [1956] A.C. 185 at p.187; *Banques Bruxelles Lambert SA v Eagle Star Insurance Co Ltd* [1995] Q.B. 375, at pp.401–403.

[19] *Overseas Tankship (UK) v Morts Dock & Engineering Co (The Wagon Mound)* [1961] A.C. 388; *Czarnikow v Koufos*, above, per Lord Reid at pp.385–387; Lord Hodson at p.411; Lord Pearce at p.413 and Lord Upjohn at p.422. The test in tort used to be whether the damage claimed, however, unforeseeable, was the direct physical consequence of the tortious act: *Polemis, Re* [1921] 3 K.B. 560 (CA). Since the last case was disapproved by the P.C. in *The Wagon Mound* it has been treated as no longer stating English or Scots law: *Doughty v Turner* [1964] 1 Q.B. 518 (CA); *Hughes v Lord Advocate* [1963] A.C. 837.

[20] *Rookes v Barnard* [1964] A.C. 1129; *Kuddus v Chief Constable of Leicestershire Constabulary* [2001] UKHL 29; [2002] 2 A.C. 122.

[21] See, e.g., *Penarth Dock Engineering Co Ltd v Pounds* [1963] 1 Lloyd's Rep. 359; *Ministry of Defence v Ashman* [1993] E.G. 144 ; *Jaggard v Sawyer* [1995] 1 W.L.R. 269; *Halifax Building Society v Thomas* [1996] 2 W.L.R. 63. An account of profits is a standard remedy for the intellectual property torts, such as breach of copyright and patent infringement. See generally, Goff and Jones, *The Law of Restitution* (7th edn, 2007) ch. 36.

[22] *Harrison v Wright* (1811) 13 East 343; *Godard v Gray* (1870) L.R. 6 Q.B. 139; *Ströms Bruks v Hutchinson* (1904) 6 Fraser 486; [1905] A.C. 515.

[23] See Treitel, *The Law of Contract* (12th edn, 2007) paras 20–121 to 20–128; Burrows, *Remedies for Torts and Breach of Contract* (3rd edn, 2004) pp.440–451.

[24] *Wall v Rederiaktiebolaget Luggude* [1915] 3 K.B. 66; *Watts v Mitsui* [1917] A.C. 227. In *Leeds Shipping Co v Société Française Bunge* [1957] 2 Lloyd's Rep. 153; affirmed [1958] 2 Lloyd's Rep. 127 (CA) in which the clause appeared in this form with "indemnity" substituted for "penalty", Pearson J. held that it was inoperative both on the reasoning of the two cases cited and also because "non-performance" did not include "mis-performance" (and the breach in question was of the latter type). The CA limited their decision to the second ground and left open the question whether the clause might be effective in the case of a refusal or failure to take any step to perform a charter.

[25] See 19th edn at p.394.

Note 2. Interest. By s.35A of the Supreme Court Act 1981, in proceedings before the High Court for the recovery of a debt or damages there may be included in any sum for which judgment is given simple interest at such rate as the court thinks fit or as rules of court may provide, on all or any part of the debt or damages in respect of which judgment is given, or payment is made before judgment, for all or any part of the period between the date when the cause of action arose and (a) in the case of any sum paid before judgment, the date of the payment; and (b) in the case of the sum for which judgment is given the date of the judgment. Section 49 of the Arbitration Act 1996 contains similar provisions relating to sums claimed in arbitration but in significant contrast to the Supreme Court Act 1981 empowers the arbitral tribunal to award compound as well as simple interest.

By the Late Payment of Commercial Debts (Interest) Act 1998 a creditor is given a right to simple interest after thirty days on an unpaid debt. By s.2 the Act applies to contracts for the supply of goods or services (other than consumer credit agreements or contracts intended to operate by way of security) where the purchaser and supplier are each acting in the course of a business. The rate of interest has been fixed at the base rate plus 8 per cent. By s.5 the interest may be remitted, wholly or in part, because of the creditor's conduct.

The above statutory provisions on interest have been necessary because, traditionally, damages could not be awarded for the general loss of use of money consequent on late payment.[26] In contrast, other losses caused by not receiving money due or receiving it late, such as interest charges paid on taking out a loan, have been recoverable as special damages where not too remote within the second "rule" in *Hadley v Baxendale*.[27] In *Sempra Metals Ltd v Inland Revenue Commissioners*[28] the House of Lords, albeit in what were technically obiter dicta, reasoned that the traditional rule should be departed from so that damages for loss of interest, including compound interest, can be awarded where proved and subject to the normal limitations of remoteness and the duty to mitigate.

Note 3. Conversion of currency. Until 1975, it was the law that an English court could only give judgment in sterling.[29] In that year the House of Lords departed from that rule so that it became possible to obtain judgment in a foreign currency and to enforce it by converting that currency into sterling at the rate current at the date of the application to enforce.[30]

The Court will normally consider the terms of the contract to see if they evidence the intention of the parties that damages should be awarded in a particular currency. If not, damages will be awarded in the currency in which the claimant's loss was felt or which

---

[26] *London, Chatham and Dover Rly Co v South Eastern Rly* [893] A.C. 429; *President of India v La Pintada Compania Navigacion SA* [1985] 1 A.C. 104. By the practice of the Admiralty Court interest on the amount of damages from the time when the claim arose is allowed: see *The Gertrude* (1887) 12 P.D. 204, affirmed (1888) 13 P.D. 105. *Cf. Smith v Kirby* (1875) 1 Q.B.D. 131; *The Kong Magnus* [1891] P. 223.

[27] *Wadsworth v Lydall* [1981] 1 W.L.R. 598; *President of India v La Pintada Compania Navigacion SA* [1985] 1 A.C. 104, 125–127. *Cf. President of India v Lips Maritime Corp (The Lips)* [1988] A.C. 395 (currency exchange losses).

[28] [2007] UKHL 34; [2007] 3 W.L.R. 354.

[29] In *United Railways of Havana, etc., Re* [1961] A.C. 1007.

[30] *Miliangos v Frank (Textiles) Ltd* [1976] A.C. 443; *Services Europe Atlantique Sud v Stockholms Rederiaktiebolag S.V.E.A. (The Folias and The Despina R)* [1979] A.C. 685. See also, e.g., *President of India v Taygetos Shipping Co SA (The Agenor)* [1985] 1 Lloyd's Rep. 155 (*cf. President of India v Lips Maritime Corp* [1985] 2 Lloyd's Rep. 180 at pp.187–188 per Staughton J., [1988] A.C. 395, at p.426, HL); *Société Française Bunge SA v Belcan N.V. (The Federal Huron)* [1985] 3 All E.R. 378; *Metaalhandel J.A. Magnus B.V. v Ardfields Transport Ltd* [1988] 1 Lloyd's Rep. 197; *A-G of the Republic of Ghana v Texaco Overseas Tankships Ltd (The Texaco Melbourne)* [1994] 1 Lloyd's Rep. 473.

most truly expresses it.[31] Where goods are delivered in a damaged condition, this will prima facie be the currency at the place of discharge.[32]

Note 4. Duty to mitigate. A claimant is under a duty[33] to mitigate its loss: that is damages will not be awarded for losses that it could reasonably have avoided.[34]

So, where a charterer refuses to load, the shipowner's measure of damages is the loss of profit on the charter (i.e. the freight to be earned less expense of earning it), against which the shipowner must give credit for what profit he can earn by a substituted employment of the ship just as a servant's damages for wrongful dismissal are the wages he would have earned under the broken contract less what he can earn elsewhere by being set free.[35] And it can be, and has been, said that he must mitigate the damages by accepting such substituted employment.[36]

Another example of the duty to mitigate loss is seen in the principle that an owner cannot claim damages for detention of his ship, if by taking a certain reasonable course he could have avoided such detention.[37] So also in *Weir v Dobell*,[38] if the claimants had not cancelled the head charterparty, and had had to load the ship at the market rate of 17s., the defendants would no doubt have been able to contend that the claimants ought to have acted reasonably, and by such cancellation of the head charterparty, have reduced the damages from 11s. 6d. to 7s. 6d. a ton. But the duty to mitigate does not oblige the party not in default to take any action which would seriously damage his commercial reputation.[39]

Some interesting questions concerning the duty to mitigate arise in the context of a repudiatory breach of contract. These require a little analysis.

A. A repudiatory breach of contract arises[40]: (i) when at the time due for performance by him one party fails to perform his part; or (ii) when before the time for his performance one party announces that he is not going to perform *and* the other party accepts such announcement as a repudiation. In the latter case until such acceptance by the other party there is no breach, and, failing such acceptance, there will be no breach until at the due time for performance a breach arises under (i). The threat to repudiate has no effect on the contract until either it is accepted by the other party or is acted on at the time of performance.[41] It follows that at any time before such acceptance the party who has so

---

[31] *The Folias* above; *A.G. of Republic of Ghana & Ghana National Petroleum Corp v Texaco Overseas Tankships Ltd (The Texaco Melbourne)*, above, noted by Knott, "The Currency of Damages in Contract" [1994] L.M.C.L.Q. 311.

[32] *Empresa Cubana Importadora de Alimentos v Octavier Shipping Co SA (The Kefalonia Wind)* [1986] 1 Lloyd's Rep. 273.

[33] As to this so-called "duty" see *Sotiros Shipping Inc v Shmeiet Solholt (The Solholt)* [1983] 1 Lloyd's Rep. 605.

[34] *British Westinghouse Electric v Underground Electric Railways Co of London Ltd* [1912] A.C. 673.

[35] See *Wallems Rederi A/S v Muller & Co* [1927] 2 K.B. 99, where the master delayed on the voyage to take in other cargo in mitigation of the shipowner's claim for dead freight.

[36] *Cf. Harries v Edmonds* (1845) 1 C. & K. 686; *Bradford v Williams* (1872) L.R. 7 Exch. 259. In *Smith v M'Guire* (1858) 3 H. & N. 554, Martin B., at p.567, suggests a doubt whether the shipowner is bound to find substituted employment for his ship, or to give credit for what he could earn on such substituted employment. This cannot be correct. Of course, the shipowner need not employ his ship unless he likes, just as a servant wrongfully dismissed may take a holiday if he likes. But if the charterer refuses to load under a charter on which the shipowner would earn £1,000, and, freight having risen when he refuses, the shipowner could at once get a cargo for the same voyage on which he would earn £1,200, clearly the shipowner's damages are only nominal, just as would be those of a wrongly dismissed servant suing for £100 as six months' salary, if it be shown that instead of taking a holiday he could have earned £120 in the same period.

[37] See *Note* 2 to Art.154.

[38] [1916] 1 K.B. 722, cited as *Case 2*, Art.193.

[39] *James Finlay & Co v Kwik Hoo Tong* [1929] 1 K.B. 400.

[40] In Sir William Anson's phrase, there is "a discharge of contract by breach."

[41] *Cf. Avery v Bowden* (1855) 6 E. & B. 953; *Heyman v Darwins* [1942] A.C. 356 at p.361. In *Howard v Pickford Tool Co* [1951] 1 K.B. 417 at p.420, Asquith L.J. said that "An unaccepted repudiation is a thing writ in water and of no value to anybody: it confers no legal rights of any sort or kind."

threatened may withdraw his repudiation and be in the same position as if he had never threatened at all.[42]

B. When there is a breach of contract by one party the damages of the other party are what he loses by the non-performance upon the due date of performance, i.e. in nearly all commercial cases nowadays, the difference between the contract price or rate and the market price or rate at the date when there should have been performance. But in the case of a breach before the due date of performance (by the acceptance of a repudiation under A (ii) above) there are two means of estimating this difference of prices or rates at the due date of performance., i.e. (i) by ascertaining at the date of the breach what are the forward prices or rates of the market for the future date of performance, and (ii) by waiting until the due date of performance and then ascertaining the spot market rates or prices.

It is conceived that, in cases in which "mitigation of damages" has been discussed, there has not been drawn a sufficiently clear distinction between two quite different questions that arise on the foregoing considerations.[43] And these are: First, when one party announces his intention to fail in future performance, is it in any case the duty of the other party to accept such repudiation and so create a breach, or has he an unfettered right, by refusing to accept, to postpone any breach until the due date for performance? Secondly, when a breach has occurred before the due date for performance (by acceptance of a repudiation), is the party claiming damages bound, or entitled, to estimate them on the basis of the forward market rates or prices for the future date of performance that are ruling at the date of the breach, or is he bound, or entitled, to wait and estimate them on the basis of spot rates or prices at the due date for performance? If he sues immediately on the breach occurring he can, of course, on the latter alternative, calculate, if at all, only on a forecast.

The answer to the first question is not as clear now as it once was. The traditional view was that the other party was never bound to accept a repudiation made before the date of performance, and so create a breach; rather, in every case, by refusing such acceptance, he could postpone any breach until the time due for performance.[44] Thus, the owner, or captain, or charterer, was not bound to accept another offer inconsistent with the charter before there had been a final breach of the charter by the charterer or shipowner, accepted by himself.[45] This principle was strikingly exemplified by *White and Carter (Councils) Ltd v McGregor*.[46] The pursuer, an advertising contractor, accepted an order from the defender's representative to display advertisements for three years. On the same day the defender asked him to cancel the contract, on the ground that the representative had made a mistake. The pursuer refused and displayed the advertisements for the full three years. The House of Lords held (by a majority of three to two) that the pursuer was entitled to recover the full contract price, and was not obliged to accept the defender's repudiation and sue for damages. The majority differed on the question whether the court had an

---

[42] *Fercometal S.A.R.L. v MSC Mediterranean Shipping Co SA (The Simona)* [1987] 2 Lloyd's Rep. 236; [1988] 2 Lloyd's Rep. 199 (CA); [1988] A.C. 788 (HL) distinguishing *Braithwaite v Foreign Hardwood Co* [1905] 2 K.B. 543. An unaccepted repudiation may nevertheless amount to a waiver excusing the performance by the other party of what would otherwise be a condition precedent; *Sinason-Teicher v Oilcakes and Oilseeds Trading Co* [1954] 1 W.L.R. 935; *Etablissements Chainbaux S.A.R.L. v Harbormaster* [1955] 1 Lloyd's Rep. 303.

[43] In *Michael v Hart* [1902] 1 K.B. 482, Collins M.R. discusses the first question at p.490, and goes on to the second question at p.491.

[44] *Frost v Knight* (1872) L.R. 7 Exch. 111; *Brown v Muller* (1872) L.R. 7 Exch. 319; *Hudson v Hill* (1874) 43 L.J.C.P. 273; *Tredegar Co v Hawthorn* (1902) 18 T.L.R. 716; *Michael v Hart* [1902] 1 K.B. 482. If, or so far as, it involves the contrary, *Wilson v Hicks* (1857) 26 L.J.Exch. 242, is wrong: *cf. Payzu v Saunders* [1919] 2 K.B. 581.

[45] *Harries v Edmonds* (1845) 1 C. & K. 686; *Hudson v Hill* (1874) 43 L.J.C.P. 273.

[46] [1962] A.C. 413. See also dicta of Lord Roskill in *Tor Line v Alltrans Group of Canada (The T.F.L. Prosperity)* [1984] 1 Lloyd's Rep. 123, at p.130: "It is trite law that an innocent party is not obliged to rescind [by accepting a repudiatory breach]". For the application of *White and Carter* to the common situation of a tenant giving up an unexpired lease, see *Reichman v Beveridge* [2006] EWCA Civ 1659.

equitable jurisdiction to relieve a defendant where the claimant had no legitimate financial or other interest in performing the contract rather than accepting damages. Lord Reid considered that there might be such a jurisdiction in appropriate circumstances although no such circumstances existed in the case before the court. Lord Hodson (with whom Lord Tucker agreed) expressed the view that equity would not intervene to assist the defendant in matters of this nature. It may be noted that the actual decision in this case was concerned with Scots law, although it was stated (*semble obiter*) that English law was the same. In practice the principle of this case will not assist the innocent party unless (i) he can obtain specific performance of the contract[47] or (ii) he can earn the remuneration due to him under the contract without the co-operation of the party who has repudiated the contract.[48]

However, in *Attica Sea Carriers Corp v Ferrostaal Poseidon Bulk Reederei (The Puerto Buitrago)*[49] the Court of Appeal distinguished *White and Carter*. On the assumption that the charterers, under a demise charterparty, were bound to repair the ship before redelivery it was held that, following repudiation by the charterers, the owners should have taken redelivery and were not entitled to insist on holding the contract open and receiving the agreed hire until the ship was repaired. But the facts were extreme in that the repairs would cost four times as much as the difference in value between the repaired and the unrepaired ship. This made the claimants' refusal to accept the repudiation particularly unreasonable. In contrast in *Gator Shipping Corp v Trans-Asiatic Oil A/S (The Odenfeld)*[50] Kerr J. applied *White and Carter* in holding that the owners of a ship had been entitled to refuse to accept a repudiation of the charterparty by the charterers. According to Kerr J. it was only on extreme facts, as in *Attica Sea Carriers*, that the principle of *White and Carter* did not apply. In a statement resembling Lord Reid's in *White and Carter* he said, "It follows that any fetter on the innocent party's right of election whether or not to accept a repudiation will only be applied in extreme cases, *viz.* where damages would be an adequate remedy and where an election to keep the contract alive would be wholly unreasonable."[51]

Lloyd J. considered the question again in *Clea Shipping Corp v Bulk Oil International Ltd (The Alaskan Trader)*.[52] After a review of the authorities, he said the following: "Whether one takes Lord Reid's language which was adopted by Orr and Browne L.JJ. in *The Puerto Buitrago*, or Lord Denning M.R.'s language in that case ('in all reason') or Kerr J.'s language in *The Odenfeld* ('wholly unreasonable . . . ') there comes a point at which the court will cease, on general equitable principles, to allow the innocent party to enforce his contract according to its strict legal terms. How one defines that point is obviously a matter of some difficulty for it involves drawing a line between conduct which is merely unreasonable . . . and conduct which is *wholly* unreasonable . . . But however difficult it is to define the point, that there *is* such a point seems to me to have been accepted."[53] In applying that approach, Lloyd J. in effect departed from *White and Carter* because, although the facts were in no sense extreme, he upheld the arbitrator's decision

---

[47] The courts will rarely, if ever, grant specific performance of the contract of affreightment: *De Mattos v Gibson* (1858) 4 De G. & J. 276; *The Scaptrade* [1983] 2 A.C. 694. The courts have power to declare that the contract is still in force, but if the wrongdoer chooses to ignore a declaratory order it cannot be enforced by specific performance. *Cf. LauritzenCool AB v Lady Navigation Inc* [2005] EWCA Civ 579; [2005] 1 W.L.R. 3686 (injunction granted to restrain breach by the shipowners of a time charterparty).
[48] *Hounslow London B.C. v Twickenham Garden Developments Ltd* [1971] Ch. 233; *Decro-Wall SA v Marketing Ltd* [1971] 1 W.L.R. 361 at pp.370, 375, 381.
[49] [1976] 1 Lloyd's Rep. 250.
[50] [1978] 2 Lloyd's Rep. 357.
[51] *ibid.* at p.374.
[52] [1983] 2 Lloyd's Rep. 645.
[53] *ibid.* at p.651.

that the relevant point had been reached so that the owners should have accepted the charterers' repudiation.

In another charterparty case, *Ocean Marine Navigation Ltd v Koch Carbon Inc (The Dynamic)*,[54] Simon J., in remitting the case back to the arbitrator, summarised the *White and Carter v McGregor* line of cases as follows: "These cases establish the following exception to the general rule that the innocent party has an option whether or not to accept a repudiation: (i) The burden is on the *contract-breaker* to show that the innocent party has no legitimate interest in performing the contract rather than claiming damages. (ii) The burden is not discharged merely by showing that the benefit to the other party is small in comparison to the loss to the contract-breaker. (iii) The exception to the general rule applies only in extreme cases: where damages would be an adequate remedy and where an election to keep the contract alive would be unreasonable."

The answer to the second question above is also not free from difficulties. In *Brown v Muller*[55] the damages were fixed at the dates for performance and not at forward prices ruling at the date of the breach, and it was said that the claimant was not in any case bound to adopt the latter alternative. In *Roper v Johnson*,[56] the damages were again fixed on prices at the dates for performance, but it was said that, if that were the reasonable course to adopt, the claimant ought to "mitigate the damages" by ascertaining them on prices at the date of the breach. In *Roth v Tayssen*[57] damages were claimed, as in the two previous cases, on prices at the date for performance. But it was held that the claimant, if he had acted reasonably, would have fixed them upon prices at the date of the breach, and that he could only claim them on the latter basis. Though the point did not arise, the principle of this last case was approved in *Nickoll v Ashton*.[58] The conclusion seems to be that the claimant must act reasonably and assess his damages (or "mitigate" his damages by assessing them) on whichever basis results in the smaller amount. Theoretically, of course, this involves him in the duty of forecast or prophecy at the date of the breach, and inasmuch as "the market" may be supposed to have at least the same power of successful prophecy it would seem to be reasonable, in any case, to fix an amount of damages on forward prices at the date of the breach. For if prices by the date for performance have become more favourable to the party who has broken the contract, that can only be because the forecast of "the market" at the date of breach has been falsified. If, therefore, at the date of the breach arising upon an accepted repudiation, the claimant in fact buys (or sells) goods for delivery at the forward date of performance, it would appear that he can claim the amount of the damages thus fixed. Where, however, a buyer did not in fact buy at the date of breach, and prices at the date for performance had fallen below the contract price, he was not allowed to claim the damages he would have sustained if he had bought forward at the date of the breach.[59]

Note 5. Date for assessment. The date for the assessment of damages is normally thought to be the date when the cause of action arose: ie the date of the breach of contract

---

[54] [2003] EWHC 1936 (Comm); [2003] 2 Lloyd's Rep. 693 at [23].
[55] (1872) L.R. 7 Exch. 319.
[56] (1873) L.R. 8 C.P. 167.
[57] (1896) 1 Com.Cas. 240, 306.
[58] [1900] 2 Q.B. 298. *Quaere* in that case whether the repudiation of the contract (if it had been one) was accepted, i.e. whether under the first question discussed above, there was a breach, by acceptance of repudiation, before the time for performance. See also *Gebruder Metalmann GmbH & Co K.G. v N.B.R. (London) Ltd* [1984] 1 Lloyd's Rep. 614.
[59] *Melachrino v Nickoll & Knight* [1920] 1 K.B. 693.

or the date of the tort (which if the tort is actionable only on proof of damage, such as the tort of negligence, will be at the date of the damage).[60]

However, this was departed from by the House of Lords in *Golden Strait Corp v Nippon Yusen Kubishika Kaisha, The Golden Victory.*[61] This concerned a seven-year charterparty. After three years, there was a repudiatory breach by the charterers. Two years later, the Iraq war broke out which, under a war clause, would have entitled the charterers to terminate the contract in any event and it was assumed that, had the contract still been on foot, they would have done so. The question that arose was whether damages should be assessed as at the date of breach on the basis of the value of a four-year remaining charterparty ignoring the outbreak of war; or as at the date of trial taking into account the known outbreak of war and hence on the basis of only a two-year remaining charterparty. By a 3–2 majority (Lords Bingham and Walker dissenting) it was held that damages should be assessed on the second basis. This is justified as more precisely measuring the claimant's known loss in a situation where the claimant had not attempted to mitigate its loss by concluding a substitute charterparty for the four-year period. The minority preferred to adhere to the date of breach rule as promoting commercial certainty.

Note 6. Contributory negligence. As a matter of statutory interpretation of the Law Reform (Contributory Negligence) Act 1945, section 1, the claimant's contributory negligence does not lead to a reduction in damages for breach of contract unless the breach was of a contractual duty of care and the defendant was concurrently liable in the tort of negligence.[62] In contrast contributory negligence is, of course, a defence leading to a reduction in damages for virtually all torts.[63]

Note 7. Optional modes of performance. "The question upon a breach of contract is what is the condition in which the plaintiffs would be if the defendant had performed the contract. Generally speaking, where there are several ways in which the contract *might* be performed, that mode is adopted which is the least profitable to the plaintiff and the least burthensome to the defendant."[64] The commonest application of this is in a contract for the sale of goods of a maximum and minimum quantity at the seller's option, and the seller fails to deliver anything: he pays damages on the minimum quantity.[65] But the possibility indicated in the word "might", italicised above, is the actual, not the theoretical,

---

[60] See, e.g., *Philips v Ward* [1956] 1 W.L.R. 471; *Dodd Properties (Kent) v Canterbury City Council* [1980] A.C. 174.

[61] [2007] UKHL 12, [2007] 2 W.L.R. 691. For another exceptional case, in which in an action for the tort of conversion damages were assessed at the date of trial rather than at the normal date of the conversion, see *Trafigura Beheer BV v Mediterranean Shipping SA* [2007] EWCA Civ 794; [2008] 1 All E.R. (Comm) 385.

[62] *Forsikringsaktieselskapet Vesta v Butcher* [1988] 3 W.L.R. 565 (affd. without discussion of contributory negligence [1989] A.C. 880 (HL)); *Barclays Bank Plc v Fairclough Building Ltd* [1995] Q.B. 214; *UCB Bank Plc v Hepherd Winstanley & Pugh* [1999] Lloyd's Rep. P.N. 963. Note that in the *Vesta* case Neill L.J. went back on his view in *Maritrans A.B. v Comet Shipping Co Ltd* [1985] 3 All E.R. 442 (which concerned the breach of a contractual duty of care to stow cargo properly) that contributory negligence *never* applies as a defence to an action for breach of contract. See generally Law Commission Report No. 219 (1993) "Contributory Negligence as a Defence in Contract".

[63] But by reason of s.11 of the Torts (Interference with Goods) Act 1977 conversion and intentional trespass to goods are exceptions. The tort of deceit is another exception: *Standard Chartered Bank v Pakistan National Shipping Corp (No 2)* [2002] UKHL 43; [2003] 1 A.C. 959.

[64] Maule J., *Cockburn v Alexander* (1848) 6 C.B. 791 at p.814; *Kaye S.S. Co v Barnett* (1931) 41 Ll.L.R. 231 at p. 239, and (1932) 48 T.L.R. 440; *Withers v General Theatre Corp* [1933] 2 K.B. 536; *The Rijn* [1981] 2 Lloyd's Rep. 267 (damages assessed against time charterers on basis of voyage in ballast and not with cargo); *Lavarack v Woods of Colchester Ltd* [1967] 1 Q.B. 278; *Paula Lee Ltd v Robert Zehil & Co Ltd* [1983] 2 All E.R. 390. *Cf. Lion Nathan Ltd v C-C Bottlers Ltd* [1996] 1 W.L.R. 1438; *Horkulak v Cantor Fitzgerald Int.* [2004] EWCA Civ 1287; [2005] I.C.R. 402.

[65] *Cf. Thornett & Fehr and Yuills, Ltd, Re* [1921] 1 K.B. 219.

possibility. The difference between the two does not arise as regards the quantity of goods procurable in the market. But if a shipowner engages under a charter to provide one of his own ships to carry not less than 1,500, and not more than 2,000 tons, and in fact the smallest ship he owns which he could use would carry 1,700 tons, he must pay damages on 1,700 not upon 1,500 tons.[66]

Sometimes the defendant will not have had a choice between alternative obligations under a contract, but rather between alternative means to perform the same contractual obligation. In this latter case, the approach to damages will generally be different, particularly where there is a considerable body of evidence as to the factors which would have influenced the defendant's conduct and those factors were not wholly within the defendant's control. In this situation, the Court will decide how, on the balance of probabilities, the defendant would have performed his obligation and award damages accordingly.[67]

Similarly, where a party to a contract has committed an anticipatory breach of the contract, but, in the events which must necessarily have happened, he would have been excused further performance of the contract when the time for performance arrived, he is liable for no more than nominal damages.[68]

Note 8. Detention under repair. Where the shipowner's claim for damages is based on delay to the ship during the repair of damage caused by the charterer's breach of contract or tortious act, the measure of damage is the amount which the ship would have earned but for the detention.[69] The onus of proving that the vessel would have been profitably employed at the relative time is on the shipowner.[70] Where a shipowner chooses a reasonable time to withdraw the ship from profitable trading for the purposes of carrying out the repairs necessary as a result of the charterer's breach, he can perform other repairs necessary for his own purposes at the same time. Provided that these do not lengthen the period of repair, they will not reduce the damages recoverable from the charterer unless it was immediately necessary to perform those repairs.[71]

---

[66] *Blane, Wright & Co v Thoresen, Lloyd's List*, June 10, 1918. See also *Thomas v Clarke* (1818) 2 Stark. 450. So in a contract to sell 10 to 15 cwt. of goods in cases, if commercially the goods were only obtainable in cases of 4 cwt. each, the damages on the failure to deliver anything must be on 12 cwt., not 10 cwt.

[67] *Ferruzzi France SA & Ferruzzi SpA v Ocean Maritime Inc (The Palmea)* [1988] 2 Lloyd's Rep. 261; *Kurt A. Becher Gmbh v Roplak Enterprises SA (The World Navigator)* [1991] 2 Lloyd's Rep. 23. This distinction is difficult to draw in practice.

[68] *The Mihalis Angelos* [1971] 1 Q.B. 164 (CA). See also *Commonwealth of Australia v Amann Aviation Pty Ltd* (1991) 66 A.L.J.R. 123 (in assessing reliance damages it was held by the majority that the *Mihalis Angelos* principle did not affect the result because there was merely a 20 per cent chance that the defendants would otherwise have validly cancelled the contract for the claimants' own breach).

[69] *The Argentino* (1889) 14 App.Cas. 519 (HL); *McGregor on Damages*, 17th edn (London: Sweet & Maxwell, 2003) paras 32–019 to 32–031. The damages awarded will usually consist of the loss of earnings during the actual period of detention, but they may in appropriate cases include loss of earnings under any engagement for another voyage for which the ship was chartered at the time of the casualty and was thereby prevented from performing: *The Argentino*, above, per Lord Herschell at p.523, and *The Soya* [1956] 1 Lloyd's Rep. 557 (CA), per Lord Evershed M.R. at p.565. The damages will not, however, include loss of earnings at a high rate under a speculative future fixture.

[70] *Carslogie S.S. Co v Royal Norwegian Government* [1952] A.C. 292 (HL). *The Soya*, above; *The City of Peking* (1890) 15 App.Cas. 438 (PC) (substitute vessel in same ownership taking the place of the damaged vessel). See also *The World Beauty* [1969] P. 12 (assessment of benefit gained by shipowner in mitigating his loss, by substituting vessel in same ownership and thereby accelerating commencement of profitable charter for damaged vessel); *The Naxos* [1972] 1 Lloyd's Rep. 149.

[71] *Elpidoforos Shipping Corp v Furness Withy (Australia) Pty Ltd (The Oinoussian Friendship)* [1987] 1 Lloyd's Rep. 258 explaining *Carslogie v Royal Norwegian Government* 84 Ll.L.R. 148 and *The Hassel* [1962] 2 Lloyd's Rep. 139; *The Ferdinand Retzlaff* [1972] 2 Lloyd's Rep. 120; *Beoco Ltd v Alfa Lavel Co Ltd* [1994] 3 W.L.R. 1179; *Sunrise Co Ltd v. The Ship Winnipeg* 77 D.L.R. (4th) 701 (Can.).

A193   **Article 193—Damages for Failure to Load**[72]

In an action against a charterer for not loading a cargo, the measure of damage is the amount of freight which would have been earned under the charter[73] after deducting the expenses of earning it and any net profit the ship may, or might, have earned during the period of the charter on a substituted voyage.[74] In calculating the net earnings on the substitute voyage, the Court will take account of the expenses of any deviation necessary to perform that voyage.[75] The deduction of the net profit on a substitute voyage reflects the claimant's duty to mitigate so there will be no such deduction if there has been no failure to mitigate.[76] Where the substitute voyage is of a longer duration than the charter voyage, no attempt will normally be made to determine the relative positions of the shipowner in the period after the date on which the charter voyage would have been completed, unless there is clear evidence that the shipowner has obtained a benefit by reason of the longer duration of the substitute charter.[77] If the expense of earning freight on a substituted voyage of the same duration is the same as on the chartered voyage, the same result is arrived at by taking the difference between the charterparty rate of freight and the market rate of freight.

As to the damages if the charter is for a named kind of cargo and the charterer ships a different kind, see above, Art.82.

Note. "To load in regular turn." Where the "regular turn" is lost through the negligence of one of the parties, he will be liable for all subsequent delay resulting from such loss.[78]

Case 1. A ship was charterered to go to X, where the charterer was either to load or to give notice that he would not load, paying at the same time £500. The ship went to X. The charterer neither loaded nor gave the notice; the ship returned by Y, making a larger freight than if she had returned

---

[72] *McGregor on Damages* (17th edn, 2003) 27–061 to 27–072. This will be the form of action if a charterer wrongfully throws up the charter under a cancelling clause: *Hick v Tweedy* (1890) 63 L.T. 765.

[73] As to method of calculation, see Art.169 and *Capper v Forster* (1837) 3 Bing. N.C. 938; *Cockburn v Alexander* (1848) 6 C.B. 791; *Warren v Peabody* (1849) 8 C.B. 800. For a complicated case of assessing damages after a fire, see *Aitken, Lilburn & Co v Ernsthausen* [1894] 1 Q.B. 773. If the charter stipulates for goods of a certain size and goods of a different size are loaded, the measure of damages will be the difference of freight involved: *Young v Canning Jarrah Co* (1899) 4 Com.Cas. 96. For special cases of damage, see *Sparrow v Paris* (1862) H. & N. 594; *Heugh v Escombe* (1861) 4 L.T. 517. Where the ship has been kept on demurrage before the refusal to load, the agreed rate of demurrage for the period of detention must be added to this: *Saxon Ship Co v Union S.S. Co* (1899) 81 L.T. 246; reversed (1900) 83 L.T. 106 (HL).

[74] *Smith v M'Guire* (1858) 3 H. & N. 554; *Staniforth v Lyall* (1830) 7 Bing. 169; *S.I.B. International S.R.L. v Metallgesellschaft Corp (The Noel Bay)* [1989] 1 Lloyd's Rep. 361 (CA). *Cf. Hyundai Merchant Marine v Dartbrook Coal* [2006] 236 A.L.R. 115 (Aust. Fed. Ct.).

[75] *Rheinoel GmbH v Hyron Liberian Co (The Concordie C)* [1985] 2 Lloyd's Rep. 55.

[76] *Petroleum Shipping v Vatis, The Riza and Sun* [1997] 2 Lloyd's Rep. 314; *UBC Chartering Ltd v Liepaya Shipping Co, The Liepaya* [1999] 1 Lloyd's Rep. 649.

[77] *ibid.*, at pp.57–58; *The Noel Bay*, above.

[78] Thus a ship chartered to load in "regular turn" lost her turn through the default of the charterer, and was detained eleven days till her turn came round again, when she was detained three days by weather before she could begin to load. *Held*, that the charterer was liable for the whole fourteen days; delay, the three days' delay being the legal and natural consequence of his first default: *Jones v Adamson* (1876) 1 Ex. D. 60; see also *Taylor v Clay* (1849) 9 Q.B. 713.

straight from X. *Held*, that the shipowner could not recover the £500, as the charterer had given no notice, but only unliquidated damages, and that as he had profited by the breach, the damages were nominal.[79]

Case 2. A chartered a ship from her owners to load a cargo at 21s. a ton with a cancelling date September 15. A sub-chartered the vessel to B to load a like cargo at 28s. 6d. a ton with cancelling date December 15. The ship was ready to load after September 15 but before December 15. B refused to load. Freights had then fallen to 17s. a ton. A cancelled his charterparty with the owners. *Held*, that A's damages against B were the difference between 28s. 6d. and 21s, not the difference between 28s. 6d.and 17s.[80]

Article 194—Damages for failure to Carry Cargo[81]   A194

In an action against a shipowner for not furnishing a ship to receive cargo under a charter, one possible measure of damage is the difference between market and charter rates of freight. This is based on the assumption that a substitute ship can be procured. If the charterer in fact charters a vessel to replace her, the excess freight he has to pay will be, prima facie, the measure of damages[82]; but he can prove the amount of his loss by giving evidence of the sum which he would have had to pay to charter another ship without actually entering into a substituted charter.[83]

Where under a charter there is a breach of a guarantee of the ship's deadweight or carrying capacity, the prima facie measure of damages is the difference between the rate of hire or freight payable on the market at the date of the charter for a ship complying with the guarantee and for one of the actual capacity of the ship chartered.[84] This is only a prima facie rule; if its application will not compensate an injured party, who has shown himself to have suffered loss of a sufficiently proximate kind, a departure from the rule is warranted.[85]

The loss of profit on cargo shut out can only be recovered either under a charter or a shipping engagement if loss of this type is sufficiently contemplated when the contract is concluded.[86] Where such a loss is contemplated, and the

---

[79] *Staniforth v Lyall* (1830) 7 Bing 169. *Bell v Puller* (1810) 2 Taunt. 285, where the shipowner was allowed to earn both charter freight and freight *aliunde*, turns on an express proviso in the charter.

[80] *Weir v Dobell* [1916] 1 K.B. 722.

[81] *McGregor on Damages* (17th edn, 2003) 27–047 to 27–053.

[82] *Featherston v Wilkinson* (1873) L.R. 8 Ex. 122; *Blackgold Trading Ltd of Monravia v Almare SpA Bi Navigazione of Genoa, The Almare Seconda and Almare Quinta* [1981] 2 Lloyd's Rep. 433. For a Scots case in which the charterers recovered this measure of damages after cancelling the charter under a cancellation clause, see *Nelson v Dundee East Coast S.S. Co* [1907] S.C. 927.

[83] Just in the same way in the sale of goods when the seller fails to deliver, the buyer need not in fact buy other goods, but may claim on the difference of market prices if he had bought.

[84] *Tibermede v Graham* (1921) 7 Ll.L.R. 250; *Sterns v Salterns* (1922) 12 Ll.L.R. 385 (two lump sum payments for consecutive voyages) *Eptanisos S.S. Co v Ministry of Supply* (1941) 69 Ll.L.R. 43; *Harrison v Board of Trade* (1949) 82 Ll.L.R. 730. See also *Heimdal A/S D/S v Questier* (1949) 82 Ll.L.R. 452, where under a lump sum charter, when the owner failed to load a full and complete cargo and substitute space could not be found for the cargo shut out, the charterer was entitled as one head of damage to the difference in lump sum freights in the market for a vessel of the capacity actually made available and for one of the capacity chartered.

[85] *Tor Line v Alltrans Group of Canada (The T.F.L. Prosperity)* [1982] 1 Lloyd's Rep. 617, at p.623. On a different point, Bingham J.'s decision was upheld by the House of Lords: see [1984] 1 Lloyd's Rep. 123.

[86] *Czarnikow v Koufos* [1969] 1 A.C. 350; *Geogos SA v Trammo Gas Ltd (The Baleares)* [1993] 1 Lloyd's Rep. 215.

failure to carry the cargo leads to delay in lifting cargo, and a consequential rise in its acquisition cost, this rise in price constitutes the prima facie measure of the shipper or charterer's recovery, unless the shipowner can prove that the shipper or charterer will in fact benefit from a corresponding rise in the price of the cargo at the port of delivery, and thereby suffer no loss.[87]

If the shipowner fails to take the whole cargo contracted for, the shipper can recover the difference between the contract and market rates of freight on the quantity not carried. Where the charterer obtains a substitute vessel, and is able to carry additional tonnage beyond that which the shipowner was obliged to carry, he will be required to bring any benefit derived from this fact into account when assessing damages.[88]

When, however, a substitute ship cannot be procured, the measure of damages payable to the charterer is the cost of replacing the goods at their port of destination at the time when they ought to have arrived, less the value of the goods at the port of shipment and the amount of the freight and insurance upon them.[89]

Case 1. A's ship was chartered by C to load coal at X and proceed to Z. A broke his contract. C chartered another vessel, at a higher freight, and purchased coal at a higher price, the first cargo being lost through the delay. *Held*, C could recover from A as damages: (1) the excess freight paid; (2) prima facie, the excess price of coal, but that A might meet this by showing a corresponding rise in the value of coal at Z.[90]

Case 2. A ship was chartered to load a grain cargo of "not less than 13,000 quarters". She only loaded 12,500 quarters. *Held*, the charterers could not recover their loss of profit under a contract for the sale of 13,000 quarters.[91]

Case 3. A's ship was chartered by C to carry 500 tons of wood pulp in September from Sweden to the U.K. C had sold the cargo to P for delivery in the U.K. A failed to send his ship to load altogether. C was unable to charter any other ship, and had to make default under his contract with P. P brought 500 tons against C, and C had to pay P £700 as the difference in price. In an action by C against A, *held* that C could recover this £700 as being the extra cost of supplying at the port of destination goods of the amount and description agreed to be carried there by A.[92]

---

[87] *The Baleares*, above.
[88] *Greenwich Marine Inc v Federal Commerce & Navigation Co Ltd (The Mavro Vetranic)* [1985] 1 Lloyd's Rep. 581.
[89] *Ströms Bruks Aktiebolag v Hutchinson* [1905] A.C. 515: followed in *Nissho v Livanos* (1941) 69 Ll.L.R. 125, where the statement in the text was approved; *Heimdal A/S D/S v Questier* (1949) 82 Ll.L.R. 452, where, in addition, the charterer recovered in respect of the value of the cargo shut out which was lost to him; *Fyffes Group Ltd v Reefer Express Lines Pty Ltd, The Kriti Rex* [1996] 2 Lloyd's Rep. 170. Query whether this rule was consistently applied in assessing the damages in *Watts v Mitsui* [1917] A.C. 227. The charterers were given the difference between the price at which five months before the shipowners' breach, they had agreed to buy the goods for shipment, and the value they would have had at the port of delivery, less the cost of freight and insurance. But the price at which they had so agreed to buy was not necessarily the value of the goods at the port of shipment when the shipowners failed to provide the ship; indeed the charterers had to pay £4,500 to their vendors to cancel the purchase. There was no evidence of any market value of the goods at the port of shipment at the date of the shipowners' breach, but if the charterers acted reasonably (and the contrary does not appear to have been contended), their action seems to show that that value was about £4,500 less than their contract price of purchase.
[90] *Featherston v Wilkinson* (1873) L.R. 8 Ex. 122. See also *The Baleares*, above.
[91] *Scaramanga v English* (1895) 1 Com.Cas. 99; *Heimdal A/S D/S v Questier* (1949) 82 Ll.L.R. 452. However, see fn.86, above.
[92] *Ströms Bruks Aktiebolag v Hutchinson* [1905] A.C. 515; *Heimdal A/S D/S v Questier*, above.

Article 195—Damages for Failure to Carry Safely, or in Reasonable Time[93]   A195

Where goods are not delivered by the vessel contracting to carry them,[94] the damages will, in the absence of special circumstances in the contract, be the market value[95] of the goods when they should have arrived, less the sums which the cargo-owner must have paid to get them, such as freight.[96] Similarly, if goods are delivered but in a damaged condition, the damages, in the absence of special circumstances in the contract, will be the difference between the market value the goods would have had on arrival, if undamaged, and their value in the damaged condition.[97] It frequently happens that the cargo-owner is compensated by his seller for short or damaged delivery by reason of his purchase being on "delivered" and not ordinary c.i.f. terms. In the case of damaged goods he can recover damages assessed on the above principles as trustees for his seller,[98] and also in cases of shortage.[99]

When the Carriage of Goods by Sea Act 1971 applies, there is by Art.IV, r.5 of its Schedule, a limit to the shipowner's liability. (See Chapter 20.)

As regards delay in delivery of goods, the ordinary measure of damages against a carrier by land is the difference between the market prices at the time when the goods should have been delivered and at the time when they were

---

[93] *McGregor on Damages* (17th edn, 2003) paras 27–002 to 27–046.

[94] *Cf. Smith v Tregarthen* (1887) 56 L.J.Q.B. 437.

[95] Where there is no market the value of the goods must be ascertained otherwise. See *The Arpad* [1934] P. 189, where it was held that the cargo-owner could not recover either in contract or tort the loss he had suffered through inability to fulfil his contract of sale to a third party, and that, on the facts, the price at which he had sold wheat five months before delivery should have been made was no evidence of the value the wheat would have had if delivered. See also *Empresa Cubana Importadora de Alimentos v Octavier Shipping Co SA (The Kefalonia Wind)* [1986] 1 Lloyd's Rep. 273 and *A.G. of Republic of Ghana v Texaco Overseas Tankships Ltd (The Texaco Melbourne)* [1993] 1 Lloyd's Rep. 471 in which, in the absence of the market value at the place of delivery, the market value at an alternative port together with the cost of on-shipment was used. See also *The Pegase* [1981] 1 Lloyd's Rep. 175 (lost resale profits awarded as damages where late delivery of goods by carrier and no available market); *Coastal (Bermuda) Petroleum Ltd v VTT Vulcan Petroleum SA (No. 2), The Marine Star (No. 2)* [1994] 2 Lloyd's Rep. 629 (lost resale profits awarded as damages for breach of contract of carriage by carrier's non-delivery where no available market). Apart from special circumstances bringing the case within the "second rule" in *Hadley v Baxendale* (1854) 9 Ex. 341 (see Art.190), the problem both in contract and tort is to assess the value the goods would have had if delivered; whether the prices at which goods have been sold for future delivery are any evidence of this will depend on the facts of each case. See also *Monte Video Gas Co v Clan Line* (1921) 37 T.L.R. 866, where shipowners carrying gas coal to a gas company delivered a different parcel of steam coal by mistake.

[96] *Rodocanachi v Milburn* (1886) 18 Q.B.D. 67; *Williams v Agius* [1914] A.C. 510; *Weir v Dobell* [1916] 1 K.B. 722, *Case* 2, Art.193, above; *A.G. of the Republic of Ghana v Texaco Overseas Tankships Ltd (The Texaco Melbourne)* [1994] 1 Lloyd's Rep. 473. See also, analagously, *Sealace Shipping Co Ltd v Oceanvoice Ltd (The Alecos M)* [1991] 1 Lloyd's Rep. 120. Overdelivery under one bill of lading will not in itself be any defence against a claim for short delivery under another bill of lading: *Nordborg (Owners) v Sherwood* [1939] P. 121.

[97] *Slater v Hoyle and Smith Ltd* [1920] 2 K.B. 11; *Bence Graphics Int. Ltd v Fasson UK Ltd* [1998] Q.B. 87; *Derby Resources AG v Blue Corinth Marine Co, The Athenian Harmony* [1998] 2 Lloyd's Rep. 410. When the receiver reasonably delays selling the damaged goods, and in consequence the market value of the replacement goods is higher the higher cost can be recovered: *Empresa Cubana Importada de Alimentos 'Alimport' v Iasmos Shipping Co SA (The Good Friend)* [1984] 2 Lloyd's Rep. 586.

[98] *Paul v National S.S. Co* (1937) 43 Com.Cas. 68. So also where the cargo-owner has been compensated by his buyer: *Obestairs Inc. v National Mineral Development Corp Ltd (The Sanix Ace)* [1987] 1 Lloyd's Rep. 465.

[99] *The Aramis* [1989] 1 Lloyd's Rep. 213; *The Arpad* (1933) 46 Ll.L.R. 182, and 51 Ll.L.R. at pp.117, 118; *Ministry of Food v Australian Wheat Board* [1952] 1 Lloyd's Rep. 297. *Cf. Den of Airlie v Mitsui* (1912) 17 Com.Cas. 117. See also s.2(4) of the Carriage of Goods to Sea Act 1992 discussed in Art.14.

delivered.[100] The same ordinary measure of damages now applies in the case of delayed delivery of goods carried by sea.[101]

In the absence of special circumstances the above measures will not be affected by the fact that the cargo-owner has sold the goods to arrive at a price higher[102] or lower[103] than the market price ruling on the (presumed) date of arrival. Special circumstances within the reasonable contemplation of the parties at the date of the contract may justify higher damages.[104]

Note. A clause is not uncommonly inserted in bills of lading to the effect "Owners not to be liable in any case beyond the net invoice cost of the goods damaged or short delivered." It has been held that such a clause means that profit only on the goods is to be excluded, and that therefore the freight (if paid or payable) is to be added to the actual invoice price of the goods.[105]

Case 1. Goods shipped on A's ship were lost through causes for which A was liable. The shippers had paid part of the freight in advance, and without A's knowledge had sold the goods to arrive for £7 2s 6d per ton. The market price of the day when the ship should have arrived was £7 7s 6d per ton. *Held*, that the shippers were entitled to recover £7 7s 6d per ton less what they must have paid to get the goods; viz. the balance of the freight.[106]

Case 2. A's master E signed bills of lading for 400 bales of cotton at Wilmington, "shipped on board the *Carbis* Bay for Liverpool". The ship could only take 165 bales, and E ordered the remaining 235 bales to be shipped on board the *Wylo*, also for L. The *Carbis Bay* arrived on October 26, the *Wylo* on October 29; between these dates the price of cotton fell. The shippers sued E under the Bills of Lading Act for damages for the non-delivery by the *Carbis Bay*. *Held*, that on such non-delivery the shippers were entitled to the market value of the goods on October 26 as damages; that they might receive the goods *ex Wylo* on October 29, in part satisfaction of such damages: but were still entitled to recover the difference in price between October 26 and 29 as damages.[107]

Case 3. F shipped on A's ship several cases containing machinery for a sawmill at Z, and described as "merchandise". A knew the general nature of the shipment. On arriving at Z one of the cases was missing, and the sawmill could not be erected till it had been replaced. *Held*, that F was entitled to the cost of replacing the missing machinery at Z, and to 5 per cent interest on such cost, for the delay, but not to damages for the estimated profits of the mill during the delay.[108]

---

[100] *Collard v S.E. Ry* (1861) 7 H. & N. 79; *Elbinger Aktiengesellschaft v Armstrong* (1874) L.R. 9 Q.B. 473; *Wertheim v Chicoutimi* [1911] A.C. 301; *Heskell v Continental Express* (1950) 83 Ll.L.R. 438.

[101] *Czarnikow v Koufos* [1969] 1 A.C. 350, not following *The Parana* (1877) 2 P.D. 118 (contract) nor *The Notting Hill* (1884) 9 P.D. 105 (claim by owners of cargo on innocent ship in tort for damages for loss of market against shipowners responsible for collision), and applying *Hadley v Baxendale* (1854) 9 Exch. 341 and *Dunn v Bucknall Bros.* [1902] 2 K.B. 614. See also *Gatoil International Inc. v Tradax Petroleum Ltd (The Rio Sun)* [1985] 1 Lloyd's Rep. 350.

[102] *The St. Cloud* (1863) B. & L. 4.

[103] *Rodocanachi v Milburn* (1886) 18 Q.B.D. 67; *Wertheim v Chicoutimi* [1911] A.C. 301; *Williams v Agius* [1914] A.C. 510; *Slater v Hoyle* [1920] 2 K.B. 11; *A-G of the Republic of Ghana v Texaco Overseas Tankships Ltd (The Texaco Melbourne)* [1993] 1 Lloyd's Rep. 471. *Cf. Bence Graphics Ltd Int. Ltd v Fasson UK Ltd* [1998] Q.B. 87.

[104] *Satef-Huttenes Albertus SpA v Paloma Tercera Shipping Co SA (The Pegase)* [1981] 1 Lloyd's Rep. 175; *Coastal (Bermuda) Petroleum Ltd v VTT Vulcan Petroleum SA (The Marine Star)* [1994] C.L.C. 1019; *The Ardennes* [1951] 1 K.B. 55 (damages based upon the fall in market price and increased import duty recovered; there was a breach of an oral warranty at the time of shipment that the ship would sail directly to London). The reverse position obtained in *British Columbia Co v Nettleship* (see *Case 3*, below) in which the bill of lading holder was limited to a claim for the cost of replacing the missing machinery plus interest thereon from the date the machinery should have been delivered until replacement at the port of discharge.

[105] *Nelson v Nelson* [1906] 2 K.B. 804.

[106] *Rodocanachi v Milburn* (1886) 18 Q.B.D. 67.

[107] *Smith v Tregarthen* (1887) 56 L.J.Q.B. 437 (*cf.* a similar claim for non-delivery in *Sargant v East Asiatic Co* (1915) 21 Com.Cas. 344).

[108] *British Columbia Co v Nettleship* (1868) L.R. 3 C.P. 499.

Case 4. C chartered A's ship to carry sugar from X to Z at which A knew there was a sugar market. He also knew C were sugar merchants. In breach of charter the ship deviated and arrived at Z nine days late on the voyage that should have taken 20 days. *Held,* C was entitled to damages for delayed delivery on the basis of the difference between the market price at Z when the ship should have arrived and the lower price prevailing when she did arrive.[109]

Article 196—Dead Freight   A196

"Dead freight" is the name given to damages claimed for breach of contract by a charterer to furnish a full cargo to a ship[110] in accordance with the charter.[111]

For such damages no lien on goods actually carried in the ship exists at common law[112]; but such a lien may be given by usage, or express contract of the parties.[113]

Case 1. A vessel was chartered to carry a full cargo of bones at so much per ton, the shipowner to have a lien on the cargo for "freight, dead freight, and demurrage". Only 386 tons were shipped; 210 tons more could have been shipped. The master claimed a lien on the cargo shipped for damages for failure to ship the 210 tons. *Held,* that the charter gave him such a lien.[113]

Case 2. A ship was chartered to load a full cargo at named freights, "but if the ship should not be fully laden, C to pay not only for the goods which should be on board, but also for so much in addition as the ship could have carried. And, in case no goods were shipped, then C should at the end of the voyage pay full freight for the vessel to A as if she had been fully loaded." A full cargo was not shipped, and the master claimed a lien on the goods carried for "dead freight" due for goods not carried. *Held,* that no such lien existed at common law.[114]

Note. It was for a long time doubtful whether the term "dead freight", in a clause in a charterparty giving a lien for dead freight, must not be confined to liquidated damages, *i.e.* damages for failure to furnish a full cargo ascertained, or at any rate ascertainable, from the charter itself. The cases of *Pearson v Göschen*[115] and *Gray v Carr*[116] supported this view. Against it was the Scots case of *McLean v Fleming*[117] decided by the House of Lords, but this was distinguished by the judges who decided *Gray v Carr.* Incidentally they pointed out the inconvenience of a lien existing for an unascertained or unascertainable amount,[118] an inconvenience which is as obvious from the commercial as from the legal point of view.

The question has become one of academic interest only[119]: for it must be taken that *Pearson v Göschen*[120] and *Gray v Carr*[121] are upon this point overruled by *McLean v*

---

[109] *Czarnikow v Koufos* [1969] 1 A.C. 350; *Dunn v Bucknall Bros* [1902] 2 K.B. 614.
[110] *McLean v Fleming* (1871) L.R. 2 Sc. & Div. 128. If the master by taking in other cargo, even though this involves delay, can reduce the shipowner's loss, he must do so, if such a course is reasonable in the circumstances: *Wallens Rederi A/S v Muller & Co* [1927] 2 K.B. 99.
[111] *Angfartygs A/B Halfdan v Price and Pierce* (1939) 63 Ll.L.R. 35; 45 Com.Cas. 23.
[112] *Phillips v Rodie* (1812) 15 East 547; *Birley v Gladstone* (1814) 3 M. & S. 205.
[113] See fn.110, above.
[114] *Phillips v Rodie,* see above.
[115] (1864) 17 C.B. (N.S.) 352.
[116] (1871) L.R. 6 Q.B. 522.
[117] See fn.110, above.
[118] *Cf. Clink v Radford* [1891] 1 Q.B. 625, per Lord Esher at p.629; Bowen L.J. at p.631; Fry L.J. at p.633. Cleasby B., however, makes the just observation that a lien for general average contribution is equally in respect of an amount that cannot be known until an adjustment has been prepared, and yet that lien has always been recognised, and does not in fact create inconvenience in its exercise: *Gray v Carr* (1871) L.R. 6 Q.B. 522 at p.530.
[119] It was discussed more elaborately in a *Note* to this Article (then Art.61) in the first six editions of this work.
[120] (1864) 17 C.B. (N.S.) 352.
[121] (1871) L.R. 6 Q.B. 522.

Fleming,[122] in view of the decision of the House of Lords in *Kish v Taylor*,[123] upholding the decision of Walton J. to the same effect.[124]

A197 ## Article 197—Damages for not Signing or Presenting Bills of Lading, etc.[125]

A clause requiring the captain to sign bills of lading within a certain time or pay a specified sum per day as liquidated damages for delay, or until the ship is totally lost or the cargo delivered, imposes a penalty, and the damages specified cannot be recovered, but only the actual damage sustained, which must be proved.[126]

Where it is the duty of the charterer to present bills of lading for signature, he must do so within a reasonable time from completion of the loading,[127] even if that is completed before the lay-days expire.[128] If the ship is detained in port by his delay in doing so, the shipowner can recover his actual loss as damages for detention and his claim is not limited to either (i) the demurrage rate fixed by the charter, or (ii) an abatement from dispatch money payable to the charterer.[20]

Where advance freight is made payable on signing bills of lading, and the shipper wrongfully delays to present bills for signature till after the ship is lost, the amount of the advance freight may be recovered as damages for failure to present bills of lading.[129]

A198 ## Article 198—Limitation of Liability

Section 185 of the Merchant Shipping Act 1995[130] provides that the Convention on Limitation of Liability for Maritime Claims 1976, as set out in Part I of Sch.7 of the Act[131] (the "Limitation Convention"), shall have the force of law in the United Kingdom.[132] The Convention provides for owners, charterers, managers or operators of ships,[133] whether seagoing or not,[134] salvors,[135] any person for whose act, neglect or default such persons are responsible,[136] to have the benefit

---

[122] (1871) L.R. 2 Sc. & Div. 128.
[123] [1912] A.C. 604; see the argument at p.612 and judgment at p.614.
[124] [1910] 2 K.B. 309. See also Bray J. in *Red "R" S.S. Co v Allatini* (1909) 14 Com.Cas. 82 at p.92.
[125] As to a charterer's liability for damages for detention of the ship at port of call for orders by his not giving orders promptly, see Arts 70 and 155, above, or by failure to give notice of cancellation promptly under a cancelling clause, see *Den Norske Africa v Port Said Salt Ass. Ltd* (1924) 9 Ll.L.R. 355. As to his liability for damages for detention of the ship from his shipping dangerous cargo, see Art.53, above.
[126] *Jones v Hough* (1879) 5 Ex.D. 115; *Rayner v Rederiaktiebolaget Condor* [1895] 2 Q.B. 289; *The Princess* (1894) 70 L.T. 388.
[127] *Oriental S.S. Co v Tylor* [1893] 2 Q.B. 518.
[128] *Nolisement Co v Bunge* [1917] 1 K.B. 160.
[129] *Oriental S.S. Co v Tylor*, above.
[130] As amended by the Merchant Shipping and Maritime Security Act 1997, s.15(1).
[131] For the text of the Limitation Convention see Appendix I, below, pp.436–444. The text of this Article is no more than a summary of the salient features of the Convention as it affects charterparties and bills of lading.
[132] s.186 re-enacts s.17 of the Merchant Shipping Act 1979.
[133] Art.1.2 of the Limitation Convention.
[134] Merchant Shipping Act 1995, Sch.7, Part II, para.2, modifying Art.1.2 of the Limitation Convention. *Cf. Tasman Orient Line v Alliance Group Ltd* [2004] 1 N.Z.L.R. 650 as to the position in New Zealand with regard to the definition of "owner" in s.85 of the Maritime Transport Act 1994.
[135] "Salvor" and "salvage operations" has an extended meaning: see Art.1.3 of the Limitation Convention.
[136] Art.1.4 of the Limitation Convention.

of a limitation of their liability[137] in respect of the aggregate of all claims subject to limitation to a sum of money calculated by reference to the tonnage of the ship.[138]

The claims which are subject to limitation of liability and which are of particular relevance to the subject matter of this work include loss of or damage to property occurring on board or in direct connexion with the operation of the ship or with salvage operations, and consequential loss resulting therefrom; claims in respect of loss resulting from delay in the carriage by sea of cargo; claims in respect of other loss resulting from the infringement of rights other than contractual rights, occurring in direct connexion with the operation of the ship or salvage operations; claims in respect of the removal destruction or the rendering harmless of the cargo of the ship, and claims of a person other than the person liable in respect of measures taken in order to avert or minimise loss for which the person liable may limit his liability in accordance with the Convention, and further loss caused by such measures.[139]

Although the provisions of the Convention do not apply to claims for salvage or contribution in general average,[140] claims to recover damages from the owner in the amount of a salvage liability to a third party are subject to the Convention.[141] A person shall not be entitled to limit his liability if it is proved that the loss resulted from his personal act or omission, committed with the intent to cause such loss or recklessly and with knowledge that such loss would probably result.[142] The "damage" which "would probably result" need not be the actual damage which resulted, provided the damage complained of was the kind of damage which would probably result; "recklessly" connotes a decision to run the risk or indifference to its existence; and the requirement of knowledge involves proof of actual knowledge in the mind of the actor at the moment that the omission occurs that the omission is taking place and that it does involve probable damage of the sort contemplated in the Article.[143]

Any person alleged to be liable may[144] constitute a fund with the High Court[145] representing the limit of his liability under the Limitation Convention, either by depositing the sum or providing an acceptable and adequate guarantee; the fund is available only for the payment of claims in respect of which limitation of liability can be invoked.[146] Where a fund has been properly constituted, any

---

[137] Including liability *in rem*: Art.1.5 of the Limitation Convention.
[138] See Arts 6 to 9 of the Limitation Convention. For the position where a shipowner has more than one vessel involved in the claim see *The Rhone and Peter A. B. Widener* [1993] 1 Lloyd's Rep. 601 (Can.).
[139] Art.2.1 of the Limitation Convention.
[140] Art.3(b) of the Limitation Convention.
[141] *The Breydon Merchant* [1992] 1 Lloyd's Rep. 373.
[142] Art.4 of the Limitation Convention.
[143] *Goldman v Thai Airways Ltd* [1983] 1 W.L.R. 1186; *S.S. Pharmaceutical Co Ltd v Qantas Airways Ltd* [1991] 1 Lloyd's Rep. 288 (Aust.), decided on similar wording in the Warsaw Convention relating to International Carriage by Air as amended by the Hague Protocol 1955. See *The Captain San Luis* [1993] 2 Lloyd's Rep. 573 as to the costs of investigating the issues of recklessness and intent.
[144] Limitation may be invoked without constituting a fund: Art.10 of the Limitation Convention.
[145] Merchant Shipping Act 1955, Sch.7, Part II, para.11.
[146] Art.11 of the Limitation Convention.

person having made a claim against the fund is barred from exercising any right in respect of such claim against any other assets of the person by or on behalf of whom the fund has been constituted,[147] and the court may stay any proceedings relating to any claim arising out of the occurrence in respect of which the fund has been constituted.[148]

The English Court characterises laws limiting the liability of shipowners and others as procedural, and in any proceedings in England will apply the English limitation rules, without regard to the rules prevailing in any other jurisdiction.[149]

---

[147] Art.13.1. The Limitation Convention makes provision for the release of a ship or other property once a fund has been constituted: Art.13.2. The shipowner is not required to show that there was no conduct barring limitation, in order to obtain the release of the ship: *The Bowbelle* [1990] 1 Lloyd's Rep. 532.
[148] Merchant Shipping Act 1995, Sch.7, Part II, para.8(2).
[149] *Caltex Singapore Pte Ltd v B.P. Shipping Ltd* [1996] 1 Lloyd's Rep. 286.

CHAPTER 20

THE CARRIAGE OF GOODS BY SEA ACT 1971

Introductory Notes

B1

THE Carriage of Goods by Sea Act 1971 continued the process of legislative control over the mutual rights and responsibilities of ship-owners and parties to bills of lading which was initiated by the Carriage of Goods by Sea Act 1924. The history of this legislation may briefly be stated as follows.[1] At common law the shipowner, whether he carried the goods under a charterparty or under a bill of lading, could modify his prima facie liability as carrier as much as he wished, and in the course of years the protective exceptions in these documents increased both in number and complexity to such an extent that a careful scrutiny of the documents became necessary in order to ascertain what rights they conferred against the shipowner. So far as charterparties were concerned this was unobjectionable; the decreased liabilities enabled the shipowner to carry at a lower rate of freight and the charterer had ample opportunity of ascertaining the terms of his contract. With bills of lading, however, different considerations arose. Not only were they contracts of carriage but they were also documents of title, which by virtue of mercantile custom and the Bills of Lading Act 1855,[2] passed freely from hand to hand as part of the currency of trade conferring on their holder both rights and liabilities. Thus consignees, bankers and others who had not been parties to the original contract and had no effective control over its terms, became interested in the bill of lading without having had any real opportunity of examining its terms or assessing the value of the security it afforded.

In the years before and immediately after the 1914–18 War, as the terms of bills of lading became more diverse, the need for standardisation became more and more insistent and an increasing demand was made on the part of importers and exporters for the imposition by legislation, on the lines of the American Harter Act 1893, of certain minimum liabilities of sea- carriers who issued bills of lading. There existed, however, a contrary body of opinion which sought to find a remedy for the merchants' grievances in the preparation of a code of rules defining the rights and liabilities of the carrier and the merchant which might be incorporated in bills of lading by voluntary agreement in the same way as the

---

[1] Rather more extensive accounts of the history of the Hague Rules may be found in the 19th edn of this work, and also in R.P. Colinvaux, *The Carriage of Goods by Sea Act*. A detailed description of the origins of the Hague-Visby Rules is contained in an article by Anthony Diamond Q.C., *Lloyd's Maritime and Commercial Law Quarterly* 225 (1978), in which many aspects of the topic are extensively discussed. See also G.H. Treitel and F.M.B. Reynolds, *Carver on Bills of Lading*, 2nd edn (London: Sweet & Maxwell, 2005); N. Gaskell et al, *Bills of Lading: Law and Contracts* (Informa Law, 2000); R. Aikens et al, *Bills of Lading* (Informa Law, 2006); Girvin, *Carriage of Goods by Sea* (Oxford: Oxford University Press, 2007).

[2] Repealed and replaced by the Carriage of Goods by Sea Act 1992.

York-Antwerp Rules of General Average 1890. In the event, the arguments in favour of legislative intervention prevailed, and a series of negotiations and discussions culminated in the formulation, during October 1923, of a draft Convention intended to form the basis of domestic legislation. This Convention was the foundation of the United Kingdom Act of 1924. Subsequently, the "International Convention for the Unification of Certain Rules of Law relating to Bills of Lading" was signed at Brussels on August 25, 1924. This differed somewhat in its provisions from the draft Convention of October 1923, upon which the 1924 Act was based.[3]

In the main the Hague Rules were for many years accepted as providing a satisfactory basis for the relationship between shipowners and cargo interests and, although the language of the Rules was strongly criticised in some quarters, the number of occasions (at least in the United Kingdom) on which it became necessary to have recourse to the courts on matters of interpretation was remarkably small. Nevertheless, a consensus developed that in some respects the language called for improvement and that there were certain aspects in which the Rules did not strike a fair balance between the respective interests. Accordingly, proposals were made for the adoption of a modified regime, whereby the scheme of the Hague Rules would be retained essentially intact,[4] subject to modifications introduced by an amending Protocol. A conference of the Comité Maritime International held at Stockholm in 1963 adopted a draft Protocol, which was later the subject of extensive amendment at sessions of the Brussels Diplomatic Convention on Maritime Law. These led to the signature of a Protocol at Brussels on February 23, 1968. The Hague Rules, as amended by the Protocol, are known as the Hague-Visby Rules.[5]

So far as concerns the United Kingdom, legislative effect was given to the Hague-Visby Rules by the Carriage of Goods by Sea Act 1971. This repealed the 1924 Act,[6] and re-enacted the Hague Rules in their modified form. The new Act came into force on June 23, 1977, but did not apply to bills of lading issued before that day.[7]

Since the 1971 Act takes the shape of adjustments to the 1924 Act, rather than a complete reconstruction of the statute law on the carriage of goods by sea,

---

[3] Strictly speaking, therefore, a reference to "the Hague Rules" denoted the rules set out in the Brussels Convention, not those embodied in the 1924 Act. They were called the Hague Rules, because they represented an amended form of a body of rules, formulated at a meeting in the Hague, and originally intended for incorporation into bills of lading as a matter of contract.

[4] This solution was far from achieving universal assent. A strong body of opinion held that the distribution of rights and responsibilities as between carrier and cargo-owner created by the Rules in their original and amended forms was outmoded and unduly favourable to the carrier. This opinion was reflected by initiatives taken, first by the United National Conference on Trade and Development, and later by the United Nations Commission on International Trade law, which culminated in the Hamburg Convention of March 31, 1978. The "Hamburg Rules" created by this Convention are set out and discussed in Appendix VI, below. It is impossible to say whether it will ever be given the force of law in the United Kingdom.

[5] For the reasons why the name Visby appears in the title, see Diamond, *op. cit.*

[6] Although the 1924 Act is no longer in force, reference to its contents is necessary for any understanding of many reported cases. In addition many countries which enacted legislation giving effect to the Brussels Convention of 1924 have not yet given statutory effect to the Brussels Protocol of 1968. Accordingly, we have for convenience set out the repealed Act in Appendix III, below.

[7] The Carriage of Goods by Sea Act 1971 (Commencement) Order 1977 (SI 1977, No. 981).

much of the commentary on the earlier Act contained in the previous edition of this work is still germane to this legislation. The expression "the Rules" denotes the Hague-Visby Rules as enacted in the 1971 Act. References to "the Hague Rules" are to the body of rules in their original unamended form. Occasionally, for the sake of clarity, we refer to the Hague-Visby Rules as "the Amended Rules".

The Scheme of the Rules

The general scheme of the Rules is as follows: Article II provides that in every contract of carriage of goods as defined in Article I, with the exception of certain special shipments dealt with in Article VI, the carrier shall be subject to the responsibilities and liabilities contained in Article III and entitled to the rights and immunities contained in Articles IV and IV *bis*. In the result: (i) the Articles impose on the carrier certain minimum responsibilities which he cannot reduce, e.g. to exercise due diligence to provide a seaworthy ship and to issue on demand a bill of lading in a particular form; (ii) responsibility for performing other operations may be divided between the carrier and the shipper, charterer or consignee in whatever manner the parties may wish, provided that no term will be effective if it is inconsistent with the main object and intention of the particular bargain. In so far as the carrier does undertake to carry out the operations he must do so properly and carefully; (iii) the Articles confer on the carrier certain maximum exceptions, which he cannot increase; (iv) the defences and limits of liability provided for in the Articles apply not only to the carrier himself, but also to his servants and agents; (v) the carrier and his servants or agents will lose the benefit of the limitation of liability conferred by the Article upon proof that the damage resulted from an intentional or reckless act or omission; (vi) the Rules are intended to regulate the right and duties of the parties to the bill of lading contract, and between one of the parties and the servants or agents of the other. The Rules do not apply to non-parties, and accordingly do not apply *ex facie* to claims against the carrier by someone who is not party to the bill of lading contract[8] albeit that the shipowner may nevertheless be able to rely on some of the defences set out in the Rules against such a claimant through the doctrine of bailment upon terms.

The Application of the Rules

Perhaps the most important single alteration brought about by the 1971 Act is that whereas under the 1924 Act the Hague Rules applied by statute only to outward voyages from the United Kingdom, under the new Act the Rules apply to a much wider variety of voyages.

---

[8] *Compania Portorafti Commerciale SA v Ultramar Panama Inc. (The Captain Gregos)* [1990] 1 Lloyd's Rep. 310.

Although the general scheme of the legislation is reasonably clear, there are a number of respects in which the application of the 1971 Act is open to doubt. These are discussed below.

To what Voyages do the Rules apply?

By virtue of the 1971 Act, the Rules apply to the following voyages—

(1) Any voyage where the port of shipment is a port in the United Kingdom,[9] whether or not the port of destination is in the United Kingdom: *s.1(3) of the 1971 Act.*

(2) Any voyage from a port in a contracting[10] state to a port in another state: *Article X(b).*[11]

(3) Any voyage from a port in one state to a port in another state,[12] where the bill of lading[13] is issued in a contracting state: *Article X(a).*

(4) Any voyage from a port in one state to a port in another state,[14] where the contract contained in or evidenced by the bill of lading provides that the Rules or legislation of any state giving effect to them are to govern the contract: *Article X(c).*[15]

(5) Any voyage, whether or not between ports in different states, where the contract contained in or evidenced by the bill of lading expressly provides that the Rules shall govern the contract: *s.1(6)(a).*[15]

(6) Any voyage, whether or not between ports in different states, where the contract contained in or evidenced by a non-negotiable document (marked as such) provides that the Rules are to govern the contract as if the receipt were a bill of lading: *s.1(6)(b).*[16]

It may be noted that categories (2), (3) and (4) apply to the carriage of goods between ports in two different states. It is submitted that the test is whether the intended carriage is international and not the actual carriage. Thus, if the goods are discharged short of their destination, at a port in the country of shipment, the Rules will nevertheless apply if the port of destination was in another country.

---

[9] i.e. Great Britain and Northern Ireland: Interpretation Act 1978, s.5, Sch.1. The application of s.1(3) of the 1971 Act may be extended by Order in Council to carriage from ports in the Isle of Man, the Channel Islands, Colonies, Associated States and certain other territories: *ibid.* s.5(1).

[10] By s.2(1) an Order in Council may certify that a state specified in the Order is a contracting state, or that a place or territory forms part of a contracting state.

[11] The port of destination need not be in a contracting state.

[12] The termini of the voyage need not be in contracting states.

[13] For a discussion of the expression "bill of lading", see commentary on Art.I, below.

[14] See fn.12, above.

[15] In practice, categories (4) and (5) overlap to such an extent that the former will rarely, if ever, be important. It is submitted that the addition of the word "expressly" in s.1(6) was not intended to have the result that an implied incorporation is sufficient for Art.X(c). Unlike the 1924 Act (s.3), the 1971 Act does not *require* the document to contain an incorporating provision. An express choice of English law would not suffice: *Hellenic Steel Co v Svolamar Shipping Co Ltd (The Komninos S)* [1990] 1 Lloyd's Rep. 541.

[16] See para.B2, below.

The categories thus summarised are those in which the Rules will apply by statute. They may also apply, independently of statute, and irrespective of the termini of the voyage, by virtue of an express incorporation in the contract of carriage.[17]

Transhipment

Problems arise in relation to transhipment bills of lading. First, do the provisions of s.1(3), relating to outward voyages from the United Kingdom, continue to apply after the goods have been transhipped at a foreign port? The position is much less clear than under the 1924 Act, but in spite of the marked difference between the language of the two statutes[18] we submit that once the rules have begun to apply, by virtue of shipment in the United Kingdom, they do so throughout the transit.[19]

Secondly, what is the position under Article X, which relates only to carriage between ports in two different states, where goods destined for a foreign port are transhipped at a port in the same state as the port of shipment? It is submitted that since the Act is concerned with establishing the rights and liabilities of the parties under the contract of carriage (see Art.II), it is the termini of the contractual carriage which should determine whether or not the Act applies. Thus, if the bill of lading is a through document in the strict sense, under which the named carrier accepts responsibility for the whole of the carriage to the ultimate port of destination, then the requirements of Article X are satisfied if the port of shipment and the port of ultimate destination are in different states. But if the document is of the type under which the shipowner assumes liability as far as the port of transhipment, and thereafter participates only as agent for the onward carrier, the Rules will not apply unless the port of transhipment is in a different state from the original port of shipment.[20]

Where the contractual voyage is from a port in a non-contracting state, the Rules will not become applicable merely because there has been a transhipment in a port in a contracting state during the voyage.[21]

To which Documents do the Rules Apply?

The scheme of the 1924 Act was straightforward. The medium was entirely contractual. The legislation was directed at the responsibilities, liabilities, rights

---

[17] See below.

[18] Section 1 of the 1924 Act read: " . . . the carriage of goods by sea in ships carrying goods from any port in Great Britain . . . " Section 1(3) of the 1971 Act reads: " . . . the carriage of goods by sea in ships where the port of shipment is a port in the United Kingdom . . . "

[19] Thus, where goods were shipped at Shoreham under a contract for the carriage from an inland depot in the United Kingdom to Jeddah, and were subsequently transhipped at Le Havre pursuant to a contractual liberty, it was held that the Rules applied throughout the operation of transhipment: *Mayhew Foods Ltd v Overseas Containers Ltd* [1984] 1 Lloyd's Rep. 317. *Cf. Art.VII*, below.

[20] For a discussion of various types of through document, see Art.180.

[21] *The Anders Maersk* [1986] 1 Lloyd's Rep. 483 (H.K.).

and immunities created by the contract of carriage. The Hague Rules, implemented by way of contractual implied terms, had no relation otherwise than to a contract of carriage (Art.II); nor indeed, apart from the special case of the non-negotiable receipt marked as such (Art.VI), to a contract which was not "covered by a bill of lading or similar document of title": Article I(b).

The 1971 Act retains Articles I(b), II and IV in their existing form, but superimposes a number of additional requirements, which define when the Hague-Visby Rules are to have "the force of law". In order to ascertain whether these Rules apply, it is now necessary to look at seven distinct provisions, some in the Act, and some in the Rules. The language employed is not consistent. The application of the Rules is variously referred to "the carriage of goods by sea" (s.1(3) and Article II); to "the contract of carriage" (ss 1(4) and 1(7), and Article I(b)); and to the document in which the contract is embodied (s.1(6)(a) and (b) and Art.X). It is not clear to what extent these differences in language reflect a real difference in intent.

Thus, for example, s.1(3) provides that the Rules are to have the force of law in relation to and in connection with the carriage of goods by sea where the port of shipment is in the United Kingdom. The Rules themselves, however, contain provisions which limit their own application by reference to the nature of the contractual document. It seems therefore that although s.1(3) is not expressed to be without prejudice to the Rules, the provisions of the Rules must be read back into the sub-section, so that carriage from a United Kingdom port is not sufficient in itself to make them applicable.

Again, when s.1(4) gives the primary definition of the type of document to which the Rules are to apply it adopts the language of Article I(b), namely "bill of lading or any similar document of title". Yet s.1(6)(a) and 1(7) and Article X refer simply to "a bill of lading". Does the latter expression tacitly comprise a "similar document of title"? With hesitation we suggest that it does, for otherwise Articles I(b), II and X cannot be reconciled.

Another problem concerns the type of "clause paramount" which is effective to make the Rules apply by operation of law, rather than contract, to contracts for voyages not made from ports in contracting states, where the bill of lading is not issued in such a state. Section 1(6)(a), dealing with bills of lading, requires an express provision that "the Rules shall govern the contract".[22] Section 1(6)(b) calls for an express provision that "the Rules are to govern the contract as if the receipt were a bill of lading". Both sub-sections are stated to be without prejudice to Article X, of which sub-section (c) requires the bill of lading to provide that "these Rules or legislation of any State giving effect to them"[23] are to govern the

---

[22] It was held in *McLarren & Co v Humber International Transport* [1982] 1 Lloyd's Rep. 301, that the words of incorporation need not provide that the contract shall be exclusively governed by the Rules, or that it is to be governed by the Rules without condition or qualification.

[23] It has been held that a reference to "the terms exceptions and immunities contained in the Brussels International Convention of April 25, 1924, and any subsequent amendments thereto", is sufficient for this purpose: *McLarren & Co v Humber International Transport*, above.

contract. It seems that these three different expressions call for three different modes of incorporation.[24]

If these views are correct, the position as regards various types of documents in common use is as follows:

(i) Bills of lading. The Rules apply by operation of law to all bills of lading[25] for shipment from United Kingdom ports, or for shipments falling within Article X(a) and (b).[26] They also apply if the bill includes a clause which applies either the Rules *simpliciter* or the legislation of any state giving effect to them.[27] Bills of lading not conforming with any of these requirements are not subject to the Rules by operation of law, although as a matter of contract parts of the Rules (for example Arts III and IV) may be applied, if the contract so provides.

(ii) A non-negotiable receipt, marked as such. If this includes a clause paramount providing that the Rules are to govern the contract "as if the receipt were a bill of lading", the contract will be subject to the Rules by operation of law, wherever the port of shipment is located. If the receipt contains a clause simply referring to the Rules (or enacting legislation) it will be subject to them as a matter of contract. In the absence of any incorporating clause, the contract will not be subject to the Rules,[28] since the document cannot be a "similar document of title" within s.1(4) and Article I.[29]

(iii) A receipt not marked as being non-negotiable, incorporating a clause paramount. This would attract the operation of the Rules by operation of law, if the receipt were accepted as a document of title in the trade in question. Otherwise, the Rules would apply only as a matter of contract.

---

[24] Although *McLarren & Co v Humber International Transport*, above, is a decision to the contrary effect, so far as concerns the words "as if the receipt were a bill of lading".

[25] A "straight" bill of lading ie. a bill of lading providing for delivery of goods to a named consignee and not to order or assigns or bearer, is a bill of lading or similar document of title within the meaning of s.1(4) and Art.1(b): *J.I. MacWilliam Co Inc v Mediterranean Shipping Co SA (The Rafaela S)* [2005] UKHL 11; [2005] 2 AC. 423 H.L. See also *"Straight Bills of Lading in the House of Lords"*, McMeel, [2005] L.M.C.L.Q. 273.

[26] The bill of lading need not actually be issued; if the bill of lading is to be issued, the contract is "covered" by it or "provides for its issue" within the definition of Art.1(b) and s.1(4) of the 1971 Act: *Parsons Corp v C.V. Scheepvaartonderneming Happy Ranger* [2002] EWCA Civ 694; [2002] 2 Lloyd's Rep. 357.

[27] But not, we suggest, where the bill of lading refers to legislation giving effect to the unamended Hague Rules (as in the case with, for example, the United States clause paramount), since s.1(1) makes it clear that "the Rules" are the Hague-Visby Rules. See also *Trafigura Beheer BV v Mediterranean Shipping Co SA (The MSC Amsterdam)* [2007] EWCA Civ. 794; [2007] 2 Lloyd's Rep. 622 where a bill of lading included a "clause paramount" which stipulated that it was subject to the Hague-Visby Rules "if compulsory applicable".

[28] But see, per *contra*, *McLarren & Co v Humber International Transport*, above.

[29] *Chan Chen Kum v Wah Tat Bank* [1971] 1 Lloyd's Rep. 439. This passage was approved by Steyn J. in *Browner International Ltd v Monarch Shipping Co Ltd (The European Enterprise)* [1989] 2 Lloyd's Rep. 185. See also *R.G. Mayor t/a Glanville Coaches v P. & O. Ferries Ltd (The Lion)* [1990] 2 Lloyd's Rep. 144 in which a similar approach was taken to the Athens Convention 1974.

(iv) A receipt or other document not marked as non-negotiable, and not incorporating a clause paramount. It is arguable that in some circumstances at least such documents might be subject to the Rules.[30]

Bills of Lading issued under Charterparties

One of the most serious difficulties which arises under the Rules in their current, as well as their original, form is to determine the position of a bill of lading issued under a charterparty.

First as to the form: Article V of the Rules (second paragraph) provides that "the provisions of these Rules shall not be applicable to charterparties, but if bills of lading are issued in the case of a ship under a charterparty they shall comply with the terms of these Rules". The reference appears to be the form prescribed by Article III, Rule 3, by which the "*carrier*" must on demand issue a bill of lading showing marks, number of packages or pieces or quality or weight, and the apparent order and condition of the goods, and to Article III, Rule 7, which deals with "shipped" bills of lading.

Where the shipper is not the charterer, it may be that no difficulty will arise; but where the charterer wishes to use the ship for his own goods, it is more than doubtful whether he will be entitled to demand the issue of a bill of lading in accordance with the provisions of these Rules.

For as between the charterer and the shipowner the operative document is the charterparty, the bill of lading being generally a mere receipt (see Art.35, above, and *Note* thereto), and there is between them no "contract of carriage" within the meaning of Article I(b) and, therefore, the shipowner is not within the meaning of Article I(a) a "carrier" (i.e. a person who "enters into a contract of carriage"), on whom alone is imposed the obligation to issue a bill of lading in accordance with Article III, Rule 3. So long, therefore, as the bill of lading conforms with the terms of the charterparty, there seems to be nothing in the Act or the Rules to compel the shipowner to issue to such a charterer a bill of lading in the form required by Article III, Rule 3. If, therefore, "the number of packages or pieces or quantity of weight" has not been inserted in the bill of lading issued, it is difficult to see how even a subsequent holder of the bill of lading will be able to claim the benefits of Article III, Rules 3 and 4, though it may be that the court will be able to give them some retroactive effect.

Secondly, as to the obligations imposed on the shipowner. At common law the operative document as between the shipowner and the charterer is the charterparty and the bill of lading issued to the charterer generally acts as a receipt and so long as it remains merely a receipt the Rules will not apply. However, as between the shipowner and subsequent "holders" of the bill of lading, apart from the present Act, the bill of lading is the operative document. Under the present Act "contract of carriage" is so defined by Article I(b) that the Rules will apply

---

[30] See Diamond, *op. cit.*, pp.34–35.

to such a bill of lading with the result that any term in it which is in conflict with Article III, Rule 8, will be rendered null and void and the carrier will incur the liabilities prescribed by the Rules. In many and in an increasing number of cases, no doubt, the chartered ship will issue a bill of lading in such a form as will incorporate the provisions of the Act. But such a bill of lading may not always be used by the ship, and, if not, the shipowner will incur to parties other than the charterer liabilities which would not have fallen upon him if the charterer had not indorsed the bill of lading to them. It would, therefore, be prudent for the shipowner in all cases where his ship is under a charter to provide in the charterparty for an indemnity from the charterer against any liability so incurred.

The Statutory Effect of the Rules

The 1924 Act provided that the Hague Rules were "to have effect" in relation to the stipulated carriage.[31]

The 1971 Act provides that the Amended Rules "shall have the force of law".[32] This change in terminology has two results.

First, it demonstrates that the Rules take effect, not merely as part of the proper law, where that law is English, but as part of the statute law of England, to which an English court must give effect, irrespective of the proper law, in all cases falling within s.1 and Article X.[33]

Secondly, the Act for the first time gives statutory force to the Rules irrespective of the termini of the voyage, where there is an express incorporation clause. This means that whereas under the previous legislation the incorporation of the Hague Rules in cases falling outside the Act gave them merely contractual effect, so that they had to be construed in conjunction with the other terms of the bill of lading, under the 1971 Act incorporation of the Amended Rules causes them to override any contradictory provisions of the bill.[34]

The Contents of the Bill of Lading

As regards the contents of the bill of lading, the 1971 Act differs from its predecessors in two respects.

In the first place, s.3 of the 1924 Act required every bill of lading, or similar document of title, issued in Great Britain or Northern Ireland which contained or was evidence of any contract to which the Hague Rules applied, to contain an

---

[31] ss.1, 3 and 4.

[32] ss.1(2), (3), (6) and (7).

[33] *The Hollandia* [1983] A.C. 565. It is therefore no longer necessary to consider the true effect of the dicta in *Vita Food Produtcts v Unus Shipping Co* [1939] A.C. 277; and *The Torni* [1932] P. 78, which related to the different legislative techniques employed by the 1924 Act and the kindred Commonwealth legislation. See also *Caltex Singapore Pte. Ltd v B.P. Shipping Ltd* [1996] 1 Lloyd's Rep. 286.

[34] By virtue of Art.III, r.8. Where the Rules are incorporated into some document other than one which attracts the operation of s.1 or Art.X, for example, where they are incorporated into a charterparty, they form part of the contract of carriage, and must be construed with, and in appropriate cases may be overruled or modified by, the other parts of that contract: see below.

express statement that it was to have effect subject to the provisions of the Rules, as applied by the Act. There is no counterpart to this provision in the 1971 Act. No doubt the omission reflects the adoption of a different legislative technique, whereby the Hague-Visby Rules are to "have the force of law" in relation to the carriage of goods from ports in the United Kingdom. Thus, so far as concerns litigation in the English and Scottish courts, in respect of cargo consigned from the United Kingdom, it makes no difference whether or not the document contains a clause expressly declaring the Rules to be applicable.[35] Nevertheless, the repeal of s.3 has left the carrier free to issue bills of lading without such a clause, and this may cause hardship to the cargo-owner if he is compelled to bring proceedings in a country which has no Hague-Visby legislation.

Secondly, although the Hague Rules and the Hague-Visby Rules contain identical provisions[36] requiring the issue of bills of lading which show the leading marks, the number, quantity or weight of the cargo, and the apparent order and condition of the goods, and also requiring bills of lading issued in the case of a ship under charter to "comply with the terms of the Rules", there is a significant difference in the status of the obligations. Under the 1924 Act[37] the Rules were to "have effect" in relation to carriage from United Kingdom ports. Now, the 1971 Act prescribes that the Rules are "to have the force of law."[38] Thus, the shipowner is obliged to issue a bill of lading in the appropriate terms. Whether the obligation is of a penal nature is perhaps of little importance, but there does appear to be a civil duty which would, if necessary, be enforced by means of injunction.

Incorporation into Charterparties

Although the Act does not apply to charterparties, some or all of its provisions may be incorporated in a charterparty.[39] The incorporating clause is frequently called a "Clause Paramount". Some forms of clause purport to incorporate the entire Act, or its foreign equivalent, into the charter.[40] Other forms incorporate only the Rules.[41] Some forms still in common use incorporate the whole or part of the Hague Rules, not the Hague-Visby Rules. Yet other forms incorporate only certain parts of the Rules.[42] The question whether the provisions thus incorporated prevail over the remaining terms of the charter depends on the construction

---

[35] See *The Hollandia*, above.
[36] In Art.III, r.3 and Art.V, respectively.
[37] s.1.
[38] ss.1(2) and (3).
[39] *Adamastos Shipping Co v Anglo-Saxon Petroleum Co* [1959] A.C. 133; *Leeds S.S. Co v Duncan Fox* (1932) 37 Com.Cas. 213; *Joseph Constantine v Imperial Smelting Corp* (1940) 66 Ll.L.R. 146 at p.148; *Chandris v Isbrandtsen-Moller* [1951] 1 K.B. 240; *Minister of Food v Reardon Smith Line* [1951] 2 Lloyd's Rep. 265.
[40] See *Adamastos Shipping Co v Anglo-Saxon Petroleum Co*, above, (consecutive voyage charter); *Seven Seas Transportation v Pacifico Union Marina Corp* [1984] 1 Lloyd's Rep. 586, 588 (time charter). It renders the charter subject to the terms of the relevant legislation in respect of all voyages, and not merely cargo-carrying voyages to and from ports in the country in question: *ibid.*
[41] In *Nea Agrex v Baltic Shipping Co* [1976] 2 Lloyd's Rep. 47 it was held that the words " . . . and also Paramount Clause are deemed to be incorporated in this charterparty" were not void for uncertainty, but on the contrary were effective to incorporate the Hague Rules (but not the Hague Rules legislation).
[42] See, e.g. *Marifortuna Naviera SA v Govt. of Ceylon* [1970] 1 Lloyd's Rep. 247.

of the whole document, and in particular on the precise wording of the clause.[43]

Construction of the Act

Since the enactment of the 1924 legislation the question as to what principles of construction should be applied to its provisions has from time to time arisen. In *Stag Line v Foscolo Mango* Lord Atkin said[44]: "In approaching the construction of these rules it appears to me important to bear in mind that one has to give the words as used their plain meaning and not to colour one's interpretation by considering whether a meaning otherwise plain should be avoided if it alters the previous law. If the Act merely purported to codify the law this caution would be well founded. I will repeat the well-known words of Lord Herschell in *Bank of England v Vagliano Brothers*."[45] (Lord Atkin then quoted the passage referred to and proceeded.) "But if this is the canon of construction in regard to a codifying Act, still more does it apply to an Act like the present which is not intended to codify the English law, but is the result (as expressed in the Act) of an international conference intended to unify certain rules relating to bills of lading. It will be remembered that the Act only applies to contracts of carriage of goods outwards from ports in the United Kingdom; and the rules will often have to be interpreted in the courts of the foreign consignees. For the purpose of uniformity, it is, therefore, important that the courts should apply themselves to the consideration only of the words used without any predilection for the former law, always preserving the right to say that words used in the English language which have already in the particular context received judicial interpretation may be presumed to be used in the sense already judicially imputed on them." Lord MacMillan, in the same case, said[46]: "As these rules must come under the consideration of foreign courts it is desirable in the interests of uniformity that their interpretation should not be rigidly controlled by domestic precedents of antecedent date, but rather that the language of the rules should be construed on broad principles of general acceptance." It is to be noted that in the earlier case

---

[43] Thus in *Seven Seas Transportation v Pacifico Union Marina Corp*, above, the charter was put together from various printed forms, together with the parties' own variations or additions. It was held that the presence of an express absolute warranty of seaworthiness did not entail that the clause paramount was ineffective to incorporate the United States Act, since it was legitimate to construe the contract as a whole and accept that some portions of it might be modified or even superseded by others. Too much weight should not be placed on the use of the word "paramount", since this may indicate merely that the Rules are intended to override only some of the express or implied terms of the charter. Thus, in *Marifortuna Naviera v Govt. of Ceylon*, above, it was held that the exceptions in the Rules did not exclude the shipowner's liability for breach of a particular term concerning notice of readiness. Contrast *Adamastos Shipping Co v Anglo-Saxon Petroleum Co*, above, where a much wider form of Clause Paramount specifically provided that the Act was to prevail over all the terms of the contract. See also *Lauritzen Reefers v Ocean Reef Transport Ltd SA (The Bukhta Russkaya)* [1977] 2 Lloyd's Rep. 744 where the charter stated "general clause paramount to apply"; *Finagra (UK) Ltd v O.T. Africa Line Ltd* [1998] 2 Lloyd's Rep. 622 where bills of lading included a special time bar provision (nine months) and also incorporated the Hague Rules; *Trane Co v Hanjin Shipping Co Ltd* [2001] 2 Lloyd's Rep. 735 (H.K. Ct.).

[44] [1932] A.C. 328, at p.343. See also *Buchanan & Co Ltd v Babco Forwarding and Shipping (UK) Ltd* [1978] A.C. 141, and *Fothergill v Monarch Airlines Ltd* [1981] A.C. 251.

[45] [1891] A.C. 107 at p.144.

[46] [1932] A.C. 328 at p.350.

of *Gosse Millerd, Ltd v Canadian Government*[47] the House of Lords, in considering the meaning of the words "in the management of the ship" in Article IV, Rule 2(a), expressly construed them according to certain decisions of the English courts prior to 1924. Lord Sumner[48] said: "By forbearing to define 'management of the ship' . . . the legislature has in my opinion shown a clear intention to construe and enforce the older clause as it was previously understood and regularly construed by the courts of law." Lord Hailsham, L.C.,[49] said: "I am unable to find any reason for supposing that the words as used by the legislature in the Act of 1924 have any different meaning to that which has been judicially assigned to them when used in contracts for the carriage of goods by sea before that date: and I think that the decisions which have already been given are sufficient to determine the meaning to be put upon them in the statute now under discussion." It is submitted, however, that the principle applied by Lord Hailsham and Lord Sumner comes within the reservation made by Lord Atkin in the concluding passage of his speech quoted above.[50] These passages and the desirability of preserving international uniformity of interpretation were stressed in the opinions delivered in the House of Lords in *Riverstone Meat Co Pty v Lancashire Shipping Co*[51] as to the meaning in Article III, Rule 1, of the "exercise of due diligence" to make the ship seaworthy. So far as we know, the desirability of preserving international uniformity of interpretation has, to date, only led English courts to have regard to decisions in English-speaking jurisdictions; unless there is evidence to the contrary the courts proceed on the basis that the broad principles of law are the same abroad as they are in England.[52]

THE CARRIAGE OF GOODS BY SEA ACT 1971

(1971 c. 19)

An Act to amend the law with respect to the carriage of goods by sea

B2 1. Application of Hague Rules as amended

(1) In this Act, "the Rules" means the International Convention for the unification of certain rules of law relating to bills of lading signed at Brussels on 25th August, 1924, as amended by the Protocol signed at Brussels on 23rd February, 1968, and by the Protocol signed at Brussels on December 21, 1972.[53]

---

[47] [1929] A.C. 223.
[48] *ibid.* p.237.
[49] *ibid.* p.230.
[50] See also, per Devlin J. in *Pyrene Co v Scindia Navigation Co* [1954] 2 Q.B. 402 at p.416.
[51] [1961] A.C. 807. See also per Viscount Simonds in *Midland Silicones v Scruttons* [1962] A.C. 446 at p.471.
[52] *Leesh River Tea Co v British India S.N. Co* [1966] 2 Lloyd's Rep. 193, at p.203.
[53] The reference to the Protocol of December 21, 1979 was introduced by s.2(1) of the Merchant Shipping Act, 1981, brought into force by SI 1983 No. 1906.

(2) The provisions of the Rules, as set out in the Schedule to this Act, shall have the force of law.

(3) Without prejudice to subsection (2) above, the said provisions shall have effect (and have the force of law) in relation to and in connection with the carriage of goods by sea[54] in ships where the port of shipment is a port in the United Kingdom, whether or not the carriage is between ports in two different States within the meaning of Article X of the Rules.

(4) Subject to subsection (6) below, nothing in this section shall be taken as applying anything in the Rules to any contract for the carriage of goods by sea, unless the contract expressly or by implication provides for the issue of a bill of lading or any similar document of title.[55]

(5) [Repealed by section 5(3) and Schedule of the Merchant Shipping Act, 1981].

(6) Without prejudice to Article X(c) of the Rules, the Rules shall have the force of law in relation to—

(a) any bill of lading if the contract contained in or evidenced by it expressly provides that the Rules shall govern the contract, and

(b) any receipt which is a non-negotiable document marked as such if the contract contained in or evidenced by it is a contract for the carriage of goods by sea which expressly provides that the Rules are to govern the contract as if the receipt were a bill of lading,[56]

but subject, where paragraph (b) applies, to any necessary modifications and in particular with the omission in Article III of the Rules of the second sentence of paragraph 4 and of paragraph 7.

(7) If and so far as the contract contained in or evidenced by a bill of lading or receipt within paragraph (a) or (b) of subsection (6) above applies to deck cargo or live animals, the Rules as given the force of law by that subsection shall have effect as if Article I(c) did not exclude deck cargo and live animals.

In this subsection "deck cargo" means cargo which by the contract of carriage is stated as being carried on deck and is so carried.

For comments on the combined effect of s.1 and Article X, see below.

---

[54] The effect of these words is to make the Rules apply to loss and damage occurring in the course of transhipment, but not before loading on the first vessel, or after discharge at the port of destination, even when the contract of carriage contemplated the performance of services ashore before such loading and after such discharge: *Mayhew Foods v Overseas Containers* [1984] 1 Lloyd's Rep. 317. *Cf.* Art.VII, below.

[55] These words cover a "straight" bill of lading: *The Rafaela S*, above.

[56] The receipt must contain words stipulating that the Rules are to govern the receipt as if it were a bill of lading: *Browner International Ltd v Monarch Shipping Co Ltd (The European Enterprise)* [1989] 2 Lloyd's Rep. 185.

B3   1A. Conversion of special drawing rights into sterling

(1) For the purposes of Article IV of the Rules the value on a particular day of [one] special drawing right shall be treated as equal to such a sum in sterling as the [International] Monetary Fund have fixed as being the equivalent of one special drawing right—

(a) for that day; or

(b) if no sum has been so fixed for that day, for the last day before that day for which a sum has been so fixed.

(2) A certificate given by or on behalf of the Treasury stating—

(a) that a particular sum in sterling has been fixed as aforesaid for a particular day; or

(b) that no sum has been so fixed for a particular day and that a particular sum in sterling has been so fixed for a day which is the last day for which a sum has been so fixed before the particular day,

shall be conclusive evidence of those matters for the purposes of subsection (1) above; and a document purporting to be such a certificate shall in any proceedings be received in evidence and, unless the contrary is proved, be deemed to be such a certificate.

(3) The Treasury may charge a reasonable fee for any certificate given in pursuance of subsection (2) above, and any fee received by the Treasury by virtue of this subsection shall be paid into the Consolidated Fund.[57]

B4   2. Contracting States, etc.

(1) If Her Majesty by Order in Council certifies[58] to the following effect, that is to say, that for the purposes of the Rules—

(a) a State specified in the Order is a contracting State, or is a contracting State in respect of any place or territory so specified; or

(b) any place or territory specified in the Order forms part of a State so specified (whether a contracting State or not),

the Order shall, except so far as it has been superseded by a subsequent Order, be conclusive evidence of the matters so certified.

---

[57] This section was inserted by the Merchant Shipping Act 1995, s.314(2), Sch.13, para.45(1), (3).

[58] At the date of going to press, Order in Council, SI 1985/443 was in force in respect of the following states or territories: United Kingdom, Belgium, Denmark, Ecuador, Egypt, Finland, France, German Democratic Republic, Lebanese Republic, Netherlands, Netherlands Antilles, Norway, Poland, Singapore, Spain, Sri Lanka, Sweden, Switzerland, Syria and Tonga. That order was amended by SI 2000/1103 by adding Croatia, Georgia and Italy.

(2) An Order in Council under this section may be varied or revoked by a subsequent Order in Council.

3. Absolute warranty of seaworthiness not to be implied in contracts to which Rules apply.   **B5**

There shall not be implied in any contract for the carriage of goods by sea to which the Rules apply by virtue of this Act[59] any absolute undertaking by the carrier of the goods to provide a seaworthy ship.

4. Application of Act to British possession, etc.   **B6**

(1) Her Majesty may by Order in Council direct that this Act shall extend, subject to such exceptions, adaptations and modifications as may be specified in the Order, to all or any of the following territories, that is—

   (a) any colony (not being a colony for whose external relations a country other than the United Kingdom is responsible),

   (b) any country outside Her Majesty's dominions in which Her Majesty has jurisdiction in right of Her Majesty's Government of the United Kingdom.

(2) An Order in Council under this section may contain such transitional and other consequential and incidental provisions as appear to Her Majesty to be expedient, including provisions amending or repealing any legislation about the carriage of goods by sea forming part of the law of any of the territories mentioned in paragraphs (a) and (b) above.

(3) An Order in Council under this section may be varied or revoked by a subsequent Order in Council.[60]

5. Extension of application of Rules to carriage from ports in British possessions, etc.   **B7**

(1) Her Majesty may by Order in Council provide that section 1(3) of this Act shall have effect as if the reference therein to the United Kingdom included a reference to all or any of the following territories, that is—

   (a) the Isle of Man;

---

[59] The words "*by virtue of this Act*" did not appear in s.2 of the 1924 Act. They make it clear that where the Rules apply by contract, rather than by statute, e.g. where they are incorporated into a charter-party, the contract when construed as a whole may subject the carrier to an absolute undertaking of seaworthiness, notwithstanding Art.III, r.1, Art.IV, r.1 and Art.III, r.8.

[60] See Carriage of Goods by Sea (Overseas Territories) Order 1982, SI 1982/1664 (British Antarctic Territory, British Virgin Islands, Cayman Islands, Falkland Islands and Dependencies, Monserrat, Turks and Caicos Islands); Carriage of Goods by Sea (Bermuda) Order 1980, SI 1980/1507; Carriage of Goods by Sea (Bermuda) Order 1982, SI 1982/1662.

(b) any of the Channel Islands specified in the Order;

(c) any colony specified in the Order (not being a colony for whose external relations a country other than the United Kingdom is responsible);

(d) ... [61]

(e) any country specified in the Order, being a country outside Her Majesty's dominions in which Her Majesty has jurisdiction in right of Her Majesty's Government of the United Kingdom.

(2) An Order in Council under this section may be varied or revoked by a subsequent Order in Council.[62]

B8   6. Supplemental

(1) This Act may be cited as the Carriage of Goods by Sea Act 1971.

(2) It is hereby declared that this Act extends to Northern Ireland.

(3) The following enactments shall be repealed, that is—

(a) the Carriage of Goods by Sea Act 1924,

(b) section 12(4)(a) of the Nuclear Installations Act 1965,

and without prejudice to section 38(1) of the Interpretation Act 1889,[63] the reference to the said Act of 1924 in section 1(1)(i)(ii) of the Hovercraft Act 1968 shall include a reference to this Act.

(4) It is hereby declared that for the purposes of Article VIII of the Rules section 186 of the Merchant Shipping Act 1995[64] (which entirely exempts shipowners and others in certain circumstances from liability for loss of, or damage to, goods) is a provision relating to limitation of liability.

(5) [Provisions for coming into force].

Subsection (4) achieves, in different words, the same effect as section 6(2) of the 1924 Act.[65]

---

[61] Subs.(1)(d) was repealed by the Statute Law (Repeals) Act 1989, Sch.1, Pt VI.

[62] See fn.60.

[63] Replaced by subs.17(2)(a) of the Interpretation Act 1978.

[64] The reference to s.18 of the Merchant Shipping Act 1979, was substituted by the Merchant Shipping Act 1995, s.314(3), Sch.13, para.45(1), (4).

[65] See para.B9, below. It is submitted that in cases governed by the Hague Rules (whether in their original or amended form) the carrier is entitled to the benefit of s.186 of the Merchant Shipping Act 1995, even in cases where the fire results from want of due diligence, and that the principle of *Virginia Carolina etc. Co v Norfolk Co* [1912] 1 K.B. 229 (see Art.116, above) does not apply.

Schedule

The Hague Rules as Amended by the Brussels Protocol 1968

Article I

In these Rules the following words are employed, with the meanings set out below:—

(a) "Carrier" includes the owner or the charterer who enters into a contract of carriage with a shipper.

"*Includes*". The use of this word suggests that the definition is not exhaustive, and, if so, the term "*carrier*" might include a freight agent or forwarding agent or carriage contractor in cases where by issuing a bill of lading he enters into a contract of carriage with the shipper. It does not include a stevedore.[66] At all events, it does not extend beyond the person who is contracting as carrier under the relevant contract of carriage. This will usually be a bill of lading, in which case the carrier is the person (whether owner of the vessel or charterer) who makes himself liable under that document. Where the bills are incorporated into a charterparty, the carrier will be the shipowner, or disponent owner, as the case may be.[67]

"*The charterer*". This, no doubt, contemplates a case in which a charterer is liable on the contract of carriage and the shipowner is not. This may arise where the charterer issues and signs his own bill of lading. In that case the owner is not entitled to the rights and immunities set out in the Rules and in particular in Article IV, nor it seems is the owner under any of the responsibilities and liabilities set out in the Rules, e.g under Article III.[68]

(b) "Contract of carriage" applies only to contracts of carriage covered by a bill of lading or any similar document of title,[69] in so far as such document relates to the carriage of goods by sea, including any bill of lading or any similar document as aforesaid issued under or pursuant to a charter party from the moment at which such bill of lading or similar document of title regulates the relations between a carrier and a holder of the same.

"*Covered by a bill of lading*". This definition includes any contract of affreightment, however informally made in its inception, the parties to which intend that, in accordance with the custom of that trade, the shipper shall be entitled to demand at or after shipment

---

[66] *Midland Silicones v Scruttons* [1962] A.C. 446.

[67] *Freedom General Shipping v Tokai Shipping Co* [1982] 1 Lloyd's Rep. 73. Thus, where the owners had been held liable under bills of lading for cargo damage, and then subsequently claimed against the charterers for an indemnity under the "Inter-Club Agreement", they were not defeated by failure to bring suit within the period of one year prescribed by Art.III, r.6, since the Rule operates in favour of "the carrier and the ship". The fact that the charterer might also have been held liable to the consignees under the bill of lading, in accordance with United States law, did not affect the position under the charterparty.

[68] *Gadsden v Australian Coastal Shipping Commission* [1977] 1 N.S.W.L.R. 575. See Art.41, above for a discussion of when bills of lading bind the charterer.

[69] These words cover a "straight" bill of lading: *The Rafaela S*, above. See also *Comalco Aluminium Ltd v Nogal Freight Services Pty Ltd*, 113 A.L.R. 677.

a bill of lading setting forth the terms of the contract.[70] To such a contract the Rules will apply even though no bill of lading is in fact demanded or issued.[71] This construction avoids the logical difficulty inherent in Article III, Rule 3[72] (which provides that the carrier shall issue a bill of lading in a certain form) if there is no "contract of carriage" until the issue of the bill of lading. It follows that a carrier may make whatever contract he pleases if it is not intended that a bill of lading should subsequently be issued, and none is issued. Article VI will only apply to that class of contract in which, according to the custom of the trade, a bill of lading is normally issued.

"*Similar document of title*". These words appear to be taken from the Canadian Water Carriage of Goods Act 1910, s.5, and their use in the present Act may have been prompted by the decision in *Diamond Alkali Co v Bourgeois*.[73] From the provisions of Article III, Rule 7, it appears that "received for shipment" bills of lading are covered by this term.[74] Sea waybills and ship's delivery orders within the Carriage of Goods by Sea Act 1992 have not at present been established judicially as documents of title by mercantile custom. It must therefore be doubtful whether they are within the Rules.

"*In so far as such document relates to the carriage of goods by sea*". Presumably this limitation was inserted in order to provide for a case where the contract evidenced by the bill of lading is for carriage of goods partly by land and partly by sea, e.g. in the case of a through bill of lading issued for the transportation of goods from Chicago to London via New York, the "*contract of carriage*" would be from New York to London and the rights and liabilities under the Rules would apply to part only of the contract between the parties.[75] Probably "carriage by sea" includes carriage on rivers and other waters where great ships go, e.g. a carriage from Quebec or Montreal to London. If not, the exception in Article IV, Rule 2(c) of perils of other navigable waters is unnecessary.

"*Issued under or pursuant to a charterparty*". These words give rise to certain difficulties. The shipowner when issuing the bill of lading to a charterer is under no obligation to incorporate the Rules, nor is he bound by them; but if the charterer indorses the bill of lading for valuable consideration it would seem that by so doing he gives a different protection to and imposes a fresh obligation upon the shipowner. Presumably, the shipowner by issuing the bill of lading to the charterer gives him implied authority so to indorse the bill of lading and so bind the shipowner. Probably, an indorsee without notice could rely upon this authority, even though the charterer had expressly undertaken not to indorse the bill of lading, and the shipowner would be liable to the bill of lading holder in accordance with the provisions of the Rules. Indeed, even if the indorsee were informed of the limitation placed upon the right to indorse, though the result might conceivably be that the stipulation would prevent the document from being a bill of lading or similar document of title, yet, if it were a bill of lading, it is difficult to see that the relationship of the shipowner to the indorsee would not be governed by the provisions of the Rules.

---

[70] *Pyrene Co v Scindia Navigation Co* [1954] 2 Q.B. 402 at p.420, following the Court of Session in *Harland and Wolff v Burns and Laird* (1931) 40 Ll.L.R. 286. See also *Vita Food Products v Unus Shipping Co* [1939] A.C. 277 at p.294; *Hugh Mack v Burns and Laird Lines* (1944) 77 Ll.L.R. 377 at p.383 (N.I.); *Canada and Dominion Sugar Co v Canadian National (W.I.) Steamships* [1947] A.C. 46 at p.57.

[71] As in *Pyrene Co v Scindia Navigation Co*, above; see particularly at p.420; see also *The Beltana* [1967] 1 Lloyd's Rep. 531 at p.533 (Sup.Ct. of W. Australia); *The Happy Ranger* [2002] EWCA Civ 694; [2002] 2 Lloyd's Rep. 357.

[72] See below.

[73] [1921] 3 K.B. 433.

[74] *Hugh Mack v Burns and Laird Lines* (1944) 77 Ll.L.R. 377 at p.383; and see Art.182, above.

[75] *Pyrene Co v Scindia Navigation Co* [1954] 2 Q.B. 402. Nevertheless, where the bill of lading permits transhipment, the Rules will continue to apply whilst the goods are ashore waiting to be loaded on board the on-carrying vessel: *Mayhew Foods Ltd v Overseas Containers Ltd* [1984] 1 Lloyd's Rep. 317.

As pointed out in para.B1, above, a prudent shipowner whose ship is under charter should see that his charterparty provides for an indemnity against any liability so incurred.

"*From the moment at which such bill of lading . . . regulates.*" These words do not apply to bills of lading generally, but only to bills of lading issued under a charterparty.[76]

"*The moment*" may apparently be: (1) if goods are shipped by a shipper other than the charterer, the time when a bill of lading is issued to such shipper[77]; (2) if the charterer ships goods and takes a bill of lading making the goods deliverable to him or to his order, the time when that bill of lading is handed to an indorsee to whom the property in the goods covered by it passes; (3) if the charterer ships goods and takes a bill of lading making the goods deliverable to a named consignee, the time when the bill of lading is delivered to the consignee.

If in case (2) the charterer, who has shipped the goods and sold them to an indorsee of the bill of lading, subsequently buys back the goods from that indorsee, it is a nice question whether he can then rely on the shipowner's absolute undertaking of seaworthiness in the charter. Probably he cannot.

Similarly, in case (3), he probably cannot rely on his right under the charter if he buys the goods from the named consignee.

This provision presents a further difficulty. Article II provides that the Rules shall apply "*under every contract of carriage*". But by Article I(b) "*contract of carriage*" is confined to contracts under bills of lading from the time the bills of lading regulate the relations of the parties. There is, therefore, no contract of carriage to which the Rules apply so long as the bill of lading is held by the charterer, and during that period presumably a bill of lading exempting the shipowner from all liability whatsoever is not subject to the Rules.

Suppose, then, such a bill of lading is issued, and the goods lost while the bill of lading remains in the hands of the charterer, and the charterer transfers the bill of lading and the property in the goods, will the indorsee of the bill of lading have the advantage of the Rules? The answer must depend on whether at the moment of indorsement the bill of lading relates back to the beginning of the loading.[78] On the whole we prefer the view that, when once the contract has become a "*contract of carriage*" within the meaning of this Rule, the Rules apply and relate back to the beginning of the carriage of the goods, i.e. the beginning of the loading.

"*Regulates the relations between a carrier and a holder*". This phrase is vague and difficult to construe. Presumably the bill of lading does regulate the relations of a carrier a consignee or indorsee to whom the property has passed, but does not regulate the relations of a carrier and the charterer's agent, or of a carrier and a mortgagee or a pledgee, until that mortgagee or pledgee presents the bill of lading and takes delivery under it.[79]

(c) "Goods" includes goods, wares, merchandise, and articles of every kind whatsoever, except live animals and cargo which by the contract of carriage is stated as being carried on deck and is so carried.

---

[76] *Pyrene Co v Scindia Navigation Co*, above.
[77] See Art.35, above, where the position of a charterer who subsequently buys the goods shipped and has the bill of lading indorsed to him is discussed.
[78] See above, para.B1.
[79] See Arts 14, 15, 35 and 36, above.

"*Goods*" as here defined excludes live animals and goods agreed to be carried, and in fact carried, upon deck. If a consignment of goods shipped under one bill of lading, which describes it as being carried on deck, is in fact carried partly on deck and partly under deck, the contract of carriage if severable may be in different terms as regards the deck cargo and the under-deck cargo, because the under-deck cargo will be subject to the Rules and the deck cargo will not.[80] If not severable the Rules will probably apply to the whole contract.[81]

If there is a clear contract for a carriage on deck, and the shipowner gratuitously carries them under deck, he will apparently increase his liabilities, because the Rules apply to the shipment. If he starts the voyage with the goods on deck and in the course of the voyage restows the goods under deck, the result appears to be that the Rules apply from the start of the voyage.

"*Stated as being carried on deck*". A clause giving liberty to carry on deck unaccompanied by anything in the bill of lading indicating that the goods are in fact being carried on deck is not such a statement as is called for by the exception. Cargo in fact carried on deck under such a liberty clause, but without any statement in the bill of lading that it is so carried, will be subject to the Act and Rules, including the obligation upon the carrier under Article III, Rule 2, carefully to stow it.[82]

(d) "Ship" means any vessel used for the carriage of goods by sea:

The Act and Rules apply in relation to the carriage of goods by hovercraft as they apply in relation to goods on board or carried by ship.[83]

(e) "Carriage of goods" covers the period from the time when the goods are loaded on to the time when they are discharged from the ship.

The function of this sub-rule is to assist in the definition of the contract of carriage by identifying the first and last operations of those which together constitute the carriage of goods by sea.[84] The words "*loaded on*" do not mean that the rights and liabilities referred to in Article II apply only to that part of the operation of loading that takes place after the goods cross the ship's rail.[81] Similarly goods are not "*discharged*" before they have been put into a lighter alongside.[85] It is clear from Article III, Rules 1 and 3, that the carrier may have obligations before the operation of loading begins.

It has not yet been decided whether the use of the word "*ship*" has the effect of excluding from the "carriage of goods by sea" to which the Rules relate the lightering of

---

[80] See, for example, *The Makedonia* [1962] 1 Lloyd's Rep. 316.
[81] See also, para.B1, above.
[82] *Svenska Traktor Akt. v Maritime Agencies (Southampton)* [1953] 2 Q.B. 295.
[83] Subject to the modifications enacted by the Hovercraft (Civil Liability) Order 1986 (SI 1986/1305).
[84] *Pyrene Co v Scindia Navigation Co* [1954] 2 Q.B. 402, per Devlin J. at p.416; and see also *Mayhew Foods Ltd v Overseas Containers Ltd* above.
[85] *Goodwin v Lamport and Holt* (1929) 34 Ll.L.R. 192. (See also *The Arawa* [1977] 2 Lloyd's Rep. 416; [1980] 2 Lloyd's Rep. 135 (CA); *Amerlux Steel Products v Mouffalize* [1958] A.M.C. 567; *Remington Rand v American Export Lines* [1955] A.M.C. 1789.) Roche J. also thought that the discharge of goods is incomplete so long as they are in a lighter and that lighter has not been fully loaded with other goods of the same cargo with which it is intended to load her; *ibid.* at p.194. *Sed quaere*, and *cf. Lindsay Blee v Motor Union* (1930) 37 Ll.L.R. 220 at p.223.

goods out to a ship at the port of loading or their removal to shore by lighter at the port of discharge.

If the carrier undertakes to perform these operations it seems possible[86] that they might be considered as part of loading and discharging respectively. If he does not, it seems probable that the Rules would have no application to these operations; the terms of Article I(d) lend some support to this view. In each case, however, it must be a question of interpreting the individual contract of carriage, to ascertain which party undertakes responsibility for the lightering.[87]

Article II   B10

Subject to the provisions of Article VI, under every contract of carriage[88] of goods by sea the carrier,[89] in relation to the loading, handling, stowage, carriage, custody, care, and discharge of such goods, shall be subject to the responsibilities and liabilities, and entitled to the rights and immunities hereinafter set forth.

"Loading... and discharge". This is the crucial Article applying the rights and liabilities in the subsequent Articles to the operations it enumerates. Article III, Rule 2[90] provides that, subject to the rights and immunities of Article IV, the carrier shall properly and carefully, inter alia, load and discharge the goods. Before the decision of the House of Lords in *Renton v Palmyra Trading Corp of Panama*[91] it was doubtful how these two provisions were to be interpreted in their application to the operations of loading and discharging.

There were three possible views: (i) the carrier, whether he wants to or not, is obliged to perform or undertake responsibility for the whole of loading and discharging; (ii) the carrier is only responsible under the Rules for that part of loading and discharging which takes place on the ship's side of the ship's rail; (iii) the carrier is only responsible for that part, if any, of either operation which it is agreed shall be carried out by or under arrangements made by him.

In *Pyrene Co v Scindia Navigation Co*,[92] Devlin J. rejected the second view[93] and preferred the third, and his choice was approved in *Renton v Palmyra Trading Corp of Panama* by Lord Morton of Henryton[94] (with whom Lord Cohen agreed[95]), and by Lord Somervell of Harrow.[96] It may therefore be taken as clear that the object of the Rules "is

---

[86] In view of the reasoning of Devlin J. in *Pyrene Co v Scindia Navigation Co* [1954] 2 Q.B. 402 at pp.417–418, adopted by the House of Lords in *Renton v Palmyra* [1957] A.C. 149 at pp.170, 173, 176.

[87] Thus, in *The Arawa* [1977] 2 Lloyd's Rep. 416, where a clause provided that "The carrier may carry the goods to or from the vessel in any... craft... and the carrier shall not be held for any... damage or delay to the goods while in such... craft... even though caused by negligence of the carrier, his agents or servants." It was held (obiter) that the discharge of the goods, for the purposes of the Hague Rules was complete when the goods were placed into lighters.

[88] *"Contract of Carriage"* is defined in Art.I(b).

[89] *"Carrier"* is defined in Art.I(a).

[90] See below.

[91] [1957] A.C. 149. For a discussion of this case see Art.127, above.

[92] [1954] 2 Q.B. 402 at p.418.

[93] Which was inconsistent with the decision of Roche J. in *Goodwin v Lamport and Holt* (1929) 34 Ll.L.R. 192.

[94] [1957] A.C. 149 at p.170.

[95] *ibid.* p.173.

[96] *ibid.* p.174.

to define not the scope of the contract service but the terms on which that service is to be performed".[97] It is also clear that even if as the result of express agreement or an agreement implied from conduct, the *risk* of the operations of loading and discharging are to fall upon the shipowner, nevertheless the *expense* of such operations may, by agreement, be placed upon the shipper or consignee.[98]

"Discharge". Wright J. considered that this word was used in place of the word "deliver" because the period of responsibility during which the Act and Rules applied ended when the operations devolving upon the ship came to an end.[99] If the view of Devlin J. be right that the Act and Rules attach to a contract or part of a contract and not to a period of time,[100] this view might perhaps be more accurately expressed by substituting for "period ... during" in the above sentence the words "contract of carriage by sea to".

The provisions of this Act have not altered the general principles of the law as it existed before the passing of the Act. A carrier who has received goods in apparent good order and has not discharged them in like good order is liable to the shipper unless he can excuse himself under Article IV, or under some other exception in his contract permitted by the Rules. It is not for the shipper in the first instance to prove negligence in the carrier.[101]

B11   **Article III**

1. The carrier shall be bound, before and at the beginning of the voyage, to exercise due diligence to—

(a) Make the ship seaworthy[102]

(b) Properly man, equip, and supply the ship

---

[97] *Pyrene Co v Scindia Navigation Co*, above, at p.418. The first view was preferred in some earlier editions of this work as being more consistent with the language of Art.III, r.2. The decision of the HL was concerned with the validity of a liberty or deviation clause altering the destination of the goods in the event, inter alia, of strikes. In *Ismail v Polish Ocean Lines* [1976] 1 Q.B. 893, a clause in a charterparty which incorporated Arts III and IV of the Hague Rules stipulated that: "Dunnaging and stowage instructions given by the charterers to be carefully followed, but to be executed under the supervision of the Master. He is to remain responsible for proper stowage and dunnage." This seems to have been interpreted, at least by Lord Denning M.R., as a case in the *Pyrene Co v Scindia Navigation Co* line of authority, whereby an express provision defining the scope of responsibility for certain operations took the liability for unsatisfactory performance of these operations outside the scope of the Rules. See also *The Saudi Prince (No. 2)* [1988] 1 Lloyd's Rep. 1. In *Jindal Iron & Steel Co Ltd v Islamic Solidarity Shipping Co (The Jordan II)* [2004] UKHL 49; [2005] 1 Lloyd's Rep. 57 the House of Lords expressed no concluded view on the issue of interpretation of Art.III, r.2 but refused to depart from the decision in *Renton v Palmyra*.

[98] A helpful summary of the scheme of the Rules is to be found in the judgment of Brandon J. in *The Arawa* [1977] 2 Lloyd's Rep. 216 at pp.424–425.

[99] *Gosse Millerd v Canadian Government* [1927] 2 K.B. 432, per Wright J. at p.434. *Trafigura Beheer BV v Mediteranean Shipping Co SA (The MSC Amsterdam)* [2007] EWCA Civ. 794; [2007] 2 Lloyd's Rep. 622.

[100] *Pyrene Co v Scindia Navigation Co* [1954] 2 Q.B. 402 at p.415. This would seem consistent with the later part of his judgment approved in *Renton v Palmyra* [1957] A.C. 149 at pp.170, 173, 174.

[101] *Gosse Millerd v Canadian Government* [1927] 2 K.B. 432 at p.435, per Wright J., and [1929] A.C. 223, per Lord Sumner at p.234; *Silver v Ocean S.S. Co* [1930] 1 K.B. 416 at p.425, per Scrutton L.J.; *cf. Bradley v Federal S.N. Co* (1927) 27 Ll.L.R. 395 at p.396 (HL).

[102] See Art.51. Once the claimant proves unseaworthiness, the burden of establishing due diligence is on the shipowner: *The Toledo* [1995] 1 Lloyd's Rep. 40; *Papera Traders Co Ltd v Hyundai Merchant Marine Co Ltd (The Eurasian Dream)* [2002] 1 Lloyd's Rep. 719. For an illustration of the importance of this burden of proof see, e.g. *Eridania SpA v Rudolf A. Oetker (The Fjord Wind)* [2000] 2 Lloyds Rep. 191; *CV Sheepvaartondernem-ing Ankergracht v Stemcor (Australasia) Ptd Ltd* [2007] FCAFC 77. See also Ezeoke, *"Allocating Onus of Proof in Sea Cargo Claims"* [2001] L.M.C.L.Q. 261.

(c) Make the holds, refrigerating and cool chambers, and all other parts of the ship in which goods are carried, fit and safe for their reception, carriage and preservation.

"*Before and at the beginning of the voyage*". The absolute undertaking of seaworthiness implied by the common law, which is abrogated by s.3 of the Act, applied not only at the beginning of the voyage, but at the beginning of each separate stage of it, the stages being marked either by the completion of a particular operation, e.g. loading, or by changes in the nature of the operation to be performed, e.g. river transit or ocean transit. Under this doctrine the shipowner was on the one hand relieved of the necessity of securing the highest degree of seaworthiness until the vessel commenced her ocean voyage, but on the other hand came under the additional obligation of securing that degree of seaworthiness when the ocean transit began even though the vessel was in fact in all respects seaworthy at an earlier stage.[99] The words here used, "*before*" and "*at the beginning of the voyage*", cover the period from at least the beginning of loading until the vessel starts on her voyage.[103] but do not relate to a period after the voyage has started,[104] such as a call at an intermediate port to load further cargo.[105] Accordingly the shipowner, who has exercised due diligence to make his ship seaworthy in all respects before she sails on her voyage, will not be held liable if the master negligently fails before entering on a new stage to remedy a defect which has developed since sailing on the voyage. As regards the supply of bunkers, the owner satisfies this Rule if he makes, before the voyage commences, proper arrangements for bunkering at usual and proper bunkering ports and, provided that the vessel sails from her first port with sufficient fuel for the first bunkering stage as fixed by the owner,[106] the failure of the master to make use of the bunkering arrangements so made by the owner would be excused under Art.IV, r.2(a).[107]

"*Due diligence . . . to make the ship seaworthy.*" The obligations arising under Art.III, r.1 are overriding.[108] The due diligence required is due diligence in the work itself by the carrier and all persons, whether servants or agents or independent contractors whom he employs or engages in the task of making the ship seaworthy; the carrier does not therefore, discharge the burden of proving that due diligence has been exercised by proof that he engaged competent experts to perform and supervise the task of making the ship seaworthy.[109] The statute imposes an inescapable personal obligation.[110]

The carrier's responsibility does not, however, begin until the ship comes into his orbit.[111] Accordingly if he has a new ship built for him or buys or charters or takes over a ship from another, he will not be liable for damage by unseaworthiness due to existing defects which could not be discovered by him, or competent experts employed by him, by

---

[103] *Maxine Footwear v Canadian Government Merchant Marine* [1959] A.C. 589 (PC).

[104] *The Makedonia* [1962] 1 Lloyd's Rep. 316; "*voyage*" means the contractual voyage from the port of loading to the port of discharge (*ibid.*).

[105] *Leesh River Tea Co v British India Steam Navigation Co* [1966] 1 Lloyd's Rep. 450, affirmed on this point at [1966] 2 Lloyd's Rep. 193.

[106] Contrast *Northumbrian Shipping Co v Timms* [1939] A.C. 397.

[107] See fn.104, above.

[108] See further the commentary under Art.IV r.2 below and *The Fiona* [1994] 2 Lloyd's Rep. 506.

[109] *Riverstone Meat Co v Lancashire Shipping Co* [1961] A.C. 807; as summarised and applied in *Union of India v N.V. Reederij Amsterdam* [1962] 1 Lloyd's Rep. 539, reversed [1962] 2 Lloyd's Rep. 336 (CA) but restored [1963] 2 Lloyd's Rep. 223 (HL).

[110] per Lord Keith of Avonholme [1961] A.C. 807 at p.871.

[111] per Lord Radcliffe [1961] A.C. 807 at p.867 and *Union of India v N.V. Reederij Amsterdam*, above. *Parsons Corp v CV Scheepvaartonderneming Happy Ranger (The Happy Ranger)* [2006] EWHC 122 (Comm); [2006] 1 Lloyd's Rep. 649.

the exercise of due diligence.[112] Nor does the carrier's obligation extend to a responsibility for the conduct of manufacturers or exporters or of shippers in their stuffing of containers and descriptions of their contents unless put on notice to do so.[113] The obligation being to exercise due diligence *"before and at the beginning of the voyage"* if a ship is unfit owing to some earlier failure of due diligence by the carrier, his servants or agents before a previous voyage, the carrier will be liable on the ground of actual or imputed knowledge continuing to the date relevant to the particular contract.[114]

The standard imposed by the obligation to exercise due diligence appears to be equivalent to that of the common law duty of care.[115] Thus, if an inspection of the vessel's machinery by or on behalf of the shipowner fails to reveal a defect, the question whether the failure amounts to want of due diligence must be answered by considering (1) whether the examination was, in the circumstances, of a character such as a skilled and prudent shipowner should reasonably have made, and (2) if so, whether the examination was carried out with reasonable skill, care and competence.[116] There is no failure of due diligence merely because precautions are not taken which subsequent experience shows to be necessary.[117]

The effect of the abolition by s.3 of the Act,[118] in relation to any contract to which the Act applies by operation of law[119] of the absolute undertaking at common law to provide a seaworthy ship and the substitution of the lesser obligation under the Rules to exercise due diligence to make the ship seaworthy has thus been summarised,[120] the carrier "will be protected against latent defects, in the strict sense, in work done on his ship, that is to say, defects not due to any negligent workmanship of repairers or others employed by the repairers, and, as I see it, against defects making for unseaworthiness in the ship, however caused, before it became his ship, if these could not be discovered by him, or competent experts employed by him, by the exercise of due diligence".

"Properly man . . . the ship". The shipowner must satisfy himself by inspection of the seaman's documents, interviews and inquiries from previous employers that he is reasonably fit to occupy the post to which he is appointed.[121] It will not necessarily be enough to rely on certificates of competence held by the seaman.[122]

"Properly . . . equip . . . the ship". Failure to provide plans of the vessel's machinery may amount to unseaworthiness.[123]

---

[112] *Angliss v P. & O.* [1927] 2 K.B. 456. The actual decision in this case, which related to defects of workmanship in a ship built for the carrier, appears, as distinct from some of the dicta in it, to have been approved by the HL in *Riverstone Meat Co v Lancashire Shipping Co* [1961] A.C. 807 at pp.841, 867, 872, 877. Since the latter decision it seems doubtful whether a shipowner can escape liability for the consequences of the erroneous approval of a fault in design by a classification society such as Lloyd's Register, either on the ground of the public and quasi-judicial positions of such societies (per Wright J. in *Angliss v P. & O.*, above, at 462), or because to go behind the certificate of such a society might lead to an almost unlimited retrogression (per Devlin J. in *Waddle v Wallsend S.S. Co* [1952] 2 Lloyd's Rep. 105 at p.130). See also, as to the position of Lloyd's surveyors, *Minister of Materials v Wold S.S. Co* [1952] 1 Lloyd's Rep. 485 at p.502.

[113] *Northern Shipping Co v Deutsche Seereederei gmbH (The Kapitan Sakharov)* [2000] 2 Lloyd's Rep. 255.

[114] *Angliss v P. & O.* [1927] 2 K.B. 456 at p.463.

[115] See per Lord Devlin in *Union of India v N.V. Reederij Amsterdam* [1963] 2 Lloyd's Rep. 223 at p.235; restoring the judgment at first instance: [1962] 1 Lloyd's Rep. 539.

[116] *ibid.* per Diplock L.J. at [1962] 2 Lloyd's Rep. 336, 345, subsequently approved on appeal at [1963] 2 Lloyd's Rep. 223 (especially per Lord Evershed at p.231).

[117] *ibid.* and see also *The Australia Star* (1940) 67 Ll.L.R. 110; A. *Mereditch Jones & Co Ltd v Vangemar Shipping Co Ltd (The Apostolis)* [1977] 2 Lloyd's Rep. 241

[118] Above, para.B5.

[119] As distinct from its application as a matter of contract: see the words "by virtue of this Act" in s.3.

[120] per Lord Keith in *Riverstone Meat Co v Lancashire Shipping Co* [1961] A.C. 807 at p.872. For an earlier and more limited summary by MacKinnon L.J. approved by the HL, see *Smith Hogg v Black Sea and Baltic General Insurance* (1939) 64 Ll.l.R. 87 at p.89.

[121] *The Makedonia* [1962] 1 Lloyd's Rep. 316; *Moore v Lunn* (1922) 11 Ll.L.R. 86.

[122] *The Farrandoc* [1967] 2 Lloyd's Rep. 276 (Canada Ex.Ct.): *contra* Noel J. *ibid.*, who held, however, that lack of proper instruction as to a seaman's duties constituted unseaworthiness.

[123] *The Farrandoc*, above.

2. Subject to the provisions of Article IV,[124] **the carrier**[125] **shall properly and carefully load, handle, stow, carry, keep, care for and discharge the goods carried.**

"*Properly*" means "in accordance with a sound system". A sound system does not mean a system suited to all the weaknesses and idiosyncrasies of a particular cargo, but a sound system under all the circumstances in relation to the general practice of carriers of goods by sea, and in the light of all the knowledge which the carrier has or ought to have about the nature of the goods.[126]

"*Load, stow, discharge*". The whole contract of carriage is subject to the Rules, but the extent to which loading and discharging are brought within the carrier's obligations is left to the parties themselves to decide.[127] Thus, if the carrier has agreed to load, stow or discharge the cargo, he must do so properly and carefully, subject to any protection which he may enjoy under Article IV. But the Rules do not invalidate an agreement transferring the responsibility for these operations to the shipper, charterer or consignee.[128]

Similarly, the obligation properly and carefully to "carry" the cargo extends only to the voyage which the shipowner has undertaken to perform, and the parties may agree upon whatever voyage they wish. Thus, a term in the contract of carriage entitling the shipowner in certain events to discharge the goods otherwise than at the named port of destination, is not inconsistent with his obligations under this Rule.[129] Moreover, it appears that the word "carry" does not even connote that the goods must be transported from one place to another, and the parties may validly agree that the shipowner shall have the liberty, in stated circumstances, to discharge the goods at the port of loading.[130]

As in the case of the obligation under Art.III, r.1, to exercise due diligence to make the ship seaworthy, the duties under this Rule are personal to the shipowner, and he cannot escape liability for damage arising for example, from lack of care for the goods, merely by proving that the master employed and acted upon the advice of a competent surveyor.[131]

The conduct of the cargo-owner may be such as to preclude him from relying on Art.III, r.2, for example where the shippers or their agents require the master to adopt an unsound method of stowage, and induce him to agree by promising an indemnity.[132]

---

[124] There are no comparable words in the American Act of 1936, see Appendix IV, below.

[125] See the note on "*due diligence*", above.

[126] *Renton v Palmyra* [1957] A.C. 149 at p.166; *Albacora v Westcott & Laurance Line* [1966] 2 Lloyd's Rep. 53; *Gatoil International Inc. v Tradax Petroleum Ltd (The Rio Sun)* [1985] 1 Lloyd's Rep. 350; *Caltex Refining Co Pty Ltd v BHP Transport Ltd (The Iron Gippsland)* (1994) 34 N.S.W.L.R. 29. *CV Sheepvaartonderneming Ankergracht v Stemcor (Australasia) Ptd Ltd* [2007] FCAFC 77.

[127] *Pyrene Co v Scindia Navigation Co* [1954] 2 Q.B. 402, per Devlin J. at p.418, approved by the HL in *Renton v Palmyra* [1957] A.C. 149 at pp.170, 173 and 174. In *Jindal Iron & Steel Co Ltd v Islamic Solidarity Shipping Co (The Jordan II)* [2004] UKHL 49; [2005] 1 Lloyd's Rep. 57, the House of Lords expressed no concluded view on the issue of interpretation of Art.III r.2 but refused to depart from the decision in *Renton v Palmyra*. See also [2005] L.M.C.L.Q. 153. It remains unclear whether the incorporation into the bill of lading of a charterparty under which loading and discharge are the responsibility of the charterer is sufficient to negate the shipowner's liability: *Balli Trading Ltd v Afalona Shipping Co Ltd (The Coral)* [1993] 1 Lloyd's Rep. 1. *Cf.: Fyffes Group Ltd v Reefer Express Lines Pty Ltd* [1996] 2 Lloyd's Rep. 171, 188.

[128] See S Baughen [2005] L.M.C.L.Q. 153.

[129] *Renton v Palmyra*, above.

[130] [1957] A.C. 149 at pp.166, 169–171, 174. A distinction must, however, be drawn between deviation clauses purporting to enable the shipowners to delay indefinitely the performance of the contract voyage simply because they choose to do so, and provisions which are applicable only in the event of certain specified emergencies. *Renton v Palmyra* [1956] 1 Q.B. 462, per Jenkins L.J. at p.502, approved [1957] A.C. 149 at pp.164 and 174. See also Art.127.

[131] *International Packers v Ocean S.S. Co* [1955] 2 Lloyd's Rep. 218; *Leesh River Tea Co v British Indian Steam Navigation Co* [1966] 1 Lloyd's Rep. 450 at p.457; *Riverstone Meat Co v Lancashire Shipping Co* [1961] A.C. 807; Art.129.

[132] As in *Ismail v Polish Ocean Lines* [1976] 1 Q.B. 893.

3. After receiving the goods into his charge, the carrier, or the master or agent of the carrier shall, on demand of the shipper,[133] **issue to the shipper a bill of lading showing, among other things—**

(a) **The leading marks**[134] **necessary for identification of the goods as the same are furnished in writing by the shipper before the loading of such goods starts, provided such marks are stamped or otherwise shown clearly upon the goods if uncovered, or on the cases or coverings in which such goods are contained, in such a manner as should ordinarily remain legible until the end of the voyage:**

(b) **Either the number of packages or pieces, or the quantity, or weight, as the case may be, as furnished in writing by the shipper:**

(c) **The apparent order and condition of the goods:**

Provided that no carrier, master or agent of the carrier, shall be bound to state or show in the bill of lading any marks, number, quantity, or weight which he has reasonable ground for suspecting not accurately to represent the goods actually received, or which he has had no reasonable means of checking.

"*After receiving, etc.*" If there be no "*Contract of carriage*" and no "*carrier*" prior to the issue of the bill of lading this Rule is reduced to confusion. This is avoided if the construction placed upon Art.I(b) by the Court of Session in *Harland and Wolff v Burns and Laird Lines*[135] is adopted.

If the goods have not been shipped but have only been "*received*" into the carrier's "*charge*" when the bill of lading is demanded, the bill of lading issued will presumably be a "received for shipment" bill of lading. As the Rules only cover the duties of the carrier in relation to loading, stowing and discharging in so far as he agrees to perform or does perform those operations[136] and do not cover what happens after discharge, a carrier may wish to protect himself by appropriate exemptions. These exemptions may be in the widest terms, e.g. "against all risks whatsoever" or "howsoever caused" and in the case of a through bill of lading may cover any time when the goods are not being carried by sea.[137]

"*Either the number, etc.*" The obligation is alternative. Therefore if the carrier issues a bill of lading showing both the number of pieces and the weight, he may qualify the

---

[133] *Secus* if no demand is made; *Vita Food Products v Unus Shipping Co* [1939] A.C. 277; *Canada & Dominion Sugar Co v Canadian National (W.I.) Steamships* [1947] A.C. 46. See also *Noble Resources Ltd v Cavalier Shipping Corp (The Atlas)* [1996] 1 Lloyd's Rep. 642 as to the position where the shipper becomes aware of a failure by the carrier to issue a bill of lading in proper terms when it is too late to object.
[134] See *Parsons v New Zealand Shipping Co* [1901] 1 K.B. 548; *Compania Importadora de Arroces v P. & O.* (1927) Ll.L.R. 63.
[135] (1931) 40 Ll.L.R. 286; see *Notes* to Art.I(b), above.
[136] See *Pyrene Co v Scindia Navigation Co* [1954] 2 Q.B. 402 and the discussion, above, of Art.I(e) and Art.II.
[137] Art.VII, below, and see comment on Art.I(b), above, as to carriage on rivers and other navigable waters.

statement as to weight as, e.g. by the words "weight unknown". Such a bill of lading will then be prima facie evidence of the number of pieces but not of the weight.[138]

4. Such a bill of lading shall be prima facie evidence of the receipt by the carrier of the goods as therein described in accordance with paragraph 3(a), (b) and (c).[139] However, proof to the contrary shall not be admissible when the bill of lading has been transferred to a third party acting in good faith.

The new words contained in the last sentence of Rule 4 have made an important change in the law, so far as concerns those cases governed by the Amended Rules. Here, the principle of *Grant v Norway*[140] does not apply and the carrier is estopped, as against a transferee of the bill, from denying shipment of the quantity or number of goods described in the bill.

It may be noted that the Rule imposes no requirement that the transfer shall be for value. Nor, indeed, does it prescribe that the transferee shall have relied on the statements in the bill when accepting the transfer. We submit that no requirement of reliance can be implied, and that accordingly the transferee is in a substantially stronger position under the Amended Rules, than he would be at common law.

By the Carriage of Goods by Sea Act 1992, s.4, the bill of lading is conclusive evidence in favour of a person who has become the lawful holder of the bill of lading (as consignee or indorsee) of the shipment of the goods against the carrier.[141]

If the bill of lading contains words such as "weight unknown", then it will not constitute prima facie evidence of the quantity shipped under this rule.[142]

5. The shipper shall be deemed to have guaranteed to the carrier the accuracy at the time of shipment of the marks, number, quantity, and weight, as furnished by him, and the shipper shall indemnify the carrier against all loss, damages, and expenses arising or resulting from inaccuracies in such particulars. The right of the carrier to such indemnity shall in no way limit his responsibility and liability under the contract of carriage to any person other than the shipper.

"*The shipper*". Under s.3(1) of the Carriage of Goods by Sea Act 1992, a person to whom rights of suit are transferred under the Act,[143] such as the lawful holder of a bill of lading or the consignee under a sea waybill, who takes or demands delivery of the goods or makes a claim under the contract of carriage against the carrier becomes subject to "the same liabilities under that contract as if he had been a party to that contract". If the

---

[138] *Pendle & Rivet v Ellerman Lines* (1928) 33 Com.Cas. 70 at p.77; *Att-Gen of Ceylon v Scindia Steam Navigation Co* [1962] A.C. 60 at p.74.

[139] Under the 1924 Act, s.5 created an exception to Article III, Rule 4 in relation to weights of bulk cargo inserted in the bill of lading pursuant to an ascertainment or acceptance by a third party, and stated in the bill of lading to be so ascertained or accepted. s.5 has no counterpart in the 1971 Act.

[140] (1851) 10 C.B. 665, discussed in Art.59, above.

[141] See Art.59.

[142] *Noble Resources Ltd v Cavalier Shipping Corp (The Atlas)* [1996] 1 Lloyd's Rep. 642; *Agrosin Pte Ltd v Highway Shipping Co Ltd (The Mata K)* [1998] 2 Lloyd's Rep. 614.

[143] See Art.14. See also s.5(5) of the Act.

guarantee referred to in this Rule is within the meaning of s.3(1) of the Act, then the person on whom liabilities are imposed by the section would, like the shipper, be deemed to have guaranteed to the carrier the marks, etc., and would therefore not only be unable to recover from the carrier for any marks, number, quantity and weight, but would also be liable for any loss consequent upon the guarantee. The Rule itself, however, seems to show an intention that the shipper only and not the consignee or indorsee should be liable under this guarantee, and the courts will probably give effect to this intention by holding that the person on whom liabilities are imposed by s.3(1), although deemed to be a party to the contract of carriage, is not the "shipper" within this Rule. If this be so, the carrier, if sued in the English Court under Art.III, r.4, by a transferee who has acted in good faith could bring in the shipper as third party.[144]

6. Unless notice of loss or damage and the general nature of such loss or damage be given in writing to the carrier or his agent at the port of discharge before or at the time of the removal of the goods into the custody of the person entitled to delivery thereof under the contract of carriage, or, if the loss or damage be not apparent, within three days, such removal shall be prima facie evidence of the delivery by the carrier of the goods as described in the bill of lading.

The notice in writing need not be given if the state of the goods has, at the time of their receipt, been the subject of joint survey or inspection.

Subject to paragraph 6 bis the carrier and the ship shall in any event be discharged from all liability whatsoever in respect of the goods, unless suit is brought within one year of their delivery or of the date when they should have been delivered. This period may, however, be extended if the parties so agree after the cause of action has arisen.

In the case of any actual or apprehended loss or damage the carrier and the receiver shall give all reasonable facilities to each other for inspecting and tallying the goods.

"*Unless notice of loss or damage . . . be given in writing.*" The first paragraph of Rule 6 appears to have no legal effect. Whether notice is given or not, the onus of proving loss or damage will lie upon the person asserting it. It was apparently intended, when the clause was first introduced, that the effect of giving notice should be to place the burden of disproving loss or damage on the carrier—which the present Rule certainly does not. Assuming, however, that the Rule has any effect, it should be observed that, although the notice must be given to the carrier or his agent at the port of discharge, the goods apparently need not be removed into the receiver's custody there, e.g. in the case of a contract of through carriage where, after the discharge from the ship, the final stage is by railway or by lighters up a river or canal. If by the time the goods have been removed into the custody of the person entitled to delivery the ship has sailed and has no agent at the

---

[144] This passage was approved by Thomas J. in *Aegean Sea Traders Corp v Repsol Petroleo SA (The Aegean Sea)* [1998] 2 Lloyd's Rep. 39.

port of discharge, it is a little difficult to see how this provision will be complied with. Possibly the agent employed for the ship will be held to continue to be agent for the purpose of receiving notice.

No provision appears to be made for total loss of the goods where there can be no "removal".

"Before or at the time of the removal of the goods into the custody". There is some ambiguity in this. The goods may no longer be in the custody of the carrier; but they may not yet be in the custody of the person entitled to the delivery thereof, e.g. if they are in a dock warehouse. Presumably the question will depend on the agency of the actual custodian, and whether he holds the goods as bailee for the carrier or for the person entitled to their delivery. On the other hand, the provision for notice within three days (i.e. "from the time of such removal") where the damage is not apparent, seems to suggest that the Rules contemplate the removal of the goods to the actual custody of the goods-owner so that he can examine them.

"Shall . . . be discharged". Article III, Rule 6, creates a time bar which extinguishes the claim and does not merely bar the remedy.[145]

"All liability whatsoever". The Hague Rules provided, before amendment, that the carrier and the ship should "in any event . . . be discharged from all liability in respect of loss or damage" unless suit was brought within the stipulated period. The text of the Hague-Visby Rules is different in two significant respects, namely, the words "in respect of loss or damage" are discarded, and the word "whatsoever" is added.

The former amendment means that it is no longer necessary to consider whether the relationship between the claim and the goods is similar to that which is required for the application of Art.IV, r.2 and Art.III, r.8.[146] The addition of the word "whatsoever"[147] makes it clear that the time limit[148] applies even where the carrier has committed a deviation[149] or the types of misconduct referred to in Art.IV, r.5(e).[150] It is also submitted that the word is also strong enough to override the wide language of Art.IV, *bis*, and to make the time limit applicable where claims are brought against the servant or agent in circumstances where he is guilty of intentional or reckless misconduct.[151]

---

[145] *Aries Tanker Corp v Total Transport (The Aries)* [1977] 1 Lloyd's Rep. 334 (HL); *Consolidated Investment & Contracting Co v Saponaria Shipping Co (The Virgo)* [1978] 2 Lloyd's Rep. 167. The plain intention is to achieve finality and to enable the shipowner to clear his books: *Linen Naviera Paramaconi SA v Abnormal Load Ltd* [2001] 1 Lloyd's Rep. 763 where the Court stated that where it is possible so to do, and where there is no consequent uncertainty as to when the one year period would expire, the Court should lean towards a conclusion in favour of the time bar.

[146] See *Adamastos Shipping Co v Anglo-Saxon Petroleum Co* [1959] A.C. 133 (Art.IV, r.2); *Renton v Palmyra* [1957] A.C. 149 (Art.III, r.8); *Freedom General Shipping SA v Tokai Shipping Co Ltd* [1982] 1 Lloyd's Rep. 73.

[147] Which does not appear in Art.IV, r.5(a) or Art.IV, r.5(h). Both paragraphs employ the expression "loss or damage to, or in connection with" goods.

[148] Unlike the monetary limit.

[149] This passage was approved in *Kenya Railways v Antares Co Pte. Ltd (The Antares No. 2)* [1986] 2 Lloyd's Rep. 633 in which the time bar was applied when there had been an unauthorised carriage of goods on deck. In the Court of Appeal [1987] 1 Lloyd's Rep. 424, the question of whether the Rules applied to a deviation proper was left open.

[150] See *Compania Portorafti Commerciale SA v Ultramar Panama Inc. (The Captain Gregos)* [1990] 1 Lloyd's Rep. 310 at p.316. One purpose of the amendment was to apply the time limit to cases of delivery without production of bills of lading, and hence to enable banks and other parties issuing letters of indemnity to regard themselves as discharged after the expiry of one year. We submit that it is at least doubtful whether the Rules apply at all to cases of this nature, or whether if they do, the words of the new Rule are strong enough to cover such a claim. But there are understandably arguments in favour of the opposite view: see Diamond, *ibid.* p.32.

[151] But see *Cheong Yuk Fai v China International Freight Forwarders (HK) Co Ltd* [2005] 4 H.K.L.R.D. 544 (Hong Kong) where it was held that the time-limit only applied where the loss or damage to the goods occurred during the period covered by the Hague-Visby Rules.

"In respect of the goods". These words may limit the operation of the Article III, Rule 6 time bar when the Rules are incorporated into a charterparty.[152]

"Unless suit is brought". The suit must be brought in a competent jurisdiction, but this need not be the jurisdiction in which the claim is ultimately decided.[153] What is required is initiation of proceedings by a claimant with title to sue[154] in respect of breach of the relevant duties under the Hague-Visby Rules. The time bar does not preclude a subsequent reformulation by amendment of the mechanism alleged to give rise to the contractual nexus,[155] but an amendment to plead a cause of action not previously pleaded is not allowed and the doctrine of "relation back" of amendments does not apply.[156]

The mere inclusion of an arbitration clause in a bill of lading to which the Rules apply does not amount to a waiver of the time limit.[157] On the contrary, the commencement of an arbitration is equivalent to the bringing of suit.[158]

"Within one year of their delivery". Where the goods in respect of which the claim is made actually arrive at a legitimate place of delivery, time starts when delivery is completed and, in all other cases, time starts when delivery of the relevant goods ought to have been delivered assuming the due performance of all contractual obligations.[159] In the former case, if, looking at all the circumstances, it can fairly be said that there was delivery under the contract of carriage, even if that contract has been varied in some respects in the light of problems that have arisen during the voyage, it will in general be appropriate to conclude (subject perhaps to the circumstances of the particular case) that there has been "delivery" within the meaning of Art.III r.6. If, on the other hand the delivery is under an entirely separate and distinct transaction it will in general be appropriate to conclude that there has been no such "delivery".[160]

---

[152] *Interbulk Ltd v Ponte dei Sospiri Shipping Co (The Standard Ardour)* [1988] 2 Lloyd's Rep. 159; *Cargill International SA v C.P.N. Tankers (Bermuda) Ltd (The Ot Sonja)* [1993] 2 Lloyd's Rep. 435; *Noranda Inc. v Barton (Time Charter) Ltd (The Marinor)* [1996] 1 Lloyd's Rep. 308; *Navigazione Alta Italia SpA v Concordia Maritime Chartering A.B. (The Stena Pacifica)* [1990] 2 Lloyd's Rep. 234. *Mauritius Oil Refineries Ltd v Stolt-Nielsen Nederlands BV (The Stolt Sydness)* [1977] 1 Lloyd's Rep. 273; *Grimaldi Compagnia di Navigazione v Sekihyo Lines Ltd (The Seki Rolette)* [1998] 2 Lloyd's Rep. 638; *Borgship Tankers Inc v Product Transport Corp Ltd (The Casio)* [2005] EWHC 273 (Comm); [2005] 1 Lloyd's Rep. 565.

[153] *The Nordglimt* [1987] 2 Lloyd's Rep. 470; *Government of Sierra Leone v Marmaro Shipping Co Ltd (The Amazonia and the Yayamaria)* [1989] 1 Lloyd's Rep. 130 (CA); *Hispanica de Petroleos SA v Vencedora Oceanica Navegacion SA (The Kapetan Markos NL)* [1986] 1 Lloyd's Rep. 211; *The Havhelt* [1993] 1 Lloyd's Rep. 523 (suit not competent where brought in breach of exclusive jurisdiction clause); *Fort Sterling v South Atlantic Cargo Shipping N.V. (The Finnrose)* [1994] 1 Lloyd's Rep. 559 (earlier proceedings struck out for want of prosecution not a competent "suit" for Art.III, r.6). *Colombiana de Seguros v Pacific S.N. Co* [1965] 1 Q.B. 101; [1963] 2 Lloyd's Rep. 479 and *The Merak* [1964] 2 Lloyd's Rep. 232 must now be read in the light of these subsequent authorities.

[154] *Transworld Oil (U.S.A.) Inc v Minos Compania Naviera SA (The Leni)* [1992] 2 Lloyd's Rep. 48. Accidental misdescription of the correct party will not invalidate the suit: *ibid.*

[155] *Hispanica de Petroleos SA v Vencedora Oceanica Navegacion SA (The Kapetan Markos NL)* [1986] 1 Lloyd's Rep. 211; *Continental Fertilizer Co Ltd v Pionier Shipping CV (The Pionier)* [1995] 1 Lloyd's Rep. 223.

[156] *The Leni*, above; *Payabi v Armstel Shipping Corp Shipping Ltd (The Jay Bola)* [1992] 2 Lloyd's Rep. 62. The suggestions to the contrary in *The Kapetan Markos*, above, *Empresa Cubana Importadora De Alimentos v Octavia Shipping Co SA (The Kefalonia Wind)* [1986] 1 Lloyd's Rep. 273 and *The Joanna Borchard* [1988] 2 Lloyd's Rep. 274 are incorrect. But see *Anglo-Irish Beef Processors International v Federated Stevedores (The Reefer Badger)* [1997] 1 Lloyd's Rep. 207 (Aust. Ct.) where the Court allowed an amendment to add a claim in contract after the expiry of the time limit; and *The Almerinda* [2002] 2 H.K.L.R.D. 197 (Hong Kong) where the Court allowed an amendment to add a *Brandt* claim.

[157] *Denny, Mott v Lynn Shipping Co* [1963] 1 Lloyd's Rep. 339.

[158] *The Merak* [1964] 2 Lloyd's Rep. 527; *Nea Agrex v Baltic Shipping Co* [1976] 2 Lloyd's Rep. 47. It makes no difference that the arbitration clause and the time limit are to be found in separate provisions; *Nea Agrex v Baltic Shipping*, above. The same principles are to be applied, when deciding when suit is brought for the purposes of Art.III, r.6, as are material to an issue under section 13 of the Arbitration Act 1996.. Where the Rules apply only as a matter of contract (e.g. when incorporated into a charterparty) the court has jurisdiction in appropriate cases to extend the time for commencing an arbitration under s.12 of the Arbitration Act 1996: *The Seki Rolette*, above.

[159] *Trafigura Beheer B.V. v Golden Stravraetos Maritime Inc (The Sonia)* [2003] EWCA Civ 664; [2003] 2 Lloyd's Rep. 201. See also *Medierranean Shipping Co SA v Sipco Inc* [2001] F.C.T. 1046 (Can.).

[160] *The Sonia*, above, at p.212.

"*This period may, however, be extended*". The last sentence of the third paragraph does not affect the position under English law. It cannot in our view be said to qualify the parties' rights to extend the time limit by agreement *before* the cause of action has arisen.

"*Cross-claims*". Where the Rules are incorporated in a charterparty and the charterer deducts a part of the freight on account of a cross-claim for cargo damage, the charterer must bring suit within the one-year period, if his deduction is to remain valid.[161]

6 bis. An action for indemnity against a third person[162] may be brought even after the expiration of the year provided for in the preceding paragraph if brought within the time allowed by the law of the Court seized of the case. However, the time allowed shall be not less than three months, commencing from the day when the person bringing such action for indemnity has settled the claim or has been served with process in the action against himself.

Since the Rules apply directly only to contracts covered by a bill of lading,[163] this new Rule is intended presumably to deal with situations where the carrier under a particular bill of lading is himself in the position of shipper or consignee under another bill of lading,[164] for instance where there has been transshipment for part of the voyage.[165] For the indemnity period in Rule 6b is to apply, it is only necessary that the contract under which the recourse claim is brought should be subject to the Rules, and it does not matter that the contract under which the underlying claim was brought was not so subject.[54]

The "*time allowed by the law of the Court seized of the case*" does not mean the time specifically provided in that system for the bringing of recourse claims under the Hague-Visby Rules, but the time provided for bringing recourse actions generally.[54]

It is submitted that the carrier has "settled the claim" when he has made a binding agreement for compromise, even if he has not yet made payment.

Presumably the words "whichever be the earlier" must be implied at the end of the Rule.

7. After the goods are loaded the bill of lading to be issued by the carrier, master or agent of the carrier, to the shipper shall, if the shipper so demands, be a "shipped" bill of lading, provided that if the shipper shall have previously taken up any document of title to such goods, he shall surrender the same as against the issue of the "shipped" bill of lading, but at the option of the carrier such document of title may be noted at the port

---

[161] *Aries Tanker Corp v Total Transport (The Aries)* [1977] 1 Lloyd's Rep. 334 (HL). The ratio decidendi of the case was that there was no right, under a voyage party, to make a deduction from freight in respect of a cross-claim for cargo damage, quite apart from any question of time bar. However, the House of Lords gave as a secondary reason for the decision the fact that there could be no equity to make a deduction in respect of a cross-claim which had become time-barred.

[162] In *Bellina Maritime SA v Menorah Insurance Co Ltd* [2002] 2 Lloyd's Rep. 575. [Is. Ct] it was held that an insurer's subrogation claim against a shipowner was not a claim for indemnity against a third party and was therefore subject to the one year time bar in Art.III r.6.

[163] Art.1(5).

[164] As, for example, where a carrier under a through bill entrusts the goods to a local carrier for carriage on part of the transit under another bill. The Rule would then apply where the cargo-owner sues the ocean carrier and the latter claims recourse against the local carrier. No doubt, if the Rules are incorporated by contract into a charterparty, and if the charterer issues his own bills, r.6, *bis* will govern any recourse claim under the charter.

[165] *China Ocean Shipping Co v Owners of "Andros", Ying Heng & Andros* [1987] 2 Lloyd's Rep. 210 (PC).

of shipment by the carrier, master, or agent with the name or names of the
ship or ships upon which the goods have been shipped and the date or dates
of shipment, and when so noted, if it shows the particulars mentioned in
paragraph 3 of Article III, the same shall for the purpose of this Article be
deemed to constitute a "shipped" bill of lading.

"*Document of title*". The difficulty arising from this vague phrase in the Factors Act
1889 was discussed at p.187 of the 17th edn of this work. What is apparently contemplated
here is that there may have been previously issued a bill of lading in the form "Received
for Shipment", and that this bill of lading instead of being surrendered, may be noted with
the name of the carrying ship.[166]

"*If it shows the particulars mentioned in paragraph 3 of Article III*". These words were
not in the Hague Rules.

8. Any clause, covenant or agreement in a contract of carriage relieving
the carrier or the ship from liability for loss or damage to or in connection
with goods[167] arising from negligence, fault or failure in the duties and
obligations provided in this Article or lessening such liability otherwise than
as provided in these Rules, shall be null and void and of no effect.[168]

A benefit of insurance in favour of the carrier or similar clause shall be
deemed to be a clause relieving the carrier from liability.

The result of this Rule may well be to make a clause in a bill of lading which exempts
the carrier from liability for which he would otherwise be liable under the Rule totally
void even in respect of operations to which the Rules do not apply. It is advisable,
therefore, in framing a clause for the protection of the carrier to confine the protection in
express terms to such operations: see the discussion of Article I(e) and II above.

"*Any clause*". It may be possible in a clause consisting of two parts to sever that part
which does not offend against the Act and merely strike out the offending part.[169]

"*Relieving . . . from liability . . . or lessening such liability . . . .*" A liberty to tranship
does not come within the prohibition of this Rule, *semble*, provided that transhipment is
reasonable and not inconsistent with "proper carriage",[170] nor does a clause providing that
all claims shall be determined at the port of destination,[171] nor does an arbitration clause,
even if it provides that if the arbitrator is not appointed within 12 months of final discharge
of the goods the claim is to be barred[172] nor a demise clause.[173] But a clause in a bill of

---

[166] See Art.182.
[167] For comment see below.
[168] In *P.S. Chellaram & Co Ltd v China Ocean S.S. Co (The Chellaram)* [1989] 1 Lloyd's Rep. 413 (N.S.W.) the
question of whether a clause restricting the shipper's right to sue the servants or agents of the carrier was void
under this Rule was considered, but no conclusion reached. It is submitted that provided nothing is done to limit
any personal or vicarious responsibility of the carrier, such a clause is not unenforceable.
[169] *Svenska Traktor Akt. v Maritime Agencies (Southampton)* [1953] 2 Q.B. 295 at p.301. See, however, *Renton v
Palmyra* [1956] 1 Q.B. 462 at pp.477, 478 (reversed on other grounds [1957] A.C. 149).
[170] *Marcelino Gonzalez v Nourse* [1936] 1 K.B. 565. If, however, the clause disclaims all liability in the carrier in
respect of the goods in the event and as from the time of transhipment, it may well be annulled by the Rule; see
Holland Colombo Trading Society v Allawdeen Segu, etc. [1954] 2 Lloyd's Rep. 45 at p.53 (PC). *Cf.: Carewins
Development (China) Ltd v Bright Fortune Shipping Ltd* [2006] 4 H.K.L.R.D. 131 (Hong Kong) where it was
held that an exceptions clause excluding liability for "misdelivery" was not affected by Art.III r.8 because the
misdelivery occurred after the period covered by the Hague-Visby Rules; *Shtutman v Ocean Marine Shipping*
[2005] F.C. 1471 (Can.).
[171] *Maharani Woollen Mills v Anchor Line* (1927) 29 Ll.L.R. 169.
[172] *The Merak* [1964] 2 Lloyd's Rep. 527.
[173] *Kaleej International Pty. Ltd v Gulf Shipping Lines Ltd* (1986) 6 N.S.W.L.R. 569.

lading requiring claims for loss or damage to goods to be made within a fixed time of discharge or of the vessel's arrival is rendered null and void by this Rule.[174] So also are clauses providing that a surveyor's certificate shall be conclusive evidence of due diligence to make seaworthy[175-176] or that the shipowner shall not be liable for incorrect delivery if special requirements as to packing or marking, going beyond adequate packing and marking under Art.IV, r.2(n) and (o), are not complied with.[177] An attempt to define "package" for the purposes of Art.IV, r.5(a) in narrow terms will also be void.[178]

Under bills of lading incorporating the American Harter Act 1893 (which by s.1 provided that it was not lawful for the shipowner to insert in a bill of lading any clause relieving him from "liability for loss or damage arising from negligence, fault, or failure in proper loading, stowage, custody, care or proper delivery of any and all lawful merchandise or property committed" to his care), it was decided in the English courts that clauses agreeing the value of goods shipped at not exceeding a certain sum per package or unit unless specifically declared were valid, in distinction to clauses exempting from liability in respect of goods of a value exceeding a certain sum per package or unit unless specifically declared.[179] This fine distinction was based on the reasoning that the Harter Act did not prevent the parties agreeing the value of the goods shipped, and if the shipowner accepted liability up to the agreed value, he was not limiting his liability. A similar point has not yet arisen in the English courts under the United Kingdom legislation, but it is submitted that by reason of Art.IV, r.5(a), which had no parallel in the Harter Act, the distinction would not be upheld and both types of clause would be held invalid unless the sum mentioned in the clause exceeded the statutory limit. Art.IV, r.5, imposes a maximum limit on the shipowner's liability unless the nature and value of goods exceeding that sum have been declared and inserted in the bill of lading. It also provides that another maximum may be agreed, provided it is not *less* than the limit stipulated in r.5(a). Clauses of the first type above mentioned would appear to lessen the maximum liability provided by Art.IV, r.5, and thus to be rendered null and void by this Rule.[180]

---

[174] *Australasian United S.N. Co v Hunt* [1921] 2 A.C. 351 (PC); *Coventry Sheppard v Larrinaga S.S. Co* (1942) 73 Ll.L.R. 256. Contrast *The Auditor* (1924) 18 Ll.L.R. 464.

[175-176] *Walters v Joseph Rank* (1923) 39 T.L.R. 255; *Studebaker Distributors v Charlton S.S. Co* [1938] 1 K.B. 459; *The Australia Star* (1940) 67 Ll.L.R. 110 at p.116; *Empresa Cubana Importado de Alimentos Alimport v Iasmos Shipping Co SA (The Good Friend)* [1984] 2 Lloyd's Rep. 586.

[177] *British Imex Industries v Midland Bank* [1958] 1 Q.B. 542.

[178] *Haverkate v Toronto Harbour Commissioners* 30 D.L.R. (4th) 125, 46 D.L.R. (4th) 767 (Can.). See also *El Greco (Australia) Pty Ltd v Mediterranean Shipping Co SA* [2004] 2 Lloyd's Rep. 537 at p.584 (Fed Ct. Aust) with regard to the number of packages or units enumerated in a bill of lading as contemplated by Art.IV r.5(c). So too a clause which does not sufficiently identify what is being carried as deck cargo: *Timberwest Forest Ltd v Gearbulk Pool Ltd* [2003] B.C.C.A. 39 (Can.).

[179] *Hordern v Commonwealth and Dominion Line* [1917] 2 K.B. 420; *Studebaker Distributors v Charlton S.S. Co* [1938] 1 K.B. 459; following the decision of the U.S. Supreme Court in *Calderon v Atlas Steamship Co*, 170 U.S. Reports 272.

[180] So decided by the High Court of Australia in *Foy & Gibson v Holyman & Sons* (1946) 79 Ll.L.R. 339, under the Australian Sea Carriage of Goods Act. See also a decision to the same effect by the US Circuit Court of Appeals (2nd Circuit) in *Pan-Am Trade and Credit Corp v The Campfire* (1946) 80 Ll.L.R. 26 (appeal to the Supreme Court was refused; see *Lloyd's List Newspaper*, December 12, 1946), on the American Carriage of Goods by Sea Act. In that case there was a partial loss only and the shipowners unsuccessfully sought to rely on a clause providing that in case of loss to goods exceeding $500 in actual value per package the value of such goods should be deemed to be $500 per package, on which basis freight was adjusted, and that the carrier's liability, if any, should be determined on the basis of a value of $500 per package *or pro rata in the case of partial loss.* A similar conclusion was reached in *Otis, McAlister & Co v Skibs-Akt. Marie Bakke* [1959] 2 Lloyd's Rep. 210 (US Circuit Court Appeal) as to a clause seeking to limit the shipowner's liability to the invoice value of the goods when the sound value at destination was less than $500 per package. See also *The "River Gurara"* [1998] 1 Lloyd's Rep. 225 where it was held in the context of the Hague Rules that a clause indirectly lessening the liability of the carrier by a redefinition of "package" was rendered null and void by Art.III r.8.

The amended Centrocon Arbitration Clause, which bars any claim if the claimant's arbitrator is not appointed within nine months of *final* discharge, is in conflict with Art.III, r.6. Accordingly, where the clause is incorporated into a bill of lading which is subject to the Rules, the nine month time limit does not apply.[181]

An express provision stipulating that the contract shall be governed by a foreign law which gives effect to the Hague Rules but not to the Hague-Visby Rules is of no effect, by virtue of Art.III, r.8, in cases governed by the 1971 Act,[182] at least to the extent that the legislation is in conflict with the Hague-Visby Rules.[183] So also is a clause conferring exclusive jurisdiction on the courts of a foreign state, but only if it is proved that, in a respect material to the claim made against the carrier, the foreign court would apply rules of substantive law less favourable to the cargo-owner than those created by the Hague-Visby Rules.[184]

"*Shall be null and void*". It is submitted that, notwithstanding the literal meaning of these words, they should be construed as nullifying the offending clause only so far as it is in conflict with the Rules—at any rate in a case where the clause is severable.[185]

"*Loss or damage to or in connection with goods*". These words are not limited in their application to physical damage only. They are wide enough to cover, for example, transhipment and storage expenses incurred by a cargo-owner in consequence of the discharge of the goods otherwise than at the port of destination.[186-187]

"*Benefit of insurance clause*". As, e.g. "shipowner to have the benefits of any insurance effected by the owner of the goods". The addition of the words "in favour of the carrier" brings the Rules into conformity with the final version of the Brussels Convention 1924.

B12   **Article IV**

1. Neither the carrier nor the ship shall be liable for loss or damage arising or resulting from unseaworthiness unless caused by want of due diligence on the part of the carrier to make the ship seaworthy, and to secure that the ship is properly manned, equipped and supplied, and to make the holds, refrigerating and cool chambers and all other parts of the ship in which goods are carried fit and safe for their reception, carriage and preservation in accordance with the provisions of paragraph 1 of Article III.

---

[181] *Unicoop Japan v Ion Shipping Co* [1971] 1 Lloyd's Rep. 541, applying *The Himmerland* [1965] 2 Lloyd's Rep. 353, 360.

[182] *The Hollandia* [1983] A.C. 585; followed in Singapore in *The Epar* [1985] 2 M.L.J. 3.

[183] In *The Hollandia*, above, the clause in question might have meant either that the foreign law was incorporated only to the extent that it applied the Hague Rules, or that the foreign law was to apply in all respects. On the former interpretation, there was no difficulty in holding that the whole of the choice of law clause was invalidated by Art.III, r.8. If the clause had the wider meaning, the question would arise whether the choice of law was entirely ineffective, or whether it continued to govern the contract of carriage, subject only to the excision of the parts which contravened the Hague-Visby Rules. The speech of Lord Diplock, at p.6, with which the remainder of the House agreed, appears to favour the latter view.

[184] It is believed that this is the correct interpretation of the leading speech in *The Hollandia*, above, at p.7. See also *The Benarty* [1984] 2 Lloyd's Rep. 245 in which a jurisdiction clause was not invalid simply because it led to the application of a more favourable limitation regime in the chosen jurisdiction because Art.VIII provides that the Rules do not affect the right to limit under such statutes.

[185] *Unicoop Japan v Ion Shipping Co*, above, at p.544 and *Svenska Traktor v Maritime Agencies* [1953] 2 Q.B. 295 at p.301; but contrast *Renton v Palmyra Trading Corp* [1956] 1 Q.B. 462 at p.476.

[186-187] *Renton v Palmyra* [1957] A.C. 149. See the discussion of similar words in Art.IV, r.2, below.

Whenever loss or damage has resulted from unseaworthiness, the burden of proving the exercise of due diligence shall be on the carrier or other person claiming exemption under this Article.

"*Neither the carrier nor the ship*". This phrase is used in para.1 and "the carrier or other person" in para.2 of this Rule. Probably the two phrases bear the same meaning, and extend the protection to the case of an action *in rem*.[188] But the reference to "the ship" in Art.IV, rr.1, 2, 5 does not have the effect of enabling the owner to invoke those rules when he is not a party to the contract of carriage, e.g. because charterer's bills of lading have been issued.[189]

"*Due diligence*". In order to harmonise the protection given by this Rule with the obligation imposed by Art.III, r.1, it would appear to be necessary to read in as a qualification to "*due diligence*" the words "before and at the beginning of the voyage". This appears to be a legitimate construction.[190]

"*Due diligence . . . to make the ship seaworthy*". Seeing that due diligence must be exercised not only by the shipowner himself but also by his servants or agents,[191] the protection given by the Rule in relation to the physical condition of the ship protects, in effect,[192] only against latent defect.[193]

"*Damage has resulted from unseaworthiness*". No onus as to due diligence is cast on the shipowner except after proof has been given by the other party of (i) unseaworthiness and (ii) damage resulting therefrom.[194]

2. Neither the carrier nor the ship shall be responsible for loss or damage[195] arising or resulting from[196]:

(a) Act, neglect, or default of the master, mariner, pilot, or the servants of the carrier in the navigation or in the management of the ship[197]:

(b) Fire,[198] unless caused by the actual fault or privity of the carrier:

---

[188] See *Gosse Millerd v Canadian Government Merchant Marine* [1928] 1 K.B. 717 (CA), per Greer L.J. at p.749, and *Hourani v Harrison* (1927) 32 Com.Cas. 305 (CA), per Atkin L.J. at p.319.

[189] *Gadsden v Australian Coastal Shipping Commission* [1977] 1 N.S.W.L.R. 575

[190] *Cf. Lockett v Cunard* (1927) 28 Ll.L.R. 81 (U.S.A.).

[191] See above, Art.III.

[192] This statement was approved in *The Antigoni* [1991] 1 Lloyd's Rep. 209 (CA) in which the theoretical possibility of a shipowner who has exercised due diligence without there being any understanding of how the vessel became unseaworthy is canvassed.

[193] See per Lord Wright in *Smith Hogg v Black Sea and Baltic* [1940] A.C. 997 at p.1001, and per Mackinnon L.J. in the same case in the CA (1939) 64 Ll.L.R. 87 at p.89; *Riverstone Meat Co v Lancashire Shipping Co* [1961] A.C. 807. For the earlier cases, which must be read with some caution in the light of the exposition of the law by the HL in the last cited case, see *Bully v British and African S.N. Co* (1925) 22 Ll.L.R. 162; *Angliss v P. & O.* [1927] 2 K.B. 456; *Brown v Nitrate Producers S.S. Co* (1937) 58 Ll.L.R. 188; *Corporacion Argentina v Royal Mail* (1939) 64 Ll.L.R. 188; *Cranfield v Tatem S.N. Co* (1939) 64 Ll.L.R. 265; *The Australia Star* (1940) 67 Ll.L.R. 110. For a case since *Riverstone Meat Co v Lancashire Shipping Co* see *Union of India v N.V. Reederij Amsterdam* [1963] 2 Lloyd's Rep. 223.

[194] *Minister of Food v Reardon Smith Line* [1951] 2 Lloyd's Rep. 265. See also *Walker v Dover Navigation* (1950) 83 Ll.L.R. 84.

[195] For comment, see below.

[196] For comment, see below.

[197] As to the meaning of these words and the decisions upon them in this provision, see Art.118. The protection might be lost if the negligence is the joint act of a member of the crew and a repairer, who is not a "servant" of the carrier; *Minister of Food v Reardon Smith Line*, above. But note that "servant" includes an independent sub-contractor: see below.

[198] For comment, see below.

(c) **Perils, dangers and accidents of the sea or other navigable waters**[199]:

(d) **Act of God**[200]:

(e) **Act of War**[201]:

(f) **Act of public enemies**[202]:

(g) **Arrest or restraint of princes, rulers or people, or seizure under legal process**[203]:

(h) **Quarantine restrictions**[92]:

(i) **Act or omission of the shipper or owner of the goods, his agent or representative**[204]:

(j) **Strikes or lock-outs or stoppage or restraint of labour from whatever cause, whether partial or general**[205]:

(k) **Riots and civil commotions:**

(l) **Savings or attempting to save life or property at sea**[206]:

(m) **Wastage in bulk or weight or any other loss or damage arising from inherent defect, quality, or vice of the goods**[207]:

(n) **Insufficiency of packing**[208]:

(o) **Insufficiency or inadequacy of marks:**

(p) **Latent defects**[209] **not discoverable by due diligence:**

(q) **Any other cause arising without the actual fault or privity of the carrier, or without the fault or neglect of the agents or servants of the carrier, but the burden of proof shall be on the person claiming the benefit of this exception to show that neither the actual fault or privity of the carrier nor the fault or neglect of the agents or servants of the carrier contributed to the loss or damage.**[210]

"Neither the carrier nor the ship shall be responsible for . . . "

---

[199] See Art.112.
[200] See Art.108.
[201] For comment, see below.
[202] e.g. pirates who are *hostes humanis generis*.
[203] See Art.110.
[204] For comment, see below.
[205] For comment, see below.
[206] See r.4 of this Article, below.
[207] See Art.111.
[208] For comment, see below; and Art.111.
[209] For comment, see below.
[210] For comment, see below.

(1) These exceptions are not expressly made conditional on the exercise of due diligence to make the ship seaworthy. Section 3 of the Act abrogates the absolute undertaking of seaworthiness and in its place Art.III, r.1, imposes in terms the obligation to exercise due diligence. That obligation, unlike the obligation in Art.III, r.2, is not subject to the provisions of Art.IV, but is an absolute obligation without exception, and therefore a carrier who has not exercised due diligence to make his ship seaworthy does not enjoy the protection of any of the exceptions in Art.IV, other than those in r.5 (where the words "*in any event*"[211] are used), if the unseaworthiness is the cause of the loss.[212] He could also in an appropriate case rely on Art.IV, r.6, which is not an exception. If unseaworthiness is proved, but it is not shown that any loss or damage was caused thereby, the shipowner can rely upon the exceptions and need not prove due diligence to make seaworthy.[213]

(2) The shipowner does not enjoy the protection of these exceptions where the loss is caused by his negligence or that of his servants or agents save in so far as protection is given under sub-headings (a) and (b).[214]

(3) If the negligence of the master is only a contributory cause of the loss, Art.IV, r.2(a) does not provide a defence.[215]

(4) The carrier will not be protected by the exceptions in this Rule in the event of a deviation not permitted by r.4 of this Article.[216]

"*Loss or damage*". The application of these words is not limited to physical loss or damage.[217] The only limitation is that the loss or damage must arise in relation to the "loading, handling, stowage, carriage, custody, care and discharge of such goods."[218] Thus, where the Rules were incorporated into a charterparty[219] for consecutive voyages to be performed within a stipulated period, the words were held to cover the loss suffered by the charterers when the unseaworthiness of the vessel reduced the number of voyages which could be completed within the stated period.[220] The words were also held to cover expenses resulting from delay in arrival at the port of loading, caused by a collision due to negligent navigation.[221] They extended to claims in the nature of a debt, as well as claims for damages.[11]

"*Fire, unless caused by the actual fault or privity of the carrier*". With this should be compared the protection given to owners of *United Kingdom* ships by s.186 of the Merchant Shipping Act 1995.[222] The present Rule extends to shipowners and charterers irrespective of nationality. It does not, however, operate if the fire has been caused by

---

[211] The same words are used in Art.III, r.6, dealing with the limitation period: see above.

[212] *Maxine Footwear v Canadian Government Merchant Marine* [1959] A.C. 589 (PC).

[213] *Minister of Food v Reardon Smith Line* [1951] 2 Lloyd's Rep. 265; *Walker v Dover Navigation* (1950) 83 Ll.L.R. 84 at p.90.

[214] As to onus of proof, see below, and the cases there cited in fn.239.

[215] *Akt. de Danske Sukkerfabrikker v S. Baghamar Cie. Nav. (The Torenis)* [1983] 2 Lloyd's Rep. 210, applying *Smith Hogg & Co v Black Sea & Baltic Insurance Co* [1940] A.C. 997. *The Fiona* [1994] 2 Lloyd's Rep. 506.

[216] *Stag Line v Foscolo, Mango* [1932] A.C. 328, and see below.

[217] *Adamastos Shipping Co Ltd v Anglo-Saxon Petroleum Co Ltd* [1959] A.C. 133.

[218] *Cf.* Art.II; per Devlin J. in *Adamastos v Anglo-Saxon Petroleum Co Ltd* [1957] 2 Q.B. 233 at p.253, approved by the HL [1959] A.C. 133 at p.157.

[219] See above, para.B1.

[220] *Adamastos v Anglo-Saxon Petroleum*, above. See also *Seven Seas Transportation v Pacifico Union Marine Corp* [1984] 1 Lloyd's Rep. 588. (Hague Rules incorporated into charter of vessel A for the purpose of lightering vessel B. Damage to vessel B through acts and ommission of the crew of A. *Held*, that the damage to B fell within Art.IV2(a), and that accordingly the owners of A were free from liability). See also *Australian Oil Refining v R. W. Miller & Co* [1968] 1 Lloyd's Rep. 448 (High Ct. of Australia).

[221] *Marifortuna Naviera SA v Govt. of Ceylon* [1970] 1 Lloyd's Rep. 247. (Charterparty expressly made shipowners liable for expenses resulting from late arrival; *held*, that the exception in Art.IV, r.2(a) applied, notwithstanding that the clause created a liability in debt, not damages.)

[222] See s.6(4) of the Act, above, para.B8.

failure to use due diligence to make the ship seaworthy[223] whereas the protection given by the Merchant Shipping Act applies even though the ship is unseaworthy, provided there has been no disqualifying conduct of the owner (or other person entitled to protection) and this protection is not diminished by the provisions of the Rules.[224] Moreover, unlike the Merchant Shipping Act 1995, the burden of establishing the absence of actual fault or privity lies on the shipper.[225]

"*Act of war*". The usual exception in British charterparties has been the "King's enemies".[226] The phrase "*act of war*" is wider in scope (e.g. it certainly includes acts of war where the carrying ship is a neutral) and is narrower than "consequences of hostilities or warlike operations" in that it includes only the direct consequences of acts of war, and not the indirect consequences such as the collision with a warship proceeding to her station in wartime.[227] It would presumably cover acts done in civil war[228] and in the course of hostilities between governments still in diplomatic relation.[229]

"*Act or omission of the shipper. . . etc.*" It has been held,[230] that this exception protects the carrier from liability where the agent of the charterer (under a contract incorporating Arts III and IV of the Hague Rules) has persuaded the master to adopt an unsound method of stowage. *Quaere* whether this exemption can apply where the effect of the shipper's intervention in the holds is to render the ship unseaworthy and the shipowner has failed to exercise due diligence to prevent this.[231]

"*Strikes or lockouts, etc.*" It has been held (obiter),[232] that Art.IV(2)(j) relieves the carrier from liability even where the result of the stoppage of labour is a failure in the proper care of the cargo while in the carrier's custody, provided always that the carrier is not personally at fault in respect of the stoppage or the damage arising from it.[232]

"*Insufficiency of packing*". This means insufficiently packed for withstanding such handling as the goods will be likely to undergo in the course of the contract of carriage, but not inability to withstand negligent handling of other goods even though those other goods are part of the same consignment.[233] It has been suggested that insufficient packing which causes the contents of a case to fall out and do damage to other goods can be relied upon by the shipowner as an answer to a claim by the owner of the goods so injured.[234] *Sed quaere*. The exception will not excuse in the case of loss by pilferage, though if he can negative negligence on his part and that of his servants and agents, the shipowner may escape from liability for pilferage under Art.IV, r.2(q).[235]

"*Latent defects*[236] *not discoverable by due diligence*". If "*latent defects*" means latent defects in the ship this is already covered by r.1, but it may bear a wider meaning and may protect the carrier if, e.g. a shore crane belonging to him breaks owing to a latent defect

---

[223] See Art.III, r.1, above; and *Maxine Footwear v Canadian Government Merchant Marine* [1959] A.C. 589 (PC). See also *A. Meredith Jones & Co Ltd v Vangemar Shipping Co Ltd (The Apostolis)* [1996] 1 Lloyd's Rep. 475 (reversed on appeal on the facts [1997] 2 Lloyd's Rep. 241).

[224] See s.6(4) of the Act, above, para.B8.

[225] *The Apostolis*, above. *The Eurasian Dream*, above.

[226] Above, Art.109.

[227] See *Richard de Larrinaga v Liverpool & London War Risks* [1921] 2 A.C. 141, and such cases as *Commonwealth Shipping Representative v P. & O.* [1923] A.C. 191; *Att-Gen v Adelaid S.S. Co* [1923] A.C. 292, and *Yorkshire Dale S.S. Co v Minister of War Transport* [1942] A.C. 691.

[228] *Curtis v Mathews* [1919] 1 K.B. 425; *Pesquerias y Secadores v Beer* (1949) 82 Ll.L.R. 501 (HL), both insurance cases.

[229] *Kawasaki Kisen, etc. v Bantham S.S. Co (No. 2)* [1939] 2 K.B. 544.

[230] By Lord Denning M.R. in *Ismail v Polish Ocean Lines* [1976] 1 Q.B. 893, but not, we believe, by the other members of the court.

[231] *Empresa Cubana Importada de Alimentos "Alimport" v Iasmos Shipping Co SA (The Good Friend)*, above.

[232] per Brandon J. in *The Arawa* [1977] 2 Lloyd's Rep. 416: (in the CA at [1980] 2 Lloyd's Rep. 135).

[233] *Silver v Ocean S.S. Co* [1930] 1 K.B. 416.

[234] *Goodwin v Lamport and Holt* (1929) 34 Ll.L.R. 192.

[235] *Potts v Union S.S. Co of New Zealand* [1946] N.Z.L.R. 276.

[236] See notes to Art.III r.1 above.

not discoverable by due diligence. Another possible meaning for these words resulting in their giving the shipowner an immunity additional to that provided in r.1 of this Article is that they cover defects which would not have been discovered by the exercise of due diligence even though the shipowner could not show that he had in fact exercised such diligence.[237]

"Any other cause arising without the actual fault or privity of the carrier, or without the fault or neglect of the agents or servants of the carrier, but the burden of proof shall be on the person claiming the benefit of this exception to show that neither the actual fault or privity of the carrier nor the fault or neglect of the agents or servants of the carrier contributed to the loss or damage."

"Any other cause". As these words are used and not "any other cause whatsoever", the exceptions in r.2(q) should be interpreted as being *ejusdem generis* as the exceptions from (a) to (p), provided there is any *genus* which will embrace all the exceptions. But it is difficult to imagine any *genus* which would embrace them all, and therefore it seems necessary to give these words the wider interpretation and thus to exclude the responsibility of the carrier in all cases where neither he nor his servants are at fault.[238]

Save in cases where negligence or privity is expressly dealt with as in Rule 2(a) and (b) it is submitted that the carrier is protected against loss or damage on proof by him that the case falls within the specific exception unless the goods-owner in his turn proves negligence.[239] Under exception (q) the onus of disproving negligence and privity is placed expressly upon the carrier.

It is not enough for the shipowner to show that the damage done was partly due to some cause for which he is excused if part of the damage is not so caused. He must show how much damage was due to the cause for which he is excused, because it is only in respect of that cause that he can claim protection. If he does not do so, he has failed to show to what extent in money his prima facie liability for the whole ought to be reduced.[240] But if part of the damage is shown to have been caused by a breach of contract by the goods owner, then it is for the goods owner to show how much of the damage was caused otherwise than by his breach of contract, failing which he can recover nominal damages only.[241]

---

[237] See per Branson J. in *Corporacion Argentina v Royal Mail Lines* (1939) 64 Ll.L.R. 188 at p.192.
[238] So held in *Potts v Union S.S. Co of New Zealand* [1946] N.Z.L.R. 276. But see *Paterson Steamships v Canadian Co-operative Wheat Producers* [1934] A.C. 538 at pp.549, 550.
[239] *The Glendarroch* [1894] P. 226; *Matheos (Owners) v Dreyfus* [1925] A.C. 654 at p.666; Greer L.J. in *Silver v Ocean S.S. Co* [1930] 1 K.B. 416 at p.435; *Albacora v Westcott & Laurance Line* [1966] 2 Lloyd's Rep. 53, per Lord Pearce at p.61 and per Lord Pearson at p.64; Roskill J. in *The Flowergate* [1967] 1 Lloyd's Rep. 1 at p.8; *A/S de Danske Sukkerfabrikker v Bajamar cia. Na. SA (The Torenia)* [1983] 2 Lloyd's Rep. 210, and the cases cited in Art.107, see also *Phillips Petroleum Co v Caboneli Naviera SA (The Theodegmon)* [1990] 1 Lloyd's Rep. 52. There is a considerable weight of authority to the contrary effect, but it may be doubted if the point has yet been fully argued in a case where it was material to the decision. Thus the principle as stated in the text was doubted in *Goodwin v Lamport & Holt* (1929) 34 Ll.L.R. 192 at p.195, but no decision was given on the point. Similarly in *Bradley v Federal S.N. Co* (1927) 27 Ll.L.R. 395 (HL) at p.396, Lord Sumner speaks of the necessity for the carrier to negative negligence, but he is not there dealing with a case where the carrier has proved an exception which prima facie protects him. See also per Wright J. in *Gosse Millard v Canadian Government* [1927] 2 K.B. 432 at pp.435–437, and in *Paterson Steamships v Canadian Co-operative Wheat Producers* [1934] A.C. 538 at p.545; per Roche J. in *Borthwick v New Zealand Shipping Co* (1934) 49 Ll.L.R. 19 at pp.23, 24; per Atkinson J. in *Phillips v Clan Line* (1943) 76 Ll.L.R. 58 at p.61, and Pilcher J. in *Svenska Traktor Akt. v Maritime Agencies (Southampton)* [1953] 2 Q.B. 295. The New Zealand courts have accepted and acted upon the statement in the text: see *Shaw, Savill v Powley* [1949] N.Z.L.R. 668.
[240] *Gosse Millerd v Canadian Government* [1929] A.C. 223, per Lord Sumner at p.241. See, also, the even stronger view of Scrutton L.J. in *Silver v Ocean S.S. Co* [1930] 1 K.B. 416 at p.430 and *cf.* Greer L.J. at p.435. See further *The Mekhanik Evgrafor and The Ivan Derbenev* [1987] 2 Lloyd's Rep. 634.
[241] *Government of Ceylon v Chandris* [1965] 2 Lloyd's Rep. 204. *C.H.Z. 'Rolimpex' v Eftavrysses Compania Naviera SA (The Panaghia Tinnou)* [1986] 2 Lloyd's Rep. 580.

"*Or without the fault . . . of the agents, etc.*" "*Or*" means "and".[242]

"*Without the fault or neglect*". It is not necessary for the carrier in order to claim the protection of the sub-rule to show the exact cause of the loss provided he shows that it was not due to negligence.[243] But it is enough that the loss is unexplained, because the onus is on the carrier to show absence of fault or negligence.[244]

"*Agents or servants of the carrier*". Agents or servants include the servants of an independent stevedore both in rr.2(a) and 2(q).[245] The dishonest act of the carrier's servants or agents (such as theft by a stevedore) is not a "cause arising without the fault or neglect of the agents or servants of the carrier" unless it takes place outside the performance of the duties entrusted to the servant or agent by the carrier.[246] Thus, the carrier cannot escape liability under r.2(q) for the theft of goods by a servant or agent charged with the custody of the goods.[247] But where a stevedore stole part of the ship's equipment, so rendering it vulnerable to the perils of the sea, the carrier was held to be protected by r.2(q).[248]

3. The shipper shall not be responsible for loss or damage sustained by the carrier or the ship arising or resulting from any cause without the act, fault or neglect of the shipper, his agents or his servants.

This Rule is expressed in very wide language.[249] The "*shipper*" means only the shipper and not the person on whom liabilities under the contract of carriage are imposed by s.3(1) of the Carriage of Goods by Sea Act 1992.[250] The shipper cannot surrender his rights. Article V[251] permits only the carrier to do so.

This Rule does not lessen the stringency of an undertaking to pay demurrage in the event of failure to load or discharge in a fixed time.[252]

4. Any deviation in saving or attempting to save life or property at sea, or any reasonable deviation shall not be deemed to be an infringement or breach of these Rules or of the contract of carriage, and the carrier shall not be liable for any loss or damage resulting therefrom.

This Rule raises some difficult questions as to deviation:

(i) In what way do the Rules affect, restrict or increase the carrier's rights as to deviation under bills of lading to which the Act applies?

Except here deviation is not dealt with anywhere in the Rules and the present Rule has only been considered in four cases in the English courts.[253] Before the penultimate of

---

[242] *Hourani v Harrison* (1927) 32 Com.Cas. 305 (CA); *Paterson Steamships v Canadian Co-operative Wheat Producers* [1934] A.C. 538 at p.549. *Leesh River Tea Co v British India Steam Navigation Co* [1966] 1 Lloyd's Rep. 450; affirmed on this point at [1966] 2 Lloyd's Rep. 193 (CA).

[243] *City of Baroda v Hall Line* (1926) 42 T.L.R. 717, a decision on the Hague Rules, 1921.

[244] *Heyn v Ocean S.S. Co* (1927) 43 T.L.R. 358; *Pendle and Rivet v Ellerman Lines* (1928) 33 Com.Cas. 70; *Herald Weekly Times v New Zealand Shipping Co* (1947) 80 Ll.L.R. 596.

[245] *Heyn v Ocean S.S. Co*, above; *Hourani v Harrison* (1927) 32 Com.Cas. 305 (CA).

[246] *Leesh River Tea Co v British India Steam Navigation* [1966] 2 Lloyd's Rep. 193, applying *Morris v Martin* [1966] 1 Q.B. 716. *Heyn v Ocean S.S. Co* (1927) 43 T.L.R. 358 must be treated as wrongly decided on this point, and *Brown v Harrison* (1927) Ll.L.R. 415 treated with reserve.

[247] *Cf. Hourani v Harrison* (1927) Ll.L.R. 334.

[248] See fn.246, above.

[249] See, too, r.6 of this Article, below.

[250] *Aegean Sea Traders Corp v Repsol Petroleo SA (The Aegean Sea)* [1998] 2 Lloyd's Rep. 39.

[251] Below, para.B14.

[252] *Leeds Shipping Co v Duncan Fox* (1932) 37 Com.Cas. 213.

[253] *Stag Line v Foscolo, Mango* [1932] A.C. 328; *Foreman and Ellams v Federal S.N. Co* [1928] 2 K.B. 424; *Renton v Palmyra* [1957] A.C. 149; *Lyric Shipping Inc. v Intermetals Ltd (The Al Taha)* [1990] 2 Lloyd's Rep. 117.

these it was possible to take various alternative views as to the effect of the Rule, which were discussed in earlier editions of this book. The law can now, it is submitted, be stated as follows:

(a) The Rule has no effect upon the right of the carrier under a liberty clause in a bill of lading in certain stated circumstances to discharge the goods at a substituted port; the exercise of such a right, if valid on common law principles, is no deviation, but is a performance of the contractual voyage.[254]

(b) Similarly a clause in a bill of lading permitting deviation from the usual, customary or reasonable route between agreed ports A and B is unaffected by the Rule in that its validity will be judged by common law principles.[255]

(c) The rights to deviate in saving or attempting to save life or property at sea or to make any reasonable deviation conferred by the Rule are additional to the rights expressly given by the bill of lading, when properly construed, or conferred at common law.[256]

(d) The words "shall not be deemed to be an infringement or breach of these Rules" were inserted *ex abundanti cautela* to preserve the carrier's rights and immunities conferred by the other Rules of Art.IV in the event of the exercise of the rights to deviate given by this Rule.[257]

(ii) Why are the words *"breach of the contract of carriage"* inserted in addition to the words *"breach of the Rules"*?

In addition to the terms incorporated into any bill of lading by the provisions of the Act and Rules, the bill of lading may contain other terms and conditions not inconsistent with the Rules (as, e.g. the imposition on the shipper of a liability to pay demurrage). The words *"or of the contract of carriage"* may import that a deviation permitted by the Rules shall not be deemed to be a breach of the contract of carriage so as to displace such additional terms, even though the contract of carriage does not expressly provide for such deviation.

(iii) What is a *"reasonable deviation"*?

Whether a deviation is reasonable or not is a question of fact for the court, which must be decided in the light of all the circumstances of the case.[258] "The true test seems to be what departure from the contract voyage might a prudent person controlling the voyage at the time make and maintain, having in mind all the relevant circumstances existing at the time, including the terms of the contract and the interest of all parties concerned, but without obligation to consider the interests of any one as conclusive."[259] A deviation may

---

[254] *Renton v Palmyra*, above. For the common law applicable, see, above, Art.127, and *Case 5* therein.

[255] Based on the approach of the courts to a "liberty" or "deviation" clause in *Stag Line v Foscolo Mango*, above, and *Foreman and Ellams v Federal S.N. Co*, above. For a similar approach in Australia, see *Thiess v Australian Steamships* [1955] 1 Lloyd's Rep. 459 (N.S.W.). The statement in the text appears also to follow from the judgments in *Renton v Palmyra* in the CA of Jenkins and Hodson L.JJ., particularly the former at [1956] 1 Q.B. 505, where he thought Rule 4 should be construed merely as giving an additional protection to shipowner. The point was left open in the HL: see per Lord Morton [1957] A.C. 149 at p.171.

[256] See per Jenkins L.J. in *Renton v Palmyra* [1956] 1 Q.B. 462 at p.505. As to the construction of "liberty" or "deviation" clauses and common law rights of deviation to save life, communicate with a vessel in distress, or as the result of necessity, see, above, Arts 127, 128.

[257] *Renton v Palmyra*, above, per Jenkins L.J. at p.506, and Hodson L.J. at p.510. See also, Lord Somervell [1957] A.C. 149 at p.175.

[258] *Stag Line v Foscolo, Mango* [1932] A.C. 328.

[259] *ibid.* per Lord Atkin, at p.343, doubting the test suggested by Wright J. in *Foreman & Ellams v Federal S.N. Co* [1928] 2 K.B. 424 at p.431, "that the reasonableness of the departure must depend upon what would be contemplated by *both parties*, having regard to the exigencies of the route known or assumed to be known to both parties". In *Danae Shipping Co v T.P.A.O.* [1983] 1 Lloyd's Rep. 499 it was held (following *Phelps, James & Co v Hill* [1891] 1 Q.B. 605, per Lindley L.J.) that the court should be slow to criticise the decision of a skilled and experienced master, or a person in a similar position, acting in good faith, that a deviation was necessary.

be reasonable even though it was planned before the voyage began or before the bill of lading was issued.[260]

(iv) What is the effect of a deviation not permitted by the Rules or the contract of carriage?

It is submitted that the position will be the same as at common law and the bill of lading holder will be able to treat the deviation as a repudiation putting and end to the contract of carriage.[261] Arguably as a matter of construction, the carrier will not be protected by the exceptions in Art.IV, r.2, nor *semble* the other statutory exceptions in his favour in the Rules.[262] But perhaps the carrier could still rely on Art.III, r.6 (third paragraph), and on Art.IV, r.5, in view of the words "*in any event*" (as to which, see further below), at any rate in a case where an English court is dealing with a bill of lading issued in the United Kingdom, and would give effect to these Rules as part of the statute law. The position is possibly different where the court is dealing with a foreign bill of lading incorporating the Rules as a matter of contract.[263]

(v) What loss or damage "*results from*" a deviation?

The Rule cannot mean "occurs after" the departure from the proper course, because in that case a carrier who had deviated permissibly would be protected from the negligence of his servants even though not in the navigation or management of the ship. Probably the intention is to protect the carrier who has deviated permissibly from all liability for which he would be excused if he were still on the customary or contractual route, e.g. from the consequences of a storm which might not otherwise have been encountered.

5(a). Unless the nature and value of such goods have been declared by the shipper before shipment and inserted in the bill of lading, neither the carrier nor the ship shall in any event be or become liable for any loss or damage to or in connection with the goods in an amount exceeding 666.67 units of account per package or unit or 2 units of account per kilogramme of gross weight of the goods lost or damaged, whichever is the higher.

(b) The total amount recoverable shall be calculated by reference to the value of such goods at the place and time at which the goods are discharged from the ship in accordance with the contract or should have been so discharged.[264]

The value of the goods shall be fixed according to the commodity exchange price, or, if there be no such price, according to the current market price, or, if there be no commodity exchange price or current market price, by reference to the normal value of goods of the same kind and quality.

(c) Where a container, pallet or similar article of transport is used to consolidate goods, the number of packages or units enumerated[265] in the bill of lading as packed in such article of transport shall be deemed the number of packages or units for the purpose of this paragraph as far as these

---

260 *Lyric Shipping Inc v Intermetals Ltd*, above.
261 *Hain S.S. Co v Tate & Lyle* (1936) 41 Com.Cas. 350, and see Art.127.
262 *Stag Line v Foscolo, Mango & Co* [1932] A.C. 328. See Art.127.
263 In the United States it has been decided that the words "in any event" do not protect in a case of unjustified deviation: *Jones v Flying Clipper* (1954) 116 Fed.Supp. 386.
264 *Cf.: El Greco (Australia) Pty Ltd v Mediterranean Shipping Co SA* [2004] 2 Lloyd's 537 (Fed. Ct. Aust). See also F.M.B. Reynolds *"The Package or Unit Limitation and the Visby Rules"* [2005] L.M.C.L.Q. 1.
265 *Cf.: El Greco (Australia) Pty Ltd v Mediterranean Shipping Co SA*, above.

packages or units are concerned. **Except as aforesaid such article of transport shall be considered the package or unit.**

(d) The unit of account mentioned in this Article is the special drawing right as defined by the International Monetary Fund. The amounts mentioned in sub-paragraph (a) of this paragraph shall be converted into national currency on the basis of the value of that currency on a date to be determined by the law of the court seized of the case.[266]

(e) Neither the carrier not the ship shall be entitled to the benefit of the limitation of liability provided for in this paragraph if it is proved that the damage resulted from an act or omission of the carrier done with intent to cause damage, or recklessly and with knowledge that damage would probably result.

(f) The declaration mentioned in sub-paragraph (a) of this paragraph, if embodied in the bill of lading, shall be prima facie evidence, but shall not be binding or conclusive on the carrier.

(g) By agreement between the carrier, master or agent of the carrier and the shipper other maximum amounts than those mentioned in sub-paragraph (a) of this paragraph may be fixed, provided that no maximum amount so fixed shall be less than the appropriate maximum mentioned in that sub-paragraph.

(h) Neither the carrier nor the ship shall be responsible in any event for loss or damage to, or in connection with, goods if the nature or value thereof has been knowingly mis-stated by the shipper in the bill of lading.

The words "in any event" in Art.5(a) are unlimited in scope so that (subject to Art.5(e)) the shipowner will be able to limit even where (for example) a cause of loss is a breach of Art.III[267] or there is a breach of the obligation to stow on deck.[268]

The new Art.IV, r.5 alters the previous law in six respects.

First, the sterling limit, coupled with a Gold Clause,[269] is replaced by a limit expressed in "special drawing rights".[270]

Second, the limit "per package or unit" is increased.

---

[266] The references to units of account were substituted for provisions relating to "Poincaré Francs" by s.2(3) of the Merchant Shipping Act, 1981, brought into force by SI 1983 No. 1906.

[267] *The Happy Ranger* [2006] EWHC 122 (Comm); [2006] 1 Lloyd's Rep. 649.

[268] *Daewoo Heavy Industries Ltd v Klipriver Shipping Ltd (The Kapitan Petko Voivoda)* [2003] 2 Lloyd's Rep. 1 However, the words "in any event" are not apt to extend the Rules period in respect of package limitation if the relevant obligations by agreement cease on discharge of the goods: *Trafigura Beheer BV v Mediteranean Shipping Co SA (The MSC Amsterdam)* [2007] EWCA Civ. 794.

[269] The Gold clause in Art.IX qualifies the £100 figure in Art.IV, r.5 of the Hague Rules with the result that the limitation figure is £100 gold value: *The Rosa S* [1989] 2 Lloyd's Rep. 574; *Brown Boveri (Australia) Pty Ltd v Baltic Shipping Co (The Nadezhda Krupskraya)* [1989] 1 Lloyd's Rep. 518 (N.S.W.); *The Thomaseverett* [1992] 2 S.L.R. 1068 (Sing.). *Cf.: Dairy Containers Ltd v Tasman Orient Line C.V. (The Tasman Discoverer)* [2004] UKPC 22; [2004] 2 Lloyd's Rep. 647 (PC).

[270] The text of r.5(d) replaces, by virtue of s.2(4) of the Merchant Shipping Act 1981, the original version, which contained a definition of "Poincaré Francs". Section 2(5) of the Act of 1981 provides that the date referred to shall be the date of the judgment in question. Section 3 of the Act of 1981 contains detailed provisions establishing when and how the sterling equivalents of the amounts in special drawing rights are to be calculated.

Third, there is now an alternative limitation based on weight, which serves to eliminate the controversy, which existed under the Hague Rules[271] as to the application of the "unit" limitation to bulk cargoes.

Fourth, sub-Rule (c) solves some, although not necessarily all, of the limitation problems which arose under the unamended Rules in relation to container transportation.[272] The difficulties which the Court may in due course have to consider to include the following—

    (1) What articles of transport are "similar to" containers and pallets?[273]
    (2) What precisely is meant by "used to consolidate" goods?[274]
    (3) In what circumstances is the number of packages "enumerated in the bill of lading as packed" in the container?[275]

Fifth, by virtue of Art.IV, r.5(e), it is provided for the first time that certain types of misconduct by the carrier will deprive him of the benefit of the limitation.[276] It is submitted that "the carrier" in this paragraph means the carrier or his *alter ego*, and does not include his servants or agents save where they are the *alter ego*.[277] It may be noted that the word "probably" sets a high standard of proof[278] and requires "recklessly" to be given a special meaning.[279]

It appears that para.(e) leaves no room for the doctrine of deviation[280] to deprive the carrier of his right to limit his liability: at any rate where the act relied upon is committed by the carrier. On the other hand, the doctrine may still operate in respect of the *exceptions* in the Rules,[281] and perhaps even in respect of the limit, where the act relied upon as a deviation is committed by the crew and not by the carrier himself.

Finally, para.(b) contains a new provision relating to the computation of damages. The purpose of this provision is not clear. One possible view is that it is intended to provide an additional upper limit to the amount recoverable, thus eliminating claims for

---

[271] As to which see the 18th edn pp.441–444 and *The Aramis* [1987] 2 Lloyd's Rep. 59.

[272] See Art.183, above and *The "River Gurara"* [1998] 1 Lloyd's Rep. 225.

[273] It is submitted that "roll on, roll off" lorries and trailers do not fall within this description.

[274] Perhaps the most obvious interpretation is "used to carry" or "used to contain". But the word "consolidate" is often employed in the trade as meaning "treat as one consignment for the purposes of calculating freight". The difficulty is most likely to arise where a forwarding agent ships the goods of several different consignors in a single container. The word in the French text is "grouper".

[275] In particular, what is the position where the bill is "said to contain" a certain number of packages? It is submitted that this is a sufficient enumeration for the purposes of this sub-Rule, even though it would probably not create an estoppel under Art.III, r.3. It would appear that both parties are bound, for limitation purposes, by an incorrect enumeration—an unsatisfactory result.

[276] Although he retains the benefit of the defences in Art.IV, and the time-bar in Art.III, r.6. The sanction is therefore less severe than the kindred provisions in the legislation governing international carriage by air and road, which deprive the carrier of *all* his protection in the event of the relevant misconduct.

[277] *Browner International Ltd v Monarch Shipping Co Ltd (The European Enterprise* [1989] 2 Lloyd's Rep. 185. It is submitted that the principle of *Riverstone Meat v Lancashire Shipping* [1961] A.C. 807 cannot be applied to this paragraph.

[278] *Cf. Goldman v Thai Airways Ltd* [1983] 1 W.L.R. 1186, a decision on similar words in the Warsaw Convention as amended at the Hague, 1956, enacted in the United Kingdom by the Carriage by Air Act 1961. It is likely to be more difficult for the cargo owner to prove that this paragraph applies than to establish "actual fault or privity" for the purposes of the Merchant Shipping Acts.

[279] The subjective element of recklessness does not normally go further than recognition that damage *may* result from the act in question: see, for example, *Reed v London & Rochester* [1954] 2 Lloyd's Rep. 463. Under r.5(e) the claimant must prove actual (not imputed or constructive) knowledge that damage of the type complained of was likely to result from the act or omission in question: *Goldman v Thai Airways Ltd*, above.

[280] For a contrary view see *Nelson Pine Industries Ltd v Seatrans New Zealand Ltd (The Pembroke)* [1995] 2 Lloyd's Rep. 290 (N.Z.). It appears that the same conclusion would have been reached whether the Rules applied as a matter of (German) Statute or contract.

[281] For the position regarding exceptions, see Art.127 and Art.IV, above. The fact that the draftsman has specifically provided that serious misconduct deprives the carrier of his right to limit might be said to imply that the other protective provisions of the Rules were not intended to be vitiated by such misconduct.

consequential loss.[282] Alternatively, the intention may have been to provide a yardstick for the calculation of damages, without necessarily providing that the sum recoverable consists *only* of the damages so calculated.[283] Whichever interpretation is correct, the application of the sub-Rule in practice is likely to give rise to difficulty.

6. Goods of an inflammable, explosive or dangerous nature to the shipment whereof the carrier, master or agent of the carrier, has not consented, with knowledge of their nature and character,[284] may at any time before discharge be landed at any place or destroyed or rendered innocuous by the carrier without compensation, and the shipper of such goods shall be liable for all damages and expenses directly or indirectly arising out of or resulting from such shipment.

If any such goods shipped with such knowledge and consent shall become a danger to the ship or cargo, they may in like manner be landed at any place or destroyed or rendered innocuous by the carrier without liability on the part of the carrier except to general average, if any.

"*Dangerous*". This probably means physically dangerous, and does not extend to those cases where the ship suffers loss owing to legal obstacles to the carriage or discharge of goods.[285]

"*May*". The shipowner can exercise his rights under this Rule even if in breach of his obligations as to seaworthiness, provided that the shipowner's breach did not cause or contribute to the loss.[286] In the case of a deviation, the Rule would be given effect to by an English court dealing with the case of a bill of lading issued in the United Kingdom as part of the statute law. Where the court is dealing with a foreign bill of lading incorporating the Rules as a matter of contract, it is unclear whether the right to an indemnity under Art.IV, r.6 would survive a deviation.[287] It is submitted that the Article should be given the same construction in a contractual context as that pertaining as a matter of statute law.

"*Innocuous*". On the wording of the clause the carrier or his master may land or destroy or render the goods innocuous at his option, and need not act reasonably in making his choice, but as the same wording is found in the last paragraph in dealing with a case where the ship has consented to receive the goods, probably he must act reasonably.

"*Shall be liable*". The shipowner's indemnity is not dependent upon his having landed, destroyed or rendered the goods innocuous.[288] The shipper's liability is not dependant on any negligence or deliberate act by him other than the act of shipment.[289]

---

[282] The words "the total amount recoverable" support this construction.

[283] The words "calculated by reference to" scarcely seem strong enough to create a limit. Contrast the much more explicit language of para.(a). Compare also the use of the same term in Art.23 of the Schedule to the Carriage of Goods by Road Act 1965.

[284] Knowledge of the carrier includes matters which the shipowner ought to know: *The Athanasia Comninos and The Georges Chr. v Lemos* (1979) [1990] 1 Lloyd's Rep. 277; *Mediterranean Freight Services Ltd v B.P. Oil International Ltd (The Fiona)* [1993] 1 Lloyd's Rep. 257.

[285] *Effort Shipping Co Ltd v Linden Management SA (The Giannis N.K.)* [1994] 2 Lloyd's Rep. 171; [1996] 1 Lloyd's Rep. 577. See also Art.53, above.

[286] See *Mediterranean Freight Services Ltd v B.P. Oil International Ltd (The Fiona)* [1993] 1 Lloyd's Rep. 257; [1994] 2 Lloyd's Rep. 506. Where the dangerous nature of the cargo and the shipowner's breach of Art.III, r.1 are concurrent causes of the damage, the shipowner will not be able to recover under Art.IV, r.6: *The Fiona*, above.

[287] See above.

[288] See *The Fiona*, above in which it was held that the words referred to causation rather than remoteness.

[289] *The Giannis N.K.* [1996] 1 Lloyd's Rep. 577.

"*Directly or indirectly*". These words indicate that recovery under the Article is not dependent on establishing that the dangerous nature of the cargo was the proximate or dominant cause of the loss.

"*Shipper*". The previous edition of this work stated that this might be read so as to include a lawful holder satisfying the requirements of s.3 of the Carriage of Goods by Sea Act 1992 but that it was submitted that it did not do so; and this statement was cited with approval in *The Aegean Sea*.[290] However, it is submitted that s.3 of the 1992 Act does indeed transfer the shipper's liability for dangerous cargo.[291]

"*With such knowledge and consent*". The absence in the second paragraph in contrast to the first, of any provision as to damages arising from the shipment of dangerous cargo, does not imply that, when such shipment takes place with the knowledge and consent of the master and damage results, the shipowner cannot make the shipper liable. The Schedule does not contain a complete code and in the circumstances mentioned the shipowner can recover damages from the shipper if his contract, apart from the Act, enables him to do so.[292]

B13   **Article IV bis**

1. The defences and limits of liability provided for in these Rules shall apply in any action against the carrier in respect of loss or damage to goods covered by a contract of carriage whether the action be founded in contract or in tort.

The principal object of this new Rule is to ensure that the cargo-owner is no better off by suing in tort than he would be if he sued in contract.[293]

It is, however, possible that the draftsman of the Rule may have unintentionally made an important alteration to English law. Where goods are carried on a chartered ship, and bills of lading are issued by the charterer, attempts have been made to circumvent the Hague Rules defences and limits by instituting proceedings directly in tort against the carrier.[294] On a literal reading of the clause, and on one possible interpretation of Art.I(a), the new Rule could be understood as conferring on the actual carrier the benefit of the Rules, even though he is not a party to the bill of lading. Although the argument might be said to gain support from s.1(3) which applies the Rules to "the carriage of goods by sea" in contrast to s.1(4) which covers the application of the rules to "any contract for the carriage of goods by sea", we submit that this is a reading which the Court is unlikely to adopt.[295]

---

[290] [1998] 2 Lloyd's Rep. 39, 70.
[291] See D. Mildon Q.C. [1999] I.J.S.L. 99.
[292] *Chandris v Isbrandtsen-Moller* [1951] 1 K.B. 240; *The Athanasia Comninos*, above; *The Giannis N.K.*, above. *Cf. The Fiona*, above. Whilst Art.IV, r.6 will prevent the implication of any inconsistent common law obligations with regard to the shipment of dangerous cargo, there are no grounds for holding that the Article would override any more onerous contractual obligations assumed by the shipper or exclude the operation of the common law in areas not covered by the Article, such as legally rather than physically dangerous cargo.
[293] The sentence was approved in *Compania Portoarfti Commerciale SA v Ultramar Panama Inc (The Captain Gregos) (No.1)* [1990] 1 Lloyd's Rep. 310. See also A. Diamond Q.C. [1978] L.M.C.L.Q. 225 at pp.248–253.
[294] It is still not clear, as a matter of English law, whether in such a case, the carrier is entitled to rely on the terms of the bill of lading, even though he is not a party to it: see *Elder Dempster v Patterson Zochonis* [1924] A.C. 522, discussed and explained in *Midland Silicones v Scruttons* [1962] A.C. 446 and *Morris v Martin* [1966] 1 Q.B. 716. See also *Compania Portorafti Commerciale SA v Ultramar Panama Inc (The Captain Gregos) (No. 2)* [1990] 2 Lloyd's Rep. 395, at pp.404–406.
[295] *Cf. Gadsden v Australian Coastal Shipping Commission* [1977] 1 N.S.W.L.R. 575 decided under Art.III, r.6 of the Hague Rules.

2. If such an action is brought against a servant or agent of the carrier (such servant or agent not being an independent contractor), such servant or agent shall be entitled to avail himself of the defences and limits of liability which the carrier is entitled to invoke under these rules.

For the first time in relation to carriage of goods by sea,[296] this Rule extends the protection of the statutory exceptions to persons other than the carrier himself.[297]

There are two important restrictions on the scope of the Rule. First, it does not purport to protect the "actual carrier" in cases where the carriage is performed by someone other than the party who issued the bill of lading.[298]

Secondly, the Rule applies only to an agent "not being an independent contractor". It is believed that the intention of these words was to exclude from the protection of the Rules persons such as stevedores.[299] The qualification appears, however, to go a good deal further than this; for it is hard to conceive of any agent, capable of being held liable in respect of carriage of goods by sea, who is not an independent contractor.[300]

The result of the Rule appears to be that the liability of the servant or agent, in cases where he is potentially liable at all, is in general[301] to follow that of the carrier; and not that the Amended Rules are read, in relation to servants or agents, as if those persons were themselves the carrier.[302]

3. The aggregate of the amounts recoverable from the carrier, and such servants and agents, shall in no case exceed the limit provided for in these Rules.

It is submitted that "recoverable" should be read as "recovered", so that judgment against an insolvent defendant would not bar recovery in full against another defendant.

4. Nevertheless, a servant or agent of the carrier shall not be entitled to avail himself of the provisions of this article, if it is proved that the damage resulted from an act or omission of the servant or agent done with intent to cause damage or recklessly and with knowledge that damage would probably result.

The wording of this Rule resembles that of Art.IV, r.5(e), but there is an important difference in its effect, in that intentional or reckless misconduct by the carrier deprives

---

[296] Similar provisons already exist in relation to the international carriage of goods by air and by road.

[297] In effect, the Rule reverses, so far as concerns Hague Rules carriage, the principle of *Adler v Dickson* [1955] 1 Q.B. 158.

[298] In other words, the actual carrier must still rely on *Elder Dempster v Paterson Zochonis* [1924] A.C. 522 as to which see Art.121. In this the 1971 Act differs from the legislation relating to the international carriage by air and by road. As to the possible effect in this context of Art.IV, *bis*, r.1, see above.

[299] And hence to preserve the effect of *Midland Silicones v Scruttons* [1962] A.C. 446.

[300] Recourse to the French text is of no help. The equivalent to "servant or agent" is *préposé*, a word elsewhere translated simply as "servant". There is no consistency in the use and translation of "*préposé*" and "*agent*".

[301] But not in every respect. If there is intentional or reckless misconduct by the servant, to which the carrier himself is not privy, the carrier may limit his liability (Art.IV, r.5(e)), but the servant may not (Art.IV *bis*, r.4). See also the comment on the latter rule, above.

[302] See the words "which the carrier is entitled to invoke". It would be hard to make sense of provisions such as Art.IV, r.1, if the servant were to be treated as the carrier for the purpose of assessing his liability.

him only of his right to limit, whereas similar conduct by the servant deprives him not only of the limit, but also of all his statutory defences, except perhaps the time bar under Art.III, r.5.[303]

B14   Article V

A carrier shall be at liberty to surrender in whole or in part all or any of his rights and immunities or to increase any of his responsibilities and obligations under these Rules, provided such surrender or increase shall be embodied in the bill of lading issued to the shipper. The provisions of these Rules shall not be applicable to charterparties, but if bills of lading are issued in the case of a ship under a charter-party they shall comply with the terms of these Rules. Nothing in these Rules shall be held to prevent the insertion in a bill of lading of any lawful provision regarding general average.

The substitution of "obligations" for "liabilities" brings the Schedule into line with the final wording of the Brussels Convention.

"*A carrier shall be at liberty to surrender, etc.*" The effect of the first paragraph of this Article is to enable the shipper to get better terms than would be obtained by relying on the Rules, e.g. in the timber trade to get the insertion of the "conclusive evidence" clause. It would seem, however, that the shipper cannot surrender the rights given to him by the Rules.

"*The provisions of these Rules shall not be applicable to charterparties.*" This Rules appears strictly to apply only to the issue of bills of lading to a shipper other than the charterer. Where bills of lading are issued to the charterer they are generally mere receipts.[304] The terms of Art.III, rr.3 and 4, are confined to cases where the goods are entrusted to a "*carrier*" or are received under a "*contract of carriage*", as defined in Art.I. Where, therefore, there is no carrier and no contract of carriage, the terms of the Rules do not apply, at any rate until the bill of lading becomes the document which regulates the relations of the parties. The Rules have, therefore, no application to a shipper who is also charterer, and it seems that such a shipper cannot demand a bill of lading in the form prescribed, because until the contract between the parties is regulated by a bill of lading there is no carrier within the meaning of the Rules.

"*General average.*" This provision was probably inserted *ex abundanti cautela*. "*Lawful*" presumably means lawful apart from the Act and Rules; e.g. Rule D of the York-Antwerp Rules 1994, would be unobjectionable.[305]

B15   Article VI—Special Conditions

Notwithstanding the provisions of the preceding articles, a carrier, master or agent of the carrier, and a shipper shall in regard to any particular goods be at liberty to enter into any agreement in any terms as to the responsibility

---

[303] The issue is canvassed without decision in *The Captain Gregos*, above. If reckless conduct deprives a servant or agent of the right to rely upon Art.III, *bis*, it would deprive him of the right to rely upon Art.IV, *bis*, r.2. It is this Rule alone which enables such a servant or agent to avail himself of any of the defences and limits available to the carrier, incuding Art.III, r.6.
[304] See the discussion in the Introductory Notes, at para.B1, above.
[305] See below.

and liability of the carrier for such goods, and as to the rights and immunities of the carrier in respect of such goods, or his obligation as to seaworthiness, so far as this stipulation[306] is not contrary to public policy, or the care or diligence of his servants or agents in regard to the loading, handling, stowage, carriage, custody, care, and discharge of the goods carried by sea, provided that in this case no bill of lading has been or shall be issued and that the terms agreed shall be embodied in a receipt which shall be a non-negotiable document and shall be marked as such.

Any agreement so entered into shall have full legal effect.

Provided that this Article shall not apply to ordinary commercial shipments made in the ordinary course of trade, but only to other shipments where the character or condition of the property to be carried or the circumstances, terms and conditions under which the carriage is to be performed, are such as reasonably to justify a special agreement.

"*Any particular goods*", i.e. as defined in the proviso, and see s.4 of the Act as to the coasting trade. As special agreements under this Article (as extended by s.4 to the coasting trade) are "*contracts for the carriage of goods to which the Rules apply*" within the meaning of s.2, it is probable that in all such agreements there is no "*absolute undertaking to provide a seaworthy ship*". It is possible, however, that, as Art.VI in effect contains provisions for contracting out of the Rules, the words "*to which the Rules apply*" in s.2 will be interpreted to mean "to which the Rules other than Article VI apply".

"*Not contrary to public policy*". We know of no decision in which any stipulation by the shipowner as to seaworthiness has been disallowed as being contrary to public policy, but there may be instances under foreign systems of jurisprudence.

"*No bill of lading has been or shall be issued*". These words can hardly mean what they literally say. It cannot be an offence against the Act to issue a document which in form would be a bill of lading. The passage presumably means "provided that any document recording the contract, which shall be non-negotiable and shall be marked as such, shall not have the legal effect of a bill of lading, but only of a receipt for the goods". If the document issued either does not embody the terms of the special agreement or is not a receipt in form, or is not marked non-negotiable, it will come under the Rules if it is in a "*bill of lading or similar document of title*".[307]

This Article is not exhaustive. There are, in addition, contracts of affreightment in which, according to the custom of the trade and intention of the parties, a bill of lading plays no part and is never issued. To such contracts Act and Rules, including Art.VI, have no application.[308] The Court of Session has suggested that Art.VI applied to those contracts of carriage which normally entitled the shipper, according to the custom of the particular trade, to demand a bill of lading setting forth the terms of the contract. In such cases the carrier may, by agreement, limit his responsibilities, if the provisions of the Article and s.4 are applicable and are complied with.

---

[306] "Stipulation" relates to "seaworthiness" and not to "any agreement": *Hugh Mack v Burns & Laird Lines* (1944) 77 Ll.L.R. 377 at p.384.

[307] See Art.I(b), above.

[308] *Harland and Wolff v Burns and Laird Lines* (1931) 40 Ll.L.R. 286; *Vita Food Products v Unus Shipping Co* [1939] A.C. 277 at p.294; *Hugh Mack v Burns and Laird Lines* (1944) 77 Ll.L.R. 377; *Canada and Dominion Sugar Co v Canadian National (W.I.) Steamships* [1947] A.C. 46 at p.57, and see *Notes* to Art.I(b), above.

"*Non-negotiable document*". As has been pointed out[309] "*negotiable*", as applied to a bill of lading, is only a popular, and not a technical expression. "*Non-negotiable*" has even less technical meaning. It is submitted that the words "*shall be a non-negotiable document*" mean that its indorsement shall have no effect under either the Carriage of Goods by Sea Act 1992[310] to transfer any rights of action or liabilities to a third party, or by mercantile custom to pass any rights in the goods.

"*Ordinary commercial shipments*". Whether a "*particular*" shipment comes within these words or not is a question of fact to be determined on the evidence. Apparently a special agreement will be justified either because of the special character or condition of the goods, or because the circumstances under which they are carried justify a special agreement. This, we think, is the intention of the proviso though it is somewhat obscurely expressed.

B16   **Article VII—Limitations on the Application of the Rules**

Nothing herein contained shall prevent a carrier or a shipper from entering into any agreement, stipulation, condition, reservation or exemption as to the responsibility and liability of the carrier or the ship for the loss or damage to, or in connection with, the custody and care and handling of goods prior to the loading on and subsequent to the discharge from, the ship on which the goods are carried by sea.[311]

B17   **Article VIII—Limitation of Liability**

The provisions of these Rules shall not affect the rights and obligations of the carrier under any statute for the time being in force relating to the limitation of the liability of owners of sea-going vessels.

This refers to s.18 of the Merchant Shipping Act 1979.[312]

B18   **Article IX**

These Rules shall not affect the provisions of any international Convention or national law governing liability for nuclear damage.

This Article is new.

B19   **Article X**

The provisions of these Rules shall apply to every bill of lading relating to the carriage of goods between ports in two different States if:

(a) the bill of lading is issued in a contracting State, or

---

[309] See Art.94, *Note 1*, above.
[310] See Art.14.
[311] See Art.III, r.8, above. See also *Mayhew Foods Ltd v Overseas Containers Ltd* [1984] 1 Lloyd's Rep. 317, in which Bingham J. was apparently not referred to this Article.
[312] See s.6(4) of the Carriage of Goods by Sea Act 1971, above.

(b) the carriage is from a port in a contracting State, or

(c) the contract contained in or evidenced by the bill of lading provided that these Rules or legislation of any State giving effect to them are to govern the contract, whatever may be the nationality of the ship, the carrier, the shipper, the consignee, or any other interested person.

For a discussion of this Article, see above. References to a contracting state include references to a state that is a contracting state in respect of the Rules without the amendments made by the Brussels Protocol of 1979 (which amends the monetary limits in Art.4, r.5) as well as to one that is a contracting state in respect of the Rules as so amended.[313]

---

[313] See s.2 of the Merchant Shipping Act 1981.

Chapter 21

JURISDICTION, CHOICE OF LAW AND LIMITATION OF ACTIONS

A199   **Article 199—Jurisdiction**

ALL divisions of the High Court have *jurisdiction* to decide disputes arising on charterparties and bills of lading,[1] but in practice this jurisdiction is exercised in the Queen's Bench Division, generally in the Commercial Court.[2] Historically, such jurisdiction was generally invoked by service of a Writ of Summons on the defendant either (i) where the defendant was within the territorial jurisdiction of the Court, *as a matter of right;* or (ii) where the defendant was out of the jurisdiction, in certain stipulated categories of cases *with permission of the Court.* That position was radically changed by the Civil Jurisdiction and Judgments Act 1982 which gave effect (by s.2) to the Brussels and Lugano Conventions on jurisdiction and the enforcement of judgments in civil and commercial matters. The Brussels Convention has now been largely superseded (save in respect of certain overseas territories of Member States) by Council Regulation 44/2001 (the "Judgments Regulation") which came into force on March 1, 2002.[3] Under the Judgments Regulation/Conventions, jurisdiction now depends principally on domicile. The High Court also possesses an Admiralty jurisdiction. Cases are generally brought in the Admiralty Court when the plaintiff is doubtful of being able to enforce a judgment *in personam* against the defendant or is unable to effect service upon the defendant out of the jurisdiction, and in either case the ship in question, or another ship owned by the defendant,[4] is within the jurisdiction of the court so as to be capable of being arrested in an action *in rem.* The case must also fall within the conditions of Admiralty jurisdiction.

The Judgments Regulation and the Brussels/Lugano Conventions. Under the Judgments Regulation/Conventions, jurisdiction depends largely on domicile. For the purposes of the Conventions, an individual is domiciled in the United Kingdom if and only if he is resident in the United Kingdom *and* the nature and circumstances of his residence indicate that he has a substantial connection with the United Kingdom, and a corporation or association is domiciled in the United Kingdom if and only if it was incorporated or formed under the law of a part of the United Kingdom and has its registered office or some other official address in the United Kingdom *or* its central management and control is exercised in the

---

[1] s.5(5) of the Supreme Court Act 1981.
[2] Proceedings in the Commercial Court are governed by the Civil Procedure Rules ("CPR") and Practice Directions. CPR Part 58 and its associated Practice Direction deal specifically with the Commercial Court. The Admiralty and Commercial Courts Guide provides further guidance with regard to the conduct of proceedings in the Admiralty and Commercial Courts. The Guide is updated from time to time. At the time of writing, the current version is the 7th edn (2006) available at *www.hmcourts-service.gov.uk/publications*.
[3] See generally Layton & Mercer, *European Civil Practice*, 2nd edn (London: Sweet & Maxwell, 2005).
[4] See below.

United Kingdom.[5] Under the Judgments Regulation, the position is similar as regards individuals[6]; but there is a new autonomous rule for the ascertainment of the domicile of a company or other legal person or association of natural or legal persons viz. such an entity is domiciled at the place where it has (a) its statutory seat or (b) its central administration or (c) its principal place of business.[7]

Under the Judgments Regulation/Conventions, persons domiciled in a contracting state, shall, whatever their nationality, be sued[8] in the courts of that state, and may be sued in the courts of another contracting state only by virtue of the rules set out in the Judgments Regulation/Conventions.[9] In particular, a person domiciled in a contracting state may in another contracting state, be sued—

(1) in matters relating to a contract, in the courts for the place of performance of the obligation in question[10];

(2) in matters relating to tort, delict or quasi-delict, in the courts for the place where the harmful event occurred[11];

(3) as regards a dispute arising out of the operations of a branch, agency or other establishment in the courts for the place in which the branch, agency or other establishment is situated[12];

(4) as regards a dispute concerning the payment of remuneration claimed in respect of the salvage of a cargo or freight, in the court under the authority of which the cargo or freight in question (a) has been arrested to secure such payment, or (b) could have been so arrested, but bail or other security has been given; but only if it is claimed that the defendant has an interest in the cargo or freight or had such an interest at the time of salvage.[13]

---

[5] ss.41 and 42 of the 1982 Act. Foreign domicile is a matter for the local law: Art.52 of the Conventions.

[6] Judgments Regulation, Art.59.

[7] Judgments Regulation, Art.60.

[8] The person who is "sued" in an action *in rem* is the person who would defend it if he were to enter an appearance: *The Deichland* [1990] 1 Q.B. 361.

[9] Arts 2 and 3 of the Conventions and Judgments Regulation.

[10] This head of jurisdiction may be invoked even when the existence of the contract is in dispute: Case 38/81: *Effer SpA v Kantner* [1982] E.C.R. 825. The place of performance is to be determined by applying the rules of private international law of the national court: Case 12/76, *Industrie Tessile Italiana Como v Dunlop A.G.* [1976] E.C.R. 1473. See also Case 14/76, *De Bloos Sprl. v Bouyer SA* [1976] E.C.R. 1497; Case 266/85 [1987] E.C.R. 239, *Sheuavai v Kreischer*; *Union Transport Plc v Continental Lines SA* [1992] 1 W.L.R. 15 (HL); and Case C-440/97 *GIE Groupe Concorde v The Master of the Vessel "Suhadiwarno Panjan"* [1999] E.C.R. I-6307.

[11] The plaintiff may sue either in the court of the place where the event giving rise to the damage occurred or in the court of the place where the damage occurred: Case 21/76, *Handelskwekerij G.J. Bier B.V. v Mines de Potasse d'Alsace* [1976] E.C.R. 1735. The place of damage is not the place of final delivery or the place where the damage was ascertained but the place where the carrier was to deliver the goods: Case C-51/97 *Reunion Europeene SA v Spliethoff's Bevrachingskantoor BV* [1998] E.C.R. I-6511.

[12] The branch, agency or establishment must be under the direction and control of the parent body: Case 139/80, *Blanckaert & Williams P.V.B.A. v Trost* [1981] E.C.R. 819; Case 14/76, *De Bloos Sprl v Bouyer SA* [1976] E.C.R. 1497. It must also have the appearance of permanency: Case 33/78. *Somafer SA v Saar-Ferngas A.G.* [1978] E.C.R. 2183. See also Case C-439/93 *Lloyd's Register of Shipping v Soc Campenon Bernard* [1995] E.C.R I-961.

[13] Art.5 of the Conventions and Judgments Regulation.

The Judgments Regulation/Conventions contain provisions enabling jurisdiction to be assumed over co-defendants, third parties and defendants to counterclaims.[14] Where proceedings involving the same cause of action[15] and between the same parties[16] are brought in the courts of different Contracting States, any court other than the court first seised[17] must of its own motion decline jurisdiction in favour of that court.[18] A court which would be required to decline jurisdiction may stay its proceedings if the jurisdiction of the other court is contested.[19] Where related actions are brought in the courts of different Contracting States, any court other than the court first seised may, while the proceedings are pending at first instance, stay its proceedings: actions are deemed to be related where they are so closely connected that it is expedient to hear and determine them together to avoid the risk of irreconcilable judgments resulting from separate proceedings.[20]

Limitation actions relating to liability arising from the use or operation of a ship may be heard by the court having jurisdiction in the action relating to the liability itself.[21]

An agreement to confer jurisdiction on the courts of a contracting state is ineffective unless it is (a) in writing or evidenced in writing; (b) in a form which accords with practices which the parties have established between themselves[22]; or (c) in international trade or commerce, in a form which accords with some usage in that trade or commerce which is "widely known" and "regularly observed" and of which the parties are or ought to have been aware.[23] Where one or more of the parties to such an agreement is domiciled in a contracting state, the chosen courts have exclusive jurisdiction. Where neither party is domiciled

---

[14] Art.6, of the Conventions and Judgments Regulation.

[15] An action seeking to have the defendant held liable for causing loss and ordered to pay damages has the same cause of action and the same object as proceedings brought by that defendant seeking a declaration that he is not liable for that loss: Case 144/86, *Gubisch Maschinenfabrik v Palumbo* [1987] E.C.R. 4861. Negative declarations are not regarded with favour by the court: in particular the court will not allow an action for a declaration that a shipowner has no right to bring a limitation action in the country of his domicile: *The Volvox Hollandia* [1988] 2 Lloyd's Rep. 361.

[16] These terms have an independent meaning: it follows that the distinctions in English law between actions *in personam* and *in rem* are not material for the interpretation of Art.21: Case C–406/92, *The Maciej Rataj* [1994] E.C.R. 5439. See also *The Deichland*, above, and *The Kherson* [1992] 2 Lloyd's Rep. 261. On this point *The Nordglimt* [1988] Q.B. 183, at 199–202 is overruled.

[17] The question when a court is first seised is a matter for the national law of the court in question: Case 129/83, *Zelger v Salinitri* [1984] E.C.R. 2397. In England the court is seised of an action when the writ is served, and not until then: *Dresser UK Ltd v Falcongate Ltd* [1992] Q.B. 502; *Neste Chemicals SA v D.K. Line SA, The Sargasso* [1994] 2 Lloyd's Rep. 6.

[18] Art.21 of the Conventions, first paragraph; Art.27 of the Judgments Regulation.

[19] Art.21 of the Conventions, second paragraph; Art.27 of the Judgments Regulation.

[20] Art.22 of the Conventions, Art.28 of the Judgments Regulation.

[21] Art.6A of the Convention, Art.7 of the Judgments Regulation.

[22] See e.g *O.T. Africa Line Ltd v Hizajy (The Kribi)* [2001] 1 Lloyd's Rep. 76.

[23] Art.17 of the Conventions, Art.23 of the Judgments Regulation. The formal requirements are to be construed strictly: Case 24/76, *Estasis Salotti v R.Ü.W.A. GmbH* [1976] E.C.R. 1831; Case 25/76, *Galeries Segoura S.P.R.L. v Bonakdarian* [1976] E.C.R. 1851; Case 73/77, *Sanders v Van der Putte* [1977] E.C.R. 2383. Mere printing a clause on the back of a bill of lading is not generally enough: the shipper must otherwise assent in writing or one or more of the other stated conditions must be satisfied: Case 71/83, *The Tilly Russ* [1984] E.C.R. 2417, *O.T. Africa Line Ltd v Hizajy (The Kribi)* [2001] 1 Lloyd's Rep. 76. But proper assent by the shipper binds indorsees: Case 71/83, *The Tilly Russ* [1984] E.C.R. 2417; Case C–159/97 *Soc Transporti Castelleti Spedizioni Internazionali SA v Hugo Trumpy SpA* [1999] E.C.R. I-1597.

in a contracting state, the courts of other contracting states have no jurisdiction unless the court or courts chosen have declined jurisdiction.[24] A bona fide agreement as to the place of performance confers jurisdiction on the courts of that place under Art.5.[25] It is doubtful whether an agreement on jurisdiction which is invalid under the Hague–Visby Rules can be an effective agreement under the Conventions.[26]

A court of a contracting state before whom a defendant enters an appearance has jurisdiction, unless the appearance was entered solely to contest the jurisdiction.[27]

The Admiralty jurisdiction of the High Court by way of an action *in rem* against a ship is not affected by the Judgments Regulation/Conventions,[28] but the applicable rules as regards *lis alibi pendens* apply to such an action.[29]

When the defendant is out of the jurisdiction. In such a case, unless the claim is within the Admiralty jurisdiction of the High Court as defined below so as to permit an action being brought *in rem* against a ship within the jurisdiction, the defendant cannot be made amenable to the jurisdiction of the High Court unless:

(i) The claim is one which the Court has power to determine under the Conventions or the Judgments Regulation and the other requisite conditions are satisfied.[30] In such cases, service out of the jurisdiction may be effected without permission of the Court; or

(ii) The claim is one falling within CPR Part 6.20 in which case it is necessary to obtain the permission of the Court to effect service out of the jurisdiction. The claims falling within CPR Part 6.20 include:

(1) A claim for a remedy against a person domiciled within the jurisdiction: CPR Part 6.20 (1).

(2) A claim for an injunction ordering the defendant to do or refrain from doing an act within the jurisdiction: CPR Part 6.20(2).

(3) A claim is made against someone on whom the claim form has been or will be served and (a) there is between the claimant and that person a real issue which it is reasonable for the court to try; and (b) the claimant

---

[24] Art.17 of the Conventions, Art.23 of the Judgments Regulation.

[25] Case 56/79, *Zelger v Salinitri* [1980] E.C.R. 89. Such an agreement may be made informally.

[26] But see Case 25/79, *Sanicentral GmbH v Collin* [1979] E.C.R. 3423; Case 150/80, *Elefanten Schuh GmbH v Jacqmain* [1982] 3 C.M.L.R. 1.

[27] Art.18 of the Conventions, Art.24 of the Judgments Regulation.

[28] See, generally, Briggs & Rees, *Civil Jurisdiction and Judgments*, 4th edn (London: LLP, 2005), chapter 8 and also *The Anna H* [1995] 1 Lloyd's Rep. 11; and see *The Deichland* [1990] 1 Q.B. 361 (vessel must actually be arrested).

[29] Case C–406/92 *The Maciej Rataj* [1994] E.C.R. 5439.

[30] See CPR Part 6.19.

wishes to serve the claim form on another person who is a necessary and proper party to that claim: CPR Part 6.20(3).[31]

(4) A claim for an interim remedy under s.25(1) of the Civil Judgments and Jurisdiction Act 1982: CPR Part 6.20(4).

(5) A claim in respect of a contract where the contract was (a) made within the jurisdiction; or (b) made by or through an agent trading as residing within the jurisdiction; or (c) is governed by English law; or (d) contains a term to the effect that the Court shall have jurisdiction to determine any claim in respect of the contract: CPR Part 6.20(5).

(6) A claim in respect of a breach of contract committed within the jurisdiction: CPR Part 6.20(6).

(7) A claim in tort where (a) damage was sustained within the jurisdiction; or (b) the damage sustained resulted from an act committed within the jurisdiction.

Thus where, for example, freight is to be paid in England, or the goods delivered in England, a case for service under (6) would arise, but the contract must expressly or by implication require performance within the jurisdiction. It is submitted that it is not enough that part of the contract as to which no breach is alleged is to be performed within the jurisdiction; the breach complained of must be of a part of a contract to be performed within the jurisdiction.[32]

Admiralty Jurisdiction of the High Court. The Admiralty jurisdiction is now[33] provided for by s.20 of the Supreme Court Act 1981 which provides in part as follows:

"20.—(1) The Admiralty jurisdiction[34] of the High Court shall be as follows, that is to say—

(a) jurisdiction to hear and determine any of the questions and claims mentioned in subsection 2.

(2) The questions and claims referred to in subsection (1)(a) are—

---

[31] This is similar—but not identical—to the former RSC Ord. 11 r.1(f). Thus, in *Massey v Heynes* (1888) 21 Q.B.D. 330 where a foreigner disputed that he was bound by a charter made by an alleged agent of his in England, leave was given to serve him under that former Rule in an action against himself on the charter, or in the alternative against the agent for breach of warranty of authority. Similarly, see *Bennett v McIlwraith* [1896] 2 Q.B. 464. But in *Flower v Rose* (1891) 7 T.L.R. 280, a writ issued against a Scots shipowner and a London broker to settle the amount of liability on a general average bond was not allowed to be served on the Scots shipowner, on the ground that the broker was colourably joined and not a proper party to the action. *Cf.: Witted v Galbraith* [1893] 1 Q.B. 577; *Multinational Gas Co v Mulnational Gas Services Ltd* [1983] Ch. 258. Further, the action is not "properly brought" if, there being no dispute of foreign law or other fact, it cannot succeed in law against the person served within the jurisdiction: it is immaterial that that person may waive a legal defence open to him: *Tyne Improvement Commissioners v Armement Anversois SA (The Brabo)* [1949] A.C. 326.
[32] *Bell v Antwerp Line* [1891] 1 Q.B. 103; *cf. The Eider* [1893] P. 119; *Thompson v Palmer* [1893] 2 Q.B. 80. These cases were decided under the former similar but not identical Rules of Court.
[33] For the historical growth of this jurisdiction see Section XIV of the 15th edn of this work.
[34] Which cannot be excluded by a clause in a contract giving exclusive jurisdiction to a foreign tribunal: *The Fehmarn* [1957] 1 W.L.R. 815; affirmed [1958] 1 W.L.R. 159 (CA). But see the text at fn.55, below.

(g) any claim for loss of or damage to goods carried in a ship;

(h) any claim arising out of any agreement relating to the carriage of goods in a ship[35] or to the use or hire of a ship[36];"

"Ship" includes any description of vessel used in navigation[37] and a reference to a ship includes a reference to a hovercraft.[38] The jurisdiction applies in relation to all ships, whether British or not and whether registered or not and wherever the residence or domicile[39] of their owners may be and in relation to all claims wheresoever arising.

Matters falling within this jurisdiction, which by s.21(1) and (4) may be exercised *in personam* or *in rem*, are, if exercised *in rem*, by s.61(1) of the Supreme Court Act 1981, assigned to the Admiralty Court of the Queen's Bench Division.

The Admiralty jurisdiction in regard to such claims may be invoked by an action *in rem* where the claim arises in connection with a ship and the person who would be liable on the claim in an action *in personam*[40] ("the relevant person") was, when the cause of action arose, the owner or charterer of,[41] or in possession or in control of, the ship. Such an action may be instituted against (i) that ship, if at the time when the action is brought the relevant person is either the beneficial owner of that ship as respects all the shares therein or the charterer of it under a charter by demise; or (ii) any other ship of which, at the time when the action is brought, the relevant person is the beneficial owner as respects all the shares in it.[42]

---

[35] The ship must be identified in or pursuant to the agreement: *The Lloyd Pacifico* [1995] 1 Lloyd's Rep. 54.

[36] These words cover claims arising out of agreements relating to the carriage of goods in a ship irrespective of whether the action is laid in contract or in tort: *The Antonis P. Lemos* [1985] A.C. 711; or whether it is for damages or indemnity or contribution: *The Hamburg Star* [1994] 1 Lloyd's Rep. 399. There must, however, be a reasonably direct connection between the agreement and the carriage of goods in, or the use or hire of the ship: *Gatoil International v Arkwright-Boston Manufacturers Mutual Insurance Co* [1985] A.C. 255. Neither a claim under a c.i.f. contract nor a claim for charter party demurrage under such a contract is within the sub-section: *Petrofina SA v A.O.T. Ltd* [1992] Q.B. 571. *Cf. The Indriani* [1996] 1 S.L.R. 305 (Sing.).

[37] Supreme Court Act 1981, s.24(1). "Goods" includes baggage: *ibid*.

[38] Hovercraft Act 1968, s.2(1). "Hovercraft" is defined in s.4(1) in terms which would extend to such a vehicle on land.

[39] *ibid*. s.1(4).

[40] "The persons who would be liable on the claim in an action *in personam*" identifies the person whose ship may be arrested and does not require a plaintiff at the outset to prove that he has a cause of action maintainable in law, but merely to show that the person whose ship is to be arrested is the person who would be liable if the action succeeded: *The St. Elefterio* [1957] P. 179. But if the owner of the ship could not be liable to the plaintiff the section does not apply: *The St. Merriel* [1963] 1 Lloyd's Rep. 63. A person can fall within these words wherever he is or is resident, since by s.21(8) it is assumed that he has his habitual residence or a place of business within England and Wales. The subsection was presumably framed with reference to the former R.S.C., Ord.11, r.1(c) and to forestall an argument that a person outside the jurisdiction might not by reason thereof in any event be liable in an action *in personam*.

[41] *Semble*, an action against a charterer under a charterparty may be brought by action *in rem* against another ship which is owned by him: see *The Span Terza* [1982] 1 Lloyd's Rep. 225, which was, however, decided on an *ex parte* application, Donaldson L.J. dissenting.

[42] Supreme Court Act 1981, s.21(4). The right to arrest sister ships was an important extension of the Admiralty jurisdiction *in rem*, since before 1956 a plaintiff was entitled to arrest only the ship to which the action related: *The Beldis* [1936] P. 51. It is now clear beyond doubt that "beneficial owner" does not include a demise charterer. As to the meaning of "beneficial owner" under similar provisions in Hong Kong, see *The Convenience Container* [2006] 3 H.K.L.R.D. 610.

Forum non conveniens.[43] The English courts have powers to prevent claims being brought in an inappropriate forum (*forum non conveniens*), and will, where necessary to prevent injustice, stay or strike out proceedings in England so that the claim may be heard in a more appropriate forum. These powers will not be exercised unless the defendant can show that there is some other available forum, having competent jurisdiction, which is clearly or distinctly the more appropriate forum for the trial of the action, i.e. in which the case may be tried more suitably for the interests of all the parties and the ends of justice. The court will look to that forum with which the action has the most real and substantial connection, e.g. on grounds of convenience or expense (such as availability of witnesses), the law governing the relevant transaction, and the place where the parties respectively reside or carry on business. If the court finds that there is no other available forum which is more appropriate it will ordinarily refuse a stay. If however it finds that there is another forum which is prima facie more appropriate, it will ordinarily grant a stay unless there are circumstances by reason of which justice requires that a stay should nevertheless not be granted. This will not depend on a mere comparison of the merits or demerits of the procedure and remedies in the two courts: thus the fact that the foreign court will not order discovery of documents, or award interest will not tell against a stay. But if, for example, the plaintiff has not acted unreasonably in allowing his claim to become time barred in the foreign court, justice will ordinarily require that the plaintiff should be allowed the benefit of having complied with the time bar in England. Where the action is stayed, the court will normally allow the plaintiff to keep the benefit of security obtained in the English court.[44] The foregoing is subject to Arts 27 to 29 of the Judgments Regulation and Arts 21 to 23 of the Conventions which contain special rules under the heading "Lis Pendens—Related Actions" to deal with the relationship between actions pending in different Judgments Regulation/Conventions States (as the case may be) where, first, the proceedings involve the "same cause of action" and, second, the cause of action is not the same, but the actions are related.[45]

It was previously held that the Conventions had no application to a case where the conflict of jurisdiction lies between the English court and the courts of a non-contracting state.[46] However, this must now be read in light of the European Court decision in *Owusu v Jackson.*[47]

Injunctions restraining foreign proceedings. The court has power, for the ends of justice, to restrain by injunction persons amenable to the jurisdiction of the

---

[43] See generally Dicey Morris & Collins. *The Conflict of Laws,*14th edn (2006) Rule 31; *Spiliada Maritime Corp v Cansulex Ltd* [1987] A.C. 460; *Akai Pty Ltd v People's Insurance Co Ltd* [1998] 1 Lloyd's Rep. 90; *Horn Linie GmbH v PanAmericana Formas E Impresos (The Hornbay)* [2006] EWHC 373 (Comm); [2006] 2 Lloyd's Rep. 44. For an illustration of a case involving an English non-exclusive jurisdiction clause, see *Import Export Metro v Compania Sud Americana de Vapores* [2003] EWHC 11 (Comm); [2003] 1 Lloyd's Rep. 405.

[44] See s.26 of the Civil Jurisdiction and Judgments Act 1982, where property has been arrested or bail or other security given in proceedings *in rem.*

[45] See *The Conflict of Laws, op cit,* Rule 31(4) and paras 12–045 to 12–066.

[46] *Harrods (Buenos Aires) Ltd, Re* [1992] Ch. 72.

[47] [2002] 1 L.Pr. 45.

English court from bringing or continuing proceedings in a foreign court, e.g. where the foreign proceedings are vexatious or oppressive. The power will however be exercised sparingly: in particular the English court will not grant an injunction simply on the ground that the English court is the more appropriate forum.[48] By contrast, the English Court will in general,[49] readily grant an anti-suit injunction to restrain a party from pursuing foreign proceedings[50] in breach of an exclusive jurisdiction agreement or an arbitration agreement.[51]

Jurisdiction clauses.[52] Where a plaintiff sues in England in breach of an agreement[53] to refer disputes to a foreign court, and the defendant applies for a stay, the English court, assuming the claim to be otherwise within its jurisdiction, is not bound to order a stay[54] but has a discretion whether to do so or not. The discretion should be exercised by granting a stay unless strong cause for not doing so is shown, the burden being on the plaintiff to show such strong cause. In exercising its discretion the court will take into account all the circumstances of the case. In particular, without prejudice to the duty of the court to look at all the circumstances, the following matters, where they arise, may properly be regarded:

(a) in what country the evidence on the issues of fact is situated, or more readily available, and the effect of that on the relative convenience and expense of trial as between the English and foreign courts;

(b) whether the law of the foreign court applies and, if so, whether it differs from English law in any material respects;

---

[48] *Société Nationale Industrielle Aerospatiale v Lee Kui Jak* [1987] A.C. 871; *Ascot Commodities N.V v Northern Pacific Shipping (The Irina A)* [1999] 1 Lloyd's Rep. 196; *Sabah Shipyard v Islamic Republic of Pakistan* [2002] EWCA Civ 1643; [2003] 2 Lloyd's Rep. 571; *Royal Bank of Canada v Centiale Raiffeisan-Boerenieen-bank* [2004] EWCA Civ 7; [2004] 1 Lloyd's Rep. 471.

[49] Though not when the case is within the Judgments Regulation/Conventions: Case C-159/02 *Turner v Grovit* [2004] I.L.Pr. 25. It has been a vexed question whether an injunction restraining foreign proceedings brought in breach of an arbitration clause falls within the Judgments Regulation/Conventions. See e.g. *Navigation Maritime Bulgare v Rustal Trading Ltd (The Ivan Zagubanski)* [2002] 1 Lloyd's Rep. 106. In *West Tankers Inc v Ras Riunione Adriatica di Sicurta SpA (The Front Comor)* [2007] UKHL 4; [2007] 1 Lloyd's Rep. 391, the House of Lords expressed the view that such an injunction did fall outside the Judgments Regulation but the question was referred for a preliminary ruling to the European Court whose decision, at the time of writing, is still awaited.

[50] In *Industrial Maritime Carriers (Bahamas) Inc v Sinoca International Inc* [1996] 2 Lloyd's Rep 585, an application for an injunction restraining the enforcement of a foreign judgment was rejected by the Court.

[51] See e.g. *The Angelic Grace* [1995] 1 Lloyd's Rep. 87; *Akai Pty Ltd v People's Insurance Co Ltd* [1998] 1 Lloyd's Rep. 90; *Donohue v Armco* [2001] UKHL 64; [2002] 1 Lloyd's Rep. 425; *The Epsilon Rosa* [2003] EWCA Civ 938; [2003] 2 Lloyd's Rep. 509. But not if the foreign proceedings are pursued solely for the purposes of obtaining security—see *The Lisboa* [1980] 2 Lloyd's Rep. 546 and contrast *The Kallang* [2006] EWHC 2825 (Comm); [2007] 1 Lloyd's Rep. 160. It is generally irrelevant that the agreement contained in the exclusive jurisdiction clause or the grant of such anti-suit injunction may offend the public policy of the foreign place: *O.T. Africa Line v Magic Sportswear* [2005] EWCA Civ 710; [2005] 2 Lloyd's Rep. 170; *Horn Linie GmbH v PanAmericana Formas E Impresos (The Hornbay)* [2006] EWHC 373 (Comm); [2006] 2 Lloyd's Rep. 44. This can potentially give rise to a "battle of jurisdictions" unless the foreign court is willing to give weight to the English judgment: see the decision of the Canada Federal Court of Appeal in *OT Africa Line Ltd v Magic Sportswear* [2007] 1 Lloyd's Rep. 85. See also: Y Baatz [2006] L.M.C.L.Q. 143.

[52] See generally, D. Joseph, *Jurisdiction and Arbitration Agreements and their Enforcement* (London: Sweet & Maxwell, 2005).

[53] For a case where the right to rely upon an exclusive jurisdiction clause was held to have been waived, see *The Thor Scan* [1999] 1 Lloyd's Rep. 940 (H.K.Ct).

[54] Unless the jurisdiction agreement is within Art.23 of the Judgments Regulation or Art.17 of the Conventions.

(c) with what country either party is connected, and how closely;

(d) whether the defendants genuinely desire trial in the foreign country, or are only seeking procedural advantages;

(e) whether the plaintiff would be prejudiced by having to sue in the foreign court because he would be deprived of security for his claim, be unable to enforce any judgment obtained, be faced with a time bar not applicable in England, or, for political, racial, religious or other reasons be unlikely to get a fair trial.[55]

Arbitration clauses.[56] Where a claim is within an arbitration agreement the defendant may apply to the court for the proceedings to be stayed so that the matter can be referred to arbitration.[57] The grant of a stay is mandatory, unless the arbitration agreement is null and void, inoperative or incapable of being performed.[58] Where there is a mandatory stay of proceedings *in personam*, the court has power to grant or to continue a freezing (*Mareva*) injunction regardless of whether the seat of the arbitration is in England or abroad.[59] Where there is a mandatory stay of proceedings *in rem* the court may (whether the arbitration is in England or abroad) order that the property arrested be retained as security for the satisfaction of any award or order that the stay of proceedings be conditional on the provisions of equivalent security.[60] Security is ordered as a matter of course, without any cross-undertaking as to damages by the plaintiff.[61]

The Hamburg Rules.[62] The Hamburg Rules contain their own rules as to jurisdiction. Article 21.1 gives the plaintiff the option of instituting an action in a court which, according to the law of the state in which the Court is situated, is competent and within the jurisdiction of which is situated one of four places:

(a) the principal place of business, or in the absence of such a place the habitual residence, of the defendant; or

(b) the place where the contract was made, provided that the defendant has a

---

[55] The judgment of Brandon L.J. in *The El Amria* [1981] 2 Lloyd's Rep. 119 contains an authoritative summary of the relevant principles, and guidelines as to the matters which may be taken into account as relevant to the exercise of the court's discretion: see *The Sennar (No.2)* [1985] 1 Lloyd's Rep. 521 (HL). See also *The Fehmarn* [1957] 1 Lloyd's Rep. 511; *The Eleftheria* [1969] 1 Lloyd's Rep. 237; *The Makjefell* [1976] 2 Lloyd's Rep. 29; *The Adolf Warski* [1976] 2 Lloyd's Rep. 241; *The Lisboa* [1980] 2 Lloyd's Rep. 546. *Cf.*: *The Jian He* [2000] 1 S.L.R. 8 (Sing.) where the application for a stay was refused.
[56] See generally, Mustill & Boyd, *Commercial Arbitration*, 2nd edn (London: Butterworths, 2001); D. Joseph, *Jurisdiction and Arbitration Agreements and their Enforcement*.
[57] Arbitration Act 1996, s.9(1).
[58] Arbitration Act 1996, s.9(4). In *Commandate Marine Corp v Pan Australia Shipping Pty Ltd (The Commandate)* [2007] 1 Lloyd's Rep 53, the Federal Court of Australia rejected an argument that the pursuit of *in rem* proceedings was inconsistent with an arbitration agreement or was a repudiation or waiver of an agreement to arbitrate.
[59] Arbitration Act 1996 ss.2(3) and 44(1), (2)(e). See generally Dicey, Morris & Collins, *The Conflict of Laws* 14th edn, paras 16–084—16–086.
[60] Civil Jurisdiction and Judgments Act 1982, s.26; Arbitration Act 1996 s.11.
[61] *Greenmar Navigation Ltd v Owners of Ship Bazias 3 and Bazias 4* [1993] 1 Lloyd's Rep. 101.
[62] See below, Appendix VI.

place of business, branch or agency through which the contract was made there; or

(c) the port of loading or port of discharge; or

(d) any other place designated for that purpose in the contract of carriage by sea.

In addition, by Art.21.2, an action can be instituted in the courts of any port or place in a Contracting State at which the carrying vessel, or a vessel of the same ownership, has been arrested. Where jurisdiction is founded by such an arrest, the defendant can have the action removed to one of the states specified by Art.21.1, provided sufficient security for the claim is furnished. By Art.21.3, the jurisdiction established by the two preceding sub-Articles is exclusive, save where, in accordance with Art.21.5, jurisdiction is designated by an agreement entered into after the claim has arisen.

By Art.21.4, once an action has been commenced in a competent court or a judgment issued by that court, no further action can be commenced unless the judgment of the court before whom the action was first instituted is not enforceable in the country in which the new proceedings are instituted.

Article 22.3 regulates the places in which arbitration proceedings may be commenced.

Article 200—Choice of Law[63]   A200

In any situation involving a choice between the laws of different countries, the law governing contractual obligations is determined by the provisions of the Rome Convention on the Law Applicable to Contractual Obligations, to which effect has been given in England by the Contracts (Applicable Law) Act 1990.[64]

The general rule is that a contract is governed by the law chosen by the parties. The choice of law will usually be expressed, but effect will be given to it if it is demonstrated with reasonable certainty by the terms of the contract[65] or the circumstances of the case.[66] The choice of foreign law by the parties, whether or

---

[63] See generally, Dicey, Morris & Collins, *The Conflict of Laws*, (14th edn) Ch.32.

[64] The Convention applies in England to contracts made after April 1, 1991: see Art.17 of the Convention and SI 1991 No. 707.

[65] e.g. by an arbitration clause providing for arbitration by English maritime arbitrators in London: *Cie d'Armement Maritime v Cie Tunisienne de Navigation* [1971] A.C. 572: see also *Hellenic Steel Co v Svolamar Shipping Co Ltd, The Komninos S* [1991] 1 Lloyd's Rep. 370 (choice of English court); *Amin Rasheed Shipping Corp v Kuwait Insurance Co* [1984] A.C. 50 (choice of standard Lloyd's insurance policy), and *Egon Oldendorff v Libera Corp* [1995] 2 Lloyd's Rep. 64 (decided under the Rome Convention).

[66] Art.3.1 of the Rome Convention. The parties can select different laws for different parts of the contract: *ibid.* This could be contrasted with the incorporation of parts of a foreign law into an English contract, when the foreign law takes effect simply as a term of an English contract, e.g. where parts of the United States Carriage of Goods by Sea Act 1936 are incorporated by reference into a charterparty. This will not of itself involve a choice of United States law to govern the contract: *Mineracoas Brasilieras Reunidas v E.F. Marine SA (The Freights Queen)* [1977] 2 Lloyd's Rep. 140; *cf. Kadel Chajkin v Mitchell Cotts* (1947) 81 Ll.L.R. 393. However, the incorporation of provisions from a foreign law which render an express choice of English law void may nullify the express choice: *Ocean S.S. Co v Queensland State Wheat Board* [1941] 1 K.B. 402.

not they have also chosen a foreign tribunal, does not however prejudice the application of English "mandatory rules", i.e. rules which cannot be derogated from by contract.[67]

Where there is no express choice of law[68] or a choice of law is not demonstrated by the terms of the contract or the circumstances of the case, the contract is governed by the law of the country with which it is most closely connected.[69] In general, it is to be presumed that the contract is most closely connected with the country where the party who is to effect the performance which is characteristic of the contract has, at the time of conclusion of the contract, his habitual residence, or, in the case of a body corporate or unincorporate, its central administration. However, if the contract is entered into in the course of that party's trade or profession, that country shall be the country in which the principal place of business is situated or, where under the terms of the contract the performance is to be effected through a place of business other than the principal place of business, the country in which that other place of business is situated.[70]

A contract for the carriage of goods, however, is not subject to this presumption. In such a contract if the country in which, at the time the contract is concluded, the carrier[71] has his principal place of business[72] is also the country in which the place of loading or the place of discharge or the principal place of business of the consignor[73] is situated, it shall be presumed that the contract is most closely connected with that country. For this purpose, single voyage charterparties and other contracts[74] the main purpose of which is the carriage of goods shall be treated as contracts for the carriage of goods.[75]

These presumptions are rebuttable, and are to be disregarded if it appears from the circumstances as a whole that the contract is more closely connected with another country.[76]

---

[67] Art.3.4 of the Rome Convention.
[68] The choice of "British law" generally invokes English rather than Scottish law: *Hirji Mulji v Cheong Yue S.S. Co* [1926] A.C. 497; *The Laertis* [1982] 1 Lloyd's Rep. 613; *The Hamburg Star* [1994] 1 Lloyd's Rep. 399; *cf. Hellenic Steel Co v Svolamar Shipping Co Ltd, The Komninos S* [1991] 1 Lloyd's Rep. 370.
[69] Art.4.1 of the Rome Convention. Exceptionally, a different law may be found to apply to a severable part of the contract: *ibid.*
[70] Art.4.2 of the Rome Convention. The presumption does not apply if the characteristic performance cannot be determined or if it appears from the circumstances as a whole that the contract is more closely connected with another country: Art.4.5.
[71] i.e. the person who, under the contract in question, undertakes to carry the goods, whether or not he performs the carriage himself.
[72] With a one-ship company, this may in practice be the place of business of the ship's managers responsible for getting charters.
[73] This would appear to refer to the person who contracts to ship the goods rather than the person who actually does so.
[74] Provided the main purpose of the contract is the carriage of goods, the presumption will apply to contracts to which reference is not specifically made in Art.4.4, such as bills of lading, sea waybills, ship's delivery orders, time charters, freight contracts and charters for more than one voyage. Schultsz, however, in North (ed.) *Contract Conflicts* (North Holland, 1982), p.185, suggests a different view with regard to time and consecutive voyage charters. A demise charter is not a contract for the carriage of goods, but for the hire of a ship.
[75] Art.4.4 of the Rome Convention.
[76] Art.4.5 of the Rome Convention. The concept of the law "most closely connected" involves looking at all the circumstances, but principally at the place of contracting, the place of performance, the places of business or residence of the parties, and the nature and subject matter of the contract: see *Bonython v Commonwealth of Australia* [1951] A.C. 201; *United Railways of Havana, Re* [1961] A.C. 1007; *Cie d'Armement Maritime v Cie*

The law applicable to a contract under the above rules governs in particular the interpretation and performance of the contract; within the limits of the powers conferred on the court by its procedural law, the consequences of breach, including the assessment of damages in so far as it is governed by rules of law; the various ways of extinguishing obligations and prescription and limitation of actions[77]; and the consequences of nullity of the contract.[78] In regard to the manner of performance and the steps to be taken in the event of defective performance regard must be had to the law of the country in which performance takes place.[79]

The existence and validity of a contract, or of any term of a contract, is to be determined by the law which would govern it if the contract or term were valid.[80] Nevertheless a party may rely upon the law of the country in which he has his habitual residence to establish that he did not consent if it appears from the circumstances that it would not be reasonable to determine the effect of his conduct in accordance with the law which would govern the contract if the contract or term were valid.[81]

A contract concluded between persons who are in the same country is formally valid if it satisfies the formal requirements of the law which governs it under the Rome Convention or the law of the country where it is concluded. A contract concluded between persons who are in different countries is formally valid if it satisfies the requirements of the law which governs it under the Rome Convention or the law of one of those countries.[82] Where a contract is concluded by an agent, the country in which the agent acts is the relevant country for this purpose.[83]

The law governing the contract under the Rome Convention applies to the extent that it contains, in the law of contract, rules which raise presumptions of law or determine the burden of proof.[84]

The Rome Convention does not restrict the application in English proceedings of English rules of law in a situation where they are mandatory irrespective of the

---

Tunisienne de Navigation [1971] A.C. 572; *Coast Lines v Hudig and Veder* [1972] 2 Q.B. 34; *Whitworth Street Estates (Manchester) Ltd v James Miller & Partners Ltd* [1970] A.C. 583; *Amin Rasheed Shipping Corp v Kuwait Insurance Co* [1984] A.C. 50.

[77] The English court will apply the limitation rule of the *lex causae*, unless the application of a foreign rule would conflict with English public policy: Foreign Limitation Periods Act 1984.

[78] Art.10 of the Rome Convention.

[79] Art.10.2 of the Rome Convention. Thus, the local law will generally determine the manner and mode of delivery: *The Sormovskiy 3068* [1994] 2 Lloyd's Rep. 266; *East West Corp v DKBS* [2002] 2 Lloyd's Rep. 182, 205. It will also generally determine, for example, what are holidays for the purpose of a demurrage clause, or whether a vessel is within the legal limits of a port.

[80] Art.8 of the Rome Convention. This Article also governs the existence and validity of the consent of the parties as to the choice of the applicable law: Art.3.4.

[81] Art.8.2 of the Rome Convention. *Egon Oldendorff v Libera Corp* [1995] 2 Lloyd's Rep. 64; *Welex AG v Rosa Epsilon Welex (The Epsilon Rosa No. 2)* [2002] EWHC 2035 (Comm); [2002] 2 Lloyd's Rep. 701; *Horn Linie GmbH v PanAmericana Formas E Impresos (The Hornbay)* [2006] EWHC 373 (Comm); [2006] 2 Lloyd's Rep. 44.

[82] Arts 9.1 and 9.2 of the Rome Convention. These Articles also govern the formal validity of the consent of the parties as to the choice of applicable law: Art.3.4.

[83] Art.9.3 of the Rome Convention.

[84] Art.14(1) of the Rome Convention. See for example, Carriage of Goods by Sea Act 1992, s.4: Art.59, above; and Art.III, r.4 of the Hague–Visby Rules: Art.60, above.

law otherwise applicable to the contract.[85] The application of a foreign law specified by the Rome Convention may however be refused only if such application is manifestly incompatible with English public policy (*"ordre public"*).[86]

The Rome Convention does not apply to arbitration agreements or agreements on the choice of court[87]; nor to the question whether an agent is able to bind a principal.[88]

Note 1. Before the enactment of the Rome Convention, it was laid down in a series of decisions that where a bill of lading incorporates various clauses of a charterparty, the law of the latter will generally govern the former.[89] It is submitted that the same result will generally follow under Art.3.1 of the Rome Convention, which provides for a choice of law where it is demonstrated with reasonable certainty by the circumstances of the case.

Note 2. The "law of the flag" was in former times presumed to be the proper law of the contract of affreightment in the absence of an expressed intention.[90] But the presumption was easily rebutted in favour of other connecting factors, such as the place where the contract was made or was to be performed,[91] and eventually became no more than a last resort, when all other factors were evenly balanced.[92] Ships nowadays are frequently registered in countries with which their owners have no real connection; moreover the owner of the ship is not necessarily the person who has contracted with the owner of the goods for their carriage.

The law of the flag could still be of relevance in the rare case where the question arises as to the authority of the master in cases of necessity for which the contract of carriage makes no provision.[93] The question whether an agent can bind his principal is outside the scope of Rome Convention,[94] and must therefore be determined on common law principles. Where the contract of carriage makes no express provision for the case of necessity, there is old authority for referring the master's authority to the law of the flag, regardless of the proper law of the contract of carriage.[95] Whether these cases hold good in modern conditions is doubtful.

---

[85] Art.7.2 of the Rome Convention. E.g. where they apply, the Hague–Visby Rules: see *The Hollandia* [1983] 1 A.C. 565.

[86] Art.16 of the Rome Convention. See also *Vita Foods Products v Unus Shipping Co* [1939] A.C. 277.

[87] Art.1.2d of the Rome Convention.

[88] Art.1.2f of the Rome Convention.

[89] *The Adriatic* [1931] P. 241; *The Njegos* [1936] P. 90; *Pacific Molasses & United Molasses Trading Co v Entre Rios Cia Na (The San Nicholas)* [1976] 1 Lloyd's Rep. 8; *Mineracoas Brasilieras Reunidas v E.F. Marine SA (The Freights Queen)* [1977] 2 Lloyd's Rep. 140; *Ilyssia Cia Na SA v Bamaodah (The Elli 2)* [1985] 1 Lloyd's Rep. 107; *Enichem Anic SpA v Ampelos Shipping Co Ltd (The Delfini)* [1988] 2 Lloyd's Rep. 599; [1990] 1 Lloyd's Rep. 107 (CA). Cf. *The Metamorphosis* [1953] 1 Lloyd's Rep. 196.

[90] e.g. *Lloyd v Guibert* (1865) L.R. 1 Q.B. 115; *The Express* (1872) L.R. A. & E. 597; *The August* [1891] P. 329.

[91] *P. & O. Co v Shand* (1865) 3 Moo. P.C. (N.S.) 272; *Moore v Harris* (1876) 1 App. Cas. 318; *Chartered Bank v Netherlands India Steam Co* (1883) 10 Q.B.D. 521; *Missouri S.S. Co, Re* (1889) 42 Ch.D. 321; *The Industrie* [1894] P. 58; *The Adriatic* [1931] P. 241; *The Njegos* [1936] P. 90.

[92] *The Assunzione* [1954] P. 150, per Hodson L.J. at p.194.

[93] See Arts 23 and 123 to 132.

[94] Art.1.2(f) of the Rome Convention.

[95] *The Gaetano e Maria* (1882) 7 P.D. 137; *The August* [1891] P. 328. See also *The Bahia* (1864) B. & L. 292; *The Karnak* (1869) L.R. 2 P.C. 505; *The Express* (1872) L.R. 3 A. & E. 597.

Limitation of Actions

Claims for damages on a charterparty or bill of lading in general are subject to the ordinary period of limitation, viz. that suit must be brought within six years of the cause of action arising. Where, however, the Carriage of Goods by Sea Act 1971 applies, a claim against a shipowner for loss or damage must be brought within one year after the delivery of the goods or the date when they should have been delivered,[96] unless otherwise extended.

---

[96] By Art.III, r.6, of the Schedule to the Act, above.

APPENDIX I

THE PRINCIPAL STATUTES AFFECTING THE CONTRACT OF AFFREIGHTMENT

The Carriage of Goods by Sea Act 1971 is printed with comments in Chapter 20, above

CARRIAGE OF GOODS BY SEA ACT 1992

Shipping documents etc. to which Act applies

1.—(1) This Act applies to the following documents, that is to say— **A1.1**

(*a*) any bill of lading;

(*b*) any sea waybill; and

(*c*) any ship's delivery order.

(2) References in this Act to a bill of lading—

(*a*) do not include references to a document which is incapable of transfer either by indorsement or, as a bearer bill, by delivery without indorsement; but

(*b*) subject to that, do include references to a received for shipment bill of lading.

(3) References in this Act to a sea waybill are references to any document which is not a bill of lading but—

(*a*) is such a receipt for goods as contains or evidences a contract for the carriage of goods by sea; and

(*b*) identifies the person to whom delivery of the goods is to be made by the carrier in accordance with that contract.

(4) References in this Act to a ship's delivery order are references to any document which is neither a bill of lading nor a sea waybill but contains an undertaking which—

(*a*) is given under or for the purposes of a contract for the carriage by sea of the goods to which the document relates, or of goods which include those goods; and

(*b*) is an undertaking by the carrier to a person identified in the document to deliver the goods to which the document relates to that person.

(5) The Secretary of State may by regulations make provision for the application of this Act to cases where a telecommunication system or any other information technology is used for effecting transactions corresponding to—

(*a*) the issue of a document to which this Act applies;

(*b*) the indorsement, delivery or other transfer of such a document; or

(*c*) the doing of anything else in relation to such a document.

(6) Regulations under subsection (5) above may—

(*a*) make such modifications of the following provisions of this Act as the Secretary of State considers appropriate in connection with the application of this Act to any case mentioned in that subsection; and (*b*) contain supplemental, incidental, consequential and transitional provision;

and the power to make regulations under that subsection shall be exercisable by statutory instrument subject to annulment in pursuance of a resolution of either House of Parliament.

Rights under shipping documents

A1.2   2.—(1) Subject to the following provisions of this section, a person who becomes—

  (*a*) the lawful holder of a bill of lading;
  (*b*) the person who (without being an original party to the contract of carriage) is the person to whom delivery of the goods to which a sea waybill relates is to be made by the carrier in accordance with that contract; or
  (*c*) the person to whom delivery of the goods to which a ship's delivery order relates is to be made in accordance with the undertaking contained in the order,

shall (by virtue of becoming the holder of the bill or, as the case may be, the person to whom delivery is to be made) have transferred to and vested in him all rights of suit under the contract of carriage as if he had been a party to that contract.

(2) Where, when a person becomes the lawful holder of a bill of lading, possession of the bill no longer gives a right (as against the carrier) to possession of the goods to which the bill relates, that person shall not have any rights transferred to him by virtue of subsection (1) above unless he becomes the holder of the bill—

  (*a*) by virtue of a transaction effected in pursuance of any contractual or other arrangements made before the time when such a right to possession ceased to attach to possession of the bill; or
  (*b*) as a result of the rejection to that person by another person of goods or documents delivered to the other person in pursuance of any such arrangements.

(3) The rights vested in any person by virtue of the operation of subsection (1) above in relation to a ship's delivery order—

  (*a*) shall be so vested subject to the terms of the order; and
  (*b*) where the goods to which the order relates form a part only of the goods to which the contract of carriage relates, shall be confined to rights in respect of the goods to which the order relates.

(4) Where, in the case of any document to which this Act applies—

  (*a*) a person with any interest or right in or in relation to goods which the document relates sustains loss or damage in consequence of a breach of the contract of carriage; but
  (*b*) subsection (1) above operates in relation to that document so that rights of suit in respect of that breach are vested in another person,

the other person shall be entitled to exercise those rights for the benefit of the person who sustained the loss or damage to the same extent as they could have been exercised if they had been vested in the person for whose benefit they are exercised.

(5) Where rights are transferred by virtue of the operation of subsection (1) above in relation to any document, the transfer for which that subsection provides shall extinguish any entitlement to those rights which derives—

  (*a*) where that document is a bill of lading, from a person's having been an original party to the contract of carriage; or (*b*) in the case of any document to which this Act applies, from the previous operation of that subsection in relation to that document;

but the operation of that subsection shall be without prejudice to any rights which derive from a person's having been an original party to the contract contained in, or evidenced by, a sea waybill and, in relation to a ship's delivery order, shall be without prejudice to any rights deriving otherwise than from the previous operation of that subsection in relation to that order.

Liabilities under shipping documents

3.—(1) Where subsection (1) of section 2 of this Act operates in relation to any   **A1.3**
document to which this Act applies and the person in whom rights are vested by virtue of that subsection—

    (*a*) takes or demands delivery from the carrier of any of the goods to which the document relates;
    (*b*) makes a claim under the contract of carriage against the carrier in respect of any of those goods; or
    (*c*) is a person who, at a time before those rights were vested in him, took or demanded delivery from the carrier of any of those goods,

that person shall (by virtue of taking or demanding delivery or making the claim or, in a case falling within paragraph (c) above, of having the rights vested in him) become subject to the same liabilities under that contract as if he had been a party to that contract.

(2) Where the goods to which a ship's delivery order relates form a part only of the goods to which the contract of carriage relates, the liabilities to which any person is subject by virtue of the operation of this section in relation to that order shall exclude liabilities in respect of any goods to which the order does not relate.

(3) This section, so far as it imposes liabilities under any contract on any person, shall be without prejudice to the liabilities under the contract of any person as an original party to the contract.

Representations in bills of lading

4. A bill of lading which—   **A1.4**

    (*a*) represents goods to have been shipped on board a vessel or to have been received for shipment on board a vessel; and
    (*b*) has been signed by the master of the vessel or by a person who was not the master but had the express, implied or apparent authority of the carrier to sign bills of lading,

shall, in favour of a person who has become the lawful holder of the bill, be conclusive evidence against the carrier of the shipment of the goods or, as the case may be, of their receipt for shipment.

Interpretation etc.

5.—(1) In this Act—   **A1.5**

"bill of lading", "sea waybill" and "ship's delivery order" shall be construed in accordance with section 1 above;
"the contract of carriage"—

(*a*) in relation to a bill of lading or sea waybill, means the contract contained in or evidenced by that bill or waybill; and

(*b*) in relation to a ship's delivery order, means the contract under or for the purposes of which the undertaking contained in the order is given;

"holder", in relation to a bill of lading, shall be construed in accordance with subsection (2) below;

"information technology" includes any computer or other technology by means of which information or other matter may be recorded or communicated without being reduced to documentary form; and

"telecommunication system" has the same meaning as in the Telecommunications Act 1984.

(2) References in this Act to the holder of a bill of lading are references to any of the following persons, that is to say—

(*a*) a person with possession of the bill who, by virtue of being the person identified in the bill, is the consignee of the goods to which the bill relates;

(*b*) a person with possession of the bill as a result of the completion, by delivery of the bill, of any indorsement of the bill or, in the case of a bearer bill, of any other transfer of the bill;

(*c*) a person with possession of the bill as a result of any transaction by virtue of which he would have become a holder falling within paragraph (*a*) or (*b*) above had not the transaction been effected at a time when possession of the bill no longer gave a right (as against the carrier) to possession of the goods to which the bill relates;

and a person shall be regarded for the purposes of this Act as having become the lawful holder of a bill of lading wherever he has become the holder of the bill in good faith.

(3) References in this Act to a person's being identified in a document include references to his being identified by a description which allows for the identity of the person in question to be varied, in accordance with the terms of the document, after its issue; and the reference in section 1(3)(*b*) of this Act to a document's identifying a person shall be construed accordingly.

(4) Without prejudice to sections 2(2) and 4 above, nothing in this Act shall preclude its operation in relation to a case where the goods to which a document relates—

(*a*) cease to exist after the issue of the document; or

(*b*) cannot be identified (whether because they are mixed with other goods or for any other reason);

and references in this Act to the goods to which a document relates shall be construed accordingly.

(5) The preceding provisions of this Act shall have effect without prejudice to the application, in relation to any case, of the rules (the Hague-Visby Rules) which for the time being have the force of law by virtue of section 1 of the Carriage of Goods by Sea Act 1971.

Short title, repeal, commencement and extent

A1.6   **6.**—(1) This Act may be cited as the Carriage of Goods by Sea Act 1992.

(2) The Bills of Lading Act 1855 is hereby repealed.

(3) This Act shall come into force at the end of the period of two months beginning with the day on which it is passed; but nothing in this Act shall have effect in relation to any document issued before the coming into force of this Act.

(4) This Act extends to Northern Ireland.

MERCHANT SHIPPING ACT 1995 (c. 21)

Liability of shipowners and salvors

Limitation of liability[1a]

185.—(1) The provisions of the Convention on Limitation of Liability for Maritime Claims 1976 as set out in Part I of Schedule 7 (in this section and in Part II of that Schedule referred to as "the Convention") shall have the force of law in the United Kingdom.   **A1.7**

(2) The provisions of Part II of that Schedule shall have effect in connection with the Convention, and subsection (1) above shall have effect subject to the provisions of that Part.

. . . [*omitted*]

Exclusion of liability[1b]

186.—(1) Subject to subsection (3) below, the owner of a United Kingdom ship shall not be liable for any loss or damage in the following cases, namely—   **A1.8**

(*a*) where any property on board the ship is lost or damaged by reason of fire on board the ship; or

(*b*) where any gold, silver, watches, jewels or precious stones on board the ship are lost or damaged by reason of theft, robbery or other dishonest conduct and their nature and value[2] were not at the time of shipment declared by their owner or shipper to the owner or master of the ship in the bill of lading or otherwise in writing.

(2) Subject to subsection (3) below, where the loss or damage arises from anything done or omitted by any person in his capacity as master or member of the crew or (otherwise than in that capacity) in the course of his employment as a servant of the owner of the ship, subsection (1) above shall also exclude the liability of—

(*a*) the master, member of the crew or servant; and

(*b*) in a case where the master or member of the crew is the servant of a person whose liability would not be excluded by that subsection apart from this paragraph, the person whose servant he is.

(3) This section does not exclude the liability of any person for any loss or damage resulting from any such personal act or omission of his as is mentioned in article 4 of the Convention in Part I of Schedule 7.

(4) In this section "owner", in relation to a ship, includes any part owner and any charterer, manager or operator of the ship.

[1a] See Art.198.

[1b] See Art.116.

[2] *Cf. Williams v African S.S. Co* (1856) 1 H. & N. 300, where a description, "248 ounces of gold dust", was held bad, as not stating value: and *Gibbs v Potter* (1842) 10 M. & W. 70, where the description "1338 hard dollars" was held good.

SCHEDULE 7[3]

CONVENTION ON LIMITATION OF LIABILITY FOR MARITIME CLAIMS 1976

PART I

TEXT OF CONVENTION

CHAPTER I. THE RIGHT OF LIMITATION

ARTICLE 1

A1.9   *Persons entitled to limit liability*

1. Shipowners and salvors, as hereinafter defined, may limit their liability in accordance with the rules of this Convention for claims set out in Article 2.

2. The term "shipowner" shall mean the owner, charterer, manager or operator of a seagoing ship.

3. Salvor shall mean any person rendering services in direct connexion with salvage operations. Salvage operations shall also include operations referred to in Article 2, paragraph 1(*d*), (*e*) and (*f*).

4. If any claims set out in Article 2 are made against any person for whose act, neglect or default the shipowner or salvor is responsible, such person shall be entitled to avail himself of the limitation of liability provided for in this Convention.

5. In this Convention the liability of a shipowner shall include liability in an action brought against the vessel herself.

6. An insurer of liability for claims subject to limitation in accordance with the rules of this Convention shall be entitled to the benefits of this Convention to the same extent as the assured himself.

7. The act of invoking limitation of liability shall not constitute an admission of liability.

ARTICLE 2

A1.10   *Claims subject to limitation*

1. Subject to Articles 3 and 4 the following claims, whatever the basis of liability may be, shall be subject to limitation of liability:

(*a*) claims in respect of loss of life or personal injury or loss of or damage to property (including damage to harbour works, basins and waterways and aids to navigation), occurring on board or in direct connexion with the operation of the ship or with salvage operations, and consequential loss resulting therefrom;

(*b*) claims in respect of loss resulting from delay in the carriage by sea of cargo, passengers or their luggage;

(*c*) claims in respect of other loss resulting from infringement of rights other than contractual rights, occurring in direct connexion with the operation of the ship or salvage operations;

(*d*) claims in respect of the raising, removal, destruction or the rendering harmless of a ship which is sunk, wrecked, stranded or abandoned, including anything that is or has been on board such ship;

(*e*) claims in respect of the removal, destruction or the rendering harmless of the cargo of the ship;

---

[3] As amended by The Merchant Shipping (Convention on Limitation on Liability for Maritime Claims) (Amendment) Order 1998, SI 1998 No. 1258 and The Merchant Shipping (Convention on Liability for Maritime Claims) (Amendment) Order 2004, 2004 SI 1273.

(*f*) claims of a person other than the person liable in respect of measures taken in order to avert or minimize loss for which the person liable may limit his liability in accordance with this Convention, and further loss caused by such measures.

2. Claims set out in paragraph 1 shall be subject to limitation of liability even if brought by way of recourse or for indemnity under a contract or otherwise. However, claims set out under paragraph 1(*d*), (*e*) and (*f*) shall not be subject to limitation of liability to the extent that they relate to remuneration under a contract with the person liable.

ARTICLE 3

Claims excepted from limitation   **A1.11**

The rules of this Convention shall not apply to:

(*a*) claims for salvage including, if appropriate, any claims for special compensation under Article 14 of the International Convention on Salvage 1989, as amended, or contribution in general average;
(*b*) claims for oil pollution damage within the meaning of the International Convention on Civil Liability for Oil Pollution Damage dated 29th November 1969 or of any amendment or Protocol thereto which is in force;
(*c*) claims subject to any international convention or national legislation governing or prohibiting limitation of liability for nuclear damage;
(*d*) claims against the shipowner of a nuclear ship for nuclear damage;
(*e*) claims by servants of the shipowner or salvor whose duties are connected with the ship or the salvage operations, including claims of their heirs, dependants or other persons entitled to make such claims, if under the law governing the contract of service between the shipowner or salvor and such servants the shipowner or salvor is not entitled to limit his liability in respect to such claims, or if he is by such law only permitted to limit his liability in respect to such claims, or if he is by such law only permitted to limit his liability to an amount greater than that provided for in Article 6.

ARTICLE 4

Conduct barring limitation   **A1.12**

A person liable shall not be entitled to limit his liability if it is proved that the loss resulted from his personal act or omission, committed with the intent to cause such loss, or recklessly and with knowledge that such loss would probably result.

ARTICLE 5

Counterclaims   **A1.13**

Where a person entitled to limitation of liability under the rules of this Convention has a claim against the claimant arising out of the same occurrence, their respective claims shall be set off against each other and the provisions of this Convention shall only apply to the balance, if any.

CHAPTER II. LIMITS OF LIABILITY

ARTICLE 6

The general limits   **A1.14**

1. The limits of liability for claims other than those mentioned in Article 7, arising on any distinct occasion, shall be calculated as follows:

(*a*) in respect of claims for loss of life or personal injury,

(i) 2 million Units of Account for a ship with a tonnage not exceeding 2,000 tons,

(ii) for a ship with a tonnage in excess thereof, the following amount in addition to that mentioned in (i):

for each ton from 2,001 to 30,000 tons, 800 Units of Account;

for each ton from 30,001 to 70,000 tons, 600 Units of Account; and

for each ton in excess of 70,000 tons, 400 Units of Account,

(*b*) in respect of any other claims,

(i) 1 million Units of Account for a ship with a tonnage not exceeding 2,000 tons,

(ii) for a ship with a tonnage in excess thereof the following amount in addition to that mentioned in (i):

for each ton from 2,001 to 30,000 tons, 400 Units of Account;

for each ton from 30,001 to 70,000 tons, 300 Units of Account; and

for each ton in excess of 70,000 tons, 200 Units of Account.

2. Where the amount calculated in accordance with paragraph 1(*a*) is insufficient to pay the claims mentioned therein in full, the amount calculated in accordance with paragraph 1(*b*) shall be available for payment of the unpaid balance of claims under paragraph 1(*a*) and such unpaid balance shall rank rateably with claims mentioned under paragraph 1(*b*).

4. The limits of liability for any salvor not operating from any ship or for any salvor operating solely on the ship to, or in respect of which he is rendering salvage services, shall be calculated according to a tonnage of 1,500 tons.

ARTICLE 7

A1.15

The limit for passenger claims

1. In respect of claims arising on any distinct occasion for loss of life or personal injury to passengers of a ship, the limit of liability of the shipowner thereof shall be an amount of 175,000 Units of Account multiplied by the number of passengers which the ship is authorised to carry according to the ship's certificate.

2. For the purpose of this Article "claims for loss of life or personal injury to passengers of a ship" shall mean any such claims brought by or on behalf of any person carried in that ship:

(*a*) under a contract of passenger carriage, or

(*b*) who, with the consent of the carrier, is accompanying a vehicle or live animals which are covered by a contract for the carriage of goods.

ARTICLE 8

A1.16

Unit of Account

1. The Unit of Account referred to in Articles 6 and 7 is the Special Drawing Right as defined by the International Monetary Fund. The amounts mentioned in Articles 6 and 7 shall be converted into the national currency of the State in which limitation is sought, according to the value of that currency at the date the limitation fund shall have been constituted, payment is made, or security is given which under the law of that State is equivalent to such payment.

ARTICLE 9

Aggregation of claims **A1.17**

1. The limits of liability determined in accordance with Article 6 shall apply to the aggregate of all claims which arise on any distinct occasion:

(a) against the person or persons mentioned in paragraph 2 of Article 1 and any person for whose act, neglect or default he or they are responsible; or

(b) against the shipowner of a ship rendering salvage services from that ship and the salvor or salvors operating from such ship and any person for whose act, neglect or default he or they are responsible; or

(c) against the salvor or salvors who are not operating from a ship or who are operating solely on the ship to, or in respect of which, the salvage services are rendered and any person for whose act, neglect or default he or they are responsible.

2. The limits of liability determined in accordance with Article 7 shall apply to the aggregate of all claims subject thereto which may arise on any distinct occasion against the person or persons mentioned in paragraph 2 of Article 1 in respect of the ship referred to in Article 7 and any person for whose act, neglect or default he or they are responsible.

ARTICLE 10

Limitation of liability without constitution of a limitation fund **A1.18**

1. Limitation of liability may be invoked notwithstanding that a limitation fund as mentioned in Article 11 has not been constituted.

2. If limitation of liability is invoked without the constitution of a limitation fund, the provisions of Article 12 shall apply correspondingly.

3. Questions of procedure arising under the rules of this Article shall be decided in accordance with the national law of the State Party in which action is brought.

CHAPTER III. THE LIMITATION FUND

ARTICLE 11

Constitution of the fund **A1.19**

1. Any person alleged to be liable may constitute a fund with the Court or other competent authority in any State Party in which legal proceedings are instituted in respect of claims subject to limitation. The fund shall be constituted in the sum of such of the amounts set out in Articles 6 and 7 as are applicable to claims for which that person may be liable, together with interest thereon from the date of the occurrence giving rise to the liability until the date of the constitution of the fund. Any fund thus constituted shall be available only for the payment of claims in respect of which limitation of liability can be invoked.

2. A fund may be constituted, either by depositing the sum, or by producing a guarantee acceptable under the legislation of the State Party where the fund is constituted and considered to be adequate by the Court or other competent authority.

3. A fund constituted by one of the persons mentioned in paragraph 1(a), (b) or (c) or paragraph 2 of Article 9 or his insurer shall be deemed constituted by all persons mentioned in paragraph 1(a), (b) or (c) or paragraph 2, respectively.

ARTICLE 12

A1.20 *Distribution of the fund*

1. Subject to the provisions of paragraphs 1 and 2 of Article 6 and Article 7, the fund shall be distributed among the claimants in proportion to their established claims against the fund.

2. If, before the fund is distributed, the person liable, or his insurer, has settled a claim against the fund such person shall, up to the amount he has paid, acquire by subrogation the rights which the person so compensated would have enjoyed under this Convention.

3. The right of subrogation provided for in paragraph 2 may also be exercised by persons other than those therein mentioned in respect of any amount of compensation which they may have paid, but only to the extent that such subrogation is permitted under the applicable national law.

4. Where the person liable or any other person establishes that he may be compelled to pay, at a later date, in whole or in part any such amount of compensation with regard to which such person would have enjoyed a right of subrogation pursuant to paragraphs 2 and 3 had the compensation been paid before the fund was distributed, the Court or other competent authority of the State where the fund has been constituted may order that a sufficient sum shall be provisionally set aside to enable such person at such later date to enforce his claim against the fund.

ARTICLE 13

A1.21 *Bar to other actions*

1. Where a limitation fund has been constituted in accordance with Article 11, any person having made a claim against the fund shall be barred from exercising any right in respect of such a claim against any other assets of a person by or on behalf of whom the fund has been constituted.

2. After a limitation fund has been constituted in accordance with Article 11, any ship or other property belonging to a person on behalf of whom the fund has been constituted, which has been arrested or attached within the jurisdiction of a State Party for a claim which may be raised against the fund, or any security given, may be released by order of the Court or other competent authority of such State. However, such release shall always be ordered if the limitation fund has been constituted.

(*a*) at the port where the occurrence took place, or, if it took place out of port, at the first port of call thereafter; or

(*b*) at the port of disembarkation in respect of claims for loss of life or personal injury; or

(*c*) at the port of discharge in respect of damage to cargo; or

(*d*) in the State where the arrest is made.

3. The rules of paragraphs 1 and 2 shall apply only if the claimant may bring a claim against the limitation fund before the Court administering that fund and the fund is actually available and freely transferable in respect of that claim.

ARTICLE 14

A1.22 *Governing law*

Subject to the provisions of this Chapter the rules relating to the constitution and distribution of a limitation fund, and all rules of procedure in connection therewith, shall be governed by the law of the State Party in which the fund is constituted.

CHAPTER IV. SCOPE OF APPLICATION

ARTICLE 15   **A1.23**

1. This Convention shall apply whenever any person referred to in Article 1 seeks to limit his liability before the Court of a State Party or seeks to procure the release of a ship or other property or the discharge of any security given within the jurisdiction of any such State.

2. A State Party may regulate by specific provisions of national law the system of limitation of liability to be applied to vessels which are:

    (a) according to the law of that State, ships intended for navigation on inland waterways;

    (b) ships of less than 300 tons.

A State Party which makes use of the option provided for in this paragraph shall inform the depositary of the limits of liability adopted in its national legislation or of the fact that there are none.

3bis Notwithstanding the limit of liability prescribed in paragraph 1 of article 7, a State Party may regulate by specific provisions of national law the system of liability to be applied to claims for loss of life or personal injury to passengers of a ship, provided that the limit of liability is not lower than that prescribed in paragraph 1 of article 7. A State Party which makes use of the option provided for in this paragraph shall inform the Secretary-General of the limits of liability adopted or of the fact that there are none.

ARTICLE 18

Reservations   **A1.24**

1. Any State may, at the time of signature, ratification, acceptance, approval or accession or at any time thereafter, reserve the right—

    (a) to exclude the application of article 2, paragraphs 1(d) and (e);

    (b) to exclude claims for damage within the meaning of the International Convention on Liability and Comepensation for Damage in Connection with the Carriage of Hazardous and Noxious Substances by Sea, 1996, or of any amendment or Protocol thereto.

No other reservations shall be admissible to the substantive provisions of this Convention.

PART II

PROVISIONS HAVING EFFECT IN CONNECTION WITH CONVENTION

Interpretation   **A1.25**

1. In this Part of this Schedule any reference to a numbered article is a reference to the article of the Convention which is so numbered.

Right to limit liability   **A1.26**

2. Subject to paragraph 6 below the right to limit liability under the Convention shall apply in relation to any ship whether seagoing or not, and the definition of "shipowner" in paragraph 2 of article 1 shall be construed accordingly.

A1.27 *Claims subject to limitation*

3.—(1) Paragraph 1(*d*) of article 2 shall not apply unless provision has been made by an order of the Secretary of State for the setting up and management of a fund to be used for the making to harbour or conservancy authorities of payments needed to compensate them for the reduction, in consequence of the said paragraph 1(*d*), of amounts recoverable by them in claims of the kind there mentioned, and to be maintained by contributions from such authorities raised and collected by them in respect of vessels in like manner as other sums so raised by them.

(2) Any order under sub-paragraph (1) above may contain such incidental and supplemental provisions as appear to the Secretary of State to be necessary or expedient.

4.—(1) Claims for damage within the meaning of the International Convention on Liability and Compensation for Damage in Connection with the Carriage of Hazardous and Noxious Sunstances by Sea 1996, of any amendment of or Protocol to that Convention, which arise from occurrences which take place after the coming into force of the first Order In Council made by Her Majesty under section 182B of this Act shall be excluded from the Convention.

(2) The claims excluded from the Convention by paragraph (*b*) of article 3 are claims in respect of any liability incurred under section 153 of this Act.

(3) The claims excluded from the Convention by paragraph (*c*) of article 3 are claims made by virtue of any of sections 7 to 11 of the Nuclear Installations Act 1965.

A1.28 *The general limits*

5.—(1) In the application of article 6 to a ship with a tonnage less than 300 tons that article shall have effect as if—

(*a*) paragraph 1 (*a*)(i) referred to 1,000,000 Units of Account; and
(*b*) paragraph 1 (*b*)(i) referred to 500,000 Units of Account.

(2) For the purposes of article 6 and this paragraph a ship's tonnage shall bc its gross tonnage calculated in such manner as may be prescribed by an order made by the Secretary of State.

(3) Any order under this paragraph shall, so far as appears to the Secretary of State to be practicable, give effect to the regulations in Annex 1 of the International Convention on Tonnage Measurement of Ships 1969.

A1.29 *Limit for passenger claims*

6.—(1) Article 7 shall not apply in respect of any seagoing ship; and shall have effect in respect of any ship which is not seagoing as if, in paragraph 1 of that article—

(a) after "thereof" there were inserted "in respect of each passenger";
(b) the words from "multiplied" onwards were omitted".

(2) In paragraph 2 of article 7 the reference to claims brought on behalf of a person includes a reference to any claim in respect of the death of a person under the Fatal Accidents Act 1976, the Fatal Accidents (Northern Ireland) Order 1977 or the Damages (Scotland) Act 1976.

A1.30 *Units of Account*

7.—(1) For the purpose of converting the amounts mentioned in articles 6 and 7 from special drawing rights into sterling one special drawing right shall be treated as equal to such a sum in sterling as the International Monetary Fund have fixed as being the equivalent of one special drawing right for—

(*a*) the relevant date under paragraph 1 or article 8; or
(*b*) if no sum has been so fixed for that date, the last preceding date for which a sum has been so fixed.

(2) A certificate given by or on behalf of the Treasury stating—

(*a*) that a particular sum in sterling has been fixed as mentioned in the preceding sub-paragraph for a particular date; or
(*b*) that no sum has been so fixed for that date and that a particular sum in sterling has been so fixed for a date which is the last preceding date for which a sum has been so fixed,

shall be conclusive evidence of those matters for the purposes of those articles; and a document purporting to be such a certificate shall, in any proceedings, be received in evidence and, unless the contrary is proved, be deemed to be such a certificate.

Constitution of fund   **A1.31**

8.—(1) The Secretary of State may, with the concurrence of the Treasury, by order prescribe the rate of interest to be applied for the purposes of paragraph 1 of article 11.

(2) Any statutory instrument containing an order under sub-paragraph (1) above shall be laid before Parliament after being made.

(3) Where a fund is constituted with the court in accordance with article 11 for the payment of claims arising out of any occurrence, the court may stay any proceedings relating to any claim arising out of that occurrence which are pending against the person by whom the fund has been constituted.

Distribution of fund   **A1.32**

9. No lien or other right in respect of any ship or property shall affect the proportions in which under article 12 the fund is distributed among several claimants.

Bar to other actions   **A1.33**

10. Where the release of a ship or other property is ordered under paragraph 2 of article 13 the person on whose application it is ordered to be released shall be deemed to have submitted to (or, in Scotland, prorogated) the jurisdiction of the court to adjudicate on the claim for which the ship or property was arrested or attached.

Meaning of "court"   **A1.34**

11. References in the Convention and the preceding provisions of this Part of this Schedule to the court are references to the High Court or, in relation to Scotland, the Court of Session.

Meaning of "ship"   **A1.35**

12. References in the Convention and in the preceding provisions of this Part of this Schedule to a ship include references to any structure (whether completed or in course of completion) launched and intended for use in navigation as a ship or part of a ship.

A1.36 *Meaning of "State Party"*

13. An Order in Council made for the purposes of this paragraph and declaring that any State specified in the Order is a party to the Convention as amended by the 1996 Protocol shall, subject to the provisions of any subsequent Order made for those purposes, be conclusive evidence that the State is a party to the Convention as amended by the 1996 Protocol.

APPENDIX II

YORK-ANTWERP RULES

Introductory Note

THE most recent revision of the York-Antwerp Rules took place in 2004. Prior to that the York-Antwerp Rules 1974 had been amended in 1990 and then revised in 1994. The 1974 Rules replaced the York-Antwerp Rules 1950, which had replaced the York-Antwerp Rules 1924, which in turn had replaced the York-Antwerp Rules 1890. The 2004 Rules, like the Rules of 1890, 1924, 1950, 1974 and 1994, have no application unless they have been expressly incorporated by contract into policies of insurance, charterparties and bills of lading, but in fact the Rules have been widely adopted and will today be found to have been incorporated in the majority of shipping documents in current use. It is, however, not unknown for parties to adopt the 1994 Rules (or even the 1974 Rules as amended) notwithstanding the publication of the 2004 Rules. **A2.1**

These Rules, having been drawn up by international agreement, are not to be presumed to have the same effect as the English common law and should not be artificially construed in an endeavour to make them conform to it. They do not constitute a complete or self-contained code, and need to be supplemented by bringing into the gaps provisions of the general law which are applicable to the contract.[1]

The most important change made by the York-Antwerp Rules 1950, was that effected by the *"Rule of Interpretation"* which precedes the lettered Rules. These lettered Rules were first introduced in the Rules of 1924 in substitution for Rule XVIII of the 1890 Rules which provided that "except as provided in the foregoing rules, the adjustment shall be drawn up in accordance with the law and practice that would have governed the adjustment had the contract of affreightment not contained a clause to pay general average according to these Rules".

Nevertheless after the introduction of the Rules of 1924 considerable doubt existed in the minds of the commercial community as to the mutual bearing of the lettered Rules and the numbered Rules. The contention on the one side was that the principles of general average were laid down in the lettered Rules, and that in any individual instance a loss could not be recovered in general average unless it fell within the principles of these Rules even though the wording of one of the numbered Rules, if it stood alone, might be sufficient to bring that loss within the ambit of general average. On the other side the contention was that a loss, although it might not come within the principles laid down in the lettered Rules, would yet be recoverable if the wording of any one of the numbered Rules standing alone was capable of being construed so as to include it. In 1929 the matter came before the English courts in the case of *The Makis*[2] when Roche J. arrived at a decision which did not exactly coincide with either of these views. It was there held that the intention of the framers of the Rules was to frame a complete code, first by setting out the general principles under the lettered Rules and then, lest there should be any doubt as to whether certain particular cases fell within the provisions of the Rules or not, by providing a solution of the doubt in the numbered Rules.

---

[1] per Pearson J. in *Goulandris Bros v B. Goldman & Sons Ltd* [1958] 1 Q.B. 74 at p.91; see also *Alma Shipping Corp v Union of India* [1971] 2 Lloyd's Rep. 494.

[2] [1929] 1 K.B. 187.

This decision was found to be generally unacceptable to the commercial interests concerned as it would have resulted in the disallowance of many items of expenditure by shipowners which under the 1890 Rules had in practice been allowed. Accordingly a market agreement was entered into (known as The Makis Agreement) to the effect that the Rules should be construed as if they contained the following provision "except as provided in the numbered Rules I–XXII inclusive, the adjustment shall be drawn up in accordance with the lettered Rules A to G inclusive". This agreement which brought the British practice into line with the practice of most, if not all, Continental countries is now embodied in the Rule of Interpretation which precedes the lettered Rules.

The effect of this Rule of Interpretation may be illustrated by reference to Rule XI(b). Under *The Makis* decision the wages and maintenance of the master, officers and crew during a period of detention in port to repair accidental damage not caused by a general average act were disallowed in general average. Under the Rule of Interpretation they would be allowed since the condition contained in the words "detained . . . to enable damage to ship caused by . . . accident to the repaired" would be satisfied notwithstanding that the case could not be brought within the principles of the lettered Rules.

The main amendments made by the introduction of the 2004 Rules are to Rules VI (salvage), XI (expenses at port of refuge), XIV (temporary repairs), XX (provision of funds), XXI (interest). In addition a new Rule XXIII has been added to provide a time bar requiring claims in General Average to be brought within one year of the General Average Adjustment or six years of the end of the common maritime adventure.

In the text below the 1994 Rules are set out alongside the 2004 Rules for comparison. In addition the changes made to the 1974 Rules by the 1994 Rules have been indicated by comment on the text or the use of italics.

York-Antwerp Rules, 1994	**York-Antwerp Rules, 2004**

A2.2 RULE OF INTERPRETATION[3]

In the adjustment of general average the following Rules shall apply to the exclusion of any Law and Practice inconsistent therewith.

Except as provided *by the Rule Paramount and* the numbered Rules, general average shall be adjusted according to the lettered Rules.

RULE OF INTERPRETATION

In the adjustment of general average the following Rules shall apply to the exclusion of any Law and Practice inconsistent therewith.

Except as provided by the Rule Paramount and the numbered Rules, general average shall be adjusted according to the lettered Rules.

A2.3 *RULE PARAMOUNT*

In no case shall there be any allowance for sacrifice or expenditure unless reasonably made or incurred.

RULE PARAMOUNT

In no case shall there be any allowance for sacrifice or expenditure unless reasonably made or incurred.

---

[3] See comment in Introductory Note, above.

York-Antwerp Rules, 1994 | **York-Antwerp Rules, 2004**

RULE A

There is a general average act when, and only when, any extraordinary sacrifice or expenditure is intentionally and reasonably made or incurred for the common safety for the purpose of preserving from peril the property involved in a common maritime adventure.[4]

General average sacrifices and expenditures shall be borne by the different contributing interests on the basis hereinafter provided.

RULE B

There is a common maritime adventure when one or more vessels are towing or pushing another vessel or vessels, provided that they are all involved in commercial activities and not in a salvage operation.

When measures are taken to preserve the vessels and their cargoes, if any, from a common peril, these Rules shall apply.

A vessel is not in common peril with another vessel or vessels if by simply disconnecting from the other vessel or vessels she is in safety; but if the disconnection is itself a general average act the common maritime adventure continues.

RULE A

1. There is a general average act when, and only when, any extraordinary sacrifice or expenditure is intentionally and reasonably made or incurred for the common safety for the purpose of preserving from peril the property involved in a common maritime adventure.

2. General average sacrifices and expenditures shall be borne by the different contributing interests on the basis hereinafter provided.

A2.4

RULE B

1. There is a common maritime adventure when one or more vessels are towing or pushing another vessel or vessels, provided that they are all involved in commercial activities and not in a salvage operation. When measures are taken to preserve the vessels and their cargoes, if any, from a common peril, these Rules shall apply.

2. A vessel is not in common peril with another vessel or vessels if by simply disconnecting from the other vessel or vessels she is in safety; but if the disconnection is itself a general average act the common maritime adventure continues.

A2.5

---

[4] This definition is wider in form than that contained in the Marine Insurance Act 1906, s.66(2), which provides that the extraordinary sacrifice or expenditure must have been made or incurred "in time of peril for the purpose of preserving the property imperilled in the common adventure"; see *Watson v Firemen's Fund Co* [1922] 2 K.B. 355, where it was held that if the peril, though reasonably believed to exist, was in fact non-existent, there could be no general average act within the meaning of this section. For a discussion of the meaning of the Rule, see *The Seapool* [1934] P. 53. See also *Athel Line v Liverpool and London War Risks Association* [1944] K.B. 87 (no general average act where master in convoy acted in blind obedience to naval orders without any knowledge of risks on which were based). The making of a contract can be a general average act, if it is intentionally and reasonably made; *Australian Coastal Shipping v Green* [1971] 1 Q.B. 456.

York-Antwerp Rules, 1994 | **York-Antwerp Rules, 2004**

A2.6 RULE C

Only such losses, damages or expenses which are the direct consequence of the general average act shall be allowed as general average.[5]

In no case shall there be any allowance in general average for losses, damages or expenses incurred in respect of damage to the environment or in consequence of the escape or release of pollutant substances from the property involved in the common maritime adventure.

Demurrage, loss of market, and any loss or damage sustained or expense incurred by reason of delay, whether on the voyage or subsequently,[6] and any indirect loss whatsoever, shall not be admitted as general average.

A2.7 RULE D[7]

Rights to contribution in general average shall not be affected, though the event which gave rise to the sacrifice or expenditure may have been due to the fault of one of the parties to the adventure, but this shall not prejudice any remedies or defences which

RULE C

1. Only such losses, damages or expenses which are the direct consequence of the general average act shall be allowed as general average.

2. In no case shall there be any allowance in general average for losses, damages, or expenses incurred in respect of damage to the environment or in consequence of the escape or release of pollutant substances from property involved in the common maritime adventure.

3. Demurrage, loss of market, and any loss or damage sustained or expense incurred by reason of delay, whether on the voyage or subsequently, and any indirect loss whatsoever, shall not be allowed as general average.

RULE D

Rights to contribution in general average shall not be affected, though the event which gave rise to the sacrifice or expenditure may have been due to the fault of one of the parties to the adventure, but this shall not prejudice any remedies

---

[5] "Direct consequences" denote those consequences which flow in an unbroken sequence from the act; whereas "indirect consequences" are those in which the sequence is broken by an intervening or extraneous cause: per Lord Denning M.R. in *Australian Coastal Shipping v Green, ibid.* at p.21. Where the general average act consists of the making of a contract, liabilities arising under the contract are direct consequences of the act (per Phillimore and Cairns L.JJ., *ibid.*) at any rate if the event which brings the liability into existence was reasonably foreseeable when the contract was made (see per Lord Denning M.R., *ibid.*).

[6] The words "whether on the voyage or subsequently" make clear what was in some countries considered uncertain under the corresponding 1924 Rule, viz. demurrage of the ship detained after completion of the voyage or the repair of general average damage is not admissible in general average. The same result had been reached in the English courts on the language of the Rule without this addition in *Wetherall v London Assurance Co* [1931] 2 K.B. 448, following *The Leitrim* [1902] P. 246 (detention for repairs during the voyage).

[7] This Rule, first introduced as part of the general Rules in 1924, reproduces with slight verbal modification the York-Antwerp Rules 1903, which had not previously been adopted by many British shipowners. For the common law rule, see Art.134(6) and fn.245, Art.134. The objects of Rule D are to keep all questions of alleged fault out of the adjustment, and to preserve unimpaired the legal position at the stage of enforcement. The first part of the Rule ensures that the adjustment is compiled on the assumption that the casualty has not been caused by anybody's fault. The second part preserves the remedies for faults, which may nullify or cut down the prima facie

York-Antwerp Rules, 1994   **York-Antwerp Rules, 2004**

---

may be open against or to that party in respect of such fault.[8]

or defences which may be open against or to that party in respect of such fault.

RULE E

RULE E   A2.8

The onus of proof is upon the party claiming in general average to show that the loss or expense claimed is properly allowable as general average.

1. The onus of proof is upon the party claiming in general average to show that the loss or expense claimed is properly allowable as general average.

All parties claiming in general average shall give notice in writing to the average adjuster of the loss or expense in respect of which they claim contribution within 12 months of the date of the termination of the common maritime adventure.

2. All parties claiming in general average shall give notice in writing to the average adjuster of the loss or expense in respect of which they claim contribution within 12 months of the date of the termination of the common maritime adventure.

Failing such notification, or if within 12 months of a request for the same any of the parties shall fail to supply evidence in support of a notified claim, or particulars of value in respect of a contributory interest, the average adjuster shall be at liberty to estimate the extent of the allowance

3. Failing such notification, or if within 12 months of a request for the same any of the parties shall fail to supply evidence in support of a notified claim, or particulars of value in respect of a contributory interest, the average adjuster shall be at liberty to estimate the extent

---

rights set out in the adjustment: see per Pearson J. in *Goulandris Bros v B. Goldman & Sons Ltd* [1958] 1 Q.B. at pp.92, 93.

[8] The effect of Rule D was considered in *Tempus Shipping Co v Dreyfus* [1931] A.C. 726; *Hain S.S. Co v Tate & Lyle* (1936) 41 Com.Cas. 350 at p.361 (HL); and *Goulandris Bros v B. Goldman & Sons Ltd*, above, a case in which the bill of lading was also subject to the Hague Rules:
The law now applicable may be summarised as follows:

    (i) A party's prima facie right to recover general average contributions in accordance with the adjustment may be defeated or diminished by the other parties' "remedies" in respect of his "faults".

    (ii) The "remedies" of the other parties include the defence that the sacrifice or expenditure was made necessary by the claimant's fault, as well as the right to counterclaim in respect of the damages caused by the fault: this is confirmed by the inclusion of the words "or defences" in the 1974 and subsequent Rules.

    (iii) The other parties may be entitled to counterclaim their proportions of the expenditure against the claimant if the loss was caused by the fault of the latter, and in such an event the court will not give judgment for the claimant, but in order to avoid circuity of action will dismiss the claim.

    (iv) A "fault" is a legal wrong which is actionable as between the parties at the time when the sacrifice or expenditure was made. A claim for contribution by a shipowner is therefore not defeated by the unseaworthiness of the ship or the negligence of the crew, if these matters are covered by exceptions in the contract of carriage. Conversely, a party may rely on a defence based on "fault", notwithstanding that his counterclaim in respect of damage resulting from the fault has become barred by lapse of time.

    For the position at common law, where the contract of affreightment does not incorporate the York-Antwerp Rules, see above, Art.136. For examples of the consideration of this rule in practice see *Sunlight Mercantile Pte. Ltd v Ever Lucky Shipping Company Ltd* [2004] 2 Lloyd's Rep. 174, *Guinomar of Conakry v Samsumg Fire and Marine Insurance Co Ltd (The Kamsar Voyager)* [2002] 2 Lloyd's Rep. 57, *Demand Shipping Co Ltd v Ministry of Food (The Lendoudis Evangelos II)* [2001] 2 Lloyd's Rep. 304.

York-Antwerp Rules, 1994 | York-Antwerp Rules, 2004

or the contributory value on the basis of the information available to him, which estimate may be challenged only on the ground that it is manifestly incorrect.

of the allowance or the contributory value on the basis of the information available to him, which estimate may be challenged only on the ground that it is manifestly incorrect.

A2.9 RULE F

Any *additional* expense incurred in place of another expense which would have been allowable as general average shall be deemed to be general average and so allowed without regard to the saving, if any, to other interests,[9] but only up to the amount of the general average expense avoided.

RULE F

Any additional expense incurred in place of another expense, which would have been allowable as general average shall be deemed to be general average and so allowed without regard to the saving, if any, to other interests, only up to the amount of the general average expense avoided.

A2.10 RULE G

General average shall be adjusted as regards both loss and contribution upon the basis of values at the time and place when and where the adventure ends.

This rule shall not affect the determination of the place at which the average statement is to be made up.

When a ship is at any port or place in circumstances which would give rise to an allowance in general average under the provisions of Rules X and XI, and the cargo or part thereof is forwarded to destination by other means, rights and liabilities in general average shall, subject to cargo interests being notified if practicable, remain as nearly as possible the same as they would have been in the absence of such forwarding, as if the

RULE G

1. General average shall be adjusted as regards both loss and contribution upon the basis of values at the time and place when and where the adventure ends.

2. This rule shall not affect the determination of the place at which the average statement is to be made up.

3. When a ship is at any port or place in circumstances which would give rise to an allowance in general average under the provisions of Rules X and XI, and the cargo or part thereof is forwarded to destination by other means, rights and liabilities in general average shall, subject to cargo interests being notified if practicable, remain as nearly as possible the same as they would have been in the absence of such

---

[9] The words "without regard to the saving if any to other interests" in this rule and in Rule XIV makes it clear that in determining to what extent "substituted expenses" are administered in general average, no account shall be taken of the benefit to other interests, e.g. the saving of a perishable cargo which might otherwise have been lost.

York-Antwerp Rules, 1994	York-Antwerp Rules, 2004	
adventure had continued in the original ship for so long as justifiable under the contract of affreightment and the applicable law.	**forwarding, as if the adventure had continued in the original ship for so long as justifiable under the contract of affreightment and the applicable law.**	
The proportion attaching to cargo of the allowances made in general average by reason of applying the third paragraph of this Rule shall not exceed the cost which would have been borne by the owners of cargo if the cargo had been forwarded at their expense.	**4. The proportion attaching to cargo of the allowances made in general average by reason of applying the third paragraph of this Rule shall not exceed the cost which would have been borne by the owners of cargo if the cargo had been forwarded at their expense.**	
RULE I. JETTISON OF CARGO	**RULE I. JETTISON OF CARGO**	**A2.11**
No jettison of cargo shall be made good as general average, unless such cargo is carried in accordance with the recognised custom of the trade.[10]	**No jettison of cargo shall be allowed as general average, unless such cargo is carried in accordance with the recognised custom of the trade.**	
RULE II. *LOSS OR DAMAGE BY SACRIFICES* FOR THE COMMON SAFETY	**RULE II. LOSS OR DAMAGE BY SACRIFICES FOR THE COMMON SAFETY**	**A2.12**
Loss of or damage to the property involved in the common maritime adventure by or in consequence of a sacrifice made for the common safety, and by water which goes down a ship's hatches opened or other opening made for the purpose of making a jettison for the common safety, shall be made good as general average.	**Loss of or damage to the property involved in the common maritime adventure by or in consequence of a sacrifice made for the common safety, and by water which goes down a ship's hatches opened or other opening made for the purpose of making a jettison for the common safety, shall be allowed as general average.**	
RULE III. EXTINGUISHING FIRE ON SHIPBOARD	**RULE III. EXTINGUISHING FIRE ON SHIPBOARD**	**A2.13**
Damage done to a ship and cargo, or either of them, by water or otherwise, including damage by beaching or scuttling a burning ship, in extinguishing a fire on board the ship, shall be made	**Damage done to a ship and cargo, or either of them, by water or otherwise, including damage by beaching or scuttling a burning ship, in extinguishing a fire on board the ship,**	

---

[10] This reproduces Rule 1 of the 1924 Rules which replaced Rule 1 of the 1890 Rules, under which jettison of deck cargo was excluded from general average in all cases.

York-Antwerp Rules, 1994 | **York-Antwerp Rules, 2004**

good as general average; except that no compensation shall be made for damage by smoke however caused *or by heat of the fire.* · | **shall be allowed as general average; except that no compensation shall be made for damage by smoke however caused or by heat of the fire.**

A2.14

RULE IV. CUTTING AWAY WRECK

Loss or damage sustained by cutting away wreck or parts of the ship which have been previously carried away or are effectively lost by accident shall not be made good as general average.

RULE IV. CUTTING AWAY WRECK

Loss or damage sustained by cutting away wreck or parts of the ship which have been previously carried away or are effectively lost by accident shall not be allowed as general average.

A2.15

RULE V. VOLUNTARY STRANDING[11]

When a ship is intentionally run on shore for the common safety, whether or not she might have been driven on shore,[12] the consequent loss or damage *to the property involved in the common maritime adventure* shall be allowed in general average.[13–14]

RULE V. VOLUNTARY STRANDING

When a ship is intentionally run on shore for the common safety, whether or not she might have been driven on shore, the consequent loss or damage to the propery involved in the maritime adventure shall be allowed in general average.

A2.16

RULE VI. SALVAGE REMUNERATION

(a) Expenditure incurred by the parties to the adventure in the nature of salvage, whether under contract or otherwise, shall be allowed in general average provided that the salvage operations were carried out for the purpose of preserving from peril the property involved in the common maritime adventure.

RULE VI. SALVAGE REMUNERATION

(a) Salvage payments, including interest thereon and legal fees associated with such payments, shall lie where they fall and shall not be allowed in general average, save only that if one party to the salvage shall have paid all or any of the proportion of salvage (including interest and legal fees) due from another party (calculated on the basis of salved values and not general average contributory values), the unpaid contribution to salvage due from that other party shall be credited in the adjustment to the party that has paid it, and debited to the party on whose behalf the payment was made.

---

[11] "Stranding" does not cover intentional running of a ship broadside against a pier: *The Seapool* [1934] P. 53.

[12] The addition of these words in the 1974 Rules changed the earlier rule, under which, if the stranding was inevitable, only loss or damage incurred in refloating the ship was allowed.

[13-14] See also *Austin Friars Co v Spillers & Bakers* [1915] 3 K.B. 586; *Anglo-Grecian Steam Trading Co v T. Beynon & Co* (1926) 24 Ll.L.R. 122; and *The Seapool*, above.

Expenditure allowed in general average shall include any salvage remuneration in which the skill and efforts of the salvors in preventing or minimising damage to the environment such as is referred to in Art. 13 paragraph 1(b) of the International Convention on Salvage, 1989 have been taken into account.

(b) Salvage payments referred to in paragraph (a) above shall include any salvage remuneration in which the skill and efforts of the salvors in preventing or minimising damage to the environment such as is referred to in Article 13 paragraph 1(b) of the International Convention on Salvage 1989 have been taken into account.

(b) Special compensation payable to a salvor by the shipowner under Art. 14 of the said Convention to the extent specified in paragraph 4 of that Article or under any other provision similar in substance shall not be allowed in general average.

(c) Special compensation payable to a salvor by the shipowner under Art. 14 of the said Convention to the extent specified in paragraph 4 of that Article or under any other provision similar in substance (such as SCOPIC) shall not be allowed in general average and shall not be considered a salvage payment as referred to in paragraph (a) of this Rule.

RULE VII. DAMAGE TO MACHINERY AND BOILERS

RULE VII. DAMAGE TO MACHINERY AND BOILERS

A2.17

Damage caused to any machinery and boilers of a ship which is ashore and in a position of peril, in endeavouring to refloat, shall be allowed in general average when shown to have arisen from an actual intention to float the ship for the common safety at the risk of such damage; but where a ship is afloat no loss or damage caused by working the propelling machinery and boilers shall in any circumstances be made good as general average.

Damage caused to any machinery and boilers of a ship which is ashore and in a position of peril, in endeavouring to refloat, shall be allowed in general average when shown to have arisen from an actual intention to float the ship for the common safety at the risk of such damage; but where a ship is afloat no loss or damage caused by working the propelling machinery and boilers shall in any circumstances be allowed as general average.

RULE VIII. EXPENSES LIGHTENING A SHIP WHEN ASHORE, AND CONSEQUENT DAMAGE

RULE VIII. EXPENSES LIGHTENING A SHIP WHEN ASHORE, AND CONSEQUENT DAMAGE

A2.18

When a ship is ashore and cargo and ship's fuel and stores or any of them are discharged as a general average act, the extra cost of lightening, lighter hire and reshipping (if incurred), and

When a ship is ashore and cargo and ship's fuel and stores or any of them are discharged as a general average act, the extra cost of lightening, lighter hire and re-shipping

York-Antwerp Rules, 1994	York-Antwerp Rules, 2004

any loss or damage *to the property involved in the common maritime adventure in consequence thereof,* shall be admitted as general average.

(if incurred), and any loss or damage to the property involved in the common maritime adventure in consequence thereof, shall be allowed as general average.

A2.19 RULE IX. *CARGO*, SHIP'S MATERIALS AND STORES *USED* FOR FUEL

Cargo, ship's materials and stores, or any of them, necessarily *used* for fuel for the common safety at a time of peril shall be admitted as general average, *but when such an allowance is made for the cost of ship's materials and stores the general average shall be credited with the estimated cost of the fuel which would otherwise have been consumed in prosecuting the intended voyage.*

RULE IX. CARGO SHIP'S MATERIALS AND STORES USED FOR FUEL

Cargo, ship's materials and stores, or any of them, necessarily used for fuel for the common safety at a time of peril shall be allowed as general average, but when such an allowance is made for the cost of ship's materials and stores the general average shall be credited with the estimated cost of the fuel which would otherwise have been consumed in prosecuting the intended voyage.

A2.20 RULE X. EXPENSES AT PORT OF REFUGE, ETC.

(a) When a ship shall have entered a port or place of refuge or shall have returned to her port or place of loading in consequence of accident, sacrifice or other extraordinary circumstances which render that necessary for the common safety, the expenses of entering such port or place shall be admitted as general average; and when she shall have sailed thence with her original cargo, or a part of it, the corresponding expenses of leaving such port[15] or place consequent upon such entry or return shall likewise be admitted as general average.

When a ship is at any port or place of refuge and is necessarily removed to another port or place because repairs

RULE X. EXPENSES AT PORT OF REFUGE, ETC.

(a) (i) When a ship shall have entered a port or place of refuge, or shall have returned to her port or place of loading in consequence of accident, sacrifice or other extraordinary circumstances, which render that necessary for the common safety, the expenses of entering such port or place shall be allowed as general average; and when she shall have sailed thence with her original cargo, or a part of it, the corresponding expenses of leaving such port or place consequent upon such entry or return shall likewise be allowed as general average.

(ii) When a ship is at any port or place of refuge and is necessarily removed to another port or place

---

[15] These words do not include the expenses of breaking ice in the approaches to the port: *Westoll v Carter* (1898) 3 Com.Cas. 112.

York-Antwerp Rules, 1994	York-Antwerp Rules, 2004

cannot be carried out in the first port or place, the provisions of this Rule shall be applied to the second port or place as if it were a port or place of refuge and the cost of such removal including temporary repairs and towage shall be admitted as general average. The provisions of Rule XI shall be applied to the prolongation of the voyage occasioned by such removal.[16]

because repairs cannot be carried out in the first port or place, the provisions of this Rule shall be applied to the second port or place as if it were a port or place of refuge and the cost of such removal including temporary repairs and towage shall be allowed as general average. The provisions of Rule XI shall be applied to the prolongation of the voyage occasioned by such removal.

(b) The cost of handling on board or discharging cargo, fuel or stores whether at a port or place of loading, call or refuge, shall be admitted as general average, when the handling or discharge was necessary for the common safety or to enable damage to the ship caused by sacrifice or accident[17] to be repaired, if the repairs were necessary for the safe prosecution of the voyage, except in cases where the damage to the ship is discovered at a port or place of loading or call without any accident or other extraordinary circumstances connected with such damage having taken place during the voyage.

(b) (i) The cost of handling on board or discharging cargo, fuel or stores whether at a port or place of loading, call or refuge, shall be allowed as general average, when the handling or discharge was necessary for the common safety or to enable damage to the ship caused by sacrifice or accident to be repaired, if the repairs were necessary for the safe prosecution of the voyage, except in cases where the damage to the ship is discovered at a port or place of loading or call without any accident or other extraordinary circumstances connected with such damage having taken place during the voyage.

The cost of handling on board or discharging cargo, fuel or stores shall not be admissible as general average when incurred solely for the purpose of restowage due to shifting during the voyage, unless such restowage is necessary for the common safety.

(ii) The cost of handling on board or discharging cargo, fuel or stores shall not be allowable as general average when incurred solely for the purpose of restowage due to shifting during the voyage, unless such restowage is necessary for the common safety.

---

[16] This paragraph does not in terms cover removal from a port of loading. Nor would it seem to cover removal from, say, a port at which the ship has made a normal call but where it is found necessary that repairs must be carried out which cannot be effected at such port: *cf.* Rule X1(b). Quaere, whether the last sentence does more than apply the first paragraph of Rule XI.

[17] Under the 1924 Rules it was held that the word "accident" must be construed in the light of the general principles laid down in the lettered Rules. Accordingly, an accident which occurred at the port of loading but did not endanger the property involved in the common adventure did not give the shipowner a claim to general average under those Rules: *The Makis* [1929] 1 K.B. 187. Now by reason of the incorporation of the "Rule of Interpretation" the result will be different, the word "accident" being given its full grammatical meaning.

York-Antwerp Rules, 1994	**York-Antwerp Rules, 2004**

(c) Whenever the cost of handling or discharging cargo, fuel or stores is admissible as general average, the costs of storage, including insurance if reasonably incurred, reloading and stowing of such cargo, fuel or stores shall likewise be admitted as general average. *The provisions of Rule XI shall be applied to the extra period of detention occasioned by such reloading or restowing.*

But when the ship is condemned or does not proceed on her original voyage, storage expenses shall be admitted as general average only up to the date of the ship's condemnation or of the abandonment of the voyage or up to the date of completion of discharge of cargo if the condemnation or abandonment takes place before that date.

(c) Whenever the cost of handling or discharging cargo, fuel or stores is admissible as general average, the costs of storage, including insurance if reasonably incurred, reloading and stowing of such cargo, fuel or stores shall likewise be allowed as general average. The provisions of Rule XI shall be applied to the extra period of detention occasioned by such reloading or restowing.

But when the ship is condemned or does not proceed on her original voyage, storage expenses shall be allowed as general average only up to the date of the ship's condemnation or of the abandonment of the voyage or up to the date of completion of discharge of cargo if the condemnation or abandonment takes place before that date.

A2.21 RULE XI. WAGES AND MAINTENANCE OF CREW AND OTHER EXPENSES BEARING UP FOR AND IN A PORT OF REFUGE, ETC.

(a) Wages and maintenance of master, officers and crew reasonably incurred and fuel and stores consumed during the prolongation of the voyage occasioned by a ship entering a port or place of refuge or returning to her port or place of loading shall be admitted as general average when the expenses of entering such port or place are allowable in general average in accordance with Rule X(a).

RULE XI. WAGES AND MAINTENANCE OF CREW AND OTHER EXPENSES BEARING UP FOR AND IN A PORT OF REFUGE, ETC.

(a) Wages and maintenance of master, officers and crew reasonably incurred and fuel and stores consumed during the prolongation of the voyage occasioned by a ship entering a port or place of refuge or returning to her port or place of loading shall be allowed as general average when the expenses of entering such port or place are allowable in general average in accordance with Rule X(a).

York-Antwerp Rules, 1994	**York-Antwerp Rules, 2004**

(b) When a ship shall have entered or been detained in any port or place in consequence of accident, sacrifice or other extraordinary circumstances which render that necessary for the common safety, or to enable damage to the ship caused by sacrifice or accident to be repaired, if the repairs were necessary for the safe prosecution of the voyage, [18] the wages and maintenance of the master, officers and crew reasonably incurred during the extra period of detention in such port or place until the ship shall or should have been made ready to proceed upon her voyage, shall be admitted in general average.[19]

Fuel and stores consumed during the extra period of detention shall be admitted as general average, except such fuel and stores as are consumed in effecting repairs not allowable in general average.[20]

Port charges incurred during the extra period of detention shall likewise be admitted as general average except such charges as are incurred solely by reason of repairs not allowable in general average.[21]

(b) For the purpose of this and the other Rules wages shall include all payments made to or for the benefit of the master, officers and crew, whether such payments be imposed by law upon the shipowners or be made under the terms of articles of employment.

(c) (i) When a ship shall have entered or been detained in any port or place in consequence of accident, sacrifice or other extraordinary circumstances which render that necessary for the common safety, or to enable damage to the ship caused by sacrifice or accident to be repaired, if the repairs were necessary for the safe prosecution of the voyage, fuel and stores consumed during the extra period of detention in such port or place until the ship shall or should have been made ready to proceed upon her voyage, shall be allowed as general average, except such fuel and stores as are consumed in effecting repairs not allowable in general average.

---

[18] This Rule is only intended to apply to the detention of a ship during the course of the voyage—so expenses arising out of delay which occurred when the ship was ordered to leave berth during the course of discharging are not recoverable—*Trade Green Shipping Inc v Securitas Bremer Allgemeine Versicherungs AG (The Trade Green)* [2000] 2 Lloyd's Rep. 451.

[19] Where, the ship being on monthly hire under a charter by which the owners pay the wages of the master and crew, the owners recover a general average contribution for such wages in the port of refuge, the charterers are not entitled to recover back any of the monthly hire they have paid: *Howden v Nutfield S.S. Co.* (1898) 3 Com.Cas. 56.

[20] This paragraph adopts the British practice whereby fuel and stores consumed in effecting repairs are not allowed in general average.

[21] This again adopts the British practice.

York-Antwerp Rules, 1994 | **York-Antwerp Rules, 2004**

Provided that when damage to the ship is discovered at a port or place of loading or call without any accident or other extraordinary circumstance connected with such damage having taken place during the voyage, then the wages and maintenance of master, officers and crew and fuel and stores consumed *and port charges incurred* during the extra detention for repairs to damages so discovered shall not be admissible as general average, even if the repairs are necessary for the safe prosecution of the voyage.

(ii) Port charges incurred during the extra period of detention shall likewise be allowed as general average except such charges as are incurred solely by reason of repairs not allowable in general average.

(iii) Provided that when damage to the ship is discovered at a port or place of loading or call without any accident or other extraordinary circumstance connected with such damage having taken place during the voyage, then fuel and stores consumed and port charges incurred during the extra detention for repairs to damages so discovered shall not be allowable as general average, even if the repairs are necessary for the safe prosecution of the voyage.

When the ship is condemned or does not proceed on her original voyage, *the* wages and maintenance of the master, officers and crew and fuel and stores consumed *and port charges* shall be admitted as general average only up to the date of the ship's condemnation or of the abandonment of the voyage or up to the date of completion of discharge of cargo if the condemnation or abandonment takes place before that date.

(iv) When the ship is condemned or does not proceed on her original voyage, fuel and stores consumed and port charges shall be allowed as general average only up to the date of the ship's condemnation or of the abandonment of the voyage or up to the date of completion of discharge of cargo if the condemnation or abandonment takes place before that date.

(c) For the purpose of this and the other Rules wages shall include all payments made to or for the benefit of the master, officers and crew, whether such payments be imposed by law upon the shipowners or be made under the terms of articles of employment.[22]

---

[22] Overtime paid to the crew during the period when wages paid are admissible is allowed in full.

York-Antwerp Rules, 1994 | **York-Antwerp Rules, 2004**

(d) *The cost of measures undertaken to prevent or minimise damage to the environment shall be allowed in general average when incurred in any or all of the following circumstances:*

(i) *as part of an operation performed for the common safety which, had it been undertaken by a party outside the common maritime adventure, would have entitled such party to a salvage reward;*

(ii) *as a condition of entry into or departure from any port or place in the circumstances prescribed in Rule X(a);*

(iii) *as a condition of remaining at any port or place in the circumstances prescribed in Rule X(a), provided that when there is an actual escape or release of pollutant substances the cost of any additional measures required on that account to prevent or minimise pollution or environmental damage shall not be allowed as general average;*

(iv) *necessarily in connection with the discharging, storing or reloading of cargo whenever the cost of those operations is admissible as general average.*

(d) The cost of measures undertaken to prevent or minimise damage to the environment shall be allowed in general average when incurred in any or all of the following circumstances:

(i) as part of an operation performed for the common safety which, had it been undertaken by a party outside the common maritime adventure, would have entitled such party to a salvage reward;

(ii) as a condition of entry into or departure from any port or place in the circumstances prescribed in Rule X(a);

(iii) as a condition of remaining at any port or place in the circumstances prescribed in Rule XI(c), provided that when there is an actual escape or release of pollutant substances the cost of any additional measures required on that account to prevent or minimise pollution or environmental damage shall not be allowed as general average;

(iv) necessarily in connection with the discharging, storing or reloading of cargo whenever the cost of those operations is allowable as general average.

RULE XII. DAMAGE TO CARGO IN DISCHARGING, ETC.

Damage to or loss of cargo, fuel or stores *sustained in consequence* of *their* handling, discharging, storing, reloading and stowing shall be made good as general average, when and only when the cost of those measures respectively is admitted as general average.

RULE XII. DAMAGE TO CARGO IN DISCHARGING, ETC.

Damage to or loss of cargo, fuel or stores caused in the act of handling, discharging, storing, reloading and stowing shall be allowed as general average, when and only when the cost of those measures respectively is allowed as general average.

A2.22

York-Antwerp Rules, 1994

York-Antwerp Rules, 2004

A2.23 RULE XIII. DEDUCTIONS FROM COST OF REPAIRS[23]

Repairs to be allowed in general average shall not be subject to deductions in respect of "new for old" where old material or parts are replaced by new unless the ship is over fifteen years old in which case there shall be a deduction of one third. The deductions shall be regulated by the age of the ship from the 31st December of the year of completion of construction to the date of the general average act, except for insulation, life and similar boats, communications and navigational apparatus and equipment, machinery and boilers for which the deductions shall be regulated by the age of the particular parts to which they apply.

The deductions shall be made only from the cost of the new material or parts when finished and ready to be installed in the ship.

No deduction shall be made in respect of provisions, stores, anchors and chain cables.

Drydock and slipway dues and costs of shifting the ship shall be allowed in full.

The costs of cleaning, painting or coating of bottom shall not be allowed in general average unless the bottom has painted or coated within the twelve months preceding the date of the general average act in which case one half of such costs shall be allowed.

RULE XIII. DEDUCTIONS FROM COST OF REPAIRS

(a) Repairs to be allowed in general average shall not be subject to deductions in respect of "new for old" where old material or parts are replaced by new unless the ship is over fifteen years old in which case there shall be a deduction of one third. The deductions shall be regulated by the age of the ship from the 31st December of the year of completion of construction to the date of the general average act, except for insulation, life and similar boats, communications and navigational apparatus and equipment, machinery and boilers for which the deductions shall be regulated by the age of the particular parts to which they apply.

(b) The deductions shall be made only from the cost of the new material or parts when finished and ready to be installed in the ship.

No deduction shall be made in respect of provisions, stores, anchors and chain cables.

Drydock and slipway dues and costs of shifting the ship shall be allowed in full.

(c) The costs of cleaning, painting or coating of bottom shall not be allowed in general average unless the bottom has been painted or coated within the twelve months preceding the date of the general average act in which case one half of such costs shall be allowed.

---

[23] This Rule was radically altered in 1974 so that now deductions in respect of "new for old" only apply to ships over 15 years old.

York-Antwerp Rules, 1994

York-Antwerp Rules, 2004

RULE XIV. TEMPORARY RE-PAIRS[24]

RULE XIV. TEMPORARY RE-PAIRS

A2.24

Where temporary repairs are effected to a ship at a port of loading, call or refuge, for the common safety, or of damage caused by general average sacrifice, the cost of such repairs shall be admitted as general average.

(a) Where temporary repairs are effected to a ship at a port of loading, call or refuge, for the common safety, or of damage caused by general average sacrifice, the cost of such repairs shall be allowed as general average.

Where temporary repairs of accidental damage are effected in order to enable the adventure to be completed, the cost of such repairs shall be admitted as general average without regard to the saving, if any, to other interests,[25] but only up to the saving in expense which would have been incurred and allowed in general average if such repairs had not been effected there.

(b) Where temporary repairs of accidental damage are effected in order to enable the adventure to be completed, the cost of such repairs shall be allowed as general average without regard to the saving, if any, to other interests, but only up to the saving in expense which would have been incurred and allowed in general average if such repairs had not been effected there. Provided that for the purposes of this paragraph only, the cost of temporary repairs falling for consideration shall be limited to the extent that the cost of temporary repairs effected at the port of loading, call or refuge, together with either the cost of permanent repairs eventually effected or, if unrepaired at the time of the adjustment, the reasonable depreciation in the value of the vessel at the completion of the voyage exceeds the cost of permanent repairs had they been effected at the port of loading, call or refuge.

No deductions "new for old" shall be made from the cost of temporary repairs allowable as general average.

(c) No deductions "new for old" shall be made from the cost of temporary repairs allowable as general average.

---

[24] *Marida Ltd v Oswal Steel (The Bijela)* [1994] 2 Lloyd's Rep. 1 (HL).
[25] This Rule is a particular illustration of the general principle as to substituted expenses stated in Rule F, and the addition of the words "without regard to the saving, if any, to other interests", brings the Rule into line with Rule F as similarly amended.

A2.25   RULE XV. LOSS OF FREIGHT

Loss of freight arising from damage to or loss of cargo shall be made good as general average, either when caused by a general average act, or when the damage to or loss of cargo is so made good.

Deduction shall be made from the amount of gross freight lost, of the charges which the owner thereof would have incurred to earn such freight, but has, in consequence of the sacrifice, not incurred.

A2.26   RULE XVI. AMOUNT TO BE MADE GOOD FOR CARGO LOST OR DAMAGED BY SACRIFICE

The amount to be made good as general average for damage to or loss of cargo sacrificed shall be the loss which has been sustained thereby based on the value at the time of discharge, ascertained from the commercial invoice rendered to the receiver or if there is no such invoice from the shipped value. The value at the time of discharge shall include the cost of insurance and freight except insofar as such freight is at the risk of interests other than the cargo.

When cargo so damaged is sold and the amount of the damage has not been otherwise agreed, the loss to be made good in general average shall be the difference between the net proceeds of sale and the net sound value as computed in the first paragraph of this Rule.

A2.27   RULE XVII. CONTRIBUTORY VALUES

The contribution to a general average shall be made upon the actual net values of the property at the termina-

RULE XV. LOSS OF FREIGHT

Loss of freight arising from damage to or loss of cargo shall be allowed as general average, either when caused by a general average act, or when the damage to or loss of cargo is so allowed.

Deduction shall be made from the amount of gross freight lost, of the charges which the owner thereof would have incurred to earn such freight, but has, in consequence of the sacrifice, not incurred.

RULE XVI. AMOUNT TO BE MADE GOOD FOR CARGO LOST OR DAMAGED BY SACRIFICE

(a) The amount to be allowed as general average for damage to or loss of cargo sacrificed shall be the loss which has been sustained thereby, based on the value at the time of discharge, ascertained from the commercial invoice rendered to the receiver or if there is no such invoice from the shipped value. The value at the time of discharge shall include the cost of insurance and freight except insofar as such freight is at the risk of interests other than the cargo.

(b) When cargo so damaged is sold and the amount of the damage has not been otherwise agreed, the loss to be allowed in general average shall be the difference between the net proceeds of sale and the net sound value as computed in the first paragraph of this Rule.

RULE XVII. CONTRIBUTORY VALUES

(a) (i) The contribution to a general average shall be made upon the actual net values of the property at

York-Antwerp Rules, 1994 | **York-Antwerp Rules, 2004**

tion of the adventure[26] except that the value of cargo shall be the value at the time of discharge, ascertained from the commercial invoice rendered to the receiver or if there is no such invoice from the shipped value. The value of the cargo shall include the cost of insurance and freight unless and insofar as such freight is at the risk of interests other than the cargo, deducting therefrom any loss or damage suffered by the cargo prior to or at the time of discharge. The value of the ship shall be assessed without taking into account the beneficial or detrimental effect of any demise or time charterparty to which the ship may be committed.

the termination of the adventure except that the value of cargo shall be the value at the time of discharge ascertained from the commercial invoice rendered to the receiver or if there is no such invoice from the shipped value.

(ii) The value of the cargo shall include the cost of insurance and freight unless and insofar as such freight is at the risk of interests other than the cargo, deducting therefrom any loss or damage suffered by the cargo prior to or at the time of discharge.

(iii) The value of the ship shall be assessed without taking into account the beneficial or detrimental effect of any demise or time charterparty to which the ship may be committed.

To these values shall be added the amount made good as general average for property sacrificed, if not already included, deduction being made from the freight and passage money at risk of such charges and crew's wages as would not have been incurred in earning the freight had the ship and cargo been totally lost at the date of the general average act and have not been allowed as general average; deduction being also made from the value of the property of all extra charges incurred in respect thereof subsequently to the general average act, except such charges as are allowed in general average *or fall upon the ship by virtue of an award for special compensation under Art. 14 of the International Convention on Salvage, 1989 or under any other provision similar in substance.*

(b) To these values shall be added the amount allowed as general average for property sacrificed, if not already included, deduction being made from the freight and passage money at risk of such charges and crew's wages as would not have been incurred in earning the freight had the ship and cargo been totally lost at the date of the general average act and have not been allowed as general average; deduction being also made from the value of the property of all extra charges incurred in respect thereof subsequently to the general average act, except such charges as are allowed in general average or fall upon the ship by virtue of an award for special compensation under Art.14 of the International Convention on Salvage, 1989 or under any other provision similar in substance.

---

[26] If a shipowner incurs expenditure at a port of refuge which is prima facie the subject of general average contributions under Rules X and XI, above, he can only claim contributions under this Rule XVII. If therefore, the adventure terminates in the loss of both ship and cargo before the completion of the voyage, he has no claim for contribution from the owners of the cargo, which being lost has no value at the termination of the adventure: *Chellew v Royal Commission* [1922] 1 K.B. 12.

In the circumstances envisaged in the third paragraph of Rule G, the cargo and other property shall contribute on the basis of its value upon delivery at original destination unless sold or otherwise disposed of short of that destination, and the ship shall contribute upon its actual net value at the time of completion of discharge of cargo.

(c) In the circumstances envisaged in the third paragraph of Rule G, the cargo and other property shall contribute on the basis of its value upon delivery at original destination unless sold or otherwise disposed of short of that destination, and the ship shall contribute upon its actual net value at the time of completion of discharge of cargo.

Where cargo is sold short of destination, however, it shall contribute upon the actual net proceeds of sale, with the addition of any amount made good as general average.

(d) Where cargo is sold short of destination, however, it shall contribute upon the actual net proceeds of sale, with the addition of any amount allowed as general average.

Mails, passengers' luggage, personal effects and accompanied private motor vehicles shall not contribute in general average.

(e) Mails, passengers' luggage, personal effects and accompanied private motor vehicles shall not contribute to general average.

A2.28 RULE XVIII. DAMAGE TO SHIP

RULE XVIII. DAMAGE TO SHIP

The amount to be allowed as general average for damage or loss to the ship, her machinery and/or gear caused by a general average act shall be as follows:

The amount to be allowed as general average for damage or loss to the ship, her machinery and/or gear caused by a general average act shall be as follows:

(a) When repaired or replaced,

(a) When repaired or replaced,

The actual reasonable cost of repairing or replacing such damage or loss, subject to deductions in accordance with Rule XIII;

The actual reasonable cost of repairing or replacing such damage or loss, subject to deductions in accordance with Rule XIII;

(b) When not repaired or replaced,

(b) When not repaired or replaced,

The reasonable depreciation arising from such damage or loss, but not exceeding the estimated cost of repairs. But where the ship is an actual total loss or when the cost of repairs of the damage would exceed the value of the ship when repaired, the amount to be allowed as general average shall be the difference between the estimated sound value of the ship after deducting therefrom the estimated cost of repair

The reasonable depreciation arising from such damage or loss, but not exceeding the estimated cost of repairs. But where the ship is an actual total loss or when the cost of repairs of the damage would exceed the value of the ship when repaired, the amount to be allowed as general average shall be the difference between the estimated sound value of the ship after deducting therefrom

York-Antwerp Rules, 1994	York-Antwerp Rules, 2004

ing damage which is not general average and the value of the ship in her damaged state which may be measured by the net proceeds of sale, if any.

the estimated cost of repairing damage which is not general average and the value of the ship in her damaged state which may be measured by the net proceeds of sale, if any.

RULE XIX. UNDECLARED OR WRONGFULLY DECLARED CARGO

RULE XIX. UNDECLARED OR WRONGFULLY DECLARED CARGO　　　　A2.29

Damage or loss caused to goods loaded without the knowledge of the shipowner or his agent or to goods wilfully misdescribed at time of shipment shall not be allowed as general average, but such goods shall remain liable to contribute, if saved.

(a) Damage or loss caused to goods loaded without the knowledge of the shipowner or his agent or to goods wilfully misdescribed at time of shipment shall not be allowed as general average, but such goods shall remain liable to contribute, if saved.

Damage or loss caused to goods which have been wrongfully declared on shipment at a value which is lower than their real value shall be contributed for at the declared value, but such goods shall contribute upon their actual value.

(b) Damage or loss caused to goods which have been wrongfully declared on shipment at a value which is lower than their real value shall be contributed for at the declared value, but such goods shall contribute upon their actual value.

RULE XX. PROVISION OF FUNDS

RULE XX. PROVISION OF FUNDS　　　　A2.30

A commission of 2 per cent on general average disbursements, other than the wages and maintenance of master, officers and crew and fuel and stores not replaced during the voyage, shall be allowed in general average.

(a) The capital loss sustained by the owners of goods sold for the purpose of raising funds to defray general average disbursements shall be allowed in general average.

The capital loss sustained by the owners of goods sold for the purpose of raising funds to defray general average disbursements shall be allowed in general average.

The cost of insuring general average disbursements shall also be admitted in general average.

(b) The cost of insuring money advanced to pay for general average disbursements shall also be allowed in general average.

York-Antwerp Rules, 1994	York-Antwerp Rules, 2004

A2.31 RULE XXI. INTEREST ON LOSSES MADE GOOD IN GENERAL AVERAGE[27]

Interest shall be allowed on expenditure, sacrifices and allowances *in* general average at the rate of 7 per cent per annum, until *three months after* the date *of issue* of the general average *adjustment,*[28] due allowance being made for any *payment on account by* the contributory interests or from the general average deposit fund.

RULE XXI. INTEREST ON LOSSES ALLOWED IN GENERAL AVERAGE

(a) Interest shall be allowed on expenditure, sacrifices and allowances in general average until three months after the date of issue of the general average adjustment, due allowance being made for any payment on account by the contributory interests or from the general average deposit fund.

(b) Each year the Assembly of the Comité Maritime International shall decide the rate of interest which shall apply. This rate shall be used for calculating interest accruing during the following calendar year.

A2.32 RULE XXII. TREATMENT OF CASH DEPOSITS[29]

Where cash deposits have been collected in respect of cargo's liability for general average, salvage or special charges such deposits shall be paid without any delay into a special account in the joint names of a representative nominated on behalf of the shipowner and a representative nominated on behalf of the depositors in a bank to be approved by both. The sum so deposited together with accrued

RULE XXII. TREATMENT OF CASH DEPOSITS

Where cash deposits have been collected in respect of cargo's liability for general average, salvage or special charges, such deposits shall be paid without any delay into a special account in the joint names of a representative nominated on behalf of the shipowner and a representative nominated on behalf of the depositors in a bank to be approved by both. The sum so deposited to-

---

[27] This Rule only governs claims for interest up to 3 months from the date of issue of the average adjustment. Thereafter interest is governed by the relevant municipal law: *Corfu Navigation Co & Bain Clarkson Ltd v Mobil Shipping Co Ltd* [1991] 2 Lloyd's Rep. 515.

[28] Despite the fact that this Rule and Rules generally contemplate that an average statement will be produced, the accrual of a cause of action for contribution to a general average sacrifice or expenditure is not postponed until the statement has been prepared so as to permit the running of time under the Limitation Act 1980: *Chandris v Argo Insurance* [1963] 2 Lloyd's Rep. 65; approved in *Castle Insurance Co Ltd v Hong Kong Islands Shipping Co Ltd* [1983] 2 Lloyd's Rep. 376; [1984] A.C. 226 (PC), but under the usual forms of Lloyd's Average bonds, time does not run until after the statement has been prepared: *ibid*. As to the ineffectiveness of the Centrocon Arbitration Clause to bar a claim for general average contributions, see *Aaby's Rederi v Union of India* [1974] 2 Lloyd's Rep. 57 (HL).

[29] It is common for cargo interests to provide a General Average Bond, often secured by way of a General Average Guarantee provided by their insurers. Note that the fact that a General Average Bond may include a choice of law clause governing the rights and liabilities arising under the bond does not, or at least not necessarily, affect the question of which system of law governs the actual underlying claim in General Average: *Galaxy Special Maritime Enterprise v Prima Ceylon Ltd (The Olympic Galaxy)* [2006] EWCA Civ 528; [2006] 2 Lloyd's Rep. 27. As to the position of insurers issuing a General Average Guarantee see *Mora Shipping v Axa Corporate Solutions Assurance SA* [2005] EWCA Civ 1069; [2005] 2 Lloyd's Rep. 769.

interest, if any, shall be held as security for payment to the parties entitled thereto of the general average, salvage or special charges payable by cargo in respect of which the deposits have been collected. Payments on account or refunds of deposits may be made if certified to in writing by the average adjuster. Such deposits and payments or refunds shall be without prejudice to the ultimate liability of the parties.

gether with accrued interest, if any, shall be held as security for payment to the parties entitled thereto of the general average, salvage or special charges payable by cargo in respect of which the deposits have been collected. Payments on account or refunds of deposits may be made if certified to in writing by the average adjuster. Such deposits and payments or refunds shall be without prejudice to the ultimate liability of the parties.

RULE XXIII. TIME BAR FOR CONTRIBUTIONS TO GENERAL AVERAGE

(a) Subject always to any mandatory rule on time limitation contained in any applicable law:

(i) Any rights to general average contribution, including any rights to claim under general average bonds and guarantees, shall be extinguished unless an action is brought by the party claiming such contribution within a period of one year after the date upon which the general average adjustment was issued. However, in no case shall such an action be brought after six years from the date of the termination of the common maritime adventure.

(ii) These periods may be extended if the parties so agree after the termination of the common maritime adventure.

(b) This Rule shall not apply as between the parties to the general average and their respective insurers.

APPENDIX III

THE CARRIAGE OF GOODS BY SEA ACT 1924

Introductory Notes

A3.1 The Carriage of Goods by Sea Act 1924 was repealed by the Carriage of Goods by Sea Act 1971, which came into force on June 23, 1977, and gave effect in the United Kingdom to the 1968 Brussels Protocol amending the Hague Rules. The text of the 1971 Act is set out, with Introductory Notes and a commentary, in chapter 20. The text of the repealed 1924 Act is set out in this Appendix, so as to enable a comparison to be made between the Hague Rules (as enacted by the 1924 Act) and the Hague-Visby Rules (as enacted by the 1971 Act). Reference to the 1924 Act may also be necessary for the understanding of many reported cases decided under the old Rules. In addition the Rules in their unamended form are frequently incorporated into charterparties contractually.

CARRIAGE OF GOODS BY SEA ACT 1924 (14 & 15 Geo. 5, c. 22)

An Act to amend the law with respect to the carriage of goods by sea.

1st August, 1924

A3.2 WHEREAS at the International Conference on Maritime Law held at Brussels in October 1922, the delegates at the Conference, including the delegates representing His Majesty, agreed unanimously to recommend their respective Governments to adopt as the basis of a convention a draft convention for the unification of certain rules relating to bills of lading:

And whereas at a meeting held at Brussels in October 1923, the rules contained in the said draft convention were amended by the Committee appointed by the said Conference:

And whereas it is Expedient that the said rules as so amended and as set out with modifications in the Schedule to this Act (in this Act referred to as "the Rules") should, subject to the provisions of this Act, be given the force of law with a view to establishing the responsibilities, liabilities, rights and immunities attaching to carriers under bills of lading:

Be it therefore enacted by the King's most Excellent Majesty, by and with the advice and consent of the Lords Spiritual and Temporal, and Commons, in this present Parliament assembled, and by the authority of the same, as follows:

A3.3 1. Subject to the provisions of this Act, the Rules shall have effect in relation to and in connection with the carriage of goods by sea in ships carrying goods from any port in Great Britain or Northern Ireland to any other port whether in or outside Great Britain or Northern Ireland.

A3.4 2. There shall not be implied in any contract for the carriage of goods by sea to which the Rules apply any absolute undertaking by the carrier of the goods to provide a seaworthy ship.

A3.5 3. Every bill of lading, or similar document of title, issued in Great Britain or Northern Ireland which contains or is evidence of any contract to which the Rules apply shall contain an express statement that it is to have effect subject to the provisions of the said Rules as applied by this Act.

4. Article VI of the Rules shall, in relation to the carriage of goods by sea in ships   **A3.6**
carrying goods from any part in Great Britain or Northern Ireland to any other port in
Great Britain or Northern Ireland or to a port in the Irish Free State, have effect as though
the said Article referred to goods of any class instead of to particular goods and as though
the proviso to the second paragraph of the said Article were omitted.

5. Where under the custom of any trade the weight of any bulk cargo inserted in the bill   **A3.7**
of lading is a weight ascertained or accepted by a third party other than the carrier or the
shipper and the fact that the weight is so ascertained or accepted is stated in the bill of
lading, then, notwithstanding anything in the Rules, the bill of lading shall not be deemed
to be prima facie evidence against the carrier of the receipt of goods of the weight so
inserted in the bill of lading, and the accuracy thereof at the time of shipment shall not be
deemed to have been guaranteed by the shipper.

6.—(1) This Act may be cited as the Carriage of Goods by Sea Act 1924.   **A3.8**

(2) Nothing in this Act shall affect the operation of sections four hundred and forty-six
to four hundred and fifty, both inclusive, five hundred and two, and five hundred and three
of the Merchant Shipping Act 1894, as amended by any subsequent enactment, or the
operation of any other enactment for the time being in force limiting the liability of the
owners of seagoing vessels.

(3) The Rules shall not be virtue of this Act apply to any contract for the carriage of
goods by sea made before such day, not being earlier than the thirtieth day of June,
nineteen hundred and twenty-four, as His Majesty may by Order in Council direct, nor to
any bill of lading, or similar document of title issued, whether before or after such day as
aforesaid, in pursuance of any such contract as aforesaid.

SCHEDULE

[NOTE: words underlined have been omitted in the 1971 rules. Words in italic have been
added by the 1971 rules.]

Rules Relating to Bills of Lading

ARTICLE I   **A3.9**

Definitions

In these Rules the following expressions have the meanings hereby assigned to them
respectively, that is to say [*words are employed, with the meaning set out below:—*]

(*a*) "Carrier" includes the owner or the charterer who enters into a contract of carriage
with a shipper:

(*b*) "Contract of carriage" applies only to contracts of carriage covered by a bill of
lading or any similar document of title, in so far as such document relates to the carriage
of goods by sea, including any bills of lading or any similar document as aforesaid issued
under or pursuant to a charterparty from the moment at which such bill of lading or similar
document of title regulates the relations between a carrier and a holder of the same:

(*c*) "Goods" includes goods, wares, merchandises, and articles of every kind whatsoever, except live animals and cargo which by the contract of carriage is stated as being
carried on deck and is so carried:

(*d*) "Ship" means any vessel used for the carriage of goods by sea:

(*e*) "Carriage of goods" covers the period from the time when the goods are loaded on
to the time when they are discharged from the ship.

A3.10 Article II

Risks

Subject to the provisions of Article VI, under every contract of carriage of goods by sea the carrier, in relation to the loading, handling, stowage, carriage, custody, care, and discharge of such goods, shall be subject to the responsibilities and liabilities, and entitled to the rights and immunities hereinafter set forth.

A3.11 Article III

Responsibilities and Liabilities

1. The carrier shall be bound, before and at the beginning of the voyage, to exercise due diligence to—

(*a*) Make the ship seaworthy:
(*b*) Properly man, equip, and supply the ship:
(*c*) Make the holds, refrigerating and cool chambers, and all other parts of the ship in which goods are carried, fit and safe for their reception, carriage and preservation.

2. Subject to the provisions of Article IV, the carrier shall properly and carefully load, handle, stow, carry, keep, care for and discharge the goods carried.

3. After receiving the goods into his charge, the carrier, or the master or agent of the carrier, shall, on demand of the shipper, issue to the shipper a bill of lading showing among other things—

(*a*) The leading marks necessary for identification of the goods as the same are furnished in writing by the shipper before the loading of such goods starts, provided such marks are stamped or otherwise shown clearly upon the goods if uncovered, or on the cases or coverings in which such goods are contained, in such a manner as should ordinarily remain legible until the end of the voyage;
(*b*) Either the number of packages or pieces, or the quantity, or weight, as the case may be, as furnished in writing by the shipper;
(*c*) The apparent order and condition of the goods:

Provided that no carrier, master or agent of the carrier, shall be bound to state or show in the bill of lading any marks, number, quantity, or weight which he has reasonable grounds for suspecting not accurately to represent the goods actually received, or which he has had no reasonable means of checking.

4. Such a bill of lading shall be prima facie evidence of the receipt by the carrier of the goods as therein described in accordance with paragraph 3(*a*), (*b*) and (*c*). *However, proof to the contrary shall not be admissible when the bill of lading has been transferred to a third party acting in good faith.*

5. The shipper shall be deemed to have guaranteed to the carrier the accuracy at the time of shipment of the marks, number, quantity, and weight, as furnished by him, and the shipper shall indemnify the carrier against all loss, damages, and expenses arising or resulting from inaccuracies in such particulars. The right of the carrier to such indemnity shall in no way limit his responsibility and liability under the contract of carriage to any person other than the shipper.

6. Unless notice of loss or damage and the general nature of such loss or damage be given in writing, to the carrier or his agent at the port of discharge before or at the time of the removal of the goods into the custody of the person entitled to the delivery thereof

under the contract of carriage, or, if the loss or damage be not apparent, within three days, such removal shall be prima facie evidence of the delivery by the carrier of the goods as described in the bill of lading.

The notice in writing need not be given if the state of the goods has at the time of their receipt been the subject of joint survey or inspection.

In any event the carrier and the ship shall be discharged from all liability in respect of loss or damage unless suit is brought within one year after delivery of the goods or the date when the goods should have been delivered.

Subject to paragraph 6bis the carrier and the ship shall in any event be discharged from all liability whatsoever in respect of the goods, unless suit is brought within one year of their delivery or of the date when they should have been delivered. This period may, however, be extended if the parties so agree after the cause of action has arisen.

In the case of any actual or apprehended loss or damage the carrier and the receiver shall give all reasonable facilities to each other for inspecting and tallying the goods.

7. After the goods are loaded the bill of lading to be issued by the carrier, master or agent of the carrier, to the shipper shall, if the shipper so demands, be a "shipped" bill of lading, provided that if the shipper shall have previously taken up any document of title to such goods, he shall surrender the same as against the issue of the "shipped" bill of lading, but at the option of the carrier such document of title may be noted at the port of shipment by the carrier, master, or agent with the name or names of the ship or ships upon which the goods have been shipped and the dates of shipment, and when so noted *if it shows the particulars mentioned in paragraph 3 of Article III,* [the same] shall for the purpose of this Article be deemed to constitute a "shipped" bill of lading.

8. Any clause, covenant or agreement in a contract of carriage relieving the carrier or the ship from liability for loss or damage to or in connection with goods arising from negligence, fault or failure in the duties and obligations provided in this Article or lessening such liability otherwise than as provided in these Rules, shall be null and void and of no effect.

A benefit of insurance or similar clause *in favour of the carrier or similar clause* shall be deemed to be a clause relieving the carrier from liability.

ARTICLE IV	**A3.12**

Rights and Immunities

1. Neither the carrier nor the ship shall be liable for loss or damage arising or resulting from unseaworthiness unless caused by want of due diligence on the part of the carrier to make the ship seaworthy, and to secure that the ship is properly manned, equipped and supplied, and to make the holds, refrigerating and cool chambers and all other parts of the ship in which goods are carried fit and safe for their reception, carriage and preservation in accordance with the provisions of paragraph 1 of Article III.

Whenever loss or damage has resulted from unseaworthiness, the burden of proving the exercise of due diligence shall be on the carrier or other person claiming exemption under this section *article*.

2. Neither the carrier nor the ship shall be responsible for loss or damage arising or resulting from—

(a) Act, neglect, or default of the master, mariner, pilot, or the servants of the carrier in the navigation or in the management of the ship:

(b) Fire, unless caused by the actual fault or privity of the carrier:

(c) Perils, dangers and accidents of the sea or other navigable waters:

(d) Act of God:

(*e*) Act of War:

(*f*) Act of public enemies:

(*g*) Arrest or restraint of princes, rulers or people, or seizure under legal process:

(*h*) Quarantine restrictions:

(*i*) Act or omission of the shipper or owner of the goods, his agent or representative:

(*j*) Strikes or lock-outs or stoppage or restraint of labour from whatever cause, whether partial or general;

(*k*) Riots and civil commotions:

(*l*) Saving or attempting to save life or property at sea:

(*m*) Wastage in bulk or weight or any other loss or damage arising from inherent defect, quality, or vice of the goods:

(*n*) Insufficiency of packing;

(*o*) Insufficiency of inadequacy of marks:

(*p*) Latent defects not discoverable by due diligence:

(*q*) Any other cause arising without the actual fault or privity of the carrier, or without the fault or neglect of the agents or servants of the carrier, but the burden of proof shall be on the person claiming the benefit of this exception to show that neither the actual fault or privity of the carrier nor the fault or neglect of the agents or servants of the carrier contributed to the loss or damage.

3. The shipper shall not be responsible for loss or damage sustained by the carrier or the ship arising or resulting from any cause without the act, fault or neglect of the shipper, his agents or his servants.

4. Any deviation in saving or attempting to save life or property at sea, or any reasonable deviation shall not be deemed to be an infringement or breach of these Rules of the contract of carriage, and the carrier shall not be liable for any loss or damage resulting therefrom.

5. *(a) Unless the nature and value of such goods have been declared by the shipper before shipment and inserted in the bill of lading,* neither the carrier nor the ship shall in any event be or become liable for any loss or damage to or in connection with *the* goods in an amount exceeding <u>£100</u>[1] *the equivalent of 10,000 francs* per package[2] or unit[3] *[or 30 francs per kilo of gross weight of the goods lost or damaged, whichever is the higher,]* or the equivalent of that sum in other currency, <u>unless the nature and value of such goods have been declared by the shipper before shipment and inserted in the bill of lading.</u>

(b) The total amount recoverable shall be calculated by reference to the value of such goods at the place and time at which the goods are discharged from the ship in accordance with the contract or should have been so discharged.

---

[1] The "Gold Clause" in Article IX qualifies this £100 figure with the result that the limitation amount is £100 gold value: *The Rosa S* [1989] 2 Lloyd's Rep. 574; *Brown Boreri (Australia) Pty Ltd v Baltic Shipping Co (The Nadezhida Krupskaya)* [1989] 1 Lloyd's Rep. 518 (Aus.); *The Thomaseverett* [1992] 2 S.L.R. 1068 (Sing.). Where the provisions of the Hague Rules apply as a result of contractual incorporation and not compulsory application by operation of law the parties are free to provide that the amount of £100 should be £100 Sterling, lawful money of the United Kingdom. This will exclude the operation of the Gold Clause and is not invalidated by Art.III r.8: *Dairy Containers Limited v Tasman Orient Line C.V. (The Tasman Discoverer)* [2004] UKPC 22; [2004] 2 Lloyd's Rep. 647.

[2] Where the shipowner provides a container to the shipper who packs it and the number of cartons which the container is said to contain is listed on the face of the bill of lading, it is each carton which is the package for the purpose of the Rule: *P.S. Chellaram & Co Ltd v China Ocean S.S. Co (The Chellaram)* [1989] 1 Lloyd's Rep. 413 (N.S.W.) and *Haverkate v Toronto Harbour Commissioners* 30 D.L.R. (4th) 125; 46 D.L.R. (4th) 767 (Can.). This is probably the case even where the number of packages is not in fact set out on the face of the bill, albeit the cargo owner would need to prove by extrinsic evidence how many packages were contained within the container: *The River Gurara* [1998] 1 Lloyd's Rep. 225.

[3] See the 18th edn at pp.441–444 and *The Aramis* [1987] 2 Lloyd's Rep. 59.

The value of the goods shall be fixed according to the commodity exchange price, or, if there be no such price, according to the current market price, or, if there be no commodity exchange price or current market price, by reference to the normal value of goods of the same kind and quality.

(c) Where a container, pallet or similar article of transport is used to consolidate goods, the number of packages or units enumerated in the bill of lading as packed in such article of transport shall be deemed the number of packages or units for the purpose of this paragraph as far as these packages or units are concerned. Except as aforesaid such article of transport shall be considered the package or unit.

(d) A franc means a unit consisting of 65.5 milligrammes of gold of millesimal fineness 900. The date of conversion of the sum awarded into national currencies shall be governed by the law of the Court seized of the case.

(e) Neither the carrier nor the ship shall be entitled to the benefit of the limitation of liability provided for in this paragraph if it is provided that the damage resulted from an act or omission of the carrier done with intent to cause damage, or recklessly and with knowledge that damage would probably result.

(f) The declaration mentioned in sub-paragraph (a) of this paragraph [This declaration], if embodied in the bill of lading shall be prima facie evidence, but shall not be binding or conclusive on the carrier.

(g) By agreement between the carrier, master or agent of the carrier and the shipper *other maximum amounts than those mentioned in sub-paragraph (a) of this paragraph may be fixed, provided that no maximum amount so fixed shall be less than the appropriate maximum mentioned in that sub-paragraph,* another maximum amount than that mentioned in this paragraph may be fixed, provided that such maximum shall not be less than the figure above named.

(h) Neither the carrier nor the ship shall be responsible in any event for loss or damage to or in connection with goods if the nature or value thereof has been knowingly misstated by the shipper in the bill of lading.

6. Goods of an inflammable, explosive or dangerous nature to the shipment whereof the carrier, master or agent of the carrier, has not consented, with knowledge of their nature and character, may at any time before discharge be landed at any place or destroyed or rendered innocuous by the carrier without compensation, and the shipper of such goods shall be liable for all damages and expenses directly or indirectly arising out of or resulting from such shipment.

If any such goods shipped with such knowledge and consent shall become a danger to the ship or cargo, they may in like manner be landed at any place or destroyed or rendered innocuous by the carrier without liability on the part of the carrier except to general average, if any.

ARTICLE IV BIS.

1. The defences and limits of liability provided for in these Rules shall apply in any action against the carrier in respect of loss or damage to goods covered by a contract of carriage whether the action be founded in contract or in tort.   **A3.13**

2. If such an action is brought against a servant or agent of the carrier (such servant or agent not being an independent contractor), such servant or agent shall be entitled to avail himself of the defences and limits of liability which the carrier is entitled to invoke under these Rules.

3. The aggregate of the amounts recoverable from the carrier, and such servants and agents, shall in no case exceed the limit provided for in these Rules.

4. Nevertheless, a servant or agent of the carrier shall not be entitled to avail himself of the provisions of this article, if it is proved that the damage resulted from an act or omission of the servant or agent done with intent to cause damage or recklessly and with knowledge that damage would probably result.

A3.14   ARTICLE V

Surrender of Rights and Immunities, and Increase of Responsibilities and Liabilities

A carrier shall be at liberty to surrender in whole or in part all or any of his rights and immunities or to increase any of his responsibilities and *obligations under these Rules* liabilities under the Rules contained in any of these Articles, provided such surrender or increase shall be embodied in the bill of lading issued to the shipper.

The provisions of these Rules shall not be applicable to charterparties, but if bills of lading are issued in the case of a ship under a charterparty they shall comply with the terms of these Rules. Nothing in these Rules shall be held to prevent the insertion in a bill of lading of any lawful provision regarding general average.

A3.15   ARTICLE VI

Special Conditions

Notwithstanding the provisions of the preceding Articles, a carrier, master or agent of the carrier, and a shipper shall in regard to any particular goods be at liberty to enter into any agreement in any terms as to the responsibility and liability of the carrier for such goods, and as to the rights and immunities of the carrier in respect of such goods, or his obligation as to seaworthiness, so far as this stipulation is not contrary to public policy, or the care or diligence of his servants or agents in regard to the loading, handling, stowage, carriage, custody, care, and discharge of the goods carried by sea, provided that in this case no bill of lading has been or shall be issued and that the terms agreed shall be embodied in a receipt which shall be a non-negotiable document and shall be marked as such.

Any agreement so entered into shall have full legal effect:

Provided that this Article shall not apply to ordinary commercial shipments made in the ordinary course of trade, but only to other shipments where the character or condition of the property to be carried or the circumstances, terms and conditions under which the carriage is to be performed, are such as reasonably to justify a special agreement.

A3.16   ARTICLE VII

Limitations on the Application of the Rules

Nothing herein contained shall prevent a carrier or a shipper from entering into any agreement, stipulation, condition, reservation or exemption as to the responsibility and liability of the carrier or the ship for the loss or damage to or in connection with the custody and care and handling of goods prior to the loading on and subsequent to the discharge from the ship on which the goods are carried by sea.

A3.17   ARTICLE VIII

Limitation of Liability

The provisions of these Rules shall not affect the rights and obligations of the carrier under any statute for the time being in force relating to the limitation of the liability of owners of sea-going vessels.

ARTICLE IX   **A3.18**

These Rules shall not affect the provisions of any international Convention or national law governing liability for nuclear damage. The monetary units mentioned in these Rules are to taken to be gold value.

ARTICLE IX   **A3.19**

These Rules shall not affect the provisions of any international Convention or national law governing liability for nuclear damage.

ARTICLE X   **A3.20**

The provisions of these Rules shall apply to every bill of lading relating to the carriage of goods between ports in two different States if:

    (a) the bill of lading is issued in a contracting State, or
    (b) the carriage is from a port in a contracting State, or
    (c) the contract contained in or evidenced by the bill of lading provides that these Rules or legislation of any State giving effect to them are to govern the contract,

whatever may be the nationality of the ship, the carrier, the shipper, the consignee, or any other interested person.

APPENDIX IV

INTER-CLUB NEW YORK PRODUCE EXCHANGE AGREEMENT[1]

A4.1   This Agreement is made on the 1st September 1996 between the P&I Clubs being members of The International Group of P&I Associations listed below (hereafter referred to as "the Clubs").

This Agreement replaced the Inter Club Agreement 1984 in respect of all charterparties specified in clause (1) thereof and shall continue in force until varied or terminated. Any variation to be effective must be approved in writing by all the Clubs but it is open to any Club to withdraw from the Agreement on giving to all the other Clubs not less than three months' written notice thereof, such withdrawal to take effect at the expiration of that period. After the expiry of such notice the Agreement shall nevertheless continue as between all the Clubs, other than the Club giving such notice who shall remain bound by and be entitled to the benefit of this Agreement in respect of all Cargo Claims arising out of charterparties commenced prior to the expiration of such notice.

The Clubs will recommend their Members without qualification that their Members adopt this Agreement for the purpose of apportioning liability for claims in respect of cargo which arise under, out of or in connection with all charterparties on the New York Produce Exchange Form 1946 or 1993 or Asbatime Form 1981 (or any subsequent amendment of such Forms), whether or not this Agreement has been incorporated into such charterparties.

A4.2   **Scope of application**

(1) This Agreement applies to any charterparty which is entered into after the date hereof on the New York Produce Exchange Form 1946 or 1993 or Asbatime Form 1981 (or any subsequent amendment of such Forms).

(2) The terms of this Agreement shall apply notwithstanding anything to the contrary in any other provision of the charterparty; in particular the provisions of clause (6) (time bar) shall apply not withstanding any provision of the charterparty or rule of law to the contrary.

(3) For the purposes of this Agreement, Cargo Claim(s) mean claims for loss, damage, shortage (including slackage, ullage or pilferage), overcarriage of or delay to cargo including custom dues or fines in respect of such loss, damage, shortage, overcarriage or delay and include:

    (a) any legal costs claimed by the original person making any such claim;
    (b) any interest claimed by the original person making any such claim;
    (c) all legal, Club correspondents' and experts' costs reasonably incurred in the defence of or in the settlement of the claim made by the original person,

but shall not include any costs of whatsoever nature incurred in making a claim under this Agreement or in seeking an indemnity under the charterparty.

(4) Apportionment under this Agreement shall only be applied to Cargo Claims where:

---

[1] See Note at the end of Art.177, above.

(a) the claim was made under a contract of carriage, whatever its form,
   (i) which was authorised under the charterparty;
   or
   (ii) which would have been authorised under the charterparty but for the inclusion in that contract of carriage of Through Transport or Combined Transport provisions,
   provided that
   (iii) in the case of contracts of carriage containing Through Transport or Combined Transport provisions (whether falling within (i) or (ii) above) the loss, damage, shortage, overcarriage or delay occurred after commencement of the loading of the cargo onto the chartered vessel and prior to completion of its discharge from that vessel (the burden of proof being on the Charterer to establish that the loss, damage, shortage, overcarriage or delay did or did not so occur); and
   (iv) the contract of carriage (or that part of the transit that comprised carriage on the chartered vessel) incorporated terms no less favourable to the carrier than the Hague or Hague Visby Rules, or, when compulsorily applicable by operation of law to the contract of carriage, the Hamburg Rules or any national law giving effect thereto;
   and
(b) the cargo responsibility clauses in the charterparty have not been materially amended. A material amendment is one which makes the liability, as between Owners and Charterers, for Cargo Claims clear. In particular, it is agreed solely for the purposes of this Agreement:
   (i) that the addition of the words "and responsibility" in clause 8 of the New York Produce Exchange Form 1946 or 1993 or clause 8 of the Asbatime Form 1981, or any similar amendment of the charterparty making the Master responsible for cargo handling, is not a material amendment; and
   (ii) that if the words "cargo claims" are added to the second sentence of clause 26 of the New York Produce Exchange Form 1946 or 1993 or clause 25 of the Asbatime Form 1981, apportionment under this Agreement shall not be applied under any circumstances even if the charterparty is made subject to the terms of this Agreement;
   and
(c) the claim has been properly settled or compromised and paid.

(5) This Agreement applies regardless of legal forum or place of arbitration specified in the charterparty and regardless of any incorporation of the Hague, Hague Visby Rules or Hamburg Rules therein.

Time Bar

A4.3

(6) Recovery under this Agreement by an Owner of Charterer shall be deemed to be waived and absolutely barred unless written notification of the Cargo Claim has been given to the other party to the charterparty within 24 months of the date of delivery of the cargo or the date the cargo should have been delivered, save that, where the Hamburg Rules or any national legislation giving effect thereto are compulsorily applicable by operation of law to the contract of carriage or to that part of the transit that comprised carriage on the chartered vessel, the period shall be 36 months. Such notification shall if possible include details of the contract of carriage, the nature of the claim and the amount claimed.

A4.4   **The apportionment**

(7) The amount of any Cargo Claim to be apportioned under this Agreement shall be the amount in fact borne by the party to the charterparty seeking apportionment, regardless of whether that claim may be or has been apportioned by application of this Agreement to another charterparty.

(8) Cargo Claims shall be apportioned as follows:

    (a) Claims in fact arising out of unseaworthiness and/or error or fault in navigation or management of the vessel:

    100 per cent   Owners

    save where the Owner proves that the unseaworthiness was caused by the loading, stowage, lashing, discharge or other handling of the cargo, in which case the claim shall be apportioned under sub-clause (b).

    (b) Claims in fact arising out of the loading, stowage, lashing, discharge, storage or other handling of cargo:

    100 per cent   Charterers

    unless the words "and responsibility" are added in clause 8 or there is a similar amendment making the Master responsible for cargo handling in which case:

    50 per cent   Chartererrs

    50 per cent   Owners

    Save where the Charterers proves that the failure properly to load, stow, lash, discharge or handle the cargo was caused by the unseaworthiness of the vessel in which case:

    100 per cent   Owners

    (c) Subject to (a) and (b) above, claims for shortage or overcarriage:

    50 per cent   Charterers

    50 per cent   Owners

    unless there is a clear and irrefutable evidence that the claim arose out of pilferage or act or neglect by one or the other (including their servants or sub-contractors) in which case that party shall then bear 100 per cent, of the claim.

    (d) All other cargo claims whatsoever (including claims for delay to cargo):

    50 per cent   Charterers

    50 per cent   Owners

    Unless there is clear and irrefutable evidence that the claim arose out of the act or neglect of the one or other (including their servants or sub-contracts) in which case that party shall then bear 100 per cent of the claim.

A4.5   **Governing Law**

(9) This Agreement shall be subject to English Law and Jurisdiction, unless it is incorporated into the charterpary (or the settlement of claims in respect of cargo under the charterparty is made subject to this Agreement), in which case it shall be subject to the law and jurisdiction provisions governing the charterparty.

APPENDIX V

Many common law jurisdictions, including most of the members of the British **A5.1** Commonwealth of Nations, have in force legislation embodying the Hague or Hague-Visby Rules.

The relevant statutes or ordinances of a number of jurisdictions are reproduced here. They are particularly valuable in considering decisions of the Courts of these jurisdictions, an increasing number of which are referred to in this work.

Care should, however, always be taken to check precisely which provisions were in force at the time of the decision under consideration. Where necessary the earlier Australian, Canadian, New Zealand, Singapore and United States statutes dealing with sea carriage will be found in earlier editions of this work.

AUSTRALIA

Carriage of Goods by Sea Act 1991 (No. 160 of 1991)

Part 1

Preliminary

1. This Act may be cited as the *Carriage of Goods by Sea Act 1991*.　　　　**A5.2**

2.—(1) Subject to subsection (2), this Act commences on the day on which it receives **A5.3** the Royal Assent.

(2) Subject to this section, Part 3 and Schedule 2 commence as provided in section 2A.

(3) If within 10 years of the commencement of this section the Minister has not tabled a statement in accordance with subsection 2A(4) setting out a decision that the amended Hague Rules should be replaced by the Hamburg Rules Part 3 and Schedule 2 and Section 2A are repealed on the first day after the end of that 10 years.[1]

3.—(1) The object of this Act is to introduce a regime of marine cargo liability that:　**A5.4**

(*a*) is up-to-date, equitable and efficient; and

(*b*) is compatible with arrangements existing in countries that are major trading partners of Australia; and

(*c*) takes into account developments within the United Nations in relation to marine cargo liability arrangements.

(2) The object of the Act is to be achieved by:

(*a*) as a first step—replacing the *Sea-Carriage of Goods Act 1924* with provisions that give effect to the Brussels Convention as amended by the Visby Protocol and the SDR Protocol, and as modified in accordance with regulations under section 7; and

(*b*) as a second step—replacing those provisions with provisions that give effect to the Hamburg Convention, if the Minister decides, after conduting a review, that those provisions should be so replaced.

---

[1] No statement was tabled within the 10 year period and section 2(a), Part 3 (which provided for the amended Hague Rules to be replaced by the Hamburg Rules) and Schedule 2 (which set out the Hamburg Rules) are taken to have been repealed on October 31, 2001. They are not, therefore, reproduced here.

A5.5 **4.**—(1) In this Act:

"amended Hague Rules" has the meaning given in section 7;

"Australia", when used in a geographical sense, includes the external Territories;

"Brussels Convention" means the International Convention for the Unification of Certain Rules of Law relating to Bills of Lading, done at Brussels on 25 August 1924;

"Hamburg Convention" means the United Nations Convention on the Carriage of Goods by Sea, being Annex I of the Final Act of the United Nations Conference on the Carriage of Goods by Sea done at Hamburg on 31 March 1978;

"Hamburg Rules" has the meaning given in section 12;

"marine insurers" means insurers who provide marine insurance, whether or not they also provide other kinds of insuarance, and includes Australian representatives of member Associations of the International Group of Protection and Indemnity Associations;

"maritime law associations" means law associations with an interest in maritime law, whether or not they are also interested in other areas of law";

"SDR Protocol" means the Protocol amending the Brussels Convention, as amended by the Visby Protocol, done at Brussels on 21 December 1979;

"Visby Protocol" means the Protocol amending the Brussels Convention, done at Brussels on 23 February 1968.

(2) A reference in this Act to a non-negotiable document includes a reference to a sea waybill.

A5.6 **5.** This Act binds the Crown in each of its capacities.

A5.7 **6.** This Act extends to all the external Territories.

PART 2

APPLICATION OF THE AMENDED HAGUE RULES ETC.

A5.8 **7.** (1) The *amended Hague Rules* consists of the text set out in Schedule 1, as modified in accordance with the Schedule of modifications referred to in subsection (2). The text set out in Schedule 1 (in its unmodified form) is the English translation of Articles 1 to 10 of the Brussels Convention, as amended by Articles 1 to 5 of the Visby Protocol and Article II of the SDR Protocol.

(2) The regulations may amend this Act to add a Schedule (the *Schedule of modifications*) that modifies the text set out in Schedule 1 for the following purposes:

(a) to provide for the coverage of a wider range of sea carriage documents (including documents in electronic form);

(b) to provide for the coverage of contracts for the carriage of goods by sea from places in countries outside Australia to places in Australia in situations where the contracts do not incorporate, or do not otherwise have effect subject to, a relevant international convention (see subsection (6));

(c) to provide for increased coverage of deck cargo;

(d) to extend the period during which carriers may incur liability;

(e) to provide for carriers to be liable for loss due to delay in circumstances identified as being inexcusable.

(3) The regulations may:

(a) amend the Schedule of modifications, but only in connection with the purposes set out in subsection (2); and

(b) amend the provisions of this Part to the extent necessary or appropriate, having regard to the modifications set out in the Schedule of modifications as in force from time to time.

(4) Before regulations are made for the purposes of this section, the Minister must consult with representatives of shippers, ship owners, carriers, cargo owners, marine insurers and maritime law associations about the regulations that are proposed to be made.

(5) For the purposes of the *Amendments Incorporation Act 1905*, amendments made by regulations for the purposes of this section are to be treated as if they had been made by an Act.

(6) In this section:

"relevant international convention" means:

(a) the Brussels Convention; or
(b) the Brussels Convention as amended by either or both of the Visby Protocol and the SDR Protocol; or
(c) the Hamburg Convention.

8. Subject to section 10, the amended Hague Rules have the force of law in Australia.   **A5.9**

9. In this Part and the amended Hague Rules, unless the contrary intention appears, a word or expression has the same meaning as it has in the Brussels Convention as amended by the Visby Protocol and the SDR Protocol.   **A5.10**

9A. A determination by the Minister, for paragraph 4 of Article 1 of the amended Hague Rules, of the limits of a port or wharf in Australia is a legislative instrument, but Part 6 of the *Legislative Instruments Act 2003* does not apply to the determination.   **A5.11**

10.—(1) The amended Hague Rules only apply to a contract of carriage of goods by sea that: **A5.12**

(*a*) is made on or after the commencement of this Part and before the commencement of Part 3; and
(*b*) is a contract:
   (i) of a kind referred to in Article 10 of the amended Hague Rules; or
   (ii) subject to subsection (2), for the carriage of goods by sea from a port in Australia to another port in Australia, being a contract that is contained in or evidenced by a bill of lading or similar document of title; or
   (iii) contained in or evidenced by a non-negotiable document (other than a bill of lading or similar document of title), being a contract that contains express provision to the effect that the amended Hague Rules are to govern the contract as if the document were a bill of lading.

(2) The amended Hague Rules do not apply in relation to the carriage of goods by sea from a port in any State or Territory in Australia to any other port in that State or Territory.

11.—(1) All parties to: **A5.13**

(*a*) a sea carriage document relating to the carriage of goods from any place in Australia to any place outside Australia; or
(*b*) a non-negotiable document of a kind mentioned in subparagraph 10(1)(*b*)(iii), relating to such a carriage of goods;

are taken to have intended to contract according to the laws in force at the place of shipment.

(2) An agreement (whether made in Australia or elsewhere) has no effect so far as it purports to:

(*a*) preclude or limit the effect of subsection (1) in respect of a bill of lading or a document mentioned in that subsection; or

(*b*) preclude or limit the jurisdiction of a court of the Commonwealth or of a State or Territory in respect of a bill of lading or a document mentioned in subsection (1); or

(*c*) preclude or limit the jurisdiction of a court of the Commonwealth or of a State or Territory in respect of:

(i) a sea carriage document relating to the carriage of goods from any place outside Australia to any place in Australia; or

(ii) a non-negotiable document of a kind mentioned in subparagraph 10(1)(*b*)(iii) relating to such a carriage of goods.

(3) An agreement, or a provision of an agreement, that provides for the resolution of a dispute by arbitration is not made ineffective by subsection (2) (despite the fact that it may preclude or limit the jurisdiction of the court) if, under the agreement or provision, the arbitration must be conducted in Australia.

PART 3[2]

PART 4

MISCELLANEOUS

A5.14   **17.** There is not to be implied in any contract for the carriage of goods by sea to which Part 2 or 3 of this Act applies any absolute undertaking by the carrier of the goods to provide a seaworthy ship.

A5.15   **18.** The provisions of this Act prevail over the provisions of Division 2 of Part V of the *Trade Practices Act 1974* to the extent of any inconsistency.

A5.16   **19.** Nothing in this Act affects the operation of:

(*a*) Division 10 of Part IV or Division 2 of Part VIII of the *Navigation Act 1912*; or

(*b*) the *Limitation of Liability for Maritime Claims Act 1989*.

A5.17   **20.**—(1) The *Sea Carriage of Goods Act 1924* is repealed.

(2) The *Sea-Carriage of Goods Act 1924*, as in force immediately before the commencement of this section, continues to apply to a contract of carriage of goods by sea after that commencement if:

(*a*) the contract was made before that commencement; and

(*b*) that Act would have applied but for the operation of subsection (1).

21. Section 2C of the *International Arbitration Act 1974* is repealed and the following section is substituted:

"2C. Nothing in this Act affects:

(*a*) the continued operation of section 9 of the *Sea-Carriage of Goods Act 1924* under subsection 20(2) of the *Carriage of Goods by Sea Act* 1991; or

(*b*) the operation of section 11 or 16 of the *Carriage of Goods by Sea Act 1991*.".

---

[2] See note 1, above.

SCHEDULE 1

THE AMENDED HAGUE RULES

Save as set out below, the Schedule is materially identical to the Schedule to the Carriage   **A5.18**
of Goods by Sea Act 1971 and is not reproduced here.

ARTICLE IV   **A5.19**

5. (*d*) The unit of account mentioned in this Article is the Special Drawing Right as
defined by the International Monetary Fund. The amounts mentioned in sub-paragraph (*a*)
of this paragraph shall be converted into national currency on the basis of the value of that
currency on a date to be determined by the law of the court seized of the case.

The value of the national currency, in terms of the Special Drawing Right, of a State
which is a member of the International Monetary Fund, shall be calculated in accordance
with the method of valuation applied by the International Monetary Fund in effect at the
date in question for its operations and transactions. The value of the national currency, in
terms of the Special Drawing Right, of a State which is not a member of the International
Monetary Fund, shall be calculated in a manner determined by that State.

Nevertheless, a State which is not a member of the International Monetary Fund and
whose law does not permit the application of the provisions of the preceding sentences
may, at the time of ratification of the Protocol of 1979 or accession thereto or at any time
thereafter, declare that the limits of liability provided for in this Convention to be applied
in its territory shall be fixed as follows:

    (i) in respect of the amount of 666.67 units of account mentioned in sub-paragraph
        (*a*) of paragraph 5 of this Article, 10,000 monetary units;

   (ii) in respect of the amount of 2 units of account mentioned in sub-paragraph (*a*) of
        paragraph 5 of this Article, 30 monetary units.

The monetary unit referred to in the preceding sentence corresponds to 65.5 milligrammes of gold of millesimal fineness 900. The conversion of the amounts specified in
that sentence into the national currency shall be made according to the law of the State
concerned.

The calculation and the conversion mentioned in the preceding sentences shall be made
in such a manner as to express in the national currency of the State as far as possible the
same real value for the amounts in sub-paragraph (*a*) of paragraph 5 of this Article as is
expressed there in units of accounts.

States shall communicate to the depositary the manner of calculation or the result of the
conversion as the case may be, when depositing an instrument of ratification of the
Protocol of 1979 or of accession thereto and whenever there is a change in either.

ARTICLE 10   **A5.20**

The provisions of this Convention shall apply to every Bill of Lading relating to the
carriage of goods between ports in two different States if:

    (*a*) the Bill of Lading is issued in a Contracting State, or

    (*b*) the carriage is from a port in a Contracting State, or

    (*c*) the contract contained in or evidenced by the Bill of Lading provides that the
        rules of this Convention or legislation of any State giving effect to them are to
        govern the contract

whatever may be the nationality of the ship, the carrier, the shipper, the consignee, or any
other interested person.

Each Contracting State shall apply the provisions of this Convention to the Bill of Lading mentioned above.

This Article shall not prevent a Contracting State from applying the rules of this Convention to Bills of Lading not included in the preceding paragaraphs.

A5.21 *SCHEDULE 2*

Schedule 2 is identical to the text of the Hamburg Rules set out in Appendix VI, below.

CANADA

Part 5

Liability for Carriage of Goods By Water

Interpretation

41. The definitions in this section apply to this Part.   **A5.23**

"Hague-Visby Rules"
"Hague-Visby Rules' means the rules set out in Schedule 3 and embodied in the
   International Convention for the Unification of Certain Rules of Law relating to Bills
   of Lading, concluded at Brussels on August 25, 1924, in the Protocol concluded at
   Brussels on February 23, 1968, and in the additional Protocol concluded at Brussels
   on December 21, 1979

"Hamburg Rules"
"Hamburg Rules" means the rules set out in Schedule 4 and embodied in the United
   Nations Convention on the Carriage of Goods by Sea, 1978, concluded at Hamburg
   on March 31, 1978.

Other statutory limitations of liability

42. Nothing in this Part affects the operation of any other Part of this Act, or section 250   **A5.24**
of the *Canada Shipping Act, 2001*, or a provision of any other Act or regulation that limits
the liability of owners of ships.

Hague-Visby Rules

Effect

43.—(1) The Hague-Visby Rules have the force of law in Canada in respect of contracts   **A5.25**
for the carriage of goods by water between different states as described in Article X of
those Rules.

Extended application

(2) The Hague-Visby Rules also apply in respect of contracts for the carriage of goods
by water from one place in Canada to another place in Canada, either directly or by way
of a place outside Canada, unless there is no bill of lading and the contract stipulates that
those Rules do not apply.

Meaning of "Contracting State"

(3) For the purposes of this section, the expression 'Contracting State' in Article X of
the Hague-Visby Rules includes Canada and any state that, without being a Contracting
State, gives the force of law to the rules embodied in the International Convention for the
Unification of Certain Rules of Law relating to Bills of Lading, concluded at Brussels on
August 25, 1924 and in the Protocol concluded at Brussels on February 23, 1968,
regardless of whether that state gives the force of law to the additional Protocol concluded
at Brussels on December 21, 1979.

Replacement by Hamburg Rules

(4) The Hague-Visby Rules do not apply in respect of contracts entered into after the
coming into force of section 45.

Report to Parliament

A5.26 **44.** The Minister shall, before January 1, 2005 and every five years afterwards, consider whether the Hague-Visby Rules should be replaced by the Hamburg Rules and cause a report setting out the results of that consideration to be laid before each House of Parliament.

Effect

A5.27 **45.**—(1) The Hamburg Rules have the force of law in Canada in respect of contracts for the carriage of goods by water between different states as described in Article 2 of those Rules.

Extended application

(2) The Hamburg Rules also apply in respect of contracts for the carriage of goods by water from one place in Canada to another place in Canada, either directly or by way of a place outside Canada, unless the contract stipulates that those Rules do not apply.

Meaning of "Contracting State"

(3) For the purposes of this section, the expression 'Contracting State' in Article 2 of the Hamburg Rules includes Canada and any state that gives the force of law to those Rules without being a Contracting State to the United Nations Convention on the Carriage of Goods by Sea, 1978.

References to "sea"

(4) For the purposes of this section, the word "sea" in the Hamburg Rules shall be read as "water".

Signatures

(5) For the purposes of this section, paragraph 3 of article 14 of the Hamburg Rules applies in respect of the documents referred to in article 18 of those Rules.

INSTITUTION OF PROCEEDINGS IN CANADA

Claims not subject to Hamburg Rules

A5.28 **46.**—(1) If a contract for the carriage of goods by water to which the Hamburg Rules do not apply provides for the adjudication or arbitration of claims arising under the contract in a place other than Canada, a claimant may institute judicial or arbitral proceedings in a court or arbitral tribunal in Canada that would be competent to determine the claim if the contract had referred the claim to Canada, where

    (*a*) the actual port of loading or discharge, or the intended port of loading or discharge under the contract, is in Canada;

    (*b*) the person against whom the claim is made resides or has a place of business, branch or agency in Canada; or

    (*c*) the contract was made in Canada.

Agreement to designate

(2) Notwithstanding subsection (1), the parties to a contract referred to in that subsection may, after a claim arises under the contract, designate by agreement the place where the claimant may institute judicial or arbitral proceedings.

SCHEDULE 3

Save for Article IV, Rule 5(d) which is identical to that in Schedule 1 to the Australian   **A5.29**
Act, this Schedule is identical to the Schedule to the Carriage of Goods by Sea Act
1971.

SCHEDULE 4

Schedule 4 reproduces the Hamburg Rules which appear in Appendi VI, below.   **A5.30**

HONG KONG

Cap 462

A5.31 An Ordinance to regulate liability in respect of the carriage of goods by sea.

Short Title

A5.32 **1.** This Ordinance may be cited as the Carriage of Goods by Sea Ordinance.

Interpretation

A5.33 **2.**—(1) In this Ordinance, unless the context otherwise requires—

"Monetary Authority" ( ) has the meaning assigned to it by section 2 of the Exchange Fund Ordinance (Cap. 66);
"the Rules" ( ) means the International Convention for the Unification of certain Rules of Law relating to Bills of Lading signed at Brussels on 25 August 1924, which was established in a single original in the French language, as amended by the Protocol signed at Brussels on 23 February 1968 and by the Protocol signed at Brussels on 21 December 1979, both of which were established in a single original in the English and French languages;
"ship" ( ) means any vessel used for carriage of goods by sea, other than a vessel which is regularly employed in trading to or from Hong Kong and which is required to be certified under the Merchant Shipping (Local Vessels) Ordinance (43 of 1999).
(2) References in this Ordinance to Articles are references to Articles of the Rules.

Application of Hague Rules as Amended

A5.34 **3.**—(1) Subject to subsection (3) the Rules as set out in the Schedule shall have the force of law.

(2) The Rules shall also apply to the carriage of goods by sea in ships where the port of shipment is in Hong Kong, whether or not the carriage is between ports in 2 different States within the meaning of Article X.

(3) Nothing in this section shall be taken as applying anything in the Rules to any contract for the carriage of goods by sea, unless the contract expressly or by implication provides for the issue of a bill of lading or any similar document of title.

(4) The Rules shall also apply to—

(*a*) any bill of lading if the contract contained in or evidenced by it expressly provides that the Rules shall govern the contract; and

(*b*) any receipt which is a non-negotiable document marked as such if the contract contained in or evidenced by it is a contract for the carriage of goods by sea which expressly provides that the Rules are to govern the contract as if the receipt were a bill of lading,

but where paragraph (*b*) applies, the Rules shall be construed and have effect—

(i) as if the following were omitted—
(A) "However, proof to the contrary shall not be admissible when the bill of lading has been transferred to a third party acting in good faith." from paragraph 4 of Article III; and
(B) paragraph 7 of Article III; and
(ii) subject to any other necessary modification.

(5) (a) If and in so far as the contract contained in or evidenced by a bill of lading or receipt referred to in paragraph (*a*) or (*b*) of subsection (4) applies to deck cargo or live animals, the Rules as applied by that subsection shall be construed and have effect as if all the words following "whatsoever" were omitted from Article I(c).

(b) In this subsection "deck cargo" (   ) means cargo which by the contract of carriage is stated as being carried on deck and is so carried.

CERTIFICATION OF CONTRACTING STATES, ETC.

4.—(1) The Chief Executive may by order certify that for the purposes of the **A5.35** Rules—

   (*a*) a State specified in the order is a contracting State, or is a contracting State in respect of any place or territory so specified; or
   (*b*) any place or territory specified in the order forms part of a State so specified (whether a contracting State or not).

(2) For the purposes of the Rules an order under this section shall be conclusive evidence of the matters so certified.

ABSOLUTE WARRANTY OF SEAWORTHINESS NOT TO BE IMPLIED IN CONTRACTS TO WHICH THE RULES APPLY

5. There shall not be implied in any contract for the carriage of goods by sea to which **A5.36** the Rules apply any absolute undertaking by the carrier of the goods to provide a seaworthy ship.

APPLICATION OF ARTICLES IV AND X

6.—(1) The date referred to in paragraph 5(*d*) of Article IV is hereby determined to be the date of the relevant judgment of the court of first instance or, in case there is an appeal, the date on which the appeal is determined.

(2) Article X shall have effect as if references therein to a contracting State included a reference to a State that is a contracting State in respect of the Rules without the amendments made by the Protocol signed at Brussels on 21 December 1979, and section 4 shall be construed and have effect accordingly.

CONVERSION OF SPECIAL DRAWING RIGHTS

7.—(1) For the purposes of Article IV the Monetary Authority may specify in Hong **A5.37** Kong dollar the respective amounts which are to be taken as equivalent for a particular day to the sums expressed in special drawing rights in that Article.

(2) A certificate given by or on behalf of the Monetary Authority in pursuance of subsection (1) shall for the purposes of that subsection be conclusive evidence of the matters stated in the certificate, and a document purporting to be such a certificate shall in any proceedings be received in evidence and, unless the contrary is proved, be deemed to be such a certificate.

(3) The Monetary Authority may charge a reasonable fee for any certificate given in pursuance of subsection (2), and every such fee shall be paid into the general revenue.

REPEALS AND SAVINGS

8.—(1) The following are repealed—   **A5.38**

   (*a*) the Carriage of Goods by Sea (Hong Kong) Order 1980 (App. III, p. BS1);

(*b*) the Carriage of Goods by Sea (Hong Kong) (Amendment) Order 1980 (L.N. 285 of 1981); and

(*c*) the Carriage of Goods by Sea (Hong Kong) Order 1982 (App. III, p. AR1).

(2) Notwithstanding subsection (1)—

(*a*) the Carriage of Goods by Sea (Parties to Convention) Order 1985 (S.I. 1985 No. 443) shall continue in force, shall be regarded as having been made under section 4(1) and shall be taken to include such adaptations and modifications (if any) as are necessary or expedient to enable this paragraph to have full effect;

(*b*) the specifications made by the Governor under section 1(5) of the Schedule to the Carriage of Goods by Sea (Hong Kong) Order 1980 (App. III, p. BS1) shall continue in force and such specifications shall be taken to include such adaptations and modifications (if any) as are necessary or expedient to enable this paragraph to have full effect.

(3) Section 23 of the Interpretation and General Clauses Ordinance (Cap. 1) applies to the repeal of the Orders mentioned in subsection (1) as it applies to the repeal (in whole or in part) of an Ordinance.

SCHEDULE

A5.39 The Schedule is identical to the Schedule to the Carriage of Goods by Sea Act 1971.

NEW ZEALAND

A5.40

INTERPRETATION

208.—(1) In this Part of this Act, "the Rules" means the International Convention for **A5.41** the Unification of Certain Rules of Law Relating to Bills of Lading signed at Brussels on the 25th day of August 1924, as amended by the Protocol signed at Brussels on the 23rd day of February 1968 and by the Protocol signed at Brussels on the 21st day of December 1979.

(2) For the purposes of Article 10 of the Rules, "State" includes each of Niue and Tokelau.

(3) A reference in this Act to a non-negotiable document includes a reference to a sea waybill.

HAGUE RULES TO HAVE FORCE OF LAW

209.—(1) The Rules, as set out in Schedule 5 to this Act, shall have the force of law **A5.42** in New Zealand.

(2) Subsection (1) of this section shall apply to carriage of goods by sea evidenced by a non-negotiable document (other than a bill of lading or similar document of title) that contains express provision to the effect that the Rules are to govern the carriage as if the document were a bill of lading.

JURISDICTION OF NEW ZEALAND COURTS

210.—(1) An agreement, whether made in New Zealand or elsewhere, has no effect to **A5.43** the extent that it purports to—

(*a*) Preclude or limit the jurisdiction of the Courts of New Zealand in respect of—
  (i) A bill of lading or a similar document of title, relating to the carriage of goods from any place in New Zealand to any place outside New Zealand; or
  (ii) A non-negotiable document of a kind mentioned in section 209(2) of this Act relating to such a carriage of goods; or

(*b*) Preclude or limit the jurisdiction of the Courts of New Zealand in respect of—
  (i) A bill of lading, or a similar document of title, relating to the carriage of goods from any place outside New Zealand to any place in New Zealand; or
  (ii) A non-negotiable document of a kind mentioned in section 209(2) of this Act relating to such a carriage of goods.

(2) Nothing in this section shall be construed as limiting or affecting any stipulation or agreement to submit any dispute to arbitration in New Zealand or any other country.

CONTRACTING PARTIES TO THE RULES

211.—If the Secretary of Foreign Affairs and Trade certifies that, for the purposes of the **A5.44** Rules or any convention relating to liability of sea carriers for loss of, or damage to, cargo,—

(*a*) A State specified in the certificate is a Contracting State, or is a Contracting State in respect of any place or territory so specified; or (*b*) Any place or territory specified in the certificate forms part of a State so specified (whether a Contracting State or not),—

then, in any proceedings, the certificate shall, in the absence of proof to the contrary, be sufficient evidence of the matters so certified.

Repeals

A5.45   **212.**—(1) The Sea Carriage of Goods Act 1940 is hereby repealed.

(2) Section 5(5) of the Carriage of Goods Act 1979 is hereby repealed.

(3) The following enactments are hereby consequentially repealed:

    (*a*) The Sea Carriage of Goods Amendment Act 1968:

    (*b*) The Sea Carriage of Goods Amendment Act 1985.

Savings

A5.46   **213.**—(1) Notwithstanding section 212(1) of this Act, the Sea Carriage of Goods Act 1940, as in force immediately before the commencement of that section, shall be deemed to continue to apply to a contract of carriage of goods by sea after that commencement if—

    (*a*) The contract was made before that commencement, and

    (*b*) That Act would have applied but for the operation of section 212(1) of this Act.

(2) Notwithstanding section 212 (2) of this Act, section 5(5) of the Carriage of Goods Act 1979, as in force immediately before the commencement of that section, shall be deemed to continue to apply to a contract of carriage of goods by sea between any place in New Zealand and any place in the Cook Islands or in Niue or in Tokelau after the commencement if—

    (*a*) The contract was made before that commencement; and

    (*b*) That subsection would have applied but for the operation of section 212(2) of this Act.

FIFTH SCHEDULE

A5.47   The Amended Hague Rules

Article 1

The schedule is in identical terms to Schedule 1 to the Australian Act.

SINGAPORE   **A5.48**

CARRIAGE OF GOODS BY SEA ACT 1978
(As Amended by the Carriage of Goods by Sea (Amendment) Act 1982 and The
Carriage of Goods by Sea (Amendment) Act 1995) (c.33)

1. This Act may be cited as the Carriage of Goods by Sea Act.   **A5.49**

2. In this Act, "Rules" means the International Convention for the unification of certain   **A5.50**
rules of law relating to bills of lading made at Brussels on 25th August 1924, as amended
by the Protocol made at Brussels on 23rd February 1968, and which are set out in the
Schedule.

3.—(1) The provisions of the Rules, as set out in the Schedule to this Act, shall have   **A5.51**
the force of law.

(2) Without prejudice to subsection (1), the provisions of the Rules shall also have
effect (and have the force of law) in relation to and in connection with the carriage of
goods by sea in ships where the port of shipment is a port in Singapore, whether or not
the carriage is between ports in two different States within the meaning of Article X of the
Rules.

(3) Subject to subsection (4), nothing in this section shall be construed as applying
anything in the Rules to any contract for the carriage of goods by sea, unless the contract
expressly or by implication provides for the issue of a bill of lading or any similar
document of title.

(4) Without prejudice to paragraph (c) of Article X of the Rules, the Rules shall have
the force of law in relation to—

> (*a*) any bill of lading if the contract contained in or evidenced by it expressly
> provides that the Rules shall govern the contract; and
> (*b*) any receipt which is a non-negotiable document marked as such if the contract
> contained in or evidenced by it is a contract for the carriage of goods by sea
> which expressly provides that the Rules are to govern the contract.

(5) Where subsection (4)(*b*) applies, the Rules shall apply—

> (*a*) as if the receipt referred to therein were a bill of lading; and
> (*b*) subject to any necessary modifications and in particular with the omission of the
> second sentence of paragraph 4 and of paragraph 7 in Article III of the Rules.

(6) If and so far as the contract contained in or evidenced by a bill of lading or receipt
referred to in paragraph (*a*) or (*b*) of subsection (4) applies to deck cargo or live animals,
the Rules as given the force of law by that subsection shall have effect as if Article I (*c*)
did not exclude deck cargo and live animals.

(7) In subsection (6), "deck cargo" means cargo which by the contract of carriage is
stated as being carried on deck and is so carried.

(8) The Minister may, from time to time by order published in the *Gazette*, specify the
respective amounts which, for the purposes of paragraph 5 of Article IV and of Article IV
bis of the Rules, are to be taken as equivalent to the sums expressed in francs which are
mentioned in paragraph 5(a) of Article IV.".

4. There shall not be implied in any contract for the carriage of goods by sea to which   **A5.52**
the Rules apply any absolute undertaking by the carrier of the goods to provide a
seaworthy ship.

5. Where under the custom of any trade the weight of any bulk cargo inserted in the bill   **A5.53**
of lading is a weight ascertained or accepted by a third party other than the carrier or the
shipper and the fact that the weight is so ascertained or accepted is stated in the bill of
lading, then, notwithstanding anything in the Rules, the bill of lading shall not be deemed

to be prima facie evidence against the carrier of the receipt of goods of the weight so inserted in the bill of lading, and the accuracy thereof at the time of shipment shall not be deemed to have been guaranteed by the shipper.

A5.54   **6.** Nothing in this Act shall affect the operation of sections 293 and 294 of the Merchant Shipping Act as amended by any subsequent Act, or the operation of any other enactment for the time being in force limiting the liability of the owners of sea-going vessels.

THE SCHEDULE

A5.55   Save as set out below, the Schedule is identical to the Schedule to the Carriage of Goods by Sea Act 1971.

ARTICLE IV

A5.57   **5.**—(*a*) Unless the nature and value of such goods have been declared by the shipper before shipment and inserted in the bill of lading, neither the carrier nor the ship shall in any event, be or become liable for any loss or damage to or in connection with the goods in an amount exceeding the equivalent of 10,000 francs per package or unit or 30 francs per kilo of gross weight of the goods lost or damaged, whichever is the higher.

(*d*) A franc means a unit consisting of 65.5 milligrammes of gold of millesimal fineness 900. The date of conversion of the sum awarded into national currencies shall be governed by the law of the Court seized of the case.

UNITED STATES

CARRIAGE OF GOODS BY SEA ACT

(*Public—No. 521—74th Congress*)

An Act relating to the carriage of goods by sea

Be it enacted by the Senate and House of Representatives of the United States of **A5.58**
America in Congress assembled, That every bill of lading or similar document of title
which is evidence of a contract for the carriage of goods by sea to or from ports of the
United States, in foreign trade, shall have effect subject to the provisions of this Act.

TITLE I

1. When used in this Act—   **A5.59**

    (a) The term "carrier" includes the owner of the charterer who enters into a contract
        of carriage with a shipper.
    (b) The term "contract of carriage" applies only to contracts of carriage covered by
        a bill of lading or any similar document of title, insofar as such document relates
        to the carriage of goods by sea, including any bill of lading or any similar
        document as aforesaid issued under or pursuant to a charter party from the
        moment at which such bill of lading or similar document of title regulates the
        relations between a carrier and a holder of the same.
    (c) The term "goods" includes goods, wares, merchandise, and articles of every kind
        whatsoever, except live animals and cargo which by the contract of carriage is
        stated as being carried on deck and is so carried.
    (d) The term "ship" means any vessel used for the carriage of goods by sea.
    (e) The term "carriage of goods" covers the period from the time when the goods
        are loaded on to the time when they are discharged from the ship.

RISKS

2. Subject to the provisions of section 6, under every contract of carriage of goods by   **A5.60**
sea, the carrier in relation to the loading, handling, stowage, carriage, custody, care, and
discharge of such goods, shall be subject to the responsibilities and liabilities and entitled
to the rights and immunities hereinafter set forth.

RESPONSIBILITIES AND LIABILITIES

3.—(1) The carrier shall be bound, before and at the beginning of the voyage, to   **A5.61**
exercise due diligence to—

    (a) Make the ship seaworthy;
    (b) Properly man, equip, and supply the ship;
    (c) Make the holds, refrigerating and cooling chambers, and all other parts of the
        ship in which goods are carried, fit and safe for their reception, carriage, and
        preservation.

(2) The carrier shall properly and carefully load, handle, stow, carry, keep, care for, and
discharge the goods carried.

(3) After receiving the goods into his charge the carrier, or the master or agent of the
carrier, shall, on demand of the shipper, issue to the shipper a bill of lading showing
among other things—

(a) The leading marks necessary for identification of the goods as the same are furnished in writing by the shipper before the loading of such goods starts, provided such marks are stamped or otherwise shown clearly upon the goods if uncovered, or on the cases or coverings in which such goods are contained, in such a manner as should ordinarily remain legible until the end of the voyage.

(b) Either the number of packages or pieces, or the quantity or weight, as the case may be, as furnished in writing by the shipper.

(c) The apparent order and condition of the goods: *Provided*, That no carrier, master, or agent of the carrier, shall be bound to state or show in the bill of lading any marks, number, quantity, or weight which he has reasonable ground for suspecting not accurately to represent the goods actually received, or which he has had no reasonable means of checking.

(4) Such a bill of lading shall be prima facie evidence of the receipt by the carrier of the goods as therein described in accordance with paragraphs (3)(a), (b), and (c), of this section: *Provided*, That nothing in this Act shall be construed as repealing or limiting the application of any part of the Act, as amended, entitled "an Act relating to bills of lading in interstate and foreign commerce," approved August 29, 1916 (U.S.C., title 49, ss.81–124), commonly known as the "Pomerene Bills of Lading Act".

(5) The shipper shall be deemed to have guaranteed to the carrier the accuracy at the time of shipment of the marks, number, quantity, and weight, as furnished by him; and the shipper shall indemnify the carrier against all loss, damages, and expenses arising or resulting from inaccuracies in such particulars. The right of the carrier to such indemnity shall in no way limit his responsibility and liability under the contract of carriage to any person other than the shipper.

(6) Unless notice of loss or damage and the general nature of such loss or damage be given in writing to the carrier or his agent at the port of discharge before or at the time of the removal of the goods into the custody of the person entitled to delivery thereof under the contract of carriage, such removal shall be prima facie evidence of the delivery by the carrier of the goods as described in the bill of lading. If the loss or damage is not apparent, the notice must be given within three days of the delivery.

Said notice of loss or damage may be indorsed upon the receipt for the goods given by the person taking delivery thereof.

The notice in writing need not be given if the state of the goods has at the time of their receipt been the subject of joint survey or inspection.

In any event the carrier and the ship shall be discharged from all liability in respect of loss or damage unless suit is brought within one year after delivery of the goods or the date when the goods should have been delivered: *Provided*, That if a notice of loss or damage, either apparent or concealed, is not given as provided for in this section, that fact shall not affect or prejudice the right of the shipper to bring suit within one year after the delivery of the goods or the date when the goods should have been delivered.

In the case of any actual or apprehended loss or damage the carrier and the receiver shall give all reasonable facilities to each other for inspecting and tallying the goods.

(7) After the goods are loaded the bill of lading to be issued by the carrier, master, or agent of the carrier to the shipper shall, if the shipper so demands, be a "shipped" bill of lading: *Provided*, That if the shipper shall have previously taken up any document of title to such goods, he shall surrender the same as against the issue of the "shipped" bill of lading, but at the option of the carrier such document of title may be noted at the port of shipment by the carrier, master, or agent with the name or names of the ship or ships upon which the goods have been shipped and the date or dates of shipment, and when so noted

the same shall for the purpose of this section be deemed to constitute a "shipped" bill of lading.

(8) Any clause, covenant, or agreement in a contract of carriage relieving the carrier or the ship from liability for loss or damage to or in connection with the goods, arising from negligence, fault, or failure in the duties and obligations provided in this section, or lessening such liability otherwise than as provided in this Act, shall be null and void and of no effect. A benefit of insurance in favor of the carrier or similar clause, shall be deemed to be a clause relieving the carrier from liability.

Rights And Immunities

4.—(1) Neither the carrier nor the ship shall be liable for loss or damage arising or **A5.62** resulting from unseaworthiness unless caused by want of due diligence on the part of the carrier to make the ship seaworthy, and to secure that the ship is properly manned, equipped, and supplied, and to make the holds, refrigerating and cool chambers, and all other parts of the ship in which goods are carried fit and safe for their reception, carriage, and preservation in accordance with the provisions of paragraph (1) of section 3. Whenever loss or damage has resulted from unseaworthiness, the burden of proving the exercise of due diligence shall be on the carrier or other persons claiming exemption under this section.

(2) Neither the carrier nor the ship shall be responsible for loss or damage arising or resulting from—

(a) Act, neglect, or default of the master, mariner, pilot, or the servants of the carrier, in the navigation or in the management of the ship;

(b) Fire, unless caused by the actual fault or privity of the carrier;

(c) Perils, dangers, and accidents of the sea or other navigable waters;

(d) Act of God;

(e) Act of war;

(f) Act of public enemies;

(g) Arrest or restraint of princes, rulers, or people, or seizure under legal process;

(h) Quarantine restrictions;

(i) Act or omission of the shipper or owner of the goods, his agent or representative;

(j) Strikes or lockouts or stoppage or restraint of labor from whatever cause, whether partial or general: *Provided*, That nothing herein contained shall be construed to relieve a carrier from responsibility for the carrier's own acts;

(k) Riots and civil commotions;

(l) Saving or attempting to save life or property at sea;

(m) Wastage in bulk or weight or any other loss or damage arising from inherent defect, quality, or vice of the goods;

(n) Insufficiency of packing;

(o) Insufficiency or inadequacy of marks;

(p) Latent defects not discoverable by due diligence; and

(q) Any other cause arising without the actual fault and privity of the carrier and without the fault or neglect of the agents or servants of the carrier, but the burden of proof shall be on the person claiming the benefit of this exception to show that neither the actual fault or privity of the carrier nor the fault or neglect of the agents or servants of the carrier contributed to the loss or damage.

(3) The shipper shall not be responsible for loss or damage sustained by the carrier or the ship arising or resulting from any cause without the act, fault, or neglect of the shipper, his agents, or his servants.

(4) Any deviation in saving or attempting to save life or property at sea, or any reasonable deviation shall not be deemed to be an infringement or breach of this Act or of the contract of carriage, and the carrier shall not be liable for any loss or damage resulting therefrom: *Provided, however,* That if the deviation is for the purpose of loading or unloading cargo or passengers it shall, prima facie, be regarded as unreasonable.

(5) Neither the carrier nor the ship shall in any event be or become liable for any loss or damage to or in connection with the transportation of goods in an amount exceeding $500 per package lawful money of the United States, or in case of goods not shipped in packages, per customary freight unit, or the equivalent of that sum in other currency, unless the nature and value of such goods have been declared by the shipper before shipment and inserted in the bill of lading. This declaration, if embodied in the bill of lading, shall be prima facie evidence, but shall not be conclusive on the carrier.

By agreement between the carrier, master, or agent of the carrier, and the shipper another maximum amount than that mentioned in this paragraph may be fixed: *Provided,* That such maximum shall not be less than the figure above named. In no event shall the carrier be liable for more than the amount of damage actually sustained.

Neither the carrier nor the ship shall be responsible in any event for loss or damage to or in connection with the transportation of the goods if the nature or value thereof has been knowingly and fraudulently misstated by the shipper in the bill of lading.

(6) Goods of an inflammable, explosive, or dangerous nature to the shipment whereof the carrier, master or agent of the carrier, has not consented with knowledge of their nature and character, may at any time before discharge be landed at any place or destroyed or rendered innocuous by the carrier without compensation, and the shipper of such goods shall be liable for all damages and expenses directly or indirectly arising out of or resulting from such shipment. If any such goods shipped with such knowledge and consent shall become a danger to the ship or cargo, they may in like manner be landed at any place, or destroyed or rendered innocuous by the carrier without liability on the part of the carrier except to general average, if any.

Surrender Of Rights And Immunities And Increase Of Responsibilities And Liabilities

A5.63 **5.** A carrier shall be at liberty to surrender in whole or in part all or any of his rights and immunities or to increase any of his responsibilities and liabilities under this Act, provided such surrender or increase shall be embodied in the bill of lading issued to the shipper.

The provisions of the Act shall not be applicable to charter parties; but if bills of lading are issued in the case of a ship under a charter party, they shall comply with the terms of this Act. Nothing in this Act shall be held to prevent the insertion in a bill of lading of any lawful provision regarding general average.

Special Conditions

A5.64 **6.** Notwithstanding the provisions of the preceding sections, a carrier, master or agent of the carrier, and a shipper shall, in regard to any particular goods be at liberty to enter into any agreement in any terms as to the responsibility and liability of the carrier for such goods, and as to the rights and immunities of the carrier in respect of such goods, or his obligation as to seaworthiness (so far as the stipulation regarding seaworthiness is not contrary to public policy), or the care or diligence of his servants or agents in regard to the loading, handling, stowage, carriage, custody, care, and discharge of the goods carried by sea: *Provided,* That in this case no bill of lading has been or shall be issued and that the terms agreed shall be embodied in a receipt which shall be a non-negotiable document and shall be marked as such.

Any agreement so entered into shall have full legal effect: *Provided*, That this section shall not apply to ordinary commercial shipments made in the ordinary course of trade but only to other shipments where the character or condition of the property to be carried or the circumstances, terms, and conditions under which the carriage is to be performed are such as reasonably to justify a special agreement.

7. Nothing contained in this Act shall prevent a carrier or a shipper from entering into **A5.65** any agreement, stipulation, condition, reservation, or exemption as to the responsibility and liability of the carrier or the ship for the loss or damage to or in connection with the custody and care and handling of goods prior to the loading and subsequent to the discharge from the ship on which the goods are carried by sea.

8. The provisions of this Act shall not affect the rights and obligations of the carrier **A5.66** under the provisions of the Shipping Act 1916, or under the provisions of sections 4281 to 4289, inclusive, of the Revised Statutes of the United States, or of any amendments thereto; or under the provisions of any other enactment for the time being in force relating to the limitation of the liability of the owners of seagoing vessels.

TITLE II

9. Nothing contained in this Act shall be construed as permitting a common carrier by **A5.67** water to discriminate between competing shippers similarly placed in time and circumstances, either (a) with respect to their right to demand and receive bills of lading, subject to the provisions of this Act; or (b) when issuing such bills of lading, either in the surrender of any of the carrier's rights and immunities or in the increase of any of the carrier's responsibilities and liabilities pursuant to section 5, title I, of this Act; or (c) in any other way prohibited by the Shipping Act 1916, as amended.

10. (Repealed by the Transportation Act 1940.) **A5.68**

11. Where under the customs of any trade the weight of any bulk cargo inserted in the **A5.69** bill of lading is a weight ascertained or accepted by a third party other than the carrier or the shipper, and the fact that the weight is so ascertained or accepted is stated in the bill of lading, then, notwithstanding anything in this Act, the bill of lading shall not be deemed to be prima facie evidence against the carrier of the receipt of goods of the weight so inserted in the bill of lading, and the accuracy thereof at the time of shipment shall not be deemed to have been guaranteed by the shipper.

12. Nothing in this Act shall be construed as superseding any part of the Act entitled **A5.70** "An Act relating to navigation of vessels, bills of lading, and to certain obligations, duties, and rights in connection with the carriage of property", approved February 13, 1893, or of any other law which would be applicable in the absence of this Act, insofar as they relate to the duties, responsibilities, and liabilities of the ship or carrier prior to the time when the goods are loaded on or after the time they are discharged from the ship.

13. This Act shall apply to all contracts for carriage of goods by sea to or from ports **A5.71** of the United States in foreign trade. As used in this Act the term "United States" includes its districts, territories, and possessions: *Provided, however*, That the Philippine Legislature may by law exclude its application to transportation to or from ports of the Philippine Islands. The term "foreign trade" means the transportation of goods between the ports of the United States and ports of foreign countries. Nothing in this Act shall be held to apply to contracts for carriage of goods by sea between any port of the United States or its possessions, and any other port of the United States or its possessions: *Provided, however*, That any bill of lading or similar document of title which is evidence of a contract for the carriage of goods by sea between such ports, containing an express statement that it shall be subject to the provisions of this Act, shall be subjected hereto as fully as if subject hereto by the express provisions of this Act: *Provided further*, That every bill of lading or similar document of title which is evidence of a contract for the carriage of goods by sea from ports of the United States, in foreign trade, shall contain a statement that it shall have effect subject to the provisions of this Act.

A5.72   **14.** Upon the certification of the Secretary of Commerce that the foreign commerce of the United States in its competition with that of foreign nations is prejudiced by the provisions, or any of them, of title I of this Act, or by the laws of any foreign country or countries relating to the carriage of goods by sea, the President of the United States may, from time to time, by proclamation, suspend any or all provisions of title I of this Act for such periods of time or indefinitely as may be designated in the proclamation. The President may at any time rescind such suspension of title I hereof, and any provisions thereof which may have been suspended shall thereby be reinstated and again apply to contracts thereafter made for the carriage of goods by sea. Any proclamation of suspension or rescission of any such suspension shall take effect on a date named therein, which date shall be not less than ten days from the issue of the proclamation.

Any contract for the carriage of goods by sea, subject to the provisions of this Act, effective during any period when title I hereof, or any part thereof, is suspended, shall be subject to all provisions of law now or hereafter applicable to that part of title I which may have thus been suspended.

A5.73   **15.** This Act shall take effect ninety days after the date of its approval but nothing in this Act shall apply during a period not to exceed one year following its approval to any contract for the carriage of goods by sea, made before the date on which this Act is approved, nor to any bill of lading or similar document of title issued, whether before or after such date of approval in pursuance of any such contract as aforesaid.

A5.74   **16.** This Act may be cited as the "Carriage of Goods by Sea Act".

Approved, April 16, 1936.

APPENDIX VI

THE HAMBURG RULES

INTRODUCTORY NOTES

THE Hamburg Rules were the product of the United Nations Conference on the Carriage **A6.1** of Goods by Sea, held at Hamburg between March 6 and 31, 1978.[1] The Conference followed a report by the United Nations Commission on Trade and Development which stated that the Hague Rules provided an unduly favourable regime to shipowner, in particular because of Article IV Rule 2(a), and that a re-drawing of risks between shipowners and shippers was necessary because shipowner were covered by liability insurance in any event.[2] In 1971, the United Nations Commission on International Trade Law began to draft the Convention. Eventually, following a diplomatic conference in Hamburg, the Convention was adopted for signature on March 31, 1978.

Article 30 of the Convention, known by the popular short title of the Hamburg Rules, provided that the Rules would come into force on first day of the month following the expiration of one year from the date of deposit of the 20th instrument of ratification. The 20th ratification was deposited in November 1991, with the result that the Rules came into effect for those countries who had acceded to them on November 1, 1992. The Rules are presently in force in 32 countries.[3] A Working Group of the United Nations Commission on International Trade Law is, however, in the process of drafting and considering a new Convention on the Carriage of Goods (wholly or partly by Sea). It is, therefore, difficult to predict whether the Hamburg Rules will ever come into force in more countries than at present.

In general, the Rules impose a more onerous regime on the shipowner. It is doubtless for this reason that the majority of ratifications have come from the developing rather than developed world. The underlying rationale of the Rules is apparent from Annex II, which states that it is the common understanding "that the liability of the carrier under this Convention is based on the principle of presumed fault or neglect", with the result that, save where the Rules otherwise provide, the burden of proof lies on the carrier. This common understanding finds its most clear expression in Article 5.1 of the Rules.

There are other significant changes from the regime created by the Hague and Hague-Visby Rules. The dual obligations of the shipowner to make the vessel sea and cargo worthy, and to properly and carefully load, carry and discharge the cargo, together with the various exceptions and immunities, are replaced by a single obligation to take all measures that could reasonably be required to avoid loss, damage or delay in delivery of the goods. The defence of negligence in the management or navigation of the vessel is not preserved.

---

[1] For an entertaining account of the gestation of the Hamburg Rules see Tetley (1979) L.C.M.L.Q. p.1. For the Hamburg Rules generally see A. J. Waldron (1979) JBL 305; O'Hare 29 I.C.L.Q. 219; the C.M.I. Colloquium on the Hamburg Rules, Vienna (1979); Selvig (1981) 12 J.M.L.C. 299; Gaskell "Damages, Delay and Limitation of Liability under the Hamburg Rules 1978".

[2] UNCTAD Report on Bills of Lading (1971).

[3] The Hamburg Rules are in force in Albania, Austria, Barbados, Botswana, Burkino Faso, Burundi, Cameroon, Chile, Czech Republic, Egypt, Gambia, Georgia, Guinea, Hungary, Jordan, Kenya, Lebanon, Liberia, Lesotho, Malawi, Morocco, Nigeria, Paraguay, Rumania, Saint Vincent and the Grenadines, Senegal, Sierra Leone, Syrian Arab Republic, Tunisia, Uganda, United Republic of Tanzania and Zambia. The Rules will come into force in the Dominican Republic on October 1, 2008.

Provision is also made for the joint liability of the contracting carrier and the actual carrier.

THE HAMBURG RULES

Final Act of The United Nations Conference on the Carriage of Goods by Sea

****

The United Nations Conference on the Carriage of Goods by Sea was held at Hamburg, Federal Republic of Germany, from Mar. 6 to 31, 1978.

A Convention was adopted by the Conference on Mar. 30, 1978 and was opened for signature at the concluding meeting of the Conference on Mar. 31, 1978. It will remain open for signature at United Nations Headquarters in New York until Apr. 30, 1979, after which date it will be open for accession, in accordance with its provisions.

The Convention is deposited with the Secretary-General of the United Nations.

The Conference also adopted a "common understanding" and a resolution, the texts of which are also annexed to this Final Act (Annexes II and III).

IN WITNESS WHEREOF the representatives have signed this Final Act.

Done at Hamburg, Federal Republic of Germany, this thirty-first day of March, one thousand nine hundred and seventy-eight, in a single copy in the Arabic, Chinese, English, French, Russian and Spanish languages, each text being equally authentic.

Annex I

United Nations Convention on the Carriage of Goods by Sea, 1978

Preamble

A6.2   THE STATES PARTIES TO THIS CONVENTION,

HAVING RECOGNIZED the desirability of determining by agreement certain rules relating to the carriage of goods by sea,

HAVE DECIDED to conclude a Convention for this purpose and have thereto agreed as follows:

Part I. General Provisions

A6.3   **Article 1. Definitions**

In this Convention:

1. "Carrier" means any person by whom or in whose name a contract of carriage of goods by sea has been concluded with a shipper.

2. "Actual carrier" means any person to whom the performance of the carriage of the goods, or of part of the carriage, has been entrusted by the carrier, and includes any other person to whom such performance has been entrusted.

3. "Shipper" means any person by whom or in whose name or on whose behalf a contract of carriage of goods by sea has been concluded with a carrier, or any person by whom or in whose name or on whose behalf the goods are actually delivered to the carrier in relation to the contract of carriage by sea.

4. "Consignee" means the person entitled to take delivery of the goods.

5. "Goods" includes live animals; where the goods are consolidated in a container, pallet or similar article of transport or where they are packed, "goods" includes such article of transport or packaging if supplied by the shipper.

6. "Contract of carriage by sea" means any contract whereby the carrier undertakes against payment of freight to carry goods by sea from one port to another; however, a contract which involves carriage by sea and also carriage by some other means is deemed to be a contract of carriage by sea for the purposes of this Convention only in so far as it relates to the carriage by sea.

7. "Bill of lading" means a document which evidences a contract of carriage by sea and the taking over or loading of the goods by the carrier, and by which the carrier undertakes to deliver the goods against surrender of the document. A provision in the document that the goods are to be delivered to the order of a named person, or to order, or to bearer, constitutes such an undertaking.

8. "Writing" includes, *inter alia*, telegram and telex.

"*Contract of carriage by sea*". Unlike the Hague and Hague-Visby Rules, the application of the Hamburg Rules is not dependent upon the issuing of a bill of lading or similar document of title. The Rules apply to any contract where goods are carried by sea in return for the payment of freight, save for charterparties or bills of lading issued to a charterer (Article 2.3). There is no definition of a charterparty in the Rules but it is submitted that this would not include a tonnage contract, even if in charterparty form.[4]

Article 2. Scope of application   A6.4

1. The provisions of this Convention are applicable to all contracts of carriage by sea between two different States, if:

(a) the port of loading as provided for in the contract of carriage by sea is located in a Contracting State, or

(b) the port of discharge as provided for in the contract of carriage by sea is located in a Contracting State, or

(c) one of the optional ports of discharge provided for in the contract of carriage by sea is the actual port of discharge and such port is located in a Contracting State, or

(d) the bill of lading or other document evidencing the contract of carriage by sea is issued in a Contracting State, or

(e) the bill of lading or other document evidencing the contract of carriage by sea provides that the provisions of this Convention or the legislation of any State giving effect to them are to govern the contract.

2. The provisions of this Convention are applicable without regard to the nationality of the ship, the carrier, the actual carrier, the shipper, the consignee or any other interested person.

3. The provisions of this Convention are not applicable to charter-parties. However, where a bill of lading is issued pursuant to a charter-party, the provisions of the Convention apply to such a bill of lading if it governs the relation between the carrier and the holder of the bill of lading, not being the charterer.

4. If a contract provides for future carriage of goods in a series of shipments during an agreed period, the provisions of this Convention apply to each shipment.

---

[4] *Cf.* Art.2.4.

However, where a shipment is made under a charter-party, the provisions of para. 3 of this Article apply.

A6.5   Article 3. Interpretation of the Convention

In the interpretation and application of the provisions of this Convention regard shall be had to its international character and to the need to promote uniformity.

PART II. LIABILITY OF THE CARRIER

A6.6   Article 4. Period of responsibility

1. The responsibility of the carrier for the goods under this Convention covers the period during which the carrier is in charge of the goods at the port of loading, during the carriage and at the port of discharge.

2. For the purpose of para. 1 of this Article, the carrier is deemed to be in charge of the goods

    (a) from the time he has taken over the goods from:
      (i) the shipper, or a person acting on his behalf; or
      (ii) an authority or other third party to whom, pursuant to law or regulations applicable at the port of loading, the goods must be handed over for shipment;
    (b) until the time he has delivered the goods:
      (i) by handing over the goods to the consignee; or
      (ii) in cases where the consignee does not receive the goods from the carrier, by placing them at the disposal of the consignee in accordance with the contract or with the law or with the usage of the particular trade, applicable at the port of discharge; or
      (iii) by handing over the goods to an authority or other third party to whom, pursuant to law or regulations applicable at the port of discharge, the goods must be handed over.

3. In paras. 1 and 2 of this Article, reference to the carrier or to the consignee means, in addition to the carrier or the consignee, the servants or agents, respectively or the carrier or the consignee.

"*The period during which the carrier is in charge of the goods at the port of loading, during the carriage and at the port of discharge*". Article 4.1 displaces the "tackle to tackle" period of responsibility of the carrier, and replaces it with a general responsibility of the carrier during the period in which he is "in charge" of the goods, as defined in Article 4.2. However, the period of responsibility only begins when the carrier takes charge of the goods at the port of loading. Where the goods are delivered to the carrier at an inland depot, the carrier may still be entitled to limit his liability to a greater extent than allowed under the Rules until such time as the goods reach the port of loading.

In circumstances in which there is transhipment outside of a port, the period of the responsibility of the transhipping carrier as actual carrier will begin when the goods are in his charge.

"*Until the time when he has delivered the goods . . . in cases where the consignee does not receive the goods from the carrier, by placing them at the disposal of the consignee in accordance with the contract*". As a result of this provision, it may be possible for the carrier to introduce a contractual provision in the bill of lading terminating his liability for

the goods at the "ship's tackle" on discharge in those cases where the consignee does not
receive the goods from the carrier.

Article 5. Basis of liability   A6.7

1. The carrier is liable for loss resulting from loss of or damage to the goods, as well
as from delay in delivery, if the occurrence which caused the loss, damage or delay
took place while the goods were in his charge as defined in art. 4, unless the carrier
proves that he, his servants or agents took all measures that could reasonably be
required to avoid the occurrence and its consequences.

2. Delay in delivery occurs when the goods have not been delivered at the port of
discharge provided for in the contract of carriage by sea within the time expressly
agreed upon or, in the absence of such agreement, within the time which it would be
reasonable to require of a diligent carrier, having regard to the circumstance of the
case.

3. The person entitled to make a claim for the loss of goods may treat the goods as
lost if they have not been delivered as required by art. 4 within 60 consecutive days
following the expiry of the time for delivery according to para. 2 of this Article.

4. (a) The carrier is liable

   (i) for loss of or damage to the goods or delay in delivery caused by fire, if the
      claimant proves that the fire arose from fault or neglect on the part of the
      carrier, his servants or agents;

  (ii) for such loss, damage or delay in delivery which is proved by the claimant
      to have resulted from the fault or neglect of the carrier, his servants or
      agents, in taking all measures that could reasonably be required to put out
      the fire and avoid or mitigate its consequences.

  (b) In case of fire on board the ship affecting the goods, if the claimant or the
carrier so desires, a survey in accordance with shipping practices must be held into
the cause and circumstances of the fire, and a copy of the surveyor's report shall be
made available on demand to the carrier and the claimant.

5. With respect to live animals, the carrier is not liable for loss, damage or delay
in delivery resulting from any special risks inherent in that kind of carriage. If the
carrier proves that he has complied with any special instructions given to him by the
shipper respecting the animals and that, in the circumstances of the case, the loss,
damage or delay in delivery could be attributed to such risks, it is presumed that the
loss, damage or delay in delivery was so caused, unless there is proof that all or a part
of the loss, damage or delay in delivery resulted from fault or neglect on the part of
the carrier, his servants or agents.

6. The carrier is not liable, except in general average, where loss, damage or delay
in delivery resulted from measures to save life or from reasonable measures to save
property at sea.

7. Where fault or neglect on the part of the carrier, his servants or agents combines
with another cause to produce loss, damage or delay in delivery the carrier is liable
only to the extent that the loss, damage or delay in delivery is attributable to such
fault or neglect, provided that the carrier proves the amount of the loss, damage or
delay in delivery not attributable thereto.

    *"The carrier is liable for loss resulting from loss of or damage to the goods, as well as
from delay in delivery, if the occurrence which caused the loss"*. It is not clear whether the
Article requires merely a causal connection between the loss, damage or delay and the

occurrence, or whether a test of remoteness of loss will apply. The better view is that the requirement of remoteness will depend upon national law.[5]

One important effect of Article 5.1 is to exclude the defence of "negligence in the navigation and management of the vessel". In addition, the carrier is made expressly liable for the negligence of his servants or agents. It is not clear whether and to what extent this liability would extend to independent contractors,[6] and whether the carrier is to be liable for the acts of "servants or agents" when acting outside the course of their employment.[7]

The Article does not place any temporal limit—such as "before and at the beginning of the voyage"—on the carrier's obligation to take all measures that could reasonably be required to avoid loss, damage or delay.

"*Unless the carrier proves*". Whilst the burden of showing that all measures that could reasonably be required to avoid an occurrence and its consequences were taken is placed on the carrier, no provision is made for who should bear the burden of establishing when the occurrence took place, and, specifically, whether it took place while the goods were in the charge of the carrier. Annex II would suggest that the burden of establishing that the occurrence took place before the goods came into his charge would rest on the carrier.

"*Delay in delivery occurs when the goods have not been delivered . . . within the time expressly agreed upon*". To circumvent the application of this Rule, a shipowner may seek to include a provision in his bill of lading allowing an extremely generous time for delivery of the goods. However, the reference to "express agreement" in Article 5.2 probably requires a genuine consensus between carrier and shipper, and it seems doubtful that a term in small print on the reverse of the bill of lading would satisfy this requirement.

"*The person entitled to make a claim for the loss of the goods may treat the goods as lost . . .* ". At first reading, this Rule might be thought to apply even in the absence of fault of the carrier. However, it is suggested that the words "the person entitled to make a claim" denote a requirement of delay for which the carrier is liable under Article 5.1 (that is to say where he is unable to show that he, his servants or agents took all measures that could reasonably be required to avoid the delay).

No provision is made for what is to happen to goods which are treated as lost. Presumably an election to treat the goods as lost involves an abandonment of such property rights in them as the claimant may have.

"*Loss of or damage to the goods or delay in delivery caused by fire*". It is not clear why the decision was taken to reverse the burden of proof in cases of loss, damage or delay caused by fire. It is suggested that this is the only effect of Article 5.4 (a), and that the use of the words "fault or neglect" rather than "all measures that could reasonably be taken" is not intended to alter the standard of care required from the carrier.[8]

"*A survey in accordance with shipping practice must be held*". It is unclear who is to bear the cost of any survey held pursuant to this Rule.

"*Where fault or neglect . . . combines with another cause*". It is submitted that this provision is not aimed at the position where there are two co-operating causes of the same loss, but rather where some part of the damage is due to a different cause from the carrier's fault or neglect.

---

[5] It would appear that a requirement for remoteness in connection with claims for loss caused by delay was considered, but not agreed upon. On this point generally see Gaskell, *op. cit.*, pp.145–6.

[6] *Cf. Riverstone Meat and Property Co v Lancashire Shipping Co* [1961] A.C. 807.

[7] Compare Arts 7.2 and 10.1 and the absence of any reference in Art.5.1 to the "scope of . . . employment".

[8] Although *cf.* the juxtaposition of these two phrases in Art.5.4(a)(ii). For a contrary view see Nicoll (1993) 24 J.M.L.C. 151 at p.154.

Article 6. Limits of liability   A6.8

1. (a) The liability of the carrier for loss resulting from loss of or damage to goods according to the provisions of art. 5 is limited to an amount equivalent to 835 units of account per package or other shipping unit or 2.5 units of account per kilogramme of gross weight of the goods lost or damaged, whichever is the higher.

(b) The liability of the carrier for delay in delivery according to the provisions of art. 5 is limited to an amount equivalent to two and a half times the freight payable for the goods delayed, but not exceeding the total freight payable under the contract of carriage of goods by sea.   \

(c) In no case shall the aggregate liability of the carrier, under both subparas. (a) and (b) of this paragraph, exceed the limitation which would be established under subpara. (a) of this paragraph for total loss of the goods with respect to which such liability was incurred.

2. For the purpose of calculating which amount is the higher in accordance with para. 1 (a) of this Article, the following rules apply:

(a) Where a container, pallet or similar article of transport is used to consolidate goods, the package or other shipping units enumerated in the bill of lading, if issued, or otherwise in any other document evidencing the contract of carriage by sea, as packed in such article of transport are deemed packages or shipping units. Except as aforesaid the goods in such article of transport are deemed one shipping unit.

(b) In cases where the article of transport itself has been lost or damaged, that article of transport, if not owned or otherwise supplied by the carrier, is considered one separate shipping unit.

3. Unit of account means the unit of account mentioned in art. 26.

4. By agreement between the carrier and the shipper, limits of liability exceeding those provided for in para. 1 may be fixed.

The limitation figures are more generous than those available under the Hague-Visby Rules, but not markedly so. It is not clear why a different test of limitation was applied to claims for delay, as opposed to those for loss of or damage to goods. Where delay itself causes loss of or damage to goods (for instance because the goods are perishable), it is submitted that the limitation provisions in Article 6.1 (a) will apply. Similarly, when there is delay, and the claimant elects to treat the goods as lost under Article 5.3, it is suggested that the limit set out in Article 6.1 (a), rather than 6.1 (b), will apply.

It is submitted that Article 6.1 (c)—which makes the limit in Article 6.1 (a) a maximum limit for "aggregate liability under both sub-paras. (a) and (b)"—would nevertheless apply where the only claim advanced was under sub-paragraph (b). In these circumstances, if liability for delay calculated in accordance with sub-paragraph (b) would exceed that applying under sub-paragraph (a) if the goods had been lost, the limit of sub-paragraph (a) would nevertheless limit the carrier's liability.

The definition of "shipping unit" (Article 6.2 (b)) avoids the controversy under the Hague Rules as to whether "unit" is a reference to freight or shipping units.

Article 7. Application to non-contractual claims   A6.9

1. The defences and limits of liability provided for in this Convention apply in any action against the carrier in respect of loss or damage to the goods covered by the contract of carriage by sea, as well as of delay in delivery whether the action is founded in contract, in tort or otherwise.

2. If such an action is brought against a servant or agent of the carrier, such servant or agent, if he proves that he acted within the scope of his employment, is

entitled to avail himself of the defences and limits of liability which the carrier is entitled to invoke under this Convention.

3. Except as provided in art. 8, the aggregate of the amounts recoverable from the carrier and from any persons referred to in para. 2 of this Article shall not exceed the limits of liability provided for in this Convention.

A6.10 ### Article 8. Loss of right to limit responsibility

1. The carrier is not entitled to the benefit of the limitation of liability provided for in art. 6 if it is proved that the loss, damage or delay in delivery resulted from an act or omission of the carrier done with the intent to cause such loss, damage or delay, or recklessly and with knowledge that such loss, damage or delay would probably result.

2. Notwithstanding the provisions of para. 2 of art. 7, a servant or agent of the carrier is not entitled to the benefit of the limitation of liability provided for in art. 6 if it is proved that the loss, damage or delay in delivery resulted from an act or omission of such servant or agent, done with the intent to cause such loss, damage or delay, or recklessly and with knowledge that such loss, damage or delay would probably result.

Article 8.1 provides that the carrier's right to limit will be lost in the event that damage resulted from an act or omission of the carrier done with the intent to cause such loss, damage or delay, or recklessly and with knowledge that such loss, damage or delay would probably result. This Article does not refer to intentional or reckless acts or omissions of the carrier's servants or agents. Article 8.2 provides that those servants or agents will lose their own entitlement to limit liability in accordance with Article 6 if the loss, damage or delay is caused by their intentional or reckless acts, but again, does not specify what the effect of such conduct is upon the carrier in an action by the shipper or consignee against the carrier for damage caused by the intentional or reckless acts of the carrier's servants or agents.

It is suggested that the carrier will not lose his entitlement to limit in such an action, albeit an action against the servants or agents would not be subject to the limits in Article 6. Nor will the intentional or reckless conduct of the actual carrier cause the carrier to lose his right to limit, notwithstanding the second sentence of Article 10.1.

The test in Article 6.1 may cause problems with regard to delay, where conduct may be undertaken in good faith but with knowledge that delay will probably result (for instance loading further cargo at an intermediate port or in a bona fide, but unreasonable, attempt to avoid a war zone or strikes). The right to limit should not be lost in these circumstances. The answer may be to require not simply knowledge that delay would probably result, but knowledge that the loss which was in fact caused by the delay would probably result. Alternatively, it might be said that the requirement of recklessness—which would appear to impose a further requirement in addition to knowledge that delay would probably result—would prevent bona fide conduct of this nature losing the carrier his right to limit.

A6.11 ### Article 9. Deck cargo

1. The carrier is entitled to carry the goods on deck only if such carriage is in accordance with an agreement with the shipper or with the usage of the particular trade or is required by statutory rules or regulations.

2. If the carrier and the shipper have agreed that the goods shall or may be carried on deck, the carrier must insert in the bill of lading or other document evidencing the

contract of carriage by sea a statement to that effect. In the absence of such a statement the carrier has the burden of proving that an agreement for carriage on deck has been entered into; however, the carrier is not entitled to invoke such an agreement against a third party, including a consignee, who has acquired the bill of lading in good faith.

3. Where the goods have been carried on deck contrary to the provisions of para. 1 of this Article or where the carrier may not under para. 2 of this Article invoke an agreement for carriage on deck, the carrier, notwithstanding the provisions of para. 1 of art. 5, is liable for loss of or damage to the goods, as well as for delay in delivery, resulting solely from the carriage on deck, and the extent of his liability is to be determined in accordance with the provisions of art. 6 or art. 8 of this Convention, as the case may be.

4. Carriage of goods on deck contrary to express agreement for carriage under deck is deemed to be an act or omission of the carrier within the meaning of art. 8.

"Only if such carriage is in accordance with an agreement". It is not clear whether a permissive provision in a bill of lading entitling the carrier to carry goods on deck would constitute an agreement recorded in the bill of lading for the purposes of Articles 9.1 and 9.2. The absence of any reference to an express agreement, in contrast to Articles 5.2 and 9.4, might suggest so, as would the absence of any requirement that such a provision appear "on the face of" rather than "in" the bill of lading.[9] Further, Article 9.2 refers to an agreement that the goods shall or may be carried on deck. Finally Article 15.1 (m) specifies that the bill of lading must include the statement that the goods shall or *may* be carried on deck, which again suggests that a permissive provision will suffice.

"The carrier must insert in the bill of lading or other document evidencing the contract of carriage by sea a statement to that effect". Where cargo is carried on deck pursuant to a trade usage or statutory rules or regulations, it would appear that no statement on the bill of lading is necessary (Article 9.2) although the wording of Article 15.1 (m) might suggest the contrary. It may be that it would be necessary to establish that the relevant usage was not simply the carriage of the goods on deck, but the carriage of goods on deck without so noting on the bill of lading.[10]

Article 10. Liability of the carrier and actual carrier   A6.12

1. Where the performance of the carriage or part thereof has been entrusted to an actual carrier, whether or not in pursuance of a liberty under the contract of carriage by sea to do so, the carrier nevertheless remains responsible for the entire carriage according to the provisions of this Convention. The carrier is responsible, in relation to the carriage performed by the actual carrier, for the acts and omissions of the actual carrier and of his servants and agents acting within the scope of their employment.

2. All the provisions of this Convention governing the responsibility of the carrier also apply to the responsibility of the actual carrier for the carriage performed by him. The provisions of paras. 2 and 3 of art. 7 and of para. 2 of art. 8 apply if an action is brought against a servant or agent of the actual carrier.

3. Any special agreement under which the carrier assumes obligations not imposed by this Convention or waives rights conferred by this Convention affects the actual

---

[9] However it is to be noted that Art.15.1 (m) appears amongst a number of matters traditionally found on the face of a bill of lading, rather than on the terms printed on the reverse side.
[10] Bauer (1993) 24 J.M.L.C. 53 at p.65.

carrier only if agreed to by him expressly and in writing. Whether or not the actual carrier has so agreed, the carrier nevertheless remains bound by the obligations or waivers resulting from such special agreement.

4. Where and to the extent that both the carrier and the actual carrier are liable, their liability is joint and several.

5. The aggregate of the amounts recoverable from the carrier, the actual carrier and their servants and agents shall not exceed the limits of liability provided for in this Convention.

6. Nothing in this Article shall prejudice any right of recourse as between the carrier and the actual carrier.

In common with the Convention Merchandises par Route (CMR), the Rules make the first carrier responsible for the acts and omissions of subsequent carriers in respect of the contractual voyage, save where the servants or agents of the actual carrier act outside the scope of their employment or where the conditions of Article 11 are satisfied. The actual carrier will be responsible for loss, damage or delay during the carriage performed by him. Whether this provision will have the desired effect of avoiding the need for the claimant "to unravel the complicated contractual relations between the charterers and the vessel owners"[11] will depend upon the ingenuity of the draftsmen of bills of lading when defining exactly what carriage the contractual carrier agrees to undertake.

"*All the provisions of this Convention governing the responsibility of the carrier*". When construing Article 10.2, a wide interpretation should be adopted to determining which are the "provisions of the Convention governing the responsibility of the carrier" so as to include those provisions dealing with limitation and time bar.

A6.13   **Article 11. Through carriage**

1. Notwithstanding the provisions of para. 1 of art. 10, where a contract of carriage by sea provides explicitly that a specified part of the carriage covered by the said contract is to be performed by a named person other than the carrier, the contract may also provide that the carrier is not liable for loss, damage or delay in delivery caused by an occurrence which takes place while the goods are in the charge of the actual carrier during such part of the carriage. Nevertheless, any stipulation limiting or excluding such liability is without effect if no judicial proceedings can be instituted against the actual carrier in a court competent under paras. 1 or 2 of art. 21. The burden of proving that any loss, damage or delay in delivery has been caused by such an occurrence rests upon the carrier.

2. The actual carrier is responsible in accordance with the provisions of para. 2 of art. 10 for loss, damage or delay in delivery caused by an occurrence which takes place while the goods are in his charge.

The requirement for a named person to be specified considerably reduces the utility of this Article so far as the carrier is concerned, as in the majority of cases it will not be possible to identify, at the time when the contract of carriage is concluded, the name of the person(s) who will be performing subsequent stages of the contractual voyage.

Where the named carrier can be identified, however, this provision is capable of application not merely to cases of transhipment, but also to the case where a charterer issues his own bill of lading as contracting party and entrusts the entire carriage to the shipowner who is named as the carrier in the bill of lading.

---

[11] Tetley, *op. cit.*, p.6.

"The burden of proving that any loss, damage or delay in delivery has been caused by such an occurrence rests upon the carrier". It is clear that the carrier will bear the burden of establishing that loss or damage occurred during the period in which the goods were in the charge of the actual carrier. Where the goods are discharged ashore, and are damaged by stevedores, before being delivered into the charge of the actual carrier, the carrier will remain liable. It might be possible to argue that the stevedores were an "actual carrier", a term defined by Article 1.2 to include "any person to whom the performance . . . of part of the carriage, has been entrusted by the carrier". However, it is most unlikely that the stevedores would be named in the bill of lading, as required by Article 11.1.

PART III. LIABILITY OF THE SHIPPER

Article 12. General rule   A6.14

The shipper is not liable for loss sustained by the carrier or the actual carrier, or for damage sustained by the ship, unless such loss or damage was caused by the fault or neglect of the shipper, his servants or agents. Nor is any servant or agent of the shipper liable for such loss or damage unless the loss or damage was caused by fault or neglect on his part.

Article 13. Special rules on dangerous goods   A6.15

1. The shipper must mark or label in a suitable manner dangerous goods as dangerous.

2. Where the shipper hands over dangerous goods to the carrier or an actual carrier, as the case may be, the shipper must inform him of the dangerous character of the goods and, if necessary, of the precautions to be taken. If the shipper fails to do so and such carrier or actual carrier does not otherwise have knowledge of their dangerous character:

(a) the shipper is liable to the carrier and any actual carrier for the loss resulting from the shipment of such goods, and

(b) the goods may at any time be unloaded, destroyed or rendered innocuous, as the circumstances may require, without payment of compensation.

3. The provisions of para. 2 of this Article may not be invoked by any person if during the carriage he has taken the goods in his charge with knowledge of their dangerous character.

4. If, in cases where the provisions of para. 2, subpara. (b), of this Article do not apply or may not be invoked, dangerous goods become an actual danger to life or property, they may be unloaded, destroyed or rendered innocuous, as the circumstances may require, without payment of compensation except where there is an obligation to contribute in general average or where the carrier is liable in accordance with the provisions of art. 5.

PART IV. TRANSPORT DOCUMENTS

Article 14. Issue of bill of lading   A6.16

1. When the carrier or the actual carrier takes the goods in his charge, the carrier must, on demand of the shipper, issue to the shipper a bill of lading.

2. The bill of lading may be signed by a person having authority from the carrier. A bill of lading signed by the master of the ship carrying the goods is deemed to have been signed on behalf of the carrier.

3. The signature on the bill of lading may be in handwriting, printed in facsimile, perforated, stamped, in symbols, or made by any other mechanical or electronic

means, if not inconsistent with the law of the country where the bill of lading is issued.

"*A bill of lading signed by the master . . . is deemed to have been signed on behalf of the carrier*". It is suggested that the purpose of this Article is to overcome the rule in *Grant v. Norway*,[12] rather than to define who the carrier is.

A6.17 ### Article 15. Contents of bill of lading

1. The bill of lading must include, *inter alia*, the following particulars:

    (a) the general nature of the goods, the leading marks necessary for identification of the goods, an express statement, if applicable, as to the dangerous character of the goods, the number of packages or pieces, and the weight of the goods or their quantity otherwise expressed, all such particulars as furnished by the shipper;

    (b) the apparent condition of the goods;

    (c) the name and principal place of business of the carrier;

    (d) the name of the shipper;

    (e) the consignee if named by the shipper;

    (f) the port of loading under the contract of carriage by sea and the date on which the goods were taken over by the carrier at the port of loading;

    (g) the port of discharge under the contract of carriage by sea;

    (h) the number of originals of the bill of lading, if more than one;

    (i) the place of issuance of the bill of lading;

    (j) the signature of the carrier or a person acting on his behalf;

    (k) the freight to the extent payable by the consignee or other indication that freight is payable by him;

    (l) the statement referred to in para. 3 of art. 23;

    (m) the statement, if applicable, that the goods shall or may be carried on deck;

    (n) the date or the period of delivery of the goods at the port of discharge if expressly agreed upon between the parties; and

    (o) any increased limit or limits of liability where agreed in accordance with para. 4 of art. 6.

2. After the goods have been loaded on board, if the shipper so demands, the carrier must issue to the shipper a "shipped" bill of lading which, in addition to the particulars required under para. 1 of this Article, must state that the goods are on board a named ship or ships, and the date or dates of loading. If the carrier has previously issued to the shipper a bill of lading or other document of title with respect to any such goods on request of the carrier, the shipper must surrender such document in exchange for a "shipped" bill of lading. The carrier may amend any previously issued document in order to meet the shipper's demand for a "shipped" bill of lading if, as amended, such document includes all the information required to be contained in a "shipped" bill of lading.

3. The absence in the bill of lading of one or more particulars referred to in this Article does not affect the legal character of the document as a bill of lading provided that it nevertheless meets the requirements set out in para. 7 of art. 1.

---

[12] (1851) 10 C.B. 665.

The requirements of Article 15.1 considerably extend those set out in Article III Rule 3 of the Hague and Hague-Visby Rules. Further, the carrier is required to specify both the number of packages or pieces and the weight of the goods.

Article 16. Bills of lading: reservations and evidentiary effect   A6.18

1. If the bill of lading contains particulars concerning the general nature, leading marks, number of packages or pieces, weight or quantity of the goods which the carrier or other person issuing the bill of lading on his behalf knows or has reasonable grounds to suspect do not accurately represent the goods actually taken over or, where a "shipped" bill of lading is issued, loaded, or if he had no reasonable means of checking such particulars, the carrier or such other person must insert in the bill of lading a reservation specifying these inaccuracies, grounds of suspicion or the absence of reasonable means of checking.

2. If the carrier or other person issuing the bill of lading on his behalf fails to note on the bill of lading the apparent condition of the goods, he is deemed to have noted on the bill of lading that the goods were in apparent good condition.

3. Except for particulars in respect of which and to the extent to which a reservation permitted under para. 1 of this Article has been entered:

(a) the bill of lading is prima facie evidence of the taking over or, where a "shipped" bill of lading is issued, loading, by the carrier of the goods as described in the bill of lading; and

(b) proof to the contrary by the carrier is not admissible if the bill of lading has been transferred to a third party, including a consignee, who in good faith has acted in reliance on the description of the goods therein.

4. A bill of lading which does not, as provided in para. 1, subpara. (k) of art. 15, set forth the freight or otherwise indicate that freight is payable by the consignee or does not set forth demurrage incurred at the port of loading payable by the consignee, is prima facie evidence that no freight or such demurrage is payable by him. However, proof to the contrary by the carrier is not admissible when the bill of lading has been transferred to a third party, including a consignee, who in good faith has acted in reliance on the absence in the bill of lading of any such indication.

Article 17. Guarantees by the shipper   A6.19

1. The shipper is deemed to have guaranteed to the carrier the accuracy of particulars relating to the general nature of the goods, their marks, number, weight and quantity as furnished by him for insertion in the bill of lading. The shipper must indemnify the carrier against the loss resulting from inaccuracies in such particulars. The shipper remains liable even if the bill of lading has been transferred by him. The right of the carrier to such indemnity in no way limits his liability under the contract of carriage by sea to any person other than the shipper.

2. Any letter of guarantee or agreement by which the shipper undertakes to indemnify the carrier against loss resulting from the issuance of the bill of lading by the carrier, or by a person acting on his behalf, without entering a reservation relating to particulars furnished by the shipper for insertion in the bill of lading, or to the apparent condition of the goods, is void and of no effect as against any third party, including a consignee, to whom the bill of lading has been transferred.

3. Such letter of guarantee or agreement is valid as against the shipper unless the carrier or the person acting on his behalf, by omitting the reservation referred to in para. 2 of this Article, intends to defraud a third party, including a consignee, who acts in reliance on the description of the goods in the bill of lading. In the latter case, if the reservation omitted relates to particulars furnished by the shipper for insertion in the bill of lading, the carrier has no right of indemnity from the shipper pursuant to para. 1 of this Article.

4. In the case of intended fraud referred to in para. 3 of this Article the carrier is liable, without the benefit of the limitation of liability provided for in this Convention, for the loss incurred by a third party, including a consignee, because he has acted in reliance on the description of the goods in the bill of lading.

The liability of the shipper under Article 17.1 is absolute, and not subject to the requirement of fault or neglect set out in Article 12.

Article 17.3 reflects the English common law position of *Brown Jenkinson & Co. Ltd. v. Percy Dalton (London) Ltd*,[13] save that it is not clear whether it will be sufficient for the purposes of Article 17.3 that a carrier forsees that a third party may be defrauded, without intending or desiring this result.

A6.20 ### Article 18. Documents other than bills of lading

Where a carrier issues a document other than a bill of lading to evidence the receipt of the goods to be carried, such a document is prima facie of the conclusion of the contract of carriage by sea and the taking over by the carrier of the goods as therein described.

PART V. CLAIMS AND ACTIONS

A6.21 ### Article 19. Notice of loss, damage or delay

1. Unless notice of loss or damage, specifying the general nature of such loss or damage, is given in writing by the consignee to the carrier not later than the working day after the day when the goods were handed over to the consignee, such handing over is prima facie evidence of the delivery by the carrier of the goods as described in the document of transport or, if no such document has been issued, in good condition.

2. Where the loss or damage is not apparent, the provisions of para. 1 of this Article apply correspondingly if notice in writing is not given within 15 consecutive days after the day when the goods were handed over to the consignee.

3. If the state of the goods at the time they were handed over to the consignee has been the subject of a joint survey or inspection by the parties, notice in writing need not be given of loss or damage ascertained during such survey or inspection.

4. In the case of any actual or apprehended loss or damage the carrier and the consignee must give all reasonable facilities to each other for inspecting and tallying the goods.

5. No compensation shall be payable for loss resulting from delay in delivery unless a notice has been given in writing to the carrier within 60 consecutive days after the day when the goods were handed over to the consignee.

6. If the goods have been delivered by an actual carrier, any notice given under this article to him shall have the same effect as if it had been given to the carrier, and any notice given to the carrier shall have effect as if given to such actual carrier.

7. Unless notice of loss or damage, specifying the general nature of the loss or damage, is given in writing by the carrier or actual carrier to the shipper not later than 90 consecutive days after the occurrence of such loss or damage or after the

---

[13] [1957] 2 Q.B. 621.

delivery of the goods in accordance with para. 2 of art. 4, whichever is later, the failure to give such notice is prima facie evidence that the carrier or the actual carrier has sustained no loss or damage due to the fault or neglect of the shipper, his servants or agents.

8. For the purpose of this Article, notice given to a person acting on the carrier's or the actual carrier's behalf, including the master or the officer in charge of the ship, or to a person acting on the shipper's behalf is deemed to have been given to the carrier, to the actual carrier or to the shipper, respectively.

Article 19.1 contains a considerable relaxation of the notification requirements of the Hague and Hague-Visby Rules. Written notice of damage which is apparent on delivery need only be given on the day following delivery in order to avoid an evidential presumption of delivery in good condition, whilst non-apparent damage need only be notified within 15 days of delivery to the consignee. Such notice must be given in writing by the consignee to the carrier.

So far as delay is concerned, there is an absolute requirement that loss or damage due to delay be notified in writing to the carrier within 60 days of the date when the goods have been handed over to the consignee. Again, it is submitted that damage caused by delay should fall within Article 19 Rules 1 and 2 rather than Rule 5.

It is not clear whether "handing over" requires actual delivery to the consignee or whether it occurs at the point in time when the carrier's responsibility under Article 4.2 (b).

Article 20. Limitation of actions   A6.22

1. Any action relating to carriage of goods under this Convention is time-barred if judicial or arbitral proceedings have not been instituted within a period of two years.

2. The limitation period commences on the day on which the carrier has delivered the goods or part thereof or, in cases where no goods have been delivered, on the last day on which the goods should have been delivered.

3. The day on which the limitation period commences is not included in the period.

4. The person against whom a claim is made may at any time during the running of the limitation period extend that period by a declaration in writing to the claimant. This period may be further extended by another declaration or declarations.

5. An action for indemnity by a person held liable may be instituted even after the expiration of the limitation period provided for in the preceding paragraphs if instituted within the time allowed by the law of the State where proceedings are instituted. However, the time allowed shall not be less than 90 days commencing from the day when the person instituting such action for indemnity has settled the claim or has been served with process in the action against himself.

The time bar is not limited to claims against the carrier, but covers any action relating to carriage of goods under the Convention.

Article 21. Jurisdiction   A6.23

1. In judicial proceedings relating to carriage of goods under this Convention the plaintiff, at his option, may institute an action in a court which, according to the law

of the State where the court is situated, is competent and within the jurisdiction of which is situated one of the following places:

(a) the principal place of business or, in the absence thereof, the habitual residence of the defendant; or

(b) the place where the contract was made provided that the defendant has there a place of business, branch or agency through which the contract was made; or

(c) the port of loading or the port of discharge; or

(d) any additional place designated for that purpose in the contract of carriage by sea.

2. (a) Notwithstanding the preceding provisions of this Article, an action may be instituted in the courts of any port or place in a Contracting State at which the carrying vessel or any other vessel of the same ownership may have been arrested in accordance with applicable rules of the law of that State and of international law. However, in such a case, at the petition of the defendant, the claimant must remove the action, at his choice, to one of the jurisdictions referred to in para. 1 of this Article for the determination of the claim, but before such removal the defendant must furnish security sufficient to ensure payment of any judgment that may subsequently be awarded to the claimant in the action.

(b) All questions relating to the sufficiency or otherwise of the security shall be determined by the court of the port or place of the arrest.

3. No judicial proceedings relating to carriage of goods under this Convention may be instituted in a place not specified in paras. 1 or 2 of this Article. The provisions of this paragraph do not constitute an obstacle to the jurisdiction of the Contracting States for provisional or protective measures.

4. (a) Where an action has been instituted in a court competent under paras. 1 or 2 of this Article or where judgment has been delivered by such a court, no new action may be started between the same parties on the same grounds unless the judgment of the court before which the first action was instituted is not enforceable in the country in which the new proceedings are instituted;

(b) for the purpose of this Article the institution of measures with a view to obtaining enforcement of a judgment is not to be considered as the starting of a new action;

(c) for the purpose of this Article, the removal of an action to a different court within the same country, or to a court in another country, in accordance with para. 2(a) of this Article, is not to be considered as the starting of a new action.

5. Notwithstanding the provisions of the preceding paragraphs, an agreement made by the parties, after a claim under the contract of carriage by sea has arisen, which designates the place where the claimant may institute an action, is effective.

A6.24   Article 22. Arbitration

1. Subject to the provisions of this Article, parties may provide by agreement evidenced in writing that any dispute that may arise relating to carriage of goods under this Convention shall be referred to arbitration.

2. Where a charter-party contains a provision that disputes arising thereunder shall be referred to arbitration and a bill of lading issued pursuant to the charter-party does not contain a special annotation providing that such provision shall be binding upon the holder of the bill of lading, the carrier may not invoke such provision as against a holder having acquired the bill of lading in good faith.

3. The arbitration proceedings shall, at the option of the claimant, be instituted at one of the following places:

(a) a place in a State within whose territory is situated:

  (i) the principal place of business of the defendant or, in the absence thereof, the habitual residence of the defendant; or

  (ii) the place where the contract was made, provided that the defendant has there a place of business, branch or agency through which the contract was made; or

  (iii) the port of loading or the port of discharge; or

(b) any place designated for that purpose in the arbitration clause or agreement.

4. The arbitrator or arbitration tribunal shall apply the rules of this Convention.

5. The provisions of paras. 3 and 4 of this Article are deemed to be part of every arbitration clause or agreement, and any term of such clause or agreement which is inconsistent therewith is null and void.

6. Nothing in this Article affects the validity of an agreement relating to arbitration made by the parties after the claim under the contract of carriage by sea has arisen.

PART VI. SUPPLEMENTARY PROVISIONS

Article 23. Contractual Stipulations   A6.25

1. Any stipulation in a contract of carriage by sea, in a bill of lading, or in any other document evidencing the contract of carriage by sea is null and void to the extent that it derogates, directly or indirectly, from the provisions of this Convention. The nullity of such a stipulation does not affect the validity of the other provisions of the contract or document of which it forms a part. A clause assigning benefit of insurance of the goods in favour of the carrier, or any similar clause, is null and void.

2. Notwithstanding the provisions of para. 1 of this Article, a carrier may increase his responsibilities and obligations under this Convention.

3. Where a bill of lading or any other document evidencing the contract of carriage by sea is issued, it must contain a statement that the carriage is subject to the provisions of this Convention which nullify any stipulation derogating therefrom to the detriment of the shipper or the consignee.

4. Where the claimant in respect of the goods has incurred loss as a result of a stipulation which is null and void by virtue of the present Article, or as a result of the omission of the statement referred to in para. 3 of this Article, the carrier must pay compensation to the extent required in order to give the claimant compensation in accordance with the provisions of this Convention for any loss of or damage to the goods as well as for delay in delivery. The carrier must, in addition, pay compensation for costs incurred by the claimant for the purpose of exercising his right, provided that costs incurred in the action where the foregoing provision is invoked are to be determined in accordance with the law of the State where proceedings are instituted.

Article 24. General average   A6.26

1. Nothing in this Convention shall prevent the application of provisions in the contract of carriage by sea or national law regarding the adjustment of general average.

2. With the exception of art. 20, the provisions of this Convention relating to the liability of the carrier for loss of or damage to the goods also determine whether the consignee may refuse contribution in general average and the liability of the carrier to indemnify the consignee in respect of any such contribution made or any salvage paid.

A6.27 Article 25. Other conventions

1. This Convention does not modify the rights or duties of the carrier, the actual carrier and their servants and agents, provided for an international conventions or national law relating to the limitation of liability of owners of seagoing ships.

2. The provisions of arts. 21 and 22 of this Convention do not prevent the application of the mandatory provisions of any other multilateral convention already in force at the date of this Convention relating to matters dealt with in the said Articles, provided that the dispute arises exclusively between parties having their principal place of business in States members of such other convention. However, this paragraph does not affect the application of para. 4 of art. 22 of this Convention.

3. No liability shall arise under the provisions of this Convention for damage caused by a nuclear incident if the operator of a nuclear installation is liable for such damage:

(a) under either the Paris Convention of July 29, 1960, on Third Party Liability in the Field of Nuclear Energy as amended by the Additional Protocol of Jan. 28, 1964, or the Vienna Convention of May 21, 1963, on Civil Liability for Nuclear Damage, or

(b) by virtue of national law governing the liability for such damage, provided that such law is in all aspects as favourable to persons who may suffer damage as either the Paris or Vienna Conventions.

4. No liability shall arise under the provisions of this Convention for any loss of or damage to or delay in delivery of luggage for which the carrier is responsible under any international convention or national law relating to the carriage of passengers and their luggage by sea.

5. Nothing contained in this Convention prevents a Contracting State from applying any other international convention which is already in force at the date of this Convention and which applies mandatorily to contracts of carriage of goods primarily by a mode of transport other than transport by sea. This provision also applies to any subsequent revision or amendment of such international convention.

A6.28 Article 26. Unit of account

1. The unit of account referred to in art. 6 of this Convention is the Special Drawing Right as defined by the International Monetary Fund. The amounts mentioned in art. 6 are to be converted into the national currency of a State according to the value of such currency at the date of judgment or the date agreed upon by the parties. The value of a national currency, in terms of the Special Drawing Right, of a Contracting State which is a member of the International Monetary Fund is to be calculated in accordance with the method of valuation applied by the International Monetary Fund in effect at the date in question for its operations and transactions. The value of a national currency in terms of the Special Drawing Right of a Contracting State which is not a member of the International Monetary Fund is to be calculated in a manner determined by that State.

2. Nevertheless, those States which are not members of the International Monetary Fund and whose law does not permit the application of the provisions of para. 1 of this Article may, at the time of signature, or at the time of ratification, acceptance, approval or accession or at any time thereafter, declare that the limits of liability provided for in this Convention to be applied in their territories shall be fixed as.

12,500 monetary units per package or other shipping unit or 37.5 monetary units per kilogramme of gross weight of the goods.

3. The monetary unit referred to in para. 2 of this Article corresponds to sixty-five and a half milligrammes of gold of millesimal fineness nine hundred. The conversion of the amounts referred to in para. 2 into the national currency is to be made according to the law of the State concerned.

4. The calculation mentioned in the last sentence of para. 1 and the conversion mentioned in para. 3 of this Article is to be made in such a manner as to express in the national currency of the Contracting State as far as possible the same real value for the amounts in art. 6 as is expressed there in units of account. Contracting State must communicate to the depositary the manner of calculation pursuant to para. 1 of this Article, or the result of the conversion mentioned in para. 3 of this Article, as the case may be, at the time of signature or when depositing their instruments of ratification, acceptance, approval or accession, or when availing themselves of the option provided for in para. 2 of this Article and whenever there is a change in the manner of such calculation or in the result of such conversion.

PART VII. FINAL CLAUSES

Article 27. Depositary   A6.29

The Secretary-General of the United Nations is hereby designated as the depositary of this Convention.

Article 28. Signature, ratification, acceptance, approval, accession   A6.30

1. This Convention is open for signature by all States until Apr. 30, 1979, at the headquarters of the United Nations, New York.

2. This Convention is subject to ratification, acceptance or approval by the signatory States.

3. After Apr. 30, 1979, this Convention will be open for accession by all States which are not signatory States.

4. Instruments of ratification, acceptance, approval and accession are to be deposited with the Secretary-General of the United Nations.

Article 29. Reservations   A6.31

No reservations may be made to this Convention.

Article 30. Entry into force

1. This Convention enters into force on the first day of the month following the   A6.32
expiration of one year from the date of deposit of the 20th instrument of ratification, acceptance, approval or accession.

2. For each State which becomes a Contracting State to this Convention after the date of the deposit of the 20th instrument of ratification, acceptance, approval or accession, this Convention enters into force on the first day of the month following the expiration of one year after the deposit of the appropriate instrument on behalf of that State.

3. Each Contracting State shall apply the provisions of this Convention to contracts of carriage by sea concluded on or after the date of the entry into force of this Convention in respect of that State.

A6.33   Article 31. Denunciation of other conventions

1. Upon becoming a Contracting State to this Convention, any State party to the International Convention for the Unification of Certain Rules relating to Bills of Lading signed at Brussels on Aug. 25, 1924 (1924 Convention) must notify the Government of Belgium as the depositary of the 1924 Convention of its denunciation of the said Convention with a declaration that the denunciation is to take effect as from the date when this Convention enters into force in respect of that State.

2. Upon the entry into force of this Convention under para. 1 of art. 30, the depositary of this Convention must notify the Government of Belgium as the depositary of the 1924 Convention of the date of such entry into force, and of the names of the Contracting States in respect of which the Convention has entered into force.

3. The provisions of paras. 1 and 2 of this Article apply correspondingly in respect of States parties to the Protocol signed on Feb. 23, 1968, to amend the International Convention for the Unification of Certain Rules relating to Bills of Lading signed at Brussels on Aug. 25, 1924.

4. Notwithstanding art. 2 of this Convention, for the purposes of para. 1 of this Article, a Contracting State may, if it deems it desirable, defer the denunciation of the 1924 Convention and of the 1924 Convention as modified by the 1968 Protocol for a maximum period of five years from the entry into force of this Convention. It will then notify the Government of Belgium of its intention. During this transitory period, it must apply to the Contracting States this Convention to the exclusion of any other one.

A6.34   Article 32. Revision and amendment

1. At the request of not less than one-third of the Contracting States to this Convention, the depositary shall convene a conference of the Contracting State for revising or amending it.

2. Any instrument of ratification, acceptance, approval or accession deposited after the entry into force of an amendment to this convention, is deemed to apply to the Convention as amended.

A6.35   Article 33. Revision of the limitation amounts and unit of account or monetary
unit

1. Notwithstanding the provisions of art. 32, a conference only for the purpose of altering the amount specified in art. 6 and para. 2 of art. 26, or of substituting either or both of the units defined in paras. 1 and 3 of art. 26 by other units is to be convened by the depositary in accordance with para. 2 of this Article. An alteration of the amounts shall be made only because of a significant change in their real value.

2. A revision conference is to be convened by the depositary when not less than one-fourth of the Contracting States so request.

3. Any decision by the conference must be taken by a two-thirds majority of the participating States. The amendment is communicated by the depositary to all the Contracting States for acceptance and to all the States signatories of the Convention for information.

4. Any amendment adopted enters into force on the first day of the month following one year after its acceptance by two-thirds of the Contracting States. Acceptance is to be effected by the deposit of a formal instrument to that effect, with the depositary.

5. After entry into force of an amendment a Contracting State which has accepted the amendment is entitled to apply the Convention as amended in its relations with Contracting States which have not within six months after the adoption of the amendment notified the depositary that they are not bound by the amendment.

6. Any instrument of ratification, acceptance, approval or accession deposited after the entry into force of an amendment to this Convention, is deemed to apply to the Convention as amended.

Article 34. Denunciation   A6.36

1. A Contracting State may denounce this Convention at any time by means of a notification in writing addressed to the depositary.

2. The denunciation takes effect on the first day of the month following the expiration of one year after the notification is received by the depositary. Where a longer period is specified in the notification, the denunciation takes effect upon the expiration of such longer period after the notification is received by the depositary.

DONE at Hamburg, this thirty-first day of March one thousand nine hundred and seventy-eight, in a single original, of which the Arabic, Chinese, English, French, Russian and Spanish texts are equally authentic.

IN WITNESS WHEREOF the undersigned plenipotentiaries, being duly authorized by their respective Governments, have signed the present Convention.

Annex II   A6.37

Common Understanding Adopted by the United Nations Conference on the Carriage of Goods by Sea

It is the common understanding that the liability of the carrier under this Convention is based on the principle of presumed fault or neglect. This means that, as a rule, the burden of proof rests on the carrier but, with respect to certain cases, the provisions of the Convention modify this rule.

Annex III   A6.38

Resolution Adopted by the United Nations Conference on the Carriage of Goods by Sea

"The United Nations Conference on the Carriage of Goods by Sea,

"*Noting* with appreciation the kind invitation of the Federal Republic of Germany to hold the Conference in Hamburg,

"*Being aware* that the facilities placed at the disposal of the Conference and the generous hospitality bestowed on the participants by the Government of the Federal Republic of Germany and by the Free and Hanseatic City of Hamburg, have in no small measure contributed to the success of the Conference,

"*Expresses* its gratitude to the Government and people of the Federal Republic of Germany, and

"*Having adopted* the Convention on the Carriage of Goods by Sea on the basis of a draft Convention prepared by the United Nations Commission on International Trade Law at the request of the United Nations Conference on Trade and Development,

"*Expresses* its gratitude to the United Nations Commission on International Trade Law and to the United Nations Conference on Trade and Development for their outstanding contribution to the simplification and harmonization of the law of the carriage of goods by sea, and

"*Decides* to designate the Convention adopted by the Conference as the 'UNITED NATIONS CONVENTION ON THE CARRIAGE OF GOODS BY SEA, 1978', and

"*Recommends* that the rules embodied therein be known as the 'HAMBURG RULES'."

INDEX

LEGAL TAXONOMY
FROM SWEET & MAXWELL

This index has been prepared using Sweet and Maxwell's Legal Taxonomy. Main index entries conform to keywords provided by the Legal Taxonomy except where references to specific documents or non-standard terms (denoted by quotation marks) have been included. These keywords provide a means of identifying similar concepts in other Sweet & Maxwell publications and online services to which keywords from the Legal Taxonomy have been applied. Readers may find some minor differences between terms used in the text and those which appear in the index. Suggestions to *sweetandmaxwell.taxonomy @thomson.com.*

(All references are to paragraph number)